AMERICAN EPOCH

*A History
of the United States
Since the 1890's*

AMERICAN EPOCH

A HISTORY
OF THE UNITED STATES
SINCE THE 1890's

by

ARTHUR S. LINK

EDWARDS PROFESSOR OF AMERICAN HISTORY
AND DIRECTOR OF THE WOODROW WILSON PAPERS
Princeton University

WITH THE COLLABORATION OF

WILLIAM B. CATTON

ASSOCIATE PROFESSOR OF HISTORY
Middlebury College

AND THE ASSISTANCE OF

WILLIAM M. LEARY, JR.

INSTRUCTOR IN HISTORY
Princeton University

THIRD EDITION

 *Alfred · A · Knopf*   *New York*

THIS IS A BORZOI BOOK,
PUBLISHED BY ALFRED A. KNOPF, INC.

© Copyright, 1955, 1967, by Arthur S. Link
© Copyright, 1963, by Arthur S. Link and William
B. Catton.
All rights reserved under International and Pan-
American Copyright Conventions. Distributed by
Random House, Inc. Published simultaneously in
Toronto, Canada, by Random House of Canada
Limited.
L. C. catalog card number: 67–12258
Manufactured in the United States of America

PUBLISHED 1955
SECOND EDITION 1963
THIRD EDITION 1967

FOR MY CHILDREN

Stanley, Jimmy, Peggy, and Billy

WHO ALREADY LOVE
AMERICAN HISTORY

PREFACE
TO
THE THIRD EDITION

THIS THIRD EDITION of *American Epoch* brings the story of events at home and abroad to mid-1966. Readers familiar with the 1963 edition will note another change in this new edition—the elimination of many old and now more or less obsolete titles in the bibliography and the updating of that section. As for the last chapter on New Frontiers and the Great Society, it can only be said that we are still very much in the midst of events discussed therein, and all judgments about these events are necessarily tentative.

Professor Catton and I take pleasure in acknowledging our indebtedness to Dr. William M. Leary, Jr., Instructor in History, Princeton University, for his work on the last chapter, the new bibliography, and the index.

The authors hope that readers will be as helpful in the future as they have been in the past in pointing out typographical and other errors. Letters should be addressed to me at the Firestone Library, Princeton, N.J. 08540.

A. S. L.

Princeton, N.J.
December 1, 1966

CONTENTS

PART I : THE PROGRESSIVE ERA AND THE FIRST WORLD WAR, 1897–1920

PART II : PROSPERITY, DEPRESSION, AND THE NEW DEAL, 1921–1941

PART III : THE SECOND WORLD WAR AND AN UNCERTAIN PEACE, 1941–1966

PHOTOGRAPHS

MAPS

PLANNED AND EXECUTED BY THEODORE R. MILLER

GRAPHS AND FIGURES

DRAWN BY THEODORE R. MILLER

PART I

THE PROGRESSIVE ERA
AND THE
FIRST WORLD WAR
1897–1920

*IN WHICH the American people sur-
mount the depression of the 1890's,
find prosperity and peace at home,
launch the progressive movement in
city, state, and nation to restore representative government and subject organized wealth to their control, and,
withal, become a world power with
dominions beyond the seas and play
a decisive role in the reshaping of a
new military balance in the world.*

CHAPTER

I

The Heritage of
the Nineteenth Century

An ANARCHIST shot President William McKinley at Buffalo, New York, on September 6, 1901, and by so doing helped to inaugurate a new era in American history. The coming to national leadership of McKinley's successor, Theodore Roosevelt, marked not only a change of Presidents but also the beginning of a new epoch for a people standing on the threshold of the most momentous century in modern history. Rash is the man who undertakes to chronicle the triumphs and failures of the American people during the past six decades. Yet knowledge of the follies and failures of history may yield wisdom and understanding for a generation ignorant of its own experiences and distraught by fear of an uncertain future.

1. *The Economic and Political Revolution, 1861–1876*

To understand our recent history we must know something about the heritage that the nineteenth century bequeathed to the twentieth. The framework of twentieth-century American society was constructed during the Civil War and Reconstruction and shaped by a revolution in industry, agriculture, transportation, and politics. The United States emerged as the leading industrial and agricultural producer of the world during the period 1861–1901. The statistics all add up to the same story of incredible growth, and multiplying the examples would merely elaborate the obvious facts of economic development. More important is an understanding of the dynamics that produced this economic revolution, for the same forces that set the revolution in progress gathered momentum after 1900 and helped to create the twentieth-century American economic society.

To begin with, the three essential ingredients—natural resources, labor, and capital—existed in abundance in the United States after 1861. The development of vast new coal fields and iron mines in western Pennsylvania, for example, provided the basis for the growing American iron and steel industry. The expanding demand for labor was amply satisfied by masses of unskilled workers from at home and abroad. And profits were sufficiently large over the long period from 1861 to 1901 to make possible a steady expansion of plant and equipment.

Moreover, a shift in the balance of power in Washington and in many of the state governments during the crisis of the Union added a new impetus to the economic revolution then in progress. Its result was to make the federal and state governments protectors and benefactors of the rising banking, industrial, and railroad interests. The Republican party in the Northeast, at least, had supplanted the Whig party as the political agent of the propertied interests, just as the Whigs had earlier supplanted the Federalists in this capacity. A tenuous alliance of the South and West in the Democratic party had held the nonagrarian interests in check before 1861 and had prevented them from using the federal government to underwrite their program. The withdrawal of the southern delegations from Congress in 1860–1, however, threw political control into the hands of the Republican agents of the business classes.

As a result, the reconstruction of the United States began even before guns were fired on Fort Sumter. The passage of the Morrill tariff law of 1861 was the first sign that control of the federal government had passed from the agricultural sections to the industrial Northeast. The industrial-financial leaders of the Republican party, under the guise of war necessity, carried forward this reconstruction of federal policies at a rapid pace—through land grants to railroads, a national banking system, introduction of contract labor from Europe and Asia, and further tariff increases.

The struggle for control of the federal government entered a new phase when the war ended and an assassin's bullet placed Andrew Johnson of Tennessee in the White House in 1865. The object of Johnson's plan of Reconstruction was to bring the former Confederate states back into the Union as speedily as possible, without changing the political control of the southern states. The Republican leaders perceived that the outcome of Johnson's plan might well be to restore dominance in the federal government to the agrarian South and West; hence they moved quickly to overturn Johnsonian reconstruction and inaugurate their own so-called Radical program. Conceived in the interest of the business classes and justified in the name of humanitarianism, Radical Reconstruction stirred passions, North and South, without effecting any lasting changes in the southern economy or social order. Negroes were enfranchised and given a varying measure of civil rights, but control of the land and other means of production was left securely in the hands of the whites. And when the Radicals, for a number of reasons, abandoned their southern program in 1877, the southern whites at once resumed sovereignty in local affairs.

Radical Reconstruction was, therefore, but an interlude in southern history. But the reconstruction of national politics that began in 1861 had fully accomplished its objectives by 1877. The business classes had executed a bloodless revolution without altering the structure of American political institutions. They had, in brief, wrested control of the political institutions from the agrarian majority and changed the character, but not the forms, of representative government in the United States.

2. *The Captains of Industry*

The transformation of the American economy was accomplished, in the final analysis, not by impersonal forces, but by men. The character and methods of the new captains of industry and transportation offer, therefore, another key to understanding politics and business during America's so-called Gilded Age from the 1870's to about 1893. The new economic leaders who rose to power during and after the Civil War were a remarkable group—sometimes ruthless and dishonest, often no worse than their fellow Americans, yet extraordinarily bold and resourceful. Like most other businessmen of their day, they conceived of economic activity as warfare, in which only the strong survived and the weak perished. It was a generally acquisitive age, and the amassing of wealth was their goal, money their standard. Monopoly, subversion of representative government, and corruption of private and public morals—these were often necessary means in the fierce struggle for wealth and power. One historian has called them Robber Barons and likened them to the freebooters of the Middle Ages who pillaged the countryside. Another writer has compared them to the gangsters of the 1920's.

The comparisons, however engaging, are essentially unfair, because, for all their faults, most captains of industry were men of enormous constructive energy and usually reflected the standards of their age. For every Daniel Drew, who bankrupted railroads for his own enrichment, there were a dozen Thomas A. Scotts, James J. Hills, and Edward H. Harrimans, who laid gleaming rails across plains and mountains to the Pacific Coast. The character, methods, and achievements of these men who used freedom to win unparalleled economic power can best be read in the career of the pre-eminent captain of industry and master monopolist, John D. Rockefeller.

Rockefeller was born in upstate New York in 1839 and moved with his family to Cleveland, Ohio, in 1853. Two years later he went to work as a bookkeeper in a commission firm. He formed a partnership in 1859 and opened a commission house to deal in agricultural products. In the same year oil was discovered in western Pennsylvania, and America's first oil boom soon developed in that area. Since Cleveland was on the main line of an East-West railroad and had direct rail connections with the oilfields after 1863, it rapidly emerged as the center of the new petroleum refining industry. Rockefeller went into the oil business in 1863, at the same time that dozens of other refineries were being built in and around the city.

Rockefeller's firm was the largest refinery in Cleveland by 1867. In that year he began his long career of sharp practices that brought eventual domination of the American oil industry. He made his first rebating agreement with the railroads. Under this arrangement Rockefeller received not only a rebate of fifteen cents a barrel on the oil that he shipped, but also a similar amount for every barrel of oil that his competitors shipped. It was not difficult for Rockefeller to prosper with such an advantage. His firm was reorganized and capitalized at $1,000,000 in 1870. He began buying other refineries in Cleveland two years later. In 1873 he acquired a large distributing company, started building his own pipelines, and purchased refineries in New York. Later he moved on to Philadelphia, Baltimore, and the Middle West and Southwest.

Rockefeller's Standard Oil Company by 1904 was refining more than 84 per cent of the crude oil in the United States, producing more than 86 per cent of the illuminating oil, and controlling 86 per cent of the export trade in illuminants. Standard's pipelines, moreover, carried nearly 90 per cent of the crude oil of the older fields and 98 per cent of the output of the new Kansas fields. So profitable was the oil monopoly that Rockefeller's wealth increased almost by a geometric ratio, and he was worth probably a billion dollars by the turn of the century.

Rockefeller was the most successful of the captains of industry, to be sure, but he was only one of many who contrived to acquire for themselves and their families large portions of the land, timber, railroads, mineral resources, and industrial wealth of the United States. The Rockefellers in oil, the Carnegies and Fricks in steel, the Morgans in banking, or the Harrimans and Hills in railroading—these were the men who had a large voice in the Republican party and usually the Democratic party as well from 1865 to 1901. They financed political campaigns and received their rewards from government in the form of utilities franchises, land bounties, freedom from taxation, or tariff protection.

3. *Consequences of the Economic Revolution*

The most significant consequence of the economic revolution was the creation of a powerful productive economy that provided in spite of its limitations an increasingly rich material life for a majority of people. Yet industrialization took place in such a way as to create extraordinary economic and social problems for twentieth-century Americans.

For one thing, freedom from public control allowed businessmen to engage in ruthless economic warfare, the end result of which was often destruction of competition and establishment of monopoly. Big business by 1901 was either monopolistic or quasi-monopolistic in many basic industries, while new enterprises were encountering grave difficulty in entering the field. Moreover, even before the turn of the century investment bankers had begun to extend their control over railroads and industries and to build interlocking financial empires. In other words, an economic oligarchy dominated the American economy by 1900.

In the second place, the economic revolution had created social problems of enormous magnitude—cities that grew too fast, where millions of people lived amid squalor and misery; the exploitation of women and children; and a whole complex of problems caused by unemployment, illness, and perilous old age. These were the human costs of rapid and uncontrolled industrialization. A growing body of thoughtful Americans realized that continuation of such unrestrained exploitation could only result in the degradation of the masses.

Finally, the manner in which the economic revolution took place meant that the American people by the turn of the century had been deprived of a large part of their great heritage of land, timber, and mineral resources by railroads and the captains of industry. Wealthy men had entered politics and dominated city, state, and federal governments to bring this about. How to recover that lost heritage, restore representative government, and subject great wealth to a measure of public control would constitute the paramount domestic challenge of the twentieth century.

4. *The Agricultural Problem, 1861–1900*

Agriculture remained the principal means of livelihood for the American people even while a new industrial and urban economy was advancing with giant strides. Moreover, American agriculture went through a revolution during the last four decades of the nineteenth century as significant as the revolution that occurred in transportation and industry. Improved transportation facilities, invention of agricultural machinery, and opening of vast new farm areas all combined to hasten the shift, which had begun in the 1850's, from subsistence agriculture to commercial agriculture, from production for home and local markets to production for the world market.

American farmers generally prospered during a period of inflation and high production during the Civil War, indeed until the late 1860's. About 1869, however, they entered a quarter-century of declining prices, during many years of which they produced at an actual loss. The result was the creation of America's most serious domestic problem from 1870 to 1897.

The most obvious causes of the farmer's steady march toward economic ruin were overproduction and declining prices, as agricultural output in the United States, indeed in all the world, far outstripped demand. For example, wheat, which brought $1.11 a bushel in 1879, sold for 49 cents in 1894; corn fell from an average of 50 cents a bushel in 1879 to 21 cents in 1896, cotton from 14 cents a pound in 1873 to 4.6 cents in 1894.

The farmer's troubles were compounded by the twin burdens of excessive freight rates and high interest charges on the money that he borrowed. Railroad freight rates, fixed on the principle of charging what the traffic would bear, were in many areas exorbitant, while discriminations in rates and services, granting of secret rebates to favored shippers, pooling agreements to eliminate competition, and improper influencing of legislatures and judges were common practices of the railroad managers. As for the burden of carrying their debt load, farmers had to pay usury instead of interest in many areas. This problem was most serious in the South, where the cotton and tobacco crops were financed by outside credit and where interest charges usually consumed profits before the crops could be harvested.

5. *The Agrarian Revolt, 1870–1890*

The consequences of the long depression in agriculture can be read clearly in the efforts that farmers made to use political instrumentalities to extricate themselves from the slough of despair. Most of the important legislative and political battles from 1873 to 1897 revolved directly or indirectly around the agrarian campaign for relief; and a political philosophy and program that would have profound significance for twentieth-century American politics emerged out of the ferment of agrarian revolt.

The Granger movement was the farmers' first organized attempt to strike back at railroads and industrial monopolies. The Grange began in Washington in 1867 as an organization designed to ameliorate the social drabness of rural life. Spreading rapidly through the West and South, it had a national membership of over 800,000 by 1875. Farmers inevitably discussed common grievances and means of remedying them when they congregated, and it was not long before they went into politics. In the Middle West, for example, they won control of legislatures in Iowa, Illinois, Wisconsin, and Minnesota and attempted to establish fair railroad rates and practices. The Granger movement fell victim to the long depression of the 1870's, but farmers had recovered their political consciousness, and a beginning toward concerted farmer political organization had been made.

Leadership in articulating and marshaling agrarian discontent passed in the 1880's from the Grange to a new and more aggressive movement— the farmers' alliances. There were a number of alliances in the late '70's and early '80's, but they had coalesced by 1890 into three powerful groups, the Northwestern Alliance, Southern Alliance, and Colored Alliance. They plunged into politics in 1890 with a vehemence that startled and frightened the business interests, captured state after state in the South and West, and sent eloquent spokesmen to state legislatures and to Congress. The agrarian revolt was spectacular in its occurrence, but more significant for the future of American politics were the Alliance leaders' political philosophy and program. Economic adversity and a sense of baffling frustration had impelled farmers to abandon *laissez faire* as the right rule of political practice and to espouse a program envisaging far-reaching governmental intervention in economic affairs. The conversion of the great masses of farmers to this new philosophy, later called progressivism, made it a political force that could not long be ignored by the two major parties.

The consummation of the agrarian revolt was the organization of the Populist party in 1892 and the effort of William Jennings Bryan and his agrarian followers to win control of the federal government in 1896. Before this last campaign occurred, however, the agrarian reformers had already sounded the death knell of *laissez faire* by their efforts to solve the railroad problem and obtain an ample supply of money and credit.

The idea of public regulation of railroads was an outgrowth mainly of the Granger movement. Illinois, Wisconsin, Minnesota, and Iowa attempted in the early 1870's to prescribe equitable rates by direct legislation and established state commissions to compel nondiscriminatory services. Except for Illinois, however, these states failed to accomplish any lasting reform. The railroad interests either regained control of the legislatures and obtained repeal of the regulatory laws or else fought the railroad commissions to a standstill in state courts. A much more promising movement for reform got under way in Georgia and California in 1879, when both states established expert railroad commissions empowered to set rates.

The failure of the so-called Granger railroad laws prompted midwestern farm organizations to come out for federal regulation. This shift was occasioned in part by the general conviction that the railroad problem was beyond the competence of the individual states. It was more immediately a result of the Supreme Court's opinion, rendered in the Wabash case of 1886, that Congress alone could regulate *interstate* rates and services. This decision simply provided the final impetus for an already strong movement for federal legislation. It came to fruition in 1887 in the adoption of the Interstate Commerce Act, which decreed that rates should be fair and just, outlawed discriminatory practices, and established the Interstate Commerce Commission. It was a landmark in American political history: the first important turning away from the *laissez-faire* philosophy that had so long prevailed among federal lawmakers. As we will see later, it soon became evident that the Commerce Act conferred no real authority on the Commission; and the railroad problem was far from being settled when the agrarian revolt of the 1890's exploded in full force.

Obtaining an adequate money supply without wrecking the national financial structure was an even more perplexing problem. Yet to embattled farmers, who saw the prices of their commodities decline, the value of their properties shrink, and the burden of their debts grow heavier, this became the vital issue of the last quarter of the nineteenth century.

The money question had its origin in the federal government's issuance of some $450,000,000 in greenbacks with no gold backing during the Civil War. The greenbacks depreciated in value and contributed to the inflation of the war period, but they also helped to make money plentiful. No sooner had the war ended than the business and banking interests demanded and obtained a reduction in the greenback currency and a return to the gold standard in 1879. One result of this deflation was a decline in per capita circulation of almost 50 per cent between 1865 and 1879; and commodity prices declined as money became dearer. Farmers who had incurred large mortgages during the prosperous years soon found themselves obliged to repay the same debts with commodities worth about half as much as when they had borrowed the money.

The debtor classes during the '70's and early '80's viewed the greenback as the means of their salvation. Then after 1882 they abandoned paper money and seized upon silver as the most likely instrument of inflation. The reason for this sudden shift in allegiance is not hard to find. So little silver was mined in the United States until about 1865 that the established ratio between silver and gold of 16 to 1 undervalued silver and drove it out of circulation as money. On the other hand, immense deposits of silver were discovered in the Rocky Mountain region during the 1860's and early 1870's. Production increased so rapidly that by 1879 the old ratio of 16 to 1 greatly overvalued silver and made it the perfect tool of inflationists. Silver, in contrast to greenbacks, satisfied the demand that the currency have a metallic basis, while coining silver at the ratio of 16 to 1 would ensure an expanded money supply and increased commodity prices without causing runaway inflation.

From the mid-seventies to about 1898, therefore, western and southern farmers demanded free and unlimited coinage of silver at the ratio of 16 to 1. Their representatives in Congress overrode a presidential veto to pass the Bland-Allison Act in 1878. It required the Secretary of the Treasury to purchase not less than two nor more than four million dollars worth of silver monthly. Farm prices rose during the early '80's, and the silver agitation subsided. But drought and hard times in the last years of the decade stimulated renewed agitation by the Alliances for free coinage at 16 to 1. So powerful was this demand that Congress in 1890 adopted the Sherman Silver Purchase Act, which provided for the purchase by the federal government of almost the entire domestic production. As it turned out, however, the economic dislocations were too fundamental to be corrected by such a simple expedient, and the farmers' plight grew infinitely worse with the coming of the Panic of 1893.

6.   *The Populist Revolt and the Battle of the Standards, 1890–1896*

The passage of the Sherman Purchase Act did not halt a sharp new downward spiral of commodity prices that began in 1891. Money was tight, credit almost inflexible, banking facilities woefully inadequate. But the national leadership of both major parties represented the industrial and banking interests, and farmers could expect little relief from either of them. In these circumstances the final revolt of the farmers developed with astonishing rapidity. The Alliances captured the Democratic party in Tennessee, Georgia, and South Carolina in 1890. By co-operating with Democrats in the midwestern and Plains states they won control of Kansas, Nebraska, South Dakota, and Minnesota as well. Next the Alliance leaders launched their own party—the People's, or Populist party—at Omaha on July 4, 1892. Thus, after nearly two decades of discontent, agrarian unrest finally took shape in political action on a national scale.

The Populist platform, the vivid preamble of which was written by Ignatius Donnelly of Minnesota, sounded the battle cry of revolt and set forth a program around which the farmers could rally. It demanded the free and unlimited coinage of silver at the ratio of 16 to 1. At the insistence of southern Alliancemen, it endorsed the so-called subtreasury plan to establish a federal commodity loan system so that farmers might borrow against their crops. It also demanded a graduated federal income tax; postal savings banks; public ownership of railroads, telegraph systems, and telephones; prohibition of alien land ownership and recovery from railroads of land illegally held; immigration restriction; the eight-hour day for industrial workers; and prohibition of the use of private armies against strikers. Finally, there were demands for measures to restore popular rule —the direct election of senators, the initiative and referendum, and the secret ballot.

The adoption of the Populist platform marked the end of an era when practically all Americans put their trust in the English Liberal ideal of a free, competitive economy, operating automatically in the general interest without decisive and planned intervention by government. The adoption of this platform heralded the coming triumph of a new progressive faith—a faith in the ability of men to overcome economic adversity and rectify social injustice by collective political action. The later progressive movement went far beyond the Populist charter in elaborating specific remedies, but the spirit, purpose, and assumptions of progressivism were inherited in large measure from the Populists, the advance guard of a new reform movement.

The Populists did not expect to win the election of 1892, but their beginning was auspicious enough. Indeed, they might well have displaced the Democratic party had the eastern, conservative element continued to dominate that party. Unforeseen events, however, wrecked the existing political alignment and destroyed Populism in the end as an independent movement.

One of the worst depressions of the nineteenth century broke out soon after the Democrat, Grover Cleveland, was inaugurated President in 1893. Cleveland was convinced that the chief cause of the depression was lack of confidence in the ability of the Treasury to maintain the gold standard, a fear induced by the Sherman Purchase Act.[1] He therefore called Congress into special session in 1893 and obtained repeal of that measure. By this action, which was accomplished with the help of Republicans, the President split his own party and embittered agrarian Democrats. Cleveland next tried to get honest tariff reform and failed. He broke a railroad strike in Chicago in 1894 by using federal troops and imprisoning the strike leaders. Finally, he further antagonized farmers and debtors by his negotiations with Wall Street bankers to keep the government on the gold standard. Cleveland saved the gold standard and disrupted the Democratic party in the process. Leaders of the southern and western majority took control of proceedings when the Democrats met in national convention in Chicago in the summer of 1896 and read Cleveland and his following out of the party. The agrarians found their new leader and presidential candidate in William Jennings Bryan, a young former congressman and editor from Nebraska, who captured the convention by defying Wall Street and demanding free and unlimited coinage of silver. The toiling producers of America—the farmers and workers—he intoned, must not be crucified upon a Cross of Gold!

Although Bryan was an ardent silverite and a low-tariff advocate, he was not yet a radical of the Populist stripe. Moreover, the Democratic platform was neither as well integrated nor as advanced as the Populist platform of 1892. But the Democrats offered enough to the more radical Populists to make fusion inevitable: tariff reform, a graduated income tax, vigorous prosecution of the trusts, and, of course, free coinage of silver. Thus Populists and Democrats in the agricultural sections, the South and West, united to capture control of the federal government from the manufacturing East.

Against the young orator from Nebraska the Republicans pitted William McKinley of Ohio, a spokesman of the business interests and a reluctant champion of the gold standard. There was much at stake, and the business community rallied behind McKinley and his campaign manager, Mark Hanna. All the influence that money could buy was brought to bear

---

[1] This Act required the Treasury to purchase 4,500,000 ounces of silver monthly and to pay for the silver, at the market price, with Treasury notes. The Secretary of the Treasury was authorized to redeem these Treasury notes "in gold or silver coin, at his discretion," but the Treasury Department consistently interpreted this provision to mean that the notes had to be redeemed "in gold or its equivalent."

ELECTION OF 1896

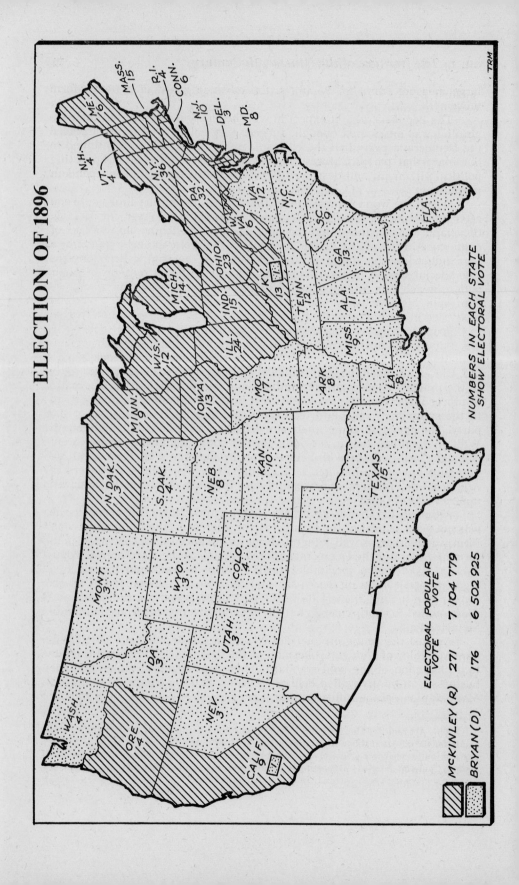

NUMBERS IN EACH STATE
SHOW ELECTORAL VOTE

	ELECTORAL VOTE	POPULAR VOTE
McKINLEY (R)	271	7 104 779
BRYAN (D)	176	6 502 925

TRM

against Bryan. Workers by the hundreds of thousands were told not to return to work after election day if the Democrats won. An enormous propaganda, depicting Bryan and his friends as anarchists, seditionists, and potential despoilers, was set in motion. In doubtful states like Indiana, Hanna spent money on a lavish scale.

With all the influence of organized wealth and respectable society marshaled against the Democrats, their defeat was almost inevitable. Worse still for their chances, Bryan's alleged radicalism solidified the urban middle classes and the more prosperous eastern and midwestern farmers in support of McKinley; and organized labor refused to join the proposed farmer-worker coalition. Even so, Bryan polled 6,503,000 votes, to 7,105,-000 for McKinley, and carried the South and many of the states west of the Mississippi. His defeat by such a narrow margin signified that the kind of progressivism he advocated would hereafter be a major force in American politics.

7. Political and Social Theories, 1865–1900

The political, industrial, and agricultural revolutions from 1865 to 1900 were accompanied by profound changes in the attitudes of thoughtful people toward government and the role that it should play in human affairs. Most of the intellectual and literary history of this period is beyond the scope of this discussion. Twentieth-century progressivism had deep nineteenth-century roots, however, and these we will attempt to describe and analyze. To put it simply, political and economic thinkers were divided roughly into two major groups from 1865 to 1900: on the one hand, persons who attempted to justify unbridled capitalism and the reign of big business; on the other, dissident voices who attempted emotionally and intellectually to justify the revolt against *laissez faire*.

The dominant economic interests found their chief justification in the theories of classical economics, the gospel of wealth, and social Darwinism. Classical economic theory was an intellectual outgrowth of the English commercial and industrial revolutions. It taught that the highest social good could be achieved only by allowing men to pursue self-interest untrammeled or unaided by governmental restrictions and favors. Economists of this school worked out an elaborate body of theory to prove this point, and a large majority of economists in the United States expounded their doctrines, at least before 1885.

The gospel of wealth accepted the classical economic assumptions and attempted to find moral and social justification for the leadership of the captains of industry. Success and the acquisition of wealth, so the argument ran, were the just rewards of industry, thrift, and sobriety, while the great mass of humanity remained poor because of their own indolence and natural inferiority. Government, the propounders of the gospel of wealth argued, should merely preserve order and protect property; it should leave control over the economy to the natural aristocracy, who won and held their leadership in competitive struggle. On the other hand, these natural aristocrats had large obligations to society, precisely because they were the stewards of the nation's wealth. To them much had been given; of them much was required—wise leadership and, above all, return of wealth to the people by lavish gifts to charity and education. To the gospel of wealth was often added the authority of the Protestant ethic of good works as being the proper response to divine blessings. Indeed, preachers often talked about the two concepts as if they were identical.

Social Darwinism, however, was probably the reigning economic and social philosophy among American defenders of the established order in the last third of the nineteenth century. As an integrated system, it was largely the product of the fertile brain of Herbert Spencer, an English political philosopher. Spencer, profoundly impressed by Darwin's findings in the field of biology, attempted to construct his system on the principles of the survival of the fittest and the evolution of organisms from the simple to the complex. Darwin had seen a fierce struggle for survival in the animal world that destroyed the weak, rewarded the strong, and produced evolutionary change. Struggle, destruction, and survival of the fit, Spencer contended, were essential to progress in human society as well. The weak stood athwart the high road to progress and had to perish. The strong survived because they were superior. As this was an elementary law of social development, it was both futile and dangerous for government to try to help the weak to survive.

Social Darwinism enjoyed great vogue even though it obviously repudiated the humane and Christian principles upon which the American democratic tradition rested. To begin with, Spencer offered to intellectuals of the period a scientific system to replace the shattered orthodox Christian cosmogony. As one historian has said, Spencer provided "a comprehensive world-view, uniting under one generalization everything in nature from protozoa to politics." [2] In the second place, Spencer's philosophy was easily understood; it made a philosopher of the crossroad sage because it confirmed his own deductions. Finally, social Darwinism was made to order to rationalize the rule of the business oligarchy. It justified economic warfare, poverty, exploitation, and suffering in the name of progress. And there was nothing that organized society, that is, government, could really do, because attempts at amelioration would only create graver social problems.

The opposite concept of positive government found its prophet in Henry George, author of *Progress and Poverty*, published in 1879, and many other tracts, and best known for his proposal of a single tax on unearned increments in land values. But the single tax was not the concept that changed men's lives and stimulated a whole host to undertake a crusade for social and economic reform. The dynamic of George's philosophy was his conviction that men could reconstruct society by collective political action. He offered confidence in a future bright with the promise of social and economic betterment. As the leading democratic philosopher of the Gilded Age, Henry George became the chief link between the reform movements of the ante-bellum period and the progressive movement of the twentieth century.

On the other hand, the task of converting American intellectuals to

---

[2] Richard Hofstadter, *Social Darwinism in American Thought, 1860–1915* (Philadelphia, 1944), p. 18.

a positive concept of the state fell mainly to a sociologist, Lester Frank Ward, who published his major work, *Dynamic Sociology,* in 1883. Ward was a social evolutionist like Spencer, but he drew a sharp difference between purposeless animal evolution and human evolution, which he said could be decisively modified by artificial control of natural phenomena. *Dynamic Sociology* was essentially an argument for controlled social and economic development. Few among his generation ever heard Ward's name, but his influence on a large school of young sociologists and economists exceeded that of any other contemporary American.

American economists could also boast of their own revolt against Spencer and William Graham Sumner, the chief American expositor of social Darwinism. Most of the young insurgents who repudiated their classical masters had been trained in the historical school of economics, either in Germany or at the new Johns Hopkins University in Baltimore. Gathering at Saratoga, New York, in the autumn of 1885, they organized the American Economic Association and adopted a statement of principles that was tantamount to a declaration of war against the classical school. Asserting that the positive intervention of the state was one of the indispensable conditions of human progress, they went on to declare that changing economic conditions must be met by changing progressive legislation.

Finally, there could be no real mass support for the new progressive concepts until the religious leaders of the United States had awakened to the challenge of social Darwinism and joined in the movement to make the industrial-financial regime responsible to the people. Accompanying the revolt against *laissez faire* among political and intellectual leaders went a humanitarian movement in American Protestantism called the social gospel, which we will review in a later chapter. So powerful was this movement that by 1900 most of the large denominations had moved well along the road toward social Christianity.

8. The End of an Era

The last four years of the nineteenth century witnessed the return of prosperity and confidence and the ending of a long era of relative isolation from international politics by the United States. A number of factors combined to produce the economic upswing. To begin with, McKinley's election in 1896 assured the business and financial communities that the federal government would continue to pursue friendly policies and would not tamper with the currency. In the second place, the Russian wheat crop of 1896–7 was short to the point of famine, and western Europe had to buy more wheat than usual in the United States. The American wheat crops of 1897 and 1898 were abnormally large; but the pressure of European buying drove the price from 78 cents a bushel in 1896 to 95 cents in 1897 and 1898. Thirdly, governmental spending and recruitment of manpower during the War with Spain in the spring and summer of 1898 added yet another stimulus. Fourthly, a spectacular increase in the world's gold production occurred at the same time to stimulate world-wide inflationary tendencies. With an increased money supply and a spurt of new industrial activity, bank clearings increased one third from 1898 to 1899, steel rails doubled in price between February and August of the latter year, and whole-sale prices increased 23 per cent between 1896 and 1900.

Extreme agrarian discontent subsided with the return of prosperity. Then the fever of imperialism and a new manifest destiny seized the American people. They righteously went to war with Spain in 1898 to save the Cubans from Spanish brutality and tyranny. They ended their short and glorious adventure a world power with a colonial empire in the Carib-bean and the Far East. The United States, by the Treaty of Paris of 1898, acquired Puerto Rico and the Philippine Islands from Spain and assumed responsibility for the government of Cuba as well. Although the Demo-crats had enough votes in the Senate to defeat ratification of the Treaty, their leader, Bryan, persuaded them to ratify the peace settlement and to try to make imperialism the paramount issue of the impending presidential campaign.

The campaign of 1900, which for a second time pitted McKinley against Bryan, was bitterly fought. The Democrats, joined by Boston and New York anti-imperialists, contended that democracy and imperialism could not coexist in the same political system, and that the United States would abandon moral leadership of the world if it went into the business of governing alien peoples. Republicans, particularly strident young ex-pansionists like Theodore Roosevelt, Henry Cabot Lodge, and Albert J. Beveridge, replied by defending "the national honor" and pointing to a new destiny for the American people. McKinley won a sweeping victory, but it is doubtful if the voters rendered any verdict on imperialism. A ma-jority of them probably voted against Bryanism and for prosperity.

At the turn of the century, therefore, Americans were both in an exu-berant and an uncertain mood. They entered the new century confident of their ability to make things work out at home, but the venture into im-perialism had raised some grave misgivings about the future of American democracy. Although a majority would probably have denied it, their long isolation was now shattered, and their government would have to play an active role in world affairs in the years to come. What the future would bring no man could foretell. But all thoughtful observers agreed that one era was dead beyond recall, and that a new epoch in America was just beginning.

CHAPTER

2

The American People
During
the Progressive Era

THE YEARS from 1897 to 1920 were a golden period of American development. They were usually prosperous years, marked by solid progress in living standards for all classes. They were, moreover, hopeful years. Americans, confident that they had the ability to set aright the social and economic injustices inherited from the nineteenth century, launched in the early 1900's a virtual crusade on all levels of government to revitalize democracy, bring economic institutions under public control, and find an answer to the twin evils of special privilege and poverty.

The progressive generation was, finally, a period when Christian moralism subdued the crass materialism of the Gilded Age, and morality and righteousness became the keynotes of politics. The YMCA movement swept through colleges and universities, and social Christianity triumphed over Calvinism, as man's first duty became love of man instead of God. Drunkenness, prostitution, the exploitation of women and children, stock watering—these and other evils were bound to fall before the reformer's trumpet blast! It did not even seem rash during this heady season to think that Americans, by participating in a world war and reconstruction, might help to usher in a new age of democracy, peace, and progress everywhere.

POPULATION CHANGE, 1900-1920

MAINE 10.7
N.H. 7.5
VT. 2.3
MASS. 37.4
R.I. 40.8
CONN. 52.1
N.Y. 42.9
PA. 36.4
N.J. 67.5
DELA. 20.5
MD. 22.1
DISTRICT OF COLUMBIA +57%
VA. 24.5
W.VA. 52.7
N.C. 35.1
S.C. 25.7
GA. 30.7
ALA. 28.4
FLA. 83.0
TENN. 15.7
MISS. 15.5
LA. 30.2
MICH. 51.5
WISC. 27.2
OHIO 33.5
IND. 16.5
KY. 12.6
ARK. 33.5
MINN. 36.3
IOWA 7.7
MO. 9.6
OKLA. 156.7
N.DAK. 102.8
S.DAK. 58.5
NEBR. 21.6
KAN. 20.3
TEXAS 52.9
COLO. 74.1
N.MEX. 84.6
WYO. 108.6
UTAH 62.1
ARIZ. 171.5
MONT. 125.9
IDA. 166.7
NEV. -6.1
WASH. 18.5
ORE. 16.3
CALIF. 130.8

POPULATION CHANGE

+ 100% AND OVER
+ 50% THROUGH 99.9%
+ 25% " 49.9%
+ 10% " 24.9%
+ 5% " 9.9%
0% " 4.9%
DECREASE

UNITED STATES AVERAGE 39.0% INCREASE

TRM

9. The American People, 1900–1920: A Demographic View

The population of the United States increased nearly 40 per cent, from 75,994,575 to 105,710,620 souls, from 1900 to 1920. Although 70 per cent of the people still lived east of the Mississippi River in 1920, the most spectacular growth had occurred in the West. The Pacific states, for example, more than doubled in numbers over the two decades, as contrasted with a growth of 43 per cent among the Middle Atlantic states.

The most striking trend in American population from 1900 to 1920 was the steadily increasing migration of people from the countryside to cities. Urban population grew nearly 80 per cent, a rate of increase six and a half times that of the rural areas. More than 40 per cent of the people lived in towns and cities over 2,500 in 1900. The percentage of town and city dwellers was 51.4 two decades later; if we include persons living in towns under 2,500, the percentage of urban population in 1920 was actually 60. As cities grew larger they began to acquire a different character, becoming more and more centers of commerce and industry, where people from outlying areas went to work and then returned to suburban homes. This trend was evidenced in the growth of the so-called metropolitan districts, that is, cities of 200,000 or over with a number of outlying suburbs, by 26.5 per cent between 1910 and 1920. By the latter date there were 32 such metropolitan districts in which 30,188,543 people, or more than 28 per cent of the total population, resided.

Most Americans—88 per cent, to be exact—were white in 1920. There were over 400,000 Indians and Orientals and 10,463,131 Negroes in the United States, but Negroes were a smaller proportion of the population in 1920 than they had been in 1900. Most Americans in 1920 were also native-born. But the numbers of the foreign-born had increased, under the impact of the tremendous immigration of the past two decades, from 10,341,276, or 13.6 per cent of the total population in 1900, to 13,920,692, or 13.2 per cent of the total in 1920. Nearly 83 per cent of the foreign-born lived either in the North or the Middle West, but 85 per cent of the Negroes lived in the South, with the highest concentration in South Carolina, Georgia, Florida, Alabama, Mississippi, and Louisiana.

As medical knowledge expanded through experience and research, Americans grew healthier every year during this period. Indeed, the progress of medicine in overcoming the ancient ravagers of mankind was spectacular. The death rate in areas where reliable statistics were kept declined between 1900 and 1920 from 17 to 12.6 per thousand for whites, and from 25 to 17.7 per thousand for non-whites. This progress was made possible in part by a sharp decline in deaths from typhoid fever and tuberculosis, in part by the practical elimination of smallpox and malaria. Moreover, a virtual physiological revolution was accomplished in the South from 1909 to 1914 through the work of Dr. Charles W. Stiles and the Rockefeller Sanitary Commission in beginning the eradication of hookworm. It had long enervated a large portion of the southern people.

In spite of great progress accomplished through utilization of new techniques, drugs, and a broadening knowledge of the causes of disease, much remained to be done in this field by the end of the First World War.

POPULATION DENSITY, 1920

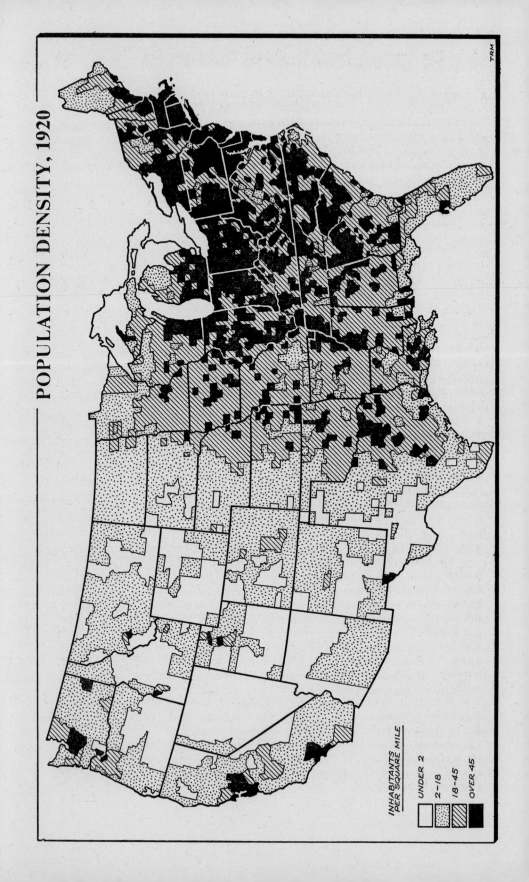

INHABITANTS
PER SQUARE MILE

UNDER 2

2 – 18

18 – 45

OVER 45

For example, one authority concluded in 1909 that the death rate could be reduced one fourth by the partial elimination of preventable diseases. Hundreds of thousands of workers were needlessly killed, maimed, or disabled each year. At the same time, a committee on the physical welfare of New York City's school children found that 66 per cent of these children needed medical care or better nourishment, 40 per cent needed dental care, 31 per cent had defective vision, and 6 per cent suffered from malnutrition.

10. *The American People: Income, Wealth, and Industry*

The most striking economic phenomenon of the first years of the twentieth century was the steady increase in the wealth and income of the people of the United States. Adjusted to fluctuations in the cost of living, the total national income increased from $36,557,000,000, or $480 per capita, at the turn of the century, to $60,401,000,000, or $567 per capita, in 1920. The economic progress of the period can also be read in the steadily increasing volume of industrial production. To state the matter briefly, while population increased by about 40 per cent during the decades 1899–1919, the number of manufacturing establishments increased 32 per cent; capital invested, more than 250 per cent; average number of wage earners, nearly 100 per cent; and value of products, 222 per cent.

The major manufacturing industries at the turn of the century were still the enterprises that furnished the basic necessities—meat packing, iron and steel, foundries and machine shops, lumbering, milling, clothing, textiles, and tobacco. By the time that the Census of Manufactures of 1919 was taken, however, there were abundant signs that a new technology, with all its implications for social life, was in process of coming into being. Industries that were either small or in their infancy in 1900—paper and printing, chemicals, and petroleum products—had burgeoned into lusty giants by 1919. The automobile industry, which had scarcely existed in 1900, now ranked second only to steel among the manufacturing industries and turned out a product valued at nearly $4,000,000,000.

Slightly more than 32,000,000 men and an additional 8,229,000 women, or a total of 40,282,000 persons, were gainfully employed in the United States in 1920. Among this working force carpenters, painters, brickmasons, printers, and other skilled and organized craftsmen enjoyed the shortest working hours and the highest wages. Workers in the building trades, for example, averaged 43.8 hours a week in 1920. But only 1,111,000 persons in manufacturing worked 44 hours a week or less in 1919, while 3,308,000 worked between 44 and 48 hours a week, 1,325,000 between 49 and 54 hours, and 2,533,149 worked 55 hours or more weekly —for an average of 52.3 hours a week.

Generally speaking, the prewar years were marked by full employment and a rising material standard of living for all classes. Yet the benefits of prosperity were not always distributed evenly, and the share of the national income received by the wealthy few was only slightly diminished on account of the high tax policies of the second administration of Woodrow Wilson. According to the best but still unreliable estimates, the richest families, constituting 1.6 per cent of the population, received 10.8 per

ECONOMIC GROWTH OF THE UNITED STATES
1899–1919

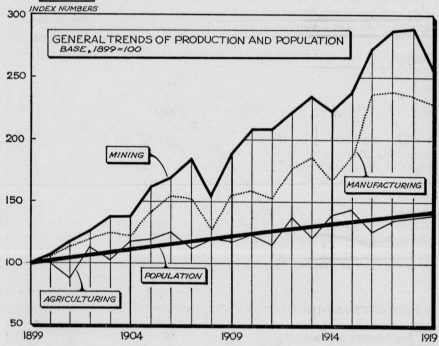

INDEX NUMBERS

GENERAL TRENDS OF PRODUCTION AND POPULATION
BASE, 1899=100

MINING

MANUFACTURING

POPULATION

AGRICULTURING

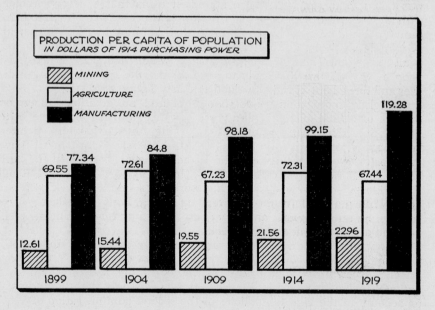

PRODUCTION PER CAPITA OF POPULATION
IN DOLLARS OF 1914 PURCHASING POWER

- MINING
- AGRICULTURE
- MANUFACTURING

1899: 12.61 | 69.55 | 77.34
1904: 15.44 | 72.61 | 84.8
1909: 19.55 | 67.23 | 98.18
1914: 21.56 | 72.31 | 99.15
1919: 22.96 | 67.44 | 119.28

THE NATIONAL INCOME, 1909-1926

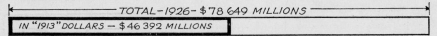

```
TOTAL-1926- $78 649 MILLIONS
IN "1913" DOLLARS — $46 392 MILLIONS
```

TREND OF NATIONAL INCOME
1913 = BASE 100

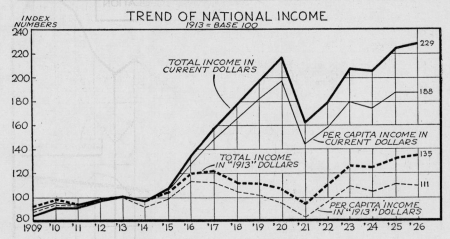

NATIONAL INCOME PER CAPITA AND PER WORKER
(IN DOLLARS)

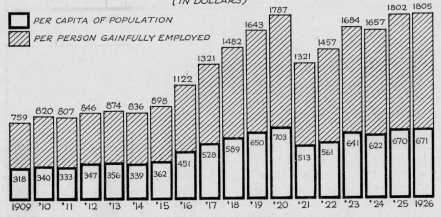

cent of the national income in 1896. More accurate figures taken from income tax returns reveal that the wealthiest 5 per cent received 14.98 per cent of the national income in 1913 and 12.34 per cent in 1920.

11. *American Agriculture Finds Stability*

American agriculture enjoyed such stability and prosperity during this period of industrial expansion as it had not known since 1865. As a result of the technological revolution that was already beginning to make its im-

pact felt, farm population decreased from 32,077,000 in 1910 to 31,556,-
000 in 1920. During the same decade, however, land under cultivation increased from 878,792,000 acres to 955,878,000, and gross farm income
rose from $7,477,000,000 to $15,907,000,000. One result of this phenomenal increase was unparalleled prosperity for farmers during a period when
what they received for the products they sold generally equaled what they
paid for the goods they purchased. Another result was a general increase
of nearly 400 per cent in the value of farm property.

This spectacular increase in the value of farm property, caused in part
by the high prices of the war period, enhanced the wealth and security of
the landowning class, but it also made the acquisition of land more difficult at the very time when the supply of free arable land was being ex-

THE GROWTH OF AMERICAN MANUFACTURES
1899–1921

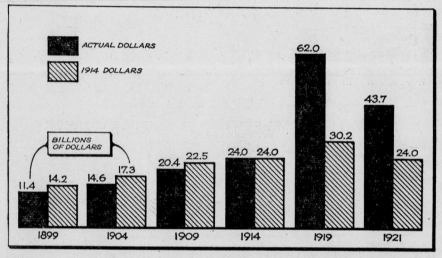

hausted. Thus, while the number of farm owners increased only slightly
(from 3,201,947 to 3,366,510) from 1900 to 1920, the number of tenants
increased by 21 per cent. More than 38 per cent of all farms were operated
by tenants in 1920, as contrasted with 35.3 per cent in 1900 and 25.6 per
cent in 1880.

Farm tenancy, especially sharecropping, was so common in the South
that its prevalence in that region evoked little comment. But the spread of
tenancy through the heartland of the Middle West during the first two
decades of the twentieth century, continuing a trend that had accelerated
in the 1890's, was so inexorable as to raise the question of whether a large
minority of midwestern farmers were not rapidly approaching a condition
of peasantry. One authority concluded in 1914 that 40 per cent of the
farms in the corn belt were operated by tenants; and in 1920 tenants
worked between 42 and 43 per cent of all farms in the immensely rich
states of Illinois and Iowa.

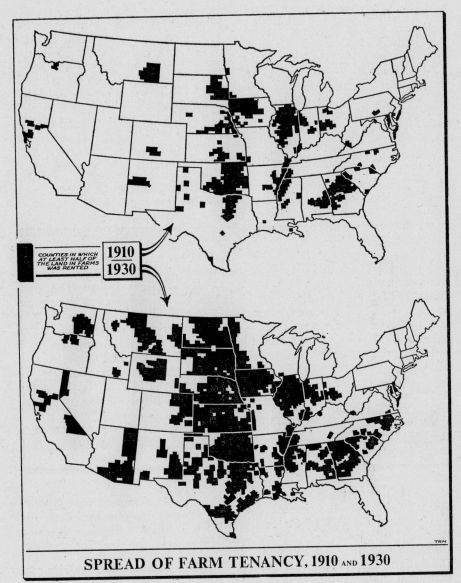

COUNTIES IN WHICH
AT LEAST HALF OF
THE LAND IN FARMS
WAS RENTED

1910
1930

SPREAD OF FARM TENANCY, 1910 AND 1930

12. *The Changing Tide of Immigration*

Immigration was the most persistent and one of the most important of the forces in American history down to the outbreak of the First World War, for the development of the United States was governed in large measure by the ebbing and onrushing tide of alien peoples to the Atlantic shores. Almost 14,000,000 immigrants came to the United States between 1860 and 1900, and over 14,500,000 followed from 1900 to 1915. The majority of immigrants after 1860 came from England, Ireland, Germany, and Scandinavia and were people akin culturally and historically to older American stock. However, an immigration of peoples heretofore unfamiliar to most Americans—Italians, Slavs, Magyars, and Jews from southern and eastern Europe—began around 1880. This so-called new immigration accounted for only 18.3 per cent of the total in the decade from 1881 to 1890, but it soon became a rushing stream. Almost 52 per cent of the immigrants were from southern and eastern Europe from 1891 to 1900, and the proportion grew to 72 per cent from 1901 to 1910. Let us examine the three major groups of "new" immigrants and see the causes for their coming to a country with a civilization so different from their own.

The Italians. Italian emigration to the United States began slowly in the 1880's and reached important proportions about 1900. More than 2,000,000 Italians came to the United States from 1901 to 1910, and an additional 889,000 entered during the four years before the war. The high mark was reached in 1907, when 286,000 passed through the gates at Ellis Island.

Italy alone among the western nations deliberately encouraged emigration and used it as an instrument of national policy to rid herself of surplus population and increase the supply of gold from abroad. The great majority of Italian immigrants came from Sicily and the southern provinces, where estates were largest and living standards were lowest. The Italian peasant, moreover, faced the unpleasant prospect of serving two years in the army as a conscript. Finally, to aggravate an already unhappy situation, the Italian birth rate was one of the highest in Europe, so that only an extraordinary death rate kept population from increasing to the point of disaster. To escape starvation and the lash of the landlord and the army officer, millions of Italians fled to the United States, Argentina, Brazil, and Uruguay.

The Slavs. The migration of the Slavic peoples of eastern Europe to the United States exceeded even the outpouring of the Italians and constituted the major element in the "new" immigration. From Austria-Hungary and Russia, which governed most of the Slavic peoples before the First World War, there came 619,000 immigrants during the decade 1881–90, 1,191,000 from 1891–1900, and over 5,500,000 from 1900–1914. As these figures include about 1,500,000 Jews, we must reckon the total Slavic immigration to the United States from 1881 to 1914 at about 6,000,000. Ranked in order of numerical importance, they were Poles, Slovaks, Croatians, Ruthenians, Czechs, Bulgarians, Serbians, Russians, and Dalmatians. Except for the Russians, they were all oppressed subjects of a dominant nationality; 95 per cent of them were peasants only a generation or two removed from serfdom. Exploited by landlords, they were poor, ignorant, and, like the Italians, were one-fourth to one-half illiterate.

The Jews. Nearly 2,000,000 Jews entered the United States in the thirty-four years from 1881 to 1915. The great bulk of them came from Russian Poland or Russia, about one fourth from Austria-Hungary, and a few from Rumania. The reasons for this great exodus, paralleled only by the movement of the Jewish people at the time of the destruction of Jerusalem and the great dispersion, are not hard to find.

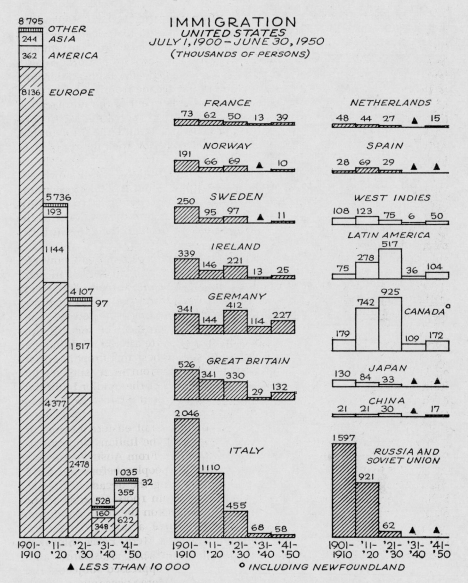

IMMIGRATION
UNITED STATES
JULY 1, 1900 – JUNE 30, 1950
(THOUSANDS OF PERSONS)

8 795 OTHER
244 ASIA
362 AMERICA
8136 EUROPE

5 736
193
1 144

4 107
97
1 517

4 377

2478

1 035
32
528
355
160
348 622

1901- '11- '21- '31- '41-
1910 '20 '30 '40 '50

FRANCE
73 62 50 13 39

NORWAY
191 66 69 ▲ 10

SWEDEN
250 95 97 ▲ 11

IRELAND
339 146 221 13 25

GERMANY
341 144 412 114 227

GREAT BRITAIN
526 341 330 29 132

ITALY
2 046 1110 455 68 58

1901- '11- '21- '31- '41-
1910 '20 '30 '40 '50

NETHERLANDS
48 44 27 ▲ 15

SPAIN
28 69 29 ▲ ▲

WEST INDIES
108 123 75 6 50

LATIN AMERICA
75 278 517 36 104

742 925 CANADA°
179 109 172

JAPAN
130 84 33 ▲ ▲

CHINA
21 21 30 ▲ 17

RUSSIA AND
SOVIET UNION
1597 921 62 ▲ ▲

1901- '11- '21- '31- '41-
1910 '20 '30 '40 '50

▲ LESS THAN 10 000   ° INCLUDING NEWFOUNDLAND

Most of the Jews had congregated in Poland during the Middle Ages because tolerant Polish kings welcomed them. Russia acquired the provinces in which the Jews were concentrated when Poland was partitioned in the eighteenth century, and the czarist government embarked upon a long and deliberate policy of persecution after 1881. Jews were forbidden to live beyond the "pale of settlement," that is to say, their original area of domicile in the western provinces. Exceptions were made in favor of those in certain occupations, but educational and other forms of discrimination reduced the numbers who could avail themselves of this privilege. Although forced to serve in the army, they could not become officers. Subjected to numerous and heavy taxes, they could never aspire to political office.

Thus the four scourges—poverty, militarism, religious persecution, and political tyranny—were in varying degrees responsible for the willingness of Italians, Slavs, and Jews to embark upon the long journey to the New World. All authorities agree, however, that the forces drawing immigrants to America—the lure of new opportunities, propaganda of steamship companies, and tall tales of recruiting agents—were more powerful than the forces driving them from their homelands. Moreover, most of the "new" immigration was made in direct response to the need for unskilled labor in the United States and was stimulated by agents of employment bureaus working closely with railroad and industrial employers.

Irish immigrants had supplied a large proportion of the unskilled laborers for work on canals and railroads and in mines and steel mills from 1846 to about 1890. As the Irish gradually moved up the economic and social ladder and the numbers of Irish immigrants declined, the Slavs and Italians followed in their footsteps and did the work that they had previously done. Only one sixth of the Italians, 3 to 5 per cent of the Ruthenians, Croatians, Rumanians, and Slovaks, and 8 to 10 per cent of the Magyars and Poles were skilled workers when they came to the United States. Invariably they went to the industrial areas of the East and Middle West and found employment on railroads, in textile factories in New England, in steel mills in Pittsburgh and Chicago, in midwestern stockyards, and in coal mines from Pennsylvania to Colorado. By 1914 they constituted the bulk of the working force in the basic industries. The Jews were as poor as other eastern European immigrants, but they brought with them a high degree of skill and experience in the trades. They congregated in the garment sweatshops of New York, Chicago, and other large cities mainly because they found Jewish employers in the clothing industry.

13.   The Social Impact of the New Immigration

The fact that the American society absorbed this transfusion of different national strains without violent reactions was testimony to its growing maturity and adaptability. Yet it was everywhere evident that the processes of social assimilation, which had on the whole worked admirably among the Germans, Irish, and Scandinavians, practically ceased to operate among the newer immigrants. Older Americans viewed them suspiciously and thought that they were an inferior people, incapable of understanding American ideals.

This hostility was evidenced in the formation in 1887 of the American Protective Association, an anti-Catholic organization much like the Know-Nothing party of the 1850's, and in the spreading fear that the "new" immigration would undermine Anglo-American institutions and eventually dilute the old American racial stock. It was reflected, also, in the absence of any governmental effort to protect the immigrant from exploitation and thievery. But the worst aspect of the record was the exploitation of these immigrants by the railroads and industries. Surveying the American scene in 1915, the Commission on Industrial Relations noted that two thirds of immigrant families lived at a subsistence level or below.

All foreigners, regardless of race, nationality, or physical and moral condition, could enter the United States before 1882. In that year the first general federal immigration act was passed, and the process of restriction was begun when, at the insistence of Californians, Chinese were excluded for ten years. The Chinese Exclusion Act was re-enacted from time to time and made permanent in 1902. No sooner had the fears of Californians been quieted regarding the prospect of a Chinese inundation than another and more alarming prospect arose—the specter of an invasion of the state by Japanese workers and farmers. There were only 2,000 Japanese subjects in the United States in 1890, but two decades later their number had increased to 110,000. A powerful and well-organized agitation for exclusion of the Japanese led in 1907 to the negotiation of an agreement between the American and Japanese governments that virtually ended Japanese immigration to the continental United States.

Thus almost complete exclusion of Orientals had been accomplished by 1907. Moreover, the doors had been shut against paupers, the sick and diseased, polygamists, prostitutes, contract laborers, anarchists, and convicts. By this time, however, the demand for a severe restriction, if not outright exclusion, of most European immigrants was mounting on all sides. Organized labor, for example, asserted that heavy immigration depressed wages and impeded the progress of unionization; and this assertion was confirmed by the federal Immigration Commission appointed in 1907. The weapon that the exclusionists advocated at this time was a literacy test. President Cleveland had vetoed a bill imposing such a test in 1897. Such a measure passed Congress in 1913 and again in 1915 only to be nullified by the vetoes of Presidents Taft and Wilson. The exclusionists in Congress finally mustered sufficient strength in January 1917 to pass an immigration bill imposing the literacy test over Wilson's veto. Thus the open door to America—for centuries the gateway of opportunity for countless millions—was partially closed.

14. *American Negroes During the Progressive Era*

The gloomiest aspect of the American social scene during the first two decades of the twentieth century was the condition of Negroes. Foreign observers could never cease to wonder how Americans could boast of democracy while denying essential democratic privileges to one tenth of the population. The great paradox was not resolved during the progressive period. In fact, the social and political status of Negroes by and large worsened, while their economic status only slightly improved.

Optimists, to be sure, could point to a few signs of progress since 1865. Demonstrating a passion for education in the face of incredible obstacles, Negroes had reduced their illiteracy rate from 95 per cent in 1865 to 44.5 per cent in 1900. And even greater progress was made during the decades 1900–20. The illiteracy rate among Negroes ten years of age and over declined from 30.4 per cent in 1910 to 22.9 per cent in 1920.

The Negro's progress toward education had been accomplished before 1900 with the help of northern philanthropists and churches and only slightly with the aid of the southern states. After 1900, however, there was an increasing awareness throughout the white South, especially in the border states, of the need for greater public aid to Negro education. Even so, no southern state by the end of the World War was making a serious effort to provide adequate or anywhere near equal educational opportunities for its Negro youth. In 1910, for example, there were only 141 Negro high schools, with a total of 8,251 pupils, in all the states from Maryland to Texas.

Meanwhile, social and political forces had been at work in the South to make the progressive era a time of profound discouragement for Negroes. For one thing, the Civil War and Reconstruction had not altered southern racial concepts or southern determination to keep Negroes in a subordinate status. For another, slavery had given way to sharecropping, so that the vast majority of Negroes found, not economic freedom, but merely another form of bondage after 1865. As a substitute for the social controls of slavery, which went by the board in 1865, the southern whites after Reconstruction had substituted a legal caste system that prohibited intermarriage and established a severe pattern of segregation for schools, public places, and transportation facilities. Informal race controls were tightened, and many a Negro suffered the extreme penalty for violating the rules of racial etiquette. Finally, many southern states in the late 1870's and early 1880's began gradually to make voting by Negroes difficult. The southern legislatures acted cautiously in this regard, however, and large numbers of Negroes voted in many southern states as late as the 1890's.

A genuine political division among southern white voters occurred for the first time since 1860 during the Populist revolt, and both Democrats and Populists bid for Negro votes. This resurgence of Negro political activity frightened both agrarian and conservative Southerners and led them to conclude that the Negro must be removed forever as a participant in southern political life. Mississippi had shown the way to disfranchise the great mass of Negro voters in 1890—by use of a literacy test, poll tax, provisions requiring an understanding of the Constitution, and long residence requirements for registration—without openly violating the Fifteenth Amendment. Then, as an aftermath of the revival of Negro political activity during the Populist upsurge, all the southern states except Maryland, Tennessee, and Kentucky disfranchised Negro voters from 1895 to 1907.

The one man who, more than any other person, brought peace between the races in the South after this bloody decade of conflict was Booker T.

Washington. His rise to leadership of the Negro people was one of the most dramatic episodes in the history of the United States. Born a slave in Franklin County, Virginia, in 1856 and educated at Hampton Institute in his native state, Washington founded Tuskegee Institute in Alabama in 1881 as a school where Negro boys and girls might learn to become useful members of southern communities as teachers, farmers, and tradesmen. Washington was recognized as the pre-eminent spokesman of American Negroes by 1895. Therefore, it came as something of an official pronouncement when, at the height of the disfranchisement movement, he counseled southern Negroes to eschew politics and learn to become good citizens. Whites all over the country quickly seized upon his program of vocational education and political quiescence for southern Negroes as a formula for racial peace.

This so-called Washington Compromise found favor especially among conservative Southerners and won their support for Negro education. But it did not operate to diminish the anti-Negro passions of the southern masses. The Populist revolt brought to the fore a new leadership of violent men. Some, like Cole L. Blease of South Carolina, were sheer demagogues; others, like Hoke Smith of Georgia, had many qualities of statesmanship. All these new leaders, however, rose to power on a wave of anti-Negroism that found expression in violence in many forms. The last sixteen years of the nineteenth century had witnessed more than 2,500 lynchings, and the century had ended with a race riot in Wilmington, North Carolina, the climax of the disfranchisement campaign in that state. This was followed in the twentieth century by other riots, the worst of which occurred in Atlanta in September 1906. Moreover, lynching continued in the twentieth century to be an important aspect of race control, as more than 1,100 Negroes fell victims, from 1900 to 1914, to mobs that often discarded the rope for the faggot.

To Negroes, however, the most frightening development of this period was the spread of southern racial concepts and techniques of violence to the North and Middle West. Southern orators like Benjamin R. Tillman of South Carolina carried the message of white supremacy to northern audiences and stimulated latent prejudices. The most effective southern propagandist was Thomas Dixon, an erstwhile Baptist minister of North Carolina, whose novels, *The Leopard's Spots* (1902) and *The Clansman* (1905), were calculated to arouse the basest racial prejudices of white readers and sold by the hundreds of thousands. *The Clansman* was made into a motion picture, "The Birth of a Nation," in 1915, and was a powerful factor in stimulating race riots in the North and Middle West during and after the First World War. These will be related in a later chapter.

It is small wonder, then, that the progressive era was a drear period for Negroes ambitious for the advancement of their race. There was, however, one ray of hope: the development of an aggressive and advanced leadership among both races. Foremost among the militant Negroes was a young scholar, William E. B. Du Bois, a native of Massachusetts with a doctor's degree in history from Harvard University. Du Bois and a small group of Negro intellectuals met at Niagara Falls, Canada, in June 1905, adopted a platform demanding political and economic equality for black men, and announced their determination to begin a new war for emancipation. Meeting the following year at Harpers Ferry, West Virginia, the site of John Brown's raid, the Niagara Movement, as the Du Bois group was called, reiterated its resolves and renewed its courage.

Progressives and champions of social justice in the North at first paid scant attention to the Niagara rebels. Then, an anti-Negro riot occurred in Springfield, Illinois, in August 1908, within half a mile of Lincoln's home, and humanitarians in the North at last awoke to the imminent threat of the southernizing of their section. The young Negro rebels and a distinguished group of white educators, clergymen, editors, and social workers met in New York City on Lincoln's birthday in 1909 and organized the National Association for the Advancement of Colored People. It was pledged to work for the abolition of all forced segregation, equal justice for Negroes, and enlarged educational opportunities for Negro children. The only Negro official of the NAACP during its formative period was Du Bois, who was director of publicity and research and editor of the Association's monthly magazine *The Crisis*. But the selection of Du Bois as official spokesman signified that the revolt against the Washington Compromise had at last found powerful support among progressives in the North and held promise for the day when the northern people would rediscover their equalitarian heritage.

15. *The Growth of American Education*

The federal Commissioner of Education could boast at the turn of the century of the steady development of educational institutions since 1890 and of an increase of 19.2 per cent in the numbers of children enrolled in public and private schools and institutions of higher learning. These general national statistics, however, obscure the details of the educational picture in the various regions. Progress in the North and Midwest, for example, had been even more substantial than they would indicate. On the other hand, the situation in the South in 1900 was so gloomy that leaders of the region wondered if there were any hope at all. Southern children on an average received three years of public schooling, as compared with an average of nearly seven years for children in the North. Southern states spent an average of $9.72 per pupil in 1900, as compared with an expenditure of $20.85 per pupil in the north central states. To use the words of a contemporary southern educator, the situation in his region was "sad beyond expression."

The general educational picture had improved perceptibly by the end of the First World War, but the most significant advances are not revealed by general statistics. To begin with, the growth of kindergartens since 1900 had evidenced the expanding influence in America of the champions of the child of preschool age. Only about 250 cities had established kindergartens in 1900. By 1920, on the other hand, there were almost 8,000 separate kindergartens, with 511,000 children enrolled. Even more important was the remarkable expansion of public high schools from 1900 to 1920. There were about 6,000 public high schools in the United States, with 500,000 pupils, in 1900. Twenty years later there were over 14,000, with some 2,000,000 students enrolled.

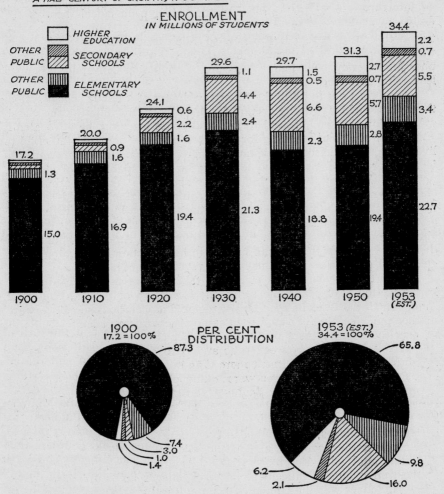

AMERICAN PUBLIC EDUCATION:
A HALF CENTURY OF GROWTH, 1900-1953

.ENROLLMENT
IN MILLIONS OF STUDENTS

HIGHER EDUCATION
OTHER PUBLIC — SECONDARY SCHOOLS
OTHER PUBLIC — ELEMENTARY SCHOOLS

PER CENT DISTRIBUTION

1900 17.2 = 100%
87.3
7.4
3.0
1.0
1.4

1953 (EST.) 34.4 = 100%
65.8
9.8
16.0
2.1
6.2

The most important educational revolution in this period occurred in the South. Under the spur of publicists like Walter H. Page and philanthropic agencies like the Southern Education Board, political leaders launched virtual crusades for education in the southern states. The result was a mass awakening from 1902 to about 1910, comparable to the educational revival that swept through the North and Middle West before the Civil War. In the short span of a decade, appropriations for school purposes by the southern states doubled, enrollment of white children increased almost a third, and average length of the school term lengthened from five to six months. Southern illiteracy, moreover, declined from 11.8 per cent of the native whites in 1900 to about 5.5 per cent in 1920, and from 44.5 per cent of the Negroes ten years of age or older to about 22.9 per cent.

A revolution in the theory and practice of education was also getting under way at this same time. Educational psychologists and experimentalists were already beginning to undermine older pedagogical theories and were stimulating a new scientific attitude toward children even as the twentieth century opened. The new so-called progressive theories gained wider acceptance in the years before the war, especially after the philosopher John Dewey, a Vermonter teaching at Columbia University, assumed leadership of the movement.

Dewey set out to fulfill the American dream of a public school system that was the chief training ground for democracy. Repudiating the classical tradition that emphasized formal and polite learning, he advocated a curriculum that had meaning for an urban age and prepared the child to live in a democratic society. He taught, moreover, that curriculum and subject matter should be adapted to the needs and capabilities of children, not of adults; that the learning process should be centered around the child's own experiences; and that "learning by doing" should supplant memorization of data that had no meaning to the child. His theories were assailed by traditionalists and sometimes violently abused by his own disciples. Even so, Dewey left such a deep imprint on American educational theory and practice that he can be said to have accomplished, almost singlehanded, one of the significant cultural revolutions of his time.

Important developments were also taking place in higher education in the United States. For one thing, the formation of the Association of American Universities in 1900 and of regional associations soon afterward marked the beginning of a concerted campaign to raise academic standards all over the country. As a result, the number of colleges and universities increased only slightly between 1900 and 1920, from 977 to 1,041, at the same time that their enrollment more than doubled from 238,000 to 598,000. Other important changes were taking place in this field: enormous improvement in facilities for graduate and specialized training; a significant development of technical education and growth of private institutions like the Massachusetts Institute of Technology and state engineering and agricultural colleges; new methods of teaching; expansion of state aid to public universities, colleges, and junior colleges; and the beginning of an important adult education movement. All Americans in 1920 could rejoice in the tremendous advancement of their colleges and universities since 1897. No longer was the United States a cultural appendage of Europe in the field of higher learning. No longer did Americans have to go to Germany for graduate training. In fact, the day was not far distant when American scholarship could claim pre-eminence in many fields.

16. *Religious Institutions and Movements*

The most important social phenomenon of the prewar period was the survival of religion after the violent storms of the last quarter of the nineteenth century. The growth of skepticism, the war between Darwinists and fundamentalists, and the spread of new philosophies like Marxian scientific materialism and social Darwinism had so promoted the growth of secularism that probably a large majority of American intellectuals by 1920 would have disavowed Christian faith. Yet Christian ethics not only survived but found wider acceptance and fuller meaning. American Protestantism largely abandoned fundamentalism and rediscovered the ancient Christian message of social justice, while the Roman Catholic Church expanded its ministry to the poor.

The years before the taking of the religious census in 1916 were a period of substantial growth in numbers, influence, and wealth for all religious groups. All told, Protestant bodies enrolled 26,205,039 members in 1916, as compared with 20,857,303 in 1906; and among Protestant denominations the Baptist and Methodist bodies were easily the most numerous and powerful. But the most spectacular religious development during the period 1890–1916 was the tremendous growth of the Roman Catholic Church in the United States, the result chiefly of the "new" immigration. This Church grew from 7,343,186 members in 1890 to 15,721,815 in 1916, for a gain of 114.1 per cent. Its greatest expansion occurred, however, before 1906. From 1906 to 1916, when Protestant bodies increased about 23 per cent, the Catholic Church grew by only 10.6 per cent.

During its period of rapid growth the Roman Catholic Church was neither torn by internal dissensions nor concerned with theological disputes. There was a movement in the late nineteenth century to "Americanize" the Catholic Church in the United States by bringing it into close co-operation with other religious groups. This effort was ended by Pope Leo XIII's firm stand in 1899 in behalf of traditional practice. Any trend toward modernism in the Church, moreover, was firmly suppressed by Pope Pius X in 1907. Thereafter, modernism simply did not exist in American Catholicism.

The decision to adhere to traditional Catholic doctrines and practices did not, however, signify any diminution of the social conscience of the Catholic Church. Catholic bishops and priests were shepherds of most of the "new" immigrants and a large portion of the submerged urban masses; they well knew what poverty and suffering were. James Cardinal Gibbons of Baltimore had been one of the leading champions of the Knights of Labor during the 1880's. His attitude was probably decisive in the issuance in 1891 of Pope Leo XIII's encyclical *Rerum Novarum,* one of the most important assertions of the rights of labor. Catholic laymen and priests like Father John A. Ryan of the Catholic University of America figured prominently in the twentieth-century movement for adoption of social and economic legislation.

For American Protestantism, on the other hand, the progressive era was a time of change on all sides. That the old divisive forces that had kept Protestant groups separated were still at work was evidenced by the steady offshooting of new sects from parent bodies. The most notable of these new movements was Christian Science, founded around the turn of the century by a remarkable Bostonian, Mrs. Mary Baker Eddy. She denied the existence of death, evil, or the material world, and worked out a new science from the Scriptures by asserting that disease did not exist. Christian Science had gained almost 100,000 adherents by the First World War and was growing rapidly. The most numerous of the new sects, however, were the various holiness, or pentecostal, bodies, most of which came out of Methodism and taught a primitive fundamentalism.

Furthermore, Protestantism was still suffering the effects of the profound division in its ranks between traditionalists, who adhered steadfastly to ancient creeds and confessions, and modernists, who ranged theologically all the way from liberal orthodoxy to outright humanism, but who usually emphasized the social mission of the church at the expense of doctrine. There could be no doubt that modernists were in the ascendancy from 1900 to 1920. The northern Presbyterian Church preserved the purity of its doctrines at the cost of expelling several of its most distinguished ministers and of losing control of its leading seminary, Union, in New York City. The Lutherans generally remained impervious to the new intellectual currents. But northern Methodists, northern Baptists, and Congregationalists were by and large captured by the modernist clergy.

In spite of these divisive forces, there were numerous signs during the first years of the twentieth century that forces drawing Protestant bodies together were at last beginning to prevail. Even the great division between traditionalists and modernists was a cohesive force, since it cut across denominational barriers and drew men together on one side or the other. Within the denominations, too, unifying forces gathered strength. The union of the northern Presbyterian and Cumberland Presbyterian bodies in 1906, for example, healed an old wound in the ecclesiastical body. Northern Baptist groups gradually came together in close co-operation, while the three principal Methodist bodies set under way a movement for unification that would come to fruition years later.

Among the denominations, moreover, subordination of minor theological differences and co-operation on various levels of church activity became the prime objective of Protestant leaders after 1900. Unity came first on the local level, in the formation of city, county, and state federations of churches, and in older organizations like the Young Men's Christian Association, the Young Women's Christian Association, the International Sunday School Association, and the American Bible Society. The dream of the champions of Protestant unity was finally realized in 1908, with the formation of the Federal Council of Churches of Christ in America. Spokesmen of thirty-three evangelical bodies and 17,000,000 members sharing common beliefs and purposes united to proclaim their faith in the ecumenical church.

The launching of the Federal Council in 1908 also signified the triumph in American Protestantism of the social gospel, a movement to revitalize the church and proclaim Christianity's message to an industrial society. It was not the first time that Protestants in America had set out to reform society. There had always been a strong, socially minded left wing of Protestantism in America, at least since the advent of Methodism in the eighteenth century. By 1865 the church had subdued the older frontier areas and overcome slavery, only to be confronted afterward by a host of new and less obvious challenges—social Darwinism, aggressive materialism, and new forms of bondage.

Perhaps a majority of urban Protestant churches during the Gilded Age fell under the control of businessmen concerned mainly with laying up treasures on earth. Perhaps their ministers glorified the captains of industry as fervently as did the college professors and editors of the day. Yet the years from 1870 to 1890 were a time also of the awakening of the social consciousness of Protestantism. An increasing number of clergymen began to measure the competitive, exploitative *Zeitgeist* by the Christian standard and found the new values wanting. Some of these pioneers found an answer in Christian Socialism; others rejected socialism but sought to resurrect the old Christian doctrine of brotherhood. In any event, a significant articulation of social Christianity emerged out of the widespread discussion of the 1870's and 1880's. It was evident by 1890 that Protestantism was changing, that it was becoming less other-worldly in outlook and beginning to view salvation in social and ethical, as well as in theological, terms.

The years from 1890 to 1920 saw the social gospel come of age. The 1890's witnessed wholesale acceptance of the theory of evolution by liberal theologians. The consequent accommodation of religion to Darwinism was accompanied by the elevation of three ancient Christian beliefs to new prominence in American religious thought. They were, first, the conviction that God is everywhere present and works through human institutions; second, belief in the fatherhood of God and the brotherhood of man; third, the view that the Kingdom of God is here now, and that the chief duty of the Church is the extension of that Kingdom. Together, these beliefs constituted a frame of reference and a point of departure for the proponents of social Christianity.

The host of social gospel preachers increased and their good works multiplied from 1890 to the end of the First World War, until it seemed that urban Protestantism had truly been transformed. At the same time, Christian Socialism became respectable and commanded the sympathy, if not the allegiance, of an increasing number of clergymen. The Salvation Army, founded by William Booth in London in 1878, spread to the United States in 1880 and, after 1890, expanded its relief and rehabilitation work among the outcasts of society. So-called institutional churches, which sponsored hospitals, missions, social and relief agencies, and boys' and girls' clubs, spread through the great cities. Finally, most of the major denominations officially recognized their social mission around 1900 by establishing commissions of social service.

Among the champions of the social gospel one man emerged as leader and spokesman—Walter Rauschenbusch, for many years professor of church history at Rochester Theological Seminary. A socialist, Rauschenbusch reserved his severest criticism for industrial capitalism, a "mammonistic organization with which Christianity can never be content." For the law of competition he proposed to substitute co-operation, collectivism, and democracy, and thus to hasten the consummation of the Kingdom of God on earth. The publication of Rauschenbusch's eloquent *Christianity and the Social Crisis* in 1907 immediately established him as the major prophet of the social gospel movement.

A year after the publication of *Christianity and the Social Crisis* the social gospel achieved fulfillment in the formation of the Federal Council of Churches, for the movement for Protestant unity had from the beginning stemmed more from social action impulses than from any desire to achieve doctrinal accord. The Council at its first meeting in Philadelphia adopted a ringing manifesto, "The Church and Modern Industry," placing official Protestantism squarely behind the movement to end exploitative capitalism through social welfare legislation and the strengthening of labor unions.

For all its power and commanding influence, the social gospel movement was a development in urban Protestantism. It was in the campaign to end the liquor traffic that urban and rural Protestants found a common outlet for mutual social energies and impulses. The later excesses of the prohibitionists and their failure to change the habits of a nation should not obscure the fact that in the beginning, at least, the temperance and prohibition movements were responses to one of the major social challenges of the time.

The crusade against Demon Rum was a child of the humanitarian awakening of the 1840's and 1850's and had culminated in the adoption of prohibition by many northern and midwestern states by 1861. The movement, however, lost its strength during the Civil War; most states repealed their prohibition laws; and it seemed that the experiment had failed. But the liquor problem grew to menacing proportions between 1860 and 1880, as investment in the liquor business increased 700 per cent, saloons multiplied in the cities, and intemperance increased everywhere. Moreover, liquor interests co-operated with vice rings and corrupt politicians, so that saloons were often fronts for houses of prostitution, and liquor dealers' associations and brewers worked hand in glove with city bosses.

The answer of the aroused church membership to this, as they thought, dire threat to home and family was immediate and emphatic. The Protestant churches, containing most of the nondrinking population, went directly into politics in the 1880's and 1890's. On the local level they smashed saloons and elected city councils opposed to the liquor dealers. On the county and state levels they organized alliances and leagues to work for local option and state-wide prohibition. Leadership in the temperance agitation in the North and Middle West was taken by the Methodists, often more socially alert than other Protestant groups. In the South, Methodists and Baptists joined hands in the movement.

The Women's Christian Temperance Union, founded by Frances Willard in 1874, was the first successful attempt to marshal the ranks of Protestantism against the liquor traffic. But effective organization of church forces on a national scale came only in 1893, with the formation of the Anti-Saloon League at Oberlin, Ohio. Methodist, Baptist, Presbyterian, and Congregational churches went into politics under the League's aegis with such determination that the division between church and state almost ceased to exist in many southern and midwestern states. The Leagues—with their general superintendents, organizers, and hosts of speakers—became the most powerful factors in politics in many states.

The goal of Anti-Saloon leaders was at first local option or state-wide prohibition. Three fourths of the American people lived in dry counties by 1917, while two thirds of the states had adopted prohibition. As the movement gained power, however, it assumed more and more the character of a religious crusade. The Anti-Saloon leaders lost sight of their original objective after 1913 and began to agitate for national prohibition by constitutional amendment. The powerful Anti-Saloon lobby in Washington obtained passage in 1913 of the Webb-Kenyon Act, which prohibited transportation of alcoholic beverages into dry states. Three years later a prohibition amendment received a majority vote, though not the necessary two thirds, in both houses of Congress. When Congress imposed prohibition on the District of Columbia in 1917, it was evident that the day was not far distant when Protestantism's crusade would culminate in nation-wide prohibition by federal amendment.

17. *The Power of the Press*

That other agency of social education, the press, grew more powerful from 1897 to 1920 and wielded greater influence among the masses of people than ever before. Indeed, one cannot recount the history of the progressive awakening without acknowledging that newspapers and magazines were in good measure responsible for generating the reform movement. And this was true because American journalism was literally transformed and re-created, because newspapers and magazines ceased to serve only the educated middle and upper classes and became a vital force in the lives of the masses.

This transformation occurred, not accidentally, but because newspaper publishers adopted new techniques to increase circulation and influence. The pioneer was Joseph Pulitzer, a Hungarian immigrant, who settled in St. Louis in 1865 and soon became active in politics and journalism. Pulitzer purchased the bankrupt *St. Louis Dispatch* in 1878 and made it a going concern. He bought the New York *World* from Jay Gould in 1883 and moved to the great metropolis. Pulitzer had soon made the *World* the first modern American newspaper. Its news coverage was generally excellent and its aggressive support of labor and reform causes made it the commanding progressive spokesman in the East. Even more important in the *World's* rise was the fact that its cartoons, features, stories, and the like made it attractive to the mass of readers.

The most spectacular development in American journalism around the turn of the century was the entry of William Randolph Hearst into the Fourth Estate. He bought the New York *Journal* in 1895 and launched a new and violent experiment in journalistic techniques. Pulitzer had made the *World* acceptable to the masses by giving them illustrations, crusades, and a modicum of sensationalism. Hearst, however, used all the techniques of yellow journalism and proved that they would pay handsomely. Pulitzer struck back by adopting Hearst's methods, and the two publishers engaged in a mad rivalry for circulation and power from 1896 to 1898. They stirred American passions against Spain, then attempting to suppress a rebellion in Cuba, to fever pitch; and they helped to drive an unwilling President to war in order to increase their circulations. After the war, however, Pulitzer repented, abandoned yellow journalism to its master, and made the *World* a model liberal, if overly partisan, newspaper.

Fortunately for the American people, the great majority of publishers followed Pulitzer rather than Hearst after 1900. Every city had its little New York *World* by 1920, and American journalism had advanced to a new level of usefulness. The Associated Press, reorganized in 1900, and the United Press, the second of its name, formed in 1907, furnished an abundance of reliable domestic and foreign news. Sunday editions added magazine sections, cartoons, and, in a few cases, book review sections, while special columns by humorists and feature writers provided entertainment.

Metropolitan dailies grew into big businesses with the enormous growth of circulation after 1900. Advertising was the main source of publishing revenue, to be sure; but as advertising followed circulation the large newspapers attained a position of security and independence in the business world that they had never known before. There is no convincing evidence that prosperity caused newspaper publishers to align themselves on the side of big business and special interests. Practically all newspapers, except the Hearst chain, whether conservative or progressive in editorial policy, tried honestly and accurately to report the news.

Along with growing circulation and wealth went consolidation and the new phenomenon of chains of newspapers under the control of single owners. The most important of these chains was the Hearst press, consisting of two magazines and nine newspapers in 1914. An even larger, if less powerful, consolidation was effected by E. W. Scripps, who by 1914 controlled thirty-four dailies, mainly in smaller cities. Another important entrepreneur was Frank A. Munsey, who in 1908 owned five large newspapers in Boston, New York, Philadelphia, Baltimore, and Washington.

All these same trends were operating to transform weekly and monthly magazines from journals of pure literature and sophisticated opinion into mass media of new ideas and originators of new movements. Technological improvements in printing made mass production of magazines possible, and this in turn stimulated the beginning in the 1890's of a number of periodicals cheap in price but often high in quality. By 1905, for example, *Munsey's Magazine, McClure's Magazine, Cosmopolitan, Collier's, Saturday Evening Post*, and *Everybody's* enjoyed circulations in the hundreds of thousands or millions. Most of these magazines became outlets for the reform literature of the early progressive period. On the other hand, older literary journals like *Century, Scribner's, North American Review*, and *Harper's* lost heavily in circulation and maintained a precarious existence. And the three leading journals of opinion, *The Nation, The New Republic*, and the Chicago *Public*, were kept alive only by generous subsidies.

The glaring contrast between the wealth of popular journals and the penury of journals of literature and comment did not signify literary decadence. On the contrary, it only emphasized the fact that middle-class Americans by 1914 were buying and reading magazines that satisfied their longing for excitement, adventure, and larger understanding of political and economic developments of the time.

18. *Main Trends in Literature*

Regenerative forces combined between 1897 and the First World War to produce a literary flowering in the United States and to lay foundations for new trends in American creative writing. It was a productive and fertile period. Traditionalism survived under new forms; a new literary genre, naturalism, reached its apogee; and literary pre-eminence passed from the East to the Middle West and, to a lesser degree, to the South.

The Victorian giants were either dead or dying by the turn of the century. Henry James, who had discovered reality in the drawing room, had escaped to the more congenial British milieu. His creative energies were almost spent by 1900. William Dean Howells lived on until 1920, a friend of many young authors; but his great work was also done. Mark Twain, the novelist of American boyhood, survived like a ghost from the nineteenth-century past until 1910. His only significant work after 1900 was *The Mysterious Stranger*, published posthumously.

For all their realism, authors like James and Howells lived in a moral universe. Realism to them meant probing into human character and mirroring life as they found it. Their subjects may have been drab or driven by greed, but they were above all else human beings with will, spirit, and purpose. Their work was taken up in the early twentieth century by a goodly company—Ellen Glasgow of Virginia, Willa Cather of Nebraska, Dorothy Canfield of Kansas and Vermont, Ole Rølvaag of Minnesota, and Edith Wharton of New York. They depicted life in the new South, the Middle West, or in New York drawing-room society in all its stark drabness, irony, and tragedy. As realists, however, they also knew the other side of the picture. And in the end they glorified the human spirit, magnified the struggle against evil, and thus carried on the humane tradition.

Meanwhile, a new literary movement, naturalism, was beginning in the 1890's to make its first impression on American writers. The leading French naturalist, Émile Zola, enunciated the philosophy of the new school. The writer, he said, must study human nature as the biologist studies the animal world and describe sheerly natural phenomena without compassion and without applying moral criteria. It was a discipline too strong for most Americans, and early so-called naturalists like Jack London, Frank Norris, Hamlin Garland, Ambrose Bierce, and Stephen Crane were more harsh realists than true disciples of Zola.

The publication in 1900 of Theodore Dreiser's *Sister Carrie*, however, marked a real turning point in American literary history. Here was a genuine effort to discover a new view of humanity based upon the findings of science, to discern a theory of existence divorced from religious beliefs. Dreiser found an answer to the search for truth in biology. Man is an animal driven by instincts to struggle for survival in an impersonal universe. In his striving for wealth, power, or sexual satisfaction, he reverts to his true animal nature, and the façade of civilization falls away. Social forces, moreover, are impersonal and drive the weak, who cannot outwardly defy social conventions, to crime and violence.

The American public was not yet ready for such strong literary fare, and Dreiser bided his time without compromising his integrity. When he published *Jennie Gerhardt* in 1911 he won, not popular acclaim, but acceptance by a wide circle of intellectuals. Dreiser's leadership of the naturalistic school was firmly secured in his publication of *The Financier* in 1912 and *The Titan* in 1914. Although naturalism had not become an obsession among American writers by 1914, it clearly commanded the allegiance of a majority of serious young writers. The day could not be far distant when it would dominate the ethos of American literature.

The years before the First World War witnessed, too, a remarkable outburst of poetic creativity. As the Victorian era gave way to the modern age, the genteel tradition survived in a simpler form; new poetic forms emerged; and poetic themes varied from the very abstruse to the homely and common aspect of life. But, withal, a real renaissance occurred, and America recovered her poetic voice.

The two poetic giants of the early years of the twentieth century, William Vaughan Moody and Edwin Arlington Robinson, were both traditionalists who wrote in the genteel manner. Moody, a professor at the University of Chicago, was an idealist outraged by the social and economic injustices of his time and by his country's venture into imperialism. His "Ode in Time of Hesitation" (1900) and "Gloucester Moors" and "On a Soldier Fallen in the Philippines," both published in 1901, were prophetic expressions of American social consciousness. Robinson, however, dealt with a simpler and more abiding theme—the individual's search for God and truth in darkness and suffering. Life and human destiny remained mysterious to Robinson; he could not fathom their secrets. Yet in the "black and awful chaos of the night," he felt "the coming glory of the Light." His first collected works, *Children of the Night,* appeared in 1897. *The Town Down the River,* published in 1910, and *The Man Against the Sky,* published in 1916, established him as the pre-eminent man of letters among a remarkable generation of poets and novelists.

Robinson was in some respects a latter-day Puritan, in others, a Transcendentalist. Such could not, however, be said of a new school of poets of the people. They came upon the literary horizon in 1912 with the publication in Chicago of *The Lyric Years,* an anthology of contemporary verse, and the printing of the first issue of *Poetry: A Magazine of Verse.* The editor of *Poetry,* Harriet Monroe, certain that traditionalism was passing, urged poets to write about contemporary life. The Chicago poets, Vachel Lindsay, Edgar Lee Masters, and Carl Sandburg, replied enthusiastically. Lindsay's "General William Booth Enters into Heaven," published in the first issue of *Poetry,* marked the beginning of his ecstatic glorification of the common people and their destiny. Masters, a Chicago lawyer who wrote poetry as an avocation, laid bare the alleged sham and moral shabbiness of small-town America in *Spoon River Anthology,* published in 1915. On the other hand, Sandburg, whose first volume appeared in 1916, magnified Chicago, the roaring, brawling butcher and steel-maker of the world. Another poet of the common people, Robert Frost, was not a Chicagoan. He was the bard of the farmers and workers of New England, and his quiet verse mirrored the staid New Hampshire countryside. The publication of his *A Boy's Will* in 1913 and *North of Boston* a year later immediately established his eminence among the "new" poets.

At the same time another revolt against the genteel tradition was brewing far to the east, among a group of American and English poets in London. These were so-called imagists, led by Ezra Pound, Amy Lowell, and later T. S. Eliot. They were striving toward a new verse form and new artistic standards. Asserting that the poet's purpose was to re-create impressions caught in the fleeting image, they rejected the metrical form and rhyming as artificial and posing obstacles to the creation of the pure image. Rejecting also romanticism as being the literary expression of a decadent humanistic culture, the imagists sought merely to re-create the impressions of everyday life.

These novelists and poets raised American literature to new eminence and gave it such standing in the western world as it had not enjoyed since the 1840's and 1850's. But none of the truly creative writers of the early twentieth century enjoyed material success or popular acclaim. Except for the few who had independent incomes or other professions, they lived in obscure poverty, like Edward Arlington Robinson, who was rescued by Theodore Roosevelt and given a sinecure in the New York Customs House, or Vachel Lindsay, who earned his bread by touring the country as a vagabond minstrel. Americans were actually reading and buying more books than ever before by the First World War; but the reading public rewarded sentimentalists and romanticists who amused and entertained them without questioning their virtue.

19. *Philosophy and the Arts*

Out of the late nineteenth-century struggle between social Darwinists and idealists emerged an American, William James, who rejected both schools and in so doing founded a philosophical system of his own. Denying the validity of all absolutes and fixed principles, and building upon the ideas of an earlier philosopher, Charles S. Peirce, James conceived a system, pragmatism, in which the truth or value of an idea or act was measured by its workability and consequences. It was a philosophy of ultimate individualism, to be sure, since each man had to establish pragmatic values for himself. It was also a philosophy that easily became the intellectual tool of progressivism, for pragmatism evaluated legislation on a basis of whether it would meet the test of practicability and benefit the greatest numbers.

The task of converting this philosophy into an instrument of progressive change fell to one of James' disciples, John Dewey of Columbia University. Whereas James had emphasized the individual, Dewey emphasized the group and sought to make philosophy an instrument of social action. As he became more and more the social prophet and advocate of a hundred causes, Dewey became less the pragmatist and more the absolutist—a believer in the absolute value of tolerance, experimentation, free expression, and democratic collectivism.

The dissent of one idealist was clearly heard in the years before the war in protest against the relativistic philosophy of James and Dewey. He was Josiah Royce, professor of philosophy at Harvard University, who published his major work, *The Philosophy of Loyalty*, in 1908. To a generation obsessed either with a mechanistic or a pragmatic view of society, Royce asserted the supreme importance of ideals. Measuring the new against the eternal, he chose the eternal and the absolute. What raised man above the level of animal was the ideal of loyalty—of devotion, selflessness, and sacrifice. These were the ideals, he said, that would give impelling quality and sense of direction to democracy.

Although they varied in method and approach, it is significant that the three leading American philosophers of the early twentieth century— James, Dewey, and Royce—all sought to formulate a creed for a democracy that would destroy the paralyzing view that mankind could not work out answers to fundamental problems. They offered hope and confidence for a world then in process of being born.

Achievement in the field of traditional music during the period under discussion was slight, although the growing number of music schools, opera houses, symphony orchestras, and civic music federations evidenced a considerable increase in popular appreciation of classical music. This was the period, also, when Victor Herbert and Sigmund Romberg, who combined the semiclassical form with popular themes, were writing their best operettas and adding dozens of songs to the American repertoire.

But the most important musical development during these years was the creation of a new music for the people: ragtime, the ancestor of modern popular music. With Irving Berlin and George M. Cohan setting the pace, a whole new school of composers burgeoned forth with tunes for musical comedies and the phonograph. The World War added a stimulus. Berlin's "Oh How I Hate to Get Up in the Morning" and Cohan's "Over There," for example, expressed the American spirit of 1917, just as "Dixie" and "The Battle-Hymn of the Republic" had done in 1861 and 1862. Negro musicians, principally in New Orleans, were also experimenting with jazz, a musical form even more rhythmic and dissonant than ragtime. Jazz had just begun its conquest of the nation by 1920.

In American painting, also, there were signs of new vigor and expanding horizons after 1897. Among the leaders of the "American" school of the late nineteenth century, Winslow Homer and Thomas Eakin survived into the twentieth century and continued to shock respectable folk with scenes of the sea and the operating room. They were joined in the early 1900's by George W. Bellows, whose scenes of the boxing ring were as realistic as they were powerful. Two Americans, John Singer Sargent and James M. Whistler, were pre-eminent among the portrait painters of the world.

The future in painting, however, belonged not to the older generation of artists but to young rebellious American followers of the French impressionists and postimpressionists, Van Gogh, Cézanne, Matisse, and Gauguin—modernists who abandoned the "imitation of nature" for painting that reflected the artist's own reactions and conceptions. A small advance guard, including Alfred Henry Maurer, John Marin, and Charles Demuth, studied in France before the First World War and brought the new postimpressionistic concepts home with them. A real turning point in the history of American art occurred in February 1913. The advance guard gathered what modern French and American paintings they could find and displayed them before a shocked public in the New York Armory. From this time forward, at least until the early 1930's, modernism in its many forms would be dominant in American artistic endeavor.

While American painters were thus responding to the dynamic artistic impulses of their time, American sculptors were raising their art to a new height. The leader of the group was Augustus Saint-Gaudens, whose wide variety of statuary, including the haunting figure, "Grief," at the grave of Mrs. Henry Adams, marked him as one of the great artists of his age. And there were other American sculptors who nearly attained Saint-Gaudens' high level of achievement during this period, like Daniel Chester

French, whose tragic figure of the seated Lincoln in the Lincoln Memorial is beloved by millions of Americans.

In the field of architecture, also, Americans demonstrated vitality and a new vision. The Victorian era of the brownstone front, gimcrack house, and "dumbbell" tenement had happily passed by 1900. New housing codes required light, ventilation, and fireproof construction in large apartment houses, and the day of tenement construction was over. In suburbs Victorian styles gave way before a craze for colonial, Dutch, and southern styles. Advanced architects condemned them as archaic, but they were a vast improvement over Victorian architectural chaos. Well before the First World War, moreover, Louis Sullivan, Frank Lloyd Wright, Ernest Wilby, and other pioneers were beginning a movement to give functional and social meaning to architectural forms.

The most notable architectural development of the period was the perfection of the skyscraper, which made possible a virtual revolution in American urban life. The first important work was done by a group of Chicago architects, Le Baron Jenney, Louis Sullivan, Daniel Burnham, and John W. Root, who by 1900 had demonstrated the potential uses to which the steel structure could be put. However, the completion of the Woolworth Building, designed by Cass Gilbert, in New York in 1912 ended a decade in which the eastern metropolis had taken leadership from Chicago in the building of skyscrapers.

CHAPTER

3

Aspects of Economic Development

PRIDE in the nation's economic growth since the end of the depression of the 1890's had in large measure given way by the end of the progressive period to foreboding among many thoughtful Americans. Along with growth had come a steady movement toward concentration of economic power in fewer and fewer hands. This movement in industry, finance, and transportation was one of the most powerful and significant forces in recent American history. For one thing, it completely transformed an economy of relatively small competitive producers into one dominated and to a degree controlled by an oligarchy of giant corporations. For another, many of the domestic problems of this century, at least before 1917, arose from the obvious necessity either of halting the movement toward monopoly or oligopoly—that is, domination of an industry by a few large producers— or else of bringing the great corporations, banks, railroads, and public service monopolies under effective public control.

No other question received as much attention or stimulated as many investigations and proposals for amelioration. Journalists, publicists, and politicians described the changes taking place: big business was becoming monopolistic, or nearly so, while the few men who dominated Wall Street were also extending their control into industry and transportation. As the statistics were plain enough for all to read, the people reluctantly agreed that the old promise of American life—the promise of equality of opportunity and a fair field for all comers—was rapidly becoming an anachronism. How to revitalize this promise—in brief, how to bring the great new aggregations of economic power under social control—this constituted progressivism's greatest challenge and dilemma.

This question, which perplexed the progressive mind and agitated the American people, is beyond the scope of the present chapter. Here we are concerned only with the development and progress of the concentration movement—how it came about and where it seemed to be heading.

20. *The Emergence of the Modern Corporation*

The most obvious yet the most important development in American industry after the Civil War was the rise of the corporation as the dominant type of industrial organization. The corporate form was used extensively before 1865 only in transportation, insurance, banking, and, to a lesser degree, in textiles. With the enlargement of industrial units, the spread of mass-production techniques, and the growth of the trust movement after 1865, however, the corporation rapidly displaced the proprietorship and partnership as the chief agency for combining capital and labor. Corporations turned out 66 per cent of all manufactured products by 1899. Ten years later the proportion had increased to 79 per cent.

The men who managed American corporations and made important decisions during the latter part of the nineteenth century usually owned the properties that they controlled. However, the domination of corporations by men who owned them gradually gave way from 1900 to 1920 in the face of a new trend: the emergence of the giant supercorporation, ownership of which was so widely dispersed that there could be no real correlation between ownership and management. In other words, one consequence of the emergence of the large corporation was the establishment in power of a professional managerial class who were only theoretically accountable to stockholders.

The most important factor stimulating the growth of the supercorporation was the movement of bankers into the transportation and industrial fields. The process first began on a large scale during and after the Panic of 1893, when J. P. Morgan & Company and Kuhn, Loeb & Company, the two leading Wall Street investment firms, set about reorganizing and consolidating bankrupt railroad properties. Morgan was so successful in rehabilitating insolvent railroads that he began to seek an opportunity to extend his control into industry. His chance came when a bitter rivalry between Carnegie and certain producers of finished steel products, with whom Morgan was associated, threatened to plunge the entire steel industry into a chaotic price war. Morgan came forward at this juncture with a plan to combine 60 per cent of the iron and steel producers into one giant corporation. The result was the creation in 1901 of the United States Steel Corporation; the retirement of Carnegie, the great freewheeling entrepreneur; and the establishment of the House of Morgan as the dominant power in the industry. This event was a turning point in modern American history, but it was only a beginning. As Morgan combined more and more industries and railroads after 1901 his power grew almost by geometric ratio. He was not merely the organizer and consolidator. He also underwrote the floating of securities that launched the new corporations on their way. And through his representatives on boards of directors, and because he controlled the sources of credit, he was able to exercise a decisive voice in the corporations' policies.

The process of banker consolidation and control did not culminate until the 1920's, but the effects of this revolution in the character, ownership, and control of large corporations was already well apparent by the outbreak of the First World War. By this date supercorporations dominated many fields of American enterprise: steel and iron, railroads, anthracite coal, agricultural machinery, copper, the telephone and telegraph, and public utilities. Hundreds of thousands of shareholders now owned these properties, but control had passed from owners to a managerial class responsible to a board of directors, who in turn were often beholden to investment bankers.

Undergirding this revolution was a body of state law that afforded a legal means of effecting consolidations and assuring managerial-banker control. New Jersey took the lead in 1888 and did a bargain counter business in charters until 1913. As New Jersey's treasury overflowed with corporation fees and taxes, other states entered the competition. The key provision in all the state corporation codes was the clause allowing one corporation to hold stock in other corporations. This was the invention of an ingenious New York lawyer, James B. Dill, and is known as the holding-company form. It was first incorporated in the New Jersey code in 1888 and was refined and clarified in 1889, 1893, and 1896. The holding-company form offered a simple means of effecting a huge combination or acquiring monopolistic control. Indeed, it soon became the legal form of practically all the giant corporations. In addition to providing a legal structure for the combinations, many state corporation codes endowed boards of directors with control over property without imposing corresponding obligations.

21. *The Consolidation Movement in Industry, 1879–1903*

The movement toward concentration of control in industry went through two major phases before the First World War: first, the trust movement, which began in 1879 and ended about 1890; second, the consolidation movement from 1897 to 1903, in which combinations were mainly constructed by using the holding-company form.

Most of the trusts of the first period of combination were organized by the manufacturers and businessmen directly involved, without the intervention of professional promoters or underwriting bankers. The trust was simply an extralegal arrangement by which competing manufacturers pooled properties to achieve monopoly. The Standard Oil Trust of 1879, superseded by the Trust Agreement of 1882, affords a good example of how this was done. First, the Trust Agreement was approved by the stockholders and owners of forty-odd oil companies, which together controlled over 90 per cent of the refining industry and an almost equal proportion of the pipe lines. Second, a valuation of the properties and assets of the member corporations was made, and trust certificates with a par value of $100 each were issued in exchange for the property on the basis of this valuation. Finally, the combined properties were managed by nine trustees elected on a basis of stock ownership. Following Standard Oil's lead, similar trusts were organized in other important branches of industry; other combinations, organized by purchase or as holding companies, were also launched in the late 1880's and early 1890's.

The use of the trust form to achieve monopoly was abandoned in the 1890's, and the combination movement came almost to a standstill for a time. The Panic of '93 was in part responsible, but even more important were the sweeping laws against conspiracies in restraint of trade enacted by Congress and many state legislatures. Few manufacturers were willing to risk heavy damages and dissolution by federal and state courts. The situation changed drastically in 1895, however, when the Supreme Court decreed that the federal antitrust law did not apply to combinations in the field of manufacturing.

The apparent removal of the formidable federal barrier to industrial combinations, the election of McKinley in 1896, and the return of prosperity in 1897 all combined to clear the way for a second consolidation movement that lasted until 1904. So great was this movement that the consolidations of the earlier period pale into insignificance. All told, not more than twelve important combinations, with a total capitalization of under $1,000,000,000, had been organized from 1879 to 1897. Yet the Census of Manufactures in 1899 reported some 185 combinations with a total capital of over $3,000,000,000. They accounted for nearly one third of the entire capitalization of all manufacturing industries in the country. A comprehensive survey of American corporations in 1904 listed 305 industrial combinations, with an aggregate capital of nearly $7,000,000,000, in operation. In addition, thirteen important combinations, with a capital of $500,000,000, were in process of reorganization; and combinations controlled fully two fifths of the manufacturing capital of the United States.

The momentum of the consolidation movement during the period 1897–1903 can best be illustrated by pointing again to the statistics. Of the 318 giant corporations in operation or in process of reorganization on January 1, 1904, 236, with a total capitalization of over $6,000,000,000, had been organized since January 1, 1898. With 95 per cent of the nation's mileage under the control of six groups, concentration in railroads had reached an even more spectacular level than in industry. Moreover, some 1,330 public service corporations had been consolidated into a few holding companies that had a combined capitalization of three and three-quarter billion dollars.

The reasons for this tremendous number of consolidations are not hard to find. Having acquired an understandable dislike of severe competition during the depression of the 1890's, manufacturers were easily persuaded that combination offered a sure means of controlling the price of their products and maintaining an orderly market. The fact that the three most important monopolies—Standard Oil, American Sugar, and American Tobacco—had prospered and paid dividends while the rest of industry struggled through destructive price wars was not lost upon the business community. Manufacturers, moreover, anticipated increased profits through the vertical integration of plants to achieve a continuous industrial process, large-scale production, the exploitation of the national mar-

ket, and the utilization of by-products. In other words, large-scale enterprises would have capital to invest in labor-saving machinery and
research, assure control of raw materials, and engage in nation-wide marketing. But certainly an important incentive to combination was the desire
to achieve stability through considerable control of prices.

The moving agent in the later consolidation movement, however, was
not the manufacturer but the professional promoter and investment
banker. He it was who brought competitors together, harmonized their
differences, and worked out schemes of financing and marketing the new
securities. A favorite method of financing the combination was to issue
bonds and preferred stock to compensate the owners of properties being
consolidated. In addition, a bonus in common stock as large as the market
would bear would be awarded to the promoter and the corporation. The
classic example of this method of financing was Morgan's financial structure for United States Steel in 1901. The corporation was capitalized at
$1,400,000,000, divided as follows: $362,000,000 in bonds, $510,000,000
in preferred stock, $508,000,000 in common stock, and $22,000,000 in
cash. As the actual value of the corporation's assets was only $682,000,-
000, all the common and about one fourth of the preferred stock—about
half the total capitalization—was pure water. Yet the Morgan firm was
able to unload these securities on the Stock Exchange and to realize a
profit of $62,000,000 as a fee for organizing and underwriting the corpora-
tion.[1]

The consolidation movement came to a halt in 1904, chiefly because
about every branch of industry susceptible of combination had been combined. But the activation of the federal antitrust law by Theodore Roosevelt and his successor, William H. Taft, was also an important factor in
bringing the movement to an end. In fact, from 1904 to 1914 the federal
government on the whole succeeded in compelling the great corporations to
comply with the antitrust law. Most of the genuine monopolies were dissolved. Other combinations, like the International Harvester Company, the
New Haven Railroad, and American Telephone and Telegraph, voluntarily
acquiesced in reorganization plans approved by the Attorney General. By
1914 the era of monopoly in American industry had passed, and a new
economic structure was emerging. It was an oligopolistic structure, in
which a few giant corporations dominated their branches of industry and
usually determined price and wage policies. We will examine this new
development in greater detail in a future chapter.

22.   *The Emergence of Financial Empires*

The savings of the middle and upper classes began to flow into banks
and insurance companies as the wealth of the United States increased during the two decades before American intervention in the First World War.

---

[1] It is only fair to add that by 1916 the directors of United States Steel, through wise
management and prudent reinvestment, had built the corporation's assets to the point
where the common stock was no longer watered.

All American financial institutions combined had assets and resources of only $9,000,000,000 in 1899. Only twelve years later the country could boast of savings and liquid capital of nearly $28,000,000,000. As a result, the entrepreneurs of the money market, the investment bankers, assumed leadership after 1897 in marshaling and allocating capital for industrial, railroad, public utility, and other forms of expansion. As we have seen, they were also the chief agents in promoting and financing the new consolidations. But the portentous fact was not the growth of American wealth, for that reflected an expanding and healthy economy; it was the startling concentration of control that took place among banks and insurance companies, and the transformation of leading investment bankers from entrepreneurs of capital into dominant forces in the American economy.

So swift were these processes of concentration that there were by 1904 two financial empires in Wall Street: the House of Morgan and the Rockefeller group. Using its profits from railroad reorganization and promotion of large corporations, the Morgan firm bought control of the National Bank of Commerce and partial ownership of the great First National Bank of New York City. From this vantage point Morgan rapidly extended his control or influence over other banks and trust companies in New York, Philadelphia, and Chicago. Moreover, the House of Morgan was represented in the counsels of United States Steel, International Mercantile Marine, International Harvester, General Electric, and other large corporations. By 1904 it controlled, besides, the Southern, Reading, Northern Pacific, Great Northern, New Haven, Erie, and other railroads, whose total mileage was over 47,000 and whose combined capital amounted to nearly one fourth of the group railroad capital in the United States. Such an empire might have satisfied a man of modest ambition. However, Morgan set out around 1900 to win the richest prize of all—the large New York insurance companies. Control of their huge resources would open an almost unlimited market for securities. Morgan won the New York Life and Mutual Life by interlocking their directors into his own system. Finally, he bought a controlling interest in the Equitable Life in 1910. These three companies had assets of nearly $2,000,000,000 by 1913 and some $70,000,000 of new money every year for investment.

On the other side of Wall Street was the far-flung Rockefeller group with its allies: the National City Bank, Hanover National Bank, Farmers Loan and Trust Company, and lesser banks; the Standard Oil Company; the Union Pacific, Southern Pacific, and nine other major railroads, managed by Edward H. Harriman; and Morgan's rival in the investment and promotion fields, Kuhn, Loeb & Company, headed by Jacob H. Schiff. The normal process of concentration had been reversed to construct this financial imperium. Industrialists in the Standard Oil monopoly had channeled their excess profits into investment and promotion.

Around the Morgan and Rockefeller empires clustered a number of smaller kingdoms. "These two mammoth groups jointly . . . constitute the heart of the business and commercial life of the nation," one financial expert wrote in 1904, "the others all being the arteries which permeate in a thousand ways our whole national life, making their influence felt in every home and hamlet, yet all connected and dependent on this great central source, the influence and policy of which dominates them all." [2]

The two groups did not always live in peace before 1907. Their rivalry for control of railroads, corporations, and insurance companies was sometimes bitter and on one memorable occasion reached the point of open war. The stakes of this battle were nothing less than control of most of the western transcontinental railroads. Morgan and his ally, James J. Hill, controlled the two northern transcontinental systems, the Northern Pacific and the Great Northern, in 1901. On the other hand, Edward H. Harriman and Kuhn, Loeb & Company controlled the central and southern systems, the Union Pacific and Southern Pacific. Neither group controlled the Burlington, the outlet to Chicago used by the Hill lines. Hill persuaded the owners of the Burlington to sell their railroad to the Northern Pacific and Great Northern in 1901, and Harriman and Schiff executed a daring flank attack by attempting to buy control of the Northern Pacific. The ensuing battle in the New York Stock Exchange drove the price of Northern Pacific common from $100 to over $1,000 a share. When the smoke had cleared it was discovered that Harriman and Schiff owned a majority of the shares of Northern Pacific, but that Hill and Morgan still controlled a majority of the voting stock. The rivals agreed to terms of peace to avert further conflict. They formed the Northern Securities Company, a holding company to control the Northern Pacific and Great Northern lines, and Harriman and Schiff were given minority representation on the board of directors. In addition, Harriman was awarded a seat on the board of the Burlington.

Morgan's pre-eminence was spectacularly revealed during the Panic of 1907, when he dramatically marshaled Wall Street's resources to prevent total demoralization of the securities markets. After this demonstration of personal power, the Rockefeller–Kuhn, Loeb group concluded that further opposition to the Morgan combination was futile. Thus, the Morgan and Rockefeller groups were merged from 1907 to 1913 into one confederated association by interlocking directorates and purchases of one another's stocks.

This confederation's power was dramatically highlighted by the careful investigation of a House subcommittee—the Pujo Committee—in the early months of 1913. This Committee found that the Morgan-Rockefeller community of interest had achieved a very considerable control of the credit resources of the nation by consolidating bank and trust companies, gaining control over insurance companies, and interlocking their directorates among the boards of railroads and industrial and public utility corporations. How widely this influence extended was illustrated by the fact that the Morgan-Rockefeller group had

> 118 directorships in 34 banks and trust companies, with total resources of over $2,500,000,000;
>
> 30 directorships in 10 insurance companies, with total assets of over $2,000,000,000;
>
> 105 directorships in 32 transportation systems, with a total capitalization of more than $11,000,000,000;

---

[2] John Moody, "The Truth About the Trusts," *Moody's Magazine* (New York, 1904), p. 493.

63 directorships in 24 producing and trading corporations, with a total capitalization of over $3,000,000,000; and

25 directorships in 12 public utility corporations, with a combined capitalization of over $2,000,000,000.

In brief, the House of Morgan and its allies on January 1, 1913, had 341 directorships in 112 banks, railroads, industries, and other corporations with aggregate resources or capitalization of more than $20,000,000,000.

The question whether a "money trust" existed as a result of the aggrandizement of power by the Wall Street bankers was hotly debated before the Pujo Committee. The Committee did not claim that the Morgan empire had established an absolute monopoly of credit. It revealed beyond cavil, however, the vast and growing concentration of control of money and credit in the hands of a few men. The significance of the Committee's findings was not lost upon the American people. How could genuine economic freedom and equality of opportunity exist in such circumstances? "This is the greatest question of all," Woodrow Wilson observed, "and to this statesmen must address themselves with an earnest determination to serve the long future and the true liberties of men."

23. *The American Railroad Empires, 1897–1914*

The same techniques of consolidation that were being used to construct the empires of industry and finance were also employed, often by the same bankers and promoters, to consolidate America's greatest single property interest, the railroads. The task of linking all sections had been accomplished by 1897, although railroad main track mileage grew at a steady pace, from 192,566 in 1900 to 256,547 in 1914, while railway capital and the volume of passenger and freight traffic practically doubled during the same period. Growth was accompanied by consolidation and an increasing degree of banker control. Leadership in the consolidation movement was taken, as we have already seen, by the Morgan firm during and after the Panic of 1893.

Morgan's dominance was soon challenged by the rise of Edward H. Harriman, easily the boldest railroad promoter of the early twentieth century. He was first associated with Kuhn, Loeb & Company in managing the Illinois Central; the group then bought control of the bankrupt and worn-out Union Pacific in 1897. Harriman personally supervised the rebuilding of this system, and it soon became immensely profitable. Harriman and Kuhn, Loeb & Company bought control of an even greater system, the Southern Pacific, in 1901. Together with several other western lines, it gave them control over most of the railroads of the Southwest and a monopoly of the transportation facilities of the entire West Coast from Canada to Mexico.

Beyond the Mississippi only three railway systems challenged the domination of that vast area by the Morgan-Hill and Kuhn, Loeb–Harriman interests. They were the Santa Fe Railroad, the Gould system, and the consolidation built around the Rock Island Railroad. The Sante Fe, financed by independent Boston and London banking interests, ran from Chicago to southern California and was never associated with the Gould or Harriman interests. The Gould system included the Missouri Pacific, the Denver & Rio Grande, the Texas & Pacific, and the Western Pacific. The Rock Island system was consolidated from 1901 to 1911 by a group of speculators out of the Rock Island, the St. Louis–San Francisco, and the Chicago & Alton.

The traffic of the East and eastern Middle West was dominated by the New York Central and Pennsylvania, allied with the Morgan interests, which controlled the Chesapeake & Ohio, the Baltimore & Ohio, and the Norfolk & Western. Under Morgan's direction, moreover, the New Haven bought control of the Boston & Maine, the trolley lines of New England, and even the Long Island Sound steamship companies. Thus, about two thirds of the nation's railroad mileage was controlled by 1906 by four gigantic communities of interest: the Morgan-Hill-Vanderbilt-Pennsylvania, the Harriman–Kuhn, Loeb & Company, the Gould, and the Rock Island groups. Obviously, the process of consolidation could not have been carried much farther.

Along with consolidation in the railroad field went banker control on a scale exceeding that prevailing in industry. It is all too clear that the bankers sought primarily their own and their stockholders' gain, though this often meant charging exorbitant rates for poor service, bankrupting railroad properties, or debauching the politics of the states. Indeed, the mismanagement of America's greatest single property interest from 1897 to 1914 reached such a point that only federal rehabilitation and operation of the railroads during the First World War saved the industry from virtual bankruptcy.

The history of the Union Pacific provides at least one good illustration of the way promoters manipulated a profitable railroad to build up a vast empire. By completely rebuilding the Union Pacific and managing it efficiently, Harriman made the line immensely profitable. But most of the cost of rebuilding was charged to operation and maintenance, while the company's excess profits were used to acquire control of the Southern Pacific and to purchase large interests in numerous other lines. All told, the Union Pacific had "invested" more than $331,000,000 in this fashion by 1907. And, while Harriman constructed his empire, Kuhn, Loeb & Company reaped huge profits as his middlemen.

Harriman repeatedly violated the antitrust law, to be sure, but he did not wreck railroad properties. The most important case of railroad mismanagement during this period involved J. P. Morgan's use of the New Haven to acquire a complete monopoly over all forms of transportation in New England. From 1903 to 1912, when Morgan pursued his relentless campaign, the capitalization of the New Haven was increased from $93,-000,000 to about $417,000,000. More than two thirds of the increased capitalization was used, not to improve or purchase railroad property, but to achieve a monopoly of all transportation facilities. New Haven directors in the process debauched politicians, bribed editors, and in the end helped to bring the economy of New England to the brink of ruin.

24. *The United States and the World Economy, 1897–1914*

Foreign trade had been the lifeblood of the American economy since colonial times. Reflecting the profound changes taking place in the domes-

FOREIGN TRADE
1900-1956

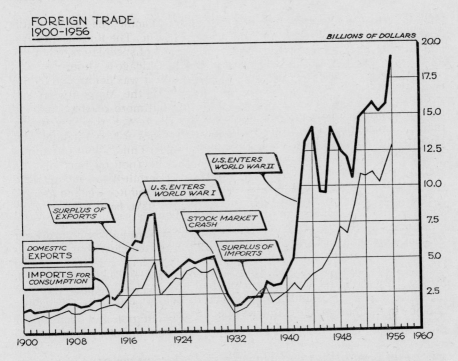

tic economy, the volume and character of foreign trade underwent important changes from 1897 to 1914. For one thing, foreign trade expanded at a faster pace during this period than at any time since the Civil War. Exports increased from $1,394,000,000 in 1900 to nearly $2,500,000,000 by 1914, while imports rose from $850,000,000 to $1,800,000,000 during the same period. Secondly, an important shift in the character of exports and imports took place. In 1900 agricultural products constituted 60 per cent of the nation's exports, manufactured products only 35 per cent. By 1914 manufactured products accounted for nearly 49 per cent of American exports. At the same time, development of new industries at home lessened American demand for manufactured goods from abroad and stimulated increased demand for raw materials like rubber, tin, and manganese.

The rapid growth of American exports of manufactured goods and capital before 1914 foretold the coming of the day when the United States would occupy a commanding position in the world economy. However, London was still the center of international exchange before 1915, and the United States continued to occupy its traditional status as debtor to Europe. In 1897 Europeans held American securities, over half of them in railroads, valued at nearly $3,500,000,000. By the eve of the First World War, European investments in the United States, direct and indirect, had more than doubled. In part this was offset by American investments abroad, but the balance of payments still ran heavily against the United States.

Nonetheless, the two most significant trends during the period 1897–1914 were the growth of American exports of manufactured goods and the rapid increase in the export of American capital abroad. The first was achieved in spite of the lack of a sizable American merchant marine, experience in doing business in foreign countries, or a well organized governmental program to support foreign trade. The growth of American investments abroad, on the other hand, took place under the guidance of experienced bankers and often with the support of the State Department.

The United States was the richest and industrially the most powerful nation in the world when it went to war with Spain in 1898. But up to this time practically every available dollar had gone into building railroads, opening the West, and constructing industries at home. American investments abroad totaled only $684,500,000 on the eve of the Spanish-American War. Yet this figure stood at $3,513,800,000 in 1914. Except for $692,000,000 invested in Europe and $246,000,000 in the Far East, American capital had not ventured far from home. American capitalists had invested $867,200,000 in Canadian mines, industries, and railroads. The encouragement given foreign investors by the seemingly stable Díaz government of Mexico from 1877 to 1911 had attracted $854,000,000 from the United States, most of which went into railroads, mines, ranches, and oil. American investments in Cuba, which was a quasi-protectorate of the United States after 1898, grew from $50,000,000 in 1897 to $200,000,000 by 1914. By the latter date Americans had also invested $136,000,000 in the other Caribbean islands, $93,000,000 in Central America, and $366,-000,000 in the more stable countries of South America.

25.   *The Conditions and Hazards of Labor, 1897–1914*

The period 1897–1914, generally speaking, was a time of relative stability and steady economic progress for labor. Except for a brief interlude in 1908, full employment prevailed during most of the period. Real earnings of all workers in manufacturing, the only group for whom we have reliable statistics, increased at the rate of 1.3 per cent annually from 1890 to 1914, for a total increase of 37 per cent for this entire period. It would have increased more had there not been a rise of 39 per cent in the cost of living for workers during the period 1897–1914.

This picture of increasing and steadier employment accompanied by a substantial increase in real wages did not encourage the friends of labor. Surveying the industrial scene in 1915, the majority members of the Commission on Industrial Relations, appointed by President Wilson to ascertain the causes of industrial unrest, observed that "a large part of our industrial population are . . . living in a condition of actual poverty. How large this proportion is can not be exactly determined, but it is certain that at least one-third and possibly one-half of the families of wage earners employed in manufacturing and mining earn in the course of the year less than enough to support them in anything like a comfortable and decent condition." [3] The social consequences of this state of affairs were ominous: children of the poor died at three times the rate of children of the middle classes; 12 to

[3] *Final Report of the Commission on Industrial Relations* (Washington, 1915), p. 10.

20 per cent of the children in six large cities were underfed and undernourished; only one third of all children enrolled finished elementary schools; less than 10 per cent of the children in public schools were graduated from high schools.

There were, even so, encouraging developments that offered hope for the future. To begin with, some progress had been made since 1897 toward reducing the hours of labor in industry and transportation. Average hours in industry fell from 59.1 a week in 1897 to 55.2 in 1914. These general averages, however, obscure the important differential in hours worked between organized and unorganized labor. The movement for shorter hours had begun in the building, printing, and other skilled and organized trades and was most successful among them. One survey, for example, revealed that in six unionized industries average weekly hours declined from 53.4 in 1897 to 48.8 in 1914. In contrast, average weekly hours in eight unorganized industries declined from 61.9 to 58.2 during the same period.

Secondly, the first real progress was made during the years from 1907 to 1914 toward reducing the hazards of labor. Statistics of industrial accidents are unreliable for this period, but an incomplete survey in 1907 revealed that at least 500,000 American workers were either killed, crippled, or seriously injured. As late as 1913, according to a more reliable survey, 25,000 workers were killed on their jobs, and another 700,000 were seriously injured.

The sporadic efforts made by several states to reduce the industrial accident rate had been unproductive before 1907. Between 1907 and 1914, however, the public awakened to the great wastage of human resources by industrial deaths and accidents. The safety movement began in 1907, when the United States Steel Corporation inaugurated a comprehensive campaign to reduce the accident toll. So successful was this program that a few other leading corporations and railroads, notably the International Harvester Company and the Chicago & North Western Railroad, instituted safety campaigns before 1914.

Thirdly, the reports of social workers and factory inspectors in many states also focused public attention on the social necessity of healthful working conditions in industry. The problem was most acute in textile mills and garment sweatshops where large numbers of women and children were employed. In fact, nowhere in the country were working conditions so incredibly bad as in the garment sweatshops of New York City, most of which were located in tenements that were literally firetraps. The Triangle Shirtwaist Factory fire on the East Side in 1911, in which 148 women lost their lives, led to the appointment of a Factory Investigating Commission and a thorough revision of New York's factory code between 1912 and 1914.

Finally, the urgency of eliminating occupational diseases like phosphorus and lead poisoning was brought home to employers and the public in a number of ways from 1900 to 1914. Medical research provided the essential knowledge, while state and national reform groups, like the American Association for Labor Legislation, carried on the necessary propaganda work. A campaign against phosphorus matches, for example, resulted in the enactment in 1912 of a federal statute forbidding their manufacture. Lead poisoning in its various forms was partially eliminated. But the greatest progress came when the American Medical Association joined hands with the American Association for Labor Legislation to begin a comprehensive campaign against industrial diseases.

26. *The Rise of the American Federation of Labor*

Nothing better illustrates the precarious position that workers occupied in the American society during the half-century between the Civil War and the First World War than the story of labor's attempts to achieve some measure of protection through organization. Organized labor passed through several phases during this long period and was confronted at times with almost insurmountable obstacles. Nonetheless, labor organizations won a larger degree of recognition than ever before in American history. And although labor's great goal—unionization of all workers—was unrealized by 1914, the necessary, solid foundations of a strong labor movement had been well laid.

There were two initial attempts at labor organization on a national scale between 1865 and the late 1880's, before the dominant pattern of unionization was established. The first, the National Labor Union, founded in 1866, was a loose aggregation of trade unions and assorted reform groups. It was practically defunct by 1872. More important was the Knights of Labor, organized in Philadelphia in 1869. It attempted to organize workers along industrial rather than craft lines, and without regard to sex or race. The union won a few spectacular strike victories and attained a membership of over 700,000 by early 1886, but it rapidly disintegrated after newspapers and employers charged it with responsibility for a serious riot in Chicago in May 1886.

While the Knights of Labor was enjoying momentary success, the leaders of the cigar makers' union, Samuel Gompers and Adolph Strasser, were building the first powerful trade union in American history. Other unions federated with the cigar makers in a Federation of Organized Trades in 1881, and the union was reorganized as the American Federation of Labor in 1886. The AF of L under Samuel Gompers, who dominated the organization until his death in 1924, for the most part spurned industrial unionism (unionism that groups all workers in a single industry into a single organization) and built upon the foundation of craft and trade unions. From its beginning, moreover, the AF of L eschewed utopianism and was avowedly opportunistic and practical in objectives.

The AF of L's lasting power was demonstrated when it weathered the defeat of the steelworkers' and miners' unions in major strikes in 1892 and 1894 and came out of the depression in 1897 with 265,000 members. From this point it soon fought its way to dominance in the American labor movement. Its membership had climbed to 548,000 by 1900. There were spectacular gains until 1904, when membership reached 1,676,000. Then membership declined under the hammer blows of an organized employer campaign until 1911, when it began slowly to mount again. It stood at a little over 2,000,000 in 1914.

Standing apart from the AF of L were the four railroad brotherhoods— the conductors, engineers, trainmen, and firemen—who since the 1880's had been the best paid workers in the country, a labor aristocracy conscious of their power and privileged position. They had won the ten-hour day throughout the country by 1910. Then the four unions, 400,000 strong, combined in 1916 to do battle for their next objective, the eight-hour day. This they won with the adoption by Congress of the Adamson Act, establishing the eight-hour day as the standard for all workers engaged in interstate railway transportation.

27. *The Progress of Unionization in the Coal Industry*

The period from the end of the Panic of 1893 to the First World War was a time of labor's first concerted striving toward the goal of industrial democracy. Many factors combined to give the AF of L opportunities and advantages that its predecessors had not enjoyed: superb *esprit de corps* accompanied by a feeling of solidarity, wise leadership, and a public opinion that was growing less hostile to the labor movement. Building largely on foundations already laid, Gompers and his colleagues from 1897 to 1914 succeeded in expanding membership and winning collective bargaining, higher wages, and shorter hours in most of the building trades and the skilled crafts. On the other hand, labor's new militancy was matched by an equally aggressive determination on management's side to prevent unionization in the mass industries. This, therefore, was the crucial question: could the AF of L carry the fight into the basic industries and triumph over great aggregations of power?

The first test came in the effort of the United Mine Workers of America, an industrial union affiliated with the AF of L, to organize the coal industry. Decisively beaten in a general coal strike in 1894, the UMW had only 10,000 members and seemed dead by 1897. Leaders of the union none the less demanded increased wages and recognition, and the operators' refusal set off a general strike in the bituminous fields that began on July 4, 1897. The strikers were well organized and magnificently led, and operators in western Pennsylvania, Ohio, Indiana, and Illinois surrendered in the following September. It was a notable victory, not merely because the miners won recognition, higher wages, and other demands, but also because it was a spur and inspiration to the entire labor movement.

Emerging from this strike well organized and over 100,000 strong, the UMW now turned its sights on the anthracite coal industry centered in five counties of northeastern Pennsylvania and controlled by nine railroad companies. The president of the UMW, John Mitchell, authorized a strike on September 12, 1900, and 150,000 anthracite miners walked out of the pits. The union had demanded recognition, establishment of labor-management committees to settle petty disputes, a wage increase, and the right to employ check-weighmen. Before the strike was over, Mitchell waived the demand for recognition and suggested that the remaining issues be arbitrated. And when the operators granted a 10 per cent wage increase and made other concessions in October 1900, Mitchell gladly called off the strike. Although the UMW won only part of its demands, it had succeeded in accomplishing its major objective—thorough organization of the anthracite industry.

The anthracite operators refused even to discuss wage rates with UMW officials in 1902, and Mitchell called a second strike that began on May 14.

Public opinion strongly favored the miners and veered even more sharply in their favor as the result of an incident that occurred in August. A citizen of Wilkes-Barre appealed in the name of Christianity to George F. Baer, president of the Reading Railroad, to end the strike by giving in to the union. Baer replied in a letter that was subsequently published that the interests of the miners would be protected, "not by the labor agitators, but by the Christian men to whom God, in His infinite wisdom, has given control of the property interests of the country."

As the strike dragged on into the autumn of 1902 coal prices skyrocketed, and people in the eastern cities thought they faced a serious coal famine. President Roosevelt summoned Mitchell and leading operators to a White House conference on October 3, 1902. While Mitchell agreed to submit the issues to arbitration and to end the strike, the operators denounced the UMW as a lawless body and declared that they would never arbitrate. This was too much for Roosevelt. He issued secret orders to the army to move 10,000 troops into the anthracite region, seize the mines, and operate them as receiver for the government. Next he sent Secretary of War Elihu Root to New York City to warn J. P. Morgan, who had close financial ties with the operators, of the impending seizure. Morgan and Root at once sketched out a plan of mediation, and the operators accepted it with the reservation that no labor official should be appointed to the arbitration commission. Mitchell approved the plan, insisting only that the President be given complete freedom in naming the arbiters. Roosevelt added a humorous touch, which he greatly enjoyed, by appointing the former Grand Chief of the Railway Conductors' Brotherhood to the commission in the capacity of "sociologist."

Roosevelt's intervention and the subsequent arbitration of the dispute was a landmark in American labor history. For the first time the federal government had looked at an industrial dispute on its merits, without automatically taking management's side. From the commission's award the miners won the nine-hour day, a 10 per cent wage increase, the right to select check-weighmen, and a permanent board of conciliation. Not until 1916 did the UMW finally win recognition from the anthracite operators. Even so, the gains from the victory of 1902 were significant indeed.

Thus, the UMW had organized the eastern and midwestern bituminous areas and the entire anthracite industry by 1903. On the troubled frontiers of coal, however, they met fierce resistance and defeat that spelled eventual disaster. West Virginia was the key to long-range success or failure, for so long as the West Virginia fields were unorganized the UMW and northern operators could never be protected from the competition of this low-wage and low-cost area. The UMW executed full-scale campaigns in 1900 and again in 1902 to organize the state and failed. Meanwhile, the task of organizing the southern area became increasingly important and difficult as new coal fields were opened in Virginia, Kentucky, Tennessee, and Alabama. The UMW launched a third great strike in West Virginia in 1912 and 1913 but was only partially successful. So long as West Virginia and other southern fields remained unorganized there could be neither stability in the coal industry nor security for the UMW.

In the meantime, the miners suffered bloodier defeats on another frontier, Colorado. A UMW strike against Rockefeller's Colorado Fuel and Iron

Company and other operators in 1903–4 ended in rout for the union and deportation of many of the strikers. Ten years later, in September 1913, the
UMW again attempted to overcome the Colorado coal companies. This time
the state was torn by violent civil war, set off when National Guard troops
attacked and burned a strikers' tent colony at Ludlow on April 20, 1914,
killing eleven women and two children.

The Ludlow Massacre and civil war in Colorado horrified the nation,
provoked investigations by a congressional committee and the Industrial
Relations Commission, and set off a wave of sympathy for the strikers. But
John D. Rockefeller, Jr., who controlled the Colorado Fuel and Iron Company, refused to surrender to the UMW. Rejecting President Wilson's plan
of settlement, he instituted a labor relations program, the chief feature of
which was the formation of a company union, which retained for management full power over policies affecting the workers. Nonetheless, the American people (and Rockefeller as well) had been taught a tragic lesson in the
consequences of industrial despotism and absentee capitalism.

28. *"As Steel Goes"*

Socialists and other left-wing elements in the labor movement often
charged that Gompers and the AF of L represented only the aristocracy of
labor and were indifferent to the necessity of organizing the basic industries
that employed the mass of workers. These critics ignored some important
facts. This was a period when organized labor progressed from impotence
to a position of considerable power, in spite of the absence of any favorable
legislation or any effective public support in behalf of the labor movement.
To say that Gompers and his leaders did not recognize the importance of
unionizing the basic industries, like iron and steel, textiles, and lumber, is
simply not true. But Gompers knew the AF of L's weakness as well as its
strength, and he knew that the time had not yet come for an all-out campaign against mass industries.

The wisdom of Gompers' view was confirmed many times during the
progressive period. For example, the UMW's leadership of the Colorado
miners in the bloody strike of 1913–14 was heroic, but the long battle was
costly, and defeat left the entire union severely weakened. The AF of L's
most discouraging and significant reversal was its failure to organize the
steel industry. All during the period under discussion steel stood as an anti-
union bastion, setting an open-shop pattern for other mass industries and
providing anti-union leadership for thousands of small manufacturers.

Carnegie had defeated the Amalgamated Iron, Steel and Tin workers,
which then included only skilled workers, during the violent Homestead
strike of 1892. When the Carnegie plants were merged into the United
States Steel Corporation in 1901 union officials decided that they now had
no alternative but to attempt to organize all steel workers, skilled and unskilled. First, however, the Amalgamated demanded that the union scale of
wages be paid in all plants of the American Sheet Steel, American Steel
Hoop, and American Tin Plate companies, all subsidiaries of United States
Steel. The directors of the corporation offered a compromise that would
have halted the progress of unionization. The union officials refused and

then, on August 10, 1901, called a general strike against all plants of the
Steel Corporation. A majority of workers walked out, but the strike for a
number of reasons was doomed from the beginning. In the end Amalgamated surrendered unconditionally. The corporation agreed to pay union
wages, but the wage rate was no longer an important issue. In return, the
union withdrew from fourteen mills, agreed neither to seek to extend its influence nor even to welcome new members, and conceded the corporation's
right to discharge workers for union activities.

Officials of United States Steel made no direct assaults upon the carcass of the Amalgamated for a time after their victory of 1901. Instead, they
instituted measures to win the loyalty of the workers: profit-sharing, begun
in December 1902; an employee-safety program, launched in 1906–7; and
finally a workmen's compensation and old-age pension program, inaugurated in 1910. Meanwhile, the American Sheet and Tin Plate Company, the
last of the unionized subsidiaries of the corporation, posted notices in June
1909 announcing that it would begin an open-shop policy on July 1. The
protests of the Amalgamated were not even acknowledged, and the union
called a second general strike against the corporation. Although the workers responded en masse throughout the far-flung steel empire and the
AF of L joined the struggle with financial support, the strikers never had
a chance. After holding out for fourteen months they surrendered on
August 23, 1910.

Thus, after 1909 the United States Steel Corporation boasted an open
shop throughout its vast domain. Moreover, the Lake Carriers' Association,
an ally of United States Steel, destroyed the Lake Seamen's Union during a
long and bitter strike from 1909 to 1912. The establishment of management's absolute authority in all branches of the steel corporation had been
accomplished by relentless warfare against the union, use of spies and
blacklisting of strike leaders, domination of local governments, and a welfare program that undermined the union's appeal. United States Steel remained the citadel of anti-unionism in the mass industries until 1937.

29.   *Left-Wing Unionism and the Rise of Socialism*

Left-wing unionism first developed on an important scale, not in the
teeming cities of the East, but in the mining regions of the western slope of
the Rockies. Here raw industrial absolutism provoked brutal retaliation by
frontier miners. The result was class warfare without ideological overtones
on a grand and violent scale. Out of this morass of class conflict an organization emerged in 1905. It was the Industrial Workers of the World, a coalition of the Western Federation of Miners, the socialistic American Labor
Union, and the Socialist Trade and Labor Alliance. Organized along industrial lines, the IWW was frankly revolutionary. Its weapons were sabotage
and strikes; its objectives, abolition of the wage system and establishment
of a proletarian commonwealth.

The IWW showed signs of coming apart at the seams within a year
after its formation. The basic difficulty was dissension between leaders of
the Western Federation of Miners, who were more interested in promoting
labor's immediate goals than in building the socialistic state, and the head

of the Socialist Trade and Labor Alliance, Daniel De Leon, a dogmatic Marxian theorist. De Leon was unceremoniously expelled in 1908, and from this time on the IWW was a champion of lower class workers without concern for pure revolutionary dogma. In the West it fought the battles of the lumbermen, migratory workers, and frontier miners. Its emphasis on the violent strike and sabotage brought it into collision with employers, the police, and the courts and prevented any systematic organizational campaigns. In the East the IWW provided leadership for unskilled workers whom the AF of L had ignored. It led a strike in Lawrence, Massachusetts, against the American Woolen Company in 1912 and won a wage increase. It took command of rebellious silk workers in Paterson and Passaic, New Jersey, and led them in a successful strike in 1912 and 1913.

While the IWW was careening from one bloody conflict to another, the political counterpart of left-wing unionism, socialism, was struggling for a program and a means of expression. The socialists were united during the 1890's in the Socialist Labor party, which De Leon ruled until his inflexible Marxist dogma provoked a rebellion by a moderate element in 1899–1900. Meanwhile, in 1897 the midwestern labor leader, Eugene V. Debs, had founded a potential rival, the Social Democratic party, dedicated to advancing public ownership of railroads, utilities, and industrial monopolies. The anti–De Leon faction in the Socialist Labor party, headed by Morris Hillquit of New York and Victor Berger of Milwaukee, joined the Debs group in Indianapolis in 1901 to launch the Socialist Party of America.

The Socialist party included visionaries and dogmatic Marxians, but it was so completely dominated by the moderates—Debs, Hillquit, and Berger —that it was more the left wing of progressivism than a revolutionary workers' party. The party had a membership of over 58,000 by 1908; four years later the figure stood at nearly 126,000. The party's influence during this period, however, was far greater than its small membership would indicate. Socialist administrations by 1912 governed Milwaukee, Schenectady, and Berkeley, California. One of the party's leaders, Victor Berger, sat in the House of Representatives and was soon joined by another Socialist from New York City's East Side, Meyer London. And the Socialist presidential candidate, Debs, polled over 897,000 votes in the election of 1912.

30. *The Counteroffensive of the Employers*

For a time at the turn of the century it seemed that the lion and the lamb might lie down together. The sign of impending industrial peace was the organization in 1900 of the National Civic Federation, founded to prove that "organized labor cannot be destroyed without debasement of the masses." The Federation's leaders included industrialists like Mark Hanna and George W. Perkins, bankers like J. P. Morgan, and labor spokesmen like Samuel Gompers and John Mitchell. For a few years the Federation rendered service to the labor movement by lending a sort of respectability to the AF of L.

That the Federation represented only a minority of employers, however, was demonstrated by a significant movement that was already on foot when the Federation was organized. It was a mass offensive of employers to

destroy unionism altogether and to establish an open-shop pattern throughout American industry. This counterattack opened in 1900 in Dayton, Ohio,
where the union movement had made considerable progress. Within two
years the local employers' association had driven the unions out of town.
Flushed with victory, propagandists went from Dayton to arouse employers
in other cities to the defense of what they called "the American Plan"—that
is, the open shop. So successful were responding employers' associations in
Chicago, Beloit, Wisconsin, and Sedalia, Missouri, that the leaders of the
open-shop crusade received appeals for assistance from employers' groups
all over the country.

Obviously, what most industrialists and businessmen wanted was destruction of the labor movement. The National Association of Manufacturers took command of the open-shop campaign in 1903 and formed the
Citizens' Industrial Association for the purpose of forming employers' associations throughout the country. The Citizens' Industrial Association also
executed a broad campaign to rally public opinion behind the American
Plan. Appealing to the average citizen's individualism and prejudices, this
propaganda defended the right of Americans to work when and where they
pleased, depicted labor organizers as agitators and socialists, and portrayed
employers as champions of free enterprise and ancient American liberties.

This counteroffensive did not destroy unionism, but it struck such a
heavy blow that the AF of L not only failed to grow but actually lost membership between 1904 and 1910. Nor can it be doubted that the Citizens' Industrial Association and its several hundred local branches succeeded in
engendering widespread popular hostility to the very concept of unionism.
President Charles W. Eliot of Harvard, for example, glorified the strike-
breaker as an "American hero," while President Woodrow Wilson of Princeton avowed himself a "fierce partisan" of the open shop.

The employers' counteroffensive would not have succeeded so well,
however, if labor had been able to come into the court of public opinion
with clean hands. The middle class would never support the labor movement until it was certain that labor sought the general good instead of class
privileges and had repudiated violence as an instrument of industrial warfare. Insofar as Gompers and his associates were able to identify unionism
with democracy and to remove the stigma of alien origin from the AF of L,
they made a lasting contribution to the advancement of American democratic institutions. Unfortunately, anti-union spokesmen during this period
were able to point with telling effect to many examples of violence, irresponsibility, and corruption among the ranks of organized labor.

31. *The Courts, Injunctions, and the AF of L in Politics*

Gompers had managed to fight off those idealists who advocated align-
ing the AF of L with the Socialist Labor party, the Populists in 1892, and the
Democrats during the great battle of 1896. It would have been difficult for
Gompers to maintain this policy of nonpartisanship in any event, given the
momentum and attraction of the progressive movement. But one event,
more than any other, was responsible for the AF of L's entry into the political arena. It was the entrance of the federal courts into labor disputes in a

decisive way. It began during the Chicago railroad strike of 1894, when the Attorney General of the United States obtained an injunction against Eugene V. Debs and other leaders of the American Railway Union for conspiring to restrain trade and obstruct the movement of mail. The theory upon which this and later injunctions were issued was that the prohibitions against restraint of trade embodied in the Sherman antitrust law of 1890 applied as much to labor and farm unions as to corporations. The effect of this doctrine, which was confirmed by the Supreme Court in 1895, was not to outlaw unions, per se, as illegal conspiracies, but to forbid union practices that might be construed to be unreasonable, or illegal, restraints upon trade.

The Sherman Act was used before 1901 less against illegal industrial combinations than labor's allegedly illegal weapons—mass picketing, the sympathetic strike, the secondary boycott, and blacklisting of goods manufactured by anti-union employers. It was the continued intervention of the federal courts after 1901 that finally compelled Gompers and the AF of L to take an active role in national politics. The immediate provocation arose out of two cases involving the boycott of nonunion products—the Danbury Hatters' case and the Buck's Stove and Range Company case.

The United Hatters of North America in 1902 called a strike against a hatmaker of Danbury, Connecticut, D. E. Loewe and Company, and declared a nation-wide boycott of Loewe's products. Officials of the company struck back by organizing the American Anti-Boycott Association and by suing the United Hatters in 1903 for triple damages of $240,000 under the Sherman Act. The Supreme Court five years later confirmed the judgment of the lower courts that the boycott was a conspiracy in restraint of trade. The district court thereupon awarded the company full damages and made members of the union personally responsible for payment of the claim. In the second case, the Buck's Stove and Range Company in 1907 obtained an injunction in a federal court ordering officials of the AF of L to end a boycott against the company's products. Gompers and the executive committee of the AF of L ignored the injunction, and a federal court sentenced them all to jail for terms ranging from six months to one year. The Supreme Court in 1914 upheld the injunction but removed the penalties on a technicality.

The effect of the rulings in these two test cases was to confirm that all of labor's strike activities fell within the purview of the federal courts, and that union leaders and members were liable to jail terms and loss of property if they defied injunctions. In short, labor might wage industrial warfare only if the federal courts approved. Obviously, the AF of L's surest means of protection against such judicial interference was to obtain amendment of the Sherman law to give labor unions immunity from its prohibitions.

The leaders of the AF of L tried in various indirect ways from 1900 to 1906 to force the desired changes in the Sherman Act, but their pressure, as contrasted with the growing political power of the NAM, was pitifully weak. Gompers and his associates decided in 1906 that the time had come to begin an all-out political campaign. First they presented to President Roosevelt and Congress a Bill of Grievances, demanding, among other things, amendment of the Sherman law and relief from judicial interference. Next, they entered the congressional campaign of 1906 and helped to elect six union members to the House of Representatives. Two years later Gompers presented the AF of L's demands to the platform committees of the Republican and Democratic national conventions. The Republicans refused to make any concessions or promises, while the Democrats adopted a disingenuous platform plank that seemed to promise substantial relief. Taking what they could get, Gompers and his colleagues openly campaigned in behalf of the Democratic ticket headed by Bryan.

The Republican victory in 1908 was only a momentary reversal, for the political situation from 1910 to 1912 seemed to offer the AF of L an opportunity finally to achieve its goal. Internal warfare split the Republican party and made certain a Democratic victory in 1912. And when the Democrats nominated a progressive, Woodrow Wilson, and reaffirmed the promises that they had made to labor four years before, Gompers and his executive committee campaigned openly and effectively for the Democratic ticket. Wilson won a sweeping victory in the Electoral College, the Democrats won control of both houses of Congress, and it seemed that labor's friends were finally in control of the federal government.

In large measure labor's hopes were realized during the period of Wilson's first administration, from 1913 to 1917. The new Secretary of Labor, William B. Wilson, was a former secretary-treasurer of the UMW; some fifteen union members sat in the House of Representatives; and the new President was considerably more susceptible to labor pressure than Roosevelt or Taft had been. The changed climate was everywhere evident in Washington —in the exposure of an NAM lobby by a congressional committee in 1913; in the forthright investigation of the Colorado coal strike in 1914 by the House labor committee and the Industrial Relations Commission; in adoption in 1915 of the Seaman's Act, sponsored by Gompers and Andrew Furuseth of the International Seamen's Union, which freed sailors from bondage to their labor contracts; in passage of the Smith-Hughes Act in 1916 (approved in 1917), providing for federal aid to state vocational education; and in passage of the Burnett immigration bill, which established a literacy test for immigrants, over Wilson's veto in 1917.

Even so, the AF of L's chief objective was still amendment of the Sherman Act to give unions immunity from prosecution for using illegal strike weapons. In this campaign Gompers and the AF of L lobby ran head on into the stubborn opposition of President Wilson and the Democratic majority in Congress. The issue first arose decisively during the preparation of new antitrust legislation, the Clayton bill, in 1914. This measure as it emerged from the House judiciary committee included no provisions for labor's benefit. Gompers and his now powerful lobby at once descended upon Congress and the White House. Labor spokesmen in the House threatened to oppose the Clayton bill, and there were many stormy conferences between the labor leaders and administration spokesmen. So firmly did the administration stand, however, that Gompers had to accept a compromise that denied the AF of L its supreme objective. The House committee added sections to the Clayton bill providing for jury trials in criminal contempt cases and circumscribing the issuance of injunctions in labor disputes. Another provision declared that neither farm nor labor unions should be construed to be illegal combinations, per se, in restraint of trade. But as the courts had repeatedly declared that labor unions were not unlawful combinations, this declaration by Congress conferred no new benefits. A final provision legalized strike activities that the courts had heretofore approved.

President Wilson and the chairman of the House committee that framed the labor sections of the Clayton bill frankly declared that the bill did not give labor unions immunity from prosecution for violating the antitrust law. But Gompers hailed the Clayton Act as labor's "Magna Charta" and announced that the AF of L had finally won freedom from judicial interference under the Sherman law. As we shall see in a later chapter, the Supreme Court thought otherwise.

CHAPTER

4

The

Progressive Movement

I T IS IMPOSSIBLE to comprehend within the bounds of a few generalizations any phenomenon so complex and far-reaching as the progressive movement in the United States. Much confusion can be avoided, however, if the reader bears several fundamental principles in mind.

To begin with, there was no such thing as *a* progressive movement. That is, there was no organized campaign uniting all diverse efforts at political, social, and economic reform. On the contrary, there were numerous progressive movements operating in different areas simultaneously. There was, for example, the effort of social workers and students of the labor question to bring state and national governments to the side of women, children, and other unprotected groups. This movement for social justice was often, but not always, independent of the movement for political reform. There was the far-reaching campaign, getting under way about 1900, to end the reign of corruption in, and to restore representative government to, the cities. Next came a movement to bring state governments out of their subservience to railroads and corporations and to make them instruments for advancing social welfare. Finally, there was a progressive movement on the national level, the main thrusts of which were attempts to subject railroads, industrial corporations, and banks to effective public control.

In the second place, the progressive movement, in its political manifestations, was essentially a revolt of the middle classes—small businessmen and bankers, prosperous farmers, editors, clergymen, and other professional groups—against a state of affairs that seemed to guarantee perpetual control to the privileged few who owned the wealth of the United States. Although it drew support from organized labor, the movement had no solid basis of popular support among the masses of workers, nor was it particularly sympathetic to labor's needs. Moreover, while leadership in the reform movement of the 1890's had been largely agrarian, extreme farm unrest subsided after 1897. Leadership in the revolt against the *status quo* passed, therefore, to the cities and small towns.

The foregoing generalization has to be somewhat qualified. In the South and West the connection between Populism and progressivism was fairly direct. In the West most Populists went into the Democratic party in 1896 and constituted the main part of Bryan's following in that region afterward. The process of assimilation was slower in the South, but the former Populists were by 1912 an important segment of a new progressive coalition vying for control of Democratic state organizations. More generally speaking, Populism's rather considerable radicalism on issues like control of railroads and industry and the money supply had a continuing effect on reform thinking and objectives.

Thirdly, the degree to which progressives were united in a common cause with well-defined objectives varied from movement to movement and from area to area. The social justice champions, for example, were organized in state and national associations and united behind common programs. Although the city and state reformers never formally combined regionally or nationally, they all faced the same problems, attacked them in much the same way, and profited from one another's experiences. In the arena of national politics, moreover, progressives in both parties often fought for the same goals.

Nonetheless, there was a profound divergence in progressive attitudes until 1916 toward the paramount questions of corporation control and of how far federal legislation should be employed for the benefit of workers and farmers. The dominant tradition of American democracy had been the Jeffersonian ideal of a neutral, umpire state giving special favors to no class or interest. Many progressives, including most Democrats, thought that the federal government should do no more than destroy the system of protection for business that the Republicans had constructed since 1861. Others, including Theodore Roosevelt and many progressive Republicans after 1908, argued that the federal government should play a positive role by directly regulating business activities and giving special protection to labor and farmers. As we shall later see, this dilemma was not resolved until 1916.

In addition, there is the problem of explaining *why* the progressive revolt happened *when* it did—during a period of economic prosperity and general social contentment. Some recent authorities have suggested that the prime dynamic force was the resentment that older established classes felt toward the *nouveaux riches* and the general fear of the middle classes that they were being ground between the rising upper and lower classes. This is what is called the "status revolution" theory of progressivism's causation. Perhaps it sheds some light. But it, like most historical theories, is too simple. The moving forces in progressivism were as complex and varied as the movement itself, and they are to be found only in the details of the historical record.

With these generalizations by way of introduction, let us now examine one of the most significant and fruitful reform movements in American history.

32. *The Social Justice Movement*

The social justice movement was the first large-scale attempt to palliate the grosser aspects of American life—the miserable living conditions of city masses, exploitation of women and children in industry, and degradation of submerged, unprotected workers. The vanguard in the movement were priests and ministers who worked in the slums. However, a separate class of social workers, usually employed by charity organizations and settlement houses, emerged in the 1890's. They constituted a growing and vociferous element in the American society after 1900. They made intensive surveys of labor conditions, causes of poverty, and means of alleviating social distress. As time passed, moreover, they became departmentalized, some concerned with care of immigrants, some with problems of labor, some with juvenile delinquency. As a recent authority has said, "By the latter part of the 1890's a start had been made toward the accumulation of social facts; after the turn of the century the study of mankind was to be carried forward with a vigor and zest that imparted a characteristic tone to the intellectual climate of the Progressive era." [1]

The leaders of the social justice movement by 1900 had gone far beyond the concept of private amelioration and were beginning to evolve ambitious new schemes of social salvation. What they now envisaged was nothing less than systematic use of state police power to accomplish rearrangement of economic relationships. In other words, state governments, and later the federal government, should enter the battle to protect the weak—first by legislation based upon investigations of social workers, next by employing social workers as agents of enforcement.

First to come under the concerted attack of the social justice forces was the old problem of child labor. It posed the most poignant challenge, for by 1900 probably 1,700,000 children under sixteen were employed in the cotton mills of New England and the South, in New Jersey berry fields, and on farms. The problem grew even worse as the textile industry advanced in the South during the early years of the twentieth century.

The attack on child labor opened simultaneously on two fronts—in the Southeast in 1901, with the introduction of child labor bills in the legislatures of the Carolinas, Georgia, and Alabama; in the North, with adoption of pioneer legislation by New Jersey, New York, and Illinois in 1903–4. The southern and northern wings of the movement came together in 1904 in the National Child Labor Committee, which had twenty-five branch committees in twenty-two states by 1910.

The accomplishments of this dedicated band constituted perhaps the greatest single triumph of the social justice movement before the First World War. In 1900 twenty-four states and the District of Columbia made

<hr>

[1] Robert H. Bremner, *From the Depths: The Discovery of Poverty in the United States* (New York, 1956), p. 85.

no provision for a minimum age for workers. But by 1914 every state but one had established a minimum age limit, usually fourteen, while many states had prohibited children between fourteen and sixteen from working at night and in dangerous occupations.

The movement for a federal child labor law did not reach serious proportions until near the end of the progressive period. Senator Albert J. Beveridge of Indiana introduced the first federal bill in 1906, but the National Child Labor Committee refused to endorse it on the ground that it was best to work for a while longer in the states. However, conditions seemed ripe for federal action in 1914, and the Committee sponsored the introduction of a bill in Congress in that year. It prohibited the shipment in interstate commerce of goods manufactured in whole or in part by children under fourteen and of products of mines or quarries where children under sixteen were employed. The measure passed the House of Representatives in 1914 but languished in the Senate while spokesmen of the NAM and southern textile interests denounced it as an unconstitutional invasion of the police power of the states. Then President Wilson pushed the bill, now called the Keating-Owen bill, through the Senate in the summer of 1916. It was the most significant victory of the social justice movement before the New Deal.

A second major objective of the social justice crusade was protection of women in industry by limiting the number of hours they might work. Illinois enacted the first enforceable eight-hour law for women in 1893—the result of the labors of Florence Kelley of Chicago's Hull House. However, the state Supreme Court nullified the Illinois statute two years later, and leadership in this campaign passed to the East. There the standard was carried by Consumers' Leagues, organizations of socially minded women. Beginning with the enactment of statutes by New York in 1896 and Massachusetts in 1900 limiting women's hours to sixty a week, the movement spread slowly to Nebraska, Michigan, Colorado, Oregon, Washington, and Tennessee. Once the United States Supreme Court ended doubt about the constitutionality of women's hours legislation, the movement gained enormous momentum. Thirty-nine states enacted hours legislation for the first time or strengthened existing laws between 1909 and 1917.

A third, and perhaps the most ambitious, social justice objective was minimum wage legislation for women workers. By enacting the first statutes of this kind from 1896 to 1909, Australia and Great Britain provided inspiration to American reformers. An even more important impetus came from governmental and private investigations in the United States from 1911 to 1914. They revealed that large numbers of women received wages entirely inadequate to maintain a decent standard of living. The National Consumers' League made minimum wage legislation part of its long-range program in 1910; the Women's Trade Union League joined the fight in the following year, and the campaign had begun.

This feminine coalition scored its first victory in 1912, when the Massachusetts legislature established a wage commission empowered to recommend minimum wages for women and to expose employers who refused to conform. The following year saw the adoption by eight midwestern and western states of statutes that went the whole way and empowered wage commissions to establish binding minimum wage rates. However, the movement lost most of its strength after 1913. During the following decade only six additional states, the District of Columbia, and Puerto Rico joined the states that sought to protect the living standard, health, and morality of women workers.

The last major objective of the champions of social welfare was establishment of public systems of industrial accident insurance. Western European nations had long since demonstrated the excellence and feasibility of such systems. In the United States, however, the common law rules relating to industrial accidents still governed the payment of damages.[2] The obvious injustice of throwing practically the entire financial burden of industrial accidents and deaths on workers and their families—for that was usually the result of the application of the common law rules—led to an early movement to abrogate or modify these doctrines. Most states by 1910 had modified the common law rules in favor of the injured worker; even so, he was little better off than before because he still had to sue to recover damages. Maryland, Montana, and the federal government experimented from 1902 to 1909 with crude and limited systems of accident insurance, but this represented all that had been accomplished to this date. A brief period of intense official investigation into the entire subject ensued between 1909 and 1913. All commissions concluded that the prevailing compensation system had collapsed and recommended enactment of accident insurance laws. A wave of protest and legislation swept over the country as the people learned the facts. Ten states established insurance systems in 1911, and twenty states, three territories, and the federal government followed suit from 1912 to 1916.

Thus it was that professional social workers, students of the labor problem, and leaders of advanced social opinion grew strong during the progressive era, emerged as a redemptive element in the American democracy, and banded together in crusades to transform an individualistic and competitive society into something approximating the welfare state. There were dozens of organizations and more campaigns for social reforms than we have space to relate. Some social justice advocates, going far beyond the objectives we have described, set on foot discussions of social security, unemployment relief, and laws designed to advance the interests of organized labor. These pioneers on the advanced social frontier failed to obtain the legislation that they advocated. They were, however, laying the necessary groundwork for a new social justice movement which would come to fruition in the 1930's. The line of descent from the social justice movement of the early 1900's to the New Deal is clear and straight.

33.   *The Supreme Court and Social Legislation*

Social justice reformers were not only beset by the opposition of employers and other representatives of selfish economic interests but also

---

[2] Briefly stated, under these common law rules the injured employee was not entitled to compensation if he had willingly assumed the risks of his job, if he was himself negligent, or if his injury had been caused by a fellow worker's negligence. Moreover, in most cases the injured employee had to sue for damages and prove that he had suffered as a direct result of his employer's negligence.

faced even more formidable opposition from yet another source—the bench and bar of the United States. The great majority of American lawyers and judges at the turn of the century had been reared on Anglo-American legal tradition that often valued liberty above justice and the rights of property above humanity. They believed firmly in the automatic operation of economic laws, cultivated strong hostility to the concept of public control, and were usually ranged on the side of railroads and large corporations.

The implications of this fact for the social justice movement become at once apparent when one recalls the peculiar power of judges in the American constitutional system. Unlike their counterparts elsewhere in the western world, American judges had established the privilege of determining whether legislation violated the provisions of written state and federal constitutions. As judges nowhere rendered decisions in an intellectual vacuum, their own preconceived notions of the proper functions of government invariably affected their legal judgments. In rendering decisions in cases involving social legislation, therefore, judges often unconsciously permitted inherited prejudices, instead of sound legal precepts, to control decisions that they made.

Proponents of social welfare legislation occasionally ran afoul of the verdicts of state judges, but federal courts, and eventually the United States Supreme Court, posed the greatest threat. This was true during the progressive period, not because federal courts always nullified state efforts at social amelioration, but because the Supreme Court in the 1880's had established the doctrine that corporations were persons within the meaning of the Fourteenth Amendment.[3] Corporations were therefore at liberty to appeal to federal courts for protection; and federal judges insisted upon reviewing state regulatory legislation to determine whether it violated the Fourteenth Amendment's dictum that no state should deprive a person of life, liberty, or property without due process of law.

It was not, however, until 1898 that the Supreme Court rendered its first important decision involving state labor legislation. In Holden v. Hardy the court in that year upheld a Utah statute establishing the eight-hour day for miners. The decision also expounded in forceful language the legal theories underlying all social legislation by the states, namely, that it was the duty of the state to protect the health and morals of its citizens; that this protection could be afforded by proper use of the police power; and, finally, that such use of the police power did not unlawfully infringe the freedom of contract guaranteed by the Fourteenth Amendment. While this decision clearly established the right of the states to limit the hours of labor in dangerous occupations, it did not affirm the constitutionality of hours legislation for any and all occupations. In fact, no one was quite sure how far the states might go in this respect until the Supreme Court set one limitation in its decision in Lochner v. New York in 1905.

The Lochner case involved the constitutionality of a New York statute limiting the hours that bakers could work to ten a day and sixty a week. Counsel for the state argued that the bakers' law protected the public's food supply. Lochner's counsel, on the other hand, replied that the law unduly violated the freedom of employer and employee to make a labor contract. A

_____

[3] For this development, see below, pp. 115–116.

bare majority of the court decided that the time had come to call a halt to improper use of the state police power. Asserting that the bakers' trade was not particularly unhealthy, the majority concluded that "Statutes of the nature of that under review, limiting the hours in which grown and intelligent men may labor to earn their living, are mere meddlesome interferences with the rights of the individual." In other words, a state could not contravene the freedom of contract unless there were obvious and compelling reasons for exercising the police power.

Worse still for the social justice reformers, the Lochner decision created grave doubt about the constitutionality of legislation restricting hours of labor merely on the basis of sex. This issue arose in 1907, when an employer challenged an Oregon ten-hour law for women. Perceiving that this was a supreme crisis in the life of the social justice movement, Mrs. Florence Kelley, chief Factory Inspector of Illinois, and Josephine Goldmark, the driving spirit in the National Consumers' League, set about to obtain a distinguished attorney to defend the Oregon statute. They turned first to Joseph H. Choate, leader of the American bar. But Choate refused, saying that he could see no reason why "a big husky Irishwoman should not work more than ten hours a day in a laundry if she and her employer so desired." On the next day Mrs. Kelley and Miss Goldmark asked Louis D. Brandeis of Boston, nationally known as "the people's attorney," to defend the law, and Brandeis gladly agreed.

Brandeis had long argued that the law had not been altered to fit the new conditions of American economic and social life. The trouble was, he said, that neither lawyers nor judges knew anything about the economic and social conditions out of which cases arose. He proposed to substitute a sociological jurisprudence in the place of a myopic legal traditionalism. As Brandeis put it, "A lawyer who has not studied economics and sociology is very apt to become a public enemy."

The Oregon case gave Brandeis an opportunity to put his sociological jurisprudence to practical use and, even better, to demonstrate it before the whole legal profession. In preparing his brief he gave only two pages to conventional legal reasoning and citation of precedents. In contrast, he used more than one hundred pages to demonstrate the economic and social consequences of long hours of work by women. By citing evidence drawn from hundreds of sources he proved that long hours were dangerous to women's health and morals and that reasonable hours produced tangible social benefits. Heretofore no lawyer had ever submitted such a brief; cases had always been argued on a basis of abstract logic and by appeal to precedents. "There is no logic that is properly applicable to these laws," Brandeis said, "except the logic of facts."

The case, Muller v. Oregon, was argued before the Supreme Court in January 1908. Plaintiff's counsel asserted that women, equally with men, were endowed with a freedom of contract that no legislature could impair. To this Brandeis again responded with a masterful array of facts. Brandeis's argument won the day even though the court was dominated by traditionalists. In upholding the constitutionality of the Oregon ten-hour law, the court for the first time admitted the need for facts to establish the reasonableness or unreasonableness of social legislation.

It was an epochal victory for the social justice movement; even more important was the fact that Brandeis's technique of marshaling economic and social data in defense of social legislation soon became ordinary legal practice. Four additional cases involving women's hours legislation reached the Supreme Court from 1908 to 1915. In each case the court adhered to the principle set forth in Muller *v.* Oregon, approving even a comprehensive California eight-hour law for women.

The Supreme Court during the period 1898–1915 also reviewed a number of state child labor laws. In no field of social legislation were reformers on surer constitutional ground, and the court consistently affirmed the right of the states to protect their children—by prohibiting work in hazardous occupations or at an age that was prejudicial to their health and morals. However, it was still a moot question before 1918 whether *Congress* could use its control over commerce to regulate the labor of children.

Obviously, the court had been profoundly influenced by the progressive upheaval. The extent of that influence was demonstrated in 1917, when the court passed on almost all forms of labor legislation. In Bunting *v.* Oregon, the justices tacitly reversed their decision in Lochner *v.* New York by approving an Oregon ten-hour law for men in industry. In Wilson *v.* New the court narrowly sustained the Adamson Act, which established the eight-hour day for railway workers engaged in interstate commerce. In Stettler *v.* O'Hara an evenly divided court upheld an Oregon statute establishing minimum wages for women. Finally, the court upheld the constitutionality of the three systems of industrial accident insurance then in effect in various states. Indeed, it seemed beyond doubt that sociological jurisprudence had at last found acceptance by the highest court of the land.

34. *The Muckrakers*

While social workers were beginning their investigations and formulating their programs, a revolution in the field of journalism was also slowly taking form. Its principal aspect was the emergence of a group of reporters, called muckrakers, who trumpeted dire warnings of changes portentous for the future of democracy. American representative government had ceased to be either representative or democratic. The old promise of equality of economic opportunity was rapidly becoming an anachronism in view of developments in business and finance. Uncontrolled railroads, insurance companies, and meat packing houses were levying tribute from the people and endangering their lives. The ideal of social equality was being destroyed on all sides by abuse of immigrants and Negroes.

These publicists who probed all the dark corners of American life did not make the progressive movement. The social justice movement and the campaign to clean up the cities and states, for example, were well on foot when they entered the battle. However, by exposing the shame and corruption of American public life the muckrakers fired the righteous indignation of the middle classes. In so doing, they helped to make the progressive movement a national uprising instead of a series of sporadic campaigns.

A medium for the muckrakers came in the 1890's with the cheap magazine.[4] *Cosmopolitan, Munsey's,* and *McClure's* were already in the field by 1900, catering to the reading habits of the middle classes. The leader of the three, *McClure's,* was the creature of S. S. McClure, an ebullient but erratic Irishman who was evolving a novel concept of the cheap magazine as the nineteenth century ended. Understanding the public excitement over the growth of railroad and industrial combinations, he decided to publish articles of contemporary economic and social significance. Giving complete freedom and generous financial support to his writers, McClure imposed only two standards—accuracy and readability.

To Ida M. Tarbell, a young writer on his staff, McClure in 1896 assigned the task of writing a history of the Standard Oil Company. He expected that her series would begin the following February. Miss Tarbell, however, spent five years in hard research and writing before her work was completed. Her *History of the Standard Oil Company,* which began in *McClure's* in November 1902 and ran for the following fifteen months, virtually took the country by storm. Although she was coldly objective and a master of the evidence, Miss Tarbell fully revealed the methods that Rockefeller and his partners had used to build the oil monopoly.

At about the time that Miss Tarbell was completing her study a courageous circuit attorney in St. Louis, Joseph W. Folk, was exposing the corruption of the local Democratic boss. McClure's managing editor, Lincoln Steffens, went to investigate, and that was how one of the best reporters of the twentieth century began his remarkable career as a muckraker. From the Missouri city Steffens went on to investigate political conditions in Minneapolis, Cleveland, New York, Chicago, Philadelphia, and Pittsburgh. He found everywhere essentially the same government by corrupt alliances of politicians and businessmen. He returned to write about them in *McClure's,* and to publish his articles in book form in 1904 as *The Shame of the Cities.* Steffens next studied political affairs in several states, and his findings were embodied in a second series in *McClure's* in 1905 and 1906, published in book form in the latter year under the title *The Struggle for Self-Government.*

The third of the trinity of McClure's great muckrakers was Ray Stannard Baker, a young journalist from the Middle West, who investigated social and economic problems. He explored the labor situation, for example, and wrote for *McClure's* a revealing account of the Colorado coal strike of 1903–4. His scholarly and convincing indictment of railroad malpractices, *The Railroads on Trial,* strengthened President Roosevelt's hand in the battle to enlarge the powers of the Interstate Commerce Commission. His *Following the Colour Line* was a pioneer study of prevailing racial attitudes, North and South.

Among other writers on the staff of *McClure's,* two were notable. Burton J. Hendrick in 1906 publicized the revelations of corruption and mismanagement among the New York insurance companies, which a commission headed by Charles Evans Hughes had brought to light the year before. George Kibbe Turner's articles in 1909 on the alliance between the

---

[4] For this development, see above, p. 40.

Chicago police and organized prostitution led to a famous vice commission's report on the midwestern city in 1911.

McClure's experiment soon proved that the public would buy a magazine devoted to serious discussions of contemporary problems, and other publishers were not long in following his example. *Collier's,* under the editorship of Norman Hapgood, led crusades against twin evils: the patent medicine fraud and the fraud of William Randolph Hearst. Charles Edward Russell's exposure of the beef trust, published in *Everybody's* in 1905, was another notable contribution.

It was inevitable, however, that the muckraking technique would be adopted by publishers and writers of dubious integrity and exploited merely for financial gain. The first of the yellow muckrakers was Thomas W. Lawson, a stock market gambler and former president of the Amalgamated Copper Company, whose series, "Frenzied Finance," in *Everybody's* in 1905, allegedly exposed the insides of the monster, high finance. His revelations of financial corruption were lurid and highly exaggerated, but they had a tremendous impact. The circulation of *Everybody's* jumped in one year from 150,000 to over 750,000; and there can be no doubt that Lawson contributed to the public demand for control of the stock market that culminated in the Pujo Committee's investigation of 1913.

It was a sure sign that muckraking was heading for the gutter when William Randolph Hearst announced in 1906 that his *Cosmopolitan* would soon publish exposures that would be "the most vascular and virile" of them all. What Hearst had in mind was a series entitled "The Treason of the Senate," which the novelist David Graham Phillips was then writing. As it turned out, Phillips combined truth, fiction, and outright prevarication. But his indictment of the Senate added a powerful impetus to the movement for direct election of senators.

35. *The Literature of Revolt*

Contemporaneous with muckraking in magazine journalism was the proliferation of a fictional literature dedicated to the cause of democracy. Social and economic criticism ran the gamut from harsh exposés to frank appeals for a proletarian revolution. Frank Norris's *The Octopus* and *The Pit* told of the Southern Pacific Railroad's domination of the politics of California and the grain speculators' control of the wheat market. The naturalist Theodore Dreiser contributed two powerful socio-economic studies, *The Financier* and *The Titan,* based on the career of Charles T. Yerkes, a traction magnate of Chicago in the 1890's. David Graham Phillips exploited the theme of the corrupting power of money in *The Great God Success* and *The Second Generation,* while his *Susan Lennox, Her Fall and Rise* analyzed the social forces that drove a country girl in the city to prostitution. Robert Herrick's *The Memoirs of an American Citizen* and *Clark's Field* were impressive portrayals of the rise of men of wealth in an acquisitive society.

Socialist literary critiques of the shortcomings of the American democracy were, if anything, even harsher than the works already cited.

Robert Hunter's *Poverty* and Ben B. Lindsey's *The Beast,* for example, indicted capitalism for making greed, exploitation, poverty, and corruption inevitable. In *The Bitter Cry of the Children* John Spargo offered a moving plea for child labor reform and a damning indictment of a system that consumed its young. Jack London, like Spargo a leader in the Socialist party, was easily the most violent literary radical of his time. His *The Iron Heel* portrayed the capitalistic system at its alleged worst. In *The War of the Classes* and *Revolution* London affirmed his faith in the ultimate triumph of the workers.

Foremost in influence among the Socialist critics was Upton Sinclair, whose most important work during the progressive period was *The Jungle,* published in 1906. It was a story of a Lithuanian immigrant in the Chicago packing houses. Intended as a plea for socialism, *The Jungle* was a moving indictment of an economic system that allegedly brought hunger and misery to great masses of people. As Sinclair later lamented, *The Jungle* appealed to the stomachs rather than the hearts of the American people. They ignored what he said about socialism but were revolted by his descriptions of the filthy conditions of the slaughtering houses. The novel was, therefore, a powerful factor in compelling passage of the Pure Food and Drug Act in 1906.

The political novelists of the first decade of the twentieth century were more prolific, if less critical of American institutions, than the socioeconomic writers. Alfred Henry Lewis' *The Boss,* based upon the career of Richard Croker of Tammany Hall, and Elliott Flower's *The Spoilsman* portrayed in fictional form the political corruption that Lincoln Steffens knew so well. Brand Whitlock, from his experiences in the government of Toledo, Ohio, added two powerful novels to the literature of exposure— *The Thirteenth District* and *The Turn of the Balance.* Booth Tarkington, in *The Gentleman from Indiana, In the Arena,* and other novels, exploited the theme of the corruption of the political life of a state by railroad and business interests.

The most popular of these political novelists was Winston Churchill of New Hampshire, whose *Coniston* and *Mr. Crewe's Career* sold by the hundreds of thousands. Churchill seemed to think that a regeneration of American politics would occur if only the sturdy, plain people turned the rascals out and elected honest men. Equally naive was William Allen White's *A Certain Rich Man,* a collection of platitudes with an incredible ending. If Churchill and White illustrated the shallowness of many of the political writers, David Graham Phillips exemplified in fictional form the strenuosity of this literary movement. In *The Plum Tree* he attempted to expose the system of corruption and special privilege everywhere in the United States.

Whether profound or shallow, these leaders of the literary revolt against the *status quo* made a considerable contribution to the progressive movement. They wrote on subjects ranging from child labor to the use of state troops to break strikes. Their achievement in highlighting corruption in politics and the darker phases of American society furnished a basis in conviction for the national effort to achieve government representative of the people and responsive to their social and economic needs.

36. *Intellectual Progressivism*

Every movement of vitality eventually reaches a point where it spawns philosophers who attempt to systematize its thought and formulate a philosophy to justify its practical program. Although the progressive movement was no exception to this rule, its intellectuals had to do more than merely construct a new philosophy. They first had to overturn the whole structure of ideas upon which the defenders of the *status quo* rested their arguments: social Darwinism and individualism; the cult of hostility to government; the belief that the Constitution was an inspired document, and that the Supreme Court was the interpreter of divine judgment; and, finally, the idea that railroad builders, financiers, and captains of industry had contributed to the nation's economic progress. These concepts had become so firmly embedded in the popular mind by 1900 that together they constituted the American creed. It had to be destroyed before progressive concepts could find wholesale acceptance.

Inherent in practically every aspect of the progressive offensive, furthermore, was the ultimate objective of planting faith in the efficacy of public measures of amelioration and control. Students of labor legislation, champions of social justice measures, and expounders of the new sociological jurisprudence, for example, were all trying to build a basis in economic and social fact for the necessity of positive government. So also were social gospel leaders, when they preached doctrines of social salvation, or sociologists, when they urged the necessity of thinking of wrongdoing in social as well as individual terms.

The most significant formulation of progressive political theory came from the pen of Herbert Croly, a New York journalist, whose major works, *The Promise of American Life,* published in 1909, and *Progressive Democracy,* published in 1914, at once established him as the chief philosopher of progressivism. Moreover, as editor of the *New Republic,* which he founded in 1914 with the financial backing of the Morgan partner, Willard Straight, Croly gathered around him most of the leading young social and economic thinkers of the time. Croly's writings provided progressives with their most cogent arguments in behalf of positive legislation.

He began by arguing that the most widely accepted American political tradition was the Jeffersonian tradition of distrust of government and extreme individualism in economic affairs. This tradition, Croly said, had become identified with democracy because Jefferson was in fact the first American democratic philosopher and leader. In contrast, the Hamiltonian tradition of strong government had been closely identified in the popular mind with special privileges for the upper classes, because Hamilton was an ardent champion of these classes. Most Americans still believed that the promise of American life could be realized only if the golden age of competition could be restored by withdrawing all special privileges to the business classes. The fact was, Croly warned, that such a policy of *laissez faire* and drift in an age of inevitable big industry and big finance could only carry the nation to an equally inevitable ruin—to aggrandizement of power by the special interests and the degradation of the masses.

Who could save the nation from such peril? How could the American dream of democracy and equality of opportunity be fulfilled? The answer, Croly said, was clear. Progressives must abandon their romantic Jeffersonian concepts and support a program of positive and comprehensive state and federal intervention on all economic fronts. This would mean, for one thing, that progressives would have to abandon opposition to class or special-interest legislation. Such a program had perhaps served a useful purpose at one time, but it was now the chief intellectual stumbling block.

The important task ahead, Croly declared, was first to define the national interest and then to achieve its fulfillment by careful planning and legislation. The important question, of course, was, who would define the national interest? Croly answered by calling for a new nationalism that would attract the leadership of the "best minds" in the task of reconciling planning and positive government with the democratic tradition.

The year 1912 saw the publication of a second significant plea for a new political positivism—Walter Weyl's *The New Democracy*. Weyl did not share Croly's mystical faith in the "national interest" and the "best minds." He was much more concerned with facts and figures, and he made self-interest the motivation for his program of social and industrial democracy. In brief, he said, a democracy could not allow large groups to be degraded and exploited because these same groups would in the end resort to violence and perhaps destroy society. Walter Lippmann's *Preface to Politics*, 1913, and *Drift and Mastery*, 1914, supplemented Croly's and particularly Weyl's arguments. Lippmann, then a young socialist in process of shedding his parlor radicalism, assumed the necessity of democratic collectivism. His major argument was for a pragmatic approach to politics, one based on science and unencumbered by so-called moral criteria.

Another important component of the intellectual attack on the conservative ideology was the discrediting of the divine-origin theory of the Constitution, which was often invoked by opponents of the direct election of senators and other neodemocratic proposals. Discontent over the undemocratic features of the Constitution was as old as the document itself, but not until the progressive period did scholars and politicians evolve the thesis that the Constitution had been written deliberately to frustrate the democratic movement.

This thesis was first systematically developed by Walter Clark, Chief Justice of North Carolina, in an address at the University of Pennsylvania Law School in 1906. The following year, in *The Spirit of American Government*, Professor J. Allen Smith of the University of Washington repeated Clark's assertion that a minority had conceived the Constitution in class interest and imposed it upon the majority in order to thwart their aspirations. Charles A. Beard, a young historian at Columbia University who had discovered Marx and Engels in England around the turn of the century, went to work to prove that the Constitution had been written to protect merchants, great landowners, moneylenders, and speculators. His findings, embodied in 1913 in *An Economic Interpretation of the Constitution*, shocked and horrified conservatives. Progressives, however, could now say that the Constitution, which had so often stood in the way of their reforms, was no more sacrosanct than any other part of the American past.

As a final blow, intellectual progressives applied the full weight of scholarship and sarcasm toward discrediting the belief that railroad build-ers, financiers, and captains of industry were heroes and contributors to American progress. The most trenchant of the critics of the moneyed classes was Thorstein Veblen, a strange quondam economics professor, whose eco-nomic theory had much greater impact in the 1930's than during his own day. His most widely read work, *The Theory of the Leisure Class*, 1899, was a biting attack against the standards and practices of contemporary American business civilization.

The most prolific of the debunkers of the plutocracy was Gustavus Myers, a socialist, who grimly set to work to discover how great fortunes in the United States had been accumulated. His *History of the Great Ameri-can Fortunes*, published in three volumes in 1909–10, confirmed the old charge that large American fortunes had been made through plunder and pre-emption of natural resources. As Myers' work came as a climax to a number of shorter exposures, he simply buried the corpse of the benevolent plutocrat.

There were, of course, many other leaders equally prominent in this extraordinary and far-reaching revolt of the intellectuals. Beginning with Lester F. Ward and the young economists who organized the American Economic Association in 1885, their numbers multiplied and their influence grew as the years passed. While we cannot measure their contribution precisely, we can surely say that their part in making the progressive movement a permanent force in American life was not small. Their great contribution lay in discrediting a conservative ideology that had strongly buttressed the *status quo*, and in formulating a philosophy for the social-welfare state. In this respect and for this reason, therefore, the intellectuals were the true leaveners of progressivism.

37. *The Shame of the Cities*

Through the agitation of political leaders and the exposures of muck-rakers, the American people, from the 1890's to about 1910, discovered that representative political institutions in their cities had broken down almost completely. Instead of being governed by representatives impartially chosen, most American cities were ruled by political machines that in their hierarchical structure resembled the modern corporation. In the bottom rank was the precinct captain, who organized a small district and dispensed small favors. Above him was the ward leader, or heeler, who was a lieuten-ant of the boss and helped to manage campaigns and run the machine. Often the ward heeler held important office, such as that of alderman or water commissioner. Together with the boss and his immediate assistants, ward leaders constituted the inner circle of the organization, called "the ring."

The head of the machine was known as the "boss," "big man," or "leader." Because of his generally unsavory reputation, he usually held no office. Almost invariably he had risen from the ranks after years of service. The boss operated like a general in charge of field forces. His orders were commands, passed down from the "ring" to its hundreds or thousands of workers. Occasionally the boss's authority was challenged by a rising politician or faction in the machine; if tensions mounted too high the organization would split into rival factions. These were exceptional cases, however, for machines were usually superbly organized and smoothly run. They were the invisible governments of great cities, affecting the well-being of millions of people.

Woodrow Wilson once declared that the prevailing form of American city government had been constructed as if to make the usurpation of power by an extraconstitutional organization inevitable. Wilson's statement was essentially correct. When city charters were granted or rewritten during the high tide of Jacksonian democracy, their framers deliberately dispersed power and responsibility among numerous agencies—the mayor, a two-house council, and sometimes independent boards and commissions. The result was not democratic government. It was a form under which responsible government was nearly impossible because the agencies for achieving it did not exist. Into the power vacuum created by this system of checks and balances and division of authority moved the kind of political machine just described. For all its sins, it did have enough cohesion and concentration of authority to govern.

The machine survived even when forms of government were changed. A more important reason for its existence and power, therefore, was the fact that it rendered service to large numbers of people. The majority of voters in 1900 did not ask whether the organization was corrupt but whether it did something for them. The machine made it a point to do things for them. Its agents met the friendless immigrant at the dock and helped him to find shelter and work. Precinct captains provided coal and food for Widow Flanagan or Mrs. Moskowitz when they were in need. There was nothing scientific about the machine's charity, to be sure. But the submerged third cared little about honesty and efficiency so long as they lived in poverty and slums. They wanted social services that the machines knew how to give and that progressives had not yet developed.

The machine survived also because it was held together by the twin cords of patronage and loyalty. The chief source of livelihood of lesser dignitaries was petty office and graft, and the boss could command a host of willing workers so long as he had favors to bestow. Loyalty and friendship also played an important role in keeping the organization intact. Organization politics, moreover, afforded social and political opportunities for immigrant and minority groups such as they could never find in "respectable" society. In fact, the machine was one of the few cohesive and unifying forces in the social chaos of metropolitan life.

The oil best calculated to lubricate the political machine was the loot that it received. On the lower levels, bribery—in the form of money paid to politicians and policemen by criminals, prostitutes, saloon keepers, and others—was extremely widespread, highly organized, and fabulously profitable. The Chicago Vice Commission reported in 1911, for example, that the annual profit from vice in that city was $15,000,000, and that one fifth of this sum was paid to the police in the form of graft.

The system of police graft was everywhere prevalent, but the most dangerous kind of bribery was the money paid by businessmen for protection, special privileges, and public rights. To begin with, the great economic interests in the cities turned "their dollars into votes and their property into political power" by buying control of the political machines. Corruption was inevitable so long as businessmen wanted exemption from equitable taxation. In addition, there were numerous opportunities in large and rapidly growing cities for bribery of another kind—purchase of franchises and contracts. New city railway lines had to be constructed; sewerage, gas, electrical, and water lines had to follow new areas of development. The boss usually had franchises and contracts at his disposal; even perpetual franchises could be bought. It was top-level bribery of this kind that was most dangerous to the public interest and most profitable to the machine.

This, therefore, was the "System," as Lincoln Steffens called it. This was the pattern of corruption that characterized American municipal politics at the turn of the century. Some cities, to be sure, outshone the others in refining the art of misgovernment. In St. Louis, for example, the Democratic boss systematically sold franchises, licenses, and exemptions to the respectable leaders of the business community. The boss of Minneapolis operated the most spectacular system of police graft in the country. In Pittsburgh two Republican leaders owned the city council and grew rich on contracts and utilities. Philadelphia presented the sorriest sight of all—a place where the citizens cheerfully acquiesced in the total subversion of representative government.

38. *The Municipal Reform Movement*

The general prevalence of municipal corruption and misrule stimulated the first important *political* development in the progressive movement—the crusade for municipal reform. It began in a sporadic way in the 1890's, with the temporary overthrow of Tammany Hall by organized reform forces in 1894, and with the formation of civic leagues in various cities. The years 1896–7, however, seem to mark a dividing line between spasmodic uprisings and widespread revolt. The first of these uprisings occurred in Chicago, where the city council was busily selling the public's most valuable rights to Charles T. Yerkes, a utilities magnate. As protests against the corrupt selling of franchises began to swell, some 232 civic leaders met in 1895, organized the Municipal Voters' League, and launched a nonpartisan campaign to clean up the city government. By pitilessly exposing the records of corrupt aldermen, the League won control of the city council in the aldermanic elections of 1896 and 1897. In the latter year, moreover, the League helped elect a progressive mayor, Carter Harrison, and Chicago was saved from the grafters, at least momentarily. So vigilant was the League in following years that Lincoln Steffens could find no evidence of a machine or of grafting on a large scale when he visited Chicago in 1903.

The reform movement in Chicago illustrated what could be accomplished by an aroused citizenry without an outstanding single leader. Elsewhere the municipal reform movement followed a similar pattern. Various nonpartisan good government leagues combined in New York City in 1913 to overthrow Tammany rule and elect a young reform mayor, John Purroy Mitchel. In Minneapolis an energetic citizens' committee and a fearless grand jury exposed the system of police graft operated by Mayor A. A. Ames and put Ames and his henchmen in prison.

The dominant pattern of municipal reform, however, was redemption through leadership of some dynamic and often colorful popular tribune. Indeed, the rise of a whole group of city reformers around the turn of the century in part signaled the beginning of the progressive revolt.

The most famous and influential member of this group was Tom L. Johnson of Cleveland. He was a successful street railway operator and steel manufacturer, who learned the secrets of monopoly at an early age. He became a convert to Henry George's philosophy in the late 1880's. Elected to Congress in 1890 and 1892, he fought vainly for free trade. He assisted Henry George in his unsuccessful campaign for the mayoralty of New York City in 1897. Returning to Cleveland, Johnson was elected mayor in 1901 on a platform demanding equal taxation and the three-cent fare on trolley lines.

Johnson gathered some of the ablest young municipal administrators in the country and moved first against the inequalities of the tax lists. He next opened fire on railroads and utilities, which owned extensive property in Cleveland but paid hardly any taxes. The state legislature doubled railroad taxes in 1903–4, while the utilities consented to a doubling of their assessments. All these battles were mere skirmishes as compared to the great campaign that Johnson waged for the three-cent fare. The climax came when Johnson and his council established competing trolley routes and invited outside capitalists to bid for them. The local traction interests appealed to the state Republican ring for protection. The state ring, in turn, appealed to the Supreme Court of Ohio; it declared that all charters of Ohio cities were void because they had been created by special legislation. With all city governments of Ohio thus destroyed, the ring called the legislature into special session to adopt a uniform municipal code. It replaced the old system of concentrated power that had prevailed in Cleveland with government by divided authorities and independent boards.

Such tactics did not daunt Tom Johnson. He kept on appealing to the people and winning mayoralty campaigns. Eventually he concluded that public ownership of utilities and traction properties was the only way to eliminate the worst source of municipal corruption. Johnson was finally beaten in 1909, less than a year before his death. But his program was saved by the election of his chief lieutenant, Newton D. Baker, as mayor in 1911. Among the whole host of city crusaders, Tom Johnson was the greatest, not only because of his dauntless spirit and determination to protect the people's interests, but also because he set new standards of efficiency for municipal administrators all over the United States. By making Cleveland "the best governed city," he proved that reformers were not necessarily incompetent and politically naive.

Such was the kind of men who led the progressive movement in the cities. All municipal reformers fought common enemies: entrenched and corrupt politicians allied with privileged business and criminal elements. They all sought the same goals: impartial government, fair taxation, regulation of public service companies, and expanded social services for the lower classes. These remained always the chief objectives. But progressives soon learned that it was not enough to throw the rascals out and inaugurate a program of economic and social reform. Politics remained; and reformers could never rest secure so long as bosses controlled the party structure. Thus inevitably progressives turned also to the task of changing the political mechanisms, in the hope that greater popular participation and control would lay a secure basis for economic and social reforms already begun.

Progressives in the cities, therefore, joined hands with other reform groups in a frontal assault on bosses and machines by establishing the direct primary for nominating candidates and adopting the short ballot, the initiative, referendum, and recall. As these campaigns were part of the progressive movement on the state-wide level, we will relate them elsewhere in this chapter.

Municipal reformers also fought hard to obtain home rule and an end to legislative interference in municipal administration. As Tom Johnson and other progressives soon discovered, city machines were invariably components of state rings. After smashing the local machine, it profited progressives little if the state ring, acting through the legislature, could nullify all their gains. This often happened because in most states city governments were creatures of the legislature and completely under its control.

Municipal reformers were not notably successful in their struggle to be free from legislative interference, because rural and small-town legislators were loath to yield control over metropolitan revenues. Four states, Missouri, California, Washington, and Minnesota, had granted home rule to cities by the turn of the century. Eight other states granted this coveted privilege from 1900 to 1914, but only two of them, Michigan and Ohio, had any large cities of consequence.

The most far-reaching progressive proposal for institutional change struck at the heart of the problem of municipal government and seemed to offer the greatest hope of saving the cities. It was the plan to abolish the old mayor-council system entirely and to substitute government by a commission of nonpartisan administrators. The commission form developed quite accidentally. A hurricane and tidal wave devastated Galveston, Texas, on September 8, 1900. With a corrupt city council utterly incapable of facing the tasks of reconstruction, leading property owners of Galveston appealed to the state legislature to assume the government of the city. The legislature responded by establishing a government by five commissioners, elected, after 1903, by the people.

The commission was so successful in rebuilding Galveston and rehabilitating its finances that the city not only retained its new form of government but also soon exported it to Houston, Dallas, Fort Worth, Austin, and El Paso. It was not long before other cities awoke to the advantages of the new system. It had often been impossible to fix responsibility for bribery on any particular individual under the old council system. Under the commission form, all responsibility, as well as all authority, was concentrated in five men, each of whom had charge of a single department.

The commission plan first won nation-wide prominence when the Iowa legislature in 1907 adopted a more elaborate version of the Texas model. The Iowa statute allowed cities over 25,000 to adopt the commission form. More important, it incorporated the initiative, referendum, and recall as part of the machinery of city politics and provided for nomination of commissioners in nonpartisan elections. At once Des Moines adopted the commission form, and thereafter it was known as the "Des Moines Idea." More than one hundred cities had adopted commission government by 1910; by the eve of the First World War the number had passed four hundred— chiefly medium-sized cities in the Middle West, New England, and the Pacific states.

Experience soon demonstrated that the commission form had inherent weaknesses that were not evident at the outset. It failed really to concentrate responsibility for administration, since there was no guarantee that the commissioners would be expert managers. Progressives slowly evolved a refinement of the commission form. The final product was the city manager plan, first adopted in its complete form by Dayton, Ohio, in 1913, after a great flood had inundated the city and the mayor and council could not cope with the emergency. This innovation preserved the best features of the commission plan and eliminated most of its weaknesses. All authority was vested in a board of commissioners, elected on a nonpartisan basis, who made laws and policies for the city. The commissioners appointed a city manager, usually a trained expert, to administer the various departments of the government, and the city manager, in turn, was responsible in all matters to the commissioners.

The new form seemed such a logical way to achieve responsible and expert administration without sacrificing the principle of democratic control that it spread rapidly and soon displaced the commission form in many cities. More than three hundred cities had adopted the city manager plan by 1923.

Thus the progressive movement in the cities stimulated the rise of a host of new leaders and the development of political institutions calculated to facilitate popular rule and responsible government. To charge, as certain critics have done, that city reformers did not abolish all evils and bring the millennium is at best naive. For the most part they were tough-minded men, who well knew that venality and corruption would survive, regardless of form of government, so long as men profited thereby. They must be judged on a basis of the obstacles that they faced and what they accomplished, not condemned for failing to change human nature or reconstruct society. Surveying the American scene at the end of the progressive period, competent authorities concluded that the municipal reformers had in large measure succeeded. The era of flagrant corruption had by and large passed. Cities were governed more efficiently than they had been a decade before, and a new class of professional municipal administrators were in training throughout the country. In short, if the city was not yet the hope of American democracy, it was no longer its nemesis.

39. *The Shame of the States*

Corruption and special privilege held sway in practically every state around the turn of the century, in the same manner and for the same purpose that they reigned in the cities. Just as the city machine was the medium through which corrupt businessmen obtained contracts, franchises, and immunities from the city government, so also was the state machine, or ring, the medium through which such favors were bought on the state level.

The boss system in the states varied greatly from state to state and from party to party. City organizations usually formed the basis for the state machine, although in rural states the county courthouse rings were the important components. In states with a tremendous concentration of population in one metropolis, the boss of the great city machine was often head of the state organization. In other states political power was more widely dispersed. In any event, party authority was concentrated in the state committee, headed by a state chairman who represented the dominant leader or leaders in the state. It was the state chairman who usually organized the legislature, controlled legislation, and made deals with railroad and corporation lobbyists.

Two states, Missouri and New Jersey, afford exaggerated but vivid illustrations of how the so-called System operated in most states of the Union at the turn of the century. In Missouri the bribery or "boodle" system worked at peak efficiency to govern the state in the interest of railroads and corporations. The corrupting agency was the lobby at the state capital, representing important railroad and business interests. The medium through which the lobby worked in this case was the party caucus in the legislature. Because the lobby bought control of the caucus, even honest legislators were caught in its net and forced to do its bidding. In Missouri, as in many other states, the lobby was the real, the living government that operated behind the façade of constitutional forms.

The control of state politics by a corporation-machine alliance reached its apogee in New Jersey. The leaders of the business and financial communities were in fact often the leaders of the dominant Republican party, and it was usually unnecessary for businessmen to corrupt legislators and state officials. The railroad lobby in 1903, for example, furnished the chief justice of the state, the attorney general, the state comptroller, the commissioner of banking and insurance, and one of the members of the state board of taxation. It was probably no coincidence that railroads at that time paid only one third of their just share of the tax burden. Moreover, both United States senators from New Jersey were interested in public utilities, while the retiring attorney general was on the boards of three public service corporations. It was not surprising that public utilities in the state enjoyed immunity from equitable taxation and public regulation.

In Missouri the methods that the business interests used were cruder and more flagrantly corrupt than those in New Jersey, but the techniques and objectives of corporation control were the same throughout the country. Who could tell how far the process of corporation dominance of state politics would go, or where it would end?

40. *The Progressive Movement in the States*

Like the municipal reform movement, the great revolt against the "System" in the states was a culmination rather than a beginning. In the

South and West, agrarian radicalism metamorphosed into progressivism from 1896 to 1900, as urban spokesmen assumed leadership in the struggle against railroad and corporation dominance. The Middle West, where the dominant GOP was firmly controlled by the vested interests at the turn of the century, was convulsed by a series of spectacular revolts from 1900 to 1908. Under insurgent leaders like Robert M. La Follette of Wisconsin, Albert B. Cummins of Iowa, and Albert J. Beveridge of Indiana, the midwestern states were transformed from bastions of conservative Republicanism into strongholds of progressivism. In the East the progressive revolt had a more decidedly urban complexion, as it often grew out of earlier campaigns in the cities. But progressivism was no less spectacular in the East than in the Middle West. Charles Evans Hughes's election as governor of New York in 1906 and 1908, and his courageous battles for the direct primary and public regulation of utilities and railroads; the New Idea movement in New Jersey, which began in 1906 as a rebellion within the Republican party and culminated in the election of a Democrat, Woodrow Wilson, as governor in 1910; and the sweeping triumph of progressivism in Ohio, with the adoption of a new constitution and the election of a Democratic progressive, James M. Cox, as governor in 1912—these developments, among others, signified the power and strength of eastern progressivism. The politics of the Pacific Coast states, too, was transformed by the triumph of such reformers as Hiram W. Johnson of California and William S. U'Ren of Oregon.

What we are dealing with here was obviously no minor phenomenon but a political revolt of national proportions and momentous consequences for the future of American politics. So successful were progressive leaders in the several states by 1912 that all observers agreed that a thoroughgoing revolution had been accomplished since 1900. In most states the power of the bipartisan machines had been shattered or at least curtailed. State governments were more representative of the rank and file and more responsive to their economic and social needs. Even more important, progressivism had spread by 1912 into the arena of national politics, subverting ancient party loyalties and causing such a political commotion as the country had not seen since 1896.

"Give the government back to the people!"—the battle cry of progressivism in the states—not only reflected the conviction that state governments had ceased to be representative but also pointed up the major objective of the movement. But how could the "System" be destroyed? What were the processes and techniques of this counterrevolution against privilege?

The first, indeed the absolutely essential, ingredient was leadership. In every state in which progressivism triumphed there was some aggressive leader who carried the fight to the people and, after winning, provided responsible and effective government. Indeed, it is now evident that the progressives' most lasting contribution to American political practice was not the mechanical changes that they instituted, but rather the fact that they awakened the American people to the necessity for responsible leadership in a democracy.

Progressive leaders in the states, moreover, made a concerted campaign to overhaul the existing structure of political institutions. If representative government had broken down under the old forms, progressives argued, then new institutions must be devised to facilitate popular control of parties and governments. Invariably, the first objective of reform leaders was inauguration of the direct primary system of nominating candidates and party officials. This objective took priority because the old system of nomination by conventions seemed to afford the bosses an easy means of perpetuating their control. Practically all city and state elective officials before 1900 were nominated at party conventions on district, county, and state-wide levels. Normally such conventions were easily bought or controlled; usually they were well-oiled cogs in the machine. Reform forces might capture the conventions and momentarily subdue the bosses, but it was an extraordinarily difficult undertaking.

The progressive remedy was simple and direct—to make it easier for voters and more difficult for bosses to control the party, by instituting a system of nominating candidates directly by the people. The direct primary apparently originated in Pennsylvania in the 1840's, but it was not used extensively on the local level until the 1890's, and then mainly in the South. Mississippi in 1902 was the first state to adopt a compulsory, state-wide primary law. Wisconsin enacted similar legislation the following year as the first major item in Governor La Follette's reform program. From this time on the system spread rapidly through all sections, so that by 1916 only Rhode Island, Connecticut, and New Mexico had failed to enact primary legislation of some kind.

State progressives usually campaigned next for a variety of institutional reforms: the short ballot, to reduce the number of elective officials and concentrate responsibility in government; corrupt practices legislation, to control and limit campaign contributions and expenditures; and the direct election of United States senators by the people instead of by the state legislatures. Progress in the field of short ballot reform was notable only in the area of municipal government, with the rapid spread of the commission and city manager forms. Practically every state adopted stringent corrupt practices laws, while Congress in 1907 and 1909 prohibited corporations, insurance companies, banks, and railroads from contributing to campaign funds in federal election contests. For many years, however, reactionary forces in the Senate would not allow a constitutional amendment for direct election of senators to pass. Many states, therefore, turned to an indirect method of electing senators directly—by requiring senatorial candidates to be nominated in primary elections and candidates for the state legislature to swear that they would vote for the senatorial candidate thus nominated by the people. The United States Senate, after a scandal involving the election of William Lorimer, Republican boss of Illinois, to that body in 1909, approved the Seventeenth Amendment for direct election in 1912. It became a part of the Constitution on May 31, 1913.

Many skeptical progressives refused to agree that the foregoing reforms sufficed. Convinced that representative government might become subverted by the forces of privilege even under the new and more democratic forms, they proposed to give the people an alternative and a last resort—the initiative and referendum.[5] The initiative and referendum were used most widely in the West, where South Dakota first adopted them in 1898. During the next ten years only Utah, Oregon, Nevada, Montana, and Oklahoma joined the experiment in direct legislation. But fifteen other states, including several in the East and South, adopted the measures from 1908 to 1915. The movement came to a virtual standstill in 1915, however, as conservatives launched a vigorous counterattack, and experience soon proved that the mass of voters were not competent to deal with technical matters of legislation.

As a further safeguard of the popular interest, progressives championed the recall, a device that afforded the voters a handy means of removing unsatisfactory elective officials. First used in Los Angeles in 1903, the recall found widest acceptance in cities that adopted the commission and city manager forms. Oregon made the recall applicable to elective state and local officials in 1908, and nine other states, most of them in the West, followed suit from 1911 to 1915. This form of recall provoked strenuous opposition from conservatives, but defenders of the *status quo* saved their choicest invectives for the recall of judges. If the people could remove judges for making unpopular decisions, then what minority and property rights would be safe from the assaults of an irrational majority? Seven states—Oregon, California, Arizona, Nevada, Colorado, Kansas, and North Dakota—adopted the recall of judges. The violent controversies over the measure at the time seem now rather pointless, as not a single judge of a superior or state supreme court has been removed since the recall of judges was first proposed. As an alternative means of protecting the right of the states to use the police power for social and economic ends, Theodore Roosevelt in 1912 proposed the recall of decisions by state courts that nullified such legislation. Only Colorado, in 1913, adopted this measure, and the Colorado supreme court in 1921 declared the statute unconstitutional.

Critics have accused progressive leaders of naively believing that representative and truly democratic government could be restored by mere alterations in the mechanics of politics. The charge reveals a profound ignorance of the progressive era. There were undoubtedly fools among the leaders of the reform movement in the states. But the great majority were realistic politicians who well knew that the changes they proposed were merely instruments to facilitate the capture of political machinery. They used these instruments, therefore, to gain and hold power. And they must be judged for what they accomplished or failed to accomplish on the higher level of substantive reform.

Their achievements in the realm of social and economic legislation were imposing indeed. We have already related the progress of the movement in the states for social justice legislation, so-called moral reform through prohibition, and development of public education. In the realm

---

[5] The initiative is a device whereby the electorate may enact legislation against the will of the legistature. Upon petition of a stipulated percentage of the voters, the legislature must consider the measure that the petitioners propose. If the legislature refuses to approve the bill it must call a special election in which the voters may enact or reject the measure. The referendum, on the other hand, is a device by which voters may nullify a measure already approved by the legislature.

of strictly economic legislation, progressive leaders in the states made substantial progress toward subjecting railroads and public service corporations to effective public control. Beginning with the Georgia railroad commission of 1879 and culminating in the adoption by the Wisconsin legislature of Governor La Follette's bill for a railroad commission in 1905, the movement for state regulation advanced steadily. Indeed, so effective had it become by 1914 that the railroad managers were then begging Congress to save them from harassment by state commissions. It was during the progressive era, too, that the movement for expert regulation by state commissions of rates and services of public service corporations and of insurance and investment companies began and reached its first culmination.

These were all important substantive reforms and together constitute an imposing record. But in assessing progressivism's achievement one should not dismiss lightly the political changes that it effected. By their emphasis on simplified forms of government, greater popular participation in and control over the electoral process, and responsible leadership, the progressive leaders transformed the theory and practice of politics in the United States. Looking back in 1913 upon his hard battles for the people as Governor of Wisconsin, Robert M. La Follette penned a fitting epilogue, not only for the progressive movement in Wisconsin, but for progressivism in many other states as well:

"This closes the account of my services in Wisconsin—a time full of struggle, and yet a time that I like to look back upon. It has been a fight supremely worth making, and I want it to be judged, as it will be ultimately, by results actually attained. If it can be shown that Wisconsin is a happier and better state to live in, that its institutions are more democratic, that the opportunities of all its people are more equal, that social justice more nearly prevails, that human life is safer and sweeter—then I shall rest content in the feeling that the Progressive movement has been successful." [6]

wwwwwwwwwwwwwww

[6] *Autobiography of Robert M. La Follette* (Madison, Wis., 1913), pp. 368–9; see also Belle Case La Follette and Fola La Follette, *Robert M. La Follette* (2 vols., 1953), I, p. 192.

CHAPTER

5

Politics and Problems
of the Republican Era

1901–1910

Iᴛ ᴡᴀs ɪɴᴇᴠɪᴛᴀʙʟᴇ that the progressive movement should soon spread
from the cities and states into the larger arena of national politics. This
was true because there is no real dividing line between state and federal
politics in the American system. It was true even more because the spread
of the railroad, financial, and industrial networks across state boundaries
created important problems with which the federal government alone
could constitutionally cope.

This and following chapters relate the impact of the progressive upheaval upon national politics and policies. At the beginning of the twentieth
century the dominant Republican party was controlled by men who frankly
urged a program of generous assistance to the business interests and who
abhorred the very concept of public regulation. Under William Jennings
Bryan, some of the minority Democrats were cautiously moving toward a
more progressive position, but they had mounted no comprehensive and
rational attack on the system of privilege. Within less than a decade, however, the progressive ferment had wrought mighty changes in the American
political scene. Advanced progressives, who sought to make the federal
government a positive, regenerative force, were a large element in the Republican party by 1910. Moreover, the Democrats were united and confident under new leadership. In brief, the progressive movement, which had

already brought important changes in federal policies, stood on the verge of culmination and fulfillment.

41. *Theodore Roosevelt and the Progressive Movement* [1]

No account of national progressivism would be complete without some note of its most extraordinary leader during its early period. Theodore Roosevelt, catapulted into the presidency by a tragic circumstance, presided over the nation's destinies during a time of agitation for and development of a national reform program. He opportunely adapted his policies to meet the changing configurations of political power. He was, however, no mere creature of circumstance, but rather a prime moving force in history.

Born on October 27, 1858, the scion of a well-to-do mercantile and banking family, he was reared in the genteel Knickerbocker traditions of New York City. Afflicted with a frail body and weak eyes, while still young he determined to make himself physically strong. He overcame his weakness by dint of exhausting labors and ever after gloried in the strenuous life and manly virtues. Whether as cowboy and gunfighter, Rough Rider during the Spanish-American War, or big game hunter in Africa, Roosevelt proved that physically he was as good as the best, and that he did not know the meaning of fear.

The urge to be always active combined with a first-rate intellect to produce a man of broad interests and intellectual creativity. Although he was not a trained historian, he wrote good history and, besides, read widely in the field of literature. A biologist and student of nature, he spent considerable time as President exposing nature-fakers who ascribed miraculous powers to animals. These were a few of his peripheral interests. His profession was the practice of politics and diplomacy, and in this calling he displayed intelligence and skill.

From his social environment and especially from his father, Roosevelt acquired a compulsion to do good for people less fortunate than himself. While most persons of his class gave money to settlement houses or home missions, Roosevelt went into politics after being graduated from Harvard in 1880. Part of his motivation must have been the strong moral sense he acquired from his Dutch Reformed religion and its Calvinistic emphasis upon righteousness. In any event, Roosevelt usually viewed political contests as struggles between the forces of good and evil and, like Wilson and Bryan, he became a preacher at large to the American people.

Background, training, temperament, and personal associations all combined in Roosevelt to produce a fundamentally cautious and conservative, rather than a doctrinaire, approach to politics. Justice to all classes, and therefore legislation in the general interest, became his guiding principle. A patrician, he viewed with righteous anger the vulgarity and materialism of the newly rich captains of industry, financiers, and railroad speculators. Yet experience and sense of justice prevented him from condemning whole

[1] Parts of the following section first appeared in Arthur S. Link, "Theodore Roosevelt in His Letters," *Yale Review*, XLIII (Summer, 1954), pp. 589–98; reproduced by permission of the editors of the *Yale Review*.

classes or accepting the socialist dictum that it was the economic system that was alone responsible for social wrongdoing. Roosevelt's conservatism, moreover, was manifested in his insistence upon continuity and his abhorrence of men who advocated unnatural change. Believing that progressive adaptation to new circumstances could not occur unless order and social stability first existed, he feared a mob as much as he feared the malefactors of great wealth.

It is proof of his complexity that Theodore Roosevelt must be reckoned a progressive in spite of his basically conservative approach to politics. On a bedrock of democratic idealism he built a structure of legislative policies the shape of which was usually determined by the pragmatic need of the hour. Experience, whether as governor of New York or President of the United States, led him to the conclusion that only organized political power, that is, government, could meet the manifold challenges that industrialism raised in city, state, and nation. For this reason he was primarily a progressive, even though he refused to be doctrinaire about his progressivism.

In the practice of politics Roosevelt was as hardheaded a realist as ever sat in the presidential chair. He was a realist because he recognized and respected power. Thus, when governor of New York, he worked with the Republican boss of that state. When he assumed the presidency in 1901 he found political power in the Republican party concentrated in the state organizations and exercised by their representatives in Congress. He did not attempt to destroy the party hierarchy; indeed, he worked with and through it. The important point is that Roosevelt not only accepted existing power structures as he found them in New York and Washington but that he also became a master politician, able to use his party for his own and the country's interests.

Indeed, in the way in which he conceded the smaller points in order to win the important objectives and mastered the political game without yielding his own integrity, Roosevelt symbolized the moral man confronted by the dilemmas of an immoral society. Doctrinaire reformers demanded the whole loaf of reform and denounced Roosevelt when he accepted half or two thirds of the loaf. Roosevelt knew that he could not transform society and politics by one bugle blast. He knew that men are usually governed by selfish motives, and that politics is fundamentally not a moral profession. Knowing these things, he tried to use selfishness to achieve a moral end— the advancement of human welfare. He also tried to strengthen altruistic tendencies whenever he found them.

These, then, were some of the features of Roosevelt's personality and philosophy. There was, however, another trait that to a varying degree dominated all the rest—his love of power, which mounted as the years passed and at times verged on megalomania. Love of his own opinions often obscured the truth in Roosevelt's mind and caused him to think that he was above the law and ordinary conventions. Yet his confidence was as much a source of strength as of danger, giving him the strength essential to leadership. Combined with intelligence and energy, it made him a superb administrator, precisely because he was bold enough to do unprecedented things.

Roosevelt enjoyed power as did no other President to his time, but he also recognized its dangers and corrupting potentialities. "There is not one among us in whom a devil does not dwell," he wrote near the end of his life. "At some time, on some point, that devil masters each of us; he who has never failed has not been tempted." Much as he enjoyed the presidency, he voluntarily gave it up. "I believe in a strong executive," he wrote in 1908; "I believe in power; but I believe that responsibility should go with power, and that it is not well that the strong executive should be a perpetual executive. . . . The Presidency . . . can only be saved from abuse by having the people accept as axiomatic the position that one man can hold it for no more than a limited time."

Personal judgments of Roosevelt will vary, but no one should make the mistake of not taking him seriously. Because he was a leader of men it was given to him to make a large contribution to the progressive movement, to the art of government in the United States, and to the diplomacy of his country. In fact, since Lincoln, only two other Presidents, Wilson and Franklin Roosevelt, have made comparable contributions.

Theodore Roosevelt's most lasting contribution to American political practice was his exercise of leadership and revitalization of the presidency. A long line of second-rate politicians had occupied the White House from 1865 to 1901. With the exception perhaps of Cleveland they were not even leaders of their own party, much less of the country. Because of the entrenched position of the Old Guard professionals in Congress, Roosevelt was never able to dominate the veterans on Capitol Hill. But he was able to bend a stubborn Congress to his will by making himself the one great popular spokesman in the country. By exploiting some of the powers inherent in the presidency, he proved that effective national leadership was possible in the American constitutional system.

Roosevelt's contributions to the science of administration alone would entitle him to distinction among the Presidents. Perceiving that the only alternative to rule by private wealth was the development of a strong, efficient administrative state, democratically controlled but powerful enough to make important economic decisions, he advanced the science of administration as no President before him had done. He and his able associates strengthened the Civil Service, put the consular service on a professional basis, modernized the army's command structure, brought the navy to an unprecedented peak of efficiency, and carried forward a scientific program of conservation of natural resources. Moreover, he helped to broaden the powers of an old agency, the Interstate Commerce Commission, and created a new one, the Bureau of Corporations. In brief, during the Roosevelt era democracy learned to become efficient.

A third contribution is almost as important as Roosevelt's development of the presidential power. It was his vindication of the national, or public, interest over all private aggregations of economic power. The open contempt that bankers, monopolists, and railroad managers displayed toward the law and the highhanded manner in which they dealt with the people filled him with loathing and anger. He retaliated by asserting the supremacy of the people over private interests in three far-reaching ways. First, he withdrew more than 200,000,000 acres of public lands to curb the plunder of a great national heritage. Second, he activated the Sherman Act and began a movement that succeeded in curbing industrial monopoly in the United States. Third, he forced adoption of the Hepburn Act of 1906, which deprived the railroads of ultimate sovereignty in the rate-making process. In the anthracite coal strike of 1902, he was prepared to go the full limit in asserting the public interest—by seizing and operating the coal mines if the operators should refuse to mediate the controversy. Such actions marked the momentous beginnings of legislation and administration that culminated in the New Deal and the democratic welfare state.

42.   *Roosevelt and the Republican Party,* 1900–1904

The leaders of the Republican party laid their plans carefully for the election of 1900. President William McKinley was of course the inevitable presidential choice of the GOP. The death in 1899 of the Vice President, Garret A. Hobart, left the second place on the ticket open and created an unusual opportunity for Thomas C. Platt, Republican boss of New York State. Platt had nominated Theodore Roosevelt, the hero of the Spanish-American War, for governor of New York in 1898 in order to win. Elected easily, Roosevelt attacked corruption with vigor, championed social legislation, and was consequently soon at odds with Platt. Hobart's death offered a dignified yet final method of getting Roosevelt out of New York. The Republican Old Guard could silence Roosevelt by elevating him to the vice presidency, and Platt would be saved the embarrassment of having to nominate him again for governor in 1900.

McKinley and his adviser, Mark Hanna, responded coldly when Platt first presented his plan. "Don't any of you realize," Hanna is later alleged to have remarked, "that there's only one life between this madman and the White House?" But Platt was so persistent that Hanna finally gave in. Roosevelt with his usual perception at once saw through Platt's scheme. He had grave misgivings about accepting his consignment to oblivion. His friends, however, suggested that he would be the logical presidential candidate in 1904, and he could think of no alternative but to accept the nomination if it were offered to him.

The Democrats nominated Bryan for a second time, and the Nebraskan made his campaign chiefly on the issues of imperialism and trust control. As we have said, Bryan soft-pedaled the silver issue and tried to make the election a solemn referendum on imperialism. As one diplomatic historian has shown, the election was more a repudiation of Bryanism and a thumping endorsement of prosperity than a popular expression on colonial policy. McKinley was elected by an even greater majority than in 1896.

Therefore, McKinley and Roosevelt were inaugurated on March 4, 1901. Platt said a pleasant good-by; Hanna stood at McKinley's right hand; and businessmen thanked God that all was right with the world. But the point of Platt's joke was lost in September 1901 when an assassin mortally wounded McKinley at Buffalo. "That damned cowboy," as Hanna called Roosevelt, was now President of the United States!

Those impatient reformers who expected Theodore Roosevelt to reorganize the Republican party and assume control of Congress at once understood neither the political situation nor the new President. The great industrial and financial interests since the Civil War had constructed an organization within the Republican party that could not be overthrown by direct assault. The pre-eminent leader of the party was Mark Hanna of Ohio, McKinley's adviser and a member of the Senate. Nearly equal in power was Senator Nelson W. Aldrich of Rhode Island, the avowed spokesman of Wall Street. Allied with Hanna and Aldrich in the upper house were John C. Spooner of Wisconsin, William B. Allison of Iowa, and Orville H. Platt of Connecticut. They and other Old Guardsmen controlled the Senate and protected the industrial, financial, and railroad interests. Furthermore, the Old Guard were firmly entrenched in the House of Representatives. The Speaker after 1902 was Joseph G. Cannon of Illinois, a thoroughgoing reactionary, who ruled the House with rural wit and an iron hand. Cannon not only appointed all committees but was also chairman of the rules committee that determined the priority of bills. It was not difficult for him to block "dangerous" legislation.

Congressional supremacy was not merely a slogan in 1901. It had been so much a reality since Lincoln's death that Presidents, except perhaps for Cleveland, had been creatures of the congressional machine. McKinley's death did not alter the configuration. Power in the Republican party still resided with the state organizations and their representatives in Congress.

Advice came to Roosevelt from all sides in the autumn of 1901 to move slowly. It was unnecessary. As he was in no position to challenge the Old Guard, Roosevelt determined to work with them for a time. He announced immediately after his accession that he would continue McKinley's policies and retain his Cabinet. Obviously, Roosevelt was feeling his way and assuring his nomination in 1904. Not yet ready to make war on the Old Guard, he came to terms with them. He went to Aldrich's home in Rhode Island in August 1902 and a short time later conferred at Oyster Bay, Long Island, with leading Republican senators. The upshot of these negotiations was Roosevelt's promise to leave the protective tariff system and monetary structure essentially undisturbed. The senators, in return, gave Roosevelt freedom of action in other matters.

The enormous agitation for railroad regulation and destruction of so-called trusts was beginning to have a significant impact on the Middle West, where a popular revolt against the policies of Hanna and Aldrich was getting under way. The first signs of this upheaval were the election of Robert M. La Follette as governor of Wisconsin in 1900, on a platform demanding the direct primary and effective railroad regulation, and the rise of Albert Baird Cummins as the dominant political leader in Iowa in 1901. Roosevelt realized far better than Aldrich and his friends the necessity of appeasing midwestern opinion. His first move was to instruct the Attorney General in February 1902 to announce that he would soon institute proceedings to dissolve the Northern Securities Company, the gigantic railroad combination that J. P. Morgan had recently formed.

The midwestern progressives could not be propitiated by this one act alone. They demanded drastic tariff reductions, federal regulation of railroad rates, and more vigorous action against the large corporations. Roosevelt made a tour through the Middle West in August 1902; the following year, in April, he returned to the region. The more he said the more it was clear that he understood and sympathized with the midwestern antagonism to Hanna and the Wall Street crowd.

This became dramatically clear in Roosevelt's first hard fight in Congress for reform legislation. It occurred in the early months of 1903 as a consequence of Roosevelt's demand for a provision, in a bill creating a Department of Commerce and Labor, for establishment of a Bureau of Corporations with full power to investigate business practices. Opposition from the big business interests was immense, but Roosevelt won his measure by stirring public opinion in a somewhat dubious manner. He confided to newspapermen that John D. Rockefeller had sent threatening telegrams to six senators in order to defeat the bill. The charge was not precisely true, but its publication provoked such a public outcry that both houses of Congress rushed through the bill for the Department of Commerce and Labor with the controverted provision still intact.

43. *The Election of 1904*

As the time for the national conventions of 1904 drew near, Roosevelt laid careful plans for winning his chief objective, the chance to be President in his own right. Quietly but surely he retired Hanna as chief dispenser of patronage and made his own alliances with dominant state organizations, especially in the South. Hanna was Roosevelt's only serious rival, but the Ohioan died on February 15, 1904, and no one stood in Roosevelt's way. Surely the old order was changing as the President made plans to seize control of the GOP. Hanna and Matt Quay, Pennsylvania Republican boss, were dead; Boss Platt had been shorn of his power over the New York State Republican organization.

Roosevelt, therefore, received the nomination at the Republican convention on June 23, 1904, without even a show of opposition. Having twice failed with Bryan, the Democrats decided to try a conservative to offset the impulsive Roosevelt. They nominated Judge Alton B. Parker of New York, an obscure and ineffectual third-rate politician. On the whole, the campaign was a drab affair. Near the end, however, Parker enlivened the contest by charging that Roosevelt was blackmailing Wall Street into supporting the Republican ticket.

The charge was false, but somehow Roosevelt became badly frightened by rumors that certain Wall Street interests were pouring huge sums into the Democratic war chest. Rejecting the suggestion that he appeal directly to the people for small contributions, Roosevelt allowed his manager, George B. Cortelyou, to raise money in the usual way.[2] The voters could

wwwwwwwwwwwwwww

[2] Edward H. Harriman, the railroad magnate, contributed $50,000 personally and collected $200,000 more from other sources. J. P. Morgan gave $150,000, and the three life insurance companies that he controlled added another $148,000. Two Standard Oil partners, H. H. Rogers and John D. Archbold, gave $100,000; and although Roosevelt demanded that this gift be returned, his managers quietly ignored his request. In all, corporations contributed nearly three fourths of the $2,195,000 collected by the Republican National Committee.

not have taken Parker's blackmail charge seriously, for they elected Roosevelt by the largest popular majority that had ever been given a presidential candidate. Roosevelt was actually stunned by the landslide. "The election results," he wrote on November 10, 1904, "are really astounding, and I am overwhelmed by them. . . . I frankly confess that I do not understand it."

44. *The Emergence of a Progressive Leader*

Events soon proved that Roosevelt had given no hostage to Wall Street by accepting its lavish contributions. On the contrary, he had won more real power with the people by 1904 than any President since Lincoln. The wine of victory exhilarated him and strengthened his determination to be the real leader of the country, the spokesman of the majority. His Annual Message of 1904 gave hints of an advanced position, but it was his address before the Union League Club of Philadelphia, delivered in January 1905, that blazoned his new progressivism. Great industries and wealth, he warned, must submit to public control; specifically, the public interest demanded effective regulation of railroad rates.

Pressure on Roosevelt from the Middle and Far West to support such causes as railroad regulation, the direct election of senators, and control of corporations mounted incessantly from this time forward. Moreover, Bryan and progressive Democrats were charging that the President talked loudly but was essentially a straddler. Roosevelt, however, did not merely give in to these pressures. Haunted by the fear that failure to appease popular demand would provoke revolution, he took personal control of the reform movement in the summer and fall of 1905. He launched an attack on the meat packers, beginning with a thorough investigation of the industry. And when Congress assembled in December 1905, he demanded a stringent railroad-regulation law, a pure food and drug law, publicity for campaign contributions, and additional conservation legislation.

The more vigorously Roosevelt asserted leadership, the more successes he won. He got a pure food and drug law; he forced the passage of a railroad-regulation bill in 1906; and he advanced the cause of conservation through executive action. Moreover, he attacked the so-called trust problem with renewed vigor, not only by many dissolution suits, but perhaps even more effectively through a number of searching exposures by federal agencies. He recognized the intensity of the midwestern demand for tariff reduction, but he never thought that the tariff was an important factor in preserving the system of privilege. He knew, also, that the country needed currency reform and more effective regulation of the banking system, but he never pressed these issues before Congress and the country.

Day in and day out during 1906 and most of 1907, however, Roosevelt gave eloquent voice to the demand for extension of public authority over great aggregations of wealth. It is easy to condemn Roosevelt for not doing more than he did—for not fighting hard for tariff and banking reform, for example. It is also easy to forget that the national progressive movement was only yet in the making, that conservative Republicans controlled Congress (in fact, there were few if any progressives in the Senate until Roosevelt's second administration), and that his leadership of the reform cause was courageous and effective.

Roosevelt was forced to restrain his reform energies during the last months of 1907 in the wake of a severe panic in Wall Street. Bankers and railroad men blamed the administration for loss of public confidence, but the panic was brought on by a world-wide credit stringency and by the very speculative excesses that Roosevelt had condemned.

Depressed economic conditions only momentarily paralyzed Roosevelt's reform impulses. He knew that the popular desire for progressive change was as strong as ever and bound to grow. Thus, while congressional leaders awaited his abdication in pleasant anticipation, Roosevelt intensified his propaganda for reform. A special message to Congress on January 31, 1908, sounded the keynote of a campaign for advanced national legislation that would culminate in a political revolt in 1912 and other consequences. Roosevelt was outraged by the Supreme Court's nullification of the federal Employers' Liability Act of 1906 and demanded new legislation; he also urged the states to adopt accident compensation systems. Moreover, he condemned the courts for using injunctions merely to protect property in labor disputes and urged Congress to empower the Interstate Commerce Commission to make a physical valuation of railroad property and supervise the financial operations of the railroads. Finally, he suggested closer supervision of corporations, either through federal licensing, "or in some other way equally efficacious"; and denounced speculators and dishonest businessmen. "The Nation," he warned, "will not tolerate an utter lack of control over very wealthy men of enormous power in the industrial, and therefore in the social, lives of all our people. . . . We strive to bring nearer the day when greed and trickery and cunning shall be trampled under feet by those who fight for the righteousness that exalteth a nation."

45.   *The Election of 1908*

Roosevelt by the end of 1907 was the spokesman for the masses of Republican voters and the real leader of his party. Even the special interests who could delay or defeat his program in Congress could not have prevented his renomination in 1908. He enjoyed being President and delighted in the thought of another four years at the helm. But he had given a pledge after the election of 1904 that he would not run again, and an inner compulsion urged him to stand by his promise.

It was the most fateful decision of Roosevelt's career and perhaps the unwisest. By refusing to heed the popular call in 1908 he denied himself the opportunity to render his greatest service to the Republican party. A Roosevelt in the White House from 1909 to 1913 might well have averted the disastrous rupture that occurred in 1912. In any event, he had the power to name his successor and was determined to use it.

The ablest member of the constellation around the President was Elihu Root, who had served as Secretary of War from 1899 to 1904 and Secretary of State since 1905. Roosevelt was sorely tempted to make this able corporation lawyer his successor, but he knew that the Middle West would never accept Root because of his Wall Street connnections. New York's reform governor, Charles Evans Hughes, was another possibility, but Hughes was strangely cold to the President's advances. Finally Roosevelt turned to William Howard Taft of Ohio, his Secretary of War, who was one of his stanchest supporters in the Cabinet. Taft had a distinguished record as federal judge, Governor General of the Philippines, and Secretary of War. He had good family connections, an eastern education, an excellent mind, and unquestioned integrity. Most important, he seemed eager to carry forward the Roosevelt policies.

Roosevelt, in January 1908, began to set all the machinery of the party organization in motion to assure Taft's nomination. Asserting publicly that the Republican convention should be free to choose its candidate, Roosevelt by the end of May was privately boasting that he had prevented his own renomination and could dictate the naming of Taft. At the Republican convention that met in Chicago in June, therefore, the Ohioan was nominated on the first ballot on a platform that promised, among other things, tariff revision and a federal system of postal savings banks.

The Democrats, meeting in Denver, turned again to Bryan in this year of Rooseveltian supremacy. Although he was by now something of a perennial candidate, the Nebraskan at least seemed able to save his party from another such disaster as it had suffered in 1904. Bryan had come a long way toward progressivism since 1896. He was not a great intellect, but he had a keen ear for the voice of the people and was free from any connection with special privilege. He made his campaign largely on the tariff and trust questions and, promising relief from indiscriminate injunctions, made a frank appeal for labor support. Taft, on the other hand, attacked Bryan as a demagogue, pledged himself to continue the Roosevelt policy of substantial justice to all classes, and promised tariff revision.

As all observers predicted, Taft won easily; but it was significant that Bryan increased the Democratic vote by a million and a third over 1904 and carried the South, Oklahoma, Colorado, Nevada, and Nebraska. More significant for the future was the marked rise of Republican insurgency, or advanced progressivism, in the Middle West. Heretofore the midwestern progressive Republican bloc in Congress had been a small minority. In the Sixty-first Congress, which would meet in 1909, they would be a powerful force in both houses.

46. *Republican Troubles Under Taft*

Roosevelt left the United States soon after Taft's inaugural to hunt big game in Africa and then to go on an extended tour of Europe. His departure was applauded in financial circles, where many men wished luck to the lions. Conservatives, generally, were sure that Taft would align himself with the Old Guard in Congress. Progressives, on the other hand, were certain that he would come to their support. As it turned out, neither group was entirely right—or wrong.

It would be unkind to say that Taft took the presidency under false pretenses. On the eve of his magistracy he thought that he was a progressive. He shared Roosevelt's belief in the supremacy of the public over the private interest. He believed in railroad regulation, was ruthlessly opposed to monopolies, and honestly wanted to continue Roosevelt's policy of preserving the nation's heritage of natural resources. In a normal period of political quietude he would have been a beloved President.

The years of Taft's reign, however, were highly abnormal. It was a time of agitation and revolt. Civil war within the Republican party impended, and open party warfare could have been averted only by bold presidential leadership. Unhappily, Taft was temperamentally unfitted to play the role that history demanded. He could not lead in a time of trouble, because leadership in such circumstances required wholehearted commitment and abandonment of the judicial quality that was dominant in his character. Taft was a philosophical progressive, but he could not get on with progressive leaders in Congress because they were too harsh in their denunciations, too impatient, too willing to experiment with untried measures.

The new President was forced to choose between the Old Guard leadership in Congress and the insurgent Republican bloc at the very outset— at the beginning of the special session which convened in March 1909 to consider tariff revision. As the Republicans now had a majority of only forty-seven in the House of Representatives, insurgent leaders concluded that the time had come to combine with Democrats to unhorse the tyrannical Speaker, Joe Cannon. When it seemed that the insurgents were bound to succeed, the Speaker appealed to Taft for help, promising to support the President's legislative program in return. Taft was in a perplexing dilemma because he did not like Cannon yet needed his co-operation. He made his first mistake: he endorsed Cannon and hinted that the insurgents should give up their campaign if they wanted a share in the patronage. In the end it was the defection of a group of southern and Tammany Democrats, not Taft's opposition, that frustrated the insurgents' *coup d'état.* Yet many progressives suspected that the President had betrayed them.

This incident only marked the beginning of the alienation of the progressives from the President. Effective White House leadership in the future could easily have repaired the damage done during the fight over the speakership. Instead of leading boldly, however, Taft soon blundered again —in a battle over tariff revision that split the Republican party in the spring of 1909.[3]

There is no doubt that Taft sincerely desired substantial tariff reductions. But he erred in the beginning by refusing to interfere in the fight in Congress and by failing to rally public opinion behind the cause of tariff reform. When he finally did intervene, moreover, he acted in such a manner as to cause midwestern insurgents, who were leading the fight for tariff reduction, to believe that he had deserted them and surrendered to special privilege. Although the President won a few noteworthy concessions, the bill that he signed—the Payne-Aldrich Act—represented a substantial victory for the eastern manufacturers. By this time—the late summer of 1909 —the Middle West was seething with rebellion. Although few men realized the fact, the doom of the Taft administration had been sealed.

Taft embarked in September 1909 upon a 13,000-mile speaking tour

[3] For details of this epochal conflict, see below, pp. 106–107.

from Boston to the West Coast to assuage the popular discontent. Instead of calming the storm, he arrayed the insurgent masses decisively against him by a series of indiscreet speeches. He publicly eulogized Nelson W. Aldrich of Rhode Island, leader of the Old Guard in the Senate. He rebuked midwestern senators who had voted against the tariff bill. And he climaxed his blunders by declaring at Winona, Minnesota, that the measure was the best tariff act that the Republican party had ever passed. After the Winona address, Midwesterners were certain that Taft had deserted to the Old Guard.

No sooner had public agitation over the Payne-Aldrich debacle quieted than a worse catastrophe completed the alienation of the progressives. This was the Ballinger affair, which grew out of a feud between the Secretary of the Interior, Richard A. Ballinger, and the chief of the Forestry Service in the Department of Agriculture, Gifford Pinchot. The root of the trouble was the fact that Pinchot was a conservationist and Ballinger was not. An investigator in the Interior Department, Louis R. Glavis, told Pinchot that Ballinger had connived with the Morgan-Guggenheim syndicate to validate certain withdrawals of Alaskan coal lands. Pinchot believed the accusation, urged Glavis to present his evidence to the President, and publicly denounced Ballinger as a traitor to conservation.

Glavis presented his indictment to the President, who accepted Ballinger's rebuttal and authorized the Secretary to dismiss Glavis for insubordination. Pinchot, however, refused to halt his attack and virtually forced Taft to remove him from the Forestry Service in January 1910. Meanwhile, the controversy had developed into a national *cause célèbre*, with conservatives defending the administration and progressives charging treachery and fraud.

The climax came when Democrats and insurgent Republicans in Congress forced an investigation of the Interior Department. A packed committee voted Ballinger a clean bill of health. But the trenchant questions asked by Louis D. Brandeis, who represented Glavis, exposed Ballinger, not as a corrupt public official, but as an opponent of conservation and a champion of the far western demand for rapid distribution of the remaining public domain. Instead of dismissing Ballinger and appointing a genuine conservationist in his stead, Taft continued stubbornly to defend him and thus exacerbated popular discontent.

Progressive Republicans in the House of Representatives were ready in the early months of 1910 to try again to shear Speaker Cannon of his dictatorial control over legislation. Aware of the impending attack, the Speaker struck back by declaring that he would fight to the end. An insurgent-Democratic coalition, led by George W. Norris of Nebraska, deposed the Speaker from the rules committee in March 1910 and deprived him of power to appoint members of standing committees. Certainly Taft secretly approved, for he well knew what a liability the Illinoisan was. Yet because he did nothing by word or deed to encourage the insurgents, the country concluded that Taft was on Cannon's side.

The misunderstanding about Taft's position in the fight against Cannon caused a final and complete break between the administration and the insurgents. They quarreled with Taft over the terms of a bill to strengthen the powers of the Interstate Commerce Commission. They accused him of conspiring with Wall Street when he proposed establishment of a postal savings system. Convinced that the insurgents were maneuvering in every possible way to destroy him politically and goaded by incessant and often unfair attacks, Taft turned fiercely against the progressives and joined the Old Guard in a powerful campaign to destroy insurgency. Taft, Aldrich, and Cannon conferred in March 1910 and formulated a plan of attack. It involved using money and patronage, first to build up strong conservative organizations in the Middle West, next to defeat insurgents for renomination in the impending spring primary elections. The plan was quickly carried out. Patronage in the midwestern states was given to supporters of the President, while Old Guard spokesmen invaded the region and exhorted voters to support administration candidates.

In fighting bitterly for their political lives, the insurgents virtually declared their independence of the party dominated by Taft, Aldrich, and Cannon. It was a momentous battle, for its outcome would determine the fate of the GOP, not only in the Middle West but in the nation as well. The railroad, industrial, and financial interests of the Midwest supported the administration almost solidly, but the people in every state supported their rebel leaders. Nothing was more indicative of the inevitable doom of the Taft administration than the failure of its anti-insurgent campaign. The flames of midwestern progressivism had grown into a raging prairie fire of insurgency. Already insurgents were talking about organizing a new party if Taft were renominated; already midwestern eyes were turning to Theodore Roosevelt for leadership in the impending battle. Before we discuss these events, however, let us turn back and see how political leadership confronted issues that agitated the American people during the Republican era.

47.   *Struggles for Tariff and Tax Reform, 1897–1913*

No public questions were more potentially explosive and at the same time more perpetually discussed after the Civil War than tariff and tax policies. The elaborate system of tariff protection and relative immunity from taxation that wealth enjoyed had become to progressives by the turn of the century the very symbol of control of the federal government by allied industrial and banking interests.

The Democrats had made a fumbling effort at tariff and tax reform during the second Cleveland administration. The outcome, the Wilson-Gorman Tariff Act of 1894, represented at best a feeble effort at downward revision and left the protective structure essentially unimpaired. But a coalition of western and southern representatives forced into the tariff bill an amendment levying a 2 per cent tax on all net incomes of individuals and corporations over $4,000.

By a strained and obviously class-conscious opinion, a bare majority of the Supreme Court ruled the income tax unconstitutional in 1895. It would be many years before progressives were strong enough to overcome the Old Guard's opposition to an income tax amendment. Meanwhile, Republicans would have spared themselves much future trouble if they had left well enough alone in tariff legislation. However, McKinley was eager to propitiate the agrarian Middle West after his close victory over Bryan in 1896 and called a special session of Congress in March 1897 to consider tariff revision. The President desired only a moderate revision of the Wilson-Gorman rates. But senators from western states held the balance of power and forced a substantial increase in duties on agricultural raw materials like wool and hides. Eastern senators, in turn, obtained increased duties on woolens, silks, and other manufactured products. The upshot of this log-rolling was the Dingley Tariff, the highest tariff in American history to that time.[4]

Manufacturing interests and western agricultural producers were able to forestall any attempt at general revision for twelve years after the adoption of the Dingley Act. Only one breach was made in the protective structure during the early progressive period: a reciprocity treaty in 1903 with Cuba, providing for mutual tariff reductions of from 20 to 40 per cent. At the same time conservatives kept an equally firm hand on tax policy. Congress imposed a moderate estate tax during the Spanish-American War. But this impost was repealed in 1902, and the federal government reverted to its usual practice of obtaining revenue almost entirely from consumption taxes—customs duties and excise taxes on tobacco and alcoholic beverages—that fell most heavily on the lower and middle classes.

Nevertheless, strong forces were at work during the first years of the twentieth century to culminate eventually in an irresistible movement for tariff and tax reform. First, the passage of the Dingley Act at the beginning of the period of frantic industrial combination lent apparent proof to the charge, often pressed by Bryan and other Democrats, that the high protective system stimulated the growth of monopolies and supercorporations at home. Second, the cost of living increased nearly one fourth between 1897 and 1907, and the average consumer saw a close relation between high tariffs and high prices, although there was often no connection between the two. Third, widespread discussion of the increasing concentration of incomes and wealth alarmed the middle class and stimulated the conviction that only income and inheritance taxes could reverse a process that seemed to threaten the future of American democracy.

The most significant factor in the beginning of a powerful movement for tariff and tax reform was the awakening of the Middle West. After an epochal struggle in 1901, Iowa Republicans nominated the progressive Albert B. Cummins for governor and wrote into their platform his proposal to remove all duties on articles manufactured by so-called trusts. Thereafter the "Iowa Idea," as Cummins's suggestion was called, became a stock feature of most midwestern state Republican platforms. Although the movement for downward revision soon became nation-wide and included many

wwwwwwwwwwwwww

[4] The Dingley Act, however, authorized the President to negotiate reciprocal agreements on certain enumerated articles, principally in the French and Latin American trade. Such agreements were later made with France, Italy, Brazil, and other nations. Section 4 of the Dingley Act, moreover, authorized the President to negotiate commercial treaties under which the American tariff might be reduced up to 20 per cent in return for reciprocal benefits. These treaties had to be approved by both houses of Congress and could not run for more than five years. The State Department subsequently negotiated eleven such treaties, none of which Congress approved.

small businessmen, the midwestern insurgents remained the most consistent advocates of tariff reform in the GOP.

Roosevelt recognized the potential danger of the popular discontent and was often tempted to take leadership of the movement for tariff revision. He failed to act for three reasons. First, he agreed with his Old Guard friends that such a move would disrupt the GOP. Second, he shrewdly struck a bargain with Speaker Cannon in late 1904 by which he agreed to jettison tariff revision in return for Cannon's promise to clear the road for a railroad-regulation bill in the House of Representatives. Third, and most important, Roosevelt thought that the tariff was a question of expediency, not of principle. In this belief he revealed progressivism's divided mind on the issue. On the other hand, both Roosevelt and Taft agreed in 1908 that the tariff question could no longer be evaded. At their insistence, a plank declaring "unequivocally for the revision of the tariff" was written in the Republican platform. Moreover, by 1908 both Roosevelt and Taft had come out squarely for graduated federal estate, gift, and income taxes.

Thus it seemed that the movement for genuine tariff and tax reform had reached a point of culmination when President Taft called Congress into special session in March 1909 to consider tariff revision. The administration's bill, sponsored by Sereno E. Payne of New York, chairman of the House ways and means committee, put a number of important raw materials on the free list and substantially reduced rates on iron and steel products, agricultural implements, sugar, and lumber. The measure included a federal inheritance tax ranging from 1 to 5 per cent. Although the Democrats made an unsuccessful effort to add an income tax amendment and then voted against the Payne bill for party reasons, they, like midwestern insurgents, were pleasantly surprised by the substantial revision that it attempted.

It was an altogether different story in the Senate. There Senator Aldrich and his finance committee took the Payne bill in hand and reported it on April 12, 1909, without the provision for an inheritance tax and with 847 amendments, the majority of which effected increases. Instead of lowering the Dingley rates, as the Rhode Island senator claimed, the Aldrich bill actually increased the *ad valorem* duties from 40.21 to 41.77 per cent. In all fairness, it should be added that Aldrich and his committee were under almost unbearable pressure for rate increases, and that the Rhode Islander acted usually under this goad, not on his own initiative.

A wave of indignation swept over the country, and especially the Middle West, as the implications of Aldrich's surrender to the special interests became clear. In the Senate a group of insurgent Republicans pledged themselves to make an open fight against the finance committee's amendments. The party rebels were Robert M. La Follette of Wisconsin, Jonathan P. Dolliver and Albert B. Cummins of Iowa, Albert J. Beveridge of Indiana, Joseph L. Bristow of Kansas, and Moses E. Clapp of Minnesota. Each took an important section of the tariff bill and discussed it in a lengthy and bitter speech. They also joined Democrats to include an income tax as a substitute for the discarded inheritance tax. So effective was their campaign that Aldrich headed it off only by accepting Taft's proposal

ABOVE: *John D. Rockefeller on his way to the oil investigation*
BELOW: *Andrew Carnegie, William Jennings Bryan, James J. Hill, and John Mitchell*

J. P. Morgan

Edward H. Harriman

Eugene Debs campaigning from the Red Special *in 1912*

Samuel Gompers

Robert M. La Follette

Louis D. Brandeis

Lincoln Steffens and Clarence Darrow

Theodore Roosevelt

Woodrow Wilson

ABOVE: *Battleships of the Great White Fleet*
BELOW: *Social Life with the Early Model T*

John Dewey

Walter Rauschenbusch

Joseph Pulitzer

Edward Arlington Robinson

ABOVE: *President Wilson reading his War Message to Congress*
BELOW: *The President leading a parade on Fifth Avenue*

The Big Four at Wilson's Paris home during the Peace Conference: Mr. Lloyd George, Signor Orlando, M. Clemenceau, and President Wilson

for a 2 per cent tax on the net incomes of corporations and by agreeing to the passage of an income tax amendment to the Constitution.

With strong administration support in the violent intraparty battle in the Senate, Aldrich put his bill across on July 8, 1909. It included the corporation income tax, restored the duties on hides, iron ore, and lumber, and greatly increased the Payne rates on a number of manufactured products. The final struggle came when the conference committee met shortly afterward. Finally bestirring himself in behalf of lower rates, Taft persuaded the committee to accept free hides and reductions in prevailing duties on shoes, lumber, coal, and iron ore. Nonetheless, the bill that the committee approved and Taft signed was a victory for the manufacturing East and an affront to the insurgent Middle West.[5]

The Payne-Aldrich debacle had profound and almost immediate repercussions. For one thing, it further widened the gulf between insurgents and the Taft administration. For another, it enabled the Democrats to capture the House of Representatives in the congressional elections of November 1910. Following hard on the heels of this disaster for the GOP, Taft proceeded further to alienate midwestern opinion by driving for reciprocity with Canada.

Confronted with an impending trade war between the United States and her northern neighbor, the State Department concluded a reciprocal trade agreement with the Canadian government in January 1911 that promised to draw the two nations into an economic union. The agreement placed all important agricultural products, industrial raw materials, and raw lumber and wood pulp on the free list. Moreover, it substantially reduced prevailing rates on many manufactured products. The President presented the agreement to Congress on January 26, 1911, for approval by joint resolution; and when the Senate refused to act before the regular session ended, Taft called Congress into special session for the first week in April.

In the subsequent battle over reciprocity that raged from April nearly to August, the recently formed alignment of progressive Republicans and Democrats against administration and Old Guard Republicans was totally destroyed. The Democrats joined Taft's friends in Congress in supporting the agreement—because it represented a tremendous victory for free trade. For the same reason the Old Guard fought the measure. The midwestern insurgents, on the other hand, accused the administration of sacrificing midwestern farm interests in order to widen the foreign market for eastern manufactured products. They fought the treaty, therefore, even more bitterly than did the Old Guard. For once Taft exerted himself strenuously and won the fight in Congress with the nearly solid support of the Democrats. The House approved the agreement on April 21, the Senate on July 22, 1911. But it seemed that Taft could not succeed, even when he did the statesmanlike thing. Canadian voters, aroused by talk in the United

[5] As the matter of tariff rates is infinitely complicated, it is almost impossible to specify the average rates of the Payne-Aldrich bill. The figure usually given by authorities is 37 per cent. The measure also established a Tariff Board to make scientific studies of various phases of the tariff question and to advise Congress and the President.

States of annexation, on September 21, 1911, repudiated the Liberal government that had negotiated the reciprocity agreement.

The anti-reciprocity coalition of insurgents and the Old Guard was short-lived. In fact, insurgents combined with Democrats even while the battle over reciprocity was raging to pass three tariff bills—a farmers' free list bill, which removed duties from about one hundred articles that the farmer bought; a wool and woolens bill; and a bill reducing duties on iron and steel products, cotton goods, and chemicals. Taft vetoed these measures on the ground that they were not "scientific." Moreover, progressive Democrats and Republicans joined hands throughout the country during 1911 and 1912 to obtain ratification of the Sixteenth, or income tax, Amendment, which Congress had submitted to the states in 1909. The first chapter in the history of twentieth-century tax reform was completed on February 25, 1913, when the amendment became a part of the Constitution. By the inauguration of the Wilson administration on March 4, 1913, therefore, the road seemed clear ahead for the fulfillment of the demand for downward tariff revision and the beginning of a democratic federal tax policy.

48. *The Railroad Problem*

Agitation for effective public control of railroad rates and services antedated the progressive movement by several decades. First came efforts by midwestern and southern legislatures during the 1870's and 1880's to institute regulation, either by statute or commission: Some of these attempts succeeded partially; others failed completely. In any event, during the 1880's the conviction grew that only Congress could deal effectively with rebating, stock watering, pools that destroyed competition, and exorbitant rates for goods and passengers in interstate commerce. Experience, and the Supreme Court's decision in the Wabash case of 1886, forbidding the states to regulate *interstate* rates, demonstrated that the really important railroad evils were beyond the jurisdiction of the states.

As a result the American people by 1886 had firmly determined to institute federal regulation and end the reign of unbridled freedom in the field of transportation. The legislative response to this overwhelming demand, the Interstate Commerce Act of 1887, was avowedly tentative in character. It specifically forbade pooling, discrimination, rebating, and higher charges for a short haul than a long one. As for rates, it declared that all charges should be reasonable and just and required railroads to publish rate schedules. Finally, the measure established the Interstate Commerce Commission, the first federal regulatory agency, to administer the law. Adoption of the Commerce Act, unenforceable though it turned out to be, marked a turning point in the exercise of federal power in the United States. For the first time the federal authority had been extended into an important area of hitherto private economic activity.

Railroad managers seemed eager to abide by the law for a brief time after the adoption of the Act of 1887. But the ICC ran head on into the refusal of railroad managers to testify when it tried to stamp out rebating, and it required years of adjudication to establish the Commission's authority to compel testimony. However, it was the Supreme Court's narrow interpretation of the Commerce Act that deprived the ICC of any real power. In the maximum freight rate cases of 1896 and 1897, the court ruled that the Commission did not have the power to fix rates. Moreover, in the Alabama Midlands case of 1897 the Supreme Court practically emasculated the prohibition against discrimination in charges for long and short hauls. Indeed, after these decisions the ICC became nothing more than a fact-finding body and openly confessed its inability to cope seriously with the problem of regulation.

The significance of these developments is, of course, at once apparent. By 1900 the whole problem of federal railroad regulation had to be fought out all over again in Congress and the country. The first amendment to the Interstate Commerce Act, the Elkins Act of 1903, was adopted, ironically enough, in response to the pleas of the railroad managers themselves. The rebating evil, they warned, had grown to such monstrous proportions that it threatened to bankrupt the railroads. Congress responded at once with the Elkins Act, which outlawed any deviation from published rates.

The "railroad senators" who framed the Elkins Act carefully avoided giving the ICC any authority over the rate-making process. Yet it was obvious on all sides that this was what the great majority of farmers and businessmen wanted most. At this high point of public agitation, Theodore Roosevelt took leadership of public opinion. In his Annual Message of December 1904 he recommended that the ICC be empowered, upon complaint of shippers, to fix maximum rates, subject to review by the courts. The House of Representatives in response passed the Esch-Townshend bill, implementing the President's suggestion, by the impressive majority of 326 to 17. Seeking to delay or postpone further action, Republican leaders in the upper house instructed the commerce committee to investigate the railroad problem during the spring and summer of 1905. As it turned out, the committee's investigation was no whitewash but rather uncovered a far-flung propaganda campaign by the railroads against federal regulation.

Armed with this new evidence of railroad misdoing, Roosevelt pressed his campaign for legislation all during the summer and fall of 1905. So enthusiastic was the popular response that even the railroad senators began to tremble. The House of Representatives quickly passed the administration's measure, the Hepburn bill, in February 1906. Although it fell short of what advanced progressives wanted, the bill went straight to the core of the railroad problem by empowering the ICC, upon complaint by shippers, to lower rates already established. It was not all that Roosevelt wanted, either, but he was certain it was the most that he could get.

The Hepburn bill was referred in the Senate to the commerce committee, the chairman of which was the multimillionaire Stephen B. Elkins of West Virginia, who, along with Aldrich, led the railroad senators. Realizing that he could not control the administration majority on the committee, Aldrich allowed it to report the Hepburn bill unamended. In order to outflank the committee, Aldrich arranged to have the fiery Democrat, Ben Tillman of South Carolina, report the bill and defend it on the Senate floor. At this stage, the astute Rhode Islander proposed amendments to cripple the bill. The most important of these endowed the courts with sweeping authority to review and nullify the ICC's rate decisions.

Debate raged for two months in the Senate over Aldrich's amendment. Roosevelt contended that judicial review should be limited solely to determining whether the ICC had exercised due process in fixing rates. He fought with unusual resourcefulness for a time. Then, when it seemed that a coalition of Democrats and administration Republicans could put the measure across without Aldrich's consent, several Democrats deserted the coalition. At this point—that is, early May 1906—Roosevelt executed a brilliant maneuver. Instead of going down to defeat with progressives who still demanded narrow court review, Roosevelt maneuvered Aldrich into accepting a compromise amendment. Framed by Aldrich, sponsored by William B. Allison of Iowa, and approved by the President, it was accepted; and the Hepburn bill became law on June 29, 1906.

Some progressives charged that Roosevelt had betrayed the cause of railroad regulation, but the verdict in this historic dispute must go to Roosevelt. The Allison amendment authorized district courts to issue interlocutory, or suspensive, injunctions against the ICC's decisions, it is true; but it also provided for speedy appeals to the Circuit and Supreme courts. Moreover, only the Circuit courts and the Supreme Court could reverse the Commission's rulings. And these high courts were instructed to pass upon such rulings with the same seriousness that they would pass upon acts of Congress, with the presumption always in favor of the ICC. Thus so-called broad court review was hedged about with such effective limitations that judicial nullification of the Hepburn Act was well nigh impossible.

Furthermore, an examination of the general provisions of the Hepburn Act emphasizes the dimensions of Roosevelt's victory. To begin with, the ICC was empowered, upon complaint, to investigate and lower rates. In other words, ultimate control over rates was taken from private hands and given to an agency of the people. The Commission, in addition, gained jurisdiction over express and sleeping car companies, switches and spurs, and pipe lines. Finally, the Act required a uniform system of cost accounting by the railroads, eliminated the old free pass evil, and required railroads to divest themselves of outside properties after 1908. The latter provision was aimed chiefly at the anthracite coal monopoly controlled by nine eastern railroads.

The effect of the broadening of the ICC's power was at once apparent. Shippers made more than 9,000 appeals to the Commission within two years, while railroad managers seemed almost in a chastened mood. Then railroad managers began suddenly to challenge the ICC in 1908, and their action in turn caused a crowding of the dockets of the Circuit courts. In addition, the railroads made general rate increases in 1909, and the masses of people realized for the first time that the Commission could deal only with specific increases, upon complaint, and lacked power to suspend or revoke general rate advances.

The railroads' resistance to regulation and the general rate increases of 1909 at once stimulated increased agitation for a further strengthening of the ICC's power. In response, President Taft, in the summer of 1909, requested Attorney General George W. Wickersham to prepare a new railroad bill. The measure that Wickersham drafted greatly enlarged the Commission's rate-making power and established a Commerce Court, which should have original jurisdiction in appeals from the rulings of the ICC. The midwestern insurgent senators were disappointed because the Wickersham draft made no provision for valuation of railroad property by the Commission, and they strongly disapproved the proposal for a Commerce Court, with power of broad review. Even so, the insurgents' opposition to the President's bill might have been less violent had it not seemed that Taft was willing to change the measure to satisfy the demands of railroad spokesmen. Taft conferred with six railroad presidents early in January 1910, even before the measure was introduced in the House, and changed the bill to allow railroads to acquire competing lines. To progressives, this looked suspiciously like collusion. And when Senator Aldrich announced that he would support the bill, they were certain that some evil scheme was being plotted.

The President's measure, introduced in the House of Representatives in January 1910 as the Mann bill, at once fell into the hands of a progressive Republican-Democratic coalition. It struck out the provision permitting mergers of competing lines, added amendments for physical valuation and equality in charges for long and short hauls, and brought telephone and telegraph companies under the jurisdiction of the Interstate Commerce Commission. Meanwhile, insurgents in the Senate had launched a violent attack on the President's bill, which the commerce committee reported without amendments. Taft made the measure a test of party loyalty, and insurgents joined Democrats and threatened to rewrite the bill altogether. After the progressive coalition struck out the provisions contrary to the Sherman Act, Aldrich turned to the Democrats. If they would support the administration's railroad bill, Aldrich said, the administration would agree to approve statehood acts for New Mexico and Arizona. As the Democrats were eager for the admission of the two territories, they sealed the bargain. Thus the progressive Republican-Democratic coalition changed into a Democratic–Regular Republican majority, and the administration's railroad bill passed the *Senate* essentially intact.

Nonetheless, the bill that emerged from the conference committee, which Taft approved as the Mann-Elkins Act, represented more a victory for the progressives than for the administration. The new legislation empowered the ICC to suspend general rate increases and revise rates on its own initiative. It also established a Commerce Court to hear appeals directly from the Commission. These provisions had been originally parts of the President's bill. On the other hand, all important progressive amendments, except the provision for physical valuation, were retained by the conference committee. Railroads were not allowed to acquire competing lines. Telephone, telegraph, cable, and wireless companies were defined as common carriers. The prohibition in the Act of 1887 against discriminations in charges for long and short hauls was strengthened. As a result of the hard fight that progressives made in support of these amendments, the Mann-Elkins Act of 1910 had become legislation comprehensive in character, not merely supplementary.

Progressives in Congress now redoubled their efforts to obtain physical valuation as the basis for rate-making by the ICC. Valuation of railroad property would enable the Commission to fix rates on a basis of the true value of railroad property, rather than on a basis of watered capitalization. This was the chief reason that progressives supported and railroad spokesmen opposed the proposal. To conservatives, moreover, physical valuation seemed to be the first step in eventual nationalization. None the less, the insurgent-Democratic congressional coalition won this last objective in the closing months of the Taft regime. The Physical Valuation Act of 1913 required the Interstate Commerce Commission to report the value of all property owned by every common carrier subject to its jurisdiction, including the original cost, the cost of reproduction new, and the cost of reproduction, less depreciation. When completed, the Act declared, such valuations were to be accepted as prima facie evidence of the worth of the property in all actions by the Commission.

49. *The Federal Antitrust Policy, 1890–1913*

Almost simultaneous with the beginning of the agitation for railroad regulation was a widespread movement to destroy the infant industrial combinations of that day, the trusts.[6] At least fourteen states and territories had written antitrust provisions into their constitutions by 1890, while thirteen others had adopted antitrust laws. Almost without exception, these were western and southern states—a reflection of the impact of the agrarian crusade against railroads and monopolies. The state antitrust crusade gained new momentum from 1890 to 1900. By the latter date forty-two states and territories attempted to outlaw monopolies, either by constitutional provision or by statute.[7]

It became increasingly obvious that sporadic and unco-ordinated action by the states could neither destroy monopoly nor restore competition, especially when New Jersey in 1888 permitted the legal incorporation of trusts as holding companies. By this date the popular agitation had reached such a high pitch that both major parties incorporated antitrust planks in their platforms. And when President Benjamin Harrison endorsed the demand for a federal antitrust law in his Annual Message of December 1889, Congress did not dare refuse to act.

Its response, the Sherman Antitrust Act of 1890, was brief and to the point. The core was embodied in Section 1. It prohibited "every contract, combination in the form of trust or otherwise, or conspiracy, in restraint of trade or commerce among the several States, or with foreign nations," and

[6] For a discussion of the origins and progress of the trust movement in the United States, see above, pp. 48–50.

[7] Practically all these states and territories prohibited restraint of trade contrary to the public interest. Some twenty-nine states prohibited suppression of competition through pools, agreements to limit quantity or divide sales territories, price-fixing agreements, and so on. A number of states, moreover, attempted to outlaw cutthroat practices, such as price cutting to destroy competition, so-called tying contracts, and discriminations in prices made for the purpose of destroying competition.

provided punishment for such misdoing. Section 7, moreover, stipulated that any person injured by illegal combinations or conspiracies might sue and recover threefold damages and the cost of the suit.

No statute ever enacted by Congress reflected more accurately an overwhelming popular demand. Yet the Sherman law, after several prosecutions by the Harrison administration, fell into neglect and general contempt until 1902. Effective enforcement of the law depended largely upon the Justice Department. But Attorneys General during the Cleveland and McKinley administrations did little to carry out the popular mandate to destroy the trusts because neither Cleveland nor McKinley had any sympathy for the objectives of the Sherman Act—except insofar as it might be applied against labor unions.

A case in point was E. C. Knight *v.* the United States, 1895, in which the government challenged the monopoly recently acquired by the American Sugar Refining Company of Philadelphia. Instead of vindicating the Sherman law, Cleveland's Attorney General, Richard Olney, presented the government's case in such a manner that the Supreme Court thought that it had to declare that the Sherman Act did not apply to combinations in manufacturing. The consequences of Olney's calculated subversion were far-reaching, but we should not fall into the common error of thinking that the Supreme Court entirely emasculated the antitrust law. As we shall later see, on every opportunity afforded by the government, that tribunal evidenced its willingness to carry out the mandate embodied in the statute.

It was obvious as the new century opened that only a President's determination to give teeth to the measure was needed to make the Sherman law a really effective measure. Theodore Roosevelt understood the dimensions of the popular fear of "trusts," abhorred monopoly, and personally resented the power that uncontrolled wealth exercised over the nation's destiny. He therefore resolved to vindicate national sovereignty by bringing great combinations to book. His chief weapons were publicity and the Sherman law. He made investigations and publicity of mergers and so-called trusts possible on a systematic scale by his victory in the fight in 1903 for establishment of the Bureau of Corporations in the Department of Commerce and Labor. The Bureau's reports on the Beef Trust, 1905, the Standard Oil Company, 1906–7, the Tobacco Trust, 1909–15, the steel industry, 1911–13, and the International Harvester Company, 1913, were widely publicized and provided basic data for antitrust proceedings.

In the form of direct attack, the Justice Department under Roosevelt instituted eighteen proceedings in equity, obtained twenty-five indictments, and participated in one forfeiture proceeding. Beginning with his first prosecution, the suit to dissolve the Northern Securities Company in 1902, Roosevelt pressed relentlessly forward against combinations. The President later in 1902 ordered prosecution of the Swift, Armour, and Nelson Morris companies—the so-called Beef Trust—for organizing the National Packing Company to acquire control of independent packing firms in the Middle West. The Supreme Court rendered a unanimous verdict for the government in 1905. But the packers continued to defy the government, and it was not until 1920 and 1921 that competition was effectively restored to the meat industry. The climax of Roosevelt's campaign came with sweeping indictments by the Justice Department of the Standard Oil Company in 1907 and of the American Tobacco Company in 1908. These two cases, the most important in the history of the antitrust movement before 1945, did not reach final settlement until 1911.

Roosevelt's contribution to the antitrust cause has been derided by most historians in spite of this effort and achievement. Their failure to understand his contribution stems, among other things, from a faulty appreciation of his objectives. Unlike some progressives, who would have limited the size of corporations, Roosevelt never feared bigness in industry—unless bigness was accompanied by monopolistic control and a disposition on the part of management to defy the public interest. Thus, he never moved against two prominent combinations, United States Steel and International Harvester, because he never had good evidence to prove they were monopolies or were illegally suppressing competition. The Taft administration later instituted dissolution proceedings against these two corporations, but the Supreme Court confirmed Roosevelt's judgment in both cases.

Roosevelt's aggressive program of publicity and prosecution was carried forward at an even more intensive pace by President Taft and his Attorney General, George W. Wickersham. When Congress refused to enact Taft's proposal for federal incorporation, a corporation commission, and legislation against stock watering, the Taft administration moved in a wholesale way against combinations. All told, Taft instituted forty-six proceedings for dissolution, brought forty-three indictments, and instituted one contempt proceeding. His two most important cases, those against United States Steel and International Harvester, ended in failure. His two most important victories, over Standard Oil and American Tobacco, were scored in proceedings that Roosevelt had instituted.

The government, after five years of legal warfare, seemingly won complete victory in 1911 with the Supreme Court's order for dissolution of the gigantic oil and tobacco monopolies. The Court implicitly repudiated the Knight decision and made it plain that the holding-company form could not be used to evade the Sherman law. And yet in both cases the government accepted dissolution plans prepared by the corporations' lawyers, plans that provided for the re-establishment of the constituent companies and a pro rata distribution of shares in the new companies on the basis of ownership of shares in the old holding companies. As time passed, the new companies did in fact emerge as independent concerns, while the tremendous expansion of the oil and tobacco industries during the First World War helped to create a new competitive situation. At the time when the dissolution decrees were issued in 1911, however, progressives indignantly protested that they were a sham and a fraud.

None the less, the primary objectives of the antitrust movement had been fairly accomplished by the end of the Taft administration. There was no longer any constitutional doubt that the federal government possessed ample power to prevent monopoly and suppress unfair trade practices in the day-to-day operations of businessmen. Because of Roosevelt's and Taft's vigorous prosecutions, moreover, the age of monopoly was over. Great corporations remained and dominated certain industries, but these oligopolies existed by the sufferance of public opinion and a government that jealously guarded their smaller competitors.

50. *The Supreme Court and Economic Policy Before the First World War*

In the American constitutional system Congress proposes and the Supreme Court disposes. The phrase is of course a hyperbole, but it points up a problem that continually perplexed progressives who were struggling to extend the boundaries of governmental power. Unlike their counterparts in other countries, American reformers in state and nation were never free to develop at will a system of administrative regulation. For one thing, they were bound by a written constitution capable of being construed as the bulwark of a *laissez-faire* policy. For another, they were restrained by the fear that a conservative Supreme Court, which insisted upon having the final word, would not tolerate the extension of governmental power that they sought to accomplish. As we will see, the courts had effected a remarkable accommodation of constitutional doctrine to most progressive regulatory concepts by 1917. In the last years of the nineteenth century, however, reformers might well have believed that such a development was impossible.

To begin with, the Supreme Court by 1900 had established the right to review all state attempts to regulate railroads and corporations. This power the court had assumed as a result of one of the most important revolutions in judicial theory in American history. It came about in the following manner. The Granger-dominated legislature of Illinois, in the early 1870's, established a schedule of charges for grain elevators, and one of the elevator owners appealed to the federal courts for redress. The Illinois statute, he averred, deprived his corporation of property without due process of law and thus violated the Fourteenth Amendment. Upholding the Illinois law in Munn *v.* Illinois, 1877, Chief Justice Morrison R. Waite declared that determination of reasonable rates was a legislative, not a judicial, function. This doctrine was reaffirmed soon afterward in a series of so-called Granger cases and seemed to be firmly established as a basic principle of American constitutional law. Yet the Supreme Court completely reversed Waite's doctrine between 1886 and 1898 and transformed the Fourteenth Amendment into an instrument for the protection of corporations and railroads against "unreasonable" regulation by the states.

It began when Roscoe Conkling, while arguing the case of San Mateo County *v.* Southern Pacific Railroad before the Supreme Court in 1882, asserted that the congressional committee that framed the Fourteenth Amendment had intended to confer federal citizenship upon corporations. As Conkling had been a member of the committee and produced its secret journal, the court listened carefully to his argument, although it did not take judicial cognizance of it. In Santa Clara County *v.* Southern Pacific Railroad, 1886, and the Minnesota Rate Case, 1889, however, the court accepted Conkling's reasoning and declared that corporations were federal citizens, entitled to protection by the Fourteenth Amendment against action of the states that would deprive them of property, or income, without due process of law. Finally, in Smyth *v.* Ames, 1898, the Supreme Court reached the last stage in its journey away from the doctrines expounded in Munn *v.* Illinois. Nebraska had established maximum charges on freight carried entirely within the state. Overturning the Nebraska statute, the court reaffirmed the federal citizenship of corporations, declared that rates must be high enough to guarantee a fair return to railroads, and warned state legislatures that the courts existed, among other reasons, for the purpose of protecting property against unreasonable legislation.

In none of these cases did the Supreme Court deny the right of the states to regulate railroads and other corporations. It only insisted that state regulation be reasonable and fair and not invade the jurisdiction of Congress. Until a body of doctrine defining due process regarding state regulation had been built, however, the effect of the court's new departure was to create a twilight zone of authority. Judges of the numerous federal district courts could prevent the states from acting; and the states had no recourse but to await the verdict of the high tribunal.

Progressives, therefore, charged that the Supreme Court had usurped the administrative function of the states and imposed its own notion of due process and reasonableness on state commissions. They resented even more bitterly the systematic manner in which the court narrowed the authority of the ICC under the Act of 1887 and even reduced that great statute to an unenforceable platitude. As we have seen, the court's decision in the Alabama Midlands Case of 1897 nullified the prohibition against discrimination in charges for long and short hauls. Moreover, in the so-called maximum freight rate cases of 1896 and 1897, the court denied that Congress had conferred rate-making authority on the Interstate Commerce Commission. In view of the absence of any specific delegation of the rate-making authority to the Commission by the Commerce Act, the court could probably not have ruled otherwise. Impatient progressives, however, found the court a more vulnerable scapegoat than Congress.

Progressives were on more solid ground when they denounced the Supreme Court's nullification of the income tax provision of the Wilson-Gorman Tariff Act of 1894. By a five-to-four decision in Pollock *v.* Farmers' Loan and Trust Company, 1895, the court reversed precedent by declaring that the income tax was in part indirectly a tax on land and would therefore have to be apportioned among the states according to population. It was easily the most unpopular judicial ruling since the Dred Scott decision of 1857. For one thing, the income tax decision effectively blocked the movement for a more democratic tax policy until a constitutional amendment could be adopted. For another, the court's majority had obviously made a political rather than a judicial judgment. Coming as it did in the same year in which the court upheld the conviction of Debs and other officials of the American Railway Union for violating the Sherman law, the income tax decision only deepened the popular conviction that the highest tribunal in the land had become the tool of railroads, corporations, and millionaires.

Popular distrust was further intensified in 1895 when the Supreme Court, in the case of E. C. Knight *v.* the United States, seemingly emasculated the Sherman Act's prohibition against industrial monopoly. That the court was actually willing to interpret the Sherman Act liberally was demonstrated, however, in a series of important antitrust cases from 1897 to 1899. In the Trans-Missouri Freight Association case of 1897, the justices affirmed that the Sherman law applied to railroads and outlawed a pool operating south and west of the Missouri River. The court reaffirmed this judgment in the Joint Traffic Association case of the following year. And in the Addyston Pipe Company case, 1899, the justices made it clear that the Sherman law applied also to manufacturers who combined in pools to eliminate price competition.

Thus by the turn of the century the Supreme Court had firmly established the rule that combinations formed directly to suppress competition in the transportation and distribution of products were illegal. Promoters of industrial combinations and their lawyers, however, continued to assume on account of the Knight decision, discussed earlier, that manufacturing consolidations did not fall under the prohibitions of the antitrust act. This illusion the court finally and completely shattered in its decisions in the Standard Oil and American Tobacco cases, rendered in 1911. Without openly repudiating the Knight decision, the tribunal declared that industrial combinations formed for the purpose of achieving monopoly were outlawed by the Sherman Act, and that the holding company form did not confer legality on otherwise illegal consolidations.

The Standard Oil and Tobacco decisions represented, therefore, a complete accommodation of legal doctrine to prevailing antitrust sentiment. But even more important was the fact that they marked the end of a long struggle within the court itself over the basic meaning of the Sherman Act. Did that statute forbid all restraints of trade, or did it prohibit only unreasonable, that is, direct and calculated, restraints? The Supreme Court's majority had consistently ruled before 1911 that the Sherman law proscribed all restraints, reasonable and unreasonable.[8] However, Justice Edward Douglas White had vigorously dissented in the Trans-Missouri Freight Association case of 1897, declaring that the framers of the antitrust law had intended to outlaw only unreasonable restraints. He reiterated his position over the years and won converts to it. He finally won a majority to his side in the Standard Oil and Tobacco cases and, as Chief Justice, wrote the "rule of reason" into American legal doctrine. The Sherman law, he declared, prohibited only unreasonable restraints of trade.

Actually, the "rule of reason" was the only standard by which the antitrust law could be enforced, as the court had tacitly admitted years before. By winning his campaign to interpret the law in the light of common law doctrine, Chief Justice White enabled businessmen to conduct normal operations without fear of reprisal, and the government to enforce the statute in good conscience. All the same, his promulgation of the new rule set off an incredible furor. The great mass of people thought that the court had drawn a distinction between reasonable, or "good," trusts and unreasonable, or "bad," trusts. A number of Democratic congressmen immediately introduced bills to outlaw White's interpretation. The Supreme Court had ruled wisely, but the Taft administration failed to explain to the people that the court's decisions in the Standard Oil and Tobacco cases and the promulgation of the "rule of reason" represented the greatest victory thus far accomplished in the long fight to destroy monopoly in the United States.

[8] In common law doctrine a reasonable restraint of trade is any restraint that is ancillary to an otherwise legal contract. Almost any form of contract involves such reasonable restraint of trade. By agreeing to sell his product to one person, for example, a manufacturer restrains trade to the extent that he cannot sell the same goods to another person. An unreasonable restraint of trade, on the other hand, occurs when businessmen enter into agreements, the objectives of which are to restrain trade. Thus conspiracies to control prices, restrict production, divide markets, and so on are unreasonable restraints of trade.

CHAPTER

6

Woodrow Wilson and the Flowering of the Progressive Movement

1910–1916

T HE YEARS FROM 1910 to 1917 were a time of culmination and fulfillment for American progressivism. We have seen how various reform movements in the cities and states came to fruition during this period. In addition, a virtual revolution took place in the more important area of national
politics. The Republican party was convulsed by internal schisms and suffered a violent rupture from 1910 to 1912; and Theodore Roosevelt attempted in the latter year to rally progressives of all parties under the ban-
ner of a third party. As the Democrats now had a reform leader of their own
in Woodrow Wilson, Roosevelt failed to build either a solid progressive phalanx or a permanent party. Instead, he split the Republican majority and enabled the Democrats to capture control of the presidency and of Congress.

But Roosevelt did more than make possible a Democratic victory in
1912. By championing an advanced program of federal economic and social
regulation, he also pointed up the major dilemma confronting American
progressives. Could national regeneration be achieved, as most Democratic
progressives thought, merely by destroying special privilege and applying

the rule of equity to all classes? Or could the promise of American life be fulfilled only through a positive program of federal intervention and participation in economic and social affairs, as Roosevelt and Herbert Croly contended?

Advocates of these two concepts of progressivism battled all during the first Wilson administration to shape the form and character of federal legislation. As the new President exercised an extraordinary control over Congress, the outcome of the conflict—in fact, the future destiny of the progressive movement—was largely in his hands. Let us now see how progressivism came to flood tide, how Wilson guided it from one channel into another, and how the basis for a later and bolder program of federal action was laid by the time the United States entered the First World War.

51. *The Disruption of the Republican Party and the Reorganization of the Democracy*

There were numerous warnings in all parts of the country during the spring and summer of 1910 that a violent storm impended in the Republican party. The most portentous was the near hurricane velocity of the insurgent revolt in the Middle West. President William Howard Taft hastily sought to make peace with his enemies and save his party from disaster after the failure of his campaign to purge midwestern progressives in the primary campaigns of 1910. The insurgents, now determined to seize control of the GOP and prevent Taft's renomination in 1912, rebuffed the President's overtures and began a search for a leader of their own.

A second signal of Republican distress was the estrangement between Roosevelt and Taft that was fully evident by the time the former President returned from Europe in June 1910. The coolness that Roosevelt felt toward his former friend was the outgrowth partly of incidents like the Ballinger affair, but above all of Roosevelt's growing conviction that Taft had allowed the Old Guard to maneuver him into a position that made the revolt of the insurgents inevitable. Roosevelt was firmly committed to the progressive cause, but he tried hard to bring the warring factions together. Feeling rebuffed by the administration when he endeavored to mediate between conservatives and progressives in New York State, the former president set out upon a speaking tour in the summer of 1910 to kindle the flames of progressivism. So enthusiastic was the popular response that he was catapulted into leadership of the rebellion against Taft and the Old Guard.

Democrats harvested the fruits of Republican dissension and popular protest against the Payne-Aldrich tariff and Ballinger affair in the congressional and gubernatorial elections of November 1910. The House of Representatives went Democratic for the first time since 1892, and Democratic governors were elected in many normally Republican states in the East and Middle West. There could be no doubt that progressive agitation was rising to flood tide, or that a Republican party dominated by Taft, Aldrich, and Cannon faced almost certain defeat in 1912.

The Republican insurgents, on the other hand, were determined to win in 1912, but to win with a ticket of their choosing and a platform embodying their objectives. Many signs pointed in 1910 and early 1911 to Senator

Robert M. La Follette of Wisconsin as the leader of the rebels, especially after prominent insurgents formed the National Progressive Republican League in January 1911 to fight for the Senator's nomination. La Follette had the support of a small and dedicated band of idealists, but the great mass of Republican progressives wanted Roosevelt. Convinced that his party faced certain defeat if Taft was renominated, and persuaded that La Follette could never be nominated, Roosevelt at last gave in to the pleas of his friends and announced his candidacy for the Republican nomination on February 24, 1912.

The battle for control of the GOP that occurred from March through May 1912 was bitter and violent. In the thirteen states that held presidential primaries, Roosevelt won 278 delegates, as compared to 48 for Taft and 36 for La Follette. On the other hand, Taft controlled the southern states, had the support of Old Guard strongholds like New York, and dominated the Republican National Committee. Consequently the Taft forces organized the national convention that met in Chicago on June 18, awarded themselves 235 of the crucial 254 contested seats, and proceeded ruthlessly to renominate the President on the first ballot on June 21.

Meanwhile, over three hundred Roosevelt delegates had stormed out of the convention and, in consultation with Roosevelt, had decided to return to Chicago and form a new party dedicated to advancing the cause of progressivism. The outgrowth of the insurgents' anger and dedication was the Progressive party, organized in Chicago on August 5 and 6, 1912. Roosevelt came in person on August 6 and delivered his acceptance speech, "A Confession of Faith." He said that he felt like a bull moose.

The high excitement of these events at Chicago should not be allowed to obscure their significance or the importance of the platform that the Progressive convention adopted. It erected mileposts that the American progressive movement would follow for the next fifty years. It was, in fact, the most important American political document between the Populist platform of 1892 and the Democratic platform of 1936. The Progressive platform of 1912 approved all objectives of the social justice reformers—minimum wages for women, child labor legislation, workmen's compensation, and social insurance. It endorsed neo-democratic demands for the initiative, referendum, and recall, the recall of state judicial decisions, nomination of presidential candidates by preferential primaries, and woman's suffrage. Finally, it demanded establishment of powerful new agencies—a federal trade commission and a federal tariff commission—to regulate business and industry. In brief, it proposed to transform state and federal governments into positive, dynamic agencies of social and economic regeneration.

A crucial struggle had also been occurring in the meantime for control of the Democratic party. Bryan remained titular head of the party, but he announced soon after the elections of November 1910 that he would not be a candidate for a fourth nomination, and a host of new leaders rose to claim his mantle. Woodrow Wilson, who had made a brilliant campaign for the governorship of New Jersey, quickly emerged as the most formidable Democratic claimant. Hard on the heels of his election in November 1910, Wilson drove ahead from one triumph to another. First he broke with the Democratic state boss who had nominated him and led a popular fight to prevent the boss's election to the United States Senate. Then, in a spectacular display of leadership, Wilson forced through an unwilling legislature a series of measures—a direct primary system, corrupt practices legislation, workmen's compensation, and effective state regulation of railroads and public utilities—that implemented the program for which New Jersey progressives had been fighting for almost a decade. As a consequence of these triumphs, many progressive Democrats throughout the country by the summer of 1911 were thanking God that they had a new leader and spokesman. For his part, Wilson threw himself into the movement for his nomination for the presidency with such vigor that it seemed at the beginning of 1912 that he would easily win leadership of the Democracy.

Wilson's apparent success made the meteoric rise of his chief rival, Champ Clark of Missouri, Speaker of the House of Representatives, all the more surprising. In contrast to the New Jersey governor, who represented the newcomer and the nonprofessional in politics, Clark was an old-line politician who had served without distinction in the House since the 1890's. Temperamentally and intellectually unfitted to be President, Clark none the less knew better than Wilson how to play the game of politics. He inherited most of Bryan's following in the West, made alliances with a number of eastern and southern state organizations, and won the support of William Randolph Hearst and his chain of newspapers.

Thus, while Wilson campaigned fervently and won not quite one fourth the delegates to the Democratic national convention, Clark negotiated shrewdly and harvested a crop nearly twice as large. To make matters worse for Wilson, Oscar W. Underwood of Alabama, chairman of the House ways and means committee and the pre-eminent Democratic tariff reformer, had entered the contest and won over one hundred southern delegates who probably would have otherwise gone to Wilson.

It was a critical moment in the life of the Democratic party and, indeed, in the history of the country, when the delegates assembled in national convention in Baltimore on June 25, 1912. As nothing less than control of the federal government was at stake, the convention was a bitter affair from the beginning. The outcome of preliminary contests over organization, in which Bryan and the Wilson forces were defeated by the conservative leaders with the help of the Clark delegates, seemed to forecast Clark's impending victory. Clark took a commanding lead in the early balloting. Then the ninety Tammany-controlled New York delegates went to the Speaker on the tenth ballot, giving him a majority—but not the then necessary two thirds.

Yet the expected and seemingly inevitable Clark landslide did not materialize; in fact, Clark lost votes on the next few ballots. Then followed a long and grueling battle in which the Wilson managers gradually undermined Clark's strength and finally won a two-thirds majority for the New Jersey governor on the forty-sixth ballot.

It has long been mistakenly assumed that Bryan's action in changing his vote from Clark to Wilson on the fourteenth ballot was the decisive factor in this miraculous conclusion. Actually, a number of other circumstances were more responsible for Wilson's victory. In the first place, the Underwood and Wilson managers at the beginning of the balloting agreed to stand together, and their solid front broke the force of Clark's main assault, on and immediately after the tenth ballot. In the second place, much

of Clark's support was more superficial than real, and the Wilson leaders
were able to capture many of the Speaker's delegates in the protracted battle that ensued. But most important was the fact that Wilson's managers
were finally able to win Roger Sullivan, Illinois Democratic boss, to their
side. Going to Wilson on the forty-second ballot, the fifty-eight Illinois votes
gave Wilson a majority for the first time and set in motion a landslide that
finally developed when the Underwood delegates came to the New Jersey
governor four ballots later.

Bryan at least did dominate the writing of the historic Democratic platform of 1912. It denounced the Payne-Aldrich tariff, promised honest downward revision, and demanded legislation to destroy so-called trusts and establish a decentralized banking system free from Wall Street control. It held
out hope for early independence to the Filipinos. Finally, it approved the
amendments for the income tax and direct election of senators and favored
exempting labor unions from prosecution under the Sherman law. Although
it was neither as advanced nor as nationalistic as the Progressive "Contract
with the People," the Democratic platform did promise at least the destruction of the system of special privileges for business that Republicans had
carefully erected since 1861.

52.   *The Campaign and Election of 1912*

A meaningful division in American politics occurred for the first time
since 1896 during the presidential campaign of 1912. The four parties and
tickets in the field offered programs that well reflected the existing divisions
of political sentiment. Although the Republican platform contained concessions to the dominant progressive sentiment, voters understood that Taft's
re-election would mean a continuation of Old Guard leadership and policies.
In extreme contrast stood Eugene V. Debs, the Socialist candidate, and his
party. Offering a program envisaging the gradual nationalization of resources and major industries, Debs campaigned as if he thought he had a
chance to win.

The campaign, however, soon turned into a verbal duel between Roosevelt and Wilson. Both men were progressives, yet they reflected in their respective programs and philosophies a significant ideological divergence in
the progressive movement. Roosevelt's program, the New Nationalism, represented the consummation of a philosophy that had been maturing in his
mind at least since 1908, if not since 1905. Like Herbert Croly, Roosevelt
urged progressives to examine their basic political assumptions and to see
that the historic American democratic creed, which was intensely individualistic, was no longer adequate for an urbanized and industrialized society. Practically, this meant, Roosevelt declared, that progressives must
abandon *laissez faire* for democratic collectivism and be willing to use the
federal government as a regulator and protector of business, industry, and
workers. It meant, in brief, that progressives must surrender their hostility
to strong government and espouse instead a New Nationalism that would
achieve democratic ends through Hamiltonian, or nationalistic, means.

In expounding this philosophy in the campaign of 1912, Roosevelt advocated a policy toward big business that was entirely at variance with the

individualistic tradition. Let us recognize, he said, that concentration and bigness in industry are inevitable in many fields. At the same time, let us subject the large corporations to comprehensive public control through a powerful federal trade commission. Let us also recognize that the great mass of American workers, especially women and children, are powerless to protect themselves, and hence let us use the state and federal governments to improve their lot—among other things by minimum wages for women, workmen's compensation, federal prohibition against child labor, and expanded public health services.

Wilson had no such well-constructed program when the campaign began. He was a recent convert to progressivism and still imbued with nineteenth-century *laissez-faire* concepts and Democratic state-rights doctrine. It taught that federal authority should be used only to destroy artificial barriers to the full development of individual energies, not to rearrange social and economic relationships or to give protection to special classes.

Thus, Wilson during the presidential campaign of 1912 promised to destroy the Republican system of tariff protection as the first step in restoring competition in industry. He followed the suggestion of Louis D. Brandeis, who became his most important adviser during the campaign, in moving next to what he called the fundamental issue of the campaign—emancipation of business and labor from monopolistic control. Wilson lashed out at Roosevelt's proposals for social legislation and control of corporations. He warned that the New Nationalism could end only with big businessmen controlling the federal government and enslaving workers. In contrast, he promised to destroy monopoly and unleash the potential energies of businessmen by restoring conditions under which competition could flourish. This he would do, specifically, by outlawing unfair trade practices and by then relying upon the courts to enforce an amended and strengthened Sherman law. This program Wilson called the New Freedom. In brief, it envisaged the destruction of special privileges, restoration of the reign of competition, and reliance for future progress on individual enterprise. On social and economic justice, Wilson was somewhat ambiguous. Since his own ideas were in flux, it is difficult to know precisely where he stood. In any event, he offered no definite program like Roosevelt's.

The most striking fact of the campaign was Roosevelt's failure to split the Democratic ranks and create a solid progressive coalition. The results, therefore, were obvious long before election day. Wilson polled 6,286,214 popular votes; Roosevelt, 4,126,020; Taft, 3,483,922; and Debs, 897,011. Although Wilson received slightly less than 42 per cent of the popular votes, his victory in the Electoral College was overwhelming because of the multiple division of popular votes. The disruption of the GOP, moreover, gave the Democrats a large majority in the House and a small but workable majority in the Senate.

The election of 1912 seems to have demonstrated that the American people were in an overwhelmingly progressive, if not rebellious, mood. Had progressive Republicans and progressive Democrats been able to unite behind a single ticket and platform, progressivism's triumph would have been even more spectacular. As it was, the Democrats would control the federal government chiefly because of the division among their opponents. Upon Wilson's ability to bring the reform program to fulfillment and unite the

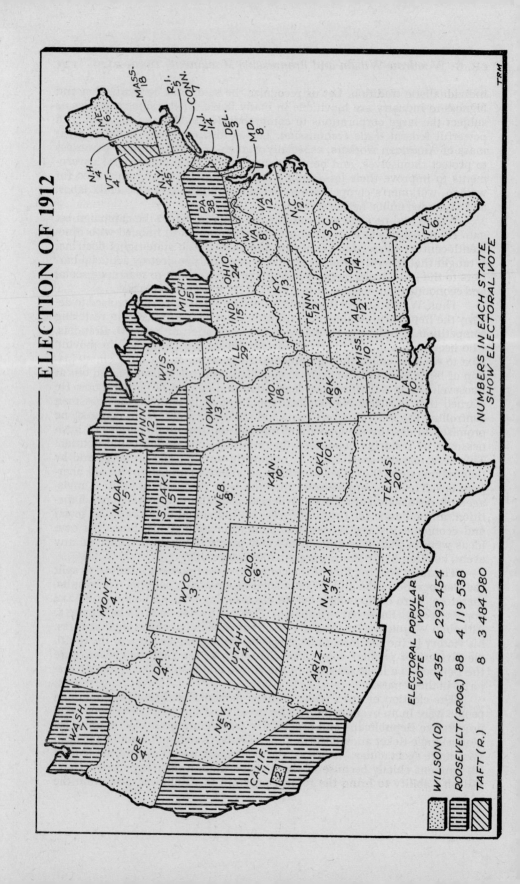

ELECTION OF 1912

NUMBERS IN EACH STATE
SHOW ELECTORAL VOTE

	ELECTORAL VOTE	POPULAR VOTE
WILSON (D)	435	6 293 454
ROOSEVELT (PROG.)	88	4 119 538
TAFT (R.)	8	3 484 980

MASS.- 18
R.I.- 5
CONN.- 7
N.J.- 14
DEL.- 3
MD.- 8
ME. 6
N.H. 4
VT. 4
N.Y. 45
PA. 38
W. VA. 8
VA. 12
N.C. 12
S.C. 9
FLA. 6
GA. 14
ALA. 12
MISS. 10
LA. 10
TENN. 12
KY. 13
OHIO 24
IND. 15
ILL. 29
MICH. 15
WIS. 13
MINN. 12
IOWA 13
MO. 18
ARK. 9
OKLA. 10
TEXAS 20
N. DAK. 5
S. DAK. 5
NEB. 8
KAN. 10
COLO. 6
N. MEX. 3
MONT. 4
WYO. 3
IDA. 4
UTAH 4
NEV. 3
ARIZ. 3
WASH. 7
ORE. 4
CAL IF. 11 2

two divergent wings would depend the future of the progressive movement in the United States.

53.   *Woodrow Wilson and the Progressive Movement*

No man in American history before 1910 had such a meteoric rise to political pre-eminence as Woodrow Wilson. Born in a Presbyterian manse in Staunton, Virginia, on December 28, 1856, he grew to boyhood in a South convulsed by Civil War and Reconstruction. After being graduated from Princeton University in 1879, Wilson studied law at the University of Virginia and tried unsuccessfully, in 1882 and 1883, to practice law in Atlanta. Disillusioned by the sharp practices of lawyers in Atlanta at that time, he entered the new Johns Hopkins University in Baltimore and won a doctor's degree in political science and history in 1886. He taught successively at Bryn Mawr College, Wesleyan University, and Princeton from 1885 to 1902. He found an outlet for his political energies in lecturing and writing, and above all in analyzing the weaknesses inherent in the structure of the national government. The basic cause of the failure of leadership in the American political system, he asserted in his most famous work, *Congressional Government*, 1885, lay in the separation of executive from legislative responsibility and leadership.

Wilson's election as president of Princeton University in 1902 gave him his first opportunity to practice the principles of leadership that had been maturing in his mind. Visualizing himself as a prime minister, he put into operation a reorganized curriculum and a new method of undergraduate instruction, the preceptorial system of discussion in small groups. As he emerged as an educational leader of national prominence, he also became increasingly articulate as a spokesman of Democratic conservatism.

Wilson probably would not have allowed his suppressed political ambitions to revive had events continued to go well for him at Princeton. He attempted in 1906 and 1907 to reorganize the social life of undergraduates by abolishing their eating clubs and substituting quadrangles, or residential colleges, in their stead. The proposal was sound intellectually and academically, but students and alumni were so bitterly opposed that the trustees felt compelled to withdraw their approval of the quadrangle plan. This first reversal was so humiliating that Princeton's prime minister nearly resigned. But the really crushing blow, the event that made Wilson willing to embark upon an uncertain political career when the opportunity arose in 1910, was his defeat in a personal controversy in 1909 and 1910 with the trustees and Dean of the Graduate School over the establishment and control of a Graduate College.

While the Graduate College controversy was at its height in the spring of 1910, George Harvey, editor of *Harper's Weekly*, persuaded the leading Democratic boss of New Jersey, James Smith, Jr., to nominate Wilson for the governorship. Wilson accepted the nomination chiefly because the situation at Princeton had become personally intolerable to him. Once in politics, however, he refused to play the role that Harvey and Smith had cut out for him. Sensing that the progressive movement in his state was at flood tide, he came out squarely behind the progressive program and, with the support of insurgent Republicans, won a startling victory in November 1910. As we have seen, he boldly seized control of the Democratic party in New Jersey, pushed a comprehensive reform program through an Assembly heretofore dominated by bosses and lobbyists, and then undertook a nation-wide campaign that carried him into leadership of the Democratic party in 1912 and the White House in 1913.

For the next four years Wilson occupied the same position with regard to the progressive movement that Theodore Roosevelt had occupied from 1905 to 1909. But changed circumstances and differences in personality made Wilson's role in the development of the movement considerably different from Roosevelt's. Unlike Roosevelt, Wilson had not helped to make the progressive movement in its early stages. In Trenton and later in Washington he was given leadership of movements ripe for fulfillment. The chief thing required of him was to act as the catalytic agent of his time—to rally and strengthen his forces, to synthesize ideas and proposals, and then to use his incomparable powers of articulation and leadership to translate these ideas into statutory realities.

Roosevelt had never really mastered the powerful and entrenched Old Guard machine in Congress. By appealing to the country he had forced Congress to act, but he never led it. In contrast, Wilson found a congressional situation in 1913 that afforded a unique opportunity for a strong executive. For one thing, there was no Democratic machine in Congress. For another, Democratic leaders, after wandering in the wilderness for twenty years, were determined to make good and to co-operate for the success of their program and party. Wilson was thus privileged to be the best and most effective kind of leader in the American system—the parliamentary leader of a co-operative congressional majority. A strong believer in party government and responsibility, Wilson prepared a legislative program, personally guided congressmen in drafting measures, and mediated among various factions when disputes inevitably arose over principles and details.

Wilson's first and most important contribution to the national progressive movement, therefore, was his strengthening and extension of the power of the presidency. By his own example he demonstrated that the President has it in his power not only to represent the majority opinion, as Roosevelt had done, but also to destroy the wall between the executive and legislative branches. His second great contribution was a more immediate one—the manner in which he used this leadership to bring the national progressive movement to legislative consummation.

Men followed Wilson because he was determined to fulfill party pledges and to act for the good of the country, and above all because he nobly articulated their own highest ideals and aspirations. Among friends and associates Wilson was usually warm and intimate. He was in most circumstances an excellent administrator who gave the widest possible rein to subordinates. But he commanded loyalty by superior intelligence and by appealing to principles and moral purposes more than to personal friendship. Wilson's leadership succeeded so long as his massive intelligence and moving eloquence survived the hazards of an increasingly demanding presidential career. Even so, his leadership was impaired by certain defects even during the heyday of his powers. The most striking of these was a tendency to value his own intuitive and moralistic judgments over conclusions deduced from an analysis of sometimes unpleasant facts. Moreover, he too often assumed that others were as high-minded as he; he was, consequently, sometimes a poor judge of men. Finally, his strong activism and urge to achieve his own solutions sometimes, although not always, prevented him from making necessary compromises.

Most historians agree that these were usually minor flaws. Wilson brought to the presidency new life and vigor informed by an almost intuitive ability to probe and understand public opinion. Perhaps better than any other president he was adept at the alchemy of transforming broad principles and traditions into statutory realities. He gave leadership in nobility of character and eloquence of language unrivaled since Lincoln, indeed, unexcelled by any president in our history. One might say, using one of his own phrases, "The light of heaven gleamed upon his sword."

54. *The New Freedom*

Wilson thought that he saw the path of progressive duty clear ahead when he took the oath of office on March 4, 1913. The Democratic party should destroy the Republican system of special privilege by revising the tariff to eliminate all features of favoritism to domestic producers, bringing national banks into effective co-operation and freeing them from Wall Street control, and working out a new code to restore competition in industry and prevent the misuse of power by large corporations. This was the heart of the New Freedom program. It was a program based squarely on the assumptions implicit in Wilson's campaign addresses of 1912, that the country could be set free by simply unleashing individual energies and strengthening the altruistic tendencies in the business community.

The first item on Wilson's reform schedule was tariff revision, for Democratic promises would be hollow so long as the Payne-Aldrich Act, that symbol of business privilege, remained in force. On the day of his inauguration, therefore, Wilson called a special session of Congress; and he went in person before the two houses on April 8. By breaking the precedent established by Jefferson, Wilson asserted his personal leadership in legislation and focused the attention of the country on Congress. Even more, he conferred frequently with Chairman Oscar W. Underwood while the House ways and means committee prepared the new tariff bill.

The measure that Underwood presented to the House on April 22, 1913, honestly fulfilled Democratic promises of tariff reform. It was not a free trade bill but rather attempted to place American industries in a genuinely competitive position with regard to European producers. All products manufactured by so-called trusts, such as iron and steel products and agricultural machinery, were placed on the free list, while most raw materials, clothing, food, shoes, and other such items were either put on the free list or given only incidental protection. The general average of the Underwood duties was about 29 per cent, as contrasted with the 37–40 per cent level of the Payne-Aldrich Act. Finally, to compensate for the anticipated loss of revenue, the ways and means committee added a provision drafted by Representative Cordell Hull of Tennessee, levying a graduated but slight tax on incomes.[1]

The Underwood bill passed the House by a thumping majority on May 8, but the battle for tariff reform had only just begun. By insisting on free sugar and free wool, Wilson had antagonized Democratic senators from states like Louisiana, Montana, and Colorado, and a change of three Democratic votes in the upper house could change a Democratic majority into a minority. It was a dangerous situation, but the President took unprecedented steps. First he applied heavy personal and political pressure on wavering Democrats. Then, on May 26, he issued a statement to the country denouncing the swarms of lobbyists who infested Washington and were hard at work to defeat tariff reform.

This bold strategy succeeded far beyond the President's expectations. In response to Wilson's indictment of the lobbyists, La Follette and other progressives in the Senate instituted a searching inquiry into lobbying and compelled senators to reveal personal property holdings that might be affected by tariff legislation. Under such penetrating publicity the opposition of Democratic senators, except for the two Louisianans, vanished, and the road was clear ahead for honest reform. In fact, by putting food and other farm products on the free list, the Senate finance committee, headed by Furnifold Simmons of North Carolina, actually reduced the Underwood rates by 4 per cent. Moreover, a threatened rebellion of progressive senators of both parties forced the finance committee to increase the levy on incomes from a maximum of 4 per cent to a maximum of 7 per cent.[2] The Senate approved the tariff bill on September 9, 1913; the House conferees accepted the Senate amendments; and Wilson signed the revised and strengthened Underwood-Simmons bill on October 3.

It was fortunate for Wilson that he emerged from this first and crucial test stronger than before, for at the moment he signed the Underwood-Simmons Act a controversy provoked by his attempt to reorganize the national banking and currency systems was brewing furiously. Practically every authority recognized the imperative need for speedy reform, lest the entire awkward banking structure collapse in another depression.[3] The trouble was that different interests and groups demanded different kinds of legislation. The banking community and conservative Republicans almost

wwwwwwwwwwwwwww

[1] The Hull provision levied a flat tax of 1 per cent on all personal and corporate incomes over $4,000 and an additional surtax of 1 per cent on incomes from $20,000 to $50,000, 2 per cent on incomes from $50,000 to $100,000, and 3 per cent on incomes over $100,000.

[2] The Senate bill, to which the House agreed, levied an income tax of 1 per cent on incomes over $4,000 and an additional surtax ranging to 6 per cent.

[3] The banking and currency systems established by the Civil War legislation were totally unfitted to the needs of a great industrial and commercial nation. For one thing, the currency was based upon the bonded indebtedness of the United States and was therefore inflexible; worse still, the national banking structure was without any effective central control or workable machinery for mobilizing banking reserves. The Panic of 1907 had prompted Congress to enact the Aldrich-Vreeland Act of 1908, which allowed banks to issue emergency currency against securities and bonds, but this measure was never meant to be a long-run solution and was devised only to meet emergencies.

unanimously supported the plan proposed by the Aldrich Commission, appointed in 1908 to study banking reform, to establish a great central bank, with branches, controlled by the dominant banking interests. The Democrats had condemned the Aldrich plan in their platform of 1912, but they were well-nigh fatally divided. The progressive faction demanded a reserve system and currency supply owned and controlled by the government. They pointed to the revelations of the Pujo committee, which investigated the so-called Money Trust in early 1913, to prove that only decisive public control could destroy the existing concentration of credit resources in Wall Street. On the other hand, conservative Democrats, still fearful of Bryan's monetary heresies, proposed a decentralized reserve system, free from Wall Street domination, but owned and controlled by private interests.

It was amid such confusing and divided counsels that Wilson tried to steer a middle course and evolve a policy that would be acceptable to all factions. He commissioned Carter Glass of Virginia, chairman of the House banking committee, to prepare a preliminary bill. As Glass was a leader of the conservative Democratic faction, he drafted a measure that would have established a system consisting of as many as twenty reserve banks, under private control and without central direction. At Wilson's insistence, Glass added a provision for a central governing board, on which bankers should have minority representation, to co-ordinate the far-flung reserve system.

The publication of the original Glass bill set off a controversy in administration circles that threatened for a time to disrupt the Democratic party. Bryan, Secretary of the Treasury William G. McAdoo, and Robert L. Owen, chairman of the Senate banking committee, led progressive Democrats in demanding a reserve and currency system owned and controlled entirely by the government. In addition, agrarian spokesmen in the House denounced the Glass bill because it made no provision for destroying the Money Trust or furnishing credit to farmers. Confronted by a seemingly impossible situation, Wilson moved serenely but decisively. Upon the advice of Louis D. Brandeis, the President decided that the bankers should be denied representation on the proposed Federal Reserve Board, and that Federal Reserve currency should be the obligation of the United States. At Bryan's urging, he allowed the agrarian faction to amend the Glass bill to provide short-term credit facilities for farmers in the new system. On the other hand, private banking interests would own and largely control the Federal Reserve banks and have a voice in an Advisory Commission that should counsel the Federal Reserve Board. Thus Wilson's mediating leadership in this first great crisis in banking reform enabled the progressive, agrarian, and conservative Democratic factions to find an acceptable compromise.

No sooner had the controversy within the administration been settled than another more violent storm burst over the country. Bankers and their spokesmen were up in arms, denouncing the revised Glass bill as harebrained, socialistic, and confiscatory. Organized banking groups and banking journals raged all during the late summer and autumn of 1913, but gradually preponderant general opinion turned in the administration's favor. The Glass bill passed the House in September by a large majority; considerably revised, it passed the Senate on December 19, and the President signed it four days later.

The Federal Reserve Act established twelve Federal Reserve Banks owned by member banks [4] and controlled by boards of directors, the majority of whom were chosen by member banks. As the central banks of their various districts, Reserve banks held a portion of member banks' reserves and performed other central banking functions. The Glass measure also created a new currency, Federal Reserve notes, issued by the Reserve banks to member banks on the basis of collateral consisting of commercial and agricultural paper and a 40 per cent gold reserve. This Federal Reserve currency was flexible, that is, it would expand or contract in volume in direct relation to the needs of the business community. Uniting and controlling in a limited fashion the entire system was a Federal Reserve Board of seven members, appointed for long terms by the president with the consent of the Senate.

It was the great merit of the Federal Reserve Act that it provided means to mobilize the major part of the banking reserves of a region, indeed of the entire country; created a new and flexible, yet absolutely sound, currency; effectively destroyed the concentration of credit resources in a few financial centers; and reinforced private control on the local level, tempered by a degree of public supervision and national co-ordination. Doctrinaire progressives like La Follette denounced the Federal Reserve Act because it did not provide for comprehensive federal control or ownership and operation of the national banking system. Yet the framers of the measure never intended to implement such far-reaching policy. In the spirit of Wilson's New Freedom they conceived a banking and currency system in which the private interest would predominate and the public interest would enjoy only a supervisory function.

55. *The Turning Point in Wilsonian Progressivism*

The Federal Reserve Act marked the high tide of the New Freedom doctrines. Wilson gave numerous evidences throughout 1913 and the early months of 1914 of his determination to adhere strictly to his limited reform program and his resolution not to surrender to the movements then on foot to commit the federal government to advanced social and economic legislation. The root of the disagreement between the President and the agrarian, labor, and social justice reformers stemmed from divergent conceptions of the proper role that the federal government should play. Like Theodore Roosevelt, advanced progressives championed measures aimed at using federal authority to benefit special, if underprivileged, classes. Thus controversy inevitably arose when Wilson invoked New Freedom concepts to thwart the demands of these powerful pressure groups.

So resolutely did the President stand in defense of the New Freedom, in fact, that for a time he obstructed or refused to encourage the fulfillment of a large part of the progressive program. We have already seen how he blocked the AF of L's campaign to obtain immunity for labor unions from application of the antitrust law to their illegal strike activities. (See above,

wwwwwwwwwwwwwwww

[4] All national banks were required to join the Federal Reserve System. State banks were free to join the system but were not compelled to do so.

pp. 66–67.) In the same manner, Wilson in the spring of 1914 prevented passage of a bill that would have established a system of long-term rural credits financed and operated by the federal government. Or, again, when the National Child Labor Committee's child labor bill passed the House in 1914, Wilson refused to fight for its approval by the Senate because he thought it unconstitutional, just as he refused to support a woman's suffrage amendment because he thought that suffrage qualifications should be determined by the states.

Three other incidents revealed the extent to which the President opposed or refused to encourage advanced progressive legislation. The first was his momentary obstruction of the movement to reduce the number of immigrants coming to American shores. Restriction, or outright exclusion, of immigration had long been an objective of the AF of L, many sociologists, and many social workers. The instrument proposed by these groups, the literacy test, was embodied in the Burnett immigration bill that passed Congress on January 2, 1915. Wilson vetoed this measure, and his veto held. Two years later, in January 1917, Congress overrode his veto of a similar bill.

The second incident was Wilson's near veto of the La Follette seamen's bill in March 1915. Initiated by Andrew Furuseth, president of the International Seamen's Union, this measure imposed rigorous safety requirements on all vessels in the American maritime trade. More important, it freed American and foreign sailors on vessels coming to American ports of their bondage to labor contracts. Wilson at first supported the seamen's bill, as it conferred no special privileges and did no more than place maritime workers on an equal footing with other workers. The State Department, however, strongly opposed the measure because it unilaterally abrogated some thirty treaties with the maritime powers. After much soul-searching, and after Senator La Follette, the measure's chief sponsor, agreed to give the State Department ample time to renegotiate the treaties, Wilson approved the seamen's bill on March 4, 1915. Obviously, it was not an administration measure.

The third incident was perhaps the most revealing. It came early in the New Freedom dispensation, when Wilson permitted his Secretary of the Treasury and Postmaster General to segregate certain Negro and white workers in their departments. This provoked such a storm of protest from Negroes and from white progressives in the North that the administration reversed what was in fact a very limited segregation policy late in 1914. The incident, nonetheless, revealed the absence in administration circles of any strong obsession with social justice, at least for Negroes.

The first important turning point or movement toward more advanced progressivism occurred in the early months of 1914 as Wilson and congressional leaders set about to prepare antitrust legislation. Advanced progressives demanded establishment of an independent trade commission armed with a kind of freewheeling authority to oversee business activities and suppress unfair trade practices. At the outset of these discussions Wilson insisted upon a solution more in accord with the New Freedom doctrine of limited intervention. His original antitrust program was embodied in two measures, the Clayton bill and the Covington interstate trade commission bill. The former enumerated and prohibited a series of unfair trade practices, outlawed interlocking directorates, and gave private parties benefit of decisions in antitrust suits originated by the government. The Covington bill created an interstate trade commission to supplant the Bureau of Corporations. The new commission would have no independent regulatory authority but, like the Bureau of Corporations, would act merely as a fact-finding agency for the executive and legislative branches.

The publication of the administration's bills provoked such an outbreak of confusing dissent that it seemed for a time that there might be no legislation at all. Because the Clayton bill failed to provide immunity from antitrust prosecution for labor unions, spokesmen of the AF of L were up in arms. Because the measure attempted to enumerate every conceivable restraint of trade, advanced progressives in both parties denounced it as futile. Because it did not attempt to destroy the oligarchical financial and industrial structure, agrarian radicals from the South and West claimed that the Clayton bill was a betrayal of Democratic pledges. Wilson was visibly shaken by these attacks, but in the confusion of voices he did not know where to turn.

When the President seemed most uncertain, his informal adviser, Louis D. Brandeis, came forward in April 1914 with an alternative that involved virtually abandoning the effort to prohibit unfair trade practices by the statutory method. Instead Brandeis proposed outlawing unfair trade practices in general terms and then establishing a federal trade commission endowed with ample authority to suppress restraints of trade whenever they occurred. Brandeis's solution had been embodied in a trade commission bill, introduced earlier by Representative Raymond B. Stevens of New Hampshire.

Although Brandeis's proposal envisaged at least something like the kind of regulation of business that Roosevelt had advocated and Wilson had at least implicitly condemned in 1912, it seemed to be the only practical answer to an otherwise insoluble problem. Thus Wilson at once made the Stevens bill the cornerstone of his new antitrust policy, and administration leaders in Congress sidetracked the Covington bill and pressed the Stevens measure instead. Wilson also lost all interest in the Clayton bill, except to maintain his inflexible opposition to granting labor unions the privilege of using illegal strike weapons. In consequence, the Clayton bill was cut adrift in the Senate, where most of its strong provisions were seriously weakened. The measure that Wilson signed on October 15, 1914, was, Senator James A. Reed of Missouri complained, "a sort of legislative apology to the trusts, delivered hat in hand, and accompanied by assurances that no discourtesy is intended." [5]

Meanwhile, the President had bent all his energies toward obtaining congressional approval of the Stevens trade commission bill. After a hard battle he won a decisive victory, for the Federal Trade Commission Act that

wwwwwwwwwwwwwww

[5] The Clayton Act forbade contracts requiring purchasers to buy from only one producer or seller, forbade corporations to purchase the stock of other corporations when the result would be substantially to lessen competition, outlawed interlocking directorates, when their existence operated substantially to lessen competition, and made court decisions in antitrust suits initiated by the government prima facie evidence in private damage suits.

he approved on September 26 committed the federal government to a policy of vigorous regulation of all business activities. In sweeping terms it outlawed but did not attempt to define unfair trade practices. Moreover, it established a Federal Trade Commission to supersede the Bureau of Corporations, armed with authority to move swiftly and directly against corporations accused of suppressing competition—first by issuing cease and desist orders and then, if that recourse failed, by bringing the accused corporations to trial.

Wilson's acceptance of what might very roughly be called a Rooseveltian legislative solution was matched to a considerable degree on the level of direct antitrust activity. Rejecting agrarian radical demands for a relentless campaign against bigness, per se, Wilson and his Attorneys General instead continued the Roosevelt-Taft policy of moving only against combinations that seemed obviously to have been in restraint of trade. For example, they continued Taft's case against United States Steel, in spite of that corporation's offer to settle out of court. What was new in the antitrust story under Wilson was the eagerness of officials of several important combinations to accept government-dictated reorganizations in order to avoid prosecution. The American Telephone & Telegraph Company, the New Haven Railroad, and the Southern Pacific Railroad, among others, accepted consent decrees proposed by the Justice Department in 1913 and 1914. The Federal Trade Commission never seemed able to fulfill the hopes of its founders during the balance of the Wilson era. It was hobbled first by incompetence and internal dissension. It had little to do during the period of American belligerence, 1917–18, as antitrust prosecutions were then generally suspended. It finally came to life in 1919–20 in a victorious campaign to destroy the old Beef Trust.

Wilson's acceptance of the Federal Trade Commission bill during the congressional discussions of 1914 was also an important turning point in the history of the American progressive movement. It was the first important sign that the President might be willing to abandon his doctrinaire New Freedom concepts and surrender to the rising progressive demands for bold social and economic legislation in other fields. Any such surrender, however, would have to come in the future, for adoption of the Clayton and Federal Trade Commission Acts in the autumn of 1914 seemed to signal the completion of the President's reform program. Wilson asserted in a public letter to Secretary of the Treasury McAdoo on November 17 that the legislation of the past eighteen months had destroyed the Republican system of special privilege and ended the antagonism between business and the public. The future, he added, would be a time in which businessmen would adapt themselves to changed conditions and the nation would enter a new era of "cooperation, of new understanding, of common purpose." In brief, the reconstructive phase of the progressive movement was over; reform would now give way to readjustment.

56. *The Triumph of the New Nationalism*

As it turned out, Wilson's forecast of future political developments was somewhat naive. By the time that the President wrote his letter to McAdoo a profound upheaval in American politics—the virtual disappearance of the Progressive party—had occurred during the congressional elections of November 3, 1914. The outbreak of war in Europe a few months before had diverted American attention from the campaign and evoked a general disposition to stand by the President. Even so, the Democratic majority in the House of Representatives was reduced from seventy-three to twenty-five, and Republicans swept back into power in key states like New York, Pennsylvania, Illinois, and New Jersey. So powerful was the tide that it seemed that a general Republican victory in 1916 was probable.

The months passed and the nation was convulsed by alarms of war with Germany and a great debate over preparedness. It was obvious by January 1916 that Theodore Roosevelt would abandon his third party and join with his erstwhile enemies to drive the Democrats from power. Democratic defeat in the impending presidential campaign was virtually inevitable if he succeeded in leading most Progressives back into the Republican camp. The urgent necessity facing Wilson and his party at the beginning of 1916, therefore, was to find some means of luring at least a large minority of the former Progressives into the Democratic ranks. This strategy offered the only possible hope of converting a normal Democratic minority into a majority in November 1916. To execute the strategy, however, Wilson and the Democratic party had to cast off the shackles of state rights and *laissez-faire* doctrines and convince still suspicious Progressives that they offered the best hope of positive economic and social reform.

Although adopting advanced progressive concepts and legislation required abandoning some of the ideological foundations upon which the New Freedom rested, Wilson did not shrink from the necessity. Moreover, it is probably accurate to say that changed convictions, growing out of his own experience during the past two years, were as much responsible for Wilson's change of course as was political expediency. Beginning in January 1916, he embarked upon a new course of action; and because his new departure seemed to offer the only hope of staying in power, most Democrats in Congress followed him willingly.

The first sign of this metamorphosis was Wilson's appointment of Louis D. Brandeis to the Supreme Court on January 28, 1916. Progressives of both parties were delighted, for Brandeis was one of the leading exponents of social and economic reform in the country. The President called the sponsors of the much controverted rural credits bill to the White House shortly afterward and told them that he would support their measure. He was as good as his word, and the Federal Farm Loan Act passed Congress in May.[6] A few months later, after the presidential campaign had begun, spokesmen of the social justice forces informed Wilson that they regarded the pending child labor and federal workmen's compensation bills as the acid tests of his progressivism. Wilson had said not a word to this point in advocacy of the measures. Now he immediately applied heavy pressure on

⁶ This measure established twelve Federal Farm Loan Banks capitalized at $750,000 each, which should extend long-term credit to farmers on a basis of land and improvements. It also created a Federal Farm Loan Board to supervise the new system.

Democratic leaders in the Senate and obtained passage of the crucial measures in August.[7]

The extent of Wilson's commitment to advanced progressivism can best be understood when we perceive the long-run significance of the Child Labor Act of 1916. By this measure, Congress for the first time used its power over interstate commerce in an important way to control conditions under which employers might operate their industries. Did this signify the beginning of a new and enlarged federal regulation under the commerce clause, as the spokesman of the NAM declared, "of any commodity produced in whole or in part by the labor of men or women who work more than eight hours, receive less than a minimum wage, or have not certain educational qualifications"? Progressives hoped and conservatives feared that it did. In any event, it seemed that a constitutional way had been found to extend federal control over all phases of the manufacturing process.

Nor did the foregoing measures alone represent the full extent of Wilson's espousal of the program embodied in the Progressive platform of 1912. Echoing a proposal Roosevelt had made in 1912, Wilson in 1916 sponsored and obtained passage of a bill to establish an independent tariff commission, allegedly to remove the tariff issue from politics. Moreover, in language that Roosevelt might have used, Wilson publicly reversed historic Democratic policy and approved the principle of rational protection for certain infant industries. He supported and won passage of a series of measures launching the federal government upon a new program of aid to the states for education and highway construction.[8] Finally, he sponsored but did not obtain adoption until January 1918 of the Webb-Pomerene bill to permit American manufacturers to combine for the purpose of carrying on export trade.

Thus it was that the exigencies of a changing political situation and changed political convictions compelled a President and party who had taken office in 1913 for the purpose of effectuating a limited reform program to sponsor and enact the most far-reaching and significant economic and social legislation in American history before 1933. Looking back in 1916 upon the development of the progressive movement since 1912, observers might well have been puzzled by the revolution that had occurred. On the one hand, Wilson and his party had tacitly abandoned the New

---

[7] Drafted by the American Association for Labor Legislation, the Kern-McGillicuddy Compensation Act established a model workmen's compensation system for federal employees. The Keating-Owen child labor bill, sponsored by the National Child Labor Committee, which became the Child Labor Act of 1916, forbade the shipment in interstate commerce of goods manufactured in whole or in part by children under fourteen, of products of mines and quarries involving the labor of children under sixteen, and of any products manufactured by children under sixteen employed more than eight hours a day.

[8] These were the Bankhead Good Roads Act of 1916, which provided federal funds to match state appropriations for interstate highways, and the Smith-Hughes Act of 1917, providing federal funds on a matching basis for vocational education in public high schools. An earlier measure, the Smith-Lever Act of 1914, provided federal money on a matching basis for agricultural extension work.

Freedom, and the President could justly claim that Democrats were also Progressives and boast that his party had enacted practically all the Progressive platform of 1912. On the other hand, Theodore Roosevelt, the great expounder of the New Nationalism in 1912, had by 1916 abandoned his platform to the Democrats and was striving mightily to defeat the party that had carried out his proposals.

CHAPTER

───

7

The Growth
of the United States
as a World Power

1898–1916

Between the end of the Napoleonic Wars in 1815 and the outbreak of the Spanish-American War in 1898 the American people enjoyed such freedom from foreign vexations as they had never known before 1815 and would not experience in the twentieth century. Not only was the United States not normally active in world politics before 1898; the American people did not want to sit in the councils of the mighty, nor engage in the scramble for colonies and concessions, nor play the game of power politics. They desired only to be let alone. They were determined to defend the Monroe Doctrine, that cornerstone of their foreign policy, to be sure. But defense of the Western Hemisphere was defense of America's splendid isolation.

Yet a people is not isolated merely by wishing to be. In fact, forces were at work during the high tide of American insularity, 1865–98, to make continued isolation soon impossible. One of them was the emergence of the United States during this period as the dominant industrial power in the world. American financiers and manufacturers were beginning to export capital and goods and to acquire markets and interests abroad that their government could not ignore. Moreover, because of their strategic economic position, the American people would find it difficult to avoid involvement in a future European war. Thus, although few Americans realized the fact in 1900, the United States had a vital stake in the peace of Europe. Secondly, swift technological advances during the half-century before the First World War were drawing the world closely together and diminishing the strategic value of America's oceanic defensive barriers. Finally, the rise of Germany as the dominant military power in Europe and Japan as an aspiring power in Asia during the last quarter of the nineteenth century upset the old balance of power upon which American security had in some measure depended.

While these great forces would in time inevitably have caused the American people to burst the bonds of provincialism, the emergence of the United States as a colonial power in 1898 was largely the result of historical accident. The Democrats who framed the Wilson-Gorman Tariff Act of 1894 had no intention of setting off a chain reaction that would culminate in war and overseas expansion. Yet by nullifying the reciprocity treaty of 1891 with Spain and placing high duties on Cuban sugar, that tariff law ruined Cuban prosperity and helped set off a revolt against Spanish rule in 1895. As the Spaniards employed brutal measures to suppress a brutally executed revolution, anti-Spanish sentiment in the United States was inflamed by such yellow newspapers as the New York *World* and New York *Journal.* President Cleveland stubbornly resisted the mounting demands for war; his successor, William McKinley, could not. After the American battleship *Maine* was mysteriously blown up in Havana harbor on February 15, 1898, the popular demand for war became irresistible. McKinley capitulated and asked Congress for a war declaration on April 11, two days after the Spanish government had surrendered to the American demand for an immediate armistice in Cuba.

57. *The Acquisition and Administration of the American Colonial Empire, 1898–1916*

The American people entered blithely upon the War with Spain only for the purpose of freeing Cuba from Spanish tyranny. Indeed, by the so-called Teller amendment to the war resolution, Congress solemnly pledged its word that the United States would not annex Cuba. Even so, a few thoughtful leaders of the war movement like Theodore Roosevelt and Henry Cabot Lodge of Massachusetts welcomed the war for the opportunity that it offered to acquire bases in the Caribbean and the Pacific. Looking toward the day when the United States would construct an isthmian canal and need naval bases to guard its approaches, they urged annexation of Puerto Rico, Spain's other Caribbean possession, and retention of naval bases in Cuba. As for the Pacific, they urged and won annexation of Hawaii a few months after the War with Spain began. As Assistant Secretary of the Navy, Roosevelt, on February 25, 1898, had instructed Commodore George Dewey, commanding the Asiatic Squadron then at Hong Kong, to prepare to attack the Spanish fleet in Manila Bay in the event that war occurred. But neither Roosevelt nor any other responsible spokesman of the administration contemplated taking the Philippine Islands.

Yet the American commissioners at the peace conference that met in Paris from October 1 through December 10, 1898, demanded and won not only Cuba's freedom and the transfer of Puerto Rico to the United States, but also the cession of Guam and the entire Philippine archipelago. The United States by this act extended its frontiers far out into the Pacific and assumed the burden of pacifying the Philippines and then defending them against future aggression.

This decision to launch the United States as a major Asiatic power was made by McKinley and his Cabinet apparently without seriously considering whether the choice was strategically sound or in accordance with the long-run national interest. Other forces and events dictated the decision. Dewey sailed into Manila harbor on May 1, 1898, and destroyed the decrepit Spanish fleet anchored there. Since a native revolt against the Spaniards was also in progress in the Philippines, it was apparent that Spanish sovereignty in the islands was doomed in any event. The German government dispatched a squadron larger than Dewey's to Manila to demonstrate German hopes of annexation. The British and Japanese governments were also concerned over the islands' fate. At the same time, Dewey's victory set off a tremendous movement in the United States for annexation. Jingoists declared that the flag should not be hauled down; church leaders expounded America's moral duty to the "little brown brothers," the Filipinos. Most important, businessmen, who had viewed the war unenthusiastically at the outset, now talked of converting Manila into a great entrepôt for the American Far Eastern trade.

As a result, McKinley instructed his peace commissioners to demand the cession at least of Luzon, the largest of the Philippine islands. But it soon became evident that the United States could not take Luzon and allow some other power to occupy the adjacent islands. Thus, on October 28 the President instructed the commissioners to demand the cession of the entire archipelago. As a consolation prize, Spain was given $20,000,000.

The immediate issue of imperialism was settled for a time after the ratification of the Treaty of Paris by the Senate in 1899 and McKinley's second victory over Bryan in 1900. The United States would continue to hold and administer the Philippines, at least until the Filipinos were ready for self-government. But the American people soon discovered that it is far easier to acquire a colonial empire than to govern it. On the outbreak of the War with Spain, Commodore Dewey and the American Consul at Singapore had helped a Philippine leader, Emilio Aguinaldo, return to Luzon to lead a revolt against the Spanish authority. Aguinaldo succeeded so well that he and his forces were besieging Manila when American troops occupied the city.

The Filipinos wanted independence, not merely a transfer of sovereignty to a new foreign master. When it became obvious that the United States intended to impose its own authority, Aguinaldo and his rebel forces raised anew the standards of revolt on February 4, 1899. So stubbornly did the Filipinos fight that McKinley eventually had to send some 70,000 troops to the islands; and before "pacification" was completed

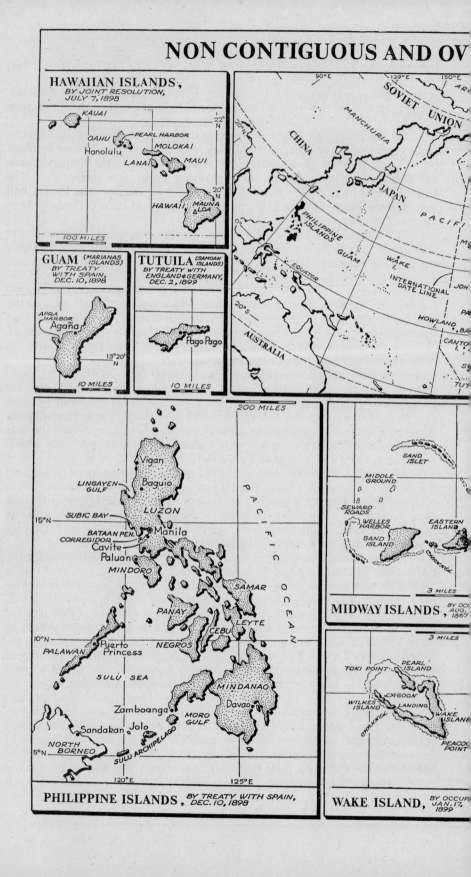

NON CONTIGUOUS AND OV

HAWAIIAN ISLANDS,
BY JOINT RESOLUTION, JULY 7, 1898

KAUAI
OAHU — PEARL HARBOR
Honolulu
MOLOKAI
LANAI
MAUI
22° N
20° N
HAWAII
MAUNA △ LOA

100 MILES

GUAM (MARIANAS ISLANDS)
BY TREATY WITH SPAIN, DEC. 10, 1898

APRA HARBOR
Agaña
13°20' N

10 MILES

TUTUILA (SAMOAN ISLANDS)
BY TREATY WITH ENGLAND & GERMANY, DEC. 2, 1899

Pago Pago

10 MILES

90°E 120°E 150°E
SOVIET UNION
CHINA
MANCHURIA
JAPAN
PHILIPPINE ISLANDS
GUAM
PACIFIC
WAKE
INTERNATIONAL DATE LINE
JOH
EQUATOR
HOWLAND
AUSTRALIA
20°S
CANTO
TUT

PHILIPPINE ISLANDS, *BY TREATY WITH SPAIN, DEC. 10, 1898*

200 MILES

Vigan
LINGAYEN GULF
Baguio
LUZON
SUBIC BAY
BATAAN PEN.
CORREGIDOR
Cavite
Manila
Paluan
MINDORO
SAMAR
PANAY
LEYTE
CEBU
NEGROS
PALAWAN
Puerto Princess
SULU SEA
MINDANAO
Davao
Zamboanga
MORO GULF
Sandakan
Jolo
NORTH BORNEO
SULU ARCHIPELAGO
PACIFIC OCEAN
15°N
10°N
5°N
120°E 125°E

MIDWAY ISLANDS, *BY OCC AUG, 1867*

SAND ISLET
MIDDLE GROUND
SEWARD ROADS
WELLES HARBOR
EASTERN ISLAND
SAND ISLAND

3 MILES

WAKE ISLAND, *BY OCCUP JAN. 17, 1899*

3 MILES

TOKI POINT
PEARL ISLAND
WILKES ISLAND
LAGOON
LANDING
WAKE ISLAND
PEACOCK POINT

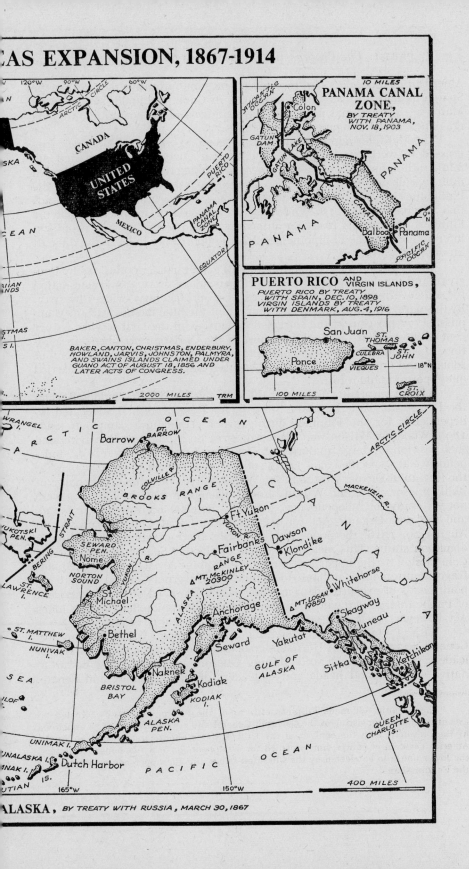

...AS EXPANSION, 1867-1914

120°W   90°W   60°W
ARCTIC CIRCLE

CANADA

UNITED STATES

...SKA

...CEAN

...RIAN ...NDS

...STMAS ...S I.

MEXICO

PUERTO RICO

PANAMA CANAL ZONE

EQUATOR

BAKER, CANTON, CHRISTMAS, ENDERBURY, HOWLAND, JARVIS, JOHNSTON, PALMYRA, AND SWAINS ISLANDS CLAIMED UNDER GUANO ACT OF AUGUST 18, 1856 AND LATER ACTS OF CONGRESS.

2000 MILES   TRM

10 MILES

PANAMA CANAL ZONE,
BY TREATY WITH PANAMA, NOV. 18, 1903

ATLANTIC OCEAN

Colon

GATUN DAM

GATUN LAKE

CANAL

PANAMA

PANAMA

Balboa Panama

9°N

PACIFIC OCEAN

PUERTO RICO AND VIRGIN ISLANDS,
PUERTO RICO BY TREATY WITH SPAIN, DEC. 10, 1898
VIRGIN ISLANDS BY TREATY WITH DENMARK, AUG. 4, 1916

San Juan

ST. THOMAS

CULEBRA

ST. JOHN

Ponce

VIEQUES

18°N

ST. CROIX

100 MILES

WRANGEL

ARCTIC   OCEAN

Barrow   PT. BARROW

ARCTIC CIRCLE

...A

...YUKOTSKI PEN.

COLVILLE R.

BROOKS   RANGE

MACKENZIE R.

Ft. Yukon

YUKON R.

Dawson

BERING STRAIT

SEWARD PEN.

Nome

Fairbanks

Klondike

ST. LAWRENCE

NORTON SOUND

YUKON R.

ALASKA RANGE

MT. McKINLEY 20300

Whitehorse

St. Michael

MT. LOGAN 19850

ST. MATTHEW I.

Bethel

Anchorage

Skagway

NUNIVAK I.

Seward

Yakutat

Juneau

...ILOF

Naknek

Kodiak

GULF OF ALASKA

Sitka

Ketchikan

...SEA

BRISTOL BAY

KODIAK I.

QUEEN CHARLOTTE IS.

ALASKA PEN.

UNIMAK I.

...NALASKA I.

...NAK I.

Dutch Harbor

PACIFIC   OCEAN

400 MILES

...UTIAN

165°W   150°W

ALASKA, BY TREATY WITH RUSSIA, MARCH 30, 1867

American commanders had resorted to the same primitive tactics that the Spaniards had unsuccessfully employed in Cuba. Aguinaldo's capture on March 23, 1901, signaled the end of resistance and the beginning of a long era of peaceful development of the islands.

The McKinley administration began even before the rebellion was suppressed to work out plans for a permanent government. A civilian administration, headed by William Howard Taft as civil governor, supplanted military rule on July 4, 1901. Then Congress passed an Organic Act for the Philippines on July 2, 1902, and established a government for the islands that survived until 1916. While the Act reflected the conviction that the Filipinos were not yet ready for autonomy, it also bore witness to American intention to give the Philippine peoples an opportunity to learn the difficult art of self-government.[1]

The results of superb administration, generous appropriations by Congress, and the determination of American leaders to lay a solid foundation for self-government in the Philippines were spectacularly evident by 1913. By this date, Filipinos constituted four out of the nine members of the Commission, 71 per cent of the classified employees in the civil service, 92 per cent of the teachers, and all governors of the Christian provinces. In addition, the Philippine government had established a splendid system of schools and other public services, dispensed impartial justice, and carried out important land reforms.

It is not surprising, therefore, that Roosevelt and Taft shuddered when the Democrats came to power in 1913, for Democrats had advocated independence for the Filipinos during every presidential campaign since 1899. Woodrow Wilson was elected in 1912 on a platform that reiterated this position. A large majority of Democrats still wanted to give independence at a specified date. On the other hand, Wilson's Secretary of War, the Bureau of Insular Affairs in the War Department, which had charge of Philippine matters, and Wilson himself all agreed that the Filipinos were not yet ready for independence. Actually, the cleavage was not profound, and the new Organic Act for the Philippines that Congress passed on August 29, 1916, the Jones Act, fell little short of giving the Filipinos dominion status. This measure created an elective Senate to supplant the Commission as the upper house of the Philippine legislature, lowered suffrage requirements, and provided that the Governor-General should appoint heads of executive departments, except the head of the Department of Public Instruction, with the consent of the Philippine Senate. The Jones Act, however, reserved ultimate sovereignty to the United States.

With a view toward hastening independence, Wilson's Governor-General, Francis Burton Harrison, co-operated with the native Nationalist leaders, Sergio Osmeña and Manuel Quezon, in transferring power to native departmental heads and to leaders of the Assembly and Senate.

wwwwwwwwwwwwwww

[1] The Organic Act made Filipinos citizens of the Philippine Islands; created an executive branch consisting of the Governor-General and a Commission, to be appointed by the President with the consent of the United States Senate; established an Anglo-American system of courts; and provided for establishment of a two-house legislature, the lower house to be elected by the Christian tribes and the upper house to consist of the Commission.

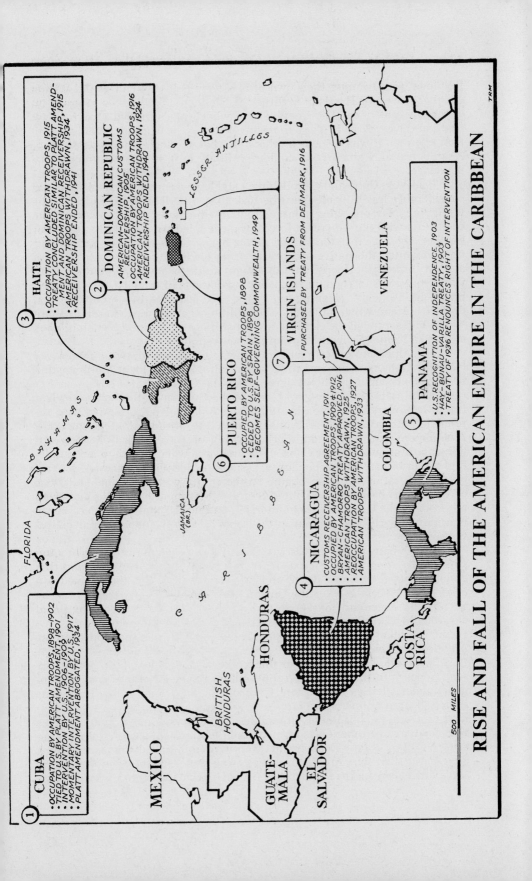

RISE AND FALL OF THE AMERICAN EMPIRE IN THE CARIBBEAN

FLORIDA

MEXICO

GUATE-MALA

EL SALVADOR

BRITISH HONDURAS

HONDURAS

BAHAMAS

JAMAICA (BR.)

CARIBBEAN

LESSER ANTILLES

COSTA RICA

COLOMBIA

VENEZUELA

500 MILES

TRM

③ **CUBA**
- OCCUPATION BY AMERICAN TROOPS, 1898–1902
- TIED TO U.S. BY PLATT AMENDMENT, 1901
- INTERVENTION BY U.S., 1906–1909
- MOMENTARY INTERVENTION BY U.S., 1917
- PLATT AMENDMENT ABROGATED, 1934

③ **HAITI**
- OCCUPATION BY AMERICAN TROOPS, 1915
- TREATY CONCLUDED SIMILAR TO PLATT AMENDMENT AND DOMINICAN RECEIVERSHIP, 1915
- AMERICAN TROOPS WITHDRAWN, 1934
- RECEIVERSHIP ENDED, 1941

② **DOMINICAN REPUBLIC**
- AMERICAN–DOMINICAN CUSTOMS RECEIVERSHIP, 1905
- OCCUPATION BY AMERICAN TROOPS, 1916
- AMERICAN TROOPS WITHDRAWN, 1924
- RECEIVERSHIP ENDED, 1940

⑥ **PUERTO RICO**
- OCCUPIED BY AMERICAN TROOPS, 1898
- CEDED TO U.S. BY SPAIN, 1898
- BECOMES SELF-GOVERNING COMMONWEALTH, 1949

⑦ **VIRGIN ISLANDS**
- PURCHASED BY TREATY FROM DENMARK, 1916

④ **NICARAGUA**
- CUSTOMS RECEIVERSHIP AGREEMENT, 1911
- OCCUPIED BY AMERICAN TROOPS, 1909 # 1912
- BRYAN–CHAMORRO TREATY APPROVED, 1916
- AMERICAN TROOPS WITHDRAWN, 1925
- REOCCUPATION BY AMERICAN TROOPS, 1927
- AMERICAN TROOPS WITHDRAWN, 1933

⑤ **PANAMA**
- U.S. RECOGNITION OF INDEPENDENCE, 1903
- HAY–BUNAU–VARILLA TREATY, 1903
- TREATY OF 1936 RENOUNCES RIGHT OF INTERVENTION

Filipinos were running their own affairs so well by the end of the Wilson era that Governor Harrison and the President urged Congress to grant independence at once. The Republicans, who now controlled Congress, refused and attempted in 1921 to restore a larger measure of American control. Even so, it was evident by this date that the logic and application of American policy since 1901 could culminate only in one solution—independence.

Pacifying Cuba and establishing a stable government in the island was considerably less difficult than the task that Americans confronted in the Philippines. For one thing, a large group of educated Cubans stood ready to co-operate with the American forces who occupied the country in 1898. For another, the fact that the United States had given a pledge of no annexation prevented the native aristocracy from leading the masses in a revolt against American troops. An American military government did heroic work from 1898 to 1902, in repairing the damage of the civil war, building roads and schools, cleaning up cities, and establishing order in rural districts. Meanwhile, in 1900, the military governor, General Leonard Wood, had arranged the election of a constituent convention, which in 1902 adopted a frame of government for the new republic.

The American government was now ready to withdraw its forces and leave the Cubans to manage their own affairs. But President McKinley and Secretary of War Elihu Root agreed that the United States bore a special responsibility to itself, the world, and to the Cubans themselves for Cuba's future behavior. Therefore, the administration resolved to draw the Cuban republic into a special relationship with the United States. The Platt Amendment to the army appropriations bill of 1901 spelled out this relationship. It stipulated that Cuba should make no treaties with other powers that might impair its independence, assume no debts it could not pay, carry on the sanitation program begun by the military government, and lease certain naval bases to the United States. Most important was a provision authorizing the United States to intervene in Cuba, if that were necessary to maintain orderly government and discharge Cuba's international obligations.

The Cubans under duress wrote the Platt Amendment into their Constitution in 1902 and signed a treaty with the United States in 1903 that embodied its provisions. Peace and prosperity reigned in the island for a brief time, especially after the Cuban-American reciprocity treaty of 1903 opened the American market to Cuban sugar. After the second national elections in December 1905, however, widespread rioting against the government broke out, and President Tomás Estrada Palma appealed for American intervention.

Roosevelt was reluctant to undertake the thankless task. He finally sent troops into the island in 1906 and established a provisional government under Charles E. Magoon, Governor of the Canal Zone. There was some talk in administration circles at this time of making Cuba a permanent protectorate, but Roosevelt repudiated it angrily. New Cuban elections were held; a government was formed; and the Americans withdrew in January 1909. The State Department afterward intervened frequently on a diplomatic level, but American troops were sent into the republic to preserve order only in 1911 and 1917. On each occasion their stay was brief.

Governing America's other major island dependencies [2] proved a relatively simple task. Hawaii, annexed by joint resolution of Congress on July 7, 1898, was made an incorporated territory on April 30, 1900, and thereafter enjoyed all territorial rights of self-government. Puerto Rico, occupied by the American army in July 1898, was given civil government by the Foraker Act in 1900 and a large measure of self-government by the Jones Act of 1917, which also granted American citizenship to inhabitants of Puerto Rico.

The chief diplomatic objective of the American government after 1900 became, as we shall see more fully in a later section, the building of an isthmian canal and establishment of its own naval supremacy in the Caribbean. As the British withdrew the larger units of their West Indian squadron in 1904–5, the United States was in fact the dominant power in the Caribbean after this date. But there was always the danger, often more illusory than real, that Germany would attempt to establish naval bases in the area, possibly by acquiring the Danish West Indies or by obtaining a base in the splendid harbor at Môle St. Nicholas in Haiti. Secretary of State Bryan tried to purchase a site for a naval base at Môle St. Nicholas in 1913. The Haitians refused to sell, but they agreed not to alienate the site to any other power. Secretary of State John Hay negotiated a treaty with Denmark in 1902 for purchase of the Danish West Indies, or Virgin Islands; but the Danish Parliament, acting, Americans suspected, under pressure from Germany, refused to ratify the treaty. When the Danish government in 1916 offered to sell the islands at the inflated price of $25,000,000, the American government concluded the deal without haggling. The islands were transferred to American sovereignty on March 31, 1917, and were governed by the Navy Department until 1931.

58. *The Panama Incident and Two Hemispheric Disputes*

The dramatic voyage of the battleship *Oregon* from Puget Sound around Cape Horn to Cuban waters in 1898 underscored the absolute strategic necessity of a canal linking the Atlantic and Pacific oceans, while the development of the West Coast and anticipation of a great American trade with the Far East highlighted the economic need. A diplomatic obstacle, however, stood athwart the achievement of what was by the end of 1898 a great national objective. That obstacle was the Clayton-Bulwer Treaty of 1850, in which the United States and Great Britain had each agreed not to construct a canal without the other's participation. The British government was now eager to win American friendship and gave up its right to participate in building the canal in the first Hay-Pauncefote Treaty, negotiated at Washington in 1900. This Treaty, however, forbade the United

[2] It should be noted that the United States by 1900 had also acquired a string of coaling stations in the Pacific beyond Hawaii: Midway Island, acquired in 1867; the Samoan Islands, occupied jointly with Germany and Great Britain from 1889 to 1899 and divided between Germany and the United States in the latter year; Guam, ceded by Spain in the Treaty of Paris of 1898; and Wake, acquired formally in 1899. All these islands were governed by naval officers under orders from the Navy Department.

States to fortify the canal. The Senate refused to ratify the Treaty without amendments providing for fortification. Indeed, it was obvious that the Americans meant to build and fortify their canal, even if they had to denounce the Clayton-Bulwer Treaty. The British, therefore, went the whole way, and the second Hay-Pauncefote Treaty, concluded on November 18, 1901, acknowledged the right of the United States exclusively to build and fortify the canal.

Discussion in Washington now centered on the proper route. President Roosevelt and a large majority of Congress favored the Nicaraguan route, and the Isthmian Canal Commission, which McKinley had appointed, officially concurred in November 1901. The House of Representatives approved the Commission's recommendation on January 9, 1902. In the meantime, however, Philippe Bunau-Varilla and William Nelson Cromwell, agents of the French New Panama Canal Company, had been working assiduously to sell their company's rights to the route across the Isthmus of Panama.[3] Faced with the possibility of losing everything, the directors of the French company hastily cut their price from $109,000,000 to $40,-000,000. Their bargain offer, the advantages of the Panamanian route, which engineers had already pointed out, and the providential eruption of a volcano in Nicaragua caused Roosevelt, the Commission, and Congress to change their minds. The Spooner Act, approved by Roosevelt in June 1902, stipulated that the Panamanian route should be used, provided that a satisfactory treaty could be concluded with Colombia, which owned the Isthmus, within a reasonable time. Otherwise, the Act declared, the Nicaraguan route should be chosen.

The State Department during the following months applied extraordinary pressure on the Colombian government to sign a treaty authorizing the construction of a Panamanian canal. The Colombian Minister left for home in disgust. Secretary Hay then concluded a treaty with the Colombian Chargé, Tomás Herrán, on January 22, 1903. It authorized the United States to build a canal across the Isthmus of Panama in return for payment of $10,000,000 and an annual rental of $250,000. Colombia agreed, moreover, not to conduct independent negotiations with the New Panama Canal Company—in other words, not to demand a share of the $40,000,-000.

The American Senate approved the Hay-Herrán Treaty on March 17, 1903. The Colombian government, however, balked. Public opinion in Colombia opposed the Treaty because it impaired the nation's sovereignty in the proposed Canal Zone, but Colombia's leaders had an additional reason for refusing to ratify the treaty. The French company's concession would expire in 1904; all its rights and property would then revert to Colombia. By delaying action for only one year, the Colombian govern-

[3] The builder of the Suez Canal, Ferdinand de Lesseps, organized a French company in 1879 for the construction of a Panamanian Canal. Over $250,000,000 had been wasted by 1889 in a vain attempt to conquer tropical diseases and the jungle, and the French company went into bankruptcy. The New Panama Canal Company was organized in 1894 to take over the assets of the bankrupt corporation. Bunau-Varilla, formerly chief engineer of the old company, was a large stockholder in the new concern. Cromwell was a prominent New York attorney with large influence in Republican circles.

ment would be in position to demand the $40,000,000 that would otherwise be paid to the French company.

The fact that the Colombian government was acting well within its rights did not seem significant to President Roosevelt. It was, he said, as if "a road agent had tried to hold up a man," and Colombians were "entitled to precisely the amount of sympathy we extend to other inefficient bandits." He made plans, therefore, to seize the Isthmus, and to justify such action by the Treaty of 1846 between the United States and New Granada (Colombia), under which the former guaranteed the neutrality and free transit of the Isthmus.

Meanwhile, Bunau-Varilla was setting plans on foot that would obviate the need for violent American action. Working through his agents in Panama, this astute Frenchman organized a Panamanian "revolution" against Colombia. The State Department took no part in these intrigues, but Bunau-Varilla informed the President and Secretary of State of the plot, and he could deduce from what they said that Colombia would not be allowed to suppress a revolution. Roosevelt, moreover, dispatched the U.S.S. *Nashville* to Colón, on the Atlantic side of the Isthmus. The *Nashville* arrived at Colón on November 2, 1903; on the following day the army of patriots rebelled at Panama City, on the Pacific side. Thereupon the commander of the *Nashville* landed troops at Colón and forbade Colombian troops in the city to cross the Isthmus and suppress the rebellion. In fact, the Colombian commander agreed to take his troops back to Colombia in return for a generous gift from Bunau-Varilla's agent.

At 11:35 in the morning of November 6 the American Consul at Panama City informed the State Department that the revolution had succeeded. At 12:51 p.m. Secretary Hay instructed the Consul to extend *de facto* recognition to the new government of Panama. Fearing that the Panamanians would now demand a share of the $40,000,000, Bunau-Varilla persuaded Roosevelt to receive him as the Minister from Panama. He signed a treaty with Secretary Hay on November 18 that conveyed to the United States, in perpetuity, a zone ten miles wide across the Isthmus. In return the United States agreed to pay $10,000,000 in cash and an annual rental of $250,000. The leaders of the new republic had no choice but to ratify this treaty.

The American government took possession of the Canal Zone on May 4, 1904, and set about preparing to excavate the great ditch. Before work could proceed, Colonel William C. Gorgas, one of the conquerors of yellow fever, had to clean up the region and subdue the fever-carrying mosquitoes. Congress approved a plan for a lock canal in 1906; Roosevelt gave responsibility to the Army Engineers in the following year. Operations proceeded smoothly under the direction of Colonel George W. Goethals. The first ship passed through the Canal on January 7, 1914. Seven months later, on August 15, 1914, the Canal was opened to the commerce of the world. The cost of the project to the United States had been approximately $375,000,000.

Many thoughtful Americans regretted the means that Roosevelt had employed to accomplish the objective even while they agreed that construction of the Panama Canal was a great boon to mankind. Criticism of Roosevelt's Big Stick diplomacy in Panama was bitter in 1903 and 1904, and the American public began to suffer from acute pangs of conscience as more details were revealed, especially by a congressional committee in 1912. On the other hand, never once did Roosevelt admit that he had perhaps acted unwisely or wrongly. Every action of his administration in the Panamanian affair, he once wrote, had been "in accordance with the highest, finest, and nicest standards of public and governmental ethics." Roosevelt grew bolder in his own defense as the years passed, until in 1911 he finally spoke the truth: "I am interested in the Panama Canal because I started it. . . . I took the Canal Zone and let Congress debate; and while the debate goes on the Canal does also."

Two other diplomatic incidents, the Venezuelan blockade and Canadian-American boundary disputes, revealed the arrogrance, strident nationalism, and growing concern for American supremacy in the Western Hemisphere that characterized Roosevelt's diplomacy during the first years of his presidency. The Venezuelan trouble began when the dictator of that republic, Cipriano Castro, refused even to acknowledge his country's indebtedness to European creditors. Great Britain and Germany, later joined by Italy, instituted a blockade of Venezuela in December 1902 after obtaining the State Department's approval. American public opinion viewed the intervention suspiciously from the beginning of the affair. It became greatly agitated when the Germans bombarded Fort San Carlos and destroyed a Venezuelan town in January 1903. Meanwhile, Castro had signified his readiness to submit the debt question to the Hague Court.

The German bombardment also caused Roosevelt to suspect German intentions. For a moment it seemed that the Berlin government would refuse Castro's offer of mediation. Roosevelt, in February 1903, at once called in the German Ambassador and told him that he had put Admiral George Dewey in charge of the Atlantic Fleet for its annual maneuvers in West Indian waters. Public opinion was so aroused, Roosevelt went on, "regretfully," that he would be obliged to use force if the Germans took any steps toward acquiring territory in Venezuela or elsewhere in the Caribbean.[4]

Roosevelt's warning was probably unnecessary, for the Germans certainly had no desire to risk a serious incident with the United States. They and the British gladly accepted arbitration to escape from a potentially dangerous situation. The Venezuelan blockade incident was significant, however, first because it emphasized the danger of any future European interventions and led soon afterward to the adoption of a new Caribbean policy by the Roosevelt administration; and second because the European powers had tacitly recognized the Monroe Doctrine and openly admitted the supremacy of the United States in the Caribbean.

The boundary dispute with Canada involved the long finger of Alaska that runs from Alaska proper down the Pacific Coast to the latitude 54° 40′. It first became acute when gold was discovered in the Canadian Klondike region in 1896. Because it seemed clear that the United States had an air-

ᴧᴧᴧᴧᴧᴧᴧᴧᴧᴧᴧᴧᴧᴧᴧᴧᴧᴧᴧᴧ

[4] It has long been a matter of intense scholarly dispute whether Roosevelt did in fact issue any such warning. I accept Roosevelt's own account, given (it seems to me) clearly enough in his letters soon after the event, and Professor Howard K. Beale's account in *Theodore Roosevelt and the Rise of America to World Power* (Baltimore, Md., 1956), pp. 399–431.

tight case, the State Department refused for several years to arbitrate the conflicting claims.[5] Roosevelt was at first inclined to let the matter rest; then he studied the case and concluded that the Canadians had completely fabricated their claim. Secretary of State John Hay, therefore, negotiated a convention with the British government in 1903 providing that six "impartial jurists of repute"—three appointed by the President and three by the King of England—meet in London and settle the question by majority vote. The tribunal convened in London in September 1903. It soon became evident that the Americans would vote as a bloc,[6] that the two Canadian members would support their country's claims, and that the decision would rest with the British commissioner, Lord Chief Justice Alverstone. Meanwhile, Roosevelt had already decided to ask Congress for authority to run the boundary line himself if the tribunal did not endorse the American claims. After the tribunal convened, Roosevelt carefully repeated this threat in conversations and letters for the benefit of the British Foreign Office. Whether Lord Alverstone was more influenced by the President's threat than by the merits of the American case, we do not know. In either event, to the disgust of the Canadians he voted consistently with the American commissioners and thus helped to cement Anglo-American friendship.

59. *The Roosevelt Corollary to the Monroe Doctrine*

On the day before the Senate ratified the Hay–Bunau-Varilla Treaty the Hague Court rendered a verdict that held significant implications for the United States. That tribunal ruled that Germany, Great Britain, and Italy, the very powers to use force against Venezuela, were entitled to first claim on payments by Venezuela to European creditors. In brief, the Hague Court's decision put a premium on intervention, at a time when American security interests in the Caribbean were being multiplied by the decision to construct the Panama Canal.

Roosevelt knew after the Venezuelan blockade affair that the United States could not thereafter tolerate European armed intervention on a major scale in the Caribbean. On the other hand, he knew also that he could not command sufficient naval power to stand off Europe by announcing a policy of nonintervention by outside powers in the Western Hemisphere. Some other way of reconciling American security needs with European economic interests in the Caribbean had to be found. The British Prime Minister, Arthur Balfour, had suggested one solution in 1902: Britain would support the Monroe Doctrine and abstain from intervention in the New World if the United States would take responsibility for seeing that the necessity for such intervention did not arise.

∿∿∿∿∿∿∿∿∿∿∿∿∿∿∿∿

[5] The Canadians claimed that the line should run thirty miles inland in a straight line from the sea and should not be adjusted to the heads of the bays and inlets. The Americans argued that the boundary should run along a line thirty miles inland from the heads of these bays and inlets.

[6] They were Secretary of War Elihu Root, Senator Henry Cabot Lodge of Massachusetts, and former Senator George Turner of Wisconsin, none of whom was either impartial or a jurist of any great repute.

A situation developed only two years later in the Dominican Republic that compelled Roosevelt to work out some kind of policy. That Caribbean republic defaulted on its foreign debt of $32,000,000 after prolonged civil war. Roosevelt was extremely reluctant to intervene. "If I possibly can I want to do nothing . . ." he wrote on February 23, 1904. "If it is absolutely necessary to do something, then I want to do as little as possible." As there was a strong probability that European powers would intervene if he did not, Roosevelt sent Admiral Dewey and the Assistant Secretary of State to the troubled republic to investigate. The latter recommended establishment of an American receivership to collect and disburse the Dominican customs. This course was soon agreed upon, and American representatives in Santo Domingo signed a protocol with Dominican officials on January 20, 1905. It stipulated that the United States should collect the Dominican customs, turn over 45 per cent of the receipts to the local government, and apply the balance for liquidation of the Dominican Republic's foreign debt. When this original agreement provoked severe opposition in the American Senate, the State Department negotiated a more restricted protocol in the following month, but it, too, failed to obtain the two-thirds vote necessary for ratification. Then Secretary Root concluded a new treaty, one less sweeping in its guarantees to the Dominican Republic, on February 8, 1907, and the Senate concurred shortly afterward. Meanwhile the President had established and operated the receivership under an executive agreement.

Roosevelt and Root put the new arrangement into operation so smoothly that neither Dominican pride nor Latin American sensitivity was offended. The American Receiver General persuaded the Dominican Republic's creditors to scale down their claims from $32,000,000 to $17,000,000, and the new debt was refunded at a lower rate of interest. More important was the fact that, since customs houses were no longer prizes to be won by successful revolutionists, the little republic enjoyed such peace and prosperity as it had never known before.

The manner in which Roosevelt solved the Dominican problem revealed that he had no real imperialistic ambitions in the Caribbean; that is, he desired neither new territories nor bases. He intervened reluctantly and in a limited way only to avert European intervention that might threaten the security of America's Panamanian lifeline. The incident was additionally important because Roosevelt seized the opportunity it afforded to announce a new Latin American policy—the Roosevelt Corollary to the Monroe Doctrine.

Roosevelt forecast his Corollary in a public letter to Secretary Root on May 20, 1904, and articulated it more fully in his Annual Message in the following December. Chronic wrongdoing by an American republic might require intervention by some civilized nation, he said on the latter occasion, and "the adherence of the United States to the Monroe Doctrine may force the United States, however reluctantly, in flagrant cases of such wrongdoing or impotence, to the exercise of an international police power." In other words, the President declared that the United States owed it to the European powers to guarantee that no cause for intervention should arise since the Monroe Doctrine prohibited European use of force in the Western Hemisphere.

As scholars have emphasized, the Roosevelt Corollary was based upon false assumptions and bad history, for no American statesman, not even Roosevelt, had ever before interpreted the Monroe Doctrine as forbidding temporary European interventions to compel Latin American states to pay debts or discharge international obligations. Roosevelt was simply invoking the sanction of a historic doctrine to justify a major and necessary change in American foreign policy: thereafter the United States would tolerate no further European interventions in the Caribbean region.

60. *Theodore Roosevelt and the New Diplomacy in Europe and Asia*

The years from 1901 to 1909 saw a perilous growth of international tension in Europe and the Far East. Germany's simultaneous determination to dominate the Continent and challenge Britain's naval supremacy brought about a diplomatic revolution in Europe by forcing Britain to seek *rapprochement,* first with France and then, in 1907, with Russia as well. In the Far East the old balance of power was upset by the rise of Japan and Russia's determination to control Korea and Manchuria. With refreshing realism and boldness Theodore Roosevelt grasped the nettle danger to help maintain the balance of power in the Far East and avert a general European war into which the United States might be drawn. That attainment of these objectives required abandonment of the traditional posture did not deter Roosevelt. He played the game of power politics as if he were a divine-right monarch, but he played it well and for the peace of the world.

Roosevelt's chief objective in European affairs was to be an impartial friend in order to help to relieve the growing tension between the *Entente* powers and Germany. Friction between France and Germany centered during the early years of the twentieth century on Morocco, where France was closing the doors to German and other foreign merchants. France's ally, Russia, became embroiled in war with Japan in 1904, and the Kaiser and his Foreign Office saw an opportunity to call France's hand and perhaps also to break the newly formed Anglo-French *entente.* The Kaiser in 1905 thereupon demanded an international conference to define the status of Morocco. The French refused, and the Kaiser appealed to Roosevelt for support. Although he was extremely reluctant to intervene, Roosevelt knew that war might break out unless the French gave in. Therefore, he brought such pressure to bear on England and France that they consented to attend a conference.

The Kaiser had won the first round. But the Germans faced a solid Anglo-French bloc, which usually had the support of the American delegates, when the conference met at Algeciras in southern Spain in early 1906. The General Act of Algeciras, signed on April 7, 1906, represented superficially a victory for commercial freedom in Morocco. However, it gave the French such control over the sultanate that they were able quietly to close the door to non-French trade. But that was in the future. At the moment when a general war seemed probable Roosevelt had intervened decisively and helped Europeans to find a peaceful alternative.

Working out a viable Far Eastern policy posed an even greater chal-

lenge to Roosevelt's skill. The basic American objectives in the Far East
had been defined by Secretary of State John Hay in the Open Door notes of
1899 and 1900—to preserve the commercial Open Door to, and the territorial integrity of, China, and to protect the vulnerable Philippines from
Japanese attack. Moreover, the American emotional investment in China
by 1905 was considerable as a result of a tremendous growth of American
missionary, medical, and educational work. Indeed, most Americans now
regarded their government as China's sole defender against allegedly
rapacious European, Russian, and Japanese imperialism.

The chief threat to the peace of the Far East in the late 1890's and
early 1900's was Russian expansion into Manchuria and Korea. In order to
halt Russian expansion, the British concluded an alliance with Japan in
1902. And when war broke out between Japan and Russia in 1904, American sympathy went to the Nipponese. Convinced that Japan was playing
America's game by curbing and offsetting a growing Russian preponderance
of power in the Far East, Roosevelt supported the Japanese, even to the
extent of warning Germany and France that he would not countenance
their going to the support of Russia.

The Japanese had won a series of spectacular victories on land and sea
by the spring of 1905, but the Empire was so exhausted that it could not
maintain a major effort much longer. The Japanese Cabinet, therefore,
appealed secretly to President Roosevelt on April 18 to offer mediatory
services. The American president was reluctant to undertake what was
bound to be a thankless task, yet he believed that a Japanese victory was
essential to maintenance of the existing power balance. Thus he invited the
belligerents on June 8 to come to a peace conference to end the "terrible and
lamentable conflict."

The conference opened at the Portsmouth, New Hampshire, Navy
Yard on August 9, 1905. The Japanese commissioners, not satisfied with
winning control of southern Manchuria, Korea, and the southern half of
Sakhalin from Russia, also demanded a huge monetary indemnity. The
latter demand caused American opinion to turn sharply against Japan, and
the Japanese leaders, realizing that they had gone too far, yielded this
point rather than risk resumption of hostilities. But the Japanese people,
ignorant of the tremendous assistance that Roosevelt had given their government, concluded that the President had denied them their indemnity.

The Treaty of Portsmouth of 1905 in effect preserved the balance of
power that Russian expansion had threatened to destroy. Russia remained
an important Pacific power, but Japan now stood as an effective counter-
poise. Whether this configuration would protect American interests in the
Far East depended upon many factors, the most important of which was the
Japanese government's future conduct. Roosevelt could not control Japanese policy; he could only try to channel it in a direction advantageous to
the United States. Even before the Portsmouth Conference opened, he sent
Secretary of War Taft, then in Manila, to Tokyo to come to an immediate
understanding with the Imperial Cabinet. Taft concluded an executive
agreement with the Prime Minister, Taro Katsura, on July 25, 1905. By its
terms the United States recognized Japan's suzerainty over Korea, and
Japan disavowed any designs on the Philippines.

The Japanese welcomed Roosevelt's recognition of their new status in the Far East, but events were developing in the United States that threatened to impair good relations between the two countries. For one thing, there was a great deal of dangerous talk about the "Yellow Peril," and the Hearst press day in and day out stimulated fears of future Japanese aggression. The most dangerous trouble, however, was brewing in California on account of Japanese immigration into that state.[7] It seemed following the Russo-Japanese War that the relatively small stream of Japanese immigrants would become a rushing tide. With Congress indifferent to the problem, Californians organized to take matters into their own hands. As the first step in an anti-Japanese campaign, the San Francisco Board of Education adopted an order on October 11, 1906, requiring the segregation of all Oriental school children.

The Japanese people, still flushed with their victory over the largest power in Europe, were in no mood to let this insult pass. The Japanese Ambassador lodged a formal protest with the Secretary of State on October 25, 1906, while irresponsible newspapers in both countries tried to stir war passions. It was a dangerous situation, but Roosevelt acted with superb caution and good sense. He did not ignore the fact that war was a possibility, but he was certain that the segregation order violated the Japanese-American Treaty of 1894, which guaranteed most favored treatment to Japanese subjects in the United States. He was determined if necessary to use the army to protect the rights of the Japanese in California; at the same time he understood that Japanese immigration was the root of the trouble and resolved to bring it to an end.

Roosevelt solved the difficulty by judicious mixture of courtesy and sternness. At his invitation the Mayor and Board of Education of San Francisco came to the White House in February 1907. Roosevelt promised to use diplomacy to stop Japanese immigration; in return, the School Board revoked the segregation order. Then the President negotiated, in 1907 and 1908, the so-called Gentlemen's Agreement with the Japanese. In this document the Imperial government promised to issue no more passports to peasants or workers coming directly to the continental United States.

In order to disabuse the Japanese of any notion that he had acted out of fear of them, Roosevelt decided in the summer of 1907 to send an American fleet of sixteen battleships on a cruise around the world—by way of the Pacific. Leaving Hampton Roads in December 1907, the fleet steamed to Australia and then to Japan, where it was received with an overwhelming demonstration of good will. From Yokohama, it sailed through the Indian Ocean, the Mediterranean, and the Atlantic, and returned to Hampton Roads on February 22, 1909. The 46,000-mile voyage had demonstrated American naval power and efficiency; more important, the fleet's visit to Japan had evoked demonstrations of Japanese-American friendship. Looking back over his administration a few years later, Roosevelt concluded that sending the fleet on its long cruise had been his most important contribution to the cause of peace.

∿∿∿∿∿∿∿∿∿∿∿∿∿∿∿

[7] There were 12,000 Japanese in California in 1900. In that year the Japanese government announced that it would cease issuing passports to laborers who wished to go to the continental United States. Japanese kept coming to California, however, at the rate of 500 to 1,000 a year until 1905.

While the fleet was on its epochal voyage the Japanese Foreign Minister instructed his Emperor's Ambassador in Washington, Baron Takahira, to open negotiations for a comprehensive understanding with the American government on all phases of the Far Eastern question. The outcome was the Root-Takahira Agreement of November 30, 1908, by which Japan and the United States agreed to help maintain the *status quo* in the Pacific, to respect each other's territorial possessions, and jointly to support the Open Door in China and the independence and territorial integrity of that country. Here indeed was a program of co-operation which, if faithfully adhered to, might provide a modus vivendi for Japanese-American peace for all time to come.

The United States was a world power in fact as well as in name when Roosevelt left the White House in 1909. By blunt and sometimes questionable diplomacy Roosevelt had established unquestioned American supremacy in the Caribbean area. By abandoning old traditions against interference in non-American affairs, he had helped to preserve the peace of Europe. And by a policy of realism, he had supported the rise of Japan and come to friendly understanding with that power. This was no mean record for a man who has often been described as an amateur diplomatist.

61. *Taft and "Dollar Diplomacy" in the Caribbean and the Far East*

William Howard Taft, who was unfitted and unwilling to be a strong leader in world affairs, deliberately abandoned Roosevelt's policy of participation in European politics, and blundered into partial reversal of Roosevelt's policy of maintaining Japanese good will. But the new President and his Secretary of State, Philander C. Knox, could not reverse Roosevelt's policy of protecting American supremacy in the Caribbean area without endangering national security. In fact, they went far beyond the limited kind of intervention that Roosevelt and Root had practiced and devised a new policy, "dollar diplomacy," to strengthen American power in the approaches to the Canal. It involved using private American banking resources to displace European concessionaires and creditors, and hence to strengthen American influence, in the Caribbean region, where, as Knox said, "the malady of revolutions and financial collapse is most acute precisely . . . where it is most dangerous to us."

Soon after taking office in 1909, Knox tried to persuade American bankers to take over the debt owed British investors by the Central American republic of Honduras. The Secretary signed a treaty with the Honduran Minister in 1911 for refunding of that country's foreign debt by American bankers and establishment of an American customs receivership. The government of Honduras, however, refused to ratify the convention. Again, in 1910, Knox persuaded four New York banking firms to invest in the National Bank of the Republic of Haiti in order to help the Negro republic to stabilize its currency.

These activities were merely a prelude to Knox's most important action in the Caribbean area, his intervention in Nicaragua. In this affair the administration first tried to use American dollars to stabilize and control

Nicaraguan finances. But it also went far beyond "dollar diplomacy" and launched a new and even more drastic policy of armed intervention. As the Nicaraguan intervention established a precedent for future American policy, it would be well to examine it in some detail.

Nicaragua at the beginning of the Taft administration was ruled by a dictator, José Zelaya, who was nursing an old grudge against the United States. He vented his spleen on the United States–Nicaragua Concession, a mining company owned by Pittsburgh capitalists, and even went so far as to make plans to offer an option on the Nicaraguan canal route to the Japanese government.

Officials of the United States–Nicaragua Concession helped to engineer a revolution against Zelaya in 1909, and the State Department sent marines to the Nicaraguan city of Bluefields to protect foreign nationals and property. As a consequence of Knox's interference Zelaya was overthrown, and Adolfo Díaz, former secretary of the United States–Nicaragua Concession, was installed as President in 1911 with the State Department's blessing.

Knox now moved swiftly to bring Nicaragua completely under American control. He signed a treaty with the Nicaraguan Minister on June 6, 1911, for refunding of the Nicaraguan foreign debt by two New York banking firms and establishment of an American customs receivership. Democrats in the Senate blocked ratification of this, the Knox-Castrillo Treaty. At the request of the State Department, however, the New York bankers advanced $1,500,000 to Nicaragua and received in return majority control of the state railways and the National Bank of Nicaragua. An American receiver-general of Nicaraguan customs was appointed by the banking houses and approved by the two governments later in the same year.

As it turned out, the new Díaz government did not have the support of a majority of Nicaraguans. In defiance of the State Department they continued to look to Zelaya and his Liberal party for leadership. The Liberals raised the standards of revolt in 1912, and Díaz would have fallen had not Taft rushed 2,700 marines to Nicaragua to suppress the uprising. So bitter was anti-Díaz and anti-American sentiment that the marines continued to occupy the country for many years.

The American intervention and occupation did not solve Nicaragua's most pressing requirement—her need for financial assistance in refunding her foreign debt and paying claims arising from the revolutions of 1909 and 1912. Chiefly to satisfy the national treasury's need for ready cash, Secretary Knox signed a treaty in 1913 with the Nicaraguan Minister for payment by the United States to Nicaragua of $3,000,000. In return, Nicaragua granted to the United States an exclusive option on its canal route, the privilege of establishing a naval base on the Gulf of Fonseca, on the Pacific side, and a ninety-nine-year lease on the Great Corn and Little Corn Islands in the Caribbean. The treaty was negotiated too late to be ratified before the Sixty-second Congress expired on March 4, 1913, and the Wilson administration inherited the unpleasant task of persuading the Senate to ratify the convention.

The objectives of "dollar diplomacy" in the Far East were nearly as ambitious as in the Caribbean. Toward the end of the Roosevelt administration a clique in the State Department headed by a young career diplomat,

Willard Straight, began to lay plans to sponsor American investment in Manchuria in order to offset Japanese influence in that province. Restrained by Secretary Root's firm hand, Straight and his colleagues came into control of Far Eastern policy when Knox took the helm at the State Department. Their opportunity to press for a more aggressive policy came in 1909, when a consortium of British, French, and German bankers signed a contract with the Chinese government to build a network of railways in central and southern China.

Straight and his friends in the Far Eastern Division easily won Knox to their side by arguing that American participation in the consortium was necessary to enable the United States to defend the Open Door and the territorial integrity of China. Accordingly, the State Department in 1909 demanded that American bankers be permitted to participate in the loan. An American banking syndicate formed by J. P. Morgan & Company was admitted to the consortium, along with Japanese and Russian bankers, in May 1911. But for various reasons the project never prospered, and President Wilson, in March 1913, announced the withdrawal of the American group.

Meanwhile, Secretary Knox pressed forward in a more reckless move— his ill-fated proposal, made in late 1909, for internationalization of Manchurian railways in order to offset growing Japanese and Russian influence in the province. The British were at this very time encouraging Japanese expansion in Manchuria in order to keep the Japanese at safe distance from the British sphere of influence; they promptly rebuffed Knox's suggestion. The Japanese, on the other hand, regarded the proposal as an attempt to undermine their influence in an area that Roosevelt had tacitly recognized as being within the Japanese orbit. In short, Knox's proposal was ill conceived and naively made. It angered the British, drove the Japanese and Russians into an anti-American bloc, and even alienated the American banking group.

The historian must conclude that, on the whole, Taft's record in foreign affairs was even more barren than in domestic politics. The most important outcome of "dollar diplomacy" in Latin America was an armed intervention in Nicaragua that lacked strategic necessity, failed to bring peace to Nicaragua, and intensified anti-American feeling in Latin America. The result of "dollar diplomacy" in the Far East was an embittering of Japanese-American relations without any benefit to the United States. For the failure of his foreign policy Taft had only himself and his Secretary of State to blame. Where Roosevelt had been wise and farsighted, Taft was indolently ineffectual; where Root had been suave, Knox was often offensive. The contrast goes far toward explaining the unsatisfactory state of American foreign relations when Woodrow Wilson took office on March 4, 1913.

62. *The New Freedom Abroad*

Humanitarians hailed Wilson's inauguration in 1913 as beginning a more idealistic era in American foreign relations. Most Democrats since

1901 had consistently condemned Roosevelt's and Taft's policies of military intervention, quasi-protectorates, and "dollar diplomacy," stood for early independence for the Filipinos, and fought for a moderate naval building program designed only to implement a diplomacy of defense.

The character and convictions of the new makers of American foreign policy also seemed to promise a new era in diplomacy. No public leader of his generation was more eloquent in articulating the liberal, idealistic international program than Woodrow Wilson. Long before he became the prime exponent of international organization and collective security, Wilson had championed a diplomacy that sought the good of mankind above the selfish interests of the United States. Moreover, Wilson's Secretary of State, William Jennings Bryan, was easily the leading opponent of imperialism and navalism and a pioneer in the movement to advance peace through arbitration and conciliation.

The first sign of a New Freedom in foreign policy was Bryan's ambitious peace plan, launched only a few months after Wilson's inauguration. It was based upon assumptions that most progressives and humanitarians of that day shared: There were no disputes among nations that could not be settled by reasonable discussion. No people in command of their reasoning faculties would allow their government to go to war if such a course could honorably be avoided. The obvious and easiest way to avoid war in the future, therefore, was to construct some machinery for peaceful settlement of disputes.

In its practical aspects, Bryan's solution was based soundly upon the experience of his predecessors in trying to steer arbitration treaties through a Senate jealous of its partial control over foreign relations. Secretary of State John Hay had negotiated a series of arbitration treaties that excluded all disputes involving vital interest and national honor. But the Senate in 1905 amended these treaties to make its consent to each arbitration necessary, and Roosevelt withdrew them. Secretary Root three years later persuaded Roosevelt to yield to the Senate's demand; he then negotiated twenty-five limited arbitration agreements in 1908 and 1909. However, the Senate rebelled again when President Taft and Secretary Knox signed new treaties with Britain and France in 1911 providing for arbitration of all "justiciable" questions, including disputes affecting national interest and honor. The upper house consented to ratification of these treaties in 1912 but exempted all important questions from possible arbitration. Taft in disgust refused to promulgate the mutilated treaties.

Bryan found a solution that he thought would achieve unlimited arbitration without arousing the Senate's suspicions. Bryan's treaties provided, not for arbitration, but for submission of all disputes to permanent commissions for investigation for a period of one year. Neither party would resort to war or increase its armaments during this interval of "cooling off." After the investigation was completed, the parties might accept or reject the commission's findings. Both countries would then be free to go to war, but Bryan was confident that hostilities could not occur in such circumstances.

Bryan signed the first conciliation treaty with El Salvador on August 7, 1913, and negotiated twenty-nine other such agreements during the following year with Great Britain, France, Italy, and lesser powers. Although realists like Roosevelt condemned Bryan's plan as worse than futile, it seems fair to say that the Secretary had constructed workable machinery that might be used if momentary crises ever menaced peace.

Further evidence of New Freedom idealism was the administration's withdrawal of the American banking group from the six-power consortium that had been formed in 1911 to finance construction of the Hukuang Railway in China. The United States, Wilson said on March 18, 1913, could not approve the loan agreement because it would lead to intolerable interference in Chinese affairs. A few weeks later, as if to emphasize his determination to cut loose from all such imperialistic conspiracies, Wilson recognized the new Republic of China without first consulting other powers.

A third example of idealistic diplomacy was Wilson's settlement of the Anglo-American dispute provoked when Congress, in August 1912, exempted American ships engaged in coastwise trade from payment of Panama Canal tolls. The British Foreign Office protested soon afterward that the exemption violated the Hay-Pauncefote Treaty's promise of equal rates for ships of all nations. Wilson had unthinkingly approved exemption during the campaign of 1912, but he concluded even before he was inaugurated that the British were right. He could not run the risk of splitting his party so long as the tariff and banking bills hung in the fire; but after these measures were safely passed, he met the Senate foreign relations committee, on January 28, 1914, reviewed the critical state of American foreign relations, and urged repeal of the exemption provision in order to restore fully cordial relations with the British government. The President reiterated his plea before a joint session on March 5, 1914, and ended with the cryptic warning that he would not know how to deal with other and more difficult problems if Congress did not grant his request. The Hearst press roared, and some Democrats in Congress threatened rebellion. But the House of Representatives approved a repeal bill on March 31, the Senate, on June 11, 1914.

Wilson's and Bryan's determination to do the moral if unpleasant thing in foreign affairs was evidenced, finally, in the treaty of reparation that they negotiated with Colombia to make amends for Rooseveltian sins of the past. In a treaty signed at Bogotá on April 6, 1914, the United States expressed "sincere regret" for incidents that had interrupted good relations between the two countries, agreed to pay $25,000,000 to Colombia for the loss of Panama, and gave the government of Colombia free use of the Canal and Colombian citizens equality of treatment with Americans in the Canal Zone. Publication of the treaty provoked an explosion of Rough Rider rage that was heard from one end of the hemisphere to the other. Roosevelt's friends in the Senate blocked ratification in 1914 and again in 1917, but the Wilson administration's intentions had been clearly demonstrated. The sight of the great government of the United States apologizing to a helpless neighbor stirred a wave of warm and cordial feeling toward the United States throughout Latin America.[8]

wwwwwwwwwwww

[8] The Harding administration negotiated a new treaty in 1921 that awarded the Colombian government $25,000,000 but omitted the specific apology.

63.   New Troubles with Japan, 1913–1917

The record of the Wilson administration's relations with Japan from 1913 to 1917 demonstrates that good intentions alone do not always suffice to settle delicate international disputes. The possibility of new difficulties was raised during the campaign of 1912, when Democrats and Progressives launched a campaign in California for a law prohibiting Japanese ownership of land. Instead of perceiving the dangers, Wilson conferred with California leaders and even volunteered a method to exclude Japanese from land ownership without violating the Japanese-American Treaty of 1911. Acting upon the President's suggestion, the California Assembly, on April 15, 1913, passed an alien bill prohibiting Japanese ownership of land in an indirect manner.

A crisis suddenly developed when news of the California Assembly's action was published in Japan. Then the California Senate exacerbated the tension on April 21 by adopting an alien land bill that was openly anti-Japanese. A rising war fever in Japan brought Wilson to his senses and compelled him to act. He first addressed a public appeal to the Californians, urging them not to make their alien land bill openly discriminatory. Next he sent Bryan to Sacramento to plead for caution. Wilson's and Bryan's supplications did not budge the California leaders from their determination to humiliate the Japanese people. The legislature on May 9, 1913, approved a bill excluding from land ownership persons "ineligible to citizenship"— words hateful to the Japanese. Governor Hiram W. Johnson signed the measure in spite of last-minute appeals from Wilson and Bryan.

For a brief moment it now seemed possible that Japan and the United States might be heading for war. The Japanese Ambassador lodged a strong protest with the State Department on May 9; Japanese public opinion was at a dangerous point of anger. So explosive was the situation that the Joint Board of the Army and Navy warned Wilson on May 13 and 14 that war with Japan was "not only possible, but even probable." The Joint Board, besides, urged the President to transfer American warships in Chinese waters to the Philippines to help avert a surprise Japanese attack.

It was a dangerous situation, but Wilson and Bryan kept their heads. Correctly assuming that the Japanese government did not want war, they rejected the Joint Board's advice and relied exclusively on diplomacy. Many notes passed between Tokyo and Washington during the remainder of 1913 and the first months of 1914. The Japanese government proposed a treaty guaranteeing the mutual right of land ownership. In reply, Wilson and Bryan promised to negotiate such a treaty when it was politically possible to obtain ratification. But that time did not come soon enough, and the new Japanese Foreign Minister, Baron Kato, abruptly terminated the negotiations in June 1914. Thus relations between the two governments were gravely unsettled when the war in Europe spread to the Far East and raised new difficulties for the United States.

As Wilson and Bryan perceived, there was now the grave danger that Japan would take advantage of Europe's adversity to extend her influence in China. When Japan entered the war on the side of the Allies and seized the German naval base and concession in the Shantung Province of China, the American leaders were disturbed but helpless to prevent such action. When the Japanese government proceeded in the early weeks of 1915 to attempt to impose a treaty embodying twenty-one demands on China, adherence to which would have made China virtually a satellite of Nippon, Wilson and Bryan first seemed partially to acquiesce. But then they entered the ensuing controversy as defenders of China, voicing their opposition to the more extreme Japanese demands in a series of statements to the press and in notes to the Japanese and Chinese governments during April and May 1915. The most important of these was a caveat that Robert Lansing, Counselor of the State Department, had drafted and that Bryan sent to Tokyo and Peking on May 11. It declared that the United States would not recognize any Sino-Japanese agreement violating the political and territorial integrity of China and the Open Door policy. The British Foreign Office had meanwhile become aroused and applied heavy pressure on the Tokyo Cabinet in favor of a policy of moderation. The upshot of these Anglo-American protests was the Japanese government's abandonment for the time being of its plan to bring China under its control.

Following this crisis the Japanese pressed forward to enhance their economic position in China by offering capital that European bankers could no longer supply. Wilson responded by reversing his position on an international bankers' loan to China. Through the State Department he announced on November 9, 1917, that the American government was contemplating creation of a new four-power consortium of American, British, French, and Japanese bankers to supply desperately needed capital to China. Actually, the American determination to offset Japanese economic expansion in China had been evident months before the announcement of November 9 and had prompted the Japanese government to ask the Washington leaders for a frank avowal of their policy. When correspondence failed to yield satisfactory understanding, the Tokyo Foreign Office sent a special envoy, Viscount Kikujiro Ishii, to Washington. Intense if intermittent discussions between Ishii and the Secretary of State, Robert Lansing, ensued between September 6 and November 2, 1917. The extent of their divergence became clear when Ishii insisted that the United States recognize Japan's paramount interest in China, in the same way that Japan had recognized the paramount American interest in Mexico. Lansing replied that Japan should reaffirm her allegiance to the Open Door and help maintain Chinese independence.

The two men were unable to come to clear and firm agreement and, as diplomats often do, used ambiguous language to make a show of accord. In an agreement signed on November 2, 1917, the United States recognized that Japan had special interests in China, especially in provinces contiguous to Japanese possessions—presumably Manchuria and the Shantung Province. In return, Japan reaffirmed her support of the Open Door and the territorial and administrative independence of China. Moreover, Japan promised in a secret protocol not to take advantage of the war situation to seek special rights in China that would abridge the interests of citizens of friendly powers.

The Japanese publicly boasted that Lansing had recognized their controlling interest in China. The report was somewhat exaggerated. The Secretary of State had refused to abandon historic American insistence upon the Open Door and the independence of China. He had used ambiguous language only to obtain a modus vivendi that would thwart Japanese claims and ambitions until the end of the war with Germany. At that time the United States presumably would be free to use its full naval and military strength to demand an acceptable Far Eastern settlement.

Looking back over the Far Eastern policy of the United States during the first four and a half years of the Wilson era, the astute observer might well have concluded in 1918 that there was little that was new about New Freedom diplomacy in this area. To be sure, Wilson and Bryan had handled the crisis over the California land law of 1913 with far less vigor and astuteness than Roosevelt and Root displayed in dealing with an earlier Japanese-American crisis. The Wilson administration, moreover, had repudiated Taft's and Knox's policy of economic penetration of China. Nonetheless, in the face of an expansive and encroaching Japanese imperialism, which threatened to upset the Far Eastern balance and establish Japan as the master of eastern Asia, the Wilson administration not only revived "dollar diplomacy" but also came to a firm defense of American interests in China. And in thus refusing to abandon the policy begun by Secretary John Hay in 1899, Wilson, Bryan, and Lansing set the stage for future and more portentous conflicts with Imperial Japan.

64. *Further Penetration of Central America and the Caribbean*

In contrast to Wilson's and Bryan's promises of a new policy of nonintervention toward Latin America stands a record of wholesale diplomatic and military interference in the affairs of neighboring states unparalleled at any time in the annals of American diplomacy. How can this contradiction between promise and performance be explained?

To begin with, the Wilson administration inherited a foreign policy aimed primarily at protecting the future Panamanian life line. This policy could not be reversed without abandoning what seemed to be the cornerstone of the American security system. Actually, the Democratic leaders believed implicitly in the necessity of preserving American supremacy in the Caribbean and Central American areas and were willing to undertake even bolder programs than their Republican predecessors had envisaged.

In the second place, although Bryan and the Democratic party had solemnly condemned so-called dollar diplomacy as insidious financial imperialism, circumstances compelled the new Secretary of State to use the very instrument that he had denounced. In the beginning, however, Bryan had other plans. To free Latin America from the snares of foreign concessionaires and bankers, he proposed a farsighted plan. It envisaged the assumption and refunding by the United States government of the external debts of the small Latin American states. But Wilson rejected this proposal as being too "radical," and Bryan concluded that he had no alternative but to continue to use private capital to consolidate American influence in a vital area.

These two points help to explain why there was no essential change in the Latin American policies of the United States in 1913. But the motives for Wilson's and Bryan's *extension* of the Roosevelt-Taft policy lay deeper than desire to protect American security interests. Wilson and Bryan were missionaries of democracy and freedom. They sincerely wanted to help less fortunate neighboring peoples to find peace and develop democratic institutions. Thus they intervened, not to subjugate and enslave, but to enlighten, instruct, and liberate.

The formulation of their program in Nicaragua shows how all these factors combined to shape and control policy. Bryan could not withdraw American troops from Nicaragua without inviting civil war and the inauguration of a bitterly anti-American regime in an area close to the Canal. He continued, therefore, to support the Knox-sponsored Díaz government, which the Nicaraguan people would almost certainly have overthrown had they been free to do so.

Having concluded that it was necessary to control the government of Nicaragua, Bryan was also willing to go the whole way and regularize Nicaragua's special relation to the United States in treaty form. Counsel for the Nicaraguan government in June 1913 presented to the State Department the draft of a document that was later known as the Bryan-Chamorro Treaty. Like the agreement that Secretary Knox had negotiated and the Senate had refused to ratify a few months before, the Bryan-Chamorro Treaty provided for an American option on the Nicaraguan canal route for $3,000,000, and for other privileges. Unlike Knox's instrument, the Bryan-Chamorro Treaty also permitted the United States to intervene in Nicaragua to preserve order, protect property, and maintain Nicaraguan independence.

Republicans hailed the administration's extension of Taft's policy. Old-line Democrats on the Senate foreign relations committee, however, refused to change their principles. The Senate approved the treaty on February 18, 1916, but only after the provision authorizing American intervention in Nicaragua's internal affairs had been removed. Actually, the deletion made no difference in State Department policy, which continued to be one of active interference in all phases of Nicaraguan politics.

The conclusion of this Treaty marked only the beginning of a further penetration of the Caribbean area that culminated in the occupation of the Dominican Republic and Haiti. This final penetration occurred, not because the Wilson administration sought imperialistic advantage or feared immediate European intervention, but rather because intervention and American control seemed the only way to save the Dominican and Haitian peoples from anarchy and sheer starvation.

The Dominican Republic by the summer of 1914 was approaching a condition of anarchy as a result of recent revolutions. Officials in the Latin American Affairs Division of the State Department argued that only full-scale military occupation would save the Dominican people from chaos. Wilson intervened, first, by trying to persuade the warring chieftains to lay down their arms, agree upon a provisional president, and allow the United States to assume control of the Dominican finances and police force. The Dominican leaders consented to the first two proposals but would not sign a treaty making their country a virtual protectorate of the United States. Wilson decided that the time for drastic action had come when the leader of the strongest rebel band launched a new revolution in 1916. Wilson gave the orders, and American marine and naval forces seized Santo Domingo on May 15, 1916, and took control of the government. And when the Dominican chieftains still refused to ratify the proposed treaty, the American naval commander established a military government on November 29, 1916. For the next six years American naval forces governed the country, built schools and roads, carried through sanitation projects, and trained a native constabulary to preserve order. Neither Dominican nationalists nor American anti-imperialists approved, but the Dominican people lived in peace and prosperity.

Haitians had also indulged frequently in the revolutionary habit, but they had contrived before 1915 to pay their external debts and escape foreign intervention and control. However, the political situation in the Negro republic grew so anarchic during 1914 and 1915 that the State Department concluded that American control of Haitian customhouses was the only possible way to remove the incentive to revolution. An excuse for intervention presented itself when a new revolution exploded in June 1915. American marines and bluejackets seized Port-au-Prince on July 28, and the commanding American naval officer took control of the Haitian government on August 9 and compelled the National Assembly to elect a pro-American, Sudre Dartiguenave, as President of Haiti. The State Department, moreover, now imposed a treaty—revised to provide not only American supervision of Haitian finances but also establishment of a native constabulary under American control—upon the puppet regime.[9]

To such extremes did the desire to protect American interests and end the reign of tyranny and anarchy in the Caribbean and Central American regions carry the administration of Woodrow Wilson. The one feature of this policy that prevented it from becoming imperialistic was the idealism that prompted Wilson and especially Bryan to adopt it. Instead of using American diplomatic and military power to promote the exclusive material interests of American citizens, Bryan guarded the interests of the people of Nicaragua, Haiti, or Cuba as vigilantly as he guarded the welfare of the American people. On numerous occasions, for example, he prevented corrupt Latin American politicians from selling special rights and resources to American bankers.

Wilson and Bryan climaxed their hemispheric policy by attempting to unite American republics in a Pan-American Alliance, binding them to respect one another's territorial integrity, guarantee one another's political independence, and settle all disputes by peaceful methods. Practically all the small states approved the proposed pact, and Brazil enthusiastically supported it. Argentina, on the other hand, was not pleased, while Chile was positively opposed to any treaty that would bind her hands in her old border dispute with Peru. As American diplomats were never able to overcome Chile's opposition, Wilson's plans for a hemispheric League of Nations collapsed.

∿∿∿∿∿∿∿∿∿∿∿∿∿∿∿∿∿∿∿

[9] When Dartiguenave balked at signing away his country's independence, Secretary of State Lansing threatened either to find a new President of Haiti or else to establish complete military government. Dartiguenave signed the treaty on September 16, 1915. It was ratified by the Haitian Senate on November 12, 1915, and by the United States Senate on February 28, 1916.

65. Wilson and the Mexican Revolution

The crucial test of New Freedom diplomacy came when Wilson sought to apply a policy of helpfulness through interference in Mexico from 1913 to 1917. As we shall see, he desired only to help the Mexicans establish a constitutional government responsive to the needs of the masses. But while helping he forgot that Mexico was a nation with a proud tradition of independence, and his efforts provoked crises that twice brought the two nations to the brink of war.

The background of the story can be briefly told. The old regime of Porfirio Díaz had been overthrown in 1911 by the reformer Francisco I. Madero. Madero tried to destroy the special privileges of the upper classes and provoked the inevitable counterrevolution. The head of the army, Victoriano Huerta, seized control of the Mexican government on February 18, 1913, and arranged the murder of the deposed President five days later. The Taft administration did not recognize Huerta as provisional President, but Britain, France, Germany, and other powers followed conventional practice in according recognition to the new regime.

This was the situation when Wilson was inaugurated in March 1913. There were appeals from representatives of American investors in Mexico to accord immediate *de facto* recognition to Huerta's government, but Wilson hesitated because of personal revulsion against Huerta and his "government of butchers." Another development caused him to hesitate further. It was the beginning of an anti-Huerta movement in the northern states of Mexico, led by the Governor of Coahuila, Venustiano Carranza. Wilson, therefore, waited to see whether Huerta could consolidate his power.

The American President had decided on a policy by the middle of June 1913. The Secretary of State informed Huerta on June 14 that the United States would attempt to mediate between Huerta's government and the followers of Carranza, called Constitutionalists, if Huerta would hold early constitutional elections and agree not to be a candidate for the presidency. President Wilson a short time later recalled the American Ambassador from Mexico City and sent John Lind, former governor of Minnesota, to confer with the Mexican leaders. Lind's objectives, in brief, were to obtain Huerta's elimination and the establishment through Wilson's mediation of a constitutional government that the United States could recognize and support.

Wilson of course assumed that the Mexicans would welcome his assistance. The fact was, however, that all factions, Constitutionalists as well as *Huertistas*, bitterly resented the President's interference and applauded when Huerta rejected Wilson's offer of mediation. Thus rebuffed, Wilson went before a joint session of Congress on August 27, 1913, explained his mediation proposal and Huerta's rebuff, and declared that the United States would adopt a policy of "watchful waiting."

During the next four or five weeks the situation in Mexico seemed to improve. Then Sir Lionel Carden, the new British Minister, arrived in Mexico City. Carden was an intimate of S. Weetman Pearson, Lord Cowdray, who had large oil interests in Mexico. As Mexico was then practically the sole source of oil for the Royal Navy, one major objective of British

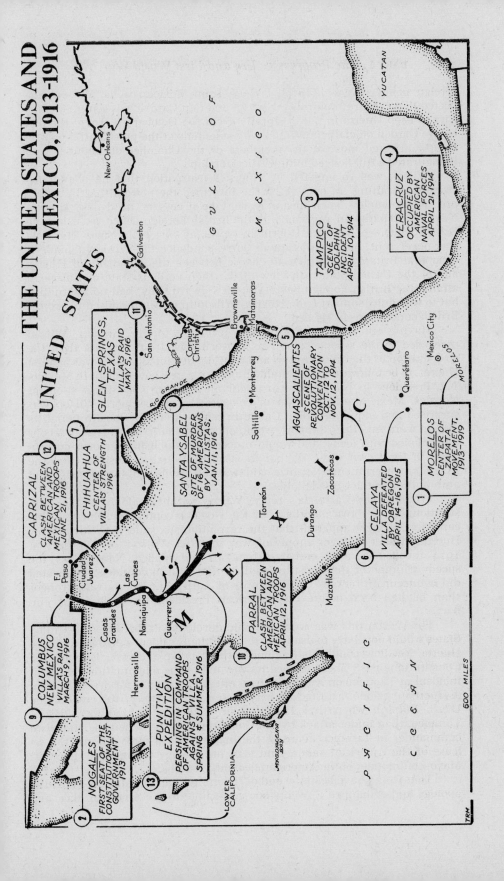

THE UNITED STATES AND
MEXICO, 1913-1916

UNITED STATES

GULF OF MEXICO

YUCATAN

New Orleans

Galveston

④ VERACRUZ
OCCUPIED BY
AMERICAN
NAVAL FORCES
APRIL 21, 1914

③ TAMPICO
SCENE OF
DOLPHIN
INCIDENT
APRIL 10, 1914

Brownsville
Matamoros

⑪ GLEN SPRINGS,
TEXAS
VILLA'S RAID
MAY 5, 1916

San Antonio

Corpus Christi

RIO GRANDE

⑤ AGUASCALIENTES
SCENE OF
REVOLUTIONARY
CONVENTION
OCT. 12 TO
NOV. 12, 1914

Mexico City
Querétaro

MORELOS

① MORELOS
CENTER OF
ZAPATA
MOVEMENT,
1913-1919

⑦ CHIHUAHUA
CENTER OF
VILLA'S STRENGTH
1916

⑫ CARRIZAL
CLASH BETWEEN
AMERICAN AND
MEXICAN TROOPS
JUNE 21, 1916

⑧ SANTA YSABEL
SITE OF MURDER
OF 16 AMERICANS
BY VILLISTAS,
JAN. 11, 1916

Monterrey

Saltillo

Zacatecas

Torreón

Durango

⑥ CELAYA
VILLA DEFEATED
BY OBREGON
APRIL 14-16, 1915

El Paso
Ciudad
Juárez

Las
Cruces

Casas
Grandes

Namiquipa

Guerrero

⑩ PARRAL
CLASH BETWEEN
AMERICAN AND
MEXICAN TROOPS
APRIL 12, 1916

Mazatlán

Hermosillo

⑨ COLUMBUS
NEW MEXICO
VILLA'S RAID
MARCH 9, 1916

② NOGALES
FIRST SEAT OF THE
CONSTITUTIONALIST
GOVERNMENT
1913

⑬ PUNITIVE
EXPEDITION
PERSHING IN COMMAND
OF AMERICAN TROOPS
AGAINST VILLA,
SPRING & SUMMER, 1916

MAGDALENA
BAY

LOWER
CALIFORNIA

PACIFIC OCEAN

600 MILES

TRM

foreign policy was to keep oil flowing from Mexican wells. Wilson suspected that Cowdray controlled Huerta, and that Carden was sent to Mexico City to keep Huerta in power. In any event, on October 10, 1913, the day before Carden officially presented his credentials at the presidential palace, Huerta arrested most of the members of the Chamber of Deputies and inaugurated a full-fledged military dictatorship.

Wilson was so angered by Huerta's usurpation that he abandoned "watchful waiting" at once. First, he informed the powers that he would proceed to employ "such means as may be necessary" to depose Huerta. Next, he prepared an angry note to the British Foreign Office, accusing the British leaders of keeping Huerta in power against his wishes. The note was never sent, but in subsequent correspondence the President made it clear that Britain would have to choose between the friendship of Huerta and of the United States. In view of the then perilous state of European affairs, the British Foreign Secretary, Sir Edward Grey, had no alternative but to withdraw support from Huerta. Wilson in return promised to protect British concessions in Mexico.

Having cut Huerta off from his principal foreign support, Wilson proceeded to the second step. This move involved nothing less than the co-operation of the United States and the Constitutionalists in a war against Huerta, to be followed by the establishment of a new government in Mexico. The President in November 1913 sent an agent to Carranza's camp at Nogales, Mexico, with an offer of co-operation and support. Wilson was surprised and indignant when Carranza replied that the Constitutionalists did not want American support, would oppose the entry of American troops into Mexico with arms, and would proceed to establish their own government in their own way. All that the Constitutionalists desired from the American government, Carranza said, was the privilege of buying arms and ammunition in the United States.

Wounded by Carranza's reply, Wilson withheld aid from the Constitutionalists for two months after the Nogales conference. But as it became increasingly apparent that the revolutionists could never overthrow Huerta without a larger supply of war matériel, Wilson, on February 3, 1914, revoked the arms embargo that Taft had applied. Nonetheless, the speedy triumph of the Constitutionalists that Wilson confidently expected did not occur. In fact, by the beginning of April 1914 Huerta was stronger than he had been before the American President lifted the arms embargo.

For Wilson this was a catastrophic development, because the United States would now have to use force to fulfill the President's pledge to depose Huerta. Yet how could this be done without provoking war also with the Constitutionalists? There seemed no way out of the dilemma until a trivial incident at Tampico on April 10, 1914, offered an excuse for drastic action. A *Huertista* colonel arrested the paymaster and several of the crew of the U.S.S. *Dolphin* when they landed their whaleboat behind the lines at Tampico, then under attack by the Constitutionalists. When the *Huertista* commander in Tampico heard of the incident he at once ordered the release of the American sailors and sent an apology to Admiral Henry T. Mayo, commander of the American fleet off Veracruz.

That would have been the end of the matter had not Mayo rejected the apology and demanded a twenty-one-gun salute to the American flag, and had not the President backed up Mayo's demand. Huerta agreed to render the salute, but only provided an American warship returned a simultaneous volley, and Wilson drew war plans with his Cabinet and military and naval advisers. Then he went before a joint session of Congress on April 20 and asked for authority to compel Huerta to respect the honor of the United States. Before Congress could act on the President's request, news arrived in Washington of the impending arrival at Veracruz of a German merchant ship, the *Ypiranga,* with a load of ammunition for the Huerta government. Without waiting for congressional sanction, Wilson on April 21 ordered the fleet to occupy Veracruz and prevent the *Ypiranga* from unloading her cargo. Veracruz was in American hands by April 22.

Wilson may have had a full-scale invasion in mind when he began the Veracruz operation, but if he did unforeseen events soon compelled him to change plans. For one thing, humanitarians in the United States were astonished by the President's belligerence and demanded that he find a peaceful solution. For another, Carranza denounced the Veracruz occupation as wanton aggression and threatened to resist the American forces if they attempted to move against Mexico City.

But how could the United States withdraw without losing face? How could war with Mexico be averted so long as American troops remained on Mexican soil? There seemed to be no answer to these questions until the Argentine, Brazilian, and Chilean envoys in Washington, on April 25, offered to mediate the dispute. In mutual relief Wilson and Huerta accepted the offer. The American and Mexican delegates met at Niagara Falls, Canada, from May 20 until July 2, 1914. As the days passed Huerta's power waned, and the Constitutionalists drove closer to Mexico City. The only significant aspect of the conference, therefore, was Wilson's effort to persuade the Constitutionalists to accept American guidance in establishing a new government. Carranza at last sent commissioners to Niagara Falls, but they made it plain that they wanted no help from the United States either in conquering or governing their country. There was nothing that Wilson could do except to acquiesce and to warn Carranza that he would tolerate no mass executions or confiscations. Huerta abdicated on July 15, 1914, after taking one parting shot at the "Puritan" in the White House; Carranza and his armies entered the City of Mexico on August 20.

Huerta's retirement, however, did not signal the beginning of peace in Mexico, for a rupture in the Constitutionalist ranks soon plunged Mexico anew into civil war. The chief cause of the schism was the rivalry between the First Chief of the Revolution, Carranza, and his most successful general, Francisco, or "Pancho," Villa, who was ignorant and unfitted for political leadership. Into this critical and delicate situation the American government moved with alacrity. The President in August 1914 sent an agent to Mexico to propose a convention of revolutionary leaders and subsequent establishment of a new provisional government which, as the agent later said, "would place Villa in control." [10] Carranza and his generals

[10] The reasons for the adoption of this ill-fated policy do no credit to Wilson's and Bryan's judgment. On the one hand, Villa had been depicted in a friendly American press as a genuine social reformer. More important, he had made it clear to Wilson that he would welcome the support and guidance of the United States. On the other hand, Carranza had already demonstrated that in no circumstances would he welcome American advice or reciprocate the friendship that Wilson had earlier proffered.

approved the American plan, and Carranza agreed to retire, provided Villa also gave up his command. That Villa had no intention of withdrawing, however, was evidenced when he declared war on Carranza three weeks before the convention was to meet.

In spite of this evidence of Villa's bad faith, the convention did assemble at Aguascalientes from October 12 through November 12, 1914. Villa controlled a majority and established a provisional government that enjoyed the limited support of the United States for a time. However, Carranza's leading generals, Álvaro Obregón and Pablo Gonzáles, withdrew and joined Carranza in his new headquarters at Veracruz, recently evacuated by the American forces.

Thus the civil war began again between the constructive wing of the Revolution headed by Carranza and the plundering elements under Villa's control. While Villa waited for the *Carrancistas* to collapse, Carranza broadened his reform program, strengthened his armies, and began a military campaign in January 1915 that drove Villa and his forces northward from the capital. Then Obregón destroyed Villa's offensive power in one great battle at Celaya in April 1915, and the bandit chieftain sought refuge in his native stronghold of Chihuahua.

The swift destruction of Villa's government compelled the Wilson administration to revert to a policy of neutrality in the Mexican conflict. At the same time, the renewal of the civil war set off a vociferous demand in the United States for intervention. For a time Wilson rebuffed these counsels and insisted that Mexicans be allowed to settle their problems in their own way. Gradually, however, his resistance weakened, and, on June 2, 1915, he warned the rival factions to compose their differences or else expect corrective measures by the United States. Two months later, furthermore, Wilson and his new Secretary of State, Robert Lansing, called in leading Latin American envoys in Washington to help formulate a plan to eliminate Carranza and create a new provisional government in Mexico.

Events over which Wilson had no control, however, again took control of his Mexican policy. In the first place, while Wilson and Lansing talked, Carranza acted. By August 1915 it was evident that Carranza's power was growing daily, and that intervention by the United States would provoke a general war with the Mexican people. Second, the United States become embroiled during the summer of 1915 in a serious diplomatic controversy with Germany over the use of submarines against Allied merchant ships. As the possibility of war with Germany increased, Wilson's and Lansing's willingness to risk military involvement in Mexico diminished. Finally, the two American leaders learned that the German government was trying to encourage a war between Mexico and its neighbor, in order to lessen American pressure against the unrestricted use of submarines. This revelation caused the Washington government to take a hard second look at plans for intervention.

The only alternative to intervention seemed to be recognition and support of Carranza. Hence Wilson swiftly reversed American policy, persuaded the Latin American envoys to co-operate, and extended *de facto* recognition to Carranza's provisional government on October 19, 1915. During the next three months relations between the United States and the *de facto* regime were friendly, and Wilson's troubles would have been at an end had no untoward events occurred. As it turned out, perplexities were just beginning.

The chief troublemaker was Villa, whose evil genius concocted mad schemes to provoke the United States to war. A band of *Villistas* stopped a train at Santa Ysabel, fifty miles west of Chihuahua City, on January 11, 1916, removed seventeen Americans, and shot sixteen of them on the spot. When this massacre failed to cause American reprisal, Villa made a bold raid on Columbus, New Mexico, on March 9, 1916, burning the town and killing nineteen inhabitants.

At once President Wilson ordered army commanders in Texas to assemble an expedition for the pursuit of Villa. At the same time he sought and seemingly obtained the consent of the leaders of the *de facto* government for the entry of an American force into Mexican territory. Finally, he sent a Punitive Expedition, under the command of Brigadier General John J. Pershing, across the border on March 18. The dispatch of the Punitive Expedition would have provoked no crisis if Villa had been quickly apprehended. However, Villa cunningly led his pursuers deep into Mexico. The Punitive Expedition had penetrated more than 300 miles into northern Mexico by April 8, 1916, but Villa was still defiantly at large. At this point the Expedition halted and gave all appearances of becoming an army of occupation.

The President refused, contrary to advice of his military counselors, to withdraw Pershing's command. He made this fateful decision chiefly because the State Department was not convinced that Carranza was either able or willing to control the bandit gangs that menaced the American border. On the other hand, the Mexican leaders were beginning to suspect that Wilson intended to occupy northern Mexico permanently. As this suspicion grew they gave less attention to pursuing Villa and more to preparing for an inevitable showdown with the United States.

Neither government wanted war, yet a situation was developing that could lead only to hostilities. A skirmish between American and Mexican troops occurred at Parral on April 12 in which forty Mexicans were killed. Such a wave of anger swept over Mexico that Carranza could do nothing less than demand prompt withdrawal of the Expedition. The Washington government refused, and Carranza took two steps preparatory to a final reckoning. First, on May 22 he addressed a bitter note to the United States government, accusing it of warlike intentions; second, he ordered his field commanders to resist the American forces if they moved in any direction but toward the border. Wilson replied by calling practically the entire National Guard to the border on June 18, and by sending a stinging rebuke to Carranza on June 20, declaring that the United States would not withdraw the Expedition and warning that any attacks on American soldiers would lead to "the gravest consequences."

The *casus belli* occurred only a few hours after the American note of June 20 was delivered in the Mexican capital. An American patrol tried to force its way through a Mexican garrison at Carrizal, in northern Chihuahua. The Mexicans lost thirty men but killed twelve and captured twenty-three Americans. As first reports to Washington told of a treacherous ambush, Wilson demanded the immediate release of the prisoners and prepared a message to Congress asking for authority to occupy northern

Mexico, action that could have resulted only in full-scale war. He did not deliver the message because newspapers on June 26 published an account of the Carrizal incident written by an American officer on the spot. It revealed that the Americans had been guilty of an aggressive attack. A wave of revulsion immediately swept through the American people; Wilson was bombarded with appeals for peace from leaders in all walks of life; and war fever passed from Washington almost at once.

The upshot of the Carrizal affair was the eventual settlement of the most troubling phase of the Mexican-American trouble. Wilson agreed when Carranza suggested on July 4 the appointment of a Joint High Commission to investigate and recommend. American and Mexican commissioners met from September 6, 1916, through January 15, 1917, and pondered all aspects of the Mexican problem. The Joint High Commission broke up without agreement on January 15, 1917. Now Wilson had to choose between surrendering to Carranza's renewed demand for withdrawal or accepting the possibility of war with Mexico. As events were now inexorably drawing the United States into the European war, the President had no alternative but to yield. The withdrawal was begun on January 27, and a nearly tragic chapter in the history of American foreign relations was happily ended.

The recalling of the Punitive Expedition and Wilson's *de jure* recognition of Carranza's new constitutional regime on March 13, 1917, marked a momentous turning point in modern Mexican history. Henceforward the Mexican people could pursue their difficult progress toward democratic institutions free from outside control. Wilson in large measure had made this great opportunity possible. Singlehanded he had prevented the European powers from coming to Huerta's aid, assisted the Constitutionalists in deposing the usurper, and stood off powerful forces in the United States that sought the downfall of the Revolution. The tragedy was that while striving for worthy objectives Wilson interfered so often and in the wrong way that he alienated the friendship of the Mexican people and aroused the deepest suspicions of their leaders.

CHAPTER

8

The Road to War

1914–1917

AMERICANS on the eve of the most frightful holocaust in history to that time thought that they were still living in a secure international community, in which a benevolent British sea dominion and a fine world balance of power would operate almost automatically to protect the Monroe Doctrine without a huge American naval and military establishment. Then things suddenly went awry in 1914. German armies destroyed the balance on the Continent; German submarines threatened to destroy British control of the seas. The established international community had collapsed, and Americans found themselves at a crossroads in their history. Upon their reactions to the First World War depended not only the fate of Europe but the destiny of the United States as well.

66. *American Neutrality, 1914–1915*

To Americans who confidently believed that a general war was virtually impossible, the outbreak of the First World War came, as one North Carolinian wrote in November 1914, "as lightning out of a clear sky." The dominant American reaction in August 1914 was relief that America was far removed from the scene of conflict, coupled with conviction that the United States had no vital stake in the outcome. Even ardent champions of the Allies approved when President Wilson issued an official proclamation of neutrality on August 4 and, two weeks later, urged Americans to be impartial in thought as well as in deed.

To be sure, many Americans were unable to follow the President's injunction all the way. The United States was deluged from 1914 to 1917 with propaganda in behalf of the opposing alliances. Probably a majority of thoughtful Americans, concluding that Germany and Austria were primarily responsible for the war's outbreak, desired an Anglo-French victory. This generalization, however, obscures some important facts. First, Americans were not nearly so naive from 1914 to 1917 as a later generation believed. Many leaders of opinion recognized the complexity of the causes of the war, and a large number of spokesmen argued that Germany, along with Great Britain, was least responsible for beginning hostilities. Second, the Germans had full and free opportunity to present their cause before the American public and did so as skillfully as circumstances would allow. Third, Allied atrocity charges against the Germans played a minor role in shaping American opinion. Fourth, American opinion was influenced not so much by propaganda as by certain obvious facts: Germany's and Austria's refusal to submit the Serbian question to arbitration, German violation of Belgian neutrality and ruthless destruction of passenger liners, and German conspiracies and intrigues against American neutrality. Fifth, the fact that a majority of Americans were pro-Allied did not mean they also wanted to enter the war. On the contrary, the overwhelming majority of Americans before 1917 desired only to live at peace with Germany.

The sudden threat and then the outbreak of war in Europe in late July and early August of 1914 set off an economic panic in the United States and compelled the Wilson administration to take drastic steps to protect the domestic economy. To prevent unloading of securities by Europeans and a panic in Wall Street, the Stock Exchange was closed on July 31. To provide tonnage to carry American products to Europe, Congress amended the ship registry law to allow foreign ships to hoist the American flag.[1] Finally, in order to protect the nation's gold reserve, the administration adopted a policy of discouraging loans by American bankers to the belligerents. The President, however, permitted Secretary Bryan to say that the administration disapproved of private loans to belligerent governments because such loans violated the spirit of neutrality.

Meanwhile, Wilson had also begun negotiations to protect American neutral trade. Since the British soon swept German raiders from the seas and began slowly but inexorably to extend far-reaching controls against neutral trade with the Central Powers, the Washington government's early difficulties were all with Great Britain. By the end of February 1915, when the British system of maritime controls was severely tightened, the British Admiralty had mined the North Sea, laid down a long-range naval blockade of Germany and neutral Europe, and seized American ships carry-

---

[1] It should be added that Congress also established a War Risk Insurance Bureau to provide marine insurance at standard rates to American shippers, and that the administration attempted to obtain passage of a bill creating a federal shipping corporation capitalized at $30,000,000 and empowered to build or purchase ships and operate them in international trade. The House approved this, the so-called ship purchase bill; but Republican leaders in the Senate successfully blocked the bill, in February and March of 1915, on the grounds that it was socialistic and that federal operation of merchant ships might provoke a serious diplomatic crisis with Great Britain.

ing certain noncontraband,[2] particularly food, to Italy, Holland, and other European neutrals for transshipment to Germany.

The crucial question during this early period of the war was whether the United States would accept the British maritime system, some aspects of which probably exceeded the bounds of international law (or what neutrals had traditionally considered to be the laws governing war at sea), or would insist to the point of war upon freedom of trade with Germany in all noncontraband materials. The reaction of the United States as the principal neutral power was complicated by the inapplicability of many traditional rules to new weapons such as the mine and the submarine. Wilson's first impulse was to insist sternly upon full respect for American commercial rights. However, his most trusted adviser in foreign affairs, Colonel Edward M. House, persuaded him to avoid provoking a serious crisis. Instead, the President used friendly persuasion to obtain British adherence to the Declaration of London.[3] But the Foreign Office refused to be bound by that Declaration, and the President acquiesced and allowed the State Department to lodge firm but friendly protests that reserved American rights for future adjudication.

This decision was virtually inevitable. The British did control the seas, and their maritime measures were essentially grounded in the beginning on traditional law and custom. Under British control of the Atlantic, American *direct* trade with Germany and Austria declined from $169,289,775 in 1914 to $1,159,653 in 1916. During the same period American trade with the Allies increased from $824,800,237 to $3,214,480,547. In short, the United States became virtually an Allied warehouse, from which munitions, food, and other vital raw materials flowed in an increasing stream. This outcome, it should be emphasized, derived from British control of the seas, not from any official American favoritism. Indeed, the United States would have been altogether unneutral had it challenged legitimate use of British sea power.

The Allied-American war trade was not the only consequence of American acquiescence in the British sea measures. The system of international exchange began to collapse as Allied, and particularly British, purchases began to assume enormous proportions in the spring and summer of 1915. As it became evident that continued adherence to Bryan's ban against loans would destroy the only important foreign trade in which Americans could then engage, the administration, including Bryan himself, began gradually to retreat. Bryan opened the door to large-scale loans on March 31,

wwwwwwwwwwwwwww

[2] Under traditional international law, goods during wartime fall into three categories: (1) absolute contraband, that is, materials destined directly for the use of military forces; (2) conditional contraband, that is, goods susceptible of being used by military forces; and (3) noncontraband, or food, raw materials, and goods destined only for use by civilians. Under traditional law, a belligerent could seize and confiscate absolute contraband, had to prove that conditional contraband was destined for military forces in order to confiscate it, and was required to allow noncontraband to pass to its enemy.

[3] This was a code of maritime warfare drawn up by representatives of the maritime powers at London in 1908 and 1909 that imposed severe limitations on the use of sea power against neutral trade. It was never ratified by the British and American governments and did not, therefore, become a part of international law.

1915, by declaring that the State Department would not oppose a $50,000,-000 "commercial credit" by the House of Morgan to the French government.

Bryan's approval of the French commercial credit partially reversed the State Department's ban on loans. The issue was raised even more squarely when an Anglo-French commission came to the United States in September 1915 to negotiate an unsecured loan of $500,000,000. The State Department announced that it had no objections to the loan, thus specifically lifting the Bryan ban, and the United States soon became the arsenal of credit as well as of war materials for the Allies. American bankers advanced an additional $1,800,000,000 to the Allied governments to finance the war trade during the next eighteen months. Unlike the first Anglo-French loan, all later loans were secured 100 per cent by high-grade American and South American securities, and none was sold by public campaign.

These were some of the ties of trade and credit that bound the United States to the Allies by the autumn of 1915. It is important that we understand why the President approved policies that operated so powerfully to the advantage of one alliance. Perhaps one decisive factor in Wilson's decision to acquiesce in the British maritime system was his conviction, shared by many Americans in 1914 and 1915, that German methods and objectives were morally reprehensible and that the triumph in Europe of Imperial Germany, militaristic and expansive, would constitute a potential threat to the security of the United States. We can only surmise that this conviction played a vital role in policy.

We can be more certain that another factor decisively shaped Wilson's neutral policies. It was the fact that he had virtually no choice but to accept British sea measures and allow the United States to become an arsenal of the Allies. The President, roughly speaking, faced the following situation in 1914 and early 1915: On one side, the Germans had used superior land power to overrun Belgium and the industrial areas of France. On the other side, Great Britain had used superior naval power to control the Atlantic and keep open her indispensable sources of supply. In accomplishing these objectives both Germany and Great Britain violated traditional international law to varying degrees but operated within a traditional framework. Because the United States was not prepared to halt the German invasion of Belgium, the President withheld any condemnation of this violation of the European treaty system. Because he had no desire to insure a German victory, the President acquiesced in the British maritime system. Only if Great Britain had been fighting for objectives that imperiled American security would Wilson have been justified in attempting to deny to the British advantages flowing from their control of the seas.

67. *The German Submarine Challenge, 1915*

So long as Germany carried on her military operations within the traditional framework there could have been no possibility of conflict with the United States. When Germany used a new weapon, the submarine, to challenge British control of the seas, however, Wilson was compelled to re-examine his whole plan of neutrality. This was necessary because the

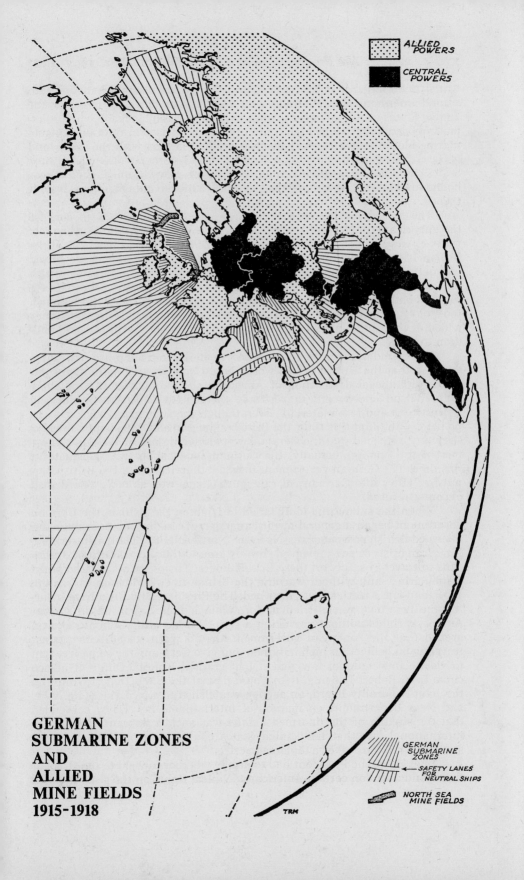

ALLIED
POWERS

CENTRAL
POWERS

GERMAN
SUBMARINE
ZONES
AND
ALLIED
MINE FIELDS
1915-1918

TRM

GERMAN
SUBMARINE
ZONES

SAFETY LANES
FOR
NEUTRAL SHIPS

NORTH SEA
MINE FIELDS

British and French governments responded to the submarine challenge with a total interdiction of all trade with the Central Powers. Hereafter the United States could no longer acquiesce in the British blockade without impairing friendly relations with Germany, nor acquiesce in the German submarine blockade without impairing friendly relations with the Allies and perhaps also guaranteeing a German victory. In other words, the United States could not be absolutely impartial in these new circumstances; it was bound to give an advantage and impose a disadvantage either way it turned.

The submarine issue arose in such a way, however, as to confuse the American people and their leaders. The German Admiralty on February 4, 1915, announced the inauguration of a submarine blockade of the British Isles. All enemy vessels in a broad war zone would be destroyed without warning; even neutral vessels would not be safe because of British misuse of neutral flags. The Imperial government, German spokesmen explained, had adopted this extreme measure in retaliation against the British food blockade. Germany would abandon her submarine blockade, they added, if the British abandoned their campaign to starve women and children.

Wilson addressed a note of reply to Berlin on February 10, 1915, warning that the United States would hold Germany to a "strict accountability" for illegal destruction of American ships and lives. At the same time, Wilson endeavored to persuade the British to lift their blockade against food and raw materials. Even though the submarine blockade was 90 per cent bluff at this time, the British agreed to allow foodstuffs to enter Germany, provided that the Germans would give up use of U-boats against merchant shipping. Actually, the German food supply was adequate at this time. The German government insisted, therefore, that the British permit free entry into Germany of raw materials as well as food. The British of course refused.

When the submarine bluff failed to frighten the British, the German government began a general terror campaign of sinking, without warning, unarmed British passenger vessels in the North Atlantic. The great German-American crisis of 1915 revolved entirely around the alleged right of Americans to travel in safety on these British liners. This issue was raised when a submarine sank without warning the British liner *Falaba* on March 28, 1915, and one American was drowned. The President and his advisers during the next five weeks tried to formulate a policy that would protect American rights without provoking a serious crisis with Germany. Bryan argued that the American government should warn its citizens against traveling on belligerent merchantmen and give Germany the same freedom to violate international law that it had granted Britain. Different advice came from Robert Lansing, then Counsellor of the State Department, and the Joint Neutrality Board, an agency established to advise the State, War, and Navy departments on matters of international law. They contended that the sinking of the unarmed *Falaba* was such a flagrant violation of international law that the United States could not avoid taking a firm stand, even if it provoked a diplomatic crisis.

In essence, the President had to decide whether to yield to the German threat and abandon certain American technical rights on the seas. It was a decision he did not want to make, and there is good evidence that he had decided not to press the *Falaba* case. However, an event occurred on May 7 that forced him to meet the German challenge to freedom of the seas —the sinking without warning of the British liner *Lusitania* off the coast of Ireland, with the death of more than 1200 noncombatants, including 128 Americans.

Americans were horrified, but few of them wanted to go to war. They applauded the President when he declared on May 10, "There is such a thing as a man being too proud to fight." Fervent appeals for peace poured into the White House. Democratic leaders in Congress warned that Wilson probably could not obtain passage of a war resolution. These appeals and warnings only strengthened Wilson's determination to find a peaceful solution. His first *Lusitania* note of May 13, 1915, invoked the rights of humanity in appealing to the Imperial German government to halt its campaign against unarmed merchantmen. The German Foreign Office replied evasively, and Wilson renewed his plea. And when the German government replied equivocally for a second time, Wilson was both conciliatory and stern in his third *Lusitania* note. He admitted that submarine operations might be conducted within traditional rules, provided that U-boat commanders warned their victims and provided for the safety of passengers and crews. On the other hand, he warned that the United States would regard a repetition of ruthless sinkings as "deliberately unfriendly." This was the language of ultimate diplomacy.

So eager was Bryan to avoid doing anything that might conceivably lead to war that he resigned on June 8, 1915, rather than sign the second *Lusitania* note. In contrast, Wilson was willing to risk war rather than yield what he thought was a deeply moral principle—respect for human life even during wartime. When a submarine sank the White Star liner *Arabic* on August 19, with the loss of two American lives, the President and his new Secretary of State, Lansing, resolved to force a showdown. This new crisis forced the German government to reveal that it had issued secret orders to U-boat commanders on June 6 to spare large passenger liners. It also prompted the German Emperor on August 26 to order total abandonment of unrestricted submarine operations against all passenger ships. Therefore, the German Ambassador in Washington informed Lansing on September 1 that unresisting liners would not be sunk without warning and without provision being made for the safety of passengers and crew.

The *Arabic* pledge preserved the peace and was a major diplomatic triumph for the President. Nonetheless, he could not have been encouraged by the perilous state of American foreign relations and the signs of disunity and confusion at home during the summer of 1915. There were numerous evidences of German conspiracies against American neutrality and of German intrigues to provoke conflict between the United States and Mexico. The secrets of the German propaganda organization came to light in August 1915, when its chief left a brief case full of documents on an elevated train in New York and the contents were published in the newspapers. Such exposures naturally intensified the anti-German sentiment that had grown by leaps and bounds since the sinking of the *Lusitania*. On the other hand, the great mass of Americans were still stubbornly op-

posed to a belligerent policy, while a minority, led by the Hearst press and
Irish- and German-American organizations, were loudly demanding an embargo on shipment of munitions to the Allies and a warning to American
citizens against traveling on Allied ships.

Meanwhile, the Washington government, after seeming to acquiesce
in the British blockade instituted in March 1915, had made it clear in a
note to the London Foreign Office on July 14, 1915, that the United
States meant to defend the rights of neutral trade. This was followed by a
long and stinging note to London on October 21. Denouncing the British
blockade as "ineffective, illegal, and indefensible," it seemed to signal the
beginning of a firm American defense of freedom of the seas against all
comers.

68.   The Diplomacy of Mediation, 1915–1916

It was not easy to know what to do in the face of strong demands at
home both for stern defense of American rights on the seas and preservation of peace almost at any price. Obviously, the surest way out of this
dilemma was to end the war by Wilson's mediation. Hope for peace ebbed
and flowed all during the period of American neutrality. In September and
December 1914, for example, the German Ambassador, Count von Bern-
storff, hinted that his government might be willing to evacuate and indem-
nify Belgium. The British Foreign Secretary, Sir Edward Grey, in turn,
intimated that the Allies would not refuse a reasonable German offer. At
Wilson's request, therefore, Colonel House went to Europe in January 1915
to explore the possibility of mediation. He found British officials willing
to discuss peace terms, provided that the Germans consented to evacuate
Belgium, disarm after the war was over, and give definite guarantees of a
future peaceful policy in Europe. But the Germans would make no promises, for they were not yet prepared to face the issue of Belgium's future.
House's first peace mission ended in failure.

The German refusal to co-operate for peace and the subsequent submarine controversy and revelations of German intrigues in the United
States convinced House and Lansing that German triumph in Europe
would gravely imperil future American security. Unlike Lansing, House
had no desire to destroy German power in Europe, for he regarded Germany as a bulwark against Russia. He concluded during the autumn of
1915 that circumstances demanded nothing less than positive action by
the United States to end the war and create a new international structure
that would safeguard American security. He thought that these goals could
be accomplished through co-operation between the United States and the
Allied governments in a drive for a reasonable peace.

House first revealed his plan to Wilson in October 1915 and with Wilson's consent broached the matter to Sir Edward Grey soon afterward.
Grey replied that the Allies might indeed be willing to consider a negotiated peace if the United States were prepared to join a postwar League of
Nations, and Wilson decided to send House to Europe for new talks. In
brief, Wilson and House envisaged close Allied and American co-operation
in forcing Germany to the peace table. If the Germans refused even to nego-

tiate, the United States would probably enter the war on the side of the Allies. On the other hand, if the German government agreed to negotiate, the United States would co-operate with the Allies at the peace conference in attempting to compel Germany to accept a reasonable settlement. Finally, if Germany withdrew from the conference and renewed hostilities, the United States would probably join the war on the Allied side.

Wilson certainly and House probably thought of armed intervention only as a last, desperate resort. They knew that there was grave danger of war if they continued to allow the German Admiralty indirectly to determine American foreign policy. They thought that the chances of obtaining a reasonable settlement through the President's mediation were good. But, they reasoned, even should the United States have to enter the war under House's plan, the nation would at least be acting on its own volition and in behalf of a cause worth fighting for—a just settlement and an effective postwar international organization. At least Americans would not be fighting merely to vindicate technical rights on the seas.

To carry forward this peace project, House arrived in London on January 6, 1916. After preliminary conferences with Grey and other British leaders, he went to Berlin and Paris, where conversations convinced him that mediation was impossible until the summer campaigns had ended. He was back in London in February and moved to bring the British to definite accord. House and Grey initialed a memorandum embodying their understanding on February 22, 1916. The President, it said, was ready to move for peace when the Allied governments gave the signal, and—although this was implied by what Grey said and was not included in the document—the Allies presumably would welcome Wilson's mediation according to the plan worked out by Colonel House.

Meanwhile, Wilson and Lansing on the other side of the water had embarked upon a separate diplomatic campaign that nearly wrecked House's negotiation, threatened to draw Germany and the United States into accord, and caused such a controversy in Congress that Wilson almost lost control of American foreign policy. The immediate background was the nearly successful conclusion in January and early February 1916 of Lansing's negotiations with the German government for settlement of the *Lusitania* affair. Even though the Germans were unwilling to admit the outright illegality of the sinking of the liner, they assumed liability for loss of American lives and offered a suitable indemnity.

The issue that set off a diplomatic and political explosion was a larger controversy over armed merchant ships. The State Department had issued regulations classifying defensively armed merchant ships as peaceful vessels months before the submarine challenge was raised. But the British not only armed merchant ships during 1915 but also ordered them to attack submarines, and Wilson and Lansing began to wonder whether it was fair to require submarines to surface before they attacked. Convinced that the American people did not want to go to war over the submarine issue, Lansing—with the President's approval—decided to try to find comprehensive understanding with the German government. On January 18, 1916, he sent the Allied governments a proposal for a new modus vivendi to govern maritime warfare. Repeating the German argument that any armed merchant ship was offensively armed in relation to the submarine, it suggested that the Allies disarm their merchant ships. More important, it warned that the American government was considering classifying armed merchantmen as auxiliary cruisers.[4]

Coming at the time when House was in London promoting intimate Anglo-American co-operation for peace, Lansing's modus vivendi struck like a bolt from a clear sky in the British capital. Sir Edward Grey remarked bitterly that the United States was proposing nothing less than destruction of the entire British merchant marine. Colonel House at once perceived the incongruity of his government's proposing a close entente with Great Britain at the very time that it was threatening to adopt a policy that might lead to Britain's defeat. House therefore urged Lansing to hold his proposal in abeyance. Before the Secretary of State could withdraw his modus vivendi, however, the German government, on February 10, 1916, announced that its submarines would sink all armed merchant ships without warning beginning on February 29.

Instead of acquiescing, Lansing declared on February 15 that the United States would *not* warn its citizens against traveling on ships armed for limited defense. Democratic leaders in Congress, baffled by this seeming reversal, and alarmed by the thought of going to war to protect Americans traveling on armed belligerent merchantmen, went to the White House on February 21 to protest. But Wilson stood firm and declared that he would hold Germany to strict account. News of the President's response provoked panic in the House of Representatives. Democratic members of the foreign affairs committee agreed unanimously to demand prompt action on a resolution offered by Representative Jeff McLemore of Texas, warning Americans against traveling on armed ships, while Democratic leaders in the House visited the President again in the morning of February 25 to warn that the McLemore Resolution would pass by a two-to-one margin. Moreover, Senator Thomas P. Gore of Oklahoma introduced an identical resolution in the upper house soon after Democratic House leaders returned from their conference at the White House.

Wilson acted with customary boldness in this great challenge to his leadership, and he won the tabling of the Gore and McLemore resolutions after a bitter parliamentary struggle. But because he refused for reasons of security to explain his stand, many Democratic leaders began to suspect that he meant to take the country into war. Actually, Wilson had repudiated Lansing's proposed modus vivendi because he realized that he would destroy completely his standing as a mediator among the Allies and give tremendous military advantage to Germany if he insisted upon its adoption.

Events soon gave Wilson an opportunity to force a final reckoning with Germany without raising the issue of armed ships. A submarine torpedoed without warning an unarmed Channel packet, the *Sussex,* with eighty casualties on March 24, 1916. After agonizing deliberation, Wilson went before a joint session of Congress on April 18 and read the terms of an ultimatum that he had just sent to Berlin: the United States would sever

---

[4] Such action by the United States government would in effect have excluded armed merchantmen from American ports, for under international law belligerent warships could stay only twenty-four hours in a neutral port and could purchase only enough fuel to reach their nearest home ports.

relations if the Imperial government did not abandon its unrestricted submarine operations against all shipping, belligerent and neutral.

Wilson's ultimatum brought to a head a controversy over submarine policy then going on in Germany between the military and civilian branches of the government. Discussion convinced the Emperor that the Admiralty did not have enough submarines to conduct a successful blockade or to justify bringing the United States into the war. He announced submission to the President's demands on May 1. The German Foreign Office informed the State Department three days later that henceforth submarine commanders would observe the rules of visit and search before sinking merchant vessels. But the note ended with a warning that Germany reserved freedom of action and might again resort to intensified submarine warfare if the United States did not compel the British to observe international law concerning neutral trade. So complete was the German surrender in this so-called *Sussex* pledge that the tension between the two governments diminished almost at once.

69. *The Preparedness Controversy, 1914–1916*

The great German-American crisis of 1915–16 had an impact on the American people more powerful than the shock caused by the war's outbreak. Among a small minority it stimulated the conviction that the United States could not safely permit the triumph of German militarism in Europe and the destruction of British sea power. Much more important was the fact that the submarine crisis caused many Americans for the first time to realize that they lived in a chaotic international community; that force, not reason, was the final arbiter in disputes between nations; and that the United States because of its military weakness was practically powerless to affect the outcome of the war in Europe or even to protect its own security.

The debate over military and naval policy began even before the submarine controversy broke out. Theodore Roosevelt, the Army League, the Navy League, the newly formed National Security League, and a small group in Congress tried vainly during the autumn of 1914 to tell the people of their military weakness. The public was apathetic, and the administration was opposed to increased armaments. Preparedness advocates were quick to seize the opportunity afforded by the submarine controversy. Beginning in the spring of 1915, they poured out articles and books in a virtual flood.

Wilson knew that he could not continue to oppose preparedness without giving the Republicans a formidable issue for the presidential campaign of 1916. However, it would be inaccurate to say that only political considerations shaped his thinking on the subject after the *Lusitania* crisis. He knew the weaknesses of the American military establishment better than most other men. He knew the disadvantage of dealing from weakness in diplomacy. He therefore shifted ground. On July 21, 1915, he requested his Secretaries of War and of the Navy to recommend programs that would satisfy the needs of national security.

The General Board of the Navy proposed adoption of a long-range construction program to give the United States naval equality with Great Britain by 1925.[5] The Army War College proposed a substantial increase in the regular army, scrapping the National Guard, and creation of a volunteer national reserve—a so-called Continental Army—of 400,000 men as the first line of defense. The President presented this as the administration's program in an address on November 4, 1915, and in so doing set off one of the most violent political controversies of the decade.

The issues went deeper than any mere difference of opinion over military policy. The great majority of American progressives were obsessed with a passion for domestic social and economic reform. They believed that wars were always caused by bankers, industrialists, and scheming diplomats. Inevitably they reacted with startled indignation to the President's proposals. To them Wilson was at best a dupe, at worst, a turncoat willing to betray the cause of progressivism and convert the country into an armed camp. Led by Bryan and numerous peace organizations, anti-preparedness spokesmen launched a campaign with a powerful appeal to workingmen and farmers.

A group of some thirty to fifty Democrats in Congress, most of them Southerners and Westerners, formed an anti-preparedness bloc to wrest control of policy from the President. Through Claude Kitchin of North Carolina, House majority leader, Democratic anti-preparedness congressmen were able to pack the key House military affairs committee when Congress met in December 1915. They were immovable when Secretary of War Lindley M. Garrison urged the most important feature of the Army's reorganization plan—abandonment of the National Guard and creation of the new Continental Army. Army spokesmen asserted that the National Guard of the states could never be effectively integrated into the national defense structure because of constitutional limitations. The military affairs committee countered with a plan to "federalize" the National Guard, that is, to subject state forces to comprehensive federal control, and to scrap entirely the Continental Army plan.

The administration and the House Democratic leaders were in hopeless deadlock by the middle of January 1916. Wilson decided to carry the issue to the people. In an extended speaking tour in late January and early February he urged preparedness as a national cause and pleaded for the Continental Army plan. He returned to Washington on February 4, however, to find his Democratic opponents more inflexible than before. Consequently Wilson yielded to the House leaders in order to obtain any legislation, and this provoked Secretary Garrison to resign on February 10. He was succeeded by the less intransigent Newton D. Baker of Cleveland, a progressive opponent of preparedness.

Garrison's resignation cleared the road, and the House adopted an army reorganization bill on March 23, 1916. It merely increased the regular army from 100,000 to 140,000 men and enlarged and brought the National Guard under control of the War Department. Then came the *Sussex* crisis. As the nation waited for word of peace or war from Berlin, preparedness champions in the Senate pushed through a measure that em-

[5] The General Board's plan envisaged construction during the first five years of ten battleships, six battle cruisers, ten cruisers, fifty destroyers, one hundred submarines, and lesser craft, at a total cost of $500,000,000.

bodied most of the War College's proposals, including a Continental Army. But the *Sussex* crisis had passed by the time that the House and Senate conferees resolved their differences in mid-May, and the measure that they approved embodied mutual concessions. The Army Reorganization bill, which Wilson signed on June 3, 1916, increased the regular army to 11,327 officers and 208,338 men; integrated the National Guard into the national defense structure and increased its authorized strength; and permitted the War Department to establish a number of volunteer summer training camps.

Meanwhile, the naval affairs committees of the two houses had been biding their time. Although most progressives in principle opposed unusual naval expansion, they concentrated their main energies on the army bill. The House on June 2, 1916, approved a bill that ignored the administration's request for a five-year building program but actually provided more tonnage than Secretary of the Navy Josephus Daniels had requested for the first year. The Senate went even further and adopted a bill on July 21 that provided for completion of the five-year building program in three years. It authorized construction during the first year of four battleships, four battle cruisers, four cruisers, twenty destroyers, thirty submarines, and a number of lesser craft. Up to this time the President had not interfered in the course of naval legislation. Now he used all his influence to persuade the House leaders to accept the Senate bill. The House capitulated on August 15, 1916, by accepting the important provisions of the Senate measure without altering a word.

The President rounded out his preparedness program three days later when the Senate approved a much revised and strengthened shipping bill. The ship purchase bill of 1915 had provided merely for federal ownership and operation of a shipping line. In contrast, the Merchant Marine Act of 1916, as the new measure was called, authorized appointment of a United States Shipping Board, empowered not only to own and operate merchant ships but also to regulate the rates and services of all vessels engaged in the interstate, coastwise, and foreign commerce of the United States. Moreover, the measure forbade the Shipping Board to purchase belligerent merchant ships, thus avoiding another pitfall of the ship purchase bill of 1915.

Thus far the President had had his way, at least in naval and merchant marine policies. The last victory belonged to the anti-preparedness radicals in finding new revenues to pay for military and naval expansion. Conservatives proposed to meet the entire cost by a bond issue and increased consumption taxes. Rejecting the suggestion of a bond issue, Secretary of the Treasury McAdoo presented a tax plan in November 1915 that threw the burden as much on the lower and middle classes as on the rich.

Spokesmen of progressive, farm, and labor groups were up in arms, demanding that the wealthy classes, whom they blamed for forcing preparedness on the country, pay the full bill. This ground swell had an immediate impact on the southern and western Democrats who controlled the House ways and means committee. Their measure, adopted by the House on July 10, was a far cry from McAdoo's proposal. It doubled the normal income tax, without lowering exemptions; raised the maximum surtax from 6 to 10 per cent; levied a tax of from 1 to 8 per cent on gross receipts of munitions manufacturers; imposed a new federal estate tax ranging from 1 to 5 per cent; and repealed special consumption taxes that had been imposed in 1914. In the Senate, midwestern progressives like George W. Norris of Nebraska and Robert M. La Follette forced even further changes,[6] so that the Revenue Act of 1916 represented a frank effort to "soak the rich." It was Populism and Bryanism finally triumphant—an important victory in the equalitarian attack on privileged wealth in the United States.

70.   *The Campaign and Election of 1916*

Not since 1910 had the American political scene seemed so confused as during the early months of 1916. The President's preparedness program and armed ship stand had nearly disrupted the Democratic party. Bryan was in a rebellious mood, threatening to bolt the party if Wilson made further warlike moves. On the other hand, Republicans were even more divided than their opponents. The eastern wing of the GOP was demanding tremendous military and naval increases, and the eastern leaders, Roosevelt, Elihu Root, and Henry Cabot Lodge, were beginning a fierce denunciation of the President for his allegedly cowardly refusal to defend American rights on the seas and in Mexico. In contrast, the great majority of midwestern Republican voters and leaders bitterly opposed further preparedness and wanted peace even at the price of abandoning rights on the seas.

Democrats closed ranks after Wilson's surrender during the battle over the army bill and after the peaceful settlement of the *Sussex* crisis. It was obvious by the middle of May that there would be no Democratic rupture, although it was not yet clear what position that party would take on foreign policy during the coming campaign. The key to the future was the alignment of former Progressives—whether they would follow Roosevelt back into the Republican party or would be won to the Democratic party by Wilson's espousal of advanced progressive measures. (See above, pp. 133–136.)

The chief task before the Republicans was to find a candidate and write a platform that would hold the conservative East without alienating the progressive, pacifistic Midwest and West. At the Republican national convention which opened in Chicago on June 8, 1916, the party managers rejected Roosevelt, who had made a hard fight for the nomination, and chose instead Charles Evans Hughes, former governor of New York and now an Associate Justice of the Supreme Court. Nomination of the progressive Hughes and adoption of a platform demanding "a straight and honest neutrality" and only "adequate" preparedness was, in the circumstances, an outright repudiation of Roosevelt's demands for a strong policy toward Germany and an effort to appease both the Middle West and the important German-American element. Roosevelt was disgruntled and disap-

wwwwwwwwwwwwww

[6] The Senate increased the surtax to a maximum of 13 per cent; levied a new tax on corporation capital, surplus, and undivided profits; increased the estate tax to a maximum of 10 per cent; and increased to 12½ per cent the maximum tax on munitions manufacturers. All these amendments were accepted by the House.

pointed, but he was so eager to avoid another four years of what he called Wilson's cowardly infamy that he disbanded his Progressive party and took to the field for Hughes.

The Democrats assembled in national convention in St. Louis on June 14. They dutifully approved the platform that Wilson and his advisers had prepared; [7] and they cheerfully renominated the President on June 15. Otherwise Wilson's plans for the convention went awry. He had planned that the convention should make "Americanism" and patriotism the keynotes of the coming campaign. Instead, the convention gave one long and tremendous ovation for peace, as delegates stormed and demonstrated when speakers extolled Wilson's success in keeping the country out of war.

The campaign that followed was full of strange surprises, but soon a clear pattern of issues emerged. Hughes tried to avoid a straightforward discussion of neutrality and was unable to attack the Democratic reforms of the past three years without seeming reactionary. He finally concentrated his main fire on Wilson's Mexican policy and alleged Democratic inefficiency. Everywhere that he spoke he made votes for Wilson by petty criticisms and failure to offer any constructive alternatives. While Hughes was thus trying to hold the Middle and Far West for the GOP, Roosevelt was barnstorming the East, calling for universal military training and heroic defense of American rights.

Wilson was unable to enter the campaign until September because of a threatened nation-wide strike for the eight-hour day by the railroad brotherhoods. He averted this catastrophe by forcing through Congress the Adamson Act, which established the eight-hour day as the standard for all interstate railroad workers. Once this crisis was over Wilson, on September 23, began a series of speeches that left Republicans dazed. Hughes, thinking that he had finally discovered an issue, denounced the Adamson Act as a craven surrender to the railroad workers. Wilson replied that the eight-hour day was the goal for which all workers should strive. Hughes denounced the Democrats for lacking a constructive program. Wilson replied by pointing to the most sweeping reform program in the history of the country.

Hughes's straddling and Wilson's bold defense of progressivism caused such a division on domestic issues as the country had not seen since 1896. The left wing of the progressive movement, including many Socialists, single taxers, sociologists, social workers, and intellectuals and their journals, moved en masse into the Wilson ranks. Most of the leaders of the Progressive party repudiated Roosevelt and came out for the President. The railroad brotherhoods, the AF of L, and several powerful farm organizations worked hard for the Democratic ticket. Finally, virtually all important independent newspapers and magazines came to Wilson's support. Thus a new political coalition that included practically all independent progressives came into being during the campaign of 1916 as a result of Wilson's

wwwwwwwwwwwww

[7] The Democratic platform made an open bid for Progressive support by promising adoption of an advanced program of federal social legislation, endorsed a neutral foreign policy, and commended the administration's program of "reasonable" preparedness. It also endorsed the proposal then being put forward by various groups for the establishment of a postwar League of Nations.

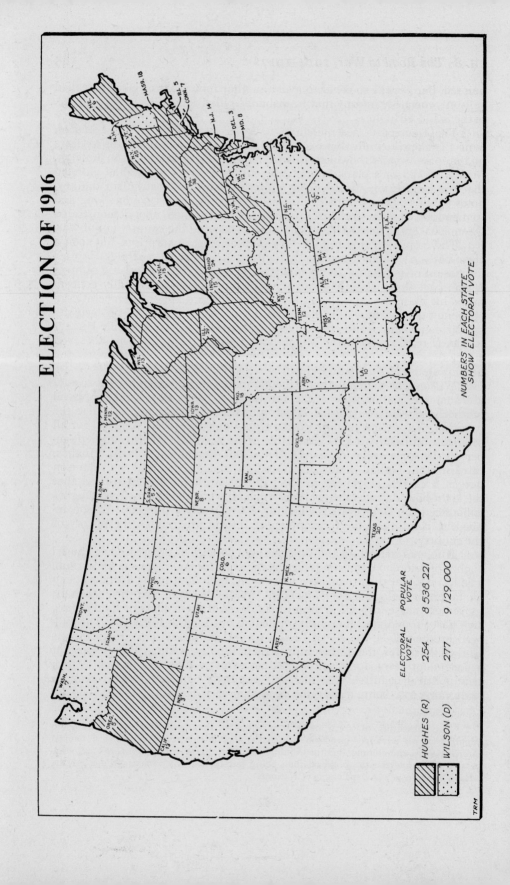

ELECTION OF 1916

WASH. 7
OREG. 5
CALIF. 13
NEV. 3
IDAHO 4
MONT. 4
UTAH 4
ARIZ. 3
WYO. 3
COLO. 6
N. MEX. 3
N. DAK. 5
S. DAK. 5
NEBR. 8
KANS. 10
OKLA. 10
TEXAS 20
MINN. 12
IOWA 13
MO. 18
ARK. 9
LA. 10
WIS. 13
ILL. 29
MICH. 15
IND. 15
OHIO 24
KY. 13
TENN. 12
MISS. 10
ALA. 12
GA. 14
FLA. 6
S.C. 9
N.C. 12
W. VA. 7
VA. 12
MD. 8
DEL. 3
N.J. 14
PA. 38
N.Y. 45
CONN. 7
R.I. 5
MASS. 18
ME. 9
VT. 4
N.H. 4

NUMBERS IN EACH STATE
SHOW ELECTORAL VOTE

	ELECTORAL VOTE	POPULAR VOTE
HUGHES (R)	254	8 538 221
WILSON (D)	277	9 129 000

TRM

and the Democratic party's straightforward espousal of reform legislation.

To interpret this campaign solely in terms of domestic issues, however, would be to miss its chief development: the fusion of progressivism with the peace cause that the President and his campaigners accomplished. Wilson was profoundly impressed by the peace demonstrations at St. Louis at the very time that he was growing suspicious of the Allies. Unhesitatingly, he took personal command of the peace movement. He charged that the Republicans were a war party, and that Hughes's election would mean almost certain war with Mexico and Germany. By implication he promised to keep the country out of war. So overwhelming was the response in the Middle West to the peace appeal that Democratic orators took up the battle cry. "He kept us out of war" became the constant refrain of campaign speeches and the chief theme of Democratic campaign literature.

It seemed at first that the President had not performed the miracle of converting the normal Democratic minority into a majority.[8] Early returns on election night, November 7, revealed that Hughes had made nearly a clean sweep of the East and of the eastern Middle West. But the tide turned suddenly in Wilson's favor as returns from the trans-Mississippi West came in. To the core of the Solid South Wilson added New Hampshire, Ohio, Kansas, Nebraska, North Dakota, Montana, Wyoming, Colorado, New Mexico, Arizona, Utah, Nevada, Idaho, Washington, and California—for a total of 277 electoral votes and a majority of twenty-three. He received 9,129,000 popular votes, as against 8,538,221 for Hughes. It was a gain for the President of nearly 3,000,000 votes over 1912.

The causes of Wilson's breath-taking victory became apparent soon after the returns were in. Democratic promises of continued peace, prosperity, and progressive policies won most independents, a large minority of former Progressives, women voters in the suffrage states, and the left-wing element that usually voted the Socialist ticket. The defection to Wilson of some 400,000 persons who had voted Socialist in 1912 was alone sufficient to give the President a majority in key states like California. These advanced progressives when added to the normal Democratic minority gave Wilson a bare majority and enabled the Democrats narrowly to control Congress for another two years.

71. *The United States Enters the War*

Let us now go back to the story of American relations with the belligerents where we left it at the end of the *Sussex* crisis. The *Sussex* pledge greatly relieved the tension in German-American relations, and events soon afterward cast a dark shadow over relations between the United States and Great Britain. To begin with, Sir Edward Grey made it plain during the spring and summer that the Allies would not welcome the President's mediation so long as they had any hope of military victory. To Wilson and House this was a crushing blow, almost a betrayal; they began to suspect that the Allies desired a vindictive peace, not a righteous settle-

<hr>

[8] Taft and Roosevelt in 1912 had received a combined vote 1,323,728 larger than Wilson's total vote.

ment. Secondly, American opinion was profoundly shocked by the British army's ruthless suppression of the abortive Irish Easter Rebellion of April 24, 1916. "The Dublin executions," observed the *New Republic*, "have done more to drive America back to isolation than any other event since the war began."

Really dangerous Anglo-American tension rose during the summer and autumn as the British intensified their economic warfare in a supreme effort to bring all neutral commerce, even shipping, under their control. These new measures included seizure of parcels in the American mails and publication of a "blacklist" of firms in the United States and the rest of the neutral world suspected of trading with the Central Powers, with which no British subject could deal in any way. Finally, the British attempted to compel American shipowners to submit to the control of the British Admiralty in return for the privilege of buying coal in British ports. Against these new infringements of American neutral rights the State Department protested in menacing language, while the President in September obtained power from Congress to use the armed forces against any nation that discriminated against American commerce.

Wilson could neither take steps to bring the British to book nor launch a peace campaign of his own so long as the nation was in the throes of a presidential campaign. Once the election was over, however, he faced a situation that demanded speedy and decisive action. Both sides were now resolved to use their most desperate weapons to break a deadlock that was consuming manpower and resources at a prodigious rate. For Great Britain this meant further intensification of economic warfare. For Germany it meant revoking the *Sussex* pledge and launching a wholesale campaign against maritime commerce.

To preserve American neutrality in the face of an all-out struggle on the seas would be virtually impossible, and yet that was what the American people wanted Wilson to do. The only way to peace and safety, the President knew, was to bring the war to an end. Yet this would be difficult to achieve in view of continued British hostility to peace negotiations. Wilson obviously had no alternative but to seek peace through co-operation with the German government, which, since the end of the *Sussex* crisis, had been urging him to take leadership in a drive for peace. The President informed House and Lansing on November 14 and 15, 1916, that he had decided to try to end the war. But what would happen, House and Lansing asked, if the Germans agreed to a reasonable settlement and the Allies refused? In that event would not the United States be driven into sympathetic alliance with Germany against the Allies? Wilson replied that he was willing to run this risk. He obviously did not think that it was very great.

While Wilson continued these discussions, civilian and military leaders in Berlin concluded that the success of their recent campaign in Rumania had created a situation favorable to a peace move. They drafted terms that would have assured German mastery of Europe; agreed that Wilson should be used only to force the Allies to the peace table and then ignored during the actual conference discussions; and resolved to begin an all-out submarine campaign if their peace move failed. When Wilson did not move quickly enough, the German government, on December 12, invited its enemies to a peace conference.

Wilson backed up the German overture on December 18 by calling upon the belligerents to define the objectives for which they were fighting. He next undertook highly secret negotiations with the German and British governments looking toward peace. The British Cabinet sent word that it was willing to negotiate on liberal terms, but the German Foreign Office was evasive and finally informed the President that it did not desire his presence at the peace table. Meanwhile, Wilson went before the Senate on January 22, 1917, to clarify the American position and to explain what kind of a peace settlement the United States would be willing to help enforce. It must be a peace among equals, he said, a "peace without victory," without indemnities and annexations.

The tragic irony was that the kind of settlement Wilson outlined was possible only if the German leaders were willing to accept a draw and co-operate with Wilson in forcing the Allies to abandon their own equally extreme objectives. Unfortunately, the men in control of the German government did not trust the American President and had abandoned all hope of peace through negotiation. They gave their answer to Wilson's appeal on January 31, 1917: after February 1 submarines would sink without warning all ships, belligerent and neutral, in a broad zone around Great Britain, France, and Italy, and in the eastern Mediterranean. The German Admiralty would allow one American ship to sail weekly between New York and Falmouth, England, provided that the ship were suitably marked.

Wilson in response broke diplomatic relations with Germany on February 3, 1917, but he was still hopeful that the Germans would not carry out their threats against American commerce. He continued to pray during the remainder of February that events would not force the nation into war. Meanwhile, demand for protective arming of American ships grew on all sides as more and more ships stayed at their berths and goods began to pile up in warehouses and on wharves. At first Wilson stubbornly refused, saying that the country was not willing to run the risk of war. However, he received a message from Ambassador Walter Page in London on February 25 that removed all his doubts as to German intentions. It was a dispatch transmitting a message, intercepted and deciphered by the British, from the German Foreign Secretary, Arthur Zimmermann, to the German Minister in Mexico City. In the event that Germany and the United States went to war, Zimmermann's message read, the Minister should propose to the Mexican government an alliance by which Mexico would join the war against the United States and receive as reward "the lost territory in Texas, New Mexico, and Arizona." Moreover, the Minister should request President Carranza to invite Japan to join the new anti-American coalition. Further indication of German intentions came on the same day that Wilson received the Zimmermann telegram, February 25. A submarine sank the British liner *Laconia* without warning off the Irish coast with the loss of American life.

Wilson on the following day asked Congress for authority, first, to arm American ships for defense and, second, to employ other measures to protect American commerce on the high seas. There was little objection in either house to giving the President authority simply to arm merchantmen. But there was overwhelming opposition to empowering him to wage an undeclared naval war. Wilson tried to force Congress's hand by giving the

Zimmermann message to the Associated Press, which published it on March 1. A tremendous surge of anger swept over the country, but a small group of western and southern radicals in the Senate stood firm. Refusing to abdicate the war-making power to the President, this "little group of willful men," as Wilson labeled them, insisted on talking the armed ship bill to death in the closing hours of the Sixty-fourth Congress.

Events from this point on led straight to war. The President announced on March 9 that he would put guns and naval crews on merchant vessels and called Congress into special session for April 16. German submarines on March 18 sank three American merchant vessels without warning and with great loss of life. The demand for war, which had heretofore been largely confined to the East, now spread to the South and West. And at this moment of excitement came the first Russian Revolution, which overthrew the autocratic government and established a liberal constitutional regime. To many Americans who had feared Russian anti-Semitism and despotism more than German militarism, the news from Petrograd ended all doubts as to the issues of the war.

The country tottered on the brink of war, but Wilson brooded in despair. The German submarine campaign was obviously succeeding; the Allies were on the verge of financial and military collapse. And yet the President hesitated. War, he told a friend, would brutalize the American people and cause them to forget that tolerance and mercy ever existed. Much of his despair stemmed from knowledge that events beyond his control were pushing the country blindly into war merely to defend American rights on the seas. In other words, the American people, without knowing what the war was about or what its outcome would be, were going to war to defend the right to be neutral!

Yet Wilson accepted the decision for war that his advisers were urging upon him. Having moved up the date for the convening of Congress, he went before the joint session on April 2 and asked for a resolution recognizing that a state of war existed as a result of actions of the Imperial government. After recounting the German aggressions against American neutrality, he tried to find moral justification for leading the American people into this "most terrible and disastrous of all wars." The world, he declared, must be made safe for democracy and led to a universal dominion of righteousness through a concert of free peoples. Thus Wilson did not urge American participation on the ground that it was essential to American security. Rather, he sounded a clarion call for a crusade to free mankind from the twin scourges of war and political oppression. There was opposition in both houses from anti-war progressives, but the Senate approved the war resolution on April 4, and the House concurred two days later.

Who willed American participation? Radicals and Socialists gave an answer in 1917 that was reiterated many times in the 1930's: The United States had been driven to war by businessmen, bankers, and munitions manufacturers. These enemies of the people had worked in devious ways to protect their profitable trade and enormous investments in an Allied victory. Moreover, this argument went on, Americans had been deceived by cunning propagandists into believing that the Allies were fighting for righteous objectives. The basic trouble, professors of international law added, was that the American government had not been truly neutral.

Obviously no such simple generalizations explain the complex causes for the decision for war in 1917. There is no evidence that bankers and businessmen affected that decision in any important way, and the effect of propaganda has been vastly overrated. In the final analysis it was Wilson, influenced by public opinion and his own conception of right and duty, who made the important decisions that shaped American policy. In the beginning he pursued a course of more or less strict neutrality that favored the Allies because the British controlled the seas. Then, as the British rejected his leadership in his drive for peace in the spring and summer of 1916, the President moved toward a policy of independent mediation. The Germans would have found a friend in the White House eager to join hands with them in 1916–17 if they had wanted a reasonable settlement and evinced a readiness to co-operate in building a peaceful and secure postwar world.

In view of the pacific state of American public opinion and Wilson's own convictions at the beginning of 1917, it is reasonable to assume that there would have been no war between Germany and the United States had the German government stayed at least technically within the bounds of the *Sussex* pledge. The German leaders knew this, just as they knew that their plan for all-out warfare against commerce would inevitably drive the United States to war. But after much doubt and conflict among themselves, they rejected American friendship and co-operation and chose to run the risks of American belligerency because they did not trust Wilson and had concluded that their only hope lay in a desperate bid for all-out victory. In German hands, in the final analysis, lay the decision for war or peace with America.

CHAPTER

9

The American Democracy at War

THE AMERICAN PEOPLE entered the First World War on a Wilsonian note of idealism, not really knowing what the struggle was about or the objectives for which their new friends and enemies were fighting. A recognition of this fact caused President Wilson to attempt to give a moral and altruistic meaning to American participation, to depict intervention in terms of the strong and pure democracy putting on the breastplate of righteousness to do battle for the Lord.

For their earlier refusal to heed all warnings that they had a vital stake in the outcome of the war, the American people paid a fearful price in divisions and doubts and organized efforts to sell the war to them. Nearly fatal was the almost utter lack of readiness for a great military and industrial effort. American unpreparedness and inability to retaliate had been the key factor in the German decision to launch unrestricted submarine warfare in 1917. More important still, the inability of the United States to throw a powerful army without delay into the battle in France prolonged the war and increased the danger of German victory.

In a stumbling manner, however, the American democracy organized for war. The industrial and military mobilization thus hastily accomplished produced the food, materials, ships, and manpower that tipped the balance and broke the deadlock on the western front in 1918. Let us now see how this was done, and at what price.

72. *Raising an Army to Save the Allies*

Neither Wilson nor his military advisers understood the weakness of the Allied military situation in the spring of 1917. Americans had assumed as a matter of course since 1914 that the Allies would win. Most Americans visualized their contribution in terms only of shipping, naval support, credit, and materials even after it was evident that the United States would enter the war. Allied war missions to Washington soon gave different advice.

Wilson and his advisers were shocked when British and French generals revealed that their governments were beginning to draw upon their last reserves. Fortunately, the Army War College had made plans for raising a large American army. The question of how this army should be raised had been hotly debated in Congress during the months preceding the adoption of the war resolution. And administration and army officials, as well as a large segment of thoughtful opinion, had agreed that conscription offered the only rational and democratic method. Even so, the selective service bill, presented to Congress soon after the adoption of the war resolution, set off a bitter struggle in the House of Representatives. Wilson insisted that conscription was essential to victory. In the end he had his way, although there was a hard struggle over age limits, sale of alcoholic beverages at or near army camps, and volunteer units. In the measure that Wilson signed on May 18, 1917, the House won its fight to set the minimum age at twenty-one instead of nineteen, as the army demanded, and the Anti-Saloon League won another victory over Demon Rum.

The issue of volunteer units set off a more violent storm because Theodore Roosevelt had already prepared to recruit a full division and to take it to France at once. The Rough Rider was fifty-eight and half-blind but still full of courage, and the French were eager to welcome his division to the western front. Wilson and Baker were determined that the army should not be plagued with political generals and were totally unmoved by Roosevelt's pleading. Roosevelt then appealed to friends in Congress to force Wilson to accept his division; but the Selective Service Act merely authorized without compelling the President to accept up to 500,000 volunteers, and Roosevelt did not get his command.

Secretary Baker, remembering the widespread rioting and bloodshed that had accompanied the draft in 1863, enlisted state and local officials in making the first registration on June 5, 1917, a nation-wide demonstration of patriotism. On that date 9,586,508 men between the ages of twenty-one and thirty-one registered without commotion, riot, or organized resistance. Congress on August 31, 1918, expanded the age limits to include all men between eighteen and forty-five. All told, draft boards registered 24,234,021 men, of whom 6,300,000 were found to be available and 2,810,-296 were inducted into the army. In addition, volunteer enlistments in the army, navy, and marine corps brought the total number of men and women under arms by November 1918 to 4,800,000.

Experience soon proved that it was easier to raise a vast new army than to equip it. Military leaders had thought and planned before 1917 in terms of an emergency force of 500,000 men. Thus the army had only

THE UNITED STATES ARMY
IN WORLD WAR I

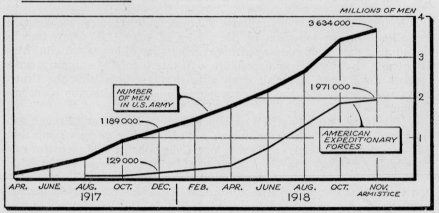

600,000 Springfield rifles, some 2,000 machine guns, and 900 pieces of field artillery on hand when the war resolution was adopted. There were ample facilities in the United States in 1917 to supply all the munitions, small arms, and machine guns that the army needed. But it was a different story with artillery and other heavy equipment, and the American army would have been miserably equipped had not British and French producers been able to fill these vital needs. American factories were converted to the production of heavy guns on a large scale, but output did not reach high gear until after the Armistice; and only 500 of the 3,500 artillery pieces used by the American forces in France were turned out in the United States. Moreover, American industry was totally unprepared to manufacture those new weapons of war, the tank and the airplane, and the much-vaunted Yankee ingenuity did not effect the miracle that circumstances demanded. Only sixty-four small six-ton tanks had been produced in the United States by the end of the war. An Aircraft Production Board, after several bad starts and crises, concentrated on a redesigned De Haviland bomber, 1,185 of which had been shipped to France by November 1918, and an all-purpose airplane engine—the twelve-cylinder Liberty motor—5,460 of which had been delivered by the end of the war.

73. *The American Military Contribution*

For commander of the projected American Expeditionary Force the President and Secretary of War ignored the most popular general, Leonard Wood, whom they regarded as an insubordinate trouble maker. They turned instead to Major General John J. Pershing, who had recently commanded the Punitive Expedition in Mexico. Arriving in Paris on June 14, 1917, to establish the headquarters of the A.E.F., Pershing quickly realized that the Allies were militarily almost bankrupt and obsessed by a passion for defense. He looked forward to the day when he would command a great fresh army that would lead the British and French out of their trenches. Pointing

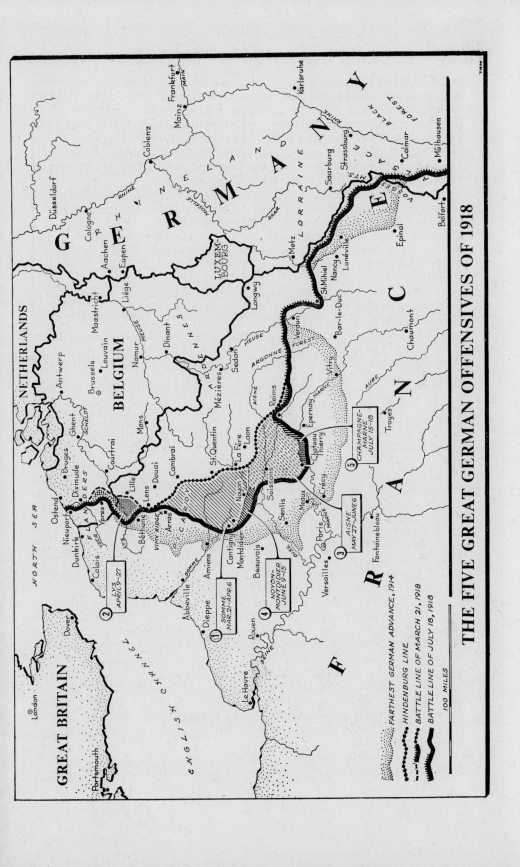

THE FIVE GREAT GERMAN OFFENSIVES OF 1918

to the obvious fact that a large American force could neither be assembled nor transported to the front for many months to come, Allied military leaders argued that available American troops should be integrated into the existing defensive structure and subordinated to Allied field commanders. However, Pershing stubbornly insisted on preserving the identity and integrity of his command and even demanded a share of the front. The French command gave him the small and quiet Toul sector east of Verdun to defend with his initial force of 14,500 men.

The Germans began a series of heavy blows in October 1917 that pointed up the urgent need of large American reinforcements and forced the Allied governments to unite effectively for the first time. Following a near rout of the Italian armies by the Germans came the triumph of the Bolsheviks in Russia, which raised the possibility that Russia would soon withdraw from the war. The Allied Prime Ministers assembled in extraordinary conference at Rapallo, Italy, in November 1917 and created a Supreme War Council to sit at Versailles and co-ordinate and direct military operations. During the next few months Pershing and President Wilson were subjected to heavy pressure by British and French leaders to permit American troops, even troops inadequately trained, to be amalgamated into their armies. The military outlook was gloomy, but Pershing refused, promising that he would have an army of a million men in France by the end of 1918.

It seemed, however, that the Germans would win the war before Pershing's reinforcements could arrive. The Imperial army hit hard at the British Fifth Army in the valley of the Somme on March 21, 1918, and rolled it back. The Allied leaders and President Wilson hastily elevated Marshal Ferdinand Foch to the post of supreme commander five days later, and Pershing offered his four divisions for use anywhere on the front. The Germans renewed their offensive against the British on April 9, captured enormous quantities of booty and 60,000 prisoners, but failed to break the British lines. The Imperial forces then turned hard against the French on May 27 and pushed to Chateau-Thierry on the Marne, only fifty miles from Paris. Foch on May 31 sent the American Second Division and several regiments of marines to bolster French colonial troops in this sector, and American troops for the first time participated in an important way. They pushed the Germans back across the Marne at Chateau-Thierry and cleared the enemy out of Belleau Wood from June 6 to 25.

The Imperial German General Staff began its last great drive—to break through the Marne pocket between Rheims and Soissons and reach Paris—on July 15. Some 85,000 Americans were engaged in this battle. The German thrust was quickly parried, and the force of the German drive was spent by July 18. Foch then began a counteroffensive against the weak western flank of the German line from the Aisne to the Marne, between Rheims and Soissons. In this engagement, which lasted until August 6, eight American divisions and French troops wiped out the German salient. British and French armies, reinforced by new American divisions, shortly afterward began offensives that did not end until they neared the Belgian frontier in November.

American soldiers began to pour into France in large numbers while Foch was mounting his offensive mainly with British and French troops.

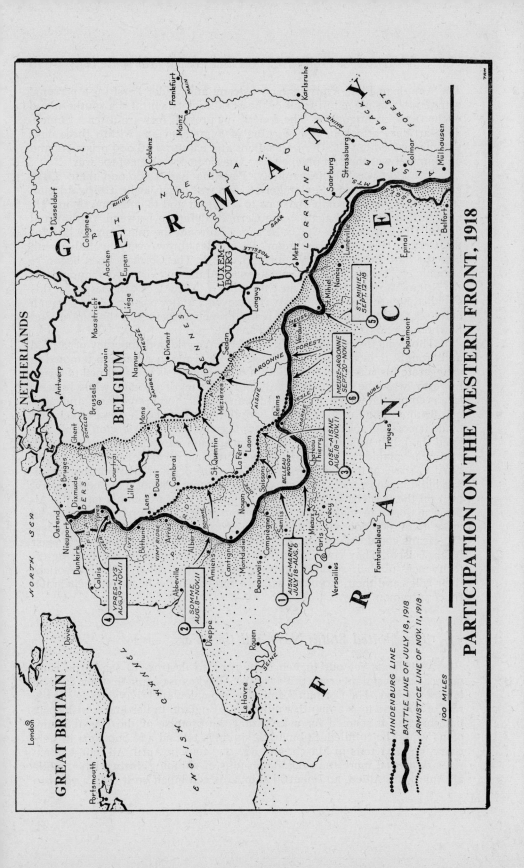

PARTICIPATION ON THE WESTERN FRONT, 1918

GERMANY

NETHERLANDS

BELGIUM

LUXEM-BOURG

FRANCE

GREAT BRITAIN

NORTH SEA

ENGLISH CHANNEL

London
Portsmouth
Dover

RHINE
Düsseldorf
Cologne
Aachen
Eupen
Maastricht
Liége
Namur
Louvain
Brussels
Antwerp
Ghent
Bruges
Ostend
Nieuport
Dunkirk
Calais
Dixmude
Courtrai
Lille
Lens
Douai
Cambrai
Arras
Béthune
Vimy Ridge
Albert
St. Quentin
Mons
Dinant
Sedan
Mézières
La Fère
Laon
Noyon
Soissons
Chateau Thierry
Reims
Verdun
St. Mihiel
Metz
Nancy
Lunéville
Saarburg
Strassburg
Colmar
Mülhausen
Belfort
Epinal
Chaumont
Troyes
Fontainebleau
Versailles
Paris
Senlis
Meaux
Crécy
Beauvais
Compiègne
Montdidier
Cantigny
Amiens
Abbeville
Dieppe
Rouen
Le Havre
Seine
Frankfurt
Mainz
Coblenz
Karlsruhe

FLANDERS
ARDENNES
ARGONNE FOREST
BELLEAU WOODS
VOSGES MTS.
BLACK FOREST
ALSACE
LORRAINE
RHINELAND

RHINE
MAIN
MOSELLE
MEUSE
SAMBRE
SCHELDT
LYS
SOMME
OISE
AISNE
MARNE
VESLE
SAAR
AUBE

① AISNE-MARNE JULY 18-AUG. 6
② SOMME AUG. 8-NOV. 11
③ OISE-AISNE AUG. 18-NOV. 11
④ YPRES-LYS AUG. 19-NOV. 11
⑤ ST. MIHIEL SEPT. 12-16
⑥ MEUSE-ARGONNE SEPT. 20-NOV. 11

100 MILES

•••• HINDENBURG LINE
〜〜 BATTLE LINE OF JULY 18, 1918
···· ARMISTICE LINE OF NOV. 11, 1918

The American First Army, 550,000 strong and under Pershing's personal command, was placed in front of the St. Mihiel salient at the southern end of the front on August 10. The Americans pressed forward after a tremendous artillery attack in the morning of September 12; within three days they had wiped out the German salient and captured 16,000 prisoners and 443 guns. It was the first independent American operation of the war.

The tide was turning rapidly. Pershing had 1,200,000 men, 2,417 guns, and 324 tanks by September 26, and was eager, as he afterward said, "to draw the best German divisions to our front and to consume them." He now hurled his force against the German defenses between Verdun and Sedan. His goal was the Sedan-Mézières railroad, the main supply line for the German forces in this sector. Both sides threw every available man into the battle that raged all during October. The German lines began to crumble on November 1; Americans reached the outskirts of Sedan and cut the Sedan-Mézières railroad on November 7. The American victory in this so-called Meuse-Argonne offensive destroyed a major portion of the German defenses and, coupled with British and French successes in the central and northern sectors, brought the war to an end.

Thus was the military strength of the American democracy organized and brought to bear in the last phases of the war. An American tempted to exaggerate his country's contribution to the victory is less inclined to boast, however, when he recalls that only 112,432 Americans died while in service, as compared with 1,700,000 Russians, 1,385,300 Frenchmen, and 900,000 Britons. The European Allies bore the brunt of the German attack and made it possible for the United States to make any contribution at all. Belated though it was, the American contribution came perhaps in the nick of time to enable the Allies to withstand the last great German assault. On April 1, 1918, at the beginning of the German drive and before the American build-up in France, the Germans had a superiority of 324,000 infantrymen on the western front. By June American reinforcements gave the Allies a majority in manpower. By November the Allied preponderance was more than 600,000 men, enough to overwhelm the German defenses. Americans could rightly say, therefore, that their contribution had at least been decisive. They could also take pride in the courage and fighting effectiveness of their soldiers. As General Pershing put it, "Their devotion, their valor and their sacrifices will live forever in the hearts of their grateful countrymen."

74. *The United States Navy and the War*

As U-boats set out in February 1917 to destroy all sea-borne commerce, the most dangerous threat to the Allied cause came first not on land but on the seas. The German Admiralty had calculated that sinkings at the rate of 600,000 tons a month would bring England to her knees within six months, and it seemed for a time that the promise of the U-boat champions would be fulfilled. Submarine sinkings totaled 540,000 tons in February, 593,841 tons in March, and 881,027 tons in April. All told, submarines destroyed more than 6,500,000 tons of shipping during 1917, while all American, Allied, and neutral shipyards combined built only 2,700,000 tons. "They will win, unless we can stop these losses—and stop them soon," Admiral Jellicoe, First Sea Lord of the Admiralty, told the American liaison admiral in London, William S. Sims, in mid-April 1917. "The British transport of troops and supplies is already strained to the utmost, and the maintenance of the armies in the field is threatened," Ambassador Page cabled the President from London on April 27. "There is food enough here to last the civil population only not more than six weeks or two months."

The adoption of the war resolution found the American navy ready and eager to join the battle. Secretary Daniels and his staff conferred with British and French admirals on April 10 and 11, 1917, and mapped out a preliminary division of duty. The American navy would defend and patrol the Western Hemisphere, while the British fleet would carry the brunt of the antisubmarine campaign in waters around the British Isles with what help the American navy could spare. American assistance was not long in coming. The first six destroyers reached Queenstown, Ireland, on May 4; there were thirty-five American destroyers stationed at that base by July 5; and 383 American craft were overseas by the end of the war.[1]

The British system of defense against submarines in April 1917 consisted of dispersing sea traffic widely and then channeling merchant ships through heavily patrolled waters around the British Isles. The system created a positive death trap for merchantmen, as there simply were not enough ships to patrol the area. To the obvious alternative—the convoy system—British naval planners and masters of merchant ships objected, arguing that convoys were slow and merchant ships could not stay in formation. But as the submarine toll mounted a minority in the British Admiralty joined Secretary Daniels and Admiral Sims in virtually demanding the use of convoys. Even after the feasibility of the plan had been demonstrated in the latter part of May 1917 by two experimental convoys from Gibraltar and Hampton Roads, the British Admiralty contended that it did not have enough warships to use the system generally. However, the American reinforcement of destroyers turned the tide in July, and convoys for merchant ships were begun.

The intensified antisubmarine campaign and inauguration of the convoy system were the two decisive factors that brought the U-boats under control. Shipping losses fell from 881,027 tons in April to half that figure in December 1917; and British losses never ran above 200,000 tons a month after April 1918. As an additional measure, the American Navy Department advocated laying a mine barrage between the coasts of Scotland and Norway to bottle up the submarines. The British Admiralty promptly rejected the plan as impractical, but the Navy Department kept at the project. With the development of a mine that was discharged when a submarine brushed against its antenna-firing device, the British gave their approval; and the two navies began the undertaking in March 1918. The North Sea barrage was still unfinished at the end of the war, but some 70,000 mines had been laid, and German difficulties had at least been compounded.

wwwwwwwwwwwww

[1] The administration immediately suspended the large building program authorized by the legislation of 1916 and adopted plans in May 1917 for the construction of 250 destroyers and 400 sub-chasers.

The American navy's next task was to transport and supply the A.E.F. The Navy Department had seven troop and six cargo ships, totaling 94,000 tons, on hand on July 1, 1917. By November 1918 it had created a Cruiser and Transport Force of 143 vessels, aggregating 3,250,000 tons, which carried 911,047 soldiers to France. In addition, every available British transport was pressed into service in the Atlantic Ferry when the need for American manpower grew acute in 1918. Slightly more than 1,000,000 soldiers were carried by British vessels. The troop carriers were so fast and closely guarded by naval escorts that only two of them, both British vessels, were sunk on the eastbound voyage.

The American navy, with more than 2,000 vessels and 533,000 officers and men in service at the end of the war, had attained unparalleled size and fighting effectiveness. By November 1918 American ships were patrolling the far reaches of the Western Hemisphere and co-operating with Japanese and British forces in the Far East, while 834 vessels and 200,000 men were either serving in European waters or else transporting troops and supplies to France. By insisting on the adoption of the convoy system and the laying of the North Sea mine barrage, American naval strategists had made a significant contribution to operations that assured an Allied-American victory at sea. By throwing its destroyers into the campaign against the submarines, the American navy perhaps turned the tide against the U-boats in the first Battle of the Atlantic. And by transporting nearly half the A.E.F. and almost all the army's cargo to France, the navy made possible the defeat of Germany in 1918 instead of 1920, as the Allied leaders had originally planned.

75. *The Triumph of a Democratic Tax Policy During Wartime*

Americans entered the First World War without the slightest conception of the costs of participation. A learned professor at Columbia University suggested that the war would cost the United States at least $10,000,-000,000 during the first year, and administration and congressional leaders smiled in unbelief. Although predictions as to long-run costs were impossible, two facts became apparent almost at once. First, the structure of international exchange would collapse and the European Allies would be in desperate straits unless Britain and France received huge credits, not a piddling few hundred million dollars. Second, the Revenue Act of March 3, 1917, which had increased taxes only slightly, was grossly inadequate to meet war needs.

Without opposition a somewhat dazed Congress approved the first War Loan Act on April 23, 1917. It authorized the Treasury to issue $2,000,-000,000 in short-term notes and $5,000,000,000 in bonds, three billions of which should be lent to the Allies. Congress recalled the controversy provoked by President Cleveland's negotiations with Wall Street bankers and also stipulated that the bonds should be sold through popular subscription. Congress added subsequent authorizations as the needs of the American and Allied governments grew, so that the government had borrowed $23,000,000,000 on a long-term basis by 1920. The Treasury staged four Liberty Loan campaigns and one Victory Loan drive after the war was over.

Out of the $33,500,000,000 that is reckoned as the cost of the war to the American people by 1920, therefore, some $23,000,000,000 was charged to future generations, and about $10,500,000,000 was raised by taxes. Determining how much should be borrowed and how much should be raised by taxes set off protracted struggles in Congress. Conservatives of both parties advocated recourse to consumption taxes, borrowing, and perhaps slight increases in income taxes. Progressives and radicals, on the other hand, believed that the wealthy classes, who had allegedly driven the country to war, should be forced to bear practically the entire costs through extraordinary income, inheritance, and excess profits taxes.

Between these two extremes stood the President, the Secretary of the Treasury, and a large majority of Congress. McAdoo at first thought that half the costs could be met by taxation; but he revised his figure downward to 35 per cent as expenditures skyrocketed. Congressional leaders finally agreed upon a new War Revenue bill, which Wilson signed on October 3, 1917. It imposed a graduated excess profits tax ranging from 20 to 60 per cent; reduced income tax exemptions from $3,000 to $1,000 for unmarried persons and from $4,000 to $2,000 for married persons; increased the normal income tax to 4 per cent for individuals and 6 per cent for corporations; and increased the maximum surtax to 63 per cent. The measure, moreover, increased excise taxes and imposed new ones on luxuries, services, and facilities. Finally, it increased the estate tax to a maximum of 25 per cent.

The War Revenue Act of 1917 imposed 74 per cent of the financial burden of the war on large individual and corporate incomes alone. Even so, radicals in the Senate denounced the bill as a betrayal of the people because it failed to confiscate all incomes over $100,000. The appalling way in which expenditures mounted during the early months of 1918 convinced Wilson and McAdoo that their radical critics had at least been partially right. The President appeared before a joint session on May 27, 1918, and urged the imposition of additional levies on incomes, profits, and luxuries. The House on September 20 passed a revenue bill to provide $8,182,000,000 of the $24,000,000,000 that the administration estimated would be required for the current fiscal year. By the time that the Senate set seriously to work on the measure, however, the war was over, and McAdoo had lowered his request for revenue from eight to six billions.

Even so, the Revenue Act of 1918, approved by the President on February 24, 1919, increased the prevailing tax burden by almost 250 per cent and put four fifths of the load on large incomes, profits, and estates. Exemptions were unchanged from the Act of 1917, but the normal tax on individual net incomes up to $4,000 was increased to 6 per cent, while all net incomes above $4,000 had to pay a normal tax of 12 per cent.[2] An additional surtax ranging up to 65 per cent brought the total tax on the largest incomes to 77 per cent. In addition, the excess profits tax was increased to a maximum of 65 per cent.

The effect of the war revenue legislation can best be seen by comparing the fortunes of the wealthy classes with those of other groups during

\\\\\\\\\\\\\\\\\\\\\\\\

[2] This rate applied only for the balance of 1918. For subsequent years the normal rate would be 4 per cent on net incomes up to $4,000 and 8 per cent on all incomes above that figure.

the war period. The average annual *real* earnings of workers in manufacturing, transportation, and coal mining were 14 per cent higher in 1917 than in 1914 and 20 per cent higher in 1918 than in 1914. A rapid increase in agricultural prices also brought new prosperity to farmers. The real income, after taxes, of all persons engaged in farming was 25 per cent higher in 1918 than in 1915, while the number of farmers earning $2,000 or more a year increased from 2 per cent of the total in 1913 to 29 per cent in 1918.

It is instructive to contrast these spectacular economic gains by the large majority of low-income receivers with the fortunes of the upper classes during the war period. To be sure, there were notable cases of "swollen" profits among certain industries, particularly munitions, shipbuilding, and steel; and the number of persons reporting incomes—*before taxes*—of between $50,000 and $100,000 increased from 5,000 in 1914 to 13,000 in 1918. But the gains of the wealthy classes as a whole were far less important than a few sensational figures would indicate. Total disbursements to owners in manufacturing, measured in terms of real income, increased hardly at all from 1913 to 1916. Real income from property increased about 30 per cent in 1917 and then fell back in 1918 almost to the level of 1916. But since the recipients of this income from property paid about seven eighths of the total personal income taxes in 1917 and 1918, it is evident that they suffered a sizable economic loss as a result of the war.

The old picture of the American upper classes fattening on the nation's misery during wartime is, to say the least, overdrawn. The effect of the tax policies shaped by a progressive administration and majority in Congress was greatly to lighten the relative share of the tax burden carried by the overwhelming majority of Americans, and sharply to increase the burdens of that small minority who had paid only slight taxes before 1916. Thus progressives could boast in 1918 that their leaders were putting democracy to work at home with a vengeance, while American soldiers were fighting to save democracy in Europe.

76.   *The Mobilization of Industry*

Preliminary groundwork for a mobilization of industry had happily been laid before the United States entered the war. Congress in the preparedness legislation of 1916 had established a Council of National Defense, composed of six Cabinet members, and the Council's working body, the Advisory Commission, made up of business, industrial, railroad, and labor representatives. The Council was armed only with limited authority, but it proceeded to take a complete inventory of America's industrial plant and then to establish, on March 31, 1917, a Munitions Standards Board.

This board was soon reorganized as the General Munitions Board and given control over the purchase and supply of ammunition for the armed forces. But the new agency never established its authority over the armed services and the Allied purchasing commissions, and it was evident by the early summer of 1917 that only a central authority, with far-reaching controls, could bring order out of the prevailing chaos. The Council of National Defense abolished the General Munitions Board on July 28, 1917, and created in its place the War Industries Board. It would serve as a clearing house for purchases, allocate raw materials and control production, and supervise labor relations.

The WIB made rapid progress in many fields of industrial mobilization, but it failed to co-ordinate military purchases because it lacked direct authority over the War and Navy departments. The Board's first chairman, Frank A. Scott, broke down under the strain and retired on October 17, 1917. Then his successor, Daniel Willard, president of the Baltimore & Ohio Railroad, left the agency on January 16, 1918. It seemed that the war effort at home was collapsing. The winter of 1917–18 was terribly severe. Heavy snows blocked the railroads so frequently that there were fuel shortages in the East and a decline in steel production.

Rumors of inefficiency led the Senate military affairs committee to begin a searching investigation of the mobilization effort in December 1917. It revealed a near breakdown in railroad transportation, confusion in the War Department, and failure to provide adequate shelter and clothing for soldiers in cantonments. "The Military Establishment of America has fallen down," exclaimed the Democratic chairman of the committee, George E. Chamberlain of Oregon, on January 19, 1918. ". . . It has almost stopped functioning . . . because of inefficiency in every bureau and in every department of the Government."

The exposures of the Chamberlain committee led Republicans to demand establishment of a coalition War Cabinet to take direction of the war effort out of the President's hands. Wilson's answer to this challenge to his leadership was as usual bold. He wrote out a measure—the so-called Overman bill—conferring on himself practically unlimited power to organize and direct the nation's resources. As Congress did not adopt the Overman bill until April, the President summoned Bernard M. Baruch, a Wall Street broker who had been Scott's and Willard's chief assistant, to the White House on March 4, 1918, and made him chairman of the WIB. Acting under his emergency war powers, the President also granted sweeping new authority to the agency to conserve resources, advise purchasing agencies as to prices, make purchases for the Allies, and, most important, determine priorities of production and distribution in industry.

Gathering about him one hundred of the ablest businessmen in the country, Baruch soon established the WIB as the most powerful agency in the government, with himself as economic dictator of the United States and, to a large extent, of the Allied countries as well. And before many months had passed the Board had harnessed the gigantic American industrial machine, mainly by instituting severe controls over the use of scarce materials, particularly steel, and brought such order into the mobilization effort that criticism almost vanished.

77. *The Mobilization of Agriculture and Fuel Supplies*

An urgent need in the spring of 1917 was an increased flow of food from the United States to provide the margin between life and death for the British, French, and Italian armies and peoples. The President on May 19, 1917, announced inauguration of a food control program under

Herbert Hoover, recently director of the Belgian Relief Commission. Hoover's agency at first acted without legal authority as a subcommittee of the Council of National Defense. However, after a lengthy and bitter debate, Congress on August 10, 1917, adopted the Lever Act, giving the President sweeping authority over production, manufacture, and distribution of foodstuffs, fuel, fertilizers, and farm implements. The measure also empowered the President to institute a limited price control over certain scarce commodities. Wilson created the Food Administration on the day that the Lever bill became law and delegated full authority to Hoover.

The most urgent task in the summer of 1917 was production and control of wheat. Bad weather and an epidemic of black stem rust had caused a sharp decline in the American crop in 1916. The domestic supply was nearly exhausted by January 1917, and the price of wheat was skyrocketing. The Lever Act fixed a minimum price of $2.00 a bushel in order to stimulate production; and the Food Administration, on August 30, 1917, offered to buy the 1917 crop at $2.20 a bushel and established the United States Grain Corporation to purchase and distribute wheat. But 1917 was another poor wheat season, and stocks of bread grains abroad fell below the danger point in early 1918. Only by loyal co-operation from American housewives and the severest economies and controls was Hoover able to find enough wheat to carry Britain and France through the winter. Nature was more bountiful in 1918, and the bumper wheat crop of that year assured a plentiful supply of bread.

The Food Administration's second major objective was increased production of hogs, as pork was another important staple in the Allied diet. The slaughtering of hogs was running 7 to 10 per cent below the figure for the corresponding period in 1916 when Hoover's agency began its work in the spring of 1917. The Food Administration solved the problem in November 1917 by setting hog prices so high—at $15.50 per hundredweight —that farmers (and hogs) outdid themselves and nearly doubled production in 1918 and 1919.

The Food Administration's third major problem was increased production of sugar, which was in exceedingly short supply in 1917, and fair distribution to consumers. Hoover after several unsuccessful attempts established the Sugar Equalization Board on July 11, 1918. It purchased the entire Cuban and American crops at a guaranteed price and resold the sugar to the British government and American refiners. No system of direct rationing was instituted, but grocers were allowed to sell only two pounds a month to each individual.

For over-all accomplishment with a minimum of confusion and direct controls the Food Administration rivaled the reorganized WIB under Baruch's direction. By appealing to American pride and patriotism Hoover persuaded people to tighten their belts on meatless and breadless days. Consequently, the United States was able to export 12,326,914 tons of food in 1917–18 and 18,667,378 tons in 1918–19, as compared with an average for the three prewar years of 6,959,055 tons. These products of the American soil were as instrumental in saving the Allies from disaster as were the American doughboys fighting in the trenches.

The basic problem with regard to fuel was encouragement of the mining of marginal coal lands that were not usually exploited in peacetime.

Empowered by the Lever Act to fix a price that would bring marginal mines into production, the President, on August 23, 1917, established the Fuel Administration, with Harry A. Garfield, president of Williams College, as administrator. The Fuel Administration obtained the increased output it demanded by pegging the price of coal at a high level, but a near breakdown in railroad transportation caused distribution to become incredibly snarled in December 1917 and January 1918. Garfield cleared the railroad lines and moved ships waiting in ports on the East Coast by ordering all manufacturing firms, except vital war plants, to operate on a limited basis for the period January 18–22, 1918, and for nine subsequent Mondays. The order set off a wave of indignant protest but got the country through the crisis.

78. *Shipping and Railroads*

The British Prime Minister, David Lloyd George, told a group of Americans in London a few days after the United States entered the war: "The absolute assurance of victory has to be found in one word, ships, in a second word, ships, and a third word, ships." And so it seemed, as submarines took a fearful toll on the seas in that gloomy April of 1917. The Washington administration, however, promised "a bridge of ships" and chartered the Emergency Fleet Corporation, a subsidiary of the United States Shipping Board, on April 16 to build ships faster than submarines could sink them.

The government's shipbuilding program began with great fanfare but soon ran afoul of adversities. In the end it was the most important failure of the American war effort. The heads of the Shipping Board and the Emergency Fleet Corporation quarreled so violently that small progress had been accomplished by July 1917. The President removed them both and gave full power to Edward N. Hurley, energetic chairman of the Federal Trade Commission. Moving with great speed, Hurley began construction of new shipyards along the Atlantic coast; they contained ninety-four shipways and were supposed to produce 15,000,000 tons of shipping. But the Emergency Fleet Corporation had delivered only 465,454 tons of *new* shipping by September 1918, while the first ship from the Corporation's largest shipyard— at Hog Island, near Philadelphia—was not delivered until December 3, 1918.

Meanwhile, the Shipping Board had moved in more fruitful directions to marshal an American merchant marine. First, it seized and put into service ninety-seven German ships in American harbors, totaling more than 500,000 tons. Second, Hurley on August 3, 1917, commandeered for the Shipping Board the 431 ships, totaling 3,000,000 tons, then under construction in private shipyards. Finally, in March 1918, he seized over half a million tons of Dutch shipping then in American ports. Through purchase, seizure, and requisition, the Shipping Board by September 1, 1918, had acquired the large fleet without which the A.E.F. could never have been transported and supplied.

Organization of American railroads was assumed during most of 1917 by a voluntary Railroads War Board. It worked in co-operation with the Council of National Defense to divide traffic and move troops and army supplies. Struggling under an extraordinary burden and lacking any unified

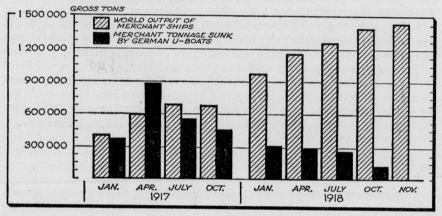

SUBMARINE SINKINGS AND SHIPBUILDING
JANUARY, 1917 TO NOVEMBER, 1918

control, the railroads seemed near collapse in December 1917, when snows blocked lines and cold weather froze switches and impeded the operation of terminals. Conditions in the eastern freight yards and ports were nearly chaotic by Christmas. Therefore, the President on December 28, 1917, put all railroad transportation under the control of a United States Railroad Administration headed by William G. McAdoo, who resigned as Secretary of the Treasury to become Director-General of the Railroads. By controlling traffic on a rational, nation-wide scale, spending more than $500,000,000 for long-needed improvements and equipment, and subordinating passenger traffic to war needs, the Railroad Administration created an efficient national transportation system that met fully the demands of the great military effort of 1918.

79. *Government and Labor During Wartime*

In no area of public policy was the Wilson administration's determination to reinforce democracy at home during wartime better illustrated than in the field of labor policy. The President and his advisers rejected proposals to conscript labor and refused to allow the machinery of the labor market to regulate wages and hours. Instead, they embarked upon what soon became a comprehensive program designed to guarantee full utilization of manpower without depriving labor of rights and living standards that it had already won.

Like most other wartime policies, the labor program evolved slowly in response to need, experience, and the administration's maturing social conscience. The War and Navy departments had the most immediate and the largest interest in uninterrupted production and could wield direct power over manufacturers and contractors. They moved quickly into the field of labor relations during the first months of the war. A Cantonment Adjustment Commission, established by the War Department on June 19, 1917, set wage and hours policies for workers engaged in constructing army camps. A Board of Control for Labor Standards, established on July 20,

1917, by Secretary Baker, regulated clothing manufacturers who supplied army uniforms. Nor was the Navy Department any less active in setting up wage commissions in navy shipyards and private firms. Even more important was the President's Mediation Commission, the driving spirit of which was Felix Frankfurter, who was also Baker's labor adviser in the War Department.

There was still a need for unified policies and national direction of the labor administration. Hence the President established the National War Labor Board on April 8, 1918, as a supreme court for labor controversies. Under the joint chairmanship of Frank P. Walsh, a distinguished labor lawyer, and former President William H. Taft, the WLB heard 1,251 cases affecting 711,500 workers. Lacking any statutory authority, the Board enforced its rulings through the President's war powers. For example, when the Smith & Wesson Arms factory at Springfield, Massachusetts, refused to accept the WLB's decision, the War Department simply commandeered the plant. On the other hand, when workers in the munitions factories in Bridgeport, Connecticut, threatened to strike rather than accept the Board's award, the President wrote a sharp letter to the Machinists' union at Bridgeport, telling members that they could either work or fight.

The members of the WLB soon discovered that they were actually more a policy-making than an arbitral body; yet they often had to decide labor policies on a basis of insufficient information and without knowing the needs of the country as a whole. To fill the need for a scientific agency to determine general policies, President Wilson created the War Labor Policies Board in May 1918. Under the direction of Felix Frankfurter the new agency undertook the gigantic task of surveying the whole labor field, standardizing wages and hours, and giving a central direction to the flow of labor. One result was the establishment in the Department of Labor of a United States Employment Service that registered over 5,000,000 workers and placed 3,700,000 of them in vital industries.

This, then, was the administrative machinery that mobilized American manpower and inaugurated the most significant and far-reaching social experiment in the history of the United States to that time. In general, the government threw its war power to labor's side and accomplished such sweeping social gains as to warrant the conclusion that a virtual revolution was effected during wartime. A few particulars will illustrate the generalization. All the various administrative boards, for example, recognized and protected the right of workers to organize and bargain collectively. As a result, total membership of the AF of L grew from 2,072,702 in 1916 to 3,260,168 in 1920, while union membership in industries engaged in war production increased at an even faster rate. Secondly, the administration compelled the adoption of the eight-hour day when it was possible to do so without disrupting industrial operations. The result was a sharp decline in the hours of labor, from an average of 53.5 per week in 1914 to 50.4 in 1920, while the proportion of wage earners in manufacturing who worked 48 hours or less a week rose from 11.8 per cent in 1914 to 48.6 per cent in 1919. Thirdly, the War and Navy departments and various labor boards worked diligently to improve conditions of labor and prevent exploitation of women and children by manufacturers with government contracts. Moreover, when the Supreme Court in 1918 invalidated the Child Labor Act of

1916, Congress responded immediately by levying a prohibitive 10 per cent tax on products manufactured in whole or in part by children under fourteen. Fourthly, the federal administrators attempted to guarantee all workers under their jurisdiction a living wage, that is, an income sufficient to provide a minimum of health and decency. In the face of a 50 per cent increase in the cost of living from 1914 to 1918, such a program involved heroic efforts to keep wages abreast of the rising level of prices. Because of full employment and the vigilance of the war labor agencies, however, the average annual *real* income of labor increased 14 per cent above the prewar level in 1917 and 20 per cent above the prewar level in 1918.

These efforts involved such federal intervention as few progressives had dreamed of before 1917. Under the spur of war necessity, an advanced element in the administration had demonstrated that public control of hours, wages, and working conditions could be effected without enslaving workers or causing undue hardship on management. The experiment was abandoned after the war, to be sure, but a precedent for future action in another dire emergency had been established.

80. *Public Opinion and the War*

President Wilson only seven days after the adoption of the war resolution signed an executive order creating the Committee on Public Information to mobilize public opinion behind the war effort. There seemed to be no doubt in administration circles about the need for propaganda to convince the American people that their cause was just.

There was still profound division in public sentiment over the question of American participation in the war. There had been no frontal attack on American territory in 1917 to solidify public opinion and convert the opposition. On the contrary, Wilson and Congress had decided to go to war only after protracted hesitation and painful deliberation. It is impossible to estimate the extent of opposition to the war resolution soon after its adoption. Probably a majority reluctantly accepted it as the only solution, but there were millions of Americans—Socialists, extreme radicals, many progressives, and tens of thousands of German and Irish Americans—who still believed that American intervention was the work of an unneutral President and great evil forces that abetted him.[3]

To convert this hostile opinion and educate all citizens to an understanding of American objectives, Wilson created the Committee on Public Information with George Creel, a progressive journalist from Denver, as head. One of Creel's first official acts was the establishment of a voluntary press censorship that worked remarkably well. He next turned to the more difficult task of making Americans war-conscious; before the war had ended he had mobilized 150,000 lecturers, writers, artists, actors, and scholars in perhaps the most gigantic propaganda campaign in American history.

[3] The Socialist party before its suppression was the only important organization that opposed the war effort. Socialist mayoralty candidates in 1917 polled 22 per cent of the popular vote in New York City, nearly 34 per cent in Chicago, 44 per cent in Dayton, Ohio, and 25 per cent in Buffalo—an impressive indication of the extent of popular feeling against participation.

As a consequence an official line was sold to the American people. One side of the propaganda glorified American participation in terms of an idealistic crusade to advance the cause of freedom and democracy throughout the world—a concept that the President reiterated in 1917 and 1918. The other side portrayed the German menace in the most lurid colors, in terms of the Hun attempting to despoil Europe and extend his dominion to the Western Hemisphere. Although the Creel Committee rejected the cruder atrocity stories, it appropriated and spread many of the official Allied atrocity charges.

The Creel Committee's efforts to make Americans war- and security-conscious came at a time when they were already distraught by rumors of disloyalty, espionage, and sabotage. The result of Creel's propaganda, and even more of the agitation of irresponsible volunteer organizations like the National Security League and the National Protective Association, was to stimulate such an outbreak of war madness as the country had never before witnessed. There were numerous spy scares, and large organizations of patriots sprang up to catch enemy agents and traitors.

Most of the hysteria was turned against German Americans, all things German, and anti-war radicals and progressives. Each state had a committee of public safety, with branches in every county and city; and in many areas these committees were not much better than vigilante groups. It was they who conducted reigns of terror against German Americans, especially in Montana, Minnesota, and Wisconsin. La Follette, as the leader of the progressives who voted against the war resolution, was burned in effigy in Madison, expelled from the Madison Club, and publicly censured by most of the faculty of his beloved University of Wisconsin. The climax came when the Minnesota Public Safety Committee demanded his expulsion from the Senate.

As one historian has shrewdly observed, the majority of Americans in their hatred of things German lost not only their tolerance but their sense of humor as well. Statues of heroes like Von Steuben and Frederick the Great were taken from their pedestals. Many states forbade the teaching of German or church services conducted in German. Sauerkraut was renamed "liberty cabbage," German measles, "liberty measles." The crowning blow came when Cincinnati ruled pretzels off free lunch counters in saloons.

81. *Civil Liberties During Wartime*

All governments try to protect themselves against enemies from within as well as from without during extreme crises. To Wilson and other administration leaders it was an absurd situation when the federal government could force men to fight and give their lives for their country and yet could not punish persons who attempted to obstruct the war effort or gave aid and comfort to the enemy without violating the law of treason.[4] The President's

wwwwwwwwwwwwwww

[4] Several Civil War statutes, still on the books in 1917, prohibited conspiracies to resist recruiting and persuade men to resist the draft; but these laws did not affect individuals. The only statute applying to individuals was the treason law, which applied only to treasonable acts, not utterances, and was extremely difficult to enforce.

answer to opponents of the war was the Espionage Act of June 15, 1917. It provided imprisonment up to twenty years and/or a fine up to $10,000 for persons who willfully made false reports to help the enemy, incited rebellion among the armed forces, or attempted to obstruct recruiting or the operation of the draft. An equivalent of censorship appeared in a section empowering the Postmaster General to deny the use of the mails to any matter which, *in his opinion*, advocated treason, insurrection, or forcible resistance to the laws of the United States.

Postmaster General Albert S. Burleson of Texas had been a staunch supporter of Wilson's policies, but he was neither tolerant nor discriminating in judgment, and he used his vast new power to establish a capricious censorship. For example, he banned the *American Socialist* from the mails soon after the passage of the Espionage Act. Two other leading Socialist publications, *The Masses* and Victor Berger's daily *Milwaukee Leader*, fell under the Texan's ban in August and October 1917. In addition, he suppressed all anti-British and pro-Irish publications and banned an issue of the single-tax organ, *The Public*, for suggesting that more revenue should be raised by taxes.

In effect the Espionage Act became a tool to stamp out dissent and radical, but never conservative, criticism. As one authority has observed, "It became criminal to advocate heavier taxation instead of bond issues, to state that conscription was unconstitutional though the Supreme Court had not yet held it valid, to say that the sinking of merchant ships was legal, to urge that a referendum should have preceded our declaration of war, to say that war was contrary to the teachings of Christ. Men have been punished for criticising the Red Cross and the Y.M.C.A." [5] A movie producer, Robert Goldstein, was sentenced to prison for ten years for displaying a movie about the American Revolution that allegedly incited hostility against an associate of the United States. The most famous case involved Eugene V. Debs, the leader of the Socialist party. Debs expressed his frank revulsion at the war in a speech before a Socialist convention in Canton, Ohio, on June 16, 1918. He was speedily brought to trial and sentenced to a term of ten years in federal prison.

In all fairness it should be said that the administration was not responsible for the excesses of this legal witch hunt. They were the outcome largely of the hysteria and maelstrom of hatred that converted district attorneys, judges, and juries into persecutors of a dissenting minority. Federal judges in the North had stood forthrightly, although usually vainly, during the Civil War in defense of civil liberties against encroachments by the military commanders. However, the federal courts provided no effective defense during the First World War against the momentary madness of the majority. None of the sedition cases reached the Supreme Court until after the war was over. But in Schenck *v.* United States, 1919, Justice Oliver Wendell Holmes, speaking for a unanimous court, upheld the Espionage Act by inventing a new constitutional doctrine. Schenck had admittedly counseled resistance to the draft. In ordinary times, Holmes said, such action would

wwwwwwwwwwwwww

[5] Zechariah Chafee, Jr., *Freedom of Speech in the United States* (Cambridge, Mass., 1941), p. 51.

have been legal. In wartime, however, Congress had power to prevent utterances that might constitute a "clear and present danger" and provoke evils that Congress had a right to prevent. Actually, Holmes was trying to limit repression of free speech by imposing the "clear and present danger" test. But the doctrine, as interpreted by other judges, destroyed the long American tradition of free and unbridled criticism of public policies.

The government's power over thought and utterance was inevitably gradually enlarged, not diminished, as the war progressed. The Trading-with-the-Enemy Act of October 6, 1917, empowered the President to censor all international communications and gave the Postmaster General sweeping powers of censorship over the foreign-language press in the United States. Still the Attorney General claimed that he lacked a means to check disloyalty and asked Congress for broader authority. Congress moved again in April and May 1918, but not so much in response to the Attorney General's request as in reaction to two developments that had shaken the country during preceding months.

The first of these was the government's suppression of the Industrial Workers of the World, a left-wing union which, as we have seen, functioned mainly among western lumbermen, miners, and agricultural workers. The IWW conducted a violent campaign during the first eight months of 1917 against the copper companies, especially the Anaconda in Montana and Arizona. The production of vital copper began to decline precipitously, and the Justice Department moved swiftly. Federal agents raided IWW offices throughout the West on September 5, 1917, and arrested the union's leaders. Nearly one hundred of them were subsequently tried, convicted, and imprisoned.

The second development was the mounting of war hysteria during the preceding winter, especially in states like Montana and Minnesota, where the IWW and German Americans were an important element. The Montana legislature met in special session in February 1918 to consider the crisis; and Governor Samuel V. Stewart signed a criminal syndicalism act on February 21 that opened a new chapter in American legal history. It prohibited any language calculated to bring the American Constitution, form of government, flag, or armed forces into disrespect or contempt.

Spurred by appeals from the West, Congress succumbed to the clamor for legislation against sabotage and sedition. The Sabotage Act, approved April 20, 1918, was aimed at the IWW and made willful sabotage of war materials, utilities, and transportation facilities federal crimes. The Sedition Act, signed by the President on May 16, 1918, was modeled after the Montana statute and supported chiefly by senators from the Rocky Mountain states. The Espionage Act had empowered the government to punish seditious utterances only if it could prove that injurious consequences would result directly from such utterances. The Sedition Act, in contrast, extended the power of the United States over speech and printed opinion, regardless of consequence. It forbade disloyal, profane, scurrilous, or abusive remarks about the form of government, flag, or uniform of the United States, or any language intended to obstruct the war effort in any way. In addition, the Postmaster General was empowered to deny the use of the mails to any person who, *in his opinion,* used the mail service to violate the Act.

All told, 2,168 persons were prosecuted and 1,055 were convicted under the Espionage and Sedition Acts, sixty-five for threats against the President, and only ten for actual sabotage. But this reckoning gives little indication of the extent to which suppression of dissent was carried out by organized groups who lynched, whipped, tarred and feathered, or otherwise wreaked vengeance on labor radicals, German Americans, or any persons suspected of disloyalty. As Wilson had predicted in April 1917, many Americans forgot mercy and tolerance and compassion. In retrospect, the war hysteria seems the most fearful price that the American people paid for participation in the First World War.

CHAPTER

10

The Great Crusade Ends in a Separate Peace

WE CAN SEE in retrospect that the participation of the United States in the First World War restored a preponderance of power to the Atlantic powers, but that Britain and France were more severely weakened by the war than was Germany. We can also see that a future preponderance of the Atlantic community depended upon the continued active participation of the United States in the western coalition. In other words, the future peace of the world depended upon the willingness of the American people to maintain a new Anglo-American-French preponderance of power, at least until a genuine world concert could come into being.

Wilson and perhaps a majority of thoughtful Americans realized this fact in 1919 and 1920. Many Americans, however, were unprepared to assume the duties of leadership that circumstances seemed to demand. When the Paris Peace Conference gave birth, not to a Wilsonian millennium, but to a settlement that seemed to embody many of the old evils that they had fought to destroy, American crusaders by the thousands turned into cynics and wished only to abandon Europe to an inevitable self-destruction. But this disillusionment over the Versailles Treaty was not the only factor in the rejection by the American people of leadership in world affairs. Historic and powerful isolationist sentiments revived in full force once the war was over and provided an ideological frame of reference to which opponents of the Treaty could appeal. Old anti-British animosities found a more virulent expression for having been suppressed during the war, while various national groups rebelled against aspects of the Treaty. But the most fatal and decisive development was the manner in which the question of a peace settlement was subordinated, by Democrats and Republicans alike, to partisan ambitions. This was the factor chiefly responsible for the failure of the Treaty in the United States.

The story we are about to relate has about it many elements of high tragedy. A concert of free peoples and the greatest aggregation of military power the world had yet seen ended in bitter and inglorious rupture, and a chain of events was set in motion that led to a Second World War.

82.   *The Formulation of the Liberal Peace Program*

The formulation of the liberal peace program illustrates the way in which thoughtful minorities affect the course of history. Groups of intellectuals and humanitarians in all western European nations not long after the outbreak of the war began to study prevention of future wars. Their remedy called for open diplomacy, an end to antagonistic balances of power, no postwar indemnities or annexations, self-determination for subject nationalities, democratic control of foreign policies, freedom of the seas, and disarmament on land. Their suggestions were causing a tremendous ferment by the spring of 1916. An American counterpart was the League to Enforce Peace, organized in June 1915. It numbered among its leaders former President Taft, President A. Lawrence Lowell of Harvard, and Hamilton Holt, editor of the *Independent,* and proposed a powerful international organization to preserve peace.

The most important moment in the peace movement came when Wilson espoused the League idea and the liberal peace program. The President had refused before 1916 to make any public comment on the causes of the war or proposals for a settlement. But in a speech before the League to Enforce Peace in Washington on May 27, 1916, he came out boldly in support of American participation in a postwar association to maintain freedom of the seas and the territorial integrity of its members. When this momentous declaration evoked much favorable comment and little criticism, Wilson incorporated the League concept in the Democratic platform and made it a leading issue in the ensuing presidential campaign of 1916.

Encouraged by a favorable popular response, Wilson next conjoined the League concept to the liberal peace program in his "Peace without Victory" speech to the Senate on January 22, 1917. He reaffirmed his belief that the American people were prepared to join a postwar League of Nations and help maintain peace. He went further, however, and for the first time outlined in general terms the kind of peace that American people would be willing to help enforce. It was a settlement giving independence to the Poles and autonomy to oppressed nationalities, guaranteeing freedom of the seas, and substituting a world community of power for the old system of a divided Europe: a peace without great indemnities and annexations, except—and this could only be inferred from the address—perhaps to return Alsace-Lorraine to France and give Russia access to the Mediterranean.

There can be no doubt that Wilson believed that this was the only kind of peace worth fighting for because it was the only kind of peace that would endure. Yet he let the opportunity pass to obtain such a settlement when he might have won it most easily—during the anxious two months before the

American war resolution. Failing to use American intervention as a bargaining weapon for peace objectives that the United States could approve, he permitted the country to drift into war merely to defend highly questionable maritime rights.

His second mistake was nearly as damaging. Wilson from the beginning of American belligerency insisted on maintaining the fiction that the United States was carrying on a private war with Germany, as an associate but not an ally of the *Entente*, presumably free to withdraw when it had won its objectives. This thinking was unrealistic, for after April 6, 1917, the United States and the Allied countries had to make war together, win together, and make peace together.

This became apparent soon after the American declaration of war, when the President and Allied leaders first discussed a possible settlement. Certainly after his talks with the British Foreign Secretary, Arthur Balfour, in late April 1917, Wilson knew the terms of some of the secret treaties that the Allied governments had concluded for the division of German and Austro-Hungarian territory and colonies. He knew also that he faced an inevitable showdown on the whole subject of peace terms. On several occasions he attempted to broach the subject with the British and French and was frightened from his efforts by warnings that such talk would cause a fatal division in the face of the impending German onslaught on the western front. Wilson comforted himself with the thought that he could *force* Britain and France to accept his terms after the war was over. "By that time," he predicted, "they will among other things be financially in our hands."

Unable, as he thought, to come to definite agreement with the Allied governments and acting in response to demands at home and abroad for a clear statement of war aims, Wilson launched his own campaign for a liberal and just peace settlement. The opening note of this campaign, the Fourteen Points, came in response to the direst catastrophe that had befallen the Allies since the beginning of the war. The Bolsheviks overthrew the socialistic Kerensky government in November 1917, appealed to war-weary peoples to put an end to the fighting, and announced their intention to expose the Allied governments by publishing their secret agreements on war aims. Failing to receive any response to these moves, the Bolsheviks opened separate peace negotiations with Germany.

Some answer had to be made. The American people, Wilson said, would not fight for "any selfish aim on the part of any belligerent." After trying vainly to persuade the Interallied Conference in Paris to formulate a reply, Wilson set himself independently to the task on January 5, 1918. Three days later he went before a joint session of Congress to announce the peace program for which the United States and the Allies were fighting. It was enumerated in fourteen points. The first five were general and called for open diplomacy, freedom of the seas "alike in peace and in war," removal of artificial trade barriers, reduction of armaments, and an "absolutely impartial adjustment of all colonial claims." Point 6 demanded the evacuation of Russia by German forces and self-determination for the Russian peoples. Points 7 and 8 called for German evacuation of Belgium and France and proposed the return of Alsace-Lorraine to France. Point 9 called for the readjustment of Italy's boundary along the clear line of nationality, Point 10 for autonomy for the subject nationalities of Austria-Hungary, Point 11 for the evacuation and restoration of Rumania, Serbia, and Montenegro, Point 12 for autonomy for the subject peoples of the Ottoman empire, and Point 13 for the creation of a free and independent Poland with access to the sea. For the end the President saved the capstone, Point 14: "A general association of nations . . . affording mutual guarantees of political independence and territorial integrity to great and small states alike."

The Fourteen Points at once became the great manifesto of the war. Enthusiastically received by liberal and labor groups in the United States and the Allied countries, they also had a powerful appeal to the German people. Wilson had promised, not the destruction of Germany, but the welcoming of a democratized Reich into the new concert of power. Although the Allied leaders used the Fourteen Points as a weapon of war, they gave no indication that they were willing to adopt them, verbatim, as a basis for peace. Nonetheless, Wilson maintained his campaign for a liberal peace all during the spring and summer of 1918.

83. *Armistice: 1918*

Wilson's opportunity to take command of armistice negotiations arose as a result of the weight of the Allied-American offensive on the western front that began in July 1918. General Ludendorff, one of the German supreme commanders, demanded on September 29 and October 1 that the Imperial civil authorities obtain an armistice immediately. A new Chancellor, Prince Max of Baden, a liberal anti-militarist, was at this moment in process of forming a new government. When the High Command warned that the army could not hold long enough to permit protracted negotiations, Prince Max appealed to President Wilson on October 3 for an armistice based on the Fourteen Points and subsequent Wilsonian pronouncements.

There were demands for driving straight to the Rhine, but Wilson resolved to end the fighting, provided an effective German surrender could be obtained. Actually, Ludendorff and the other German leaders hoped to use the supposedly simple Wilson to win the respite that they needed in order to prepare defense of the Fatherland. Wilson's reply to Prince Max's appeal revealed that the President understood German purposes. The United States was ready to consider peace negotiations, Wilson wrote on October 8, but only if the Central Powers would evacuate Belgium and France and give adequate guarantees that they would not resume hostilities—in other words, if Germany was prepared to admit defeat. Furthermore, Wilson added, he would negotiate only with a responsible, legitimate civilian government, not with the military masters of Germany.

Prince Max replied on October 12, assuring Wilson that he spoke in the name of the German people, accepting the Fourteen Points, and suggesting that a mixed commission be established to supervise the evacuation of France and Belgium. The President responded on October 14. Rejecting the suggestion of a mixed commission, he made it clear that the only kind of armistice that he would approve was one that guaranteed the present supremacy of the American and Allied armies. This note fell like a bolt in Berlin. The German commanders were now all for fighting to the last man. At the same time, it was evident that the morale of the German people was destroyed beyond repair, and the civilian government finally took control. Prince Max informed Wilson on October 20 that Germany accepted the President's conditions.

Convinced that the German peace appeal was sincere, Wilson replied on October 23 that he would transmit that appeal to the Allied governments and discuss with them the question of an armistice. Among the Allied-American prime ministers and commanders only Pershing opposed the cessation of hostilities on satisfactory military terms. Agreement on the military and naval terms had been reached by the evening of November 4 by the Supreme War Council, the Interallied Naval Council, Colonel House, representing President Wilson, and the British, French, and Italian premiers. In the meantime, events were transpiring within Germany that made acceptance of almost any terms by the German authorities inevitable. Wilson's message of October 23 to Prince Max had contained the hint that a German Republic would fare better at the peace conference than an Imperial Germany. Feeling in civilian and military circles reached such a point that the Emperor abdicated and fled to Holland on November 8. The lowering of the Imperial standards so shattered the army's morale that Germany was afterward incapable of waging even a purely defensive war.

Meanwhile, discussions in the Allied camp had brought Allied and American differences over peace terms sharply into the open. Believing that he had now or never to win Allied approval of his peace program, Wilson sent Colonel House to Paris to force a showdown with the Allied premiers. At the first conference on October 29 the Allied spokesmen claimed that they did not know what the Fourteen Points were. House read them. David Lloyd George, the British Prime Minister, refused point blank to accept Point 2 regarding freedom of the seas; the French and Italian leaders concurred. House replied that the President might feel compelled to lay the matter before the American people and make a separate peace if his colleagues refused to accept the Fourteen Points. He reiterated this warning on the following day and headed off a whole host of French and Italian objections.

The Allied leaders surrendered for the moment in the face of this threat, but not until the President had agreed that the British might reserve freedom of action on Point 2, and that the Germans should be told that they would be required to pay reparations for all civilian damages caused by their aggression. The Supreme War Council approved the compromise on November 4. On the following day Wilson informed the German government that Marshal Foch was ready to receive its representatives. German delegates met the French Marshal and a British naval representative in Foch's headquarters in a railroad car in Compiègne Forest on November 8. At 5:15 on the morning of November 11 they signed articles providing for a rapid withdrawal of the German armies beyond the right bank of the Rhine, surrender of a huge quantity of matériel and 150 submarines, and withdrawal of the German surface fleet to the Baltic.

Thus the end of the war saw no such capitulation of the German forces as the Allied armies could have soon compelled. It saw, instead, agreement by both sides to quit fighting on terms that would prevent Germany from renewing hostilities and, more important, on the basis of a solemn Allied-American pledge that Germany could expect a peace based upon the Fourteen Points and subsequent Wilsonian pronouncements with the two reservations noted.

84. *Preliminaries to the Peace Conference*

The President would need the full support of the American people in the months following the Armistice if he were to win the peace settlement that he had set his heart upon. But he could have overwhelming support at home only if he continued to be the spokesman of the entire country, of Republican moderates as well as Democrats of good will. In this situation, which demanded adroit and national leadership, Wilson so failed to unite the country that it was doubtful whether he spoke for a majority of his people when the peace conference opened.

He made his first mistake even before the guns were silenced on the western front, at the close of the hotly contested off-year congressional campaign. Importuned on all sides by Democratic congressional and senatorial nominees for individual endorsements such as he had given many times before, Wilson decided to issue a blanket appeal to the country. Instead of asking voters to elect candidates who would support him regardless of party affiliation, he made a frankly partisan appeal for a Democratic Congress on October 25, 1918. "The return of a Republican majority to either House of the Congress," he added, "would . . . certainly be interpreted on the other side of the water as a repudiation of my leadership." It was an invitation to disaster. By attempting to make political capital out of foreign policy, Wilson outraged the numerous Republicans whose support had made his war measures possible and threw the question of the peace settlement into the arena of partisan discussion. Even worse, Wilson had declared that he would stand repudiated in the eyes of the world if the people did not vote the Democratic ticket. He had asked for a vote of confidence when he should have known that such a vote is impossible in the American constitutional system.

It is ironical that Wilson's appeal probably had little effect on the outcome of the elections on November 6. Other factors—business resentment against high taxes, disaffection of western wheat farmers because the administration had put ceilings on wheat prices and allowed cotton prices to rise uncontrolled, all the large and petty irritations that stemmed from the war, and the normal inclination of a majority to vote Republican—these, rather than Wilson's ill-timed and futile appeal, accounted for the Republican victory.[1]

Whether or not he stood repudiated by his own people, President Wilson had to proceed. He went ahead unperturbed, sustained by the conviction that he was the representative, not only of the great majority of Americans, but of forward-looking people everywhere. Wilson announced on November 18, 1918, that he would go to the peace conference in Paris as head of

wwwwwwwwwwwwww

[1] In the next, or Sixty-sixth, Congress, the Republicans would outnumber the Democrats in the House of Representatives 237 to 190 and have a majority of two in the Senate.

the American delegation. Believing as he did that only he could prevail against the forces of greed at Paris, and that the fate of the liberal international program depended upon his presence at the peace conference, Wilson thought that he had no choice in the matter. He went to Paris because stern duty called him there, and whether his decision was a mistake is at least debatable.

Wilson's choice of the peace commissioners was, as things turned out, more of a blunder. The commissioners, in addition to the President, were Colonel House, Secretary of State Lansing, General Tasker H. Bliss, a member of the Supreme War Council, and Henry White, an experienced Republican diplomat. All of them were able men, but circumstances demanded more than mere ability. Other considerations aside, political necessity demanded appointment of a peace commission that was broadly representative, for Wilson would fail in the critical period after the peace conference if he could not command the support of the Senate and a large minority of Republicans. Wilson understandably ignored the Senate, because he knew that he would have to include Henry Cabot Lodge of Massachusetts, who would be the new chairman of the foreign relations committee, if he appointed any senators at all. Personal relations between the President and Senator Lodge were already so bad that Lodge's appointment was out of the question. On the other hand, it is difficult to understand why Wilson ignored certain other prominent Republicans, notably William H. Taft, who might have worked loyally with him at Paris. The answer lies perhaps in Wilson's growing realization that the important work would, perforce, have to be done by the heads of government at the conference, and in his belief that he would need a group of advisers whom he could trust absolutely. But by refusing to take prominent Republicans to Paris Wilson offended the great body of moderate Republicans and lent credibility to the charge then current that he intended to maintain an exclusive Democratic monopoly on peacemaking.

85. *The Versailles Compromise*

Wilson, the peace commissioners, and a large body of technical experts sailed from New York aboard the *George Washington* on the morning of December 4, 1918. The voyage was a tonic to the President and afforded him an opportunity to reflect soberly on the task ahead. Already he was beginning to think that the burden of delivering Europe from the tyranny of history would fall mainly on his own shoulders. The American delegation, he told the assembled experts on board, would be the only disinterested spokesmen at the conference; the Allied leaders did not even represent their own people. "Tell me what's right and I'll fight for it," he promised.

The situation in Europe did not, however, portend easy sailing for one who wished merely to fight for the right. England was in the throes of a parliamentary campaign that found Lloyd George and his Conservative-dominated coalition obliged to give hostages to the aroused passions of the electorate. The French were in a state of postwar shock and clamoring for fearful retribution. Italians expected compensation for their losses in the form of large accretions of Austrian territory. Germany was torn by revolt, and the old Austro-Hungarian Empire had already crumbled. Moreover, the meeting place of the Conference, Paris, was a hotbed of anti-German hatred. The crippling terms that the Germans had imposed on the Russians in the treaty of Brest-Litovsk in March 1918 could be used to put aside arguments in favor of greater leniency. At the same time, consideration of long-term issues was handicapped by the immediate fears of the spread of Bolshevism into central and even western Europe.

Wilson first made triumphal tours of Paris, London, and Rome. He then returned to Versailles on January 12, 1919, for discussions with the Allied leaders, who made plans for the first Plenary Session that met six days later. So unwieldy was the conference that important questions were referred to a Council of Ten representing Great Britain, France, Italy, the United States, and Japan, while the detail work was divided among sixty commissions on which the small nations were represented. In order to hasten the conference's work, the Council of Ten was abolished on March 24, and the so-called Big Four—Wilson, Lloyd George, Premier Georges Clemenceau of France, and Prime Minister Orlando of Italy—began a long series of private discussions. At the same time, the Council of Five, consisting of the foreign ministers of the five great powers, was established to discuss matters of subordinate importance.

A treaty for Germany had been hammered out and presented to the government of the new German Republic by the end of April. The German Foreign Secretary appeared before a Plenary Session to receive the Treaty on May 7; the German delegates presented a comprehensive reply on May 29; the German National Assembly at Weimar approved the Treaty on June 23. The formal ceremony of signing was held on June 28, 1919, in the Hall of Mirrors of the Versailles Palace, where the German Empire had been proclaimed forty-eight years before.

This chronology ignores the thousand small details and the writing of treaties with other Central Powers. What concerns us most at this point, however, is what Wilson accomplished by his labors at Paris. How did his liberal peace program fare, in spite of the high passions that pervaded the deliberations? The answer is that Wilson accomplished less than he fought for and a great deal more than his critics later admitted. The Versailles Treaty was a compromise between the Fourteen Points and what the Allied, and especially the French, peoples demanded.

The foremost problem was security against future German aggression in the West. Foch and Clemenceau proposed to tear the west bank of the Rhine from Germany and create buffer states under French control. Wilson resisted this demand with Lloyd George's assistance. Instead, France had to be satisfied with the return of Alsace-Lorraine, which was in accord with the principle of self-determination and the Fourteen Points; the permanent demilitarization and a fifteen-year occupation by Allied forces of the west bank of the Rhine; and an Anglo-French-American treaty of mutual defense against Germany. It was this promise of a triple defensive security treaty that persuaded Clemenceau to abandon his demand for the creation of buffer states in the Rhineland. Finally, the German army and navy were so severely limited in size that a future German war of aggression was to be impossible. On the whole, Wilson, Lloyd George, and Clemenceau succeeded in erecting an intelligent defensive structure which, if maintained

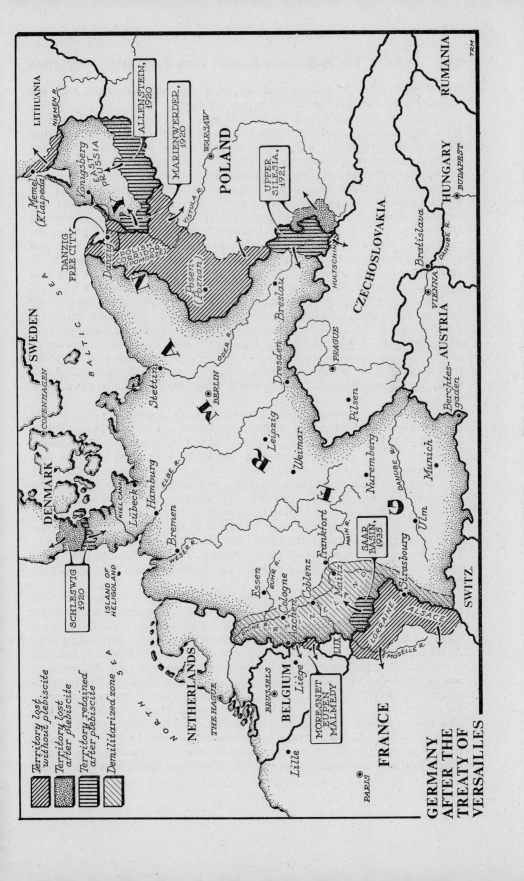

GERMANY
AFTER THE
TREATY OF
VERSAILLES

in full vigor, might have preserved the peace of Europe. Certainly it did not violate the Fourteen Points in any important way.

Secondly, Wilson found the spokesmen of Britain, the British Dominions, Japan, and Italy determined that Germany should not recover her overseas colonies. In the face of their inflexible position, he gave in, but not without gaining important concessions. For one thing, although Japan received title to German economic rights in the Shantung Province, she promised to return that province to the political control of China. For another, the former German colonies were not awarded outright to new masters, but were made mandates of the League of Nations and given in responsible trusteeship to Great Britain, the Dominions, and Japan. Whether this arrangement represented the "absolutely impartial adjustment of all colonial claims" that Wilson had demanded in Point 5 would in large measure depend upon the development of the mandate system. We can now see that approval of the mandate system marked the end of western colonialism.

A third major problem was the creation of a Polish state that would have access to the sea and include former German and Austrian territory inhabited mainly by Poles, without violating unduly the principle of self-determination. Wilson and Lloyd George stood firm against Clemenceau and the Polish representatives to win a settlement that vindicated the Fourteen Points. Poland was given a corridor to the Baltic, while Danzig, her outlet to the sea, was made a free city under the administration of the League of Nations.

The fourth important issue—how much Austrian territory Italy should receive—involved the validity of the secret Treaty of London of 1915. It had brought Italy into the war and promised her the Trentino, the Austrian Tyrol, and a strip of the Dalmatian coast. Wilson was impressed by the plea that control of the Brenner Pass in the Tyrol was absolutely essential to Italian security. He therefore agreed that this area, which contained 200,-000 Germans, should go to Italy. The Italians also demanded a long strip of the Dalmatian coast, including the important Port of Fiume. Wilson passionately objected, going so far as to appeal to the Italian people over the heads of their government. He argued that Fiume was the only possible outlet to the sea for the new state of Yugoslavia, and he pointed to the Treaty of London, which awarded the port to Yugoslavia. He won his case by main force.

In the struggle over the fifth great issue, reparations, Wilson made his most important concessions. He had agreed during the pre-Armistice negotiations that Germany should be compelled to pay for all civilian damages incurred by the Allied countries during the war—alone a staggering sum. At the conference he agreed that Germany should also be forced to bear the cost of separation allowances and pensions for Allied veterans. Although he was ill at the time and acted through Colonel House, the President later approved Article CCXXXI of the Treaty, in which Germany acknowledged *legal* responsibility for all losses incurred by the Allied governments and peoples during the war. Wilson agreed, besides, that the Allies might occupy the Rhineland until the potentially astronomical reparations bill was finally paid. Nor was this all. In compensation for wanton destruction of French mines by the retreating German armies, France was given ownership of the mines in the Saar Province of Germany, and the territory was to be governed by a League of Nations commission for fifteen years. The people of the Saar might vote to join the Fatherland at the end of that period. Finally, the Treaty compelled the Germans to pay to Britain, France, and Belgium twenty billion gold marks' worth of reparations in kind—merchant shipping, coal, livestock, and the like. Inexplicably, Wilson made hardly any effort to prevent this, the grossest violation of the Fourteen Points and the Pre-Armistice Agreement with Germany.

In Wilson's mind, however, the first, last, and overriding issue was the creation of an international organization to create a concert of world power and preserve the peace. He insisted from the outset of the conference that the Covenant, or constitution, of the League of Nations be firmly embedded in the Treaty, and that execution of the Treaty be entrusted to the League. Clemenceau was not opposed to the League, but he contended that the organization would be helpless to maintain peace unless it had a powerful army and navy at its command. Convinced that such a proposal was politically impossible, Wilson and the British delegates created a League that would depend upon the wholehearted support of its leading members for its effectiveness. As Clemenceau thought that he had obtained security for his beloved France by other means, he was willing to let Wilson write any kind of Covenant he desired.

Wilson must have looked back over his labors at Paris and remembered the tense sessions, the bitter complaints of Orlando, the barbed remarks of Clemenceau, and the compromises that he inevitably had had to make. He was nonetheless certain that he had helped to write a Treaty and create a postwar peace structure that would endure. He knew that the Treaty was not perfect, but he was sure that time would heal many wounds, and that the United States could obtain modifications within the League of Nations.

Critics, contemporary and historical, have castigated Wilson in general for failing to win the liberal peace program at Paris, in particular for bargaining all his Fourteen Points away in order to win a League of Nations. Such criticism can come only from one who has never bothered to read the Fourteen Points, for that document was actually honored more in the observance than in the breach. Wilson's chief failures—on the colonial question and reparations—were perhaps inevitable. But the damage done was not irreparable, given forceful American leadership in the League of Nations and the Reparations Commission. Wilson failed to vindicate the principle of freedom of the seas only because he finally realized during the conference that freedom of the seas was a part of the old system of neutrality, and that neutrality would be impossible in future wars. As he said, there could be no neutrals in the new system of collective security.

Wilson's critics, not content with exaggerating his failures, have also minimized his difficulties. He did not write the Treaty alone but in collaboration with three astute and determined negotiators. To be sure, Wilson could have withdrawn from the conference, as on one occasion he seriously threatened to do. But the results of American withdrawal would have been even worse than an unsatisfactory settlement. Furthermore, Wilson's difficulties at Paris were compounded by virulent opposition to his peace program in the United States. Senator Lodge, for example, did not lighten the

President's burdens by writing to Clemenceau that Wilson did not speak for the American people, who, Lodge declared, desired a harsh and punitive settlement.

Finally, the historian must ask what kind of a peace treaty would have been written if Wilson had not been at Paris and had not won British support for most of his principles. Wilson and Lloyd George together prevented the dismemberment of Germany and compelled a redrawing of the map of Europe that did not unnecessarily violate the principle of self-determination. As the spokesman of the only disinterested nation represented at the conference, Wilson emerged from the fiery trial with the greatest stature precisely because he was able to accomplish so much in spite of stupendous obstacles.

86.   First Phases of the Treaty Fight

There were signs long before the end of the Peace Conference that Wilson would encounter strong opposition in the Senate if he insisted on incorporating the League Covenant in the Treaty. The President returned briefly to Washington in the latter part of February 1919 and conferred with the members of the House and Senate foreign relations committees in an effort to meet the rising criticism. Many senators, he learned, objected because the Covenant contained no explicit recognition of the Monroe Doctrine, did not specifically exclude internal affairs from the jurisdiction of the League, and made no provision for the right of a member nation to withdraw. On March 4, 1919, just before Wilson was to return to France, moreover, Senator Lodge presented to the upper house a round robin drawn up by Republican leaders warning that the Covenant, "in the form now proposed," was unacceptable. It was signed by thirty-nine senators or senators-elect, considerably more than the one third plus one necessary to defeat ratification.

Wilson did not turn the other cheek but was defiant in response. When he brought the Treaty back with him, so he boasted at the Madison Square Garden on March 4, the Covenant would be so embedded in the Treaty that the two could never be separated. Back in Paris, however, Wilson obtained changes in the Covenant to meet all the criticisms noted above. Returning to the United States on July 8, he formally presented the Treaty to the Senate two days later. "Our isolation was ended twenty years ago," he declared. ". . . There can be no question of our ceasing to be a world power. The only question is whether we can refuse the moral leadership that is offered, whether we shall accept or reject the confidence of the world."

Wilson spoke confidently of the great new role of "service and achievement" that lay ahead for the American people, whose destiny had been disclosed by the very hand of God. His poetic phrases, however, suggested a unanimity that did not exist. No one could yet say how large a part of the population critics of the Treaty represented, but they were already well organized and exceedingly vociferous by the time that Wilson returned to the United States. Leading the opposition were a small group of extreme isolationists in the Senate, chief among whom were Hiram W. Johnson of California, William E. Borah of Idaho, and James A. Reed of Missouri. These irreconcilables, as they were called, were convinced that membership in the

League would violate wise historic policy, and they pledged themselves to keep America free from the entanglements of Europe. Even though sincere conviction, and not petty hatred of Wilson, caused them to raise the standards of battle, they fought bitterly and unscrupulously. Their chief weapons were misstatements, perversions of fact, and false alarms.

Perhaps even more bitterly opposed to the Treaty were the so-called hyphenates, their newspapers, and their chief journalistic allies, the Hearst publications. German Americans protested that the Treaty was a base betrayal of the Pre-Armistice Agreement. Italian Americans were sulking over Wilson's refusal to award Fiume to Italy. But the most virulent opposition came from the Irish Americans. They were up in arms because Wilson had refused to press the cause of Irish independence at Versailles or throw the support of the United States behind the Irish rebellion then in progress.

These opponents were powerful, but the President might yet have triumphed if all Americans who believed in the liberal international program had stood together. Unfortunately for Wilson, such a solid phalanx did not materialize. In the first place, many cautious liberal internationalists—like Elihu Root and Henry L. Stimson, who put their faith in international law and arbitration—feared that Wilson was going too far too fast in breaking with ingrained American traditions. In the second place, many independent progressives and radicals, who had followed Wilson during the war and shared his noble dream of a new world order, drew back in revulsion when the terms of the Treaty were published. "The European politicians who with American complicity have hatched this inhuman monster," exclaimed the *New Republic*, the leading liberal internationalist journal, "have acted either cynically, hypocritically, or vindictively." The *Nation* and other such liberal journals were equally bitter.

The greatest obstacles to ratification of the Treaty, however, were personal and partisan rivalries and prejudices, old traditions of apartness, and the absence in 1919 and 1920 of any popular conviction that membership in the League was essential to American security. Germany had been decisively beaten and disarmed; Russia was in chaos. No war clouds darkened the horizon; no nation menaced the peace and security of the United States. Men might warn of the perils of the future, but who would believe them when it was obvious there could never be another war?

After Wilson presented the Treaty to the Senate on July 10, the vortex of the struggle over ratification shifted to the upper house, which in the past had upset the plans of less distinguished Presidents than Woodrow Wilson. A fairly distinct alignment was already evident by midsummer of 1919. There were some twelve to fifteen bitter-end isolationists, mainly Republicans, who would vote against the Treaty in any form so long as it contained the Covenant. They were a small minority, but they dominated the foreign relations committee and were able to influence the committee's chairman, Lodge, by their frequent threats to bolt the Republican camp. On the other hand, at least forty-three of the forty-seven Democrats would follow Wilson's lead, while the great majority of the forty-nine Republicans favored ratification after making certain reservations to safeguard American interests. Most of these were what were called strong reservationists. Thus considerably more than the necessary two thirds in the Senate favored ratification of the Treaty and membership in the League. The main task of statesmanship in the months ahead would be to find common ground upon which this preponderant majority could stand.

Much, of course, would depend upon the ability of leaders of both parties to suppress partisan ambitions and prejudices and pull together for the common good. The Republican leader in the Senate was Henry Cabot Lodge, a Boston Brahmin, long an intimate of Theodore Roosevelt, and a man of some intellect. Although he had supported a postwar League in 1915 and 1916, Lodge reversed himself after Wilson linked the League plan with the concept of a "peace without victory." Exactly where he stood on the League of Nations in the summer of 1919, it is impossible to say. One historian has recently suggested that Lodge was not an irreconcilable but rather that he was intent upon taking leadership in the Treaty struggle out of Wilson's hands and winning credit for ratification for himself and the Republican party.

Lodge's position was, admittedly, extraordinarily difficult. As leader of his party in the Senate he had to preserve some semblance of harmony among the three Republican factions—the irreconcilable isolationists, the so-called mild reservationists, and the majority who favored strong reservations. Naturally he was buffeted about and appeared all things to all men. But never during the Treaty fight or afterward did he act like a sincere friend of the League or a statesman who was able to exalt the national interest above his consuming personal hatred of Wilson and the Democratic party. On the contrary, moving from one calculated step to another, he acted as if his chief purpose was to embarrass the President and prevent ratification of the Treaty.

Public sentiment in July 1919 was running so strongly in favor of the Treaty that Lodge knew that he could not defeat it outright. Thirty-two state legislatures and thirty-three governors had endorsed the League. Leaders of the League to Enforce Peace were now actively campaigning for unconditional ratification, and a poll of the nation's press indicated that an overwhelming majority of newspapers favored American membership in the League. It was evident to the Massachusetts senator, therefore, that he must work indirectly—first, by packing the foreign relations committee with enemies of the League; second, by appending such strong reservations to the Covenant that the President would refuse to accept them.

Meanwhile, Lodge desperately needed time to allow the opponents of the League to agitate. Time he easily obtained, by reading aloud all of the 264 pages of the Treaty, which consumed two weeks, and then by holding public hearings on the Treaty for another six weeks. In the meantime, the bitter-enders, liberally supplied with funds by the steel manufacturer Henry C. Frick and the banker and aluminum monopolist Andrew W. Mellon, flooded the country with anti-League propaganda.

Opponents of the Treaty were gaining momentum by September 1919. At the same time, a series of convulsive strikes had diverted Wilson's attention and prevented him from giving his customary leadership to the League forces. It is true that he had appeared before Lodge's committee on August 19 and conferred individually with some twenty Republican senators, most of them "mild reservationists," in an effort to detach them from their party. But the more he conferred with senators the more he realized that the situation was passing out of his control. In these circumstances Wilson decided upon bold steps. First, he announced on September 3 that he would not oppose interpretive reservations that did not impair the integrity of the Covenant or require new diplomatic negotiations. Second, he decided to carry his fight for the League to the people. He would purify the wells of public sentiment poisoned by the irreconcilables; he would tell the people the truth about their stake in preserving peace through the League of Nations.

No act of his public career so dramatically demonstrated Wilson's sincerity as his decision to undertake this campaign. His health had been poor since he narrowly escaped a stroke at Paris. He was now weak and exhausted, and his physician warned that a long speaking tour might take his life. He gladly took the risk, however, thinking that he could arouse such a ground swell of support for the League that his senatorial opponents could not resist it. He traveled more than 8,000 miles through the Middle and Far West for three weeks in September and delivered some thirty-seven addresses. The strain on his meager physical resources was great, but the total effect of his outpouring to the people of the West was magnificent. The deeper Wilson moved into the West the larger and more enthusiastic the crowds became. In fact, the irreconcilables were so alarmed by the President's triumphal procession that they sent their two best speakers, Senators Johnson and Borah, to trail him.

The effects of the strain began to tell on Wilson even before the tour was half over. He began to have blinding headaches and to show signs of exhaustion. He delivered one of his longest and most important speeches at Pueblo, Colorado, on September 25. "It always seems to make it difficult for me to say anything, my fellow citizens, when I think of my clients in this case," he exclaimed. "My clients are the children; my clients are the next generation. . . . I intend to redeem my pledges to the children; they shall not be sent . . . [to France]." After this address the President was so near collapse that his physician canceled the remaining speeches and sped the presidential train straight to Washington. Wilson suffered a stroke on October 2, 1919, that paralyzed the left side of his face and body, and for days his life hung in a precarious balance.

87. *The Triumph of Partisanship*

Meanwhile, the battle in the Senate had begun when the foreign relations committee reported the Treaty on September 10, 1919, with forty-five amendments and four reservations. The Democrats defeated all the amendments with the help of some twelve Republican "mild reservationists." Thereupon Lodge, on November 6, presented for his committee a series of fourteen reservations. Most of them merely underlined existing provisions of the Covenant and provided that the United States could take no action in important matters without the consent of Congress. The fourth reservation reserved control over all domestic affairs exclusively to the United States; the fifth removed all questions arising under the Monroe Doctrine from the jurisdiction of the League; the sixth declared that the United States withheld assent from the articles of the Treaty relating to Shantung. The most important reservation, the second, had been suggested by Elihu Root on

June 21, 1919. It asserted that the United States assumed no obligations under Article X of the Covenant to preserve the territorial integrity or political
independence of any country, interfere in controversies between nations, or
use its armed forces to uphold any article of the Treaty for any purpose, unless Congress by joint resolution so provided. The Senate approved twelve of
Lodge's reservations, including the second, after a bitter partisan battle and
added two others.

The next move was up to the ailing President and his Democratic colleagues in the Senate. Colonel House and other friends of the League begged
Wilson either to compromise on Lodge's terms or else to accept the Senator's
reservations entirely, if that were necessary to get the United States into the
League. Gilbert M. Hitchcock of Nebraska, Democratic leader in the Senate, was allowed to visit Wilson in his sickroom on November 7 and 17. He
found the President determined never to surrender and disposed to compromise only on his own terms—by accepting reservations that he thought did
not impair the obligations of the United States under the Covenant. Furthermore, in a public letter to Hitchcock, actually drafted by Hitchcock,
Wilson declared on November 18 that the Lodge reservations provided for
nullification, not ratification, of the Treaty. He virtually ordered Democratic senators to vote against them.

The first showdown came when the Senate voted on the Treaty on the
following day, November 19, 1919. On a resolution to ratify with the Lodge
reservations, the irreconcilables combined with a nearly solid Democratic
phalanx to defeat ratification by a vote of fifty-five nays to thirty-nine ayes.
A Democratic resolution to ratify without any reservations failed immediately afterward by a vote of fifty-three nays to thirty-eight ayes. Obviously,
Wilson's strategy of splitting the "mild reservationists" from the Republican
bloc had failed.

Yet it was apparent from the two test votes that seventy-seven senators,
considerably more than the necessary two thirds, favored ratification with
or without reservations. What chance was there for compromise between
the two factions? It was clear after the first Senate vote that Lodge would
never surrender and that Wilson would have to compromise largely on the
Senator's terms if he wanted ratification. Colonel House advised the President to wash his hands of responsibility and let the Senate decide; William J. Bryan urged immediate ratification, even with reservations, and
most Democratic senators privately agreed. The French and British leaders
were, if anything, more frightened by the prospect of the Treaty's defeat
than were Wilson's friends. The British government sent Sir Edward Grey
(now Viscount Grey of Fallodon), former Foreign Secretary, as a special
Ambassador to Washington to plead for compromise. The President, however, refused to see Grey and was angered when the Viscount later issued a
public statement declaring that the League would fail without the United
States, and that the Allies would accept the Lodge reservations without requiring a reopening of negotiations.

Public sentiment in the United States, moreover, refused to accept the
Senate's vote on November 19, 1919, as final. Leaders of the League to Enforce Peace, now called the League of Free Nations Association, appealed
for ratification with necessary reservations; newspaper spokesmen were up
in arms. Spokesmen of twenty-six organizations representing some 20,-

000,000 members on January 13 and February 9, 1920, demanded that Lodge and Wilson compromise their differences. But the aged and weary man in the White House paid scant heed to this ground swell, if, indeed, he knew much about it. He tried to find some constitutional way to challenge his senatorial foes to resign and go before their constituents on the issue of the League. In this plan he would have resigned if his opponents were returned to the Senate. Failing for technical reasons to work this out, Wilson made another proposal in a public letter to Democrats assembled at a Jackson Day dinner in Washington on January 8, 1920. He was certain, Wilson asserted, that the overwhelming majority of Americans desired prompt ratification without crippling reservations. If, however, the Senate refused thus to ratify, then the presidential election of 1920 would be a "great and solemn referendum" in which the voters could decide the issue. Wilson probably meant this more as a threat than as a proposal to be taken seriously. He apparently still believed that the Senate in the final showdown would not dare to reject the Treaty entirely.

In the face of what seemed to be an overwhelming demand at home and abroad for ratification, the Senate agreed to reconsider and began debate anew in mid-February 1920. While Democratic leaders tried desperately to find common ground with the Republicans, the President, now vastly improved in health and mental vigor, hurled blast after blast at the Lodge reservations and even intimated that he would refuse to proclaim the Treaty if the Senate adopted them. The Treaty came up for vote on March 19. One reservation, favoring Irish independence, had been added by the Democrats in an effort to embarrass Lodge, while the second reservation regarding Article X had been made even more sweeping than before.

Practically all Democratic senators desperately wanted to accept the reservations. But a majority of them were literally too afraid of Wilson to oppose him; and twenty-three Democrats joined the irreconcilables to defeat approval by a vote of thirty-five nays to forty-nine ayes. A change of only seven Democratic votes would have put the United States in the League of Nations! To end the state of hostilities, Congress adopted a joint resolution on May 15, 1920, repealing the war resolutions against Germany and Austria-Hungary and reserving to the United States all rights under the Treaty of Versailles. Wilson vetoed this resolution on May 27, declaring that he would not be party "to an action which would place ineffable stain upon the gallantry and honor of the United States."

It was the end, although the tragedy was prolonged during the "great and solemn referendum" that was no referendum at all. Who was responsible for American refusal to enter the League of Nations and for the "ineffable stain" of a separate peace? Certainly Lodge and his Republican friends shared a large measure of guilt for one of the most tragic episodes in American history. Had they been less interested in the election of 1920 and more concerned with their country's good they would have suppressed personal and partisan ambitions and met the champions of the League halfway. In addition, the irreconcilables, who used every device to defeat ratification, shared a large part of the blame, for their unscrupulous propaganda helped to confuse the public about the implications of American membership in the League.

On the other hand, Wilson, too, was partly responsible. Perhaps because of his hatred of Lodge, perhaps because he believed to the end that the people would force the Senate to his terms, perhaps because his illness had impaired his statesmanship, he also refused to compromise. He ignored the advice of his best counselors and threw away the only possible chance for ratification. He therefore shared responsibility for breaking the heart of the world. Moreover, those Democratic senators who voted against ratification with reservations out of fear of Wilsonian wrath served neither the national interest nor the cause of international peace.

Whatever the causes for the great betrayal of 1919–20, the consequences remained. The American people were perhaps not yet ready to assume leadership in world affairs, but their leaders denied them an opportunity even to learn the duties of leadership or to grow in wisdom and experience. More important were the catastrophic effects of the American rejection on the infant League and on the future development of European politics. Given American leadership in the postwar era, the League might have developed into the association of free peoples of which its founders had dreamed, and become more efficient in dealing with the maladjustments of European society.

CHAPTER

II

Demobilization and the Triumph of Normalcy

1918–1920

ALL POSTWAR PERIODS in American history have been times when partisanship runs at fever pitch and passions generated by the war drive people to acts of violence. So it was during the years following the Armistice, as war hysteria found new victims in "Reds," foreigners, Jews, Negroes, and Catholics. As if further to confuse the domestic scene, labor unrest during 1919 and 1920 was at its highest peak since the 1890's. Politically, the postwar era was marked by extraordinary partisanship. Centering at first on the struggle over ratification of the Versailles Treaty, this partisan conflict culminated in 1920, when a reunited Republican party smashed the Wilsonian progressive coalition and swept into control of the federal government. The election results were convincing evidence that the people were determined to put an end to the division of control in the federal government and to return, as the Republican candidate in 1920 said, to "normalcy," to the good days of prosperity and peace.

88. Demobilization, 1918–1920

Just as it had adopted the war resolution without any effective preparation for a great war effort, the American government found itself on

November 11, 1918, without any plan for demobilization and reconstruction. Indeed, the sudden and unexpected German collapse came at a time when American leaders were planning, not for peace, but for an invasion of Germany in 1919.

The President aptly described the manner in which demobilization took place in his Annual Message to Congress in December 1918: "The moment we knew the armistice to have been signed we took the harness off." And that is about what happened. The A.E.F. was brought home and quickly demobilized. Various war agencies began to wind up their affairs. For example, the War Industries Board, refusing to believe there were any problems of demobilization that the business world could not solve, abandoned its control of industry once the fighting stopped. "The magnificent war formation of American industry was dissipated in a day," writes the Board's chief historian.

Everyone, it seemed, expected the country to return quickly to normal without benefit of governmental controls and planning. However, by the time that Wilson returned from Paris for the first time, in February 1919, prices were rising fast, and large-scale unemployment and industrial conflict seemed inevitable. Unable to obtain legislation from the lame-duck session, Wilson prepared for the impending crisis as best he could. Calling governors and mayors to the White House on March 3, he warned them of the dangers ahead. In addition, he established an Industrial Board to co-ordinate the efforts of various governmental purchasing agencies to hold the line on prices. The Industrial Board, however, had neither statutory authority nor prestige in the business world. It disbanded in May 1919, after the Railroad Administration refused to permit it to fix prices for steel.

For the most part, therefore, the administration was powerless to meet the larger problems of postwar inflation, business readjustment, and industrial conflict. On the other hand, the period 1919–20 was not as chaotic or unproductive as this generalization might suggest. For one thing, there were specific problems of demobilization so urgent that Congress could not ignore them. For another, the last two years of the Wilson era witnessed congressional approval of significant measures that brought several phases of the progressive movement to final culmination.

The first requirement was the most urgent—to provide funds to liquidate the war effort at home, care for wounded soldiers and sailors, bring the A.E.F. back from France, and provide relief for Europe. In spite of demands for immediate tax reduction, the lame-duck session courageously adopted a War Revenue bill in February 1919 that increased the tax burden, especially on business and the upper classes. (For the provisions of this measure see above, p. 201.)

The second problem was the disposition of the railroads still being operated by the Railroad Administration at the beginning of 1919. While McAdoo recommended a five-year experiment in public operation and Congress deliberated during the summer of 1919, a movement for nationalization gained the support of AF of L unions and the railroad brotherhoods. It was the so-called Plumb Plan, suggested by Glenn E. Plumb, a lawyer for the brotherhoods, to nationalize the railroads and give the workers a share in their management and profit. Wilson took no part in the controversy. He simply announced on December 24, 1919, that he would return the railroads to their owners on March 1, 1920, unless Congress decided otherwise.

Congress responded with the Transportation Act of 1920, drawn largely by two midwestern progressive Republicans, Representative John J. Esch of Wisconsin and Senator Albert B. Cummins of Iowa, and approved February 28, 1920. The Transportation Act was perhaps the most significant measure of the immediate postwar era because it marked the complete fulfillment of the movement for thoroughgoing federal control of railroads. Stopping only short of nationalization, the Act gave the ICC complete control over rates, even those set by state commissions; authorized the Commission to supervise the sale of railroad securities and expenditure of the proceeds; permitted railroads to pool traffic in the interest of economy; and empowered the ICC to consolidate existing lines into a limited number of systems.

A third issue was disposition of the huge fleet of merchant vessels that the Shipping Board had purchased, confiscated, or built during and after the war. No one wanted to junk a merchant marine that totaled some 15,000,000 tons by 1920; yet Congress was unwilling to embark upon a long-range program of public operation. A compromise solution was embodied in the Merchant Marine Act of 1920. It directed the Shipping Board to sell as many vessels as possible to corporations of predominantly American ownership and authorized the federally owned Merchant Fleet Corporation to open new shipping lines and operate surplus vessels. As it turned out, the Shipping Board's low prices on easy terms and guarantees against operational losses to private firms lured considerable private capital into the shipping industry and kept a sizable merchant marine afloat in the 1920's. By 1930 the privately owned American merchant marine totaled over 7,000,000 tons.

Four measures—the General Leasing and Water Power acts of 1920 and the woman's suffrage and prohibition amendments—rounded out the postwar legislative program and revealed that the reform spirit was by no means dead. The General Leasing Act kept large naval oil reserves from private exploitation but empowered the Secretary of the Interior to lease other public lands containing mineral and oil deposits to private parties on terms that safeguarded the public interest. The Water Power Act established a Federal Power Commission, composed of the Secretaries of War, the Interior, and Agriculture. It could license the building and operation of dams and hydroelectric plants on navigable rivers and non-navigable streams in the public domain. Experience soon proved that effective federal control of electric rates and services was almost impossible under this legislation. Even so, it marked the beginning of federal regulation of an expanding electric power industry.

We will reserve our discussion of national prohibition for a later chapter. The point here is that Congress acted promptly and, it thought, effectively to implement what many progressives hailed as the greatest triumph for morality since the abolition of slavery. Another important objective of the progressive movement, woman's suffrage, also came to fruition at this time. Congress approved the Nineteenth Amendment, which forbade denying the right to vote on account of sex, in June 1919; it went into effect in August 1920.

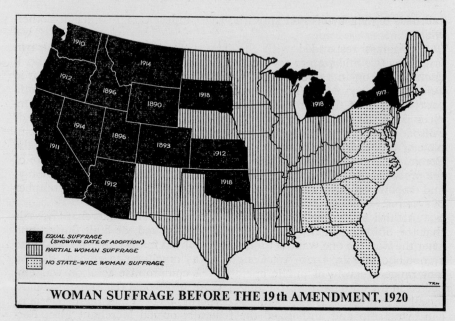

EQUAL SUFFRAGE
(SHOWING DATE OF ADOPTION)

PARTIAL WOMAN SUFFRAGE

NO STATE-WIDE WOMAN SUFFRAGE

WOMAN SUFFRAGE BEFORE THE 19th AMENDMENT, 1920

89. *Postwar Inflation and Labor Troubles*

Leaders in Washington and the states prepared during the early months of 1919 as best they could to cope with the mass unemployment that they thought would follow demobilization. The crisis that they anticipated never came. To be sure, industrial production declined slightly from October 1918 to July 1919, and unemployment reached a level of 3,000,000 in February 1919. But economic distress was acute at no time during these months. Then a boom got under way during the summer of 1919, and industrial production was well above the wartime peak by the following October.

A number of forces—continued heavy governmental spending, release of pent-up consumer demand and savings, rapid resumption of industrial and home construction, increased production of automobiles, and continuation of exports financed in part by American loans to the Allied governments—contributed to the postwar boom. In face of what seemed to be insatiable demand prices began rising in the spring of 1919 and continued to mount until the autumn of 1920. Prices of manufactured goods rose from 198.4 in 1918 (100 representing average prices in 1913) to 239.5 in 1920, while prices of processed farm products increased from 201.1 to 241.9 during the same period. To put it more comprehensively, the cost of living rose to 77 per cent above the prewar level in 1919 and to 105 per cent above the prewar level in 1920.

The postwar inflation's chief significance lay in the fact that it combined with other forces to set off an unprecedented outbreak of labor troubles. All told, during 1919 there were 2,665 strikes involving more than 4,000,000 workers, as organized labor fought to preserve wartime gains and embarked upon ambitious new projects of unionization.

The wave of strikes began four days after the Armistice, when the Amalgamated Clothing Workers in New York and Chicago struck for the forty-four-hour week and a 15 per cent wage increase. Victory for the union was followed by adoption of the new wage and hours scale in the entire clothing industry. Then in rapid succession followed strikes by textile workers in New England and New Jersey, a general strike in Seattle, strikes by New England telephone operators and by telegraph operators throughout the country, by the printers' union, the longshoremen of New York, and switchmen in the Chicago railroad yards. Practically all these strikes, and hundreds of others, succeeded, and organized labor was able not only to hold its own against rising prices but also to win an increase in real income.

This outbreak of industrial unrest, however, occurred at a time when the American people were disturbed by a new hysteria—the so-called Red scare. Most of the strikes of 1919 were waged successfully in spite of a growing popular suspicion that they were being provoked by Communist agents and would culminate in a general labor uprising. On the other hand, organized labor's most important effort in 1919, the AF of L's drive to establish collective bargaining in the steel industry, ran afoul of the "Red" hysteria.

The United States Steel Corporation had stood since 1901 as the chief barrier to unionization of the basic industries. Encouraged by the friendly attitude of federal authorities and what they thought was a sympathetic public opinion, the AF of L convention directed its executive committee in June 1918 to undertake "one mighty drive to organize the steel plants of America"—the first attack in a new general offensive against the mass industries. The union's president, Samuel Gompers, appointed a National Committee for the Organizing of the Iron and Steel Industry on August 1, with William Z. Foster, a left-wing syndicalist, as secretary.

Foster and his committee organized the steel workers all during late 1918 and early 1919, and the reorganized steel workers' union claimed a membership of 100,000 by June 1919 and was ready to test its strength in battle. Although the union included a minority of the steel workers, no impartial observer could doubt that it voiced the protests of the overwhelming majority against old and rankling grievances. Steel workers lived everywhere under the tyranny of petty bosses, and even mild complaints often brought prompt dismissal. Moreover, about half the iron and steel employees worked from twelve to fourteen hours a day, an additional quarter worked between ten to twelve hours daily, and a minority worked twenty-four hours a day every other Sunday.[1] Wage rates were so low in 1919 that 60 per cent of all steel workers and their families lived below or barely above a minimum subsistence level.

Union officials presented their demands—recognition, the eight-hour day, "an American living wage," and reinstatement of workers discharged for union activities—to Judge Elbert H. Gary, head of United States Steel, in August 1919. Gary refused to negotiate, and some 343,000 workers in the plants of United States Steel went on strike on September 22. Three

---

[1] The average work week in the steel industry in 1919 was 68.7 hours, as compared with a work week of 67.6 hours in 1910.

days later the walkout spread to plants of Bethlehem Steel. The ensuing struggle was marked by widespread violence in which eighteen strikers were killed, by the use of state and federal troops to prevent picketing, and by stern suppression of civil liberties in all strike districts except West Virginia. Perhaps the most significant aspect of the conflict was management's use of new propaganda techniques learned during the war. By raising and reiterating the false alarm of Bolshevism, management and the vast majority of newspapers diverted public attention from the workers' grievances to the false issue of communism. As a result the workers lost the support of public opinion in this most crucial battle.

With a large segment of public opinion and most state officials arrayed against them, the strikers could not win, for the steel companies had emerged from the war with full treasuries and resources adequate for a long struggle. The first break came when United States Steel officials imported tens of thousands of strikebreakers and put them to work under military guard. For example, the large United States Steel works at Gary, Indiana, were operating at 75 per cent capacity by November. The struggle dragged on into January 1920, when it was officially ended by the unconditional surrender of the AF of L.

While the steel strike was getting under way a police strike in Boston gave further evidence of deep social unrest and incidentally catapulted an obscure Governor of Massachusetts into the vice-presidency of the United States. The police of Boston, like most other public employees during the postwar inflation, were struggling to survive on prewar salaries. When city authorities refused to raise wages and correct other grievances, the policemen's organization, the Boston Social Club, obtained a charter as an AF of L local in August 1919 and threatened to strike. A hastily appointed Mayor's Citizens' Committee was conciliatory and proposed a settlement that would have granted most of the union's demands, except recognition. The Police Commissioner, however, not only rejected the proposed settlement but also summarily dismissed nineteen leaders of the local.

Thus goaded, the policemen abandoned their posts on September 9, 1919. A volunteer force of prominent citizens and Harvard students was unable to control the gangs of looters that menaced the city, and Governor Calvin Coolidge called out the Boston companies of the National Guard and took personal command. The strike was quickly broken; the rebel policemen were dismissed; and a new police force was assembled. And when Gompers appealed to Coolidge to persuade the Boston authorities to reinstate the strikers, the Governor replied with a cryptic rebuke that made him at once nationally famous: "There is no right to strike against the public safety by anybody, anywhere, any time."

The last important strike of the immediate postwar era, the short-lived bituminous coal strike of November 1919, was notable in that it provoked the first test of strength between the federal government and the new president of the United Mine Workers of America, John L. Lewis. Of all workers in the country bituminous miners probably had best grounds for discontent. The UMW had concluded a no-strike agreement—the so-called Washington Agreement—with the Fuel Administration in August 1917. Although anthracite miners later received substantial wage increases, bituminous miners received none. The UMW contended after the Armistice that the Washington Agreement was dead; government spokesmen, however, pointed to the fact that the Agreement would not expire until March 31, 1920.

Agitation among bituminous miners mounted in the spring and summer of 1919, and UMW officials were able to end an insurgent strike in Illinois in August only by extreme threats. The UMW met in national convention in Indianapolis in the following month and adopted a bold program demanding immediate abrogation of the Washington Agreement, a six-hour day and five-day week, and wage increases of 60 per cent. And when the operators refused to negotiate until the Washington Agreement had expired, Lewis called a nation-wide bituminous strike for November 1. Meanwhile, Attorney General A. Mitchell Palmer had tried vainly to persuade the UMW to cancel the strike order, which, he claimed, was in violation of the Lever Act.

Faced with a complete shutdown of the mines, Palmer obtained one injunction on November 8 from the federal district court in Indianapolis ordering Lewis and other UMW officials to cease all strike activity. Shortly afterward he obtained another injunction commanding union officials to cancel their strike order by November 10. "We cannot fight the government," Lewis declared as he called off the strike. Nonetheless, the miners refused to go back to work until the government, a month later, ordered an immediate 14 per cent wage increase and established an arbitration commission to consider the union's demands. The commission after extended hearings awarded the miners another 27 per cent increase in pay without changing the hours of work.

90. *The First Red Scare*

The triumph of the Bolshevik revolution in Russia in November 1917, the ensuing spread of communism into Germany, Hungary, and other parts of Europe, and especially the formation in Moscow on March 2, 1919, of the Third International, or Comintern, as it came to be known, dedicated to stimulating immediate world proletarian revolution, set off a wave of new hysteria in the United States. No other development of the postwar era so well reflected the insecurity of the American people as their reactions to fantastic rumors of an equally fantastic Bolshevik uprising in their midst.

An early sign of the excited state of public opinion was the trial of Victor Berger, Socialist congressman from Milwaukee, for conspiracy under the Sedition Act. Re-elected to the House in November 1918 after his indictment, Berger was tried in Chicago in the following December, convicted, and sentenced to prison for twenty years. He was released on bail pending appeal (the government finally dropped all charges against Berger in 1922), but denied his seat in the lower house when Congress met in special session in May 1919. Re-elected in a special election in December 1919, Berger was again denied his seat in January 1920.[2]

~~~~~~~~~~~~~~~~~~~~~~~

[2] He was re-elected to the House in 1922, seated promptly when Congress convened, and served until his death in 1929.

Berger's conviction was the first manifestation of hysteria that developed in response to a series of events during the following months into the first Red scare. Workers in Seattle staged a general strike on February 6, 1919, that brought industry to a standstill and seriously crippled operation of utilities and transportation services. Asserting that the strike was the work of Bolsheviks and the IWW, Mayor Ole Hanson trumpeted that it was the first step in a nation-wide workers' uprising. At the same time, committees of the United States Senate and the New York legislature began investigations of Bolshevik activities, while the Justice Department rounded up fifty-three alien Communists on the West Coast on February 11 and shipped them to New York for deportation. A week later a naturalized citizen was quickly acquitted in Indiana for killing an alien who had shouted, "To hell with the United States!"

The climax came with the discovery in April of a plot to assassinate governors, judges, Cabinet members, and other public officials. A large bomb was found in Mayor Hanson's mail on April 28; the following day the maid of Senator Thomas W. Hardwick of Georgia had her hands blown off when she opened a package in the Senator's Atlanta home. Immediate investigation in the New York Post Office uncovered sixteen bomb packages addressed to such persons as Attorney General Palmer, Postmaster General Burleson, Justice Oliver Wendell Holmes, J. P. Morgan, and John D. Rockefeller. Some twenty other missiles were discovered elsewhere in the mails. In addition, the residences of Attorney General Palmer, two judges, and others were partially destroyed, with loss of two lives, by bombs in eight cities later in the spring.[3]

Popular retaliation came quickly and indiscriminately. The California legislature outlawed membership in organizations that advocated use of violence. In the wake of the investigations of its Lusk Committee, the New York legislature enacted similar, if less drastic, legislation.[4] Some four hundred soldiers and sailors invaded the offices of the New York *Call*, a Socialist daily, and beat up several May Day celebrants. In other parts of New York, and in Boston and Cleveland, there were clashes between May Day paraders and servicemen and police. The most serious outbreak occurred in the lumber town of Centralia, Washington, on Armistice Day. Members of the newly organized American Legion attacked the local headquarters of the IWW, and four of the attackers were killed in the ensuing fracas. In swift reprisal enraged townspeople lynched one of the defenders; police officials raided IWW headquarters throughout the state, arresting more than one thousand leaders of the union; and eleven IWW members involved in the Centralia affair were soon afterward convicted of murder and sentenced to long prison terms.

Scare headlines and sensational newspaper reports magnified these

[3] The worst outrage, incidentally, occurred more than a year later, in September 1920, when a wagonload of explosives was set off in front of the offices of J. P. Morgan & Company in New York City. Thirty-eight people were killed, more than 200 were injured, and property damage ran to more than $2,000,000.

[4] Vetoed by Governor Alfred E. Smith, the New York anti-Communist bill was re-enacted and signed by Smith's Republican successor in 1921.

events and stimulated a widespread public alarm,[5] and never was a great nation so afraid of phantom invaders and so agitated by groundless fears. To be sure, there was widespread labor unrest during 1919. But there was no evidence of any important Communist infiltration of labor unions, and all the great strikes of 1919–20, except perhaps the Seattle general strike, were caused by usual grievances. The end of wartime restraints saw a revival of the radical press, but this spoke as always for an infinitesimal fraction of the people. The IWW was struggling for rebirth in the Northwest and along the Pacific Coast, and there were a few anarchists, some of whom probably perpetrated the bomb outrages, in the large cities. These disparate and fractional groups offered no threat to the public safety that ordinary law enforcement agencies could not have controlled.

Any threat would have had to come, therefore, from the newly organized Communist parties, the alleged spearheads of the revolution. One of them, the Communist Labor party, breaking away from the national Socialist convention in Chicago, was formed on August 31, 1919. It had between 10,000 and 30,000 members by the end of the year. Another, the Communist Party of America, was organized on September 1. It had a membership of between 30,000 and 60,000 by the end of 1919.

The danger of social upheaval in 1919 now seems exceedingly remote in view of the extreme weakness of these parties of the Left. The Wilson administration, however, acted as if the menace were dire and launched such a campaign against civil liberties as the country had not witnessed in peacetime since 1799. The organizer and leader of this campaign was the Attorney General, A. Mitchell Palmer of Pennsylvania, who thought that he had a good chance to become the next resident of the White House. Palmer not only set the entire Federal Bureau of Investigation to work ferreting out Communists and boring into their organizations; he also urged Congress to adopt a measure that went so far as to punish persons guilty even of inciting sedition.

When Congress refused to enact Palmer's sedition bill, the Attorney General struck out on his own private campaign. The Labor Department had rounded up some 249 known Russian Communists and shipped them to Finland, on December 21, 1919. But Palmer was after bigger game. Without informing the Secretary or Assistant Secretary of Labor of his plan, Palmer obtained warrants for the arrest of some three thousand alien members of the Communist and Communist Labor parties from a subordinate official in the Labor Department. Thousands of federal agents and local police executed a gigantic simultaneous raid on Communist headquarters throughout the country on the night of January 2, 1920. Some four thousand persons, many of them non-Communists and American citizens, were hurried off to jails and bull pens in thirty-three major cities in twenty-three

wwwwwwwwwwwww

[5] One good index of the state of public opinion was the adoption by state legislatures in 1919 and 1920 of laws outlawing display of the Red flag, prohibiting membership in organizations that advocated the violent overthrow of the government, and forbidding seditious utterances. Thirty-four states and two territories enacted such statutes in 1919; two states adopted such legislation in 1920.

states. Persons visiting prisoners in Hartford, Connecticut, were arrested on the ground that they, too, must be Communists.

Eventually one third of the victims were released for lack of evidence. American citizens suspected of membership in a Communist party were turned over to local authorities for indictment and prosecution under state syndicalism laws. But for the aliens it was a different story. Outraged by Palmer's procedure, Secretary of Labor William B. Wilson, a stout Scotch-Irish Presbyterian, took charge of the deportation proceedings and saw that justice was done. Only 556 aliens, all of them proved members of the Communist party, were deported.

Palmer continued to warn of gigantic Red plots, but he executed no more raids. The scene now shifted to the states, with investigations by the Lusk Committee of the New York legislature and the subsequent expulsion of five Socialist members of the New York Assembly on April 1, 1920, for no crime except membership in the Socialist party; the arrest and conviction of two anarchists, Nicola Sacco and Bartolomeo Vanzetti, for the alleged murder of a paymaster in a South Braintree, Massachusetts, shoe factory; and the growth everywhere of demands for conformity. As we shall see in a later chapter, the postwar era bequeathed to the 1920's a heritage of hatred and hysteria that permeated and disturbed every aspect of life and thought.

91.   *Troubled Race Relations*

This summer of the first Red scare was also a time of tribulation for American Negroes, as postwar intolerances found yet other victims and another form of expression. Tensions burst into the most awful outbreak of interracial warfare in the history of the United States. Let us look first at the causes of this violence on America's most troubled social frontier.

To begin with, a decline in immigration from a little over 1,218,000 in 1914 to 327,000 in 1915 created a scarcity of unskilled labor and stimulated the first large-scale migration of Negroes from the southern countryside to northern and midwestern industrial centers. This stream of black workers swelled in response to increased demands in 1917 and 1918. The several hundred thousand Negroes who went to the North found no warm welcome awaiting them. Forced to crowd into the worst areas, they became the object of the suspicion and hatred of white unskilled workers, most of them immigrants themselves, who resented Negro competition and mores.

At the same time, Negro-white relations were considerably worsened by the Negroes' participation in the war. Some 400,000 Negroes served in the armed forces, about half of them overseas to be accorded an equality they had never known in their native South. White Southerners were terrified at the thought of so many Negro men learning the use of firearms and the ways of equality. They were prepared in 1919 to use the rope and the faggot to remind returning Negro veterans that the Great Crusade had been no war for racial democracy in the South.

Thirdly, while the war heightened anti-Negro sentiments, North and South, the Negro people of America and their spokesmen were beginning to demand higher wages, immunity from violence, and larger participation in politics. The National Association for the Advancement of Colored People, now under control of the militant element, was especially active during the war. One of the NAACP's leaders, William E. B. Du Bois, convoked a Pan-African Congress in Paris during the Peace Conference to speak for Negroes throughout the world.

These tensions burst into wholesale violence in the South as white men resorted to traditional weapons to intimidate the Negro communities. Lynchings increased from thirty-four in 1917 to sixty in 1918, and to more than seventy in 1919. Ten Negro veterans, several of them still in uniform, were lynched in 1919; fourteen Negroes were burned publicly. Southern white terrorism also found expression in a form more ominous than these individual acts of violence—in the rapid spread, especially through the Southwest, of the newly revived Ku Klux Klan, about which more will be said later. The Klan grew during 1919 from insignificance into a thriving organization of more than 100,000 members with cells in twenty-seven states. Defying law enforcement officials, hooded Klan night riders flogged, tarred, and hanged their victims in many southern and southwestern communities.

Even worse travail awaited Negro Americans in the outbreak of the most fearful race riots in American history. They began in July 1919 in Longview, Texas, and spread a week later to the nation's capital, where mobs composed principally of white servicemen pillaged the Negro section. The worst riot broke out in Chicago on July 27, 1919, after an altercation between whites and Negroes on a Lake Michigan beach. Mobs roamed the slum areas of the city for thirteen days, burning, pillaging, and killing, with the National Guard unable to subdue them. Fifteen whites and twenty-three Negroes were dead when it was over; 178 whites and 342 Negroes were injured; and more than 1,000 families were homeless. During the next two months major riots broke out in Knoxville, Omaha, and Elaine, Arkansas, and the final count by the end of 1919 revealed some twenty-five riots, with hundreds dead and injured and property damages running into the millions.

Negroes and liberal whites were dismayed and reacted in varied ways. The NAACP and other militant Negro groups counseled resistance and undertook a public campaign against lynching. It culminated in the passage by the House of Representatives of the first anti-lynching bill in 1921. This measure was endorsed by twenty-four governors and an overwhelming northern opinion, but it was defeated by a southern filibuster in the Senate. The most significant reaction in the South was the first substantial awakening of the southern conscience and the organization in Atlanta in 1919 of the Commission on Interracial Co-operation. It would become the spearhead of a growing southern liberal movement in the 1920's and 1930's.

The mass of Negroes, however, were not inspired by anti-lynching campaigns or encouraged by the beginning of an organized southern effort to combat racial intolerance. They were simply overwhelmed by the events of 1919 and ready to follow any leader who promised escape. Such a Moses was Marcus Garvey, a Jamaican, who organized his Universal Negro Improvement Association in 1914 and moved to New York City two years later. A chauvinist and charlatan, Garvey urged Negroes to be proud of their allegedly superior race and culture and follow him back to Africa to build a "free, redeemed and mighty nation." In the racial upheaval of the postwar years Garvey's schemes stimulated visions of a grand new destiny in the minds of countless Negroes. Claiming 4,000,000 followers in 1920 and 6,000,000 in 1923, Garvey proclaimed himself provisional president of an African Empire in 1921 and raised funds to buy a Black Star steamship line and carry his people home. The empire crumbled in 1923, however, when the black Moses was convicted in federal court of using the mails to defraud and sentenced to the Atlanta penitentiary for a five-year term. American Negroes, obviously, would not go back to Africa, but the fact that so many of them rallied to Garvey's standard was pathetic evidence of their despair.

92. *The Election of 1920*

Politicians began their quadrennial preparations for the coming presidential campaign during this season of social conflict and racial unrest. It was obvious by the beginning of 1920 that any passable Republican candidate would win the presidency, and there was much activity in the GOP camp. However, the commanding figures who had led the party since 1900 were absent or in retirement. Theodore Roosevelt, who might have had the nomination by default, had died on January 6, 1919. Charles Evans Hughes, the party's nominee in 1916, adamantly refused to run and would not even participate in the national convention.

Into the fight for leadership, therefore, rushed a number of lesser dignitaries. General Leonard Wood, who had inherited most of Roosevelt's following, made the most formidable campaign for the Republican nomination. Wood was forthrightly independent of party bosses, intensely nationalistic, and a champion of universal military training. Nearly as popular was Frank O. Lowden, former congressman and Governor of Illinois in 1920, who had the support of the business and farm interests of the Middle West. On the periphery were Senator Hiram Johnson of California, vainly trying to rally the old insurgents; Senator Robert M. La Follette of Wisconsin, always a hopeful but never a successful contender; Herbert Hoover, who announced that he was a Republican and would accept the nomination; and a number of favorite sons, including the distinguished Nicholas Murray Butler of New York and the nondescript Warren G. Harding of Ohio.

The outcome was, therefore, by no means certain when the Republicans met in national convention on June 8, 1920. The Wood and Lowden managers battled fiercely to a standstill during the first four ballots on Friday, June 11. Fearing an impasse, Chairman Henry Cabot Lodge adjourned the convention at seven o'clock, in order, he said, to give the leaders a chance to think. Managers and leaders had little time for reflection during the ensuing hectic hours. The Wood leaders tried unsuccessfully to win the Johnson delegates and refused to make entangling alliances with party bosses and oil lobbyists. At the same time, another group was gathering in the suite of National Chairman Will H. Hays at the Blackstone Hotel. It included Hays and a clique of powerful senators and their allies, among them being Lodge, Senator Frank B. Brandegee of Connecticut, George

Harvey, caustic New York editor, and other party regulars. They wanted, not Wood or Lowden, but a President whom they could control. Their opportunity to name the candidate seemed to be at hand on account of the Wood-Lowden deadlock.

The senatorial clique in the now-legendary "smoke-filled" room in the Blackstone continued their search all during the evening of Friday, June 11. They eliminated the strong dark horses, like Charles Evans Hughes and Governor Henry J. Allen of Kansas, one by one. Then they settled upon Senator Warren G. Harding of Ohio, a party hack who met all the qualifications of a perfect dark horse. Harding had many friends, particularly among delegates to the convention, and no enemies in the party, had voted for the Lodge reservations, and, most important, was controllable. The decision was made and relayed to other party leaders by eleven o'clock on Friday night. Harvey called Harding to the "smoke-filled" room at about two o'clock on Saturday morning, told him of the decision, and asked if there was any reason why the party should not nominate him. After meditating privately in an adjoining room for ten minutes, Harding returned to reply that there was no reason why he should not be President.

The senatorial clique was, of course, proceeding on the assumption that the Wood and Lowden forces would never combine. As it turned out, it was a safe enough gamble. The deadlock continued for four more ballots on Saturday morning, June 12, until Chairman Lodge recessed the convention in the early afternoon. Then, while the Wood and Lowden managers negotiated to no avail, Harvey and the senatorial clique, for reasons that are still obscure, tried to rally the party behind Will Hays. The effort failed, and Harding was nominated on the tenth ballot soon after the convention reassembled Saturday afternoon. The main reason seems to have been that leaders and delegates realized that he was the one candidate who could now be nominated without a grueling, disruptive battle. For Vice President the senatorial clique had settled upon Senator Irvine L. Lenroot of Wisconsin. However, the weary delegates in an unexpected burst of independence nominated Governor Calvin Coolidge, hero of the recent Boston strike.

The Republican platform gave notice of the GOP's intention to destroy Wilsonianism and all its works. It promised tariff increases, tax reductions, immigration restriction, vigorous aid to farmers, and, by implication, an end to further federal social legislation. On the League issue the framers made room both for irreconcilables and Republican League men. The platform condemned Wilson's League but approved membership in the World Court and "agreement among nations to preserve the peace of the world."

Meanwhile, the Democrats had been engaged in a preconvention contest even more confused than the struggle that preceded the Republican convention. The chief cause of the Democratic uncertainty was the President himself, for Wilson acted very much like a receptive if silent candidate after his partial recovery during the early months of 1920. He dismissed Secretary of State Lansing and took charge of the government in February. He attended well-publicized Cabinet meetings and took long rides in his automobile. And just before the Democratic convention met in June he called photographers to the White House and gave an important interview to Louis Seibold of the New York *World*. All available evidence indicates that the President hoped that he might be chosen to lead a campaign for the League of Nations, and that he intended to resign once the Treaty had been ratified.

Wilson's potential candidacy cast a long shadow over the aspirations of his son-in-law, William G. McAdoo, the chief contender for the Democratic nomination. As a gesture of filial respect, McAdoo "withdrew" from the race on the same day, June 18, that Wilson's interview appeared in the New York *World*. McAdoo's strongest rival was the Attorney General, A. Mitchell Palmer, who was still beating drums for Americanism. Among the favorite sons, Governor James M. Cox of Ohio had the greatest potential strength, even though President Wilson thought that his candidacy was "a joke." Three times elected governor of a doubtful state, Cox had an excellent progressive record, had survived the Republican victory of 1918, and was more acceptable to the city bosses than McAdoo or Palmer because of his opposition to prohibition.

Because of the division in the Wilsonian ranks, the Democratic convention that opened at San Francisco on June 28 was no less confused than its Republican counterpart. As events turned out, Wilson had no influence over the convention's choice. He had made plans to have his name presented and his nomination effected by acclamation once a deadlock occurred. But this stratagem was never executed because a group of the President's close friends met in San Francisco on July 3–4 and agreed that a third nomination would kill both Wilson and the Democratic party. The Irish bosses who controlled the delegations from Massachusetts, New York, New Jersey, Indiana, and Illinois held the balance of power and, in the end, named the candidate in the same manner that the senatorial clique had done at Chicago, or at least had tried to do until events took control out of their hands. The McAdoo and Palmer forces fought to a standstill for thirty-seven weary ballots. Palmer released his delegates on the thirty-eighth ballot; but as most of them went to Cox, a McAdoo drive fizzled, and Cox was named on the forty-fourth roll call on July 5. Cox's choice for running-mate was Franklin D. Roosevelt of New York, Assistant Secretary of the Navy, a prominent Wilsonian and League supporter.

Meanwhile the convention had adopted a platform that sidestepped the prohibition question, extended sympathy to Ireland, and promised tax reductions and independence for the Philippines. On the all-important League issue the platform was at the same time straightforward—reflecting Wilson's demands—and evasive—reflecting the arguments of Democrats who wanted to accept the Lodge reservations. We advocate immediate ratification of the Treaty without crippling reservations, the platform declared; but we do not "oppose the acceptance of any reservations making clearer or more specific the obligations of the United States to the League associates." Wilson was pleased because adoption of this plank signified the defeat of William J. Bryan's campaign for a plank demanding speedy ratification even with the Lodge reservations.

In spite of the convention's straddle, Cox and Roosevelt labored heroically during the ensuing campaign to make the election a "great and solemn referendum" on the League and to warn voters that the reactionary business interests would control the government if Harding won. Harding's managers, on the other hand, wisely decided that the less that he said the

ELECTION OF 1920

NUMBERS IN EACH STATE
SHOW ELECTORAL VOTE

	ELECTORAL VOTE	POPULAR VOTE
HARDING (R)	404	16 152 000
COX (D)	127	9 147 000

TRM

better his chances would be. Hence Harding made no long tours like Cox
but rather stayed at home in Marion, Ohio, and greeted delegations on his
front porch. He was a perfect tool in the hands of his advisers as he talked
about getting away from nostrums and back to "normalcy," a general association of nations based on justice, which the United States might join,
and the like. It was impossible to judge from his sonorous homilies just
where Harding stood on any specific issue. Isolationists were certain that
he would keep the country out of the detested League. In contrast, a group
of thirty-one distinguished pro-League Republicans, including Charles
Evans Hughes and Elihu Root, assured voters that Harding's election was
the first necessary step in ratification with reservations.

Harding's ambivalent speeches and the statement of the thirty-one so
confused the voters that it is doubtful if the League was even an important
issue in the campaign. It was evident long before election day that the
Republicans were capitalizing on an accumulation of grievances going
back all the way to the progressive legislation of 1916 and the adoption of
the war resolution. The disparate elements opposed to Democratic policies
—the Irish and German Americans, Negroes, industrialists and businessmen in rebellion against high taxes and policies favorable to labor, champions of civil liberty, independent progressives outraged by the Treaty and
the Palmer raids, and midwestern and Plains farmers then undergoing a
severe depression—moved en masse into the Republican camp.

The result of the combining of the dissident elements with the normal
Republican majority was the most smashing electoral triumph since the
re-election of James Monroe in 1820. Harding received 16,152,000 popular
votes, or 61 per cent of the total; won all the states outside the South, for
an electoral vote of 404; and even broke the Solid South by carrying Tennessee. With only 9,147,000 popular and 127 electoral votes, Cox was the
worst beaten Democratic candidate since Stephen A. Douglas. The Republican sweep in the senatorial and congressional contests—there would
be Republican majorities of twenty-two in the Senate and 167 in the House
in the next Congress—was nearly as impressive as Harding's own majority.

This landslide did not signify a repudiation of the League but rather
revealed the confusion and growing popular apathy over that issue. It did
not signify a repudiation of progressivism or any great collapse of idealism
among the people. It signified, rather, the triumph of the combined forces
of dissent and protest. Wilson had created a majority Democratic coalition
in 1916 composed principally of Southerners, middle and far western anti-
war progressives and farmers, and workingmen throughout the country.
Wilson's policies after 1916 consistently alienated independents, anti-war
progressives, and, most important, western farmers. By destroying the
Wilsonian coalition in 1920, these groups not only registered their protests
against Wilson's alleged betrayal of their interests, they also destroyed the
only political alliance capable of carrying on progressive policies in a
systematic way. And unwittingly they turned the next administration over
to their traditional enemies—the business elements that once again were
in control of the Republican party.

PART II

==

PROSPERITY, DEPRESSION, AND THE NEW DEAL
1921–1941

IN WHICH *the American people reject world leadership, find unrivaled prosperity, are beset with new intellectual and social tensions, struggle vainly to prevent the Great Depression from engulfing themselves and the world, and go on to restore democracy at home while they are overwhelmed by events abroad.*

CHAPTER

12

Aspects of Economic Development

1920–1940

THE DECADE 1919–29 was a period of rapid economic development that brought the standard of living of the American people to a level hitherto unknown in history. Even so, the economic progress of the twenties lacked the over-all solidity of economic growth from 1900 to 1914. The prosperity of the twenties was more urban than general, confined to some industries more than to others. More dangerous still was the fact that the resources of commercial banks were used to finance a runaway speculative boom in real estate and the stock markets.

Yet these were signs seen only by the wisest economists. By the autumn of 1929 the American people were basking in the golden glow of prosperity but standing on the brink of the greatest depression in their history. Perhaps it was just as well that they did not know the perils and tests that lay ahead in the 1930's.

93. The American People, 1920–1940

These were two decades of revolutionary changes affecting the growth, distribution, and composition of the American people. The decline in the birth rate, which had begun a century before, became really precipitous after 1915. It fell from 30.1 per thousand in 1910 to 27.7 in 1920, and to

POPULATION CHANGE, 1920–1940

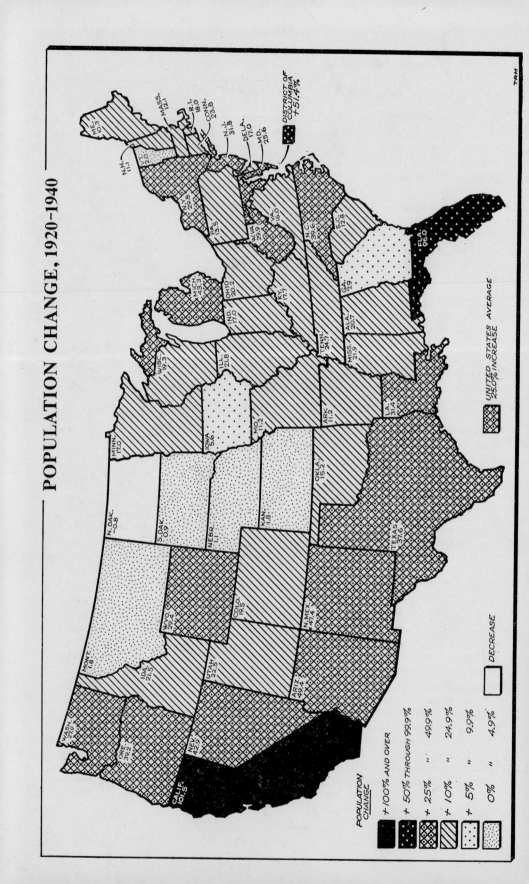

MAINE 10.3
N.H. 1.1
VT. 2.0
MASS. 12.1
R.I. 18.0
CONN. 23.8
N.Y. 25.6
N.J. 31.8
DELA. 17.0
MD. 25.6
DISTRICT OF COLUMBIA +51.4%
PA. 13.5
W.VA. 29.9
VA. 16.0
N.C. 39.3
S.C. 12.8
MICH. 43.3
OHIO 20.2
IND. 17.0
KY. 17.7
GA. 7.9
ALA. 20.7
WISC. 19.3
ILL. 21.8
TENN. 24.7
MISS. 21.9
FLA. 96.0
MINN. 17.0
IOWA 5.6
MO. 11.2
ARK. 11.2
LA. 31.4
N.DAK. −0.8
S.DAK. 0.9
NEBR. 1.1
KAN. 1.8
OKLA. 15.2
TEXAS 37.6
MONT. 1.8
IDA. 21.5
WYO. 2.0
COLO. 19.5
N.MEX. 47.4
WASH. 22.9
ORE. 39.2
NEV. 42.9
UTAH 21.5
ARIZ. 49.4
CALIF. 101.5

UNITED STATES AVERAGE 25.0% INCREASE

POPULATION CHANGE

+ 100% AND OVER
+ 50% THROUGH 99.9%
+ 25% " 49.9%
+ 10% " 24.9%
+ 5% " 9.9%
0% " 4.9%

DECREASE

TRM

21.3 in 1930; and the population increase from 106,466,000 souls in 1920 to 123,188,000 in 1930 was at a rate of 16.1 per cent, as compared to 21.2 per cent for 1900–10. Population experts found abundant reasons for this steady decline—urbanization, the virtual end of immigration, greater education of the masses, the so-called emancipation of women, and a growing determination not to imperil personal living standards by having too many children.

With the onset of the depression the birth rate fell even further and hovered between 18.5 and 19 per thousand during the last half of the 1930's. Mothers were not having enough children between 1930 and 1940 even to maintain the population, much less to add to future numbers. Studying the statistics at the end of the decade, demographers took a gloomy view of the future of population growth in the United States. On the basis of seemingly irrevocable trends, they projected curves that forecast further steady decline in rate of growth until a peak population had been reached between 1960 and 1980, after which decline in total numbers would set in.

The results of the Census of 1940 seemed fully to justify these predictions. From 1930 to 1940 the population of the United States increased from 123,188,000 to 132,122,000 souls. The rate of increase of 7.2 per cent was less than half the rate of the preceding decade and about one third the rate from 1900 to 1910. Offsetting the declining birth rate to some degree, however, was a nearly phenomenal improvement in the health of the American people caused by new medical and surgical techniques, more effective public health services, and wider consumption of vitamins, fresh vegetables, and milk. The death rate in areas furnishing reliable statistics fell from 17.2 per thousand in 1900 to 13 per thousand in 1920, and to 10.8 per thousand in 1940. Life expectancy for both sexes increased from 47.3 years in 1900 to 62.9 years in 1940.

Americans in 1940 were more than ever white and native born. The 12,865,518 Negroes and 588,887 Indians, Orientals, and other nonwhites enumerated by the Census of 1940 together represented 10.3 per cent of the total population, as compared to 12 per cent in 1920. The severe restriction and selection of European immigration effected by the legislation of the 1920's (see pp. 329–331) had already begun markedly to alter the composition of the white population. The 11,594,896 foreign-born persons in the United States in 1940 constituted only 8.7 per cent of the total population, while 15 per cent had been foreign born in 1910. Total net immigration declined from a prewar peak of 3,015,301 for the period 1911–15 to 68,789 for the entire decade of the 1930's. As these figures include Canadians and Mexicans unaffected by restrictions, they fail to convey the full impact of the quota system established by legislation in the twenties on immigration from Europe. One example must suffice. Italian stock in the United States increased in numbers from 727,844 to 3,336,941 from 1900 to 1914. In contrast, net Italian immigration was only 224,000 from 1920 to 1924, while 27,000 more Italians left than entered the United States from 1925 to 1929. Obviously, the operation of the quota system meant the eventual elimination of the foreign-born as an important element in the American population.

Among other important demographic changes that took place in the

POPULATION DENSITY, 1940

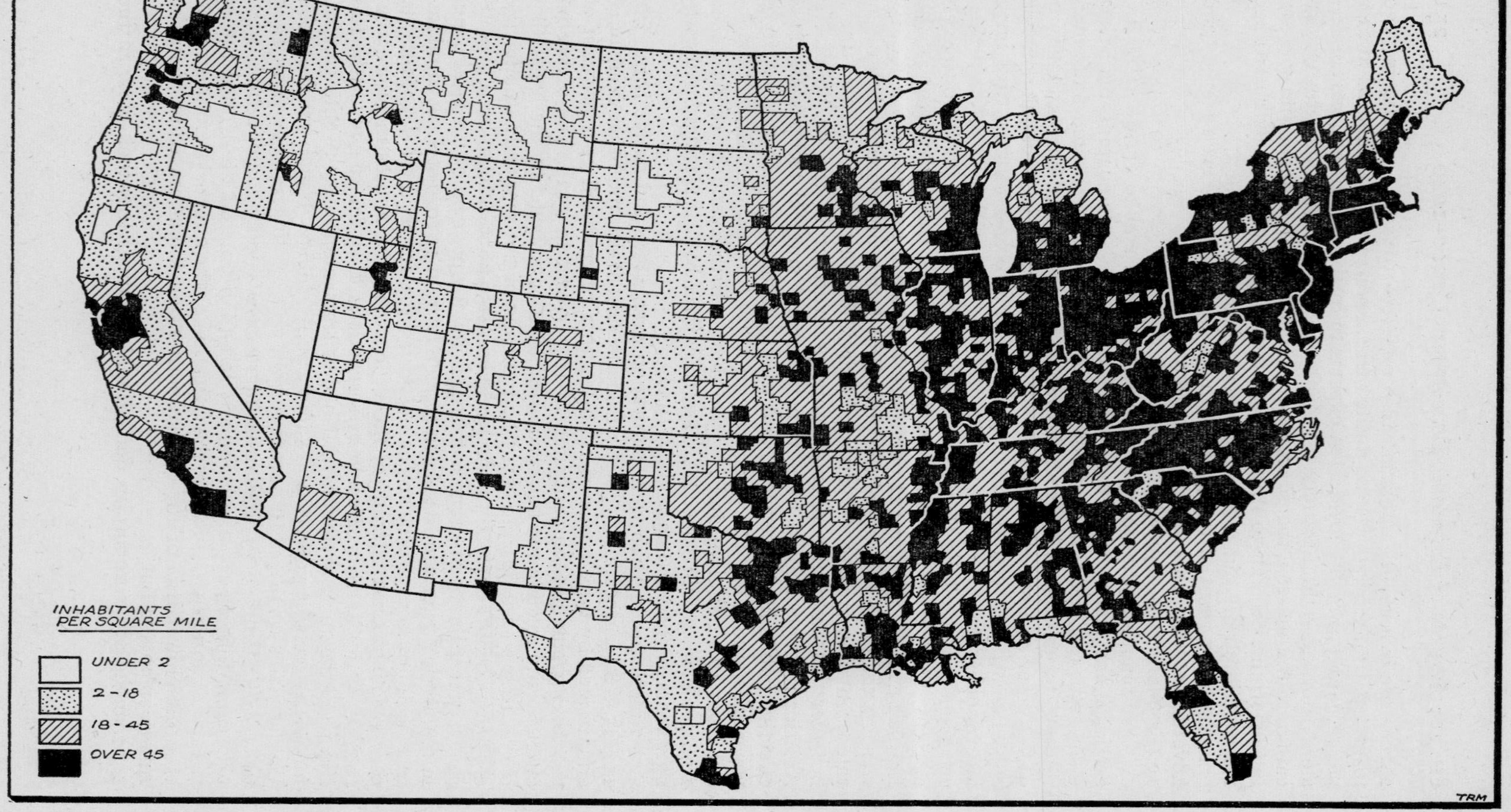

INHABITANTS
PER SQUARE MILE

UNDER 2
2 - 18
18 - 45
OVER 45

1920's and 1930's, the most notable were the practical surcease of the westward land movement, the decline in farm population, and, above all, the acceleration of the growth of cities and towns. Continued land settlement from 1900 to 1920 caused the entire area west of the hundredth meridian to grow at a much faster pace than the older sections. However, growth in the West from 1920 to 1940 depended more upon industry, oil, the tourist trade, and highly specialized agriculture than upon general farming. California, Washington, Oregon, Texas, and Arizona grew rapidly, but the remaining agricultural states of the West either lost population or else increased by less than 10 per cent.

This phenomenon was merely additional evidence of the most important internal demographic change of the decade—the increasing movement from the countryside to the cities. The American farm population suffered a loss of 10,184,000 by internal migration from 1920 to 1940. It was so tremendous a movement that total farm population sustained a net loss of 1,134,000 persons during the two decades, in spite of a high birth rate among farm people. One of the most important changes in the American social fabric during the first four decades of the twentieth century can be read in the following sentences. In 1900 nearly 60 per cent of the American people lived in the country and in small towns under 2,500. By 1940 43.5 per cent of the people lived in rural areas, while only 23 per cent actually lived on farms.

One direct consequence of this massive movement was the accelerated growth of American cities, particularly in the 1920's. The five cities of 1,000,000 inhabitants or over, for example, alone absorbed more than one third the total urban increase of 14,600,000 during the decade. The so-called satellite cities surrounding the metropolises grew at twice the speed of nonsatellite cities of similar size. Movement to the cities was momentarily reversed during the early thirties, as nearly 2,000,000 unemployed and homeless people returned to farm homes for food and shelter. But the exodus to the cities began again with the return of prosperity between 1935 and 1937. In 1940 the Census Bureau could count 140 so-called metropolitan districts, in which 48 per cent of the people lived. This represented an increase of 9.3 per cent for the decade of the 1930's alone.

A final significant internal population change was a steady migration of Negroes from the South to the North and Middle West, which had begun on a large scale around 1915. In 1920, 85 per cent of all Negroes lived south of the Mason and Dixon Line, which was only 7 units lower than the corresponding percentage on the eve of the Civil War. By 1940 nearly 24 per cent of Negroes lived outside the South, and this was merely the beginning of a movement that would grow hugely in volume in the 1940's and 1950's.

94. *The American People, 1920–1940: Income, Wealth, and Industry*

The prewar American economy was stimulated from 1914 to 1917 by an extraordinary European demand for food and war materials, and from 1917 to 1919 by continued European purchases, enormous federal war expenditures at home, and a concomitant expansion in bank credits. Then followed, as we have related in a preceding chapter, a dizzy postwar period of inflation and intense economic activity, stimulated chiefly by a further increase in exports and a high domestic demand for clothing, household goods, automobiles, and housing.

Actually, the postwar boom of 1919–20 was more apparent than real, except in agriculture. National income, adjusted by the cost of living, declined from $64,500,000,000 in 1918 to $57,884,000,000 in 1920, and the index of production in the basic industries fell correspondingly. Yet the decline during 1920 was not precipitous in manufacturing or trade, nor was it marked by any large number of business failures. The greatest shock was the collapse in farm prices that began in the late spring and reached panic proportions during the autumn.

The recession had become a full-fledged depression by the spring of 1921. American foreign trade declined in value from $13,500,000,000 in 1920 to less than $7,000,000,000 in 1921; wholesale prices declined 21 per cent; and unemployment reached a peak of 4,754,000. Actually, a general readjustment to a lower world price level was taking place. Recovery set in at the beginning of 1922 and was steady on all fronts until 1927. Then a slight recession was followed by an intensification of economic activity that continued until 1929. This was the period that contemporary economists called the "New Economic Era," when it seemed that production, prices, and wages had reached an equilibrium and a high plateau upon which the economy might run indefinitely. Such hopes were obviously overly confident, but the 1920's were none the less a time of marked advancement on most economic fronts.

To begin with, there was a steady increase in the wealth and incomes of the American people during this decade. Total national wealth, which had been $192,000,000,000 on the eve of the First World War, reached an estimated $367,000,000,000 in 1929. Adjusted by the cost of living, total national income increased from $65,093,000,000, or $620 per capita, in 1919, to $82,810,000,000, or $681 per capita, a decade later. The spectacular improvement in the material well-being of the American people during the first decades of the twentieth century becomes apparent when we recall that the adjusted per capita income in 1900 was $480.

These generalizations illustrate the over-all economic progress of the twenties but fail to indicate internal maladjustments that made the prosperity of the period ephemeral for large elements. We can, therefore, obtain a more meaningful picture of the state of the nation during the New Economic Era by seeing the important changes in the relative economic status of the major groups that occurred from 1923 to 1929.

As we have already seen, farmers suffered a severe deflation in 1920 and 1921. In spite of some recovery in prices from the depression level of 1921, farmers never regained the fine relative balance that they had enjoyed in 1914 and 1919. The share of agriculture in the national private production income had been 22.9 per cent in 1919; it was 12.7 per cent in 1929.

In contrast, the condition of most workers in industry substantially improved in almost all aspects during the 1920's. Over the decade 1919–29 there was a rise in annual real earnings of 26 per cent; it was perhaps the largest decennial increase up to that time. During the period of greatest expansion, 1923–9, the number of wage earners increased only about .5 per cent, but average hourly wages increased 8 per cent, average real earnings increased 11 per cent, while the average work week decreased from 47.3 to 45.7 hours. (For a detailed discussion of the decline and tribulations of organized labor in the 1920's, see below, pp. 308–312; for the revival of the labor movement in the 1930's, see below, pp. 401–404, 435–440.)

EMPLOYMENT AND PAYROLLS OF PRODUCTION WORKERS
IN MANUFACTURING
1920-1940
BUREAU OF LABOR STATISTICS INDEXES, WITHOUT SEASONAL ADJUSTMENT, 1947-1949=100
PER CENT, MONTHLY

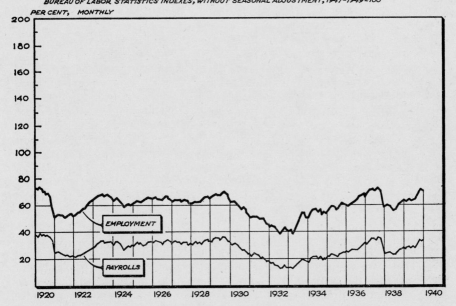

A basic stimulant of prosperity in the 1920's was expansion in the construction industry after 1918. Stable costs and a continued high demand, especially for residential construction, enabled the industry to record one large gain after another from 1922 to 1928, when it began to slacken. The estimated value of construction, based on the value of materials used, rose from a little over $12,000,000,000 in 1919 to a peak of nearly $17,500,000,000 in 1928. The industry paid 7.5 per cent of all wages and salaries in 1926 and nearly equaled agriculture and transportation in importance.

Manufacturing enjoyed an even more significant expansion during the prosperity decade. The number of manufacturing establishments declined through consolidation and elimination of small producers from 274,598 in 1919 to 210,959 in 1929; the number of wage earners declined during the decade from 9,041,311 to 8,838,743. At the same time, there was an increase of 64 per cent in manufacturing output, chiefly because of a 40 per cent increase in labor's productivity. The following table illustrates the general character of the shifting pattern of production:

THE TEN LEADING AMERICAN INDUSTRIES,
RANKED ACCORDING TO VALUE OF PRODUCTS,
1919 AND 1929

	1919	VALUE OF PRODUCT (IN THOUSANDS		1929	VALUE OF PRODUCT (IN THOUSANDS
RANK	INDUSTRY	OF DOLLARS)	RANK	INDUSTRY	OF DOLLARS)
1.	Food and allied industries	$12,748,348	1.	Food and allied industries	$12,023,589
2.	Textiles and textile products	9,210,933	2.	Textiles and textile products	9,243,303
3.	Iron and steel and products	5,887,844	3.	Iron and steel and products	7,137,928
4.	Transportation equipment, including automobiles	5,627,623	4.	Machinery	7,043,380
5.	Machinery	4,768,673	5.	Transportation equipment, including automobiles	6,047,209
6.	Chemicals and allied products	3,803,753	6.	Chemicals and allied products	3,759,405
7.	Forest products	3,113,460	7.	Petroleum and coal products	3,647,748
8.	Leather and its products	2,613,217	8.	Nonferrous metals and products	3,597,058
9.	Nonferrous metals and products	2,519,032	9.	Forest products	3,591,765
10.	Petroleum and coal products	2,289,170	10.	Printing, publishing, and allied products	3,170,140

These are statistics of dollar volume of production and therefore partially obscure the important growth of certain segments of the economy. Thus the actual production of automobiles increased 255 per cent from 1919 to 1929; of chemical products, 94 per cent; of rubber products, 86 per cent; of printing and publishing, 85 per cent; of iron and steel products, 70 per cent. On the reverse side, production of coal and railroad equipment sharply declined, while production of leather, food, tobacco, and textile products increased at a slower pace.

On the surface the American people had never seemed so economically healthy as in 1929. And yet their prosperity was so unevenly divided that it could not long continue without some adjustment. This was true primarily because such an increasing share of the national income was going to industry and finance that workers relatively lost ground, and farmers suffered an absolute retrogression. For example, corporate profits and dividends increased 62 and 65 per cent, respectively, from 1923 to 1929, while workers enjoyed an 11 per cent increase in real income. Such a large portion of the national income was being funneled off at the top by receivers in restricted geographical areas by the end of the prosperity decade that the men and women on America's assembly lines and farms were finding it difficult to purchase what they produced. For example, there were indications by 1928 of overproduction in residential housing and automobiles.

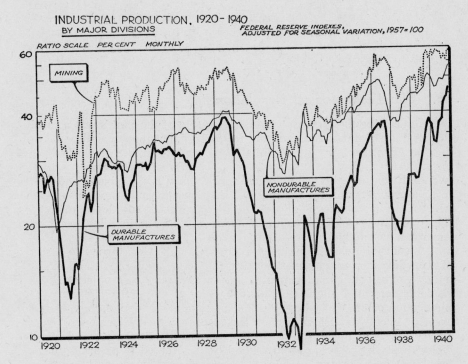

INDUSTRIAL PRODUCTION, 1920-1940
BY MAJOR DIVISIONS

FEDERAL RESERVE INDEXES, ADJUSTED FOR SEASONAL VARIATION, 1957=100

RATIO SCALE   PER CENT   MONTHLY

MINING

NONDURABLE MANUFACTURES

DURABLE MANUFACTURES

This fundamental maladjustment is dramatically revealed by the following analysis: There were nearly 27,500,000 families in the United States in 1929. Nearly 6,000,000 families, or more than 21 per cent of the total, had incomes less than $1,000; nearly 12,000,000, or more than 42 per cent, had incomes under $1,500; nearly 20,000,000 families, or some 71 per cent, had incomes under $2,500, the sum estimated as being necessary for a decent living standard. On the other hand, the 36,000 wealthiest families received an aggregate income in 1929 nearly equal to the total income received by the 11,653,000 families receiving less than $1,500 a year. Or, to put it another way, 16,000,000 families, or nearly 60 per cent of the total number, received an aggregate income of $18,300,000,000. These families, experts estimated, were living either on or below a subsistence level. In contrast, the remaining 11,000,000 families, or 40 per cent of the total, received an aggregate income of $58,900,000,000.

Since we will relate the course of the Great Depression, the slow progress toward economic recovery, and other changes affecting industry, wage earners, and farmers in the 1930's in some detail in later chapters, a few summary generalizations about economic trends in the 1930's must suffice at this point. The years between the onset of the Great Depression and 1940 were a time of retrogression and despair such as the American people had rarely known in their long history, followed by painful and slow recovery. Briefly stated, recovery from the depression was already fairly complete before the great defense spending of 1941 opened a new era in American economic history. The gross national product, measured in constant 1953 dollars, declined from $175,900,000,000 in 1929 to $123,400,-

000,000 in 1933 and then gradually increased to $205,700,000,000 in 1940. At the same time, per capita disposable income,[1] measured in 1953 dollars, declined from $1,059 in 1929 to $728 in 1933 but recovered steadily to $1,130 by 1940.

95. *The Technological Revolution*

Underlying the increased industrial output of the 1920's was a revolution in industrial management and technology that made possible the production of larger numbers of units by a smaller number of workers at a lower cost. Of all the causes of America's industrial development in the twentieth century, the technological revolution was most basic and therefore most significant, for the mass production age could never have come without the techniques it afforded. Like other economic developments of the 1920's and 1930's, the technological revolution had its roots deep in the American past and its greatest impact after 1920.

A young industrial engineer, Frederick W. Taylor, turned to a study of scientific shop management during the 1880's and 1890's and evolved a theory of scientific management. It was that engineers by objective analysis could determine the reasonable capacities of men and machinery. The publication of his "Piece-Rate System" in 1895 and "Shop Management" in 1903 at once established him as the leading industrial engineer in the United States, if not in the world. So successful were Taylor and his disciples that scientific management had been accepted to a varying degree by almost every branch of business and industry by the early 1920's. It had, moreover, become an integral part of the curricula of engineering and business schools that were now busy graduating a new generation of managers.

Meanwhile, another and equally important development had been maturing—mass production by the assembly line technique and production of interchangeable parts by automatic precision machinery.[2] The use of interchangeable parts had begun in the late eighteenth century,[3] but the introduction of the assembly line, or progressive line production, technique was a twentieth century phenomenon, first developed by Henry Ford in the automobile industry from 1908 to 1914. From 1908 to 1913 Ford used a stationary assembly line. In 1913 and 1914, however, he reorganized the assembly process in a revolutionary way—by introducing the moving assembly line, which reduced labor required for assembly of an automobile chassis from fourteen to less than two man-hours. In the effort to increase production during the First World War, the assembly line technique was applied to shipbuilding, the manufacture of airplane engines, and the production of munitions. The new method was firmly established in many branches of industry by the early 1920's.

wwwwwwwwwwwwwww

[1] That is, income left after taxes and Social Security payments.

[2] A whole series of inventions between 1865 and 1900, particularly the micrometer caliper and other measuring devices, the automatic turret lathe, and hard alloys for cutting purposes, contributed to this development.

[3] By 1900, for example, interchangeable parts were being used in the manufacture of firearms, agricultural machinery, sewing machines, typewriters, and bicycles.

THE INCREASE OF PRODUCTIVITY IN THE UNITED STATES, 1891–1950, BY DECADES

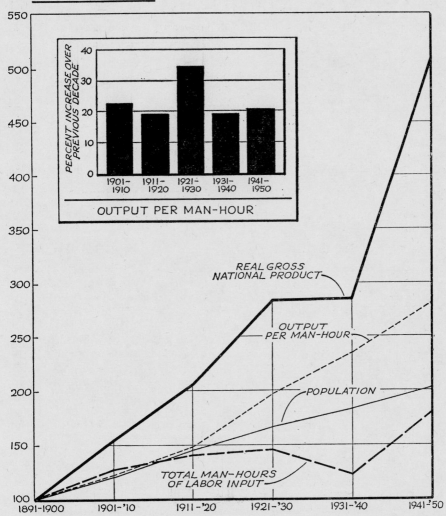

Another important component of the technological revolution was industrial research. It had been carried on crudely in the United States before the First World War but did not reach an important position until the 1920's. The establishment of the Mellon Institute of Industrial Research at Pittsburgh in 1913 marked the first systematic beginning. The creation of the National Research Council by the National Academy of Sciences in 1916 marked the first effort to stimulate and organize research on a national scale. The war of course gave the largest stimulus, and by 1920 many corporations had established independent research laboratories. By 1927 at least one thousand corporations were carrying on either independent or co-operative research for improvement of product or service,

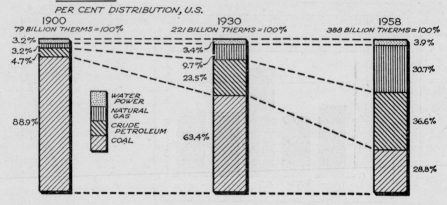

SOURCES OF ENERGY IN THE UNITED STATES
1900–1958

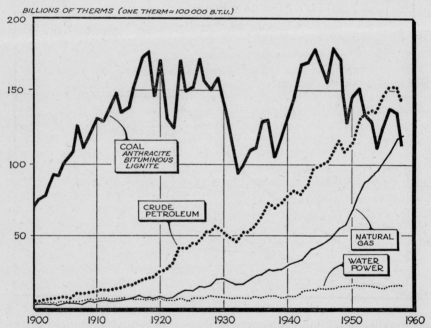

reduction of production costs, development of by-products and new products, and the like. Data on total expenditures in 1927 are unavailable, but 208 firms reported expenditures aggregating nearly $12,000,000. This was a significant beginning, but industrial research was still in its infancy. By 1937, for example, American industrialists were spending $180,000,000 annually for research; four years later the figure stood at $510,000,000.

A fourth aspect of the technological revolution paid largest dividends in human health and happiness. It was the growing acceptance and application of the theory that conditions affecting the health, comfort, and safety of workers had a direct influence on production and productivity. So successful was the safety-in-industry campaign before the First World War that practically every factory erected during the 1920's was constructed according to modern safety standards, while many old factories were modernized in this regard. A study of industrial accidents about 1928 revealed that only 10 per cent of them were caused by lack of mechanical safeguards.

The fifth and also the most basic factor in the increased productivity and output of the 1920's was a phenomenal growth in power per worker. During the decade 1919–29 horsepower per worker increased nearly 50 per cent in manufacturing, 62 per cent in agriculture, 60 per cent in mines and quarries, and 74 per cent in the railroad industry. In manufacturing, much of this increase was made possible through a threefold increase in the use of electric power; [4] in agriculture, through the first important use of tractors. [5]

By 1929 the technological revolution had gone so far as to cause observers to think that they were living in an age of miracles. That revolution, in its first culmination from 1919 to 1929, caused a gain of productivity of 40 per cent in manufacturing and of 26 per cent in agriculture— as contrasted with gains in productivity from 1899 to 1909 of 7 per cent in manufacturing and 6 per cent in agriculture.

The technological revolution slowed perceptibly in the 1930's, chiefly because of a severe decline in investment for new capital equipment and the absence of new technological breakthroughs. Indeed, general productivity decreased sharply between 1929 and 1933. For the decade as a whole, however, general output per man-hour increased about 20 per cent; and productivity in manufacturing and agriculture increased about the same percentage. Such progress as occurred in spite of the depression was not, to be sure, spectacular. However, the American people, without realizing the fact, were standing in 1940 on the threshold of the most fantastic stage of the further technological revolution.

96. *The Rise of New Industries*

Several industries, in their infancy when the decade began, emerged to positions of key importance during the 1920's. They were not only dynamic economically, in that they stimulated other segments of the economy. They were also prime movers of a revolution in living habits and social attitudes that was taking shape by 1929 and would come to full flower after the Second World War.

The Rise of the Automobile. The historian feels almost at a loss for words to relate the story of the rise of the automobile or to convey some

---

[4] Seventy per cent of all industries were electrified by 1929, as compared with 30 per cent in 1914.

[5] The horse and mule yielded to the tractor grudgingly, however. In 1919 there were 26,436,000 horses and mules and 147,600 tractors in the United States. A decade later 19,476,000 horses and mules and 852,989 tractors were in use on American farms.

intimation of its economic and social significance in recent American history. As two students of American sociology have put it, "It is probable that no invention of such far reaching importance was ever diffused with such rapidity or so quickly exerted influences that ramified through the national culture, transforming habits of thought and language."

Europeans experimented for almost a century with self-propelled carriages, until Carl Benz, a German, built the first automobile powered by a gasoline engine in 1884. Charles and Frank Duryea of Springfield, Massachusetts, and Henry Ford of Detroit built the first successful gasoline-driven carriages in the United States in 1892–3. At about the same time a number of other men were experimenting with automobiles driven by steam and electricity. There were some 8,000 automobiles in the United States by the turn of the century. Some 181 companies entered the field during the next quarter century; but three major concerns, Ford, General Motors, and Chrysler, accounted for 83 per cent of the output by 1930.

Henry Ford was the leader all during this period. After experimenting with low-priced cars, he introduced the Model T in the autumn of 1908. By concentrating on this single unlovely but enduring model, and by introducing the assembly line process and scientific management, Ford realized his dream of producing automobiles for the masses. The price of Ford cars dropped after introduction of the assembly line from $950 to $290. Ford's closest rival in the fierce struggle for supremacy was the General Motors Corporation, organized by William C. Durant in 1908. It fell under the control of the DuPont and Morgan interests in 1921 and produced a wide number of lines, ranging from the luxurious Cadillac to the low-priced Chevrolet. A third but much smaller competitor was the Chrysler Corporation, organized in 1923, which acquired Dodge Brothers in 1928 and Plymouth in 1929.

Meanwhile, the automobile industry had emerged as the largest single manufacturing industry in the United States. Production of automobiles increased from 4,000 in 1900 to 1,518,061 in 1921, to 4,794,898 in 1929. Production declined to 1,103,557 in 1932 and then increased steadily to nearly 4,000,000 in 1937. By 1940 there were nearly 32,500,000 automobiles, trucks, and busses in operation in the United States. In 1919 the automotive industry employed 343,115 workers, who earned $491,122,-000 in wages and turned out products valued at two and a third billion dollars. In 1939 the industry employed 398,963 workers, paid $646,406,-000 in wages, and manufactured products with an aggregate value of $4,047,873,000. Its importance in the economy as a whole can be seen by the fact that in 1929, for example, it used 15 per cent of the steel and four fifths of the rubber processed in the United States, employed 7.1 per cent of the manufacturing wage earners, paid 8.7 per cent of the manufacturing wages, and produced 12.7 per cent of the total product value of all manufacturing concerns.

Indeed, it is no exaggeration to say that manufacture of automobiles was in large measure responsible for the intense economic activity of the 1920's. According to one estimate, it gave employment, directly or indirectly, to 3,700,000 persons by 1929. Use of the automobile gave rise to construction and maintenance of hard-surfaced highways, operation of garages and filling stations, maintenance of tourist camps to accommodate the millions of Americans who annually took to the roads in the 1920's, operation of fleets of motor trucks and busses, and the like. County, state, and federal authorities were spending nearly $2,500,000,000 annually by the end of the 1930's for construction, maintenance, and financing of highways and bridges alone.

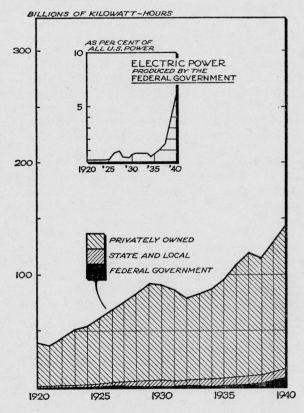

ELECTRICAL POWER PRODUCTION
IN THE UNITED STATES
1920–1940

Electric Power, Machinery, and Appliances. In a later chapter (pp. 331–334) we will note the rise of the electric power industry, but it might be well at this point briefly to summarize the story. The electric power industry from 1900 to 1929 rose from comparative insignificance to become the second most important economic interest in the United States. Production increased from 6,000,000,000 kilowatt hours to nearly 117,000,-000,000; capital invested in the industry grew to nearly $12,000,000,000, and total income to nearly $2,000,000,000. Growth was slower in the 1930's, but in 1940 production was nearly 180 billion kilowatt hours; capital invested stood at $15,500,000,000; and total income was nearly

264   PART II: *Prosperity, Depression, and the New Deal, 1921–1941*

$3,000,000,000. Only 16 per cent of American homes were electrified in 1912; nearly 79 per cent used electric power by 1940.

Almost overnight, also, the manufacture of electric turbines, motors, supplies, and appliances grew into an industry of the first importance. The decade 1919–29 was the period of greatest growth, as the value of products of this industry increased from $997,968,000 to $2,300,916,000. In 1939 the industry's products were valued at $1,730,000,000. Even by the late thirties the appliance industry was still in its infancy and was just beginning to venture into large-scale production of stoves and refrigerators. In 1939 the entire value of electrical appliances manufactured was only $145,700,000.

The Radio Industry. Most inventions basic to the construction of radio transmitters and receivers had been perfected before the First World War, but it was not until 1919 that the federal government lifted its ban on the private operation of sets. A great new industry came into being during the next decade. The General Electric and Westinghouse companies organized the Radio Corporation of America in 1919, obtained control of patents by cross-licensing agreements, and began to manufacture radio parts on a small scale. In response to tremendous demand RCA began to manufacture receivers and parts on a large scale in 1922. Patents on tubes expired at about this same time, and a number of other concerns entered the field. Radio soon became a virtual obsession of the American people, and the production of sets increased by leaps and bounds. In 1921 sales of radio parts totaled a mere $10,646,000. By 1939 the industry produced nearly 11,000,000 radios with a total product value of $276,000,000; and census reporters discovered the following year that 28,500,000 American families, or 80 per cent of the total number, had radio sets—an increase of 100 per cent since 1929.

Meanwhile, radio broadcasting had evolved from a sport into a big business. The first regular broadcasting station was KDKA at East Pittsburgh, which began daily operation on November 2, 1920. The number of stations grew to 562 between 1920 and 1924. In the latter year RCA organized the National Broadcasting Company, arranged with the American Telephone & Telegraph Company to transmit programs over telephone lines, and began the first nation-wide broadcasting service. Three years later the Columbia Broadcasting System was established on a similar nation-wide scale.

The Aviation Industry. Although two Americans, Wilbur and Orville Wright, built and flew the first successful airplane at Kitty Hawk, North Carolina, on December 17, 1903, leadership in aviation soon moved across the Atlantic. With the outbreak of the war Europeans swiftly developed the flying machine as a powerful fighting weapon. When Congress adopted the war resolution in 1917, however, the American army had no combat planes and only a few inefficient observation craft. The government at once began a gigantic program to train thousands of pilots and established the Aircraft Production Board to build thousands of engines and aircraft.

The United States had twenty-four plants capable of producing 21,000 planes annually when the Armistice was signed. But the government hastily canceled its orders, and the entire industry practically collapsed.

European governments kept their aviation industries alive through gen-erous mail subsidies, but it was many years before Congress followed suit. The Post Office Department established daily airmail service between New York and Washington with its own planes and pilots in 1918; six years later it began regular airmail service between New York, Chicago, and San Francisco. In the following year, 1925, Congress authorized the Post Office Department to let contracts for carrying mail to private com-panies; in 1926 it enacted the Air Commerce Act, vesting control of com-mercial aviation in the Commerce Department.

As a result of this legislation scheduled commercial air service first began in 1926, and eighteen airlines had carried 5,782 passengers over routes totaling 3,715 miles by the end of their first year of operation. By 1930 the aviation industry was firmly established with 122 airlines in operation over routes covering nearly 50,000 miles. Technological progress was painfully slow during the following decade. The slow and inefficient Ford trimotor aircraft gave way to the all-metal twin-engined Douglas DC-3 in 1936; then came the production of the huge Boeing flying boat on the eve of the Second World War. By 1940 there were 22 airlines in the United States carrying 3,185,000 passengers over routes totaling 94,000 miles.

The Motion Picture Industry. The story of the rise of the motion pic-ture industry from humble beginnings to a position of major importance in American life is one of the great sagas of the twentieth century. Thomas A. Edison and others by 1896 had constructed machines capable of taking motion pictures and projecting them on a screen. For the next few years short feature films were shown in vaudeville houses, and the first movie that told a story, "The Great Train Robbery," was produced in 1903.

The motion picture industry had its first real beginning in 1905— when a Pittsburgh promoter rented a warehouse and displayed one-reel shows for a nickel. Within two years there were some 5,000 "nickelodeons," as these first movie theaters were called, in all parts of the country. From this time on progress in technique and technology was substantial, and promoters began constructing large and ornate theaters on the eve of the First World War.

Rapid technological developments, the most important of which were sound movies, brought the industry to full maturity by the end of the 1920's. By 1930 the motion picture industry had a capital investment of some $2,000,000,000 and gave employment to 325,000 persons. In every town and city there were motion picture theaters—some 23,000 of them, with a seating capacity of approximately 11,300,000. During 1930 total weekly attendance averaged perhaps 115,000,000, and total admissions ran to $1,500,000,000. Motion pictures had become so important a part of American social life that even the depression did not halt the growth or im-pair the prosperity of the industry.

97. *The Age of Big Business*

In spite of antitrust crusades, the consolidation movement in industry proceeded inexorably, through Democratic and Republican administrations, through eras of reform and reaction.[6] It slackened from 1904 to 1917, but revived on a large scale at the end of the First World War. A few statistics will illustrate the general trend. The assets of the two hundred largest nonfinancial corporations totaled $26,000,000,000 in 1909, $43,-718,000,000 in 1919, and $81,074,000,000 in 1929. The startling fact was that the growth of the two hundred giants had been two and one half times faster than the growth of smaller corporations during the period 1909–29, and three times faster during the years 1924–8. These two hundred corporations by 1929 controlled 49 per cent of all corporate wealth and received 43 per cent of the corporate income. Or, to illustrate the degree of concentration in another way, the largest 1,349 corporations had a combined income in 1929 of about $7,000,000,000, while all the rest had an aggregate income of only $1,740,000,000.

For various reasons, chief of which were the depression and a political climate unfavorable to big business, the merger movement virtually ceased, and the movement toward concentration in industry was slightly reversed in the 1930's. Five per cent of corporations received 85 per cent of total corporation income in 1930. The figure declined to 81 per cent in 1935 and stood at not quite 84.5 per cent four years later.

The favorite instrument of consolidation in the 1920's was the holding company, which enabled an individual or group of men with comparatively small resources to control a utility or railroad empire.[7] Samuel Insull, the Chicago utilities magnate, was most adept at the game. Indeed, so far-flung and complicated was his utilities network by 1930—it had combined assets of $2,500,000,000 and produced one eighth of the electric power in the United States—that it is doubtful whether even he understood its structure. Oris P. and Mantis J. Van Sweringen of Cleveland were other masters of the technique. Beginning by controlling the Nickel Plate Railroad before the First World War, they used the holding company de-

---

[6] Industrial expansion from 1900 to 1929 was in large measure financed by the savings of the rank and file of people, rather than by the investments of a few promoters and industrial leaders. The result was a wide spread in the ownership of America's factories, banks, railroads, and insurance companies and a consequent separation between ownership and management. The 4,000,000 owners of corporate stocks in 1900, for example, grew to a mighty throng of 20,000,000 by 1930.

This divorcement of ownership from control in industry, which began around 1900, reached major proportions in the 1920's, as the component parts of the dissolved "trusts" developed into independent concerns and as more and more companies sold stock to the public. Consequently, there developed a significant managerial revolution, in which control passed from single owners or partners, and even from boards of directors, to a salaried bureaucracy, highly trained in production and distribution. In fact, American industry was so thoroughly bureaucratized by 1929 that the large majority of routine decisions were made by plant managers and shop foremen even in corporations controlled by owners.

[7] The technique is known as pyramiding and works in the following manner: Using a small investment a promoter might organize a holding company and gain control of it by owning a majority of the voting common stock. By using the proceeds from the sale of the bonds, preferred stock, and nonvoting common stock of this first holding company, the organizer would buy control of operating utility companies. And by following the same method the promoter might pyramid one holding company on top of another almost indefinitely.

vice from 1925 to 1929 to acquire control of the Chesapeake & Ohio, the Pere Marquette, the Erie, and the Missouri Pacific railroads.

The American industrial economy had obviously become highly consolidated by the end of the 1930's, but not to the degree that the bare statistics might imply. Actually, few vestiges of industrial monopoly remained by 1940,[8] while many important industries, notably textiles, clothing, furniture, and bituminous coal, remained fiercely competitive. On the other hand, oligopolies, that is, oligarchies of a few large producers, dominated many branches of industry. For example, in 1937–8 ten large companies controlled approximately 88 per cent of the total productive capacity of the steel industry; three corporations controlled 90 per cent of the automobile output; four meat packing concerns produced 70 per cent of the product of that industry; the four largest rubber companies turned out 80 per cent of the automobile tires; four tobacco companies produced 85 per cent of the cigarettes.

This trend toward oligopoly, however, did not necessarily signify a diminution of competition. On the contrary, it meant restoration of competition in several important branches of industry. In 1901, for example, United States Steel controlled about 60 per cent of the steel ingot capacity of the country. That corporation grew steadily, so that its net assets totaled nearly $2,500,000,000 in 1929. But its rivals grew even faster; and United States Steel controlled only 40 per cent of the total steel ingot capacity of the industry in 1937. At the time of its dissolution in 1911, the Standard Oil Company of New Jersey enjoyed a virtual monopoly over the refining of petroleum in the United States. The dissolution of the holding company into its constituent corporations was followed by the gradual emergence of these companies as independent concerns. Meanwhile, tremendous new amounts of capital entered the oil refining field, and all the former members of the Standard Oil Trust combined did only about 50 per cent of the oil business of the country in 1930. In retailing, also, the rise of mail-order houses and chain stores, which did 25 per cent of the retail business in 1935, gave a powerful stimulus to competition in the distribution field. In thousands of small towns the hegemony of the local merchant was destroyed. Now he had to compete, and competition often meant drastically lower prices for consumers.

One could multiply these examples to show that the trend toward oligopoly from 1910 to 1940 actually strengthened competition in many branches of industry in which competition had not existed before 1910. The important phenomenon in this regard, however, was the manner in which competition itself changed during the three decades before 1940. Historic price competition remained in many branches of industry and was always a potential threat in others. But producers in a given branch of industry tended more and more to follow the price leadership of the largest

---

[8] The Texas Gulf Sulphur Company and the Freeport Sulphur Company controlled virtually the entire sulphur production of the United States, while the Aluminum Company of America enjoyed a monopoly in the production of bar aluminum, and the United Shoe Machinery Company was virtually the sole producer in its field. But these were the only important industrial monopolies remaining by 1940, and the aluminum monopoly was soon to be broken.

manufacturer and to concentrate on improving and advertising their products.

98. *The Regulation of Business, 1919–1939*

During the ten years following the Armistice there was considerable diminution of the antitrust energies of the Justice Department.[9] But to say that this decline of regulation occurred merely because the Harding and Coolidge administrations were friendly to the business world would be to reduce a complicated subject to a crude generalization. We can under- stand the evolution of federal control of business during the 1920's only if we bear a few fundamental facts in mind.

The first and most important is the fact that the main thrust of the antitrust movement before 1917 was aimed only at destroying monopoly and preventing the subversion of competition. As Wilson and Theodore Roosevelt often affirmed, the antitrust campaign was not aimed at bigness, per se, or even at oligopoly—so long as large producers did not use their power to destroy competitors. There was a strong trend away from mo- nopoly toward competition from 1911 to 1930, while large corporations practically abandoned the old and now outlawed methods of destructive competition. Consequently, the problem of regulation was considerably different in the 1920's from what it had been in the early progressive period.

The second fundamental fact is that the Harding-Coolidge policy of beneficent regulation represented the maturing of policies begun by the Wilson administration. The authors of the Federal Trade Commission bill intended that the FTC should prevent destructive competition and the growth of monopoly, it is true. But they also envisaged the Commission as the protector of small business and friend and champion of all legitimate business enterprise. The FTC had failed to become a strong arbiter of busi- ness affairs by 1921. This was true in part because Wilson had appointed conservatives to the Commission, in part because the chief objective of governmental control had changed from destruction of monopoly to pres- ervation of competition and conditions in which industry could expand and grow. The tremendous expansion of the American economy from 1919 to 1929, strengthening of competition through the growth of oligopoly, and emergence of new industries seemed to confirm the wisdom of the moder- ate Wilsonian program. It also lessened the tension between the rank and file of the people and the business community.

The most important problems of business control in the 1920's stemmed from the rapid growth of new concepts and practices in the busi- ness world. They involved a diminution of price competition and empha-

[9] That is, as compared with the antitrust activities of the Roosevelt and Taft ad- ministrations. Actually, the Harding-Coolidge record of antitrust action surpassed the record of the Wilson administration. Under Wilson, the Justice Department entered twenty-seven consent decrees and instituted ninety-seven criminal and equity cases under the antitrust laws. Under Harding and Coolidge, the Justice Department entered forty-eight consent decrees and instituted 130 criminal and equity proceedings.

sized close co-operation in purchasing, selling, and price-fixing through trade associations, that is, organizations of producers in competitive industries. Some 2,000 of these trade associations were in operation by 1921.

It was many years before various governmental agencies and departments could agree upon common policy toward this new co-operation. The FTC had given open endorsement to the trade associations before 1921, especially during the war. Many progressives, notably Justice Louis D. Brandeis, hailed the new co-operation as the salvation of small business enterprise. And Secretary of Commerce Herbert Hoover sponsored the formation of trade associations in the 1920's and approved their activities. On the other hand, the FTC and Justice Department from 1921 to 1925 sought to prevent such collusion as the Commerce Department was encouraging, and they were sustained by the Supreme Court.

The appointment in 1925 of former Representative William E. Humphrey of Washington as chairman of the FTC, however, gave conservative Republicans control of the Commission and resulted in an important shift in the agency's attitudes and tactics. Thereafter, at least until 1933, the Commission encouraged trade associations and approved agreements by businessmen to eliminate cutthroat competition in advertising and pricing. At the same time, the Commerce Department helped trade associations find a way to circumvent the court's ban against exchange of information. Manufacturers submitted information on costs, production, and sales to the Department, and the Department assembled the information and distributed reports among producers in various fields. The court approved this new procedure in 1925 on the ground that it involved no conspiracy to fix prices or limit production.

The FTC's change of front in 1925 provoked bitter criticism from agrarian spokesmen in Congress, who asserted that the agency had become the tool of big business. Actually, it was simply fulfilling one of the major purposes of its founders—regulation of competition to prevent ruthless, cutthroat practices that had been the chief weapons of would-be monopolists in the past. In brief, the FTC tried to suppress fraudulent advertising, illegal price cutting, and commercial bribery without attempting to destroy the oligarchical structure of the American industrial economy.

This was the policy, too, of the Hoover administration from 1929 to 1933. Even though the succeeding Roosevelt regime vastly enlarged the federal government's general regulatory activities, it sought until about 1936 to achieve its objectives by direct control, not by the more indirect route of antitrust action. But with the failure of its first direct efforts, the Roosevelt administration in 1937–8 launched a searching inquiry into the concentration of economic power, and the Justice Department began a series of antitrust prosecutions reminiscent of the days of Theodore Roosevelt. We will say more about this in a later chapter (below, pp. 430–431).

99. *Trends in Banking and Finance, 1919–1940*

Industrial growth during the period 1919–29 was accompanied by a rapid accumulation of the financial resources of the American people. Bankers, security promoters and salesmen, and managers of other financial institutions had never before been as numerous or prosperous and had never received such a large share of the national income.[10] Nor had the financial structure of the country ever seemed more solvent. As we shall see, however, there were forces at work changing the character of the banking structure and undermining its foundations.

From 1919 to 1929 the total number of banks in the United States declined from 29,767 to 25,568. Although there were a number of significant mergers during the twenties, the principal reason for the decline was the steady failure of banks in rural areas and in Florida following the collapse of a land boom in that state in 1926. All told, 5,714 banks closed their doors from 1921 through 1929. On the other hand, total bank capital and surpluses increased nearly 100 per cent from 1919 to 1929, while total banking resources grew from $47,615,400,000 to over $72,000,000,000.

The statistics afford numerous other evidences of the steady accretion of American financial wealth during the decade. For example, life insurance companies, which had now emerged as the chief depositories of the people's savings, grew in resources much faster than the banks. Life insurance income and policies in force increased nearly 300 per cent from 1919 to 1929, and the aggregate resources of life insurance companies grew from $6,759,000,000 to $17,482,000,000. Americans during the same period also increased their savings in banks from $13,040,000,000 to $28,218,000,000 and in building and loan associations from $2,126,620,000 to $8,695,154,000.

Along with expansion came a relentless movement toward consolidation and the growth of large financial institutions. By 1929, for example, 250 banks, or 1 per cent of the total, controlled more than 46 per cent of the nation's banking resources, while some 273 chains controlled 18 per cent of total banking resources. In addition, there were a number of mergers in Wall Street that greatly concentrated the banking resources of the nation's financial center.

Such consolidations were spectacular, but the most important financial trend of the 1920's was a profound change in the character and functions of great commercial banks. The chief function of commercial banks in the past had been to make short-term loans to care for the needs of industry, commerce, and agriculture. The high prosperity of the period from 1922 to 1929 caused corporations to rely increasingly upon profits and proceeds from the sale of securities for expansion or even for current needs. Thus new capital issues increased from a total of $3,577,000,000 in 1921 to a record high of $10,183,000,000 in 1929, while business concerns piled up surplus cash reserves in the form of time deposits that increased from $3,500,000,000 in 1921 to nearly $9,000,000,000 by 1929.

As a consequence, bank loans during the prosperity decade did not keep pace with the rising level of economic activity, and there was no inflation either of bank credit or of the money supply.[11] Coming at a time

---

[10] In 1919 financial institutions earned 2.2 of the total private production income. A decade later finance's share had increased to 4.6 per cent.

[11] National banks increased their loans and discounts from $11,980,000,000 in 1921 to $14,811,000,000 in 1929; the total money in circulation actually declined slightly during the period—from $4,911,000,000 in 1921 to $4,746,000,000 in 1929.

when banking resources were greatly expanding, this phenomenon caused the managers of great commercial banks to look elsewhere than to business and industry for ways to use idle money. Consequently, they increased bank purchases of stocks and bonds by two thirds and expanded bank loans against real estate by about 350 per cent. Most important, they allowed surplus funds to be used to finance the most reckless speculative campaign in American history. Loans to brokers against stocks and bonds stood at the astounding total of $8,500,000,000 by the autumn of 1929.

The role of commercial banks in abetting stock speculation did not end at this point, for practically all large commercial banks established investment affiliates, hired thousands of salesmen, organized huge speculative campaigns, and did a flourishing business so long as the upward surge continued. For example, these security affiliates participated in the floating of $19,000,000,000 of issues in 1927.

Meanwhile, the great financial leaders—Kuhn, Loeb & Company, the House of Morgan, and their allies—not only survived but also prospered and grew larger during the New Economic Era. They continued to dominate the financial operations of the railroads, in spite of the efforts of the Interstate Commerce Commission to break their control. They took leadership in organizing and underwriting utility holding companies. They continued to play a major role in marketing securities and wielded a certain influence through interlocking directorships in industrial corporations. And yet events and developments of the twenties changed and greatly weakened the Morgan–Kuhn, Loeb & Company imperium. The elder J. Pierpont Morgan had dominated Wall Street through sheer will power until his death in 1913. His son, J. Pierpont Morgan, Jr., was no such dominant leader, and control in the House of Morgan shifted to partners and became institutionalized in various departments. But it is doubtful that the elder Morgan could have retained during the 1920's the power that he wielded before 1913. There was too much competition in the money markets as new financial centers emerged and old ones grew in power. Corporations were too independent and prosperous. Finally, there was too vast a growth of the financial machinery to allow continued domination by Wall Street or by one man, even if that man were the great J. Pierpont Morgan.

The story of the fortunes of banks and bankers during the following decade is an altogether different one. We need only to sketch the outlines here, as we will come back to this subject. (See pp. 368–9, 391–5.) First came the frightening attrition of the depression and the near collapse of the banking structure in 1933. Heroic federal reorganization and massive assistance had saved the system by 1935 and provided new safeguards for the future. Meanwhile, the American people were slowly rebuilding their ravaged financial resources. By 1940 there were only 15,076 banks in operation (as compared with 25,568 in 1929), but they had total resources of nearly $80,000,000,000 (as compared with $72,000,000,000 in 1929).

CHAPTER

13

Social and Cultural
Main Currents

1920–1940

THE AMERICAN SOCIETY between the Spanish-American and First World wars was bound together by common moral and political standards, and it was an exciting and hopeful time. The two decades between the Armistice and the Second World War were also a period of social and intellectual ferment. But it was ferment of a different kind, marked by changes in moral standards, the rise of new faiths among intellectuals, and the flowering of a literary revolt against the polite tradition in letters. To what degree this revolt of the intellectuals affected the masses it is impossible to say. It was, however, surely significant that a large segment of molders of thoughtful opinion repudiated traditional values and thereby destroyed the ideological unity of the prewar period.

As we shall see, however, the 1920's and 1930's were decades of social and artistic accomplishment, as well as a time of revolt and repudiation. The period witnessed the first important beginnings of American literary criticism; achievements that gained new eminence for American literature; a flowering of American scholarship and research; and development of new vogues in music, art, and architecture. In addition, Americans poured out money to improve and expand public schools and construct the most extensive system of higher education in the world. Finally, churches not only survived but grew in social usefulness. Thus, the twenties and thirties, far from being barren of social and cultural accomplishment, were a time of enduring achievement and bright promise for the future.

100. *The Revolution in Morals and Customs*

The most astonishing aspect of the revolution in manners and moral standards that occurred after 1918 was the rapidity with which forces that had long been eroding historic Christian standards suddenly destroyed that code among an influential element. In its ethical aspects the Christian system taught respect for parental authority, idealized the husband-father as the master of the family, and required premarital chastity and marital fidelity. This code provided the basic way of life for most Americans before the First World War. It was often violated, to be sure; but most middle-class Americans accepted it as a standard practically and morally sound even if unattainable.

The postwar rebellion was first evidenced by a revolt among young people, especially among "flaming youth" on college and university campuses, against the rules governing sexual relations. Wartime excitement broke down the barriers, but other forces kept them down during the 1920's and 1930's. For one thing, the automobile extended the possibilities of love-making far beyond the sitting room. For another, the increased drinking among middle-class women and young people that accompanied prohibition played a large role in weakening inhibitions. But even more important was the phenomenal spread of the teachings of Sigmund Freud, a Viennese psychoanalyist, whose writings were popularly misinterpreted to mean that the main cause of maladjusted personality was the suppression of the sexual desire, and that a free expression of the libido, or sexual energies, promoted mental health.

Whatever the causes—and we have mentioned only the most important—the breakdown of the Christian moral standard was widespread. F. Scott Fitzgerald's *This Side of Paradise*, a story of undergraduate life at Princeton, and Charles C. Wertenbaker's novels about students at the University of Virginia undoubtedly drew exaggerated pictures. But "petting," promiscuity, and drinking among college students became to a degree fashionable. High school students, too, indulged in the new freedom on such a scale as to shock their parents.

Indeed, if there was any single striking social phenomenon of the twenties and thirties, it was the popular obsession with sex. While highbrows read James Branch Cabell's erotic novels and applauded Eugene O'Neill's powerful dramas written around Freudian themes, the common people found excitement in a new form of literature, the confession magazines, which featured lurid stories by fallen women or high school girls who had "gone wrong." [1] The motion pictures, also, played upon the sex theme, and it was revealing that the maidenly Mary Pickford was supplanted as "America's sweetheart" by the voluptuous Clara Bow, the "It" girl of the 1920's, and by the equally voluptuous Jean Harlow in the 1930's.

wwwwwwwwwwwww

[1] *True Story*, the most successful of these new periodicals, began with a small circulation in 1919 and approached the 2,000,000 mark seven years later.

A second manifestation of the revolution in morals and manners was the rise of new forms of ballroom dancing. The waltz and more decorous forms gave way to the fox trot, the Charleston, and, late in the thirties, the "jitterbug." To defenders of older forms the modern dance was simply another evidence of the general breakdown of sexual standards; and church groups launched heroic but vain attacks upon what they called the "syncopated embrace." The modern dance, exclaimed the Reverend John William Porter of Kentucky in his tract, *The Dangers of the Dance* (1922), is based upon and stimulates the sexual instinct. "If this be not true, why is it that women do not dance with women, and men with men? . . . The mix-up is the magnet. A man dancing with a man is about as satisfactory as near-beer to the old drunkard." The elders cried in vain, however, and parents were dancing quite as fast and as artfully as their children before the 1930's had ended. American morality seemed destined to survive in spite of the close embrace and frenzied rhythm of the new dance forms.

The most important aspect of the revolution in social life in the long run was the change in the status of women. Political equality was achieved with adoption of the Nineteenth Amendment, and the twenties and thirties saw women not only voting but also holding offices high and low.[2] Although female spokesmen claimed that employers still discriminated against women in wages and salaries, women found far larger economic opportunities after 1920 than ever before. There was a sharp decline in the number of women employed in farming, and virtually no increase in the number in domestic service. On the other hand, the rapid expansion of female employment in industry, public schools, service trades and professions, and business enterprise more than compensated for the decline in other fields. By 1940 the 14,160,000 women gainfully employed constituted 25 per cent of the entire working force of the nation, as contrasted with 17.7 per cent in 1900.

This expansion of economic opportunities for middle-class women was the factor largely responsible for the revolution in feminine attitudes and manners that began in the early 1920's. Masculine supremacy had been based upon man's economic leadership in the family. It rapidly deteriorated as spinster sisters moved into apartments of their own, unmarried daughters went into school teaching or office work, and wives gained independence either by going to work or threatening to do so. As a consequence, women married at a later age, had fewer children, and were more willing to dissolve the marriage bonds. The number of divorces per 100 marriages increased from nine in 1914 to an apparently stable level of around seventeen from 1936 through 1940.

The outward signs of the so-called emancipation were even more

[2] There were, for example, two women governors and one female United States senator during the 1920's. Mrs. Miriam A. ("Ma") Ferguson served as Governor of Texas from 1925 to 1927. Mrs. Ferguson represented her husband, former Governor James E. Ferguson, who had been impeached and removed from office in 1917. Her administration did not bear out feminine claims that women in office would purify politics. Mrs. Nellie T. Ross succeeded her husband upon his death in 1924 as Governor of Wyoming and served until 1927. Mrs. Rebecca L. Felton of Georgia, appointed to the United States Senate in 1922 after the death of Thomas E. Watson, was the first woman senator. She served for only a short time.

frightening to persons who believed in the old way of life. As the barriers fell on all sides women began smoking cigarettes and, what seemed worse to traditionalists, demanded and asserted the right to drink with men. As women went to work in larger numbers they began to discard historic badges of femininity and, ironically, sought to make themselves over in the image of man. The first casualty of feminine independence was the traditional dress that covered the neck and arms and assiduously hid the ankles from masculine view. The average skirt was about six inches from the ground in 1919. From this time on the ascent was spectacular, until the skirt had reached the knees or even above by 1927. At the same time women discarded their corsets and de-emphasized the upper reaches of their anatomy, usually with fearful results. Finally, to complete the de-feminization, women sheared their tresses and wore their hair straight and short. But there was one curious exception to this trend. The shorter skirts and hair became the more women used cosmetics—lipstick, rouge, and mascara. It seemed as if the face had become the last refuge of femininity.

The revolution in morals and customs had run its full course by 1930. There now seemed to be certain signs of returning sanity. Experience soon taught that free expression of the libido produced not mental health but psychological and moral degeneracy. After trying to look and act like men, women finally admitted that there were, after all, certain physical differences between the sexes. They discovered that they did not have to yield their beauty in order to retain the large measure of independence they had won. Most men accepted the new order; in fact, many husbands abandoned authority and responsibility for the rearing of children to their wives. If, as Frederick Lewis Allen has observed, the American people were beginning by 1929 to build a new code on the shambles of the old system and learning to live gracefully again, then that effort would consist mainly of salvaging the enduring values of the Christian system.

While most Americans in the 1930's learned to live with sex without completely losing their heads about it, they also enlarged and made permanent the revolution in mores governing the family that had begun after the First World War. The general acceptance during the thirties of the code exalting happiness as the supreme objective of marriage, permitting divorce for often trivial reasons, and, above all, giving women and children equality with men in family relationships signified that the new code had become the cornerstone of American social life.

101. Main Currents in American Thought

Deep and sometimes bitter currents of intellectual unrest converged and swelled into a revolt of considerable proportions in the early 1920's. It is not difficult to understand why this happened. Intellectuals had made a deeply personal commitment to the democratic cause during the progressive period. Most of them, like the group that wrote for the *New Republic*, had answered Wilson's call for an application of progressive ideals to international life during the war. The dream was shattered after Versailles and the subsequent treaty fight. Like the Confederate veteran on the way home from Appomattox, who said he would be damned if he ever loved another country, many intellectuals were damned if they would ever love another ideal.

As it turned out, the reaction against the Versailles settlement was merely the beginning of the disillusionment. Intellectual progressives, who had advocated extension of governmental authority before the war, saw that same authority being used after 1918 to deprive a minority of the privilege of deciding whether they would drink alcoholic beverages. Intellectual progressives had glorified the people and championed adoption of democratic political reforms before 1917. But the people in the 1920's were demanding and enforcing conformity of thought, joining anti-democratic organizations like the Ku Klux Klan, and even attempting to forbid the teaching of evolution in public schools in many states.

Many intellectuals concluded that the old assumptions about the innate virtue of people and the desirability of more democracy were wrong and turned in anger and disgust against the democratic ideal. Thus during the 1920's there developed an intellectual leadership at war with the middle classes, separated from the people, tired of crusades and talk about moral idealism and service. Turning from pursuit of social and economic justice, they sought refuge in developing individuality through sexual freedom, esoteric literary and artistic forms, or bitter attacks upon domestic developments. Some of them, but not a large number, repudiated democracy altogether and hailed the Soviet Communist system as the answer to a dying bourgeois democracy. The importance of the defection of intellectuals from the progressive movement can hardly be overestimated. It was as if the spark plugs had been removed from the engine of reform.

In essence, the revolt of the intellectuals was a rebellion against what they thought was the cant, hypocrisy, and low cultural level of American life. "This so-called 'moral idealism,'" cried Harold Stearns in 1921, "is merely what any good psychiatrist would immediately recognise as the morbid perversities which conventionally accompany a deeply dissatisfied human life." The young intellectual of the early twenties simply did not like the society in which he thought he lived. He objected to the "morbid perversities"—the anti-intellectualism of small towns, the "shoddy, cheap" newspapers that gave more space to baseball than to the theater, the demand for conformity, the emphasis upon utilitarian virtues, the "democracy of mountebanks." He felt rejected, unwanted, and overborne by the crowd. He wanted freedom to experiment, to drink, to dream, to write like James Joyce and paint in cubes. If he was impecunious he sought fellowship in Greenwich Village in New York City; if he had an independent income he moved to the Left Bank in Paris to find freedom and cultural refreshment with fellow expatriates.

It will perhaps suffice to illustrate the revolt by pointing to Henry L. Mencken, the chief intellectual rebel of the decade. A native of Baltimore, Mencken received his literary training as a reporter for the Baltimore *Sun*, wrote an excellent study of the American language, and briefly edited a "little" magazine, *The Smart Set*, with George Jean Nathan. Then, in collaboration with Alfred A. Knopf, Mencken and Nathan began publication in 1922 of *American Mercury*, a monthly addressed to the intellectual rebels.

Mencken's observations on the American scene were barbed and pungent, and *American Mercury* soon became the Bible of the "lost generation." Mencken ridiculed idealism, democracy, organized religion, prudery, cant, prohibition, and ignorance. To him, morality and Christian marriage, for example, were absurdities; patriotism was imbecilic; the American people were mainly a vast collection of peasants, boobs, and hillbillies. It was ironic and revealing that such a purveyor of intellectual snobbishness and anti-democratic views should have become, as Walter Lippmann observed in 1927, the most powerful influence on the contemporary generation of educated people.

To stop at this point, however, would be to give the impression that American intellectuals did nothing but scoff and condemn during the 1920's. Actually, the intellectual rebellion was a phenomenon that passed quickly. Intellectual prodigals returned in huge numbers to their democratic household in response to the challenges of the 1930's. We will discuss this revival of faith in a later chapter (below, pp. 446–448). Moreover, the twenties and thirties witnessed the flowering of many fields of intellectual endeavor. It was, for example, a period adorned by important accomplishments in the social sciences. Historians abandoned preoccupation with political institutions and advanced scholarship deep into the frontiers of intellectual, social, and economic history. This advance, aided by the expansion and growing endowments of the country's academic institutions, gave American historiography a breadth that no single European country could match. Sociologists broke loose from the subjective, inductive method, developed new objective criteria, and launched new studies of ecology, urbanization, population, and race relations. The study of anthropology in the United States became an integral part of university curricula rather than an avocation of museum scholars. Social psychology became an independent discipline. A host of economists abandoned preoccupation with economic "laws" and set to work to analyze, describe, and dissect the American economic system. (For further details, see below, pp. 446–448.)

American accomplishment in the physical sciences during the 1920's and 1930's was on the whole perhaps less impressive than in the social sciences, mainly because the most important theoretical work was still being done by Europeans. The twenties saw the culmination and complete acceptance of new theories of matter, energy, and the structure of the universe fully as revolutionary in meaning as the Copernican and Newtonian theories had been. Robert A. Millikan of the California Institute of Technology and Arthur H. Compton of the University of Chicago won Nobel prizes in 1923 and 1927 for contributions to the new concepts, and Ernest O. Lawrence of the University of California won the prize in 1939 for inventing the first cyclotron, or atom smasher. But leadership in theoretical physics still rested with Europeans like Albert Einstein, Niels Bohr, and Enrico Fermi.

On the other hand, American chemists made extraordinary progress in a seemingly more practical field—production of synthetic chemical fibers, plastics, and products from coal and oil. In biology, Americans like Edmund B. Wilson, T. H. Morgan, and H. J. Muller enlarged man's knowledge of heredity, mutations, and transmission of characteristics from one generation to the next. Following the lead of Europeans, American psychologists abandoned the study for the laboratory, there to attempt to discover the biological bases of human behavior. The 1920's and 1930's witnessed no spectacular discoveries in the field of medicine, but they were marked by steady advancement in knowledge, improvement of medical schools, construction of great medical centers, development of new X-ray and surgical techniques, and growth of the branch of medicine devoted to treatment of mental illness.

102. *The Triumph of Naturalism in Literature*

The conjunction of circumstances and intellectual currents at the end of the First World War produced one of the most significant literary developments in American history—the flowering of the naturalistic revolt against the genteel and Christian traditions in literature among a new group of writers called the "Lost Generation." Frank Norris, Theodore Dreiser, Jack London, and Edgar Lee Masters had raised the standards of the revolution before the war and pointed the way. To the historian, the significant fact was the incredible vogue of the new standards among both writers and readers in the 1920's. For a time it seemed as if literary America had repudiated all ideals and values of the past.

In trying to discern the causes for such revolutionary changes in literary standards the historian sees through a glass darkly. Yet writers not only create; they also reflect the intellectual and spiritual standards and voice the perplexities and doubts of their time. The "Lost Generation" of the 1920's were creatures of an age characterized on the higher levels of thought by determinism in the physical sciences and relativism in ethics. Naturalism in literature—the study of man as a biological creature entirely enthralled to environment in an amoral universe—was nothing more than the literary reflection of a science that had removed the Creator from the universe, reduced man to a laboratory case study, solemnly declared that human emotions stemmed from the viscera, and avowed that the sexual act was on the same level as eating and drinking. The disillusionment of the "Lost Generation" was, moreover, reflected in a dozen other currents of national thought.

In any event, the converging of naturalistic concepts with the sharp moral deterioration that followed the war set the literary revolution in motion. Inevitably there was a spate of war novels and plays depicting the misery of trench warfare and the complete moral and spiritual bankruptcy of the soldiers. Among the early war novels the most notable was John Dos Passos's *Three Soldiers*, published in 1921. Its theme was aptly expressed by one of the leading characters: "This ain't a war, it's a goddam madhouse."

Combining protest against Victorian prudery with a lusty naturalism, Ernest Hemingway wrote a series of stories and novels that set new standards of style in fictional writing. His most notable work during these years, *A Farewell to Arms*, 1929, summarized a decade of revulsion against the sham idealism of the war. But in a number of earlier short stories and novels—*The Sun Also Rises*, 1926, and *Men Without Women*,

1927, for example—he voiced the "Lost Generation's" revolt against allegedly false ideals.

Meanwhile, naturalism as a literary form found its apogee in a number of other American writers. Sherwood Anderson, in *Winesburg, Ohio*, 1919, *Poor White*, 1920, *Many Marriages*, 1922, and other novels and stories, attempted to unmask what he alleged to be the perversities of the small-town Middle West. Anderson, however, had too deep a sympathy with his tragic characters to be a true naturalist. More faithful to naturalistic standards were Ring Lardner and Erskine Caldwell. Their stories about small-town and country people of the Middle West and South were marked by a morbid interest in the diseased in mind and body. And it was fitting that in this decade of naturalism Theodore Dreiser, one of the founders of the movement in the United States, should have written his most popular work. His *An American Tragedy*, published in 1925, was even more perfectly mechanistic than *Sister Carrie, Jennie Gerhardt, The Financier*, and *The Titan* had been.

Preoccupation with sex, which they often glorified as the primal drive, was characteristic of all the naturalists and quasi-naturalists. There was, however, considerable difference in emphasis. To writers like Dreiser and Sherwood Anderson, sex was only one of the important drives that determined man's behavior. But there was a group who played upon the sexual theme almost to the point of obsession. One of these was James Branch Cabell, author of *Jurgen*, 1919, *Figures of Earth*, 1921, and *Something About Eve*, 1927, whose vivid symbolism drew the fire of professional defenders of American morality. More indirect was F. Scott Fitzgerald, a superb storyteller and one of the most talented writers among the "Lost Generation." In *This Side of Paradise*, 1920, *The Beautiful and Damned*, 1922, and *The Great Gatsby*, 1925, Fitzgerald chronicled the moral and spiritual dissolution of the "Lost Generation," to whom, as he said, all gods were dead, all wars fought, all faiths shaken.

As the decade drew to a close a southern rebel gave promise of offsetting the "Lost Generation's" extreme negation. He was Thomas Wolfe, a North Carolinian, whose *Look Homeward, Angel*, published in 1929, was the expression of a young tortured soul in rebellion against the materialism of his mother and, as it seemed to him, the narrow provincialism of his home town of Asheville. But Wolfe was no naturalist. He was too adolescent, too romantic, too fond of life to be always morbid and introspective, as his later novels, *Of Time and the River*, 1935, *The Web and the Rock*, 1939, and *You Can't Go Home Again*, 1940, revealed.

The most widely read and universally acclaimed American novelist of the 1920's, Sinclair Lewis, stands almost alone as the connecting link between muckraking novelists of the progressive era and social novelists of the New Deal period. He could be harsh and almost captious in depicting the drabness of small-town midwestern life, the provincialism and smugness of the business booster, and the moral sham and materialism of his time. *Main Street*, 1920, *Babbitt*, 1922, *Arrowsmith*, 1925, *Elmer Gantry*, 1927, and *Dodsworth*, 1929, presented caricatures of types of middle-class Americans and won for their author in 1930 the first Nobel Prize in literature ever awarded an American.

Traditionalists not only survived in spite of the seemingly irresistible vogue of naturalism and negation, but also waged a rear-guard action against the younger generation. It is interesting that most of the novelists among the traditionalists were women. Edith Wharton continued writing her satires of the life and manners of the New York aristocracy. Dorothy Canfield Fisher defended morality and integrity. Ellen Glasgow of Richmond continued her series on life among Virginians high and low. But the greatest of these gentle realists was Willa Cather, who found nobility and spiritual grandeur in human tragedy and divine grace. Her *Death Comes for the Archbishop*, 1927, was not only her finest work but also one of the American novels of the 1920's most likely to endure.

In literary criticism the traditionalists were more articulate and aggressive. The leaders in a new humanistic movement, Paul Elmer More, Irving Babbitt, William C. Brownell, and Stuart P. Sherman, met their antagonists, Mencken, Van Wyck Brooks, and Harold E. Stearns, in a great battle of the books. The neo-humanists not only condemned the naturalists' disdain of graceful style and form; they also boldly championed the Christian ethic and Western cultural tradition. And if they did not convert the writers of the twenties they founded a school and laid the foundations for a later broad humanistic revival in letters. Thus on both sides there was an energy and activity that made the twenties exciting, creative, and fertile.

Nor did the poetic revival, which had begun so auspiciously during the years before the First World War, abate. Among the poets of the people, Vachel Lindsay and Edgar Lee Masters produced little of consequence; but Robert Frost and Carl Sandburg did not lose their voice during the twenties. In *New Hampshire*, 1923, and *West-Running Brook*, 1928, Frost again expressed his deep love of nature and a sharpened sympathy for man. Edwin Arlington Robinson, after securing his reputation with *The Man Against the Sky*, 1916, continued his search for meaning in a trilogy based upon the Arthurian legend, *Merlin, Lancelot,* and *Tristram*, 1917–27. He was, in the eloquent words of one critic, "the solitary poet who absorbed into his thought and art the best of the old in American poetry and became the first of his generation to understand, however darkly, the new." [3]

Meanwhile, leadership among the young intellectual poets who called themselves imagists was shared by two American expatriates, Ezra Pound and T. S. Eliot. Pound had deserted the imagist group in London before the war, spent four years in Paris, and finally settled in Rapallo, Italy. During the 1920's and 1930's he wrote seventy-one *Cantos*, brilliant word pictures often devoid of meaning. Although isolated from British and American friends, he continued to have great influence on young poets.

T. S. Eliot, born in St. Louis and educated at Harvard, moved to London after the outbreak of the war. Convinced that poetry should convey a sense of the complexity of life, Eliot wrote poetry difficult to understand. But the shimmering imagery of his words hid certain profound convictions, especially a belief that life without faith is vain foolishness. *The Waste Land*, 1922, Eliot's most important work of the decade, revealed the proportions of his break with the imagists on account of his conviction that

wwwwwwwwwwwwww

[3] Stanley T. Williams, "Edwin Arlington Robinson," in Robert E. Spiller *et al., Literary History of the United States* (New York, 1953), p. 1170.

the word image was futile unless it conveyed essential meaning about life.

Robinson Jeffers was one poet who more accurately reflected the dominant naturalistic temper among American writers. He wrote romantic poetry before the war and then, in the mid-twenties, turned savagely against humanity. His *Tower Beyond Tragedy* and *Roan Stallion*, 1925, and *The Women at Point Sur*, 1927, expressed the conviction that violence, sexual perversion, and inhumanity characterize all human behavior, and that the natural world alone has grandeur and dignity.

Convincing proof of the continued vitality of the poetic tradition in the United States was the rise of a generation of young new poets in the 1920's and 1930's. There was, for example, Pound's and Eliot's disciple, Hart Crane. A group of southern regionalists at Vanderbilt University— John Crowe Ransome, Robert Penn Warren, Donald Davidson, and Allen Tate—combined romantic love of the southern past with experiments in new forms. Edna St. Vincent Millay's sonnets expressed the youthful revolt against Victorian manners. Archibald MacLeish began a distinguished literary career by voicing the dominant mood of discontent. Or, again, there was the experimentalist, E. E. Cummings, whose strange style almost obscured the simple romantic themes of his poems, and Conrad Aiken, William Carlos Williams, Marianne Moore, and Wallace Stevens, among a host of others. The most widely read of the young poets, Stephen Vincent Benét, found his theme in the great crisis of the Union. His *John Brown's Body*, 1928, an epic poem, depicted the passions and experiences of the American people during the Civil War more convincingly than most social histories have done.

The most significant literary development of the 1920's was the flowering of a native American theater. It began around 1915, when young intellectuals established little theaters at Provincetown, Massachusetts, and New York City, and began to experiment for their own pleasure. The New York group reorganized in 1919 under the name of The Theatre Guild, acquired a theater of its own, and began presenting the plays of contemporary European dramatists.

The most distinguished member of the Provincetown group was Eugene O'Neill, whose *Bound East for Cardiff* was first produced by the Provincetown Players in 1916. O'Neill emerged during the next six years as the only American dramatist of any consequence to that time. Then, in *Desire Under the Elms*, 1924, *Strange Interlude*, 1928, and *Mourning Becomes Electra*, 1931, he turned to Freudian themes in an attempt to understand human motivation.

O'Neill was beyond cavil the pre-eminent American dramatist of his generation, but he was joined by such a goodly company after 1922 that almost overnight an American drama of genuine literary significance came into being. Moreover, the American public evinced an encouraging interest in the stage and a willingness to accept experimental forms. It was reflected not only on Broadway, but on college campuses and in little theater groups in a hundred American cities. This renaissance first began with the production of Elmer Rice's *The Adding Machine* in 1923. Then followed Maxwell Anderson's and Laurence Stallings' *What Price Glory?*, Sidney Howard's *They Knew What They Wanted*, and John Howard Lawson's *Processional* in 1924–5. From this beginning progress was rapid.

Although S. N. Behrman and Philip Barry enlivened the theater with sophisticated comedies and Paul Green and Hatcher Hughes tried vainly to stimulate interest in folk drama, the large majority of young playwrights simply mirrored the contemporary determinism, disillusionment, and preoccupation with sex. Not until the depression would the stage become a sounding board for the American social conscience.

103.   *Writers in Turmoil, 1929–1941*

American fictional writing during the years between the Great Depression and the Second World War reflected the violent crosscurrents of thought and challenges to democracy that confused the American mind. To begin with, the rebels of the "Lost Generation," who had discarded the genteel tradition and joined in warfare against what they considered smug idealism and prudish cant, lived on into the thirties. However, their revolt had lost much of its meaning by 1933, and the standards of a new rebellion were being unfurled by other insurgents. There was the tragic spectacle of F. Scott Fitzgerald, caught in the moral and cultural collapse of which he had written so poignantly. His final works, *Tender Is the Night*, 1934, and *The Last Tycoon*, 1941, were artistically distinguished but revealed a neurotic mind sickened by the corruption that he thought damned American life.

Ernest Hemingway and Sinclair Lewis gave further evidence of the bewilderment that confused and enfeebled the survivors of the "Lost Generation." In a series of books—*Death in the Afternoon*, 1932, *Winner Take Nothing*, 1933, and *The Green Hills of Africa*, 1935—Hemingway violated his own literary standards and nearly renounced human values. Then, alarmed by the challenge of fascism, he replied in 1940 with his most popular novel, *For Whom the Bell Tolls*. In the place of repudiation he now substituted devotion to a cause, the fight of the Spanish Loyalists. But his political ideology was confused, and his characters were out of place. *For Whom the Bell Tolls* marked the end of the "Lost Generation," not its rebirth.

The work of Sinclair Lewis after 1930 illustrated in a different way the deterioration of the "Lost Generation." Lewis was superbly effective so long as he held a mirror to the absurdities of middle-class thought and manners. But after 1930 he searched for new themes and evidenced less hostility toward society. His *It Can't Happen Here*, 1935, depicted the triumph of fascism in America and forecast the salvation of democracy by the middle class. Neither this nor his final novels, written in the forties, displayed the trenchant power that had characterized his work in the twenties.

In contrast, the late twenties and the thirties saw the rise of the brightest star in the whole twentieth-century American literary constellation. He was William Faulkner of Oxford, Mississippi, who had begun to write in the twenties but who had been culturally too isolated (or intellectually too independent) to be a member of the "Lost Generation." Faulkner from his lonely outpost sought to find the meaning of life through reconstruction of the southern past, through the heroes and villains and plain people caught in the vortex of a society in dissolution. From reading his earlier novels—such as *The Sound and the Fury*, 1929, *Light in August*, 1932, and *Absalom! Absalom!*, 1932—it is difficult for the layman to know whether Faulkner rejected completely the value structure of the past or used a powerful symbolism to reaffirm old values. But in a later volume—*The Unvanquished*, 1938—Faulkner began to exhibit clearer signs of the high purpose that underlay his important novels of the forties and fifties. (See below, pp. 636–637.)

Meanwhile, the 1930's witnessed an astounding rebirth of the social and economic novel in America that equaled if it did not exceed the outpouring of the years before the First World War. The mass of human suffering during the depression stimulated despair, while the hope of salvation either through destruction or reform of capitalism stimulated both a cathartic analysis of the American system and a political climate in which such analysis could flourish.

The most loquacious and perhaps the bitterest critic of American capitalism among the fictional writers of the thirties was John Dos Passos. In his trilogy, *U.S.A.—The Forty-Second Parallel*, 1930, *Nineteen-Nineteen*, 1932, and *The Big Money*, 1936—Dos Passos used a variety of literary techniques to reconstruct the panorama of American life from 1900 to 1929. In a second trilogy—*Adventures of a Young Man*, 1939, *Number One*, 1943, and *The Grand Design*, 1948—he continued the story through the depression and the New Deal.

Writing in the same vein but on a less panoramic scale and perhaps with less bitterness was James T. Farrell. His *Young Lonigan*, 1932, *The Young Manhood of Studs Lonigan*, 1934, and *The Judgment Day*, 1935, recounted the moral and spiritual disintegration of a lower middle-class Irish neighborhood in south Chicago. Another social novelist, John Steinbeck, protested against the injustices of an economic system that allegedly degraded workers and sharecroppers to the level of animal existence. His greatest work, *The Grapes of Wrath*, 1939, was a moving odyssey of the flight of a sharecropper family, the unforgettable Joads, from Oklahoma to California. In this and other novels Steinbeck emerged as a social novelist of the first rank and also as the writer who best understood the tragedy of the lower classes of his time.

The bitterest critics of the depression decade were the so-called proletarian writers—Marxists, Communists, and fellow-travelers—who used the novel as propaganda to hasten the conversion of the middle classes to revolutionary ideals. The politically devout among them magnified the sins of capitalism, glorified the "little people," and heralded the coming triumph of the disinherited. The "deviationists" used proletarian themes but would not surrender their artistic integrity to the commissars of Union Square. To a varying degree, Dos Passos, Farrell, and Steinbeck were proletarian writers and the most distinguished members of this group. The Negro naturalist, Richard Wright, was briefly a party member. His *Native Son*, 1940, and *Black Boy*, 1945, showed considerable talent if a strong penchant for unrelieved violence. The majority of proletarian writers, however, were important for their economic and social criticism, not for their literary prowess.

Not all the writers of the thirties were angry and raucous. There were survivors from the genteel past: Willa Cather, who published one of her most important books, *Shadows on the Rock*, 1931, and one of her most poignant tales, *Sapphira and the Slave Girl*, in 1940; Ellen Glasgow, who continued her satires on life in Virginia; and the southern writers, Elizabeth Madox Roberts and Katharine Anne Porter. And there were three new novelists, Pearl S. Buck, John P. Marquand, and Robert Penn Warren, who enriched the literature of the thirties and helped keep alive the traditions of graceful writing and moral purpose.

Judged sheerly by popular standards, the most important literary development after 1930 was the emergence of the historical novel as a mature literary form. Many of the historical novelists of the thirties simply romanticized the past and wrote cheap literature. On the other hand, a large minority, including Margaret Mitchell, Kenneth Roberts, Walter Edmonds, and Conrad Richter, illustrated the timelessness of human experience in graceful prose. Margaret Mitchell's *Gone with the Wind*, 1936, for example, was not only an epic of a civilization destroyed and struggling to live again, but also something of a literary masterpiece.

It was evident by the Second World War that a great era in American fictional writing had ended. It had begun with the revolt of the naturalists before 1917, flowered in the twenties with the rise of the "Lost Generation," and culminated in the thirties in the literature of the people and the search for a symbolic expression of human tragedy in the writings of William Faulkner, Robert Penn Warren, and other authors. But what new school would take their places? What would become of American literature after the old gods were dead?

104. *The Flowering of Poetry and the American Drama in the 1930's*

There were crosscurrents and new moods in American poetical writing after the brilliant renaissance of the period 1910–27. Some of the old masters and practitioners of more conventional forms survived in the thirties. For example, the dean of American poets, Edwin Arlington Robinson, confirmed his supremacy during the period between the completion of his Arthurian trilogy in 1927 and his last work, *King Jasper*, published in 1935. His death in that year deprived America of her greatest poet since Walt Whitman. Robert Frost, whose reputation was already well established by 1930, continued to write with deceptive simplicity about nature and man's struggles. Carl Sandburg, another of the "new" poets of the earlier renaissance, affirmed his faith in American destiny in *The People, Yes*, published in 1936. Edna St. Vincent Millay, a lyrical poet of some power who had begun her work in the early twenties, came to full artistic maturity in the 1930's, particularly in *Fatal Interview*, 1931.

These latter-day traditionalists had some followers in the thirties. There was Stephen Vincent Benét, who continued to voice American democratic idealism in *Litany for Dictatorships*, 1936, *Nightmare at Noon*, 1940, and *Western Star*, 1943, the year of his untimely death. Moreover, the challenge of depression at home and the rise of fascism abroad stimulated a brief outburst of democratic and leftist poetry in the 1930's. Muriel Rukeyser's *Theory of Flight*, 1935, and *U.S. 1*, 1938; Kenneth Fearing's

Poems, 1935; and Archibald MacLeish's *Public Speech,* 1936, *America Was Promises,* 1939, and other works, were poetic counterparts of the fictional "literature of the people."

Despite these survivals of more or less traditional poetry, the most important fact about American poetic thought and writing in the 1930's was the growing influence of the imagist school established by Ezra Pound before the First World War and dominated by T. S. Eliot in the twenties and thirties. Converted to Anglo-Catholicism in the late twenties, Eliot turned to religious themes. His later notable poems, *Ash Wednesday,* 1930, and *Four Quartets,* 1943, and his plays, *Murder in the Cathedral,* 1935, and *The Cocktail Party,* 1950, sought to convey the meaning of life and the universe.

The imagist revolt had long since become a mature movement with elaborate standards by 1940. We can now see that its emphasis upon imagery, symbolism, and intellectual quality produced a "new" poetry which, in its attempt to re-create the complexity of human experience, often went beyond the ability of the average reader to comprehend and enjoy. But many great poets have done this. The significant contribution of the modern poets was, in the words of one historian of the school, the triumph of "sincerity over sham, of naturalness over affectation, of a striking turn toward precision, analysis, and structure; of a wider range of conception and idea; of a deeper apprehension of meaning." [4]

We have earlier seen how a host of young playwrights, notably Eugene O'Neill, created an American drama in the decade following the Armistice. O'Neill's creative energies waned in the early thirties (even though he wrote perhaps his most powerful play, *The Iceman Cometh,* during this period), and leadership passed to other playwrights. Indeed, so voluminous, varied, and excellent was the outpouring after 1930 that it seemed the drama had become the chief form of American literary expression. Maxwell Anderson, who had made his literary debut earlier in the twenties, turned to writing historical tragedies in poetic verse. His *Elizabeth the Queen,* 1930, *Mary of Scotland,* 1933, and *Valley Forge,* 1934, established him as perhaps the leading American dramatist of the 1930's. S. N. Behrman and Philip Barry continued to enliven the stage with penetrating social satires that often said more than audiences understood. Marc Connelly depicted Negro folkways and religious thought in *The Green Pastures,* 1930, one of the most beautiful plays of the decade. Thornton Wilder expressed the theme of man's survival in spite of evil, ignorance, and war in *Our Town,* 1938, and *The Skin of Our Teeth,* 1942.

These and a host of other playwrights celebrated the foibles and follies as well as the enduring values of American life, but they were creative artists rather than social critics. Of greater significance to the political historian of the thirties was the work of a large group who used the stage as a sounding board for all kinds of ideologies and social and political protest. There were, most notably, the leftists—Elmer Rice, John Howard Lawson, and especially Clifford Odets, the most frankly Marxian of them— who joined in the Theater Union and Group Theater to write fierce de-

[4] Louise Bogan, *Achievement in American Poetry, 1900–1950* (Chicago, 1951), p. 106.

nunciations of the sins of capitalism. Some of them were also subsidized by the Federal Theater Project, an enterprise of the New Deal's relief agency, the Works Progress Administration. It was discovery of a number of Communists and Communist sympathizers that prompted Congress unceremoniously to end the Theater Project's life in 1939. The most talented social playwright, Lillian Hellman, demonstrated great power in her *The Children's Hour*, 1934, and then turned to propaganda in *The Little Foxes*, 1939, and *Watch on the Rhine*, 1941. Of different political faith was Robert Sherwood, who best reflected the changing temper of the non-Marxist intellectual during the thirties. His *The Petrified Forest*, 1934, reflected the pessimistic view of its day that reason was ineffectual as compared with brute force. His *Idiot's Delight*, 1936, was one of the most eloquent pieces of antiwar propaganda during the high tide of pacifist sentiment. In response to the challenges of Nazism and Communism, however, Sherwood replied with two ringing affirmations of faith in man and democracy—*Abe Lincoln in Illinois*, 1938, and *There Shall Be No Night*, 1940.

105.   *The Growth of American Music, Art, and Architecture*

Americans who, at the end of the First World War, lamented the absence of any strong musical and artistic traditions and bemoaned the public's indifference to these important manifestations of culture might well have been encouraged by developments between the Armistice and the Second World War. One of the happiest cultural developments in the period was the flowering of the musical tradition in the United States. This fact was manifested particularly in the spread of music by the phonograph and radio and in growth of music education, symphony orchestras, and choral groups. It was manifested, additionally, in the phenomenal public response to one of the most interesting cultural experiments of the 1930's—the establishment of a Federal Music Project by the New Deal's relief agency, the Works Progress Administration.

The Project's orchestras gave a total of about 150,000 concerts which were heard by more than 100,000,000 persons between 1935 and 1940. Statistics on musical activity in 1940 do not seem to exist, but in 1930 practically every elementary and high school in the United States offered some form of musical training, and there were 35,000 orchestras in public schools alone. At the same time, there were in the United States seventy-three permanent symphony orchestras, fifty-five chamber music groups, and 576 choral societies. Even more important was the development during the twenties and thirties of music schools and conservatories. There were probably more able music teachers in the United States than in Europe by the outbreak of the Second World War.

This musical awakening stimulated a love for music among millions of Americans, provided a broad economic base for the musical profession in the United States, and gave rise to a host of young composers. Between 1865 and 1917 America had produced a number of serious composers—Edward MacDowell, Edgar S. Kelley, Frank van der Stucken, Charles M. Loeffler, to mention a few of them. Except for MacDowell, however, their works made slight impression on the American musical public. In contrast,

American music critics and listeners were celebrating the accomplishments of their serious composers by 1940.

Deems Taylor was easily the most popular of this group. His *Through the Looking Glass*, written from 1917 to 1919, sparkled with wit and brilliance. His *The King's Henchmen*, completed in 1927, was produced at the Metropolitan Opera House and won enthusiastic acclaim. Ernest Bloch, a Swiss composer who came to the United States in 1916, abandoned Jewish themes to write *America*, a symphony built around American musical traditions. Howard Hanson, director of the Eastman School of Music at Rochester, New York, was perhaps the most gifted and technically competent of the composers of the twenties. His opera, *Merry Mount*, based upon an old American story, was produced by the Metropolitan Opera Company in 1934.

This small if distinguished group continued to compose in the classical tradition and were joined in the thirties by a larger company. Notable among the new American composers were four romanticists of great virtuosity, Douglas Moore, Virgil Thomson, Samuel Barber, and William Schuman; William Grant Still, who drew upon the American Negro past for haunting melodies; and the modernists, Aaron Copland and Roy Harris.

Important though the above work was, American musicians during the twenties and thirties made their most original contribution to the musical tradition by developing an old form, folk songs, and elaborating a new one, jazz. In the nineteenth century folk music voiced the yearnings of the slave, the patriotism and ideals of Northerners and Southerners during the Civil War, and other more homely aspects of life. The form and themes of folk music changed in the early twentieth century from haunting melodies to so-called ragtime, from themes of country and small-town life to themes reflecting an urban civilization.

This was even more true in the twenties and thirties, as hundreds of popular song writers like Cole Porter and George Gershwin expressed the folly and wisdom, gaiety and pathos of the time. A significant popular musical development of the thirties was the emergence of swing music, a refinement of jazz through elaborate arrangement and the use of larger orchestras. There were dozens of swing leaders in the thirties, among them being the great Glenn Miller and Tommy Dorsey; but the "King of Swing" was the incomparable Benny Goodman, whose clarinet set the viscera of jitterbugs afire. Especially noteworthy were musical plays, like Jerome Kern's and Oscar Hammerstein II's *Show Boat*, 1927, which gave birth to many of the best songs of the period. Gershwin climaxed his long career in 1935 with *Porgy and Bess*, based upon a play about Negro life in Charleston by Du Bose Heyward. It was perhaps the greatest American opera; certainly it was destined to be sung as long as men love music. During the same period Richard Rodgers and Lorenz Hart enlivened the musical stage with carefree comedies. Noteworthy also was the rise of the Negro "blues" songs, best exemplified by W. C. Handy's "Memphis Blues" and "St. Louis Blues." But the most important musical development of the period 1920–40 was the phenomenal spread of Negro jazz, which had originated in the early years of the century in New Orleans and made its way to Chicago by 1916. A highly sophisticated musical form, jazz spread rapidly over the country, especially after Paul Whiteman demonstrated the wide potentialities of the new form in the early twenties, and Gershwin combined the syncopation of jazz with the symphonic form in *Rhapsody in Blue*, 1927, and *An American in Paris*, 1928.

We have seen that the period 1900–20 witnessed the first important beginnings of American public interest in painting and sculpture. The years between 1920 and 1940 saw the full maturing of a genuine appreciation. This phenomenon was manifested in many ways: in increased artistic creativity, the introduction of art subjects in public schools and college curricula, the immense popularity of the WPA's Federal Art Project between 1935 and 1939, and especially the establishment of art museums in all sections of the country, not merely in New York, Boston, Chicago, and Philadelphia. The most notable of the new museums was the National Art Gallery in Washington, built in the late thirties as a gift of the Pittsburgh banker and industrialist, Andrew W. Mellon. It rapidly emerged as one of the great galleries of the world.

American painters during the twenties continued more to follow the Continental lead than to develop techniques and forms of their own. The reaction against impressionism, in the form of movement toward intellectualized abstraction and primitivism, which had got under way in France just before the World War, came to full flower in Europe and America after 1920. At the same time, abstraction metamorphosed into cubism, surrealism, and other "modern" forms among an advanced artistic guard. Among the notable exponents of abstraction in the United States were John Marin, Max Weber, Maurice Prendergast, and Charles R. Sheeler. Not all American artists of the twenties abandoned the concrete for the newer intellectual forms. A large group persevered in the realistic tradition and left a memorable graphic record of various aspects of American social life. George Bellows continued to paint powerful scenes of the ring. Edward Hopper, Rockwell Kent, Ernest Lawson, John Sloan, and other artists of the so-called Ash Can School painted "drunks and slatterns, pushcart peddlers and coal mines, bedrooms and barrooms." These artistic rebels shocked many genteel folk but left a vivid pictorial record of the seamy side of American life.

The impact of the depression, conflict of ideologies, and threat of war in the thirties stimulated a strong continuation of artistic realism dedicated to the people.[5] The most significant manifestation was the development of an aggressively "American" school that drew its inspiration from the region and sought to portray every aspect of American life on canvas. The three leaders of the new regional school were John Steuart Curry, Grant Wood, and Thomas Hart Benton, whose scenes of life in Kansas, Iowa, and Missouri recalled the grandeur as well as the reality of midwestern life. But the names of the "American" school were legion: artists of the calm New England countryside, of southwestern desert isolation, of Negro life, of decaying plantations, of the Bowery and Skid Row and chaos of city

[5] To be sure, the abstract painters and surrealists survived in the thirties, as was evidenced by the work of Walter Quirt, George L. K. Morris, and Stuart Davis. But they suffered a relative decline in artistic influence and found it increasingly difficult to justify their work in social terms.

life, of workers, farmers, and other plain people. The great artistic re-discovery of America gained new momentum, moreover, when the WPA established an Art Project in 1935, hired thousands of artists, good and bad, to paint murals in post offices and courthouses, and sponsored various projects of instruction in art and the handicrafts.

Then there was a second large and more vocal group among American realists, who combined attachment to the local scene with devotion to radical ideologies. Leaders of the political avant-garde met in annual Artist Congresses from 1936 to 1940 and turned out a flood of propaganda on canvas. Their main themes were oppression of labor, lynching and abuse of the Negro, and wicked capitalists conspiring to drive the world to war. There were, for example, William Gropper's and Joseph Hirsch's savage caricatures of American politicians, Robert Gwathmey's pictures of the South, and Ben Shahn's scenes of capitalistic-police oppression in the coal regions. As one authority has observed, "Too many of these lynchings, prairie wagons, and barroom carousels possessed an energy that was simply of the nerves and muscles." [6]

In sculpture one trend of the twenties and thirties was away from the idealistic realism of the prewar masters like Augustus Saint-Gaudens and Daniel Chester French toward abstract symbolism and primitivism. It was exemplified in the work of William Zorach, Arnold Ronnebeck, Robert Garrison, and others. On the other hand, Trygve Hammer, Gaston Lachaise, and Jo Davidson did memorable work in the realistic tradition, while the most widely acclaimed sculptor of the period, Gutzon Borglum, chiseled massive realistic monuments on Stone Mountain in Georgia and Mount Rushmore in South Dakota.

In architecture the two decades from 1920 to 1940 saw the culmination of a revolution no less significant than that in other fields. The modern functional school founded by Louis Sullivan and Frank Lloyd Wright finally came to dominance among American architects and began to find some acceptance by the rank and file of the people. It is true that progress in the movement to free Americans from their prison walls of stone and cement must have seemed painfully slow to the pioneers. As late as the mid-thirties modern homes were still architectural curiosities. The federal government was pouring hundreds of millions of dollars into massive marble mausoleums in Washington and elsewhere. In addition, Gothic and colonial styles still prevailed in the construction of college and public school buildings.

The first important sign that the tide had turned toward functionalism came with the construction in the 1930's of Rockefeller Center and the McGraw-Hill and *Daily News* skyscrapers in New York City and of modern garden-type apartment projects throughout the country by the Federal Housing Authority. Moreover, Hitler's lash or the fear of tyranny drove many of Europe's best functional architects to America before 1939. They were not only a generative force in themselves but also helped to strengthen liaison with other European functionalists. The most important turning point was the planning and construction of the New York World's Fair of

wwwwwwwwwwwww

[6] Oliver W. Larkin, *Art and Life in America* (New York, 1949), p. 450.

1939–40, for it gave functionalists an opportunity to introduce advanced design to millions of Americans. Especially noteworthy was Norman Bel Geddes' General Motors Building with its "Futurama" of a new America.

Of equal significance was the movement for city planning and the development of great parkway systems to facilitate traffic between the city and outlying areas. The movement to establish city planning commissions actually began in 1905 but did not gain momentum until after 1914. There were only seventeen such agencies before 1914; more than 750 planning commissions were established between 1914 and 1930. In the wake of this development followed campaigns to zone cities into exclusively industrial, commercial, and residential areas, to improve building codes, and to clean up slums—in other words, to clear away the jungle growth in American city life.

106. *The Great Age of Motion Pictures*

The years from 1915 to 1930 saw that new and immensely popular art form—the motion picture—come to first maturity. The artistic possibilities were first demonstrated by David W. Griffith's "The Birth of a Nation," produced in 1915. Although it was a piece of anti-Negro propaganda, it was a milestone in motion-picture history. Griffith surmounted the limitations and conventions of the stage by using large numbers of actors, panoramic scenery, the close-up, the fade-out, and the switch-back. He subsequently produced other great historical films, notably "Intolerance"—as penance for "The Birth of a Nation." Cecil B. de Mille used thousands of actors and spectacular sets and scenery in his religious dramas, "The Ten Commandments," "The Flood," and "The King of Kings." Other spectacles like "The Covered Wagon," "The Four Horsemen of the Apocalypse," "The Big Parade," "Quo Vadis," and "Ben Hur" employed diverse themes but used all the new artistic techniques and helped make the twenties a memorable motion-picture decade. Moreover, as Hollywood salaries lured many of the best actors of the period from the legitimate stage, acting became an art that the masses of people, rather than the privileged few, could enjoy. Charlie Chaplin and Harold Lloyd, for example, were not only the pre-eminent film comedians of the twenties; they were superb creative artists as well.

Progress was, if anything, swifter in the late twenties and the thirties than it had been in the preceding decade. After the perfection of sound movies from 1926 to 1929 and of Technicolor in 1935 there were no technical developments of importance until the 1950's. But there was considerable improvement in technique, form, lighting, and use of music. And Hollywood continued to attract most of the best actors and actresses in America and Europe by the lure of fabulous salaries. Moreover, during the thirties Walt Disney perfected the animated cartoon and demonstrated its versatility in full-length productions like "Snow White and the Seven Dwarfs" in 1938 and "Fantasia" in 1940.

The 1930's will rank in the final history of the motion pictures as Hollywood's golden decade, at least during the first half century of the industry's existence. There were films for every taste and mood, ranging from superb comedies like "It Happened One Night," 1934, and "The Philadelphia Story," 1940, to epic dramas like "Mutiny on the Bounty," 1936, and "Gone with the Wind," 1939. Charles Laughton, Paul Muni, Walter Huston, James Stewart, Victor McLaglen, Frederic March, Gary Cooper, and a whole galaxy of stars raised motion pictures to new artistic heights. For lovers of nonsense there were the incomparable Laurel and Hardy and the Marx brothers, whose series have not been equaled since for sheer hilarity. For devotees of social satire there were Charlie Chaplin's "City Lights," 1931, "Modern Times," 1936, and "The Great Dictator," 1940, and Orson Welles's caricature of William Randolph Hearst, "Citizen Kane," 1941.

The thirties were a memorable decade, above all, because Hollywood for a brief time addressed itself to serious social questions and became almost an echo of the American social conscience. During a time when democracy was everywhere under attack Paul Muni recalled the traditions of freedom and justice in "Juarez" and "The Life of Émile Zola," while Raymond Massey embodied the living Emancipator in "Abe Lincoln in Illinois." In addition, a whole series—"I Am a Fugitive from a Chain Gang," "Dead End," "Black Legion," "The Grapes of Wrath," and "Fury," for example—revealed cancerous growths in the body of American social life. Finally, the federal government contributed two memorable documentary films, "The River" and "The Plow That Broke the Plains." They depicted America's wastage of human and natural resources and pointed the way toward social redemption through democratic collective action.

107. *School and Church in the Twenties and Thirties*

Progress in expanding and improving free education had been steady and substantial from the Civil War to 1920. The prosperity of the twenties, however, stimulated such achievement as had not been recorded in any earlier comparable period. Then came heavy blows in consequence of diminished revenues during the depression (for an account of which, see below, p. 371), followed by slow but steady recovery to new heights in the late 1930's. The following generalizations illustrate the main trends: The number of pupils enrolled in public schools from 1920 to 1940 increased from 21,578,000 to nearly 25,500,000. Total expenditures for education in the United States grew during the same two decades from $1,036,000,000 to $2,344,000,000, the number of teachers from 680,000 to 875,000, and expenditure per pupil from $53.52 to $88.09. Moreover, illiteracy declined during the same period generally from 6 per cent of the total population to 2.9 per cent, and among nonwhites, mainly Negroes, from 23 per cent to 11.5 per cent.

The goal of free education for all children in elementary schools had been fairly accomplished by 1920, and, except for expansion in kindergartens and schools for Negro children, progress accomplished in the elementary field from 1920 to 1940 came more from improved instruction, longer terms, and the like, than from any great expansion in sheer numbers. For one thing, state departments of education assumed responsibility for licensing teachers and began to require completion of a four-year college course as a prerequisite for a teaching certificate. For another, the "progressive" methods advocated earlier by John Dewey and others found wider acceptance as schools of education broke away from the formal classical tradition. Traditionalists bemoaned the neglect of genteel subjects, but increased emphasis upon experimentation and participation by children, as well as widespread use of workshops, laboratories, and other material equipment, were certainly well adapted to the capacities of children. They were also indispensable instruments of mass education.

Americans made their greatest relative progress during the two decades under discussion in secondary and higher education. The number of children enrolled in public high schools increased 200 per cent, from 2,200,000 to 6,601,000, from 1920 to 1940. And along with growth came important changes in curriculum as high schools ceased to prepare children exclusively for college. Thus, only 16 per cent of high school pupils studied Latin in 1934, as contrasted to nearly 50 per cent in 1910. On the other hand, music, manual training, home economics, typewriting, agricultural science, and other vocational subjects, most of which had not even been offered in 1910, were beginning to overshadow the so-called classical offerings. Accelerated by the Smith-Lever and Smith-Hughes Acts of 1914 and 1917, which provided federal support for agricultural and vocational education, this movement toward more practical training for the large majority of high school students who would not go to college was a frank recognition of the state's enlarged social responsibilities.

The prosperity of the 1920's, and especially the great increase in high school enrollment, in turn stimulated an unprecedented expansion of American colleges and universities. The following statistics illustrate the general trends: From 1920 to 1940 there was an increase in the number of students enrolled from 598,000 to 1,494,000, of instructors from 48,600 to 147,000, of total endowments from $556,350,000 to $1,686,000,000, and of total receipts exclusive of new capital funds from $199,922,000 to $715,211,000.

This extraordinary growth raised serious new problems concerning the role of higher education in a democracy and inevitably compelled college and university leaders to modify methods and objectives. In short, colleges and universities ceased to prepare students almost exclusively for the professions and became also training schools where young men and women prepared for careers in industry, business, and other walks of life. This fact did not signify any diminution of advanced professional training, research, and writing. On the contrary, graduate schools grew even more rapidly than undergraduate departments,[7] while the growth of medical, law, and other professional schools was substantial if not as spectacular.

Although the state universities grew faster in enrollment and income during the twenties and thirties, private colleges and universities continued to provide leadership in academic innovation. Harvard, Swarthmore, and a number of other institutions followed Princeton's earlier example and introduced the tutorial system and honors programs. Following a plan

wwwwwwwwwwwww

[7] For example, there were 16,000 students enrolled in graduate schools and 615 Ph.D. degrees conferred in 1920; in 1940 there were 106,000 graduate students enrolled and 3,290 Ph.D. degrees conferred.

proposed by Woodrow Wilson in 1906, Harvard and Yale constructed undergraduate colleges, in which upper-classmen and faculty members lived together. At Rollins College in Florida Hamilton Holt abandoned the lecture system for the conference method of instruction, while Arthur E. Morgan introduced the so-called in-and-out system at Antioch College in Ohio, in which students alternated between attendance at college and work outside. There were of course retrogressive trends—periodic assaults upon freedom of teaching by religious and nationalistic groups, attempts by reactionary trustees to control academic policies, and the like. Such efforts to bring higher education under reactionary religious and economic control, however, were the exception rather than the rule. College and university faculties by and large enjoyed greater respect and freedom than ever before in American history.

How fared the churches, the other great agencies of moral and social enlightenment, during this period? Protestant, Roman Catholic, and Jewish churches continued to grow in membership and wealth during the decades between the religious censuses of 1916 and 1936. Increasing urbanization and use of the automobile caused elimination of many small rural churches and consolidation of others, and church construction proceeded at a much slower pace than the growth in the general population. But church membership in the United States increased more rapidly than the population—from a total of 41,927,000 to 55,807,000, or by 33 per cent, during a time when population increased by 27 per cent; and churches increased expenditures from $328,810,000 to $518,954,000, or by about 27 per cent. But these are only rough figures and do not reveal the significant exceptions. Growth was extraordinarily rapid from 1916 to 1929; church membership increased hardly at all during the depression years from 1929 to 1940. It was a time of such precipitous relative decline as to lead certain observers to conclude that the church in America was a dying institution.

As much as during the early years of the twentieth century, the United States was predominantly a Protestant country in the 1920's and 1930's. Total Protestant membership grew from 25,848,000 in 1916 to 31,251,000 in 1936, Catholic membership from 15,722,000 to 19,914,366 over the same two decades. Roman Catholics constituted 37.5 per cent of all church members in 1916 and only 36 per cent in 1936 because of the more accurate reporting of Jewish congregations. Among the more than two hundred Protestant bodies in 1936, the Baptists, with nearly 9,500,000, and various Methodist bodies, with an aggregate of some 7,000,000, continued to command a large superiority in numbers and to account for the greatest increases in membership.

Meanwhile, the 1920's had witnessed the almost complete triumph of liberalism among leaders of American Protestantism. Frankly embracing evolution and the higher criticism, many liberals abandoned theological exegesis for the Social Gospel and hopefully looked toward the early establishment of the Kingdom of God among men. The liberal minority became probably a majority during the 1920's, at least among the Methodist and Congregational churches. One survey in the late twenties revealed that liberal ideas prevailed among a large minority of ministers and among a large majority of all Protestant seminary students.

Protestant thought was convulsed in the 1930's, and the tide began to turn against liberalism as a consequence of one of the most important intellectual upheavals since the Reformation—the rise of so-called neo-orthodoxy, or reformulated biblical theology. It began in Europe. The Swiss theologians Karl Barth and Emile Brunner, surveying the wreckage of the World War and the failure of the League of Nations in the twenties and early thirties, indicted liberalism for glorifying man instead of God and for forgetting that man's sin produced perpetual crises in history. They were modernists insofar as higher criticism and evolution were concerned, but they were thoroughly orthodox in their emphasis upon the sovereignty and majesty of God, the sinfulness of man, and God's loving grace in justification and election in Jesus Christ. Barth's *Commentary on Romans*, published in 1919, was the fire bell that awakened Europe.

These European theologians of crisis were only faintly heard in the United States during the confident twenties, but they gained many American disciples in the thirties. The great leader of neo-orthodoxy in the United States was Reinhold Niebuhr of Union Theological Seminary in New York City. His *Moral Man and Immoral Society*, 1932, *Reflections on the End of an Era*, 1934, *Beyond Tragedy*, 1937, and *The Nature and Destiny of Man*, 1941–3, epitomized the neo-orthodox indictment of shallow liberalism and pointed to the return in the United States to the Church's historic knowledge of God and man.

Many American liberals refused to go the whole way but confessed that liberalism had obviously failed in the face of crisis. For example, Harry Emerson Fosdick, pastor of the Riverside Church in New York City, in an epochal sermon in 1935 repudiated humanism and called for a return to biblical theology. In addition, the thirties saw a marked revival in interest in the writings of Luther and Calvin; the discovery of the Danish existentialist, Sören Kierkegaard; and stronger emphasis on the Atonement and the concept of the Church as the Body of Christ.

The Social Gospel was undergoing decline, reconstruction, and revival in a new form while this reformulation of American Protestant theological understanding was taking place. The Social Gospel survived in the twenties, to be sure; but, ironically, it declined during the heyday of the liberalism that had given it birth. The depression, world crisis, and neo-orthodoxy all converged in impact to produce a radical revival and transformation of American Protestant social thought and energies. Older Social Gospel thought survived and was manifested in advanced pronouncements on poverty, the rights of labor and racial minorities, economic justice, and so on. But Protestant social thought was responding more and more to the neo-orthodox doctrines that repudiated utopianism and viewed the Church more as the saving remnant in an immoral society than as the remaker of the social order. This was the conviction popularized by Niebuhr under the name of "Christian realism."

It was not all erosion and decline, for the decades 1920–40 witnessed one of the Social Gospel's greatest triumphs of the twentieth century —the Roman Catholic Church's official endorsement and espousal of its cause. This occurred, most specifically, when the American bishops took command of the inchoate social justice groups within the Church during the First World War and then, in 1919, endorsed a platform entitled "Social Reconstruction: A General Review of the Problems and Survey of Remedies." Prepared by Father John A. Ryan, a prophetic sociologist at the Catholic University of America, it was a ringing document that endorsed unionization, collective bargaining, and worker participation in industrial ownership and management. Soon afterward the bishops established the National Catholic Welfare Council and a special committee of the American hierarchy to co-ordinate the Church's social thought and work. It was the beginning of what would become a vast enterprise by the end of the 1930's.

Meanwhile, there were numerous signs that forces drawing Protestants together continued to be far stronger from 1920 to 1940 than old antagonisms keeping them apart. The only disruptive elements in Protestantism after 1920 were the extreme fundamentalists, who insisted upon verbatim acceptance of historic creeds, and a lunatic fringe that included a wide variety of apostles of discord. More than offsetting them was a powerful ecumenical movement toward either organic union or close fellowship among the major Protestant bodies. In 1931, for example, the Congregational and Christian churches combined; in 1939 the three main Methodist bodies healed old wounds and formed the largest single Protestant denomination; and movements for union within Presbyterian and Lutheran bodies seemed to be gaining ground. Throughout the thirties, moreover, the Federal Council of Churches of Christ in America continued to speak for a large majority of American Protestant churches.

108. *Trends in American Journalism, 1920–1940*

Newspapers grew in size and circulation from 1920 to 1940 and continued to rival schools and churches as the chief instruments of mass education and the dissemination of ideas. At the same time, there were signs that earlier trends were culminating in the 1920's and 1930's to alter the character and practice of journalism and newspaper publishing in the United States.

For one thing, there was a striking trend toward consolidation in ownership, a consequent decline in the number of newspapers published, and the further extension of the influence of the metropolitan press through rural areas. Daily newspapers declined in number from 2,325 in 1920 to 1,903 in 1933 and then increased to 1,998 in 1940; the number of weekly newspapers shrank from 12,876 in 1920 to 4,218 in 1933 and increased to 6,212 in 1939. "Among 2,000 dailies in the United States in 1937, more than 300 were controlled by 60 chains and more than 100 by 6 chains." [8] By 1940 there were twenty-five cities over 100,000, including Providence, Omaha, St. Paul, Louisville, Des Moines, and Oklahoma City, with single newspaper ownership. In addition, Atlanta, Baltimore, Buffalo, Denver, Kansas City, Minneapolis, and New Orleans had only two ownership groups.

Among the large newspaper publishers, William Randolph Hearst was still the leader for most of the period. He added twenty-seven dailies to his

wwwwwwwwwwwwwwww

[8] U.S. Temporary National Economic Committee, *Competition and Monopoly in American Industry* (Washington, 1940), p. 61.

newspaper realm from 1914 through 1929 and owned in addition two wire news services, King Features, six magazines, a newsreel, a motion picture company, and a weekly supplement. Abandoning his simulated progressivism of the prewar period, Hearst became openly reactionary in the twenties and thirties and was as stridently nationalistic as ever. Hard hit by the depression, he was forced to severe retrenchment and controlled only seventeen dailies by 1940. The Scripps-McRae chain, which published twenty-three newspapers in 1914, became the Scripps-Howard chain in 1922 and absorbed an additional eighteen dailies from 1921 through 1929. It still controlled nineteen dailies in 1940 and had surpassed the Hearst chain in strength. In upstate New York Frank E. Gannett established a chain of fifteen dailies, while James M. Cox, Democratic presidential candidate in 1920, went into the newspaper business in 1923 and bought control of a newspaper chain in Ohio, to which in the 1930's he added the Atlanta *Journal* and the Miami (Florida) *News*.

As newspapers declined in number and fell increasingly under outside control, they inevitably became capitalistic enterprises often representing investments of several million dollars. In form and content, however, most American newspapers changed little after 1920. For the most part they used standardized news and features, became decidedly less partisan in politics, and grew more dependent upon advertising for revenue. Newspaper advertising revenues alone totaled $2,088,000,000 in 1940. In other words, running a great newspaper became a highly institutionalized and departmentalized function, and often a highly profitable business. Consequently, the editor not only lost his independence but also the great prestige he had once enjoyed as a tribune of the people. Old-fashioned editors like Josephus Daniels of the Raleigh *News and Observer* and William Allen White of the *Emporia* (Kansas) *Gazette* survived; but they were prototypes of a vanishing race of men who once dominated their newspapers and made them extensions of their personalities.

A majority of newspapers continued to adhere to the traditions of public service and honest and dignified reporting established earlier by Joseph Pulitzer and Adolph S. Ochs, but the most notable journalistic development of the 1920's was the rise of the so-called tabloid. Imitating Lord Northcliffe's *Daily Mirror* of London, Robert R. McCormick and Joseph Medill Patterson in 1919 established the New York *Daily News*, a morning newspaper of sixteen four-column pages. Featuring sensational sex and crime stories and filled with pictures and features, the *News* attained the largest circulation in the country in 1924. Hearst was embittered because the owners of the *News* surpassed him in the art of yellow journalism and established his own tabloid in 1924, the New York *Daily Mirror*. And when Bernarr Macfadden entered the competition a few months later with the New York *Graphic*, there began such a frenzied newspaper war as New Yorkers had not seen since Hearst and Pulitzer fought it out in 1898. Meanwhile, tabloids spread to numerous other cities, causing the worst wave of yellow journalism in modern American history. However, a public reaction against journalistic obscenity set in about 1929, and tabloids gradually changed into small newspapers with little news and many pictures, features, and cartoons. By 1940 there were nearly fifty tabloids in existence, many of them being in smaller cities.

Throughout the twenties and afterward weekly and monthly magazines remained an important medium of opinion, news, and entertainment. The two chief organs of progressive ideas, the *Nation* and *New Republic,* maintained their subsidized existence. The *Saturday Evening Post, Collier's,* and the women's magazines combined light fiction with articles of contemporary interest and continued to enjoy mass circulations.

A new kind of weekly, *The New Yorker,* edited by Harold Ross until his death in 1951, entered the field in 1925. Urbane, witty, and even scholarly at times, it, more than any other magazine of the period, maintained the high literary standards of American magazine journalism. Also new in concept and even more successful in terms of circulation was the *Reader's Digest,* launched by DeWitt Wallace in 1922. It provided busy readers the so-called best of magazine writing in capsule form. On the other hand, journals like *Outlook, World's Work,* and *Independent,* which appealed to more limited audiences by combining serious fiction with news and opinion, declined in the 1920's. Faced with a sharp rise in paper and printing costs and unable to adapt themselves to new mass reading habits, these journals passed from the American journalistic scene during the depression.

Meanwhile, the most important revolution in magazine publishing since the advent of the popular magazine in the 1890's, the rise of the weekly news and picture magazines, was taking shape in the brain of Henry Luce, the most daring magazine publisher since S. S. McClure. Luce in 1925 began publication of *Time,* a weekly devoted exclusively to news in concise form, cryptic style, and ostensibly from an objective political viewpoint. It became the leading American news weekly within a decade. Luce opened a new field in 1930 with the publication of *Fortune,* a monthly addressed to business leaders and intellectuals. But his greatest triumph came with the publication in 1936 of *Life,* a weekly news-picture magazine, which enjoyed immediate success. The subsequent rise of rival magazines like *Newsweek* and *United States News,* founded in 1933, and *Look,* founded in 1937, only emphasized the dimensions of the journalistic revolution that Luce had accomplished by 1940.

CHAPTER

14

Tensions of the 1920's

A NUMBER of developments combined at the end of the war to intensify old religious, social, and ideological discords and to cause new insecurities. The clash of scientific materialism and materialistic evolution with religious orthodoxy stimulated a remarkable fundamentalist counterattack. Patriotic organizations revived the strident nationalism and intolerance of the war period and inflamed religious prejudices. The Protestant majority attempted to suppress the traffic in alcoholic beverages and ended by outraging intellectuals, embittering the urban masses, and provoking a campaign of resistance to federal authority. The changing fortunes and turmoil of organized labor further reflected the social tensions racking American life.

Few were unaffected by the tensions and conflicts we are about to describe, but withal democracy survived its periodic testing. Perhaps the foibles and failures of the American people in the 1920's will afford hope for the future to a generation distraught by new insecurities.

109. *The Anti-Evolution Crusade*

The anti-evolution crusade was the last organized uprising of fundamentalist America against materialistic concepts that seemed to remove God from the process of creation, deny His dominion over human affairs, and attempt to destroy an ethical system based upon divinely revealed moral law. It was fitting that William J. Bryan, spokesman of rural, Protestant America, should have taken leadership in a movement that drew most of its recruits from rural areas. The spread of scientific materialism and especially of the belief in the material origins of man presented a personal challenge to Bryan. Investigation convinced him that evolutionary teaching caused students first to lose faith in the verbal inspiration and inerrancy of the Scriptures and later to repudiate Christianity altogether. What Bryan dreaded most was the possibility of atheistic evolutionists being graduated from the colleges, invading public schools as teachers, and undermining the Christian faith of American school children.

He sounded the first note in his campaign to purge public schools and colleges with addresses at the University of Wisconsin in April 1921 and before the General Assembly of Kentucky in January 1922. "They have taken the Lord away from the schools," he cried again and again. "Shall teachers paid by taxation be permitted to substitute the unproven hypothesis of scientists for the 'Thus saith the Lord' of the Bible, and so undermine the faith of the children of Christian taxpayers?" The answer, of course, was obvious: legislators should forbid the teaching of evolution in public schools and institutions of higher learning. Bryan soon made his campaign a nation-wide crusade. He turned his monthly magazine, *The Commoner,* into a fundamentalist sheet. He spoke before state legislatures through the South and Middle West. He carried his fight to the General Assembly of the northern Presbyterian Church, there failing to win adoption of an anti-evolution resolution in 1923. But he had succeeded in beginning one of the liveliest controversies of the decade; legislatures in many states were already being pressed to enact anti-evolution laws.

Bryan's campaign had significant reverberations in the Middle West, but it met with strong popular support and a measure of success only in the South. Leadership and support for the movement in that region came largely from Baptists and Presbyterians. There was, however, no uniformity of religious opinion in the so-called Bible Belt. Baptists, for example, were badly split by the evolution issue, while the Methodist Episcopal Church, South, and the Episcopal Church taught theistic evolution and refused to be drawn into the controversy.

But Bryan's call to battle in 1921 was answered by a large number of southern fundamentalists. There was, for example, the Reverend J. Frank Norris of Fort Worth, Texas, the *enfant terrible* of the southern Baptist church, who undertook a reign of terror against science teachers at Baylor University in Waco and published a weekly newspaper, *The Searchlight,* devoted to exposing atheists and evolutionists. Or there was the Reverend T. T. Martin, an itinerant Baptist evangelist, author of *Hell in the High Schools,* one of the leading anti-evolution tracts. They and their cohorts carried on vigorous campaigns in most southern and southwestern states from 1921 to 1925. At the same time, liberal leaders in church, school, and journalism met the fundamentalists head on, fought courageously for academic freedom, and, on the whole, won the first round.

In fact, the only state in which the anti-evolutionists had won a decisive victory by 1925 was Tennessee.[1] Academic circles in the United States
wwwwwwwwwwwwwww

[1] The fundamentalists, however, won qualified victories in Florida, North Carolina, and Texas. Without forbidding the teaching of evolution, the Florida legislature in May 1923 adopted a resolution advising that "Darwinism, Atheism, and Agnosticism" should not be taught as truths in the public schools of the state. The North Carolina State Board of Education on January 22, 1924, forbade the teaching in public schools of any form of evolution affirming that man descended from a lower order of animals. The State Textbook Board of Texas in October 1925 ordered the deletion of all references to evolution in books adopted for public schools in the state.

were shocked in the spring of 1923 by the dismissal from the University of Tennessee of a professor of genetic psychology for using James Harvey Robinson's *Mind in the Making*. Five other professors were dismissed at the end of the college year for teaching the evolutionary hypothesis. An anti-evolution bill was introduced in the Tennessee legislature two years later, and Bryan and a powerful Baptist lobby descended upon Nashville. The legislature and governor surrendered by approving a measure forbidding any teacher in the state's schools and colleges to teach any theory denying the biblical account of creation or asserting that man had descended from a lower order of animals.

The American Civil Liberties Union at once offered to finance defense of any Tennessee teacher who would test the constitutionality of the statute. A young high school biology teacher in Dayton, John Thomas Scopes, volunteered, and a friendly test case was begun in May 1925. When the state's counsel invited Bryan to join the prosecution, the Commoner accepted joyfully, declaring, "This is a matter for the nation." At the same time, the famed trial lawyer, Clarence Darrow, joined the defense counsel, thus setting the stage for one of the great forensic battles of the century.

The little mountain town of Dayton, Tennessee, was crowded with evangelists, traveling performers, and newspaper correspondents from all over the United States and the Western world as the opening day of the trial, July 14, 1925, drew near. Bryan was greeted by huge crowds and ovations; he responded by promising a campaign to amend the Constitution to prohibit the teaching of evolution anywhere in the United States. The presiding judge, John T. Raulston, did his best to preserve a semblance of decorum. But the proceedings soon degenerated into a public circus after the court obligingly adjourned to a vacant lot in order to accommodate the huge crowds. Raulston refused to admit expert testimony concerning the validity of the Darwinian hypothesis, and the trial became a verbal duel between the agnostic Darrow and the fundamentalist Bryan.

It did not take long to prove that Scopes had violated the law, since he admitted as much. The Supreme Court of Tennessee later rescinded the small fine that Raulston had imposed but upheld the conviction and the anti-evolution law. But the anticlimax came on July 26, 1925, a few days after the Scopes trial, when Bryan died, from exhaustion and overeating, at the scene of his attempt to defend the faith.

The Scopes trial and Bryan's death stimulated a momentary revival of the anti-evolution crusade—especially after the formation of the Supreme Kingdom, the Bible Crusaders, the Bryan Bible League, and other fundamentalist organizations. The Supreme Kingdom was modeled after the Ku Klux Klan and dedicated to winning an anti-evolution constitutional amendment. It functioned in sixteen states, published a monthly magazine, *Dynamite*, and established a rest home in Florida for "those who grow old in the war against evolution." The Bible Crusaders, under T. T. Martin, was the best organized and most formidable of all the anti-evolution organizations. It formed mobile squadrons that went from one state capitol to another. It descended upon the Mississippi legislature in 1926, for example, and obtained passage of an anti-evolution law before the liberal forces of the state could counterattack. It struck next at Louisiana, was turned back, and then moved to North Carolina. The fight that ensued was bitter and prolonged, but liberal spokesmen struck back hard and prevented passage of an anti-evolution bill in 1927.

Defeat in North Carolina seemed to break the back of the entire fundamentalist crusade. In one state after another—in Georgia, Kentucky, Florida, South Carolina, and Oklahoma—anti-evolutionists met with subsequent defeats. They had one last, curious triumph in Arkansas. After the Arkansas legislature several times had refused to adopt an anti-evolution bill, fundamentalists obtained adoption of their measure in 1928 by using the initiative to bypass the legislature. For the first time in the history of the world the sovereign people by direct legislation decreed that Darwin was wrong!

Thus ended one of the most significant and also one of the most tragic social movements in American history. Southern Protestants who participated in the anti-evolution crusade thought that they were fighting to preserve the best features of the American heritage—a belief in the spirituality of the universe and in the God-like character of man. Instead, they tended to identify organized religion with bigotry and ignorance instead of freedom and learning. In several states and many communities fundamentalists instituted witch hunts and inquisitions, the effects of which were felt for many years. On the other hand, the anti-evolution movement had one beneficial effect. Its great challenge to academic freedom revealed the South's intellectual backwardness and compelled the rising body of southern liberals to take a firm stand against intolerant obscurantism. Their victory in most states was, therefore, all the more significant for the future.

110. *The Growth of Nativism and Intolerance*

There were, unhappily, numerous other manifestations of a growth of intolerance, bigotry, and chauvinism among all classes and in all sections during the decade following the First World War. There was fear of "Reds," an intensification of anti-Semitism, organized campaigns against Roman Catholics, and legislation practically to end immigration from southern and eastern Europe. It seemed for a time that champions of arrogant nationalism and religious bigotry spoke for virtually the entire American people.

Fear of communism came out in different ways. Following policy set by the Wilson administration, Republican administrations refused to enter into diplomatic relations with the Soviet Union. The New York legislature, in order to prevent the dissemination of revolutionary propaganda, in 1921 required all nonchurch private schools to obtain approval of their curricula by the Board of Regents. When the Socialist party's Rand School refused to apply for a license, the state began proceedings to close that institution.[2] State officials in California carried on a ruthless campaign from 1919 to 1924 to destroy the Industrial Workers of the World; and 504 persons were arrested, and 264 alleged subversives were tried under the

wwwwwwwwwwwww

[2] After the election of Alfred E. Smith as governor in 1922, this legislation was repealed, and proceedings against the Rand School were dropped.

state's criminal syndicalism law for committing sabotage and advocating the violent overthrow of the government.

The case that aroused the most violent controversy involved two obscure Italian-born anarchists, Nicola Sacco and Bartolomeo Vanzetti. Arrested in 1920 for the alleged murder of a paymaster in South Braintree, Massachusetts, Sacco and Vanzetti were tried the following year by a judge, Webster Thayer, who publicly vented his contempt for anarchism and allowed the state's attorney to make the defendants' radicalism a cornerstone of his case. Sacco and Vanzetti were convicted and sentenced to death, but radical and liberal groups throughout the United States and Europe believed that the two men had been sentenced, not for murder, but for anarchism.[3] In spite of mass demonstrations abroad and fervent appeals at home, Governor A. T. Fuller allowed Sacco and Vanzetti to die in the electric chair on August 23, 1927.

Anti-Semitism, always a latent menace, was exacerbated by the identification of many Jewish radicals, first with opposition to the war, and then with the Communist party and other radical groups. It was also intensified by the fact that many Jews were recent immigrants, as yet not "Americanized" during a decade when a great majority demanded unquestioning adoption of American manners and customs. It was, moreover, nurtured and used as a rallying cry by leaders of the Ku Klux Klan, who resurrected discredited charges of an international Jewish conspiracy to control the world. These charges were echoed by Henry Ford's newspaper, the *Dearborn Independent*, until Ford was threatened with court action and repudiated the accusation.

An uncritical nationalism, stimulated by postwar disillusionment and bitter European criticisms of American life, also seized millions, if not a majority, of Americans during the twenties. Officials in New York and Chicago, agitated by the Hearst newspapers and the *Chicago Daily Tribune*, investigated textbooks to root out works that failed properly to glorify the American past and damn the British. Oregon and Wisconsin forbade use of history texts that defamed American heroism in the Revolution and the War of 1812, while organizations like the American Legion, the Daughters of the American Revolution, and the Ku Klux Klan maintained a steady pressure for "one hundred per cent Americanism." And nationalism often shaded into racism, as Madison Grant and Lothrop Stoddard, among others, in their *Passing of the Great Race* and *The Rising Tide of Color*, popularized the contemporary view that the Nordic type was inherently superior to other so-called races.

The most sinister development of the 1920's was the rise in many states of the Knights of the Ku Klux Klan, the American counterpart of Italian Fascists and German Nazis. The Klan was organized by William J. Simmons, a former lay preacher and history teacher, under a blazing cross on Stone Mountain near Atlanta in the autumn of 1915, and was modeled after the hooded organization that had terrorized the South during Recon-

∿∿∿∿∿∿∿∿∿∿∿∿∿

[3] It might be added that this belief has grown into a firm conviction since 1921 among lawyers and historians who have studied the case.

struction. Simmons had established a few chapters in Georgia and Alabama by the end of 1919, but loss of membership seemed to threaten his organization with early extinction.

Two expert organizers, Edward Y. Clarke and Mrs. Elizabeth Tyler, rescued the Klan from oblivion early in 1920. Simmons had constructed an imposing empire headed by himself as Imperial Wizard, but with only a few thousand subjects of dubious loyalty. Recognizing the rich financial opportunity at hand, Clarke and Mrs. Tyler increased the initiation fee to $10.00 and established an imperial promotion department, known as the imperial kleagle, with door-to-door solicitors and heads of state promotion departments.

The Klan gained 100,000 new members in 1920 by a vigorous promotional campaign. The impractical Simmons was ousted as Imperial Wizard in 1922 and replaced by Hiram W. Evans, a Texas dentist with a bent for making money. The Klan's spectacular growth now ensued. It moved first into the Southwest and stirred violent political storms. The venerable Texas statesman, Charles A. Culberson, who had served in the United States Senate for twenty-four years, was defeated for renomination in 1922 by a Klan-supported candidate because of his opposition to the Klan. Civil War nearly ensued in Oklahoma when Governor J. C. Walton put the state under martial law on September 15, 1923, and called all citizens into military service in his campaign to exterminate the organization. The Klan-dominated legislature retaliated by impeaching Walton and removing him from office on November 18, 1923.

From the Southwest the Klan penetrated rapidly into California and Oregon. A Klan-supported governor and legislature were elected in the latter state in 1922 and proceeded to attempt to destroy Catholic parochial schools. Moving at the same time into the Middle West, Klan organizers soon gained a large constituency in this stronghold of democratic idealism. In Indiana, for example, the leading klansman, David C. Stephenson, captured control of the Republican state organization, cowed Indiana's two senators into submission, and helped to elect his henchman, Ed Jackson, to the governorship in 1924.[4]

In summary, the Klan at the peak of its strength in 1925 had a membership throughout the country, but chiefly in the Southwest, Far West, and Middle West, of approximately 5,000,000. At one time or another and to a varying degree, it controlled or had powerful influence in the governments of Texas, Oklahoma, Arkansas, California, Oregon, Indiana, Ohio, and other states. Wherever it went it carried bigotry, violence, and corruption and, as we shall see, posed a dire threat to democracy.

Klan membership was drawn largely from lower-middle-class old American stock, chiefly in small towns and cities, who were intensely sus-

wwwwwwwwwwwww

[4] Stephenson's downfall, however, came swiftly. After a sordid affair in which he kidnaped and assaulted a secretary and caused her to commit suicide, Stephenson was convicted of second-degree murder on November 14, 1925, and sentenced to life imprisonment. His crony, Jackson, was indicted for bribery in September 1927, and the Klan was disgraced and destroyed as a political and social force in Indiana.

picious of anything foreign or different and responded to bombastic expressions of patriotism. As only native-born white Protestants were allegedly "racially" capable of comprehending Americanism, the Klan excluded Catholics, Jews, Negroes, and most aliens. The same sort of people who followed demagogues, went to revival meetings, and tried to suppress the teaching of evolution joined the Klan.

The Klan's chief appeal outside the South was anti-Catholicism. Its program in the Middle and Far West was devoted almost exclusively to destroying parochial schools, thwarting the Catholic hierarchy's alleged plot to capture the United States, and preventing the Pope from moving the Holy See to Georgetown. If there was any single issue on which small-town, Protestant Americans could be easily aroused, it was this Catholic issue. Thus the Klan gained members and power by appealing to historic fears and perpetuating a strong anti-Catholic tradition that went back to the colonial period of American history.

The Klan was not officially anti-Semitic, but in practice it was almost invariably so, because Jews were not only not Protestants but were also, for the most part, aliens from southern and eastern Europe. However, the Klan stood openly for white supremacy and for keeping the Negro "in his place." Indeed, the most important impetus for the rise of the Klan in the South was fear among whites of returning Negro veterans and the troubled condition of race relations from 1919 to 1921.

Aside from its anti-Catholic program, the Klan's strongest attraction was its ritual, secrecy, and regalia, and the fact that for a time it was a going concern. Americans have always been a nation of joiners with strong penchant for high-flown ritual. The Klan also allowed its members to wear weird-looking white robes and hoods; and any ordinary person could pay his ten dollars, become an exalted Knight of the Ku Klux Klan, and parade in exciting anonymity.

Because the imperial headquarters exercised absolutely no control over the klaverns, or local chapters, Klan tactics varied from community to community. The coming of the Klan to the Southwest in 1920–21, for example, was accompanied by a wave of murders, floggings, kidnapings, and other outrages. And thus it went, though on a lesser scale, wherever the Klan penetrated. Klan leaders piously protested that criminals using the Klan costume were always responsible for the outrages. Klan opponents replied that the Klan was essentially a lawless, terroristic organization, whose chief purpose was the subversion of orderly constitutional government.

Fascism was triumphant in Italy at the end of the 1920's, and the forces of reaction were gathering strength in Germany. In the United States, on the other hand, the Ku Klux Klan stood exposed and discredited, its membership reduced to perhaps 100,000. For this failure of fascism in the United States the American people had to thank their traditions, a free press, and courageous leaders all over the country. Progressive editors, politicians, clergymen, and other public spokesmen everywhere recognized the Klan for what it was. They took the Klan's measure and threw themselves into what seemed in the beginning a losing fight. They triumphed in the end because they fought to preserve traditions that the overwhelming majority of Americans, even most klansmen, cherished.

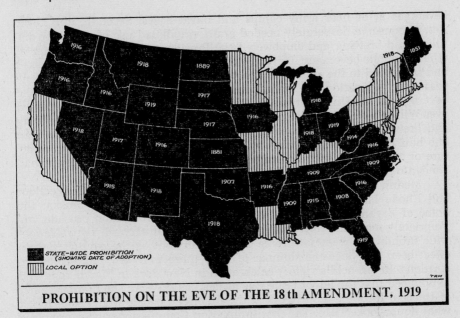

PROHIBITION ON THE EVE OF THE 18th AMENDMENT, 1919

Legend: STATE-WIDE PROHIBITION (SHOWING DATE OF ADOPTION); LOCAL OPTION

111. *Prohibition: The "Noble Experiment"*

The prohibition movement had gained such momentum by the eve of American participation in the First World War that the day could not be far distant when Anti-Saloon leaders would campaign for a constitutional amendment outlawing the manufacture and sale of alcoholic beverages in the United States.[5] By the end of 1914 fourteen states had adopted prohibition; and by the end of 1918 over three fourths of the people lived either in dry states or counties. Prohibition, obviously, was not the product of sudden impulse or wartime hysteria. On the contrary, it was an important component of the modern reform movement and demonstrated better than any other aspect of that movement the naive progressive faith in the efficacy of legislation in accomplishing fundamental social change.

On the other hand, the Anti-Saloon League might never have won the Eighteenth, or prohibition, Amendment had not the entrance of the United States into the war coincided with the high tide of prohibition agitation. Many champions of local option and state rights had consistently opposed such far-reaching extension of federal authority as national prohibition would compel. But Anti-Saloon spokesmen succeeded in identifying prohibition with patriotism, and these conservative voices were momentarily stilled. Consequently, the dry leaders were able to carry the government and people from one step to another in their relentless campaign.

To begin with, the Anti-Saloon lobbyists forced adoption of an amendment to the Conscription Act of 1917 forbidding the sale of alcoholic

[5] For the origins of the prohibition movement, see above, pp. 38–39.

beverages at or near army camps and naval bases. Secondly, the Lever Act, to conserve desperately needed grain, prohibited use of grain for distilling and brewing and empowered the President to ban manufacture of other alcoholic beverages. Thirdly, Congress on December 18, 1917, passed and submitted to the states the Eighteenth Amendment. It prohibited, one year after ratification, the manufacture, sale, or transportation of alcoholic beverages in the United States. Fourthly, Congress in October 1919 passed over Wilson's veto the Volstead Act extending the wartime ban on distilling and brewing, defining alcoholic beverages as any containing more than one half of 1 per cent alcohol by volume, and prohibiting the manufacture or sale of any such beverages after the Eighteenth Amendment had gone into effect in January 1920.

Meanwhile, in a wave of idealism all the states except Connecticut and Rhode Island approved the Eighteenth Amendment. Nebraska, the home of Bryan, one of the prime leaders of the prohibition crusade, appropriately made the thirty-sixth ratification on January 16, 1919. Nationwide prohibition went into force a year later; but as the country had in effect been dry since the summer of 1917 there were few protest demonstrations. Bryan held a victory celebration in New York in March 1920 and announced that the liquor issue was as dead as slavery. The Commissioner of Internal Revenue predicted that the American people would soon forget what liquor looked like. The first Prohibition Commissioner later promised that no liquor would be manufactured, "nor sold, nor given away, nor hauled in anything on the surface of the earth or under the earth or in the air."

Of course it did not turn out that way. Strict enforcement was impossible unless the government put a million agents in the field and sternly suppressed personal liberty. Partial enforcement was possible only if a large majority of the people were determined to exterminate the liquor traffic. There was probably a considerable decline in drinking and the liquor traffic in rural and strongly Protestant areas, where public opinion generally supported state and federal enforcement authorities. In fact, prohibition was accompanied by a sharp decline throughout the country in the measurable results of drinking—arrests for drunkenness and deaths from alcoholism.

The difficulties of enforcement were, however, enormous from the outset. The politically dry majority in Congress followed the advice of the Anti-Saloon League throughout the twenties in making appropriations and tightening enforcement laws. Even so, such provisions were hopelessly inadequate without the full support of local officials and public opinion. There were only 1,520 agents in the Prohibition Bureau in 1920 and 2,836 ten years later. As a consequence, enforcement was spasmodic, largely ineffective in areas where public opinion was hostile to the Eighteenth Amendment, and often violent and corrupt because of the bad character and strong-arm methods of many agents.

The two chief obstacles to enforcement were the determined resistance of large and important segments of the population and the fanaticism of dry leaders. Probably a majority of people in states with large foreign-born populations—like Massachusetts, New York, New Jersey, Maryland, Illinois, Ohio, and Wisconsin—would have voted against prohibition in a national referendum. Certainly the overwhelming majority in the large cities, native and foreign-born alike, thought that they had an inalienable right to drink. Consequently, neither local nor state officials, nor the masses of people in these states and cities, supported enforcement. Instead, they rallied behind organizations like the Association Against the Prohibition Amendment and political leaders like Governor Albert C. Ritchie of Maryland and Governor Alfred E. Smith of New York, committed to repeal of the Eighteenth Amendment.

In the main, prohibition might have succeeded had dry leaders realized that most opposition to the Eighteenth Amendment stemmed from the ban on the sale of beer and light wine. Immediately after ratification of the Amendment, the legislatures of Wisconsin, Massachusetts, New York, Maryland, and New Jersey adopted laws outlawing saloons and sale of hard liquors but permitting sale of light beer. Instead of accepting this slight deviation from perfection, Anti-Saloon lobbyists forced adoption of the Volstead Act and successfully challenged the constitutionality of the beer laws of these states. Inevitably officials and masses of people in the "wet" states not only refused to respect prohibition but began a relentless war against the dry regime.

The consequences of prohibition, that "noble experiment" in federal social control, were as remarkable as the difficulties that the effort raised. For one thing, prohibition brought in its wake a series of social innovations among the "wet" minority. Speakeasies instead of saloons, hip flasks at football games, "bathtub" gin, and the cocktail party—these were some of the social side products of the Eighteenth Amendment. Another phenomenon was an increase in drinking by women. Saloons before the war had been exclusively male preserves in which no respectable woman would be seen. In contrast, mixed drinking in the home and speakeasy became the rule after 1919—another sign of the emancipation of the so-called weaker sex.

The most disastrous consequence of prohibition was the tremendous increase in bootlegging that followed adoption of the Eighteenth Amendment. Bootlegging in turn encouraged organization of underworld gangs that went into rackets of various kinds, bought control of city governments, and seriously threatened democratic government in American cities during the 1920's and early 1930's. Prohibition alone was not responsible for this development. Organized vice and gambling had long been the curse of American cities; and gangsterism, racketeering, and organized blackmail developed almost in direct proportion to the speed of the automobile and the ease with which criminals could purchase weapons of wholesale slaughter like the Thompson submachine gun. Even so, bootlegging was the chief livelihood and source of income of the gangs.

The truth of this generalization can be demonstrated by a brief recital of the rise of the Capone gang in Chicago, the most important underworld association of the twenties. The story begins in 1920, when young Alphonse, or Al, Capone moved to Chicago after serving a brief apprenticeship in the Sicilian underworld of New York City. He was soon not only master of his own gang but also the leading bootlegger and gambling and vice operator in the Chicago area, with a gross income by 1927 of $60,-000,000 a year. Ironically, most of Capone's income from bootlegging came from the sale of beer. With a private army of from 700 to 1,000 gangsters he ruthlessly crushed rivals who dared to challenge his sovereignty; and Chicago witnessed pitched battles and mass gang killings that made its name a byword in the civilized world. Capone was toppled from his high eminence only when a Treasury agent worked his way into the organization and obtained evidence that led to the gangster's conviction and imprisonment for federal income tax evasion in 1931.

Opposition to the Eighteenth Amendment, sporadic and unorganized at the beginning of the 1920's, mounted after New York repealed its enforcement laws in 1923 and the Democratic party in the eastern states assumed leadership of the anti-prohibition movement. Republicans continued from 1920 through 1932 to support the "noble experiment," as Herbert Hoover characterized the prohibition effort, without any important division in their ranks. On the other hand, Democrats were so badly split over prohibition, among other issues, that they practically ceased to be a national party in the twenties.

The end of the "noble experiment" came not long after the people had seemingly sweepingly endorsed it in the presidential election of 1928. President Hoover soon after his inauguration appointed a commission headed by former Attorney General George W. Wickersham to investigate the problems of enforcement. The commission's report, presented in 1931, revealed what most informed Americans already knew—that the whole process of enforcement had broken down, and that it was virtually impossible to impose aridity upon a determined minority. Moreover, the conviction grew and was shared by many persons who originally had approved the experiment that prohibition simply was not worth the political and social costs—among others, the disruption of the Democratic party, subversion of the right of the states to control social customs, widespread contempt for law that prohibition had bred, and, most important, the stimulus that it gave to organized crime and bootlegging.

By 1932 problems of relief and recovery from the depression overshadowed all other issues. In that year a reunited Democratic party came out frankly for repeal of the Eighteenth Amendment and resumption of state control over the liquor traffic. The deed was quickly done after the smashing Democratic victory in November. The lame-duck session in February 1933 passed and submitted to the people the Twenty-First Amendment. It repealed the Eighteenth Amendment and prohibited the transportation of liquor into any dry state or territory. The same Congress also legalized the sale of light beer in March 1933. Three fourths of the states had ratified the Twenty-First Amendment by the following December, and the "noble experiment," so auspiciously begun, was over.

112. *The Decline of Organized Labor, 1920–1932*

As we have seen earlier, the postwar decade was in the main a time of prosperity and economic advancement for American workers. This generalization, however, obscures the important exceptions, for economic sickness in the textile and coal mining industries stimulated labor tensions of fierce intensity that culminated in numerous outbreaks of industrial warfare. Moreover, in spite of steady employment and increases in real wages, the 1920's witnessed a steady decline in the numbers and power of organized labor, a decline that was sharply accelerated by the Great Depression.

For the anomalous phenomenon of the decline of organized labor during a prosperous period, both employers and trade union leaders were responsible. To begin with, state manufacturers' associations and the NAM began a vigorous campaign in 1920 to restore the open shop through the "American Plan." [6] Invoking sentiments of individualism and winning the support of the American Bankers' Association and the National Grange, open-shop associations in every city and state pressed the attack with considerable success. Management's offensive in the twenties had another side—a positive, constructive effort, called "welfare capitalism," aimed at eliminating causes of industrial unrest by substituting co-operation for conflict in the field of industrial relations. Accepting the relatively new concept, first expounded by Henry Ford, of full production and consumption through high wages, advanced industrialists took labor policy out of the hands of tyrannical foremen, established expert departments of labor relations, and sought to win labor's good will by recreational programs, profit sharing, stock distribution, group health and life insurance programs, and even plans for retirement benefits. Such employers, in addition, usually established an elaborate system, ranging from shop grievance committees to company unions, by which workers might voice complaints and seek rectification of injustices.

All employers in the 1920's did not approve these new concepts and practices, but it was significant for the future that a large majority of the men who determined the policies of great corporations began to think of the needs and aspirations of their workers. For the most part, organized labor heartily reciprocated management's good will. In fact, when management accepted the principle of collective bargaining, labor leaders often went to unusual lengths to prove that co-operation was more profitable than conflict. A union-management plan adopted in the shops of the Baltimore & Ohio Railroad in 1922–3, for example, so improved efficiency and reduced labor unrest that the Chicago & North Western Railroad, Milwaukee Road, and Canadian National Railway adopted it soon afterward. The Amalgamated Clothing Workers of America willingly assumed responsibility for shop discipline, encouraged plans to increase efficiency, and even lent money to clothing manufacturers in distress.

With several notable exceptions, tensions between management and organized labor after 1921 lessened perceptibly in the wake of these developments. The average number of strikes per year declined from 3,503 for the period 1916–21 to 1,304 during the years 1922–5, and to 791 from 1926 through 1930. In addition, the AF of L became increasingly "conservative," in the sense that its leadership accepted "welfare capitalism" when it was accompanied by recognition and the right to bargain collectively. The AF of L, moreover, fought hard and successfully to prevent

[6] This was the name given to the open-shop movement by a conference of the leaders of twenty-two state manufacturers' associations in Chicago in January 1921.

Communist infiltration. Most important, it generally refused to launch movements to organize the great basic industries.

It was little wonder, therefore, that liberal critics of the AF of L and the railroad brotherhoods charged that organized labor had ceased to speak for the great mass of workers and had become a bulwark of the established order. It was little wonder, also, that organized labor not only did not grow but instead declined precipitously in numbers and influence during the 1920's. Trade union membership declined generally from 5,034,000 in 1920 to 2,857,000 in 1932, while membership in the AF of L fell from 4,079,000 to 2,532,000. Part of this loss resulted from the AF of L's failure to consolidate gains hastily made from 1917 to 1920; part of it was caused by the employers' counteroffensive; and a small part stemmed from losses incurred by unemployment during the depression. But the most important factor was unaggressive and timid leadership.

The violent experiences of workers in coal mining and textiles during the decade 1920–30 stand in striking contrast to the generalizations of the foregoing discussion. These two industries remained highly competitive, unstable, and plagued by overproduction and dislocations resulting from the movement, especially by textile manufacturers, into the low-wage area of the South. Frontier social conditions still prevailed to a large degree in mining areas and mill towns. Low wages and attempts by employers to preserve an industrial absolutism stimulated efforts at unionization. In turn these organizational campaigns were accompanied by the kind of violent warfare that had often characterized the American industrial scene before the First World War.

The United Mine Workers of America emerged from the bituminous coal strike of 1919 superficially defeated but actually strengthened by the award of the Bituminous Coal Commission and by simultaneous negotiations with the anthracite operators. Along the frontier of the bituminous industry in West Virginia and eastern Kentucky, however, an outbreak occurred that ended in disastrous defeat for the UMW. The union's attempt to organize mines in West Virginia in 1919 and 1920 provoked fierce resistance by operators and pitched battles between striking miners and imported guards. The governor declared martial law in the strike area, and state and federal troops momentarily stopped the fighting. Then violence broke out anew in 1921, after the miners organized an army of 4,000 men and began to invade the strike zone. The uprising quickly collapsed when President Harding dispatched 2,100 troops to the area, and state authorities arrested the strike leaders on charges of treason, murder, and conspiracy.

The West Virginia civil war marked the beginning of a decade of conflict in the troubled coal fields. Negotiations for new contracts with bituminous and anthracite operators failed in early 1922, and President John L. Lewis of the UMW called miners out in the greatest coal strike in American history to that time. There was no violence until the Southern Illinois Coal Company, in Williamson County, Illinois, imported strike-breakers and attempted to resume operations on June 21, 1922. The killing of two strikers by mine guards brought swift retaliation at Herrin. There enraged miners charged a stockade and slaughtered nineteen strikebreakers. Tempers subsided after the Herrin Massacre, and a test of endurance between the UMW and the operators then followed. In the late summer the operators gave in.

Although Lewis forced the operators to renew their contracts in 1924, a series of catastrophes soon befell and nearly wrecked the UMW. For one thing, increased competition from nonunion operators in the South and West forced northern and midwestern operators to cut wages. For another, progressive and Communist elements in the UMW began a vigorous campaign in 1926 to destroy Lewis' allegedly dictatorial and corrupt control. Although the movement failed, it seriously weakened the UMW and led to the formation of two rival unions, the reorganized United Mine Workers and the Communist-controlled National Miners' Union. Lewis saved the UMW and preserved a semblance of collective bargaining in the coal industry by accepting wage reductions during contract negotiations in 1927. But by 1929 the once proud UMW was so weakened, both from within and from without, that it would be helpless to cope with problems raised by the depression.

Tensions and conflicts also plagued the textile industry during the 1920's. New England manufacturers, pleading southern competition and depressed economic circumstances, cut wages about 20 per cent in 1921. They attempted to raise hours and impose another 20 per cent wage cut early in the following year. This provoked a series of strikes by the United Textile Workers and left-wing unions that forced a restoration of the old wage and hour scales. The conflict shifted to Passaic, New Jersey, three years later, after the large woolen textile mills in that city cut wages 10 per cent in September 1925. A United Front Committee under Communist leadership began a strike in January 1926 that soon spread to all the large mills and engendered such disturbances as northern New Jersey had not seen since the IWW's Paterson strike of 1912. After the Communists withdrew from leadership in the strike, the United Textile Workers took control and brought it to a successful conclusion in March 1927.

Northern textile workers staved off wage reductions after 1921 by such violent reprisals. But the rise of southern manufacturers to dominance in the industry and the movement of New England mills to the South in the 1920's posed a serious long-range menace to union wages in the North. Obviously, safety for northern workers lay only in eliminating the sectional wage differential—by unionizing southern mills and imposing a uniform national wage scale.

The United Textile Workers, after a brief and unsuccessful attempt to organize the southern mills in 1919, invaded the South again in 1927 and 1928. They found the mass of workers bitter and resentful over long hours, low wages, the "stretch-out," and above all, high profits. They found, also, a virtual textile barony allied with local police and state officials ready to use any means to prevent unionization. It is not surprising that one of the bloodiest outbreaks of labor violence in recent American history ensued.

The disturbances began in March 1929, when more than 5,000 rayon textile workers in Elizabethton, Tennessee, struck against a low wage scale. Local vigilante groups combined with company guards, state troops, and the courts to drive the United Textile Workers organizers from the mills. A month later the Communist-controlled National Textile Workers'

Union began a strike against the largest cotton mill in Gastonia, North Carolina, the center of the textile industry. The strike collapsed after the conviction, in October 1929, of seven of the Communist leaders for the second-degree murder of the Gastonia chief of police. At the same time, a Textile Workers strike in Marion, North Carolina, ended with the slaughter of five and the wounding of nineteen unarmed pickets by a sheriff's posse. The United Textile Workers made their most formidable effort at the Riverside and Dan River Mills in Danville, Virginia, in the autumn of 1930. The owners stubbornly refused either to bargain with the union or to submit to arbitration, and the strikers had to surrender to avoid starvation.

Although the decade ended with labor tension running at its highest point since 1919, there were a few signs that official and public opinion was finally beginning to veer strongly in labor's favor. For one thing, the 1920's saw federal endorsement of the principle of genuine collective bargaining between railroads and their employees. The Transportation Act of 1920 had established a Railroad Labor Board that soon proved its uselessness, especially after it failed to prevent a nation-wide strike of railway shopmen in 1922. Congress in 1926 therefore adopted the Railway Labor Act. It created effective mediation and arbitration machinery and, more important, virtually compelled railroads to eschew company unionism and deal responsibly with the independent brotherhoods. Then in 1930 the Senate refused to confirm the nomination of Circuit Court Judge John J. Parker to the Supreme Court, in part because Parker had upheld the use of injunctions to prohibit union organizers from attempting to unionize workers who had signed a "yellow dog" contract.[7] Finally, Congress in March 1932 adopted the Anti-Injunction Act sponsored by Representative Fiorello La Guardia of New York and Senator George W. Norris of Nebraska. This measure made "yellow dog" contracts unenforceable in federal courts; forbade issuance of injunctions against a number of hitherto outlawed union practices; and guaranteed jury trials in cases involving violations of criminal injunctions. Altogether it was not a revolution in federal policy, but it did herald more important changes that would occur after 1932.

wwwwwwwwwwwwww

[7] An agreement between employer and employee by which the latter promised not to join a union in return for the privilege of employment.

CHAPTER

15

The Survival of Progressivism: Politics and Problems of the Harding-Coolidge Era

For MANY YEARS American historians assumed that the return of Republican rule in 1921 signified the end of the progressive movement and ushered in an era in which reactionaries controlled the federal government. Then came progressivism's revival and redemption under Franklin D. Roosevelt. Recent research and re-examination of the Republican era is only now beginning to reveal that the traditional picture is somewhat overdrawn.

To be sure, Presidents Harding and Coolidge and their spokesmen in Congress were avowed champions of business and financial enterprise. Believing that American prosperity depended upon the well-being of the upper classes, they sponsored tariff and tax policies to promote special interests, brought federal administrative agencies into close co-operation with the business community, and opposed measures that would have discouraged investment or carried the government into new areas of regulation.

But to stop at this point would be to give a grossly distorted view of American politics in the 1920's. Conservative Republicans gained and held power in the executive branch only because of the peculiar character of the American political system, and only because progressives were divided, not because they were few in number. When the progressive coalition of 1916 was destroyed in 1920, progressives reverted to their traditional voting habits in the national elections of 1920, 1924, and 1928 and were never able to combine to capture the presidency. On the other hand, they combined in Congress to control the legislative branch during practically all the 1920's, thwart a conservative executive leadership on several important issues, and push through a remarkable progressive program, the most advanced parts of which were nullified by presidential vetoes. In addition, progressivism survived on the local and state levels, particularly in movements for administrative efficiency and expansion of state educational and social services. Even the movement for social justice survived. As one authority has written, "The 1920s were not conducive to public action for social reform; but hundreds of social workers were prepared, nevertheless, to maintain their alliance with social reformers. The assumption that the reformers were driven from the field is not valid—they remained on the firing line, beat tactical retreats when necessary, engaged in flank attacks, waited for the breaks, and never for a moment surrendered the initiative. Frustrated and rebuffed, often ridiculed, sometimes despised, they kept alive and vital the crusade for social action, and thus formed a viable link between prewar progressivism and the New Deal." [1]

Thus, as the following sections will attempt to reveal, the political development of the period 1920–8 refuses to accommodate itself to sweeping generalizations or pat theories. As we shall see, there were numerous conflicts, crosscurrents, and elements of confusion; but withal progressivism not only survived as an articulate expression of social and economic aspiration but also widened its horizons.

113. *The Harding Debacle*

What a contrast the incoming President made with the outgoing Chief Executive as they rode to the Capitol on March 4, 1921! There was Wilson, aged and infirm, a living mind in a dying body, still full of high hopes and stronger than ever in his convictions. At his side sat Warren G. Harding, majestic in countenance but awed and still dazed by the trick that fate had played upon him in Chicago in June 1920.

The new President was born at Caledonia, Ohio, on November 2, 1865, and owned and edited the *Star*, in the small town of Marion, Ohio, for a number of years. Driven by an ambitious wife, he served two terms, rather effectively, in the State Senate and one as lieutenant governor and was his party's unsuccessful candidate for governor in 1910. At the urging of his wife and his friend Harry M. Daugherty, Harding ran for the United States Senate in 1914 and was elected by a large plurality. He was his party's keynoter in the national convention of 1916. Realizing his own limitations, he was skeptical about running for the Republican presidential nomination. But ambition overcame his scruples. He permitted his friend

<hr />

[1] Clarke A. Chambers, "Creative Effort in an Age of Normalcy, 1918–33," *The Social Welfare Forum, 1961* (New York, 1961), p. 254.

Daugherty to conduct an undercover campaign; he was popular with the delegates; and he accepted the nomination when it came to him almost by default in June 1920. (See above, pp. 242–243.)

A man of average mental endowment can fulfill the duties of the presidency if his will power and character fortify his determination to rule wisely. It was an unkind act of fate, however, that made Harding President, for he had only average talents, no will power, and a striking inability to discriminate between right and wrong. Easygoing and affable, he drank too much and possessed an uncanny ability to draw men utterly unworthy of his confidence into his personal circle. There is also strong evidence that Harding was adulterous.

The contrast between Wilson and Harding was no more vivid than the dissimilarity between the outgoing administration and many of the men surrounding the new President. Most of the members of the Wilson circle were able and honest public servants. They had carried the nation through a great war effort and spent billions of the public money, and hardly any of them had been guilty of theft or of using their office for private gain. In contrast stands a record of fraud and corruption in high places during the brief Harding regime unparalleled since the Grant era. Not all the thieves who moved in on the public treasury in 1921 were from Ohio, but the ringleaders were. Let us look briefly at the men Harding appointed to office—the so-called Ohio Gang—as well as the more honorable leaders of the administration.

The "Ohio Gang" was as avaricious a group as ever moved in high circles in Washington. The leader was Harding's old Ohio crony, the unsavory politician and lobbyist Harry M. Daugherty, whom the new President made Attorney General. As Secretary of the Interior, Harding appointed his old Senate intimate, Albert B. Fall of New Mexico. The President made "Ed" Scobey, a crony from Ohio and former Sheriff of Pickaway County, Director of the Mint; Daniel R. Crissinger, a second-rate lawyer from Marion, Comptroller of the Currency and afterward Governor of the Federal Reserve Board; Charles R. Forbes, a smooth-talking friend of brief acquaintance, head of the Veterans' Bureau; and Thomas W. Miller, prominent in the American Legion, Alien Property Custodian. These were the leaders of the "Ohio Gang."

The opportunity to honor old friends and enjoy them as drinking and poker companions warmed the President's heart. But when he was about halfway through his list Harding resolved to find the best men in the Republican party for the remaining and most important posts. Thus he chose Charles Evans Hughes as Secretary of State; Andrew W. Mellon, Pittsburgh industrialist and banker, as Secretary of the Treasury; former Senator John W. Weeks of Massachusetts as Secretary of War; Henry A. Wallace, a distinguished Iowa farm editor, as Secretary of Agriculture; Herbert Hoover as Secretary of Commerce; and James J. Davis, a Pennsylvania labor leader, as Secretary of Labor. These able men not only lent distinction to the new administration but also saved their departments from the pillaging of the "Ohio Gang."

During his brief tenure Harding presided over the government of the United States with outward dignity. He abdicated leadership of legislative and foreign policies to Congress and his Cabinet, but this was what the leaders of the Republican party wanted him to do. On the other hand, he performed three acts of his own that revealed the generous side of his nature and indicated a certain courage. The first was his pardoning, in 1921, of Eugene V. Debs, who had spent three years in the Atlanta penitentiary and polled over 900,000 votes as Socialist candidate for President in 1920. The second was his bringing the heads of the steel industry to the White House in 1922 and persuading them to institute the eight-hour day. The third was his defiance of the American Legion lobby in his veto of the soldiers' bonus, or adjusted compensation, bill in 1922. On important matters of policy, however, Harding was ignorant and confused and yielded where pressure was strongest.

Meanwhile, the President's cronies were engaging under his myopic eyes in a mad scramble for bribes and as much loot as they could lay their hands upon. Scandal was inevitable. The first one involved Jesse Smith, an old-time friend of Daugherty's, who had moved to Washington with the Attorney General. Smith soon became the liaison between the Department of Justice and violators of the prohibition laws, income tax evaders, and "fixers" of all kinds. Rumors of Smith's behavior reached Harding, and the President told Daugherty that his friend had to go back to Ohio. Smith went home for a while but could not endure the exile. He returned to Daugherty's apartment and killed himself on May 23, 1923.

Smith's suicide was the first event in a chain that culminated in exposure of several enormous scandals. The first to come to light involved the Veterans' Bureau, established by Congress in August 1921, under the direction of Charles R. Forbes. Harding had a profound concern for disabled veterans, especially for those afflicted with mental illness and tuberculosis. Forbes was a bustling, energetic person with a convincing tongue, who gave the impression of an efficient administrator. He supervised the building of hospitals and the expenditure of hundreds of millions of dollars, and Harding was pleased by these visible signs of progress. Unhappily, Forbes could not resist the temptation to make money on the side, and he stole or squandered nearly $250,000,000 before he left office.

Daugherty learned about the corruption in the Veterans' Bureau late in 1922 and passed the bad news on to Harding. The President learned part of the truth from Forbes himself and permitted him to go abroad and resign on February 15, 1923. Rumors soon reached the Senate; it began an investigation on March 2. Twelve days later the legal adviser to the Veterans' Bureau, Charles F. Cramer, committed suicide. This broke the case, and the Senate committee pressed on to expose the full extent of defalcation in the Bureau. Forbes was convicted of defrauding the government in 1925 and sentenced to a two-year term in Leavenworth penitentiary.

Meanwhile, Secretary of the Interior Albert B. Fall had been executing one of the most daring criminal forays in American history. He persuaded President Harding in 1921 to transfer control over naval oil reserve lands at Elk Hills in California and Teapot Dome in Wyoming from the Navy Department to his own jurisdiction. Soon afterward, on April 7, 1922, Fall secretly leased Teapot Dome to the Mammoth Oil Company, owned by Harry F. Sinclair. The Secretary leased Elk Hills to the Pan-American Petroleum Company, owned by Edward L. Doheny, on April 25.

News of the leases leaked out at once. Responding to an early Senate inquiry, Fall declared that he had leased Teapot Dome to Sinclair in the interest of national preparedness and was about to lease Elk Hills to Doheny. The Senate public lands committee, spurred on by Thomas J. Walsh of Montana, began an investigation in October 1923 that was continued the following year by a special commission. These investigations revealed that Sinclair had given Fall $223,000 in government bonds, $85,000 in cash, and a herd of cattle for his ranch at the time that the lease for Teapot Dome was negotiated; and that Doheny had also "lent" $100,000 to Fall at the time that the lease on Elk Hills was being signed.

Eventually—in 1927—the government won its suit to cancel the leases, while Doheny, Sinclair, and Fall were tried for conspiracy to defraud the government and acquitted, although Sinclair spent terms in jail for contempt of Congress and tampering with a jury. Fall was convicted of bribery in October 1929, fined $100,000, and sentenced to a year's imprisonment. After many delays the former Secretary went to jail in July 1931, thus becoming the first corrupt Cabinet member in American history to receive something like his just reward.

Attorney General Daugherty was suspected of complicity in several frauds. But all during the furor raised by the revelations of the oil scandal in 1923 and 1924 he not only refused to resign but also turned the FBI on senators and other public leaders who were unearthing details of the corruption. Then a scandal involving the return of the American Metal Company to its German owners by the Alien Property Custodian, Thomas W. Miller, broke early in 1924. It came out that a highly placed New York Republican who engineered the deal had paid $50,000 to Miller and another $50,000 to Jesse Smith, and that Smith had deposited his share in an account that he held jointly with Daugherty. President Coolidge dismissed Daughtery when he refused to testify before a Senate committee of investigation in March 1924. Daugherty was brought to trial in New York in 1926 but again refused to testify, saying that his personal relations with President and Mrs. Harding made it impossible for him to do so. After deliberating nearly three days the jury disagreed because Harding's good name seemed to be at stake. The following year Miller was tried, convicted, and sent to jail.

114. The Death of President Harding

Harding made plans early in 1923 for a speaking tour through the West and a vacation in Alaska. Before he left Washington on June 20 the President had learned enough about the corruption of his friends to make him sick at heart and to fill him with presentiment of impending doom. "My God, this is a hell of a job," he told William Allen White shortly before he left on his western trip. "I have no trouble with my enemies. . . . But my damned friends, my God-damn friends, White, they're the ones that keep me walking the floor nights!" [2]

wwwwwwwwwwwwww

[2] *The Autobiography of William Allen White* (New York, 1946), p. 619.

Harding was physically exhausted and mentally depressed all during the long trip across the continent. The trip to Alaska brought no rest. The President returned to Seattle on July 27 and stood bareheaded under the sun to make a speech. He faltered several times, and members of his party feared that he would collapse. That same evening Harding suffered intense pain. His physician said that he had ptomaine poisoning from eating spoiled crabs. The presidential party went to San Francisco on July 29. Harding insisted on walking unaided from the station to his car, but he went to bed at once and developed pneumonia on the following day. Just when it seemed that he was on the road to recovery he suffered a stroke and died on August 2, 1923. As the funeral train bearing the President's body made its way slowly across the country, millions of Americans paid their respects to the man they thought Harding had been.

It was not long, however, before Americans learned the details of the various scandals, read the accusations of Harding's alleged mistress, Nan Britton, and heard absurd rumors that Harding had been poisoned by his wife. In consequence, the deflation of Harding's reputation came at once, not slowly. The people forgot his simplicity and kindliness and remembered only that he had connived with thieves and sheltered scoundrels. And during a later period, when the Republican leadership of the twenties stood discredited in the public mind, "normalcy" became a term of opprobrium, and the scandals of the Harding era, compounded with the ones of the Great Depression, became a heavy liability to the GOP.

115. *The Anomaly of American Politics, 1921–1928*

Those business leaders and men of wealth who poured nearly $8,000,-000 into the Republican campaign coffers in 1920 soon realized part of the expected return on their investment. Through the powerful Senate clique they controlled the President and had a decisive voice in shaping federal policies, both administrative and legislative. The time seemed ripe for complete fulfillment of the business-sponsored program—economy, drastic tax reductions, and sound financing; a return to tariff protection; control of federal regulatory agencies by men friendly to business interests; and an end to quasi-socialistic experiments launched during the war. At the very moment that conservatives were enjoying the election returns on November 2, 1920, however, disruptive economic forces were at work that soon robbed them of many of the legislative fruits of victory. During the autumn and winter of 1920–1 agricultural prices were falling hard and fast, and a political rebellion, nearly equal in strength to the insurgent revolt of 1910–12, was brewing.

Congress met in special session in April 1921, business leaders thought, to take the country back to "normalcy." If the President had controlled the enormous Republican majorities in both houses he could have put his program across with ease. As it turned out, the agrarian revolt developed so rapidly that conservatives could not command even a bare majority for measures to which the agrarian insurgents objected.

A month after the special session convened, a group of midwestern farm spokesmen in Congress, led by Senators William S. Kenyon of Iowa and Arthur Capper of Kansas, met in the Washington offices of the new and powerful Farm Bureau Federation to consider the agricultural crisis. Agreeing upon a program of extensive legislation, they at once organized the so-called Farm Bloc for nonpartisan action. By combining with southern Democrats the Midwesterners were able not only to put a part of their program across but also to block the administration's efforts at substantial tax reductions. Later sections cover this story in some detail.

Agricultural prices recovered slightly during the following year, 1922, and business and industry began to recuperate from the sharp depression of 1921. But returning prosperity only stimulated progressive discontent. Republican insurgents made almost a clean sweep in the Republican primary campaigns through the Middle and Far West in the spring and summer of 1922. This was discouraging to administration leaders, but the results of the congressional election in November were even more discouraging. Republican majorities in the Senate and House were reduced to eight and eighteen respectively, and so many insurgents were elected that the administration lost its small measure of control over Congress.

The congressional election of 1922 not only stimulated hopes of a general progressive revival but also heartened leaders of the Farm Bloc in Congress. When the lame-duck session convened in December 1922, Midwesterners organized a new and stronger bloc and adopted a platform that appealed as much to independents and workers as it did to farmers. Insurgent leaders insisted that they were merely protesting against conservative Republican policies, not contemplating a campaign to unite the disparate progressive elements in a third party. And yet there were numerous signs even as they spoke that the rebellion among farmers and organized workers was growing to such large proportions that a nation-wide independent movement might be possible in 1924.

The most important sign was the sudden revival of the Non-Partisan League after 1919. Organized among wheat growers of North Dakota in 1915, the Non-Partisan League advocated a program that was remarkably advanced for its day—state ownership and operation of farm credit agencies, warehouses, and grain elevators; minimum wages; and stringent control of railroads, banks, and private businesses. Capturing the state government of North Dakota in 1916, League organizers moved into Minnesota, Iowa, Montana, Idaho, and other states in 1917 and 1918. The League joined with a number of radical remnants in 1920 to form the Farmer-Labor party and took second place in Minnesota, South Dakota, and Washington.

As the sharp agricultural and industrial depression of 1920–2 intensified discontent, leaders of the railroad brotherhoods called a Conference for Progressive Political Action to meet in Chicago in February 1922 for the purpose of considering independent political action. Represented at this first conference were the brotherhoods and many other unions, the Non-Partisan League, the Socialist party, and numerous splinter groups. Instead of launching a third party, the Conference decided to endorse congressional and senatorial candidates and to await the outcome of the fall elections.

Encouraged by the success of insurgent Republican and Farmer-Labor candidates in this canvass, Senator Robert M. La Follette of Wisconsin convoked an assemblage of progressive politicians, editors, and labor leaders in Washington in December 1922. The Conference for Progressive Political Action met shortly afterward for a second time in Cleveland. The upshot of these two gatherings was agreement to campaign for La Follette's nomination on the Republican ticket in 1924 and, that failing, to launch a third party.

"The Midwest," said William Allen White, "is on the rampage again"; and, remembering the insurgent revolt of 1910, progressives believed that a second upheaval impended. Much, of course, depended upon the Democrats, for the insurgents alone could never capture the government. If the Democrats could find a strong new leader and unite behind a progressive program, they might win independents, the labor vote, and insurgents, and rebuild their party into the powerful progressive coalition it had been in 1916.

This is what the Democrats did in 1932. In 1923 and 1924, however, the Democracy offered little hope of ever again becoming an effective instrument of the progressive movement. It had become so fragmentized since 1920 that it had ceased to be a national party. The majority element, southern Methodists and Baptists, demanded vigorous enforcement of the Eighteenth Amendment. On the other hand, Democratic organizations in the northern cities represented wet constituencies who demanded repeal of that Amendment. Southern and midwestern Democrats either supported or feared the Ku Klux Klan, while most northern Democrats were Catholics or foreign-born citizens, opposed to all the Klan stood for. Finally, these two wings of the Democracy were hopelessly divided on leading questions of the day. Southerners still supported the League of Nations; the northern Irish bosses wanted to forget the issue. Southerners demanded radical aid to farmers but were unfriendly to labor, uninterested in social reform, and anti-Negro. Northern Democratic organizations opposed radical farm support but sponsored advanced labor legislation and were beginning to develop strength among Negro voters.

The unbridgeable gulf separating southern and northern Democrats was revealed at the Democratic national convention that met in New York City from June 24 to July 10, 1924. During the preconvention contest former Secretary of the Treasury William G. McAdoo had won the support of the South and West and, although he openly repudiated it, the endorsement of the Ku Klux Klan. He might have won the nomination had he not become linked to the Teapot Dome scandal as Edward L. Doheny's lawyer. This cost him heavily in support among progressives. His chief and only serious rival was Alfred E. Smith, Governor of New York, a Roman Catholic opponent of prohibition and the Klan. He had the support of Irish- and Catholic-dominated eastern and midwestern machines. For an incredible number of weary ballots the McAdoo and Smith forces fought it out and revealed in their struggle the tensions that divided their party. Smith's spokesman, Franklin D. Roosevelt, offered after the ninety-third ballot to withdraw Smith's name if McAdoo would also withdraw. McAdoo refused, and the struggle went on. Then on the one hundred and third ballot the convention turned to John W. Davis, former Ambassador to Great Britain and now a lawyer for corporation and banking interests. As a sop to the agrarian element, the convention chose Governor Charles W. Bryan of

Nebraska, brother of the former Secretary of State, as Davis's running-mate.

The Democrats found it as difficult to agree upon a platform as upon a candidate. The worst fight centered around a resolution sponsored by the Smith forces condemning the Klan as un-American. It failed by a vote of 543 to 542. Nor could Northerners and Southerners agree on prohibition: the platform merely scolded the Republicans for failing to enforce the Eighteenth Amendment. Refusing to approve American membership in the League of Nations, the convention called for a public referendum on the issue. Except for denouncing the Republican Fordney-McCumber tariff of 1922 and promising independence to the Philippines, the Democratic platform differed little from its Republican counterpart.

In the meantime, insurgent Republicans had been pressing their campaign to capture the Republican party. The futility of this endeavor had become so apparent by the spring of 1924, however, that La Follette withdrew from presidential primaries in Montana, North Dakota, and Michigan. Control of the party had passed to Harding's successor, Calvin Coolidge, a dour, taciturn man, who was even more intimately associated with big business than Harding had been.

Coolidge and his conservative allies completely dominated the Republican convention that opened in Cleveland on June 10, 1924. Only the Wisconsin and South Dakota delegates objected when the President was nominated almost by acclamation on the first ballot. Rejecting a progressive platform submitted by the Wisconsin delegation, the convention adopted instead a document promising economy, tax reduction, and limited aid to farmers, and approving American membership in the World Court.

Soon afterward, on July 4, the insurgent Republicans and their Conference for Progressive Political Action allies, representing organized labor, disgruntled western farmers, Socialists, and independent progressives, met in Cleveland.[3] The Communists, who had tried to control the Conference for Progressive Political Action, were unceremoniously excluded. Agreeing that both major parties were hopelessly corrupt and reactionary, the delegates formally organized the Progressive party, nominated La Follette for President,[4] and adopted a brief platform demanding nationalization of railroads, public ownership of water power and development of a great public utilities system, abolition of the use of injunctions in labor disputes, the right of Congress to overrule decisions of the Supreme Court, and direct nomination and election of the President.

La Follette made a strenuous campaign, appealing chiefly to midwestern farmers and urban workers. But he was hampered by lack of funds, a gradual withdrawal of AF of L support, refusal of most midwestern Republican leaders to support his party, and most of all by a considerable increase in farm prices a month before the election. President Coolidge took practically no part in the contest, but the other Republican

wwwwwwwwwwwww

[3] The principal organized groups represented at the Progressive convention were the Socialist party, the Farmer-Labor party, the Non-Partisan League, the railroad brotherhoods, and the AF of L.

[4] The National Committee later named the Montana Democrat, Senator Burton K. Wheeler, as La Follette's running-mate.

leaders were generously supplied with funds [5] and made a vigorous campaign. Republicans practically ignored Davis and Bryan and concentrated heavy fire against La Follette, who, they said, was un-American and a front for the Third International. Davis tried to make a campaign on the issues of corruption and Coolidge's intimate association with big business, but his appeals were lost in the anti-Red clamor.

The question whether La Follette would draw enough votes away from Coolidge to throw the election into the House of Representatives was answered emphatically on election day, November 4, 1924. Coolidge received 15,725,000 popular and 382 electoral votes; Davis, 8,387,000 popular and 136 electoral votes; and La Follette, 4,823,000 popular votes and the thirteen electoral votes of Wisconsin.

Outwardly the results constituted a thumping endorsement of the Coolidge policies of *laissez faire* and do-nothingism. Actually, few presidential elections in American history have meant so little. La Follette had frightened numerous voters from Davis to Coolidge in his effort to unite progressives. But it was not La Follette's candidacy that caused the Democratic debacle. It was internal dissension, failure to adopt a boldly progressive platform, Davis's inherent weakness as a leader of the forces of discontent, and his failure to appeal to the urban, Catholic, and immigrant voters that wrecked Democratic hopes in 1924. The fact that only 52 per cent of the voters went to the polls was striking proof of Democratic failure to rally the people behind either a candidate or a platform.

The following four years were a prosperous interlude during which Coolidge asserted no leadership in legislation and set about quietly to gain control of the regulatory agencies. The Republicans controlled the Sixty-ninth Congress from 1925 to 1927 by large majorities and the Seventieth Congress during the following two years by a slight margin, but they were constantly at war with one another and with the President. The Farm Bloc in Congress regrouped after La Follette's death in 1925 and put across two advanced progressive measures in 1927 and 1928—the McNary-Haugen farm relief bill and a measure for governmental operation of the Muscle Shoals dam—both of which were nullified by Coolidge's vetoes. They are discussed in greater detail in a later section in this chapter.

We have thus reviewed in outline the anomalous pattern of American national politics from 1920 to 1928. The pattern was anomalous because conservative administrations, seemingly overwhelmingly endorsed by the American people in 1920 and 1924, were counterbalanced by progressive coalitions in Congress that perpetuated the progressive tradition in legislative policy. How this came about will become more apparent as we discuss the legislative problems and policies of the period in detail.

116. *Tariff, Tax, and Bonus Battles of the Twenties*

The first item on the Republican agenda after the election of 1920 was upward revision of the tariff, chiefly to meet the demands of midwestern

---

[5] According to the best estimates the Republicans spent nearly $6,000,000, the Democrats, $1,614,762, and the Progressives, $236,963.

agrarian congressmen then in panic over declining farm prices. In the lame-duck session of the Sixty-sixth Congress in the winter of 1920–1, eastern Republicans gladly joined Midwesterners in adopting an emergency tariff bill that imposed high duties on meat and major farm staples. Wilson vetoed this measure on March 3, 1921, warning that farmers needed new markets for their products, not futile tariff protection.

When the Sixty-seventh Congress met in special session on April 11, 1921, however, midwestern leaders obtained the immediate re-enactment of the emergency tariff bill, and Harding signed it on May 27. In the meantime, Chairman Joseph W. Fordney of Michigan and his ways and means committee set to work to overhaul the Underwood rates. The measure that Fordney reported on June 29, and the House approved three weeks later, incorporated the emergency increases for agricultural products and effected moderate increases in rates on most industrial products. The Senate finance committee, headed by Porter J. McCumber of North Dakota, deliberated during the summer and autumn of 1921 and reported the Fordney bill with over two thousand amendments in April 1922. After some wrangling it was adopted by the two houses and approved by the President on September 19, 1922.

The Fordney-McCumber Tariff Act to a degree revived the historic Republican policy of economic nationalism. It represented, first of all, a clear-cut victory for the newly formed Farm Bloc, as duties on farm products—including reindeer meat and acorns—were higher than the Payne-Aldrich rates, while agricultural implements, wagons, and boots and shoes remained on the free list. For the rapidly expanding chemical industry, the Act provided the protection that it needed to withstand the destructive competition of the German dye trust. For producers of silk and rayon textiles, toys, chinaware, cutlery, guns, and other items produced more cheaply by the Japanese and Germans, the measure offered almost prohibitive duties. Finally, for the great mass of industrial products the Act provided only moderate protection in order to equalize differences in cost of production at home and abroad. The average ad valorem rate for all schedules was 33 per cent, as contrasted to the 26 per cent average of the Underwood-Simmons Tariff Act of 1913.

As it turned out, the Fordney-McCumber Act was not nearly so disastrous to foreign trade as Democrats said it would be. The protection afforded agricultural products was more illusory than real except for sugar and wool. The protection given the chemical industry was important, but it represented fulfillment of a policy promised by the Wilson administration in 1916. The chief significance of the Act of 1922 lay in the fact that its framers attempted to carry on the Underwood policy of fixing rates for the mass of industrial products so as to equalize differences in costs of production in the United States and abroad. In addition, the Tariff Commission, established in 1916, was instructed to study relative production costs and recommend changes to the President, who might then raise or lower rates by as much as 50 per cent.

Although Democrats voted against the Fordney-McCumber bill, the measure was such a satisfactory compromise that for the next four years, at least, the tariff issue ceased to be important in national politics. Mean-

while, Harding and Coolidge also left well enough alone. Upon recommendation of the Tariff Commission, they made thirty-seven unimportant
changes in rates. On the other hand, when the Commission suggested
lowering the sugar duty in 1924, Coolidge discreetly buried the report.

The great majority of businessmen were clamoring more for reduction in federal expenditures and drastic tax cuts than for a return to a
McKinley-type protection in 1921 and 1922. As the first step toward economy, Congress in May 1921 enacted the nonpartisan Budget and Accounting Act, establishing a Director of the Budget in the executive department
and a Comptroller General as a watchdog for Congress to oversee expenditure of funds. As the first step toward tax reduction, spokesmen of
the industrial and banking interests in the GOP insisted that Harding name
Andrew W. Mellon as Secretary of the Treasury. Although he had never
heard of Mellon, Harding did as his advisers requested.

What Mellon's appointment signified was clear to all who knew him.
Head of the aluminum monopoly and of a financial-industrial empire, he
was the personification of the American self-made man and seasoned reactionary. His philosophy was honest and simple. Believing in the sacredness
of debts, he demanded full payment by the former Allied governments of
their debts to the United States. Sharing the Hamiltonian trickle-down
theory of prosperity, he advocated low taxes on wealth and noninterference
by government in business affairs.

Businessmen during 1920 had launched a powerful campaign against
the excess profits tax and extremely high surtaxes that still prevailed
under the War Revenue Act of 1918–19. (See above, p. 201.) Mellon
reiterated these demands to the special session of 1921, recommending
repeal of the excess profits tax, a slight increase in the corporation tax,
reduction of the combined normal and surtaxes on incomes from a maximum of 73 per cent to 40 per cent for 1921 and 33 per cent thereafter,
repeal of war luxury taxes, and imposition of a new federal tax on automobiles. The House of Representatives and the Senate finance committee
approved a bill embodying Mellon's program. In the Senate, however, midwestern Republicans joined Democrats to write a tax measure of their
own. Commanding a solid majority, these "wild asses of the desert," as
insurgents were derisively called at the time, defied the House of Representatives, the President, and the Secretary of the Treasury and warned
that there would be no tax legislation at all unless their bill prevailed. The
President signed their measure on November 23, 1921.

The Revenue Act of 1921 was significant, not only because it attested
to the power of the combined Farm Bloc and the Democratic minority, but
even more because it gave evidence of the strong survival of advanced
progressive tax theories. The measure repealed the excess profits tax
entirely—progressives and conservatives alike agreed that it was an unnecessary burden on business during peacetime. But the insurgent senators won all their demands in the critical battle over the income tax. The
Act of 1921 continued the rates under the War Revenue Act for the balance
of 1921, set the maximum surtax thereafter at 50 per cent, increased the
tax on net corporation incomes from 10 to 12½ per cent, and left estate
taxes unchanged.

Meanwhile, the American Legion had launched a campaign to force Congress to provide additional compensation for men who had served in the armed forces while civilians enjoyed wartime prosperity at home. A measure to provide "adjusted compensation" passed the House in May 1920 but was killed by the Senate finance committee. But the agitation for adjusted compensation redoubled; and Chairman Fordney of the House ways and means committee introduced a revised "bonus" bill in March 1922. It provided payment of twenty-year endowment policies to veterans on a basis of $1.00 a day for service in the United States and $1.25 a day for service overseas. Even after the measure passed both houses by large majorities, Harding vetoed it on September 19, 1922. The veto was not overridden.

The tax reduction of 1921 caused a decrease the following year of $1,500,000,000 in ordinary federal revenues; yet Mellon was able to reduce the national debt by almost two billions and to report a surplus of $310,-000,000 on hand at the end of the fiscal year. He reopened the tax battle in December 1923, therefore, by urging Congress to cut the maximum surtax on incomes from 50 to 25 per cent, decrease proportionately the normal tax on small incomes, and reduce drastically the federal estate tax. However, insurgent Republicans and Democrats in Congress took control once more. Their Revenue Act of 1924 cut the maximum surtax from 50 to 40 per cent and halved the normal tax on small and middle incomes. To compensate for these reductions, they increased the maximum estate tax from 25 to 40 per cent and imposed a new gift tax. President Coolidge and Secretary Mellon were disgusted, but the President signed the measure on June 2, 1924. In a second display of defiance, Congress in the spring of 1924 re-enacted the adjusted compensation bill over Coolidge's indignant veto.

Drastic tax reduction remained the chief objective of the business and propertied classes. They poured nearly $6,000,000 into Republican coffers in 1924 to elect Coolidge and a friendly Congress; and they began a strong propaganda after the election to stimulate a clamor for tax reduction. The insurgent-Democratic coalition finally surrendered control of fiscal policy to the administration when the Sixty-ninth Congress met on December 7, 1925. The country was so prosperous and the needs of the Treasury were relatively so slight that only a tremendous increase in expenditures for public works, housing, and farm relief would have justified maintenance of the prevailing high tax structure. Such a program was far beyond the ken of most progressives at the time.

The Revenue Act that Congress adopted on February 12, 1926, therefore, reduced the normal tax on small incomes, cut the maximum surtax from 40 to 20 per cent, abolished the gift tax, and slashed the estate tax in half. One further tax measure—the Revenue Act of 1928, which left income taxes undisturbed but slightly reduced corporation and consumption taxes—rounded out Mellon's fiscal program. He had failed only to obtain complete repeal of the federal estate levy. Organized wealth and its political allies, nevertheless, had succeeded for a time in repudiating the democratic tax policy inaugurated by the anti-preparedness radicals of 1916. (See above, pp. 183–184.)

117. *The Farm Problem, 1920–1928*

The most important domestic economic problem of the 1920's was the agricultural depression that began in the summer of 1920 and continued intermittently until 1935. Most of the farmers' troubles were caused by overextension, inflation, and too much spending during and immediately following the war. This development would not have had serious consequences if the prices of agricultural products had remained at the high level of 1919, for the farmers' position relative to the rest of the economy had not changed since 1914. However, the farmers' happy world came tumbling down when foreign demand decreased sharply in 1920 and the government withdrew price supports from wheat on May 31, 1920. By the autumn of 1921 the price of wheat had dropped to approximately 40 per cent of its highest price in 1920, that of corn to 32 per cent, and that of hogs to 50 per cent.

Farm prices recovered slightly between 1921 and 1929, but they were never high enough to make agriculture a really profitable enterprise. In fact, except during 1925 and 1929 farmers operated at a net capital loss during the entire period 1921–9. A few statistics must suffice. Total net farm income declined from $10,061,000,000 in 1919 to $9,009,000,000 in 1920 and to $4,138,000,000 in 1921. It increased slightly to $5,081,000,-000 in 1922 and ran between six and seven billions from 1923 through 1929. Farmers received 16 per cent of the national income in 1919 and only 8.8 per cent a decade later.

The first sharp decline in agricultural prices coincided with the return of the Republican party to national power and, as we have seen, stimulated the formation of the Farm Bloc in Congress. By operating as a nonpartisan pressure group, the Farm Bloc took control of agricultural policy between 1921 and 1924 and pushed through Congress the most advanced agricultural program in American history to that time.

We have already discussed the adoption of high tariff protection for agricultural products. It was the least important item in the Farm Bloc's program. A more urgent goal in 1921 was legislation to subject meat packers and stockyards to rigorous federal control. The Federal Trade Commission had made a thorough investigation in 1920. It stimulated widespread demand for federal ownership and operation of the stockyards; and Attorney General A. Mitchell Palmer had compelled the packers shortly afterward to accept a consent decree that ended their control over the stockyards. All that remained was to preserve competition in the packing industry and maintain close public scrutiny over the stockyards. These objectives the Farm Bloc accomplished in August 1921 with adoption of the Packers and Stockyards Act. It empowered the Secretary of Agriculture to issue cease and desist orders to preserve competition among packers and compel commission merchants and stockyards to charge only reasonable rates.

This was not all that the Farm Bloc won during the hectic special session of 1921. First, Congress extended for three years the life of the War Finance Corporation, established in 1918 to supply capital for war industries, and authorized it to lend up to $1,000,000,000 to stimulate the

THE ECONOMIC FORTUNES OF AMERICAN FARMERS:
CASH INCOMES AND PRICES
1910-1940

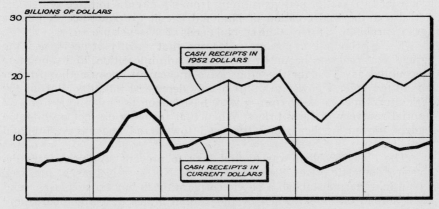

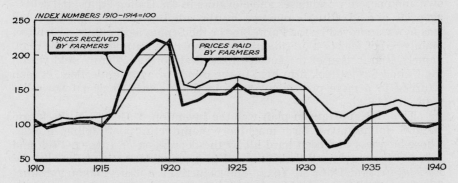

export of agricultural commodities. Second, the lending operations of the Federal Farm Loan System were expanded by increasing the capital of the land banks, established in 1916. Thirdly, the Farm Bloc obtained passage of the Grain Futures Act, which gave the Secretary of Agriculture sweeping control over the grain exchanges. In addition, Congress in 1922 added an agricultural representative to the Federal Reserve Board and approved the Capper-Volstead bill exempting farm co-operatives from prohibitions of the antitrust laws.

The Farm Bloc's most important triumph in the early twenties was the enactment in March 1923 of the Agricultural Credits Act—the culmination of a searching inquiry into the farm problem by a joint congressional commission established in 1921.[6] This measure established twelve

---

[6] The farmer's long- and short-term credit needs, the commission revealed, had been amply satisfied by the Federal Reserve and Federal Land Bank systems. What the farmer needed most, therefore, was an intermediate credit system enabling him to borrow against his products and land for periods running from six months to three years. With such new credit resources, farm spokesmen argued, co-operatives could withhold surpluses from the market during periods of deflation and thus prevent violent price fluctuations.

Intermediate Credit Banks, capitalized by the Treasury and operated in conjunction with the Federal Land Banks, to make loans to organized groups of farmers for periods running from six months to three years. The Act also authorized creation of National Credit Corporations, or private agricultural banks, to serve the special needs of livestock producers.

These were all important measures that greatly strengthened the agricultural program begun by the Wilson administration, and they must be counted as gains for the progressive movement because they further committed federal power to uplift a now depressed minority. But all the agricultural measures of 1921–3 were based upon the assumption of substantial recovery in farm prices. When that recovery did not occur farm leaders moved further along the road toward advanced governmental participation.

The chief problem was to find how to prevent surpluses from depressing domestic prices. Senator George W. Norris of Nebraska suggested a plan in 1921 to establish a public corporation to buy up surpluses, send them abroad on ships owned by the United States Shipping Board, and own and operate warehouses and elevators in the United States and selling agencies abroad. Bitterly opposed by the administration, the Norris bill was never approved by the Farm Bloc or the Senate agriculture committee, mainly out of fear of a presidential veto. But the idea inherent in the plan, namely, segregation of the surplus from that portion of crops sold within the United States, took firm hold in the minds of agrarian leaders. It soon returned in a more pretentious form in the McNary-Haugen farm relief plan.

The McNary-Haugen plan was the invention of George N. Peek and Hugh S. Johnson, two farm machinery manufacturers of Moline, Illinois, whose business had been hard hit by the depression of 1920–1. Peek and Johnson first explained their proposal in a pamphlet entitled *Equality for Agriculture*, published in 1922. The objective—a "fair exchange value" for farm products—would be achieved by segregating the exportable surplus so that the domestic market would not be governed by world prices. How this would be done can be illustrated by a familiar example. The United States during the 1920's annually produced about 800,000,000 bushels of wheat, of which about 650,000,000 bushels were consumed at home. If the world price were $1.00 a bushel, then in a free market American farmers would receive $800,000,000 for the wheat crop. Let us assume, however, that the Peek-Johnson plan were in operation. In this event, a federal board would buy the entire wheat crop at a price that would yield a "fair exchange value," presumably the world price plus the tariff on wheat, which after 1924 would have totaled $1.42 a bushel. Farmers would thus receive a gross of $1,136,000,000 for 800,000,000 bushels of wheat. The board would sell the surplus of 150,000,000 bushels abroad at the world price of $1.00, and its loss of 42 cents a bushel, or $63,000,000, would be assessed in the form of an "equalization fee" against the farmers. Thus under the plan farmers would receive a net of $1,073,000,000 for the crop, instead of $800,000,000 if the wheat had been sold in a free market at world prices.

The Peek-Johnson proposal seemed such an easy and sensible way of assuring equitable farm prices that it was embodied in the form of the

McNary-Haugen bill in 1924. It was endorsed by more than 200 farm
organizations and many state legislatures and chambers of commerce
throughout the Middle West and Northwest. Violently opposed by eastern
Republicans and President Coolidge, the measure was defeated by the
House on June 3, 1924. This first defeat, however, only spurred farm
leaders to redouble their propaganda and seek new allies. Midwesterners
won the support of southern farm organizations in 1926 by including
cotton, tobacco, and rice in the proposed system; and a southern-western
coalition pushed a revised McNary-Haugen bill through Congress in
February 1927. Coolidge replied on February 25, with a caustic veto message denouncing the measure as unconstitutional special-interest legislation. Re-enacted in May 1928, the McNary-Haugen bill drew a second veto
from the President.

Organized farmers, therefore, failed to commit the federal government to the most advanced farm program yet seriously proposed. But they
failed only because the eastern business wing of the GOP dominated
the presidency. Actually, by 1929 the Farm Bureau Federation and other
organizations in the forefront of the agricultural relief movement had
scored one of the most important victories in the history of American
progressivism. They had succeeded in promoting a new unity among
farm leaders throughout the country. More important, they had compelled
the conservative majority in the Republican party to approve a federal
farm program that included strict control of grain exchanges, stockyards,
and packing houses, support for agricultural co-operatives, and credit
facilities on every level. From this advanced program there could be no
turning back; in fact, the pathway of progressivism pointed straight ahead
to other advanced measures built upon the foundations laid during the
1920's.

118. *The Triumph of the Movement for Immigration Restriction*

One of the oldest objectives of a certain segment of the progressive
movement was exclusion of Oriental immigration to the West Coast and
restriction of the numbers of Europeans who came to the United States
before the First World War. Rightly or wrongly, leaders of organized
labor believed that large-scale immigration depressed the domestic labor
market and impeded the progress of unionization. Additionally, many
sociologists and social workers believed that the immigration of eastern
and southern Europeans created grave social problems. Finally, most
"new" immigrants were either Catholics or Jews, and their coming aroused
fear among Protestant Americans, especially in the rural areas, of a
Catholic and Jewish inundation.

Restrictionists sought to accomplish their objective first by imposing
a literacy test in 1917, which they thought would exclude large numbers
of peasant immigrants from eastern Europe. But the literacy test was only
a slight deterrent, as immigrants who went to the trouble to seek a new
home were also willing to learn enough to pass a simple test in reading and
writing. Some 1,235,000 immigrants poured into the ports in 1920–1, and
American consuls warned that millions more were preparing to leave
war-ravaged districts.

EFFECTS OF THE QUOTA ACTS
ON SOURCES OF IMMIGRATION

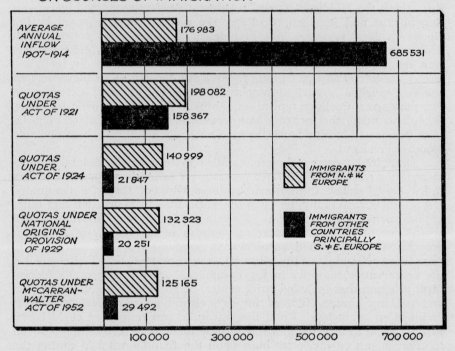

Labor leaders and social workers found so many new allies in 1920 and 1921 that the movement for restriction became irresistible. For one thing, many leaders of communist and other radical groups were eastern Europeans; and employers, heretofore the chief opponents of restriction, now joined the movement for new legislation. For another, the Ku Klux Klan was beginning a powerful campaign aimed at Jews and Catholics. It is only fair to say, however, that the restrictionists probably would have succeeded without the assistance of the extreme nativistic element, for the preponderant majority had decided to end the historic policy of free and almost unlimited immigration.

Congress, therefore, acted with dispatch in 1920 and 1921. The House approved a bill sponsored by Representative Albert Johnson of Washington to suspend immigration for one year. It was amended in the Senate to limit the number of immigrants to 3 per cent of the various foreign-born elements in the United States in 1910 and approved by Congress in the closing days of the lame-duck session. When Wilson refused to sign the bill, congressional leaders swiftly pushed it through the special session, and Harding approved the measure on May 19, 1921. The number of immigrants declined in consequence from 805,228 for the fiscal year ending June 30, 1921, to 309,556 during the following fiscal year.[7]

----

[7] It should be noted, however, that neither this measure nor the National Origins Act of 1924 limited immigration from any countries of the western hemisphere.

Warren G. Harding

Andrew Mellon

President Hoover opening the baseball season, 1932

ABOVE: *Sacco and Vanzetti*
BELOW: *The Ku Klux Klan*

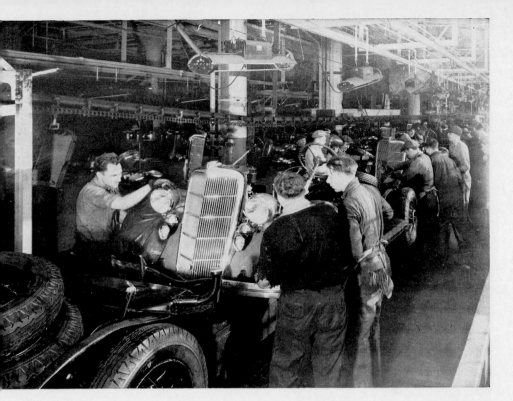

ABOVE: *Assembly line at Ford's River Rouge Plant*
BELOW: *The tractor displaces the horse*

Helen Breaker

Ernest Hemingway   Eugene O'Neill

Sinclair Lewis and his first wife in a Model T

President Coolidge in the Black Hills

Al Capone and the Law

Wall Street, October 24, 1929

Apple sellers in New York, 1931

ABOVE: *A Hooverville—Grant's Tomb, Riverside Church, and uptown New York skyline in background*

BELOW: *Breadline, 1932*

Franklin D. Roosevelt

The magazine of the USS Shaw explodes at Pearl Harbor

The reduction effected was obviously drastic, but restrictionists and especially champions of religious and nationalistic bigotry were still not satisfied. Congress responded in 1924 with a new and comprehensive immigration statute that satisfied even the exclusionists. Known as the National Origins Act, it prohibited Oriental immigration and limited the total number of European immigrants to 2 per cent of the foreign-born according to the census of 1890. The latter stipulation reduced the total number of immigrants to 164,000, discriminated heavily in favor of Great Britain, Ireland, and Germany, and cut the flow of Italians, for example, to less than 4,000 a year. The Act provided, additionally, that immigration should be further reduced to a maximum of 150,000 after July 1, 1927, apportioned on a basis of the national origins of the American people in 1920.

The application of the new quota system based upon the national origins of the American people was postponed beyond 1927 because of the difficulty of determining what those origins were; but the quotas finally went into effect on July 1, 1929. Moreover, President Herbert Hoover drastically reduced the quotas in 1931, so that more foreigners left the United States than entered in 1932. The number of immigrants in any one year during the thirties never exceeded 100,000, while the total net immigration for the entire decade was only 68,789.

119. *The Power Controversy of the Twenties*

The survival of progressivism in the 1920's was nowhere more significantly illustrated than in battles that progressives waged, first, to obtain either municipal ownership and operation of electric power facilities or effective state regulation of the electric industry and, second, to commit the federal government to the operation of important power projects. If progressives in the 1920's did little more than awaken the public and lay the foundations for future action, they gave further evidence that success in great movements comes only after decades of hard struggle.

Compared to the railroads, the electrical industry was still young in the 1920's, but its rise had been spectacular. Production of electric power increased from 6,000,000,000 to 117,000,000,000 kilowatt hours between 1902 and 1929. Expansion had been accompanied by consolidation of small operating companies into large systems, and of large systems into great holding company aggregations. By 1930 eleven well-defined holding company groups controlled 85 per cent of the installed capacity of the industry.

The movement to regulate this vast private interest, the second most important industry in the country, went through the same stages and encountered the same obstacles as did the earlier movement for railroad regulation. The establishment of public utility commissions with rate-making authority in Virginia in 1901 and in Georgia, Wisconsin, and New York in 1907 marked the beginning of the movement on the state level. In spite of public apathy caused by high-pressure utilities propaganda and a downward trend in rates, many state commissions effected a reasonable degree of control over rates and services. On the other hand, probably a majority of the state commissions were timid and incompetent and controlled more often than not by the utilities interest. Therefore, progressives in the 1920's not only sought to strengthen state commissions but also joined a movement for municipal ownership of power plants and distribution facilities.[8]

Like the railroads decades before, power companies during the twenties fought to protect their privileged position, preserve immunity from effective regulation, and prevent public ownership. They executed a gigantic advertising campaign that cost between $28,000,000 and $35,000,-000 a year to influence public opinion and indirectly control the editorial policies of hundreds of newspapers. They sometimes bought control of leading dailies. "Information Bureaus" working in practically every state on orders from the textbook committee of the National Electric Light Association brought pressure on school boards to force abandonment of civics texts that condemned stock-watering and exorbitant rates and mentioned the benefits of regulation or public ownership. Moreover, the power interests quietly hired a number of college professors for public lectures, subsidized the General Federation of Women's Clubs, influenced bankers through judicious use of deposits, bribed leaders of farm organizations, and worked relentlessly to control local and state politicians and commissions.

The first serious attempt at federal regulation was the adoption of the Water Power Act of 1920, enacted after a long controversy over policy for the licensing of dams on public lands, reservations, or navigable rivers. This measure created a Federal Power Commission, composed of the Secretaries of War, Interior, and Agriculture. It was empowered to license hydroelectric projects on sites within the jurisdiction of the federal government. Such leases ran for fifty years, but the government might purchase the entire property at net cost at the expiration of the lease. In addition, the Commission was authorized to regulate the rates, services, and financial operations of companies operating under its license, unless such companies were subjected to state regulation.

The Federal Power Commission licensed 449 projects with 2,489,978 installed horsepower capacity between 1920 and 1930. Because of inadequate staff and the pressure of private interests, however, it did practically nothing to protect the public interest. At President Hoover's request, Congress created a new and independent Federal Power Commission in 1930 but refused to endow it with additional authority because of fear that the President would pack the new agency with men friendly to the power interests. As Hoover soon justified congressional suspicions, effective federal regulation was postponed until the inauguration of an administration less concerned with protecting private enterprise in the production of electricity.

More significant than these largely ineffective efforts at federal regulation was the development of an organized campaign during the 1920's to commit the federal government to large hydroelectric projects in the Tennessee Valley, the Columbia River watershed, the Southwest, and on

[8] By 1930 Los Angeles, Seattle, Tacoma, and some 2,000 other cities and towns owned generating plants or distribution facilities.

the St. Lawrence River. These regional developments, progressives asserted, would assure an abundance of cheap power for millions of consumers and also provide "yardsticks" for rates throughout the country. Only one of the proposed projects was begun during the Republican era—Hoover, or Boulder, Dam [9]—but around another proposed development centered one of the most crucial battles of the twenties. It was the struggle for control of a large federally owned dam and nitrogen plants at Muscle Shoals, Alabama, which in time became the focus of the entire controversy over public ownership and operation of power plants.

The background goes back to 1916, when Congress empowered the President and War Department to construct a plant to manufacture nitrates and thus make the United States independent of German and Chilean supplies. Two nitrate plants, with a combined annual capacity of more than 40,000 tons, were built in 1918 at a cost of over $80,000,000 at Muscle Shoals, on the Tennessee River in Alabama. At the same time, the War Department began construction at this site of the gigantic Wilson Dam to provide electric power for the nitrate plants. The war's end found the nitrate plants completed but not yet in production and the dam about three-quarters finished.

Soon after Harding's inauguration the new Secretary of War announced that he would urge Congress to appropriate funds to complete the dam if some private company would lease the Muscle Shoals properties and guarantee a fair return on the government's investment. A number of power companies and industrial corporations submitted bids during the next two years, but it was the proposition made by Henry Ford, the automobile manufacturer, that excited the greatest enthusiasm. He offered to lease the Muscle Shoals facilities for one hundred years, to pay an annual rental of $1,500,000, and to produce at least 40,000 tons of nitrates annually for cheap fertilizers. He also promised to build a city seventy-five miles long in the Tennessee Valley and to devote the entire development to the welfare of the American people.

Ford's proposal was enthusiastically supported by the Harding and Coolidge administrations and farm groups, and the House of Representatives, on March 10, 1924, approved a bill authorizing acceptance of Ford's bid. The Muscle Shoals offers had been referred in the Senate to the agriculture committee, headed by George W. Norris. The Nebraska senator had already concluded that Ford, the power companies, and other industrialists were deceiving the people in an attempt to steal one of the

ᵐᵐᵐᵐᵐᵐᵐᵐᵐᵐᵐᵐ

[9] The passage of the Boulder Dam Project Act by Congress in December 1928 represented a compromise between private power interests and the southwestern states and municipalities in a long battle for control of the water and water power resources of the lower Colorado River.

The Act provided for the construction of a dam 726 feet high and 1,244 feet long in the Black Canyon of the Colorado River on the Arizona-Nevada boundary. The cost of the dam and power plant, $108,000,000, was to be repaid out of revenues from the sale of electricity. (Actually, the power facilities were to be leased to private companies.) In addition, the Act authorized the building of the so-called All-American Canal to divert water from the Colorado River to the Imperial and Coachella Valleys in California. The cost of this seventy-five-mile canal, $38,500,000, was to be paid by the users of the water.

nation's greatest natural assets—the potentially enormous hydroelectric resources of the Tennessee Valley. As early as 1922 a bold alternative had begun to take shape in Norris's mind: creation of a public corporation to control the waters of the Tennessee Valley—and afterward of other such watersheds—for flood control and production of vast quantities of cheap electric power.

Norris's first move was to push a bill through Congress in 1922 for completion of Wilson Dam; his second, to persuade the Senate agriculture committee, in May 1924, to approve a bill for governmental operation of the Muscle Shoals properties. When the Nebraskan presented his measure to the Senate on December 3, 1924, Senator Oscar W. Underwood of Alabama countered with a substitute providing for private operation. The battle was joined. The ship of state, Norris exclaimed, referring to Coolidge's support of the Underwood bill, was "headed straight for Wall Street" and carried "a deed of conveyance . . . for one of the greatest inheritances of unborn generations of American citizens."

Norris's invective was biting, but it could not stem the tide. The Senate approved the Underwood bill on January 14, 1925; two weeks later a conference committee met to iron out differences between the Senate and House measures. Just when it seemed that the Senate would approve the conference report, Norris, on February 19, made what was probably the most important parliamentary point of order in American history. He protested that the conference committee had improperly added new provisions to the Muscle Shoals bill. The point of order was sustained, and Norris was able to prevent a vote by threat of filibuster when the conference committee reported a proper bill on February 26, 1925. Norris did not relax his vigilance during the next two years. Indeed, he won new allies among the southern senators and the Senate's approval, on March 13, 1928, of his bill for governmental operation of the Muscle Shoals power plant. Insurgent Republicans and Democrats in the House soon afterward adopted a measure that was in many respects superior to the Norris bill. It provided for creation of a federal corporation to operate Wilson Dam and the nitrogen plants, as well as for construction of an additional dam at Cove Creek, Tennessee, to ensure flood control and a steady flow of water through the Muscle Shoals turbines. It was this House measure that Congress approved in the latter part of May 1928.

The issue was now clearly drawn between private interests and advocates of public power, and spokesmen of a large part of the business community appealed to Coolidge to prevent such a far-reaching experiment in socialism. Coolidge did not disappoint his friends; he gave the Muscle Shoals bill a pocket veto. In spite of President Hoover's open opposition, Norris and the progressive coalition adopted a second Muscle Shoals bill in February 1931. Hoover replied on March 3 in a veto message that was a ringing defense of private enterprise. Thus the fight to launch one of the most significant progressive experiments in American history was again momentarily defeated by a conservative President. Even so, Norris and progressives in Congress had saved Muscle Shoals and the water power resources of the Tennessee Valley for the American people. The time was not far distant when this aspect of the progressive movement would come to fruition.

120. *The Supreme Court and Social and Economic Policy, 1918–1929*

The conflict between conservative and progressive theories in the postwar decade was as evident in the Supreme Court as in the political arena. On the whole, conservative views prevailed in the judicial arm, chiefly because Chief Justice Edward D. White and a majority of the old conservative justices had refused either to die or to resign and allow Wilson to appoint a progressive majority.[10] On the other hand, the two great progressive jurists, Oliver Wendell Holmes and Louis D. Brandeis, remained on the bench during the twenties, and Harlan F. Stone, appointed by Coolidge in 1925, shocked his conservative friends by joining Holmes and Brandeis in numerous dissents.

The court had validated a whole series of advanced social and economic legislation from 1908 to 1917. (See above, pp. 74–75, 117.) Then, beginning with the child labor case in 1918, discussed below, reaction against advanced progressivism set in and was enormously strengthened by the appointment of a new conservative majority between 1921 and 1930. So retrogressive, in fact, was the new court that on occasion it tended to be blindly reactionary in cases involving economic and social policies. This attempt to turn back the progressive tide provoked violent attacks by reform groups and numerous proposals to curb the court's authority. The causes for progressive anger can best be demonstrated by a discussion of the trend of the court's decisions in the fields of civil rights, social and economic legislation, the legal status of organized labor, and limitations on the regulatory power of the state and federal governments.

The decade from 1919 to 1929 was no time of triumph for defenders of the American tradition of civil rights. On the contrary, the prevailing demand for conformity and suppression of radical ideas was in part reflected in a series of Supreme Court decisions that destroyed old judicial barriers against assaults on the right of free expression. In Schenck *v.* United States and two other decisions rendered in 1919, a unanimous court agreed that the government had the right to suppress sedition during wartime, on the ground that sedition constituted, to quote Justice Holmes's famous words, a "clear and present danger" to national security. In Abrams *v.* United States, 1919, and other cases, Holmes and Brandeis tried to persuade their colleagues to accept a narrow interpretation of the "clear and present danger" doctrine. But the bars were down, and the two dissenters pleaded in vain for a return to the old freedom. Moreover, in Gitlow *v.* New York, 1925, and Whitney *v.* California, 1927, the court—with Holmes and Brandeis again eloquently dissenting—upheld criminal anarchy and syndicalism laws of New York and California. The effect of these decisions, in brief, was to give federal and state officials practically unlimited discretion in determining what constituted a "clear and present danger."

[10] Wilson appointed only three justices during his eight years as President. Harding appointed a Chief Justice and three associate justices during his two and a half years as President.

In contrast, the court exhibited more boldness in protecting racial and religious minorities. It overturned in 1923 state wartime statutes forbidding the use of foreign languages in schools.[11] In a momentous decision two years later—Pierce *v.* Society of Sisters—the court unanimously outlawed a Klan-sponsored Oregon statute to destroy parochial schools by requiring all children between eight and sixteen to attend public schools. Finally, when the Texas legislature excluded Negroes from the Democratic primary and soon afterward authorized the Democratic state committee to exclude Negro voters, the court, in 1927 and again in 1932, nullified the statutes on the ground that they obviously violated the Fourteenth and Fifteenth amendments.[12] In other cases, however, the court vacillated between firm defense of civil rights and willingness to condone new means of violating them. On the one hand, it condemned illegal seizure of evidence; on the other, it sanctioned admission of evidence obtained by wiretapping, approved western state statutes excluding Orientals from land ownership, and upheld denial of citizenship to immigrants who refused to take an oath promising to bear arms in defense of the United States.

As for social and economic policies, it would be an exaggeration to say that the Supreme Court set out willfully during the period under discussion to overturn the whole body of progressive state and federal statutes. But on two important frontiers of the social justice movement the court not only called a halt to reform but also completely nullified gains already made. The first controversy involved the constitutionality of the Child Labor Act of 1916. By a five-to-four decision in Hammer *v.* Dagenhart, 1918, the court declared that the Act involved an unconstitutional invasion of the police powers of the states. In other words, Congress could not use its power over interstate commerce to regulate the conditions of labor. Congress in 1919 levied a prohibitive tax on products manufactured in whole or in part by children, and the court, in Bailey *v.* Drexel Furniture Company, 1922, again applied its veto. Congress, the majority declared, could not use the taxing power to accomplish an unconstitutional regulation.

The court's inflexible opposition to any form of *federal* regulation of hours, wages, and the conditions of labor—for such opposition was clearly implied in the child labor decisions—was discouraging enough to social justice reformers with ambitious plans for extensive federal regulation through the commerce power. Even more disheartening was the court's destruction of all *state* efforts to regulate the wages of women workers. The case of Adkins *v.* Children's Hospital, involving the constitutionality of a District of Columbia minimum wage statute for women, came before the new conservative Supreme Court in 1923. Felix Frankfurter defended the statute by marshaling economic and social data to prove a direct connection between the wages that women received and their health and morality. Justice George Sutherland, speaking for the majority, dismissed

[11] In Meyer *v.* Nebraska, 1923, and Barteis *v.* Iowa, 1923, both involving the use of German in parochial schools.

[12] In 1935, however, the same conservative court, in Grovey *v.* Townsend, allowed the Democratic state convention of Texas to exclude Negroes from party membership and the privilege of voting in the party primary election.

this argument as irrelevant. He also resurrected the decision in Lochner *v.* New York to affirm that state efforts to regulate the wages of grown women violated their freedom to make a labor contract. Indeed, Herbert Spencer or William Graham Sumner could not have been more eloquent in defense of *laissez faire.*

Progressives were enraged by this reversion to obsolete interpretations and launched propaganda that seriously weakened the court's prestige and did not subside until the justices in the late 1930's specifically repudiated Hammer *v.* Dagenhart and Adkins *v.* Children's Hospital. Meanwhile, another long and bitter controversy erupted when the court denied that the labor provisions of the Clayton Act of 1914 had conferred any substantial new benefits and privileges on labor unions. The question, in essence, was: Did the Clayton Act give unions immunity from prosecution and injunctions against methods of industrial warfare—the secondary boycott, the "blacklist," and mass picketing, among others—which the federal courts had earlier outlawed under the Sherman Act?

The Supreme Court in a number of decisions in the 1920's ruled that the Clayton Act had neither conferred upon labor unions immunity from prosecution for violating the antitrust laws nor legalized labor practices that were illegal before the Clayton Act was adopted. Although the majority correctly interpreted the intentions of the framers of the Clayton Act (see above, pp. 66–67), Justices Holmes, Brandeis, and John H. Clarke dissented and lent authority to the AF of L's contention that organized labor had been unjustly deprived of the benefits of its "Magna Charta."

Continuing a policy begun in the 1880's, the Supreme Court during the 1920's insisted on wielding the power to review state action regulating economic enterprises. Generally speaking, however, Supreme Court policy concerning state regulation was neither capricious nor reactionary. The court readily acknowledged the right of states to regulate businesses clothed with a public interest. At the same time, it insisted that such regulation be nondiscriminatory and according to due process of law. Railroad regulation, both state and federal, had become in practice thoroughly institutionalized by the 1920's. But state regulation of public utilities was not as well developed by precedent and experience, and there was considerable confusion over the proper constitutional basis for rate-making. State commissions usually determined rates on a basis of original cost; during the prosperous twenties, on the other hand, public utilities companies contended that the cost of reproducing the properties was the proper basis. Although the court usually accepted the latter contention before 1933, it did not evolve any definite formula for determining the basis for a fair return.

As for federal regulation, there occurred a relentless expansion of the federal power during the 1920's, in spite of the conservative temper of the men who determined Republican policies and controlled the Supreme Court. In Massachusetts *v.* Mellon, 1923, the court upheld the system of federal grants-in-aid to the states and repudiated Massachusetts's argument that such grants unduly infringed the police power of the states because of conditions attached to acceptance of such grants. The result of the decision was a significant erosion of state sovereignty. Moreover, in all cases in which the United States could demonstrate that the regulated activity was interstate in character the Supreme Court sanctioned an expansion of federal authority. In Stafford *v.* Wallace, 1922, for example, the court upheld the Packers and Stockyards Act, which subjected the meat packing industry to strict federal control. While nullifying the Grain Futures Act in 1923, because Congress had used the taxing power to regulate grain exchanges, the court declared that Congress might use its commerce power to accomplish the same result. When Congress established the Federal Radio Commission and gave it complete control over the airways, the court agreed in 1933 that such regulation was proper and constitutional.

Moreover, the Supreme Court's interpretation of the antitrust laws in the 1920's was consistent and straightforward. In United States *v.* United States Steel Corporation, 1920, and United States *v.* International Harvester Company, 1927, for example, the court declared that mere bigness was no violation of the antitrust laws. In a number of cases involving the activities of trade associations, the court outlawed any practices that might lead to price-fixing or restriction of production. In dealing with cases arising from the efforts of the Federal Trade Commission to suppress unfair trade practices, the court always insisted upon the privilege of determining what an unfair trade practice was. It was true, as progressives lamented, that such broad review seriously hampered the work of the Commission. Progressives forgot, however, that the framers of the Federal Trade Commission Act of 1914 had explicitly given the court broad review over the Commission's actions in order to prevent the Commission from ever becoming arbitrary, capricious, or independent of judicial limitations.

CHAPTER

16

Foreign Relations
of the 1920's

THE DEVELOPMENT of American foreign policy during the years between the Armistice and the Great Depression presents an anomaly between the popular desire for extrication from entangling obligations on the one hand and the necessary adoption of measures of co-operation on the other. In brief, the United States in the 1920's largely abandoned isolation and sought to strengthen and protect the peace structure of the world. At the same time it sought the advantages of peace without being willing to assume obligations to preserve peace. And in some measure because of this fact, new aggressors were able to make a hollow mockery of these vain efforts in the following decade.

Events of the thirties lay in the distant future, however, as the Harding administration set about in the spring of 1921 to extricate the United States from obligations that Wilson had assumed. First, the new President made it clear that the United States would not join the League of Nations—"We do not mean to be entangled," he declared in his inaugural address. Second, the administration moved to end the state of war between the United States and the Central Powers. Soon after Congress, on July 2, 1921, approved a joint resolution declaring the war with Germany at an end, the new Secretary of State, Charles Evans Hughes, negotiated separate peace treaties with Germany, Austria, and Hungary. They gave the United States the benefits without the responsibilities of the Versailles Treaty.

By concluding a separate peace with Germany, the Harding administration made it clear that the United States would assume no responsibility for enforcing the peace it had helped impose. Meanwhile, however, a crisis of dangerous magnitude involving the United States, Great Britain, and Japan was nearing culmination just as Harding took office. Let us now examine the causes of this menace to peace and see how the new administration met the first challenge to its leadership and courage.

121. *War Clouds over the Pacific*

The reader will recall that Japanese-American relations on the eve of America's entrance into the First World War were troubled, and that the effort of Viscount Ishii and Secretary of State Lansing to come to comprehensive understanding on all aspects of the Far Eastern question in October and November 1917 had brought no real relief from the tension. (See above, pp. 159–161.) Events following negotiation of the Lansing-Ishii Agreement only further embittered relations. For one thing, in order to prevent Japanese economic domination of northern China and Manchuria, Wilson revived the international banking consortium that he had roundly condemned in 1913. For another, as a result of the Russian Revolution and ensuing civil war, Japanese and American troops had been brought face to face in Siberia. The American and Allied governments agreed in the summer of 1918 to send an expedition to Vladivostok to rescue a sizable Czech army from the Bolsheviks. President Wilson dispatched an expedition of 9,000 men under General William S. Graves to Vladivostok in August 1918. At the same time, the Japanese army sent some 73,000 troops and controlled all the strategic centers of eastern Siberia within a short time. Perceiving that the Japanese meant to seize the Russian Maritime Province, Lansing at once brought heavy pressure on Tokyo for withdrawal of most of its troops.

Japanese-American relations were further embittered at the Paris Peace Conference. Wilson was maneuvered into opposing a Japanese demand for inclusion of a provision in the League Covenant affirming the principle of racial equality. Failure of the demand greatly embittered public opinion in Japan. Even more exacerbating were the controversies between Wilson and the Japanese delegates over disposal of the former German-owned Marshall, Mariana, and Caroline islands and the Shantung Province of China, all of which Japan had occupied in 1914. The Marshall, Mariana. and Caroline islands lay directly athwart the sea lanes between Hawaii and the American outposts in Guam and the Philippines. The Japanese, by fortifying their new island possessions, could render American protection of the Philippines virtually impossible. Unable to win British and French support, Wilson had to agree that the disputed islands should be mandated to Japan but never fortified.[1]

Although he realized the strategic importance of this concession, Wilson made a much harder fight to force the Japanese out of the Shan-

wwwwwwwwwwwwwww

[1] Wilson, however, refused to concur in the conference's decision to mandate the island of Yap to Japan. Yap, which lay west of Guam and the Carolines, was an important center for the Pacific cables. Wilson entered a reservation to protect American rights in the island.

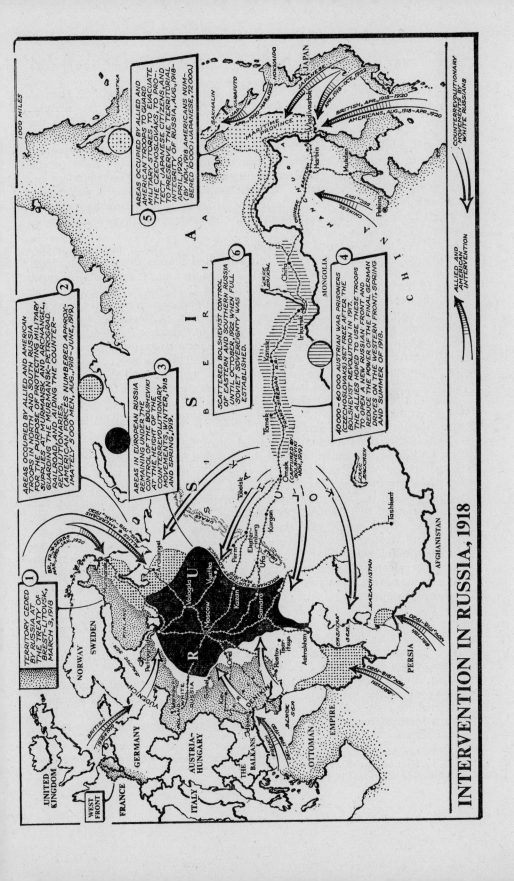

INTERVENTION IN RUSSIA, 1918

① TERRITORY CEDED BY RUSSIA AT THE TREATY OF BREST-LITOVSK, MARCH 3, 1918

② AREAS OCCUPIED BY ALLIED AND AMERICAN TROOPS IN NORTH AND SOUTH RUSSIA FOR THE PURPOSE OF PROTECTING MILITARY SUPPLIES AT MURMANSK AND ARCHANGEL, GUARDING THE MURMANSK-PETROGRAD RAILROAD, AND AIDING THE COUNTER-REVOLUTIONARIES. (ALLIED AND AMERICAN FORCES NUMBERED APPROXIMATELY 15,000 MEN, AUG.1918–JUNE,1919.)

③ AREAS IN EUROPEAN RUSSIA REMAINING UNDER THE CONTROL OF THE BOLSHEVIKI AT THE HEIGHT OF THE COUNTERREVOLUTIONARY MOVEMENTS, WINTER, 1918 AND SPRING, 1919.

④ 40,000–60,000 AUSTRIAN WAR PRISONERS (CZECHOSLOVAKS) SET FREE AFTER THE BOLSHEVIST REVOLUTION AND HEADED TO USE THESE TROOPS TO OPEN A NEW RUSSIAN FRONT AND REDUCE THE POWER OF THE FINAL GERMAN DRIVES ON THE WESTERN FRONT, SPRING AND SUMMER OF 1918.

⑤ AREAS OCCUPIED BY ALLIED AND AMERICAN TROOPS TO GUARD MILITARY STORES, TO EVACUATE THE CZECHOSLOVAKS, TO PROTECT JAPANESE CITIZENS, AND TO PRESERVE THE TERRITORIAL INTEGRITY OF RUSSIA, AUG.,1918–APRIL,1920. (BY NOV. 1918 AMERICANS NUMBERED 10,000; JAPANESE, 72,000.)

⑥ SCATTERED BOLSHEVIST CONTROL OF EASTERN AND SOUTHERN RUSSIA UNTIL OCTOBER, 1922, WHEN FULL SOVIET SOVEREIGNTY WAS ESTABLISHED.

→→→ ALLIED AND AMERICAN INTERVENTION

⟹ COUNTERREVOLUTIONARY MOVEMENTS BY WHITE RUSSIANS

tung Province than out of the Marshalls, Marianas, and Carolines. He was fighting from a position of extreme weakness, however, for Britain, France, and even China had earlier agreed that Japan should retain the former German leasehold on Kiachow Bay and former German economic interests in the Shantung Province. Supported by a rising anti-Japanese sentiment in the United States, the President pressed his fight to the verge of disrupting the conference; he gave in only at the last moment because he had no alternative. Nonetheless, American opinion was bitter, and the Japanese left the conference convinced that Wilson had tried to thwart their legitimate expansion and challenge their predominant position in the Far East.

The event that made the tension immediately dangerous was the development of a naval race among the United States, Britain, and Japan at the end of the war. The United States was, ironically, immediately most responsible. The Navy Department shelved its plans to build the great new fleet authorized by Congress in 1916 upon American entry into the war in 1917 and concentrated on construction of destroyers and anti-submarine vessels. The United States had but sixteen battleships at the end of the war, as compared with Britain's forty-two. However, the Navy Department soon after the Armistice prepared to resume construction of the ships authorized in 1916,[2] completion of which would give the United States a dreadnought and battle cruiser fleet nearly equal to Britain's. In addition, the Department presented plans to Congress in December 1918 for a second three-year building program to give the American navy definite superiority over the British fleet.

Actually, the President permitted introduction of the second three-year building program in order to increase his bargaining power with the British at the peace conference. He cheerfully abandoned it in return for British support for the League of Nations. However, the Navy Department's General Board in December 1919 presented a new one-year program for construction of two battleships, one battle cruiser, and lesser craft, completion of which would give the United States command both of the Atlantic and western Pacific. Rebuffed by Congress, the General Board returned the following year to urge a new three-year program. Although Congress rejected this latest recommendation in 1920–1, the Navy's plans for a fleet as large and powerful as the British had considerable support in the American press.

The fear of an uncontrollable upsurge of navalism in the United States alarmed British leaders as no other event had done since Germany in the 1890's set out to challenge the mistress of the seas. "Great Britain would spend her last guinea to keep a navy superior to that of the United States or any other Power," Prime Minister Lloyd George had told Colonel House; and the British government in March 1921 revealed plans to resume construction on a large scale. Japanese leaders were equally alarmed. The Diet by 1920 had authorized a construction program to give the Empire a force of twenty-five capital ships by 1927. More immediately dis-

[2] Ten dreadnoughts and six battle cruisers were authorized by the naval bill of 1916; in addition, the Navy Department had not yet completed construction of three dreadnoughts authorized in 1914 and 1915.

turbing to the Japanese than the threat of new American naval construction was the stationing by the end of 1919 of an American fleet in the Pacific nearly as powerful as the entire Japanese navy, together with development of plans by the Navy Department to enlarge naval bases in Hawaii and the Philippines and to fortify Guam.

122. *The Washington Conference*

The naval race would have gone merrily on if the naval chieftains had had their way. But they did not have their way because moderate opinion in the United States, Britain, and Japan rose against a senseless arms rivalry. In no country was this popular uprising more powerful than in the United States. The old anti-preparedness bloc in Congress revived after the Armistice and forced drastic cuts in the naval programs of 1919 and 1920. Then the anti-navy elements coalesced in the winter of 1920–1 into a strong movement for an international conference for naval disarmament. The Senate on May 25 and the House on June 29, 1921, overwhelmingly approved a resolution introduced by Senator William E. Borah of Idaho requesting the administration to begin negotiations with Britain and Japan looking toward disarmament.

Meanwhile, achievement of a naval agreement with the United States had become one of the principal objectives of the British Foreign Office. The British were as anxious as ever to maintain naval superiority, but the prospect of an arms race with the United States caused His Majesty's Government to count the costs, both financial and political, of attempting to maintain sea supremacy. Convinced that the costs were exorbitant, the British Foreign Office informed the State Department that it would make the first move for disarmament if the Washington government did not. Harding and Secretary Hughes, on the same day, July 8, 1921, that this message reached Washington, agreed that action could no longer be postponed. After preliminary overtures met with friendly responses, Hughes issued formal invitations on August 11 to Britain, Japan, China, France, Italy, Belgium, the Netherlands, and Portugal, all with interests in the Far East, to join the United States in a conference at Washington in November 1921.

Hughes next set to work to find a disarmament formula that would neither impair American security nor threaten the security of Japan and Great Britain. Rejecting the General Board's suggestion that the United States should agree to halt construction after the building program already authorized was completed, Hughes concluded that the only hope lay in persuading the powers to agree to abandon present building plans and set definite limits for capital ships based roughly upon existing strength. Hughes made these points vigorously when the conference assembled for its first session on November 12, 1921. The only way to end the naval race, he asserted, was to end it now, not sometime in the future. He then outlined a bold plan for a ten-year holiday in construction of capital ships, to be accompanied by agreement to set the maximum capital tonnage of the United States and Britain at 500,000 tons and of Japan at 300,000 tons. This could be accomplished, Hughes said, if the United States scrapped 845,740 tons, the British 583,375 tons, and the Japanese 448,928 tons of capital ships already built or under construction.

The British, American, and Japanese delegates announced agreement on all essential points on December 15, and observers concluded that Hughes's troubles were over. However, he ran into a host of difficulties when he tried to persuade the French and Italians to accept a maximum of 175,000 tons of capital ships. The French were offended by their exclusion from the three-power discussions and an offensive remark by Hughes about their inability to pay their debts. They demanded a quota of 350,000 tons of heavy ships. Only by marshaling world opinion and appealing over the heads of the French delegates to Premier Aristide Briand was Hughes able to persuade the French to agree to his proposed limit.

Thus the Five Power Naval Treaty, signed in Continental Hall on February 1, 1922, not only ended the naval armaments race in capital ships but also preserved a balance of power in the Far East that left the relative security of the great powers unimpaired. Under the Treaty the naval powers agreed to abandon capital ship construction for ten years, to follow with a few exceptions Hughes's proposal for destruction of existing tonnage, and to limit auxiliary craft to 10,000 tons and aircraft carriers to 27,000 tons.[3] In addition, Japan, the United States, and Great Britain promised not to fortify further their outlying island possessions in the western Pacific.

The Five Power Naval Treaty was the first agreement in modern history by which major powers undertook disarmament of any kind. It represented a remarkable triumph of reason over selfish nationalism, but it was not enough. The naval arms race had in large measure reflected America's quest for security in the Pacific and Japan's fear of future American encroachments. Any agreement for naval disarmament would soon prove worthless unless the causes for mutual distrust were removed and the three major powers were willing to forgo aggression in the future.

Such an understanding was achieved at Washington because Britain and the United States desired only to preserve a *status quo* that safeguarded their interests in the Far East, but above all because the existing government of Japan sought the friendship of the democracies of the West. To Americans the chief obstacle to a comprehensive understanding was the Anglo-Japanese Alliance, which obligated Britain to assume a benevolent neutrality toward Japan in the event of a Japanese-American war. Months before the Washington Conference met, when renewal of the Alliance was under consideration, Hughes had brought strong pressure upon the British Foreign Office for abrogation or modification of the treaty. The Dominion governments were even more insistent upon abrogation than was the United States.

Japan and Britain were willing to abrogate the Alliance, which had now seemingly outlived its original purpose of restraining Russian expansion in the Far East, provided they could obtain a new triple alliance that included the United States. Hughes rejected this proposal and insisted

---

[3] Each signatory, however, was permitted to convert two capital ships to aircraft carriers as large as 33,000 tons. This provision was inserted to permit the American navy to convert the battle cruisers *Lexington* and *Saratoga* into carriers.

upon bringing France into the new understanding. The outcome was the Four Power Treaty, presented to a plenary session of the conference on December 10, 1921, by Senator Henry Cabot Lodge of the American delegation. It pledged Britain, America, Japan, and France to respect each other's possessions in the Pacific area and to confer jointly if disputes among them or aggression by nonsignatories threatened the peace. The Treaty provided also that the Anglo-Japanese Alliance would be abrogated upon ratification of the Four Power pact.

The question of China's status and of Japan's intentions toward that so-called republic still remained unanswered. Under steady Anglo-American pressure the Japanese yielded their imperialistic ambitions and approved an agreement that reaffirmed the historic American policy of the Open Door and noninterference. It was the Nine Power Treaty, signed on February 6, 1922, by representatives of the United States, Britain, Japan, France, Italy, China, the Netherlands, Belgium, and Portugal. It pledged the signatories to respect the sovereignty, independence, and integrity of China; to give China full opportunity to establish a stable government; to uphold the Open Door in China; and to refrain from seeking special rights and privileges in China that would impair the rights of friendly states.

Nor was this all, though it represented the most sweeping affirmation of self-denial that Japan had yet made. Hughes meanwhile had been hard at work on the Japanese and Chinese delegates to effect a direct settlement of the Shantung question. Actually, the Japanese were more reasonable than the Chinese; and the Treaty concluded on February 4, 1922, conceded everything that Hughes had asked—restoration of full Chinese sovereignty over Shantung and the sale by Japan to China of the Shantung Railroad. Finally, as if to demonstrate their determination to liquidate all sources of potential trouble, the Japanese promised to evacuate Siberia, conceded the American demand for special cable rights on the island of Yap, and joined the United States in abrogating the Lansing-Ishii Agreement.

It became fashionable in the United States years later to condemn the Harding administration for surrendering naval supremacy and failing to obtain ironclad guarantees against future disturbers of the peace. Such criticism, however, ignores some large historical facts. First, the Five Power Naval Treaty required the United States to yield only potential naval supremacy. Actual naval supremacy could have been achieved only if the American people had been willing to maintain a long and costly arms effort. But the evidence is overwhelming that the people and Congress were not willing, for Congress refused until 1938 even to maintain the fleet at the authorized treaty strength. Second, although the absence in the Washington treaties of any enforcement machinery undoubtedly weakened them, enforcement would have involved the giving of guarantees that the Senate would never have approved. In spite of the omission of any such guarantees, the Senate, in consenting to ratification of the Four Power Treaty in March 1922, insisted upon declaring that the United States had made "no commitment to armed force, no alliance, no obligation to join in any defense."

The expressed determination of the American people to avoid a naval rivalry and even the suggestion of binding obligations to preserve the peace was a compelling historical reality to which Hughes had to yield. But by yielding he obtained for his country parity in capital ships with Great Britain and considerable supremacy over Japan under an agreement that ended the most dangerous phase of the naval race for a decade. He cleared the air of suspicion and distrust and won the abrogation of the Anglo-Japanese Alliance. Best of all, he helped to erect a new peace structure for the Far East that seemed to make it possible for Britain, the United States, and Japan to live and work together in mutual trust and respect.

123. *The Japanese-American Crisis of 1924*

Relations between Japan and the United States were unusually cordial for a short time after the Washington Conference, especially when a great earthquake in 1923 evoked an outpouring of American aid to the stricken Japanese people. Then a catastrophic event in 1924 renewed the Yellow Peril agitation in the United States and poisoned the wells of sentiment against the United States in Japan. It was the adoption by Congress of legislation specifically prohibiting Japanese immigration.

Japanese immigration to the United States had been regulated since 1907 by the Gentlemen's Agreement.[4] Although the Agreement had worked reasonably well, it ended neither Japanese immigration nor agitation on the Pacific Coast for frank and total exclusion. When the House immigration committee in 1923 began work on a permanent immigration bill to supplant the emergency measure of 1921, the AF of L, American Legion, and other organizations joined Californians in what seemed to be an overwhelming demand for statutory exclusion. News of the impending legislation prompted the Japanese Embassy to remind the Secretary of State of the dangers it would raise. In turn, Hughes urged House leaders to put Japanese immigration on the quota basis, permitting only 246 Japanese to enter a year. On the high ground of national interest he pleaded against insulting the Japanese people by an open and invidious exclusion. The House committee disregarded this solemn advice and reported a bill forbidding the immigration of persons "ineligible to citizenship"—words hateful to the Japanese.

This was the situation in March 1924, when the Secretary of State called in the Japanese Ambassador, Hanihara, and asked him to write a letter summarizing his government's attitude toward the Gentlemen's Agreement. This Hanihara did on April 10; but he warned in closing that "grave consequences" would follow enactment of the House immigration bill. Hughes read the letter before it was published and unwisely let the words "grave consequences" pass without comment. Published in the press with Hughes's approval, Hanihara's letter provoked a storm of comment. The aged Senator Lodge exclaimed that it was a "veiled threat" to the United States; he persuaded the Senate to reject an amendment tacitly extending the Gentlemen's Agreement. The senators approved the House bill

~~~~~~~~~~~~~~~~~~~~~

[4] For the negotiation and provisions of this Agreement, see above, p. 153.

71 to 4 on April 16, 1924, and Coolidge reluctantly signed it after vainly attempting to persuade the conference committee to delete the controverted provision.

It is no exaggeration to say that Congress by this action virtually nullified all the progress that Hughes and Japanese leaders had made since 1921 in restoring cordial relations between their two countries. "Our friends in the Senate have in a few minutes spoiled the work of years and done a lasting injury to our common country," Hughes wrote in disgust on April 24, 1924. Unfortunately, reaction in Japan fully justified the Secretary's gloomy observation. The day upon which the immigration law went into effect was a day of national mourning and humiliation, and millions of Japanese lived thereafter in shame and anger.

124. *The United States and the World Economy, 1919–1929*

While international political developments in the early 1920's refused to permit a reversion to isolation, the American people were projected into the arena of world affairs by still another force—the dissipation of European economic power during the war and sudden emergence of the United States as the chief source of capital for so-called backward areas and the debt-ridden countries of Europe. American citizens by 1914 had invested some $3,500,000,000 abroad but still owed to Europe a net debt of $3,-686,000,000. As a consequence of the disgorging of 70 per cent of British- and French-owned American securities between 1914 and 1919, the aggregate investment of foreigners in the United States was reduced from a little over seven to nearly four billion dollars. During the same period *private* American investments abroad increased to nearly $7,000,000,000. On December 31, 1919, therefore, foreigners owed Americans a net *private* debt of nearly three billions. In addition, European governments owed the United States $10,351,000,000 borrowed during the war and post-Armistice periods.

This fundamental shift in the world's economic balance of power demanded bold American leadership in establishing a workable system of international exchange. Unfortunately, the American leaders and people were too inexperienced to be farsighted in meeting this, the most important economic challenge of the postwar era. Instead of insisting upon mutual cancellation of all intergovernmental debts and reparations—the most disturbing factors in the postwar international economy—the United States insisted on full payment of war debts. Instead of lowering tariffs to enable Europeans to pay their private debts in goods, Congress increased tariff rates. Instead of using the resources of the federal government to stabilize European economies, administrations from Wilson to Hoover withdrew as completely as possible from making important international economic decisions and threw the burden of readjustment on private bankers.

The result was by no means international economic chaos. Private bankers constructed a new system of international exchange that worked remarkably well. But given the balance of payments situation, the new system was bound to be entirely dependent upon the maintenance of a high

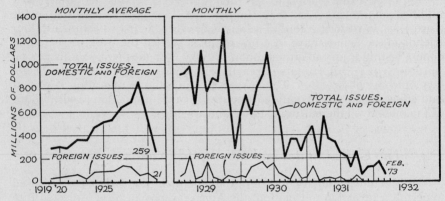

FOREIGN INVESTMENTS BY AMERICAN CITIZENS, 1919–1932

SECURITIES PUBLICLY OFFERED, EXCLUDING REFUNDING ISSUES

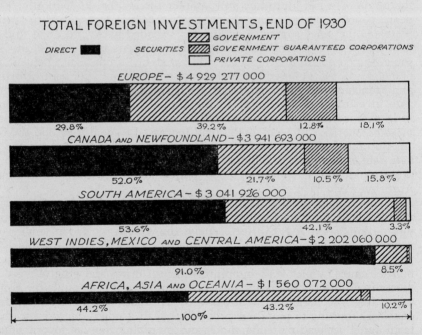

TOTAL FOREIGN INVESTMENTS, END OF 1930

level of American export of capital for successful operation. During the
1920's the United States bought raw materials and other goods on the
world market in large quantities—imports in the peak year totaled $4,-
463,000,000. On the other hand, Americans consistently sold more abroad
than they bought, the excess ranging from a low of $375,500,000 in 1923
to a high of slightly over $1,000,000,000 in 1928.

The manner in which foreigners found dollars to meet trade deficits
and pay their war debts to the United States in 1929 was typical for the

decade. The United States in that year had a "favorable" trade balance of $842,000,000 and received additionally about $800,000,000 from payments on war debts. Europeans met this aggregate deficit of $1,642,000,-000 in a variety of ways—by the expenditure of $500,000,000 by American tourists abroad, the remittance of $200,000,000 to Europe by immigrants in the United States, and by dollar earnings from the carrying trade, foreign investments in the United States, and the like. The remaining deficit was supplied by American investments abroad of $1,037,000,000. Thus foreign bankers and merchants actually accumulated a surplus of $508,-000,000 in 1929. And so it went throughout the 1920's. By the annual export of about $1,000,000,000 between 1919 and 1930 American bankers and businessmen supported the huge volume of American foreign trade and the world economy as well. The fatal weakness of the system was that its maintenance depended upon a continuing flow of American dollars in

INTERNATIONAL PAYMENTS OF THE UNITED STATES, 1927

PRINCIPAL CONSTITUENTS

VISIBLE ITEMS	SERVICES	SECURITIES TRANSACTIONS
MERCHANDISE	COMMERCIAL	INTEREST AND CURRENT ITEMS
GOLD	PERSONAL	CAPITAL MOVEMENT

EXPORTS AND OTHER CREDITS, $9 115 000 000

PER CENT   55.2   4.3 3.7 3.7   11.8   21.3

IMPORTS AND OTHER DEBITS, $9 121 000 000

PER CENT   49.2   2.5 3.3 12.5 3.1   29.4

the form of purchases and investments abroad. As long as the system lasted, however, it seemed to work admirably and well.

125. *American International Economic Policy, 1919–1930*

The Harding, Coolidge, and Hoover administrations followed the policy begun by the Wilson administration of withdrawing the federal government from the realm of international economic activity. At the same time, the State and Commerce departments worked vigorously and often successfully to protect economic interests abroad and to expand the frontiers of American foreign trade and investments. One notable victory was the Nine Power Treaty, which for a time preserved an area of freedom for American merchants and capitalists in China. Another was the State Department's effort to prevent confiscation of American mining and oil properties in Mexico by the government of that country. More important, perhaps, was Secretary Hughes's fight to break the monopoly over Middle Eastern oil reserves that the British, French, and Dutch governments had established at the end of the World War. Seven American oil companies were given a quarter share in the future exploitation of oil in Iraq in 1925 as a result of Hughes's intervention. In all these and other economic aspects of diplomacy the State Department continued the well-established policy of opposing special concessions and exclusive rights for Americans and insisting only upon equal commercial opportunity abroad.

The most perplexing international economic issues of the 1920's were war debts and reparations, and the stubborn refusal of American leaders to work out an enlightened solution disturbed the economies of Europe and engendered antagonisms that persisted until the Second World War. The United States lent the Allied governments a little over $7,000,-000,000 during the war and an additional $3,250,000,000 in cash and supplies during the months immediately after the Armistice. But this was only one aspect of the complicated structure of intergovernmental debts. The British, for example, had lent more than $4,000,000,000 to seventeen creditor nations; the French had lent to ten nations.

Allied leaders began a concerted campaign at the end of the war for cancellation of all intergovernmental debts as the first step in restoring a healthy international economy. As for Allied war debts to the United States, Europeans pointed out that practically every dollar borrowed had been spent in America for food and munitions; that Europeans had contributed their sons and Americans their money in a common cause; and that, in any event, American tariff and shipping policies prevented Europeans from paying these war debts in goods and services, the only kind of payment they could offer.

In retrospect, these arguments seem realistic, reasonable, and morally sound. To Americans of the 1920's and 1930's, however, they represented a shocking attempt to escape a just debt. When the British at Versailles suggested either mutual cancellation of intergovernmental debts or else a linking of reparation and war debt payments, Wilson replied coldly. His insistence upon full payment without any reference to reparations receipts established a policy to which all administrations from Harding to Franklin D. Roosevelt adhered.

Congress established a World War Foreign Debt Commission in February 1922 to negotiate long-term funding agreements with the European debtors. The British, with their reputation for financial integrity at stake, agreed in June 1923 to pay $4,600,000,000 in principal and accrued interest over a sixty-two-year period at 3 per cent for the first decade and 3½ per cent thereafter. The French and Italians, however, at first refused to acknowledge either the moral or financial validity of their indebtedness to the United States. The State Department retaliated by imposing a ban on all private loans to citizens and governments in default; and the French and Italians finally surrendered under this pressure in 1925 and 1926.[5] In the same manner the smaller nations of Europe were brought to terms.

---

[5] The Italians reached agreement with the War Debt Commission in November 1925. The Italian debt was funded at $2,042,000,000, at two fifths of 1 per cent interest, to be paid in installments over a sixty-two-year period. The French acknowledged an indebtedness of $4,025,000,000, at an average interest rate of 1.64 per cent, to be paid over a sixty-two-year period. The French Chamber of Deputies did not ratify this agreement until July 1929.

Thus did the United States bludgeon Europeans into obligating themselves for a debt that they could never possibly pay from their own resources through normal channels of exchange. In the end a solution was found, but not before the American government had intervened decisively though unofficially to help settle the most perplexing issue of all—Germany's reparations payments, upon which the entire structure of intergovernmental payments was based. Let us review briefly the background of this story.

The Reparations Commission on May 1, 1921, presented to the German Republic a reparations bill of $33,000,000,000, in addition to the total Belgian war debt and the costs of the armies of occupation. The German government was forced at the point of a gun to accept responsibility for this sum; it tried to make payments but had to default in 1922. The French retaliated by occupying the Ruhr, the center of German industry and coal mining. Thereupon the Germans inaugurated a program of passive resistance that soon resulted in a spectacular inflation of the German currency. The German government was bankrupt by the end of 1923, and the Reich tottered on the brink of total economic ruin. Alarmed by the prospect of chaos in central Europe, Secretary Hughes intervened to find a way out of the impasse. With British support he negotiated patiently with the French government and persuaded the Reparations Commission to attempt to work out a plan of reparations payments based upon Germany's capacity to pay.

The upshot was the appointment by the Reparations Commission in November 1923 of a committee upon which two Americans, Charles G. Dawes and Owen D. Young, served unofficially. This, the so-called Dawes Committee, submitted a plan in April 1924 that saved Europe from financial collapse. It provided elaborate financial machinery to collect and distribute reparations payments, established a schedule of payments that Germany could bear, and arranged for a gold loan of $200,000,000 by American bankers to the German government to stabilize the German currency on a gold standard. A new committee of experts, headed by Owen D. Young, re-examined the reparations question in 1929, set the total bill at a little more than $2,000,000,000 exclusive of interest, and provided for an end of payments by 1988.

The significant point of this somewhat complicated story is the manner in which the American government and private bankers participated to help establish a system of intergovernmental debt and reparations payments that worked so long as the dynamic factor in the system continued to operate. That dynamic factor was private American loans to the central government, states, municipalities, and corporations of Germany totaling some $2,500,000,000 from 1924 to 1930. During the same period Germany made reparations payments under the Dawes Plan totaling nearly $2,000,-000,000, while the former Allies in turn paid to the United States $2,606,-000,000 on their war debt accounts, or about the same amount that American bankers had lent to Germany. Thus, in spite of the refusal of the State Department ever to admit the fact, payment of war debts under this complicated structure became contingent upon the payment of reparations by Germany. They in turn depended upon the flow of dollars from the United States.

126. *The Further Search for Peace, 1924–1930*

Peace was the prevailing passion of the American people in foreign affairs in the 1920's. A small but influential minority of public leaders continued to agitate for entrance into the League of Nations, but probably a majority preferred to advance the cause through less entangling means —disarmament, membership in the World Court, co-operation with the League, treaties outlawing war, and the like. After the Washington Conference the popular obsession with peace continued unabated, while events in Europe—the settlement of the reparations imbroglio, the Locarno treaties of 1925, and Germany's admission to the League in 1926— raised bright hopes for the future. But the American peace sentiment was conceived in naïveté concerning European affairs and born of a romantic delusion as to the manner in which the United States could best serve mankind. Americans wanted peace, to be sure, but they were unwilling to assume obligations to enforce an international system. Moreover, as the Immigration Act of 1924 revealed, Americans were not yet ready to forgo nationalistic prejudices that impaired international friendship. It is against this background climate of opinion that we must consider the further search for peace without obligations.

One significant manifestation of this search was the campaign for American membership in the World Court waged by Presidents and Secretaries of State from Harding and Hughes to Roosevelt and Cordell Hull. It was a project upon which both advanced and cautious internationalists could agree, for the Permanent Court of International Justice was an agency apart from the League, and membership did not involve any obligation to help enforce the court's decisions. Hughes won Harding's approval for membership in February 1923 and began a campaign to stimulate public discussion. Sentiment was so aroused by the summer of 1924 that both major parties endorsed membership, and the House of Representatives adopted a resolution approving a membership protocol in March 1925. Bitter-end isolationists like Senator Borah failed to prevent passage of the resolution by the Senate on January 27, 1926, but they forced adoption of a reservation restricting the right of the court to render advisory opinions. When the member nations refused to accept the reservation, Presidents Hoover and Roosevelt, in 1930 and 1935,[6] again vainly urged membership in the court. Meanwhile, a number of distinguished Americans, including Charles Evans Hughes, John Bassett Moore, and Frank B. Kellogg, had served as judges on the tribunal.

A second manifestation of the American search for peace in the 1920's was the gradual change in official policy toward the League of Nations. The State Department during the early months of the Harding ad-

wwwwwwwwwwwwww

[6] Isolationists made an especially bitter campaign against American membership in the World Court in 1934-5. In spite of an outpouring of public support, the Roosevelt administration was unable to muster a two-thirds majority when the Senate, by a vote of fifty-two yeas to thirty-six nays, refused to approve a membership protocol on January 29, 1935.

ministration had not only refused to co-operate with the League's non-political agencies but had also failed, either accidentally or deliberately, even to acknowledge communications from the League's Secretariat. Evidence indicates that Hughes was trying to avoid giving offense to Senate isolationists while devising a means by which the United States might co-operate with the League's humanitarian endeavors.

In any event, the Secretary of State launched a new policy of co-operation in the spring and summer of 1922 by sending "unofficial observers" to speak for the United States in various League agencies and commissions. This policy developed rapidly, and the American government co-operated in conferences to control the traffic in arms, women, and opium, in the work of the Reparations Commission, in the League Health Organization, and in the International Labor Organization. Senator Borah and other irreconcilables charged that the Harding, Coolidge, and Hoover administrations were taking America into the League through the back door. In a sense the charge was justified, for the United States by 1930 had participated in some forty League conferences and had five permanent representatives stationed at Geneva, Switzerland, headquarters of the League. Even more important, the State Department had constructed machinery for co-operation with the League Council in any crisis menacing the peace of the world.

Even so, there were few indications by the late twenties that the American people were willing to undertake responsibilities for preserving the peace in times of crisis. This fact was vividly revealed by the peculiar American peace movement that culminated in the signing of the Kellogg-Briand Pact in 1928. American peace organizations voiced the passion for peace during the early twenties but could not agree on the most crucial issue, American membership in the League of Nations. It fell to Salmon O. Levinson, a Chicagoan interested in the peace cause, to devise a program upon which all the disparate and sometimes warring peace elements could unite—a program to outlaw war as an instrument of national policy. Levinson's crusade, begun in 1921, became somewhat formidable when he won the support of Nicholas Murray Butler and James T. Shotwell, two officials of the Carnegie Endowment for International Peace.

Shotwell visited the French Foreign Minister, Aristide Briand, in Paris in March 1927 and suggested that the French government could best allay American fears of French militarism by taking leadership in the movement to outlaw war. Perceiving an opportunity to draw the United States and France together in a sympathetic alliance, Briand on April 6, 1927, addressed an open letter to the American people, proposing that the two countries join hands in a pact forever outlawing war between them. Briand's message went virtually unnoticed in the American press until Butler called attention to it in a letter published in the *New York Times* on April 25. At once the various peace organizations and Senator Borah took up the hue and cry for a peace pact.

Secretary of State Frank B. Kellogg, who had succeeded Hughes in March 1925, had little more than contempt for the "fools" and "pacifists" leading the outlawry movement. He planned at first to ignore Briand's appeal. Then on May 21, 1927, the young American flier Charles A. Lindbergh landed his *Spirit of St. Louis* outside Paris after making the first nonstop solo flight from New York. Lindbergh's feat provoked such a demonstration of Franco-American friendship and so stimulated the peace forces in America that the administration had to capitulate. Unwilling to sign a bilateral pact with France, which they regarded as a negative military alliance,[7] Coolidge and Kellogg suggested on December 28, 1927, that France and the United States invite other powers to join them in a treaty renouncing war as an instrument of national policy. It was not altruism that motivated the explosive Secretary of State; it was a desire to appease the American peace forces who, Kellogg thought, had been playing Briand's game.

Kellogg's counterthrust came as an alarming move to Briand, who well knew that France's security rested upon her willingness to go to war to preserve her dominant position in Europe. Negotiations went smoothly, however, once the State Department made it clear that the proposed pact should outlaw only aggressive war and not legitimate defensive efforts. Representatives of all the great powers except Russia, which later ratified, signed the Pact of Paris in the French capital on August 27, 1928. "The High Contracting Parties," it read, "solemnly declare in the names of their respective people that they condemn recourse to war for the solution of international controversies, and renounce it as an instrument of national policy in their relations with one another."

Although idealists romanticized the significance of the Pact of Paris and cynics sneered at what they called an "international kiss," its negotiation constituted another milestone along the road away from isolation for the American people. To be sure, the Treaty established no enforcement machinery and would be only as effective as the signatories made it. But it was not meaningless. For one thing, by outlawing aggressive war it changed international law in an important way. For another, it brought the United States, however tenuously, into the peace system established by the Treaty of Versailles and the Locarno treaties. While the American government assumed no legal obligations under the Pact of Paris to defend that peace system, it did assume large moral obligations to co-operate with the League in the event that some aggressor violated the Pact. As Briand wisely observed, the Pact was "a beginning, not an end."

127.   Continued Efforts at Naval Disarmament

The Five Power Treaty of 1922 ended the rivalry in the construction of battleships and aircraft carriers; and for a short time after the Washington Conference it seemed that the signatory powers would also refrain from expanding their fleets of cruisers, destroyers, and submarines. However, Great Britain launched a new construction program in 1924 by laying keels for five heavy cruisers of 10,000 tons each. The following year she adopted a program for building nine 10,000-ton and seven 8,000-ton cruisers. The Japanese countered by beginning work on four heavy cruis-

---

[7] In other words, an alliance requiring the United States to remain neutral in the event that France had to go to war under her far-flung military alliance system.

ers, while the American Congress in December 1924 authorized the President to undertake, prior to July 1, 1927, construction of eight 10,000-ton cruisers. Obviously, the major naval powers stood by 1927 on the verge of another costly naval race that threatened to upset the fine balance established so auspiciously at Washington.

In response to urgings by the House of Representatives and peac organizations in the United States, President Coolidge issued a hasty call on February 10, 1927, for a five-power naval disarmament conference to meet at Geneva that same year. Alleging that they preferred to work for general disarmament through the League, the French refused to attend; and French refusal gave the Italians good excuse for staying away. Thus only the three major naval powers sent delegates to the conference that met at Geneva from June 20 to August 4, 1927. Negotiations went badly from the outset because the State Department had made no diplomatic preparations for the meeting. The British were willing to accept parity in heavy cruiser tonnage with the United States. But the two delegations were never able to agree upon the limitation of light cruisers, and the conference broke up in complete disagreement.

Public opinion in the United States and Britain refused to accept the Geneva failure as final, despite the passage by Congress in February 1929 of a second and larger cruiser bill. The coming to power of the Hoover administration in the United States and the Labour Cabinet under Ramsay MacDonald in Great Britain in 1929 raised new hopes of Anglo-American accord, as MacDonald and the new American Ambassador, Charles G. Dawes, set to work to prepare the way for understanding. By July 26, 1929, the two governments had agreed on equality in combat strength, to be determined in all categories of fighting ships.

Only minor details remained for discussion, therefore, when Hoover invited MacDonald to visit the United States for final talks preparatory to calling a new five-power naval conference. The two men met at the President's fishing camp at Rapidan, Virginia, and agreed to end "all competitive building"; and the Prime Minister, speaking before the Senate on October 7, ended all doubts about British willingness to go all the way. On that same day the British government invited the other four naval powers to send delegates to a conference in London the following year.

It opened on January 21, 1930. The American, British, and Japanese representatives readily agreed to extend the construction "holiday" on capital ships for five years and to scrap a total of nine battleships. However, Japanese insistence upon greater cruiser strength than the 10:10:6 ratio would allow threatened for a time to disrupt negotiations. In the end the Japanese accepted a compromise by which they obtained a 10:10:6 ratio for heavy cruisers, a 10:10:7 ratio for light cruisers and destroyers, and equality in submarines. In addition, the delegates fixed a definite tonnage quota based upon these ratios for cruisers, destroyers, and submarines.[8]

\wwwwwwwwwwwww

[8] Under this quota the United States was awarded 325,000 tons of cruisers, 150,000 tons of destroyers, and 52,700 tons of submarines; Great Britain, 339,000 tons of cruisers, 150,000 tons of destroyers, and 52,700 tons of submarines; Japan, 208,850 tons of cruisers, 105,500 tons of destroyers, and 52,700 tons of submarines.

It was not all harmony and good feeling. The French, worried as to what parity with Italy would mean locally in the Mediterranean, refused to accept any limitation unaccompanied by an Anglo-American guarantee of security. When President Hoover flatly refused to make any such commitment, the French—and the Italians also—refused to approve the important provisions of the naval treaty completed on April 22, 1930. Consequently, the British insisted upon insertion of a so-called escalator clause permitting the signatories to expand their fleets if their national security should be threatened by the naval construction of some outside power.

Coming at the end of a decade of popular agitation, the London Treaty was a striking victory for the peace movement [9] and further evidence of the determination of the British and American peoples to live in close friendship. As President Hoover declared in 1930, the alternative to naval agreement was mutual "suspicion, hate, ill-will and ultimate disaster." The British, American, and Japanese governments chose mutual trust instead, at least for a moment, in this, the last successful effort to preserve the peace system of the postwar era.

128. *Toward a New Latin American Policy*

Relations between the United States and Latin America were at probably their bitterest point in hemispheric history when Harding took office in 1921. American troops stationed in Nicaragua were sustaining a minority government in that country. American naval commanders were running the governments of the Dominican Republic and Haiti. And the State Department and the government of Mexico headed by Álvaro Obregón were not even on speaking terms.

It is ironic that Republican administrations of the 1920's, allegedly the special protectors of American investors, should have reversed Wilsonian interventionism and set in motion liquidation of a good part of the American imperium in the Caribbean area. For this phenomenon a number of factors were responsible. First and most important was the elimination of every threat to American security in the approaches to the Panama Canal. This meant that the American government could afford to be more relaxed about revolutions and debt repudiations after 1920. A second factor was the accidental injection of Latin American policy as an issue in the campaign of 1920, when Franklin D. Roosevelt, Democratic vice presidential candidate, indiscreetly boasted that the United States would control twelve Latin American votes in the League Assembly and inaccurately bragged that he had written the Haitian constitution. This provoked Harding to give a sweeping pledge of nonintervention toward Caribbean republics.

A third and certainly not unimportant factor was the character and attitude of the new Secretary of State in 1921, Charles Evans Hughes. He viewed with abhorrence the Wilsonian assumption that Americans knew

wwwwwwwwwwwwww

[9] We should note one other important article of the Treaty—Part IV, which outlawed unrestricted submarine warfare against merchant shipping and which France and Italy, as well as the three great naval powers, approved.

more about the good government of neighboring countries than leaders of those countries knew, and he determined to withdraw American power as fast as circumstances would permit. The new Secretary was also fortunate in finding an able young career diplomat, Sumner Welles, at the Latin American desk in 1921. Welles left the Department in the following year but returned on several occasions to help implement the policy of withdrawal.

The first testing ground of the new policy was the Dominican Republic. Convinced that Dominicans were ready to resume self-government, Hughes superintended the holding of elections and the formation of a native government from 1922 to 1924. After the inauguration of President Horatio Vásquez on July 12, 1924, the American occupation forces were gradually withdrawn; and, except for the American customs receivership, Dominicans were once again masters in their own house. Planning to restore self-government also to the Haitians, the Secretary sent a special commissioner to the black republic in 1922 to work with local leaders. When the commissioner warned that renewed anarchy would follow American withdrawal, and a special Senate committee confirmed his findings, Hughes had to postpone the day of liberation.

Nicaragua, however, seemed at last ready to stand on its own; and Hughes withdrew the United States marine guard at Managua in August 1925, after the Liberal, Carlos Solórzano, won the presidency in 1924. Immediately afterward, the Conservative leader, Emiliano Chamorro, forced Solórzano out of office and installed himself in the presidential palace. When the United States withheld recognition, the Nicaraguan Congress, in October 1926, elected Adolfo Díaz, another Conservative and long-time friend of the United States, to the presidency. Secretary of State Kellogg unwisely accorded immediate recognition.

At this point the exiled Liberal Vice President, Juan B. Sacasa, returned to Nicaragua and raised a general revolt against the Díaz government. In response to frenzied appeals from Díaz, President Coolidge dispatched some 5,000 marines to suppress the uprising early in 1927. The President's action evoked a storm of protest in the United States; and Coolidge sent Henry L. Stimson to Nicaragua to mediate. Stimson by tact and patience persuaded the Liberals to give up the fight. In return, Stimson guaranteed a fair presidential election—under American military supervision—and compelled Díaz to admit Liberals to his Cabinet.

The result of Stimson's mediation became apparent when the Liberals, General Moncado and Sacasa, were elected to the presidency in 1928 and 1932. The United States had used military force from 1909 to 1927 to keep unpopular but pro-American Conservative governments in power, in defiance of the wishes of a large majority of Nicaraguans. When Stimson offered impartiality in return for the co-operation of the Liberals, he was in effect reversing the historic policy of the State Department. American troops remained in Nicaragua to help the government suppress the bandit leader, Augusto Sandino, and were gradually withdrawn from 1931 to 1933.

Setting the withdrawal from the Dominican Republic, Haiti, and Nicaragua in motion was easy as compared with the task of re-establishing Mexican-American relations on a friendly basis. The high tension between the two countries provoked by Wilson's interventions was increased during the war by American charges that Mexico was a hotbed of German espio‑ nage, and especially by Carranza's decree of February 19, 1918, applying Article XXVII of the Mexican Constitution of 1917. This highly contro‑ verted provision vested ownership in the Mexican people of all subsoil rights to oil and mineral properties acquired by foreigners before 1917 and, moreover, required foreign owners of such properties to obtain new concessions from the revolutionary government. Vigorous protests from the United States and Great Britain forced Carranza to postpone operation of the decree.

A revolution led by General Álvaro Obregón deposed Carranza and put Obregón and a less anti-American group in power in Mexico City in April 1920. The Wilson administration refused recognition because Obregón would not promise to respect American holdings in Mexico, and diplo‑ matic relations were thus in a ruptured state when Hughes assumed of‑ fice. By firm but cordial dealing, Hughes won all his demands [10] and recog‑ nized the Obregón regime in 1923. The accession to the presidency in 1924 of Plutarcho Elias Calles, however, brought a more radical wing of the revolutionary party to power, and relations between Mexico and the United States suddenly worsened. Calles threatened to overturn the Mexican‑ American agreement of 1923 by requiring American owners of oil lands to exchange their titles for fifty-year leases. He also launched a bloody cam‑ paign against the Catholic Church that greatly inflamed Catholic opinion in the United States.

Relations were brought to a crisis point early in 1927 when Secretary of State Kellogg foolishly charged that the Calles government was working with Russian agents to establish a "Mexican-fostered Bolshevik hegemony intervening between the United States and the Panama Canal." Although Kellogg's sensational charge stimulated a serious war scare, the State Department was actually then preparing a new campaign to win Mexican friendship. President Coolidge inaugurated this campaign in September 1927 by sending Dwight Morrow, a partner of Morgan & Company and a man of extraordinary tact and ability, as Ambassador to Mexico City. By offering genuine friendship, Morrow won the affection of the Mexican people. By his shrewd handling of Calles, he also won a compromise settle‑ ment of the oil lands dispute, a surcease of the anticlerical campaign, and a new Mexican-American accord.

Republican leaders not only retreated from empire in the Caribbean area but also set in motion repudiation of the Roosevelt Corollary to the Monroe Doctrine, which Theodore Roosevelt had devised in 1904 to justify a policy of intervention (see above, pp. 149–151). Hughes began the rever‑ sal in 1923 by attempting to explain to the American people that the Mon‑ roe Doctrine was exclusively a policy of self-defense. It neither infringed the independence of any American state, he said, nor warranted interfer‑

---

[10] They were compensation for or return of American-owned land seized by the revolutionary government before May 1, 1917; validation of the title to mineral and oil properties owned by Americans in Mexico before 1917; and the establishment of a joint commission to consider claims of American losses suffered during the Revolution.

ence by the United States in the affairs of neighboring countries.[11] That such interpretation did not imply American abandonment of the alleged right to intervene, however, was dramatically revealed at the Pan-American Conference at Havana in January 1928. There Hughes, as head of the American delegation, stubbornly refused to yield to overwhelming Latin American demand that his country give an unequivocal pledge of nonintervention.

Even so, there were numerous signs from 1928 to 1933 that the United States could not long maintain its traditional position in face of a growing Latin American demand. President-elect Hoover made a good will tour of Latin America in early 1929; a short time later he promised never to intervene to protect American property rights abroad. He courageously honored this promise, even when the depression set off a wave of revolutions and debt repudiations throughout Latin America. It was little wonder, therefore, that relations between the United States and Latin America were on a more cordial basis when Hoover left office than they had been at any time since 1901. The Good Neighbor policy of the Franklin Roosevelt administration was possible only because preceding Republican administrations had laid the groundwork in theory and practice for the American retreat from dominion through force.

[11] This position was later affirmed by the State Department in a *Memorandum on the Monroe Doctrine*, prepared by J. Reuben Clark in 1928 and published in 1930. The *Memorandum* did not renounce the alleged right of the United States to intervene but pointed out that such intervention could not be justified by the Monroe Doctrine.

CHAPTER

17

Hoover and
the Great Depression

1929–1932

THE GREAT DEPRESSION brought an end to a long era of economic expansion and social progress since the 1890's. There had been momentary recessions in 1907, 1913, and 1921, to be sure; but these reversals had never been severe enough or long enough to shake the deeply rooted popular confidence in the American economic system or generate any comprehensive national discontent.

It would be inaccurate to say that the depression that began in 1929 destroyed the faith of the American people in the essential worth of the capitalistic system or the enduring value of democratic institutions. However, the Great Depression caused widespread suffering and profound discontent among all classes in all sections, and this in turn revived the American progressive movement in full strength. Thus the chief consequence of the Great Depression was not the havoc that it wrought for a decade. It was, rather, the impetus that it gave for completion of the metamorphosis in popular attitudes regarding the role of government in the economy that had been in progress for nearly half a century.

The depression not only caused deflation at home but also stimulated the withdrawal of American capital from abroad, and this culminated in the collapse of the international economy in 1931. In this chapter we will attempt to tell why and how this happened, and why political leadership seemed incapable of overcoming this most serious international crisis since the First World War.

129. *The Election of 1928*

As we have seen, the conflicts over the Klan, race and religion, and prohibition so rent the Democrats that they ceased to be an effective opposition from 1924 to 1928. That these same tensions would weaken the Democracy during the campaign of 1928 became apparent long before the national convention met in Houston, Texas, on June 26, 1928. Governor Alfred E. Smith of New York had emerged as the only Democrat of presidential stature and had won most of the non-southern states during the preconvention campaign of 1928. But he had failed utterly to win any popular support in the South on account of his Roman Catholicism, Tammany connections, and avowed opposition to prohibition. Indeed, all signs pointed to a southern rebellion of large proportions if the northern and western majority insisted upon nominating the New York governor and standing for repeal of the Eighteenth Amendment.

After praying, drinking, and struggling in the Houston convention, Southerners concurred in Smith's nomination only after the northern managers had agreed to yield their demand for a platform plank favoring repeal of the controverted Amendment. Without this concession, the southern politicians warned, they could not hold their constituents in the party. Ignoring these warnings, Smith notified the convention that although he would enforce the prohibition laws if elected, he also reserved the right to advocate and work for repeal of the Volstead Act and perhaps also of the Eighteenth Amendment.

Meanwhile, the Republicans had met at Kansas City on June 12 and nominated Secretary of Commerce Herbert Hoover, the most distinguished representative of the business leadership of the Harding-Coolidge administrations and a pre-eminent champion of individualism and regulated and orderly private enterprise. During the ensuing campaign Hoover reiterated his frank opposition to all advanced progressive proposals like pegging of agricultural prices, public power projects, and special-interest legislation in organized labor's behalf. Time and again, also, he reiterated his conviction that only a continuation of the Harding-Coolidge policies could make prosperity permanent. "We in America today are nearer to the final triumph over poverty than ever before in the history of any land," he exclaimed in his acceptance speech. "The poorhouse is vanishing from among us. We have not yet reached the goal, but, given a chance to go forward with the policies of the last eight years, we shall soon, with the help of God, be in sight of the day when poverty will be banished from this nation."

Smith had a moderately progressive platform upon which to campaign [1] and a distinguished record as a champion of civil rights and social

[1] The Democratic platform promised farm relief without specifying details, approved collective bargaining and an anti-injunction act, demanded strict control of hydroelectric power, and promised immediate independence to the Philippines. It did not

legislation. But progressives who expected him to revive and rally their scattered forces must have been badly disappointed. He advocated federal operation of Muscle Shoals and development of power projects in the West and accepted the principle of the McNary-Haugen plan. But otherwise Smith's campaign was thoroughly conservative in tone. He discussed almost exclusively the evils of prohibition and religious bigotry, while his peripheral remarks were aimed at convincing voters that a Democratic victory would not endanger prosperity. For chairman of the Democratic National Committee, Smith chose John J. Raskob, a prominent Catholic layman, chairman of the finance committee of General Motors, and an official of other corporations and banks. Only a year before he had given his party affiliation as Republican and his occupation as "capitalist." Moving Democratic headquarters to the General Motors Building in New York City, Raskob boasted proudly whenever a banker or corporation official came out in support of Smith.

Smith campaigned gallantly, but his obstacles were nearly insuperable. His attacks on prohibition cost more votes in the South and Middle West than they gained in the East. The fact that he was a devout Roman Catholic stirred bigots and Protestant leaders who feared the aggrandizement of Catholic power. Republicans and Hoover Democrats in the South blamed the New Yorker for all the misdeeds of Tammany Hall. Social snobs whispered that Smith and his wife would not grace the White House because they had risen from New York City's Lower East Side.

This invocation of religious bigotry and social snobbishness and the charge that Smith would restore saloons and debauch American youth had a powerful appeal all over the country. But the campaign to defeat the Democratic nominee assumed the proportions of a religious crusade in the South. Throughout that region Protestant clergy and laity were up in arms, chiefly because of Smith's opposition to the Eighteenth Amendment. This is not to say that Catholicism was not a campaign issue in the region. Catholicism was a powerful issue, but it was used more by the Republican managers and the remnant of the Klan than by Bishop James Cannon, Jr., of the Methodist Episcopal Church, South, who formally organized southern opposition to Smith.

Cannon's organization broke the Solid South and carried Virginia, North Carolina, Tennessee, Florida, Kentucky, Oklahoma, and Texas for Hoover. Even so, the results of the election would not have been measurably different had Smith been a Baptist deacon and a stanch supporter of the Eighteenth Amendment. Outside the South, Smith carried only Massachusetts and Rhode Island. His combined popular vote was 15,016,443, as compared with Hoover's 21,392,190. Yet there were signs of things to come in the election returns of 1928. For one thing, Smith carried the twelve largest cities—in contrast to Cox's and Davis's failure in the metropolitan areas in 1920 and 1924—and ran impressively in all counties in which Catholics and recent immigrants were significant elements. Sec-

vvvvvvvvvvvvvvvvvvvvvvvvvvvvvvvvvvvvvvvvvvvvvvvvvvvvvvvvvvvvvvvvvvvvvvvvvvvvvvvvvvvvvvvvvvvvvvvvvvvvvvvvvvvvvvvvvvvvv

mention the League of Nations or demand drastic tariff reductions. The Republican platform approved prohibition and the protective tariff and promised sane farm relief without artificial price supports.

ondly, Smith ran far better in the midwestern farm states, particularly in the wheat belt, than any Democrat had done since the election of 1916. Whether these new currents would produce a tide, only the future could reveal.

The truth was that the prevailing prosperity, more than the liquor and religious issues, was the decisive factor in the election. There was still acute unrest in the farm areas, especially in the western Middle West. In Minnesota, Nebraska, North Dakota, Wisconsin, and Washington insurgent Republicans, who violently opposed the conservative leadership of their party, were elected by large majorities. These were signs for the future, to be sure; but a large majority of Americans in the autumn of 1928 apparently desired only continuation of the leadership and policies that had seemingly accomplished economic stability and offered the promise of even better times ahead.

130. *Underlying Causes of the Depression*

The American people in November 1928 almost self-consciously reveled in the prospects of the economic millennium that lay just around the corner. The campaign had been scurrilous and unpleasant; but it had been a passing if necessary episode in the march of the people toward their economic destiny. As the year 1929 opened, all seemed well with the Republic: the government was in safe hands, and a great engineer, pledged to abolish poverty and carry on policies that had made America prosperous, would soon occupy the White House. Except for a speculative boom in Wall Street, there were few obvious signs of impending disaster. And yet more discerning eyes could see subtle signs of weakness in the economy, apart from the dangerous stock market boom. In themselves these weaknesses did not set off the depression. But once the stock market collapse destroyed business confidence and caused huge withdrawals of capital, the subsidiary economic strains combined to prolong and intensify the severity of the depression.

The first and perhaps the most important maladjustment of the 1920's was the unstable nature of the international economy, stemming from a complex of difficulties reviewed in an earlier chapter. (See above, pp. 347–351.) The outpouring of American dollars helped western Europe to meet its trade deficits and war debt and reparations obligations; and Europe's recovery from 1925 to 1930 in turn stimulated American prosperity. But the fundamental weakness of the new international exchange system—Europe's financial dependence upon the United States—proved fatal when the wellsprings of American credit dried up.

In the second place, the long depression in agriculture that began in 1920 impoverished American farmers and caused them to operate at a net capital loss during most of the decade. (See above, p. 326.) The effects of this agricultural depression were everywhere apparent—in the decline in farm incomes, values, and purchasing power, and in the failure of thousands of country banks. Even conservative Republican leaders admitted that the situation could not long continue without impoverishing the nation. Farmers dragged the rest of the nation with them in their decline when nothing really effective was done after 1929 to halt the downward plunge of farm prices.

A third maladjustment was the lack of any proper balance between private and public control of financial institutions and practices. The fundamental weakness here was a rigid gold standard that tied the government's hands in controlling the money supply. Moreover, the Federal Reserve Board, perhaps because of statutory ambiguities, had not emerged with really decisive authority in the banking world. Finally, there were no state or federal agencies with power to prevent the stock market excesses and malpractices that abetted speculation.

In other ways, too, the American political economy was badly out of joint by 1929. Large segments of American industry were concentrated and bureaucratized and able to maintain wages and prices at artificially high levels for a time after the depression began. Abnormally high industrial profits and a federal tax policy that favored the rich also aggravated an unequal distribution of incomes that gave 26 per cent of the national income to the top 5 per cent of income receivers in 1929. (See above, pp. 256–257.) These internal maladjustments were beginning to impair the health of the economic system at least two years before the stock market crash occurred. Even so, the development that threw the financial machinery out of gear and set off the cumulative forces of dissolution was the stock market boom that ended in the crash of October 1929.

131. *The Wild Bull Market: Boom and Bust*

The speculative craze that seized a large minority of the American people in 1927 was by any reckoning one of the most remarkable developments in the nation's history. It seemed as if the mania for quick profits had infected everyone from bank presidents to street-corner grocers and school teachers.

One of the most startling aspects of the wild bull market was the suddenness with which it developed. In response to increased business activity and rising profits, trading on the New York Stock Exchange increased from 236,000,000 shares in 1923 to 451,000,000 in 1926, while the average price of twenty-five representative industrial stocks rose from $108 to $166 a share, or about 54 per cent. This forward movement represented only the normal response of the market to higher earnings in industry. Then a tremendous upward surge of the market began in 1927. Brokers' loans—that is, loans with stock for collateral—increased from a little over $3,000,000,000 in January 1927 to nearly $4,500,000,000 by the end of December. The volume of shares traded on the New York Stock Exchange rose from 451,000,000 in 1926 to 577,000,000 in 1927.

Obviously, a boom was developing; and conservative bankers, sensing a disastrous inflation of stock prices, urged caution. During the early weeks of 1928 it seemed briefly that the market might break. Instead, it held firm when Treasury officials and President Coolidge declared that the volume of brokers' loans was not too great, and that the country had never been more soundly prosperous. Thus reassured, a group of the largest operators on the Stock Exchange, on March 3, 1928, opened a gigantic buying campaign in

CH. 17: *Hoover and the Great Depression, 1929–1932*   365

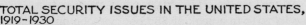

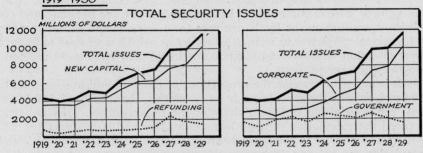

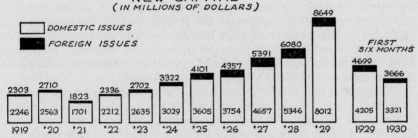

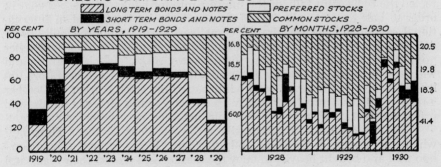

the stock of General Motors and the Radio Corporation of America. As the price of these and other stocks rose, the fever spread, and the wild bull market had begun.

The first phase of the speculation lasted until nearly the middle of June 1928, when prices declined slightly. Rallies alternated with declines during the next sixteen months, but prices always recovered and surged to new heights. The boom was totally out of control by the beginning of 1929. Industrial issues were then selling at more than sixteen times their earnings, although the traditional safe ratio was ten to one.

A few summary statistics will illustrate the dimensions of the stock market inflation that occurred from 1927 to September 1929. The market value of all stocks listed on the New York Stock Exchange increased from $27,000,000,000 in 1925 to a peak of $87,000,000,000 on October 1, 1929. The average price of common stocks increased nearly 300 per cent, and the volume of trading on the Exchange rose from 454,000,000 shares in 1925 to 1,125,000,000 shares in 1929. Brokers' loans, which were used to finance the speculation, rose from $3,500,000,000 in January 1926 to $8,500,000,-000 on September 30, 1929.

It is easier to describe the proportions of the wild bull market than to say precisely why the speculative fever developed when it did. Certainly the large commercial banks bore a share of the responsibility. They not only financed the speculation through loans to brokers and individuals but also participated directly in the market through active trading, underwriting of speculative issues, and formation of investment trusts and pools. The United States Treasury, by its approval of an unsound inflation, gave an early impetus to the speculative movement. The Federal Reserve Board did try vainly to check the runaway boom by selling governmental securities and increasing the discount rate. But it was too late. Speculation was so profitable by the summer of 1928 that money was flowing into New York from London and Paris and from the treasuries of American corporations. Banks with surplus cash paid no heed to the Federal Reserve Board's warnings and proceeded blindly to abet the speculation.

The boom had reached such irrational proportions by the summer of 1929 that some kind of readjustment, if not a collapse, was inevitable. Prices could not rise forever, and the financial structure was so precarious that even a slight recession would set off a panic. The first storm signals came from London, when the Bank of England, on September 26, 1929, raised the rediscount rate, or the interest rate for banks, to 6½ per cent in order to halt the outward flow of gold and protect the pound in international exchange. The withdrawal of at least several hundred millions of dollars from New York to London caused prices to decline on September 30; but the market rallied during the next two weeks. Then dissolution and withdrawal began on October 15, gradually at first, as large operators unloaded discreetly. However, total panic seized the stock market on October 24, 1929, "Black Thursday." Nearly 13,000,000 shares changed hands, and prices fell so rapidly that tickers could not keep pace with their descent.

The panic subsided momentarily in the afternoon of "Black Thursday" when J. P. Morgan & Company and other large banks formed a $240,000,-000 pool and bought heavily to buoy the market and protect their loans and investments. Thousands of brokers and hundreds of thousands of petty speculators had been ruined by the end of the day, to be sure. But Treasury officials, leading economists and bankers, and the metropolitan press all hastened to assure the public that the decline in stock prices would have a salutary effect by freeing more money for genuine investment purposes. "The fundamental business of the country, that is, production and distribution of commodities," said President Hoover on October 25, "is on a sound and prosperous basis."

Hoover's reassurance was echoed a hundred times in the inner circles of Wall Street. Nonetheless, the bankers let prices slide when the bottom dropped out of the market again on October 29. Nearly 16,500,000 shares changed hands in the wildest trading in the New York Stock Exchange's history, and the average price of fifty leading stocks declined almost forty points under the pressure. Rallies alternated with declines during the remaining weeks of 1929 and afterward, but the declines were always greater than the subsequent advances, until it seemed as if there could be no end except a final smashup of the entire financial system.

132. *The Progress of the Depression, 1929–1932*

The tremendous decline in stock values—a loss of some $40,000,000,-000 during the last four months of 1929 alone—set off intricate forces that interacted to carry the United States into the depths of industrial and financial stagnation. The essential fact was that American prosperity was in large measure dependent upon the smooth functioning of the basic cogs of the economic machinery—world trade, investment in capital plant and equipment, the construction industry, and production of automobiles. The oil that lubricated this economic machinery was confidence that goods could be sold and investments would yield a profitable return.

The stock market crash did not at once utterly destroy but it did severely shake the confidence of the business community, weaken financial institutions, slow down industrial expansion, and cause a diminution in American purchases and investments abroad. The practical withdrawal of the American dollar props from beneath the foundations of the international economy in turn precipitated a severe financial crisis in Europe in 1931. Europeans met this crisis only by adopting policies that virtually destroyed the system of international exchange. The European collapse in turn caused further strain on American banks and deepened the industrial and business depression. Thus the forces of dissolution gained power and momentum like a great avalanche as they interacted to speed the downward plunge.

The progress of the depression and its effect on the basic generative components of the economy are revealed by the following statistics: New capital issues, representing the investment of the American people in industrial, railroad, public utility, and other stocks and bonds, declined from $10,000,000,000 in 1929 to $7,000,000,000 a year later, to $3,000,000,000 in 1931, and to a little over $1,000,000,000 in 1932. Obviously, not enough new capital was being invested by 1932 even to maintain the domestic industrial plant. Foreign capital issues, governmental and corporate, declined from a high of nearly $1,500,000,000 in 1928 to a paltry $88,000,000 in 1932. American imports of goods and raw materials dropped from $4,463,000,000 in 1929 to $1,343,000,000 in 1932, exports from $5,347,-000,000 to $1,667,000,000. At home the two basic industries of construction and automobiles declined even more alarmingly.

The progressive slowing down of these important cogs in the economic machinery of course had an immediate and catastrophic effect on all other segments of the economy—the stock market, the financial and business communities, railroads, industrial production and employment, and agriculture. The depression's course can be at least partially comprehended when we examine its impact on these major aspects of economic life.

We might begin our review with a survey of the decline of stock prices.

THE PROGRESS OF THE GREAT DEPRESSION, 1929–1933

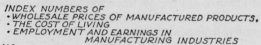

INDEX NUMBERS OF
- WHOLESALE PRICES OF MANUFACTURED PRODUCTS,
- THE COST OF LIVING
- EMPLOYMENT AND EARNINGS IN MANUFACTURING INDUSTRIES

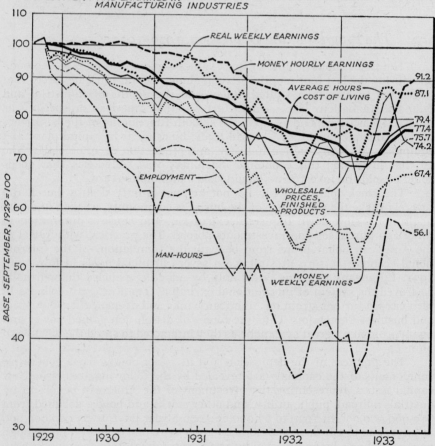

Twenty-five representative industrial stocks fell from an average closing price of $366.29 a share in 1929 to $96.63 a share in 1932. The decline in other shares was even more severe. From 1929 to 1932 twenty-five railroad stocks declined in average closing prices from $136 to $22 a share, twenty public utilities stocks from $142 to $28 a share, and the stock of twenty New York banks from $358 to $68 a share.

Another barometer of economic decline was the increasing frequency with which banks and business firms went under. There were 659 bank failures, involving deposits of nearly $250,000,000, in 1929; in the following year 1,352 banks, with deposits of $853,000,000, failed. In 1931, when the European financial crisis intensified the crisis, a total of 2,294 banks, with aggregate deposits of nearly $1,700,000,000, closed their doors. The

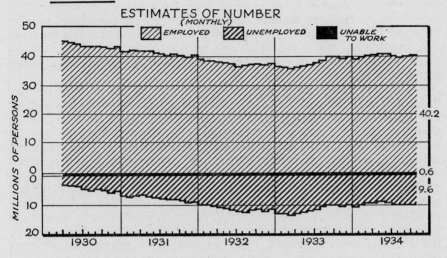

EMPLOYMENT AND UNEMPLOYMENT
IN THE UNITED STATES
1930–1934

ESTIMATES OF NUMBER
(MONTHLY)

EMPLOYED   UNEMPLOYED   UNABLE TO WORK

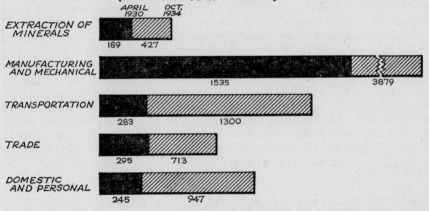

ESTIMATES OF UNEMPLOYED IN SPECIFIED INDUSTRIES
(IN THOUSANDS OF PERSONS)

APRIL 1930   OCT. 1934

EXTRACTION OF MINERALS   189   427

MANUFACTURING AND MECHANICAL   1535   3879

TRANSPORTATION   283   1300

TRADE   295   713

DOMESTIC AND PERSONAL   245   947

process of financial dissolution was finally halted in 1932, after the Reconstruction Finance Corporation reinforced the sagging financial structure. Only 1,456 banks, with deposits of nearly $750,000,000, failed in that year. Equally dismal was the record of 109,371 commercial failures, with aggregate liabilities of nearly $3,000,000,000, from 1929 through 1932, and a decline in the net profits of all private corporations from $8,400,000,-000 in 1929 to −$3,400,000,000 in 1932.

This plummeting provoked an even more serious crisis among the railroads. Already beginning to feel the effect of competition from the trucking industry in 1929, they staggered under heavy blows, and such great systems as the Wabash, Chicago & North Western, Missouri Pacific, Milwaukee, and New Haven, with an aggregate of some 45,000 miles, passed into receivership from 1929 to 1933. Moreover, only timely federal assistance saved other large systems from bankruptcy. As freight shipments and carloadings declined approximately 50 per cent from 1929 to 1932, net railroad operating income fell from $1,262,636,000 to $325,332,-000. In addition, railroads laid off men by the hundreds of thousands, reduced the work week of employees, and practically stopped buying new equipment.

The cumulative momentum of the depression can perhaps best be illustrated by the statistics on industrial production and unemployment for the period under discussion. By the last quarter of 1930 industrial production in the United States was 26 per cent below the peak level of 1929. By midsummer of 1932 the production curve had declined 51 per cent below the level of the peak year. In response, unemployment grew by the month and year: 3,000,000 in April 1930, 4,000,000 in October 1930, almost 7,000,000 in October 1931, nearly 11,000,000 a year later, and from 12,-000,000 to 14,000,000 during the first months of 1933. Moreover, workers fortunate enough to find or retain employment suffered severely from wage reductions, especially after 1931. Total labor income from 1929 to 1933 fell from $53,000,000,000 to $31,500,000,000; manufacturing wages, from nearly $12,000,000,000 to approximately $7,000,000,000.

American farmers, already in desperate economic straits by 1929, lost more in cash income and general economic standing during the depression years than any other important group. Gross farm income shrank from $11,941,000,000 to $5,331,000,000 between 1929 and 1932.

The dimensions of the economic misfortune that befell the American people from 1929 to 1933 can perhaps be comprehended by the following summary view: National income declined from $87,800,000,000 in 1929 to $40,200,000,000 in 1933; adjusted for the cost of living, per capita income declined from $681 to $495. Salaries decreased 40 per cent, dividends nearly 57 per cent, and manufacturing wages 60 per cent. The total picture of these years of the locusts, therefore, is one of extreme deflation everywhere except in the debt structure. As the American people struggled to save their financial system, interest payments on long-term debts declined only 3.3 per cent from 1929 to 1933.

133. *The Social Impact of the Depression*

The social impact of the depression could be seen in all aspects of life. The first place affected was the home, to which women formerly employed returned by the hundreds of thousands, even though the incidence of unemployment was less among women than among male workers. Most middle-class families had to dispense with domestic servants; and women responded to "live at home" appeals by gardening, canning, making soap, and the like.

Americans sometimes acted curiously under the impact of shattered hopes. They practically stopped buying new automobiles, to be sure, but they stubbornly refused to give up their old ones; and gasoline consumption increased slightly from 1929 through 1933. Jewelry sales declined precipitously; but women would not give up silk and rayon hosiery or even radios, for "soap operas" were just coming into vogue. And never would people give up smoking. Cigarette consumption, in fact, rose steadily during the depression years, as if the nervous strains engendered by distress demanded a sedative.

One of the most unfortunate social effects of the depression was its impact on family relationships and marriage and birth rates. Tens of thousands of families were forced to double up in homes and apartments, and tensions between fathers and sons increased as the latter found it impossible to find work. Young people out of work married later and had fewer children. Thus the number of marriages declined from 1,233,000 in 1929 to 982,000 in 1932, while the birth rate declined from 21.3 per thousand in 1930 to 18.4 in 1933. Moreover, as family tensions mounted in the first two years of the depression, the number of divorces per 1,000 marriages increased from 163 in 1929 to 173 in 1931.[2]

Schools and colleges were of course profoundly affected, but Americans struggled successfully to maintain school plant, equipment, and salaries until 1932. The tide began to turn in that year, and the retreat had turned into a rout on all educational fronts by the end of the school year 1933–4. Expenditures for school purposes declined from $1,844,000,000 to $1,500,000,000, or about 18 per cent, from 1930 to 1934. But in many states the decrease exceeded 30 per cent, and in Michigan and Mississippi it was 41 and 52 per cent, respectively. During the same period, capital outlay for new school buildings declined 84 per cent; many rural counties reduced school terms from one fifth to one half; all states except Rhode Island decreased salaries, and the decreases in rural southern and western states ran as high as 43 per cent and averaged more than 30 per cent.

Colleges and universities experienced even greater adversity. Total enrollment in institutions of higher learning declined 8.5 per cent throughout the country between 1931 and 1934. Generally speaking, state colleges and universities were hardest hit, suffering a 31 per cent decline in income from state appropriations, as compared with a 19 per cent decline in income from endowments owned by private institutions.

Perhaps the most important, because it was the most lasting, social effect of the depression was the way it caused a shift in responsibility for alleviating social distress from private to public agencies and resources. City and state governments formed emergency relief administrations almost at once and took over the burden of relief and public health services from old philanthropic agencies. In spite of early optimism, excellent administration, and the co-operation of federal authorities, the cities and states could not meet the relief emergency after 1931. Staggering under financial burdens they could not bear, forced to default on obligations and pay public employees in scrip, the cities and states simply could not borrow the money necessary to meet the elementary needs of the unemployed. Appeals for private support yielded only paltry sums; "give-a-job" campaigns, "block aid" programs, and so on, were largely futile.

ᴧᴧᴧᴧᴧᴧᴧᴧᴧᴧᴧᴧᴧᴧᴧᴧᴧᴧ

2 There was, however, a sharp decline in the number of divorces to 163 per 1,000 marriages in 1932.

The impossibility of using only private, city, and state resources to meet the crisis had been amply demonstrated by social workers and statisticians by the winter of 1932. The destitute congregated in cardboard shacks in so-called Hoovervilles on the edges of cities across the nation; hundreds of thousands of the unemployed roamed the country on foot and in boxcars in futile search of jobs. There was perhaps little outright starvation, but there was much hunger; and the malnutrition rate among patients admitted to certain community health centers in New York City and Philadelphia increased 60 per cent. Nor were hunger and malnutrition confined to the great cities, for five-cent cotton meant a lean diet of salt pork and hominy for southern poor whites and Negroes, and unemployment in the mining areas brought destitution unequaled on a large scale anywhere in the cities.

134.   Rumblings of Social Discontent

Americans were baffled by the anomaly of a country with abundant resources, the largest force of skilled labor, and the most productive plant in the world being unable to find the right formula for getting the wheels of industry turning once again. Moreover, it was difficult to understand why millions of people should go hungry in a country groaning under the burden of huge food surpluses. The people, as they are wont to do during periods of economic distress, searched for scapegoats and soon concluded that speculators and bankers in Wall Street had been responsible.

This discrediting of an economic leadership hitherto warmly admired did not, of course, occur all at once. Until the summer of 1931 probably a majority of the people believed the assurances of Republican spokesmen and financial leaders, who since the stock market crash had predicted that the economic system would soon right itself again. However, the European collapse caused more banks to fail and bread lines to lengthen, and the Senate banking committee in the winter of 1931–2 exposed corruption and malfeasance in the banking community. Consequently, public confidence in the economic leadership and the Hoover administration sagged and then nearly collapsed during the summer of 1932.

The rumblings of discontent grew from a scarcely audible whisper into a mighty chorus after the spring of 1931. In the late summer of 1931, for example, a commission of the Federal Council of the Churches of Christ in America prepared a statement to be read from pulpits on Labor Sunday. It was one of the most sweeping indictments of American capitalism ever drawn by a middle-class group. The bishops of the Protestant Episcopal Church seconded the Federal Council's indictment in a pastoral letter demanding that employers abandon the profit motive for the ideal of service to mankind.

Many businessmen, alarmed by the menace of revolutionary upheaval and moved by the misery of the lower classes, abandoned faith in automatic mechanisms and began to doubt the worth of an economy in which there could be so much abundance and misery at the same time. One of the most startling proposals for amelioration, in fact, came from Wall Street. It was a suggestion by Gerard Swope, president of the General Electric

Company, that industrial leaders co-operate to increase production and protect workers against unemployment and poverty. Swope's warning that government would surely assume this responsibility if industry did not was echoed by the banker-industrialist, Owen D. Young, and by the president of the United States Chamber of Commerce.

Nor were labor spokesmen any less disturbed. Leaders of the AF of L during the first two years of the depression had supported the President's plan to prevent strikes for higher wages. They had also waited patiently for the return of prosperity. But unrest among AF of L members was so great by the autumn of 1931 that spokesmen of organized labor could no longer remain silent. The executive committee of the AF of L prepared a statement in October 1931 declaring that the prime cause of the depression had been the unequal distribution of wealth and incomes and calling upon President Hoover to convoke a great national economic conference to consider ways and means of combating the foe from within.

These protests and proposals were, of course, more a reflection of the important ideological upheaval that was transforming popular attitudes toward government and the economy than manifestations of any disposition toward social violence. Signs of dangerous social eruption, actually, were few. There were hunger marches and a serious riot of unemployed persons in Dearborn, Michigan, in the spring of 1932. Embattled farmers organized to prevent mortgage owners from profiting by foreclosure. (See below, p. 405.) But the only outbreak that threatened to get out of hand was the descent of the so-called Bonus Expeditionary Force of some twelve to fourteen thousand unemployed and homeless veterans on Washington in May and June 1932. They demanded passage of a bill providing immediate full payment of the bonus by the issuance of $2,400,000,000 in paper money, built a shanty town on Anacostia Flats outside the capital, and threatened to sit it out all summer. The Senate, under strong presidential pressure, refused to approve the bonus bill, and about half the marchers went home when Congress appropriated funds to provide transportation. But some five or six thousand veterans, many with wives and children, remained: gaunt representatives of the millions of destitute in every state and section.

Then a riot occurred on July 28, 1932, when police attempted to clear a throng of bonus marchers out of a construction area. Two veterans were killed, and several policemen were injured. The District commissioners warned that they could not preserve order without extensive use of force, and President Hoover at once called upon the army to control the situation.[3] The Army Chief of Staff, General Douglas MacArthur, assembled a formidable small army with machine guns and tanks, dispersed the bonus marchers from Anacostia Flats and, accidentally or deliberately, burned the shanty town. The very "institutions of our Government" would have been severely threatened, MacArthur declared, if the President had not acted decisively.

No doubt the General exaggerated the dimensions of the threat. To be sure, there was much talk of revolution if Hoover should be elected again,

---

[3] In a public statement issued on July 28, 1932, President Hoover declared that Communists and persons with criminal records were stirring the bonus army to violence.

but it never got beyond street corners. Actually, the wonder is that there were so few organized uprisings like the "Bonus March," that people suffered so much without losing their sense of humor or falling prey to Communist and fascist agitators. The American democracy survived one of its severest testings only because the people never lost hope of finding a democratic solution through new political leadership.

135.   *Hoover and the Crisis of American Capitalism*

No man ever came to the presidency with broader experience in world and domestic affairs than Herbert Clark Hoover. He was a self-made man, whose success story should become as much a part of the American legend as Horatio Alger's tales of boys who made good. Born of Quaker parents at West Branch, Iowa, in 1874, Hoover migrated in his youth to Oregon, attended the newly established Stanford University, and was graduated with a degree in mining engineering in 1895. He proved to be resourceful and hard-working, in fact, a sheer genius at running large enterprises. Rising from one high position to another, Hoover had won an international reputation and amassed a large personal fortune by 1914. During the first years of the World War Hoover did an extraordinary job as head of the Belgian Relief Commission. He was called to Washington to direct the Food Administration when his country entered the war. His reputation was so great by 1920 that he was seriously mentioned for the Democratic presidential nomination. The movement foundered when he decided that he was a Republican.

He was appointed Secretary of Commerce by Harding in 1921 and served in this post until his nomination for the presidency in 1928. Hoover was the chief spokesman of free regulated enterprise, mass consumption, and welfare capitalism during a decade when the businessman was the hero of the urban middle classes. He was never intimate with professional politicians, but the popular demand for his nomination in 1928 was so overwhelming that the professionals had to submit.

Hoover must have idealized the presidency as the culmination of his long career of service to the people of the world. As one historian has put it, "Hoover the engineer would be the symbol of the coming age of material fulfillment, as Jefferson had been of democracy and Lincoln of emancipation." With supreme confidence that his administration would witness the maturing of humanitarian capitalism, he entered the White House with such popular approval as few Presidents have ever enjoyed. He left office, on the other hand, rejected and despised as few Presidents have ever been, his name an article of common sneering and associated with horse-drawn carts and assemblages of human misery.

What was wrong? How can we account for this almost total deflation of a great reputation? Why was it that a great engineer and expert in alleviating human suffering should have failed to provide the leadership and techniques so desperately needed in this interval of domestic crisis?

In the first place, Hoover was as inept at politics as he was superb at administration. He had grown accustomed to obedience during a long career of holding positions of command. In his rigorously honest and orderly mind he probably had contempt for mere politicians, for men who consulted only the popular will. Thus, when it came to dealing with Congress, and particularly with a hostile Congress from 1931 to 1933, he was poorly equipped for effective leadership. He could command men's respect in times of prosperity but not their love and devotion to a great vision during times of adversity.

Hoover's chief handicap, however, was a rigid, unyielding mental quality that made it difficult for him to adapt to new circumstances and undertake unusual experiments. Out of long experience and careful thought he had come to certain convictions concerning government and the economy. He was no *laissez-faire* economist of the classical school. He approved regulation of business enterprise clothed with the public interest, and he championed order and efficiency in business rather than destructive competition. On the other hand, he believed fervently that American progress and prosperity depended upon private initiative and striving. Thus he opposed all measures, like federal operation of Muscle Shoals, that would diminish private energies or impede private investment and enterprise. Out of a sincere belief in democracy and the inherent goodness of the American people Hoover just as strongly opposed any measures that would transfer responsibility for social alleviation from localities and states to the federal government.

With Hoover these principles constituted not only a political philosophy but a religious faith as well. During his own lifetime the American system of comparatively free enterprise, powered by private initiative and what he called "rugged individualism," had worked the greatest material miracle of the modern age. Free capitalism, unhampered by binding controls, had brought a good material life within the reach of the average man. Hoover saw no reason why it should not continue to carry the masses ever upward toward a higher standard of living. When the stock market crash set off a business depression, he refused to believe that the downswing was anything more than a passing phase in the business cycle, like the Panic of 1907 or the depression of 1921–2.

Once the recession of 1929–30 turned into a full-fledged depression in 1931, Hoover was forced to recognize that complete economic ruin would ensue without positive and unprecedented action by the federal government. Abandoning momentarily the main tenets of his philosophy, he approved ambitious measures to save the economy. At the same time, he never lost confidence in the inherent soundness of American economic institutions or in the altruism of businessmen and bankers. Recovery was bound to come, he was certain, if only the federal government did not destroy business confidence by tampering with the gold standard or launching wild measures of control.

136. *The Hoover Policies: Agricultural Stabilization*

Disturbed by the rising insurgency in the Middle and Far West, Hoover and other GOP spokesmen during the campaign of 1928 promised sane farm relief and upward revision of the tariff rates on agricultural products. Hoover soon after his inauguration called the Seventy-first Congress into special session for April 15, 1929, to redeem these campaign pledges. Farm leaders still contended that only the McNary-Haugen or some other price-fixing plan would give agriculture parity with industry, and they had long since ceased to believe that higher tariff rates would mean higher agricultural prices at home. But the President had his way, and Congress approved his two measures for farm relief—the Agricultural Marketing Act of June 15, 1929, and the Hawley-Smoot Tariff Act of June 17, 1930.

The draft of the Agricultural Marketing bill that Hoover presented to Congress provided a remedy that would not, the President explained, undermine the initiative of the individual farmer or involve the government in any schemes of price control. It created a nonpartisan Federal Farm Board and gave it the use of a revolving fund of $500,000,000. This money would be lent to agricultural marketing co-operatives, to enable them to market products efficiently, build warehouses, and hold farm products in the event of a price decline. In order to win the support of the Senate, however, the President made one concession that changed the character of the proposed stabilization program. It was an amendment authorizing the Federal Farm Board to establish corporations to stabilize farm prices through direct intervention in the market.

The Agricultural Marketing Act, therefore, launched the federal government upon the most ambitious program of agricultural stabilization and support in American peacetime history to that date. The Federal Farm Board from 1929 to 1931 organized producers of major staples into national co-operatives and established corporations to stabilize farm prices through large-scale market operations. By lending to co-operatives and buying wheat and cotton in large quantities, the Board maintained domestic farm prices a little above the world price level until the summer of 1931. However, the financial crisis in Europe that same year caused a sudden shrinking of foreign markets for American agricultural exports, and dumping by Russia, Argentina, and Australia drove prices to fantastically low levels. From this point on the Board was powerless to prevent the collapse of the price structure at home. Wheat, which sold at an average price of $1.04 a bushel in 1929, declined to 67 cents in 1930, and then plummeted to 39 cents in 1931 and 1932. Corn fell from 80 cents to 32 cents a bushel from 1929 to 1932, cotton from 17 cents to 7 cents a pound, and tobacco from 18 cents to 11 cents a pound.

The Federal Farm Board might well have achieved its chief objective of underwriting efficient and economical marketing during a time of relative stability or rising farm prices. Its program was launched instead at the onset of a great depression, with a consequent demoralization of commodity markets throughout the world. It was doomed to futility, chiefly because the Board had no authority to compel farmers to limit production to achieve domestic price stability. The Board used persuasion to achieve reduction of wheat and cotton acreage in 1930; it undertook a more strenuous campaign to achieve a general 30 per cent reduction in staple crops in the following year. But for every farmer who co-operated there must have been one who increased his plantings. The index of agricultural production fell two points in 1930, but only because of a severe drought; production in 1931 exceeded even that of 1929.

The members of the Federal Farm Board recognized their inability to cope with the situation as early as 1931. Having lost some $354,000,000 in market operations bv the summer of 1932, the Board openly admitted its helplessness. Finally, on December 7, 1932, it urged Congress to establish an effective system for regulating acreage and production as the only alternative to continued agricultural bankruptcy. Hoover's ambitious experiment obviously failed; but out of failure came experience and a profound conviction that co-operation and voluntary action would not suffice. The transition from the Hoover stabilization program to the bolder and more advanced New Deal measures was as natural as it was inevitable.

Hoover's program of tariff relief for agriculture was an even greater fiasco than his ill-fated effort at price stabilization. Although the tariff had not been a partisan issue in the campaign of 1928, Hoover appealed to Congress in 1929 to give agriculture the same measure of protection that domestic manufacturers already enjoyed. His intentions undoubtedly were excellent, but all the old lobbies and pressures set diligently to work once work on a tariff bill began. The result was the Hawley-Smoot tariff bill of 1930, which provided about seventy-five increases for farm products and 925 for manufactured commodities.[4]

As a device for supporting domestic agricultural prices, the Hawley-Smoot Tariff was completely futile, except, perhaps, with regard to meat and dairy products. Moreover, its sheerly economic effect on foreign trade was probably unimportant. Its psychological impact abroad, however, was unfortunate, as it seemed to signal an intensification of economic nationalism in the United States just at the moment when the world desperately needed enlightened leadership. One thousand members of the American Economic Association pointed out this elementarv fact in an urgent appeal to the President to veto the Hawley-Smoot bill. Their warning was justified if unheeded. The British, for example, adopted protection and a system of imperial preference in 1932. Germany in the following year embarked upon a program of autarky that severely damaged world trade. The passage of the Hawley-Smoot bill was not responsible for the international economic demoralization that occurred in 1931 and afterward, but its enactment set a bad example for the rest of the world.

137. *The Hoover Policies: Combating the Depression*

Hoover moved with a new kind of presidential boldness during the first and relatively mild phase of the depression that lasted from October 1929 to the spring of 1931. He met with railroad presidents on November 19, 1929, and obtained their promise to proceed with normal construction. Calling leaders of finance, industry, and trade to the White House two days later, Hoover frankly warned them that a serious recession would follow in the wake of the storm in Wall Street. The leaders of American

[4] This measure increased the average level of agricultural duties from 20 to 34 per cent and the general average of all duties from 33 to 40 per cent. As a result of the Hawley-Smoot Act, moreover, the average ad valorem duties on imports subject to the tariff increased from 26 per cent for the period 1921–5 to 50 per cent for the period 1931–5.

business responded to Hoover's urgent pleading by agreeing to maintain production and refrain from severe wage reductions, provided labor leaders would co-operate by withdrawing demands for wage increases. On the same afternoon the President obtained a promise of full co-operation from labor leaders. The following day, November 22, Hoover met with leaders in the construction industry and won their promise to maintain current wages and hours standards. Then on November 23 he called upon governors and mayors throughout the country to join the federal government in increasing expenditures for public works. In addition, the President met again with larger groups of business and labor leaders in December and warned them that responsibility for averting a major catastrophe was primarily theirs.

It seemed by the spring of 1930 that Hoover's program of co-operation had carried the country through the worst phase of the storm. Bankers had reduced brokers' loans from eight and a half to three billion dollars; the index of industrial employment, which had stood at 99 in December 1929, dropped only two and a half points during the next four months. A nation-wide census of unemployment taken in the following April revealed that only 2,500,000 workers were unable to find jobs. Congressional action in the spring of 1930, authorizing expenditure of $145,000,000 for rivers and harbors improvements, $530,000,000 for public buildings, and $75,000,000 for highways, also had a steadying effect.[5] Moreover, employers were honoring their pledges not to cut wages and workers their promise not to strike.[6]

Then, beginning in May and June 1930, employers began slowly to reduce production, at first without seriously cutting wages. From April to November 1930 the index of industrial employment fell from 96.3 to 84.6 and of payrolls from 97.7 to 76.8. When unemployment reached about 4,000,-000 in October, Hoover appointed a Committee for Unemployment Relief and called upon city and private agencies to redouble their relief efforts. Moreover, he ended immigration and declared that he would ask Congress for larger appropriations for public works.

Meanwhile, Democratic leaders had begun the congressional campaign of 1930 with such confidence as they had not felt since Wilson's first administration. Aided by a mounting public fear and by a "smear" campaign against Hoover personally, the Democrats made a much better showing in the November elections than they had done two years before.[7] The election was no landslide or mass repudiation of Hoover's leadership. Yet by giving control of the legislative branch to the President's political foes

<hr>

[5] Actually, federal expenditures for public works totaled $493,000,000 in 1930, as compared with $384,000,000 in 1929. State and municipal expenditures totaled $2,838,-000,000 in 1929 and $3,054,000,000 in 1930.

[6] Only 7 per cent of firms reporting to the Bureau of Labor Statistics reduced wages during 1930.

[7] The Democrats elected seventeen governors, the Republicans twelve. The GOP lost some forty seats but retained control of the House of Representatives by a plurality of one. When the Seventy-second Congress met in December 1931, however, enough Republican incumbents had died to give control to the Democrats. The new Senate consisted of forty-eight Republicans, forty-seven Democrats, and one Farmer-Laborite; but so many Republican senators were midwestern insurgents that an insurgent-Democratic coalition easily controlled the upper house.

on the eve of a presidential election, it divided responsibility in the federal government and led inevitably to bitter wrangling.

In fact, there were numerous manifestations of tension between Hoover and the progressive bloc in Congress even during the lame-duck session of the Seventy-first Congress that sat from December 1930 to March 1931. Progressives, Republican and Democratic, demanded that the President abandon voluntarism and meet the crisis boldly—by a federal relief program, part payment of the veterans' bonus, and development of the Muscle Shoals facilities. Hoover replied that private and local relief resources were still ample and set himself sternly against any projects for direct federal relief. He successfully vetoed the Norris bill for federal operation of Muscle Shoals, but Congress overrode his veto of a bill allowing veterans to obtain half the value of their certificates in cash.

At the same time, it seemed again that the President's policies had turned back the depression tide and set the nation on the road to recovery. Indices of employment, payrolls, and production steadied in February 1931 and then rallied slightly until about the first of June. Bank failures abated; unemployment slackened. To many observers these encouraging developments signified that the recession was nearly over.

Unhappily, the second and catastrophic phase of the depression was now about to begin in the United States as the result of a financial panic in Europe that paralyzed the international economy. Central European and South American countries had been borrowing heavily in short-term loans since 1927 to compensate for a drying up of the sources of long-term credit.[8] French bankers, who held large sums of German and Austrian short-term notes, demanded immediate payment, partly for political reasons, in March 1931. To avert bankruptcy, Germany and Austria appealed to London and New York for aid. British bankers did what they could, but it was not enough, and the *Kreditanstalt* of Vienna, the largest bank in Austria, was "reorganized" on May 11, 1931. Its virtual failure stimulated such heavy withdrawals of gold from Germany that the Republic was unable by June to meet reparation payments, much less its short-term obligations. Desperately, almost pathetically, the aged President of Germany, Paul von Hindenburg, appealed personally to Hoover on June 18 for immediate assistance.

Hoover and his advisers, meanwhile, had been contemplating proposing a one-year moratorium on all intergovernmental debt and reparations payments. As these obligations would total about $1,000,000,000, any attempt to force payment would bankrupt Germany and cause the entire international economy to collapse. Hoover proposed the moratorium on June 21, 1931, after delaying too long for fear of political repercussions. Britain and Germany accepted at once; but the French government balked for two weeks, and further withdrawals from Germany compelled the German government to adopt severe measures to stave off repudiation.

wwwwwwwwwwwwww

[8] By March 1931 Germany alone had more than $4,000,000,000 in short-term debts outstanding. Normally, short-term loans are made to finance business and trade operations. The Germans, however, had invested the money in a variety of nonliquid assets. Any crisis leading to demand for payment of these obligations would, therefore, immediately imperil the entire German financial structure.

No sooner had the German crisis passed than French bankers began withdrawing large sums of gold which they had earlier deposited in British banks. The Bank of England negotiated a short-term gold loan in France and the United States on August 1 and another in the United States at the end of the month. But the withdrawals were so heavy that the Bank of England defaulted on gold payments on September 21, 1931, and the British Cabinet took the government off the gold standard. Within six months only the United States, France, Italy, Belgium, Holland, and Switzerland remained committed to payment in gold.

The financial crises of the spring and summer of 1931 virtually destroyed the existing system of international exchange and trade and set off a sharp depression in western Europe. More significant for our story was the effect of the European crisis in deepening the depression in the United States. For one thing, before the European crisis erupted, British, French, and other European nationals and banks had deposited some $1,500,000,-000 in gold in American banks, and American banks in turn had lent out most of this money. Europeans demanded payment of most of this gold when their own crisis came in the spring of 1931, and American depositories had to call in domestic loans. In the second place, American banks held more than $1,000,000,000 of German short-term trade paper and bank acceptances. Fear that these obligations could not be paid caused American bankers further to call loans to amass liquid reserves. Third, the panic in Europe prompted foreigners to unload large quantities of securities on the New York Stock Exchange. Finally, devaluation and demoralization of exchange caused a virtual stoppage of foreign trade, the consequences of which were catastrophic for the commodity markets.

These and other factors combined during the summer of 1931 to destroy all the encouraging progress toward recovery that the American economy had made since January and to plunge the country deeper into depression. Contraction of loans set off panic, hoarding of cash, and "runs" by depositors; bankers in turn had to contract further. Dumping of securities drove the price of stocks and bonds to new depths. The loss of foreign markets caused agricultural prices to fall to very low levels. Above all, fear seized the American business and financial communities. Men began hoarding instead of spending; employers cut production and wages; investors tried to recover money instead of investing it. The downward spiral is well illustrated by the following table:

1931	INDEX OF EMPLOYMENT (MONTHLY AVERAGE 1923–1925 = 100)	INDEX OF PAYROLLS (MONTHLY AVERAGE 1923–1925 = 100)	NUMBER OF BANK FAILURES
May	80.1	73.4	91
June	78.4	69.7	167
July	77.0	66.2	93
August	77.1	65.9	158
September	77.4	63.4	305
October	74.4	61.3	522
November	71.8	58.1	175
December	71.0	57.6	358

It was obvious by the late summer of 1931 that unrestrained liquidation could lead only to total collapse of the American financial structure.
Now President Hoover moved more boldly than before. Still hoping to defeat the depression by the voluntary co-operation of the business community, he called some thirty leading New York bankers and insurance
executives to a secret conference on October 4, 1931. He wanted the banks
to form an emergency credit pool of $500,000,000 and the insurance com-
panies to agree not to foreclose mortgages when creditors were in honest
straits. Moreover, he warned that he would call Congress into special session if the financial leaders did not co-operate. The warning sufficed to
bring early compliance. The bankers formed the credit pool soon afterward
and organized the National Credit Corporation to administer it. Moreover,
the President met with congressional leaders of both parties on October 6
and won their promise of support in the impending Seventy-second Congress.

Hoover outlined the recovery program upon which he had been working since September when Congress convened in early December. It proposed drastic reductions in administrative expenditures and an expansion
of federal public works; expansion of the lending powers of Federal Farm
Banks; creation of a system of home-loan banks to prevent foreclosures;
and a gigantic emergency reconstruction corporation to strengthen the entire economy. Fear of national collapse had obviously forced the President to abandon old assumptions about the sufficiency of voluntary measures and to support a program that implied more extensive federal
intervention that had ever been attempted in peacetime. But he had come
to this position reluctantly. He had accepted the proposal for an emergency reconstruction agency only after the National Credit Corporation
had collapsed, and only under heavy pressure from New York bankers and
particularly Eugene Meyer, a member of the Federal Reserve Board and
author of the idea.

The next seven months were marked by bitter wrangling between
the President and Congress and among the leaders of the two houses. While
unemployment mounted and huge withdrawals of gold by French banks
threatened to drive the country off the gold standard, Congress delayed
urgently needed legislation for weeks and months. Many Democrats acted
as if they feared recovery would come before the presidential election in
November 1932. Other Democrats and progressive Republicans supported
Hoover's program but also demanded that the government extend as much
relief to farmers and the unemployed as it gave to financial institutions
and railroads. But Congress in spite of wrangling and delay had approved
a comprehensive recovery program by the time that it adjourned in July
1932.

The main cog of the recovery machinery was the Reconstruction Finance Corporation (RFC), chartered by Congress on January 16, 1932,
with a capital of $500,000,000 and authority to borrow up to $1,500,000,-
000 more in tax-free obligations. The RFC opened offices in thirty cities
and set to work immediately to save banks, railroads, building and loan associations, and other financial institutions. In all, the RFC lent $1,500,000,-
000 during 1932 to more than 5,000 concerns, restored a large measure of

public confidence, and successfully halted the undermining of the financial structure.

Through other measures the President and Congress co-operated to strengthen the financial machinery. Thus, the Glass-Steagall Act of February 27, 1932, made government bonds and new classes of commercial paper acceptable as collateral for Federal Reserve notes. This measure not only permitted the Federal Reserve Banks to expand the currency but, more important, released $1,000,000,000 in gold to meet foreign withdrawals. The Federal Home Loan Bank Act of July 22, 1932, established home loan banks with a total capital of $125,000,000 to enable building and loan associations, savings banks, and insurance companies to obtain cash without foreclosing on home owners. In addition, an Act of January 23, 1932, provided more capital for Federal Land Banks.

On the whole these were nonpartisan measures, adopted after a minimum of bickering. Conflicting relief proposals, however, engendered bitter controversies between the administration and Democratic and progressive Republican leaders in Congress. Many of the progressives were frank inflationists, who proposed to extend direct aid to the unemployed by printing paper money. Hoover blocked their efforts at almost every turn. A case in point was the controversy provoked by the agitation for full and immediate payment of the so-called bonus. The House of Representatives on June 15, 1932, approved a measure sponsored by Wright Patman of Texas for full payment of the bonus with $2,400,000,000 in newly printed money. The Senate rejected the Patman bill on June 19 under threat of a presidential veto.

Progressives also demanded adoption of a large-scale public works and direct relief program, to be financed through borrowing; and Congress, in early July 1932, adopted the Garner-Wagner relief bill providing direct aid to individuals and a vast expansion of public works. Hoover was not callous to the sufferings of the unemployed, but he insisted that relief was a local problem, and that the federal government could serve best by working through the cities and states. It came as no great surprise, therefore, when he vetoed the Garner-Wagner bill on July 11, calling it "impractical," "dangerous," and "damaging to our whole conception of governmental relations." Congress then followed his advice and adopted a new relief bill on July 16. It authorized the RFC to lend $300,000,000 to states whose resources were exhausted and an additional $1,500,000,000 to states and municipalities for self-liquidating public works.

To repeat the old allegation that Hoover fiddled while the country burned would merely add undue dignity to an important part of the American political mythology. Hoover was surely no old-fashioned conservative, no social Darwinist, willing to let the depression run its full course in the confidence that the automatic machinery of the economy would eventually start the wheels to roll again. On the contrary, he was a cautious progressive, whose campaign for recovery was grounded ideologically on the assumption that only strong federal leadership and action could carry the country through the storm. His philosophy and policies, especially during 1931 and 1932, represented a turning point, a transition toward a future characterized by increasing federal participation in economic affairs.

It was Hoover's personal misfortune that he lost the confidence of a large majority of the American people at the very time that he was going to greater lengths to combat depression than any President before his time. This was true in part because he had the bad luck to be President during a time of widespread social and economic misery. It was true even more because he saved the financial structure but stubbornly refused to countenance measures to help individuals in distress. In the minds of most Americans Hoover's program seemed inadequate and too heavily weighted in favor of the upper classes. Moreover, the majority of people were beginning to demand, not a holding action, but a thoroughgoing overhauling of the economic machinery. Hoover still talked as if it would do merely to revive the business machinery of the 1920's. In contrast, millions of Americans were turning their eyes toward a new and, they hoped, brighter future in which they, not businessmen and bankers, would make important economic decisions.

CHAPTER

18

The First New Deal:

Experiment

in Compromise

THE HOOVER ADMINISTRATION had seemingly halted the most destructive attrition of the depression by the summer of 1932, but most Americans were now somewhat weary of the President's talk about prosperity being just around the corner. Farmers in debt, workers without jobs, and bankrupt businessmen demanded bolder federal action than Hoover was willing to approve. Rejecting the President and the now discredited business leadership, the disparate forces of discontent came together in a new coalition in November 1932 and voted to entrust the government of the United States to a new leader and a party long out of power.

The consequence was a new era in American political history—the Age of Franklin D. Roosevelt. A word of warning should perhaps be said at the outset. The key to understanding this period lies in the realization that there was no single set of Roosevelt policies carried out according to a prearranged plan. There were, roughly speaking, two New Deals, two reform programs. Given historical circumstances at the time, the second was an inevitable extension of the first. The First New Deal, from 1933 to 1935, marked a transition from a cautious progressivism, such as Wilson and Hoover had espoused, to new programs with expanded social and economic horizons. In the Second New Deal, from 1935 to 1939, the American progressive movement found fulfillment. We will pause briefly at the beginning of the following chapter to try to see what all this implied for American political traditions.

138. *The Election of 1932*

While Republican fortunes declined in direct ratio to the intensity of economic distress after 1930, Democratic leaders looked forward with growing confidence to victory in the presidential election of 1932. Alfred E. Smith of New York was still titular head of the Democratic party, but a number of other contenders entered the preconvention contest as hopes of victory multiplied. Among the Democratic aspirants, Franklin D. Roosevelt was easily Smith's most dangerous rival. Elected Governor of New York in 1928, Roosevelt was re-elected in 1930 by 725,000 votes, the largest majority ever given a gubernatorial candidate in his state. The magic of this majority at once made him a leading contender for the Democratic nomination in 1932. But the situation in New York was discouraging, for Tammany Hall, the New York City Democratic organization, was still loyal to Smith. Therefore, Roosevelt's managers—Louis M. Howe, his secretary, and James A. Farley, a former Smith lieutenant who had come into the Roosevelt camp in 1929—began to build support for the New York Governor in the South and West. They succeeded so well that they had amassed a majority of the delegates, but not the then necessary two thirds, by the time that the Democratic national convention opened in Chicago on June 27, 1932.

Smith's only hope of stopping Roosevelt was coalition with other favorite sons—Newton D. Baker of Ohio, Governor Albert C. Ritchie of Maryland, and particularly Speaker John Nance Garner of Texas, who had the support of the California and Texas delegates. The anti-Roosevelt managers maneuvered desperately, but Farley played a shrewd game. Instead of showing his full strength on the first ballot, he held off part of his delegates and added them to the Roosevelt column on the second and third ballots in order to create the impression of a landslide. But the expected landslide did not occur on the third ballot, and Farley turned in desperation to the Texas and California delegates. Garner could not have taken his chances for the presidency very seriously; he was certainly eager to avoid a futile deadlock. When consulted on Friday evening, July 1, he swung Texas and California into the Roosevelt column and precipitated the landslide on the fourth ballot. Only Smith's Tammany followers refused to make the nomination unanimous. Garner was named as Roosevelt's running-mate, perhaps as a reward—there is some evidence of a bargain—more certainly because he was from the Southwest and a powerful figure in the party.

Flying to Chicago to accept the nomination in person, Roosevelt went down the planks in the platform, endorsing them one by one. "I pledge you, I pledge myself, to a new deal for the American people," he concluded on a high note of dedication. ". . . This is more than a political campaign; it is a call to arms." Roosevelt's promises of work, security, and a fairer distribution of incomes encouraged the country, but what it foretold no man could say. Moreover, a reading of the Democratic platform would neither have yielded knowledge nor provided inspiration. Indeed, in view of later New Deal policies, it was a poor prophecy.[1]

The Republicans had meanwhile assembled at Chicago on June 14 and renominated President Hoover on the first ballot. The Republican convention was a gloomy conclave, and it seemed that the delegates knew they were going through necessary motions. Most of the speeches and a good part of the platform [2] were devoted to proving that the depression was the product of outside forces, and that Hoover had met the enemy on home ground and conquered him through bold measures of relief and reconstruction.

In the ensuing campaign Republican leaders fought like men with their backs to the wall, but their effort was hobbled from the outset by its defensive character. First, they tried to restore public confidence in the President, by portraying him as a shy but kindly man; as the pilot who had kept eternal vigil on the bridge, fighting through the storm; as the great engineer, whose genius would lead the people to safety. Second, Republicans tried to absolve their party of responsibility for the depression, convince the voters that they were capable of bringing recovery, and restore public confidence in the GOP as the party of all the people, not merely of the business and financial interests.

Hoover also campaigned vigorously. But he spoke gravely, recounting the things that he had done to combat the depression, "the battles on a thousand fronts, . . . the good fight to protect our people in a thousand cities from hunger and cold." To the unemployed he declared that he would mobilize the nation's resources rather than permit a single person to starve. To farmers he promised enlarged tariff protection and additional federal credit. To investors he promised maintenance of the gold standard. To the country at large he promised abundance if the Republicans won. And he warned that grass would grow "in the streets of a hundred cities, a thousand towns" if Roosevelt were elected.

In sharp contrast to Hoover's unencouraging defense was Roosevelt's brilliant campaign. He said many things about economy and a balanced budget that he must have regretted afterward. But with the help of his advisers, called the "Brain Trust," Roosevelt also forecast at least the shadow of future New Deal policies. Thus at Topeka, Kansas, he sketched

wwwwwwwwwwwwww

[1] The Democratic platform was brief but neither radical nor bold. Among other things, it demanded repeal of the Eighteenth Amendment; promised to balance the budget and reduce federal expenditures by 25 per cent; demanded the removal of government from all fields of private enterprise, "except where necessary to develop public works and natural resources." It also promised to maintain "at all hazards" a sound currency and reform the banking system; advocated lending money to the states to care for the unemployed; endorsed unemployment and old-age insurance "under state laws"; and promised lower tariffs and "effective control of crop surpluses" without specifying the nature of such controls.

[2] The Republican platform, among other things, advocated economy, emergency relief loans to states unable to cope with the unemployment crisis, maintenance of the gold standard, and banking reform. It endorsed co-operative efforts by farmers to control agricultural production and maintenance of tariff protection. And it approved a constitutional amendment to allow the states to resume control of the liquor traffic.

ELECTION OF 1932

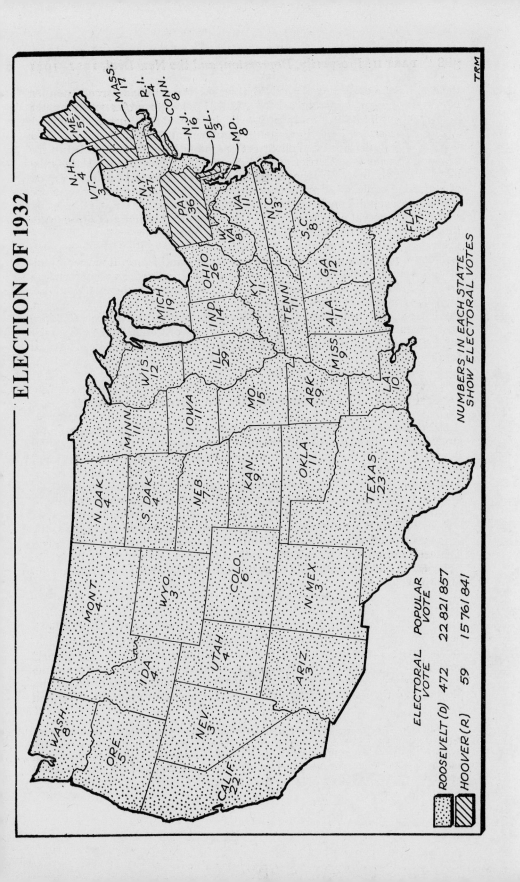

NUMBERS IN EACH STATE
SHOW ELECTORAL VOTES

	ELECTORAL VOTE	POPULAR VOTE
ROOSEVELT (d)	472	22 821 857
HOOVER (R)	59	15 761 841

TRM

the outline of a crop control measure that farm leaders had agreed upon. At Portland, Oregon, he promised federal hydroelectric projects. Before the Commonwealth Club of San Francisco he demanded that businessmen work together to assure full production and employment. To millions of investors who had been fleeced by Wall Street operators he promised to bring the stock exchanges under strict control. To the unemployed he declared that he was "utterly unwilling that economy should be practiced at the expense of starving people." Strange to say, organized labor was the only group to which Roosevelt did not promise some specific benefit.

Any Democrat could probably have won in that autumn of depression. But there can be no doubt that Roosevelt's contagious smile, reassuring voice, and ability to inspire confidence helped to make the election of 1932 one of the most impressive mandates in American history. Retaining business and a large middle-class support, Hoover received 15,761,841 votes and carried Pennsylvania, Connecticut, Delaware, Maine, New Hampshire, and Vermont. In contrast, Roosevelt received 22,821,857 popular votes, carried the electoral votes of the rest of the states, and helped give the Democrats staggering majorities in both houses of Congress. Certainly the revolution of 1932 was as sweeping as any Democrat could have wished for.[3]

139. *Franklin D. Roosevelt and the Progressive Movement*

No man, except perhaps Washington, Lincoln, and Truman, ever assumed the duties of President with more baffling problems than Franklin D. Roosevelt. But if the tasks were overwhelming, the opportunity for bold leadership was also great. That opportunity arose not only from the weakness of the Republican opposition and the strength of Roosevelt's forces in Congress after 1932. It arose even more importantly because of the strong survival in the 1930's of the progressive movement, especially in its economic and social manifestations. Divided and thwarted in the 1920's, the various components of progressivism came tentatively together in 1932. Roosevelt's most urgent political task, therefore, was to weld disparate groups that had not been able to co-operate effectively for long into a solid majority coalition.

This task proved deceptively easy in the dire emergency of 1933, for practically all classes and interests demanded action. Once the worst phase of the depression had passed, however, large conservative and business elements deserted the New Deal coalition, and Roosevelt had to fashion a new alliance and a new program. Abandoning many of his early policies, he resurrected the Jacksonian alliance of farmers and workingmen in 1935, added to it the social justice forces and the mass of the unemployed, and then set in motion the most far-reaching program of federal

---

[3] In spite of a vigorous campaign and a comprehensive program for combating the depression, the Socialist candidate, Norman Thomas, polled only 884,781 votes. The Communist candidate, William Z. Foster, enjoyed considerable support in intellectual and literary circles. But he also failed utterly to profit by the prevailing discontent and polled a mere 102,991 votes.

social and economic legislation in American history. It was ironic that Roosevelt in 1932 neither foresaw nor planned this culmination of the American progressive movement. And yet when necessity compelled a new departure he took firm control of the progressive forces and won congressional approval for a program that satisfied their historic demands. This, in brief, was his chief contribution to the progressive movement in the United States.

What manner of man was he who guided the destinies of the American people from the Great Depression to victory in global war and became almost the personal embodiment of the democratic movement? Walter Lippmann's classic observation, written in January 1932—that Roosevelt was a "pleasant man who, without any important qualifications for the office, would very much like to be President"—was undoubtedly overdrawn. Even so, it would have required a soothsayer in 1932 to predict the shape of things to come.

Roosevelt came up the easy way, at least before 1921. Born at Hyde Park, New York, on January 30, 1882, the son of James and Sara Delano Roosevelt, Franklin received a proper education at Groton and Harvard without demonstrating ambition or much intellectual promise. After being graduated from Harvard in 1904, he moved to New York City, studied in a desultory way at the Columbia University Law School, married his distant cousin Anna Eleanor Roosevelt in 1905, and settled down in 1907 for a comfortable career with a prominent New York law firm.

Following the example of his uncle-in-law and fifth cousin, Theodore Roosevelt, Franklin went into politics in 1910. He accepted the Democratic nomination for the State Senate in a Hudson Valley district that had gone Republican in every election but one since the Civil War. By virtue of hard campaigning and a split in the Republican party he won his first election. He led a small group of anti-machine Democrats at Albany in 1911 in a fight to prevent the election of the Tammany leader, William F. Sheehan, to the United States Senate. Seeming success in this first skirmish brought Roosevelt a measure of national publicity; soon afterward he organized the anti-Tammany Democrats in support of Wilson's candidacy for the presidential nomination in 1912.

Roosevelt was appointed Assistant Secretary of the Navy in 1913 by Wilson at the suggestion of Josephus Daniels (who remembered that Theodore Roosevelt had used the same office as a stepping stone to the presidency). The young New Yorker was an able administrator and popular in the second rank of the Wilson circle from 1913 to 1920, even if he agreed more with Theodore Roosevelt than with Wilson and Secretary Daniels on issues like preparedness and intervention in the European war. Coming to friendly terms with the new young leaders of Tammany Hall, Roosevelt supported Alfred E. Smith in Smith's first bid for the governorship in 1918. Indeed, he won the Democratic vice presidential nomination in 1920 because he was the leading New York Wilsonian acceptable to Tammany.

Roosevelt lost the election, to be sure, but he gained invaluable experience, a host of friends, and a position of considerable prominence in Democratic councils. In brief, he was rapidly changing from a patrician reformer into a practical politician with a bright future. Then disaster struck in August 1921, when an attack of polio laid Roosevelt low. Courageously he fought to regain his strength and use of his withered legs; slowly, painfully he won a partial victory. Meanwhile, his wife and his devoted secretary and adviser, Louis M. Howe, stayed by his side and helped him to extend his influence among Democratic politicians through voluminous correspondence.

Roosevelt had recovered sufficiently by 1924 to nominate Smith for the presidency at the Democratic convention in New York's Madison Square Garden. He had discarded his crutches in public and had achieved maximum recovery when he placed Smith's name before the national convention at Houston in 1928. The New York leaders during the succeeding months begged Roosevelt to accept the gubernatorial nomination and pleaded that his name would greatly strengthen the national ticket in the state. At first he declined, saying that he needed another year for complete recovery and thinking that 1928 was a Republican year. But he could not refuse when Smith appealed to him on a personal basis. Roosevelt surprised friends and opponents by his vigor during the campaign of 1928; except for Smith he was the best vote-getter that the Democrats had. But the greatest surprise came on election day. Smith lost New York by a narrow margin, but enough Republicans voted for Roosevelt to put him in the Governor's chair by a plurality of 25,000.

We have seen how Roosevelt won the presidency in 1932 and established himself as the spokesman of a large part of the American people. During the fateful years of his tenure he abandoned old policies and adopted new ones, and he emerged with greater stature in the contemporary public eye during war than in peace. But throughout the conflict and turmoil he remained remarkably the same man.

Roosevelt's personality was extraordinarily complex; he had many sides, and the whole is not equal to the sum of its parts. Personally, he was urbane and witty; yet for all his patrician upbringing he had a deep affection for people as individuals, not en masse. This was true in part because his long illness and fight for recovery purged him of any social snobbishness that he might once have had. It stirred a deep compassion in his heart for the physically afflicted and troubled in spirit. Moreover, he so much wanted people to like him that he often gave the impression of duplicity because he found it difficult to disagree with a good friend. Finally, in spite of his great courage in times of national peril, he rarely had the heart to dismiss a loyal but incompetent friend. On this account he was often a poor administrator,[4] although it must be added that Roosevelt's canny refusal to permit any subordinate to exercise too much power was the chief cause of the administrative snarls that vexed his regime.

Roosevelt's religious beliefs underlay all his attitudes toward men and society. He believed in a personal God, an absolute ethic, and the essential goodness of his fellow men. Hence his views toward government and what government should do for people stemmed from his belief in decency, justice, and fair play. To his friends he was playful, radiant, and warm, and few could resist his charm, which he used in the confidence that he

<hr />

[4] But see the extended analysis in Arthur M. Schlesinger, Jr., *The Coming of the New Deal* (Boston, 1959), pp. 533–52.

could "get through" to any person. Toward his enemies, on the other hand, he could appear vain, deceptive, petty, and vindictive.

Intellectually, Roosevelt was at once naive and sophisticated. He was not widely read in literature, preferred to obtain information from conversation rather than from study, and gave the impression of relying upon intuition more than hard thinking in solving difficult problems. The latter he himself characterized as "playing it by ear." He was not a particularly original thinker, but he had great capacity for learning and for thinking in broad terms, and a flexibility that freed him for experimentation. In economic matters Roosevelt displayed considerable virtuosity in assimilating, mastering, and reducing complex data. But he was not as competent in economic theory and was often at the mercy of advisers in formulating economic policies.

In spite of all his shortcomings, Roosevelt won such affection and loyalty from the American people as few Presidents have earned. He was the champion campaigner of American history, the President for life after 1932. In brief, Roosevelt succeeded, first, because he was able to communicate—either in person, over the radio, or in newsreels—directly with individuals and to radiate his warmth and confidence into the hearts and minds of all manner of men. He succeeded, secondly, because he was able to articulate great ideals in simple language, in other words, to express the hopes and aspirations of the average man in homely yet moving words. He succeeded, above all, because he possessed an uncanny ability to know and understand what the majority of people wanted and the courage to defy powerful forces of privilege and fight for measures of social and economic justice. By his character and the techniques of his leadership he restored the presidency nearly to the high eminence that it had enjoyed under Woodrow Wilson.

140. *Interregnum: The Banking Panic and the Change of Government*

The event that gave the new administration its tremendous emergency power was the practical collapse of the banking structure of the United States in the last months of Hoover's tenure. Most of the country's banks, especially the great metropolitan institutions, had stood impregnable during the first phase of the depression. Aggregate banking resources declined only $2,000,000,000—from a total of $72,172,500,000 to $70,209,000,000 —from June 1929 to June 1931. Then American banking strength began to give way after the European collapse in the summer of 1931. Total banking resources declined from $70,209,000,000 to $57,245,100,000 between June 30, 1931, and June 30, 1932, while bank deposits shrank nearly $9,000,000,000.

Thus by the summer of 1932 the forces of dissolution had eroded and were beginning to imperil the very foundations of American capitalism. Whatever the cause, fear spread and grew into panic in January 1933. The strain of runs and heavy withdrawals was too great for the banks to bear. The first sign of crisis came on October 31, 1932, when the Governor of Nevada declared a twelve-day banking holiday in his state to avert the failure of an important chain of banks. Governor Huey P. Long closed the banks of Louisiana on February 4, 1933; ten days later the Governor of Michigan declared a banking moratorium for a week. Then state after state succumbed during the ensuing three weeks, until the climax of the crisis came in the early morning on March 4, when Governor Herbert H. Lehman closed New York banks for two days. Banks were either closed or doing business under severe restrictions in forty-seven states when Roosevelt was inaugurated.

Meanwhile, President Hoover had been trying to win Roosevelt's approval for policies that would stabilize the financial situation and restore public confidence. Hoover in private conference and by letter exhorted the President-elect to announce that he would balance the budget, maintain the dollar at its current value in gold, and co-operate with European powers in stabilizing currencies and exchange rates. Roosevelt refused, not only because he had already decided to inflate the currency, but also because he suspected that Hoover was trying to transfer some of his own unpopularity to the incoming administration. Thus irreconcilable differences over policy prevented effective teamwork between the two men, although Treasury officials worked loyally with the Secretary of the Treasury—designate and his subordinates.

Throughout all the turmoil Roosevelt was hard at work constructing an administration. For Secretary of State he chose Senator Cordell Hull of Tennessee, probably the most influential Democrat in the upper house. As Secretary of the Treasury Roosevelt wanted Senator Carter Glass of Virginia, author of the Federal Reserve bill and former head of the Treasury under Wilson, whose financial orthodoxy would reassure the banking interests. Glass, however, refused because Roosevelt would not promise to eschew inflation. The post went instead to William H. Woodin of New York, president of the American Car & Foundry Company, a heavy contributor to the Democratic party, and a friend of Raymond Moley, head of the "Brain Trust." Woodin was succeeded by Henry Morgenthau, Jr., in 1934. The secretaryships of Agriculture and of the Interior went to two midwestern progressive Republicans, Henry A. Wallace of Iowa and Harold L. Ickes of Chicago, who had helped swing their section to Roosevelt during the campaign. By selecting Frances Perkins, a social worker with long experience in New York, as Secretary of Labor, the President-elect honored women and accorded signal recognition to the men and women who had been pressing the cause of social and labor reform. The important job of dispenser of the patronage, otherwise known as the Postmaster General, went to the astute Jim Farley, while the remaining Cabinet appointees were an assortment of party hacks and wheelhorses. They were George H. Dern, Secretary of War; Homer S. Cummings, Attorney General; Claude A. Swanson, Secretary of the Navy; and Daniel C. Roper, Secretary of Commerce.

The men who stood close to Roosevelt and made important decisions with his approval were not the Cabinet, although a few Cabinet members were in the charmed inner circle. They were Roosevelt's unofficial advisers —the earlier "Brain Trust," now considerably enlarged in number: Raymond Moley, A. A. Berle, Jr., Rexford G. Tugwell, Hugh S. Johnson,

George N. Peek, Louis M. Howe, Samuel I. Rosenman, and others. All of them were given posts in various agencies and the White House.

It was a gloomy day, March 4, 1933, when Franklin Delano Roosevelt took the oath as President of the United States. The economic machinery of the country was almost at a standstill, and people looked toward Washington for some word of hope. The new President struck at the frights and anxieties of the last three years and called out defiantly: "This great Nation will endure as it has endured, will revive and will prosper. So, first of all, let me assert my firm belief that the only thing we have to fear is fear itself." He was ready, he declared, to assume supreme command, and he called upon the people to follow him as if he were their commander in chief in battle. There were many urgent tasks ahead, Roosevelt continued. People had to be put to work; the banking, credit, and currency systems had to be overhauled and strengthened; the nation had to learn to use its resources wisely. If Congress failed to provide adequate remedies, he warned, he would ask Congress for "broad Executive power to wage a war against the emergency, as great as the power that would be given to me if we were in fact invaded by a foreign foe."

The meaning of this pronouncement was not lost upon the people of the United States as they sat huddled around their radios. They knew little about the finely spun rationalizations of the orthodox economists and understood even less the abstruse mathematical logic of the new school who talked of managed currency. They did not have to know or understand these things in order to sense that this day, March 4, 1933, was a fateful moment in the nation's history. One order was dead beyond recall. Another, ill defined and uncertain though it was, had been born.

141. *Financial Reinforcement and Reform Under the New Deal*

So desperate was the crisis on March 4, 1933, and so frightened were congressmen and the people, that Roosevelt possessed a power unprecedented in American peacetime history. Had he harbored imperial ambitions, he probably could have obtained dictatorial powers from Congress. Had he been a socialist, he might have nationalized the banks and set the country upon the road toward extreme collectivism. However, Roosevelt was neither a fascist, socialist, or communist. He was simply an old-fashioned American—as he once put it, simply "a Christian and a democrat"—with traditional views on the benefits of the system of private enterprise and ownership of property. He believed that the capitalistic system was worth saving. And the manner in which he and his helpers accomplished this objective revealed the true character of the First New Deal.

The hope for national salvation, Roosevelt thought, lay in quick action to overcome the menace of national economic collapse. He closed all banks on March 6, 1933, for a four-day period and forbade all gold payments and exports. Congress met in a special session on March 9 and within four hours enacted the Emergency Banking bill that Moley, Woodin, and spokesmen of the banking community had agreed upon. The Emergency Banking Act revealed that the administration had decided to restore and strengthen private ownership and management in the financial field. It authorized Federal Reserve banks to issue currency against bank assets, empowered the RFC to provide liquid funds to banks by buying their preferred stock, directed Treasury officials to supervise the reopening of banks,[5] and forbade hoarding and export of gold.

Coupled with the Economy Act, approved March 20, which drastically reduced federal expenditures in an effort to balance the budget, swift Treasury action under the Emergency Banking Act at once restored the confidence of the business classes. Roosevelt explained what the government was doing and appealed for public confidence in the banking system in his first "fireside chat," or direct radio talk, with the American people on March 12. The response was immediate. By the first week in April more than a billion dollars in currency had flowed back to the banks; hoarders had returned gold to the Federal Reserve banks; and Treasury officials had had to issue only a small amount of new Federal Reserve currency.

The worst crisis was over, and now the Treasury began the immense task of strengthening weak banks and eliminating unsound ones. First, the RFC between March 1933 and July 1935 extended more than $1,000,000,-000 in aid to 6,468 banks that were deemed essentially sound. Second, Treasury and state officials liquidated 2,352 banks, with aggregate deposits of $2,756,946,000, during the same two-year period. Hence the administration strengthened and restored to private hands the most vital and sensitive part of the capitalistic economy. As Moley observed, "The policies which vanquished the bank crisis were thoroughly conservative policies. The sole departure from convention lay in the swiftness and boldness with which they were carried out." [6]

In fulfilling his promise to reform the financial system the President merely encouraged a bipartisan congressional determination that the speculative debacle of 1929 should never happen again. Thus the Glass-Steagall Act, or Banking Act of 1933, sought to prevent banks from using the resources of the Federal Reserve System for speculation—chiefly by compelling the absolute divorcement of commercial banks from their investment affiliates.[7] Moreover, the Truth-in-Securities Act of 1933 and the Securities Exchange Act of 1934 left operation of stock exchanges in private hands but compelled all underwriters and brokers to furnish complete information regarding the true value of securities being offered for sale and the arrangements under which the sale was being made. To the Securities and Exchange Commission (SEC), a nonpartisan agency established by the Act of 1934, was entrusted the task of preventing and helping to punish misrepresentation and fraud.

vvvvvvvvvvvvvvvvvvvvvv

[5] Treasury officials divided banks into four classes, on a basis of relative soundness. Over half the banks, with 90 per cent of all deposits, were given a clean bill and allowed to reopen by March 15, 1933.

[6] Raymond B. Moley, *After Seven Years* (New York, 1939), p. 155.

[7] For a discussion of the growth of these investment affiliates and their contribution to the speculation of the late 1920's, see above, pp. 270–1, 366. At the insistence of southern and western Democrats, the Banking Act of 1933 also established the Federal Deposit Insurance Corporation which insured deposits, first up to $2,500, then up to $5,000 in 1935, and finally up to $10,000 after the Second World War.

Administration leaders set to work after the banking crisis had been liquidated to prepare a comprehensive measure to supplant the temporary Banking Act of 1933. The result, the Banking Act of 1935, was the first fundamental overhauling of the Federal Reserve Act since its adoption in 1913. In contrast to the Wilsonian legislation, which had diffused power within the Federal Reserve System and given little initiatory authority to the central board, the Act of 1935 concentrated enormous power in the central board, now called the Board of Governors. The Board now had *direct* authority over discount, or interest, rates, reserve requirements, and open market operations of Federal Reserve Banks. In addition, a number of highly technical provisions established new classes of securities and commercial paper against which Federal Reserve currency might be issued.

Roosevelt's own contribution to this edifice of financial reform—the Holding Company Act of 1935—was the center of a long and bitter battle in Congress and the country. Ambitious monopolists had used the holding company device during the 1920's to create far-flung and often irrational public utilities systems. (See above, pp. 266–267.) Conservatives and New Dealers alike approved the President's plan to bring holding companies under rigorous federal control, but controversy arose when Roosevelt insisted upon incorporating a provision imposing the "death sentence" upon the gigantic holding companies.

The battle over the President's bill raged in Congress all during the spring and summer of 1935. Administration spokesmen stirred hot resentment in their efforts to force congressmen and senators into line. The utilities companies spent hundreds of thousands of dollars in a spectacular lobbying campaign that also backfired. The upshot was a compromise, embodied in the Public Utility Holding Company Act of August 28, 1935. It gave the SEC complete supervisory control over financial operations of holding companies, compelled destruction of the giant utilities empires within five years, but allowed small holding companies controlling single, integrated operating systems to survive. It was, altogether, a substantial victory for the President.

The task of reforming the country's financial institutions was now fairly complete. To progressives the changes that had been accomplished during the past two years were good because they transformed financial operations from a private into a quasi-public business. At long last the populistic demand for complete federal control of banks, stock markets, and the money supply had been satisfied.

Two other aspects of the First New Deal's program to save the capitalistic structure remain to be noted here: the effort, first, to enable homeowners to refinance and adjust their debt burdens and, second, to spur a revival of private home construction through federal support of the mortgage market. The first objective was accomplished by the establishment on June 13, 1933, of the Home Owners Loan Corporation (HOLC). Authorized to borrow up to $2,000,000,000, later increased to $4,750,000,000, the HOLC refinanced mortgages of home owners in dire peril of foreclosure. The agency lent more than $3,000,000,000 to more than 1,000,000 home owners and assumed about one sixth of the entire urban mortgage load during its three years of life. Secondly, to stimulate the nearly defunct housing construction industry,[8] Congress on June 28, 1934, established the Federal Housing Administration (FHA), which insured mortgages for new construction and home repairs. The FHA played a large role in the resumption of private home construction by providing a system of long-term repayment at low interest rates. Between 1934 and 1940 it insured 2,300,000 loans totaling $945,000,000 for home repairs and 554,000 loans totaling $2,300,000,000 for new construction.

142.   *The Problem of Recovery and an Unsuccessful Experiment*

The philosophy underlying the administration's recovery program was compounded of a curious mixture of pessimism about the future of the economy and naive faith in the ability of government to work miracles by easy solutions. Roosevelt and his advisers accepted the then popular view that the American economy had reached a stage of full maturity, that the closing of the agricultural frontier, restriction of immigration, and sharp decline in the birth rate had removed the self-generating forces from the economy. The age of expansion and confidence, when businessmen invested in the future and expanded economic frontiers, was allegedly over. Indeed, Roosevelt several times observed, the American industrial plant was overbuilt because it could produce more than people could consume.

The chief task ahead, therefore, was to conserve human and natural resources, restore prices to a level that would yield profits to farmers, manufacturers, and businessmen, and assure fair distribution of goods and incomes. This could be accomplished, not by stimulating foreign trade and encouraging new investment, but by close co-operation among workers, farmers, businessmen, and government to raise prices, increase purchasing power through shorter hours and higher wages, and limit production to actual needs.

This is not to say that Roosevelt took the helm with any grand plan for recovery, for his most elaborate undertakings, the National Recovery Administration and the Public Works Administration, which we will soon discuss, were afterthoughts and improvisations. The administration's original program was aimed chiefly at stimulating recovery by raising the prices of agricultural products through restriction of output and by increasing the general price level through controlled inflation.

Roosevelt took the first step toward controlled inflation on March 6, 1933, by prohibiting redemption of currency in gold coin and export of gold without the Treasury's approval. Subsequent presidential decrees and acts of Congress nationalized gold and forbade fulfillment of private and public contracts calling for payment of debts in yellow coin. This action took the country off the traditional gold standard at home but retained a gold bullion backing for the currency and allowed limited gold payments in international exchange.

The dollar had fallen in value by mid-May 1933 to 85 cents in gold on international exchanges. Wholesale prices in the United States were rising

~~~~~~~~~~~~~~~~~~~~

[8] Urban home construction numbered only 60,000 units in 1933, as compared with 900,000 units in 1925.

as a result, and the entire economy seemed on the verge of invigoration. Having apparently set recovery in motion, would the President now agree to stabilize the gold content of the dollar, or would he embark upon a course of frank inflation?

This was perhaps the most important question confronting the administration in the late spring of 1933. On the one hand, an overwhelming majority of Congress favored outright inflation through the issue of paper currency.[9] On the other hand, an international conference would meet in London in June 1933 to lower tariffs, stabilize currencies, and find other means to stimulate a revival of international economic activity. Thus the President was caught in an embarrassing dilemma by the end of May. He had pledged support to the London Conference, yet he was not willing to stabilize the gold content of the dollar and forgo the advantages of further inflation.

By the time that the London Conference met,[10] Roosevelt had been converted to the so-called commodity dollar theory and had decided upon further inflation. Advocates of the "commodity dollar" argued that the best hope for sound recovery lay in devaluing the dollar to its purchasing power of 1926. This could be done, they said, by decreasing its gold value by 43 per cent. Such inflation, these economists further contended, would not only stimulate production through substantial price increases but would also enable the American people better to carry their debt burdens.

Before acting, however, the President first waited to see how far the dollar would fall naturally in the exchanges and whether the recovery that had set in would last. The dollar had depreciated about 30 per cent by October, and commodity prices had risen 19 per cent. Meanwhile, the country had gyrated from depression to near recovery and back to depression again, as the following statistics reveal:

1933	MANUFACTURING PRODUCTION *	EMPLOYMENT *	PAYROLLS *	WHOLESALE PRICES ‡
March	56	58.8	37.1	60.2
April	65	59.9	38.8	60.4
May	77	62.6	42.7	62.7
June	93	66.9	47.2	65
July	101	71.5	50.8	68.9
August	91	76.4	56.8	69.5
September	83	80	59.1	70.8
October	65	79.6	59.4	71.2

* Monthly average 1923–5 = 100
‡ 1926 average = 100

[9] It required all the President's influence to restrain these congressional demands, but he won control over monetary policy with the passage of the Thomas Amendment to the Agricultural Adjustment Act of May 12, 1933. The Thomas Amendment authorized but did not require the President to increase the money supply by six different methods, including the printing of $3,000,000,000 in paper currency, free coinage of silver at 16 to 1, lowering of Federal Reserve requirements, and devaluation of the gold content of the dollar up to 50 per cent.

[10] For Roosevelt's "torpedoing" of the London Economic Conference, see below, pp. 459–461.

Resolved to try any expedient rather than permit the nation to suffer through another winter of subdepression, Roosevelt decided that the time had come to put the "commodity dollar" theory to work. He announced his decision in a "fireside chat" on October 22, 1933. Three days later he instructed the RFC to purchase gold, then selling at $29.80 an ounce, at $31.36 an ounce.[11] The President gradually increased the price of gold during ensuing months until he had finally achieved the "commodity dollar," theoretically equal in purchasing power to the dollar of 1926. Now willing to stabilize, he persuaded Congress to establish a new gold reserve standard.[12] Then on January 31, 1934, he set the price of gold at $35.00 an ounce and the gold content of the dollar at 59.06 per cent of its pre-1933 value. Not long afterward he approved a Trade Agreements Act and permitted Secretary Hull to undertake a vigorous campaign to expand foreign trade. (For details, see below, pp. 467–468.)

The most important thing that can be said about Roosevelt's efforts to achieve recovery through monetary manipulation was that they failed to accomplish their announced objective. Prices refused to rise significantly because devaluation was not accompanied by a large increase either in the money supply or in bank credit, and because the European nations quickly adjusted their currencies to the inflated American dollar. Moreover, the costs of devaluation were so great as to overshadow any temporary benefits. For one thing, devaluation in part cost the President the friendship of a number of close advisers and alienated conservative Democrats. Worse still, European leaders interpreted Roosevelt's refusal in 1933 to stabilize the dollar and his subsequent devaluation as a declaration of economic warfare. Inevitably, they retaliated in kind.

After stabilizing the dollar, however, the President eschewed any further financial legerdemain. Perhaps he realized that recovery could not be bought so cheaply; certainly he began to recognize his mistake in thinking that the depression was almost entirely domestic in origin and that recovery could come without a vigorous revival of foreign trade. In any event, his economic policies were hereafter aggressively internationalistic: tariff reductions, international currency stabilization, and revival of foreign trade were the order of the day.

143.   *The NRA: Unsuccessful Experiment in a Planned Economy*

Perhaps the most interesting and revealing fact about the Roosevelt administration when it came into power was its utter lack of any plan for industrial recovery other than devaluation. The first stimulus came from organized labor and its spokesmen in Congress. Senator Hugo L. Black of

[11] The pre-1933 price had been $20.67 an ounce.

[12] In the Gold Reserve Act, adopted on January 30, 1934. This measure impounded in the Treasury all gold in Federal Reserve Banks, authorized the President to set the gold content of the dollar at between 50 and 60 per cent of its pre-1933 value, made gold bullion an unredeemable reserve against Federal Reserve notes, and established from the "profits" of devaluation a fund of $2,000,000,000 to be used to stabilize the dollar in international exchanges.

Alabama in December 1932 introduced a bill sponsored by the AF of L to limit hours of labor in industry to thirty a week. Roosevelt's advisers regarded the Black bill as a dangerous threat to recovery, but they were so engrossed in the banking crisis that they paid scant attention to the congressional situation. Then the Senate passed the measure on April 6, and the President commissioned Secretary Perkins to prepare an administration alternative. Miss Perkins went before the House labor committee a few days later, half-heartedly approved the thirty-hour principle, and suggested addition of provisions for minimum wages and federal control of production. By this time leaders of the business community were up in arms, and Roosevelt asked Raymond Moley to find out what they wanted.

Business spokesmen were ready with an answer, for the Chamber of Commerce of the United States had been at work on a recovery plan since 1931. It proposed creation of a national council of industrialists and businessmen who would work through trade associations to control production, raise prices, and stabilize wages. It was the business community's old dream of "self-regulation" brought to full maturity.

While Congress debated the Black bill, Moley and two other "brain trusters," Hugh S. Johnson and Rexford G. Tugwell, set to work to reconcile the Chamber of Commerce plan with the principle of federal control. Moley and Johnson presented a draft of their recovery bill to the business leaders when the Chamber of Commerce met in Washington on May 3, 1933. Although it included substantial concessions to labor, the Chamber of Commerce approved it as the only practical alternative to the Black bill. Thus fortified, the administration presented its measure, the National Industrial Recovery Act (NIRA), to Congress on May 15, 1933.

It was one of the most pretentious pieces of legislation ever presented to Congress to that time. Its objectives were to end cutthroat competition, raise prices to a profitable level by limiting production to actual needs, and guarantee a reasonable work week and a living wage to labor. These aims would be accomplished through the adoption of codes for all branches of industry and business by committees representing management, labor, and the public. In the event of irreconcilable disagreement, the President might intervene and impose a code of his own making. Section 7a of the bill—added, incidentally, at the demand of Secretary Perkins and William Green, president of the AF of L—affirmed labor's right to organize and bargain collectively. All these provisions were included in Title I of the measure. Title II, which appropriated $3,300,000,000 for a public works program, was incorporated in the measure at the last minute.

The two houses held slipshod hearings and debates on the bill for several weeks. A few senators were skeptical; but business, labor, and the administration united in a solid front, and Congress willingly concurred. Roosevelt signed, as he called it, "the most important and far-reaching legislation ever enacted by the American Congress" on June 16, 1933. On the same day he established the National Recovery Administration (NRA) and named Hugh S. Johnson as Administrator.

Johnson plunged into work with great energy and bustle. To provide for the interim period before specific codes could be drawn up, he proposed adoption of a blanket code. And to spur compliance he permitted employers who co-operated to display the Blue Eagle—the NRA emblem—and sponsored Blue Eagle parades reminiscent of the preparedness, draft, and war-loan parades of the Wilson era. Almost 2,500,000 employers with 16,-000,000 workers had signed the blanket code within a few weeks. The NRA was on its way.

Now began the laborious task of preparing individual codes to fit the needs of every industry and trade in the United States. Theoretically the code-making process involved mutualization of the interests of management, labor, and the consuming public. In actual practice it was the trade associations, dominated usually by their large members, that wrote the codes in the first instance. After hasty reviews by the Code Analysis Division and various advisory boards, these codes were adopted as bodies of law governing the industries or trades involved.

From October 1933 to early 1935, when the code-making process was completed, the NRA approved 557 basic codes and 208 supplementary codes. All of them contained provisions confirming labor's right to organize and establishing minimum wage and maximum hours scales. But business leaders, in making these concessions, obtained far-reaching benefits from the government: price stabilization,[13] production controls,[14] and outlawry of allegedly unfair competition. More important, business leaders won the right to govern themselves, for each code was administered by a code authority, almost invariably composed of trade association officials representing the large corporations. Finally, businessmen won another long-sought objective—exemption from antitrust prosecution for restrictive practices heretofore deemed illegal by the courts.

In the beginning this "self-regulation" of industry went smoothly on the surface, so long as the NRA gave free rein to businessmen. By the spring of 1934, however, Johnson had assembled his own staff of experts to run the NRA. They soon discovered the obvious fact that the codes discriminated against small producers, especially in pricing and sales policies. But the codes were already written and in force. All that the NRA staff could do was to try to compel code authorities to implement the broad objectives of the NIRA. This effort brought the NRA into increasingly frequent and bitter conflict with business leaders. As if to compound the NRA's perplexities, the inchoate opposition of small businessmen and manufacturers to codes written and administered by big business swelled into a mighty storm of protest in the early months of 1934. Actually, there is little evidence that small businessmen were much injured by the codes; they objected mainly to their provisions for minimum wages and prevention of sharp practices. To palliate this discontent, Roosevelt on February 19 appointed a National Recovery Review Board, headed by the famed criminal lawyer, Clarence Darrow, to investigate and recommend. Darrow instead

wwwwwwwwwwwwwww

[13] Although the NRA tried to discourage outright price-fixing, the bituminous coal, petroleum, and lumber codes contained schedules of minimum prices; most of the codes forbade sales below cost; and over half the codes required establishment of the open-price system, that is, a system of prices openly published and adhered to.

[14] Production control was achieved in various ways in the codes. The petroleum, copper, and lumber codes, for example, set definite production limits and assigned quotas to individual producers. The cotton textile code limited mills to two eight-hour shifts daily. Other codes forbade the expansion of plant without approval of the code authority.

of trying to evaluate impartially dealt with the NRA as if he were the prosecutor in a murder trial.

The fortunes of the NRA fell hard and fast after his pillorying. In the face of mounting criticism the President asked Johnson to resign, abolished the office of National Recovery Administrator, and, on September 27, 1934, created a National Recovery Board composed of representatives of management, labor, and the public. Any overhauling of the codes themselves, however, had to await congressional action, as the NIRA's life of two years would soon expire. The Supreme Court ended the discussion before Congress could respond to the President's request for extension of the NIRA. It declared the measure unconstitutional on May 25, 1935.

Economists and historians agree that although the NRA brought substantial benefits to workers (discussed in the following section), it failed to achieve many of the objectives of the Act that gave it birth. What was wrong? Why did so hopeful an experiment fail to come off? In the final analysis the NRA failed because it was based upon false assumptions about human nature and the American economy. The framers of the NIRA assumed, for example, that businessmen would use "self-regulation" to promote the general interest. As any good Calvinist could have predicted, businessmen used the NRA for other purposes, and they fought the NRA when they could not control it. Secondly, the NIRA was based upon the assumption that full production and employment could be achieved by outlawing price competition and either limiting or discouraging full production. Here was the basic contradiction and the most egregious error. What the United States needed in 1933 was new investment and a massive increase in production. Because the NRA discouraged both prerequisites of prosperity it impeded rather than stimulated recovery. Finally, the NIRA failed because it attempted to achieve something like a planned economy without conferring any powers necessary to attain this objective. It gave no power to the NRA, for example, either to determine desirable production goals for the entire economy or to compel manufacturers to meet them. Looking back, old "brain trusters" like Tugwell have said that the NIRA might have been the first step toward development of rational economic planning. Perhaps hindsight has brought the wisdom that administration leaders seemed to lack at an earlier time.

144. *Relief, Labor, and the First New Deal, 1933–1934*

In no area of federal action was the basically emergency character of the First New Deal more fully revealed than in the matter of relief policies. So long as Roosevelt's original advisers had the President's ear, the administration rejected long-range comprehensive plans and followed Hoover's policies of public works and indirect relief through the cities and states.

From the outset, however, Roosevelt was more responsive to the needs of the millions in distress than Hoover had been. For example, Roosevelt personally devised a new plan to save both human and natural resources. It was the Civilian Conservation Corps (CCC), authorized by Congress in late March and put into operation on April 5, 1933. The CCC, with an initial grant of $300,000,000, enrolled 250,000 young men from relief families [15] in some 1,500 camps. They worked under the direction of the War Department at reforestation, flood control, and soil conservation. The CCC had reached a maximum strength of 500,000 by 1935. More than 2,750,000 youths had served in the Corps when the project was ended in 1942.

The administration's primary concern in the spring of 1933 was the plight of the 15,000,000 unemployed and the survival of the nearly 6,000,-000 persons on city and state relief rolls. In response to the President's appeal, Congress approved the Federal Emergency Relief Act, signed on May 12, 1933. It appropriated $500,000,000, one half of it to be given outright to impoverished states and the balance to other states on a basis of one federal dollar for every three dollars spent by states and municipalities. Creating the Federal Emergency Relief Administration (FERA), Roosevelt appointed Harry L. Hopkins, chairman of the New York Temporary Emergency Relief Administration, as Administrator. The President while doing this made it clear that he agreed with Hoover that relief was primarily the responsibility of the cities and states.

Actually, Roosevelt regarded these measures as stopgaps to keep people from starving until recovery had set in. The administration's ace in the hole was a gigantic public works program to be launched with the NRA to stimulate depressed industries, mainly construction, not immediately affected by the main recovery program. Title II of the NIRA, which established the Public Works Administration (PWA) and appropriated $3,300,-000,000 for the program, gave specific authorization.

The effect might have been invigorating had this huge sum been poured immediately into the economy. As it turned out, the President unwittingly prevented any such result. Fearing that Johnson was too unstable to spend the money wisely, the President separated the PWA from the NRA and gave control of the former to Secretary of the Interior Ickes. He was a cautious, honest man, determined that not one cent of the $3,300,000,000 should be stolen or wasted. Thus he insisted upon scrutinizing the details of all projects. His loving care bore fruit eventually in the form of new highways, hospitals, university buildings, municipal water works, and the like. But it prevented the PWA from being a great spur to recovery in 1933. Thus the President faced a critical situation in September of that year. The false boom of the spring and summer had ended; the PWA was mired in red tape; and millions of families faced the coming winter with no hope of employment.

It was during this crisis that Harry Hopkins first had decisive influence in the administration. He saw the President on about November 1 and urged him to launch a vast new program of work relief—a kind of primitive public works on a direct basis—for 4,000,000 of the unemployed. Readily concurring, Roosevelt created the Civil Works Administration (CWA) on November 8, appointed Hopkins as Administrator, and took $400,000,000 from PWA funds to get the program under way. Within

---

[15] Men between the ages of eighteen and twenty-five, who were in need and capable of performing hard labor, were eligible. They received subsistence and $30 a month, $25 of which was sent to their families.

thirty days the CWA was a thriving concern and a means of living for 4,000,000 men and their families.

It seemed for a time that Roosevelt's approval of the CWA signified capitulation to what were then considered to be radical doctrines—that every man was entitled to a job, not merely a dole, and that it was the federal government's duty to provide work if private industry did not. Then, in response to the advice of conservative Democrats and bitter Republican criticism of waste, Roosevelt told Hopkins in mid-January 1934 that he would have to end the CWA. Hopkins obtained an additional $450,000,000 from Congress in February to carry the agency through the winter, but he liquidated his CWA projects in March and April. The burden of relief for the balance of 1934, therefore, fell again on the FERA, for which Hopkins had obtained an additional $500,000,000 from Congress on February 15.

An experimental approach and indecision over general objectives also characterized the First New Deal's labor program. Administration leaders sincerely wanted to help labor, and they succeeded to some degree. To begin with, incorporation of labor provisions in all NRA codes won immediate gains that organized labor in its then weakened position could not have won on its own. The forty-hour week was established by codes covering 13,000,000 workers, while the average work week for all industries fell from 43.3 hours in June 1933 to 37.8 hours in the following October. All codes, moreover, contained provisions outlawing child labor and establishing minimum wages, ranging generally from 30 to 40 cents an hour. Finally, adoption of the codes helped to stimulate an increase in the index of factory employment from 62.6 in May 1933 to 80 in September and in the index of payrolls from 42.7 to 59.4 during the same period. But little change in hours and wages occurred between October 1933 and May 1935, when the NRA was ended, in spite of an increase of 14 per cent in manufacturing output during this same period.

More important to labor in the long run was Section 7a of the Recovery Act. It asserted that workers should have the right to organize and bargain collectively "through representatives of their own choosing," outlawed the "yellow dog" contract, and declared that workers should not be required to join a company union as a condition of employment. Experience soon demonstrated that Section 7a was more an affirmation than a grant of essential protection. Nonetheless, it marked an epochal turning point: for the first time the federal government endorsed organized labor's historic objectives in general legislation.

Under the aegis of Section 7a, the AF of L roused with new hope and vigor. AF of L membership increased from 2,127,000 to 3,045,000 between 1933 and 1935, while membership in all unions grew from 2,857,000 to 3,728,000 during the same two years. It was substantial growth. A minority of employers, particularly in the building trades and the coal and garment industries, tried faithfully to honor Section 7a. For the most part, however, management was as determined as ever to prevent unionization, and employers by the thousands defied the NRA in labor disputes and harassed it by frequent appeals to the courts. More important, employers somewhat frantically organized company unions as a foil to independent unionism. Some 2,500,000 workers were organized in company unions by 1935.

Labor's striving and management's continued determination to preserve the open shop inevitably collided; and a wave of bloody strikes followed adoption of the NRA codes. Most of the disputes of 1933 and 1934 were not protracted, but they were exceedingly numerous and frequently violent, particularly in the southern textile region. To help bring peace to the industrial world, the President, on August 5, 1933, established a mediation commission to co-operate with the NRA. It was the National Labor Board, composed of distinguished labor leaders and industrialists, with Senator Robert F. Wagner of New York as chairman.

The National Labor Board settled many disputes during the ensuing year by common sense, persuasion, and an ability to find a compromise. More important was the fact that a group of public leaders studied, for the first time since 1915, the whole problem of industrial relations and discovered the full extent of management's opposition to the very principle of collective bargaining. They also learned that many employers would use almost any method, including the use of labor spies and force, to prevent unionization.

The experience convinced Senator Wagner that the movement for unionization could never succeed until the federal government came strongly to labor's support. When an employer refused to recognize a union or to bargain in good faith, for example, there was nothing that the National Labor Board could do but appeal to the NRA and the courts for uncertain redress. Following a wave of strikes in the spring of 1934, the President abolished the National Labor Board and established the National Labor Relations Board, a three-man commission empowered to hold elections to determine the right of unions to conduct collective bargaining. Wagner vainly tried to persuade the President and Congress to give the new Board authority to prevent so-called unfair practices by management. Lacking such authority, the National Labor Relations Board was even less successful in settling disputes than its predecessor had been.

The First New Deal's labor policies in part represented the fulfillment of the most advanced objectives of the social justice program—abolition of child labor, minimum wages, and maximum hours. Long overdue though they were, these reforms were not enough. In the final analysis, industrial democracy could be achieved only by the workers themselves, not by a beneficent government. In refusing to give the protection and positive support that organized labor needed for the full success of its movement, the President acted in the spirit of compromise that permeated the First New Deal.

145. *Toward Agricultural Stability, 1933–1935*

Farmers everywhere were on the verge either of despair or rebellion by the spring of 1933, but in no section was agrarian discontent so intense and dangerous as in the corn belt of the Middle West. Radical farm sentiment there found expression in the so-called Farm Holiday Association, organized by the fiery president of the Iowa Farmers' Union, Milo Reno. Its objective was to persuade farmers to withhold agricultural products from the market until prices equaled cost of production. Mobs of farm strikers in August 1932 tried to prevent food from entering Sioux City and

Des Moines. Representatives from most of the midwestern and Plains states met in a national convention of the Farm Holiday Association in the Iowa capital on March 12–13, 1933, and threatened to call a nation-wide strike if the new Roosevelt administration did not meet its demands by May 3.

Actually, the farmers' most immediate concern was not low prices but the threat of foreclosure. Farm owners everywhere in the Middle West banded together to save their farms, either by direct action or through their state governments. The legislature of Minnesota enacted a two-year moratorium on foreclosures; the Governor of North Dakota forbade forced sales of farm properties. Vigilante committees threatened to shoot bank or insurance agents and went en masse to foreclosure sales and bought back properties for nominal sums. The most famous outbreak occurred at Le Mars, Iowa, when some six hundred enraged farmers dragged a foreclosing judge from his bench and beat him into unconsciousness on April 27, 1933.

The Roosevelt administration acted quickly in this crisis to save the farmers and avert the likelihood of even more violent revolt. The President consolidated all federal agricultural credit agencies into the Farm Credit Administration on March 27, 1933; Congress provided abundant new credit shortly afterward.[16] Moreover, Congress in response to radical farm demands adopted the Frazier-Lemke Farm Bankruptcy Act on June 28, 1934; it enabled farmers to recover lost property on easy terms.

These, however, were all stopgaps. The major need was a long-range program for agricultural recovery. Here the difficulty lay not in originating measures but in persuading agricultural spokesmen to unite upon a common plan. The National Farmers' Union and the Farm Holiday Association, speaking for tenants and subsistence farmers, demanded direct relief and inflation and opposed production controls. On the other hand, the more influential spokesmen of large farmers—the Farm Bureau Federation and the National Grange—had settled by the beginning of 1933 upon the so-called domestic allotment plan. It called for federal payments to farmers who cooperated in limiting the production of basic staples.

The new Secretary of Agriculture, Henry A. Wallace, began a series of conferences with farm leaders on March 6, 1933. The outcome was the Agricultural Adjustment Act, approved by Congress on May 10, 1933, and signed by the President two days later. It was easily the most ambitious agricultural legislation in the history of the country, but all its major features had long been discussed and advocated by important farm groups. Thus it represented, not a new departure, but a logical culmination of policies begun by the Wilson administration and carried forward by subsequent Republican Presidents and Congresses.

Lest there be misunderstanding as to the intentions of the framers, the Act announced their objectives in clear language: to establish and maintain such a balance between production and consumption of agricultural

⌁⌁⌁⌁⌁⌁⌁⌁⌁⌁⌁⌁⌁⌁

[16] The Emergency Farm Mortgage Act of May 12, 1933, for example, authorized emergency loans to save farmers in immediate peril. Within less than two years the Farm Credit Administration had refinanced one fifth of all farm mortgages in the United States. The Farm Credit Act of June 16, 1933, moreover, established a system of production credit corporations to extend short-term loans to farmers and livestock producers.

commodities that farm income would have the same relative purchasing power that it had enjoyed during the stable parity period from 1909 to 1914. To achieve so-called parity prices, the Act authorized the imposition of various production controls [17] on major staples. The money to finance the program would come from taxes on the processing of agricultural commodities and customs duties on certain enumerated commodities.

While farm leaders and administration spokesmen were agreeing upon the domestic allotment plan, the Agricultural Department received frightening reports of bountiful crops for the coming summer and autumn of 1933. In response, Wallace and George N. Peek, the new head of the Agricultural Adjustment Administration (AAA), sent agents through the South and Southwest to persuade farmers to plow under 10,000,000 acres, or one fourth, of the cotton crop in return for benefit payments. The AAA in addition bought 220,000 sows and over 6,000,000 pigs for immediate slaughter. A similar destruction of part of the wheat crop was averted only by weather reports indicating that there would be drastic natural reductions in that staple.

Cotton farmers plowed under with a vengeance, but they fertilized the remaining crop so heavily that total output in 1933 was 13,047,000 bales, as compared with 13,002,000 bales in 1932. In the following year, therefore, Congress adopted the Bankhead Cotton Control Act, approved April 21, 1934. It permitted the AAA to assign marketing quotas and imposed a prohibitive tax on cotton sold in excess of the quotas.[18] Cotton production fell in consequence to 9,636,000 bales in 1934, and to 10,638,000 bales in 1935.

The AAA meanwhile used its vast powers in other ways to restrict production and restore prices. After the "plow under" and the slaughter of the pigs, the AAA set production goals for 1934 in the major staples and sent out 100,000 agents to persuade farmers to sign contracts. In addition, the AAA established the Commodity Credit Corporation on October 18 to enable cotton and corn producers to borrow against their crops and hold them until prices rose to higher levels.

The AAA worked almost an economic miracle through these and other measures until the Supreme Court called a halt in January 1936. In the case of cotton and tobacco, the effects of the AAA program were direct and calculable. Cotton production, for example, was cut one third during the period 1933 to 1935; had controls and price supports not been in effect the price of cotton would not have risen much above the depression level. The effects of the AAA program on corn, wheat, and livestock are more difficult to calculate, but it seems likely that the droughts of 1933 and 1934 caused vastly greater reductions than could ever have been accomplished by crop controls. It was as if nature co-operated with the AAA to end for a time the problem of uncontrollable surpluses in the basic food commodities.

Whatever the cause, farmers were well on the way toward stability and parity by the end of 1935. Net farm income rose from $1,928,000,000 in

[17] Among them were benefit payments for voluntary crop reduction, commodity loans to farmers who co-operated, marketing agreements and quotas, export subsidies, and purchase of surpluses by the Department of Agriculture.

[18] The Kerr-Smith Tobacco Control Act, also approved in 1934, gave the AAA similar powers of control over tobacco growers.

1932 to $4,605,000,000 in 1935, with startling results. For one thing, the ratio of farm prices to prices that the farmer paid for manufactured goods rose from 58 per cent in 1932 to 88 per cent in 1935.[19] For another, moderate prosperity and increased governmental credit enabled farmers not only to hold their own in the battle against bankruptcy but even to turn the tide for the first time since 1920—by reducing the total farm mortgage load from $9,630,768,000 in 1930 to $7,584,459,000 in 1935.

In the long run, however, the economic results of the first AAA program were not as significant as its political implications. Representatives of the urban majority in Congress, acting on the assumption that a bankrupt agriculture could mean only an impoverished economy, converted agriculture into a subsidized industry by taxing consumers and diverting a portion of the national income to the farming minority. To be sure, the organized farmers who benefited most from the AAA program were a powerful pressure group, able almost to impose demands on the two parties. Even so, the first AAA stemmed as much from genuine progressive convictions concerning government's duty toward submerged groups as from considerations of political advantage.

∿∿∿∿∿∿∿∿∿∿∿∿∿∿∿∿

[19] 100 equals the ratio prevailing during the parity period 1909–14.

CHAPTER

19

The Second New Deal:
The Culmination of
American Progressivism

THE FIRST NEW DEAL coalition of businessmen, workers, and farmers came apart at the seams in the spring and summer of 1934. A large part of the business and industrial leadership came out against the administration's program, while the masses of voters—workers, farmers, and unemployed—rallied more overwhelmingly to Roosevelt's support in the congressional election in the autumn of 1934 than they had done two years before. Roosevelt had neither foreseen nor desired the realignment in American politics that occurred as the nation divided roughly into a Right and a Left during the last months of 1934 and the early part of 1935. Yet the realignment occurred, and spokesmen of labor, the unemployed and destitute, and the aged were beginning campaigns to commit the federal government to new and often absurd schemes. Indeed, it was evident by January 1935 that the administration would have to undertake measures to allay the forces of discontent or else run serious risk of being overwhelmed by those forces.

Roosevelt moved with remarkable agility swiftly to construct a new coalition and program in order to bring the political situation under his control. Gradually discarding conservative advisers, he gathered a new retinue of rasher friends and espoused a program designed to ameliorate the misfortunes of the masses through deficit spending, redistribution of wealth, and the most far-reaching program of social and economic legislation in American history. This was the Second New Deal, the full flowering of social justice progressivism.

This shift was certainly leftward in one sense. The First New Deal was grounded in large measure upon technocratic assumptions about the possibilities of national planning through the NRA, among other agencies. The effort collapsed both in constitutional theory and in practice. The Second New Deal, for all its concern for legislation to help disadvantaged groups, was based at least in practice upon the assumption that competition was still the life of trade, and that it was government's *main* duty to regulate in order to prevent the imposition of shackles upon private economic energies.

Actually, it is extremely risky to try to fit either the First or Second New Deal in any Procrustean bed of ideology. The NIRA in one sense marked a radical departure from the main traditions in American political economy. Yet it represented the triumph of a movement for "self-regulation" in the business community itself that was at least as old as the second administration of Theodore Roosevelt. Whatever radical departures it might have implied were more than offset by the First New Deal's conservative reinforcement of the financial sector, even though this effort also brought final satisfaction of the old Populist demand for popular control over banks and the money supply.

It seems safest to conclude in retrospect that both New Deals moved inexorably toward fulfillment of the main historic objectives of the American progressive movement. There were deviations like the NIRA, to be sure. They did not survive for long. Much of the First New Deal did survive: financial reform and restructuring, expanded federal relief activity, the Tennessee Valley Authority's experiment in regional planning (to be discussed in a later chapter), the federal agricultural program launched in 1933 and later overhauled, and an inchoate policy of support of labor, among other things. To this foundation the Second New Deal added a vast new structure of advanced legislation and policies, as we will soon see. It is somewhat far-fetched to say that this culmination marked any important deviation from main traditions. Every single important policy both of the First and Second New Deals had deep roots in the progressive tradition.

146. *Launching the Second New Deal*

The normally conservative middle and upper classes began to judge the First New Deal by conventional standards and to turn receptive ears toward its critics once the worst phase of the depression was over in 1934. Herbert Hoover, for example, had taken to the American road to warn that the foundations of constitutional government were being undermined by the federal government's steady encroachment upon the rights of the states. The developments that turned the industrial and business classes decisively against the administration, however, stemmed mainly from the NRA. On the one hand, small businessmen rebelled against codes that favored big business. On the other hand, when the NRA tried to bring the code authorities under some measure of public control, the great industrial leaders turned sharply against the administration. Moreover, practically all manufacturers, large and small, resisted when the National Labor Board endeavored to implement Section 7a of the NIRA.

The conservative revolt took shape with the formation in August 1934 of the American Liberty League. Its voices were those of conservative lawyers and Democratic politicians led by Alfred E. Smith and John W. Davis, but its financial support came from certain big business interests, notably the Du Pont family. It opposed New Deal bureaucracy and capricious presidential tyranny and championed state rights, "free enterprise," and the "American" system of the open shop. In their zeal to turn back the tide of progressivism, Liberty Leaguers entered the congressional campaign of 1934 to help elect conservatives of both parties.

Roosevelt viewed this revolt of the business community at first as the opposition of a small minority. Much more disturbing to him and his political advisers was the rising tide of opposition to the First New Deal program from disgruntled reformers and demagogic leaders. The frightening thing was the fact that the New Deal had obviously failed to bring hope to sharecroppers, tenant and subsistence farmers, the unemployed, and especially indigent old people. These lower-class elements seemed ready in their desperation to follow any crackpot with a plan.

One of the first movements on the non-Communist Left was the campaign of the muckraking novelist, Upton Sinclair, to end poverty in California. Championing a radical program of high state income and inheritance taxes and a $50 monthly pension to indigent persons over sixty,[1] Sinclair won the Democratic gubernatorial nomination in California in 1934. His End Poverty in California movement, called EPIC, soon disintegrated, but its momentary success was a signal of mass dissatisfaction.

At the same time a more important movement came out of California. It was the so-called Townsend Plan, the creation of the generous Dr. Francis E. Townsend of Long Beach. He proposed that the federal government pay $200 monthly to all unemployed persons over sixty. Townsend's proposal spread like wildfire among the destitute aged; there were thousands of Old Age Revolving Pension, or Townsend, clubs by 1935, and the good doctor claimed 5,000,000 followers.

More disquieting to the administration were movements being promoted from 1933 to 1935 by the Reverend Charles E. Coughlin and Senator Huey Pierce Long. Coughlin was a Roman Catholic priest in a Detroit suburb who fell to discussing politics and economic issues in radio sermons around 1930. His animadversions against bankers and Republican leaders were soon more popular than his religious messages. Advocating a program of far-reaching socialization of industry and credit, Coughlin at first supported the New Deal. However, he soon fell out with Roosevelt over monetary policies and turned his National Union for Social Justice against the New Deal in 1935. Coughlin claimed 9,000,000 followers—an absurdly exaggerated estimate—at the height of his influence.

Huey P. Long was a much more dangerous menace. He was not a mere

---

[1] Sinclair described his program in *I, Governor of California, and How I Ended Poverty* (Los Angeles, 1933). He sold almost 1,000,000 copies and partially financed his gubernatorial campaign from the proceeds.

demagogue of the anti-Negro, anti-Catholic type. Rising out of the poverty of the piney woods section of northern Louisiana, he won a reputation in the early 1920's because he addressed himself realistically to the needs of the lower classes of his state. Elected Governor of Louisiana in 1928, Long redeemed his promises to the common people. Elected to the United States Senate in 1930, he continued to dominate the government of his state as completely as if he had remained at Baton Rouge. So powerful was his hold over the lower classes that he established a dictatorship in 1934–5, organized a private army of storm troopers, and could declare, "I am the law." His henchmen were enormously corrupt, but he was still the idol of the common people of Louisiana when an assassin's bullet cut short his career on September 8, 1935.

Long's significance on the national scene lay chiefly in the fact that he was the chief agitator of lower-class protest against the First New Deal compromise. Long, like Coughlin, was an ardent Roosevelt supporter in 1932. But the Louisianan turned savagely against the administration and set out to win control of the Democratic party when Roosevelt refused to nationalize banks, expropriate wealth, and knuckle under to Long's patronage demands in 1933. Organizing the Share Our Wealth Society in that same year, Long promised to make every man a king. His methods were simple enough. He would give every family a homestead worth $5,000 and an annual income of $2,500, and he would confiscate large fortunes to provide this bounty to the poor.[2]

President Roosevelt in late 1934 and early 1935 launched a program frankly designed to provide larger security and incomes for the masses. This sudden leftward shift, if such it may be called, was one of the really significant turning points in twentieth century American politics. It occurred, not because the President "planned it that way," but in response to the developments just discussed. In these circumstances Roosevelt converted challenge into opportunity. First, he accepted leadership of the new progressive coalition of farmers, workers, the lower middle classes, and the unemployed that came into existence during the congressional campaign of 1934. Second, he reconstituted his program to satisfy the basic aspirations of these various groups.

The catalyst was the election of a Congress eager to implement a comprehensive reform program in November 1934. As the election results were in part interpreted as an emphatic mandate for a work relief program, the prestige of Harry L. Hopkins, the chief advocate of that program, increased enormously. "Boys—this is our hour," Hopkins told his friends in the FERA soon after the election. "We've got to get everything we want—a works program, social security, wages and hours, everything—now or never." [3]

ммммммммммм

[2] A survey published by the magazine *Fortune* in July 1935 revealed the extent to which Long's attack on the wealthy reflected widespread popular opinion. When asked whether they believed that the government should permit a man who had investments worth more than $1,000,000 to keep them, "subject only to present taxes," 45.8 per cent of the persons polled replied in the negative. In the Middle West 54.6 per cent and on the Pacific Coast 54 per cent of all persons queried replied in the negative.

[3] Robert E. Sherwood, *Roosevelt and Hopkins, an Intimate History* (New York, 1948), p. 65.

Hopkins joined Roosevelt soon after Thanksgiving at Warm Springs, Georgia, and apparently won his approval for "everything." Then the President launched the Second New Deal in his Annual Message to Congress on January 4, 1935. Dismissing the achievements of the past two years, he declared that the mandate of the people in the recent election was clear: The time had come to fulfill a bold new social mission and to subordinate profits and wealth to the general good. This he proposed to accomplish, first, by ending the dole; second, by putting the 3,500,000 able-bodied persons on relief rolls to work in new programs of slum clearance, rural housing, rural electrification, and expanded public works; and, third, by inaugurating a comprehensive social security program to reduce the hazards of unemployment and old age.

147. *The WPA: The Second New Deal as the American Social Conscience*

Advanced progressives hailed the President's full-fledged conversion to the cause of social justice, while Congress for the most part responded eagerly to the administration's suggestions from 1935 to 1937. The outcome of this converging of reform impulses was the enactment of legislation that marked the full flowering of the humanitarian-progressive movement and the construction of at least the framework of the welfare state. We can best see what the Second New Deal intended and accomplished by looking at the details of its program.

The first item—the work relief program—was authorized by Congress and the President on April 8, 1935, with the adoption and signing of the Emergency Relief Appropriation Act, providing nearly $5,000,000,000 for the fiscal year 1935–6. It was launched by the President on May 6, 1935, with the establishment of the Works Progress Administration (WPA) and allied agencies. Secretary of the Interior Harold L. Ickes was made head of the WPA planning division, but to Harry Hopkins went the real power. He was appointed WPA administrator and directed to transfer unemployables and indigent persons to local relief rolls. More important, he was authorized to begin small work projects designed to put as many as 5,000,000 jobless men and women to work.

Actually the number of workers on WPA rolls never reached this large figure. The average monthly number from 1935 to 1941 was 2,112,000, and the peak of WPA employment was 3,238,000 in November 1938. The agency, along with co-operating sponsors, spent $11,365,000,000 on some 250,000 projects ranging in size from large airports to stone walls on university campuses. The bulk of WPA money, 78 per cent to be exact, went for public construction and conservation. The balance was expended for a variety of community projects which, on the theory that professional people also had to eat, enrolled musicians, actors, writers, artists, and even historians.

In addition, Hopkins and his colleagues used their broad authority in ambitious experiments that well exemplified the humanitarian impulses of the Second New Deal. The first of these new agencies of social reform was the Resettlement Administration (RA), which the President established as an independent agency under Tugwell in the Department of Agriculture on May 1, 1935. The AAA, FERA, and Subsistence Homesteads Division of the Interior Department had bought submarginal land in 1934 and established nearly one hundred small-farm co-operative communities. They were not a great success. Officials in the RA were eager to push bold schemes involving the rehabilitation of almost a million lower-class farmers and the removal of 500,000 farm families from submarginal land. Congressmen, especially Southerners, suspected however that the RA was bent upon collectivization and kept up such a steady attack that the agency's efforts never got beyond the experimental stage.[4]

Secondly, the President established the Rural Electrification Administration (REA) on May 11, 1935, to provide loans and WPA labor for extension of power lines into rural areas not served by private companies. In spite of opposition by the private power interests, the REA made such a successful beginning that its authority and resources were greatly expanded in 1937.

Thirdly, the administration embarked upon a long-range program to benefit young people with the establishment of the National Youth Administration (NYA) in the WPA on June 26, 1935, and with a doubling of appropriations for the Civilian Conservation Corps. The NYA was designed to keep high school and college students off the labor market as well as to enable them to enlarge their knowledge and skills. Some 750,000 high school, college, and graduate students were earning from $5 to $30 a month by 1939–40 as typists, laboratory and library assistants, tutors, and the like.

All these developments were sure signs of the rise of Harry Hopkins's star, of the triumph of the social worker over the businessman, in the Roosevelt inner circle. Believing that it was government's duty to provide jobs if private industry could not,[5] Hopkins regarded the WPA not as a stopgap but as a means of fulfilling society's obligations to its citizens. Roosevelt's approval of the work relief concept also committed the administration to a program of pump-priming by deficit spending on a huge scale. Although Congress increased income and estate taxes in 1935, the administration did not attempt to redistribute the national income through drastic tax increases but financed the WPA program mainly through borrowing.[6]

The WPA's accomplishments, however, were substantial and to progressives far outweighed the costs. It helped to build a reservoir of trained

〜〜〜〜〜〜〜〜〜〜〜〜〜

[4] The RA during its two years of independent existence purchased 5,000,000 acres of submarginal land and resettled 4,441 families on farms and in thirty-one homestead communities. In addition, it built three so-called Greenbelt towns, experiments in planned suburban communities for low-income city workers, near Washington, Cincinnati, and Milwaukee.

[5] Contemporary surveys of public opinion indicated that an overwhelming majority of Americans at the time shared Hopkins's conviction. In a *Fortune* poll, published in July 1935, for example, 76.8 per cent of all persons queried agreed that "the government should see to it that every man who wants to work has a job." Even 46.6 per cent of the prosperous and 69 per cent of the upper middle-class persons replied in the affirmative.

[6] The Hoover administration operated at a total deficit of $3,844,010,531 during 1931 and 1932; the Roosevelt administration accumulated a total deficit of $25,279,670,735 from 1933 through 1940. The gross national debt increased from $18,170,000,000 in 1929 to $23,350,000,000 in 1932, and to $52,848,000,000 in 1940.

manpower just before the time when the United States needed every skilled hand in a struggle for survival. Most important from the social point of view, the WPA greatly relieved the discontent of the millions of persons formerly on the dole. For the first time many of them felt that they had a stake in society and believed that the government was conscious of their material and spiritual needs.

Considered in sheerly economic terms, WPA expenditures contributed importantly to substantial progress toward recovery between 1935 and 1940. Politically, the WPA helped fasten the control of the Democratic party on the country, although not usually in the manner that Republicans alleged. To be sure, local politicians used WPA staffs and funds, and their activities became so flagrant during the congressional and senatorial campaign of 1938 that Congress intervened the following year to put an end to

THE NATIONAL DEBT
1910 – 1960

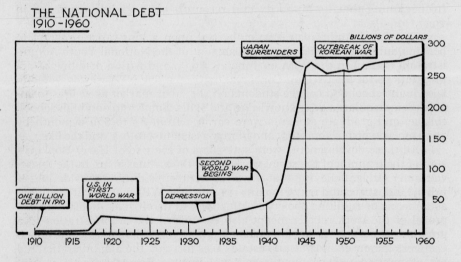

them.[7] The chief political significance of the WPA was the fact that workers on WPA rolls and their families rarely voted against an administration that had befriended them.

148. *Expanding the Second New Deal, 1935–1936*

For all its immediate and long-run significance, the work relief program was the most ephemeral phase of the Second New Deal. Let us now look at other measures adopted at the high tide of progressivism, measures that more permanently altered American social and economic institutions.

The first was the Social Security bill, prepared in 1934 by a nonpartisan Committee on Economic Security and presented to Congress in January

[7] With the passage of the Hatch Act, forbidding federal office-holders below the policy-making level from participating actively in political campaigns or soliciting or accepting contributions from WPA workers.

1935. Spokesmen for the Townsend Plan assailed the bill because it did not transfer title to the country to old people. Representatives of the AF of L objected because the measure provided for contributions by workers; the president of the National Association of Manufacturers, because it levied a payroll tax on employers. The upshot was that Congress approved the bill with only minor amendments, and the President signed it on August 14, 1935. "If the Senate and the House of Representatives in this long and arduous session had done nothing more than pass this Bill," he told a happy assemblage at the White House as he signed the measure, "the session would be regarded as historic for all time."

For old people the Social Security Act provided two kinds of assistance. First, the federal government offered to share equally with the states the burden of caring for persons over sixty-five who would have no opportunity to participate in the new old-age insurance program.[8] Second, the Act established a nation-wide system of old-age insurance, participation in which was compulsory except for public servants, domestic servants, farm and casual workers, merchant seamen, and employees of educational, religious, and philanthropic institutions.[9] Benefit payments ranging from $10 to $85 a month would begin in 1942.

The Social Security Act nominally left the establishment of unemployment insurance systems to the states but actually gave state governments no alternative but to co-operate. It imposed on employers an unemployment tax beginning at 1 per cent of all payrolls in 1936 and rising to a permanent level of 3 per cent after 1937. However, employers might pay 90 per cent of the tax to approved state unemployment compensation commissions; and most of the balance paid directly into the federal Treasury would be returned to the states to finance the administration of their systems. On the other hand, states that failed to establish unemployment compensation systems would lose all the taxes paid by employers within their jurisdiction. Needless to say, all states had complied within two years and provided a schedule of benefits that met minimum federal standards and afforded protection for some 28,000,000 workers.[10]

Finally, the measure offered federal aid to the states on a matching basis for the care of the crippled, the blind, and dependent mothers and children, and for public health services. It also established a nonpartisan Social Security Board to administer the entire system.

Roosevelt and the authors of the Social Security Act knew that the measure was experimental and inadequate; they were also confident that

ᴧᴧᴧᴧᴧᴧᴧᴧᴧᴧᴧᴧᴧᴧᴧᴧᴧᴧᴧ

[8] The federal contribution was limited to $15 monthly per person but was increased to $20 in 1939. Some 2,000,000 persons were receiving assistance under this provision by 1940, and combined federal and state payments averaged $20 a month per person.

[9] Employees and employers were required to pay at the rate of 1 per cent each on all wages under $3,000 a year from 1937 through 1939, 1½ per cent each from 1940 through 1942, 2 per cent each from 1943 through 1945, 2½ per cent each from 1946 through 1948, and 3 per cent each after 1948. The measure contemplated the accumulation of a reserve fund invested in government bonds, which would total some $47,-000,000,000 by 1980 and make the system self-sustaining.

[10] Unemployment benefits varied in different states and sections. Maximum weekly payments ran $15–$18 a week, while duration of payments ranged from twelve to twenty-six weeks in any single year.

the system would be strengthened and enlarged with the passage of time.[11] To the end of his life the President regarded Social Security as the New Deal's "supreme achievement." And who could gainsay him? Between 1935 and 1939, when the system was launched and strengthened, the administration and Congress effected a lasting revolution in American public policy. Discarding ingrained traditions of self-help and individual responsibility, they set the United States upon the high road leading to the welfare state.

The question of new labor legislation also arose during the early months of 1935, but there was no such unanimity of administration and congressional opinion regarding wise labor policy as had prevailed during the drafting of the Social Security bill. Senator Robert F. Wagner was working almost singlehandedly in Congress for passage of his labor disputes bill to give unions federal protection. But the President opposed the measure, saying that he preferred to obtain protection for labor through renewal of the NIRA.

The Senate under administration pressure voted to renew the NIRA. Then it approved the Wagner bill on May 16, 1935. There seemed to be a strong possibility of a presidential veto if the House approved the measure. Less than two weeks later the Supreme Court declared the code system of the NIRA unconstitutional. In response, the President reversed himself on the Wagner bill (actually, he had indicated on May 24 that he favored the bill), persuaded House leaders to bring it to the floor, and signed the measure on July 5 after the House of Representatives had speedily approved it.

The Wagner, or National Labor Relations, Act reaffirmed the principles set forth in the now defunct Section 7a. But the Wagner Act was specific and strong where Section 7a had been vague and weak. By making virtually impossible the organization of company unions and outlawing so-called unfair practices,[12] it deprived employers of their most formidable antiunion weapons. By establishing a nonpartisan National Labor Relations Board (NLRB) empowered to issue cease and desist orders and compel obedience from employers, the Act provided machinery for its own enforcement. Finally, by setting forth the explicit conditions under which unions should be entitled to recognition,[13] it threw the power of the federal govern-

wwwwwwwwwwwww

[11] This, of course, did occur. In response to widespread criticisms, congressional leaders and the Social Security Board undertook a study in 1937 looking toward revision of the Social Security Act. The upshot was legislation in 1939 completely overhauling the old-age retirement program by (1) extending the Act's coverage to include 1,600,000 additional workers, (2) advancing the date of the beginning of retirement benefits from 1942 to 1940, (3) increasing monthly payments to persons who had been insured for a short time, (4) providing benefits for wives and dependent children of retired workers, as well as survivors' benefits for widows and dependent children when insured workers died before reaching sixty-five, and (5) continuing the old-age payroll tax of 1 per cent each on workers and employers until 1943.

[12] For example, interference with employees in the exercise of guaranteed rights, discharge or blacklisting of employees for union activities, and discrimination against employees who brought charges against the company.

[13] A union was entitled to recognition by the employer as the sole bargaining agent when it won—usually in a secret election conducted by the NLRB—majority support among workers in an industry, company, shop, or craft.

ment behind a union seeking to compel an employer to bargain in good faith. The measure did not of course attempt to deal directly with substantive questions of hours, wages, and so on.

Congress seemed to assume that a strong labor movement was the surest safeguard of democracy in an industrial society and the best counterbalance to big business. In any event, the Wagner Act rather decisively brought the power of the federal government to bear in the industrial struggle in order to redress the balance between the two opposing forces. Coming at a time when the advance guard of the AF of L were making plans to organize the basic industries, the Wagner Act and the NLRB straightway became the charter of liberty and shield of the American labor movement.

Work relief, Social Security, and legislation to reinforce the labor movement were only the beginning of a new program designed to increase and strengthen public control over business and industry and benefit the masses of people. The fact that the Supreme Court invalidated the NIRA just at the moment when the President and his advisers were formulating these new measures meant that they could decide what features of the NRA experiment were worth salvaging. We have seen how Roosevelt abruptly espoused the Wagner Act in order to re-enact and reinforce Section 7a. Earlier, after the Supreme Court had invalidated Section 9c of the NIRA, which established special controls for the oil industry, the President in February 1935 had approved the Connally Act prohibiting shipment in interstate commerce of oil produced in violation of interstate compacts. With adoption of the Guffey-Snyder Coal Conservation Act in August 1935, the administration salvaged the bituminous coal code and re-established the NRA coal code authority in a different form.[14] Another measure, the Alcohol Control Act of August 29, 1935, re-enacted the provisions of the NRA liquor code and vested enforcement in the Treasury Department. Refusing to approve a general wages and hours bill, on the ground that such a measure was probably unconstitutional, Roosevelt instead supported and signed the Walsh-Healey Act on August 30, 1936. It attempted indirectly to establish fair labor standards for manufacturing and the construction industry.[15] To preserve the sections of the NRA codes that prohibited destructive competition, Congress in 1936 and 1937 enacted the Robinson-Patman Act, which out-

∿∿∿∿∿∿∿∿∿∿∿∿∿∿∿∿∿

[14] This measure established a National Bituminous Coal Commission composed of representatives of management, labor, and the public and empowered to control production and prices of the raw material. The Act, moreover, guaranteed collective bargaining in the coal industry and stipulated that when wages and hours agreements were signed by the miners' union and producers of two thirds of the national tonnage, such agreements should go into effect in the entire industry. The Supreme Court declared the Guffey-Snyder Act unconstitutional in 1936, on the grounds that the labor provisions conferred legislative authority on the Coal Commission, and that a tax levied by the Act on non-co-operating producers resulted in an unconstitutional regulation of an industry that was not interstate in character. Omitting the provisions to which the Court had objected, Congress re-enacted the Guffey-Snyder Act in April 1937.

[15] The Walsh-Healey Act required the inclusion, in all federal contracts involving the expenditure of $10,000 or more, of provisions limiting hours to eight a day and forty a week, prohibiting child labor, and empowering the Secretary of Labor to set minimum wages.

lawed differential pricing of commodities, and the Miller-Tydings Act, which legalized the setting of "fair trade" prices by manufacturers, below which a retailer could not sell.

To these measures for regulation were added other more important substantive reforms during 1935 and 1936. We have seen how the Banking Act of 1935 established strong federal control over the Federal Reserve System and how the President obtained destruction of the public utility giants and strict federal control of the smaller holding companies. In addition a rash of measures from 1935 to 1940 strengthened and extended the federal regulatory authority in many fields. The Federal Power Act of 1935 enlarged the jurisdiction and rate-making authority of the Federal Power Commission. The Motor Carrier Act of 1935 and the Transportation Act of 1940 brought trucking concerns and domestic water carriers under the regulation of the ICC. The Merchant Marine Act of 1936 created a new Maritime Commission and authorized it to help create an American merchant marine. And the Civil Aeronautics Act of 1938 established a Civil Aeronautics Authority, later called the Civil Aeronautics Board, to regulate the operations and services of airlines.

These were all nonpartisan measures of reform and regulation, and, except for the Holding Company Act, they excited little opposition. More indicative of the Second New Deal's social and economic purposes was Roosevelt's campaign in 1935 to democratize the federal tax structure. Roosevelt replied to his critics on the Left on June 19, 1935, by calling upon Congress to increase the tax burden on the upper classes and large corporations in order to check the growing concentration of economic power, reduce "social unrest and a deepening sense of unfairness," and encourage the wider distribution of wealth. Congress with astonishing alacrity wrote most of the President's suggestions into the wealth tax bill, or the Revenue Act of 1935, and Roosevelt signed it on August 30. It left the normal income tax unchanged but increased the surtax to the highest rates in American history,[16] increased the federal estate tax to a maximum of 70 per cent, and imposed a graduated income tax on net corporation income.[17] Leaders of the business community denounced the Revenue Act of 1935 as a sophisticated version of the Share Our Wealth plan, but Roosevelt was undaunted.

149.   *The Election of 1936*

Republican leaders must have surveyed the political scene during the early months of 1936 with considerable dismay. Not since Andrew Jackson's day had the Democratic party been so firmly entrenched and so popular with the masses. Probably never before had there been such a dearth of able leadership in the GOP. Hoover was still revered by his friends, but all

wwwwwwwwwwwwww

[16] The Revenue Act of 1935 increased the surtaxes only on net incomes over $50,000, rising in a graduated scale from a surtax of 31 per cent on net incomes over $50,000 to 75 per cent on incomes over $5,000,000.

[17] The Revenue Act of 1934 had levied a flat tax of 13¾ per cent on the net incomes of all corporations, large and small. The Act of 1935 levied a graduated tax of from 12½ to 15 per cent, depending on the size of net corporation income.

Republicans knew that he would be a millstone around the party's neck if he were nominated. Senator William E. Borah of Idaho, a quadrennial candidate since 1912, was willing, but he was too old and erratic to suit the powers that controlled his party. Senator Arthur H. Vandenberg of Michigan had miraculously survived the Democratic landslide of 1934, but he was not anxious to challenge the occupant of the White House. The only really serious candidate was Governor Alfred M. Landon of Kansas, who had also survived the Democratic landslide of 1934 and had the support of William Randolph Hearst and his chain of newspapers.

Republican delegates assembled in Cleveland on June 9, 1936, and applauded Hoover's strictures against the New Deal without any thought of nominating him. Instead, they named Landon on the first ballot on June 11 and afterward nominated Frank Knox, publisher of the *Chicago Daily News*, as his running-mate. Orators denounced the New Deal in the generalities of campaign rhetoric. But the Republican platform did not threaten to destroy the New Deal reform structure, except to revise the corporation tax structure and the Trade Agreements Act of 1934, which empowered the President to make tariff agreements. (See below, pp. 467–468.) On the contrary, Republicans in 1936 reaffirmed their own progressive tradition by promising to provide better relief, farm subsidy, and labor programs.

The Democrats met in Philadelphia on June 23, 1936, in a convention that was riotous and triumphant. So prevalent was the good feeling that Roosevelt and Garner were nominated by a mighty shout on the first ballot. Southern Democrats, in a moment of exhilaration or perhaps intoxication, even agreed to abrogate the historic party rule that required a two-thirds majority for a presidential nomination.

The Democratic platform was a frank reiteration of the social ideals of the Second New Deal and a recital, with emphatic endorsement, of the good works of the Roosevelt administration. Declaring that "government in a modern civilization has certain inescapable obligations to its citizens," the platform promised more rural electrification and a stronger farm program, public housing, additional legislation to protect workers, and vigorous enforcement of the antitrust laws. The foreign policy planks, like those of the Republican platform, reflected the then dominant isolationist temper and the popular determination to avoid, as the Democrats said, "being drawn, by political commitments, international banking, or private trading, into any war which may develop anywhere."

Both candidates conducted dignified and strenuous campaigns. Landon spoke forcefully and made it clear that he approved the basic features of the New Deal program, but he did not fire the public imagination or inspire much confidence. On the other hand, Roosevelt was at his magnificent best as a campaigner and phrase-maker in this battle. His acceptance speech was a declaration of war against "economic royalists" who had supposedly regimented and enslaved the people in an "industrial dictatorship." It was also a new call for dedication to the cause of democracy. "This generation of Americans," Roosevelt concluded, "has a rendezvous with destiny. . . . We are fighting to save a great and precious form of government for ourselves and for the world." Taking nothing for granted, the President stumped the country as if his election were in doubt; the themes of social and economic democracy ran strongly through all his speeches. Frankly acknowledging that he had the support of workers, farmers, young people, and the unemployed, he promised to continue the fight against "business and financial monopoly, speculation, reckless banking, class antagonism, sectionalism, war profiteering."

Two developments of the campaign were significant because they indicated long-range realignments. One was the development of a vigorous political consciousness among organized labor and the participation of the major unions in an all-out effort to return the Democrats to power. The leaders in labor's first important political crusade since 1924 were George L. Berry of the AF of L and John L. Lewis and Sidney Hillman, two spokesmen of the newly formed CIO. They organized Labor's Non-Partisan League in April 1936, raised some $1,000,000, half of which came from Lewis's United Mine Workers, and turned their unions into momentary political machines. The second significant development in 1936 was the shift of a majority of Negro leaders and newspapers in northern and midwestern states from the GOP to the Democracy. For the first time in American history, a majority of Negro voters supported a Democratic candidate in 1936.

It was obvious by mid-October that Landon simply did not have a chance, in spite of the fact that more than two thirds of the metropolitan newspapers supported him, and the *Literary Digest* poll indicated that he would win by a comfortable margin. Even so, most observers were startled by the magnitude of the Democratic victory on November 3. Landon won 16,679,583 popular votes and carried only Vermont and Maine for a total of eight electoral votes. Representative William Lemke, radical farm leader from North Dakota, running on a Union party ticket supported by Dr. Townsend, Father Coughlin, and Huey Long's successor, the Reverend Gerald L. K. Smith, polled nearly 900,000 votes. The Socialist Norman Thomas and the Communist Earl Browder trailed far behind. In contrast, Roosevelt won 27,751,597 popular and 523 electoral votes and carried huge Democratic majorities with him in the greatest sweep since 1920. The verdict of the people was unmistakable: it was an emphatic mandate for continuation of the Second New Deal.

150. *The Supreme Court Controversy*

High Democratic spokesmen uttered veiled threats against the Supreme Court during the presidential campaign of 1936 for overturning New Deal measures, but the President gave no indication ther. that he intended to bring the court before the bar of public opinion. Nor was there any strong hint of an impending attack in Roosevelt's Annual Message of January 6, 1937, or in his second inaugural address, delivered on January 20. Yet he presented a plan for judicial reorganization to Congress on February 5, the purpose of which was nothing less than to bring the Supreme Court under popular control. We cannot understand Roosevelt's motive and purpose unless we understand also the gravity of the constitutional crisis that he thought compelled him to take this dangerous step.

As one authority has put it, "five willful Supreme Court Justices . . . had in fact contrived well-nigh complete absence of the power to govern" by the early months of 1937.[18] In short, the court's majority had nearly paralyzed the executive and legislative branches. Responsibility for this situation lay primarily with the court, not with the President or Congress. Four of the justices—James C. McReynolds, George Sutherland, Willis Van Devanter, and Pierce Butler—were reactionaries who lived in a nineteenth-century world of social Darwinism and liberty of contract. They were so consistently hostile to advanced progressive legislation that they were popularly called the "Four Horsemen." In a small minority were the three progressive justices, Louis D. Brandeis, Benjamin N. Cardozo, and Harlan F. Stone. Somewhere between the reactionaries and the progressives stood the Chief Justice, Charles Evans Hughes, and Owen J. Roberts, who often voted with the "Four Horsemen."

A majority of the court seemed capable before 1935 of recognizing an emergency when they saw one, but what soon became prodigious judicial nullification began in January 1935. In the so-called hot oil cases,[19] the court invalidated Section 9c of the NIRA on January 7, on the ground that it conferred improper legislative authority upon the President to regulate the petroleum industry. More alarming to the administration was the court's decision,[20] rendered on May 6, in a five-to-four verdict, which nullified the Railroad Retirement Act of 1934. The majority alleged, first, that the government had deprived railway companies of property without due process of law by compelling them to contribute to pensions for their employees and, second, that Congress's control over interstate commerce did not warrant such interference in labor relations. The Social Security bill then pending was also surely unconstitutional if this was true.

These two decisions constituted a kind of prelude to "Black Monday," May 27, 1935, when the court set a new record in judicial review. In Louisville Joint Stock Land Bank *v.* Radford, it nullified the Frazier-Lemke Farm Mortgage Act, on the ground that it deprived creditors of property without due process of law. In Humphrey's Executor *v.* United States, the majority reprimanded the President for removing William E. Humphrey, a reactionary Republican, from the Federal Trade Commission and laid down a new constitutional rule of considerable importance.[21] The most fateful decision on this fateful "Black Monday" was rendered in A. L. A. Schechter Corporation *v.* United States. In this decision all the justices agreed that the NIRA was unconstitutional, on the grounds that the statute conferred essential legislative authority on the President, and that the corporation involved in the case was engaged only in intrastate commerce.

Stunned by the Schechter decision, the President went to the root of the issue in a press conference on May 31. He pointed out that the court's objection to a plenary grant of legislative power to the Executive could be easily

---

18 A. T. Mason, "Charles Evans Hughes: An Appeal to the Bar of History," *Vanderbilt Law Review,* VI (December 1952), p. 10.

19 Panama Refining Co. *v.* Ryan and Amazon Petroleum Corporation *v.* Ryan.

20 Railroad Retirement Board *v.* Alton Railroad.

21 Namely, that independent regulatory commissions were arms of Congress, not of the Executive, and that the President could not remove their members except for reasons stipulated by Congress.

overcome. The danger, he said, lay in the court's narrow view of interstate commerce as consisting only of goods in transit.[22] How could the federal government seek to remedy *any* national economic problem if this "horse and buggy" definition of interstate commerce prevailed?

The court answered the President's query after a period of anxious waiting in a series of epochal decisions that emphatically confirmed the Schechter doctrine. Justice Roberts, speaking for himself, Hughes, and the "Four Horsemen" in United States *v.* Butler on January 6, 1936, held that the Agricultural Adjustment Act of 1933 was unconstitutional. It was a strained decision, but its meaning was clear: production of agricultural commodities was local activity, not interstate commerce; therefore Congress could not use the taxing power to regulate agriculture. Then an even clearer reaffirmation of the Schechter doctrine came on May 18, 1936. Justice Sutherland, in Carter *v.* Carter Coal Company, rendered an opinion invalidating the Guffey-Snyder Coal Conservation Act. The mining of coal, Sutherland asserted, was obviously not interstate commerce, and Congress could not use the taxing power to regulate an industry over which it had no constitutional control. Having thus denied the federal government jurisdiction over manufacturing, mining, agriculture, and labor conditions, the conservative majority went all the way on June 1, 1936, and denied to the *states* the right to regulate hours and wages. This decision, rendered by Justice Butler in Morehead *v.* New York *ex rel.* Tipaldo, nullified a New York State minimum wage law for women and children by resurrecting the doctrine enunciated in Adkins *v.* Children's Hospital in 1923.[23]

Only a blind man could fail to see that the country was in an intolerable constitutional situation by the summer of 1936. The Supreme Court had wrecked several key New Deal enterprises. It seemed certain that the justices would soon invalidate the Social Security and Wagner Acts; and the President and Congress knew that they proceeded with further reform legislation only at the risk of additional judicial reversals. Nor was this all. Inferior federal courts were also hard at work in a campaign of judicial nullification and obstruction. They issued no less than 1,600 injunctions against federal administrative officials before 1937; for intermittent periods they paralyzed such important agencies as the NLRB and the SEC.

The President must have concluded that the reckoning could no longer be postponed after the people gave him their emphatic mandate in the election of 1936. He submitted a Judiciary Reorganization bill on February 5, 1937. It empowered him to appoint a new federal judge whenever an incumbent failed to retire within six months after reaching the age of seventy. The number of additional judges would be limited to fifty, and not more than six of them could be named to the Supreme Court. Roosevelt explained in an accompanying message why he desired to enlarge the federal courts. He pointed to the crowded dockets and delay in judicial business caused by insufficient and infirm personnel; described the confusion created by hun-

---

[22] For this obsolete definition of interstate commerce, Chief Justice Hughes had gone back to the notorious Knight decision of 1895, for which see above, p. 113.

[23] In this decision the court had ruled that minimum wage laws violated the freedom of contract guaranteed by the Fourteenth Amendment.

dreds of injunctions issued by inferior courts; and frankly asserted that the courts needed new blood and a modern outlook.

The whole plan was of course grounded upon Roosevelt's assumption that he could control the huge Democratic majorities in both houses of Congress. Republicans and spokesmen for the Liberty League charged that the President aimed to destroy the Constitution and establish a personal dictatorship. The Chief Justice himself entered the fray, by addressing a public letter on March 21 to a Senate leader denying Roosevelt's allegation that the Supreme Court was behind in its work. Roosevelt must have expected and discounted this opposition. What surprised, even stunned him was the violent opposition that developed within his own party. Conservative Democrats in the Senate like Carter Glass of Virginia and Walter F. George of Georgia joined progressives like Burton K. Wheeler of Montana in open rebellion.

For this nearly catastrophic rupture, Roosevelt was himself in large measure responsible. In his cocksureness he had not taken Democratic leaders into his confidence before submitting the Judiciary Reorganization bill. He allowed Postmaster General Farley to use the patronage stick too bluntly after the controversy had begun. Worst of all, he refused to listen to compromise proposals that might have succeeded. "All his sagacity seemed to desert him," one contemporary has written of the President; "he was arrogant to those who counseled caution, disbelieving when they warned him of defeat, and neglectful until too late of their alternative suggestions." [24] Consequently, he lost control of Congress for the first time since 1933. Then his Majority Leader in the Senate, Joseph T. Robinson of Arkansas, died at the height of the struggle on July 14, 1937. It was a hopeless battle by this time, and Roosevelt informed the new Majority Leader, Alben W. Barkley of Kentucky, that he would accept a compromise to which all Democrats could agree.

It was not congressional opposition and Robinson's death alone that caused Roosevelt and his friends to abandon the fight. Equally decisive was an extraordinary and sudden change in the opinions of the Supreme Court that took place while the court controversy raged. We may never know conclusively why this change occurred. There are indications that Chief Justice Hughes persuaded Justice Roberts to stand with the progressives in validating several important reform statutes then being tested. Only by such strategy, Hughes might have urged, could the court save itself from debasement at the hands of the Executive.

It can be said with greater confidence that Hughes and Roberts acted during the court fight more like political strategists than consistent interpreters of the Constitution. The court rendered judgment on a minimum wage statute of the State of Washington in the case of West Coast Hotel *v.* Parrish on March 29, 1937. Roberts had joined the "Four Horsemen" only a year before to invalidate a similar New York law. Now he joined Hughes and the progressives to approve the Washington statute in sweeping lan-

ʌʌʌʌʌʌʌʌʌʌʌʌʌʌʌʌʌʌʌ

[24] Rexford G. Tugwell, *The Democratic Roosevelt, A Biography of Franklin D. Roosevelt* (Garden City, N.Y., 1957), p. 403.

guage that left room for almost any reasonable form of state wages and hours legislation.

The crowning irony came when the new progressive majority upheld the Wagner Act in National Labor Relations Board *v.* Jones and Laughlin Steel Corporation on April 12, 1937. Here the issue was essentially the same as in the Schechter, Butler, and Carter Coal Company cases: Did the power of Congress to control interstate commerce include the power to control the actual production of commodities? In the Jones and Laughlin decision the Chief Justice in effect reversed the earlier decisions without openly admitting that any change in interpretation had occurred. Congress's control over interstate commerce was absolute, Hughes declared, and included power to encourage and protect such commerce. The peaceful movement of goods was essential to the life of the nation, he concluded. Hence Congress might even prescribe the labor relations prevailing at factories in which goods were manufactured. In addition, the court approved the Social Security Act on May 24, 1937, in three decisions [25] by Justices Stone and Cardozo that upheld the compulsory features of the unemployment and old-age retirement systems.

Thus the President had lost the proverbial battle and won the war when he abandoned the Judiciary Reorganization bill in mid-July 1937. Moreover, Justice Van Devanter, an implacable foe of New Deal legislation, retired on June 1, thus allowing Roosevelt to buttress the new progressive majority on the supreme bench.[26] Now that the constitutional crisis was resolved in favor of broad interpretation, the advocates of compromise, Vice President Garner and Majority Leader Barkley, came forward with a new Judiciary bill that denied the President power to enlarge the courts but conceded badly needed procedural reforms. The Judicial Procedure Reform Act, which Roosevelt signed on August 26, 1937, empowered the Attorney General to participate in cases involving the constitutionality of federal statutes when they were first tried before district courts. It also made provision for moving such cases, when they went against the government, from district courts directly to the Supreme Court and severely circumscribed the right of federal judges to stay the execution of federal laws.

151.   *Additions to the New Deal: 1937*

The President reaffirmed his determination to broaden and complete the reform structure of the Second New Deal on several notable occasions following the election of 1936. His Annual Message of January 6, 1937, and his second inaugural address of January 20 were clarion calls to Congress for aid to the millions of people in city and country on low incomes, the "one-third of a nation ill-housed, ill-clad, ill-nourished," over whom disaster hung like a pall. "The test of our progress," he declared in his inaugural, "is

---

[25] Carmichael *v.* Southern Coal Company, Charles C. Steward Machine Company *v* Davis, and Helvering *v.* Davis.

[26] Congress had enacted a Supreme Court Retirement Act, approved March 1, 1937, which permitted justices to retire at full pay after reaching the age of seventy.

not whether we add more to the abundance of those who have much; it is whether we provide enough for those who have too little."

Roosevelt presented his new program cautiously during the early months of 1937 in step with changing circumstances. Thus in his Annual Message of January 6 he merely asked Congress to consider measures for public housing, aid to tenant farmers, and broader social security coverage. On January 12 he submitted a plan for reorganization of the Executive Department that had been prepared by a committee of distinguished political scientists. On February 5 he added his plan for reorganization of the judiciary. This was as far as he could go until the constitutional crisis had been resolved. But he moved quickly to round out his program once the Supreme Court had executed its reversal in March and April. On May 24 he urged Congress to "extend the frontiers of social progress" by enacting legislation establishing minimum wages and maximum hours in American industry. Finally, on July 12 he asked Congress to re-establish the AAA.[27]

This, then, was the administration's program to complete the Second New Deal. Unfortunately for the President, the Judiciary Reorganization bill consumed much of Congress' energies during the spring and early summer of 1937, disrupted the party's ranks, and gave conservative Democrats in both houses an excuse for defying the President's leadership on other questions. They combined with the Republican minority to defeat the Executive Reorganization bill by charging that it was a twin of the Judiciary Reorganization bill and another step toward presidential dictatorship.[28] The Senate approved the administration's wages and hours, or Fair Labor Standards, bill on July 31, 1937, but conservative Democrats and Republicans on the House rules committee prevented the House from voting on the measure. The President's proposal for a new agricultural act received scarcely any attention from the lawmakers.

~~~~~~~~~~~~~~~~~~~~~

[27] Congress had adopted the Soil Conservation and Domestic Allotment Act a month after the Supreme Court's invalidation of the Agricultural Adjustment Act on January 6, 1936. The former was a hastily drawn and unsatisfactory substitute. It simply appropriated $500,000,000 to be paid to farmers who diverted part of their land from staple to soil-building crops.

It was the time of the great "dust bowl" in the Southwest and Plains states, and the nation had been profoundly alarmed by the spectacle of millions of tons of topsoil being blown away in the parched area. The epic documentary film, "The Plow That Broke the Plains," had further dramatized the urgent need to save American soil resources. Thus the conservation program under the legislation of 1936 evoked widespread popular approval and support by farmers, two thirds of whom signed contracts with the Department of Agriculture to plant soil-building crops. However, the Soil Conservation Act was woefully inadequate as a means of crop control because the Agriculture Department had no power under its provisions to compel co-operation by the recalcitrant minority. Severe drought in the corn and wheat belts continued in 1936, and there were consequently no grain surpluses. But, as we shall see, return of good weather and prosperity in 1937 stimulated the planting and harvesting of huge cotton, wheat, corn, and tobacco crops and demonstrated the need for new and more effective controls.

[28] The Senate passed a revised reorganization bill in 1938, but conservatives in the House, led by the reactionary chairman of the rules committee, John J. O'Connor of New York, defeated it. Finally, both houses approved a new administration Reorganization Act in 1939. It deprived the President of power to reorganize the independent regulatory agencies but permitted him to appoint six administrative assistants and to reorganize and consolidate a number of lesser agencies.

Even so, the first session of the Seventy-fifth Congress that sat from January to September 1937 left a memorable record of achievement: the Judicial Procedure Reform Act; the Guffey-Vinson Bituminous Coal Act, which re-enacted most of the provisions of the Guffey-Snyder Act; and, most important, the Bankhead-Jones Farm Tenancy Act and the Wagner-Steagall National Housing Act. The last two measures were landmarks in the history of federal policy.

The Bankhead-Jones Farm Tenancy Act was the outgrowth of the investigations of the President's Committee on Farm Tenancy. Its report, issued in February 1937, revealed that more than half the farmers in the South, nearly a third in the North, and one fourth in the West were sharecroppers or tenants. Highlighting the poverty and misery of this important segment of the farm population, the report also took serious notice of a new group of the rural destitute—the hundreds of thousands of migratory farm workers and displaced cotton sharecroppers from the Southwest, the "Okies," who were moving en masse to California in search of jobs.

To turn back the tide of tenancy the Committee suggested a remedy in keeping with the spirit of the Second New Deal. It proposed that the Resettlement Administration (RA) be reorganized as the Farm Security Administration (FSA). The FSA should help enterprising tenants to become landowners, refinance and rehabilitate small farmers who were in danger of losing their lands, promote withdrawal of submarginal land, and help migratory workers. With the support of southern Democrats keenly responsive to the needs of small farmers and white tenants, the Bankhead-Jones Act, embodying the Committee's recommendations, became law on July 22, 1937.

The FSA was the social conscience of the Second New Deal in action on the rural front from 1937 until the end of the Second World War.[29] It established some thirty camps that accommodated from 12,000 to 15,000 migratory families, helped farmers scale their debts, organized rural medical and dental care groups, sponsored co-operative leasing of land and purchase of machinery by tenants and small farmers, and carried on homestead projects already begun by the RA. Moreover, the FSA had lent over $800,000,000 in short-term rehabilitation loans by June 1944 to 870,000 farm families. Finally, it lent nearly $260,000,000 to 41,000 families—on a forty-year basis at 3 per cent interest—between 1937 and 1946 for purchase of farms.

The Wagner-Steagall National Housing Act, approved September 1, 1937, was the culmination of several years of planning and investigation by various agencies of the government. Large-scale public housing was one objective of the PWA from 1933 to 1937; and despite Secretary Ickes's caution, the PWA Housing Division by 1937 had constructed fifty-one projects in thirty-six cities with new homes for 21,700 families. The housing program launched by the Wagner-Steagall Act of 1937, on the other hand, reflected the administration's determination to meet the housing problem comprehensively and not as part of a public works and recovery program. This measure established the United States Housing Authority (USHA) in

[29] Congress created a new Farmers' Home Administration in August 1946 and transferred to it the functions of the FSA.

the Interior Department, with a capital of $1,000,000 and authority to borrow up to $500,000,000, increased to a total of $1,600,000,000 in 1940.

The USHA did not go into the construction business, as the PWA had done, but worked through public housing agencies in all important cities—by lending up to 100 per cent of the costs of housing projects on a long-term basis, making annual subsidies to local agencies, and establishing standards of cost, construction, and eligibility of tenants.[30] All told, before 1941, when the USHA turned to providing housing for defense workers, the agency lent over $750,000,000 to local housing authorities for 511 projects with a total of 161,162 units. It was, obviously, only the beginning of what would perforce be a long campaign to destroy slums and provide adequate housing for America's urban poor. Those progressives and humanitarians who did not expect the millennium to come overnight were encouraged by the beginning that had been made.

152. Recovery, Recession, and the Last Surge of Reform, 1937–1938

Health began to return to the ailing American economy between 1933 and 1936, but the wounds of the depression were so deep that recovery was at best slow. National income rose from nearly $42,500,000,000 in 1933 to $49,000,000,000 in 1934, and to $57,100,000,000 in 1935. The indices of production, employment, and payrolls in manufacturing [31] rose from 56, 62.3, and 38.3, respectively, in March 1933 to 104, 94.2, and 80.5, respectively, in December 1935. The trend was unmistakably upward. Even so, the basic cogs of the economic machinery were still running feebly by 1936.

All indices of economic activity began to rise sharply in the spring of 1936. Removal of NRA restrictions on production perhaps gave one stimulus. Certainly increased farm income and enormous federal expenditures for work relief beginning in the spring of 1935 and payment of the bonus in 1936 all had an important impact. From May 1936 to September 1937 the index of employment rose from 96.4 to 112.2—higher than the peak figure in 1929—while the payroll index increased from 84 to 109, and the index of industrial production rose from 101 to 117 during the same period. Disposable per capita income, measured in 1952 dollars, increased from $906 in 1935 to $1,048 in 1937. It had been $1,045 in 1929.

There was a speculative upsurge on the stock markets, but the upswing from 1935 to 1937 was essentially sound [32] because it was based on in-

ᴗᴗᴗᴗᴗᴗᴗᴗᴗᴗᴗᴗᴗᴗᴗᴗᴗ

[30] Residents of public housing projects, for example, had to be from among the lowest third of income receivers. The average income of all families living in USHA projects on December 31, 1941, was $837 a year; the average rental of all USHA units was $12.64 a month.

[31] Monthly average, 1923–5 = 100.

[32] It was not caused, for example, by monetary or bank credit inflation. The volume of money in circulation increased only slightly, from $5,567,100,000 in 1935 to $6,447,100,000 in 1937; total bank loans increased from $20,419,300,000 to $22,698,-200,000 during the same period.

creased investment and production and larger purchasing power through higher wages and public spending. Instead of welcoming the return of prosperity and making certain that the volume of credit was equal to business needs, however, the administration acted as if it feared prosperity. The Board of Governors of the Federal Reserve System, assuming that another runaway boom was in the making, increased reserve requirements of member banks drastically in 1936 and again in 1937, while Federal Reserve Banks took sharp action on their own to prevent monetary and bank credit inflation. In addition, the President made plans drastically to cut the work relief program, reduce other federal expenditures, and balance the budget in 1939. Consequently, WPA rolls were reduced from 3,000,000 to 1,500,-000 workers between January and August of 1937.

Credit restrictions, reduced federal expenditures, and other factors combined in September and October 1937 to cause a severe slump that set the indices tumbling and threatened to wipe out all gains toward recovery that the country had made since 1935. There was grave danger that price rigidity accompanied by widespread wage cutting would accentuate the downward spiral, and that farm prices would fall to subdepression levels because of extraordinarily large production in 1937. Roosevelt therefore called Congress into special session on October 12, 1937. Then in a "fireside chat" and message to Congress on November 15 he presented a program to halt the recession and complete the Second New Deal. That program included a new and comprehensive agricultural act, legislation to abolish child labor and establish minimum wages and maximum hours, revision of the antitrust laws to root out monopolistic control over prices, and reorganization of the Executive Department. He was willing, he added, to give businessmen an opportunity to increase production and end unemployment. "If private enterprise does not respond," he warned, "government must take up the slack."

Profoundly frightened by the prospect of returning depression during an election year, Democrats in Congress closed ranks and set to work with resolution and dispatch. The most urgent necessity was legislation to prevent the complete collapse of agricultural prices. Drought and soil conservation contracts had kept farm production in 1936 at the lowest point since the First World War, except for the drought year of 1934. High prices stimulated tremendously increased plantings in 1937, however, and the return of good weather made possible the harvesting of the largest aggregate yield in American history.

It was simply to avert agrarian catastrophe that Congress enacted and the President signed a new Agricultural Adjustment Act in mid-February 1938. It provided up to $500,000,000 for soil conservation payments annually to farmers who co-operated in restricting production. In addition, marketing quotas might be applied to cotton, wheat, corn, tobacco, and rice if production exceeded normal requirements and two thirds of the producers of each crop voted to institute such controls. To achieve parity for agricultural prices, the Act of 1938 provided a number of devices. All farmers were eligible for soil conservation payments, but producers of cotton, rice, wheat, corn, and tobacco were granted even larger assistance. First, they were also eligible for parity, or price-adjustment, payments whenever Congress appropriated funds for this purpose.[33] Second, the Commodity Credit Corporation was authorized to make loans ranging from 52 to 75 per cent of the parity price—increased to a maximum of 85 per cent in 1941—on the five leading staples. This provision not only established a floor below which prices could not fall but also enabled the Agriculture Department to store up surpluses in good years for use in years of drought and shortage.

A provision for wider distribution of surplus farm products gave some evidence that the administration had shifted from a philosophy of scarcity to a new policy of abundance. The Act authorized the Surplus Marketing Administration to buy food surpluses and distribute them to families on state relief rolls, to furnish food for school lunch programs, and in other ways to subsidize persons on relief and the WPA.[34] Finally, the measure included provision for export subsidies to stimulate the sale of American agricultural products abroad.

The Second World War soon ended the farm problem for a time, but there can be little doubt that the second AAA brought stability to American agriculture during the interim years 1938 to 1941. Huge surpluses threatened to depress prices to the level of 1932 when the measure went into effect. The Agriculture Department averted a rural depression in the critical years of 1938 and 1939 by vigorous action on many fronts and helped farmers to return to the near-prosperity level of 1937 in 1940.[35]

Meanwhile, the widespread wage cutting that occurred during the first months of the recession of 1937 prompted the administration to muster all its strength to force passage of the Fair Labor Standards, or wages and hours, bill. This measure had run afoul of the opposition of many groups, among them being the AF of L, since its adoption by the Senate in July 1937. Administration leaders prepared a new measure that won labor's support. Then the rules committee refused to allow the House of Representatives to consider the bill. But extraordinary administration pressure coupled with a public appeal by the President on April 30 resulted in House approval of the bill on May 23, 1938. The Senate concurred, and the President signed the measure on June 25.

The Fair Labor Standards Act was the last of the great New Deal measures and joined the Social Security and National Labor Relations Acts to round out a comprehensive structure of advanced labor legislation. In spite of certain necessary concessions, the Fair Labor Standards Act represented the culmination of perhaps the most important aspects of the social justice movement. First, it established a minimum wage of 25 cents an hour, to go into effect at once and to be gradually increased to 40 cents. Second, it lim-

wwwwwwwwwwwwwww

[33] Congress appropriated $212,000,000 in 1938, $225,000,000 in 1939, and $212,-000,000 in 1940 to bring farm income up to the parity level.

[34] The most interesting and widely used method was the so-called Food Stamp Plan, begun experimentally in Rochester, New York, in May 1939 and soon put into effect in all important cities. The Food Stamp Plan was an arrangement under which relief families received fifty cents' worth of free surplus food for every dollar they spent for food in any grocery store.

[35] Cash farm income, including governmental payments, was $9,176,000,000 in 1937, $8,130,000,000 in 1938, $8,658,000,000 in 1939, and $9,120,000,000 in 1940.

ited hours of labor to forty-four a week, to be reduced within three years to forty a week, and provided for payment at the rate of time and a half for overtime work. Third, it forbade shipment in interstate commerce of any goods manufactured in whole or in part by children under sixteen. Finally, it created a Wage and Hour Division in the Department of Labor to supervise application of the new law. Thus the Act abolished the worst sweatshops and ended the exploitation of children even though it left many workers unprotected. Nearly 13,000,000 persons were protected by the Wage and Hour Division by April 1939; an additional 700,000 workers, chiefly in the South, received immediate pay increases when the minimum wage was increased from 25 to 30 cents in October 1939.

Meanwhile, the President waited to see whether the economy would recover without new efforts at pump priming. The economic situation steadily worsened instead of improving during the winter of 1937–8, as the following table reveals:

1937	INDEX OF EMPLOYMENT IN MANUFACTURING	INDEX OF PAYROLLS IN MANUFACTURING	INDEX OF PRODUCTION
October	110.3	104.9	102
November	104.2	93.3	88
December	97.7	84.6	84
1938			
January	91.0	75.4	80
February	91.6	77.7	79
March	91.2	77.8	79

Therefore, the President sent a special message to Congress on April 14, 1938, announcing a loosening of credit restrictions, demanding a drastic revival of deficit spending, and calling upon business and labor to unite in a common war against the recession.

A frightened Congress hastily responded by making some $3,000,000,-000 immediately available to expand the WPA, launching a huge public works program in conjunction with the states, and increasing the activities of the FSA, CCC, and other agencies. Expanded bank credits and renewed pump priming reversed the tide almost at once. Indices of manufacturing production, payrolls, and employment started upward beginning in July and August 1938; recovery to the near-prosperity level of 1937 was almost complete by the end of 1939.

The last surge of New Deal reform was the inauguration by the administration and Congress in the spring and summer of 1938 of the most intense antitrust campaign since the presidency of William Howard Taft. Thurman Arnold of the Yale Law School, an ardent foe of monopoly, was appointed head of the Antitrust Division of the Department of Justice and given large new appropriations and increases in staff. He set 215 major investigations and ninety-two test cases to sharpen federal antitrust policy in motion within a short time. In addition, the President sent a special message to Congress on April 29, 1938, calling for a thorough study of the concentration of economic power and its effect on the American system of free enterprise. "The liberty of a democracy," he warned, "is not safe if the people tolerate the growth of private power to a point where it becomes stronger than their democratic state itself."

Congress responded on June 16, 1938, by creating the Temporary National Economic Committee (TNEC), composed of members of Congress and representatives of various Executive agencies. For seventeen months, from December 1, 1938, to April 26, 1940, the TNEC called some 552 witnesses, including bank presidents, corporation officials, and distinguished economists, and heard testimony that filled thirty-one volumes. In addition, TNEC economists wrote forty-three monographs covering almost every phase of American economic life.

The result was such a stock-taking of the American economy as had never before been attempted. It seemed at first that the administration contemplated some drastic new form of public control over business, industry, and finance. Such plans, however, did not long survive if they ever existed. The TNEC, after taking mountains of testimony, submitted a final report on March 31, 1941, that was neither original nor bold. It recommended only traditional remedies like strengthening the antitrust laws and reform of the patent system. By the date of the publication of the final report, of course, the administration was more concerned with preparations for war than with sweeping reform of the economic system.

153. *The Passing of the New Deal*

The administration's reform impulses and plans came to an abrupt halt in the early months of 1939 as the result of portentous developments in Europe and Asia and political reversals at home. Hitler's triumph at Munich in September 1938 and his subsequent partition of Czechoslovakia in March 1939 convinced Roosevelt that the Nazi menace to European and American democracy demanded a stronger foreign policy and preparation for possible conflict. Moreover, Japan's invasion of China in 1937 and threat of future expansion seemed to raise threats to American security in the Far East. In brief, the President believed that a world-wide cataclysm impended in the near future, and that his chief duty was now the protection of American security.

A firm defense of American interests, however, would almost inevitably require a radical alteration of the policy of strict nonintervention embodied in the neutrality legislation from 1935 to 1937. (See below, pp. 470–474.) Such a reversal could not be accomplished unless Roosevelt had a strong majority in Congress, but the Democratic party was split wide open on foreign policy. Midwestern and western Democrats were ardent supporters of Second New Deal domestic policies. But they, like their Republican counterparts, were determined to avoid any action that might conceivably lead to American participation in a Second World War. Eastern Democrats generally supported progressive measures and, except for representatives of Irish-American districts, were willing to support a stronger foreign policy. Southern Democrats were the most vociferous champions of defense and co-operation with Britain and France. But they were growing acutely fearful that the administration's advanced reform measures would impinge upon race relations in their region. Roosevelt might have to call a halt to further reform legislation in order to win their support for a stronger foreign policy. He might even have to jettison Midwesterners and Westerners and try to build a new coalition of Southerners and internationally minded Easterners. The implications of such a new departure for continuation of the Second New Deal were clear enough.

Political developments in 1938 emphasized this dilemma and revealed that the Second New Deal coalition of Midwesterners and Easterners was beginning to crumble. The first sign came in December 1937 and January 1938 during struggles in Congress over the proposed Ludlow Amendment and the Wagner–Van Nuys anti-lynching bill.[36] The President addressed a strong plea to Congress for defeat of the Ludlow resolution on January 6, and the House defeated it by a vote of 209 to 188 four days later. But Roosevelt must have perceived the significance of the alignment on the measure: three fourths of the Republicans and a majority of midwestern and western Democrats combined in support of the proposed amendment, while an overwhelming majority of southern and eastern Democrats voted against it. The conflict over the anti-lynching bill came to a head in the Senate at the same time. Although Roosevelt probably approved the measure in principle, he said no word in condemnation when southern senators by filibuster prevented a vote.

The development that decisively compelled Roosevelt to make peace with the conservatives in order to build strength for his foreign policy was the failure of his campaign to purge conservative southern Democrats in the primary campaigns during the summer of 1938. The President announced his determination to participate in the Democratic primary campaigns on June 24 and threw himself into the fight during the next two months. What Roosevelt said to Southerners was honest enough. Citing the *Report on Economic Conditions of the South,* issued on August 12, 1938, by a committee of leading southern educators, clergymen, editors, and businessmen, he declared that conditions that made the South "the Nation's No. 1 economic problem" could be remedied only by united progressive action in which Southerners played a leading part.

As was perhaps inevitable, the President's intervention boomeranged. Two stanch southern progressives, Representative Lister Hill of Alabama and Senator Claude W. Pepper of Florida, had won notable victories in earlier primary campaigns in which Roosevelt took no part. In contrast, not a single southern conservative was dislodged by Roosevelt's attempted purge. In fact, it was the general consensus that only Roosevelt's opposition saved old Senator "Cotton Ed" Smith of South Carolina from defeat.

The outcome of the congressional elections in November, moreover,

––––––––––––––––––––

[36] Introduced by Representative Louis Ludlow, Democrat of Indiana, this proposed amendment required majority approval of a war resolution in a national referendum, except in the event of an invasion of the United States or its territories. It had the support of numerous church and pacifist groups and apparently of a large majority of the American people.

The Wagner–Van Nuys anti-lynching bill made lynching a federal crime and allowed families of lynch victims to sue counties in which the lynching occurred for damages running to $10,000. It was supported by the National Association for the Advancement of Colored People and by liberal labor, church, and political groups in all sections except the South, where sentiment was divided.

left Roosevelt no alternative but to end his civil war and draw his party together in a solid front. The Republicans made enormous gains in the Middle and Far West and, by gaining seven seats in the Senate and eighty in the House, became a formidable power for the first time since 1932. Roosevelt would desperately need the support of Southerners on foreign policy in the next Congress. He would not be able to run the risk of driving them into alliance with the Republicans by further antagonism on domestic issues.

Therefore the President in effect announced the end of the great reform movement of the Second New Deal in his Annual Message to the Seventy-sixth Congress on January 4, 1939. Pleading only for continuation of deficit spending until full recovery had returned, he asked for no new reform legislation and declared: "We have now passed the period of internal conflict in the launching of our program of social reform. Our full energies may now be released to invigorate the processes of recovery in order to preserve our reforms." The major theme of this address, in fact, was the enormity of the totalitarian threat to religion, democracy, and international peace.

Thus it came about that the forward motion of progressivism came to a halt in the early uncertain months of 1939. And yet it would be erroneous to conclude that the failure of the "purge," the Republican revival, or even the increasing peril of the international situation alone accounted for the President's decision to abandon the fight for further reform legislation. More important was the fact that with one exception—development of new regional hydroelectric projects like the Tennessee Valley Authority— the President and his party had by 1939 brought to full completion the progressive program first formulated by agrarian, social justice, and labor progressives from 1897 to 1917 and then enlarged in the 1920's and 1930's. In other words, progressives had nearly reached the limits of achievement within the framework of their ideology. It embodied a faith in the middle way, in regulation and activity on behalf of disadvantaged classes, rather than in socialistic ownership of the means of production. Progressives in the years after the Second World War would find that their own ideological limitations made it difficult for them to do more than round out and strengthen the structure of the Second New Deal.

"As a Nation we have rejected any radical revolutionary program," Roosevelt observed in 1938. "For a permanent correction of grave weaknesses in our economic system we have relied on new applications of old democratic processes." And what student of American history could disagree with this judgment on the whole New Deal effort? The chief significance of the reform legislation of the 1930's was its essentially conservative character and the fact that it stemmed from half a century or more of discussion and practical experience and from ideas proposed by Republicans as well as by Democrats.

CHAPTER

20

The New Deal and the American People

OLD PROGRESSIVES must have been as much astonished as gratified in 1941 by all the changes they had seen. Most important was the profound metamorphosis in popular attitudes toward the federal government that had occurred in the four decades after 1900. By 1941 most Americans agreed that the federal government should be the most powerful organized force in their democracy: a guarantor of solvency to farmers, a beneficent protector to workers, a friend in adversity to tenant farmers and the unemployed, and a powerful safeguard as well as a regulator to businessmen and bankers.

Historians might argue that popular acceptance of progressive assumptions represented more a pragmatic response to obvious need than a reasoned acceptance of an elaborate ideology. Nonetheless, analysts were quick to perceive the significance of the institutional changes wrought by the New Deal legislation and the new spirit that permeated the American democracy by 1941. We have noted many of these changes in agriculture, industry, finance, and politics in the preceding two chapters. Now let us look at other and in the long run perhaps more important effects of the New Deal: how the intellectual and political upheaval of the 1930's affected the labor movement; promoted the growth of bold concepts concerning the development of regional resources, constitutional interpretations, and the treatment of minority groups; and stimulated the expansion and maturing of the progressive ideology.

154. *Labor's Civil War*

The labor movement experienced its most spectacular growth from 1933 to 1941 and finally won its old and hitherto elusive goal of unionization of the mass industries. Unhappily for labor, this triumph was accomplished at the cost of a bitter civil war that split the ranks of organized labor and left deep scars for years to come. It grew out of a division among the leaders of the AF of L over immediate tactics and fundamental philosophy. Leadership in the union had fallen to cautious men after the death of Samuel Gompers in 1924. They were convinced that craft or trade unionism offered the only solid basis for the American labor movement, and they abhorred the concept of industrial unionism, that is, organization of all workers in a given industry into one big union. The experience of the Knights of Labor and the IWW, they argued, proved that industrial unions were inherently unstable and inevitably fell prey to radical agitators.

In opposition stood a small but aggressive minority among the leaders of the AF of L. One was John L. Lewis, gifted with a stentorian voice, leonine appearance, and command of a virile Elizabethan vocabulary. He had built his United Mine Workers (UMW) into the most powerful union in the United States by 1935. Another was Sidney Hillman, one of the founders and president of the Amalgamated Clothing Workers. A third was David Dubinsky, head of the International Ladies' Garment Workers. These and other leaders argued that labor's hope lay in meeting strength with strength—by organizing mass industries on a mass, or industrial, basis and by attempting to bring the great body of Negro workers into the ranks of organized labor.

The AF of L convention voted in 1934 under strong pressure from Lewis, Hillman, and Dubinsky to charter so-called federal, or industrial, unions in the automobile, cement, aluminum, and other mass industries. But the conservatives had no intention of allowing the infant unions to grow into lusty giants and seize control of the AF of L. In fact, no sooner were the new unions launched than the old craft unions began to raid them.

The struggle came to a head at the AF of L convention in October 1935. Then Lewis bluntly proposed that craft unions should have no jurisdiction over workers in mass industries and made a ringing plea for a great campaign to organize unskilled workers. The majority of the convention rejected this resolution on October 16. Lewis and other leaders of eight AF of L unions met in Atlantic City on November 10 and formed the Committee for Industrial Organization, allegedly to help the AF of L unionize the basic industries. President William Green and the AF of L executive council struck back in January 1936, ordering the CIO to disband. The rebels defiantly welcomed new allies and laid plans for unionization campaigns. Then the AF of L executive council suspended ten unions in August 1936 and expelled them in March 1937. Moreover, the executive council announced in the following May that it would undertake an intensive organizational campaign of its own in the basic industries.

Ensuing months saw a bitter struggle for control of the masses of unorganized workers and CIO triumphs on almost every front. Beginning with 1,800,000 members in March 1937, the new union could claim a membership of nearly 3,750,000 six months later. Peace negotiations with the AF of L in October 1937 failed to yield an agreement satisfactory to Lewis. At the conclusion of these negotiations the rebel leaders finally declared their independence of the parent organization and reorganized the CIO soon afterward as the Congress of Industrial Organizations.

155. *The Progress of the CIO*

Meanwhile, the CIO had begun its offensive against the mass industries in June 1936 with the formation of the Steel Workers' Organizing Committee (SWOC) under Philip Murray, a lieutenant of Lewis in the UMW. The SWOC campaigned in the steel industry for over seven months, and discontented workers everywhere broke away from company unions and joined the CIO. In the past company managers could always rely upon the military assistance of the states and the moral support of the federal government. In that year of New Deal grace, 1936, however, the Washington administration was openly friendly to the workers, while the Democratic Governor of Pennsylvania promised relief assistance if a strike should occur.

It soon became evident that the executives of United States Steel, if not other captains of the industry, preferred surrender to a long and costly strike. Myron C. Taylor, chairman of the board of directors of United States Steel, held a series of private conferences with John L. Lewis beginning in December 1936. They led to friendly understanding and agreement by officials of the corporation to recognize the SWOC. Consequently, Benjamin Fairless, president of the Carnegie-Illinois Steel Company, a United States Steel subsidiary, signed on March 2, 1937, what was perhaps the most important contract in American labor history—important because it signified surrender of the corporation which since 1901 had taken leadership in the movement to block unionization of the basic industries. All the rest of United States Steel's subsidiaries had signed similar contracts within a short time. They granted recognition, a 10 per cent wage increase, the forty-hour week, and time and a half for overtime work.

It was on epochal victory, and Murray and the SWOC expected the remainder of the steel companies, known collectively as Little Steel, to come to terms quickly. Several of them, notably Inland Steel, made no effort to break the strike; but the leaders of the Bethlehem Steel, Republic Steel, and Youngstown Sheet and Tube companies fought back with all the force they could command. Republic Steel officials in Massillon, Ohio, organized a small army of deputies that killed two strikers in a wanton attack on July 11, 1937. Police in South Chicago killed ten and wounded scores of strikers at the Republic Steel plant on Memorial Day, 1937.

So violent was Little Steel's counterattack that the SWOC's momentum was almost entirely halted. Inland Steel agreed to recognize the union in July 1937, but the other companies held out. In pre–New Deal days this would probably have been the end of the story, at least until the workers organized for another bloody battle. Now, however, the workers' new ally, the federal government, went into action. First, a Senate subcommittee, headed by Robert M. La Follette, Jr., of Wisconsin, conducted a thorough investigation into all aspects of the strike during the spring and summer of 1938. It reported numerous violations of the Wagner Act and the civil liberties of the strikers by the steel companies, local police, and the National Guard. It also discovered that the companies maintained corps of spies and *agents provocateurs*, and it revealed that the same companies had collected arsenals of guns, tear gas, and ammunition for use against strikers.[1] Second, the NLRB moved into the case upon appeal of the SWOC and compelled the Little Steel companies to recognize and bargain in good faith with the SWOC in 1941. By the end of that year, therefore, the steel workers' union, now 600,000 strong, stood triumphant throughout the entire industry.

The key automobile industry became the CIO's next target, although the union's leaders did not plan it that way. The AF of L had chartered some 100 local unions in the automobile industry in 1933 and 1934 and launched the United Automobile Workers in August 1935. But the UAW declined rapidly in membership and strength because it did not have effective leadership and support from the AF of L. Then Homer Martin, an industrial unionist and former Baptist preacher, gained control of the UAW in May 1936 and took it into the CIO. The following summer and autumn saw an intensive and successful unionization campaign among workers in General Motors and Chrysler plants. The workers were so determined to win full recognition that the national CIO leaders could not refuse to support them, even though their chief concern now was the impending strike in the steel industry.

Martin invited officials of the General Motors Corporation to a bargaining conference in December 1936. When company spokesmen declined, workers in the Fisher Body Plant in Cleveland sat down by their machines on December 28. Within a few days the sit-down strike had spread through key General Motors plants. There had been minor sit-down strikes before, but none so well organized and on such a spectacular scale as this one. Company officials for the most part did not dare molest the occupying forces, for fear that violence would lead to destruction of machinery. But there was one pitched battle on January 11, 1937, when police tried to prevent the delivery of food to strikers inside Fisher Body Plant No. 1 at Flint, Michigan. Strikers in this melee turned back the police, reopened food lines, and retained possession of the plant.

General Motors officials called upon the recently inaugurated Governor of Michigan, Frank Murphy, to use the National Guard to dislodge the trespassers. But Murphy was a rare phenomenon for Michigan in those days—a Democrat, elected with the support of labor, who sympathized with the objectives if not the methods of the strikers. Instead of using force, he tried to conciliate. Mediation conferences in Lansing and Washington failed to bring peace. Then the corporation appealed to Circuit Court Judge Paul V. Gadola on January 29, 1937, for an injunction ordering the

[1] It is only fair to add that the La Follette subcommittee was grossly partial to the cause of the strikers in its investigation and report. The subcommittee, for example, made no effort to investigate the companies' plea that they were seeking merely to protect their own property and the right of nonunion members to work.

strikers from the plants. Gadola signed an injunction on the following day ordering all strikers from the property of General Motors under pain of a $15,000,000 fine and imprisonment if they refused. "Unarmed as we are, the introduction of the militia, sheriffs, or police with murderous weapons will mean a blood bath of unarmed workers," the strikers replied. ". . . We have decided to stay in the plant." Judge Gadola ordered the sheriff to arrest the strikers; the sheriff refused and appealed to Governor Murphy. Murphy in turn refused to use the National Guard and redoubled his efforts at mediation.

After days of tense negotiations, during which President Roosevelt brought enormous pressure to bear upon General Motors officials, the corporation finally surrendered on February 11, 1937. The UAW won all its demands except the closed shop—dismissal of the injunction proceedings, recognition of the union as the sole bargaining agent for the workers, and collective bargaining looking toward agreement on hours and wages.

Flushed with their victory over General Motors, UAW leaders moved next against the smaller Chrysler Corporation and applied sit-down and mass picketing techniques at eight Chrysler plants on March 8, 1937. Judge Allen Campbell of Detroit ordered the arrest of CIO leaders and 6,000 sitting strikers (they had defied his earlier injunction), and the workers prepared to resist. But public opinion throughout the country by this date was growing alarmed by a wave of sit-down strikes in many branches of industry and was turning sharply against the new technique.[2] Governor Murphy announced that he would enforce the injunction; at the same time he succeeded in bringing Walter P. Chrysler and John L. Lewis together in high-level peace talks. The upshot was an agreement altogether favorable to the UAW. Lewis called the strikers out of Chrysler plants on March 24, and the corporation surrendered on April 6 on the terms to which General Motors had recently agreed.

Henry Ford had always repelled the suggestion that workers should participate in the determination of company policies. Ford had the lowest wage scale of any of the major automobile producers in 1937; he also had the most efficient "service department," a collection of labor spies and company police dedicated to destroying any incipient union. The UAW began an organization campaign in the Ford Company soon after Chrysler capitulated, but it was badly managed and failed to win the workers in Ford's huge River Rouge plant. However, the UAW was consistently successful among smaller producers like Packard and Hudson; by September 1937 the union had over 300,000 members and boasted bargaining agreements with every automobile producer except Ford.

Meanwhile, personal rivalry between factions headed by Homer Martin on the one side and Richard T. Frankensteen, R. J. Thomas, and Walter Reuther on the other came to a head in 1937–8 and split the UAW. Backed by the CIO, Thomas and Reuther won the support of an overwhelming majority, whereupon Martin carried his followers into the AF

‸‸‸‸‸‸‸‸‸‸‸‸‸‸‸‸

[2] Some 500,000 workers were engaged directly in sit-down strikes from September 1936 through May 1937 and forced the shutting down of other plants employing 600,000 workers. The peak came in March 1937, when nearly 200,000 workers participated in sit-down strikes.

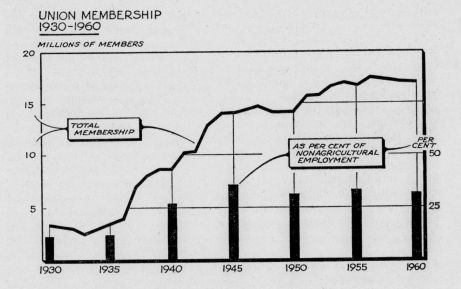

UNION MEMBERSHIP
1930-1960

MILLIONS OF MEMBERS

TOTAL MEMBERSHIP

AS PER CENT OF NONAGRICULTURAL EMPLOYMENT

PER CENT

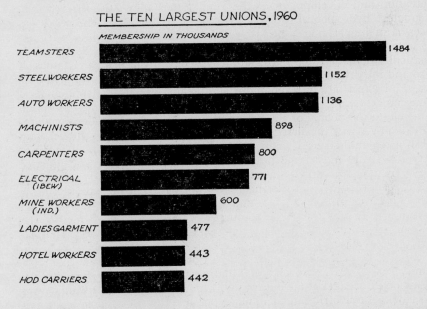

THE TEN LARGEST UNIONS, 1960

MEMBERSHIP IN THOUSANDS

TEAMSTERS	1484
STEELWORKERS	1152
AUTO WORKERS	1136
MACHINISTS	898
CARPENTERS	800
ELECTRICAL (IBEW)	771
MINE WORKERS (IND.)	600
LADIES GARMENT	477
HOTEL WORKERS	443
HOD CARRIERS	442

of L. The UAW–CIO went on with the full support of the NLRB to organize the Ford workers in the autumn of 1940; in the following spring it conducted a strike that soon won complete recognition.

Meanwhile, CIO unions had won the right to bargain for workers in most of the other basic industries. An uprising of rubber workers in Akron, Ohio, in February 1936 led to the formation of the United Rubber Workers Union and the CIO's rapid conquest of the rubber industry. The

United Textile Workers Union organized the textile mills of the North and made a heroic but generally unsuccessful effort to penetrate the southern area in 1937 and 1938. Harry Bridges organized longshoremen on the Pacific Coast into a powerful CIO union. And so it went in dozens of other industries, until by the time that the United States entered the Second World War the CIO had some 5,000,000 members, the AF of L had grown to a membership of 4,569,000, and independent unions could count an additional 1,000,000. By this date 28.2 per cent of all workers in nonagricultural employment were unionized, as compared to 11.5 per cent in 1933. In short, labor was well on its way toward achieving the organization of all important American industries and its long-sought goal of equality with management in the determination of labor policies. Offsetting and to a degree counterbalancing the power of big business now stood big labor, a new institution brought into being not merely by labor's own efforts but also because the federal government had thrown its moral and legal support to labor's side during the critical period of the CIO's life.

156.   *The TVA and the Concept of the Region*

No New Deal enterprise so fired the imagination of progressives as the creation and development of the Tennessee Valley Authority (TVA). The greatest hydroelectric project in history, it harnessed the water resources of an area 40,000 square miles in size and made possible utilization of vast quantities of electric power in a once impoverished region. It dramatically demonstrated man's ability to control the primeval forces of nature and repair the damage done to the good earth during two centuries of wasteful exploitation. Even more significant was its conception as a regional undertaking and operation by a nonpartisan agency as much responsible to the people of the region as to its owner, the federal government. The TVA was the first really significant experiment in public planning on a regional scale. Its concepts and techniques might well prove to be the New Deal's most important contribution to the theory and practice of government in the United States.

The reader will recall the struggle for control of Wilson Dam at Muscle Shoals, Alabama, in the 1920's, and how Senator George W. Norris of Nebraska helped save the power resources of the Tennessee Valley for the American people. (See above, pp. 332–334.) Progressives bided their time and enlarged their objectives even while their plans for federal development were being thwarted by Presidents Coolidge and Hoover. Their opportunity came with Roosevelt's nomination and election in 1932, for the new Democratic leader came out for public power projects that would serve as yardsticks for electric rates and make possible the wider consumption of power. The President-elect visited the Tennessee Valley in January 1933 in company with Norris. Roosevelt's fertile imagination must have been excited by the opportunities that unfolded as he stood on Wilson Dam.

He converted opportunities into objectives on April 10, 1933, when he asked Congress to establish a Tennessee Valley Authority, "a corporation clothed with the power of Government but possessed of the flexibility and initiative of a private enterprise," to plan for the full development of the natural resources of the valley. Congress responded quickly by creating the TVA, a corporation controlled by a three-man board and endowed with sweeping authority subject to the general supervision of the President and Congress.

The TVA directors conceived their first task to be control of the Tennessee River and its tributaries to stop erosion, prevent floods, and improve navigation. With liberal appropriations from Congress, the TVA organized a construction force of 40,000 men and began "one hell of a big job of work," as a local carpenter described it. The Authority designed and constructed twenty new dams and improved five existing ones between 1933 and 1952; poured two and one half times as much concrete as went into the Panama Canal; and used enough material to build thirty-five Hoover or ten

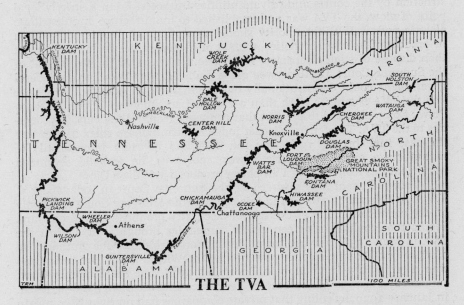

THE TVA

Grand Coulee Dams. By 1960 the Authority's investment stood at two billion dollars.

The result was the completion of a nearly perfect system of water control in one of the areas of heaviest rainfall in the United States. There were no more floods in the Tennessee Valley once the TVA dams were completed; and TVA engineers could also greatly reduce the flood menace in the Ohio and Mississippi valleys by holding back the Tennessee and its tributaries. In addition, the TVA created an inland waterway 652 miles long with a minimum depth of nine feet, connecting the interior of the South with the Great Lakes, Ohio River, and Missouri-Mississippi River systems. Traffic on the Tennessee River increased from 32,000,000 ton-miles in 1933 to 2,000,000,000 ton-miles in 1960, as barges brought grain from Minneapolis, automobiles from Detroit, and steel from Chicago into the recesses of the South.

Flood control and development of navigation required technical planning on a regional scale, to be sure, but the TVA directors viewed their

task in the broader terms of helping the people of the region to stop erosion
and recover the valley's lost fertility. To accomplish this goal, the TVA
used facilities at Muscle Shoals to produce phosphatic fertilizers and
distributed them through the AAA. It also conducted a demonstration program to teach farmers how to prevent erosion and rebuild soil and worked
with the CCC in the reforestation of hundreds of thousands of acres of
gullied lands. The results were unexpectedly gratifying. Cash receipts from
farming increased 196 per cent in Tennessee from 1929 to 1948, as compared with an increase of 170 per cent for the country as a whole.

It is well known that the TVA also became one of the major producers
of electric power in the United States. Progress toward this goal was, however, slow in the beginning, in large measure on account of persistent obstruction by the courts and private utilities interests. From a strictly legal
point of view, the TVA was not established to manufacture and distribute
electric power. If the Authority should manufacture electric power as a
by-product of its main activities, the Act of incorporation declared, it might
then dispose of such electricity. This of course was said for the benefit of
the Supreme Court, for there was grave doubt in 1933 whether the federal
government could constitutionally engage in such an activity. No sooner
had the TVA begun its work than a group of stockholders in the Alabama
Power Company sued to prevent that company from selling certain properties to the TVA. The federal district judge in Birmingham ruled in deciding
the case in February 1935 that the TVA had no right intentionally to
manufacture and sell electric power; moreover, he forbade seventeen
municipalities from buying TVA power produced at Wilson Dam.

This judgment was reversed by the Supreme Court in Ashwander *v.*
T.V.A. in February 1936. But in this decision the Supreme Court ruled only
on the constitutionality of the sale of electricity produced at Wilson Dam.
Seeing the loophole, nineteen utility companies brought suit against the
TVA in May 1936, praying for an injunction forbidding the Authority to
produce or distribute electric power except at Wilson Dam. The companies
won a temporary injunction in December 1936, but the Supreme Court
summarily disposed of the case in Tennessee Electric Power Co. *v.* T.V.A.
in January 1939, by ruling that private companies had no right to complain
of competition by the government. The leader of the utility interests,
Wendell L. Willkie, president of the Commonwealth & Southern Corporation, gave up the fight after this rebuff. He sold the entire facilities of the
Tennessee Electric Power Company to the TVA in August 1939 at his own
price of nearly $79,000,000.

Commonwealth & Southern's withdrawal marked the end of private
enterprise in the utilities field in the Tennessee Valley, for numerous
smaller operating companies had either already sold out to TVA or soon
followed Commonwealth & Southern's example. With the completion of
new dams and particularly with the building of steam plants in the 1950's,[3]
the TVA's revenues from the sale of electric power increased from $2,306,-
000 in 1938 to $95,000,000 in 1952 and to $237,540,000 in 1959, and the
Tennessee Valley emerged as the largest producer of electric power among

[3] By the end of 1959, 66 per cent of TVA electricity was produced by steam plants,
34 per cent by turbines in the dams.

the regions of the United States. Over the period 1933–59 total generating capacity in the valley increased from 800,000 kilowatts to 11,386,710 kilowatts, while actual production of electricity increased from 1.5 billion to 63.4 billion kilowatt hours.

President Roosevelt, on June 3, 1937, urged Congress to plan for six additional regional authorities.[4] He was thinking, however, more in terms of future than of immediate development. Meanwhile, the administration pushed forward in a more limited way with other regional projects. One was Hoover Dam and the All-American Canal, completed in 1936 with the aid of PWA funds at a total cost of about $165,000,000, with an installed capacity in 1960 of 1,245,000 kilowatt hours. Another was Grand Coulee Dam on the Columbia River in Washington, the largest masonry structure in the world, completed in 1942 at a cost of $435,734,000, with a total power capacity in 1960 of 1,974,000 kilowatt hours. A third was the great earthen Fort Peck Dam on the Missouri River in Montana, completed in 1939 and used principally for flood control. Whether these projects should constitute the basis for new regional developments like the TVA would be one of the major issues confronting the American people in the years after 1945.

157. *The New Deal in the Supreme Court*

Although it was the last branch of the federal government to fall under New Deal influence, the Supreme Court effected a profound and rapid revolution in constitutional interpretation after 1937. Sweeping away all doubt about the constitutionality of advanced social and economic legislation, it became the chief practitioner of sociological jurisprudence, gave a larger degree of freedom to state and federal regulatory agencies than they had enjoyed before 1937, and added strong new safeguards for the protection of civil liberties, labor, and minorities. This revolution in American law occurred in the first instance because Roosevelt was privileged by virtue of his long tenure and the advanced age of incumbent judges to appoint virtually a new federal judiciary, from district courts to the supreme tribunal. By the end of 1941, for example, the President had appointed the Chief Justice and seven of the eight Associate Justices of the Supreme Court.

Convinced that the Constitution must serve the needs of an urbanized and industrialized democracy, the members of the "Roosevelt court" completed and clarified the constitutional revolution begun by the unreformed court in 1937. In a series of cases from 1938 to 1942 testing the constitutionality of the TVA's power operations, the Fair Labor Standards Act, the Holding Company Act of 1935, the second Railroad Retirement Act, the second Agricultural Adjustment Act, and other measures, the court gave Congress virtually unlimited authority under the interstate commerce

ʌʌʌʌʌʌʌʌʌʌʌʌʌʌʌʌʌʌʌʌ

[4] In the following areas: the Atlantic Seaboard; the Great Lakes and the Ohio Valley; the Missouri River and the Red River of the North; the drainage basins of the Arkansas, Red, and Rio Grande rivers; the basin of the Colorado River; and the Columbia River Valley.

clause. The key decision in this epochal series was rendered by Justice Harlan F. Stone in United States *v.* Darby in 1941, testing the constitutionality of the Fair Labor Standards Act. It was a decision that buried the last vestiges of the theory that the Tenth Amendment had limited the national commerce power. The new court, while accepting the principle of stringent federal regulation, also gave to federal and state administrative agencies broad new freedom to act in the public interest—a reversal of the old court's insistence on imposing judicial criteria on the regulatory agencies.

The New Deal court made its most important contribution in the development of broad federal protection of religious, civil, and political liberty and defense against arbitrary police authority. Chief Justice Hughes had already firmly laid the basis for new safeguards in the 1930's, in decisions establishing the doctrine that because of the adoption of the Fourteenth Amendment no state could deprive a person of any of the basic rights guaranteed by the first ten Amendments.[5] The significant fact was the way in which the New Deal court, with Hughes still its spokesman until his retirement in 1941, expanded the concept of basic liberties guaranteed by the Fourteenth Amendment.

To begin with, the court reaffirmed Hughes's earlier condemnation of so-called third-degree methods of obtaining confessions by beating and torture and applied this ban against all subtler forms of torture as well. Again, the court majority went to the defense of Jehovah's Witnesses, a fanatical sect that disavowed loyalty to any earthly state, by ruling in 1943 that local or state authorities could not require children of Jehovah's Witnesses to salute the flag in school, since such action violated the Witnesses' religious scruples and liberty. The court also nullified local ordinances requiring religious groups to obtain licenses to conduct open-air services or distribute literature.

Negroes, who had most often been denied civil rights on account of race, benefited most from the court's increased vigilance. As a result of decisions cited above, they enjoyed a larger degree of personal safety and the right to a fair trial in which members of their race would participate. It was perhaps more important that the new court opened wide the gates to political and educational opportunities for Negroes and confirmed their right to live and travel as citizens of a great democracy, not as servants of a master class.

On the educational front the court took the first step toward abandoning the legalism which, under the "separate but equal" concept, had permitted southern states to maintain segregated educational facilities for Negroes for three quarters of a century. Chief Justice Hughes set in motion

---

[5] In Stromberg *v.* California and Near *v.* Minnesota, both rendered in 1931, Hughes invalidated a California statute forbidding the display of the red flag and a Minnesota censorship law, on the ground that the measures contravened fundamental civil rights guaranteed by the Fourteenth Amendment. In another decision in the second Scottsboro case in 1935—Norris *v.* Alabama—involving the conviction of seven Negroes for rape, Hughes reversed the conviction on the ground that Negroes had been excluded from the jury that convicted the Scottsboro boys. Exclusion on grounds of race, Hughes asserted, was a denial of the citizen's right to a trial by a jury of his peers.

the reversal that would end in repudiation of the theory that separate public schools, colleges, and universities for Negroes could in fact be equal in the case of Missouri *ex rel.* Gaines in 1938. In this decision the court simply required the University of Missouri Law School to admit a Negro student because the state had not provided separate but equal facilities for Negroes. In the forties, as we shall see in a later chapter, the New Deal court handed down a series of decisions that removed many of the legal roadblocks on the Negro's avenue to full citizenship, preparing the way for the spectacular advances—social, political, economic, educational—made by the nation's Negro inhabitants during the 1950's. (See below, pp. 769–771, 776–786.)

Nearly as important were decisions that freed organized labor from the bonds imposed by the courts under the Sherman Antitrust Act. The fundamental issue was whether labor unions, in the conduct of industrial warfare, might employ methods that restrained interstate commerce. The Roosevelt court formulated a new doctrine in Apex Hosiery Co. *v.* Leader, 1940, and United States *v.* Hutcheson, 1941, that labor unions might restrain commerce when such restraint was incidental to achievement of legitimate objectives. The Apex and Hutcheson rulings reversed earlier decisions and gave organized labor its long-sought immunity from prosecution under the antitrust laws, except when unions sought directly to restrain commerce through monopolistic and restrictive practices or attempted to defy the government when it was an employer.[6]

Although the Roosevelt court well deserved its reputation for progressivism, it was never a "rubber stamp" court, as many New Deal critics averred. And it was far from being a unanimous or even a personally harmonious court. Chief Justice Hughes had contrived by masterful mediation to subordinate personal differences among the justices; but his successor, Harlan F. Stone, apparently failed to prevent differences of opinion from developing into violent personal antagonisms. In any event, the Roosevelt court had divided into two distinct and sometimes hostile factions by the time of Stone's death on April 22, 1946.[7] In the beginning, at least, divisions arose out of genuine differences of constitutional opinion. One faction, led by Justice Felix Frankfurter, was willing to give local authorities and state legislatures the benefit of the doubt in borderline cases involving civil rights. The other, whose chief spokesmen were Justices Hugo L. Black and William O. Douglas, insisted upon a more rigid defense of civil rights based upon principles embodied in the Bill of Rights. On the other hand, Frankfurter and his friends evinced a readiness to impose

---

[6] For example, in United States *v.* United Mine Workers of America, 1947, the Supreme Court upheld a district court judge's injunction ordering John L. Lewis and the UMW to terminate a strike against the coal industry, then technically operated by the United States. In this important decision the court ruled that the Norris Anti-Injunction Act did not apply when the United States was the employer. Again, in United States *v.* Petrillo, 1947, the Supreme Court upheld an Act of Congress of 1946 that made it unlawful for the musicians' union to attempt to compel radio stations to employ more musicians than they actually needed.

[7] President Truman appointed Fred M. Vinson of Kentucky to succeed Stone. Vinson died on September 8, 1953, and was succeeded by Governor Earl Warren of California, appointed by President Eisenhower.

judicial criteria in cases involving state economic legislation, while the Black-Douglas faction were willing to accept almost any form of state control over economic affairs. These differences in interpretation were exacerbated as the years passed by intemperate outbursts in which one faction accused the other of betraying civil liberties or of promulgating foolish doctrines. Unfortunate though this development was, it should not be allowed to obscure the fact that the New Deal court sat during a critical period of peace and war and left a lasting impact on the American political system and ideology by its overhauling of constitutional interpretation concerning governmental power and civil and religious freedom.

158.   *The Return of the Prodigals: Intellectuals and the New Deal*

It is difficult to recount the impact of the New Deal on American intellectuals without seeming to exaggerate. Yet reflection confirms the conviction that the hope of reform and redemption under Roosevelt's leadership stirred intellectuals as they had not been roused since 1917. Political thinkers, professors in various disciplines, editors, and socially minded lawyers, clergymen, and writers threw off the torpor and cynicism that had ruined their influence and separated them from the middle classes in the 1920's. They reclaimed their high position as leaveners of progressivism and chief interpreters of the American democratic tradition. In a sense this was the natural response of a sensitive group to challenges to democracy raised at home by the depression and abroad by the rise of totalitarianism. The significant fact, however, was that Roosevelt personally drew large numbers of intellectuals, particularly professors, into governmental service and used them to construct his program of reform and rehabilitation.

This was true in the first two years of the New Deal, when the "Brain Trust" wrote much of the emergency legislation, and when the President called into the public service men like William O. Douglas of the Yale Law School and Dean James M. Landis of the Harvard Law School to serve as chairmen of the SEC. It was true on a much broader scale when Roosevelt utilized the services of trained scholars and experts to formulate and carry out the important measures of the Second New Deal. A mere listing of the host of men and women who left university and foundation posts to launch and direct the Social Security, Farm Security, and kindred agencies would require more space than we could give.

Intellectuals working with the administration did more than staff New Deal agencies. They were organized in various President's committees on social security, farm security, executive reorganization, natural resources, the problem of southern poverty, and the like, and they issued reports that stirred thoughtful Americans to the necessity for action in these fields. Sociologists and economists working with the National Resources Planning Board surveyed the problem of population redistribution and other such subjects. A large group of economists working in conjunction with the TNEC revealed the concentration of control in American industry, exposed the quasi-monopolistic practices of big business, and pointed the way ahead to reform. Historians co-operated with the special Senate subcommittee headed by Senator Gerald P. Nye of North Dakota in exorcising war.

The result of these manifold labors was such a thoroughgoing examination of every phase of American economic and social life as the country had not experienced since the early years of the progressive period. In other words, professors and other intellectuals were the muckrakers of the 1930's and catalysts of the latter reform movement. They had greater resources than the earlier muckrakers had, and their audience was different, but their task and accomplishment were much the same. It is not surprising that a generation of intellectuals should have regarded the New Deal Era as a time bright with the hope of good things.

The 1930's were a time also when social scientists, under the impact of the depression crisis, discarded old concepts and matured new ones to justify a broad expansion of public authority. Following the trail blazed years before by the iconoclastic Thorstein Veblen, economists analyzed American economic institutions critically and apart from a priori assumptions about the nature of economic activity. These institutional economists taught the necessity of governmental participation in economic affairs. The disciples of John Maynard Keynes, a British economist, for example, evolved a theory of governmental compensatory spending to prevent or end depressions and adduced intricate mathematical formulas to buttress an otherwise common-sense theory. The institutional economists of the 1930's were collectivists to the degree that they recognized the interdependent character of the economy and the necessity for a larger measure of public participation in economic affairs. But, like their earlier counterparts in the United States, they believed not in utopian socialism but in democratic capitalism controlled in the interest of all the people.

A group of political scientists working in an allied field abandoned the ivory tower of abstract principles to discover how and why the American political system actually functioned. It was the sociologists, however, who won the largest audience and had the most significant impact on the thoughtful American public. They were learned, sophisticated, and "scientific," to be sure. But like the muckrakers they performed the task, indispensable to the preservation of democracy, of laying bare the unpleasant facts of American social life. The most important new developments in this field accurately reflected the major concerns of the Second New Deal—the South and the concept of the region, the Negro, and rural poverty. Led by Howard W. Odum and Rupert B. Vance of the University of North Carolina, southern sociologists courageously examined their region's institutions and social structure. This cathartic self-analysis was too strong for many proud Southerners. To a growing body of young progressives, however, it seemed the first step toward a healthy reconstruction. Moreover, Southerners joined other sociologists in an almost frantic drive to understand and destroy the bases of racial prejudice. The culmination of this campaign was a co-operative study financed by the Carnegie Corporation of New York and synthesized by the Swedish sociologist, Gunnar Myrdal, in a huge volume entitled *An American Dilemma: The Negro Problem and Modern Democracy,* published in 1944.

Progressive intellectuals in the New Deal era made their most lasting contribution by expanding the horizons of democratic ideology to encompass fundamentals that earlier progressives had often ignored. New Deal progressives assumed that the political institutional structure was essentially sound and made few suggestions for political change. They gave major attention to economic justice and security, advanced concepts of civil liberty, and experiments in compensatory spending and planning. The pioneers in the progressive movement had been principally concerned with constructing new forms for democracy and with bringing uncontrolled property under public control. It fell, therefore, to the latter-day progressives to broaden the horizons and objectives of the movement to include programs for the benefit of hitherto neglected disadvantaged groups: Negroes, the unemployed, tenants and sharecroppers, industrial workers, and the like. The dimensions of their accomplishment can be seen in the social and economic legislation of the Second New Deal. The significance of this accomplishment lay in the fact that the great majority of Americans, Republicans and Democrats alike, accepted and approved the new ideals of social welfare democracy.

159. *The Survival of the Democratic Faith*

The 1930's were a time of severe testing for democracy throughout the world, as Fascism, Nazism, and militarism grew audacious, and the democracies trembled in fear of aggression and war. At the same time, the totalitarian powers used all weapons of modern psychological warfare in a great campaign to capture the minds of men. The American democracy was throughout the decade a vast free market place where contenders peddled their ideological wares, often by deceit and cunning but always with such freedom as befits a democracy.

On one side were a crowd of fascist and Nazi-financed demagogues and their organizations, whose themes ranged from social justice to violent anti-Semitism. The Reverend Charles E. Coughlin, Catholic priest of Royal Oak, Michigan, quickly emerged as the pre-eminent leader of the fascist forces after Huey P. Long's death in 1935. Coughlin discarded his social justice disguise in 1938, came out frankly as a pro-Nazi and anti-Semite, and formed the Christian Front in 1939 to unite the widely scattered anti-democratic organizations. The Christian Front had mobilized strong-arm gangs in cities throughout the country by the autumn of 1939, and Coughlin counted his followers by the hundreds of thousands and his audience by the millions.

Working for the same objectives and using the same anti-Semitic, anti-Communist propaganda were a group of lesser fascist demagogues. There was, for example, the mystical megalomaniac, William Dudley Pelley, who organized the Silvershirt Legion, a counterpart of Hitler's Brown Shirts, in 1933. Lawrence Dennis, author of *The Coming American Fascism* and other works, was the intellectual leader and principal adviser of the fascist groups. Long's chief organizer, the Reverend Gerald L. K. Smith of Shreveport, Louisiana, moved to Detroit, converted the "Share Our Wealth" organization into the Committee of One Million, and began a campaign against Jews, Negroes, and Communists. Smith's counterpart in the Middle West was the revivalist, the Reverend Gerald B. Winrod of

Wichita, Kansas. He learned the secrets of the "international Jewish conspiracy" in Nazi Germany in 1934 and 1935 and was as violently anti-Catholic as anti-Semitic. In the Northeast Fritz J. Kuhn, a naturalized German American and veteran of Hitler's Munich beer-hall *putsch* in 1923, formed the *Amerikadeutscher Volksbund* in 1936. As *Bundesführer* he hailed the day when the swastika would replace the Stars and Stripes.

There were, besides, dozens of lesser evangels of fascism and religious hatred. They flooded America with Nazi propaganda, nurtured anti-Semitic passions, and formed an important component of the large isolationist faction after 1939. They had the support of a small but vocal element in Congress, and they reached a combined audience running into the millions. They were potentially dangerous, but they failed to subvert democracy or to become anything more than a lunatic fringe. Most of them were sheer money-makers rather than conspirators working under the control of the Nazi government. Factionalism and personal rivalries prevented the little *führers* from uniting. Most important, practically the entire civil and religious leadership of the United States recognized the rabble-rousers for what they were and effectively neutralized their propaganda.

The Communist movement in the United States, on the other hand, was better organized, used a more insidious propaganda, and was part of a vast international conspiracy directed and controlled by the Soviet government. Its menace to American democracy varied, however, according to changing circumstances and party lines. The Communist party in the United States was torn during the 1920's by the struggle for power between Joseph Stalin and Leon Trotsky then going on within the Soviet Union. Stalin, after winning absolute power in Russia in 1927–8, called the leaders of the American section to Moscow, removed the Trotskyites, and established a party hack, Earl Browder, as secretary general of the party.

This purging of the Trotsky element weakened American Communism at the time when the depression offered some opportunity to the party. Communists tried to bore into the AF of L unions and were turned back. They then organized rival but unsuccessful unions in the clothing, coal, textile, and other industries and thus earned the undying hatred of most American labor leaders. They also tried to organize the unemployed, and probably had a hand in the bonus riots in Washington in 1932. The net effect of all these efforts was only to confirm the dominant popular conviction that Communism was at war with American institutions. Party membership, which stood at 8,000 at the beginning of the depression, was only 12,000 in 1932 and, after two years of vigorous recruiting, only 24,000 in 1934. William Z. Foster, the party's presidential candidate in 1932, polled a mere 102,991 votes.

One of the chief causes for Communist failure during the depression years was the inability of American comrades to develop an ideology and a program of their own. They were forced to follow tactics and a party line dictated by the Comintern, or Communist International. International Communism from 1928 to 1935 was in its so-called third period, in which Stalin adhered to exaggerated notions of world revolution in order to diminish Trotsky's influence. Convinced that the depression would culminate in the downfall of capitalism in the West, the Russian dictator declared war on labor unions and democratic leaders who seemed to offer the best hope of recovery and reform. In the United States this assault was directed chiefly at the New Deal, which the Communist party declared in 1934 was "the aggressive effort of the bankers and trusts to find a way out of the crisis at the expense of the millions of toilers . . . [and] a program of fascization and the most intense preparations for imperialist war."

Stalin obviously made a bad guess as to the outcome of the world depression. The consequences of his policy were particularly tragic in Germany, where Communist refusal to co-operate with the Social Democrats was a decisive factor in Hitler's rise to power in 1932–3. The German fascists did not collapse as Stalin expected, but soon won complete control of the Fatherland and began to prepare for an all-out struggle with Russia. Stalin too late perceived the enormity of his blunder and effected a swift and complete reversal of policy. He announced the new line at the seventh Comintern meeting in Moscow in the summer of 1935. Hereafter Communists should take leadership in a movement to contain fascism by co-operating in so-called Popular Front organizations with democratic and "anti-fascist" forces in political parties, labor unions, and even church groups.

This reversal gave Communists in the United States their first opportunity to try a policy of co-operation with an infiltration of progressive organizations. Quietly putting revolutionary doctrines and heroes in temporary storage, Communists now proclaimed the slogan, "Communism is Twentieth Century Americanism," disclaimed any intention forcibly to subvert the Constitution, and made a bold bid for the friendship of old-line groups. Their chief aim after 1935 was not rapid expansion of party membership but infiltration and control of labor unions, writers' groups, Popular Front organizations with mass memberships, and, finally, the federal government itself.

Communists scored their most important successes on the labor front. To be sure, they were in no way responsible for events that led to the split in the AF of L and the formation of the CIO in 1935. But Lewis, Hillman, and other CIO leaders needed thousands of trained organizers and accepted such support as the Communists could give, without asking questions about Communist motives. As a consequence, Communists by 1938 controlled several major unions, including the electrical workers, the West Coast longshoremen, and the seamen, and were in strategic positions in the powerful UAW. Moreover, two fellow travelers if not party members, Lee Pressman and Len De Caux, were highly placed in the leadership of the CIO as, respectively, general counsel and editor of the *C.I.O. News*. Even more important, the general counsel and a member of the NLRB, Nathan Witt and Edwin S. Davis, were strong Communist sympathizers if not card-bearing party members during the period of the critical struggle between the CIO and AF of L from 1935 to 1940. They seemed to have no difficulty persuading the Board to render opinions favorable to the CIO as against rival AF of L unions or employers.

To a large group of writers Communist doctrine and propaganda either appealed with the force of a new religion or else held out the hope of genuine co-operation to halt the spread of fascism and anti-Semitism at home and abroad. Many so-called intellectuals were sickened by the plight of the lower classes in the United States and inspired by the seeming material progress and social stability of the Soviet Union during the depression period. Hence a number of distinguished American novelists, including Sherwood Anderson, Erskine Caldwell, and Granville Hicks, publicly supported Foster for President in 1932. Moreover, left-wing writers and artists banded together in John Reed clubs to nurse the cult of proletarian literature from 1932 to 1935. The John Reed clubs metamorphosed into the League of American Writers in 1935. It held annual conferences until 1939 and included a hard core of Communists and a host of momentary co-operators like Ernest Hemingway, Richard Wright, Archibald MacLeish, Upton Sinclair, and James T. Farrell. Left-wing actors also banded together in the Group Theater, Theater Union, and Theater Collective to enjoy the bohemian life and salve their social consciences by producing plays of Clifford Odets, John Howard Lawson, Elmer Rice, and other "proletarian" playwrights.

Communist leaders executed their most ambitious schemes in trying to gain control of large segments of public opinion through the formation of more general "front" organizations. In these, distinguished non-Communist progressives lent their names and energies to bodies actually controlled by a Communist minority. Three such "front" organizations were the American League for Peace and Democracy, which claimed an affiliated membership of over 7,000,000, the American Student Union, and the American Youth Congress, which won the sponsorship of Mrs. Eleanor Roosevelt and pretended to speak for nearly 5,000,000 young people.

On the political front Communists pursued a two-pronged campaign from 1935 to 1939: first, to bore into and gain control of independent non-Communist political groups and, second, to build a powerful machine within the federal government to influence federal policies and carry on political espionage. In both its aspects this campaign met with some success. The Communists put a ticket, headed by Browder, into the field during the campaign of 1936; under cover, they worked hard for Roosevelt. Only in New York City, however, did they gain any power in an important political party.[8]

More successful was the Communist effort to establish a conspiratorial underground in Washington. The leader of the principal group was Harold Ware, who had managed a large collective farm in Russia in the early 1920's. Ware organized a Communist cell soon after Roosevelt's inauguration that included a number of party members strategically placed in various departments and agencies. Several of the conspirators and co-operators, notably Alger Hiss, Harry Dexter White, Julian Wadleigh, and Nathan

[8] This was the American Labor party, formed by labor leaders and Socialists to support the Democratic cause in 1936. Communists entered the ALP at the outset but kept well under cover for a number of years. However, Sidney Hillman, the CIO's chief political spokesman, joined forces with the Communists in 1944 to capture the ALP and drive the anti-Communist right wing from control of the party. The right-wing group, headed by George S. Counts and David Dubinsky, thereupon seceded and formed the American Liberal party. The complete measure of Communist control of the American Labor party became evident after Hillman's death in 1946, when the devout admirer of Stalin, Representative Vito Marcantonio, became state chairman of the party.

Witt, rose to positions of high responsibility and carried from their offices thousands of documents to be photographed and passed on to the head of the Soviet underground, Colonel Boris Bykov. Witt and later John Abt became leaders of the cell after Ware's death in an automobile accident in 1935.

The American Communist movement began to lose strength in 1937, suffered mortal blows in 1938 and 1939, and had shrunk to its hard conspiratorial core by 1941. For this swift decline in prestige American comrades could only blame the actions of their Soviet masters and the fundamental democratic convictions of the great body of American intellectuals. Several thousand Americans, many of them non-Communists but imbued with the Popular Front psychology, fought on the Loyalist side in the Spanish Civil War from 1936 to 1939. Many young idealists saw Communists at work, conspiring to control the Loyalist government and betraying and killing comrades-in-arms to achieve this goal. John Dos Passos, one of the most distinguished of the Popular Front novelists, was thus disillusioned by what he saw in Spain.

Also shattering to illusions were the purges, trials, and executions from 1936 to 1938 by which Stalin eliminated his closest friends and rivals and established a ruthless monolithic dictatorship. A commission of anti-Communist intellectuals headed by John Dewey made a thorough investigation of the trials and published their findings in 1938 under the title *Not Guilty*. The crowning disillusionment came when the Soviet government signed a Non-Aggression Pact with Hitlerite Germany in August 1939. Communists changed at once from ardent "anti-fascists" into apologists for Nazism and vehement opponents of any form of support for Britain and France in their war against Germany. Thus events on the international scene ripped off the democratic disguise of American Communism and revealed the true character of the movement for all to see and know the truth.

What shall we say about American Communism's significance in the 1930's—its strength, its hold over American intellectuals, and the danger that it posed to the American democracy? In brief, how red was the so-called Red Decade? It was not as red as the above discussion might indicate. To begin with, few Popular Front Americans actually embraced the Communist ideology, for historical materialism and a philosophy of class warfare were doctrines abhorrent to people imbued with the Christian-democratic tradition. It must be remembered, also, that the Communists succeeded only to the degree that they were able to identify Communism with democracy and resistance to brutal aggression. For example, many Americans joined Writers' Leagues and Leagues Against War in the sincere belief that the Soviet Union was the only power willing to take effective measures to halt aggression and turn back the tide of anti-Semitism.

However, the significant fact was not the momentary alignment of these Americans but the proof, furnished by events of the 1930's, that Communism could not prosper when the channels of exposure and criticism were kept open. Because of free debate and objective reporting of events, practically all Americans affected by the concept of a Popular Front recognized the character of international Communism and then rallied courageously to the defense of the democratic ideal. The American democracy survived in the face of the Communist assault, moreover, because the reforms of the Second New Deal healed the wounds of the body politic and gave proof that democracy could effect fundamental institutional changes without recourse to revolution, purges, and executions.

CHAPTER

21

The United States
and the Collapse of the
International Structure

1931–1938

W E COME NOW to that time of trouble when aggressors in Europe and the Far East made a mockery of the peace structure so hopefully constructed during the Versailles Conference and the 1920's. Depression, fear, mutual suspicion, and a guilt complex arising from the alleged injustices of the Versailles settlement destroyed the democratic coalition, prevented the western democracies from finding a new modus vivendi for collective defense, and so paralyzed the peoples of Britain, France, and the United States that they were impotent in the face of the rising tide of aggression.

It was an ironic circumstance that an overwhelming majority of the people of the world, with unrivaled resources and technology and a great superiority in military and naval power, should have been unable to curb aggression because unwilling to run the risk of war! Why this was so will perhaps become evident as we review events of the 1930's and relate the part that the American people played in the unfolding tragedy.

160. *Stimson, Hoover, and the Manchurian Crisis*

The first important assault upon the post-World War peace structure occurred when Japan occupied Manchuria and made war on China in 1931–2, and the western powers with interests in the Far East failed to co-operate in any effective measures to halt Japanese aggression. The background of the Manchurian episode can be briefly told. The Japanese government enjoyed such large privileges in southern Manchuria after the Russo-Japanese War that the province soon became an economic colony of the island empire, although it remained technically under Chinese political jurisdiction. The Japanese Imperial government by and large attempted to protect its interests in Manchuria by a policy of friendship with China and the great powers. Such a peaceful policy, however, could prevail only so long as China and the western powers acknowledged Japanese supremacy in Manchuria. All Japanese, liberals and militarists alike, regarded the province as the economic lifeline of the Empire and the bulwark against Russian expansion.

Two developments in the 1920's excited Japanese fears for the safety of Manchuria and strengthened the clique who had long been clamoring for a "positive" policy of direct action. One was the resurgence of Soviet Russia as a Far Eastern power after Russian withdrawal from northern Manchuria and the Maritime Province following the Bolshevik revolution. Sun Yat-sen, leader of the Chinese Nationalist party, the Kuomintang, joined forces with the Chinese Communists and the Soviet government in 1924 in a drive to conquer and unite his country. Sun's successor, Chiang Kai-shek, succeeded in this campaign. Then he broke with the Chinese Communists in 1927 and next endeavored to oust the Russians from northern Manchuria. The result was an undeclared war between China and Russia in 1929. Soviet armies invaded northern Manchuria and compelled the Chinese to respect the Sino-Soviet treaty of 1924 providing for joint Chinese and Russian control of the Chinese Eastern Railway that ran from Siberia to Harbin and Vladivostok. At the same time, the Soviet government was busily engaged in constructing huge air and naval bases at Vladivostok that pointed at the heart of Japan.

The return of Russian power to the Far East made the Japanese all the more determined to reinforce southern Manchuria as a barrier against Soviet expansion. But the development that incited Japan to "positive" action was the spread of Chinese nationalism into Manchuria and Chiang Kai-shek's attempt to control that province. A number of minor incidents had increased the tension to the breaking point by 1931. The Japanese Army, taking control of policy out of the hands of the Foreign Minister, attacked and occupied Mukden, Changchun, and other Manchurian cities on September 18–19, 1931.

The blow was well timed, for Britain and the United States were then struggling to stave off international economic collapse. China appealed to the League of Nations for protection on September 21, 1931, and the whole world turned to Britain and the United States. The British were in general opposed to strong measures against Japan and waited to see what policy the Washington government would follow.

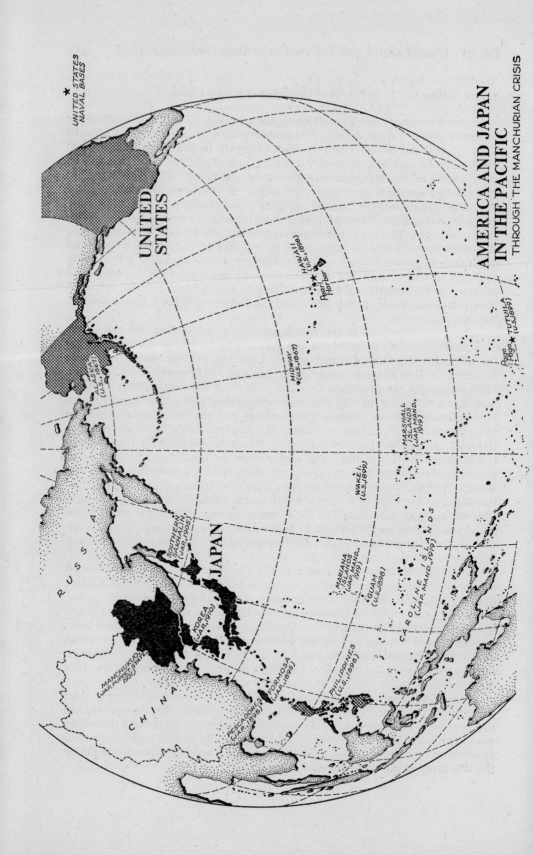

AMERICA AND JAPAN
IN THE PACIFIC
THROUGH THE MANCHURIAN CRISIS

UNITED STATES
NAVAL BASES

UNITED
STATES

RUSSIA

JAPAN

CHINA

ALASKA
(U.S.,1867)

SOUTHERN
SAKHALIN
(JAP.,1905)

KOREA
(JAP.,1910)

MANCHUKUO
(JAP. PUPPET STATE
1931)

FORMOSA
(JAP.,1895)

PESCADORES
(JAP.,1895)

PHILIPPINES
(U.S.,1898)

GUAM
(U.S.,1898)

MARIANA
ISLANDS
(JAP. MAND.,1919)

CAROLINE ISLANDS
(JAP. MAND.,1919)

WAKE I.
(U.S.,1899)

MARSHALL
ISLANDS
(JAP. MAND.,
1919)

MIDWAY
(U.S.,1867)

HAWAII
(U.S.,1898)
Pearl
Harbor

TUTUILA
(U.S.,1899)
Pago
Pago

Secretary of State Henry L. Stimson moved cautiously during the first weeks following the outbreak of the crisis because he assumed that strong American action might embarrass the Japanese Cabinet in bringing the Army under control. Stimson called in the Japanese Ambassador on September 22 and reminded him that the United States had a profound concern for the integrity of China. Yet the Secretary of State opposed appointment of a commission of inquiry by the League Council, refused to agree that Japan had violated the Kellogg-Briand Pact, and warned the League Council that the United States would not co-operate in imposing economic sanctions against Japan.

The Tokyo Foreign Office talked of direct negotiations with China and withdrawal, but the Imperial Army drove steadily forward and consolidated its hold over all southern Manchuria. The moderate Cabinet gave way in December to a Cabinet that supported the Army, and Japanese forces occupied Chinchow, the last Chinese stronghold in Manchuria, on January 2, 1932. Now Stimson had to admit that his policy had failed.

Still it was not easy to know what the United States and the League of Nations should do. Stimson now believed that Japanese militarists and imperialists had ruthlessly violated treaties and destroyed the entire security system erected at the Washington Conference. He was now eager to rally Britain and America in defense of China, even if that meant economic sanctions and possible war. However, no statesman ever faced more discouraging obstacles than Stimson did in late 1931 and early 1932. He had to content himself with expressing his government's abhorrence of Japanese aggression while he knew that he could do nothing to bring the Japanese to book.

The reasons for Stimson's predicament are now well known. To begin with, evidence was overwhelming that the American people strongly condemned Japanese ruthlessness but even more strongly opposed any measures that might conceivably lead to war. The same public spokesmen—like Senator William E. Borah, the *Christian Century*, the *Nation*, and the *New Republic*—who were loudest in condemning Japan advised complete withdrawal of American forces from China. If this overwhelming popular resistance to warlike moves had not been enough, then President Hoover's inflexible determination to avoid the risk of war would have proved an insurmountable barrier to forceful action. Stimson suggested as early as October 1931 that the United States might have to co-operate with the League in imposing sanctions against Japan. Hoover was startled and concluded that his "able Secretary was at times more of a warrior than a diplomat." The President learned through personal inquiry in London that the British government would not support the United States in a strong policy. He was convinced that the American people did not want war, and that the imposition of sanctions would goad Japan into a war which the United States might have to fight alone. He therefore sternly vetoed Stimson's plan for economic measures in early 1932.

There were, the President thought, moral weapons in the arsenal of diplomacy. He suggested that Stimson should revive the doctrine of nonrecognition of territorial and political changes effected by military force, which Secretary Bryan had first enunciated in 1915 at the time of the crisis over Japan's twenty-one demands upon China. (See above, pp. 159–160.)

Stimson, however, first turned to Britain and France for support. When London replied with a pointed rebuff, Stimson issued an identical warning to Japan and China on January 7, 1932: the American government would recognize no changes in the Far East brought about by force which impaired the treaty rights of the United States and the independence and administrative integrity of China.

It was perhaps courageous, but it was not immediately successful. The British Foreign Office refused to concur, while the Japanese Foreign Office replied with "elegant irony" to the State Department on January 16, 1932. Then less than two weeks later, on January 28, the Japanese fleet and marines invaded Shanghai in retaliation against a Chinese boycott, wantonly bombarded the city, and killed thousands of civilians. The Shanghai attack strengthened Stimson's hand but pointed up the fatal weakness of his method. On the one side the British Foreign Secretary now joined Stimson in vigorous diplomatic condemnations of this new Japanese aggression. On the other, when Stimson suggested imposing economic sanctions, Hoover refused even more emphatically than before. Hoover declared that the Chinese could defend themselves, and that it would be folly to fight for Asia. Thus Stimson once again was forced back to use of moral weapons. In a long public letter to Senator Borah on February 23, 1932, he reiterated the American position in order to keep the record clear.

It was a triumph for Stimson when the Assembly of the League of Nations, with the Japanese representative abstaining, unanimously adopted a resolution on March 11, 1932, incorporating almost verbatim the Bryan-Stimson doctrine of nonrecognition. Events in the Far Eastern crisis now moved swiftly to conclusion. A League commission of inquiry presented a report naming Japan as the aggressor, and the League Assembly on February 24, 1933, called upon Japan to observe the Covenant and return Manchuria to China. The Japanese replied by withdrawing from the League.

These are the bare facts of this episode. Their meaning is still not altogether clear. This much, at least, can be said by way of conclusion: The policy of the United States and the League of Nations was far from being realistic, however one views the merits of the case. If the Japanese attack on Manchuria was a gross violation of the Covenant and the Nine-Power Treaty, then only willingness to go to war, not moral exhortation, would have sufficed to bring the Japanese to book. If the Japanese were justified in securing their hold on Manchuria, then wisdom would have demanded a policy of acquiescence. Hoover and Stimson in effect simply perpetuated a policy that had long been irrelevant to the facts of international life in the Far East. More than this, they gave a simple moral gloss to an enormously complicated situation. Without knowing it, they staked out a policy that would eventually culminate in war between their country and Imperial Japan.

161.   The United States and the Collapse of European Stability, 1931–1933

We have seen how President Hoover issued his plan for a one-year moratorium on all intergovernmental debt and reparations payments in the late spring of 1931, and how this move eased the strain on the international economy. (See above, p. 379.) The late summer or autumn of 1931 was clearly the time for the President to urge a mutual cancellation of all intergovernmental debt and reparations obligations. As Stimson argued at the time, such a move would have removed a huge incubus from the international economy, restored European confidence, and won a host of friends for the United States.

Hoover was personally willing to extend the moratorium until the worst of the depression had passed, but he regarded Europe's debts to the United States as sacred obligations and would never consent to cancel them or connect them officially with Germany's reparations obligations. In this matter he, not Stimson, spoke for the vast majority of Americans and Congress. The latter voiced its emphatic opposition to any reduction or cancellation of the war debts by joint resolution on December 23, 1931.

The truth was, however, that Germany could not pay reparations in 1932, and most of the European debtors were thus unable to meet their debt payments to America without running the risk of bankruptcy. Europeans consequently did what they had to do. Representatives of the western and central European powers, meeting in Lausanne, Switzerland, in June 1932, reduced Germany's reparations obligations to $714,000,000 and tacitly agreed that this sum would never have to be paid. However, this final settlement would go into effect only when the nations in debt to the United States and one another had reached a "satisfactory settlement" of the war debts question. Stimson urged a graceful acceptance of the inevitable, but Hoover condemned the Lausanne agreement and continued to apply diplomatic pressure on Europe.

The denouement of this story can be briefly told. Germany ceased reparations payments altogether after the Lausanne Conference. Then when the time for renewal of semiannual payments to the United States came in December 1932, Britain, Czechoslovakia, Italy, Finland, Latvia, and Lithuania met their obligations, while France, Greece, Poland, Belgium, Estonia, and Hungary defaulted. Britain, Italy, Czechoslovakia, Rumania, Lithuania, and Latvia made token payments on the following June 15, 1933, while the remaining debtors, except Finland, again defaulted. Congress replied on April 13, 1934, with the Johnson Act. It forbade any American citizen or corporation to lend money to any nation in default on its debt payments to the United States. When the Attorney General ruled that token payments did not meet the requirements of the Johnson Act, all of America's debtors except Finland defaulted in 1934 and afterward.

However, there seemed to be some hope in the early months of 1933 that American and western European leaders would unite in the forthcoming World Economic Conference to attack two other impediments to international economic recovery—high tariffs and unstable currencies. President Hoover had taken leadership in calling the conference, and the new President, Roosevelt, promised co-operation. Prime Minister Ramsay MacDonald of Great Britain, former Premier Edouard Herriot of France, and other spokesmen from Europe descended upon Washington in late April and early May for preliminary conversations with Roosevelt and his economic advisers. The upshot of these discussions was a firm American refusal to discuss suspension of war debt payments, agreement that the con-

THE INTERGOVERNMENTAL DEBT SITUATION ON THE EVE OF THE LAUSANNE CONFERENCE

TOTAL RECEIPTS AND PAYMENTS STIPULATED IN DEBT ADJUSTMENT AGREEMENTS
IN MILLIONS OF DOLLARS

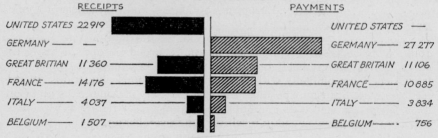

RECEIPTS		PAYMENTS
UNITED STATES 22 919		UNITED STATES —
GERMANY — —		GERMANY — 27 277
GREAT BRITIAN 11 360		GREAT BRITAIN 11 106
FRANCE 14 176		FRANCE 10 885
ITALY 4 037		ITALY 3 834
BELGIUM 1 507		BELGIUM 756

TOTAL DEBTS DUE UNITED STATES
ACCORDING TO FUNDING AGREEMENTS, 1923–1926

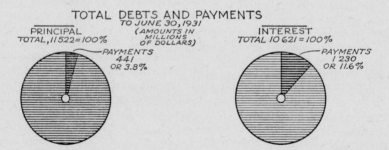

	MILLIONS OF DOLLARS	PRINCIPAL	INTEREST	MILLIONS OF DOLLARS	RATE PER CENT
GREAT BRITAIN	4 600			6 506	3.306
FRANCE	4 025			2 823	1.640
ITALY	2 042			366	0.405
BELGIUM	418			310	1.790
OTHER	438			617	—

TOTAL DEBTS AND PAYMENTS
TO JUNE 30, 1931

PRINCIPAL
TOTAL, 11 522 = 100%

(AMOUNTS IN MILLIONS OF DOLLARS)

INTEREST
TOTAL 10 621 = 100%

PAYMENTS
441
OR 3.8%

PAYMENTS
1 230
OR 11.6%

ference should meet in London in June 1933, and vague assurances by Roosevelt that the United States would co-operate in lowering tariff barriers and stabilizing currencies.

Once again the United States had an opportunity to take bold leadership in formulating a program to repair the ravages of the depression. Once again the American government refused the opportunity, because Roosevelt had no intention of agreeing to the first necessary step, currency stabilization, unless the dollar had fallen sufficiently in value to stimulate a considerable price increase at home and an increase of American exports abroad. A large American delegation, headed by the new Secretary of State, Cordell Hull, sailed for London on May 31, 1933; but they sailed in deepest ignorance of the President's intentions and in confusion among themselves.

Hull believed that his government should agree to lower its tariffs and peg the dollar at its then present value in gold; moreover, he thought that Roosevelt agreed with him. On the other hand, a majority of the delegates opposed tariff reductions and were confused on stabilization.

The conference opened on June 12 and got off to a bad start when Prime Minister MacDonald raised the war debts question. Roosevelt after a week of indecisive debate sent his economic adviser, Raymond Moley, to London with a tentative proposal to stabilize the dollar, then worth $4.00 to the British pound, at between $4.05 and $4.25 to the pound. But while Moley was on the high seas the dollar began to fall rapidly in value, until it reached $4.38 to the British pound on June 28. Roosevelt was delighted by this development. He was convinced that further depreciation of the dollar was essential to recovery at home, and so he decided to end the agonizing debate at London. Therefore, he sent his "Bombshell Message" on July 3 to the conference announcing that the United States could not agree to immediate currency stabilization. Hull kept the conference alive for another three weeks by heroic efforts, but all the delegates knew that further talk was futile.

American unwise economic policy was matched in the political field by Washington's attitude toward the important question of disarmament. Various commissions of the League worked on the problem from 1921 to 1926; and the United States joined the European powers from 1926 to 1931 in a League Preparatory Commission to draft a treaty for land disarmament. The World Disarmament Conference finally met despite French fears and hesitations at Geneva on February 2, 1932, amid alarming developments in Asia and Europe. The Japanese had attacked Shanghai only a few days before, while the Nazi party, frankly committed to rearmament and repudiation of the Versailles Treaty, was growing daily in Germany. Yet the stronger the Nazis grew, the more inflexible the French became in their opposition to disarmament.

The conference from February 2 to June 21, 1932, intermittently discussed a French proposal for an international army and compulsory arbitration, and American proposals for abolition of offensive armaments like tanks and bombing planes. President Hoover tried to end what seemed to be the hopeless deadlock by using the same techniques of shock and surprise that Secretary Hughes had employed successfully at the Washington Naval Conference. The head of the American delegation presented Hoover's startling plan on June 22, 1932. It proposed the immediate abolition of all bombers, tanks, large mobile artillery, and instruments of chemical warfare, and the reduction of all land and naval forces by approximately one third. Hoover's proposal revived the conference; and American, British, and French leaders soon afterward promised revision of the Versailles Treaty and equality in land armaments to Germany. But these concessions came too late to save the future peace of Europe. Hitler became Chancellor of Germany on January 30, 1933. Roosevelt renewed Hoover's plea for action on May 16 and promised American participation in a new collective security system on May 24, but Hitler withdrew his delegations from the World Disarmament Conference and the League of Nations on October 14, 1933.

One development in 1933—American recognition of the Soviet Union

—at first seemed a positive step in the direction of common action to prevent aggression. The Washington government since 1917 had consistently
withheld diplomatic recognition from the Moscow regime, chiefly because
it refused to honor the debt of the tsarist government to the United States,
confiscated American-owned property, denied religious freedom to Americans in the USSR, and waged covert warfare against American institutions
through the Comintern and its branch in the United States. However, international circumstances made an abrupt change in Russian policy imperative by 1933. In that year Russia feared a Japanese attack against the Maritime Province, and Soviet authorities now wanted American friendship
and the right to purchase supplies on credit in the United States in the event
of war with Japan.

The President informed the Soviet government on October 10, 1933,
that he would receive a commissioner to explore "all questions outstanding
between our countries." The Russian Foreign Minister, Maxim Litvinov,
arrived in Washington on November 7 to open negotiations. The upshot was
an agreement embodied in a formal exchange of notes on November 16,
1933. In return for American recognition the Soviet government promised
to abstain from propaganda activity in the United States, guarantee religious freedom and fair trials to Americans in the Soviet Union, and
negotiate a settlement of the tsarist debt to the United States.

The Washington administration, eager to promote full economic intercourse with the Soviet Union, established an Export-Import Bank on February 12, 1934, to facilitate exchange. Secretary Hull's bright hopes of friendship and mutual accommodation were soon blasted, however, by Russian
failure to honor pledges given on November 16, 1933. Negotiations over a
debt settlement failed because the Russians refused to acknowledge the
interest on the debt; consequently the State Department blocked the extension of any credits to the Soviet Union. More damaging to Russian-American relations was the Kremlin's refusal to call off the dogs operating in the
guise of the American Communist party. Relations between the two governments were formally correct but hardly cordial before 1941.

162.   *The Good Neighbor Policy, 1933–1936*

Franklin D. Roosevelt and Cordell Hull came into control of American
foreign policy at a time when the forces of international anarchy seemed
about to engulf the New World as much as the Old. With courage and unflagging consistency they repudiated Wilsonian missionary interventionism, completed the Hoover-Stimson reversal of the Roosevelt Corollary
(see above, pp. 357–359), and then went on to construct an edifice of inter-
American friendship and peace. Let us see how this so-called Good Neighbor policy [1] developed and what its larger consequences were.

wwwwwwwwwwwww

[1] Roosevelt in his first inaugural dedicated the United States to the policy of the
good neighbor in foreign affairs generally. He reiterated the phrase a few weeks later,
in an address on Pan-American Day, and applied it specifically to the Latin American
policy of the United States. The slogan at once caught the popular fancy and was thereafter associated only with the administration's Latin American policy.

Hughes, Stimson, and Hoover had taken the first steps, but much remained to be done in 1933 to put the relations of the United States with its Latin American neighbors on a really cordial footing. For one thing, although the Hoover administration had tacitly repudiated the Roosevelt Corollary, it had steadfastly refused to surrender the alleged right to intervene in the internal affairs of the Caribbean republics. No Latin American could take seriously its professions of friendship so long as the United States maintained this position.

Moreover, tragic circumstances were conspiring in Latin America in 1932 and early 1933 to present the new administration with perplexing difficulties in its search for unity and peace in the Western Hemisphere. In the first place, American trade with Latin America had declined from $2,079,817,000 in 1929 to $573,814,000 in 1932. The effect was to blast the foundations of Latin American prosperity and cause wholesale economic disorganization, bankruptcy, and repudiation. Secondly, the peace of the New World was threatened by dissension from within as Roosevelt came into office. The so-called Chaco War between Paraguay and Bolivia was raging intermittently in the jungles, a border conflict between Colombia and Peru threatened to explode into full-scale war, and unrest was rising in Cuba against the brutal dictatorship of Gerardo Machado.

Roosevelt's and Hull's determination to establish a genuine Pan-American accord was put immediately to test as a result of these and other developments. When the League of Nations offered to mediate the Peruvian-Colombian border dispute, for example, the State Department approved and, in May 1933, appointed a member of the commission that settled the controversy a year later. Soon afterward, on August 7, 1933, the State Department concluded an agreement with Haiti for withdrawal of American marines from the Negro republic by October 1, 1934. The real test of the new administration's sincerity came when a revolution against the Machado government broke out in Cuba in the spring of 1933. There were numerous demands for American intervention, but Roosevelt and Hull stubbornly resisted them. The State Department stood by patiently without taking sides, until a second army coup, led by Fulgencio Batista, established a new government in late 1933 and early 1934.

These developments were a prelude to the Seventh Inter-American Conference that met in Montevideo, Uruguay, in December 1933. Hull was not sanguine over the prospect of establishing hemispheric solidarity at Montevideo, for anti-American feeling was still rife throughout Latin America, and the Argentine Foreign Minister, Doctor Saavedra Lamas, seemed determined to turn the conference into an anti-American rally. He tried to embarrass the United States just a short time before the Montevideo Conference was to open by inviting all nations to join Argentina in signing an anti-war and nonaggression pact. One of its provisions bound the signatories to refrain from any kind of intervention in the affairs of other states.

Hull arrived in Montevideo early in December 1933 to be greeted by an angry reception from the local press and deep hostility among many of the Latin American delegates. First he called upon all the Foreign Ministers in their hotel suites. Next he told the Argentinian Foreign Minister that the United States stood ready to renounce any right it once claimed to intervene in the affairs of sister states and would be happy to approve the Argentine nonaggression pact. Within a short time Saavedra Lamas gave his reply: Argentina would co-operate with the United States in working for peace and economic unity in the Western Hemisphere.

Hull's actions assured the entire success of the Montevideo Conference, and the result of the newly found spirit of friendship was the signing of a number of important inter-American treaties. The most important was the Convention on Rights and Duties of States. It represented a sweeping triumph for Latin American jurisprudence on such important issues as recognition of *de facto* governments, equality of states, nonintervention, the sovereignty of states in dealing with foreign nationals, inviolability of territory, and territorial changes effected by forceful means.

The months following the Montevideo Conference were a critical period. Any refusal by the United States to observe the letter and spirit of the Convention on Rights and Duties of States would have destroyed all the progress thus far made. For the second time Cuba became the testing ground of the Good Neighbor's sincerity, for the Cubans demanded abrogation of the Cuban-American Treaty of 1903 that embodied the Platt Amendment and gave the United States a legal right to intervene in the internal and external affairs of the republic. Hull hastened to honor his promises after recognizing the government of Carlos Mendieta, who came to power with Batista's support on January 18, 1934. He signed a treaty on May 29, 1934, formally abrogating the Platt Amendment and ending all special American rights in Cuba, except the right to maintain a naval base at Guantánamo.[2] In addition, Hull moved soon afterward to restore the basis of Cuban prosperity, the sugar trade, which had been hard hit by the Hawley-Smoot Tariff[3] and the depression. The tariff on Cuban sugar was reduced by 25 per cent in May and by an additional 40 per cent in August. As a result, American trade with Cuba increased nearly 100 per cent during the next year.

There still remained three Caribbean countries—Haiti, the Dominican Republic, and Panama—in which the United States might intervene by treaty right to protect property and maintain order. By special agreement with the Haitian government, American marines were withdrawn from Port-au-Prince on August 15, 1934, instead of on October 1, 1934, as the treaty of 1933 had stipulated. Moreover, the Washington government allowed the Haitian-American Treaty of 1916, which had made Haiti a semiprotectorate of the United States, to expire in 1936 and relinquished its control over Haiti's financial affairs. Panama and the United States concluded a treaty in 1936 that ended the American right to intervene in Panamanian affairs granted in the Panamanian-American Treaty of 1903.[4] The Dominican-American Treaty of 1924, which had continued the Ameri-

[2] Ratifications were exchanged on June 9, 1934, and the Cubans held a three-day festival to celebrate.

[3] American imports from Cuba declined in value from $207,421,000 in 1929 to $90,059,000 in 1931.

[4] A special article provided, however, that the two nations would consult with each other and take action to protect the Canal should war or aggression endanger its security. The United States Senate approved the treaty in 1939, but only after the Panamanian government had agreed that in emergencies the United States might act first and consult afterward.

can receivership of the Dominican customs after the withdrawal of American troops and which did not expire until 1945, was abrogated by a new treaty between the two countries in 1940, and the receivership was ended in 1941.

Thus did the United States gracefully surrender rights and privileges that few nations in the history of the world have voluntarily given up once they obtained them. No act of the Roosevelt administration better illustrated its good faith than the execution of this retreat from empire in the Caribbean region, for more was involved in this withdrawal than sheerly strategical considerations. By 1930 Americans had invested over $1,000,-000,000 in Cuba, $87,000,000 in the Dominican Republic, $29,000,000 in Haiti, $47,000,000 in Panama, and $13,000,000 in Nicaragua. None of these countries was noted for political stability. Even so, the United States gave up a treaty right to intervene for the protection of property interests because such a surrender had to be made in order to convince Latin America that the Good Neighbor meant what he had said at Montevideo.

It is only fair to add that the Roosevelt administration was not motivated by sentimental altruism but rather by a desire to protect the security of the people of the United States. Roosevelt and Hull believed that only a policy of nonintervention would win the friendship of Latin America. They further believed that Latin American friendship was essential to the security of the United States. Hence they adhered firmly to nonintervention, even when that policy involved possible capital losses by American citizens. Their action came none too soon, for events in Europe and Asia demanded concerted co-operation for peace by the American republics.

The Eighth Inter-American Conference was scheduled to meet in Lima, Peru, in 1938, but the international situation was so foreboding by 1936 that the State Department did not dare to wait to sound a warning against potential Nazi aggression in the New World. At Roosevelt's suggestion, therefore, a special inter-American conference assembled at Buenos Aires in December 1936. The President went in person to Buenos Aires and opened the conference on December 1 to emphasize the seriousness of the international crisis heightened by the recent outbreak of civil war in Spain.

The delegates made easy progress on matters about which there was no disagreement. A new treaty—an Additional Protocol Relative to Non-Intervention—pledging the American republics not to intervene "directly or indirectly" in the affairs of neighboring states, for example, was signed by representatives of all twenty-one republics. On the overshadowing issue of mutual defense against aggression, however, Hull and the American delegation ran head on into the opposition of the Argentine Foreign Minister, Saavedra Lamas. Hull presented the American plan on December 7. It envisaged establishment of a permanent Inter-American Consultative Committee to determine whether a state of war existed among two or more American republics; imposition of a Pan-American embargo on credit and war materials in the event such a war did occur in the hemisphere; and consultation among the American republics in the event of any outside threat to hemispheric security. Saavedra Lamas bitterly opposed the American plan and offered an alternative that envisaged close Pan-American co-operation with the League of Nations.

Rather than disrupt the conference, the American and Argentine delegations accepted a compromise offered by the Brazilians. It was embodied in a Convention for Collective Security and a Convention to Co-ordinate, Extend and Assure the Fulfillment of Existing Treaties. These treaties omitted Hull's suggestion for a permanent consultative committee, but they pledged the signatories to consult with one another in the event that war threatened the peace of the hemisphere; to refrain from hostile action against one another for six months while consultation was in progress; and to adopt a common neutrality in the event that war should break out. The Convention for Collective Security was weakened by the inclusion, at Argentina's insistence, of a reservation giving each signatory freedom to refuse to join in mutual consultation in the event that war outside the hemisphere threatened the peace of the Americas. Hull, nonetheless, was convinced that a beginning toward mutualization of the Monroe Doctrine had been made. Finally, the delegates at Buenos Aires proclaimed their unity and peaceful purposes in a Declaration of Principles of Inter-American Solidarity and Co-operation. It pledged the American republics to peaceful settlement of all disputes and outlawed territorial conquest, collection of debts by force, and intervention by one state in the affairs of another.

Thus the Roosevelt administration had laid the groundwork for friendship and mutual defense in the Western Hemisphere by the time that Hitler's threats had imperiled hopes for peace in Europe. We shall see in the following section, moreover, how the Washington administration reinforced political unity with measures of economic support and refused to use even the threat of force to protect American property interests in Latin America. Let us now examine another phase of the American retreat from empire during the 1930's—the ironic way in which domestic self-interest combined with old anti-imperialistic impulses to impose independence upon the Filipinos.

Following the award of near-autonomy to the Philippines by the Jones Act of 1916, President Wilson recommended full independence in 1920. President Harding, committed to a more cautious policy, sent a commission in 1921 headed by General Leonard Wood and former Governor General W. Cameron Forbes to Manila to investigate. The commission advised that American withdrawal would constitute a "betrayal of the Philippine people . . . and a discreditable neglect of our national duty." Wood stayed on as Governor General and thoroughly antagonized local leaders by his insistence upon prerogative. The new Governor General after Wood's death in 1927, Henry L. Stimson, quickly won the confidence of Filipino politicians.

All Filipino leaders continued in the 1920's publicly to demand immediate independence and privately to wonder whether independence was worth losing the free American market for Philippine sugar and other agricultural products. The Philippine-American trade had reached $183,000,000 in value by 1930, and almost two thirds of the people of the islands were dependent upon it for the highest standard of living in the Orient. Moreover, fear of an expansive Japan after 1931 caused Filipino leaders to count the blessings of American protection and conclude that dominion status in an American Commonwealth was safer than a perilous independence.

Ironically, it was the depression that gave the greatest impetus to the movement for the independence that most Filipino leaders privately opposed by 1932. Western beet sugar growers, American investors in the Cuban sugar industry, southern cotton growers, and dairymen throughout the country were determined to end the competition from Philippine sugar and cocoanut oil. Their spokesmen in Congress on January 17, 1933, adopted over Hoover's veto an act for Philippine independence after a ten-year transition period, provided that the Filipinos established a republican form of government. The Philippine legislature rejected the Act and sought dominion status instead. But Congress was adamant, and the Filipino leaders had to accept the Tydings-McDuffie Act of March 24, 1934. It was almost an exact replica of the Independence Act of 1933. Filipino voters and President Roosevelt subsequently approved a Philippine Constitution drafted by a constitutional convention in 1934 and 1935; Manuel Quezon became first President of the Commonwealth of the Philippines in 1935; and July 4, 1946, was set as the date for launching the Philippine Republic.

163. *The Good Neighbor in Foreign Economic Policy*

Roosevelt tried to ride two horses at the same time during the first year of his presidency. On the one hand, he pursued a thoroughly enlightened policy of co-operation and friendship with foreign countries on the political level. On the other hand, he experimented with nationalistic economic measures. The President would obviously have to make up his mind and co-ordinate his political and economic foreign policies. He would either have to pursue a course of political and economic autarky, such as Germany embarked upon in 1933, or else he would have to stabilize the dollar, lower tariffs, and make serious efforts to reopen the channels of international trade.

From the beginning, Roosevelt's Secretary of State, Cordell Hull, was obsessed with the conviction that the United States could never find prosperity and friendship abroad unless it was willing to act like a good neighbor in foreign economic affairs. He saw his suggestions for currency stabilization and a reciprocal trade program go unheeded for almost a year while proponents of economic nationalism had the President's ear. But he waited patiently, and Roosevelt was ready to stabilize the dollar and conclude his little experiment in autarky by the end of 1933.[5] With the White House's blessing, therefore, Hull and his assistants set to work on a reciprocal trade bill in January 1934. It empowered the President to negotiate trade agreements, which would go into effect without congressional approval, and to raise or lower existing Hawley-Smoot rates by as much as 50 per cent in order to obtain concessions from other countries. All tariff reduc-

〰〰〰〰〰〰〰〰〰〰〰

[5] As we have seen, he stabilized the price of the dollar on January 31, 1934. Moreover, in October 1936 the American, British, and French governments agreed to stabilize their currencies, use large stabilization funds to maintain the value of these currencies in the international exchanges, and adopt a common gold standard for purposes of international trade.

tions made by the United States would apply to all nations that accorded the benefits of their lowest tariff rates to the United States. The Trade Agreements bill passed Congress easily, and the President signed the measure on June 12, 1934. "Each stroke of the pen," Hull afterward recalled, "seemed to write a message of gladness on my heart."

The State Department concluded its first trade agreement with Cuba on August 24, 1934, and began negotiations with other nations soon afterward. It had concluded trade agreements by the end of 1936 with Belgium, Sweden, Holland, Canada, France, Switzerland, Finland, and six Latin American nations as well. American exports to these countries increased 14 per cent during 1936, as compared with an increase in exports to other nations of only 4 per cent.

Congress renewed the Trade Agreements Act for a second three-year period in 1937, and Hull's chief objective now became a trade agreement with Great Britain and a breakdown of the imperial preference barriers that Britain and the Dominions had erected in 1932. He achieved some success in the British-American and Canadian-American trade agreements signed at the White House on November 17, 1938. The Trade Agreements Act was renewed again in the spring of 1940. By this time Hull had negotiated agreements with twenty-one nations, including all the leaders of the democratic bloc. They covered nearly two thirds of the total foreign commerce of the United States.

Hand in hand with the reciprocal trade program went policies to reconcile the broad political objectives of the Good Neighbor policy with the protection of American investments in Latin America. To begin with, the Roosevelt administration merely continued Hoover's policy of refusing to use force or the threat of force to protect American investments in Latin America. Actually, outright confiscations of American property in the 1930's were rare and were largely confined to Bolivia and Ecuador, both of which had irresponsible dictators during the period. Next, the Washington government established a second Export-Import Bank in March 1934 to stimulate foreign trade with Latin America and other countries. The bank lent some $66,000,000 from 1934 through 1938, most of which went to help stabilize Latin American currencies and exchange rates. Because of Hull's fierce opposition to barter deals, however, the bank never became an important direct factor in expanding the commerce of the Western Hemisphere.

This, in brief, was the Good Neighbor policy at work in the economic field; it was usually unspectacular and generally ignored by the public. However, one case, the Mexican expropriations of American-owned land and oil properties, exploded rather violently in the 1930's, involved the fate of property worth many millions of dollars, and put the principles of the Good Neighbor to severe test.

Beginning in 1934 the Mexican government of Lázaro Cárdenas began to expropriate land holdings of American citizens in Mexico. Secretary Hull followed the advice of the extraordinarily popular Ambassador in Mexico City, Josephus Daniels, in refusing to deny Mexico's right to expropriate. But through Daniels the Secretary of State did apply pressure on Mexico City to obtain fair compensation to former owners. The controversy over land expropriations, heated though it threatened to become, was of minor importance as compared to the storm set off when the Mexicans moved against the British and American oil companies within their territory.

As we have seen, the attempt of the Mexican government to claim ownership of foreign-held oil properties had provoked a near rupture in Mexican-American relations in the 1920's, a rupture healed only when the Mexicans agreed in 1928 that foreign oil companies might retain possession of properties acquired before 1917. (See above, pp. 357–358.) Cárdenas did not openly repudiate this agreement but rather began a flanking movement against the British and American companies soon after his accession in 1934. This campaign culminated in demands by the government-sponsored union of oil workers in 1936 that would have crippled, if not bankrupted, the companies. They refused to surrender, and the Mexican government thereupon declared that an "economic conflict" existed and ordered them to comply. The Mexican Supreme Court upheld the government's decree, and the companies made a counterproposal that won Cárdenas's approval. Then the companies made the fatal mistake of demanding that Cárdenas put his approval in writing. Outraged by what he considered to be a slur on the national honor, the Mexican President told his people on March 15, 1938, that the government had decided to nationalize the oil industry and expropriate the property of the large foreign companies.

Loud was the protest in the United States and Great Britain from the oil companies. Their spokesmen claimed that the expropriated properties had a potential value of $450,000,000. The British Foreign Office protested in such a way as to cause the Mexican government to hand the British Minister his passports. Reaction in Washington was only slightly less violent, and for a time it seemed that Secretary Hull might hurl his own stern demands. But under pressure from Daniels—and perhaps because of President Roosevelt's direct intervention—the Secretary of State began negotiations that culminated on November 19, 1941, in a general settlement of the land and oil claims,[6] conclusion of a Mexican-American trade agreement, and a promise by the United States to help stabilize the peso and obtain loans for Mexico through the Export-Import Bank.

Thus Roosevelt and Hull, with Daniels's vital help, turned the expropriation affair to the advantage of the people of the United States. By refusing to interfere in a controversy that was essentially Mexican in character, they won the lasting friendship of the Mexican people and a valuable ally during the Second World War. More important, they convinced most Latin Americans that there were no strings attached to the Good Neighbor policy.

[6] The Mexican government promised to pay a total of $40,000,000 during the next fourteen years to satisfy all American general and agrarian claims. By the agreement on the oil issue, the United States and Mexico appointed a joint commission of experts to determine the value of the expropriated American oil properties. Both governments agreed, however, that oil in the ground was the property of the Mexican people. The joint commission reported on April 17, 1942, that the value of the expropriated American property was $23,995,991, plus interest of some $5,000,000. The American companies grudgingly accepted the award, which, incidentally, was apparently a fair one, after the State Department told them they must accept it or receive no compensation at all.

164. American Disillusionment and the Triumph of Isolationism

Roosevelt understood well enough the consequences to the United States of the breakdown of the international system in Europe and Asia. But he was so acutely sensitive to political and popular pressures from 1932 to 1938 that he was more often a captive of public opinion than an audacious leader. There were signs during these years that the administration might have pursued a different course had the public been willing to approve collective action for peace. The important facts, however, were the determination of the American people to avoid international commitments and participation in all future wars, and the administration's refusal to run perhaps fatal risks by flouting the popular will.

As we have earlier observed, isolationism—the feeling of apartness coupled with a belief in the degeneracy of Europe and the unique virtue of American institutions and motives—had been one of the oldest traditions and perhaps the dominant ideological force in American history. The American people caught the internationalist vision for a brief moment during the First World War. But events at Versailles and afterward turned American idealism into disgust and confirmed traditional beliefs about Europe's congenital perversity.

Moreover, intellectuals in the 1920's nursed a nagging guilt feeling about American participation in the war and peace conference. American historians set to work as European archives were opened to discover the causes of the war; many concluded that Germany had been among the powers least responsible for the tragedy. This "new" history soon mushroomed into the cult of so-called revisionism. If Germany had not been primarily responsible for the war, the revisionists argued, then the Versailles Treaty was a monstrous fraud and injustice, and the American people had been tricked into fighting for an unworthy cause.

This belief, popular among American intellectuals during the late 1920's, was fired by sensational exposures after 1932 and spread rapidly among the masses of people. The House foreign affairs committee conducted an investigation of the arms traffic and its allegedly sinister influence in world politics in 1933. In April 1934 the Senate approved a resolution for a special investigation of the munitions industry offered by Senator Gerald P. Nye, an extreme isolationist Republican from North Dakota. Nye himself was appointed chairman of the investigating committee.

What ensued was not a restrained inquiry but rather a ruthless investigation to prove the old progressive thesis that wars are always primarily economic in origin. The committee's report grossly exaggerated the influence of bankers and businessmen and distorted the causes for America's entry into the First World War. Its charges were soon echoed by a number of so-called revisionist historians, among them being Charles A. Beard, Walter Millis, and Charles C. Tansill. Their writings along with the Nye committee's report set off a virtual wave of hysteria among thousands of thoughtful Americans. They resolved that such tragic mistakes should not happen again.

Thus the dominant temper of the American people in the mid-1930's was even more doggedly isolationist than before. A whole raft of books by scholars, journalists, and professional pacifists played upon the antiwar theme and reiterated the assertion that Americans could make their best contribution by staying out of Europe's troubles and strengthening democracy at home. High school and college students organized Veterans of Future Wars, joined pacifist movements like the Fellowship of Reconciliation, and vowed that they would not fight if the nation went to war again. A wave of pacifism swept over the clergy. It was little wonder that nearly two thirds of the people questioned in a Gallup poll in April 1937 said that American participation in the First World War had been a mistake.

So strong was the popular feeling by 1935 that neutrality legislation of some kind was inevitable; the only question was whether Congress would take control of foreign policy out of the President's hands. Senator Key Pittman of Nevada, chairman of the foreign relations committee, introduced a resolution on August 20, 1935, prohibiting, "upon the outbreak or during the progress of war between, or among, two or more foreign States," the export of arms and munitions from the United States. It also made it unlawful for American ships to carry arms for or to any belligerent and empowered the President to warn American citizens against traveling on belligerent ships. The President had no discretion and no authority under this resolution to discriminate in favor of the victims of aggression. The Senate approved the bill on August 21. The best that Hull could do was to persuade the House to amend the measure by limiting the life of the mandatory arms embargo provision to six months. Thus amended, the Pittman Resolution was quickly adopted by Congress and approved by the President with some misgiving on August 31, 1935.

165. *The United States and the Ethiopian Crisis, 1935–1936*

While Congress sought to outlaw American participation in future wars, events in Europe and Asia began to spell the end of international stability and make a hollow mockery of American hopes. The year 1935 opened on an international situation dangerous for the peace of the world. In the Far East the Japanese were pushing forward in northern China. In Europe Hitler was feverishly rearming Germany in defiance of the Versailles Treaty, while Benito Mussolini, Italian dictator, was laying plans to conquer Ethiopia.

Hitler made the opening move on March 16, 1935, by denouncing all provisions of the Versailles Treaty for German disarmament and inaugurating conscription. The British, French, and Italian governments had the power to compel German compliance with the Treaty, but they contented themselves with verbal protests. All hope for decisive Allied action faded when the British government concluded a treaty with the Nazis on June 18, 1935, conceding to Germany equality in submarines and the right to build a surface fleet 35 per cent the size of the Royal Navy.

Meanwhile, a skirmish between Italian and Ethiopian troops on December 5, 1934, had given Mussolini the pretext for picking a quarrel with Haile Selassie, Ethiopian "Lion of Judah." Mussolini rejected mediation by the League and launched an invasion from Eritrea and Italian Somaliland on October 3, 1935. President Roosevelt applied an arms embargo two days later, and the State Department waited to see what the League would do. The League Council under strong British pressure condemned Italy as the aggressor on October 7; the League Assembly voted four days later to impose economic sanctions. Then the British moved their main fleet to the Mediterranean, and it seemed that the stage was at last set for a real test of the collective security system.

Britain and France, however, preferred compromise rather than showdown. The League's sanctions against Italy went into effect on November 18; but the embargo did not include oil and coal, without which the Italian fleet and war machine could not function. Actually, the President and Secretary of State would have been prepared to co-operate in stern measures of economic coercion had the League given the lead.[7] But Pierre Laval, French Foreign Minister, feared that such action would drive Italy into the arms of Germany. He therefore blocked all suggestions for an oil embargo. And while the League debated, Mussolini completed his conquest of Ethiopia on May 9, 1936.

Meanwhile, consultation with Democratic leaders had convinced Hull that Congress was determined to enact permanent neutrality legislation to supplant the Pittman Resolution, which would expire on February 29, 1936. They also led the Secretary to believe that the Senate would not give the President discretionary authority to apply the embargo only against aggressors. Hull tried to persuade Senator Pittman and Representative Sam D. McReynolds, chairman of the House foreign affairs committee, to introduce a bill extending the nondiscretionary arms embargo but adding provisions for a virtual embargo on the export of essential raw materials and extension of credits to belligerents. Isolationists led by Senators Hiram Johnson, William E. Borah, and Gerald P. Nye counterattacked furiously, charging that Hull's measure was aimed at Italy and designed to strengthen the League system of sanctions. The attack was so effective that the Senate foreign relations committee refused even to report Hull's measure. Instead, Congress extended the provisions of the Pittman Resolution to May 1, 1937, and added amendments that gave the President discretionary power in finding that a state of war existed, prohibited extension of war loans and credits to belligerents, required the President to apply the neutrality legislation in the event other nations went to war after hostilities had begun, and exempted any American republic at war with a power outside the Western Hemisphere.

166. *The United States and New Aggressions in Europe and Asia, 1936–1937*

Mussolini's successful defiance of the League revealed England's and France's fatal timidity and indecision—caused in large part by the conviction that they would get no help from America in the event of war—and

---

[7] On November 15, 1935, for example, Hull announced the institution of a "moral," or voluntary, embargo against the shipment to Italy of coal, oil, cotton, and other raw materials in excess of normal Italian purchases in the United States.

cleared the road for new assaults on the peace structure by Germany, Italy, and Japan. Indeed, Hitler denounced the Locarno treaties and sent his troops into the demilitarized Rhineland on March 7, 1936, at the height of the Ethiopian crisis. Hitler and Mussolini joined hands eight months later, on October 25, in the so-called Rome-Berlin Axis, which afterward metamorphosed into a political and military alliance between the two dictators. Then the Germans and Japanese joined forces in an Anti-Comintern Pact on November 16, 1936, and the stage was at last set for a new alliance of the militaristic-imperialistic nations to destroy the old balance of power.

The leaders of the Soviet Union recognized the new coalition as a dire threat to the security of their own regime and appealed to the western democracies for stern collective action to contain fascism. The British and French, however, feared the Communist threat from within as much as the fascist danger from without; were obsessed by fear of a general war, which they would have to fight without even a modicum of support from the United States; and hopefully assumed that satisfaction of legitimate German and Italian complaints would preserve the peace of Europe. Had the American government been able to provide the necessary leadership and rally the Atlantic powers in this time of crisis, the world might have been spared the worst tragedy in the history of mankind. Lacking American support, the dominant western powers stood by helplessly from 1936 to 1939 while Germany and Japan marched from one triumphant conquest to another.

No sooner had the Ethiopian crisis ended than Europe's peace was again threatened by the outbreak of civil war in Spain on July 18, 1936. The conflict was in the beginning simply a Spanish affair—a revolt of the army under General Francisco Franco, supported by great landowners, the Roman Catholic Church, and the business classes, against a Popular Front government. However, Spain soon became an arena in which Spanish, Italian, and German fascists joined battle against an incompatible coalition of democrats and Communists.

Before the civil war developed into this international contest, the British, French, German, Italian, Russian, and other European governments applied a policy of seemingly strict nonintervention to prevent the Spanish cauldron from boiling into a general war. Representatives of twenty-seven European powers on September 9, 1936, established a Non-Intervention Committee in London to prevent men and supplies from going to either side; and the Committee established a naval blockade of Spain in March 1937. But the Committee's efforts were totally futile, as the Italians, Germans, and Russians made a laughingstock of the blockade, and the Italian government openly boasted of its aid to Franco.

The American government in the meantime had joined the British and French in applying a policy of nonintervention. The Neutrality Act of 1936 did not apply to civil wars, but the State Department imposed a "moral" embargo against the export of arms and war materials as a means of strengthening the Non-Intervention Committee. Then, when a dealer in second-hand airplanes sought to export some 400 airplane engines to the Loyalist government in December 1936, the administration hastily requested Congress to apply the arms embargo to Spain. A joint resolution granting the President's request passed with only one dissenting vote in both houses on

January 6, 1937. It became law two days later with the President's approval. Even after the true character of the civil war became evident and a large body of opinion favorable to the Loyalists, or the forces of the legitimate government, developed in the United States, the administration, fearful of alienating Catholic opinion, blocked all efforts at repeal of the joint resolution. Thus Franco destroyed the Spanish democracy with the open support of Germany and Italy and secured his dictatorship in 1939 while the western democracies stood by.

Moralists debated, and critics of the administration afterward denounced American policy toward the Spanish civil war as a betrayal of the democratic cause. Perhaps it was, but it would have been extremely difficult if not impossible for the Roosevelt administration to have pursued a different course. The nonintervention policy was made in London and in Paris, not in Washington. It is doubtful that the American people at the outset would have countenanced aggressive support of the Loyalists and defiance of the international blockade. It was probably too late for American assistance to have done much good by the time that American opinion had veered sharply in favor of the Loyalist cause. There seems to be little reason to challenge Hull's assertion that the Washington government had no alternative but to follow Britain and France in what was obviously a mistaken policy.

The overriding American determination to avoid entanglement in European troubles was again demonstrated in the late winter and spring of 1937, when Congress adopted a new and permanent neutrality law to supplant the temporary measure of 1936. Hull knew that he could not prevent legislation, and so he worked quietly and to a degree successfully to win larger discretion for the Executive in the enforcement of the new statute. Approved by Congress on April 29 and signed by Roosevelt on May 1, 1937, it authorized the President to determine when a state of war existed or a civil war threatened the peace of the world. If the President should find that such international or civil wars existed, an embargo against the export of arms, ammunition, and credits would go immediately into effect. In addition, a "cash and carry" provision, to run for two years, empowered the President to require belligerents who purchased nonmilitary commodities in the United States to pay cash for such goods and to transport them in their own vessels.

It was a fateful time for a great nation thus to bind its hands. The Japanese were completing plans for a war against China, and Hitler was contemplating the seizure of Austria and Czechoslovakia at the very time that Congress approved the "permanent" Neutrality Act. Let us look briefly at these events.

The Japanese Army, after absorbing Manchuria and Outer Mongolia in 1932 and 1933, began a campaign to wrench the five northern provinces of China from the control of the Nationalist government at Nanking. At the same time, the Nationalist leader, Chiang Kai-shek, consolidated his administrative power and strengthened his armed forces in preparation for the inevitable showdown. A minor clash between Chinese and Japanese troops at the Marco Polo Bridge near Peking on July 7, 1937, gave the Japanese Army an excuse for launching full-scale war. Instead of submitting, however, the Chinese fought back; thus what the Japanese military leaders thought would be a mere "incident" quickly settled into a long and bloody war.

The Washington government was not surprised by this renewal of Japanese aggression, but it was in no position in the summer of 1937 to do anything to thwart it. Hull circulated a note on July 16 in which he implicitly condemned the Japanese and called upon the powers to reaffirm allegiance to the principles of international morality. Next the President dispatched 1,200 marines to Shanghai on August 17 to reinforce the 2,200 American soldiers already stationed in China.

In order to stir public support for a stronger policy, Hull persuaded the President to include a plea for international co-operation in an address he had agreed to deliver in Chicago on October 5. But Roosevelt, going far beyond the draft prepared by the State Department, appealed to the American people to see the facts of international life and implied that peace-loving nations might have to quarantine aggressors to prevent the spread of international anarchy. Roosevelt hoped that the slogan, "Quarantine the Aggressors," would catch the public fancy, as the phrases "New Deal" and "Good Neighbor Policy" had done. Instead, the quarantine speech stirred such violent reactions that it probably injured the movement for a larger degree of collective action.

On the day following the President's address the League Assembly adopted reports condemning Japanese aggression and suggesting that a conference of the signatories of the Nine Power Treaty meet to consider proper measures of redress. The British strongly endorsed the suggestion as they feared a Japanese threat to their far-flung interests in the Orient. Secretary Hull also approved and recommended Brussels as the meeting place. What might have become the first great experiment in forceful co-operation against aggression, however, was wrecked before it could be launched—by the overwhelming American determination to avoid the risk of war, and by the President's refusal to defy this popular will. Press polls revealed a two-to-one congressional majority against co-operation with the League in applying sanctions against Japan. Roosevelt beat a quick retreat from the advanced position of his quarantine address. For example, he assured the country in a "fireside chat" on October 12 that the purpose of the Brussels Conference was settlement of the Sino-Japanese war by agreement and co-operation, obviously not to propose use of strong measures of economic warfare.

The British and French leaders probably had no more heart for risky policies than Roosevelt and Hull. To Anthony Eden, British Foreign Secretary, it was obvious that the Brussels Conference would take no effective action, anyway. Hence he maneuvered to throw the onus for its failure on the United States. Eden had a long talk at Brussels with the American delegate at the conference on November 2, 1937. His Majesty's Government, Eden declared, was prepared to stand shoulder to shoulder with the United States and would co-operate in any measures against Japan. But Britain would go only so far as the United States and would "base her policy upon American policy during the present crisis." Other delegates demanded that the Americans take leadership in formulating a program of action when the conference opened on the following day. The Washington government could not lead because it believed that it was impotent in the face of public opinion at home. Since no one dared to act the conference adjourned on November 24 after adopting a pious reaffirmation of the principles enunciated in the Nine Power Treaty.

The Japanese gave their answer on December 12 by bombing and sinking the United States gunboat *Panay* and three Standard Oil tankers in the Yangtze River near Nanking. The chief reaction in the United States was a loud demand for withdrawal of all American forces in China,[8] and Japan was allowed to apologize and pay an indemnity on December 23, 1937.

167.   *The President's Plan and Its Aftermath*

At the time that he made his quarantine address Roosevelt was contemplating some bold stroke—perhaps a meeting of the leaders of the great powers at sea—to prepare the way for the Brussels Conference. Undersecretary of State Sumner Welles on October 6, 1937, sent the President a memorandum embodying a program—the calling of a world conference in which the powers would seek to reconstruct international law and find a basis for political and economic co-operation. Roosevelt approved and contemplated summoning the diplomatic representatives on Armistice Day. He postponed action when Hull strenuously opposed the plan on the ground that Japan and the European dictators would of course pay lip service to peace and brotherhood, and that their seeming concurrence would lull the democracies into a false sense of security.

Significant events in Europe soon afterward caused the President to take up his plan again. The British government embarked upon a policy in November 1937 aimed at appeasing Germany's legitimate grievances and establishing a new European accord. Lord Halifax, speaking for the Cabinet, described the new British policy in conversations with Hitler in Berlin; Hitler in turn promised sincere co-operation. Roosevelt learned of this development and decided to launch his campaign for a new international modus vivendi in order to support Britain's attempt to come to an understanding with Germany.

First, however, the President sent a secret message describing his plan to Prime Minister Neville Chamberlain on January 11, 1938. In delivering the message to the British Ambassador, Welles warned that "all the progress which had been made in Anglo-American co-operation during the previous two years would be destroyed" if the British Cabinet did not co-operate.[9] Chamberlain replied on January 13 without consulting the absent Eden that the President's proposal would interfere with his, Chamberlain's, plan to appease Germany and recognize Italy's conquest of Ethiopia in return for certain guarantees. This news that Britain intended to condone Mussolini's conquest of Ethiopia dumbfounded the Washington administra-

wwwwwwwwwwww

[8] In a Gallup poll taken in January 1938, 70 per cent of the persons queried said that they favored total American withdrawal from the Far East. Four months before only 54 per cent of the persons queried in a similar poll had favored such withdrawal.

[9] The quotation is from Winston S. Churchill, *The Gathering Storm* (Boston, 1948), pp. 251–2.

tion, and Roosevelt and Hull both replied in words that scarcely concealed their disgust.

Eden meanwhile had returned to London and virtually forced Chamberlain to inform the President on January 21, 1938, that the British government would cordially co-operate in his plan but could not take responsibility for its failure. We do not know whether Roosevelt would have acted had circumstances not changed drastically soon afterward. In any event, Eden resigned on February 20, primarily in protest over Chamberlain's Italian policy, while Hitler occupied and annexed Austria to Germany on March 12 and 13. In consequence the President's plan sank out of sight.

The prospect for peace was now obviously uncertain, and the Washington administration began seriously to consider the naval and military impotence of the nation. The President and Congress had slightly augmented the army's feeble strength since 1933 but had not provided enough new naval construction to maintain the fleet even at the strength authorized by the London Treaty of 1930. The Japanese had denounced the Washington Naval Treaty in December 1934. American, British, French, and Japanese delegates had met in London early in 1936 to discuss continuation of the naval agreement, and the Japanese had withdrawn when the Atlantic powers would not grant equality to the Imperial fleet.

A renewal of Japanese construction in 1937 and especially the outbreak of the Sino-Japanese War in the same year convinced the President that the time had come for the United States to look to its own defenses. He sent a special message to Congress on January 28, 1938, urging an immediate increase of 20 per cent in expenditures for naval construction. Pacifists all over the country decried the President's request as beginning a new arms race. Nonetheless, Congress in May 1938 approved the Vinson Naval Expansion Act authorizing the expenditure over the next decade of some $1,000,000,000 to create a navy presumably strong enough to meet the combined fleets of Japan, Germany, and Italy.

The adoption of the naval expansion bill was one sign, among others, of profound changes that were taking place in American opinion by the spring of 1938. The American people were still determined to avoid participation in Asia's and Europe's wars. Even so, most thoughtful Americans were beginning to perceive the enormity of the rising Nazi menace and were willing at least to admit the necessity for strong defenses against potential threats to the security of the Western Hemisphere.

CHAPTER

22

The Second Road to War

1938–1941

Hitler brought Europe to the brink of war soon after his seizure of Austria in late winter of 1938 by threatening to seize the German-speaking Sudeten provinces of Czechoslovakia. The British and French rejected Russian co-operation and submitted to Hitler's demands during this so-called Munich crisis. They thus postponed war but lost a powerful ally. Then Hitler's hasty betrayal of his Munich pledges and attack against Poland in September 1939 caused the two western democracies to stand up and fight to prevent Nazi power from overwhelming all of Europe.

The policies demanded by the American people and followed by their government between September 1939 and June 1940 were certainly neither bold nor helpful to the western democracies. But it is easy to criticize in retrospect and to forget how divided and distraught the American people were in this time of crisis, and how the administration could not lead where Congress and the people would not follow. The important fact was that Americans, or a majority of them, rallied behind the President in bold if belated efforts once they understood the dimensions of the Nazi threat.

While the Washington government sought to help stem the Nazi tide in the West by measures short of war, it used stern diplomacy to turn back the rising tide of Japanese imperialism that threatened to engulf the Far East. At any time during the period from 1939 to December 1941 the American leaders could have come to terms with the Japanese government —by accepting Japanese control of China and Japanese demands for leadership in the Orient. The supreme tragedy was that by 1941 the situation had passed beyond the point of reasonable solution. As compromise on any terms that did not violate everything the American people had stood for in the Far East seemed impossible by 1941, the two nations reached the point where diplomacy could not harmonize fundamentally divergent objectives.

In the following chapter we will tell how the American government and people, haltingly at first, but boldly afterward, emerged from the chrysalis of isolation and assumed a position of decisive power in the affairs of mankind.

168. *From the Munich Crisis to the Outbreak of War*

After the annexation of Austria Hitler began a campaign for incorporation of the German-speaking Sudeten provinces of Czechoslovakia into Greater Germany, prepared defenses along the French border, and made plans for a campaign in the East. Prime Minister Chamberlain and his new Foreign Secretary, Lord Halifax, had meanwhile concluded that the best hope for peace lay in autonomy for the Sudeten Germans. Chamberlain, therefore, attempted to mediate between the Czech government and Konrad Henlein, spokesmen of the Sudeten Germans. These negotiations failed because Henlein rejected autonomy and demanded the union of the Sudetenland with Germany.

War seemed inevitable. Chamberlain flew to Germany for a personal meeting with Hitler on September 15, 1938, there to learn that Germany would accept nothing less than cession of the Sudetenland. Chamberlain and the French Premier, Edouard Daladier, knuckled under and agreed that Czechoslovakia must surrender to the *Führer's* demands. The Czech leaders had no alternative but to submit. Then Hitler rejected Chamberlain's arrangement for the transfer of the disputed provinces, and it seemed that the British and French governments would accept war rather than further humble themselves.

The overwhelming majority of the people of western Europe and the United States, however, continued to hope for peace even in the blackest days of the September crisis. Roosevelt responded to promptings from Paris and London by appealing on September 26 to Chamberlain, Daladier, Hitler, and President Eduard Beneš of Czechoslovakia to compose their differences peacefully. He urged Mussolini on the following day to use his influence with Hitler for peace and also dispatched a special message to Berlin. Chamberlain in a last ditch plea on September 27 suggested that Hitler, Daladier, Mussolini, and he meet personally to find a solution. The world was surprised when Hitler accepted and relieved when the four leaders met at Munich on September 29 and quickly agreed to a scheme for the dismemberment of the Czech Republic.

Chamberlain and Daladier by a stroke of the pen confirmed Hitler's supremacy over his generals, who had opposed his recent reckless moves; made Germany absolutely dominant on the Continent; weakened the attractiveness of a western alignment for the Soviet leaders; and demonstrated their own incompetence as diplomats. All that they received in return was Hitler's unctuous promise that he would make no more territorial demands in Europe, respect Czech sovereignty, and settle all future disputes by peaceful negotiation.

Roosevelt had acted as an unhappy partner in appeasement, but he was never guilty of believing that the Munich Agreement offered any hope for peace in Europe. On the contrary, he began to reorient his domestic and foreign policies soon afterward in preparation for the conflict that he was certain would ensue. To begin with, he abandoned his "purge" of conservative Democrats, called a halt to the reform energies of the New Deal, and began a campaign for speedy rearmament in the autumn of 1938. Hitler announced an expansion of German military strength on October 9. Roosevelt countered two days later by announcing a $300,000,000 increase in American spending for defense purposes and calling upon his military advisers to plan for huge increases in aircraft production. In his Annual Message to Congress and his Budget Message on January 4 and 5, 1939, moreover, he asked for one and a third billion dollars for the regular defense establishment and an additional $525,000,000, most of it for airplanes. These appeals fell upon receptive ears, for the Munich tragedy had opened the eyes of millions of Americans to the Nazi danger to world peace, while violent anti-Jewish pogroms in Germany in November 1938 had revealed anew the brutal character of the Nazi regime.[1] Thus Congress responded by increasing the military and naval budgets by nearly two thirds and by authorizing the President to begin accumulating stockpiles of strategic raw materials for use if war occurred.

In addition, the Washington administration intensified its campaign to strengthen the collective security system in the Western Hemisphere. This was now a more urgent and difficult task than during the early years of the Good Neighbor policy, for the German government had begun a tremendous economic and propaganda campaign aimed at establishing German hegemony in Latin America. Nazi agents had organized National Socialist parties among German immigrants in Brazil and Argentina, threatened economic reprisals against any Latin American nation that dared to co-operate with the United States, and engaged in wholesale military espionage under the cover of German steamship and air lines.

Roosevelt and Hull therefore determined to form a solid hemispheric anti-Nazi front at the Pan-American Conference that opened at Lima, Peru, on December 9, 1938. Hull, as chairman of the American delegation and chief advocate of hemispheric solidarity, had the cordial support of most Latin American governments. As during the Buenos Aires conference two years before, however, the Argentine delegation seemed determined either to dominate or wreck the proceedings. Hull marshaled a nearly solid Latin American opinion and conducted patient negotiations with the President and Foreign Minister of Argentina. The result was unanimous approval of the Declaration of Lima on Christmas Eve. It reaffirmed the twenty-one American republics' determination to resist jointly any Fascist or Nazi threat to the peace and security of the hemisphere.

The President's chief objective during the uneasy months following Munich was repeal or drastic amendment of the Neutrality Act of 1937.

---

[1] It would be difficult to exaggerate the importance of the American reaction to this outbreak of terrorism against the Jews of Germany. Leaders of both parties joined in expressing the revulsion of the American people, while Roosevelt recalled Ambassador Hugh Wilson from Berlin in protest.

Roosevelt was so eager to avoid giving isolationists an issue during the early months of 1939 that he moved for repeal of the arms embargo through negotiation rather than by direct attack. Hull was in constant communication with Key Pittman, chairman of the Senate foreign relations committee, urging him to take leadership in repealing the arms embargo, that "incitement to Hitler to go to war." But Pittman warned that a repeal measure could not pass, and Roosevelt and Hull momentarily gave up the fight and concentrated on measures for stronger defense.

The international situation suddenly deteriorated two months later to the point where war seemed inevitable. Hitler sent his armies into the Czech capital on March 15, 1939, and took control of what remained of unhappy Czechoslovakia. The dictator's cynical violation of an agreement upon which the ink was hardly dry caused such a profound revulsion of sentiment in Great Britain that Chamberlain was forced to abandon appeasement. The Prime Minister almost at once began negotiating treaties guaranteeing the independence and territorial integrity of countries believed to be next in Germany's line of march—Poland, Rumania, Greece, and Turkey.

Reaction in Washington to Hitler's latest move was nearly as violent as in London. Speaking for the President on March 17, Acting Secretary of State Sumner Welles condemned Germany's "wanton lawlessness" and use of "arbitrary force." On the same day the President decided not to recognize the destruction of Czechoslovakia and to continue to deal with the Czech Minister in Washington. Accompanying this strong talk now went even stronger administration action to obtain revision of the neutrality statute. In order to win Senator Pittman's support, Roosevelt and Hull accepted a compromise measure—introduced by Pittman on March 20—that extended the "cash and carry" provision but amended it to include arms, ammunition, and other war materials.

The President ventured all his prestige in the fight to obtain either passage of the Pittman bill or outright repeal of the arms embargo, but the campaign was to no avail. Roosevelt called House leaders to the Executive Mansion on May 19 and declared that repeal of the arms embargo might prevent war and would certainly make an Axis victory less likely if war occurred. In addition, he persuaded King George VI and Queen Elizabeth to pay a state visit to the United States in June in order to stimulate Anglo-American friendship. But Congress would not budge; both houses decisively refused to approve measures of revision. Then the President invited Senate leaders to the White House on July 18 for a frank discussion of the European situation. All senators present but one thought that revision of the Neutrality Act was impossible, and Vice President Garner turned to Roosevelt and said: "Well, Captain, we may as well face the facts. You haven't got the votes, and that's all there is to it." The President replied that he had done his best, and that the Senate would have to shoulder responsibility for refusing to take action to protect the nation's security.

Roosevelt and Hull worked as best they could meanwhile to restrain Germany and Italy. For example, the President warned the Italian Ambassador on March 22, 1939, that the United States would extend aid to Britain and France in the event that war broke out and promised that he would cooperate with Mussolini in any effort for peace. When the Italians occupied Albania on April 7, Roosevelt countered a week later by appealing publicly to the two dictators to demonstrate that they did not want war. "Are you willing to give assurance that your armed forces will not attack or invade the territory or possessions" of Europe and the Middle East, the President bluntly asked. If Hitler and Mussolini were willing to give such assurances for a reasonable period, Roosevelt continued, he would take leadership in a movement for disarmament and equal access by Germany and Italy to the trade and natural resources of the world. Roosevelt's message bolstered British and French courage and threw the German and Italian leaders into a paroxysm of rage.

169.   *The Impact of the War upon the American People*

Leaders of Europe engaged in last-minute negotiations during the summer of 1939 in preparation for Armageddon. Chamberlain and Daladier by signing the Munich Pact had not only isolated Russia but had also intensified Russian suspicions that they were trying to turn Hitler eastward. The British and French premiers, once they had abandoned appeasement, appealed to the Kremlin to sign an alliance to contain Nazism. The Russians demanded as their price a guarantee of the security of all of eastern Europe and the Baltic states and acknowledgment of Russia's right in certain circumstances to occupy this broad zone stretching from Finland to Bulgaria.

While Chamberlain and Daladier were negotiating, Stalin and his new Foreign Minister, Vyacheslav Molotov, were simultaneously sounding out the possibilities of agreement with Germany. Hitler was glad to make temporary concessions to prevent Russia from joining his adversaries in the West. The upshot of these negotiations was the signing of a Nazi-Soviet treaty of nonaggression in Moscow on August 23, 1939. The published terms provided simply that Russia and Germany would refrain from attacking each other. The secret provisions provided that in the event of a territorial rearrangement in eastern Europe, Russia should have Finland, Estonia, Latvia, eastern Poland, and the Rumanian province of Bessarabia, while Germany might annex Lithuania [2] and western Poland.

Hitler was now protected against the danger of a two-front war and increased his demands on Poland. Chamberlain warned that Britain would go at once to Poland's aid if Germany attacked but offered to discuss the Polish question, and Roosevelt added a new appeal for peace. Hitler responded by sending his armies into Poland on September 1; two days later Britain and France declared war on the Reich. Thus the chips were finally down for a last play after four years of intolerable tension.

Most Americans had seen that war was inevitable and took the outbreak of hostilities in stride. The President issued an official proclamation of neutrality on September 5, 1939, and put the Neutrality Act into force,[3] as he was bound to do; but he did not ask the people to be impartial in

wwwwwwwwwwwwwww

[2] By subsequent negotiation Germany exchanged Lithuania for Polish territory.

[3] Thus the arms embargo went into effect, causing an immediate cancellation of Anglo-French war orders worth $79,000,000. Belligerents, however, were free to buy raw materials and food, although the Johnson Act prevented extension of credits to the British and French governments.

thought as well as in deed, as Wilson had done in different circumstances in 1914. "This nation will remain a neutral nation," Roosevelt declared on September 3, "but I cannot ask that every American remain neutral in thought as well. Even a neutral has a right to take account of facts. Even a neutral cannot be asked to close his mind or his conscience."

The Washington administration moved swiftly to strengthen the defenses of the Western Hemisphere by arranging for a conference of the Foreign Ministers of the American republics. They met at Panama City on September 23 and agreed with surprising unanimity upon common neutrality regulations and mutual consultation in the event that a transfer of territory from one European power to another threatened the security of the New World. The most striking work of the conference was the adoption of the Declaration of Panama, marking out a broad zone 300 miles wide around the Americas, excluding Canada and European colonies, into which the belligerents were forbidden to carry the war. It was, actually, only a verbal prohibition and had no practical effect.

The President's primary objective, however, was still repeal of the arms embargo provision of the Neutrality Act. He called Congress into special session to plead earnestly for repeal on September 21. His main theme was maintenance of American neutrality, for he shared the prevalent view that Britain and France could defeat Germany if only they could obtain weapons of war. As if to prove that he believed that neutrality was desirable, he urged Congress to prohibit American ships from entering European war zones and to apply the "cash and carry" principle to all European purchases in the United States.

The request was modest and thoroughly neutral, but it stirred isolationists to frenzied activity. Senator Borah in a radio broadcast repeated the old American dictum that European wars were caused by "the unconscionable schemes of remorseless rulers" and warned that lifting the arms embargo would be tantamount to taking sides in a war in which American interests were not involved. Other isolationist leaders in Congress joined the attack, while the battle was squarely joined in the country at large. Pacifists, who argued that the only way to prevent war was to have nothing to do with the instruments of destruction, were joined by Communists, who charged that Britain and France were fighting to preserve imperialistic capitalism. Former President Hoover contributed the suggestion that the United States forbid only the export of offensive armaments. Colonel Charles A. Lindbergh, popular air idol of other days, warned that the American people had no stake in the war and should keep their hands clean. On the other side, in support of the President, was ranged a powerful new combination of southern and eastern Democrats in Congress. They were joined in the country at large by such preparationist Republicans as Stimson and Frank Knox, a vast majority of the business interests and the metropolitan press, and a large segment of the intellectual leadership of the country.

It was evident by the middle of October that the tide had turned in the President's favor. Meanwhile, Senator Pittman had drafted a new neutrality bill that lifted the arms embargo and imposed severe restrictions on American shipping. Pittman persuaded the foreign relations committee to report the measure favorably on September 28. Congress approved the Pittman bill after a month of debate, and the President signed it on November 4, 1939. It afforded considerable advantage to the democratic allies. But its provisions forbidding American ships to trade with belligerent countries and American citizens to travel on belligerent vessels also reflected the high tide of the American determination to avoid the kind of controversies over neutral rights that had led to involvement in the First World War.

Meanwhile, Hitler's armies had overrun Poland before the French could mount an offensive on the western front, and the Russians had shocked the world by joining the Germans in devouring Poland. The Germans built their offensive power for a drive in the West during the following months, while the British and French acted as if the war could be won merely by waiting for the Nazi regime to collapse. This so-called phony war lulled Americans even more than the British and French into believing that the Germans could never win.

American attention was diverted from the western front by a Russian invasion of Finland in November and December 1939. A hot wave of anger swept over the American public, but the administration acted cautiously. Roosevelt indignantly denounced the "dreadful rape of Finland" and castigated the Soviet Union as "a dictatorship as absolute as any other dictatorship in the world." The State and Treasury departments instituted an effective "moral" embargo on the export of war supplies to the Soviets. But beyond this action the administration would not go. Roosevelt and Hull perceived that the marriage between Germany and Russia was incompatible and simply refused to do anything to cement the alliance of the two totalitarian regimes.

Meanwhile, the months passed without any eruption on the western front, and the thoughts of Roosevelt and most Americans turned inevitably toward the peace that they all desired. Their hope, however, exceeded the possibilities of the time. What they wanted was a postwar world founded upon international justice and close co-operation for peace. The President and State Department co-operated with private foundations in launching studies and sponsoring public meetings to achieve new understanding and stimulate public discussion. But what point was there in talking about peace so long as Hitler dominated the Continent, skeptics in the administration asked. Roosevelt was undaunted and decided in early February 1940 to send Sumner Welles to London, Paris, Rome, and Berlin to sound out the possibilities of a just and lasting settlement. Welles went on his mission and soon discovered what he and every informed person already knew—that Hitler would agree to no settlement which Britain, France, and the United States could approve, and that the ultimate decision would have to be made on the battlefield.

170.   *The Menace of a Nazi Victory*

The "phony war" ended on April 9, 1940, as Hitler sent his armies into Denmark and Norway, and German airplanes and *Panzer* divisions struck hard at Belgium, Holland, and northern France on May 10. It is difficult to describe the terror that swept over the American people as this blitzkrieg (lightning war) developed. All Americans except a few diehard isolationists recognized that a Germany completely dominant in Europe would pose a dire threat to their peace and security. And now it was about to happen, the catastrophe that only a week before had seemed impossible. There was France, her poorly equipped armies reeling and scattering under the impact of Nazi power; there was the British expeditionary force, driven to the sea at Dunkirk and forced to execute a nearly impossible evacuation.

The immediate threat to American security was the possibility that Hitler might claim Iceland and Greenland, both of which commanded the American sea lanes to Britain, by virtue of his conquest of their mother country, Denmark. Roosevelt refused to order the occupation of Iceland but was obviously pleased when the British occupied it on May 10. Greenland, however, was too close to the United States and Canada to be ignored. Roosevelt declared on April 18 that the island enjoyed the protection of the Monroe Doctrine. The Washington administration refused a request by Greenlanders that it assume a temporary protectorate. Instead, it furnished military supplies and established a Greenland Patrol by the Coast Guard.

Chamberlain resigned on May 10, 1940, the day before the Germans hurtled into the Low Countries, and Winston Spencer Churchill, long the chief British opponent of appeasement, took the helm as Prime Minister. He had nothing to offer the people of the Empire but "blood, toil, tears, and sweat" and the hope of ultimate victory. Churchill sent a cable to Roosevelt when the blitzkrieg was in its fifth day in which he frankly acknowledged the likelihood of German conquest of Europe and asked the President to proclaim a state of nonbelligerency, lend Britain forty or fifty old destroyers, and supply several hundred aircraft and quantities of ammunition. Roosevelt had to reply that the moment for such action was not opportune since Congress would have to approve a transfer of the destroyers.

Roosevelt had determined even before he received Churchill's urgent plea to ask Congress to hasten the nation's armament campaign.[4] This he did in a special message on May 16, 1940, warning Americans that their own security would be gravely imperiled if an enemy should seize any outlying territory, and calling for production of 50,000 planes a year and large new expenditures for the armed forces. Moreover, after the Allied collapse on the western front, he asked Congress on May 31 for an additional $1,000,000,000 for defense and for authority to call the National Guard and reserve personnel into active service.

Meanwhile, Roosevelt had also been trying to bolster French morale and to dissuade Mussolini from joining Hitler. Mussolini was deaf to such appeals and rushed to join the Nazis in devouring the carcass of France on June 10. This act of aggression gave the President an opportunity to say in clear and ringing words what the United States would do. In an address at the University of Virginia on the same day that Italy entered the war, Roosevelt announced the end of American isolation and the beginning of a new phase of nonbelligerency. Hereafter the United States would "extend to the opponents of force the material resources of this nation." Moreover, he voiced American indignation at Mussolini's treachery in the now famous in-

---

[4] The War Department had made plans for increasing the army's strength to 500,000 men by July 1941, to 1,000,000 by January 1942, and to nearly 2,000,000 by July 1942; for production of 50,000 aircraft a year; and for manufacture of vast numbers of tanks and guns.

dictment, "On this tenth day of June, 1940, the hand that held the dagger has struck it into the back of its neighbor."

This was the week in which France was tottering on the brink of ruin. German armies entered Paris on June 12. The government of Paul Reynaud, who had succeeded Daladier as Premier on March 21, gave way on June 16 to a government headed by the aged Marshal Henri-Philippe Pétain. He surrendered to the Germans on June 22. The supreme moment of decision had now come for the President and his advisers. Hitler stood astride the Continent. Italian entry into the war seemed to presage early Axis control of the Mediterranean and North Africa. The British army was stripped of virtually all its heavy equipment after the Dunkirk evacuation. Churchill had warned in repeated messages that the British Isles might be overrun without immediate American assistance, and that a successor government might have to surrender the fleet in order to save the realm. Should the Roosevelt administration assume that the British were lost, abandon aid to them, and prepare to defend the Western Hemisphere? Or should it strip American defenses in the hope the British could survive?

Not only isolationists but many "realistic" Americans demanded adherence to the former course. They were joined by the Joint Planners of the War and Navy departments, who warned on June 27, 1940, that Britain might not survive and urged the President to concentrate on American defenses. It was the kind of advice that military leaders, who think in terms of the worst contingencies, have to give. But Roosevelt decided to gamble on Britain. In this decision he had the support of his new Secretaries of War and of the Navy, Henry L. Stimson and Frank Knox, whom he had appointed on June 20 to gain Republican support for the defense effort. Roosevelt rejected Churchill's ambitious proposals for turning the United States into a gigantic arsenal for Britain, but he ordered the War and Navy departments to "scrape the bottom of the barrel" and turn over all available guns and ammunition to private firms for resale to Britain.[5] In addition, officials of the War, Navy, and Treasury departments conferred with a British Purchasing Mission and promised to deliver 14,375 aircraft by April 1942. Roosevelt's decision to gamble on British survival was the most momentous in his career to this time, for he acted in the certain knowledge that war with Germany was probable if Britain should go down.

171.   *The Great Debate*

The fall of France and the seeming imminence of British defeat shocked the American people and stimulated much wild talk of an immediate German invasion of the Western Hemisphere. Such panic, however, soon subsided. More significant was the way the threat of Nazi victory intensified the great debate over American foreign policy that had been in progress since the Munich crisis. Upon the outcome of this controversy would depend the fate of the world.

---

[5] Some 970,000 rifles, 200,500 revolvers, 87,500 machine guns, 895 75 mm. guns, 316 mortars, and a huge quantity of ammunition were shipped to Britain from June to October 1940.

Hitler's destruction of Czechoslovakia had convinced a small but influential minority of Americans that the United States would live in deadly peril if Nazism ever enveloped Europe. Soon after the outbreak of the war they formed the Non-Partisan Committee for Peace through Revision of the Neutrality Law, with William Allen White of Kansas as chairman. The Non-Partisan Committee had branches in thirty states by the end of October 1939. Its propaganda was a decisive factor in swinging public opinion behind repeal of the arms embargo provision. The Committee quietly disintegrated during the "phony war" but reorganized on May 17, 1940, as the Committee to Defend America by Aiding the Allies. The Committee had over six hundred local branches within a few months and had taken leadership in a nation-wide campaign to combat isolationism and stimulate public support for the government's policy of all aid short of war.

The Committee's success was reflected in the transformation in public opinion that occurred during the summer of 1940. When the public opinion polls revealed in July that probably a large majority favored aid to Britain, the Committee next worked to generate public support for a transfer of destroyers to the British.[6] A Gallup poll in mid-August indicated that a majority of the people would approve if the President followed the Committee's lead. In addition, White and other Republican leaders in the Committee headed off an isolationist bloc in the Republican national convention and obtained a platform plank approving aid to "all peoples fighting for liberty."

It was inevitable that this movement to draw America closer to the war's orbit would not go unchallenged by isolationist leaders. Their ranks were considerably thinned by the fall of France, but isolationists—or non-interventionists, as they preferred to call themselves—were still a powerful if incongruous group by the autumn of 1940. They included pro-Nazi spokesmen like Father Coughlin, Gerald L. K. Smith, and William Dudley Pelley and subtle defenders of fascism like Anne Morrow Lindbergh, whose *The Wave of the Future* argued that Germany was bound to triumph. A large body of midwestern businessmen joined their ranks mainly out of hatred of the New Deal. Old progressives like Senators Burton K. Wheeler and Gerald P. Nye still identified co-operation with England with the machinations of Wall Street. Many Protestant ministers and idealists had embraced a philosophy of nonresistance. The Hearst newspapers, the *Chicago Tribune*, the *New York Daily News*, the *Washington Times-Herald*, and other newspapers lent editorial support. Co-operating also were the Socialists, led by Norman Thomas, who still thought of war in economic terms, and the Communists, who had become increasingly pro-Nazi after the signing of the Nazi-Soviet Non-Aggression Pact.

Isolationists organized a number of committees at the height of the debate over foreign policy in the summer and autumn of 1940, but their leading organization was the America First Committee. It was incorporated in September 1940 with Robert E. Wood, chairman of the board of Sears, Roebuck and Company, as national chairman. The America First movement soon included thousands of patriotic Americans who sincerely believed that

ᴧᴧᴧᴧᴧᴧᴧᴧᴧᴧᴧᴧᴧᴧᴧᴧᴧ

[6] The President told White about the contemplated destroyer transfer at a conference on June 29, 1940, and won White's and the Committee's support for the project.

defense of the Western Hemisphere and nonintervention in Europe's war were the only course of safety for the United States. But the America First Committee also had the support of all pro-Nazi groups in the country.

The debate between proponents of strong support for Britain and the noninterventionists did not end until Japanese bombs fell on Pearl Harbor, but it was evident that the former had won the battle for control of the American public mind long before this date. The public opinion polls showed the metamorphosis that occurred: In September 1939 some 82 per cent of persons queried thought that the Allies would win; by July 1940 only 43 per cent were sure that Britain would win. More important, the propor-

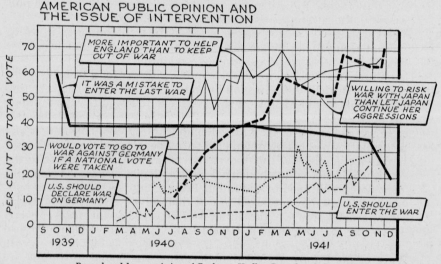

Reproduced by permission of Professor Hadley Cantril and the Public Opinion Research Project of Princeton University.

tion of Americans who believed that a German victory would menace their security increased from 43 per cent in March 1940 to 69 per cent in July 1940. All through the period 1939–41 an overwhelming majority of Americans queried indicated a desire to avoid active participation in the war. The important fact was that this same majority approved strong assistance to Britain; and by the spring of 1941 a majority of persons polled favored extending such aid even if it led to hostilities with Germany.

The President, administration leaders, and the Committee to Defend America played a significant role in this erosion of isolationist sentiments, but events in Europe and the Far East from 1939 to 1941 played an even more significant part. The American people supported the administration in a strong policy and accepted the risk of war, not to defend obsolete neutral rights or to engage in a second crusade for democracy, but rather to defend their own security and freedom. The tragedy was that it required the momentary triumph of Hitler and the near defeat of the British Empire to awaken the American people to the simple facts of international life.

172.   The Presidential Election of 1940 and the World Crisis

Meanwhile, the crisis of the spring and summer had no less an impact upon the national conventions and presidential campaign of 1940 than upon popular attitudes regarding the American stake in an Allied victory. It seemed certain at the beginning of the year that either Senator Robert A. Taft of Ohio, Senator Arthur H. Vandenberg, or young Thomas E. Dewey of New York—all of them ardent noninterventionists at the time—would win the Republican presidential nomination. Almost at the last moment Wendell L. Willkie of Indiana, president of the Commonwealth & Southern Corporation and an old antagonist of the TVA, had entered the preconvention campaign. For all his "big business" connections, Willkie was a former Democrat who approved most of the New Deal reform measures. More important, he had long supported the President's program of aid to Britain. Willkie would not have had a chance in more normal times, but the Republican convention opened in Philadelphia on June 24 amid the panic created by the French surrender two days before. Willkie's managers were able to execute a miraculous whirlwind campaign in the fear and excitement of the time. They won his nomination on June 28 by marshaling the young progressive and internationalist element in the GOP. They won a second notable victory over the diehard isolationist bloc with adoption of a platform approving "prompt" and "realistic" defense and aid to victims of aggression.

The nomination of the rugged, popular Willkie—the first colorful Republican candidate since 1904—compelled President Roosevelt to come to some decision concerning the Democratic nomination. Roosevelt probably intended all along to run for a third term, for he made his nomination inevitable by refusing to support another candidate and by failing to discourage efforts in his own behalf. In any event, he sent a message on July 16 to the Democratic national convention, which had opened in Chicago the day before, saying that he had no desire to remain in office and wanted the convention to be free to make a choice, but implying that he would accept the nomination if the convention insisted. Few of the party bosses wanted Roosevelt, but there was nothing that they could do except nominate him on the first ballot. The delegates rebelled, however, when the President insisted upon Secretary of Agriculture Henry A. Wallace as his running-mate. Roosevelt's spokesman, Harry Hopkins, was able to force the Iowan upon an unwilling party only by using the most ruthless methods.

The President delivered his acceptance speech by radio to the convention early in the morning of July 19 and then did not make another campaign address until September 11. In the meantime he gave all his energies to more urgent problems: military, air, and naval expansion, which he obtained easily from Congress; approval of the Burke-Wadsworth bill for selective service, which he won in September with Willkie's support; and defense of the northern reaches of the hemisphere, which he enhanced with the establishment in August of a Canadian-American Permanent Joint Board on Defense.

There was the danger at this time that the Nazis might seize the French islands in the Caribbean, Guadeloupe and Martinique. The Washington government first warned Berlin against trying any such stratagem; then it arranged for a conference of the Pan-American Foreign Ministers to meet at Havana on July 21, 1940, to consider countermeasures. Hull won unanimous approval at Havana, on July 27, of a declaration that an attack on any American republic was an attack against all of them, as well as adoption of a convention providing that an Inter-American Commission for Territorial Administration should take temporary control of any European possessions in the New World about to be transferred to another sovereignty. Moreover, the Washington government after the Havana Conference began for the first time seriously to plan for large-scale economic and military aid to the Latin American countries.

The most urgent necessity confronting the administration during this summer of campaign and crisis, however, was devising some means of transferring forty or fifty destroyers [7] to Britain for antisubmarine operations and assistance in defense of the British Isles against the invasion that Hitler planned for mid-September of 1940. The chief obstacle was an amendment to the naval appropriations bill that Congress had adopted on June 28. It forbade the President to transfer defense equipment to a foreign power unless the Army Chief of Staff and the Chief of Naval Operations first certified that the equipment was not essential to the national defense.

Roosevelt found a way out of this dilemma, after the Nazis had begun a great air assault against Britain preparatory to the invasion. The upshot was an agreement signed in Washington on September 2, 1940. The United States gave fifty destroyers to the British government in return for a formal pledge that Britain would never surrender its fleet and ninety-nine-year leases on air and naval bases on British territory in Newfoundland, Bermuda, and the Caribbean. Because the agreement vastly enhanced the security of the Western Hemisphere, General George C. Marshall, Army Chief of Staff, and Admiral Harold R. Stark, Chief of Naval Operations, could in good conscience approve it, as the amendment of June 28 required. Churchill, however, rebelled at the idea of a "deal" and insisted upon giving outright the leases for American bases in Newfoundland and Bermuda. Isolationists were up in arms, but criticism in Congress was remarkably restrained. It was too obvious that a large majority of Americans approved, even though the destroyer-bases agreement meant the end of formal neutrality and marked the beginning of a period of limited American participation in the war. Henceforth the extent of that participation would bear a direct relation to German strength and British needs.

While Roosevelt was thus engaged, Wendell Willkie had undertaken a one-man campaign against a silent opponent. He was ebullient and confident during the early weeks of the campaign in his strictures against Democratic inefficiency and a third term. He was fatally handicapped, however, by his own basic agreement with most of Roosevelt's domestic and foreign policies. Willkie apparently realized around the first of October that he might be defeated. In desperation, because he badly wanted to win, he jetti-

ᴧᴧᴧᴧᴧᴧᴧᴧᴧᴧᴧᴧᴧᴧᴧᴧᴧᴧ

[7] They were to be supplied from a reserve of 172 destroyers built during the First World War, which the Navy Department had reconditioned and returned to service.

The Yalta Conference: Prime Minister Churchill, President Roosevelt, Premier Stalin, and high ranking Allied Officers

ABOVE: *Surrender at Rheims*
BELOW: *Surrender in Tokyo Bay*

The mushroom cloud at Nagasaki, 1945

Harry S. Truman

William Faulkner

Arthur Miller

John L. Lewis

T. S. Eliot

ABOVE: *Candidate Eisenhower*
BELOW: *Candidate Stevenson receives congratulations from President Truman*

ABOVE: *President Eisenhower at the ill-fated Paris Summit Conference of 1960*
BELOW: *Richard M. Nixon accepts the Republican nomination in 1960*

ABOVE: *The inauguration of John F. Kennedy*
BELOW: *President Johnson, standing before statue of Abraham Lincoln in Capitol Rotunda, speaks on voting rights bill*

soned his progressive, internationalist advisers and accepted the counsel of the Old Guard professionals. They "begged Willkie to abandon this nonsense about a bipartisan foreign policy—to attack Roosevelt as a warmonger—to scare the American people with warnings that votes for Roosevelt meant wooden crosses for their sons and brothers and sweethearts." [8]

The more Willkie played upon the war issue the more his campaign caught fire, and Democratic managers throughout the country were appalled lest the rising antiwar tide sweep the Republican candidate into the White House. Appeals begging Roosevelt to tell the country that he stood for peace poured into the White House. In response, the President reversed his field. He assured voters in a speech at Philadelphia on October 23 that he had made no secret agreement to involve the United States in the war, "or for any other purpose." He made a grand tour of New York City on October 28, climaxed by an evening address in the Madison Square Garden. Reviewing his long efforts to strengthen the nation's defenses, he warned that Americans could keep war from their shores only by stopping aggression in Europe. This, however, was the "realistic" way to preserve the peace that all Americans desired.

The Madison Square Garden address was in the main a forthright enunciation, but it neither reversed the rising Willkie tide nor quieted the fears of Democratic politicians. The President on October 30 began a tour of New England, to be climaxed by a speech in Boston during the evening. He was inundated all during the day by telegrams warning that defeat impended unless he gave more explicit pledges to maintain peace. For once the great campaigner seemed unsure of himself. At the last minute he included the following promise in his Boston address: "I have said this before, but I shall say it again and again and again: Your boys are not going to be sent into any foreign wars. . . . The purpose of our defense is defense." Roosevelt made it clear in the same speech that he considered defense of Britain to be defense of the United States as well; obviously, he had no intention of involving the country in a "foreign" war.

It was evident by the late evening of election day, November 5, that the President had won again, although the margin of his victory was considerably smaller than it had been in 1936. He received 27,243,000 popular and 449 electoral votes, as compared with 22,304,400 popular and 82 electoral votes for Willkie. In addition, the Democrats retained large majorities in both houses of Congress. The Socialist and Communist candidates, Norman Thomas and Earl Browder, received 100,264 and 48,579 popular votes, respectively.

Roosevelt's victory was greeted with restrained rejoicing in Britain and studied indifference in Berlin and Rome. It was not so much that the British leaders thought that Willkie was an isolationist; it was rather that, as the London *Economist* put it, they preferred Roosevelt's known vices to Willkie's unknown virtues. At home, the President's victory was interpreted as a mandate for continued defense and full support of Britain. Thus reinforced

[8] Robert E. Sherwood, *Roosevelt and Hopkins, An Intimate History* (New York, 1948), p. 187.

ELECTION OF 1940

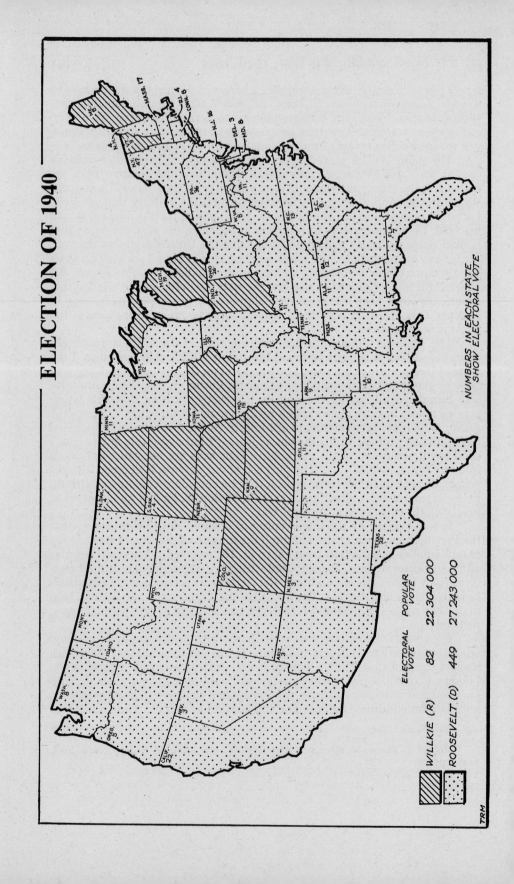

NUMBERS IN EACH STATE
SHOW ELECTORAL VOTE

	ELECTORAL VOTE	POPULAR VOTE
WILLKIE (R)	82	22 304 000
ROOSEVELT (D)	449	27 243 000

TRM

by a third commission from the American people, Roosevelt could begin to co-operate with Churchill in laying bold plans for the coming defeat of Nazi Germany.

173. *Lend-Lease: Implementing Nonbelligerency*

The chief concern of British and American leaders by the autumn of 1940 was the danger that the entire flow of American goods would be cut off as a result of the exhaustion of British dollar reserves. Out of their total dollar resources of $6,500,000,000 at the beginning of the war, the British had spent $4,500,000,000 in the United States by November 1940. By the latter date they were ready to place new orders for American airplanes, armored equipment for ten divisions, and cargo ships. But the Neutrality Act of 1939 required cash payment for all supplies, and the British were nearing the end of their ability to pay. Roosevelt and Treasury officials well knew that the entire system of American aid would soon collapse unless some solution was quickly found.

The President embarked upon a cruise of the Caribbean aboard the cruiser *Tuscaloosa* on December 2, 1940, when the crisis seemed darkest. A navy seaplane landed alongside the ship on the morning of December 9 and delivered a long letter from Churchill. The Prime Minister wrote as a partner in a common cause, not as a supplicant. He reviewed the naval and military situations and emphasized the grave danger of the growing submarine threat. That threat could be overcome, and Britain could mount air and land offensives, Churchill continued, only if American shipping and naval forces helped to keep the North Atlantic sea lanes open, and only if the British had enough American aircraft, especially heavy bombers, "to shatter the foundations of German military power." Moreover, Churchill went on, the time was approaching when Britain could no longer pay for shipping and other supplies. He was confident, he concluded, that the President could find the means to implement a common effort for victory.

Roosevelt pondered Churchill's message for two days and then apparently resolved to act swiftly. On December 17, the day after his return to Washington, he intimated to reporters the plan that had taken shape in his mind. Brushing aside suggestions that the United States either lend money to the British or else give them military supplies, he told a homely parable about a man who lent his neighbor a garden hose—without first demanding payment for it—in order to help put out the fire in his neighbor's house. Then, in a "fireside chat" on December 29, the President told the people frankly what he had in mind. Britain and the British fleet, he declared, stood between the New World and Nazi aggression. Britain asked for war materials, not for men. "We must be the great arsenal of democracy," he concluded. ". . . I call upon our people with absolute confidence that our common cause will greatly succeed."

Public reaction was immediate and overwhelmingly favorable. Roosevelt reiterated the danger from Nazi aggression in his Annual Message on January 6, 1941, and asked Congress "for authority and for funds sufficient to manufacture additional munitions and war supplies of many kinds, to be turned over to those nations which are now in actual war with aggressor nations." These, he went on, would be paid for, not in dollars, but in goods and services at the end of the war. Finally, he voiced a fervent hope for a postwar world built upon freedom of speech and of worship, and freedom from want and fear.

The President's measure, called the Lend-Lease bill, was drafted by Treasury officials during the first week in January 1941 and approved by administration and congressional leaders on January 9. It was introduced in Congress on the following day. Noninterventionists immediately charged that the purposes of the bill were to take the country into war and, as the *Chicago Tribune* said, to "destroy the Republic." But administration spokesmen and a host of leaders from all walks of life countered effectively in congressional hearings, and public opinion unmistakably supported them. The House approved the Lend-Lease bill on February 8, the Senate, on March 8. The President signed it on March 11, 1941. Roosevelt on the following day asked Congress for $7,000,000,000 for Lend-Lease production and export; Congress complied two weeks later.

No man could doubt what the enactment of the Lend-Lease Act signified. "Our blessings from the whole British Empire go out to you and the American nation for this very present help in time of trouble," Churchill wrote to Roosevelt on March 9, 1941. "Through this legislation," the President told Congress on March 12, "our country has determined to do its full part in creating an adequate arsenal of democracy." Actually, Roosevelt's characterization was an understatement. Adoption of the Lend-Lease Act converted the United States from a friendly neutral, which sometimes helped more than the rules of traditional neutrality permitted, into a full-fledged nonbelligerent, committed to pour out all its resources if need be to enable Britain to bring Germany to her knees. If there had ever been any doubts before that the American people would falter or refrain from taking the risk of war, those doubts were now resolved.

The Washington government, having committed itself to underwriting a British victory, was not willing to watch Nazi submarines prevent the delivery of goods vital to German defeat. German depredations on British and neutral shipping from the beginning of the blitzkrieg to the end of 1940 had been staggering enough,[9] but the spring of 1941 witnessed an even more powerful German attack. The Nazis extended their war zone on March 25, 1941, to include Iceland and the Denmark Strait between Greenland and Iceland and sent swarms of new submarines into the North Atlantic (they hunted their prey in "wolf packs"). They also used surface vessels in daring raids and threw a large part of their air force into the battle to choke off the stream of supplies flowing from American to British ports. The Germans destroyed 537,493 tons of merchant shipping in March 1941; 653,960 in April; 500,063 in May. As Churchill repeatedly warned, the outcome of the Battle of the Atlantic might well determine the entire course of the war.

To the President, therefore, the choice did not seem to lie between action and inaction but rather among various means of participating in the Battle of the Atlantic. Consequently, on March 25 and April 2, 1941, he au-

---

[9] British, Allied, and neutral shipping losses totaled 3,139,190 tons from May through December 1940.

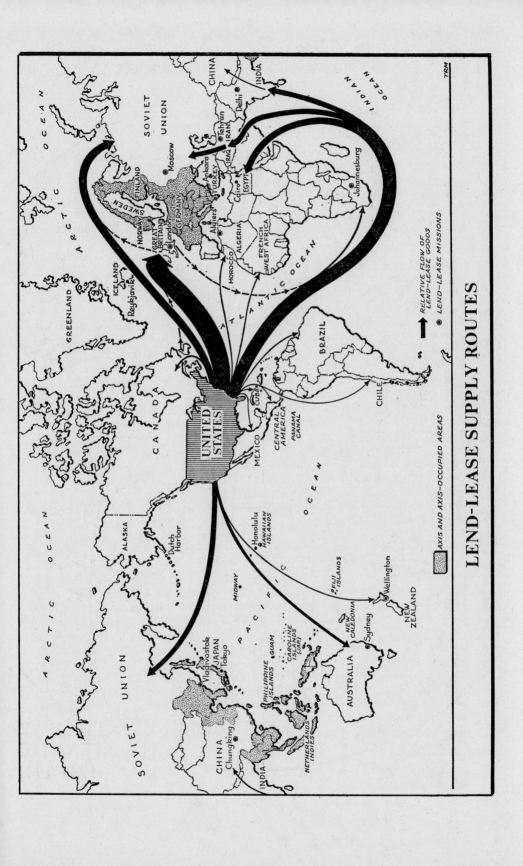

LEND-LEASE SUPPLY ROUTES

RELATIVE FLOW OF
LEND-LEASE GOODS

● LEND-LEASE MISSIONS

▓ AXIS AND AXIS-OCCUPIED AREAS

TRM

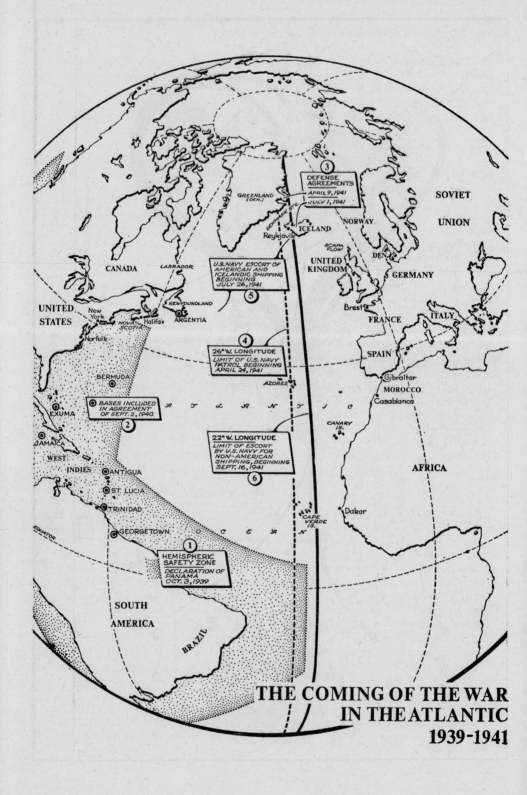

THE COMING OF THE WAR
IN THE ATLANTIC
1939-1941

thorized American naval yards to repair British vessels; on March 28 he transferred ten Coast Guard cutters to the British fleet to assist in antisubmarine operations; on March 31 he had the Coast Guard seize thirty Axis and thirty-five Danish merchant ships in American ports. It was bold action, but it was not enough to clear the sea lanes. Secretary Stimson urged Roosevelt to order the navy to convoy British and Allied merchant ships all the way from American to British ports.

The President rejected Stimson's advice but decided on April 10 to extend the American Neutrality Patrol far out into the Atlantic—to longitude 25° west, a line between Brazil and the west coast of Africa in the south and slightly west of Iceland in the north. American naval vessels would search out, but not attack, Nazi submarines and warn British vessels of their presence within the area between the American coast and longitude 25° west.[10] In addition, the President issued a proclamation on April 10 removing the area of the Red Sea from the list of war zones forbidden to American ships.

Isolationists in Congress were meanwhile pressing the charge that Roosevelt had begun an undeclared naval war by ordering American vessels in the patrol area to convoy British ships and attack Nazi U-boats. A German submarine torpedoed an American freighter, the *Robin Moor*, in the South Atlantic on May 21. The President had a "fireside chat" with the people six days later and told them what their navy was doing in the North Atlantic. He said that German control of the Atlantic would imperil American security, and he revealed that the Nazis were sinking ships twice as fast as British and American shipyards could replace them. The hope of victory, he continued, lay in increasing shipbuilding and in helping to reduce losses at sea. To accomplish the latter objective, he explained, "Our patrols are helping now to insure delivery of the needed supplies to Britain." He ended by warning that "all additional measures necessary to deliver the goods" would be taken, by calling upon industry and labor to redouble their efforts, and by declaring an unlimited state of national emergency.

174. *The Invasion of Russia*

An overwhelming majority of Americans had thought no better of the Russians than of the Nazis ever since the Soviet Union sealed its pact of friendship with Hitlerite Germany and then seized eastern Poland, absorbed the Baltic states, launched an aggressive war against Finland, and afterward tore the province of Bessarabia from Rumania. This anti-Russian tension was increased during the period from August 1939 to June 1941 by efforts of American Communists to cripple defense production through strikes in airplane factories and otherwise to impair American solidarity. Congressional vexation at such subversion took form in the Smith Act in the spring of 1940. It made it unlawful for any group to advocate or teach the

wwwwwwwwwwww

[10] This was the substance of orders issued by Roosevelt to Admiral Ernest J. King on April 19–21, 1941. The Navy began intensified patrol activities on April 24, 1941. Meanwhile, the State Department on April 9 concluded an agreement with the Danish Minister in Washington, authorizing the United States to build naval and air bases on Greenland.

violent overthrow of government in the United States, or for any person to belong to such a group.

We now know that the Soviet leaders would have probably been prepared to come to agreement with Hitler for a division of Europe and the Middle East. Conversations between Hitler and Molotov in Berlin in November 1940 failed to bring agreement, but only because Hitler thought the Russians wanted too much. He was enraged by Russian demands and ordered preparations on December 18, 1940, for an invasion of Russia in the coming spring. Hitler launched his attack against the Soviet Union in the early morning hours of June 22, 1941. The Washington government reacted circumspectly, for the American public probably welcomed a showdown battle between the dictatorships, while Roosevelt's military advisers warned that Russia would collapse within three months and that any aid given to the Soviet armies would only fall into Hitler's hands.

Meanwhile, Roosevelt used the breathing space afforded by the German attack to strengthen home defenses and the American position in the North Atlantic. The most urgent defense necessity in the early summer of 1941 was extension of the terms of service of the 900,000 men drafted in the preceding autumn. The defense effort would have practically collapsed if the men had been allowed to go home at the end of their one-year term. The President, therefore, permitted General Marshall to ask Congress on July 3 to extend the term of service and also to remove the provisions in the Selective Service Act of 1940 that prohibited sending draftees outside the Western Hemisphere. Marshall's request stirred a hornet's nest of opposition, not only from isolationists but from administration supporters in Congress as well. Marshall explained that the army had no desire to send a new A.E.F. and pleaded that extension of the draft was essential to national security. The Senate extended the term of service by six months on August 7, 1941. On the other hand, the struggle in the House of Representatives was bitter, and long in doubt until that body approved extension by a vote of 203 to 202 on August 12.

While this controversy was in its first stage the President moved decisively to strengthen American control of the North Atlantic sea lanes. Negotiations among Roosevelt, Churchill, and the Prime Minister of Iceland culminated in the occupation of Iceland by American marines on July 7, 1941, and the inauguration of United States naval escorts for convoys of American and Icelandic ships between the Atlantic Coast and Iceland on July 26. Thus by one stroke the character of American naval operations in the North Atlantic was changed drastically. Henceforward the American navy would not merely patrol the area between Iceland and the United States but would destroy "hostile forces" that threatened American and Icelandic shipping in that broad expanse of water.

175. *The Atlantic Conference and the Brink of War*

Harry Hopkins, Lend-Lease administrator and now Roosevelt's closest confidant, left Washington on July 13, 1941, for London to pave the way for a personal meeting between Roosevelt and Churchill. Roosevelt not only wanted to renew acquaintance with the "Former Naval Person"; he also wanted the military and naval leaders of both countries to co-ordinate plans for future operations. At Roosevelt's explicit instruction, Hopkins warned Churchill that there should be no talk of economic or territorial deals, or of American participation in the war. Churchill was delighted and agreed to come to a secret meeting "in some lonely bay or other" on August 9.

Hopkins flew next to Moscow for conversations with Stalin and other Soviet leaders. From Stalin the American envoy heard the news that the Russian armies would withstand the first Nazi onslaught and take the offensive during the coming winter. Hopkins also learned that the Kremlin would welcome Lend-Lease aid and facilitate its delivery, and that the Russian government desired American entry into the war above all other things and "would welcome the American troops on any part of the Russian front under the complete command of the American Army."

Hopkins was back in London in time to join Churchill and his party aboard the new battleship, *Prince of Wales*, for the journey to the rendezvous with Roosevelt off Argentia, Newfoundland. The President arrived aboard the cruiser *Augusta,* and the two leaders met on the American vessel on the morning of August 9.[11] The British tried to obtain some commitment of American support if Japan attacked British possessions in the Far East. In this, as in all other matters discussed, Roosevelt and his advisers refused to make any promises of a military or naval character.

The most important work of the Argentia meeting was the approval, after some stiff argument about Britain's imperial policy, by Roosevelt and Churchill on August 12 of the joint declaration known as the Atlantic Charter. It was the product of careful thought and patient negotiation and recorded Anglo-American agreement on "certain common principles" on which the two governments based "their hopes for a better future for the world." These principles were no territorial aggrandizement, no territorial changes that did not accord with the wishes of the people involved, the right of all peoples to choose the form of government under which they lived, economic collaboration in the postwar world, and the right of all peoples to live in peace and in freedom from fear, want, and aggression.

News of the Argentia conference and the text of the Atlantic Charter were published in the press on August 15 and provoked isolationist editors and politicians to new outbursts. But the overwhelming majority of Americans believed Roosevelt's assurances that he had made no commitment to intervene actively and approved the idealistic aspirations embodied in the Atlantic Charter. Obviously, the preponderant majority continued to approve giving aid to Hitler's enemies and to hope that the United States would not have to enter the "shooting war." Roosevelt probably shared these sentiments. Like the great majority of his fellow countrymen, he continued to hope for peace while announcing policies that could be attained only by full-fledged American participation in the war.

The President set about to provide greater assistance to Russia soon after his return from Argentia. This undertaking was made immensely difficult by the opposition of isolationists, the Catholic press, and many anti-

‧‧‧‧‧‧‧‧‧‧‧‧‧‧‧‧‧‧‧‧‧

[11] It was, incidentally, their second meeting. They had met casually in London on July 29, 1918.

Communist Americans. Even though he was uncertain of public and congressional reaction, Roosevelt began discussions that led to an Anglo-American-Soviet conference in Moscow in late September 1941 and an Anglo-American promise to furnish $1,000,000,000 worth of aid to Russia before June 30, 1942. When Congress, while voting a new $6,000,000,000 appropriation for Lend-Lease production and export in October, rejected an amendment forbidding extension of aid to Russia, Roosevelt declared the Soviet Union eligible for Lend-Lease assistance on November 7.

More significant for the immediate future, however, was Roosevelt's decision further to relieve the British position in the North Atlantic. The President decided at Argentia to allow British and Allied vessels to join American convoys between the United States and Iceland. This was done unofficially before the end of August, although orders to this effect were not issued until September 13.

Roosevelt pondered the best way to break the news of this new policy to the people. Then a German submarine attacked the destroyer *Greer* south of Iceland on September 4, after the *Greer* had joined a British airplane in trailing the U-boat. The incident gave the President the "provocation" he needed to justify a change of policy. In a radio address on September 11, he declared in seeming seriousness that the attack on the *Greer* was part of a Nazi plan to control the Atlantic, in preparation for an assault upon the Western Hemisphere. The time for active defense had come, he added; hereafter American ships and planes would protect all ships within the area between the United States and Iceland. Moreover, he continued, he had ordered the army and navy to shoot on sight at all German and Italian war vessels in the American patrol area.

The President's speech was in effect a declaration of an undeclared naval war against Germany—the perhaps inevitable outcome of the adoption of the Lend-Lease Act and the American decision to get supplies through the troubled waters to Great Britain. Not only did a large majority of Congress and the public approve this forward step; the majority also approved when Roosevelt finally asked Congress on October 9, 1941, to revise the Neutrality Act of 1939. He requested permission to arm American merchantmen and indirectly suggested that Congress should permit American ships to enter war zones and belligerent ports. While debate on these proposals proceeded, a German submarine torpedoed the destroyer *Kearny* on the night of October 16–17, with the loss of eleven lives. A fierce debate ensued in both houses, and isolationists made a determined last stand. But the Senate on November 7 and the House on November 13 voted to allow merchantmen to arm and to pass through the war zone to British ports.

Meanwhile the undeclared naval war in the North Atlantic proceeded. A submarine sank the destroyer *Reuben James* with the loss of 115 lives on October 31, but there was no such general agitation for war as had followed German attacks on American ships in early 1917. The American people now clearly understood their immediate task—to deliver supplies to Britain and Russia regardless of the peril. They assumed that task not gladly, for they knew that it involved the risk of war, but with grim determination and still fervent hope that somehow they could avoid full-scale participation.

176. *Futile Negotiations with Japan, 1938–1941*

Relations between the United States and Japan were in a state of suspended hostility between the adjournment of the Brussels Conference of 1938 and the outbreak of the German-Polish crisis in the spring of 1939. During this period the military clique in the Tokyo government were pressing for an alliance with Germany to offset Soviet and American power. The Japanese Army was also undertaking extensive military operations against Russian forces along the Manchurian border. The army's hopes for an alliance with the Nazis were momentarily blasted by the Nazi-Soviet Pact in August 1939; meanwhile, however, the Imperial government undertook a diplomatic campaign to force the British to recognize Japanese conquests in China. The Chamberlain government surrendered to Japanese demands on July 24, 1939, by recognizing that the Japanese army was supreme in the areas it occupied.

The announcement of this agreement galvanized the American government's determination to play a stronger role in the Far East. Therefore, the President sent to Tokyo on July 26 the necessary six months' notice of the possible abrogation of the Japanese-American commercial treaty of 1911. It was no idle warning but a stern threat that after January 26, 1940, the United States might deny to the Japanese access to the source from which they obtained more than half the raw materials, especially iron, steel, and oil, for their war machine.

The threat of full-scale war with Russia and economic retaliation by the United States restrained the extreme militarists in Japan and prevented the Imperial government from embarking upon new conquests following the outbreak of war in Europe. Instead, the Japanese ended the border conflict with Soviet forces in September and next launched a strenuous effort to liquidate the "China Incident." Moreover, the Japanese Foreign Office opened negotiations with the State Department in December 1939 to prevent imposition of the threatened American embargo. These talks ended in a stalemate because neither government would recede on the basic issue of China. The Washington administration simply reaffirmed its traditional position and declared that for the time being it would not end the export of American war supplies.

Japanese-American official relations were relatively quiescent during the early months of 1940, especially after a new moderate government under Admiral Mitsumasa Yonai came to power in Tokyo on January 14, 1940. In the United States, however, public opinion was moving strongly toward the application of an embargo. In fact, sentiment in Congress was so vociferous that administration leaders suppressed it only with difficulty.

The State Department's policy of threatening economic retaliation might well have succeeded had not Germany's triumph in western Europe convinced the Japanese military leaders that the power of Britain, France, and the Netherlands was gone, and that henceforth they would have to deal only with the United States. Army leaders and expansionists were excited by the opportunity to seize or fall heir to French Indo-China and the Netherlands East Indies and by the hope of an alliance with Germany. They caused

THE COMING OF THE WAR
IN THE PACIFIC, 1939-1941

1000 MILES

ARCTIC OCEAN

ALASKA (U.S.A.)

SOVIET UNION

S I B E R I A

Yakutsk

Novo-Sibirsk

LAKE BAIKAL

KAMCHATKA

SEA OF OKHOTSK

Irkutsk

Chita

SAKHALIN

KARAFUTO

Ulan Bator

MONGOLIA

INNER MONGOLIA

MANCHUKUO

Harbin

Khabar-ovsk

ETOROFU

KURILE IS. (JAP.)

Peking

Mukden

Vladivostok

⑥ DEPARTURE OF PEARL HARBOR STRIKING FORCE NOV. 26, 1941

Tientsin

Dairen

KOREA

SEA OF JAPAN

NORTH

SINKIANG

HUANG HO

TIBET

CHINA

Nanking

Shanghai

Tokyo

Lhasa

Chungking

YANGTZE

EAST CHINA SEA

JAPANESE EMPIRE

① BOMBING OF PANAY DEC. 12, 1937

PACIFIC OCEAN

BURMA ROAD

Foochow

BONIN IS. (JAP.)

INDIA (BR.)

Amoy

SALWEEN

Canton

⑬ HONG KONG FALLS DEC. 25, 1941

FORMOSA

RYUKYU ISLANDS

Hanoi

HAINAN

② OCCUPIED BY JAPS FEB. 10, 1939

SOUTH

BURMA (BR.)

Rangoon

IRRAWADDY

④ JAPS OCCUPY N. INDOCHINA SEPT. 22, 1940

⑧ JAP LANDINGS DEC. 10, 1941

LUZON

MARIANAS (JAP.)

FRENCH INDOCHINA

PHILIPPINE IS. (U.S.A.)

PACIFIC

THAILAND

Bangkok

⑤ JAPS OCCUPY S. INDOCHINA JULY 24, 1941

⑨ JAP LANDINGS DEC. 10, 1941

GUAM (U.S.A.)

MEKONG

CAMRANH BAY

Saigon

③ JAPS OCCUPY SPRATLY I. MAR. 13, 1939

(JAPANESE MANDATE)

OCEAN

YAP

KRA ISTHMUS

⑫ JAP LANDINGS DEC. 24, 1941

MINDANAO

PALAU

CAROLINE IS.

⑦ JAP LANDINGS DEC. 8, 1941

BR. N. BORNEO

⑪ JAP LANDINGS DEC. 20, 1941

MALAY STATES (BR.)

⑩ JAP LANDINGS DEC. 16, 1941

SARAWAK (BR.)

SUMATRA

BORNEO

⑭ SINGAPORE FALLS FEB. 15, 1942

CELEBES

(AUSTR. MANDATE)

I N D I A N

Batavia

D U T C H   E A S T   I N D I E S

NEW GUINEA

PAPUA (AUSTR.)

OCEAN

JAVA

(PORT.) TIMOR

Darwin

AUSTRALIA

TRM

the fall of the Yonai Cabinet on July 16, 1940, and created a new government headed by Prince Fumimaro Konoye, with the boastful Yosuke Matsuoka as Foreign Minister and the ardent expansionist, General Hideki Tojo, as Minister of War.

The new Cabinet, as a first step toward achieving a "new order in Greater East Asia," demanded and after some negotiation obtained from the Vichy government the right to build airfields and station troops in northern Indo-China. As a second and more important step, Konoye, Tojo, Matsuoka and other leaders approved a program for future action on July 27 and September 4, 1940. It envisaged conquest of British, French, and Dutch Far Eastern possessions *if circumstances permitted* and a military alliance with Germany if Hitler approved these plans of conquest. The bargain was struck following the arrival of a new German Ambassador in Tokyo on September 7. It was formally sealed in Berlin on September 27, 1940.[12]

The Washington government moved cautiously to apply such counter-pressure as would not provoke an immediate Japanese thrust into the South Pacific. First, it applied an embargo on the export of aviation gasoline, lubricants, and prime scrap metal to Japan on July 26, 1940. Then, after the Japanese occupied northern Indo-China, the American government announced extension of a new $25,000,000 loan to China on September 25.[13] On the following day it decreed an embargo on the export of all types of scrap iron and steel. Following this action came a virtual embargo in December on the export of iron ore and pig iron, certain chemicals, certain machine tools, and other products. Churchill was encouraged to reopen the Burma Road, the chief supply route between Nationalist China and the outside world, on October 8, 1940.[14] The Japanese protested, but the Washington government's firm stand and rumors of Anglo-American naval cooperation in the Pacific [15] caused the Konoye government to beat a momentary diplomatic retreat.

[12] This was the Tripartite Agreement, or Triple Alliance, in which Japan recognized German and Italian leadership in Europe, Germany and Italy recognized Japan's leadership in the establishment of a "new order" in Greater East Asia, and the three signatories agreed to co-operate militarily, politically, and economically "if one of the three Contracting Powers is attacked by a Power at present not involved in the European War or in the Chinese-Japanese conflict."

[13] Moreover, Roosevelt announced on November 30, 1940, after the Japanese had recognized a puppet Chinese government in Nanking, that the United States would extend a $100,000,000 loan to Nationalist China. This assistance, incidentally, came in the nick of time to save Chiang Kai-shek's government at Chungking from collapse.

[14] The British government had closed the Burma Road in response to Japanese threats on July 12, 1940.

[15] The Washington government, alarmed by the conclusion of the Tripartite Pact, also began in the late autumn of 1940 to consider joint British, American, and Dutch planning for defense of the Western Pacific. Discussions between Washington and London culminated in elaborate Anglo-American staff discussions from January 27 to March 27, 1941, and in British-American-Dutch-Commonwealth staff discussions in Singapore from April 21 to April 27, 1941. During both conferences, known respectively as ABC-1 and ADB, the American representatives refused to make political or military commitments. Instead, they simply joined potential allies in making tentative plans for common action in the event that a Japanese attack forced the United States into the war.

It should be added that the American conferees at the ADB Conference named

The United States by a policy of implicit threatening had, therefore, prevented the Japanese from striking while Britain and America were in direst peril following the fall of France. Even so, it was evident by the beginning of 1941 that Matsuoka and his following of militarists and expansionists had been only momentarily checked. In a speech before the Diet on January 26, 1941, the Foreign Minister frankly stated the impossibility of reconciling Japanese aspirations with American policy. "There is nothing left but to face America," he declared. ". . . Japan must demand America's reconsideration of her attitude, and if she does not listen, there is slim hope for friendly relations between Japan and the United States."

Matsuoka's blunt talk, however, hid the fact that Japan was not yet prepared to engage the western democracies. There was still the danger that the Soviet Union would strike in the north if Japan turned southward; and there was still the faint hope that somehow the United States might be frightened into acquiescing in Japanese plans. In order to safeguard Japan's long exposed northern flank, Matsuoka made a pilgrimage to Berlin, Rome, and Moscow in March and April 1941. Hitler urged that Japan strike immediately at Singapore. Foreign Minister Ribbentrop, intimating that a German-Russian conflict was no longer inconceivable, promised that Germany would attack Russia if the Soviets attacked Japan after she was involved in war with Britain and America. Matsuoka was pleased but not entirely satisfied by these assurances. His supreme objective—a pledge of Soviet neutrality—he obtained in Moscow on April 13, in a Neutrality Pact in which Japan and Russia promised to remain neutral if either power were attacked by one or more countries.

Meanwhile, the Konoye government had begun secret discussions with the Washington government on the other side of the world in a desperate effort to see if any ground for accommodation existed. The background of these negotiations was somewhat odd. An American Catholic bishop and priest discussed the problem of Japanese-American relations with certain Japanese leaders in Tokyo in December 1940. In consequence Premier Konoye asked them to convey a startling message to President Roosevelt—that Japan would for all practical purposes nullify the Tripartite Pact, withdraw its troops from China, and discuss closer economic relations with the United States. The two Catholic emissaries delivered the message to the President in the latter part of January 1941. They were followed soon afterward by two unofficial Japanese representatives, who urged that Roosevelt and Konoye could come to a comprehensive agreement [16] in a personal meeting. After this, they said, the Emperor would dismiss Matsuoka. Hull doubted that Konoye could carry through, but he began discussions in March 1941

certain circumstances—notably a Japanese attack on British and Dutch possessions—in which the United States would enter the war. General Marshall and Admiral Stark, however, refused to approve the ADB report because it contained this commitment.

[16] As elaborated in a proposal brought to the State Department on April 9 by a messenger from the Imperial Army, the Japanese proposed withdrawal of Japanese troops from China by agreement between China and Japan, reaffirmation of the Open Door policy, merger of the Chinese Nationalist regime with the Japanese puppet government in Nanking, resumption of normal economic relations between Japan and the United States, and an American loan to Japan.

with the new Japanese Ambassador, Admiral Kichisaburo Nomura, who had meanwhile been brought into the secret discussions. Hull did not reject the Japanese proposal, which had been put into writing in language much less promising between April 2 and April 5 as a "Draft Understanding." The Secretary of State simply countered on April 16 with a four-point program that embodied traditional American demands concerning China and disavowal of expansion by forceful means.

The Japanese leaders were encouraged by Nomura's report that Hull was eager to negotiate and failed utterly to see the significance of the Secretary's four-point program because of the Ambassador's incompetence. Instead, they gained the impression that the "Draft Understanding" was *the American government's own proposal*. A Liaison Conference in Tokyo on April 21, 1941, decided to continue the discussions and to defer making definite reply until the return of Matsuoka from Moscow. The Foreign Minister was infuriated by the negotiations that had proceeded during his absence. Japan's destiny lay with Germany and in expansion, he argued; strength, not weakness, would prevent the United States from interfering. He countered on May 7 with the suggestion that Japan and the United States sign a neutrality pact. Hull at once rejected the proposal as a carte blanche for Japanese seizure of British, French, and Dutch far eastern possessions. Matsuoka next submitted to the State Department on May 12 a revised and remarkable proposal for a comprehensive understanding. It provided that the United States would cut off aid to Britain, urge Chiang Kai-shek to come to terms with Japan, resume normal trade relations with Japan, and end its ban on Japanese immigration.

Matsuoka's proposal was obviously unacceptable, but Roosevelt and Hull agreed to continue the negotiations, chiefly to buy time in the hope that moderates in the Tokyo government would depose the unruly Foreign Minister. Hull restated the American position on May 31 and more fully on June 6 and 21, therefore, and proposed that the Japanese agree that American aid to Britain was defensive in character and that the Tripartite Pact would not apply if such aid led to a German-American clash. At this moment, when it seemed that the opponents of war with the United States might gain the upper hand in Tokyo, the German attack on Russia removed the threat of Soviet interference and encouraged the Japanese leaders to decide to occupy all of Indo-China, perhaps preparatory to an attack on Singapore.

The German assault on Russia also momentarily disrupted the desultory Japanese-American talks then in progress. Matsuoka apparently wanted to end the negotiations altogether and loudly demanded that Japan strike at once at the Soviet Union. But he carried his arrogance too far and was deposed on July 16 and replaced by the more moderate Admiral Teijiro Toyoda. As the Washington government knew from intercepted Japanese messages to Berlin,[17] the Cabinet shake-up did not mean any immediate change in Japanese policy. In fact, the Imperial government presented a demand to Vichy on July 14 for the immediate occupation of land, air, and naval bases

wwwwwwwwwwwwwwww

[17] Experts in the American government had earlier deciphered the Japanese diplomatic code.

in southern Indo-China by Japanese forces. It was the first step in a general program adopted at an Imperial conference on July 2. Under its provisions Japan would attempt to conclude the "China incident," avoid war with the USSR for the time being, and advance southward (this provision was intentionally vague) even at the risk of war with the United States and Great Britain.

The Washington government reacted swiftly and violently. The United States, Hull told Nomura on July 23, 1941, could only conclude that the occupation of southern Indo-China was the prelude to further Japanese conquests and could see no point in further discussions. On the following day, after Vichy had surrendered to the Japanese demands, the President received the Japanese Ambassador, hinted that he was contemplating an embargo on the export of oil to Japan, and warned that a Japanese attack on the Dutch East Indies would result in serious consequences. On the other hand, Roosevelt continued, if Japan would withdraw from Indo-China he would take leadership in a movement to neutralize that French colony and help Japan to find access to raw materials.

The President, however, was done with mere parleying. He impounded all Japanese funds in the United States, closed the Panama Canal to Japanese shipping, and called the Philippine militia into active service on July 26. Moreover, on August 1 he forbade the export to Japan of a number of vital materials, including oil that could be refined into aviation gasoline, while the British and Dutch governments applied similar sanctions.

This decisive retaliation put the Tokyo authorities in the dilemma of having to choose between a modified retreat or a desperate war with the United States. Although some extremists welcomed the prospect of war, the naval leaders were reluctant to risk hostilities and frankly admitted that the Empire would probably be defeated in a protracted conflict. The Cabinet, therefore, maneuvered to find a solution that would include both Japanese occupation of southern Indo-China and peace with the United States. Premier Konoye proposed on August 7 that the President meet him in personal conference to discuss means of relieving the tension. Roosevelt gave his reply on August 17, after his return from the Atlantic Conference. If Japan made any further aggressive moves the United States would take all necessary steps to safeguard American security. However, if the Japanese government sincerely desired to come to agreement along lines already laid down by the United States, then the American government would be willing to resume the exploratory discussions disrupted by the Japanese occupation of Indo-China.

Konoye, faced squarely with the choice of war or agreement with the United States, now moved desperately to persuade the President to join him in a personal conference. Foreign Minister Toyoda reiterated Konoye's proposal to Ambassador Joseph C. Grew on August 18, while Konoye ordered a ship to stand in readiness to take him to the meeting. Then Nomura presented the Imperial government's reply on August 28 to the American note of August 17: The Japanese government would withdraw its troops from Indo-China as soon as the "China Incident" was settled; it would not undertake expansion southward or make war on the Soviet Union unless attacked; and it agreed that the principles set forth in the American note were "the prime requisites of a true peace." In a subsequent note of clarification dated September 4 the Japanese government made perhaps its most important offer, namely, that Japan would not feel bound by the Tripartite Pact to go to war if the United States became involved in a defensive war with Germany.

Roosevelt was so pleased by the Japanese response that he was ready to give immediate consent to the proposal for a conference. But Hull urged caution and insisted that the two governments agree upon *the fundamental issue of China* before the chiefs of state met. Despite warnings from Tokyo that only some bold stroke could restrain the war party, the President accepted the State Department's view that Japan would not attack and that a policy of continued firmness would force the Imperial government to surrender. Thus Roosevelt replied on September 3 that he would be glad to confer with Konoye, but that basic differences, particularly on China, would have to be cleared up first.

The President's reply in the circumstances spelled the doom, not only of the projected conference, but of peace as well. Whether the momentous decision was wise or foolish will be long debated by historians. Defenders of the administration have argued that agreement on important issues was impossible, and that in any event Konoye could not have forced the army to make the concessions necessary to preserve the peace. On the other hand, Roosevelt's antagonists have maintained that the administration rejected Konoye's invitation in order to goad Japan into attacking the United States. At least on the point of the administration's intentions the records are full and revealing. They indicate that the President and State Department, far from desiring war, were convinced the Japanese could not undertake hostilities and would retreat in the face of a firm American policy.

In view of the primacy of the Nazi danger and the likelihood that the United States would soon be drawn into the European war, American policy in the Far East might well have been directed at one objective only—maintenance of peace with Japan on any terms short of countenancing further Japanese aggressions in the southwest Pacific. Such a policy might have necessitated unfreezing Japanese assets, lifting the embargo on export of oil and metals, and easing the pressure on Japan to withdraw immediately from China. There is considerable evidence that such concessions by the United States at this time—that is, early September 1941—would have enormously strengthened the Japanese moderates and might have sufficed to preserve the status quo and gain precious time.

Roosevelt and Hull were influenced by a group of Sinophiles in the State Department into believing that Japan would not fight, and that it would not matter much if she did. Instead of making any concessions they continued to press demands for Japanese withdrawal from China, demands that were impossible in the circumstances. The time might have come when the United States and Britain could have forced a showdown on China without having to go to war.[18] But that time would be after the defeat of Ger

mmmmmmmmmmm

[18] From a sheerly strategic point of view, the continuation of the Sino-Japanese War served Anglo-American interests by keeping large Japanese forces occupied, draining Japanese resources, and deterring the Japanese from expanding into the southwestern Pacific. Perceiving the rather obvious fact that involvement in China in part prevented the Japanese from expanding northward, the Soviet leaders played a skillful game of

many, when the two democracies were invincible, not in the late summer of 1941, when they were weak, and when wisdom demanded a policy of delay.

177.   *Pearl Harbor*

Events following the delivery of Roosevelt's reply of September 3 confirm the thesis that the effect of American policy was to strengthen the extremists and perhaps tip the balance in Tokyo in favor of the war party. An Imperial Conference met for a showdown on policy on September 6, soon after receipt of the President's reply. The Army Chief of Staff urged immediate preparations, if not a decision, for war. The Navy Chief of General Staff agreed that Japan might have to resort to hostilities to avoid economic destruction as a consequence of the American embargo. Emperor Hirohito, however, demanded that negotiations be continued in the hope of peaceful understanding. The Imperial Conference ended in agreement to continue military preparations, to be completed by the end of October, and to seek for the last time American acquiescence in the minimum Japanese program.[19]

Premier Konoye met secretly with Ambassador Grew during the evening of September 6, immediately after the Imperial Conference, and reiterated his desire for a personal meeting with Roosevelt. Konoye renewed his invitation on September 22, and Grew added a plea for acceptance. Hull replied on October 2, again declaring that the two governments must agree on fundamental issues, principally China, before a general conference could succeed. To Konoye, Washington's final refusal spelled the doom of his efforts to prevent war. He and the navy leaders tried to persuade the army chieftains that Japan could not defeat America and had to evacuate China as a prerequisite to peace. The army adamantly refused and insisted that there was no recourse but war. Then Konoye sent a special emissary to Washington to plead the absolute necessity for some kind of speedy agreement. Japan was even willing to evacuate China, the messenger told Welles on October 13.

But the situation in Tokyo was passing out of Konoye's control. The Premier had a long conference with high military and naval officials on October 12 and argued in behalf of agreement to withdraw from China. But the War Minister, General Tojo, instantly vetoed the proposal. Further discussions revealed that the Premier and the army group had reached an im-

preserving peace with Japan while at the same time sending a modicum of supplies to Nationalist China to make certain that the Japanese would have to continue their now useless war in China.

[19] This the Imperial Conference defined as (1) Anglo-American agreement to close the Burma Road, cease all aid to Nationalist China, and not obstruct a settlement of the "China incident" by Japan, (2) Anglo-American agreement to make no offensive preparations in the Far East, and (3) Anglo-American agreement to resume normal trade relations with Japan and assist Japan in her negotiations with Siam and the Netherlands Indies. In return Japan would (1) agree not to use Indo-China as a base for offensive operations except against China, (2) withdraw troops from Indo-China after establishment of peace in the Far East, (3) guarantee the neutrality of the Philippines, (4) refrain from war against Russia unless attacked, and (5) agree to clarify Japanese obligations under the Tripartite Pact.

passe, and Konoye resigned on October 16. As his successor the Emperor named Tojo himself, after the General had promised that he would continue negotiations.

The fall of the Konoye government only intensified the conflict in Tokyo between the army and the antiwar group. The Emperor, supported by the navy, demanded reconsideration of the provisions for early military operations adopted at the Imperial Conference on September 6. Debate proceeded from mid-October through November 5. The new Foreign Minister, Shigenori Togo, tried to find a solution for the evacuation of China, but the army would not yield and insisted that war was preferable to the gradual economic ruin of the Empire. Togo did persuade the army to agree to one last effort at compromise with the United States. The military chieftains agreed on November 5 but won the Emperor's consent to preparations for immediate attack if the negotiations had yielded no agreement by about November 25. On November 5 the army and navy also issued war orders, to go into effect in early December if diplomacy had failed.

As a consequence negotiations proceeded anew in Washington between November 7 and December 7. The repetitious details need not be given here. It suffices to say that neither government retreated from its irrevocable position on the key issue of China, and that the American leaders continued the discussions mainly in the hope of deferring the conflict that they now thought was practically inevitable.

The utter hopelessness of the deadlock was further revealed after a special Japanese envoy, Saburu Kurusu, arrived at the White House on November 17. After talking with Roosevelt and Hull, Kurusu and Nomura were unable to persuade their government to agree to a stopgap proposal providing for immediate evacuation of southern Indo-China, which the United States was willing to accept. Then Nomura on November 20 presented what was in fact Japan's final offer, actually, in Japanese eyes, an ultimatum. It was not entirely impossible as a basis for bargaining; [20] indeed, Foreign Minister Togo was confident that it would provide the basis for agreement.

Actually, Roosevelt had already drafted in his own hand a proposal for a temporary modus vivendi not entirely dissimilar from the Japanese proposal, except that the President's draft also provided for Japanese neutrality in the event of American hostilities in Europe. Thus the State Department, after receiving the Japanese note of November 20, drafted a counterproposal of its own, to run for three months. Its crucial provisions embodied mutual pledges against military action in the South Pacific, a Japanese promise to evacuate southern Indo-China "forthwith," an American promise to restore normal trade relations with Japan, and a statement

 wwwwwwwwwwwww

[20] It included (1) Japanese-American agreement not to invade any area in Southeast Asia and the South Seas, except for Indo-China, (2) Japanese-American co-operation in guaranteeing mutual access to raw materials in the Netherlands Indies, (3) resumption of normal Japanese-American trade relationships, (4) American promise to put no obstacle in the way of Japan's attempts to make peace with China, (5) Japanese promise to withdraw from all of Indo-China upon conclusion of a Sino-Japanese peace, and (6) Japanese promise to withdraw from southern to northern Indo-China upon the conclusion of this agreement.

to the effect that the United States would "not look with disfavor upon the inauguration of conversations between the Government of China and the Government of Japan directed toward a peaceful settlement of their differences."

We will never know whether the American proposal could have saved the peace of the Pacific. Roosevelt and Hull decided not to submit the modus vivendi as a consequence of two events on November 25—receipt in Washington of news of the movement of Japanese troopships off Formosa, and the violent reaction of the British and Chinese governments to the proposed modus vivendi. The Chinese frankly warned that adoption of the modus vivendi would cause a collapse of their resistance. Receipt of a cable from Churchill on that same day evidently clinched Hull's decision to abandon the project. Hull called in Nomura and Kurusu on the following day, November 26, and formally rejected the Japanese proposal of November 20. He then proceeded to read the text of a draft "Mutual Declaration of Policy" and "Steps to be taken by the Government of the United States and by the Government of Japan." The "Mutual Declaration" was a reaffirmation of the principles that Hull had somewhat tediously enunciated many times. The proposed "Steps to be taken" provided for Japanese evacuation not only of Indo-China *but of China as well*, and for support of the Nationalist government by the Japanese.

To say that Hull's note was an ultimatum is not quite correct. But in the circumstances it was hardly responsive and, taken as American rejection of the Japanese proposal of November 20, it spelled the doom of the negotiations. Receipt of Hull's note in Tokyo on November 27 stunned the Japanese leaders, who concluded that it signified American insistence upon war. The Japanese deferred final decision until Nomura and Kurusu had conferred with President Roosevelt on November 27. When news of the President's refusal to consider any modus vivendi reached Tokyo, an Imperial Conference on December 1 decided on hostilities. To responsible Japanese leaders an uncertain war, which they really did not expect to win, seemed the only way to avoid slow economic strangulation or humiliating surrender that would spell Japan's end as a great power.

Meanwhile, Japanese preparations for probable conflict had been proceeding on the assumption that one must be prepared to fight if diplomacy fails. A carrier task force left the Kuriles on November 25 to attack the great American naval base in Hawaii, Pearl Harbor, while large army forces were poised in southern Indo-China to strike at Malaya. The Washington leaders knew from intercepted messages only that the Japanese would attack somewhere soon. They recognized that an assault on the Philippines and Guam was possible, but they concluded that Tokyo would avoid such direct provocation to the United States. Thus the American government was more concerned on the eve of war over what to do in the event of a Japanese attack on Malaya and the Dutch East Indies than with immediate defense of American territory. When news of the movement of large Japanese forces against Malaya reached Washington on December 6, Roosevelt dispatched an urgent personal appeal to Hirohito, warning that the present tension could not last much longer and urging him to take some action to dispel the threat of war.

The Japanese reply to Hull's note of November 26 began to come to

Washington over the wires in the afternoon of Saturday, December 6. The first sections, which were decoded by early evening, revealed Japan's rejection of the note; the final section, which announced termination of the negotiations, was in the President's hands by the morning of December 7. The attack on Pearl Harbor had already occurred, and first reports from the stricken base had reached Washington by the time that Nomura and Kurusu were able to deliver the message to Hull.

Meanwhile, American military and naval commanders in the Pacific had been duly but not strenuously warned on November 24 and 27 that surprise Japanese attacks were likely. Like their superiors in Washington, however, they expected the Japanese to strike at Malaya, not at them. The commanders in Hawaii, Admiral Husband E. Kimmel and General Walter C. Short, were unconcerned as the "day of infamy" approached. Kimmel had concentrated virtually his entire fleet in Pearl Harbor; fearing sabotage, Short had disposed his airplanes and antiaircraft guns in such a manner as to make successful defense impossible. Neither commander had established an effective air patrol. Thus the carrier task force under Admiral Chuchi Nagumo approached Hawaii from the northwest undetected.

The first wave of Japanese airplanes, 189 in number, attacked airfields at 7:55 a.m. on December 7, 1941, and then struck the fleet anchored in the harbor. A second wave of 171 Japanese planes followed at 8:50. The navy and marine corps were unable to get a single plane off the ground. An army fighter squadron at Haleiwa, which the Japanese overlooked, got a few planes into the air and destroyed several of the attackers. A few anti-aircraft batteries were operating by the time of the second major assault. And several naval craft were able to get into action and attack Japanese submarines. Otherwise, the Japanese were unopposed and raked and bombed at will. When the last planes turned toward their carriers at about 9:45 the great American bastion in the Pacific was a smoking shambles. Practically every airplane on the island of Oahu was either destroyed or disabled. All eight battleships in Pearl Harbor were disabled—two of them, *Oklahoma* and *Arizona*, were destroyed or sunk. Three cruisers and three destroyers were heavily damaged or destroyed. And 2,323 men of both services were dead. The cost to the Japanese was twenty-nine airplanes, five midget submarines, and one fleet submarine.

First reports of the attack came to Washington at about two in the afternoon, while later news told of other Japanese attacks on the Philippines, Hong Kong, Wake Island, Midway Island, Siam, and Malaya, and of a Japanese declaration of war against the United States and Great Britain. After Cabinet meetings in the afternoon and evening, the President called congressional leaders to the White House and reviewed dispatches he had received. He appeared before the two houses on the following day, December 8, excoriated the "unprovoked and dastardly attack by Japan," and asked Congress to recognize the obvious state of war that existed. It was done within an hour and with only one dissenting vote in the House of Representatives. Roosevelt had deliberately avoided mention of Germany and Italy in his war message, in order to leave the decision for full-fledged war for the time being to Hitler. The *Führer* was delighted by the Pearl Harbor attack and responded to the Japanese request for a German declaration of war against the United States on December 11. Mussolini followed suit at once. The President and Congress reciprocated during the afternoon of the same day.

Words are inadequate to describe the shock and indignation that the American people felt as they heard the news of the Japanese attack over their radios on the afternoon of Pearl Harbor day. They did not know that their armed forces had suffered the most humiliating defeat in American history by a foreign foe, or the desperate circumstances that impelled the Japanese to undertake a suicidal war. The American people only thought that they had been treacherously attacked. And in their anger they forgot all the partisan quarrels and debates over foreign policy that had so long divided them and resolved with firm determination to win the war that the Japanese had begun. The agony of doubt was over; the issue was now fully joined. The American people had embarked, not gladly upon a second crusade, but grimly upon a war for survival.

PART III

═══

THE
SECOND WORLD WAR
AND AN
UNCERTAIN PEACE
1941–1966

*IN WHICH the American people
emerge triumphant after fighting on
two fronts in the greatest war in
history, strengthen the New Deal
structure, and achieve unprecedented
economic heights at home, only to
discover that the quest of peace and
security abroad is unending.*

CHAPTER

23

The Second World War: The American Home Front

Not since the dark days of the Revolution had the American people confronted so dire a military menace or so staggering a task as during the Second World War. Within a few months after Japanese bombs fell on Pearl Harbor, the ensign of the Rising Sun floated triumphantly over all the outposts and bastions of the far Pacific region, while Hitler and his armies stood poised to strike at the Middle East and join forces with the Japanese in India.

It was perhaps fortunate that the American people in December 1941 little knew how long the war would last and what the costs would be. However, they had certain advantages that made victory possible: courageous allies, unity unprecedented in American history, enormous resources and industrial capacity, superb political and military leadership, and, most important, determination to win. These factors combined from 1941 to 1945 to achieve miracles of production that made earlier American war efforts look small by comparison.

The astonishing thing, however, was the fact that Americans could engage in total war without submitting to the discipline of total war at home. To be sure, the war intensified certain social tensions and created new problems of adjustment; but the mass of Americans took the war in stride, without emotional excitement or hysteria.

178. Mobilizing Manpower for War

The adoption of the war resolutions by Congress found the United States in the midst of a sizable rearmament campaign, the momentum of which was daily increasing. Planners in the War and Navy departments had faced up to the long-run requirements for defeat of the Axis and presented a Victory Plan to the President in September 1941. In addition, thanks to the extension of the terms of service of the draftees of 1940, the American army in December 1941 was already a formidable force of about 1,600,000 men, a majority of whom had recently been seasoned in battle maneuvers.

All these preparations saved precious time. Meanwhile, Congress, soon after approving the war declarations, ordered the registration of all men between the ages of twenty and forty-four for war service and of men

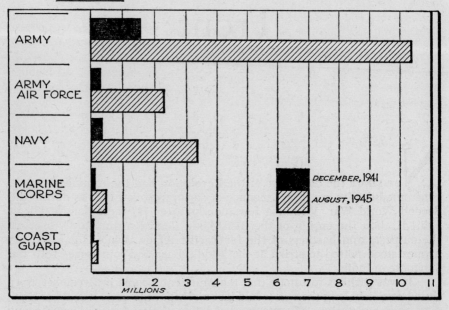

EXPANSION OF U.S. ARMED FORCES
1941–1945

between forty-five and sixty-five for potential labor service, and extended the terms of all servicemen to six months beyond the duration of hostilities. The drafting of men beyond the age of thirty-eight was soon abandoned; on the other hand, the President on November 13, 1942, signed an amendment to the Selective Service Act lowering the draft age to eighteen.

All told, draft boards registered some 31,000,000 men, of whom 9,867,707 were inducted into service. Including volunteers, a total of 15,145,115 men and women served in the armed services before the end of the war—10,420,000 in the army, 3,883,520 in the navy, 599,693 in the marines, and 241,902 in the Coast Guard. It was an immense mobilization, yet by European standards it was far from being a total one. The Soviet Union mobilized 22,000,000 men and women, Germany, 17,000,000, and the British Empire, 12,000,000.

Housing and training the huge American force was a task of incredible size. There was first the job of building new army and Air Forces camps, posts, and bases at home and expanding old ones. The army had provided housing for nearly 5,000,000 men in the United States by the end of March 1943, when three fourths of the army's home construction projects were completed. Then came the task of training men for combat in New Guinea jungles, Bavarian Alps, and African deserts, as well as in the French and German countryside. The training, of course, occurred in stages: thirteen weeks in basic training, twenty-six weeks' additional training after the soldier was assigned to a division, and a final thirteen weeks in maneuvers and field exercises.

Because the first offensive blows could be delivered from the air, the Army Air Forces were authorized at the outset of American participation to increase their strength to two and one-third million men and were given highest priority on manpower and materials. When the Japanese attacked Pearl Harbor the AAF had 292,000 men and 9,000 planes, 1,100 of them fit for combat. When the Japanese surrendered in August 1945, the AAF had enlisted 2,300,000 men and women and had 72,000 planes in service.

The third branch of the army, the Services of Supply, had grown in strength by the end of the war to over 1,750,000 men and executed its prodigious task with a minimum of hardship to the civilian population. The Services of Supply alone operated between 1943 and 1945 a fleet of 1,537 ships, paid out over $22,000,000,000 in pay and allowances, processed more than $75,000,000,000 in army contracts, managed 3,700 posts or cantonments in the United States, transported 7,370,000 men and 101,-750,000 tons of cargo, and administered a far-flung medical service.

Thanks to the wealth, technology, and industrial and agricultural capacity of his country, the American soldier was the best-paid, best-clothed, and by 1943 the best-equipped fighting man in the world. In that year, for example, Americans achieved not only a quantitative but also a decided qualitative superiority in fighter planes and bombers. Even in areas of research in which the Germans had a head start, such as atomic fission, American scientists and engineers had won decisive advantages by 1945. On the battlefield the best American weapons were the light semi-automatic Garand rifle and the multiple-driven truck. They combined to give a superiority in firepower and mobility that the Germans were never able to overcome in spite of general equality in machine guns, mortars, rocket-launched missiles, and artillery.[1]

wwwwwwwwwwwwwww

[1] In certain categories, however, the Germans retained a marked advantage. The German 88-mm rifle, for example, was superior to the American 90-mm rifle. Use of a smokeless, flashless powder gave the German infantryman a great advantage over his American foe, who had to use powder that exposed his position every time he fired. Moreover, the American medium Sherman tank was no match from 1943 to 1945 for the heavy German Tiger and Panther tanks. Not until production of the heavy Pershing tank in the winter of 1944–5 were American armored divisions able to meet German *Panzer* forces on equal terms.

In the meantime, the navy, marines, and Coast Guard had grown from relative weakness after the Pearl Harbor disaster to dimensions of gigantic strength at the time of the Japanese surrender. On December 7, 1941, the navy had a complement of 337,349 men, in addition to 66,048 in the Marine Corps and 25,336 in the Coast Guard. By the summer of 1945, the navy's manpower had increased to 3,408,347 officers and men, the Marine Corps' to 484,631, and the Coast Guard's to 170,480. Before Japanese bombs disabled or sank part of the Pacific Fleet at Pearl Harbor, the navy had in operation some 4,500 ships, including seventeen battleships, seven fleet carriers, eighteen heavy and nineteen light cruisers, 200 destroyers and torpedo boats, and 114 submarines. By the end of 1945 the navy had grown to more than 91,000 ships of all sizes, including twenty-four battleships, two large cruisers, twenty-nine fleet carriers, seventy-three escort carriers, twenty-three heavy and forty-five light cruisers, 489 destroyers and torpedo boats, 500 escort vessels, and 274 submarines.

Finally, there was mobilization of women for war service: the Women's Auxiliary Corps, which grew in size to 100,000 and sent 17,000 WACs overseas; the navy's counterpart, the WAVEs, who numbered about 86,000 at the end of the war; and the Coast Guard's SPARs and the Marine Corps' Women's Reserve. Working as stenographers, clerks, technicians, cryptographers, and the like, female contingents not only performed indispensable functions but released over 200,000 men for service on battle fronts.

179. *The Price of Victory*

Measured in human costs, the price of victory in the Second World War came high to the American people—253,573 dead, 651,042 wounded, 114,205 prisoners, and 65,834 men missing. In all theaters to the Japanese surrender, the army suffered 943,222 casualties—201,367 killed, 570,783 wounded, 114,205 prisoners, and 56,867 missing; the Navy, Marine Corps, and Coast Guard, 141,432 casualties—52,206 killed, 80,259 wounded, and 8,967 missing. Relative to total numbers, the 36,700 airmen who died in combat made the greatest sacrifice, but the infantry divisions, with only one fifth of total army personnel, suffered 70 per cent of all army casualties. For the men who died, however, Americans and their allies exacted a fearful retribution. Germany and Italy suffered 373,600 dead and lost 8,108,983 prisoners to the Allies on the Western Front alone. The Japanese gave up 1,093,000 battle dead in areas outside China.

For their relatively low death lists, Americans in large measure could thank the medical corps of the several services. Although American soldiers lived and fought in deserts and jungles as well as in the temperate zones, the death rate from nonbattle causes was no higher than the rate for similar groups at home. And for the sick and wounded there was extraordinary care, while use of sulfa drugs, penicillin, and whole blood brought such healing and relief from wounds and shock as would not have been possible a decade before. The result was to cut the rate of deaths from disease and battle wounds in half from the rate of the First World War. Almost 59 per cent of the soldiers wounded in the Second World War were returned to battle duty. Moreover, increased use of psychiatry enabled the Medical Corps to return from 40 to 60 per cent of the battle-shock cases to combat and another 20 to 30 per cent to limited duty. Finally, for the maimed and psychologically ill, the army established twenty-five convalescent centers. They offered training in new skills and helped to prepare the permanently disabled for useful civilian life.

180. *"Scientists Against Time"*

In the last analysis the war was won as much in the laboratory and on the testing ground as on the battlefield. American scientists at the outset of the war lagged far behind the Germans in research in atomic fission, jet propulsion, and rockets, and behind the British in work on jet propulsion, radar, and other electronic devices. Alarmed by the prospect of his country entering the war scientifically unprepared, Dr. Vannevar Bush, president of the Carnegie Institution of Washington, persuaded the President in June 1940 to establish the National Defense Research Committee (NDRC), with representatives from the defense departments, universities, and private industry. Then Roosevelt reorganized the government's research program in June 1941 by creating the Office of Scientific Research and Development (OSRD). Bush was director of the OSRD, with power to approve or veto all projects and initiate research.

Bush and his colleagues had accomplished a full mobilization of scientific personnel and facilities by the autumn of 1941. Let us look briefly at some of the most significant results of this great effort—the development of radar and electronic devices, rockets for combat use, the proximity fuse, and, finally, the atomic bomb.

Work on radar, or radio detection, had been in progress in the United States, Britain, and Germany since the early 1930's, but it was the British who first perfected radar and put it to large-scale use during the great German air assault of 1940–1. Radar sets in patrol planes enabled the British and American navies to bring the German submarines under control.[2] Radar in fighters enabled the air forces to launch powerful night interceptors; in bombers, it provided a generally accurate bombsight. As the basis of a new method of fire-control, it gave eyes to guns as well as to airplanes and ships. The American armed services alone had received $3,000,000,000 worth of radar equipment and $71,000,000 worth of Loran, a long-range navigational aid, by July 1945.

The outbreak of the war found research in the field of rocket warfare well advanced in Britain and Germany and practically nonexistent in the United States. But NDRC scientists had a sizable research program under way by the end of 1941. One of the first results was the "bazooka," a tube rocket-launcher perfected in 1942, which could be operated by two infantrymen and discharged a rocket powerful enough to destroy a tank. Subsequently, scientists developed an incredible variety of rocket-launchers

[2] Perhaps even more effective in anti-submarine operations was so-called sonar, or underwater sound detection apparatus, developed by the NDRC in conjunction with the Harvard Underwater Sound Laboratory.

and rockets for use in land combat and anti-aircraft operations, by air-planes, and in ship-to-shore bombardments. What this meant in terms of increased firepower can perhaps best be illustrated by the fact that a single fighter plane carrying rockets could discharge a salvo as heavy as a de-stroyer's, while "a squadron of Grumman Hellcats carrying Tiny Tims [an 11.75-inch aircraft rocket] packs a punch comparable to a broadside from a division of heavy cruisers." [3]

The Germans, on the other hand, made the greatest progress in rocket missiles and scored their greatest success with the V-1 flying bomb and the V-2. The latter was a rocket that flew 3,400 miles an hour and carried a warhead of one ton of explosives. The V-1 traveled so slowly that Allied anti-aircraft gunners and fighters could shoot it down, but no defense against the V-2, except the capture of the sites from which it was launched, was ever found.

One of the most brilliant scientific achievements of the war was the development, exclusively by the OSRD, of the proximity fuse. It was a miniature radio set in the head of the shell that detonated it by proximity to the target. Proximity fuses were first used by the navy against Japanese aircraft in 1943 and next in quantity against German V-1 bombs in 1944. Fearing that the Germans would recover an unexploded shell and put the fuse into production, the Joint Chiefs of Staff did not allow the ground forces in Europe to use the new weapon until December 1944. Put into use against the Germans in their Ardennes counteroffensive, the proximity fuse compounded the effectiveness of American artillery and proved dev-astating against German ground troops.

The mobilization of American scientists paid numerous other divi-dends—among them the development of more powerful explosives and fire bombs, of DDT and other weapons in the warfare against insects and vermin, of advanced techniques in the use of blood plasma and whole blood, of penicillin, and of new and deadly gases, which were never used. But the greatest triumph of American scientific and production genius was the development of the atomic bomb. The perfection of this weapon marked an epochal turning point in history.

The Danish physicist Niels Bohr startled a group of American physi-cists assembled in Washington on January 26, 1939, by announcing that two Germans at the Kaiser Wilhelm Institute in Berlin had recently ac-complished atomic fission in uranium. Nuclear physicists had long under-stood the structure of the atom and known that atomic fission was theoreti-cally possible. But the deed had now been done, and the road was open for the development of a bomb more powerful and deadly than the world had ever dreamed of. The grave danger was that the Nazis would produce atomic bombs and literally conquer the world. Therefore, Professor Enrico Fermi of Columbia University, Professor Albert Einstein of the Institute for Advanced Study, and others indirectly persuaded the President to begin a small research program. It was not until 1940, however, that work began in earnest. Research at Columbia, California, and other universities had confirmed the possibilities of atomic fission through a chain reaction by

[3] James Phinney Baxter 3d, *Scientists Against Time* (Boston, 1946), p. 46.

the summer of 1941. The chief problem now was to find a fissionable element in sufficient quantity. Earlier experiments had proved that the uranium isotope, U-235, was fissionable; but since U-235 was an infinitesimal part of uranium, the chances were remote of ever accumulating enough of the element to manufacture atomic bombs. This problem was solved by Dr. Ernest Lawrence of the University of California at Berkeley, who used a huge cyclotron, or "atom smasher," to convert the plentiful uranium element, U-238, into a new element, plutonium, which was as fissionable as U-235 and much easier to obtain in quantity.

The next objective became a chain reaction in uranium, that is, the almost simultaneous fission of the uranium atoms through a chain bombardment by neutrons. A group of physicists under the direction of Dr. Arthur H. Compton built the first atomic pile, or apparatus, under the stadium at Stagg Field of the University of Chicago. They produced the first controlled chain reaction on December 2, 1942. Production of an atomic bomb was now possible, provided a means of production could be devised. But what a problem it was! "The technological gap," writes one physicist, "between producing a controlled chain reaction and using it as a large scale power source or an explosive is comparable to the gap between the discovery of fire and the manufacture of a steam locomotive."

OSRD turned the problem over to the Manhattan District of the Army Engineer Corps, headed by General Leslie R. Groves, on May 1, 1943. Drawing upon the combined resources of the OSRD, universities, and private industries, Groves pushed the project with incredible speed. Oak Ridge, Tennessee, eighteen miles west of Knoxville, and Hanford, Washington, were selected as sites for two plutonium producing plants because of the availability of water and electricity. Work on the bomb itself was begun in the spring of 1943 at a laboratory built on a lonely mesa at Los Alamos, outside Santa Fe, New Mexico. Here a group of American, British, and European scientists under direction of Dr. J. Robert Oppenheimer worked night and day to perfect the bomb. They began the final assembly of the first atomic bomb on July 12, 1945, and tension mounted as the fateful day of testing drew near. Nearly $2,000,000,000 had been expended in an effort which yet might fail. The bomb was moved to the air base at Alamogordo and successfully detonated at 5:30 a.m. on July 16. A searing blast of light, many times brighter than the noonday sun, was followed by a deafening roar and a huge mushroom cloud; and relief mixed with a feeling of doom filled the minds of the men who watched the beginning of a new era in human history.

181.   *American Industry Goes to War*

The story of how changing agencies mobilized the American economy for staggering tasks is a tale full of confusion and chaos, incompetence and momentary failure, political intrigue and personal vendetta, but withal one of superb achievement on many home fronts. Government and industry accomplished one of the economic miracles of modern times before it was too late—the production of a stream of goods that provided a high standard of living at home and also supplied the American armed forces with all and the British, French, and Russians with a large part of the resources and matériel for victory.

The task during the first period of industrial mobilization, from August 1939 until about the end of 1941, was the comparatively easy one of utilizing idle plants and men to supply the inchoate American armed forces and the British. The President in August 1939 established the War Resources Board, headed by Edward R. Stettinius, Jr., of the United States Steel Corporation, to advise the administration on industrial mobilization. It soon fell victim to labor and New Deal critics, who charged that it was dominated by Morgan and Du Pont interests.

This was, of course, the time of the "phony war," when Allied victory seemed assured and the necessity for total economic mobilization seemed remote. Nevertheless, the War Resources Board, before its dissolution in October 1939, prepared an industrial mobilization plan that envisaged dictatorial economic authority for a single administrator in the event that the United States entered the war. Roosevelt rejected this plan and asked the former chairman of Wilson's War Industries Board, Bernard M. Baruch, to prepare another. Baruch presented a plan that met all Roosevelt's objections to the War Resources Board's proposal and provided for gradual transition to a total war economy.

Roosevelt, for reasons still unknown, suppressed the Baruch plan and permitted the partial mobilization effort of 1939–40 to drift aimlessly. The fall of France, however, galvanized the President into action, inadequate though it was. Calling for vast new defense appropriations and the production of 50,000 planes a year, he re-established the Advisory Commission to the old and nearly defunct Council of National Defense on May 28, 1940. It was charged with responsibility for getting defense production into high gear. In addition, Congress on June 25 authorized the RFC to finance the building of defense plants and, in the Revenue Act of October 8, 1940, permitted businessmen to write off construction costs over a five-year period.

The Advisory Commission abdicated control over priorities to the Army-Navy Munitions Board and had lost all control of industrial mobilization by December 1940. Roosevelt still stubbornly refused to institute the kind of mobilization plan that Baruch had earlier suggested. Instead, on January 7, 1941, he established the Office of Production Management (OPM), headed by William S. Knudsen of the Advisory Commission and Sidney Hillman of the CIO. It was directed to co-operate with the President and defense secretaries in stimulating and controlling war production. In addition, an Office of Price Administration and Civilian Supply, established on April 11, would work to protect consumers' interests.

The OPM went to work to improve the priorities system, to co-ordinate British and American orders, and especially to help automobile manufacturers prepare for conversion to production of tanks and planes. The result was a gradual shift during the spring and summer of 1941 to a wartime economy. Shortages of electric power, aluminum, steel, railroad rolling stock, and other materials became acute. The priorities system nearly broke down, and internal bickering and public criticism mounted. Roosevelt attempted another superficial reorganization. He suspended the OPM on August 28, 1941, but left an OPM Council. Then he created a Supplies Priorities and Allocation Board, headed by the Sears-Roebuck executive,

Donald M. Nelson, and added other agencies, many of which overlapped in a confusing way. The central force in the new apparatus, however, was the Supplies Priorities and Allocations Board, for it had the power to determine and allocate requirements and supplies for the armed forces, the civilian economy, and the British and the Russians.

The President at last attempted to establish a comprehensive economic mobilization on January 16, 1942, by creating the War Production Board (WPB), under Donald Nelson, to take supreme command of the economic home front. Nelson was an excellent technician, "big, jovial, and self-possessed"; but he failed to meet the test of leadership. He continued to allow the military departments to control priorities; consequently, he never established firm control over production. He permitted the great corporations to obtain a practical monopoly on war production, and this caused a near scandal when the facts were disclosed by a special Senate committee headed by Harry S. Truman of Missouri. Finally, he allowed industrial expansion to get out of hand and occur in the wrong areas.

American industry was booming by the autumn of 1942, but chaos threatened. Alarmed by the prospect, Roosevelt brought Justice James F. Byrnes to the White House as head of the new Office of Economic Stabilization on October 3 and gave him supreme command of the economic effort.[4] One of Byrnes's first moves was to force adoption of a plan that established such complete control over allocation of steel, aluminum, and copper that the priorities difficulty vanished almost at once. Then Roosevelt in May 1943 created the Office of War Mobilization, a sort of high command with control over all aspects of the economy, with Byrnes as Director or "Assistant President." Representative Fred M. Vinson of Kentucky succeeded Byrnes as head of the Office of Economic Stabilization. The home front was at last well organized and under control.

182. *The Miracle of Production*

In spite of all its shortcomings, the American industrial mobilization did succeed far beyond any reasonable expectations. Few persons in 1939 could visualize the potentialities of full employment of manpower, resources, and capital and plant. Still fewer persons knew the proper formula for shifting the economic machinery into high gear. It was the vast expansion of federal expenditures and availability of billions of public capital for investment that invigorated the economy in 1940. And it was the continued high level of federal expenditures, coupled with a program of high taxes and co-operation between labor and management, that effected the miracle of American production from 1941 to 1945.

We can gain some understanding of the total achievement by considering the general performance of the American economy from 1939 through 1945. Measured by depression standards, 1939 was a relatively prosperous year. Gross national product stood at $91,300,000,000—higher

---

[4] Nelson remained as head of the WPB until August 1944, when the President sent him to China to advise Chiang Kai-shek on economic matters. He was succeeded by Julius A. Krug.

in real dollars than during the boom year of 1929. On the other hand, the gross national product had risen, in 1939 dollars, to $166,600,000,000 by 1945. Moreover, from 1939 to 1945 the index of manufacturing production increased 96 per cent, of agricultural production, 22 per cent, and of transportation services, 109 per cent. Contrasted with the performance of the economy during the First World War, when the total national output increased hardly at all, this was a remarkable achievement.

The keys to success in the industrial effort were the conversion of practically the entire American durable goods industry to war production and the application of mass production techniques to manufacture of instruments of warfare. The automobile and automotive parts industries, for example, converted entirely to war production after Pearl Harbor and alone accounted for 20 per cent of the entire output. The electronics and appliance industries made radar equipment, proximity fuses, machine guns, materials for the atomic bomb, and a thousand other items of destruction.

American war production in 1941 was a mere trickle, only $8,400,-000,000 in value. It totaled $30,200,000,000 in value in 1942 and equaled that of Germany, Italy, and Japan combined. American factories by 1944 were producing twice the volume of the Axis partners. A few illustrations will give point to the generalizations. The American airplane industry employed 46,638 persons and produced 5,865 planes in 1939. At the peak of production in 1944, the industry employed 2,102,000 persons and turned out 96,369 aircraft. All told, American factories from Pearl Harbor to the end of the war produced 274,941 military aircraft, 34,500 of which went to the Allies under Lend-Lease.

The war was won as much on the seas as in the air, and production of merchant ships in the United States was an essential ingredient of Allied victory in the battle of supply. The construction of merchant shipping, which had totaled only 1,000,000 tons in 1941, rose from 8,000,000 tons in 1942 to a peak of over 19,000,000 tons in 1943, and, as the need diminished, declined to nearly 16,500,000 tons in 1944 and nearly 8,000,000 tons from January through July of 1945. All told, from July 1, 1940, to August 1, 1945, American shipyards produced a total of 55,239,000 tons of merchant shipping—a tonnage equal to two thirds of the merchant marines of all Allied nations combined.

Perhaps the most remarkable example of the miracle of production was the creation, almost overnight, of a new synthetic rubber industry. Japanese conquest of Malaya and the Netherlands East Indies deprived the United States of 90 per cent of its natural rubber supply at a time when the total stockpile of rubber in the United States amounted to only 540,000 tons and normal consumption exceeded 600,000 tons annually. Total imports could not exceed 175,000 tons during 1942, and the rubber shortage threatened to hobble the entire war effort.

Nelson and the WPB wrestled unsuccessfully with the problem for months, until Undersecretary of the Navy James V. Forrestal took the matter directly to Harry Hopkins and the President. The upshot was Roosevelt's appointment on August 6, 1942, of a special committee headed by Bernard M. Baruch to investigate and recommend. The Baruch committee reported on September 10, warning that the war effort and civilian economy might collapse if a severe rubber shortage occurred. It urged nation-wide gasoline rationing, a thirty-five mile speed limit, and immediate construction of a vast industry to produce rubber synthetically from petroleum. Roosevelt acted at once, appointing William M. Jeffers, president of the Union Pacific Railroad, as Rubber Director in the WPB on September 15, 1942. Jeffers ruthlessly cut his way through the existing priorities system. He had brought into existence by the end of 1943 a synthetic rubber industry that produced 762,000 tons in 1944 and 820,000 tons in the following year.

183. *The Greatest Tax Bill in History*

Americans accustomed to normal federal expenditures of about $8,000,000,000 annually during the 1930's found it difficult to comprehend the magnitude of federal spending during the Second World War. Federal expenditures aggregated $321,212,605,000 from 1941 to 1945. It was a sum roughly twice as large as all previous federal expenditures from 1789 to 1941 and ten times as great as during the First World War. A large part, some 41 per cent, of the money for the war effort came from tax receipts. They totaled nearly $131,000,000,000 during the fiscal years 1941–5. The balance was raised by borrowing from individuals, banks, and corporations. Such borrowing, in turn, increased the gross national debt from $49,000,000,000 in 1941 to $259,000,000,000 in mid-1945. Treasury of-

EXPENDITURES OF THE UNITED STATES GOVERNMENT, 1914–1952

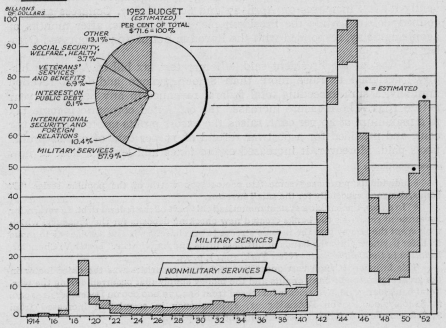

ficials made extraordinary efforts to induce individuals and nonbanking institutions to purchase war bonds in order to reduce inflationary pressures and provide revenue without creating new money. Individuals and non-banking institutions purchased nearly $100,000,000,000 worth of war bonds.[5] The Treasury had to call upon Federal Reserve and commercial banks to take an additional $87,500,000,000 in federal securities.[6]

Meanwhile, the administration and Congress had joined hands to revolutionize the tax structure. On the one hand, the President, Congress, and a vast majority of Americans, rich and poor alike, agreed that the few should not profit from the sacrifices of the many, and that there should be no new millionaires as a result of the defense and war efforts. On the other hand, it became increasingly evident that it would be hopelessly inadequate to use the income tax as a tax principally on wealth, and that the costs of the war would have to be borne in part also by the lower and middle classes.

The administration's tax program evolved gradually in response to the Treasury's need for funds and the necessity for curbing inflation. For example, Congress approved two Revenue Acts in 1940 that increased income and corporation taxes and imposed an excess profits tax graduated to a maximum of 50 per cent. Congress again increased old taxes in 1941 and devised new means of finding revenue. Even so, the income tax still touched only the small minority with upper middle- and upper-class incomes. The turning point came when the President presented his Budget Message to Congress on January 5, 1942. Personal incomes were increasing so much faster than the available supply of consumers' goods that inflation threatened to disrupt the economy. Roosevelt therefore proposed a $7,000,000,000 increase in the tax burden; he appealed even more urgently for tax increases on April 27 and September 7. Congress and the country debated while the President pleaded. Congress, after months of agonizing delay, responded with the Revenue Act of 1942, approved October 21.

It was, as the President said, "the greatest tax bill in American history," designed to raise more than $7,000,000,000 additional revenue annually, a sum exceeding total federal revenues in any peacetime year before 1941. The measure increased the combined corporate income tax to a maximum of 40 per cent, raised the excess profits tax to a flat 90 per cent, and provided for a postwar refund of 10 per cent of excess profits taxes paid. Moreover, it increased excise taxes and levied a host of new

<hr />

[5] Individuals purchased some $40,000,000,000 worth of the popular series "E" bonds, designed especially for the small investor.

[6] "In effect, the banking system monetized this part of the federal debt. In return for government securities the banks created new checking deposits for the Treasury, which then spent the money into the income stream to purchase goods and services or to make transfer payments into the hands of business firms and individuals." Lester V. Chandler, *Inflation in the United States* (New York, 1951), p. 73.

This infusion of such vast quantities of federal securities was the chief factor in the great expansion of bank credits and the money supply that occurred during the war. Total bank loans and investments increased from $54,177,000,000 on December 31, 1940, to $140,277,000,000 on December 31, 1945; money in circulation increased from $7,848,000,000 to $26,746,000,000 during the same period.

ones, and stiffly increased estate and gift taxes. The revolutionary feature of the Revenue Act of 1942, however, was its broadening of the income tax to tap low incomes as well as practically to confiscate large ones. Only 13,000,000 persons had paid federal income taxes in 1941; in contrast, some 50,000,000 persons were caught in the net cast in 1942.[7] The difficulty of collecting income taxes from 50,000,000 persons by the conventional method of individual returns led to the adoption, in 1943, of a measure requiring employers to collect the tax by payroll deductions.

FEDERAL EXPENDITURES AND RECEIPTS, 1939-1953

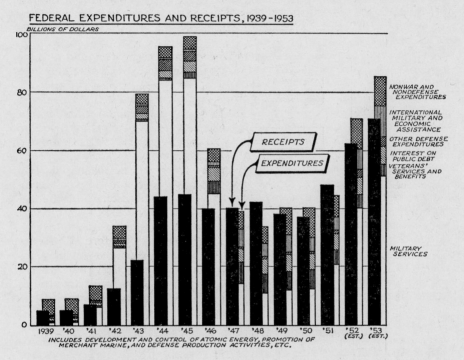

INCLUDES DEVELOPMENT AND CONTROL OF ATOMIC ENERGY, PROMOTION OF MERCHANT MARINE, AND DEFENSE PRODUCTION ACTIVITIES, ETC.

Meanwhile, personal incomes, governmental expenditures, and inflationary pressures continued to mount. The President therefore came back in his Budget Message of 1943 to demand an increase of $16,000,-000,000 in the federal tax load. Treasury officials later lowered the request to $10,500,000,000. Even so, congressional leaders rebelled and adopted a Revenue Act in early February 1944 that yielded additional revenue of only $2,200,000,000, chiefly by increasing the excess profits tax to 95 per cent

~~~~~~~~~~~~~~~~~~~~

[7] Specifically, the Act of 1942 lowered exemptions to $500 for single persons and $1200 for married persons and increased the normal income tax from 4 to 6 per cent. On top of this normal tax came a surtax ranging from 13 to 82 per cent and a Victory tax of 5 per cent, collected at the source on all incomes above $624 a year. The Act of 1942 promised that part of the Victory tax would be refunded after the war, but Congress revoked this pledge in 1944. A married person with two dependents and a net income of $500,000 paid $344,476 in federal income taxes in 1941; he paid $439,931 under the Act of 1942. A married person with two dependents and a net income of $3,000 paid $58 in the first instance and $267 in the second.

and by heavy increases in excise taxes. The President replied on February 22 with a veto so stinging that his spokesman in the Senate, Alben W. Barkley of Kentucky, resigned his post as Majority Leader. The Senate Democratic caucus promptly and unanimously re-elected Barkley, and an angry House and Senate overrode the veto by enormous majorities on February 24 and 25, 1944.

From this time forward administration and congressional leaders were concerned, not with increasing the tax burden, but with simplifying

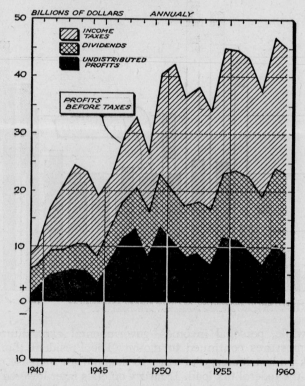

CORPORATE PROFITS, TAXES, AND DIVIDENDS, 1940–1960

the withholding system and planning for the reconversion that would soon come with the end of the war. Congress approved the Individual Income Tax Act in May 1944. It repealed the Victory tax, substituted an increase in the normal tax, and permitted some 30,000,000 taxpayers with incomes under $5,000 to file a simplified tax return. Moreover, Congress in July 1945 approved a Tax Adjustment Act to aid business during the reconversion period. It provided for refunds or reductions in corporation taxes during the next two years of about $5,500,000,000.

In retrospect, perhaps the most significant aspect of the tax program from 1941 to 1945 was the way it reflected the nation's conviction that a war for survival should not become a war for the enrichment of the few. There could be no "swollen fortunes" when the federal income tax reached a maximum of 94 per cent of total net income, to say nothing of state income and local property taxes. Indeed, the nation's top 5 per cent of income receivers suffered their severest relative economic losses in the history of the country during this period. Their share of disposable income declined from 25.7 per cent in 1940 to 15.9 per cent in 1944.[8] And with an excess profits tax of 95 per cent and corporation income taxes reaching a maximum of 50 per cent, there were few cases of "swollen profits." Net corporation income was $9,400,000,000 in 1941 and 1942, increased slightly in 1943 and 1944, and fell back to $8,500,000,000 in 1945. Dividends increased hardly at all during the same period.

184. *Combating Inflation on the Home Front*

Aside from the mobilization of fighting men and the maintenance of a steady flow of materials to the battle fronts, perhaps the most important problem at home was prevention of a runaway inflation that would compound the costs of the war and increase the burdens of many classes. To state the problem in its simplest terms, inflationary pressures existed after 1941 because the volume of disposable personal income greatly exceeded the supply of goods and services available for civilian consumption at the prevailing price level. Disposable personal incomes rose from $92,000,-

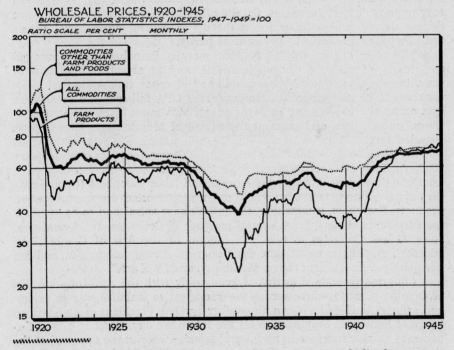

WHOLESALE PRICES, 1920-1945
BUREAU OF LABOR STATISTICS INDEXES, 1947-1949 = 100

RATIO SCALE PER CENT   MONTHLY

COMMODITIES OTHER THAN FARM PRODUCTS AND FOODS

ALL COMMODITIES

FARM PRODUCTS

[8] The relative status of the top 1 per cent of income receivers declined even more. Their share of disposable income declined from 11.5 per cent in 1940 to 6.7 per cent in 1944.

000,000 in 1941 to $151,000,000,000 in 1945, but the supply of civilian goods and services, measured in constant dollars, rose from $77,600,000,-000 to only $95,400,000,000 during the same period.

The danger of inflation stalked the home front because of this "inflationary gap." Wholesale prices had risen some 170 per cent during and immediately after the First World War. Administration leaders were determined that such a catastrophe should not occur again. They understood the enormous complexity of the problem and knew that economic stabilization could not be achieved by imposing a few direct controls. What ensued, therefore, was a comprehensive and fruitful experiment in stabilization that involved a broad extension of the federal authority over almost every aspect of economic life.

The most obvious weapon against inflation and the first to be tried was control of prices and rents. It will be recalled that Roosevelt, while reorganizing the defense mobilization machinery, had established an Office of Price Administration and Civilian Supply (OPA), headed by the explosive Leon Henderson, to work in conjunction with the Office of Production Management. Henderson had no real power and was helpless to control prices during 1941. Consequently, retail prices were rising at the rate of 2 per cent a month by February 1942. The President pleaded for new authority, and Congress responded with the Emergency Price Control Act of 1942. It empowered the Price Administrator to fix maximum prices and rents in special areas and to pay subsidies to producers, if that were necessary to prevent price increases. On the other hand, the powerful farm bloc denied the Price Administrator authority to control agricultural prices until they had reached 110 per cent of parity.

The OPA during the next three months launched a two-pronged campaign—to stabilize prices piecemeal, and to establish a system of rationing for tires, automobiles, gasoline, and sugar and, somewhat later, for shoes, fuel oil, and coffee. Moreover, the OPA followed the President's lead on April 28 by issuing its first General Maximum Price Regulation. It "froze" most prices and rents at their level of March 1942. Events soon revealed large loopholes in the stabilization program. The most obvious was the ban on a ceiling for food prices until they reached an extraordinary level. As food prices continued their inexorable rise—they increased a total of 11 per cent during 1942—organized labor redoubled its demands for pay increases that in turn would mean higher prices for manufactured products. Somehow, somewhere, the inflationary spiral had to be stopped, the President exclaimed in a special message to Congress on September 7, 1942. "I ask Congress to take . . . action by the first of October," he added. ". . . In the event that the Congress should fail to act, and act adequately, I shall accept the responsibility, and I will act."

Congress responded swiftly if grudgingly with the Anti-Inflation Act of October 2, 1942, empowering the President to stabilize wages, prices, and salaries at their levels on September 15. The President established an Office of Economic Stabilization on the following day, October 3, and forbade any further increase in wages and salaries without the approval of the Stabilization Director, James F. Byrnes. In addition, he "froze" agricultural prices at their level on September 15 and extended rent control to all areas of the country.

PERSONAL INCOME, CONSUMPTION, AND SAVING, 1940–1961

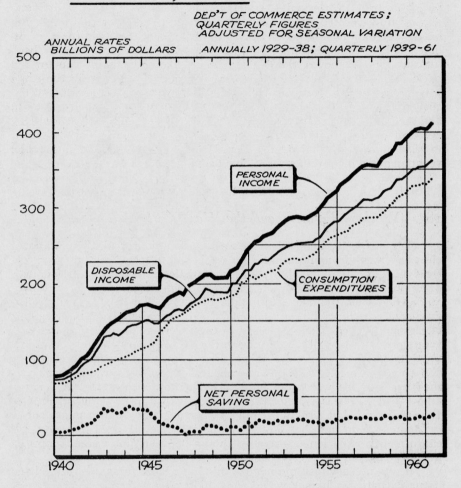

DEP'T OF COMMERCE ESTIMATES:
QUARTERLY FIGURES
ADJUSTED FOR SEASONAL VARIATION

ANNUAL RATES
BILLIONS OF DOLLARS   ANNUALLY 1929-38; QUARTERLY 1939-61

PERSONAL INCOME

DISPOSABLE INCOME

CONSUMPTION EXPENDITURES

NET PERSONAL SAVING

It was a heroic beginning, but even rougher storms lay ahead. The OPA administrator, Leon Henderson, had never been popular with Congress and the public. Roosevelt permitted him to resign in December 1942 and appointed Prentiss S. Brown, former senator from Michigan, in his stead. Unfortunately, business, farm, and labor groups took his appointment as a signal for an all-out campaign against stabilization. Congress tried to open a large hole in the dike in March 1943 by approving a bill to exclude subsidy and parity payments in determination of parity levels for agriculture. Roosevelt vetoed the measure on April 2, pointing out that it would increase the cost of living by more than 5 per cent. At the same time, labor spokesmen, particularly John L. Lewis of the United Mine Workers, were growing restive under a formula by which workers had been allowed a 15 per cent wage increase in 1942, and were threatening to break the no-strike pledge they had given after the Pearl Harbor attack.

It was a dangerous situation, but the President acted decisively on April 8 by ordering the stabilization agencies to "hold the line" against any further unwarranted price and wage increases. Nor was this all. Lewis called a general coal strike on May 1 in defiance of the "hold the line" order. The President seized the coal mines and virtually ordered miners back into the pits. Moreover, the OPA began an aggressive campaign to "roll back" food prices. It culminated in a 10 per cent reduction in the retail prices of meat, coffee, and butter on May 7. The tide had turned, and the cost of living increased less than 1.5 per cent between the spring of 1943 and the summer of 1945. The Consumer Price Index had increased by 28.3 per cent during the entire period 1940–5. This was a remarkable record in view of the power of organized pressure groups and inevitable public vexation at the inconveniences of direct controls.

185. Workers, Farmers, and the War Effort

The nearly insatiable demands of the American and Allied war machines created new opportunities for workers and solved most of the problems of the depression. The following statistics give the over-all picture: The number of civilian workers increased from about 46,500,000 to over 53,000,000 from 1940 to the middle of 1945. The chief factor in this expansion was the addition of about 7,000,000 workers from the reservoir of the unemployed. Their numbers, in turn, were augmented by 3,800,000 young persons, most of them between the ages of fourteen and seventeen; nearly 2,000,000 women over thirty-five, who doffed aprons for overalls; about 1,000,000 elderly people; and about 600,000 young war wives. To all these workers the war boom brought such prosperity as they had never known before. The Consumer Price Index advanced 23.3 per cent between 1941 and 1945, but weekly earnings of persons employed in manufacturing increased 70 per cent. Much of this increase occurred, however, because men worked longer—average hours per week increased from 40.6 in 1941 to 45.2 in 1944—and benefited from overtime pay.

It was no easy task to mobilize this huge labor force, restrain labor's natural desire for higher wages, and bridle irresponsible labor leaders. Indeed, the administration never did achieve comprehensive control over manpower resources. The President created the War Manpower Commission (WMC) in April 1942 and appointed former Governor Paul V. McNutt of Indiana to direct the flow of workers into war industries. The WMC gradually evolved coercive measures that prohibited workers in defense industries from leaving their jobs without approval of the United States Employment Service. This system worked reasonably well, but it did not solve the more important problem of recruiting new workers and shifting workers from nondefense to war industries. One solution, of course, was national service legislation to draft men for war work. The CIO and AF of L bitterly opposed such legislation, but the manpower shortage seemed so critical by the end of 1943 that the President finally came out in support of a national service act in his Annual Message in January 1944. The House

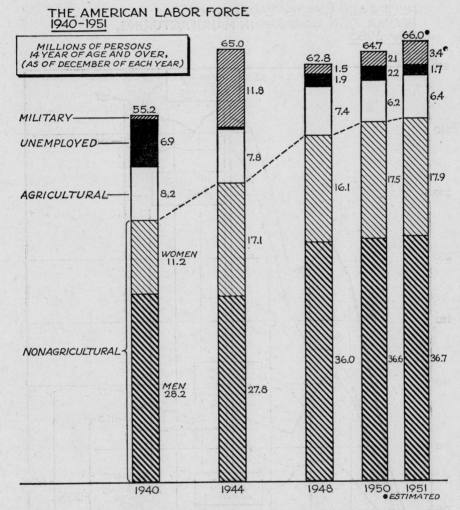

THE AMERICAN LABOR FORCE
1940–1951

MILLIONS OF PERSONS
14 YEAR OF AGE AND OVER,
(AS OF DECEMBER OF EACH YEAR)

MILITARY

UNEMPLOYED

AGRICULTURAL

NONAGRICULTURAL

1940 — 55.2; 6.9; 8.2; WOMEN 11.2; MEN 28.2

1944 — 65.0; 11.8; 7.8; 17.1; 27.8

1948 — 62.8; 1.5; 1.9; 7.4; 16.1; 36.0

1950 — 64.7; 2.1; 2.2; 6.2; 17.5; 36.6

1951 — 66.0•; 3.4ᵉ; 1.7; 6.4; 17.9; 36.7

• ESTIMATED

approved a labor draft bill in December 1944, but Germany collapsed before the Senate could act on the measure.

Much more important and difficult was the task of preventing strikes and reconciling labor's natural desires for economic advancement and union security with the general objective of winning the war without runaway inflation. This gigantic and at times nearly impossible task was entrusted to the War Labor Board (WLB), created by the President on January 12, 1942. The WLB was established simply to settle labor disputes, but it soon discovered that mediation was impossible without a complete edifice of labor policy. Inevitably, therefore, the WLB emerged as a powerful policy-making body in the war economy.

To the leaders of organized labor the fundamental issue was protection of the right of collective bargaining. The WLB stood firm in defense of labor's rights under the Wagner Act, even the right to the closed shop

HOURS AND WEEKLY EARNINGS OF
PRODUCTION WORKERS IN MANUFACTURING,
1939–1950

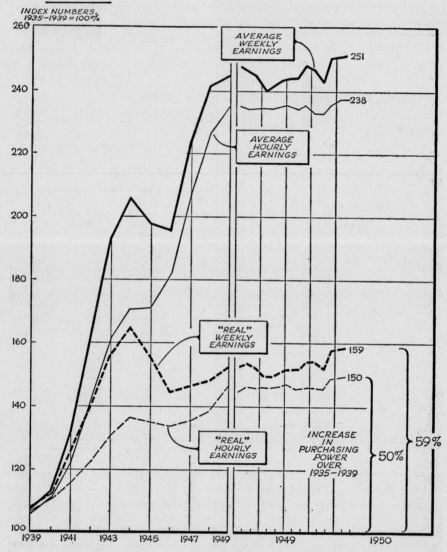

when a majority of workers voted in favor of it. Moreover, it applied a compromise—the so-called maintenance of membership plan—that protected unions in rapidly expanding war plants.[9] It was not all that labor

[9] Under this arrangement unions retained their membership and the right to bargain for all workers during the life of a bargaining contract. On the other hand, new workers coming into an industry or plant were not required to join the union as a condition of employment.

leaders wanted, but it gave them security against raids by employers and rival unions. In fact, union membership expanded under its aegis to nearly 15,000,000 by the end of the war.

The thorniest problems of wartime labor administration were inexorable demands for higher wages and strikes to enforce such demands. Here the issue lay not between labor and management, for management enjoyed guaranteed profits and was usually eager to increase wages in order to hold and attract labor, but rather between the public interest and com-

WORK STOPPAGES IN THE UNITED STATES, 1935-1951

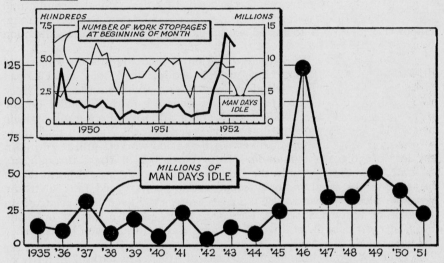

NUMBER OF STOPPAGES
BY MAJOR ISSUES INVOLVED

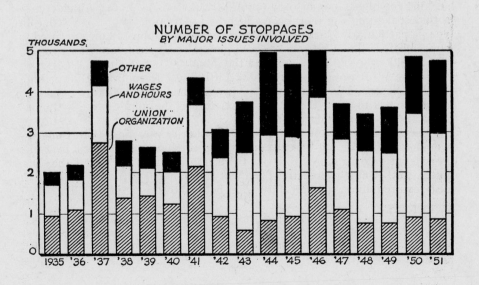

bined private interests. The WLB defended labor's right to enjoy a standard of living "compatible with health and decency." It also endorsed union demands for equal pay for Negroes and women and elimination of sectional differentials. On the other hand, it also asserted that workers should be content to maintain and not improve their standard of living during wartime. In theory most labor leaders concurred; the trouble was that they could never agree with the WLB on what that standard of living was. The rise in the cost of living during the early months of 1942 precipitated the first crisis. The WLB responded on July 16, 1942, with the so-called Little Steel formula. It granted most workers a 15 per cent wage increase to offset a similar increase in the cost of living since January 1, 1941. But employers began to award pay increases that exceeded the Little Steel formula, and the President, under authority of the Stabilization Act of October 2, 1942, empowered the WLB to forbid increases that imperiled the stabilization program.

Meanwhile, the WLB's determination to hold the line on wages had driven a minority of labor to irresponsible action. The AF of L and CIO had given a no-strike pledge soon after Pearl Harbor and promised to "produce without interruption." Responsible labor leaders kept this promise for the most part, but a few reckless leaders and a minority of the rank and file accumulated a sorry record during the Second World War. All told, there were 14,731 work stoppages involving 6,744,000 workers and resulting in the loss of 36,301,000 man-days from December 8, 1941, through August 14, 1945. To cite only the bald record, however, would be to do an injustice to the great majority of workers who remained faithful to the no-strike pledge. Most work stoppages were short-lived and occurred in defiance of union leadership. Moreover, they caused a loss of only one ninth of 1 per cent of total working time—a record that even British labor did not exceed.

Even so, it was difficult for the mass of Americans to think in terms of averages when they saw workers in airplane factories and shipyards striking for higher pay or over union jurisdiction. Two major incidents—a coal strike and the near occurrence of a nation-wide railroad strike in 1943—particularly alarmed the American people. John L. Lewis refused to appear before the WLB and called a general coal strike on May 1, 1943. The President seized the mines, but the miners struck again on June 11 because the WLB would not break the Little Steel formula and grant high wage increases. Miners returned to work when Roosevelt threatened to ask Congress to draft them, but Lewis forced the administration to surrender by threat of a third strike.[10]

Lewis's cynical defiance of federal authority was more than Congress would tolerate. In hot resentment it approved and re-enacted over the President's veto on June 26, 1943, the Smith-Connally, or War Labor Disputes, Act. It empowered the President to seize any struck war plant. It also required unions to wait thirty days before striking, and to hold a secret

[10] Under the agreement concluded between Lewis and Secretary of the Interior Ickes the miners received normal wage increases under the Little Steel formula. In addition, they received pay increases to compensate for reduced lunch periods and for time spent going to and from the pits.

vote of the workers before a strike was executed. Actually, it was useless legislation, which prevented no strikes and only gave an additional weapon, the strike threat, to labor leaders. More indicative of the rising anti-labor sentiment was the enactment by many state legislatures of laws to prevent certain union practices and to subject unions to a measure of public regulation.[11] We can say in summary, therefore, that although labor gained in union strength and improved living standards during the war, such gains were often purchased at the price of labor's greatest asset, the good will of the American people at large.

For agriculture, the war boom brought new problems but also a stability and prosperity unknown since 1919. Net cash income from farming increased from $2,300,000,000 to $9,458,000,000 from 1940 to 1945, or by more than 300 per cent. Under the stimulus of heady prosperity, farmers not only painted their houses and barns and enjoyed a higher standard of living; they also reduced their total mortgage and debt loads and added $11,000,000,000 to their savings. At the same time, tenancy declined sharply in the nation as a whole, from a national average of 38.7 per cent in 1940 to 31.7 per cent in 1945.

Two factors—increased production and higher prices, both of them stemming from vastly increased demands at home and abroad—made possible this return of agriculture to its long-sought position of parity in the American economy. Agricultural prices more than doubled between 1940 and 1945. During the same period, the index of all farm production rose from 108 to 123, while increases in food crops were even more spectacular. Incredible though it sounds, this expansion was accomplished in spite of a declining farm population and without any significant increase in acreage planted and harvested.[12]

186. *Public Opinion, Civil Rights, and War*

Never before had Americans gone to war with such determination and unity as during the Second World War. Significant opposition to the war effort simply did not exist after the Pearl Harbor attack. And because disloyalty was rare, there were no volunteer leagues of patriots, no committees of Public Safety, no high-powered propaganda campaigns and war madness. This is not to say that the government abandoned control over news and expressions of opinion,[13] or was not ready to act ruthlessly to

~~~~~~~~~~~~~~~~~~~~~~~~

[11] For example, these laws forbade the closed shop, mass picketing, secondary boycotts, and the like, and required unions to file financial reports and obtain licenses for labor organizers.

[12] The total number of agricultural workers declined from 11,671,000 in 1940 to 10,873,000 in 1945. On the other hand, the index of productivity in agriculture increased from 112 in 1940 to 136 in 1945 because of increased use of tractors, trucks, and other machinery. Two factors making possible larger yields without significant increases in acreage were a large expansion in the use of fertilizers and the spread of hybrid corn.

[13] Some kind of censorship, for example, was inevitable. The President entrusted censorship of war news to the War and Navy departments and the FBI on the day after the Pearl Harbor attack. Then, following passage by Congress of the first War Powers Act on December 18, 1941, the President established an Office of Censorship,

suppress dangerous dissent. For example, the Justice Department at the President's command convened a special grand jury in Washington in July 1941 and laid before it and two succeeding grand juries voluminous evidence on the far-flung network of Nazi and fascist organizations in the United States. The upshot was the indictment under the Smith Act of thirty leading seditionists for conspiring to establish a Nazi government in the United States and incite disloyalty among the armed forces. The trial proceeded for more than seven months in 1944 until the judge died, apparently a victim of the badgering of defense attorneys. The seditionists were indicted a second time in 1945, and government attorneys rushed to Germany to obtain new evidence. However, the Circuit Court of Appeals of the District of Columbia ended the fiasco in November 1946 by dismissing the indictment on the ground that the government's proceedings were a travesty of justice.

The government was scarcely more successful when it tried to imprison individual champions of Nazism and opponents of the war. The critical test arose when the Justice Department invoked the Espionage Act of 1917 against one Hartzel, who published a diatribe against American participation in the war in 1942 and mailed copies to army officers. The Supreme Court, in Hartzel v. United States, 1944, made enforcement of the Espionage Act virtually impossible by declaring that the government had to prove specific intent to obstruct the war effort before it could obtain convictions under the law. Again, when the government obtained the conviction of twenty-four leaders of the German-American Bund for violating the Espionage Act, the court reversed the conviction on the ground of insufficient evidence of criminal intent. And when the government brought denaturalization proceedings against German-born leaders of the Bund, the court made it plain that it would permit denaturalization and deportation only if the government could clearly prove that the defendants had taken the oath of allegiance to the United States with reservations.

Actually, the government knew that the assorted crackpots who made up the Bund and other pro-Nazi organizations were no menace, for the FBI had penetrated these groups and placed their leaders under surveillance. Espionage and sabotage, however, were different matters, and the Justice Department moved swiftly and sternly in dealing with them. The FBI broke a small Nazi espionage ring in 1938, destroyed the major Nazi network in 1941, and was prepared to move against potential spies and saboteurs on the eve of American entrance into the war. The FBI had taken more than 1,700 enemy aliens into custody within less than three days after the

with Byron Price, executive news editor of the Associated Press, as director. Roosevelt next established the Office of War Information (OWI) on June 13, 1942, with Elmer Davis, veteran correspondent and commentator, in charge. The OWI happily never became a second Creel committee. It produced motion pictures and published pamphlets and posters reminding Americans of their duty and depicting the dangers of an Axis victory. On the other hand, it did not spread manufactured atrocity stories—the truth was horrible enough—or attempt to engender hatred of the enemy. Indeed, such hatred, especially for the Japanese, already existed in full measure and was fanned by the radio, press, and motion pictures. The overseas branch of the OWI also broadcast daily programs to the Axis peoples.

Pearl Harbor attack.[14] By such effective countermeasures the Justice Department completely destroyed the elaborate German intelligence and sabotage systems, with the result that not a single known act of sabotage was committed in the United States after December 7, 1941.

Deprived of its underground in America, the German High Command resorted to audacious plans. It trained two teams of saboteurs—they were Germans who had lived in America and American citizens of German descent—and sent them by submarines in May 1942 to destroy the American aluminum industry and blow up bridges and railroad facilities. One team landed on Long Island, the other on the Florida coast. The eight invaders were captured almost immediately by the FBI, tried by special military commission, sentenced to death, and executed on August 8.[15] The father of one of the saboteurs, Hans Haupt of Chicago, was also convicted of treason for hiding his son and given life imprisonment. Another German American, Anthony Cramer, was convicted of treason for assisting one of the saboteurs.[16]

The one great blot on the administration's otherwise excellent civil liberties record during the war was the detention and forced removal of Japanese Americans from the West Coast to internment camps in the interior. It was the greatest single violation of civil rights in American history. The issue was not the arrest of Japanese subjects who were potential saboteurs, for they were rounded up immediately after the Pearl Harbor attack. It was the loyalty of some 41,000 Japanese ineligible to citizenship and 71,000 Nisei, or American citizens of Japanese ancestry. The General Staff declared the West Coast a theater of war in the panic following December 7, 1941, and newspapers and political leaders in California began a widespread campaign for removal of all Japanese Americans, whether citizens or not. The demand was taken up in Washington by the congressional delegations from the Pacific Coast states, and was seconded by the commanding general on the West Coast, John L. De Witt. The President on February 19, 1942, authorized the army to take control. General De Witt soon afterward ordered removal of *all* Japanese Americans from an area comprising the western third of Washington and Oregon, the western half of California, and the southern quarter of Arizona. Some

---

[14] All told, the Justice Department arrested some 16,000 enemy aliens during the war, one fourth of whom were imprisoned.

[15] The President commuted the sentences of two saboteurs who gave evidence to life imprisonment in one case and thirty years' imprisonment in the other.

[16] The Supreme Court reversed Cramer's conviction in 1945 on the ground that the government had not proved that he gave aid and comfort to the enemy within the meaning of the treason clause. However, the court upheld Haupt's conviction in 1947. Only one other person was tried for treason during the war. He was a Detroit Bundsman, Max Stephan, who was sentenced to death in 1942 for helping a German prisoner of war to escape. The President commuted his sentence to life imprisonment one day before the execution was to take place. However, the Justice Department obtained indictment of a number of turncoat Americans—among them Ezra Pound, the poet, Robert H. Best, a former foreign correspondent, Mildred Gillars, known to servicemen as "Axis Sally," and Mrs. Iva d'Aquino, better known as "Tokyo Rose"—who broadcast for the Axis during the war. Most of them were apprehended at the end of hostilities, convicted of treason, and sentenced to long prison terms. Pound, however, was declared insane and incarcerated in St. Elizabeth's Hospital in Washington.

110,000 Japanese and Nisei were ruthlessly ejected from their homes, herded into temporary stockades surrounded by barbed wire, and then transported to ten relocation centers established by the War Relocation Authority in western deserts and the swamplands of Arkansas. Eventually some 18,000 persons suspected of disloyalty were confined in a camp at Tule Lake, California, while the remainder were allowed to find new homes or go to colleges in the Midwest and East. Some 36,000 chose resettlement during the war.

The most disappointing aspect of the whole affair was the Supreme Court's refusal to vindicate the principle of civilian supremacy or defend elementary civil rights. A divided court, in Korematsu *v.* United States, rendered in December 1944, apologetically approved the evacuation on the ground that military leaders were justified in taking extreme measures against persons on account of race to protect the national security, even though the situation was not serious enough to justify imposition of martial law. The meaning of the decision was clear and foreboding: In future emergencies no American citizen would have any rights that the President and army were bound to respect when, *in their judgment,* the emergency justified drastic denial of civil rights.

187. *Negroes and the Home Front*

The Second World War was a time of unrest and new striving on America's troubled frontier of Negro-white relations. There were race riots, and national discriminations like continued segregation in the armed services and separation of Negro and white blood in Red Cross blood banks. Racial tensions rose to the danger point in the South as Negroes acquired a measure of financial independence and social self-respect. Yet, withal, Negroes emerged from the war with a larger measure of economic and political security than they had ever enjoyed.

Increased racial tensions during the First World War had produced mass riots, a wave of lynchings, and such degradation as Negroes had not suffered since about 1900. The social and economic upheavals of the Second World War increased tensions, to be sure, and sometimes with disastrous results. The South was swept by rumors that Negro men planned to appropriate white women when white soldiers were gone; that Negro women had formed "Eleanor Clubs," named for Mrs. Roosevelt, and vowed never again to work in white kitchens; and that Negroes were gathering ice picks for a mass uprising. Southern fears were further stimulated by the presence of nearly 1,000,000 Negroes in the armed services, and by the obvious determination of Negroes everywhere to fight rather than accept conventional insults. In the words of a southern sociologist, "The South and the Negro, in the early 1940's, faced their greatest crisis since the days of the reconstruction." [17]

The most dangerous racial tension, however, developed in industrial areas outside the South, as a result of the sudden immigration of nearly

[17] Howard W. Odum, *Race and Rumors of Race* (Chapel Hill, N.C., 1943), p. 4.

1,000,000 southern Negroes in search of jobs and new social opportunities. There were numerous minor clashes in many cities, and New York escaped a major race riot in early 1944 only because of the quick action of its mayor and police force. Tensions flared into large-scale rioting in Detroit, home of Gerald L. K. Smith and other Negro-baiters. A fight between a Negro and a white man on June 20, 1943, led to other clashes. Soon mobs of whites were roaming the Negro section, killing and burning as they went. By the time that federal troops had restored order, twenty-five Negroes and nine whites had been killed.

This was the dark side of an otherwise bright picture, for the Second World War was a time also of great advancement for American Negroes. Negroes in the South enjoyed greater acceptance and security and larger political and economic opportunities than ever before. Lynching, long the extreme form of southern race control, became almost an historic phenomenon, as the number of Negroes thus done to death declined from five in 1942 to one in 1945. A distinguished body of southern leaders, Negro and white, met in Atlanta in 1944 and organized the Southern Regional Council to combat prejudice and misunderstanding by concerted action in communities and states. Equally significant was the growth during the war of an advanced equalitarian movement outside the South. Assuming the proportions almost of a crusade, this campaign against Jim Crow won many triumphs, the most important of which was a growing concern for civil rights by the major parties.

Negroes made greatest progress during the war, in both the North and the South, on the economic front. Of all groups they had suffered most during the depression; nor did the defense boom of 1940-1 bring relief, as employers stubbornly refused to hire black workers. The administration moved slowly, until A. Philip Randolph, president of the Brotherhood of Sleeping Car Porters, called upon 50,000 Negroes to march on Washington to protest. Randolph called off the threatened march; but he did so only after Roosevelt had issued his epochal Executive Order 8802 on June 25, 1941. It directed that Negroes be admitted to job training programs, forbade discrimination in work on defense contracts, and established a Fair Employment Practices Committee to investigate charges of discrimination on account of race.

The FEPC made progress slowly and performed its most effective service during 1942 and 1943 by conducting hearings on discrimination in most of the large cities of the country. It set to work more vigorously when the President, in May 1943, reorganized the agency, expanded its budget, and directed that anti-discrimination clauses in contracts be enforced. Establishing fifteen regional offices, it heard some 8,000 complaints and conducted thirty public hearings from 1943 to 1946. The results were unexpectedly gratifying. Nearly 2,000,000 Negroes were at work in aircraft factories, shipyards, steel mills, and other war plants in the South and elsewhere by the end of 1944.[18]

The millennium had not come for American Negroes when the war

---

[18] In addition, New York, New Jersey, and Indiana established Fair Employment Practices Commissions, while many cities set up anti-discrimination boards.

ended in August 1945. To men of good will, however, the steady enlargement of economic, social, and political opportunities for Negroes during
the war years was perhaps the most encouraging development on the
American home front. Negroes in 1945 could look forward to a postwar era
full not only of struggle but also of hope for a new era in which they might
stand erect as free men and citizens of the great democracy.

CHAPTER

24

The Second World War: Diplomatic and Military Aspects

T HE AMERICAN PEOPLE were destined to play a leading and decisive role in the military operations that brought victory for the United Nations in 1945. In this chapter we will follow the Allies on the long and tortuous road from defeat to victory. Since the war was won not only in the factory and on the battlefield but around the conference table as well, we will also note how Roosevelt and Churchill forged the bonds of Anglo-American unity, drew the Russian leaders into close association, and gave such an effective demonstration of allied co-operation in wartime as the world had rarely seen before.

188. The Formation of the Grand Alliance

American and British leaders gathered in Washington soon after the Pearl Harbor attack to lay plans for combined conduct of the war. Prime Minister Winston S. Churchill arrived in Washington on December 22, 1941, for a week of conferences known by the code name of ARCADIA. These discussions continued on the military level until January 14, 1942. This was a time when Allied military fortunes were at their lowest ebb since the fall of France, but negotiations proceeded smoothly and yielded complete agreement on all important points: American production goals for 1942 and 1943, pooling of Anglo-American munitions and their disposal by a joint Munitions Assignment Board, and immediate establishment of a Combined Chiefs of Staff in Washington and a combined British, American, and Dutch command in the Pacific. ARCADIA's most important work was reaffirmation of the earlier staff decision to defeat Germany first since that nation was the stronger enemy and controlled industry and manpower superior to the Japanese. Therefore the Allies would launch their first major offensives against the Continent and conduct holding operations in the Pacific until Nazi power had been subdued.

On the diplomatic level, moreover, Roosevelt and Churchill worked in complete harmony for the formation of a grand coalition of the Allies. The fruit of their labor was the Declaration of the United Nations, signed at the White House on New Year's Day, 1942, by Roosevelt, Churchill, Maxim Litvinov for the USSR, and representatives of twenty-three other nations at war with the Axis. The signatory powers reaffirmed the principles set forth in the Atlantic Charter, pledged their full resources to the defeat of the Axis nations with which they were at war, and promised one another not to make a separate peace.

The most uncertain link in the new Allied chain was Russia. By hearty co-operation, the USSR could hasten victory and help lay the groundwork for postwar co-operation; by making a separate peace, on the other hand, Russia could postpone the hope of Allied victory perhaps indefinitely. The President's and Prime Minister's most pressing diplomatic problem during the early months of 1942 was Russian territorial ambitions in Europe and a Russian demand that Britain and the United States guarantee those ambitions in advance. The Kremlin presented the first installment of its demands during a visit of Foreign Secretary Anthony Eden to Moscow in December 1941. Stalin then requested Britain's immediate approval of Russia's absorption of the Baltic states and parts of Finland, Poland, and Rumania. He warned, moreover, that conclusion of a British-Soviet alliance would depend upon British endorsement of his territorial claims.

The issue came to a head when the Soviet Foreign Minister, Molotov, arrived in London on May 20, 1942, to press Russian territorial and military demands. Churchill and Eden had been strengthened by a warning from Washington that the United States might publicly denounce any Anglo-Russian agreement conceding Stalin's ambitions. They stood firm and persuaded Molotov to sign, on May 26, a general twenty-year Treaty of Alliance that included no references to boundaries. "This was a great relief to me," Churchill writes, "and a far better solution than I had dared to hope." As we shall see, it was not the end but only the beginning of a long and bitter controversy that helped to split the Grand Alliance after the war.

189. *The Ebb Tide of Allied Military Fortunes*

Axis victories were so swift and far-reaching during the first six months of 1942 that it seemed that the United Nations might lose the war before they could begin fighting. The Japanese, following air attacks on Brit-

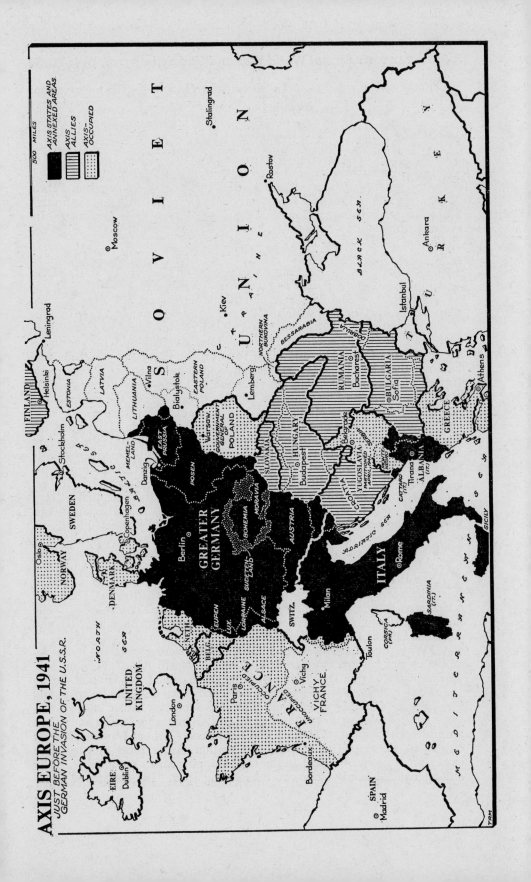

AXIS EUROPE, 1941
JUST BEFORE THE GERMAN INVASION OF THE U.S.S.R.

500 MILES

AXIS STATES AND ANNEXED AREAS

AXIS ALLIES

AXIS OCCUPIED

EIRE
Dublin

UNITED KINGDOM

London

NORTH SEA

NORWAY
Oslo

SWEDEN
Stockholm

DENMARK
Copenhagen

FINLAND
Helsinki

Leningrad

ESTONIA

LATVIA

LITHUANIA

MEMEL-LAND

Danzig

EAST PRUSSIA

POSEN

Vilna

Bialystok

GENERAL GOVERNMENT OF POLAND

EASTERN POLAND

S O V I E T

Moscow

U N I O N

Kiev

Stalingrad

Rostov

Lemberg

NORTHERN BUKOVINA

BESSARABIA

DOBRUJA

BLACK SEA

Berlin

GREATER GERMANY

BOHEMIA

MORAVIA

SUDETEN-LAND

SLOVAKIA

HUNGARY

Budapest

CROATIA

Belgrade

PARTITIONED SERBIA

YUGOSLAVIA

RUMANIA

Bucharest

BULGARIA

Sofia

GREECE

Athens

Istanbul

T U R K E Y

Ankara

NETH.

BELG.

EUPEN

LUX.

LORRAINE

ALSACE

AUSTRIA

SWITZ.

Milan

ITALY
Rome

CATTARO

Tirana

ALBANIA

MONTE-NEGRO

ADRIATIC SEA

SARDINIA
(IT.)

CORSICA
(FR.)

Toulon

SICILY

F R A N C E

OCCUPIED

Paris

Bordeaux

VICHY FRANCE

Vichy

SPAIN
Madrid

M E D I T E R R A N E A N   S E A

TRM

ish and American possessions on December 7, launched sea-borne invasions of Hong Kong, Malaya, the Philippines, and lesser islands. They were free to roam and strike almost at will, for the once mighty Anglo-American Pacific naval power was nearly gone by the end of 1941. Guam, a lonely American outpost in the Marianas, fell on December 11, 1941; Wake Island, on December 23; Hong Kong, on Christmas Day. Meanwhile, Japanese forces pressed forward in conquest of Malaya, Burma, and the Philippines. Singapore, the great British naval base in the Far East, surrendered on February 15, 1942, to a Japanese force that came down from the north through Malaya. Most of Burma fell in March and April 1942, while Ceylon and India were threatened by a large Japanese naval force that momentarily controlled the Indian Ocean and the Bay of Bengal in April.

In the Philippines General Douglas MacArthur, with a force of 19,000 American regulars, 12,000 Philippine Scouts, and 100,000 soldiers of the new Philippine army, fought a desperate delaying action. When Japanese troops threatened Manila, MacArthur declared the capital an open city, moved to Corregidor, and withdrew his troops into the Bataan Peninsula for a hopeless but gallant last stand. MacArthur was transferred to Australia on March 17, 1942. His successor, General Jonathan Wainwright, continued the fight from Corregidor and other forts off the tip of the peninsula and held out there until disease, starvation, and superior enemy forces made further resistance impossible. He surrendered his force of 11,574 men on May 6; some 75,000 American and Filipino troops, left on the peninsula to defend the entrance to Manila Bay, had surrendered on April 9.

Meanwhile, large new Japanese forces were poised in Malaya and the Philippines by the end of December 1941 to strike at Borneo, the Celebes, New Guinea, and the Dutch East Indies. Only the small American Asiatic Fleet and a few Dutch and British cruisers stood athwart the path of Japanese conquest of the Indies. In the Battle of Macassar Strait, January 24, 1942, American destroyers executed a daring night attack against a Japanese convoy and forced it to turn back. But in the subsequent engagements, known as the Java Sea campaign, the Allies lost their entire naval force, except for four American destroyers that made their way to Australia. The Japanese by the end of March 1942 were in possession of the East Indies, had pushed into New Britain and the Solomon Islands, and were in position to strike at Port Moresby, the Allied base in southern New Guinea, and at Australia itself. In little more than three months they had gained control of a vast area extending from the Gilbert Islands in the Central Pacific west and south through the Solomons and New Guinea to Burma. India and Australia lay virtually undefended.

Events almost as catastrophic for the Allies were transpiring in the Atlantic, on the eastern front in Russia, and in North Africa. German submarines came perilously close to winning the Battle of the Atlantic during 1942. Hitler's undersea raiders ranged up and down the Atlantic coast and penetrated the Caribbean and Gulf of Mexico. Moreover, Allied convoys carrying Lend-Lease supplies to Murmansk and Archangel in Russia had to run a murderous gauntlet of U-boats and land-based German bombers. Nearly one fourth the ships that traveled this perilous Arctic route in 1942 were sunk. But everywhere Allied and neutral shipping losses mounted fearfully and aggregated nearly 8,000,000 tons during 1942. "The disaster of an in-

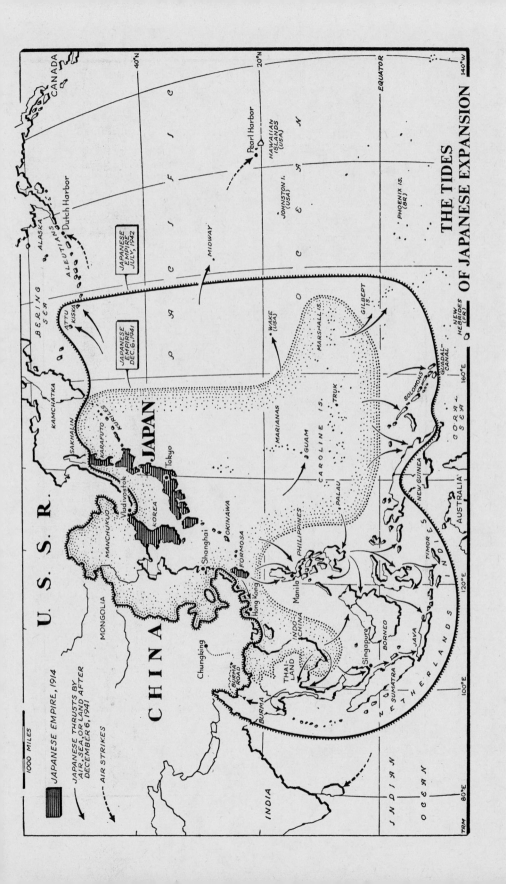

THE TIDES
OF JAPANESE EXPANSION

1000 MILES

JAPANESE EMPIRE, 1914

JAPANESE THRUSTS BY
AIR, SEA, OR LAND AFTER
DECEMBER 6, 1941

AIR STRIKES

JAPANESE EMPIRE
JULY, 1942

JAPANESE EMPIRE
DEC. 6, 1941

CANADA

ALASKA

Dutch Harbor

ALEUTIANS

ATTU

KISKA

BERING SEA

KAMCHATKA

SAKHALIN

KARAFUTO

KURILES

JAPAN

Tokyo

Vladivostok

KOREA

OKINAWA

Shanghai

FORMOSA

Hong Kong

Manila

INDO CHINA

PHILIPPINES

PALAU

CAROLINE IS.

TRUK

GUAM

MARIANAS

MARSHALL IS.

WAKE (USA)

MIDWAY

Pearl Harbor

HAWAIIAN
ISLANDS
(USA)

JOHNSTON I.
(USA)

PHOENIX IS.
(BR)

GILBERT
IS.

GUADAL-
CANAL

SOLOMONS

NEW GUINEA

NEW
HEBRIDES
(FR)

CORAL SEA

AUSTRALIA

TIMOR

EAST INDIES

JAVA

BORNEO

SUMATRA

Singapore

THAI-
LAND

BURMA

BURMA
ROAD

Chungking

C H I N A

MONGOLIA

MANCHUKUO

U. S. S. R.

INDIA

NETHERLANDS

INDIAN OCEAN

PACIFIC OCEAN

EQUATOR

40°N

20°N

80°E

100°E

120°E

160°E

140°W

TRM

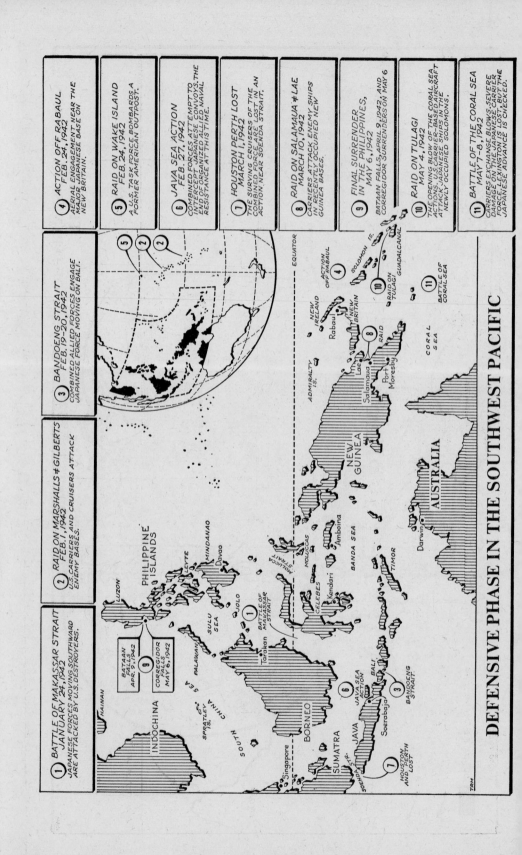

① **BATTLE OF MAKASSAR STRAIT**
JANUARY 24, 1942
JAPANESE FORCES MOVING SOUTHWARD ARE ATTACKED BY U.S. DESTROYERS.

② **RAID ON MARSHALLS & GILBERTS**
FEB. 1, 1942
U.S. CARRIERS AND CRUISERS ATTACK ENEMY BASES.

③ **BANDOENG STRAIT**
FEB. 19-20, 1942
COMBINED ALLIED FORCES ENGAGE JAPANESE FORCE MOVING ON BALI.

④ **ACTION OFF RABAUL**
FEB. 24, 1942
AERIAL ENGAGEMENT NEAR THE MAJOR JAPANESE BASE ON NEW BRITAIN.

⑤ **RAID ON WAKE ISLAND**
FEB. 24, 1942
A U.S. TASK FORCE BOMBARDS A FORMER AMERICAN OUTPOST.

⑥ **JAVA SEA ACTION**
FEB. 27, 1942
COMBINED FORCES ATTEMPT TO INTERCEPT JAPANESE CONVOYS. THE END OF ORGANIZED ALLIED NAVAL RESISTANCE AT THIS TIME.

⑦ **HOUSTON PERTH LOST**
MARCH 1, 1942
THE SURVIVING CRUISERS OF THE COMBINED FLEET LOST IN AN ACTION NEAR SOENDA STRAIT.

⑧ **RAID ON SALAMAUA & LAE**
MARCH 10, 1942
CARRIERS ATTACK ENEMY SHIPS IN RECENTLY OCCUPIED NEW GUINEA BASES.

⑨ **FINAL SURRENDER IN THE PHILIPPINES,**
MAY 6, 1942
BATAAN FALLS, APRIL 9, 1942, AND CORREGIDOR SURRENDERS ON MAY 6

⑩ **RAID ON TULAGI**
MAY 4, 1942
THE OPENING BLOW OF THE CORAL SEA ACTIONS. U.S. CARRIER-BASED AIRCRAFT ATTACK JAPANESE SHIPS IN THE NEWLY OCCUPIED SOLOMONS.

⑪ **BATTLE OF THE CORAL SEA**
MAY 7-8, 1942
CARRIERS EXCHANGE BLOWS. SEVERE DAMAGE IS INFLICTED ON EACH FORCE. LEXINGTON IS LOST, BUT THE JAPANESE ADVANCE IS CHECKED.

DEFENSIVE PHASE IN THE SOUTHWEST PACIFIC

definite prolongation of the war," to quote Churchill's phrase, threatened to upset Allied plans for military operations.

Meanwhile, the Germans had mounted a large offensive to drive through North Africa, cut the Suez Canal, and penetrate Arabia and the Middle East. General Erwin Rommel, the "Desert Fox," opened the campaign in Libya on May 26. The British, after several sharp defeats, retreated to El Alamein in Egypt, only seventy-five miles from Alexandria, to regroup and reinforce their shattered Eighth Army. The German lines were overextended by July 1, and Rommel's *Afrika Corps* was too exhausted to press the offensive.

MERCHANT SHIPS SUNK
BY GERMAN SUBMARINES
NOVEMBER 1941 *TO JUNE* 1943

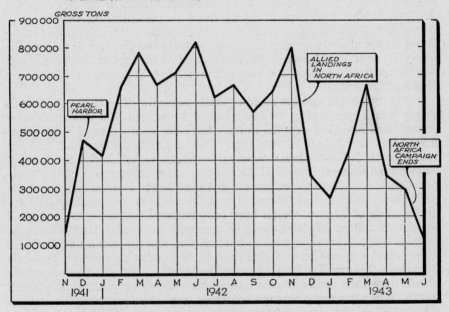

These reversals during the spring and summer of 1942 had a nearly fatal impact on the Grand Alliance when the hard-pressed Russians demanded assistance in the form of a second front in the West. The issue first arose prominently when Molotov arrived in Washington on May 29, 1942, for conferences mainly of a military nature with the President and his advisers. Stalin wanted, Molotov declared, an Anglo-American invasion of western Europe strong enough to draw forty German divisions from the eastern front. Without a second front in 1942, he continued, Germany might deal the USSR a mighty, crushing blow. "If you postpone your decision," he concluded in ominous words, "you will have eventually to bear the brunt of the war." Roosevelt turned to General Marshall for an answer. Marshall replied that there were enough men and supplies for the undertaking; the chief problem was to obtain adequate shipping for an expeditionary force without cutting off supplies to the Soviet Union.

Molotov returned to Moscow with only the President's promise that the United States would do everything possible to launch a cross-Channel invasion in 1942. The Germans drove deeper into southeastern Russia and penetrated the Caucasus, and the pressure from Moscow for relief in the West increased. At this point the President and his advisers began to consider the feasibility of an Anglo-American thrust at the northern coast of France, known by the code name SLEDGEHAMMER, as a means of averting total disaster in eastern Europe. This was the issue that dominated the conferences among Roosevelt, Churchill, and their chiefs of staff that began in Washington on June 21. Churchill stubbornly opposed any limited diversionary attempt. He admitted that the British would have six or eight divisions available for an invasion by September; they would participate if the Americans could guarantee the success of the undertaking. But were there not other ways, perhaps an invasion of North Africa, in which combined Anglo-American forces could attack more successfully? In the midst of these heated deliberations came news of Rommel's threatened drive into Egypt. It diverted the conferees' attention from the coast of France to the imperiled area, enabled Churchill to drive home his arguments for a North African invasion, and caused him to hurry home to face his critics in the House of Commons.

The President and his military staffs moved swiftly to bolster British defenses in Egypt during the last week of June 1942. But this crisis soon passed, and Roosevelt decided to have the issue of the second front determined once and for all. He sent Harry Hopkins, General Marshall, and Admiral Ernest J. King, American naval commander, to London on July 16. They joined General Dwight D. Eisenhower, now commander of the European Theater of Operations, and other Americans in London on July 18 for preliminary conferences. Marshall and Eisenhower were enthusiastic for an invasion of France, which they contemplated beginning on a limited scale until a large offensive could be mounted. But British staff officers refused to budge from their adamant opposition; and American naval officers agreed that a cross-Channel operation in September or October would be dangerous. Informed of the stalemate, Roosevelt replied that his spokesmen should now insist upon offensive operations somewhere, preferably in North Africa. When it seemed that the conferees would also postpone decision on GYMNAST, as the North African operation was then called, the President replied that plans must be made at once, and that landings in North Africa should occur no later than October 30, 1942. "It was one of the few strategic decisions of the war in which the President overrode the counsel of his military advisers." [1] Churchill agreed, and there now remained only the task of preparing for TORCH—the new code name of the North African operation —and the unpleasant job of telling Stalin why his western Allies could not open a second front in 1942.

~~~~~~~~~~~~~~~~~~~~~~~~

[1] Leo J. Meyer, "The Decision to Invade North Africa (TORCH)," in K. R. Greenfield (ed.), *Command Decisions* (New York, 1959), p. 129.

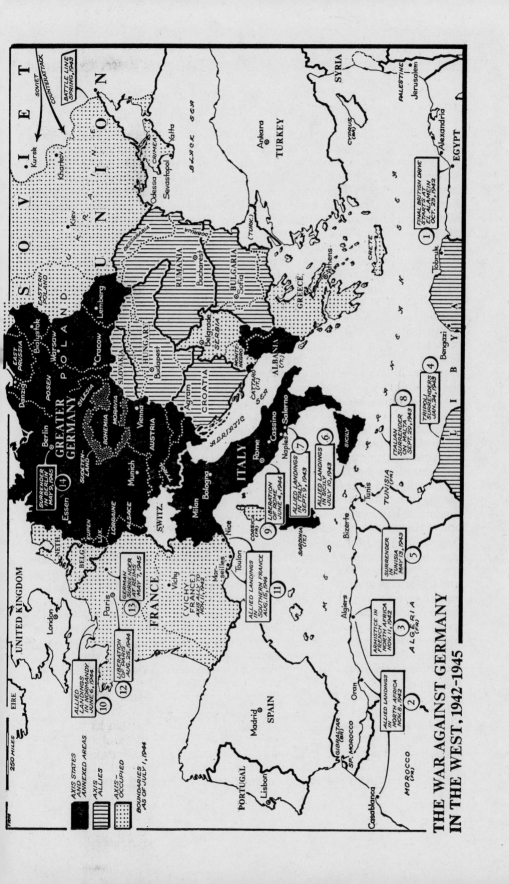

THE WAR AGAINST GERMANY
IN THE WEST, 1942–1945

250 MILES

AXIS STATES
AND ANNEXED AREAS

AXIS
ALLIES

AXIS-
OCCUPIED

BOUNDARIES
AS OF JULY 1, 1944

1 FINAL BRITISH DRIVE STARTS AT EL ALAMEIN OCT. 23, 1942

2 ALLIED LANDINGS IN NORTH AFRICA NOV. 8, 1942

3 ARMISTICE IN FRENCH NORTH AFRICA NOV. 11, 1942

4 TRIPOLI SURRENDERS JAN. 24, 1943

5 SURRENDER IN TUNISIA MAY 13, 1943

6 ALLIED LANDINGS IN SICILY JULY 10, 1943

7 ALLIED LANDINGS IN ITALY SEPT. 9, 1943

8 ITALIAN SURRENDER ON MALTA SEPT. 29, 1943

9 LIBERATION OF ROME JUNE 4, 1944

10 ALLIED LANDINGS IN NORMANDY JUNE 6, 1944

11 ALLIED LANDINGS IN SOUTHERN FRANCE AUG. 15, 1944

12 LIBERATION OF PARIS AUG. 25, 1944

13 GERMAN SURRENDER AT RHEIMS MAY 7, 1945

14 SURRENDER IN BERLIN MAY 9, 1945

UNITED KINGDOM

EIRE

London

NETH.

BELG.

Eupen

Lux.

FRANCE
(VICHY FRANCE)
AXIS ALLY TO NOV. 11, '42

Paris

SWITZ.

LORRAINE

ALSACE

Nice

Vichy

Marseilles

Toulon

CORSICA (FR.)

SARDINIA (IT.)

SPAIN

Madrid

PORTUGAL

Lisbon

GIBRALTAR (BR.)

SP. MOROCCO

MOROCCO (FR.)

Casablanca

Oran

Algiers

ALGERIA (FR.)

TUNISIA (FR.)

Tunis

Bizerte

GREATER GERMANY

Berlin

Essen

Munich

Vienna

BOHEMIA

MORAVIA

SUDETEN-LAND

SILESIA

AUSTRIA

TIROL

EAST PRUSSIA

Danzig

POSEN

POLAND

Warsaw

Bialystok

Cracow

Lemberg

EASTERN POLAND

SLOVAKIA

HUNGARY

Budapest

Agram

CROATIA

SERBIA

Belgrade

MONTE-NEGRO

CATTARO (IT.)

ALBANIA (IT.)

ITALY

Milan

Bologna

Rome

Cassino

Naples

Salerno

SICILY

ADRIATIC SEA

RUMANIA

Bucharest

BESSARABIA

DOBRUJA

BULGARIA

Sofia

GREECE

Athens

CRETE

(TURK.)

BLACK SEA

CRIMEA

Odessa

Sevastopol

Yalta

Kiev

Kharkov

Kursk

SOVIET UNION

SOVIET COUNTERATTACK

BATTLE LINE SPRING, 1943

TURKEY

Ankara

SYRIA

CYPRUS (BR.)

PALESTINE

Jerusalem

Alexandria

EGYPT

LIBYA

Bengazi

Tobruk

190.   *The Tide Begins to Turn*

Events of the autumn of 1942 began for the first time to bring some hope to the embattled United Nations. The American navy and marines finally stemmed the onrushing tide of Japanese conquest and began their slow and painful progress on the road to Tokyo. The Anglo-American Allies began a campaign in North Africa that ended the Nazi threat to the Middle East and culminated in an invasion of Sicily and Italy in 1943. The Russians finally held firm on the banks of the Volga and then began a counter-offensive that would not cease until Soviet armies had captured Berlin.

The American Pacific Fleet, commanded by Admiral Chester W. Nimitz, had regrouped and given warning even during the high tide of Japanese expansion. Two carrier task forces executed raids on the Marshall and Gilbert Islands and Wake Island in January and February of 1942, while planes from the carriers *Lexington* and *Yorktown* hit ports in New Guinea during March. A spectacular blow came on April 18, when United States Army medium bombers under Colonel James Doolittle took off from the carrier *Hornet* to raid Tokyo. But the most decisive engagement during this defensive phase was the Battle of the Coral Sea, May 7 and 8, when planes from *Lexington* and *Yorktown* turned back a large Japanese force moving around the southeastern coast of New Guinea to attack Port Moresby.

The Japanese, shocked by the raid on Tokyo and unaware that the planes had come from a carrier, concluded that the Americans had launched the attack from one of the outlying islands in the Central Pacific. To avoid repetition of this air attack, they decided to extend their perimeter and sent a large armada and invasion force against Midway Island, an outpost guarding the Hawaiian Islands, in a bold bid to cut American communication lines in the Pacific and perhaps establish bases in the islands themselves. Nimitz, warned of this attack by intercepted Japanese code messages, had moved his carriers and cruisers into the Central Pacific, and one of the most decisive battles of the Pacific war raged with incredible fury from June 3 to June 6. Dive bombers and B–17s from Midway joined with dive bombers and torpedo planes from *Enterprise, Hornet,* and *Yorktown* to sink four Japanese carriers, a heavy cruiser, and three destroyers, and to damage one heavy cruiser and two destroyers. In contrast, the Americans lost only *Yorktown* and a destroyer. The Battle of Midway was, to quote Admiral King, the "first decisive defeat suffered by the Japanese Navy in 350 years." It not only removed the threat to the Hawaiian Islands but also restored the balance of naval power in the Pacific. It was, moreover, convincing proof of the importance of naval air power, for warships in this battle, as in the Battle of Coral Sea, did not exchange a single salvo during the engagement.

Now it was the Americans' turn to go on the offensive. The Japanese had recently moved into the southern Solomon Islands and were building an airfield on Guadalcanal, which imperiled the Allied position in the entire South Pacific and the line of communication to Australia. Assembling a large South Pacific force of warships, transports, and marines in New Zealand, Admiral Robert L. Ghormley attacked Tulagi and Guadalcanal in the Solomons on August 7 and soon won control of Tulagi and the airfield

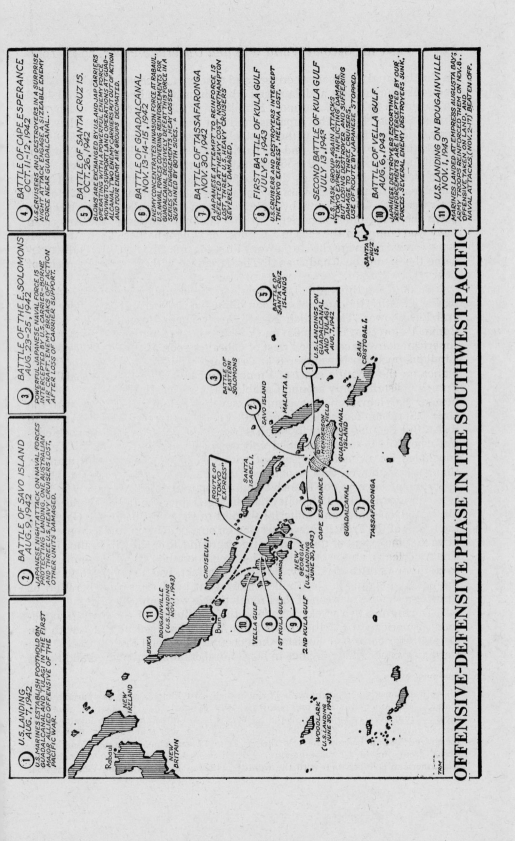

① U.S. LANDING
AUG. 7, 1942
U.S. MARINES ESTABLISH FOOTHOLD ON GUADALCANAL AND TULAGI IN THE FIRST MAJOR U.S. LANDING. OPENS "OFFENSIVE OF THE PACIFIC WAR.

② BATTLE OF SAVO ISLAND
AUG. 9, 1942
JAPANESE NIGHT ATTACK ON NAVAL FORCES PROTECTING LANDING. ONE AUSTRALIAN AND THREE U.S. HEAVY CRUISERS LOST, OTHER UNITS DAMAGED.

③ BATTLE OF THE E. SOLOMONS
AUG. 23-25, 1942
POWERFUL JAPANESE NAVAL FORCE IS INTERCEPTED. AND TURNED BACK. OUR AIRCRAFT ENEMY BREAKS OFF ACTION AFTER LOSS OF CARRIER SUPPORT.

④ BATTLE OF CAPE ESPERANCE
OCT. 11-12, 1942
U.S. CRUISERS AND DESTROYERS IN A SURPRISE NIGHT ENGAGEMENT SMASH A SIZEABLE ENEMY FORCE NEAR GUADALCANAL.

⑤ BATTLE OF SANTA CRUZ IS.
OCT. 26, 1942
BLOWS ARE EXCHANGED BY U.S. AND JAP CARRIERS OPERATING WITH A POWERFUL ENEMY FORCE MOVING TO SUPPORT LAND OPERATIONS AT GUADAL-CANAL. LOSSES ARE HEAVY ON BOTH SIDES OF ACTION AND FOUR ENEMY AIR GROUPS DECIMATED.

⑥ BATTLE OF GUADALCANAL
NOV. 13-14-15, 1942
ENEMY CONCENTRATES INVASION FORCE AT RABAUL. U.S. NAVAL FORCES COVERING REINFORCEMENTS FOR GUADALCANAL DECISIVELY DEFEAT THIS FORCE IN A SERIES OF ENGAGEMENTS. HEAVY LOSSES SUSTAINED BY BOTH SIDES. A

⑦ BATTLE OF TASSAFARONGA
NOV. 30, 1942
A JAPANESE ATTEMPT TO REINFORCE IS DEFEATED AT HEAVY COST. NORTHAMPTON LOST. THREE U.S. HEAVY CRUISERS SEVERELY DAMAGED.

⑧ FIRST BATTLE OF KULA GULF
JULY 6, 1943
U.S. CRUISERS AND DESTROYERS INTERCEPT THE TOKYO EXPRESS. HELENA LOST.

⑨ SECOND BATTLE OF KULA GULF
JULY 13, 1943
U.S. TASK GROUP AGAIN ATTACKS TOKYO EXPRESS, INFLICTING DAMAGE, BUT LOSING ONE DESTROYER AND SUFFERING DAMAGE TO THREE CRUISERS. USE OF ROUTE BY JAPANESE STOPPED.

⑩ BATTLE OF VELLA GULF
AUG. 6, 1943
JAPANESE DESTROYERS ESCORTING REINFORCEMENTS ARE INTERCEPTED BY OUR FORCES. SEVERAL ENEMY DESTROYERS SUNK.

⑪ U.S. LANDING ON BOUGAINVILLE
NOV. 1, 1943
MARINES LANDED AT EMPRESS AUGUSTA BAY; ARMY TROOPS REINFORCED THEM ON NOV. 8. OFFENSIVE TAKEN ON LAND, AND NAVAL ATTACKS (NOV. 2-17) BEATEN OFF.

OFFENSIVE-DEFENSIVE PHASE IN THE SOUTHWEST PACIFIC

on Guadalcanal. A Japanese cruiser and destroyer force surprised the Allies and sank four cruisers and damaged other ships in the Battle of Savo Island on August 8 in one of the most humiliating defeats ever suffered by the United States Navy. The Japanese did not know what damage they had done, and they withdrew without attacking the Allied transports. But they soon returned with troops, and the battle raged on Guadalcanal and for control of the air and seas in the Solomons area during the next six months. The issue was long in doubt, as the Japanese enjoyed an advantage in land-based aircraft from their base in Rabaul in New Britain. They reinforced their troops on Guadalcanal by nightly runs on the so-called Tokyo Express, down the slot from Bougainville to Guadalcanal. However, the American navy won control of the seas in a number of violent battles. Then American army forces, relieving the battle-worn First Marine Division, gradually overcame the enemy on Guadalcanal. The Japanese withdrew on the night of February 7–8, 1943.

In the meantime, Allied planners and diplomats had been at work preparing TORCH, the Anglo-American offensive in North Africa under General Eisenhower. The British Eighth Army opened an offensive against Rommel's forces at El Alamein on October 24, 1942, and three great Anglo-American convoys converged west of Gibraltar soon afterward. They struck simultaneously on November 8 at Oran and Algiers in Algeria and Casablanca on the Atlantic coast of French Morocco. They encountered heavy French resistance only around Casablanca. Marshal Henri-Philippe Pétain, head of the Vichy French government, severed diplomatic relations with the United States on November 9 and called upon his forces in North Africa to resist. But Pétain's deputy in North Africa, Admiral Jean Darlan, took control when the Germans invaded unoccupied France on November 11. He concluded an armistice agreement with the Allied supreme commander, General Eisenhower, that recognized Darlan's control and promised the cooperation of some 50,000 French colonial troops in North Africa.[2]

American and British policy had diverged since the fall of France. Britain had given moral and material support to General Charles de Gaulle as the leader of the French forces carrying on outside France, and as representative to some extent of the growing underground resistance in France itself. The Americans, on the other hand, had regarded the De Gaullist movement as a minor military auxiliary. Roosevelt, in fact, was to continue to resist the political claims of De Gaulle's movement until after the liberation of France, when the reaction of the French people was unmistakable.

During the two weeks following the conclusion of the Darlan agreement, American and British units from Algiers engaged in a race with the Germans for control of Tunisia, then occupied by small French forces. The Germans reached the province in large numbers first and poured additional

~~~~~~~~~~~~~~~~~~~~

[2] Eisenhower's agreement with Darlan nearly cost him his post as supreme commander. The Americans had brought with them General Henri H. Giraud, who had escaped from German captivity, in the hope that he could command the loyalty of all French forces in North Africa. When Giraud failed to win that support, Eisenhower recognized Darlan because he was the *de facto* French chief of state. Nonetheless, liberal groups in the United States and Britain were outraged by what they charged was American collaboration with the worst reactionary elements in the Vichy regime.

men, tanks, and planes into North Africa, and the ensuing campaign became a crucial test of strength. Fighting began in earnest on February 11,
1943. It mounted in intensity as General Sir Bernard Montgomery's British
Eighth Army in the east and Eisenhower's combined armies in the west
gradually closed the jaws of a gigantic vise on the Germans. The result was
a complete Allied victory, signaled by German surrender on May 12, which
cost the Axis fifteen divisions, and 349,206 men killed and captured, 250
tanks, over 2,300 airplanes, and 232 ships. In contrast, the Allies suffered
70,000 casualties in a campaign that hardened their troops and opened the
Mediterranean once again to Allied shipping.

In the meantime, Roosevelt, Churchill, their political advisers, and the
American and British Chiefs of Staff had met at Casablanca for a full-dress
conference in January 1943. The Chiefs of Staff talked about operations to
be launched after the Tunisian campaign had ended, as soon as the confer-
ence opened on January 12. These discussions continued after Roosevelt ar-
rived on January 14. The upshot was a decision, agreed to reluctantly by the
Americans, first, to invade Sicily in order to secure complete control of the
Mediterranean and advanced air bases and, second, to defer the invasion of
France at least until 1944. General Marshall argued strenuously for a cross-
Channel invasion in 1943, but without success.

Roosevelt and Churchill also plunged into French politics at Casablanca. Darlan had been assassinated on December 24, 1942, and the De
Gaullist Free French group in London and the supporters of General Giraud, Darlan's successor, were contending for the right to speak for the
French nation. All that the President wanted was co-operation in the common cause of liberation, and agreement that the French people should decide the question of sovereignty after the war was over. To obtain this co-
operation, Roosevelt and Churchill persuaded the austere and sensitive De
Gaulle to come to Casablanca on January 22, meet with Giraud, and work
out plans for future co-operation.

The work of the conference completed, Roosevelt and Churchill held a
joint press conference at Casablanca on January 24 in which they reviewed
their work and looked forward to victories ahead. But more important was
Roosevelt's declaration, made after previous consultation with Churchill,
that the Allies would insist upon the unconditional surrender of the Axis
enemies. "It does not mean the destruction of the population of Germany,
Italy, and Japan," he explained, "but it does mean the destruction of the philosophies in those countries which are based on conquest and the subjuga-
tion of other people." It was, as one critic afterward said, one of the "great
mistakes of the war." It hardened the German popular will to resist and
shut the door to negotiations by an anti-Hitler faction. Worse still, it virtually precluded a negotiated settlement of the Pacific war, the one conflict
that might well have been terminated by negotiation.

191.   1943: *The United Nations on the Offensive*

The Anglo-American victory in Tunisia in May 1943 marked the beginning of new and more powerful air, sea, and land offensives by the United
Nations in almost every sector of the globe. In brief, the tide had already

definitely turned, and henceforward progress toward victory was steady if often slow and costly.

The decisive turning point of the European war in 1942–3 occurred when the Russians held Stalingrad from September to November 1942 against furious German attacks. Then the Russians launched a counter-offensive that destroyed or captured a large German army in the blazing city on February 2, 1943. From this point on, the Soviet armies pressed forward along the entire length of the eastern front. The Red armies by October 1943 had driven across the Don Basin deep into the Ukraine and stood on the east bank of the Dnieper River, poised for a winter offensive that would drive through the Ukraine into Rumania. One decisive factor in the Soviet victories was the stream of Lend-Lease supplies from the United States. They grew from a trickle in 1941 to a mighty torrent in 1943, after the development of new supply routes obviated the necessity of using the perilous North Atlantic route to Murmansk.[3]

The year 1943 also witnessed the turning of the tide in the Battle of the Atlantic, "the dominating factor all through the war." The Germans had more than one hundred U-boats constantly at sea by the spring of 1943. But the Anglo-American Allies had finally found the means to victory—aggressive offense through new methods of detection, air patrols both from land bases and escort carriers, and fast destroyers and destroyer escorts to protect the convoys. The turning point came from March through May 1943, when U-boat sinkings in the Atlantic declined from 514,744 tons in the former month to 199,409 tons in the latter month, and the number of submarines destroyed rose from twelve to forty. Thereafter Allied control of the Atlantic and Mediterranean grew increasingly secure, in spite of desperate German efforts. Allied shipping losses averaged not more than 150,000 tons monthly from August 1943 through March 1944. They had declined to 27,297 tons by May. Not a single Allied ship was torpedoed in the summer of 1944, when the invasion of France was launched. And for decreasing results the Germans paid such a high price—237 submarines sunk in 1943, 241 in 1944, and 153 during the first four months of 1945—as to make their underseas campaign a useless drain on resources and manpower.

Allied power increased so swiftly in the Pacific from March 1943 to March 1944 that the two major commanders in the area, Admiral Nimitz and General MacArthur, were able not only to overwhelm or neutralize the Japanese bastions in the Central and South Pacific, but also to launch new offensives that pierced the outer perimeter of Japanese defenses.

The objective of the first great offensive was Rabaul in New Britain Island, the most important Japanese air and naval base in the Southwest Pacific area. The Allied attack was two-pronged. First came a tortuous drive up the New Guinea coast from Port Moresby to Hollandia by American and Australian ground forces, paratroops, and the American Fifth Air Force and Seventh Fleet—all under MacArthur's general command. The enemy had

ᴧᴧᴧᴧᴧᴧᴧᴧᴧᴧᴧᴧᴧᴧᴧᴧᴧᴧᴧᴧ

[3] The new supply routes ran through Iran into southern Russia. Lend-Lease supplies worth $4,250,000,000 went from the United States to Russia from October 1941 to January 1944. They included 7,800 planes, 4,700 tanks and tank destroyers, 70,000 trucks, and huge quantities of ammunition; equipment for an oil refinery and a tire factory; and large quantities of food and clothing.

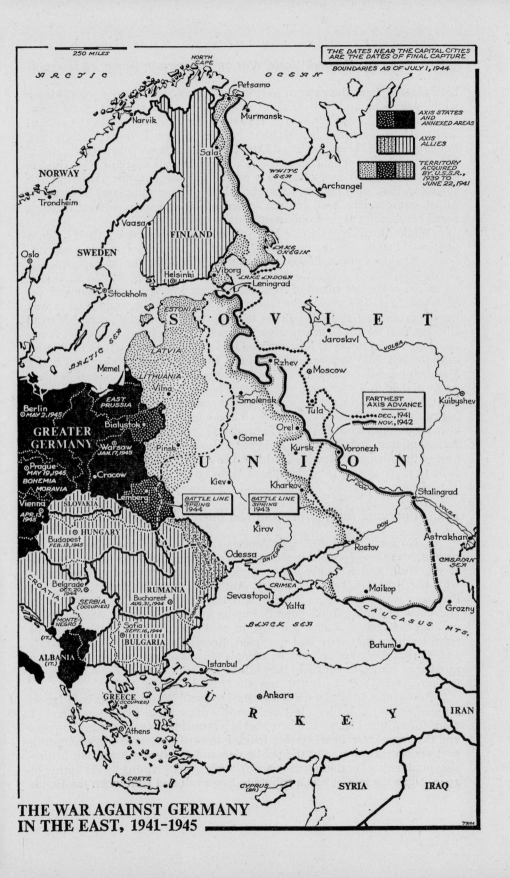

THE WAR AGAINST GERMANY
IN THE EAST, 1941-1945

been cleared from the eastern part of the island by February 1944. Meanwhile, American and New Zealand ground forces and strong air and naval forces under Admiral William F. Halsey began a drive through the central and northern Solomon Islands that carried to New Georgia on June 30, Bougainville on November 1, and the Green Islands on February 15, 1944. Finally, with the occupation of the Admiralty Islands north of New Guinea on February 29, 1944, Rabaul was cut off from communication with the Japanese base of Truk, and its encirclement was complete. Thereafter, Allied commanders were content to reduce Rabaul to impotence through aerial bombardment, without attempting to capture it.

While Allied forces under MacArthur were thus securing their hold on the South Pacific, the forces under Admiral Nimitz launched two major offensives in the Central Pacific that cracked the outer rim of Japanese defenses in that area. A new Central Pacific Force, including marine and army units, under the command of Admiral Raymond A. Spruance, attacked Tarawa and Makin islands in the Gilberts on November 20, 1943. Makin was lightly garrisoned and fell quickly to army troops; but the Second Marine Division that invaded Tarawa after an inadequate bombardment met fierce resistance from Imperial Marines and had to fight for every inch of ground until the last defenders were wiped out on November 24. Striking next at the Marshall Islands, army and marine divisions rooted out Japanese defenders on Kwajalein, Roi, Namur, and Eniwetok between February 1 and 19, 1944. Next the American navy steamed into the enemy's interior defenses in daring raids against Truk on February 16 and against Saipan in the Marianas, only 1,350 miles from Tokyo, on February 21, 1944. Meanwhile, in May and August of 1943, combined sea and ground forces far to the north had reconquered the Aleutian islands of Attu and Kiska, occupied by the Japanese in June 1942 during the fateful Battle of Midway.

192. *Planning for Victory and the Surrender of Italy*

No sooner had the Anglo-American Allies taken the offensive than they began to look forward to victory and an uncertain postwar future. Roosevelt, Hull, and Hopkins began exploratory discussions in Washington with the British Foreign Secretary, Anthony Eden, in March 1943. The President was reluctant to approve Russia's absorption of the Baltic states and parts of Finland and Poland, but he agreed that there was probably nothing the United States and Britain could do to dislodge the Russians from territory that they had occupied. Roosevelt and Eden emphatically agreed that Germany should be completely disarmed and broken into a number of states. In addition, they talked in a general way about the organization of a postwar security agency, the United Nations.

Roosevelt and Hull were determined to avoid Wilson's mistake of ignoring congressional leaders and assiduously drew them into discussions of plans for a United Nations. There had been considerable debate in Congress and the press since Pearl Harbor looking toward American leadership in a postwar organization, and the public demand for strong American leadership in planning for the future was obviously overwhelming by the spring of 1943. None the less, it was a tribute to Roosevelt and Hull when the House

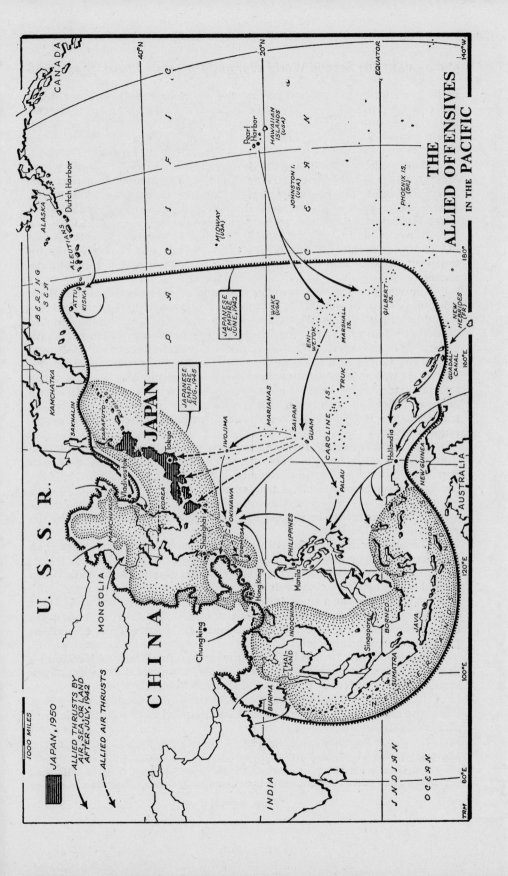

THE
ALLIED OFFENSIVES
IN THE PACIFIC

of Representatives on September 21 and the Senate on November 5 approved by overwhelming majorities the Fulbright and Connally Resolutions pledging the United States to membership in an international organization, "with power adequate to establish and to maintain a just and lasting peace."

Meanwhile, Churchill and his advisers arrived in the United States on May 11, 1943, for another grand conference on war strategy known as TRIDENT. In brief, the conferees agreed that the British should seize the Azores Islands to provide new air and naval facilities,[4] approved plans for a tremendous increase in the aerial bombardment of Germany, instructed Eisenhower to plan for an invasion of Italy after the conquest of Sicily, set May 1, 1944, as the date for OVERLORD—the new code name for the invasion of France—and mapped plans for new offensive operations in the Pacific.

The war in the Mediterranean erupted again according to the Allied schedule soon after the TRIDENT conference. A huge Anglo-American armada disgorged 160,000 troops, 600 tanks, and 1,800 guns on the beaches of Sicily on July 10, 1943. The British Eighth Army under General Montgomery and the American Seventh, under General George S. Patton, had routed the Italian and German defenders and overrun the island by August 17. It was an important turning point, for a group of Italian conspirators persuaded King Victor Emmanuel to connive at the deposition and arrest of Mussolini on July 25 [5] and formed a new government under Marshal Badoglio. He proceeded to open negotiations looking toward the surrender of Italy.

This sudden turn of events raised new perplexities for Roosevelt and Churchill—whether to negotiate with the Badoglio government, as Eisenhower and other Allied leaders requested, or to demand unconditional surrender in accordance with the Casablanca declaration. The situation was so uncertain that the President, the Prime Minister, and their respective entourages met in Quebec on August 17, 1943, for a conference known by the code name of QUADRANT.

The new Italian government made secret contact with the Allies. The Italians were eager to surrender but insisted that the Allies protect Rome, the King, and the government from the Germans, who had meanwhile taken control of most of Italy. Roosevelt and Churchill agreed to send an air-borne division to capture the airfields around Rome, and the armistice was signed on September 3. By the time that preparations for an air-borne assault on Rome were completed, however, the Germans had surrounded the city in force and seized the airfields.

Meanwhile, the British Eighth Army crossed the Straits of Messina on September 3 and began the invasion of the Italian mainland, known as operation AVALANCHE. A week later a British air-borne division seized the large Italian naval base at Taranto, while the United States Fifth Army, under the command of General Mark Clark, landed in the Gulf of Salerno

^^^^^^^^^^^^^^^^^^^^^

[4] The British Cabinet, however, won permission from the Portuguese government to establish these bases, and thus the projected invasion never came off.

[5] A German parachute force rescued Mussolini on September 12, 1943. He then established a new Fascist government at Lake Como under German protection.

south of Naples. The Fifth Army occupied Naples on October 7 in spite of furious German counterattacks and pushed northward to the Volturno River. Meanwhile, British forces had cleared the central and eastern sections of the Italian boot. Allied forces had pushed to a winter line south of Cassino by January 1, 1944.

A long and bloody campaign for Italy still impended, but the Italian surrender and successful invasion of Italy yielded large dividends to the Anglo-American Allies. It brought the surrender of the Italian fleet and guaranteed complete Allied control of the Mediterranean. It gave the Allies advanced air bases from which to bomb the Balkans and Central Europe. It consumed some of Hitler's best divisions. Most important, it gave the British and Americans the incalculable advantage of being on the offensive.

193. Slow Progress Toward Accord with Russia

The conferees at Quebec turned to other urgent problems after approving final arrangements for the Italian surrender. For example, they reaffirmed May 1, 1944, as the date for OVERLORD; agreed to launch an invasion of the Toulon-Marseilles area in southern France in conjunction with OVERLORD; and established a Southeast Asia Command in Burma under Lord Louis Mountbatten. Moreover, Hull and Eden discussed postwar plans for Germany and approved the draft of a Four-Power Declaration—to be submitted to the coming conference of Foreign Ministers in Moscow—pledging America, Britain, Russia, and China to work for establishment of an effective postwar security organization. The conference was over on August 24, and Churchill accompanied Roosevelt back to Washington and stayed with him intermittently during the next three weeks. During this time the Badoglio government surrendered, and the Allies began their invasion of the Italian mainland.

Soon afterward, Secretary Hull made the arduous air journey to Moscow for the conference of Foreign Ministers that opened in the Russian capital on October 18. Before this time no one in Washington or London knew what Russian postwar ambitions were, except for the territorial demands that Stalin had outlined to Eden in December 1941. Hull, Molotov, and Eden discussed immediate and postwar problems in Moscow from October 18 to 30, 1943, with so little disagreement that future accord seemed assured. They agreed, for example, upon a plan for the postwar treatment of Germany that the State Department had prepared and the President had tentatively approved. Indeed, Molotov declared that it expressed Stalin's views and had his complete endorsement.[6] They agreed,

⁶ As this plan eventually became the cornerstone of Allied postwar policy toward Germany, it would be well to examine it in some detail. It called for the unconditional surrender of Germany by whatever government exercised power at the end of the war. An Inter-Allied Control Commission would supervise the surrender and occupation of Germany by Soviet, American, and British troops. During the occupation the Control Commission would undertake to destroy all vestiges of Nazism and take necessary steps to encourage establishment of a democratic government and restore freedom of religion, speech, the press, and political activity. Moreover, Germany should be denied a standing army and general staff and prohibited from manufacturing any war materials or air-

moreover, that Austria should be reconstituted an independent nation and regarded as a liberated and not an enemy state, while Hull persuaded Stalin and Molotov to sign the Four-Power Declaration. In addition, at a state dinner on October 30 Stalin told Hull the welcome news that Russia would join the war against Japan after the defeat of Germany. Finally, the conferees approved the draft of a three-power declaration on war crimes, which was issued over the signatures of Roosevelt, Stalin, and Churchill in Moscow on November 1. It promised swift and terrible punishment, not only for the leaders of the Nazi government, but for all Germans guilty of atrocities.

There were differences over Poland,[7] but the Moscow Conference was nonetheless a resounding success. To be sure, no one in the West knew absolutely whether Russia would co-operate in the postwar era, but such co-operation now seemed at least possible. As one milestone along the road to Allied unity, the conference prepared the way for the next—a personal meeting of the Big Three.

Roosevelt had long wanted to meet with the Russian leader, and he had invited Stalin before the Moscow Conference to join him and Churchill at Ankara, Bagdad, or Basra in Iraq. Stalin replied that he would go only to Teheran, since he could maintain personal control over his High Command from the Iranian capital. The President agreed and left Hampton Roads on the new battleship *Iowa* on November 13, 1943, for the long journey to Cairo. There he conferred with Churchill, Chiang Kai-shek, Lord Mountbatten, and General Stilwell from November 23 to 27 on the situation in Burma and China. Most of these discussions revolved around an Allied drive in Burma to open supply lines to China, and a Chinese offensive in northern China.[8]

The President and his party next flew from Cairo to Teheran on November 27. Roosevelt for security reasons moved into a villa in the Russian compound on the next day. The Big Three thrashed over practically all outstanding military and political problems during the next four days. These included military operations in Italy; an Anglo-American invasion of the Istrian peninsula and of southeastern Europe, suggested by Churchill; and

craft of any kind. The Hull plan was vague on future German boundaries, except to say that East Prussia should be separated from the Reich. Finally, Germany should be required to pay reparations in goods, equipment, and manpower, but not in money.

[7] The Kremlin had severed diplomatic relations with the Polish Government-in-Exile in London, because the Poles had demanded that the International Red Cross investigate a German charge that the Russians had murdered 8,000 to 10,000 Polish officers in 1939 and buried their bodies near Smolensk. Moreover, the Russians were beginning to deal with a group of Polish Communists in the Soviet Union. In Moscow, Hull urged the Russians to restore relations with the Polish government in London, but Molotov made it clear the Kremlin would deal only with a Polish government it could control.

[8] The Allies opened this campaign in December 1943, when General Stilwell's Chinese divisions moved from Ledo against Japanese forces in northern Burma, and British forces moved down the southwestern coast of Burma in January 1944. Japanese counterattacks against Chittagong and Imphal, both in India, were eventually repulsed but delayed British liberation of Rangoon and southern Burma until the spring of 1945. To the north, however, Stilwell's American and Chinese forces were more successful and assured completion of the new supply line to China, the Ledo Road. It was opened in January 1945.

American plans for offensive operations in the Pacific, during discussions of which Stalin again promised that Russia would join the war against Japan after Germany's surrender.

The Russians were most concerned about OVERLORD and seemed desperately anxious to pin Roosevelt and Churchill to a definite time and place for the great invasion. Stalin pressed Roosevelt to name a supreme commander for OVERLORD and implied that he would believe that the operation would come off only after the President had named the commander. Roosevelt had long wanted General Marshall, for whom he had warm affection and respect, to have the honor of leading the liberation of Europe; but he wisely refused to follow the impulse to give Stalin an immediate answer. As it turned out, Roosevelt and his advisers concluded that Marshall could not be spared from his vital post in Washington. The President decided on his return from Teheran to name Eisenhower as supreme commander of OVERLORD.

The Big Three also discussed the future of Germany and plans for postwar collaboration. They now seemed to favor partition. Stalin emphasized the danger of future German resurgence and added that he did not think that the State Department plan submitted at the Moscow Conference was severe enough. Roosevelt outlined his plan for a future United Nations organization, which would assume responsibility for preventing wars and aggression. During all these conversations the utmost frankness and usually a spirit of cordiality prevailed. In fact, the President was convinced that he had broken through the wall of suspicion and distrust surrounding Stalin, won Russian trust and friendship, and laid the basis for fruitful collaboration in the future. His feeling was well expressed in the concluding sentences of the Declaration of Teheran, issued on December 1: "We came here with hope and determination. We leave here, friends in fact, in spirit, and in purpose."

The President said good-by to Stalin after a final dinner on December 2, paid a short visit to American troops of the Persian Gulf Command, and then went to Cairo for conferences with Churchill and Turkish leaders about Turkey's entrance into the war. In addition, Roosevelt and Churchill and the Combined Chiefs of Staff held conferences of tremendous military importance from December 4 to 6. Thus the end of the year 1943 found the Allies on the offensive on all fronts, Allied unity existing in fact as well as name, and Anglo-American leaders completing plans for final assaults against Germany and Japan.

194. *The Allied Air Offensives in Europe, 1940–1945*

Superiority in the air passed to the British after the failure of the German air *Blitz* against England in 1940–1. The RAF Bomber Command conducted a limited number of night raids against selected industrial and transportation targets in Germany from 1940 to early 1942. Results were so unsatisfactory that the new chief of the Bomber Command, Sir Arthur Harris, executed a complete change in British bombing tactics—from the target system to mass bombing of industrial areas in order to disrupt the German economy and lessen the will of the German people to fight. The first 1,000-

plane RAF raid, against Cologne on May 30, signaled the beginning of the new campaign. It was followed in 1942 by others against centers in the Ruhr, Bremen, Hamburg, and other German cities. This was only a small beginning, for less than 50,000 tons of bombs fell on Axis Europe in 1942, and German war production and civilian morale were not visibly impaired.

Meanwhile, the United States Eighth Air Force had established bases in England in early 1942 and joined in the air war on August 17, 1942. The offensive power of the Eighth Air Force grew and was reinforced by the Ninth Air Force and the Fifteenth Air Force, and the Americans became a powerful factor in the air campaign during the summer of 1943. While the British continued their devastating night attacks, the Americans used their heavier armored Flying Fortresses and Liberators in daring daylight raids— until extremely heavy losses in a raid on Schweinfurt on October 14, 1943, convinced American commanders that further large daylight operations must await production of long-range fighters to protect the bombers. All told, American and British bombers dropped 206,188 tons of bombs on European targets in 1943.

A new phase in the air campaign began in February 1944. The arrival in England of substantial numbers of long-range American fighters made resumption of daylight raids possible. The introduction of radar bombsights had already greatly increased the accuracy of night bombing. And there was a use of increasingly heavy bombs and a rapid build-up of the Eighth and Fifteenth Air Forces. The Americans first began a systematic campaign to destroy the German aircraft industry. Then the attack shifted in March to French and Belgian marshaling yards, railroads, and bridges. Then, after the invasion of France, the American AAF and the British RAF began a coordinated and relentless "round-the-clock" assault upon German synthetic oil and chemical plants. Some 8,000 to 9,000 Allied planes turned to the task of paralyzing the German transportation system in February 1945. Finally, the air forces joined the advancing Allied armies in April in reducing the German nation to utter impotence and ruin.[9]

The over-all dimensions of the Anglo-American air effort in Europe are so enormous as to stagger the imagination: 1,442,280 bomber and 2,686,-799 fighter sorties, which dropped 2,697,473 tons of bombs on Germany and Nazi-occupied Europe and cost the Allies some 40,000 planes and 158,000 personnel. Fortunately, the intensive investigations of the United States Strategic Bombing Survey, conducted in the immediate postwar period, have given us some indication of the results achieved. In general, Anglo-American strategic bombing, especially in the last year of the war, was

[9] The increasing fury of the air assault can be read in the following statistics of tonnage of bombs dropped on Axis Europe in 1944 and 1945:

YEAR	QUARTER	TOTAL TONNAGE DROPPED
1944	First	114,360
	Second	333,556
	Third	403,808
	Fourth	349,810
1945	First	369,687
	April	111,462

decisive in three particular ways. It destroyed or impeded development of German productive capacity, nearly paralyzed transportation in France, Belgium, and the Reich, and caused a massive breakdown of morale among the German people. To state the matter briefly, the entire German economy was so near collapse by March 1945 as a consequence of Allied air raids that German war production would have practically ceased by May 1945, and the German armies would have had to cease fighting by June or July, even without the Allied invasion of Germany. All told, Allied bombs dropped on Germany killed 305,000 persons and wounded 780,000 others, destroyed or damaged 5,500,000 homes, and deprived 20,000,000 persons of essential utilities. By the beginning of 1944, according to a poll taken by the Strategic Bombing Survey immediately after the war, some 77 per cent of the German people were convinced that the war was lost; and by May 1945 most Germans had lost all will to continue the uneven struggle.

195.   *Victory in Europe: To the Westwall*

General Dwight D. Eisenhower, Supreme Commander, Allied Expeditionary Forces, arrived in London on January 15, 1944, with orders from Roosevelt and Churchill to "enter the continent of Europe and, in conjunction with the other Allied Nations, undertake operations aimed at the heart of Germany and the destruction of her armed forces."

Never was so stupendous a task defined in so few words! The Combined Chiefs of Staff and various technical staffs in Britain and America had been hard at work on OVERLORD since 1942. Planning for the actual invasion and subsequent operations proceeded apace in Eisenhower's London headquarters after mid-January 1944. As a prelude to OVERLORD the strategic air offensive shifted from Germany to France and Belgium on March 6. The effect of this assault was to paralyze almost completely the invasion area and the region through which the Germans would have to move reinforcements and supplies.

The appointed time, June 5, 1944,[10] for which the world waited now approached rapidly. The great invasion armada was delayed by a sudden storm and put out to sea early in the morning of June 6. The Germans expected the invasion to come in the Pas de Calais area, where the English Channel is narrowest. Instead, the Allies struck at five beaches along a sixty-mile stretch of the Cotentin Peninsula in Normandy. First there were furious air and naval bombardments of the invasion area and beaches. Next came the landing of three air-borne divisions behind the German lines a few minutes after midnight on June 6. Finally, the sea-borne troops hit the beaches at 7:30 in the morning. German resistance was generally light; but American invaders met a fierce defense on Omaha Beach, suffered heavy casualties, and overcame the Germans, as General Omar N. Bradley has written, only by "guts, valor, and extreme bravery."

The German commanders, Field Marshals Rommel and Karl von Rundstedt, hampered by constant air attacks that made it impossible to move re-

wwwwwwwwwwwwww

[10] The date for the launching of OVERLORD was postponed from May 1 to the more unfavorable first week in June 1944 because of a shortage of landing craft.

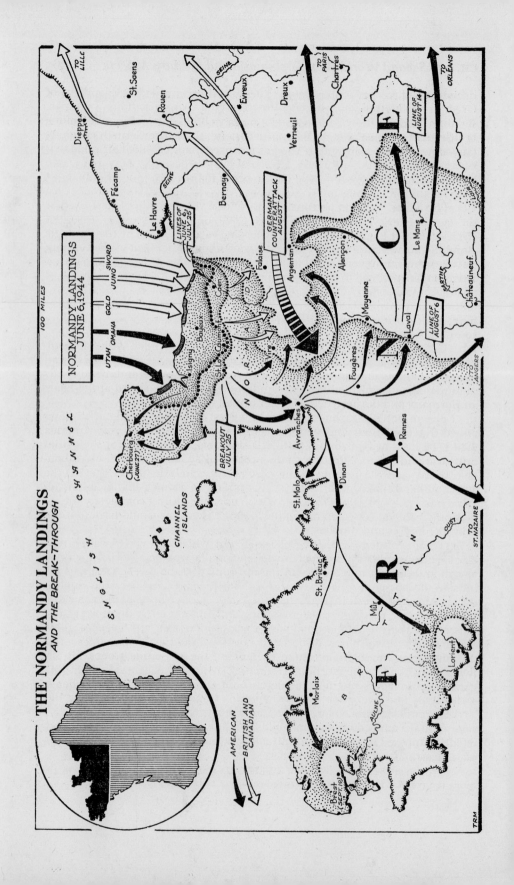

THE NORMANDY LANDINGS
AND THE BREAK-THROUGH

100 MILES

ENGLISH CHANNEL

NORMANDY LANDINGS
JUNE 6, 1944

UTAH OMAHA GOLD JUNO SWORD

LINES OF JULY 25

BREAKOUT JULY 25

GERMAN COUNTERATTACK AUGUST 7

LINE OF AUGUST 6

LINE OF AUGUST 14

AMERICAN
BRITISH AND CANADIAN

CHANNEL ISLANDS

NORMANDY

BRITTANY

FRANCE

TO LILLE
TO PARIS
TO ORLÉANS
TO ANGERS
TO ST. NAZAIRE

St. Saens
Dieppe
Fécamp
Le Havre
Rouen
Évreux
Dreux
Chartres
Verneuil
Bernay
SEINE
SEINE
Falaise
Caen
Bayeux
Isigny
Cherbourg (JUNE 27)
St. Lo
Argentan
Alençon
Le Mans
Mayenne
Laval
Châteauneuf
SARTHE
LOIR
Fougères
Avranches
St. Malo
Dinan
Rennes
St. Brieuc
Morlaix
Brest (SEPT. 19)
Lorient
BLAVET
OUST
AULNE
TRM

inforcements by day, mistook the Normandy invasion as a screen for a larger invasion in the Pas de Calais. They were not able to bring up their reserve divisions in time to prevent the Allies from securing and capturing a bridgehead in Normandy. The Allies within two weeks after D-Day had landed more than 1,000,000 troops with enormous quantities of supplies in a broad sector along the Normandy coast. They had also captured Cherbourg, Caen, and St. Lô, "eaten the guts out of the German defense," and were poised for a grand sweep through northern France.

The battle of the breakthrough began on July 25, with a lightninglike thrust by General Patton's Third Army into Brittany and a breakthrough to Avranches and Falaise by the American First Army and the British Second Army. Soon the battle for Normandy turned into the battle for France. The German Seventh Army in the area between Falaise and Argentan was under orders to "stand firm." It was surrounded and partially destroyed or captured during a furious battle from August 19 to 23. The Allies completed the liberation of France in blitzkrieg fashion while the surviving German armies moved back to their Siegfried Line. The American Seventh Army invaded southern France on August 15 and joined the race for the German frontier. Paris fell to French and American troops ten days later. American and British armies by mid-September had captured Brussels and Antwerp, occupied Luxembourg, and crossed the German border at Aachen.

The Allies were on the move on other fronts as well. They had tried vainly to break the German lines in southern Italy. Then they tried to turn the German flank on January 22, 1944, by landings at Anzio and Nettuno on the Italian western coast, only thirty-six miles from Rome. This effort failed. But the British Eighth Army and the American Fifth Army pushed northward in the spring, joined the beleaguered divisions on the Anzio beachhead, and captured Rome on June 4, 1944. Under heavy Allied pressure and harassment, the Germans pulled back to their Gothic Line, which ran across Italy some 150 miles north of Rome. There they managed to stabilize the fighting around September 1, 1944.

Meanwhile, the Russians, during the spring of 1944, began offensives along the entire eastern front fully as important in the Allied strategy as the Anglo-American sweep across France. One Russian drive on the northern sector forced Finland to sue for peace on August 25. The greatest Russian offensive, however, opened on June 23 to coincide with the Anglo-American drive in the West. Soviet armies captured the German stronghold of Vitebsk and then broke through to the Baltic on August 1. Five Russian armies in the central sector rolled into Poland, reached the Vistula River in late July, captured Warsaw on January 17, 1945, and reached the Oder River, only forty-five miles from Berlin, the following month. Farther to the south, two Red armies overran Rumania in August 1944. Then they marched into Bulgaria, captured Belgrade on October 20, and entered Budapest in February 1945.

It was obvious to almost everyone by the autumn of 1944 that the German military situation was hopeless. Germany was now a beleaguered fortress awaiting final destruction because her fanatical master preferred complete destruction to unconditional surrender. Some high German officers, foreseeing inevitable ruin under Hitler's leadership, in co-operation with certain anti-Nazi groups perfected plans to take control of the German government and assassinate Hitler. Their agent left a time bomb in Hitler's headquarters on July 20, 1944. Thinking Hitler dead, the conspirators proceeded to take first steps to seize control of the army and government. Unfortunately, Hitler was only injured by the bomb's blast. He rounded up the opposition with the support of loyal troops, executed about 5,000 persons after drumhead trials, and sent another 10,000 enemies to concentration camps. In consequence, the war would proceed to its bitter end.

196. *The Campaign and Election of 1944*

We must interrupt our story to give some attention to the political scene in the United States. The President tried hard and on the whole successfully to draw Democrats and Republicans together in the common war effort. Politics of course persisted. The Republicans made a hard fight to win control of Congress in 1942. They failed, but they made such sweeping gains in the elections on November 3 that the GOP's victory in 1944 seemed at least possible.[11] Especially significant for the future was the election of Thomas E. Dewey as the first Republican governor of New York since 1920, and the fact that there would be Republican governors in 1943 in twenty-six states that cast 342 of the 531 electoral votes.

Actually, what occurred in the federal and state elections in November 1942 was not merely a Republican revival but also a strong conservative upsurge. The significance of the upheaval became apparent after the organization of the Seventy-Eighth Congress in January 1943, when many southern Democrats joined Republicans to form a majority coalition and seize control of legislative policy. This coalition gave the President aggressive support in all matters relating to the war and postwar policies. In domestic matters, however, they proceeded as fast as they could to destroy certain parts of the New Deal.

Politicians in both camps began preparations for the coming national conventions and presidential campaign while the conservative coalition and the President engaged in frequent verbal duels during the winter and spring of 1944. Wendell L. Willkie was still titular head of his party, but he had no support among party leaders and had become so closely identified with the Roosevelt administration as to lose his status as leader of the opposition. He withdrew from the preconvention campaign after suffering an impressive defeat in the Wisconsin presidential primary in April. Meanwhile, Willkie's chief rival, Governor Dewey, was fast emerging as the new Republican leader. Ambitious and able, Dewey had many assets: youth and vigor, a reputation for efficiency, moderate liberalism, and, most important, proved ability as a vote-getter in the crucial Northeast.

Dewey had to contend after Willkie's withdrawal only with favorite sons, the most important of whom, Governor John W. Bricker of Ohio, was put out of the serious running by William Allen White's quip that he was

---

[11] The Democrats elected 222 and the Republicans 209 members of the House—a Republican gain of forty-seven seats. The Republicans, moreover, gained nine seats in the Senate.

"an honest Harding." The presidential nomination went to Dewey on the first ballot when the Republican convention met in Chicago on June 26, and Bricker was pacified by the vice-presidential nomination. The convention adopted a platform that was aggressively internationalistic and essentially progressive in tone.[12]

Democratic leaders in the early summer of 1944 found themselves in the predicament of men with no control over their party's presidential nomination. Many old-line bosses and most southern conservatives bitterly resented Roosevelt's leadership and would have preferred to nominate some conservative. But Roosevelt again frustrated his enemies by waiting until July 11, only a week before the Democratic convention opened, to say that he would accept a fourth nomination. "All that is within me," he wrote in a public letter to National Chairman Robert E. Hannegan, "cries out to go back to my home on the Hudson River. . . . But as a good soldier . . . I will accept and serve."

The President's announcement settled the matter, for the rank and file of Democrats wanted him to run, and no party leader dared deny him the opportunity of leading his people from war into peace. The great, and, as it turned out, crucial struggle revolved around the nomination of a vice-presidential candidate. This battle was bitter and created divisions in the party that persisted for years afterward. Vice President Henry A. Wallace enjoyed the support of the advanced progressive wing and large elements in the CIO. But he was almost unanimously opposed by party bosses, Southerners, and many moderates who suspected that he was temperamentally unfit for the presidency and hopelessly inept in political leadership. Roosevelt endorsed Wallace publicly but refused to insist upon his nomination. In fact, the President had apparently promised the succession to Byrnes and actually tried to obtain the nomination for the South Carolinian.

The President's plans, however, were upset on the eve of the convention by a newcomer in high Democratic councils, Sidney Hillman, a vice president of the CIO and former co-director of the defense effort. Alarmed by the rising tide of anti-labor sentiment and the failure of workers to go to the polls in 1942, Hillman organized the Political Action Committee (PAC) of the CIO in 1943. His purpose was not only to rally workers and progressives but also to win new bargaining power for labor within the Democratic party. The PAC was so powerful by the spring of 1944 that it frightened labor-baiting Representative Martin Dies from the Texas Democratic primary campaign and was instrumental in defeating two other members of Dies' un-American activities committee for renomination.

Hillman now used his power in a more spectacular way. He virtually vetoed Byrnes's nomination by warning the President that the South Carolinian was unacceptable to labor and northern Negroes. Edward J. Flynn,

wwwwwwwwwwww

[12] The Republican platform roundly condemned the Roosevelt administration's alleged inefficiency, waste, excessive centralization, and destruction of private enterprise. However, it made it clear that Republicans had no fundamental quarrel with Democrats on domestic issues by promising to strengthen the New Deal's labor, Social Security, and agricultural programs. All in all, it was the most significant endorsement of the Roosevelt policies yet written.

Democratic leader of New York, warned that Byrnes was also unacceptable to Catholics because he had left the fold and joined the Episcopal
Church. The President concluded that his assistant must give way to a compromise candidate. He therefore declared that either Senator Harry S. Truman or Justice William O. Douglas would be an agreeable running-mate;
and he agreed with Hillman that the PAC should shift its support from Wallace to Truman when it became obvious that Wallace could not be nominated. In any event, Roosevelt declared in his final instructions to National
Chairman Hannegan, the party managers must "clear it with Sidney," that
is, must win Hillman's approval for any vice-presidential candidate.

The issue was actually settled during the three days before the Democratic convention opened in Chicago on July 19, 1944. Hillman declared
that he would fight Byrnes's nomination to the bitter end, and the President
on July 17 asked the South Carolinian to withdraw. Byrnes's withdrawal
narrowed the field to Wallace, who still enjoyed the PAC's seeming support,
and Truman, upon whom administration and party leaders had finally
agreed. During the balloting for the vice-presidential nomination on July 19
and 20, Wallace led on the first ballot and Truman won on the third, as the
leaders had planned. The convention had nominated the President on the
first ballot a short time before. The Democratic platform promised continuation of progressive policies at home and vigorous American leadership
abroad in the postwar era.

Dewey campaigned hard under tremendous handicaps during the ensuing summer and autumn. He was beaten before he started by smashing
Allied victories in Europe and the Pacific, a general reluctance to change
governments in the midst of the world crisis, and above all by his own general agreement with basic administration policies. This latter handicap
forced him to make criticisms that could only sound captious. Dewey's chief
advantage was Roosevelt's failing health and a growing suspicion that perhaps the President was incapable of managing affairs of state. This suspicion increased after he delivered an address at Bremerton, Washington, and
was halting and ineffective. However, Roosevelt came back in a speech before the Teamsters' Union in Washington on September 23 that convinced
millions of voters that he was still the champion campaigner. He followed
this masterpiece with strenuous tours and speeches in Chicago, Wilmington, Delaware, New York City, and New England.

This aggressive campaign gave Roosevelt the initiative that he had
seemingly lost. He also recovered lost ground by committing himself
squarely to a full resumption of progressive policies in the postwar era. Almost as decisive was the PAC's success in getting workers to the polls. In the
election on November 7, Roosevelt received 25,602,505 popular and 432
electoral votes; Dewey, 22,006,278 popular and ninety-nine electoral votes.
The Democrats lost one seat in the Senate, but they gained twenty seats in
the House, all but four of them in the large cities, and captured governorships in Ohio, Massachusetts, Missouri, Idaho, and Washington. The most
important outcome of the election was not the continuation of Democratic
control but rather the fact that Americans of both parties were now irrevocably committed to assume the leadership in world affairs that they had so
often rejected before 1941. For better or for worse, there could be no turning
back on the high road to international responsibility.

ELECTION OF 1944

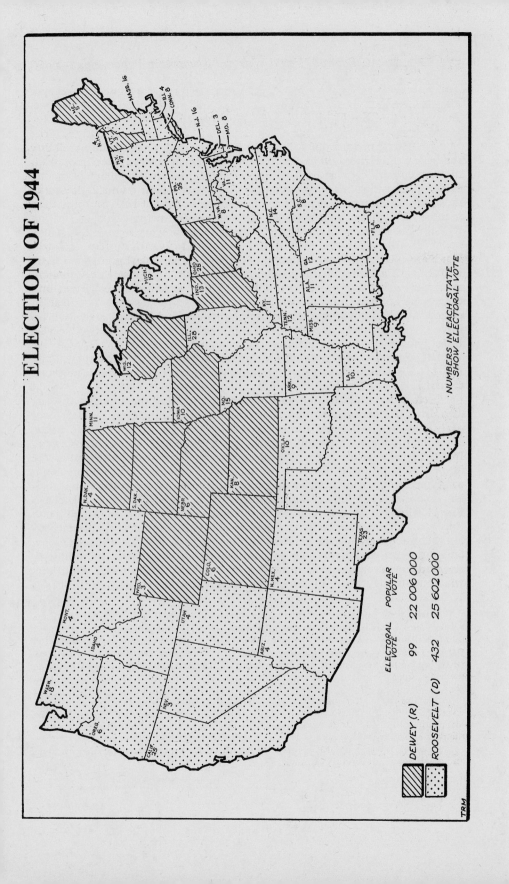

NUMBERS IN EACH STATE
SHOW ELECTORAL VOTE

	ELECTORAL VOTE	POPULAR VOTE
DEWEY (R)	99	22 006 000
ROOSEVELT (D)	432	25 602 000

TRM

197.   *Yalta: The High Tide of Allied Unity*

The rapid progress of Allied and Russian armies raised the possibility that war in Europe might end before the three great powers had come to definite agreement on plans for future collaboration. Indeed, there was little evidence that the American leaders yet knew even their own minds on the most important aspect of postwar planning, a policy for the control of Germany.[13] More disturbing, however, were signs of growing Allied dissension that threatened to split the Grand Alliance and prevent organization of a postwar United Nations. British, American, and Russian delegates met at Dumbarton Oaks in Washington in September 1944. They agreed on a basic structure for a United Nations but could not agree upon certain fundamental aspects of voting procedure. Following this the State Department and the British Foreign Office engaged in heated controversies over organization of a new Italian government and the methods and objectives of British intervention in Greece. The most dangerous potential source of trouble was Russian policy in eastern Europe, especially in Poland.

Roosevelt's thoughts inevitably turned toward another meeting of the Big Three to discuss matters that could be settled only on the high level. Churchill and Stalin were agreeable, although Stalin insisted that he could not leave Russia because he was personally directing the Russian armies. The three leaders soon agreed upon Yalta in the Crimea as the place and early February 1945 as the time of the conference.

The Yalta meeting would obviously be the last Big Three conference before the surrender of Germany, and the President and the new Secretary of State, Edward R. Stettinius, Jr.,[14] went to unusual effort, first, to formulate an American program and, second, to come to firm agreement with the British before the Big Three met. Stettinius took his staff to Marrakech in French Morocco for a briefing session from January 26 to 29, 1945. Then they went to Malta for conferences with Churchill and Eden on January 31 and February 1. Roosevelt arrived with his party aboard the cruiser *Quincy* on February 2, and it was soon evident that recent Anglo-American difficulties had not impaired his intimate relationship with Churchill. Stettinius was much encouraged, moreover, by the great improvement in the Presi-

[13] American confusion on this aspect of postwar policy was revealed during a heated controversy in the Washington administration in the late summer of 1944 around the so-called Morgenthau Plan. Prepared by Harry Dexter White in the Treasury Department and presented by Secretary of the Treasury Henry Morgenthau, Jr., it proposed to give parts of Germany to Poland, Russia, Denmark, and France and to divide the remaining rump, strip it of all industrial capacity, and convert it into a large "goat pasture." Roosevelt approved it over the violent opposition of Hull and Secretary of War Stimson. Moreover, at a conference with Churchill in Quebec from September 11 to 16, 1944, the President was so insistent that Churchill reluctantly agreed to consider the Morgenthau Plan as a basis for postwar German policy. Yet the President had dropped the plan altogether within six weeks.

[14] Cordell Hull resigned because of ill health on November 21, 1944, after thirteen and a half years as Secretary of State.

dent's physical appearance. He appeared more cheerful and calm than at the time of his fourth inaugural and "always . . . mentally alert and fully capable of dealing with each situation as it developed."

The Anglo-American-Russian conferees assembled at Yalta on February 3 and 4, 1945, for the opening of the conference called ARGONAUT on the latter day. The Big Three discussed almost every conceivable problem related to the future of Europe, Asia, and the United Nations from February 4 through 11. In addition, the Foreign Ministers and military and naval leaders of the three powers worked behind the scenes to smooth out minor differences and lay the groundwork for major understandings. It was easily the most harmonious tripartite conference, for Stalin and Molotov seemed determined to meet their guests at least halfway. Without following the conferees in their long deliberations, let us now summarize their major agreements and decisions.

a. *Germany.* The discussions relating to Germany revolved around the question of dismemberment, reparations, future Allied control, and French participation in the Inter-Allied Control Commission. The conferees approved dismemberment in principle and agreed to consider details in future negotiations. However, they agreed that northern East Prussia, including Königsberg, should go to Russia; that Poland should annex the southern half of East Prussia; that Russia should annex certain former eastern Polish provinces; and that Poland should receive territory in eastern Germany as compensation.[15] As for reparations, the Russians proposed exacting a total bill of $20,000,000,000, half of which should be paid to the USSR. Roosevelt and Churchill would not approve any fixed sum. But they agreed to accept the Russian proposal as the basis for future negotiations and to establish a Reparations Commission with headquarters in Moscow. The Russians withdrew their objection to French participation in the occupation of Germany, and Stalin agreed also that France should have a seat on the Control Commission. As the several occupation zones had already been drawn by the European Advisory Commission in London, there was no discussion of this matter at Yalta.

b. *The Governments of Poland and Eastern Europe.* The crucial question was Poland's political future. Stalin and Molotov said quite frankly that they would not tolerate a Polish regime unfriendly to the USSR. They insisted that Britain and the United States recognize a provisional Polish government in Lublin that Russia had sponsored and recognized. Roosevelt and Churchill adamantly refused. Then Stalin suggested that the Lublin government be enlarged to include some of the leaders of the London Government-in-Exile that the western powers supported. Roosevelt and Churchill again refused. Stalin finally agreed that the Lublin government should be reorganized to include Polish democratic leaders at home and

---

15 Roosevelt and Churchill refused to agree to a definite cession of this territory to Poland. However, the American and British leaders agreed at the Potsdam Conference in July 1945 that the Poles should occupy the region between the Oder-Neisse rivers and the old eastern German boundary, pending settlement of the boundary by a future peace conference. The Poles at once proceeded to incorporate the territory, expel the German population, and settle the region with Poles.

abroad, and that free elections should be held at an early date to determine the future government of the country. Roosevelt made it clear that the British and American ambassadors in Warsaw would judge whether this pledge had been honestly kept.

The three powers pledged themselves to assist the peoples of other so-called liberated countries of eastern Europe to establish, through free elections, democratic governments responsive to popular will.[16]

c. *The Organization of the United Nations.* The Russians conceded practically everything for which Americans had fought at the Dumbarton Oaks Conference in discussions at Yalta over organization of the United Nations. First, they accepted the American formula for voting in the Security Council.[17] Second, the Soviets withdrew their demand for sixteen votes in the General Assembly and received in return additional representatives and votes for the Ukraine and White Russia.[18] Third, Stalin agreed to Roosevelt's proposal that all nations at war with Germany by March 1, 1945, might become members of the United Nations.

d. *The Far East.* By secret agreement between the Americans and Russians, which Churchill approved but did not help make, and which was not published until February 11, 1946, Stalin agreed to bring Russia into the war against Japan within two or three months after the surrender of Germany. In return, the President approved the transfer of the Kurile Islands from Japan to Russia, recognized Russian control of Outer Mongolia, and agreed that Russia should recover all rights and territory lost at the end of the Russo-Japanese War.[19] Finally, Stalin agreed to recognize Chinese sovereignty over Manchuria and to conclude a treaty of friendship and alliance with the Nationalist government of China.

Millions of words have since been spoken and written about the Yalta agreements. Critics have called them base appeasement of Russia, betrayal of Poland and eastern Europe to Soviet imperialism, and useless surrender to Communism in the Far East—all by a mentally incompetent President

∿∿∿∿∿∿∿∿∿∿∿∿∿∿∿

[16] It should be added that Churchill and Eden had had conferences with Stalin in Moscow over the future of the Balkans in October 1944. They agreed that during the coming months Russia should have predominance in Rumania and Bulgaria, that Britain should have predominance in Greece, and that the two countries would share responsibility in Yugoslavia and Hungary. Churchill tried to make it clear, however, that the arrangement provided merely a temporary modus vivendi to prevent a conflict of British and Russian forces during the period of German withdrawal and should not be construed to authorize interference in the domestic affairs of the Balkan states. In any event, the Yalta agreements superseded the Churchill-Stalin agreement.

[17] The main issue here was whether the permanent members of the Security Council, that is, the great powers, should have the right to veto consideration of disputes to which they were a party. The Americans fought against use of the veto in such circumstances and overcame Russian objections at Yalta. The right of the great powers to use the veto in all important matters was not involved, for Americans and Russians alike insisted upon having veto over any proposed *action* by the Security Council.

[18] In return, Stalin and Churchill agreed that the United States might have three votes in the General Assembly if it so desired.

[19] This commitment involved (a) transfer of the southern half of Sakhalin from Japan to Russia, (b) internationalization of the port of Dairen and safeguarding of "the pre-eminent interests of the Soviet Union in this port," (c) restoration of the Russian lease on Port Arthur as a naval base, and (d) joint Soviet-Chinese operation of the Chinese Eastern Railroad and the South Manchuria Railroad.

who was hoodwinked by the wily Stalin. Defenders have replied that the agreements were wise, necessary, and "realistic."

The charge that Roosevelt was mentally incompetent is most easily disposed of. Roosevelt was obviously tired at Yalta and exhausted afterward by the strain of the grueling sessions and of his long journeys. But there is no evidence that he was not in full possession of his mental faculties during the conference itself.[20] The consensus of historical judgment rather emphatically supports the conclusion that Roosevelt and Churchill achieved nearly everything that circumstances permitted. They undoubtedly knew the risks they were running in the agreements on Poland and eastern Europe. They knew also that they had no alternative but to accept a compromise and hope that the Russians would honor it. The Russians were already in eastern Europe. The United States and Britain might conceivably have driven them out, but neither the Anglo-American peoples nor soldiers would have tolerated even the suggestion of a long and bloody war to save Poland or Rumania from Communist domination. These were the two prime historical realities with which Roosevelt and Churchill had to reckon, and from which Stalin could benefit, at Yalta. The Anglo-American leaders obtained important concessions from Stalin in spite of them. Future conflicts with the Soviet Union developed, not because the Russians honored the Yalta agreements, but precisely because they violated them.

We now know that Roosevelt concluded the secret far eastern agreement with Stalin because he and his military advisers believed that the Japanese would not surrender unconditionally without invasion and occupation. Moreover, no one yet knew whether the atomic bomb would explode or what damage it would do. Acting on the advice of his military advisers, Roosevelt made the agreement with Stalin, he thought, in order to prevent the death of perhaps 1,000,000 American men in bloody campaigns in Japan and on the Asiatic mainland. To avert this catastrophe, the President virtually let Stalin name his own price for Soviet participation. Actually, Soviet Far Eastern policy was neither determined nor defined at Yalta. It is a fair assumption that the Russians would have entered the war against Japan and re-established themselves as a major far eastern power whether the Americans liked it or not.[21]

Critics of the Yalta agreements tend to forget that the Russians, also, made substantial concessions. They agreed to participate in a United Nations that would certainly be controlled by the Anglo-American bloc; to give France a share in the control of Germany; and to respect the integrity of the peoples of eastern Europe. They seemed determined to act reasonably and to meet Churchill and Roosevelt halfway on all important issues. Roosevelt and Churchill, therefore, acted in the only manner that was historically pos-

ᜠᜠᜠᜠᜠᜠᜠᜠᜠᜠᜠᜠᜠᜠᜠᜠ

[20] It might be well in passing to mention the charge that Alger Hiss, who was a member of the State Department staff at Yalta, and had been an agent for the Soviet spy ring in the 1930's, was the principal author of the Yalta agreements. It has never been demonstrated that Hiss had any influence in determining any important decisions at the conference.

[21] It might be added, also, that Chiang Kai-shek, who was not informed until much later of the details of the far eastern agreement, was delighted by the Russian promise of a treaty of alliance because he thought that it meant Soviet neutrality in the Nationalist government's war with the Chinese Communists.

sible. As Churchill put it, "Our hopeful assumptions were soon to be falsified. Still, they were the only ones possible at the time." [22]

198. *Victory in Europe: Triumph and Tragedy*

We now come to the portentous spring of 1945, when the triumph of the onrushing Allied and Russian armies was overshadowed by the larger tragedy of ruthless Soviet domination of eastern Europe and the failure of the American leadership to understand and perhaps act in time to restrain Communist imperialism.

The British and American armies approached the Siegfried Line in September 1944. Having rejected General Montgomery's plan for concentrating on an all-out thrust across the north German plain, Eisenhower made an effort to turn the northern flank of the German defenses by landing three air-borne divisions to capture bridges across the Meuse, Waal, and Rhine rivers. This effort failed when the British 1st Airborne Division was unable to hold a bridge across the Rhine at Arnhem, and the Allies were denied the opportunity to make a rapid drive across the north German plain. Instead, they brought up reinforcements for a winter campaign through the heavy German defenses manned by armies now regrouped and strengthened.

While American and British armies were probing along the length of the Siegfried Line, Hitler laid plans for one final gamble—a counteroffensive through the weak center of the Allied lines in the Ardennes Forest. This he hoped would split the enemy's forces and carry to Liége and perhaps Antwerp. Bad weather in late November and early December enabled Von Rundstedt, the German commander, to bring up his forces in secret. They struck furiously in the Ardennes on December 16 and scored heavily until Allied counterattacks forced them to withdraw. The Battle of the Bulge, as the German offensive is commonly known, was over by January 1945. Hitler's gamble had cost him his last reserves of aircraft and some of his best divisions.

In fact, the German army in the west was so weakened by ruinous losses in the Ardennes counteroffensive that it could no longer prevent the Allied armies from advancing to the Rhine. Forces under Field Marshal Montgomery captured Cleves, in the north, on February 12. Cologne fell to the American First Army on March 6. Troops of the French First and the American Third and Seventh armies had cleared the Saar and Palatinate areas in the south by March 25. Meanwhile, American troops by an unbelievable stroke of good luck captured the Ludendorff Bridge across the Rhine at Remagen on March 7 before it could be demolished. They quickly established a bridgehead on the other side of the river.

Anglo-American armies were now poised along the Rhine for a final drive into the heart of Germany, and Russian armies were massed on the Oder River for an assault upon Berlin. But new tensions between the western democracies and Russia gave warning of troubled times ahead. For one thing, the Russians in February 1945 had ruthlessly imposed a Communist

---

[22] Winston S. Churchill, *Triumph and Tragedy* (Boston, 1953), p. 402.

ALLIED OFFENSIVES TO THE RHINE
1944-1945

GREAT BRITAIN

NORTH SEA

NETH.

Norwich

Ipswich

London

Dover

Brighton

Portsmouth

Boulogne

Dunkirk

Calais

Abbeville

ENGLISH CHANNEL

Cherbourg

Le Havre

Rouen

St.Lo

Caen

Falaise

Avranches

Rennes

Laval

Le Mans

Lorient

St. Nazaire

Nantes

Angers

BREAKOUT
AT ST.LO
JULY 25,1944

Amiens

Compiegne

Amsterdam

The Hague
Rotterdam

WAAL
MAAS

Arnhem

Münster

Essen
Dortmund

Düsseldorf
Cologne

Kassel

BELG.

Ghent

Antwerp
Brussels

Lille

Cambrai

Dinant

Bonn

Aachen

BATTLE LINE
DECEMBER 15
1944

GERMANY

REMAGEN
BRIDGE
MAR.7,1945

Coblenz

Frankfurt

Mainz

Mannheim

Karlsruhe

Strasbourg

Colmar

Freiburg

Basel

BATTLE OF
THE BULGE
DEC. 1944

Bastogne

Sedan

LUX.

SAAR

Verdun

Metz

Nancy

Belfort

Besançon

Bern

SWITZ.

Evreux

Paris

Chartres

SEINE

Orléans

LOIRE

Tours

Bourges

Nevers

Reims

Sens

Epinal

Dijon

SAÔNE

Sombernon

Bourg

Geneva

ITALY

Turin

Savona

FRANCE

La Rochelle
Rochefort

Limoges

Vichy

Clermont
Ferrand

Lyon

Grenoble

Montélimar

RHONE

Sisteron

Bordeaux

GARONNE

Toulouse

Montpellier

Narbonne

Avignon

Marseille

Toulon

Nice

St.Raphaël

St.
Tropez

Bayonne

Pamplona

Perpignan

LANDINGS
IN SOUTHERN FRANCE
AUGUST 15, 1944

SPAIN

Lérida

Barcelona

AMERICAN

BRITISH AND
CANADIAN

FRENCH

TRM

100 MILES

government on Rumania. For another, Anglo-American negotiations with a German general for surrender of German forces in Italy had caused Stalin to address a letter to Roosevelt virtually accusing him and Churchill of treacherously negotiating for surrender of all German forces in the West so that British and American armies could occupy Berlin before the Russians.

Even more ominous were Russian actions in Poland. It was bad enough that the Russians had refused to honor the Yalta agreement to reorganize the puppet Lublin government. Even worse, they had also refused to allow American and British observers to enter Poland and had proceeded to liquidate the leaders of the democratic parties in that unhappy country. It was plain that Stalin would tolerate no Polish government that he could not completely control; indeed, he admitted as much in correspondence with Churchill. The Polish dispute was nearing the point of open rupture by mid-March, but Roosevelt was now so weak that he had lost his grasp and could not take leadership in opposing Soviet violations of the Yalta agreements. Actually, Poland was irretrievably lost to Communist imperialism, as Stalin's blunt replies to Churchill's vigorous protests revealed.

Poland was lost, but not yet Prague and Berlin, if the Allies resolved to act quickly and send their armies hurtling across Germany. Churchill perceived clearly enough that "Soviet Russia had become a mortal danger to the free world." He pleaded all through April and early May with his American colleagues to push as rapidly as possible toward the two central European capitals. Even more important, he proposed that the Allies stay in force on this forward eastern line until the Russians had honored earlier promises.[23]

The reasons for failure to attempt to seize strong outposts in Central Europe can best be seen in an account of military and political events. The combined Anglo-American armies began their crossing of the Rhine on March 24. Montgomery's forces in the north and Bradley's in the center had converged by April 1 to encircle the Ruhr and trap more than 250,000 German troops. General Montgomery was all for driving straight to Berlin. But Eisenhower, for what seemed to be sound military reasons, decided to "push his main force from the Kassel-Frankfurt area to the Elbe, split the German forces, cut off Berlin from the so-called 'National Redoubt' area [the Bavarian mountains, where Hitler was reputed to be preparing for a last stand], and then turn his forces directly to the north and to the southwest of the Elbe. These maneuvers would enable him to seize ports on the North Sea and the Baltic and also clean up the area to the south before the enemy could assemble a force there."[24]

Eisenhower relayed this decision to Stalin directly on March 28. Stalin was pleased, but Churchill was so distressed that he appealed personally to

[23] The Big Three at Yalta had approved the occupation zones drawn earlier by the European Advisory Commission, but Roosevelt and Churchill had made no agreement anywhere to stop their armies at any certain point. Churchill argued that Russian violations had already invalidated the Yalta agreements. He proposed to occupy as much of the Soviet zone of Germany and of Czechoslovakia as possible, and to stay there until the Russians lived up to the agreement on Poland and consented to a real integration of the occupation administration in Germany.

[24] Forrest C. Pogue, "The Decision to Halt at the Elbe," in K. R. Greenfield (ed.), *Command Decisions* (New York, 1959), p. 378.

Roosevelt to join him in ordering the Supreme Commander to move against Berlin. "I deem it highly important," the Prime Minister wrote to Eisenhower on April 2, "that we should shake hands with the Russians as far to the east as possible." Eisenhower, however, argued that his plan was sound on military grounds; and he had the firm support of other American field generals. "I could see no political advantage accruing from the capture of Berlin that would offset the need for quick destruction of the German army on our front," Bradley writes. "As soldiers we looked naïvely on this British inclination to complicate the war with political foresight and nonmilitary objectives." [25]

The vanguard of the American army reached the Elbe, only fifty-three miles from Berlin. The Russians were still on the banks of the Oder, thirty to forty miles from the German capital. Churchill now redoubled his pleading, but his voice was no longer heard in Washington. Roosevelt was tired and unable to stand any longer at the helm. He wanted rest and recovery, not a new quarrel with the Russians. He went to Warm Springs early in April to renew his strength before opening the San Francisco Conference of the United Nations on April 25. On April 12 he complained of a terrific headache, lost consciousness, and died at 4:35 p.m. of a massive cerebral hemorrhage.

Roosevelt's growing weakness and death came at a fateful time in the history of the world. The new President, Harry S. Truman, had been utterly unprepared by his predecessor. Eisenhower had submitted a plan for further action to the Combined Chiefs of Staff on April 7. He proposed pushing through to the Elbe near Leipzig and then turning northward to the Baltic coast in order to prevent the Russians from occupying any part of the Danish peninsula. He added that he saw no point in making Berlin a military objective, but that he would cheerfully accept the Combined Chiefs' decision on this matter. The Combined Chiefs did not discuss the question of Berlin. President Truman supported Eisenhower's proposal. Even Churchill agreed on April 19 that the Anglo-American forces were "not immediately in a position to force their way into Berlin." Eisenhower informed Stalin of his plan on April 21, adding that he intended to send forces not only northward but also southward into the Danube Valley. He sent General Patton into Bavaria on the following day.

Even at this late date Eisenhower could have captured Prague with ease, and Churchill pleaded for action that "might make the whole difference to the post-war situation in Czechoslovakia." Eisenhower in response decided to send Patton into Prague and so informed the Soviet High Command. But he called Patton back after receiving a vehement protest from Stalin. Thus while the Americans waited the Russians occupied Prague on May 9.

Meanwhile, Hitler remained in Berlin, confident that a miracle would yet save the Third Reich. He was heartened by Roosevelt's death and certain that the western Allies and Russia would soon turn against each other. But *Götterdämmerung* was near. Marshal Georgi K. Zhukov began a massive offensive across the Oder on April 15 that reached the suburbs of Berlin a week later. American and Russian troops met on the Elbe near Torgau on

ᴠᴠᴠᴠᴠᴠᴠᴠᴠᴠᴠᴠᴠᴠᴠᴠ

[25] Omar N. Bradley, *A Soldier's Story* (New York, 1951), pp. 535-6.

April 27. Italian Partisans captured and shot Mussolini on the following day. Hitler married Eva Braun in his bunker in Berlin and appointed Admiral Karl Doenitz his successor on April 29. He committed suicide on the next day, and his body was burned in the garden of the Reichschancellery.

Nothing remained but to end the war as quickly as possible. Nearly 1,000,000 German troops in northern Italy and Austria surrendered on May 2. Two days later German troops in northwest Germany, Holland, Schleswig-Holstein, and Denmark laid down their arms. Then Colonel General Alfred Jodl surrendered unconditionally the remnants of the German army, air force, and navy at Eisenhower's headquarters at Rheims at 2:41 a.m. on May 7. All hostilities ceased at midnight May 8, 1945. Churchill did not exaggerate when he wrote: "The unconditional surrender of our enemies was the signal for the greatest outburst of joy in the history of mankind." But the rejoicing throngs in Britain and America knew only of the triumph and nothing of the tragedy that overshadowed the world. "I moved amid cheering crowds," Churchill remembers, "or sat at a table adorned with congratulations and blessings from every part of the Grand Alliance, with an aching heart and a mind oppressed by forebodings." [26]

199. *Victory in the Pacific*

American ground, naval, and air power in the Pacific was overwhelmingly preponderant by the early summer of 1944. The American navy, for example, was now five times stronger than the Imperial fleet. The time had come to close in on the stronghold of the enemy's inner ring. Admiral Raymond A. Spruance with a huge force of ships, aircraft, and troops moved against the strongly held Marianas, about 1,350 miles south of Tokyo. After a bitter struggle, in which the Japanese defended fanatically, the three principal islands in the group, Saipan, Tinian, and Guam, fell before the overpowering assault. While Americans were invading Saipan a large Japanese force of nine aircraft carriers, five battleships, and other ships sailed from the Philippines to intercept the invaders. Over 500 Japanese airplanes attacked and slightly damaged a battleship and two carriers on June 19, 1944. But the Japanese lost 402 airplanes and pilots, the core of their naval aviation. Pursuing American submarines and aircraft caught up with the Japanese fleet on June 20. They sank three Japanese carriers and two destroyers and severely damaged one battleship, four carriers, and other craft in the first Battle of the Philippine Sea on that date. American naval and ground forces then attacked the Western Caroline Islands in September, overpowering fierce resistance on Peleliu, Angaur, and Ngesebus islands, and neutralizing the main Japanese garrisons on the islands of Babelthuap and Yap.

While Admiral Nimitz's forces were clearing the Central Pacific route to the Philippines, General MacArthur farther in the Southwest Pacific was making final preparations for an invasion of the islands. First came an Allied drive in April and May 1944 that cleared the northern coast of New

---

[26] The quotations are from W. S. Churchill, *Triumph and Tragedy*, pp. 548 and 456.

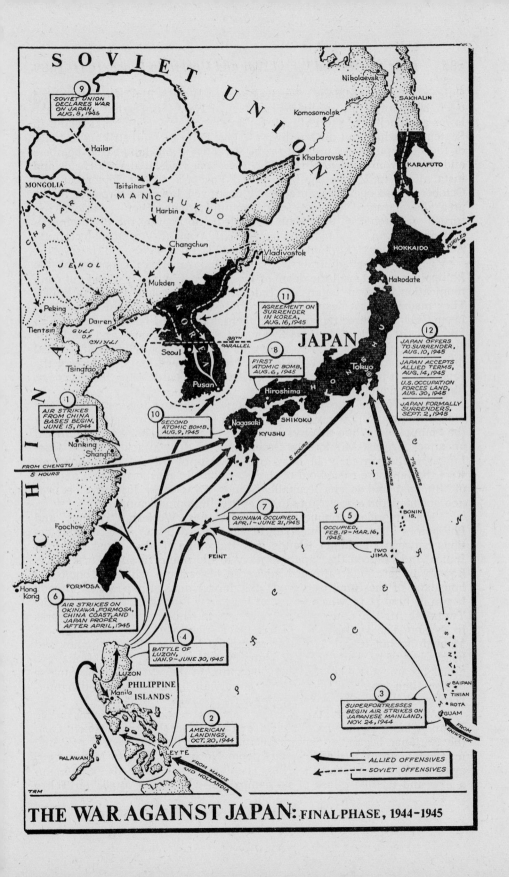

THE WAR AGAINST JAPAN: FINAL PHASE, 1944–1945

(9) SOVIET UNION DECLARES WAR ON JAPAN, AUG. 8, 1945

(11) AGREEMENT ON SURRENDER IN KOREA, AUG. 16, 1945

(8) FIRST ATOMIC BOMB, AUG. 6, 1945

(12) JAPAN OFFERS TO SURRENDER, AUG. 10, 1945 / JAPAN ACCEPTS ALLIED TERMS, AUG. 14, 1945 / U.S. OCCUPATION FORCES LAND, AUG. 30, 1945 / JAPAN FORMALLY SURRENDERS, SEPT. 2, 1945

(1) AIR STRIKES FROM CHINA BASES BEGIN, JUNE 15, 1944

(10) SECOND ATOMIC BOMB, AUG. 9, 1945

(7) OKINAWA OCCUPIED, APR. 1 – JUNE 21, 1945

(5) OCCUPIED, FEB. 19 – MAR. 16, 1945

(6) AIR STRIKES ON OKINAWA, FORMOSA, CHINA COAST, AND JAPAN PROPER AFTER APRIL, 1945

(4) BATTLE OF LUZON, JAN. 9 – JUNE 30, 1945

(2) AMERICAN LANDINGS, OCT. 20, 1944

(3) SUPERFORTRESSES BEGIN AIR STRIKES ON JAPANESE MAINLAND, NOV. 24, 1944

ALLIED OFFENSIVES — SOVIET OFFENSIVES

FROM CHENGTU 5 HOURS

5 HOURS

3¾ HOURS

7½ HOURS

FROM MANUS AND HOLLANDIA

FROM ENIWETOK

FEINT

TRM

Guinea; next, amphibious offensives against Wakde, Biak, Noemfoor, and other islands off the northwestern coast of New Guinea that cleared the lower approaches to the Philippines; finally, capture of Morotai Island in September, which put the Southwest Pacific Forces within striking distance of the Philippines. As prelude to the great invasion, land-based bombers and planes from carriers of the Third Fleet scourged Japanese airfields and installations in Mindanao, Luzon, and Formosa during September and October. These operations practically destroyed Japanese airpower in the area and disrupted Japanese sea communications. Then Americans returned on October 20 to redeem their pledge to liberate the Philippines— with an invasion of Leyte Island by the Sixth Army, the Seventh Fleet under Admiral Thomas C. Kinkaid, and the Third Fleet under Admiral Halsey.

The Japanese admirals well knew that American conquest of the Philippines would spell the doom of the Empire, because it would cut communication between Japan and Indochina, Malaya, and the East Indies. They made one last desperate effort to destroy the American invaders in Leyte Gulf. The three naval engagements that ensued between October 24 and 25—the Battle of Surigao Strait, the Battle off Samar, and the Battle off Cape Engaño, collectively known as the Battle for Leyte Gulf—ended disastrously for the Japanese. In this greatest naval battle in history the Japanese lost practically their entire fleet—three battleships, four carriers, nine cruisers, and eight destroyers.

The threat of Japanese naval intervention was forever ended, and MacArthur could now press forward with his overwhelming campaign in the Philippines. While the invasion of Leyte was at its height, he launched an attack against Mindoro in December and then attacked Luzon from Lingayen Gulf in early January 1945. Not until July 5, 1945, however, were the Japanese rooted out of the mountains of northern Luzon and out of Mindanao and dozens of smaller islands. All told, the Japanese lost over 400,000 men and 9,000 planes in the entire Philippines campaign.

The American conquest of the Marianas, Western Carolines, and Philippines blasted the inner rim of Japanese defenses, cut communications between the home islands and Indochina, Malaya, and the East Indies, and reduced the Japanese navy to the size of a single task force. Equally important, it afforded advanced bases from which to bomb the homeland of the Empire. Indeed, the air war against Japan had already begun in June 1944, when a force of large new B-29 Superfortresses of the Twentieth Air Force, operating from bases in China, attacked steel works in Kyushu. The Twentieth Air Force made subsequent raids on Japan and Manchuria, but its operations were limited because all its supplies and bombs had to be flown over the Himalayan Hump from India. A massive attack became possible only with the capture of the Marianas. The capture of Iwo Jima later yielded bases for American fighter planes and fighter-bombers that joined in the increasing aerial assault.

All told, American planes dropped about 160,000 tons of bombs on the Japanese home islands from November 1944, when the bombardment from the Marianas began, to September 1945, when the war ended. Air commanders concentrated their attack from November 1944 to March 1945 against Japanese aircraft factories. Then, on March 9, the Air Force began a new and terrible phase of its campaign—a firebomb attack on Tokyo that destroyed sixteen square miles of the city and caused 185,000 casualties. It was followed soon afterward by similar fire raids on Nagoya, Osaka, and Kobe. Thereafter the Air Force alternated saturation bombing of some sixty-six civilian areas with attacks on industrial and military targets.

Although the tonnage of bombs dropped on Japan was about one ninth of that dropped on Germany, the physical destruction in Japan almost equaled that in Germany. American bombs killed 330,000 Japanese civilians and injured nearly 500,000; moreover, they destroyed 2,510,000 buildings and 40 per cent of the built-up areas of sixty-six cities. The effects on the Japanese war economy were equally devastating. Air attacks by July 1945 had reduced the productive capacity of Japanese oil refineries by 83 per cent, of aircraft engine plants by 75 per cent, of electronics and communication equipment plants by 70 per cent, and of munitions factories by some 30 per cent. For a nation with an industrial capacity only 10 per cent that of its chief enemy, these losses were fatal.

Let us now turn back to the last phase of the relentless American drive by land and sea toward Japan. While MacArthur was bringing the Philippines campaign to its climax, marine divisions invaded Iwo Jima, 750 miles south of Japan, on February 19, 1945. The Japanese defenders had made the island virtually one vast pillbox. They fought so courageously that the Iwo Jima operation was the bloodiest in the history of the United States Marine Corps. However, the entire island, with its two airfields, was in American hands by March 16. Next came a larger attack, beginning April 1, by marine and army forces against Okinawa, a large island in the Ryukyus only 350 miles southwest of Japan. The Japanese and American leaders both knew that the fall of Okinawa would spell the early doom of the Empire. The defenders, therefore, fought fanatically during the battle that raged from April 1 to June 21 and lost nearly 111,000 dead and 9,000 prisoners. The most spectacular aspect of the Japanese defense was the unrelenting and often effective *kamikaze,* or suicide, attacks by Japanese aircraft against American warships and transports. All told, the Japanese lost some 4,000 aircraft, 3,500 of them in *kamikaze* attacks, during the Battle of Okinawa.

By this time the main question was whether Japan would collapse internally before the Americans had launched their final invasion of the island empire. We have noted the terrible devastation wrought by the Superfortresses from Saipan. They were joined in February 1945 by thousands of planes of the Third Fleet and in April by fighter-bombers from Iwo Jima and Okinawa. American battleships and heavy cruisers joined in the attack in mid-July by shelling steel works, synthetic oil plants, and other industrial targets on the mainland and by heavy attacks upon Japanese shipping. But Japan was suffering most from a combined sea, air, and mine blockade that had reduced her once large merchant fleet to ineffectiveness and deprived her people of food and her industries of vital raw materials.[27]

[27] Japan entered the war with 6,000,000 tons of merchant shipping and constructed an additional 4,100,000 tons between 1941 and 1945. Of this total of 10,100,000 tons, the Japanese lost 8,900,000—54.7 per cent to submarines, 16.3 per cent to carrier-based planes, 14.5 per cent to land-based planes, 9.3 per cent to mines laid by B-29s, 4 per cent to marine accidents, and less than 1 per cent to surface gunfire.

Indeed, it had been evident to certain Japanese leaders since the autumn of 1943 that they were fighting a losing battle, and that the Imperial government should seek peace, even at the cost of giving up China, Korea, and Formosa. On July 18, 1944, soon after the American invasion of the Marianas, a moderate group led principally by the naval chieftains forced Tojo to resign and established a new Cabinet under General Kuniaki Koiso. An important element in the new government, led by Navy Minister Mitsumasa Yonai and allied with officials in the Imperial Court, were determined to end the war as quickly as possible. The Emperor threw his full support to the peace party in February 1945. After the invasion of Okinawa on April 8, he appointed Baron Kantaro Suzuki as Premier and ordered him to end the war. Suzuki, however, did not control the army. It was determined to fight to the bitter end and threatened to revolt if the Cabinet moved for peace. Thus the Cabinet began secret discussions in May with the Russian Ambassador, Jacob Malik, looking toward Russian mediation. In addition, the Emperor appealed directly to the Soviet government in June and July to help arrange peace talks with the United States.

This was the situation when Truman, Churchill, Clement Attlee, soon to be Churchill's successor, and Stalin met at Potsdam on July 17, 1945, for the last conference of the Big Three. Truman almost certainly knew about the Japanese peace overtures even before the Potsdam Conference met; in any event, Stalin soon gave full information about them. The President was not inclined to take the overtures seriously. He did not trust the Japanese, and his military advisers believed that Japan would not surrender until Allied forces had invaded and occupied Japan. He therefore approved a discouraging Soviet reply to Tokyo.

Meanwhile, word had come to the American leaders at Potsdam on July 16 that an atomic bomb had been exploded in New Mexico. Knowing that the bomb was a reality (there were materials on hand to assemble two additional bombs at once), and that its use might avert the necessity of a long and bloody campaign in Japan, Truman now concentrated on a public warning to Japan. It was the Potsdam Declaration issued on July 26 under Truman's, Churchill's, and Chiang Kai-shek's signatures. It promised stern justice to Japanese war criminals and enforcement of the Cairo Declaration stripping Japan of all conquests. But it also held out the hope of generous treatment of a Japan purged and reformed. "The alternative for Japan," it concluded, "is prompt and utter destruction."

The leaders of the Suzuki government in Tokyo agreed to accept the Potsdam Declaration but could not persuade the army leaders to surrender. When Suzuki, on July 28, declared, only for home consumption, that the Potsdam Declaration was "unworthy of public notice," President Truman and his advisers took this as a refusal and decided to use the atomic bomb.[28] The decision was made largely on military grounds. The Japanese were doomed, to be sure, but they still had large supplies of weapons and an

[28] This decision to use the bomb if the Japanese refused to surrender was actually made at Potsdam on July 22, after intensive discussions among Truman, American military leaders, and Churchill, and after earlier discussions in the War Department and among the scientists involved in the Manhattan Project.

army of 2,000,000 in the home islands. An invasion would surely have succeeded only at great human costs on both sides.

Thus a lone B-29 flew over Hiroshima on August 6 and dropped the first atomic bomb used in warfare. It leveled 4.4 square miles of the city and killed between 70,000 and 80,000 persons. On the same day President Truman announced the news to the world and "warned the Japanese that if they did not surrender they could expect 'a rain of ruin from the air, the like of which has never been seen on this earth.' " [29] Still the Japanese army refused to surrender. Then, on August 9, news came to Tokyo that Russia had entered the war,[30] and that the Americans had dropped a second atomic bomb on Nagasaki. When hurried conferences failed to yield agreement to accept the Potsdam ultimatum, the Emperor made the decision for peace. The Cabinet informed the Washington government on the following day that it accepted the Potsdam terms, provided that the status of the Emperor would not be changed. The military and naval chieftains balked when Washington replied on August 11 that the Emperor must be subject to the Supreme Commander of the Allied Powers. But the Emperor insisted, and the Suzuki government formally accepted the Allied demands on August 14. The Emperor at once prepared records of an Imperial Rescript ordering his armed forces to surrender; and the Cabinet, after suppressing an insurrection of army fanatics, sent emissaries to General MacArthur to arrange the details of surrender. A great Allied fleet entered Tokyo Bay on September 2. Soon afterward Foreign Minister Mamoru Shigemitsu and a representative of the Imperial General Staff signed articles of surrender on board the battleship *Missouri*. General MacArthur and representatives of the Allied powers accepted on behalf of their respective governments.

∧∧∧∧∧∧∧∧∧∧∧∧∧∧∧∧∧∧∧

[29] Louis Morton, "The Decision to Use the Atomic Bomb," K. R. Greenfield (ed.), *Command Decisions*, p. 407.

[30] The conferees at Potsdam had given careful attention to Russian plans for participation. American leaders still welcomed Russian intervention even though they were by no means as eager for it as they had been earlier.

CHAPTER

25

The American Economy

1940–1960

I T IS a forbidding task to relate in one chapter the swift emergence of the American people from the worst depression in their history to an unprecedented level of prosperity. Even more formidable is the attempt to describe the new economic society which Americans had achieved by mid-century. Yet it is a story worth the telling, for we cannot meet the problems of the future unless we understand the past and present. And the future is already here.

200. The American People, 1940–1960

One of the most significant developments in the postdepression decades was a demographic revolution, beginning in the early 1940's, which dramatically reversed the steadily declining birth rate of the previous twenty years and confounded the gloomy predictions made by population experts before the Second World War. (See above, pp. 249–251.) With the advent of selective service and the war in 1940–1 the birth rate began to rise sharply, declining momentarily in 1944–5 because of the absence of millions of men in Europe and Asia. Then, as veterans returned to build homes and begin families, the birth rate resumed its rapid increase—from 19.4 per thousand in 1940, to 23.3 in 1946, to a peak of 25.8 in 1947. Demographers were even more suprised when the postwar years witnessed no real decline in the new high rate, but rather a leveling off within a range only slightly below the 1947 peak. After dropping slightly to 24.1 in 1950,

POPULATION CHANGE, 1940-1960

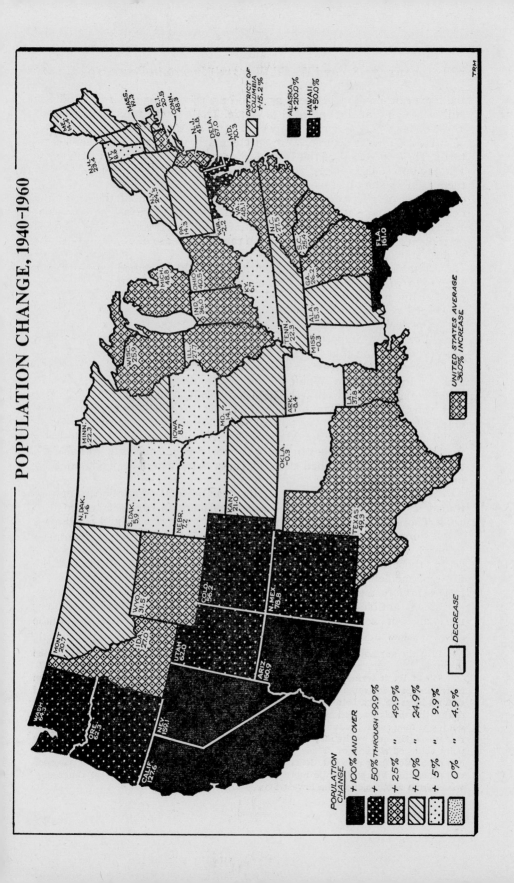

ME. 4.4
N.H. 23.4
VT. 8.6
MASS. 19.3
R.I. 20.15
CONN. 48.3
N.Y. 24.5
N.J. 45.8
DELA. 67.0
MD. 70.3

DISTRICT OF COLUMBIA +15.2%

ALASKA +200.0%

HAWAII +50.0%

PA. 14.3
W.VA. -2.2
VA. 40.1
N.C. 27.5
S.C. 25.4
GA. 26.2
FLA. 161.0

MICH. 48.8
OHIO 40.5
IND. 36.0
ILL. 27.7
KY. 6.7
TENN. 22.3
ALA. 15.3
MISS. -0.3

WISC. 25.9
IOWA 8.7
MO. 14.1
ARK. -8.4
LA. 37.8

MINN. 22.3
N. DAK. -1.6
S. DAK. 5.9
NEBR. 7.2
KAN. 21.0
OKLA. -0.3
TEXAS 49.3

MONT. 20.7
IDAHO 27.0
WYO. 31.5
COLO. 56.2
N. MEX. 78.8

WASH. 62.3
ORE. 62.3
NEV. 159.1
UTAH 63.0
ARIZ. 160.9
CALIF. 127.6

UNITED STATES AVERAGE 36.0% INCREASE

POPULATION CHANGE

+ 100% AND OVER
+ 50% THROUGH 99.9%
+ 25% "   " 49.9%
+ 10% "   " 24.9%
+ 5%   "   " 9.9%
+ 0%   "   " 4.9%

DECREASE

TRM

the birth rate hovered between 25.0 and 25.3 from 1953 to 1957 and was still above 24.0 at the end of the decade. The average rate for the period 1940–60 had not been equaled since the early 1920's.

The results, of course, were spectacularly reflected in the census returns. The population of the United States expanded from 132,122,000 to 151,325,000 souls between 1940 and 1950. No previous ten-year period in the nation's history had recorded so large a numerical increase, and the rate of increase of 14.5 per cent was more than twice that of the preceding decade. Even more startling were the figures for the 1950's. The Census of 1960 reported a new record increase of 28,000,000 Americans since 1950, a total population of 179,323,000, and a rate of increase of 18.5 per cent, the highest since the decade 1900–10.

Certainly the war and postwar prosperity, which seemed to offer secure futures to young Americans, was an important factor in this remarkable change. But prosperity does not alone explain the increase, for prosperity during the 1920's had been accompanied by a steady decline in birth rates, while the depression alone was not responsible for the further decline after 1929. Even more important was a pervading change in social values—a growing conviction that families of three and four children were "normal" and desirable, in contrast to the socially correct family of one and two children in the thirties. Whatever the causes, the results of the rise in the birth rate after 1940 were wonderful to behold—an annual crop of babies that warmed the hearts of manufacturers of washing machines and diapers,[1] and a whole new set of calculations concerning America's future social and economic needs and capacities. Whether the future would bring further significant changes in the birth rate, no one could say, although in the fifties the unchastened demographers were again at work on their projections.[2]

Along with the increase in birth rates and total population went continued improvement in the health of the American people from 1940 to 1960. There was a steady growth in concern for the mentally ill of all ages. Admissions to mental hospitals increased from 158,253 in 1940 to 296,359 in 1956, while the number of beds in mental hospitals considerably exceeded those in general hospitals by the latter date. Further advances in the fields of medicine and surgery, better diet, continually expanding public health services, and above all a vast array of new drugs—like sulfanilamide, penicillin, antibiotics, and cortisone—all combined to render impotent many ancient enemies of mankind. The use of penicillin, for example, made

　　[1] Nearly 4,250,000 babies were born in 1959, as compared with a paltry 2,200,000 in 1930.

　　[2] Actually, it seemed that the American population would continue to grow at an increasing rate for some time to come. The net reproduction rate, or intrinsic rate of natural increase, is a better index than the crude birth rate. The net reproduction rate during the 1930's hovered around 981, which meant that the American population was not in the long run reproducing itself. From 1944 to 1949, however, the net reproduction rate was 1,385, and by the middle fifties it had climbed past 1,700—far higher than any point achieved since 1900. Their confidence in the continued upward trend in American population fully restored, demographers have recently predicted a total of 210,000,-000 Americans by 1970, while more advanced estimates for the year 2000 range anywhere from 230,000,000 (the lowest figure) to nearly 300,000,000.

possible the virtual eradication of venereal diseases. The perfection and widespread availability of the famous Salk vaccine by the late fifties had greatly reduced the ravages of the dread poliomyelitis. The use of sulfa drugs, penicillin, and other antibiotics reduced the number of deaths from influenza and pneumonia from 65.5 per 100,000 in 1940 to 32.5 in 1959. Typhoid, diphtheria, malaria, and childbirth fever practically disappeared, while three times as many Americans died from automobile accidents in 1958 as from tuberculosis, which had been the greatest single cause of death in 1900. Consequently, the death rate decreased from 10.8 per thousand in 1940 to 9.6 in 1950, and to 9.5 in 1960,[3] while the average life expectancy for white males increased from forty-six years in 1901 to sixty years in 1940, and to sixty-six years in 1958. Thus Americans in the period 1940–60 were growing older and younger at the same time. But as they grew older they faced new perils as the diseases of old age—heart diseases, cancer, arteriosclerosis, and mental illnesses—took an increasing toll and moved into first rank as the undisputed enemies of American life.

By 1960 it appeared that one long-range trend in the racial composition of the American people—the slowly declining percentage of non-white to total population—had at least temporarily been reversed. This was a result primarily of the precipitous drop in the death rate among Negroes and other non-white Americans, as rising educational and living standards and increased medical and health facilities enabled this segment of the populace to escape the diseases attendant upon poverty and ignorance. The number of non-whites rose from slightly over 16,000,000 in 1950 to nearly 20,-500,000 in 1960—an increase of 26.7 per cent, as compared with an increase of 18.5 per cent for the American people as a whole. Nearly 19,-000,000, or 92 per cent, of the non-white inhabitants were Negroes. The ratio of non-whites to total population increased from 10.5 per cent in 1950 to approximately 12 per cent in 1960.[4]

The percentage of foreign-born Americans continued to register a decline in the period 1940–60. Ninety-three of every one hundred Americans were native-born in 1950—the highest proportion ever recorded—and the sheer number of the foreign-born was lower at mid-century than at any time since 1890. By 1960 the percentage of foreign-born had dwindled to five per cent. This figure would have been even smaller had not Congress consented under presidential and public pressure to liberalize slightly the immigration laws after the Second World War. By the War Brides

〰〰〰〰〰〰〰〰〰〰〰

[3] Even more spectacular and gratifying was the decline in the death rate among Negroes, from 13.8 per thousand in 1940 to 11.2 in 1950, and to an estimated 9.9 in 1959—only slightly above the national rate, as opposed to a Negro death rate 50 per cent higher than the national rate in 1900 and nearly 30 per cent higher as recently as 1940.

[4] Better standards of health, education, and income account for the 25 per cent increase in America's Negro population between 1950 and 1960, and for much of the 46.5 per cent increase in the number of American Indians. Part of the latter figure, however, is accounted for by the admission of Alaska to the Union in 1958; and the admission of Hawaii in 1959 similarly explains much of the sizeable increase—42 and 58 per cent, respectively—in the numbers of Japanese and Chinese in this country. Over half a million Indians, more than 460,000 Japanese, and nearly a quarter of a million Chinese were enumerated by the Census of 1960.

Act of 1946 and the Displaced Persons Act of 1948, amended in 1950 to remove discriminations against southern and eastern Europeans, Congress permitted some 1,500,000 quota immigrants to enter the country from 1946 through 1958. This total, which does not include some 1,000,000 non-quota arrivals from other New World countries, was the largest number of immigrants admitted in any comparable period since the early 1920's. But it was small as compared with the number who would have come had the gates at Ellis Island been opened wide.

To stop at this point in our survey of the American people would be to overlook the revolutionary internal changes that occurred in the population from 1940 to 1960. The defense and war crises and the high prosperity of the postwar years stimulated such astounding movements of people as the country had not seen since the high tide of the westward land movement. While the Northeast, the Plains states, and parts of the South grew in population more slowly then the nation as a whole, other areas recorded spectacular gains from 1940 to 1960. The area north of the Ohio and east of the Mississippi increased by 40 per cent, the South Atlantic states by nearly 50 per cent, the Mountain states by 66 per cent, and the Pacific states by an amazing 110 per cent—as compared with a national population increase of 33 per cent over the same period.

Expanding economic opportunities accounted for most of the large gains in such states as Michigan, New Jersey, Delaware, Maryland, Washington, and Texas, but it is significant that by far the most impressive growth took place in states that offered not only new jobs but a pleasanter mode of existence. The enormous gains in New Mexico (80 per cent), Arizona (160 per cent), Nevada (170 per cent), and above all in California (127 per cent) and Florida (160 per cent), are traceable primarily to mild and healthful climate and an attractive array of recreational facilities—national parks and mountain resorts in the West and Southwest generally, lush night clubs and casinos in Nevada, and year-round sunshine and warmth in Arizona, California, and Florida. A booming tourist trade in these states reflected the higher incomes and increased leisure time that more and more Americans were enjoying in the prosperous postwar years. And the fact that California, Arizona, and Florida were becoming vast, permanent Meccas for invalids and retired persons offered further dramatic evidence that Americans in the fifties were healthier and wealthier than ever before, and wiser at least in their heightened interest in planning for a comfortable retirement. This latter concern, of course, was natural enough for a nation in which the number of people aged sixty-five and over increased from 9,000,000 in 1940 to nearly 16,000,000 in 1960.

The most important population change of the forties and fifties was the continued movement from countryside to cities and the further decline in farm population. The latter shrank in absolute numbers, from 1940 to 1960, from over 30,000,000 to less than 21,000,000, a drop of nearly one third, while the percentage of Americans living in urban areas increased from 56 to 75 over the same period. The United States had truly become a nation of city dwellers by 1960.

The most significant phenomenon of urban growth was the further expansion of the suburban areas adjacent to the central cities of the so-called metropolitan districts. The Census in 1940 counted 140 such dis-

POPULATION DENSITY, 1960

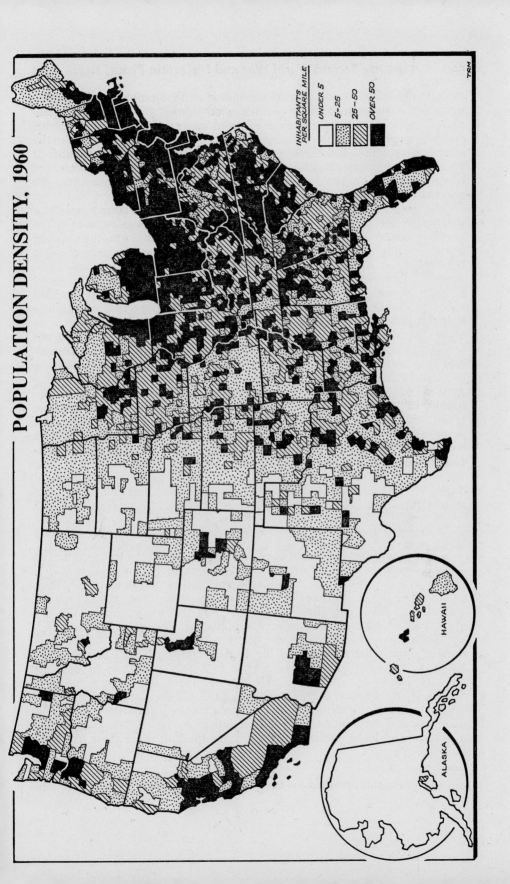

INHABITANTS
PER SQUARE MILE

UNDER 5

5 – 25

25 – 50

OVER 50

HAWAII

ALASKA

tricts, containing 48 per cent of the nation's inhabitants. By 1960 there were 211 metropolitan districts with a combined population of nearly 112,000,000, or 62 per cent of the national total. Over 75 per cent of this enormous urban increase between 1940 and 1960 was registered in the suburban as opposed to the central portions of the metropolitan districts. With the exception of cities that continued to expand their corporate boundaries, such as Los Angeles and Houston, all of the largest American cities either suffered actual losses in population or barely held their own during the fifties. But the complex of suburbs around them grew at a staggering rate and sprawled steadily further into the once rural adjacent areas. No break in the pattern seemed likely; the typical American in the latter half of the twentieth century was not merely a city-dweller, but a suburbanite.

One other important internal population trend remains to be noted here—the acceleration of the movement of Negroes from the South to the North and other sections. The number of Negroes living outside the South increased from a little over 3,000,000 in 1940 to almost 5,000,000 in 1950, and to well over 7,000,000 in 1960. Actually, if the non-southern total is expanded to include the Negro populations of Maryland, Delaware, Missouri, and the District of Columbia—as it ought to be, since the Negroes living in those areas were largely city-dwellers, enjoying the same increased economic and social opportunities that existed farther North—the number of Negroes living outside the South in 1960 stood at over 8,500,000, or 45 per cent of the total. This reflected a migration of truly awesome proportions. Since 1940 the southern Negro population had increased by a bare 10 per cent, while the number residing outside the South had multiplied two and a half times.

201.   *The American People, 1940–1960: Income, Wealth, and Industry*

The years from the end of the Great Depression to the inauguration of John F. Kennedy were, by and large, a time of such growth in industry, wealth, and incomes as the American people had not hitherto experienced, even during the boom times of the 1920's. Recovery from the depression was already fairly complete before the great defense spending of 1941 opened a new era in American economic history. The gross national product, enormously stimulated by the heavy volume of defense and war production during the first half of the forties, increased (in constant 1960 dollars) from $233,800,000,000 in 1940 to $369,100,000,000 in 1945. At the same time, per capita disposable income,[5] measured in the same 1960 dollars, increased from $1,274 in 1940 to $1,669 in 1945. In the latter year, moreover, unemployment was at an almost irreducible minimum; and individuals and corporations had accumulated savings of $48,500,000,000, and state and local governments surpluses totaling more than $10,000,-000,000.

~~~~~~~~~~~~~~~~~~~~~~~

[5] That is, income left after taxes and Social Security payments.

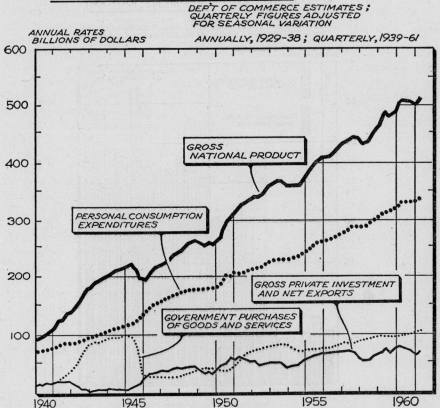

GROSS NATIONAL PRODUCT, 1940-1961

DEP'T OF COMMERCE ESTIMATES;
QUARTERLY FIGURES ADJUSTED
FOR SEASONAL VARIATION

ANNUAL RATES
BILLIONS OF DOLLARS
ANNUALLY, 1929-38; QUARTERLY, 1939-61

GROSS NATIONAL PRODUCT

PERSONAL CONSUMPTION EXPENDITURES

GROSS PRIVATE INVESTMENT AND NET EXPORTS

GOVERNMENT PURCHASES OF GOODS AND SERVICES

Even so, economists and public leaders were obsessed in 1945 by the fear of economic storms ahead when private industry converted from war to civilian production. Rarely had learned predictions been so far from the mark, for the nation stood on the verge, not of a postwar depression, but an era of unprecedented economic expansion and lasting achievement. There was pent-up consumer and local governmental demand, accompanied by huge savings, a continuation of large-scale federal spending and an easy monetary policy, a high level of foreign trade financed in part by an out-pouring of billions of American dollars, and a resumption of construction on an intensified scale. All these forces combined in 1945 and afterward to confound the prophets of gloom and drive the economy forward at a dizzy speed.

The gross national product, in 1960 dollars, declined from its ab-normal war peak to a level of about $320,000,000,000 in 1946 and 1947. It then rose steadily until the Korean War stimulated a new outburst of activity culminating in a gross national product of $425,000,000,000 in 1953. A continued expansion in civilian production, together with the high level of defense spending that remained a significant element in the Ameri-

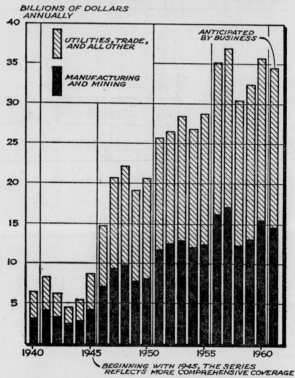

BUSINESS EXPENDITURES ON
NEW PLANT AND EQUIPMENT, 1940-1961

*FEDERAL RESERVE ESTIMATES THROUGH 1944,
DEPARTMENT OF COMMERCE, AND SECURITIES
AND EXCHANGE COMMISSION ESTIMATES, 1945-1961*

*BILLIONS OF DOLLARS
ANNUALLY*

*UTILITIES, TRADE,
AND ALL OTHER*

*MANUFACTURING
AND MINING*

*ANTICIPATED
BY BUSINESS*

*BEGINNING WITH 1945, THE SERIES
REFLECTS MORE COMPREHENSIVE COVERAGE*

can economy even after the Korean truce in 1953, resulted in a steady rise
in gross national product during the rest of the decade. The figure stood at
an unprecedented $503,000,000,000 in 1960. In spite of considerable in-
flation after 1945 and the imposition of new income and corporate taxes in
1950 and 1951, aggregate disposable income, measured in constant 1960
dollars, declined only slightly in 1946 and 1947 and rose steadily afterward until it reached a peak of $354,200,000,000, or $1,969 per capita,
in 1960—an increase of over 66 per cent since 1940.[6]

To be sure, inflation was a constant threat to economic stability all
during the postwar years. It first developed during the war because dis-

---

[6] The tonic of prosperity affected almost every segment of the economy and spurred,
from 1946 through 1960, an investment of over $400,000,000,000 in new plant and
equipment and of nearly $59,000,000,000 in farm equipment and construction. It also
stimulated the building of nearly 17,000,000 nonfarm private homes and apartment
houses (at a total cost of over $216,000,000,000) and the building of thousands of
schools, hospitals, and other public nonmilitary facilities (at a total cost of over $151,-
000,000,000).

WHOLESALE PRICES, 1940-1961
BUREAU OF LABOR STATISTICS INDEXES, 1947-1949=100

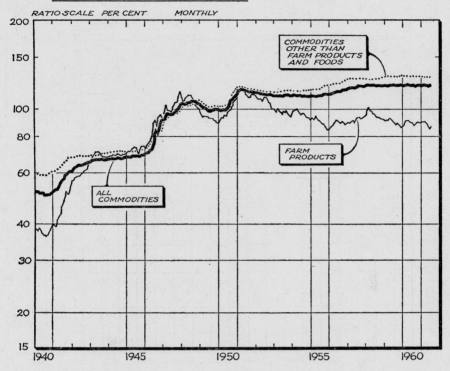

posable personal income grew at a much faster rate than the supply of food and civilian goods. It reached critical proportions in 1946–7, when the federal price control program collapsed and a series of strikes pushed prices inexorably higher. The general consumer price index (1947–9 = 100) rose from 76.9 in 1945 to 102.8 in 1948. It seemed that the tide had turned and that prices had reached a stable plateau in 1949. Then the outbreak of the Korean War in 1950 set the price indices off on a second inflationary spiral, until the general consumer price index reached a peak of 114.4 in 1953. For the next two years prices held fairly steady at about this level, only to begin another slow, uninterrupted climb in 1956 that brought the price index to an all-time high of 126.4 at the end of the decade.

In spite of inflation and its consequent hardships upon certain classes, the years from 1945 to 1960 were a time of unparalleled material prosperity for the mass of the American people. While population increased about 28 per cent during that period, the gross national product, in constant dollars, increased over 56 per cent, and total *disposable* personal income increased over 53 per cent, despite severe tax increases in 1950 and 1951. During the same period, moreover, the civilian labor force grew from 55,250,000 to nearly 67,000,000 persons, and the number of business firms increased from 3,242,000 to 4,659,000.

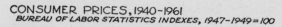

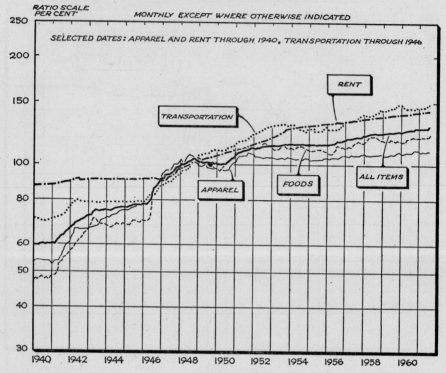

CONSUMER PRICES, 1940–1961
BUREAU OF LABOR STATISTICS INDEXES, 1947–1949 = 100

RATIO SCALE
PER CENT   MONTHLY EXCEPT WHERE OTHERWISE INDICATED

SELECTED DATES: APPAREL AND RENT THROUGH 1940, TRANSPORTATION THROUGH 1946

RENT

TRANSPORTATION

ALL ITEMS

APPAREL   FOODS

The foregoing generalizations fail to indicate the relative shifts in income distribution that occurred after 1940. As we have seen in an earlier chapter, farmers experienced incredible prosperity during the war years 1940–5, when net farm income, measured in 1960 dollars, almost doubled —from $10,449,000,000 to $19,347,000,000. Measured in these same dollars, net farm income stayed at about the same level through 1948 and then began an irregular downward plunge that continued throughout the fifties. Net farm income had shrunk (in 1960 dollars) to $12,549,000,000 in 1954, and to $11,073,000,000 in 1960. The plight of agriculture was not quite so acute as these figures would indicate, since total farm income was being divided among a far smaller agrarian population in 1960 than in the forties.[7] The decline in the number of farmers, however, did not keep pace

wwwwwwwwwwwwww

[7] The number of farms declined 37 per cent, from 5,859,000 in 1945 to 3,704,000 in 1959; and the farm population dwindled steadily after 1947, from 27,100,000 in that year to 21,170,000 in 1959. Moreover, the greatest decreases during the fifties occurred among the smaller and less remunerative farms. In 1945 there were 5,100,000 units under 260 acres in size, representing 88 per cent of all farms, and only 2,900,000 such units in 1959, representing 78 per cent of the total. Farms 260 acres or larger actually showed an absolute as well as a percentage increase, from 750,000, or 12 per cent, in 1945, to over 800,000, or 22 per cent, in 1959.

EMPLOYMENT AND PAYROLLS OF
PRODUCTION WORKERS IN MANUFACTURING, 1940–1961
BUREAU OF LABOR STATISTICS INDEXES, WITHOUT SEASONAL ADJUSTMENT, 1947–1949=100

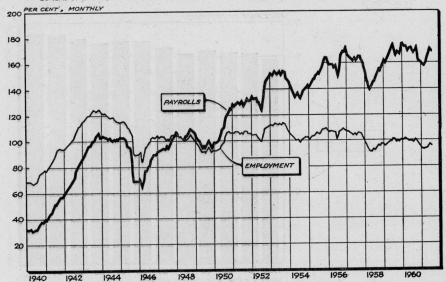

HOURS AND EARNINGS OF PRODUCTION WORKERS
IN MANUFACTURING, 1940–1961
BUREAU OF LABOR STATISTICS DATA, WITHOUT SEASONAL ADJUSTMENT

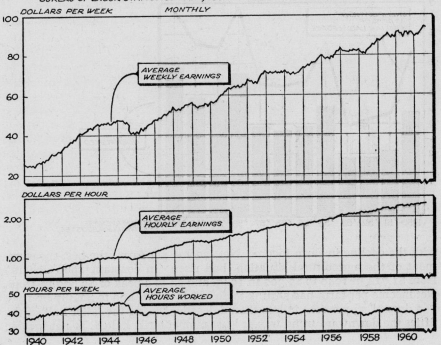

EMPLOYMENT AND UNEMPLOYMENT
IN THE UNITED STATES
1950–1961

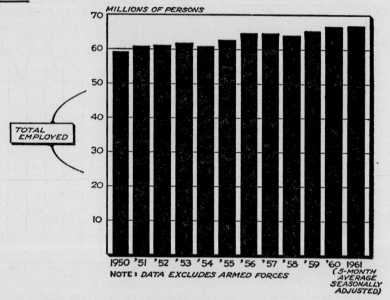

NOTE: *DATA EXCLUDES ARMED FORCES*

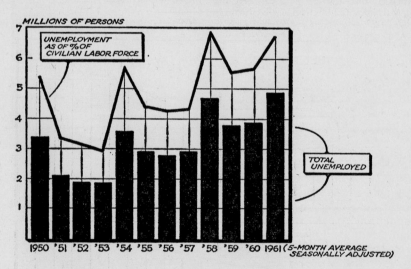

with the decline in farm income. Net income per farm, the best measurement of the agricultural situation, had risen (in constant 1960 dollars) from $1,714 in 1940 to $3,302 in 1945, and on to a peak of $3,677 in 1946. Net income per farm had shrunk to $2,916 by 1950, and to $2,487 by 1955 —a drop of 33 per cent in less than a decade. During the latter half of the fifties the downward trend was at least momentarily halted, as net income per farm hovered around $2,500 in 1956 and 1957, shot up to $2,982 in 1958, and declined less sharply to $2,640 in 1960.

The fact remained that farmers' real income decreased 28 per cent between 1946 and 1960, while the real income of most other Americans was on the rise. The chief cause of agrarian distress in the postwar years was not declining prices, which were maintained above or only moderately below the parity level by federal support,[8] but steadily rising costs. Increased farm expenses, in terms of equipment, machinery, labor, and taxes, reduced the farmer's net share of his gross income from 49 per cent in 1946 to less than 30 per cent in 1959.

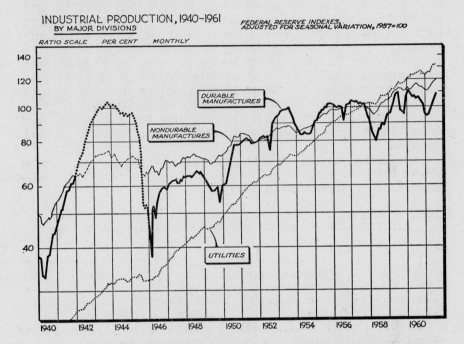

INDUSTRIAL PRODUCTION, 1940–1961
BY MAJOR DIVISIONS

FEDERAL RESERVE INDEXES,
ADJUSTED FOR SEASONAL VARIATION, 1957=100

RATIO SCALE   PER CENT   MONTHLY

DURABLE MANUFACTURES

NONDURABLE MANUFACTURES

UTILITIES

In contrast was the steady improvement, in spite of inflation and higher taxes, of the economic status of most workers in industry, mining, construction, transportation, and other fields. This was due, basically, to the fact that employment and income from 1940 to 1960 expanded faster than the population and the increase in prices and taxes. For example, the net spendable *real* income of the average industrial worker with three dependents increased more than 60 per cent from 1939 through 1960, as compared with a rise in real labor income of 26 per cent during the prosperous decade 1919–29.

wwwwwwwwwwwwww

[8] The parity ratio, or percentage ratio of prices received for all farm products to prices paid by the farmer, fluctuated above 100 every year from 1945 through 1952, then dropped to 92 in 1953, and declined slowly but steadily for the balance of the decade to 80 in 1960.

As the decade of the fifties wore to a close, however, the problem of slowly rising unemployment even in the midst of prosperity had become an increasing source of alarm to economists and labor experts. The economy underwent three recessions between the end of the Korean War and 1960, and the residue of unemployment, in terms of both absolute numbers and percentage of the labor force, was higher after each recovery than before the recession began. In 1947 there were 2,325,000 unemployed, representing 3.8 per cent of the civilian labor force. These figures dropped during the Korean War, rose to 3,578,000 and 5.6 per cent during the recession of 1954, and recovered somewhat from 1955 to 1958—the percentage, however, remaining above 4 per cent. They rose again in 1958 to 4,681,000 and 6.8 per cent, dropped slightly to 3,813,000 and 5.5 per cent in 1959, and climbed again to 4,206,000 and 6.1 per cent by March 1960, with further increases in store before recovery began in the spring of 1961. The major cause, obviously, for a slowly rising rate of unemployment even in times of prosperity and increased production, was higher efficiency per worker as a result of technological advances and automation. It raised the question, by no means answered in 1960, as to whether the twin goals of higher productive efficiency and nearly full employment were basically compatible. It promised to be one of the major problems confronting the United States in the 1960's.

The forties and fifties were also a time of dynamic change in the pattern of industrial production. The following table illustrates the major changes in that pattern from 1939 to 1958:

THE TEN LEADING AMERICAN INDUSTRIES, 1939 AND 1958

1939		1958	
	VALUE ADDED BY MANUFACTURING (IN MILLIONS		VALUE ADDED BY MANUFACTURING (IN MILLIONS
RANK INDUSTRY	OF DOLLARS)	RANK INDUSTRY	OF DOLLARS)
1. Food and kindred products	$3,485	1. Food and kindred products	$17,151
2. Primary metal industries	2,169	2. Transportation equipment, including automobiles	16,397
3. Machinery, except electrical	2,037	3. Machinery, except electrical	14,193
4. Chemicals and allied products	1,819	4. Primary metal industries	11,265
5. Textile mill products	1,818	5. Chemicals and allied products	12,623
6. Printing and publishing	1,765	6. Electrical machinery	9,362
7. Transportation equipment, including automobiles	1,773	7. Fabricated metal products	9,153
8. Fabricated metal products	1,401	8. Printing and publishing	7,795
9. Apparel	1,386	9. Apparel	6,289
10. Electrical machinery	941	10. Paper and allied products	5,855

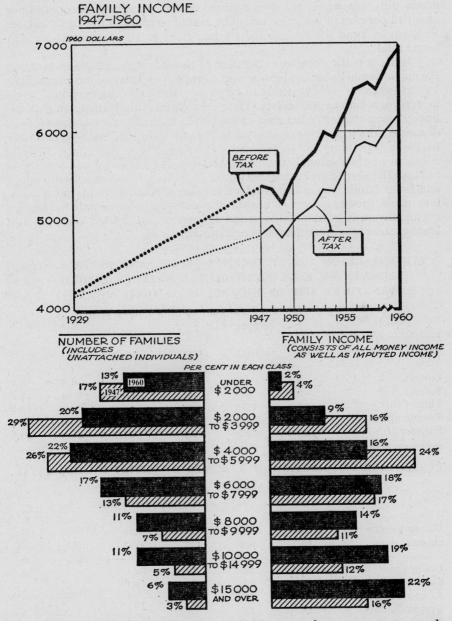

FAMILY INCOME
1947–1960

1960 DOLLARS

7 000

6 000

BEFORE
TAX

5 000

AFTER
TAX

4 000

1929   1947   1950   1955   1960

NUMBER OF FAMILIES
*(INCLUDES
UNATTACHED INDIVIDUALS)*

FAMILY INCOME
*(CONSISTS OF ALL MONEY INCOME
AS WELL AS IMPUTED INCOME)*

PER CENT IN EACH CLASS

NUMBER OF FAMILIES	CLASS	FAMILY INCOME
13% (1960) / 17% (1947)	UNDER $2 000	2% / 4%
20% / 29%	$2 000 TO $3 999	9% / 16%
22% / 26%	$4 000 TO $5 999	16% / 24%
17% / 13%	$6 000 TO $7 999	18% / 17%
11% / 7%	$8 000 TO $9 999	14% / 11%
11% / 5%	$10 000 TO $14 999	19% / 12%
6% / 3%	$15 000 AND OVER	22% / 16%

These statistics of dollar value added by manufacture convey a crude sense of the fundamental shifts in industrial production, but they obscure the dynamic growth of certain segments of the industrial economy, which we will examine in a later section. They also fail to indicate one of the most important developments in recent American history—the startling growth of industry in the South after 1939, which transformed that region in a dozen different ways. All the southern states combined accounted for about 12 per cent of the value added by manufacturing in the United States in 1939; by 1958 the southern share had risen to 20 per cent of a much larger total.

What was the economic condition of the American people in 1960, at the end of twenty years of almost uninterrupted expansion and prosperity? The answer one gives depends in large measure upon the economic goals he sets for a democratic society. The goal of most Americans is an expanding economy that affords a rising standard of living for the masses without destroying the incentives to unusual talent and industry. The best, certainly the most elementary, measurement of progress toward this goal is the distribution of the national income among the major groups of income receivers. The seemingly inexorable tide of concentration of incomes in fewer and fewer hands was at last reversed in the period after 1939, and the nation made greater progress toward the democratic economic goal than during any earlier comparable period at least since the Civil War. The following tables best illustrate the generalization:

PERCENTAGE OF MONEY INCOME, BEFORE AND AFTER TAXES,
RECEIVED BY EACH FIFTH OF THE NATION'S FAMILIES,
RANKED BY SIZE OF INCOME, 1941, 1947, AND 1957

Family units ranked by income	Per cent of total money income					
	BEFORE TAX			AFTER TAX		
	1941	1947	1957	1941	1947	1957
Lowest fifth	3.5	4.0	4.8	3.7	4.3	5.1
Second fifth	9.1	9.8	11.3	9.5	10.4	11.8
Third fifth	15.3	15.4	16.3	15.9	16.2	16.8
Fourth fifth	22.5	22.6	22.3	23.2	22.8	22.7
Highest fifth	49.6	48.2	45.3	47.7	46.3	43.6

PERCENTAGE DISTRIBUTION OF FAMILIES BY MONEY INCOME LEVEL,
1941, 1947, AND 1957

Money income classes	Per cent of all family units					
	1941		1947		1957	
	Before tax	After tax	Before tax	After tax	Before tax	After tax
Under $500	14	14	4	4		
$500–$1,000	17	17	8	9	14	14.9
$1,000–$1,500	15	16	17	18		
$1,500–$2,000	15	15				
$2,000–$3,000	21	22	17	19	10	11.0
$3,000–$4,000	9	9	17	17	12.5	13.9
$4,000–$5,000	4	3	12	12	13.1	14.8
$5,000–$7,500			15	13	25.6	25.2
$7,500–$10,000	5	4	5	4	12.4	10.2
$10,000 and over			5	4	12.4	10.0

PERCENTAGE OF DISPOSABLE INDIVIDUAL
INCOME RECEIVED BY —

Year	Top 1 per cent	Top 5 per cent
1919	12.2	24.3
1929	18.9	33.5
1940	11.5	25.7
1945	7.4	16.8
1946	7.8	17.9
1950		21.4
1958		20.2

To be sure, Americans had not achieved the millennium by 1960, nor even yet begun to reach the limits of economic fulfillment. Poverty still existed. In 1958 over 14 per cent of all American families and 36 per cent of Negro families received less than $2,000 annual income.[9] Millions of old persons suffered heavily during the inflation. And there still remained some 650,000 families on marginal and eroded farms, with annual cash incomes of less than $1,200. The fact remains, however, that the majority of Americans were no longer living in poverty or near subsistence by 1960. From 1944 to 1958 the number of families and unattached individuals with annual incomes below $4,000 decreased from 29,000,000, or over 70 per cent of the total, to less than 20,000,000, or 36 per cent. Those with annual incomes in excess of $6,000 increased from less than 5,000,000, or 12 per cent, in 1944, to nearly 25,000,000, or about 40 per cent, in 1958. Here was surely one of the most significant economic and social revolutions of modern times.

202. *The Further Technological Revolution*

A further revolution in technology was in large measure responsible for the economic progress of the United States following the Great Depression. It increased the productivity of labor in mines and factories and on farms, emancipated the housewife from numerous drudgeries, and destroyed unskilled labor's ancient slavery to the pick and shovel. It also culminated in new industries and inventions that made Jules Verne look like a good prophet. We have discussed in an earlier chapter the principal factors in the first technological revolution of the period 1900–40—increasing horsepower per worker, application of principles of scientific

[9] It should be pointed out, however, that of all major groups in the United States Negroes made the greatest relative economic progress after 1940. Negro farm tenancy in the South declined over 70 per cent from 1940 to 1959, while Negro farm ownership in the South declined only 26 per cent in the face of a 50 per cent decrease in the total number of southern farms. The proportion of Negroes employed in relatively menial and unskilled tasks declined from almost 71 per cent of the total Negro labor force in 1948 to 58 per cent in 1961. Though still far below the national average, the proportion of Negroes employed in clerical and sales work increased by over 100 per cent, in professional and technical occupations by 100 per cent, in skilled and supervisory work by 15 per cent, and in nonhousehold service occupations by 30 per cent, from 1948 to 1961.

PER CAPITA PERSONAL INCOME, 1960

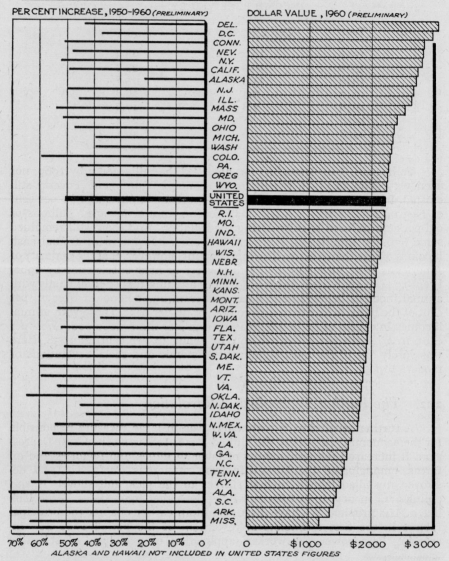

PER CENT INCREASE, 1950–1960 *(PRELIMINARY)*   DOLLAR VALUE , 1960 *(PRELIMINARY)*

DEL.
D.C.
CONN.
NEV.
N.Y.
CALIF.
ALASKA
N.J.
ILL.
MASS
MD.
OHIO
MICH.
WASH
COLO.
PA.
OREG
WYO.
UNITED STATES
R.I.
MO.
IND.
HAWAII
WIS.
NEBR
N.H.
MINN.
KANS.
MONT.
ARIZ.
IOWA
FLA.
TEX.
UTAH
S. DAK.
ME.
VT.
VA.
OKLA.
N. DAK.
IDAHO
N. MEX.
W. VA.
LA.
GA.
N.C.
TENN.
KY.
ALA.
S.C.
ARK.
MISS.

70% 60% 50% 40% 30% 20% 10% 0   0 $1000 $2000 $3000

ALASKA AND HAWAII NOT INCLUDED IN UNITED STATES FIGURES

management to industrial and business operations, the assembly line technique of mass production, use of interchangeable parts, and research and development of new inventions and techniques. These were also the chief components of the further technological revolution after 1940; the chief differences between the two phases were differences in degree and speed.

If the true measure of the technological revolution is horsepower, then the extent of the revolution after 1940 was startling indeed. Total energy produced from mineral fuels and water power increased 60 per cent from

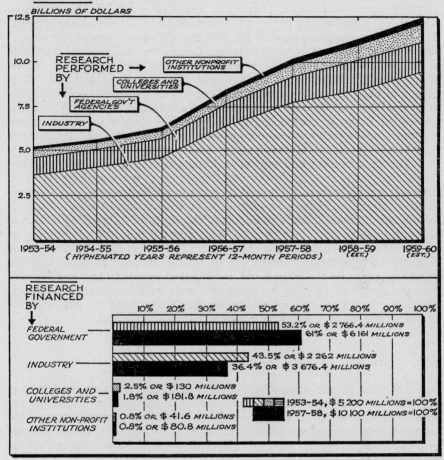

RESEARCH IN THE UNITED STATES
1953-1960

BILLIONS OF DOLLARS

RESEARCH PERFORMED BY →

OTHER NONPROFIT INSTITUTIONS
COLLEGES AND UNIVERSITIES
FEDERAL GOV'T AGENCIES
INDUSTRY

1953-54   1954-55   1955-56   1956-57   1957-58   1958-59 (EST.)   1959-60 (EST.)
(HYPHENATED YEARS REPRESENT 12-MONTH PERIODS)

RESEARCH FINANCED BY ↓

FEDERAL GOVERNMENT — 53.2% OR $2 766.4 MILLIONS / 61% OR $6 161 MILLIONS

INDUSTRY — 43.5% OR $2 262 MILLIONS / 36.4% OR $3 676.4 MILLIONS

COLLEGES AND UNIVERSITIES — 2.5% OR $130 MILLIONS / 1.8% OR $181.8 MILLIONS

1953-54, $5 200 MILLIONS=100%
1957-58, $10 100 MILLIONS=100%

OTHER NON-PROFIT INSTITUTIONS — 0.8% OR $41.6 MILLIONS / 0.8% OR $80.8 MILLIONS

1940 to 1959. The production of electric power alone increased over 340 per cent, while the increase of horsepower in automobiles, airplane engines, farm and industrial tractors, diesel locomotives, and a thousand gadgets was incalculable but enormous.

There was, besides, the spread of scientific management to practically every business and industry and, more important, the wider application of the assembly line method of mass production. The further use of the assembly line and interchangeable parts proceeded slowly during the depression years and then came to full flowering during the defense and war crises from 1940 to 1945, especially in the shipbuilding and airplane industries. Moreover, the introduction of electronic measuring devices enabled automatic machine tools to produce engines of almost perfect quality and practically eliminated the need for hand tooling.

Another significant factor in the technological revolution after 1940 was a rapid acceleration in research devoted to industrial and military needs. From its first important beginnings during the First World War, industrial research developed slowly in the twenties and expanded rapidly even during the depression years. But this was merely the beginning of what would soon become perhaps the most important American enterprise. The federal government entered the field in a decisive way with the organization of the National Defense Research Committee in 1940 and the Office of Scientific Research and Development in 1941. The number of professional scientists employed in research grew, between 1941 and 1945, from 87,000 to 119,000, while expenditures grew from $900,000,000 to $1,520,-000,000. Both private and public research continued to expand once the war ended. By 1959, 277,000 scientists—over one third of all scientists and engineers in the country—were engaged in research projects, expenditures for which aggregated well over $10,000,000,000.

The far-reaching and pervasive impact of the technological revolution after 1940 is at once obvious and impossible to measure fully. We can, however, partially measure one of its most important results, the increase in the productivity of labor in several fields. During the 1930's productivity in industry increased about 20 per cent. The index of industrial production went up 150 per cent from 1940 to 1958, and the output per man-hour in all manufacturing increased by 55 per cent. The most spectacular increase occurred in agriculture. Output per man-hour actually declined between 1929 and 1935; on the other hand, it increased by a startling 220 per cent between 1939 and 1960, as the horse and mule gave way to the tractor and new inventions like the corn picker, the hay loader, and the cotton picker displaced hundreds of thousands of hired hands and tenants.[10]

203.   *The Rise of New Industries*

The rise of the automobile, chemical, radio, aviation, and motion picture industries was beginning to cause a significant revolution in the American way of life in the 1920's. That revolution proceeded apace but unevenly in the depressed thirties; it came to full flowering in the postwar era, as mass production reached a level that would have been considered fantastic in the 1920's.

The Continued Pre-eminence of the Automobile. The automobile continued to enjoy its pre-eminence as the chief single dynamic factor in the American economy. Production of passenger cars and trucks declined from the prosperity peak figure of 5,358,000 in 1929 to 1,371,000 in 1932; returned to a prosperity level of nearly 5,000,000 in 1937; and then ceased almost altogether during the war years. Pent-up consumer demand in the postwar era, however, stimulated unprecedented production, which culmi-

wwwwwwwwwwwwwwww

[10] The mechanization of agriculture proceeded at a prodigious rate between 1940 and 1959. The number of farm tractors tripled—the average by the late fifties was substantially more than one tractor per farm. The number of trucks on farms also tripled. The number of grain combines increased by more than 400 per cent, of corn pickers by 600 per cent, and of forage harvesters by over 1000 per cent. The number of farms with milking machines increased from 175,000 to 610,000. The manufacture of the cotton picker, which seems destined to revolutionize southern agriculture, did not begin commercially until 1949. About 11,500 cotton pickers were in use by the autumn of 1952.

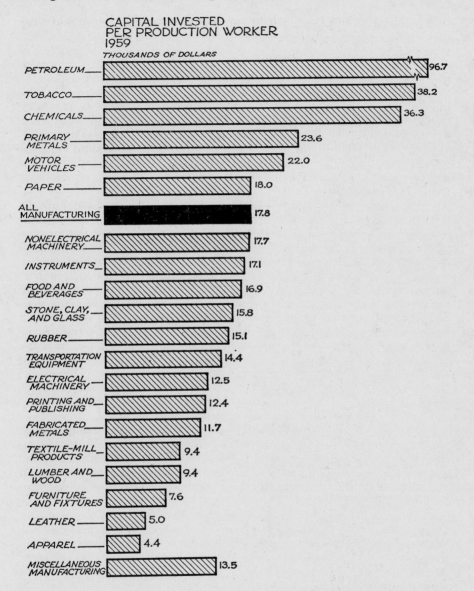

CAPITAL INVESTED
PER PRODUCTION WORKER
1959
THOUSANDS OF DOLLARS

PETROLEUM	96.7
TOBACCO	38.2
CHEMICALS	36.3
PRIMARY METALS	23.6
MOTOR VEHICLES	22.0
PAPER	18.0
ALL MANUFACTURING	17.8
NONELECTRICAL MACHINERY	17.7
INSTRUMENTS	17.1
FOOD AND BEVERAGES	16.9
STONE, CLAY, AND GLASS	15.8
RUBBER	15.1
TRANSPORTATION EQUIPMENT	14.4
ELECTRICAL MACHINERY	12.5
PRINTING AND PUBLISHING	12.4
FABRICATED METALS	11.7
TEXTILE-MILL PRODUCTS	9.4
LUMBER AND WOOD	9.4
FURNITURE AND FIXTURES	7.6
LEATHER	5.0
APPAREL	4.4
MISCELLANEOUS MANUFACTURING	13.5

nated in the manufacture in 1950 of 8,003,000 cars and trucks. Annual factory sales of cars and trucks averaged nearly 7,000,000 throughout the 1950's.

The number of automobiles and trucks on highways increased from 32,035,000 to 67,422,000 from 1940 to 1958. And with this increase went steady growth of the petroleum industry, filling stations, and garages; expenditure of billions of dollars for construction and maintenance of highways—over $5,300,000,000 in 1958 alone; and a vast expansion of tourist courts and motels to serve the millions of Americans who took annually to

the roads.[11] It is not too much to say that the economy would have collapsed if by some magic the automobile had been removed from the American scene.

As the automobile multiplied, it became larger, faster, more powerful,
and gaudier. Such devices as automatic transmission became standard
equipment on most American models after the war and combined with
power steering, power brakes, and high-horsepower engines to make the
American automobile easier to drive, faster accelerating, and more lethal
than ever before. In the fifties, too, the relatively staid prewar models
blossomed spectacularly in a burst of chromium ornamentation, two- and
three-tone color combinations in bathroom shades, soaring tailfins, enormous red tail lights, "wrap-around" windshields, and other eye-catching
features.

Toward the end of the decade a reaction set in, noted hopefully by
some as the harbinger of a new automotive era. Increasing numbers of
Americans suddenly discovered that the cheaper, smaller, more economical,
less ostentatious European cars had much to recommend them. The fast-
growing popularity in this country of such makes as the Volkswagen,
Renault, Fiat, Hillman, Peugeot, and other European products forced
Detroit to respond with smaller and more economical models of its own.
The so-called compact, whether of domestic or foreign manufacture, had
won a secure place on the American highway by 1960 and was exercising a
healthy influence on every feature of automotive design. The trend toward
smaller and more practical cars was the first indication, perhaps, that the
people were beginning to reshape their attitudes toward the automobile and
even attempting to control the massive problems it had created. There was
also growing concern over the steady deterioration of commuter rail lines
and the patent failure of new urban expressways to keep pace with the
chronic, stifling traffic snarls in every metropolitan area.[12]

The Age of Chemicals. Although the automobile clung tenaciously to
its claim to leadership in the American economy, the most significant development of the late thirties and the postwar era was the growth of the
chemical industry and its sudden spawning of countless new and related
industries. Indeed, the chemical industry in all its aspects was by 1960 "the
premier industry" of the United States, a "great, yeasty force at the center of

᠁᠁᠁᠁᠁᠁᠁

[11] A few statistics will illustrate the economic significance of the industries that
serve the automobile owner. In 1957 the manufacturers of tires and tubes employed
71,000 workers, who added $1,067,000,000 in value by manufacture. In 1958 there were
some 85,000 automotive dealers that employed over 700,000 persons; 206,755 service
stations that employed 465,550 persons and sold products valued at $14,228,000,000;
and 56,377 tourist camps and motels.

[12] Urban planners were predicting in growing chorus that continued unrestricted
use of the automobile would soon bring complete paralysis and ultimate decay to the
central core of every major American city. Experiments in one-way streets, fringe parking, downtown malls for pedestrians only, tax relief and other forms of aid for commuter railroads, and new transit projects were among the remedies being proposed or
tried in the 1950's. The urgency of the traffic problem, of course, was merely one manifestation of what must obviously become a prime object of national concern in the
years ahead: the chaotic, unplanned "urban sprawl" resulting from the proliferation
of suburbs and the too rapid growth of metropolitan areas, with attendant problems
in government, finance, health, crime, and the very viability of the American city.

the economy," which produced at least one fifth the total national industrial product.

It received its first important stimulus when the United States was cut off from German supplies during the First World War and domestic manufacturers and the federal government first turned on a large scale to production of organic chemicals, dyes, and nitrogen. Domestic manufacturers secured their independence with tariff protection in the twenties and were turning out a product valued at $3,232,556,000 by 1929. There was a slight decline during the depression, but production began to climb again in 1936 and rose steadily afterward. The chemical industry turned out a total product valued at nearly $4,000,000,000 by 1939.

The American chemical industry concentrated before 1940 almost exclusively upon old-line products—rayon and organic chemicals for industrial, farm, and medicinal uses. However, the manufacture of nylon, a synthetic yarn derived chemically from coal, air, and water, by Du Pont in December 1939 was the harbinger of the new chemical age that lay beyond the horizon. The basic chemical industry—and the following statistics give an incomplete picture, because they account only for the production of basic raw materials—employed 743,000 workers and added $12,623,000,-000 in value to products by manufacture by 1958. It was an increase since 1939 of 168 per cent in workers employed, of 600 per cent in value added by manufacture, and of 300 per cent in actual volume of production. The most significant development in the field after 1939 was the sudden growth of a whole complex of new synthetic industries—plastics, synthetic rubber, synthetic fibers, detergents, drugs, insecticides, and so on—built upon chemical processes and production.

The Electrical Era. As we have seen, the enormous increase in the manufacture of electric power after 1940 was one of the prime forces spurring the progress of the further technological revolution. One important consequence of this tremendous expansion was the growth of two relatively new industries—appliances and electronics. They vitalized the American economy in the forties and fifties as the automobile industry had done in the twenties, and together effected profound changes in the American way of life. The appliance age materialized suddenly after 1945. Overnight, it seemed, a host of new products came on the market in an unending stream. There were air conditioners, electric blankets, dehumidifiers, electric and gas clothes dryers and automatic washing machines, home freezers, electric dishwashers and garbage disposal units, power lawn mowers, and a hundred other such gadgets.[13]

Even more startling was the sudden burgeoning of the electronics industry during and after the war. As the editors of *Fortune* observed in July 1951, "Electronics has in progress more revolutions of profound impact upon industrial society than any technology" and would "someday crowd the dynamically expanding chemical industry as premier industry in the second half of the century."

[13] By January 1960, for example, 3,200,000 homes had motor-driven dishwashers, 4,800,000 had food waste units, 47,100,000 had electric washing machines, 11,200,000 had home freezers, 9,000,000 had clothes dryers, and 6,500,000 had room air conditioners. Nearly 50,000,000 American homes had electric refrigerators by 1960.

The electronics industry produced mainly radios, radio parts, and communications equipment during the 1930's, and its product value barely exceeded $500,000,000 in 1939. The industry came of age with revolutionary new discoveries during the war and immediately afterward and was turning out a product valued at $6,500,000,000 by 1958. So numerous and baffling were the new inventions that we can only mention the most important of them: power rectifiers and electronic controls, gauges, selectors, and counters; micro-wave relay systems for the transmission of sound and television waves; electronic computers—the "mechanical brains" that could perform elaborate tasks of computation and even correct their own mistakes; and the transistor, which was a simple substitute for the vacuum tube.

The prime mover in the electronics revolution was television, the perfection of which from 1945 to 1948 gave rise to the fastest growing major industry in the postwar era. Production of television sets increased from 7,000 in 1947 to 6,000,000 in 1952 and remained at about the latter annual figure throughout the 1950's. By January 1960 there were television sets in 45,500,000 American homes, or nine out of every ten. At the same time there occurred a parallel growth of television stations, from ten in 1946 to 517 in 1960, and of television revenues from $658,000 to over $1,000,-000,000.

New Metals and Fuels. The primary development in the metals field after 1940 was the rise of new or relatively new metals. The production of the most important of these, aluminum, swelled from 286,642 tons in 1940 to nearly 2,000,000 in 1959. In addition, there was magnesium, another lightweight metal, production of which grew some thirty times between 1940 and 1959, and titanium, an entirely new metal in 1949, which seemed well on the way toward displacing lead in the manufacture of paint.

Two important changes in fuels were the introduction of fuel oils and the widespread use of natural gas for home and business heating. While residential consumption of coal declined from 85,000,000 tons in 1940 to 29,000,000 in 1959, the sales of fuel oil to home and business users increased from a value of $125,925,000 in 1939 to $1,771,000,000 in 1958. Moreover, the value of natural gas consumed by residential, commercial, and industrial users increased from $872,000,000 in 1940 to $5,085,000,-000 in 1959. The postwar demand for natural gas gave rise to an unprecedented outburst of pipeline construction. In fact, so frenzied was the activity in this field that virtually a great new industry came rapidly into being after 1945. The gas utilities industry had assets of $21,425,000,000 in 1958, an increase since 1940 of 300 per cent; by 1959 the total gas main and pipeline mileage (not including petroleum pipelines) was nearly 600,-000.

The Aviation Transport Industry Comes of Age. Rapid technological change after 1940 made possible man's nearly complete conquest of the air. In the postwar era, a number of sleek new four-engined airliners made their appearance—among them, the Douglas DC–4, DC–6, and DC–7, the Boeing Stratocruiser, and the graceful Lockheed Constellation and Super Constellation—carrying up to 100 passengers or more. The successful adaptation of the jet engine to commercial aircraft in the 1950's, and the steadily increasing employment of jet transports by the end of the decade, enabled American air travelers to journey at speeds averaging two and three times faster than the best achievements of the prewar carriers. Concurrent developments in electronics, moreover, enabled pilots to fly as easily at night as in daytime and to land safely even when the ceiling was zero.

Expansion in air transportation service occurred in direct ratio to technological change. Air travel at home and overseas was not only commonplace by 1959 but also a real threat to railroads and shipping lines. Forty-five scheduled air carriers flew routes at home and abroad totaling 325,000 miles, carried over 114,000,000 passengers and a half billion ton-miles of freight, employed 160,000 persons, and collected nearly two billion dollars in revenues.

204. *Concentration and Competition in the American Economy*

It would little profit a democratic society if economic growth were accompanied by inexorable concentration of wealth and ownership of the means of production in the hands of an irresponsible few. Was the inevitable tendency of capitalism toward monopoly, restricted production at high prices, and aggrandizement of economic and political power by the few? We have already noted that the depression decade witnessed a slight reversal of the seemingly inevitable trend toward concentration, and a virtual cessation of the far-reaching merger movement of the 1920's. (See above, pp. 265–267.) It is more difficult to generalize about this subject in the period after 1940. There is much to suggest that the return of prosperity during and after the war was accompanied by a renewal of the trend toward concentration. But the pace was slower and less inexorable than before 1929, and a substantial degree of competition was maintained or even enlarged in most segments of the economy. If this latter statement did not apply to the inherently monopolistic areas—government, transportation, communications, and utilities—it was certainly true of such competitive fields as mining, construction, finance, services, and trade.[14]

[14] The challenge of concentration was far from absent. In the field of food marketing, for example, a threat to competition appeared in the 1950's of sufficient scope to call for investigation and hearings by a Senate subcommittee in 1959. The findings revealed that the fifteen largest food chains had increased their proportion of total food sales from 23 per cent in 1948 to nearly 30 per cent in 1958; that chains with 11 or more stores had upped their proportion from 29 per cent to 37 per cent in the same period; and that during the decade 1948–58 some 315 chains, embracing a total of 2,238 stores, had been acquired by 83 larger aggregations. The National Association of Retail Grocers was sufficiently alarmed by this trend to warn against what it called "undue concentration of economic power in retail food distribution."

A Federal Trade Commission report in 1955 pointed up a similar development in the hotel business, noting that the Department of Justice had filed a complaint on April 27, 1955, asking that the acquisition of the Statler chain (second largest in the country) by the Hilton Hotels Corporation (the largest) be found in violation of Section 7 of the Clayton Act. It was obvious that thorough investigations and vigorous enforcement of the antitrust laws were needed to safeguard the healthy functioning of competition in the American economy, in 1960 as much as in 1910. The startling revelation in 1960 of illegal price-fixing on an enormous scale in the electrical industry, involving billions of dollars, gave further warning that care and attention were needed.

It was also true, by and large, of agriculture, but the dominant trend in this sector of the economy, traditionally the most fiercely competitive of all, was clearly toward elimination of marginal and smaller farms, while the lion's share of agricultural profits went increasingly to a relatively small number of well-entrenched, highly mechanized commercial farms.[15] By the fifties, moreover, the traditionally individualistic way of life of the American farmer had completely disappeared. The successful farmer now operated through a vast, complex network of co-operative associations, which corresponded in general purpose and function to the corporate organization in commerce and industry.[16] In approach, method, and general outlook the successful farmer had become a modern businessman.

Manufacturing was even more complicated and difficult to describe. Some of the statistics certainly indicate a renewal of the trend toward concentration. The proportion of total corporate assets owned by the 139 largest manufacturing concerns between 1931 and 1947 fell from 50 per cent to 45 per cent, but the figure had risen again to nearly 53 per cent by 1958. The supercorporations—those with assets in excess of $100,000,000 each—were larger, more numerous, and of greater importance to the economy than ever before. There were 113 such giants in 1947, owning 46 per cent of all manufacturing plant, property, and equipment, and 40 per cent of total manufacturing assets in the United States. The number had increased to 286 by 1958. They owned 67 per cent of all manufacturing plant and equipment and 62 per cent of total manufacturing assets. Data on the share of production controlled by the largest producers in specific industries are, on the whole, inconclusive. They indicate that small producers gained at the expense of the largest corporations in certain industries while the reverse was true in others.[17] It should also be noted that a new

~~~~~~~~~~~~~~~~~~~~~~~~

[15] In 1959, 44 per cent of American farms sold less than $2,500 worth of farm products. Nearly four fifths of these were so-called part-time and part-retirement farms, where the operator derived a portion of his income from nonfarm sources. The remainder, some 350,000 units, constituted the primary source of income for the families in question. The point is that farms with less than $2,500 annual income declined by nearly 50 per cent between 1944 and 1959, while farms with incomes in excess of $10,000—the large commercial farms—increased from 438,000 in 1944 to 800,000 in 1959, or more than 80 per cent. Clearly, the share of total farm income realized by these large commercial units was disproportionate and growing.

[16] There were in 1959 some 10,000 agricultural marketing and purchasing co-operatives, with total membership of nearly 7,500,000, plus hundreds of land bank associations, credit associations, rural credit unions, rural electric co-operatives, mutual irrigation companies, dairy-herd improvement associations, and other organizations.

[17] A few examples must suffice to illustrate this point. In the manufacture of aircraft engines, for instance, the proportion of the product shipped by the four largest producers fell from 72 per cent in 1947 to 62 per cent in 1954. For other aircraft equipment the share controlled by the four largest concerns dropped in the same period from 37 per cent to 20 per cent. On the other hand, in steel works and rolling mills the "big four" increased their share of total shipments from 48 to 54 per cent. In the automobile industry the three major companies, whose share of total production had declined from 86 per cent in 1935 to 78 per cent in 1948, produced 95 per cent of American automobiles in 1958. (This predominance was partly offset, toward the end of the fifties, by the increasing share of the American automobile market captured by foreign manufacturers, who accounted for 10 per cent of total sales in this country in 1958—as opposed to less than one tenth of 1 per cent three years earlier.) In many important

merger movement gained momentum after 1945, reaching such large proportions in the latter half of the 1950's as to approach the scope of the far-
reaching movement of the 1920's.[18] Many important industries—such as
automobiles, aluminum, tires, meat products, cigarettes, liquors, and copper smelting and refining—were dominated by three or four large producers.[19] Thus, on the surface, oligopoly—that is, control by the few—
seemingly prevailed in most important branches of manufacturing.

However, there is grave danger in arriving at a priori conclusions from
obvious facts. For one thing, the thirty-seven industries in each of which
four companies sold 75 per cent or more of the total product, together accounted for only 9 per cent of the manufacturing output. And the eighty-
seven other industries in which four companies sold between 50 and 75
per cent of the product only accounted for an additional 18 per cent.[20] In
the second place, the dominance of an industry by four or eight large concerns did not necessarily signify the absence of competition, as an examination of the development of the automobile, steel, agricultural implements,
oil, and other industries would reveal.

Indeed, there seems little reason to doubt the conclusion of Richard B.
Heflebower, one of the wisest students of this problem: "Competition out-
weighs monopoly by a wide margin in the American economy today."
Historic price competition remained in the 1960's a powerful force in
distribution and in many branches of industry characterized by a large
number of producers. So-called oligopolistic growth since 1900 had usually
meant the growth of large rivals at the relative expense of corporations
once totally dominant in their respective fields. And often the decline of
price competition had been offset by the rise of competition in quality,

branches of industry there was no appreciable change in the share of the large producers during the 1950's.

[18] The following figures indicate this trend: Some 2,235 manufacturing and mining
concerns were absorbed by larger companies from 1920 to 1924, and the number of
such acquisitions rose to 4,583 in 1925–9. The figure declined to 1,687 in 1930–4,
and to 577 in 1935–9. During the war years, 1940–4, 906 such mergers were recorded,
after which a sharp rise began. There were 1,505 acquisitions in 1945–9, 1,424 in
1950–4, and 2,665 in 1955–9—the highest number since the merger heyday of the
1920's.

The figures for total corporate assets acquired by merger are far from complete, but
scattered estimates suggest that some $5,200,000,000 in aggregate assets were absorbed
by the acquiring companies from 1940 to 1947, another $5,000,000,000 from 1951 to
1954, and over $4,000,000,000 from 1954 to 1956, with the sharpest postwar increase
in the merger movement just beginning. On the other hand, it must be added that big
business grew far more through normal expansion than through mergers in the period
1940–60. In any case, more detailed and thorough statistical studies of the merger
movement are needed before its significance and scope can be assessed.

[19] In 1954 there were thirty-seven industries in which four large firms produced
at least 75 per cent of the output, eighty-seven others in which four large firms produced between 50 and 75 per cent (out of a total of 367 industries as classified by the
Census Bureau). Eight large producers dominated the steel, electrical, and aircraft
industries.

[20] However, the share of total value added by manufacture accounted for by the
largest corporations showed a significant increase from 1947 to 1954: the share contributed by the 50 largest companies rose from 17 to 23 per cent; that of the 200 largest,
from 30 to 37 per cent.

design of products, and advertising. Moreover, the rise of powerful combinations of retailers, themselves not monopolies, had operated to restore competition not only among retailers but also among the so-called manufacturing oligopolies. By manufacturing, or threatening to manufacture, products themselves, combinations like Sears Roebuck, Montgomery Ward, A & P, and numerous other chains had restored vigorous competition in most consumers' goods. As one economist has put it, "The formula for competition is simple: add one part of Sears Roebuck to twenty parts of oligopoly." Finally, technological change in American industry had been too rapid and far-reaching since 1930 to permit would-be monopolists to stand still and attempt to exercise an imperial sway.

Nor should we ignore the role of the federal government in the development of an expansive and essentially competitive economy. The government was transformed after 1929 into incomparably the most powerful economic force in the nation. It took control of the money supply and interest rates out of the hands of private bankers and emerged as the single greatest spender, with far-reaching control over contracts and prices. It entered the capital markets through the RFC, the Export-Import Bank, and a hundred other agencies. It broke the aluminum monopoly and destroyed the utility holding company empires. It assumed a large share of responsibility for industrial research and entered the fields of production in electricity, synthetic rubber, and atomic energy. It encouraged business enterprise through programs of subsidization, chiefly by allowing depreciation for tax purposes.

In addition, the Washington government, after the end of the ill-fated NRA experiment, began the most concerted and successful antitrust campaign since the heyday of the crusade under Theodore Roosevelt and Taft. (See above, pp. 430–431.) Expansion in the work of the Antitrust Division of the Justice Department and the Federal Trade Commission was, moreover, accompanied by a virtual revolution in judicial opinion concerning restraint of trade. It finally gave the federal government power to destroy not only monopoly, but oligopoly as well. The Supreme Court, in a series of decisions from 1911 to 1927, had laid down the rule that a corporation was not illegal under the Sherman law merely because it was large. This doctrine prevailed until 1945, when Justice Learned Hand of the Court of Appeals delivered a verdict in United States *v.* Aluminum Company of America.[21] The government had asked for Alcoa's dissolution on the grounds that the company, because it controlled 90 per cent of the production of bar aluminum and had used illegal methods to maintain its predominance, was *ipso facto* a monopoly. Affirming the allegations of past unfair trade practices, Hand declared that Alcoa was a monopoly because its control of the market was so large as to give it the benefits of a monopoly.

An even more significant decision was the one rendered by the Supreme Court in American Tobacco Company *v.* United States in 1946. The Antitrust Division had instituted criminal proceedings in 1940 against the American Tobacco, R. J. Reynolds, and Liggett and Myers tobacco companies, alleging that the big three had conspired to control the price of leaf

wwwwwwwwwwwww

[21] The Supreme Court had failed to obtain a quorum to hear the case and allowed Justice Hand to render the decision.

tobacco and cigarettes. The government was able to prove in subsequent court hearings that the companies had paid and charged identical prices for the two products, but it failed to prove that the defendants had conspired to maintain common prices. The court brushed aside the companies' pleas that they had never conspired to set prices and sustained the conviction of the District Court. The crime of monopoly, the Supreme Court declared in its epochal decision, consisted as much in possession of power to suppress competition and raise prices as in commission of illegal acts. Moreover, the court added, the government did not have to prove the existence of collusion to set prices if such collusion could be reasonably inferred from market conditions.

The government finally won in the Tobacco decision the power for which it had been struggling at least since Taft's administration—the ability to strike at oligopolies as well as monopolies. It did not follow that the government desired or intended to force the atomization of the American industrial structure. The important fact was that the government now possessed effective recourse against the most common oligopolistic practice in the American economy, collusion to eliminate price competition.

The government scored another legal triumph in the immediate postwar era in the successful culmination of its long battle against the basing-point system of pricing.[22] The Supreme Court dealt a deathblow to this instrument for the elimination of price competition in a series of decisions from 1945 to 1948, but most notably in decisions in 1948 involving the steel and cement industries. Finally, Congress also took a hand in 1950, plugging an old loophole in the Clayton Act by prohibiting the purchase of the assets of one corporation by another when such purchase would tend to lessen competition or lead to monopoly.

The main question after 1950 was no longer whether the government possessed sufficient power to maintain competition, but how it would use the sweeping authority that the Supreme Court had said that it possessed. It was easier to ask the latter question than to answer it. "Liberal" antitrust economists still suspected bigness and continued to urge relentless measures to preserve economic freedom. They were challenged by a new school of "realists" in the 1950's. These critics argued, in language that Theodore Roosevelt and Herbert Croly would have approved, that abstract theories had little relevance to the modern American economy. That economy was inevitably composed of big units—supercorporations, big government, big labor unions, and so on. The principal objective, they said, should be to preserve a fine balance of countervailing power so that no single group could alone make important economic decisions. This was part of the argument in John Kenneth Galbraith, *American Capitalism, The Concept of Countervailing Power* (1952); David E. Lilienthal, *Big Business: A New Era* (1953); and A. A. Berle, Jr., *The 20th Century Capitalist Revolution* (1954).

[22] This was the system of adding freight charges from a certain base point to the point where the sale was made, regardless of where the product was manufactured. A good example was the "Pittsburgh-plus" system used in determining the price of steel products. Buyers of steel in Chicago had to pay freight charges on steel from Pittsburgh to Chicago, even though the steel involved was actually produced in Gary, Indiana, only a few miles away.

It is not surprising that officials charged with enforcement of the anti-trust laws were sometimes confused over means and ends in the fifties. There was also a noticeable decline in antitrust fervor during the Eisenhower administration, the very years when the merger movement seemed to be accelerating greatly. For one thing, the money and personnel available for the Antitrust Division of the Justice Department steadily shrank under Eisenhower, as did the number of actions instituted. They averaged forty-three a year during the Eisenhower era, as contrasted to forty-six a year under Truman. And yet the Antitrust Division maintained a certain momentum and won several notable victories between 1953 and 1961. It blocked the merger of the Bethlehem Steel Company and the Youngstown Sheet and Tube Corporation and forced the great Du Pont empire to divest itself of ownership of a large block of the stock of General Motors Corporation. In a more spectacular action it brought twenty-nine manufacturers of electrical equipment to trial in 1960 for conspiring to rig prices, and forced them to plead no contest. Seven vice presidents of General Electric, Westinghouse, and other concerns went to jail for short terms in February 1961. The FTC was also active during the period under discussion, particularly in attempting to prevent deceptive advertising. However, it was evident by 1961 that the Eisenhower majority on the FTC had come a long way toward condoning many policies, especially in pricing, that had been condemned earlier as restraints of trade.

The Supreme Court left no doubt throughout the 1950's that it still adhered to the doctrine enunciated in the Alcoa decision of 1945, namely, that possession of power to control the market could be as illegal as exercise of this power. Several significant decisions reinforced this doctrine in the 1950's. The landmark was United States *v.* E. I. Du Pont de Nemours and Company, 1957. Du Pont had purchased 23 per cent of the stock of the General Motors Corporation in 1917. The court, in compelling Du Pont to divest itself of General Motors shares, laid down three propositions with far-reaching implications for antitrust interpretation. First, the antitrust laws applied to vertical integrations, that is, to mergers of concerns that were not directly competitive. Second, the government need prove only that mergers resulted in foreclosure of only a "substantial share" of the market. Third, the legality of mergers or acquisitions is to be measured "by conditions existing at the time suit is brought, rather than at the time of acquisition." [23]

205. *Organized Labor in the Postwar Era*

The years from 1945 to 1960 were a time of tumult, change, significant achievement, and grave new challenges for organized labor in the United States. On the one hand, it was an unquestioned fact that organized labor finally won security and equality of bargaining power with management in the postwar era. This victory was evidenced by a rise in union membership from 14,600,000 in 1945 to over 18,000,000 a decade later, and by the firm

[23] Richard B. Wilson, "The Eisenhower Antitrust Policy: Progressivism or Conservatism?" *Rocky Mountain Law Review*, XXXII (February 1960), p. 13.

establishment of strong unions in all major fields of manufacturing, mining, transportation, and construction.

Labor's rise to its new position in the postwar era was not achieved without a struggle. The war's end found its leaders resentful against a stabilization program that had supposedly deprived workers of deserved wage increases. They were also fearful of inflation, large-scale unemployment, and depression in the reconversion period. Yet they were determined not only to hold but also to enlarge the gains that labor had made since 1940.

A wave of strikes began soon after the Japanese surrender in August 1945. At one stage during the first months of peace nearly 2,000,000 workers in a variety of industries were simultaneously on strike, in what seemed the gravest industrial crisis in American history. The crucial stage came from November 1945 to January 1946, when 180,000 auto workers, some 200,000 electrical workers, and 750,000 steel workers struck for a 30 per cent wage increase. In contrast to the riotous strikes of the mid-thirties, these postwar strikes were mild affairs because management and labor eschewed violence and appealed to the public for support. When presidential fact-finding boards recommended wage increases of 19½ cents an hour, General Motors and leaders in the steel and electrical machinery industries compromised on an increase of 18½ cents, thereby setting the pattern for most of American industry.

Meanwhile, new and more violent eruptions impended in the coal and railroad industries. John L. Lewis, president of the United Mine Workers, was demanding not only the 18½ cent hourly increase but also a number of so-called fringe benefits. When the operators refused, miners throughout the country walked out of the pits on April 1, 1946, and the government seized the mines soon afterward.

Lewis achieved most of his goals in the ensuing settlement, but in October he demanded shorter hours and another wage increase and threatened a second strike if the government did not surrender by November 20. Negotiations failed; the strike was called; and Lewis and his union were fined for contempt by a federal judge on December 4 for defying a temporary restraining injunction. With the miners back at work pending an expected reversal of the decision, the Supreme Court in March 1947 reduced the fine but upheld the contempt conviction, and Lewis duly withdrew the strike order. But he won a new contract that conceded all his demands when the mines were returned to their owners in the following June.

The country was also rocked by a nation-wide railroad strike and events that followed in its wake. The failure of protracted negotiations over wages and working rules led the Engineers and Trainmen to call a strike. The President seized the railroads on May 17, 1946, and offered a compromise settlement that eighteen unions accepted. The Engineers and Trainmen, however, would not yield, and walked out on May 23. For the first time in its history the nation was threatened by almost total paralysis. The President on May 25 asked Congress for drastic, almost dictatorial, power to save the country, after the strikers had ignored his appeal.[24]

<hr />

[24] Specifically, Truman requested Congress to empower him to declare a state of national emergency whenever a strike imperiling the national safety occurred in a vital

Actually, the leaders of the Engineers' and Trainmen's brotherhoods had given in three minutes before Truman appeared before the joint session, and the crisis was over.

The autumn of 1946 witnessed a second squaring off between labor and management, induced in large measure by price increases that wiped out all of labor's gains during the preceding year. There were numerous small strikes but no major ones, because the big unions resorted more to persuasion and appeals to public opinion than to direct action. Negotiations in the major industries were protracted but not bitter. The break came in mid-April 1947, when the automobile and steel companies con-

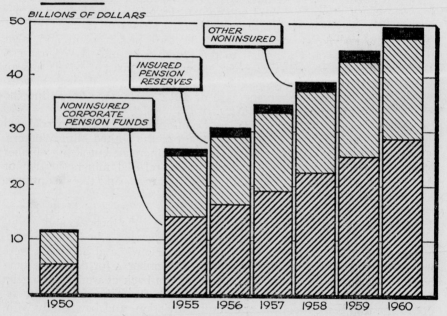

CORPORATE PENSION FUNDS
BOOK VALUE OF ASSETS AT END OF YEAR
1950–1960

ceded a fifteen-cent hourly wage boost and set the pattern for the balance of industry.

The peaceful settlements of the spring of 1947 marked a decisive turning point in labor relations during the postwar era. Afterward there occurred third, fourth, and fifth rounds of wage increases, but management evinced a willingness to raise wages so long as the increases could be passed on to consumers in the form of higher prices. The number of workers in-

industry under federal control. Workers who persisted thereafter in striking would lose all employment and seniority benefits and would be drafted into the army. Moreover, union leaders would be fined and imprisoned if they persisted in strike activities. The House approved a measure embodying these demands, but the Senate refused to act once the danger had passed.

volved in strikes, which stood at an all-time high of 4,600,000 in 1946, declined to 2,170,000 in 1947 and to 1,960,000 in 1948. And with returning peace came a new spirit of mutual accommodation and epochal innovations in collective bargaining contracts.[25]

However, the increased inflation and economic activity that followed outbreak of the Korean War in 1950 stimulated further wage demands, strikes in which 4,843,000 workers were involved, and inevitable wage increases. Congress made a gesture toward economic stabilization in August 1950 by approving the Defense Production Act empowering the President to establish price and wage controls. But the President's authority was so circumscribed that the price and wage stabilization boards he established in January 1951 could do little more than oversee and approve price and wage increases.

The last great strike of the Truman era occurred while the two major parties were preparing for the national conventions of 1952 and ended in a significant testing of the presidential authority. A breakdown in wage negotiations in the steel industry threatened to lead to a nation-wide strike. President Truman seized the steel plants on April 8, 1952, in order to prevent an interruption of the flow of steel to defense plants. The workers got a wage increase from the government, but the Supreme Court intervened on June 2 by ruling that the seizure was illegal in the absence of statutory authority. The President then withdrew, and a strike ensued for fifty-four days, until both sides compromised their differences in an agreement signed at the White House on July 24, 1952.

Although organized labor attained unprecedented power and the status of an established institution during the postwar era, it also suffered

~~~~~~~~~~~~~~~~~~~~~~

[25] The two-year contract between General Motors and the UAW, concluded in 1948 and renewed for a five-year period in 1950, contained two of the most important innovations in collective bargaining in the postwar era. The General Motors contract provided, first, for an upward or downward revision of wage rates every three months according to a schedule based upon the consumers' price index and, second, for automatic annual wage increases ranging from 2 to 2½ per cent, in order to give workers the benefit of increases in productivity. Over 1,000,000 other workers shared the benefits of the so-called escalator clause and the annual improvement provision by 1951. Another major innovation in bargaining contracts was the widespread adoption of so-called welfare provisions. The musicians' union and the UMW won such provisions in 1944 and 1946, respectively, but the important turning point in industry came in October 1949, when a brief strike by the steel workers won pensions and health insurance for the workers in the steel industry in lieu of a wage increase. By 1958 more than 19,000,000 workers were covered by pension plans to supplement the Social Security system, and perhaps as many enjoyed the benefits of medical and life insurance purchased by their employers.

Another significant milestone in the field of collective bargaining was reached in 1955, when the United Auto Workers signed contracts with the automobile, farm machinery, and aircraft manufacturers providing for a guaranteed annual wage—or supplementary unemployment benefits, as the device came to be called. The agreement provided for company payments to its unemployed workers, in sufficient amount, when added to state unemployment compensation, to guarantee those workers a fixed percentage of their normal annual wage when fully employed. The steel, rubber, aluminum, and maritime workers obtained supplementary unemployment benefits on the UAW model in 1957.

heavy losses in popular support and adverse state and federal legislation.[26] Chief responsibility for this anomalous development lay not with management, despite its campaign to enlarge employers' rights and restrict union prerogatives, but with the leaders of the labor movement. Their efforts to break the economic stabilization program during the war, their undemocratic procedures and refusal to accept responsibility for the fulfillment of contracts, and their failure to move decisively against "featherbedding" and racketeering in the unions all contributed to the profound change in public sentiment that occurred after 1940. But the major cause of the change was the growing popular conviction that big labor, irresponsible and uncontrolled, was potentially as dire a menace to the general interest as uncontrolled and irresponsible big business.

This new sentiment was naturally reflected in the attitude of Congress, where a coalition of conservative Democrats and Republicans worked assiduously in 1945 and 1946 on legislation designed to curb labor's power.[27] Their chief aim was to rectify the alleged unbalance in favor of labor established by the Wagner Act, and they moved quickly to accomplish a thoroughgoing revision of the New Deal statute when their strength was augmented by the Republican sweep in the congressional elections of 1946. The Hartley bill, approved by the House on April 17, 1947, was sweeping, severe, and vindictive—an obvious effort to break the labor movement. The anti-labor forces in the Senate, led by Robert A. Taft of Ohio, were equally determined to reduce union power but were unable to win approval for their most ambitious objectives, notably the prohibition of industry-wide bargaining. The Taft-Hartley, or Labor-Management Relations, bill, approved by both houses in June 1947, represented a compromise between what the foes of organized labor wanted and labor's friends were willing to concede. It outlawed the closed shop and certain "unfair" union practices —refusal to bargain in good faith, secondary boycotts, jurisdictional strikes, exaction of pay for work not performed, and the like. It permitted employers to sue unions for breach of contract, to petition the NLRB for elections to determine the bargaining agents, and to speak out during organizational campaigns. It provided for "cooling-off" periods and use of the injunction by the President in strikes imperiling the national health or safety. Finally, the measure required unions to register with and submit

\\\\\\\\\\\\\\\\\\\\\\\

[26] In 1947, for example, more than thirty states enacted legislation prohibiting secondary boycotts, jurisdictional strikes, and sometimes strikes in vital industries.

[27] Their first solution was the Case bill, approved by the House on February 7 and by the Senate on May 25, 1946. It provided for "cooling-off" periods before important strikes could occur, outlawed secondary boycotts and union interference with interstate commerce, and allowed employers to sue unions for breach of contract. Although the President vetoed this measure on June 11, 1946, he did approve a series of bills in 1946 and 1947 to outlaw a number of allegedly unfair union practices—"featherbedding," especially in the musicians' union; racketeering or interference with interstate commerce; and union demands for payment for past portal-to-portal work time. The Portal-to-Portal Act of 1947 was adopted in response to the Supreme Court's ruling in the so-called Mt. Clemens Pottery case in June 1946. The court ruled that workers were entitled to pay for time spent in preparing for their job as well as for time spent going to their jobs after they had reached the place of their employment. At once unions filed thousands of suits to recover back pay under the ruling.

annual financial reports to the Secretary of Labor, forbade union contributions to political parties, and prohibited certification of unions until their officers had filed affidavits that they were not Communists.

Whether the Taft-Hartley Act was a wise attempt to restore balance to the field of industrial relations or whether, as President Truman declared in his unsuccessful veto message on June 20, 1947, it contained "seeds of discord which would plague this nation for years to come," we will not attempt to say. The power of the unions grew during the years following the measure's adoption, while management demonstrated even greater willingness after 1947 than before to accept unions and work with them in good faith.

Organized labor not only grew in bargaining power in spite of the Taft-Hartley Act but also passed from awkward adolescence into at least the first stage of maturity after 1947. Symbolic of the change was the rise of what one sociologist has called the "new men of power"—a young and socially minded union leadership better trained in law and labor economics than in the art of industrial warfare. The election of Walter P. Reuther as president of the CIO after the death of Philip Murray in 1952 was a notable victory for the progressive element in that union. Symbolic also of labor's maturing was the notable lessening of tension between unions and management, as union leaders adopted the objectives of "welfare capitalism" and made a determined and successful effort to purge their ranks of Communists.[28]

Typical of the constructive goals sought and achieved by the new order of labor leaders in the fifties was the merger of the AF of L and the CIO into a single, giant federation. Such a proposal had been under discussion for years, always postponed but never forgotten. Thoughtful spokesmen from both camps began to plan more earnestly for the project in the face of identical political and economic goals and the lessened importance of issues that once divided the two organizations.

A steadily widening area of co-operation preceded and made possible the actual merger. The AF of L and the CIO joined during the Korean War in setting up a United Labor Policy Committee to advise the government on labor questions and work out manpower, wage, production, and price agreements for unions during the national emergency. A common desire to effect repeal of the Taft-Hartley Act and obtain the election of state and national candidates favorably disposed toward labor brought the two organizations into close working harmony on the political front. The most significant step toward merger was taken in 1954, after months of preparation, when nearly all of the constituent unions of both the AF of L and the CIO concluded a two-year no-raiding agreement, thus virtually ending the biggest single cause of friction between industrial and craft unions competing for membership within a single plant or industry.[29]

[28] The AF of L had never tolerated Communist infiltration. The CIO, which had allowed such infiltration in the late thirties and during the war, finally expelled the electrical workers' union, the farm equipment workers' union, and nine other Communist-dominated unions in 1949 and 1950, and set about to organize new CIO unions in the industries involved.

[29] Constant "raiding" of each other's members by competing AF of L and CIO unions had led to a frequent outbreak of so-called jurisdictional strikes in various industries. These purely intralabor quarrels were widely condemned by union leaders

Functioning concurrently with the negotiations that led to the no-raiding agreement was a joint unity committee of AF of L and CIO representatives, hard at work on specific plans for effecting the merger. Indispensable guidance and leadership in both these important projects were provided by the two new presidents, the dynamic Walter Reuther of the CIO and the burly, tenacious George Meany, who had succeeded William Green as president of the AF of L upon the latter's death in the fall of 1952. Only labor's innermost circles knew whether the merger talks were making any real progress. Then on February 9, 1955, the joint unity committee made the dramatic announcement that it had reached full agreement on all major details for the union of the two great organizations. Ratification of the proposed new constitution by the AF of L and CIO executive committees was surprisingly rapid, and both memberships gave overwhelming endorsement to the plan at their December conventions. For its name the new organization simply combined the titles of the two parent bodies, and the AFL-CIO came officially into being in December, 1955, at the Seventy-first Regimental Armory in New York. Meany was president and Reuther vice president of the new organization. Nearly 90 per cent of America's 17,750,-000 organized workers had become members of a single, massive federation.

For the balance of the decade organized labor continued to strengthen its position along the lines laid down in the immediate postwar years. Unions obtained new rounds of moderate wage increases at a fairly steady rate—boosts averaging between five and ten cents an hour were granted to over 7,000,000 workers each year from 1956 to 1960. The adoption of pension plans, paid vacations, and other fringe benefits proceeded apace. On the whole, labor and management met at the bargaining table in a mutual spirit of restraint, accommodation, and good will. Recurrent strikes, especially in the major industries, continued to excite public attention, but the obvious trend during the fifties was toward settlement of more and more labor disputes by negotiation, mediation, and arbitration rather than by strike.[30] In the general field of social welfare legislation, labor stepped up its political pressure for broader Social Security coverage, a higher minimum wage, more public housing, and related issues, and could point to a considerable degree of legislative progress in many of these areas. (See below, pp. 766–767.)

Despite its many gains, organized labor was sorely beset by a variety of problems in the late 1950's. The one that attracted most public notice was

themselves as wasteful, costly, and unnecessary for labor, and an undeserved burden for management.

[30] A comparison of the turbulent period 1945–52 with the more stable period 1953–60 points up the general improvement in labor-management relations. The average number of strikes per year in the former period was over 4400, as opposed to an annual average of 3968 from 1953 to 1960. An average of nearly 3,000,000 workers per year, representing 8.6 per cent of the labor force in occupations and industries normally subject to strike, were involved in strikes from 1945 to 1952, as opposed to an average of less than 2,000,000 workers per year, or 4.6 per cent of the "strike-prone" labor force, in the period 1953–60. The most significant difference was in the number of man-days of idleness caused by strikes, which averaged 49,200,000 per year from 1945 to 1952, less than 31,700,000 per year from 1953 to 1960.

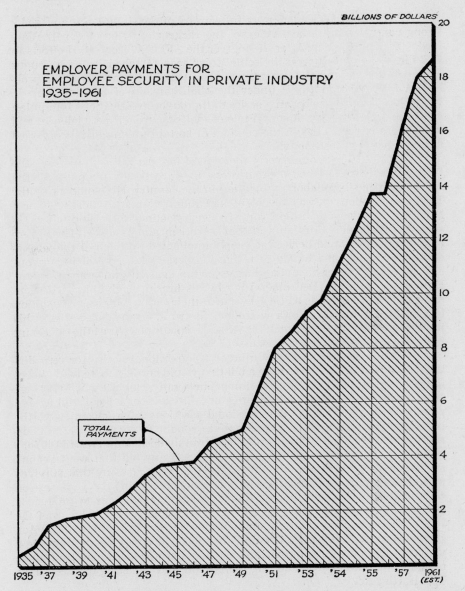

BILLIONS OF DOLLARS

EMPLOYER PAYMENTS FOR
EMPLOYEE SECURITY IN PRIVATE INDUSTRY
1935–1961

TOTAL
PAYMENTS

1935 '37 '39 '41 '43 '45 '47 '49 '51 '53 '54 '55 '57 1961 (EST.)

that of corruption, fraud, and dishonesty in the affairs of certain unions. Swollen membership, high wages, the union shop, and the enormous and growing pension funds now being administered by the unions all created opportunities for varied and large-scale illegality, and a few union leaders succumbed to these temptations. Racketeers and other criminal elements had long been involved with certain of the more vulnerable and less disciplined labor organizations, most notably the International Longshoremen's Association.

AF of L and CIO leaders were fully aware of the situation and waged a strong campaign to reform or expel the racket-ridden unions in the late forties and early fifties. After the merger the AFL-CIO intensified efforts in this direction. But success in some areas was matched by conspicuous failure in others, and the government soon took active notice of the problem. A Senate committee [31] under the chairmanship of Senator John L. McClellan of Arkansas began a series of thorough investigations into union affairs in January 1957. A sordid tale of malfeasance, crime, violence, and other gross irregularities in the conduct of certain union officials emerged from the reams of testimony.

The McClellan committee's most shocking disclosures involved the International Brotherhood of Teamsters, the largest and undoubtedly the most powerful single labor aggregation in the country. High officials in the Teamsters' Union, it was revealed, had indulged systematically, almost blatantly, in misuse of union funds, rigged elections, extortion, close association with racketeers, and acts of terrorism and violence. The Teamsters' president, David Beck, was deeply implicated in much of the wrongdoing and was finally forced to resign his post in the face of indictment and ultimate conviction upon charges of tax evasion and grand larceny. He was succeeded in December 1957 by his brash, tough-minded lieutenant, James R. Hoffa. The AFL-CIO voted at their December 1957 convention to oust the Teamsters. Hoffa welcomed the rupture and boasted that his union possessed power to break the AFL-CIO and replace it as the dominant force in the American labor movement.

Public anger and alarm reinforced congressional desire for remedial legislation. The attempt to frame a bill that would correct undoubted abuses in the labor movement, however, immediately ran afoul of the whole range of more basic questions concerning organized labor's legal rights and powers. The approaching congressional elections of 1958 injected the issue into partisan politics. Conservatives sought to combine the anticorruption measure with broader provisions frankly designed to restrict labor's ordinary privileges. Liberals staunchly opposed any bill that went beyond the issues of corruption and malfeasance. The only measure that survived partisan wrangling and obstruction to become law during the 1958 session was totally inadequate.[32] It took Congress another full year to produce a stronger bill that majorities in both Houses could accept. This was the Labor-Management Reporting and Disclosure, or Landrum-Griffin, Act, signed by President Eisenhower on September 14, 1959. Besides making a variety of anti-corruption provisions, the new statute placed new limitations upon labor's power by broadening the boycott and picketing clauses in the Taft-Hartley Act.[33]

wwwwwwwwwwwwww

[31] The select committee on improper activities in the labor or management field.

[32] This was the Welfare and Pension Plans Disclosure, or Douglas-Kennedy-Ives, Act, signed by the President on August 28, 1958. It confined itself to requiring detailed disclosure of all employee welfare and pension plans.

[33] The Landrum-Griffin Act extended the definition of a secondary boycott—which the Taft-Hartley Act had outlawed—to include coercing an employer to prevent his transacting business with another employer. The new act also defined picketing against a company where another union was lawfully recognized as an unfair labor practice

Along with the problem of corruption, which brought the labor movement into growing public disfavor and raised the threat of increased governmental supervision over union activities, came a distinct reversal of the
twenty-year growth trend in union membership. The number of organized
workers had increased between 1935 and 1945, under the spur of New
Deal legislation and wartime prosperity, from about 3,700,000 to almost
15,000,000. Thereafter, union membership expanded slowly but steadily to
a peak of nearly 18,500,000 in 1956. By 1958, however, the figure had declined to just over 18,000,000, where it hovered for the rest of the decade.
It appeared that the great period of expansion in the ranks of organized
labor had come to a definite close.

The reasons for the decline, once again, stemmed from the great
prosperity of the postwar years. It was true that opposition to union organization in the South had stiffened, helping to impede progress in this area,
but the major causes were of a different sort. Even in industries and areas
where unions were well entrenched, there was found to be a lessened
interest in union membership on the part of unorganized workers. This
was chiefly because the higher wages and increased benefits won by unions
since 1945 had perforce been extended by management to unorganized
workers as well. Of even greater significance was the steady shift in the
American labor force from blue-collar to white-collar occupations, where
the task of union organization has always been more difficult. Technological advances steadily reduced the demand for unskilled and semi-
skilled workers in manufacturing, mining, and transport; and technological and other changes after 1945 helped to create new white-collar and
professional jobs in trade, finance, government, and above all in the service
industries.[34]

If occupational shifts posed new organizational problems for the labor
movement, technological advance was generally recognized as posing the
gravest challenge of all—especially since most labor leaders basically approved the improved efficiency and lessened drudgery that industrial labor-
saving devices made possible. In practical terms, however, labor feared that
the too rapid spread of automation and other technological improvements
would work undue hardships upon the thousands of workers whose jobs
were yearly being supplanted by the machine. Consequently, even the more
progressive union leaders sought to cushion the impact of automation by

and allowed the states to assume jurisdiction whenever the National Labor Relations
Board refused to act in a labor dispute.

The anti-corruption provisions of the Landrum-Griffin Act attempted to safeguard
democratic procedures in union elections by means of a Labor Bill of Rights, subjected
union officials found guilty of misusing union funds to fine and imprisonment, made
forcible interference with the rights of union members a federal crime, and struck at
racketeers by prohibiting certain types of criminal offenders from holding union office
for five years after their release from prison.

[34] A few figures will demonstrate the dramatic changes in the composition of the
American labor force. Between 1940 and 1957 the population increased 30 per cent, the
number of blue-collar workers by only 16 per cent, and the number of white-collar
workers by fully 64 per cent. To put it another way, in 1940 over 62 per cent of the
nonfarm labor force was in the blue-collar category; by 1957 this proportion had declined to 54 per cent, and the future trend was clearly toward a further steady increase
in the white-collar category.

demanding that employers help in relocating and even retraining displaced workers. The tendency in some unions was to demand labor contracts that fully protected the jobs of their members, even if this forced employers to retain what they regarded as unnecessary men on the payroll.

So widespread had these concerns become by the late 1950's that the question of "work rules" and "featherbedding" [35] replaced wages and fringe benefits as the key items in most labor disputes. Management, of course, insisted in the name of economy and efficiency upon the right to cut labor costs by installing automative devices as it saw fit, while unions demanded job protection and employer responsibility for displaced workers.[36]

One of the largest and costliest strikes in American history—the great steel strike of 1959—was fought essentially over the issue of work rules. The dispute grew out of protracted negotiations between the steel companies and David McDonald's United Steelworkers over a new wage contract in the spring of 1959. The industry, more determined than in former years to resist another round of wage increases, denied labor's claim that steel profits were high enough to afford the proposed increase without raising prices. Before the usual compromise could be reached, the companies demanded a modification of existing work rules, and union resistance stiffened immediately; wages were negotiable, but work rules were not. The talks broke down completely in mid-July. Thereupon 500,000 steel workers, in factories producing 85 per cent of the nation's steel, banked furnaces and left the plants.

All subsequent efforts to break the impasse and reach agreement were in vain. Neither side would budge from its position. Both labor and management, obviously, were ready for a showdown on the all-important work-rules issue, and the strike became a gigantic endurance contest—unmarred by the violence that had attended the historic steel struggles of 1892, 1919, and 1937, but waged with equal determination and even greater persist-

wwwwwwwwwwwwwww

[35] "Work rules" is the term applied to the complex system of defining, grading, and classifying all jobs in a given establishment, a matter over which labor unions naturally wish full jurisdiction in the interest of protecting members from arbitrary layoffs. "Featherbedding" is the opprobrious term for maintaining unneeded workers on the payroll, at union insistence, even after their jobs have been or could be eliminated by mechanization.

[36] Automation had its greatest impact in the mining and transportation industries. The application of mechanical processes revolutionized—and saved—the American coal industry after 1940. Although the increasing use of rival fuels after the Second World War led to a marked decline in domestic coal consumption, coal was able to retain a substantial share of the market by drastically cutting production costs—especially payrolls. The figures tell a graphic story. Coal production declined from 512,000,000 tons in 1940 to 431,000,000 in 1958, or by about 15 per cent; the number of miners decreased from 530,000 to 223,000, or by nearly 60 per cent. Output per man-hour in the coal mines more than doubled during these years.

Automation also brought particular concern to the transport workers and longshoremen. "Containerization," a new concept for transferring certain cargoes from ship to truck or train without breaking bulk, promised to effect revolutionary savings in the time and labor cost of this operation. And the spread of mechanical devices on the railroads to all phases of the industry enabled the roads to carry 40 per cent more traffic in 1958 than in 1940 with almost 20 per cent fewer employees. Railroads had eliminated 200,000 jobs in that eighteen-year period without substantially decreasing the size of their physical plant.

ence. The entire economy began to feel the effects as existing steel supplies dwindled to the vanishing point by the end of the summer. Some 225,000 other workers were laid off as industries dependent on steel were forced to cut back production schedules.

The Eisenhower administration was reluctant to take strong action,[37] but public concern and the threat of economic paralysis made further delay impossible as the strike moved into its fourth month. The President invoked the emergency provisions of the Taft-Hartley Act on October 9. Announcing that the national health and safety would be impaired by continuance of the steel strike, Eisenhower appointed a special board of inquiry. The board reported ten days later that it could find no basis for a settlement. Then the President ordered the Department of Justice to seek an eighty-day injunction against the steelworkers' union, under the terms of the Taft-Hartley Act. The injunction was granted on October 20 by the federal district court in Pittsburgh. The Supreme Court, by a vote of 8 to 1, sustained the injunction on November 7 after some litigation, and the steelworkers promptly returned to the plants.

The strike was over, but the issue that prolonged it was far from settled. While the national economy gradually recovered as steel once again became available, the union announced its intention to resume the strike as soon as the eighty-day injunction expired. At the end of the year, as this expiration date approached, the two sides appeared as far from agreement as ever, and only a dramatic last-minute intervention by Vice President Richard M. Nixon and Secretary of Labor James P. Mitchell averted a resumption of the strike. Nixon finally persuaded the reluctant steel companies that a second strike would only result in an enforced governmental settlement and stringent legislation that would please no one. Consequently, the steel companies came to terms with the union on January 5, 1960, and the danger of another costly walkout was ended.

The agreement represented a fairly complete victory for the steelworkers. In addition to granting a substantial wage hike and increased pension and insurance payments, the industry agreed to maintain existing work rules and to co-operate in establishing joint committees under neutral chairmen for the purpose of studying human relations and work conditions within the industry.

The steel settlement may prove to be labor's most significant victory in the entire postwar era. Management had fought this strike hard, and the outcome of the dispute, together with the attention that it focused on the basic problem of work rules and automation, suggested not only that labor's rights would continue to be upheld in the matter, but also that the

[37] The government did, of course, employ a variety of persuasive maneuvers. In August the Department of Labor reviewed conditions in the industry and published a report calling attention to the fact that both wages and prices in the steel industry had risen more since 1945 than in most areas of the economy—facts which labor and management each hailed as supporting its position in the dispute, with agreement as remote as ever. During September Eisenhower first pleaded for "intensive, uninterrupted, good faith bargaining," then offered to name a nongovernmental fact-finding board if both sides requested it (the companies refused), and finally conferred separately with union and industry spokesmen at the White House to persuade them to renew the talks. They did so on October 2, but to no avail.

problem would hereafter receive the sort of intensive, co-operative, planned study that it deserved.[38] The American economy would obviously continue to mechanize at a fast rate. The United Steelworkers had helped to establish the principle that it must not lose sight of the human element in the process. At the same time, the strike demonstrated that the Taft-Hartley Act provided woefully inadequate machinery for permanent settlement of serious labor disputes.

On balance, then, the position of organized labor at the end of the 1950's remained strong, and was perhaps healthier than ever before. Despite gloom in high labor circles, labor's major bulwarks—the right of exclusive bargaining, compulsory union membership, and various legal immunities—remained intact. The labor movement faced the future in 1960 with a confidence strongly tempered by sober caution and a heightened awareness of the problems that lay ahead. Its workers possessed a higher living standard and greater economic security than ever before in American history. Its leadership on the whole was making substantial progress toward the high level of maturity and restraint demanded by the times.

206. *Americans and Their "Mixed" Economy in the 1960's*

What, then, was this American economy past mid-century? Was it capitalistic in the traditional sense? Was it a welfare economy fatally weakened by "creeping socialism"? The American people were confused by a welter of conflicting claims and charges and groped for understanding.

Much of the popular confusion stemmed from the effort to apply old economic theories to new economic conditions. In 1960 it was futile to attempt to describe the American economy in terms of conventional capitalism. Only reactionary Americans and the Kremlin's propagandists would make that mistake. It was equally futile to attempt to impose a socialistic pattern upon an economic system as complex and dynamic as the American one.

By the end of the 1950's the American economy was neither capitalistic nor socialistic, competitive nor monopolistic, business-controlled nor laboristic. It was a "mixed" economy, a combination of many elements. Manufacturers, bankers, and businessmen still retained control over a large share of the important economic decisions. Yet their control was restrained or shared by other important groups—the federal and state governments,

[38] Other victories for labor on the question of automation and work rules were registered in 1959. The Pacific Maritime Association, after long negotiations with West Coast longshoremen, agreed in July to pay $1,500,000 into a fund to compensate workers for hours lost due to the container method of unloading vessels. In their turn, the longshoremen agreed to furnish "competent personnel" to man all labor-saving devices on the waterfront. In another automation dispute, the Meat Cutters and Packinghouse Workers secured a contract with Armour & Company that created a fund for the establishment of a joint committee to study the problems of relocation, retraining, and job opportunities for technologically displaced employees in that industry. And transport workers won a work-rules dispute with the Pennsylvania Railroad after a twelve-day strike in September 1960.

A HALF CENTURY OF PUBLIC WELFARE

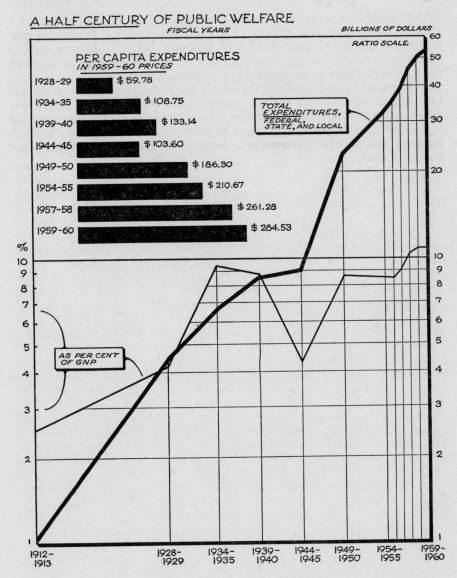

FISCAL YEARS

BILLIONS OF DOLLARS

RATIO SCALE

PER CAPITA EXPENDITURES
IN 1959–60 PRICES

1928–29	$ 59.78
1934–35	$ 108.75
1939–40	$ 133.14
1944–45	$ 103.60
1949–50	$ 186.30
1954–55	$ 210.67
1957–58	$ 261.28
1959–60	$ 284.53

TOTAL EXPENDITURES, FEDERAL, STATE, AND LOCAL

AS PER CENT OF GNP

labor unions, farm groups, and organized consumers. The American economy was indubitably a "free" economy, yet political agencies and not the market determined the price of agricultural commodities; manufacturers were not "free" to ride roughshod over workers or determine wage and hours policies. The United States was not a "welfare state" in the European sense, yet the federal and state governments sponsored far-reaching programs of social security and assistance to the poor.

In retrospect, we can see that the institutional reforms of the New Deal and underlying forces at work since 1933 had transformed a monolithic economic society dominated by the business-financial elements into a virtually new economic society of great countervailing forces, as one economist has called them—industry, business, banking, finance, organized labor, and agriculture—each of them struggling for a larger share of the national income, each appealing to the political power.

Americans moving toward the end of the twentieth century might not understand the subtleties of their contemporary economic order, but most would agree that it was a far better system than the monolithic order of 1929. The vast majority, regardless of political faith, liked their "mixed" economy and desired government to continue to assume responsibility for making it work.

CHAPTER

===

26

Social and Cultural Trends

1940 – 1960

FROM 1940 TO 1960 the American people experienced much—total war and dubious peace, recurrent international crises always overhung with the threat of nuclear holocaust, and a steadily expanding prosperity that made rapid change and continuous adjustment normal features of American life. It is of course impossible to encompass the total American social and cultural experience during these two eventful decades within the confines of a single chapter, but we can gain some insight into the meaning and significance of the changes that occurred by looking at specific manifestations of social and cultural development, for in every case the microcosm reflected the whole.

207. *Social Trends from Depression to Prosperity*

The most sweeping and important changes in the American social scene were stimulated in the first instance by the demographic and economic revolutions of the period after 1940. The decline of the agricultural and rural populations, which we noted in the preceding chapter, was not as rapid as the destruction by science and technology of the rural way of life of long hours, backbreaking toil, and primitive living conditions. Even more important was the complete triumph of the city over the country and small town in customs, manners, and habits of thought.

The growth of large cities from 1940 to 1960 was dwarfed by the development of small cities and suburban areas. The central cities of the metropolitan districts grew during these years by only 25 per cent while the

A NATION OF CITY DWELLERS, 1960

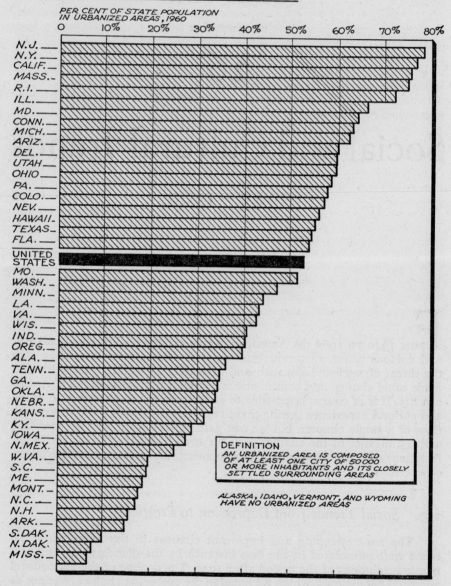

PER CENT OF STATE POPULATION IN URBANIZED AREAS, 1960

DEFINITION
AN URBANIZED AREA IS COMPOSED OF AT LEAST ONE CITY OF 50,000 OR MORE INHABITANTS AND ITS CLOSELY SETTLED SURROUNDING AREAS

ALASKA, IDAHO, VERMONT, AND WYOMING HAVE NO URBANIZED AREAS

outlying suburbs grew by fully 100 per cent. Everywhere along the fringes of cities large planned communities of small single-family homes and garden-apartment developments with their own shopping centers mush-roomed; and former city-dwellers not only found a new way of life in suburbia but also became increasingly conservative as property owners and members of integrated communities.

The effect of prosperity was greatly to enlarge the middle classes. The result was a society in which the great mass of industrial workers and their leaders thought and acted as members of the middle class, not as an impoverished proletariat, and in which skilled workers often enjoyed higher incomes than teachers and white-collar workers.

What changes time wrought as this drive toward equality gained powerful momentum after 1939! By 1960 the effects were evident on all sides—in the gradual disappearance of city slums, blighting poverty, the old leisure class, and the servant class, and the relative decline of what was once called High Society.

The drive toward equality had its greatest impact in changing old American attitudes and practices toward large groups formerly outside the main stream of social life—southern and eastern Europeans, Jews, Negroes, and other minority groups. Only an ignorant optimist would claim that Americans had reached a state of social blessedness by mid-century. The significant fact, however, was that the American society had made greater progress toward the democratic ideal during the three decades after 1929 than during any comparable period at least since Reconstruction. By the postwar era practically all leaders in church, school, press, labor, law, and government had joined in a campaign to square American practices with principles. It was a crusade on many levels, but it operated most spectacularly in the troubled area of Negro-white relations. (For details, see below, pp. 768–771, 776–786.)

Meanwhile, what happened to American customs, manners, and morals during the years of war and postwar fear and crisis? It is difficult to generalize about the social attitudes and behavior of millions of people, and yet there were significant changes.

The trend during the two decades after 1940 was for Americans to marry at an earlier age and to dissolve marriages at a much higher rate than in former years. The median age of American males at time of marriage declined from 24.3 years in 1940 to 22.3 years in 1959, that of women, from 21.5 years to 20.2. Understandably, the war brought hasty marriages and a startling increase in the divorce rate. It culminated in a peak of nearly thirty-one divorces for every 100 marriages in 1945. The rate declined slightly afterward, but not greatly; and throughout the fifties, at a remarkably steady rate, fully one fourth as many people were breaking the marriage bonds as were getting married.

Defenders of the family often bewailed the prevalence of divorce without understanding its causes—the weakening of religious sanctions, the widespread conviction that unhappy marriages were better dissolved than endured, the increased economic independence of women, and, above all, the fact that public and private organizations had taken over many of the functions associated with the rearing of children.

The tempo of American life accelerated in an incredible way during the defense and war crises. Millions of men and women, many of whom had never been outside their counties, were suddenly dispersed to remote corners of the globe. Millions of civilians left the shelter of their native communities to work in war industries. Indeed, the wonder is that the social system withstood the shock so well, without major riots or upheavals.

Prosperity in the postwar era further accelerated the tempo of life and heightened certain tensions. The return of millions of veterans put an almost unbearable pressure on housing facilities, although the supply of new houses and apartments had largely relieved the strain by 1952. More significant was the faster pace that resulted from the proliferation and integration of private activities. By 1951 there were at least 200,000 organizations of every conceivable kind and purpose in cities, towns, and countryside: labor unions, Parent-Teachers' Associations, church groups, Community Chests, organizations of farmers and businessmen, all of them institutionalizing and integrating voluntary activities. The philanthropic agencies alone mobilized 2,000,000 volunteers and raised $3,000,000,000 for good works in 1949. Americans eleven years later were giving a staggering total of some $9,000,000,000 for all charitable causes.

Surveying the national scene in the middle of the twentieth century, Americans might well have been encouraged by the progress their generation had made toward the eradication of social and economic injustices and the lessening of racial tensions. Yet in the midst of plenty and apparent progress there was gloom and fear of the future.

A good measure of the prevailing pessimism stemmed from the experiences of the adult generation and from profound changes in recent religious thought. The depression had left deep scars and bitter memories, and millions of older Americans in the postwar period lived in fear that prosperity could not last. The Second World War and revelations of Nazi and Communist cruelty ended fatuous dreams of automatic moral improvement, while the threat that a third world conflagration would bring mass if not total extermination hung like a pall over the minds of men.

It was enough to make even the most optimistic shudder, but it was not all. In the thirties the American democracy had survived the assaults of demagogues of the right and left and of purveyors of racial and religious prejudices; during the war Americans had found a kind of unity and domestic peace through common sacrifice. But old and new threats to democracy arose at home in the postwar era. A wave of corruption swept over the nation, engulfing leaders in private organizations and in government on every level. Fear of Communist infiltration, stimulated by ambitious demagogues, seized millions of Americans and spurred a fierce attack on civil liberties and nonconformity unprecedented since the early 1920's. (For details, see below, pp. 657, 682–7, 742–6.) There were ugly recrudescences of hostility between Catholics and Protestants over the issues of religious freedom and state support of parochial schools, about which more will be said later (below, pp. 663–4, 767–8, 869).

Worst of all, organized crime and racketeering flourished alarmingly and threatened the integrity of many businesses, labor unions, and municipal governments. Crime syndicates, using techniques learned during prohibition and copying the organizational methods of modern business, became multipurpose enterprises of large scope and influence. The most disturbing aspect was the way organized crime infiltrated a host of normally legitimate businesses. Large profits made in traditional criminal activities— bootlegging, gambling, prostitution, narcotics, and the "policy," or "numbers," racket—were channeled by enterprising syndicates into many promising new areas. They engaged heavily in black-market operations during the Second World War and again during the Korean conflict. They steadily enlarged their influence in certain labor unions, exploiting both workers and employers by a system of corruption, extortion, and violence that became a national scandal in the 1950's. (For details, see above, pp. 622–624.) Liquor, real estate, and automobile agencies, restaurants and taverns, night clubs, hotels, the garment industry, vending machines, bakeries, laundries, and the stock market were among the businesses that attracted organized crime in the prosperous years after 1945. Syndicates invariably sought to achieve monopoly or near-monopoly in every field that they entered, "stabilizing" highly competitive retail and service industries in ruthless fashion.

In many towns and cities racketeers conducted their affairs with impunity and wielded much political power and influence, sometimes by corrupting police and other officials, but more often by lavish campaign contributions and other political favors. Organized crime took on the trappings of respectability as it prospered and found new and varied sources of wealth. The swaggering gangster of the 1920's gave way to the self-effacing, conservatively dressed leader who lived quietly in a fine suburban home.

The social order was also menaced by increased juvenile delinquency, alcoholism, and the bootlegging of narcotics, especially to young people. The dislocations and tensions of the war years, overcrowding in schools, the rapidly changing character of urban and suburban neighborhoods after 1945, racial and ethnic tensions, and the declining number of part-time and unskilled jobs available to young workers as a result of automation all contributed to a rise in juvenile criminal activity. Delinquent gangs roamed city streets, making lurid headlines with their violent pitched battles and assaults on persons and property. The number of youths arrested for such crimes as theft, manslaughter, rape, and even homicide mounted ominously and seemed to suggest a dangerously maladjusted and rebellious generation, while drug addiction among the same group also increased.

And yet full-scale revelations of these darker phases of American life brought not only alarm but new public and private efforts at amelioration. For example, the special Senate committee to investigate crime in interstate commerce, commonly known as the Kefauver committee, dramatized the glaring shame of the cities as Lincoln Steffens had done in journalistic fashion fifty years before. A similar service was performed by a thorough Senate investigation of criminal activities in the labor and management fields beginning in 1957. The arrest and subsequent trial of more than sixty well known racketeers and criminal leaders from all over the country at a "gangland meeting" in Appalachin, New York, in 1957 further revealed the scope and nature of organized crime in the United States.

The result of these national disclosures was a wave of crime investigations and popular uprisings against politicians allied with racketeers in many cities and states. The federal government advocated more stringent legislation and invited greater co-operation among federal, state, and local authorities in prevention and detection of crime. Attorney General Robert F. Kennedy proposed creation of a national crime commission in 1961, and Congress passed laws in that year prohibiting interstate wire services from sending gambling information and forbidding gamblers and illegal narcotics dealers from use of the mails and interstate transportation facilities for business purposes. As for the liquor problem, there was actually less drinking per capita in 1960 than in 1915. The problem simply seemed larger because of the increased attention given it by scientists, educators, and organizations like Alcoholics Anonymous, and because of the spread of so-called social drinking. Narcotic addiction, due to the heightened activity of international and federal agencies, actually decreased each year during the late 1950's. And intensive study of juvenile delinquency by a host of organizations—states, churches, welfare agencies, the National Education Association, and a special White House Conference on Children and Youth in 1960—was at last giving this complex problem the kind of serious attention it deserved.

208.   *Main Currents in American Fiction, 1940–1960*

It is difficult, if not impossible, for the historian to pass more than tentative judgment on the literary and artistic achievements of his own day. By the end of the second decade after Pearl Harbor, however, a review of the literature of the war and postwar years permitted one or two generalizations. To begin with, it seemed apparent that the quality of American fictional writing after 1940 did not compare with that of the preceding generation. The Second World War marked the close of a great literary epoch, and no unmistakable signs of a revival could be detected twenty years later. With some exceptions, young authors seemed neither as talented nor as clear of purpose as their predecessors of the twenties and thirties, and—again with one or two exceptions—the giants of that earlier day spoke with declining power after 1940.

The latter exceptions, of course, were Ernest Hemingway and William Faulkner, who maintained and even strengthened their undisputed position as masters of American fiction. Both writers continued to display the expert craftsmanship that had marked their prewar novels, but for Hemingway, at least, the forties and fifties were less productive years. Between his triumph with *For Whom the Bell Tolls* in 1940 and his characteristically violent and mysterious death in a shooting accident in 1961, Hemingway produced only two major works. One of these, *Across the River and Into the Trees,* 1950, was a disappointment, full of unlikely dialogue and shallow philosophizing and carping criticism that amounted almost to a parody of his earlier writing. The other was a striking and highly successful short novel, *The Old Man and the Sea,* 1952, for which he received the Pulitzer Prize in 1953. In this powerful tale of an aging fisherman adrift in the Gulf Stream, battling for his own survival while he stalked a great fish, all of the author's unique force and skill were once more in evidence. And the emphasis, as one critic has observed, was again upon "the heroism of the solitary individual, set against a hostile universe, which Hemingway has always celebrated." As a study in the basic human qualities of compassion, courage, and endurance, *The Old Man and the Sea* offered a measure of reassurance, if not hope, to the uneasy postwar generation. Hemingway received the Nobel Prize for literature in 1954.

These same basic human qualities were also the primary concern of William Faulkner, despite the themes of violent conflict, decadence, and greed that pervaded so much of his work. His reputation as America's foremost living novelist became firmly established after 1945 and endured until his death in 1962. In all of his major novels Faulkner probed the meaning of life through a many-sided portrayal of southern society, with its tensions between a meaningful but archaic past and a rapidly changing present, and between the established but often degenerate older families and the rapacious, petty, materialistic instincts of the rising poor whites. The inescapable racial antagonism added malign tensions of its own. Readers could not be sure from his novels of the twenties and thirties whether Faulkner was affirming or denying the values of the past. But in the impressive array of later works—*The Hamlet,* 1940, *Go Down, Moses,* 1942, *Intruder in the Dust,* 1948, *Requiem for a Nun,* 1951, *A Fable,* 1954, *The Town,* 1957, and *The Mansion,* 1959—Faulkner's purpose emerged with greater clarity. It was, as he said in accepting the Nobel Prize for literature in 1950, to reaffirm the eternal worth of human beings and the dignity of the human spirit. For all his preoccupation, which at times seemed almost morbid, with the bitter antagonisms and dark violence that he saw in southern life, Faulkner insisted that his ultimate message was one of hope. "I believe that man will not merely endure," he said. "He will prevail. He is immortal . . . because he has a soul, a spirit capable of compassion and sacrifice and endurance."

The other major voices of the Lost Generation were muted or still in the postwar years. Fitzgerald died in 1940, a tragic victim of his own disenchantment with American life. Sinclair Lewis survived until 1951, but his later writing never recaptured the quality of his great achievements of the twenties. In his last novels, from 1943 to 1947, Lewis returned to old themes and took up a new one, racial prejudice; but withal he demonstrated, in the words of one critic, "a continuous decline of powers and an irritable indecision concerning the meaning of what he is doing."

John Steinbeck and John Dos Passos were both productive throughout the forties and fifties, but neither could scale the heights that they had once achieved. Although Steinbeck received the Nobel Prize for literature in 1962, none of his postwar novels duplicated the power and scope of *The Grapes of Wrath;* and Dos Passos permitted bitterness and petulance to warp his work. Disillusioned by what he regarded as the failure of the New Deal to do more than bureaucratize American life, Dos Passos swung from his cautious, skeptical Marxism of the thirties to a highly unskeptical and extreme conservatism in the forties and fifties. He was still concerned, as in his greatest work, *U.S.A.,* with the place of the individual in modern society. The menace was no longer heartless capitalism but expanding world communism and its unwitting—or perhaps purposeful—ally, the welfare state. Hypnotized by this belief, he gradually lost his power to capture, as he once had done, the entire mood and tempo and harsh impact of twentieth-century American society. His second trilogy, *District of Columbia* (*Adventures of a Young Man,* 1939, *Number One,* 1943, *The Grand Design,* 1948), though a vivid and often moving account of America during the depression years, was weakened by its distorted treatment of the New Deal. His novels of the fifties betrayed a growing alienation from the realities of modern life and a visible disaffection with "the People" whom he had once championed so eloquently. Clearly, the survivors of the Lost Generation could not lead a literary revival in the sixties.

Indeed, it was far from apparent at the end of the Eisenhower years that a genuine literary revival had yet begun. One of the most gifted of the postwar writers, Ross Lockridge, Jr., whose *Raintree County*, 1948, gave promise of richer development, cut himself off by suicide. Already established authors, such as Robert Penn Warren, J. P. Marquand, and John O'Hara, continued to produce competent, readable, and often penetrating novels, but they blazed no new trails in form, viewpoint, or subject matter. The same was true, essentially, for a highly talented group of southern writers, many of whose novels were among the most sensitive and carefully fashioned works to appear after 1945. This southern local-color school consisted, for the most part, of women writers who maintained the genteel tradition and high literary standards established by such earlier novelists as Ellen Glasgow, Willa Cather, Katherine Anne Porter, and Dorothy Canfield Fisher. Among the outstanding postwar writers in this tradition were Caroline Gordon, Carson McCullers, Eudora Welty, Harper Lee, Joan Williams, and Reynolds Price. Presenting realistic and finely drawn sketches of southern society, past and present, their books did not depend for their effectiveness upon obscurity or brutality; and they were, unlike so much contemporary fiction, a genuine pleasure to read.

There was also an outburst of war fiction, including a few books of more than passing interest. Perhaps the best in this category were three probing portrayals of military life in which war formed an incidental backdrop for a study of complex human relationships among men in uniform. They were James Gould Cozzens' *Guard of Honor*, 1948, James Jones' *From Here to Eternity*, 1951, and William Styron's *The Long March*, 1956. There were also the neo-Hemingways, to borrow a name—Alfred Hayes, John Horne Burns, Norman Mailer, and Irwin Shaw—who wrote powerfully of war's horrors and brutality. But they were too intense and "stultified and frozen in a helpless attitude of horror" to be effective; and they did not give promise of founding a school. There were other young writers, like John Hersey, Herman Wouk, and James Michener, who found courage and nobility in the great tragedy. But few of these writers, whether despairing or hopeful, had demonstrated by 1960 that they could transcend or even equal the quality of their war novels.

Much of the postwar writing was vigorous and forceful, but it reflected indecision and a failure to find intellectual and moral bearings. The overriding concern, in one form or another, was a familiar one in twentieth-century American literature: the attempt to discover how the isolated individual might survive in an increasingly impersonal and complex society. Some, like Nelson Algren, Saul Bellow, and John Updike, wrote with eloquent but harsh and despairing realism about tormented, sordid lives and seemed to conclude that the answer was ultimate stagnation or defeat. There were the so-called beatniks, of whom the leader and probably the ablest writer was Jack Kerouac—angry nonconformists who claimed solace in the mystical doctrines of Zen Buddhism and made a point of rejecting society and its conventions with desperate abandon and much posing. The need for Christian redemption in a world of lost innocence was part of the message of John Howard Griffin, although his recurrent fascination with eroticism suggested, at the very least, a lack of conviction. American writers had discovered the central problem, but few had advanced solutions that were not negative or confused.

Somewhat more positive, or at least more sharply focused, were the writings of two of the ablest novelists of the fifties, James Gould Cozzens and J. D. Salinger. They were poles apart in style and tone, but both were expert craftsmen who explored human relationships with care and skill. Cozzens was no newcomer; he had written five able novels in the thirties and early forties. But he did not achieve wide recognition until *Guard of Honor* appeared in 1948, or fame until his most ambitious novel, *By Love Possessed*, was published in 1957. The latter was an elaborate fictional treatise on justification by faith—on the failure of man to achieve moral or social virtue by ordinary morality. Its Christian symbolism was lost upon most of its readers. The sum of Cozzens's works, in the opinion of one critic, "marked by a steady increase in power, complexity, and formal mastery, must convince us that Mr. Cozzens is that almost unknown phenomenon in American letters, the artist with staying-power and the capacity to grow." [1]

While Cozzens pointed up human imperfections in order to show the need for living in faith, Salinger seemed to be asking youth to denounce these imperfections and retain or regain the purity of childhood through mystical religious experience. He explored this theme with a masterful rendition of the idiom, dialogue, and thought processes of intelligent but bewildered and rebellious young people in search of meaning and truth, in *The Catcher in the Rye*, 1951, in a related series of *New Yorker* short stories, and in *Franny and Zooey*, 1961. "What we have in these stories," a critic has noted, "is a writer who is concerned primarily with the nature of religious experience . . . above all, with the trust that a man's life is ultimately measured not by what he does, but by the pureness-in-heart with which he does it." [2]

There was, certainly, an abundance of talent and promise in the literary field at mid-century, and no cause for gloom about the future of American fictional writing. Nevertheless, from the vantage point of the early sixties not even the ablest of the postwar writers could be said to have founded a movement or opened vistas that seemed to lead in promising directions. The enormous complexity and uncertainty of the postwar world had inspired a babel of literary voices but, as yet, no recognized literary prophet or even an unfailingly convincing spokesman.

209. *Poetry and the American Drama*

On the whole, American poetical writing in the postwar era displayed greater excitement, virtuosity, and sense of direction than were apparent in American fiction. The best poetry revealed a noticeable vigor and vitality and a sustained interest in experimental forms and combinations of words. The influence of Ezra Pound and T. S. Eliot, who had cast long shadows

[1] Louis O. Coxe, "A High Place," *Critique*, I (October, 1958), p. 50.
[2] *New York Herald Tribune Book Review*, September 17, 1961, p. 3.

across the field of modern poetry since the First World War, continued to be felt. This was true both in the field of experimentation, which helped to give American verse its dynamic quality, and in the continued vogue of obscurity, which had long been the delight of most critics and the despair of laymen. Much recent poetry, after the fashion of Pound and Eliot, demanded repeated rereading and careful thought and study, with no guarantee that such assiduous attention would yield meaning. The very obscurity of some of the modern poets reflected the basic inability of words to convey the writer's full meaning. In a deeper sense it symbolized the essential isolation of the individual, "the man so far away from society that he no longer cares to talk with his fellows."

In a variety of directions American poetry was exhibiting a new-found maturity, a quiet self-assurance, and a sense of having come of age. An English critic noted, for example, that American poets had not only discovered the classics but had learned how to use classical and biblical allusions in ways that were fresher and less stylized than those employed by English poets. The same critic noted less "aggressive nativeness" on the part of American verse writers than in earlier years, and deeper awareness of the cultural values and traditions of other lands. In the poems of writers like Robert Penn Warren, John Malcolm Brinnin, and Robert Lowell could be seen a thoughtful quest, relatively new in America, for identity with one's ancestors. Many American poets, of whom Warren and Delmore Schwartz were typical examples, carefully seasoned their rhetoric with wit, their romantic elegies with irony, their self-pity with self-mockery; and the results were often effective. Thoughtful readers soon learned to appreciate the wide-ranging themes and varied styles of young poets such as Karl Shapiro, Randall Jarrell, and Robert Lowell, who began to publish during the Second World War, or the well-knit form and inner logic in the poems of Stanley Kunitz and Theodore Roethke, whose careers had begun a few years earlier. Three well-established poets of the preceding generation, all in the Eliot tradition—Marianne Moore, William Carlos Williams, and e. e. cummings—continued to display their diverse talents in the postwar era.

If the ordinary reader remained baffled by the remote allusions and cryptic imagery of the more radical experimentalists, he could take comfort from the fact that by no means all modern poetry was obscure. At least five young poets who had begun to achieve eminence by mid-century— Phyllis McGinley, William Meredith, Reed Whittemore, Louis O. Coxe, and Richard Wilbur—chose to communicate with more directness, clarity, and emotion. Robert Frost, the venerable dean of American verse, continued to charm and captivate a wide circle of readers. Frost, up to his death at eighty-eight in 1963, retained all his unique New England magic, controlled but exuberant energy, and dry humor and sympathetic wisdom. His enduring place in American letters was attested by a special Senate citation in 1950, four Pulitzer prizes awarded between 1924 and 1943, and his reading of one of his own poems at President Kennedy's inauguration in 1961. Frost was too kindly and cheerful to adopt the gray note of gloom and doom for mankind, but his sympathy never lost its sharp satiric edge, and he had no cures to offer. "Every poem," he said, "is an epitome of the great predicament; a figure of the will braving alien entanglements."

In striking juxtaposition at mid-century stood another venerable writer, Wallace Stevens, who in the opinion of many critics was one of the greatest of modern American poets. Stevens like Frost began writing verse before the First World War. Unlike the New Englander, he did not win recognition beyond a small circle of critics and poets until a few years before his death in 1955. He was intuitive rather than rational, and he could write with eloquent simplicity about nature and the seasons and "gusty emotions on wet roads on autumn nights . . . the bough of summer and the winter branch." But Stevens was also, far more than Frost, a constant experimentalist in the Eliot-Pound tradition, a believer in bizarre words (often of his own invention) and obscure allusions, too difficult to follow in many of his verses for any save the most erudite and persevering. However, he won a large and devoted following among the generation that came of age after 1950. Those who took the trouble discovered that much beauty, force, love of life, and profundity were contained in his poems and critical essays.

American dramatic output declined somewhat in the forties and fifties from its pinnacle of great achievement in the thirties. There were many musical plays and light comedies in the war and postwar years, but only three new playwrights of any literary consequence: William Inge, Tennessee Williams, and Arthur Miller. Inge, a master of realistic plot and dialogue, reported the ordinary tragedies and tensions of middle-class life with sympathetic insight. He achieved four notable successes on Broadway with *Come Back, Little Sheba*, 1950, *Picnic*, 1953, *Bus Stop*, 1955, and *The Dark at the Top of the Stairs*, 1957.

Williams, whose skillfully constructed plays established him as one of the most expert dramatists of the twentieth century, both captivated and shocked his audiences by liberally infusing his plots with sex and violence. These items were always relevant to his theme, but as time went on he showed an increasing tendency to probe to the very depths of human depravity, psychic disorder, and abnormality. Many critics who could not deny the powerful impact of his plays began to feel that he had carried his sympathy for the degenerate and the perverted to a repellent extreme. Nevertheless, his long succession of plays included many theatrical landmarks: *The Glass Menagerie*, 1945, *A Streetcar Named Desire*, 1947, *Summer and Smoke*, 1948, *The Rose Tattoo*, 1951, *Camino Real*, 1953, *Cat on a Hot Tin Roof*, 1955. This impressive array was followed by four other dramas—*Orpheus Descending*, 1957, *Suddenly Last Summer*, 1957, *Sweet Bird of Youth*, 1959, and *Period of Adjustment*, 1960. None of these equaled the excellence of the earlier works, and there was reason to suspect by the end of the fifties that Williams' powers were at least temporarily on the wane. But the widespread critical praise accorded to *Night of the Iguana*, 1961, indicated that he had recaptured all of his unique dramatic mastery.

Arthur Miller was concerned both with social and psychic anxieties. He fully shared the pervasive moral uneasiness of the postwar world and attacked and laid bare a variety of social ills. His plays—which included *All My Sons*, 1947, *Death of a Salesman*, 1949, *The Crucible*, 1953, and *A View From the Bridge*, 1955—were eloquent if somewhat strident protests against materialism, dehumanized efficiency, and conformity.

The brooding genius of Eugene O'Neill survived miraculously in the postwar era. His productivity was slowed by illness, but he completed four plays after 1940—*The Iceman Cometh*, 1946, *A Moon for the Misbegotten*, 1947, *Long Day's Journey Into Night*, 1956, and *A Touch of the Poet*, 1957. O'Neill continued his intensive probing of human character, still convinced, in the words of one critic, "that the only subject worth writing about was the eternal tragedy of Man in his glorious, self-destructive struggle." [3]

Three or four good playwrights do not make a dramatic revival. Whether television, with its large financial rewards for quick plays, was responsible for the postwar decline, or whether playwrights, like novelists, were floundering in their search for new themes, we cannot say. In any event, there were few hopeful signs in the early 1960's of any important rebirth of drama in the United States.

210. *Art, Architecture, and Music*

The forties and fifties saw the full maturing of American endeavor in the fine arts. Indeed, development of artistic efforts and public appreciation was so rapid that one observer could conclude in 1960 that the American people had become obsessed by a passion for art and "culture."

The dominant trend among American artists during the decade after 1918 had been a movement away from realism toward abstraction, cubism, and surrealism. By 1960, after a brief revival of artistic realism during the depression years, the trend of the twenties had re-established itself more firmly than ever before. Realism, though often of the "symbolic" variety, retained many adherents after 1940, as did primitivism, but the overriding emphasis was upon varieties of abstract expressionism or "non-objective" painting, and the continued power and strength of the artistic revival in the United States found its major outlet in that direction.

The realists were mainly represented by artists of the prewar period who remained productive in the forties and fifties. Viewers who found neither sense nor satisfaction in the work of the abstractionists could still enjoy the "stoical sentimentality" of Edward Hopper, the precise style and emotional detachment of Charles Sheeler, the bright colors, dreamlike overtones, and "sharp-focused naturalism" of Andrew Wyeth, or the nostalgic, fantasy-touched landscapes of Charles Burchfield. Among the younger non-abstract painters who achieved prominence after the Second World War were Constance Richardson, who adhered to the objective tradition; Morris Graves and Kenneth Callahan, who painted in a highly subjective, imaginative style; and John Wilde, Elwyn Chamberlain, and Robert Vickrey, whose symbolic realism, "carrying as it does observation to a point of extreme intensity, invades the territory of surrealism." It should be noted that even among the realists the subjective overtones of fantasy, dream, haunted imagery, and hallucination were much in evidence, suggesting that the world of the artist was a troubled one, concerned with a reality that lay below the surface.

wwwwwwwwwwwwwww
[3] Willard Thorp, *American Writing in the Twentieth Century* (Cambridge, 1960), p. 107.

Similar tendencies were evident in the work of the abstractionists, whose vogue was triumphant in the postwar years. In the words of one authority, "Artists have set themselves the task to create a wholly 'nonobjective' world, without reference to any forms of nature. Alone with their self-consciousness, they try to make themselves understood (if they have not, as some have, abjured communication altogether) by muffled visions and unknown imagery from the subconscious. . . . Painting in the United States, since the close of the 1939 war, has been haunted by apparitions: the ghosts and demons of Stone Age man have risen to stalk into the twentieth century." [4]

The retreat from objectivity was manifest in a number of ways. To begin with, some abstractionists attempted to transcend reality by distorting or even "pulverizing" the normal vision of nature and, by so doing, to reveal what they regarded as its true essence. Others tried to "translate the tumult of the emotions" directly on to their canvas, abandoning images altogether in favor of color and movement. On the extreme fringe was a group that turned away from the very principles and logic of abstract art itself and employed a sort of stream-of-consciousness style, claiming that the picture painted itself and arrived at ends the artist could not foresee when he began.

Many spectators, viewing the works of the abstract expressionists in the Museum of Modern Art or in Frank Lloyd Wright's new Guggenheim Museum in New York City, were horrified or amused. They could see in most of the new pictures little more than the results, to use Ruskin's classic phrase, of a "pot of paint flung at the canvas." For other observers the best abstractionists offered much more. They could derive aesthetic pleasure from contemplating the repeated designs of elegant swirls of color dripped on canvases by Jackson Pollock, or the "huge, apparently random patches of color" in the works of Clyfford Still, or the diffuse, rectangular shapes and mood-evoking color contasts of Mark Rothko, to name three of the most prominent and influential among the American abstract school.

The best artists were clearly trying to say something important. Their large epic canvases, their attempts to distill rather than merely to describe, their absorption with mood and emotion, and their wide-ranging choices of unconventional themes and methods were often eloquent expressions of the disordered modern age in its quest for ultimate meaning. Finally, by rejecting conformity and concentrating on the bold, the experimental, and the right to express themselves, new American artists reaffirmed a much needed faith in the individual, and in art itself. "In an age that has tended to think only of American materialism," one English critic has noted, "the action painter, the abstract expressionist, call him what you will, must be saluted. He has kept alive a faith in the perennial qualities of disinterested values; he stands out as an upholder, in his own setting and in his own fashion, of *l'art pour l'art*. For that, if for nothing else, his contemporaries and posterity have every reason to be grateful to him." [5]

In the field of architecture, pre-eminence and recognized world leader-

[4] E. P. Richardson, *Painting in America* (New York, 1956), p. 409.

[5] *The American Imagination: A Critical Survey of the Arts from the Times Literary Supplement* (London, 1960), p. 110.

ship passed to the United States during the 1950's. "For the young European architect," an English authority observed, "an American Grand Tour is becoming as important as the Italian was to the eighteenth-century English gentleman; apart from the buildings, he finds there a wider public interest in his subject than he is used to, an atmosphere of excitement that heralds something important taking place, and . . . a searching criticism which is an aspect of self-confidence." [6] This same observer noted that the three essential conditions for great architecture—a prosperous building industry, creative freedom, and conspicuous expenditure—were uniquely combined in postwar America. The results were gratifying and suggested that a new architectural tradition of lasting importance was already taking shape. A host of talented American architects reached out boldly for the forms that would both enrich and serve the complex industrial society in which they lived. To be sure, they were powerfully influenced by the theory and practice of such pioneering giants as Frank Lloyd Wright, Walter Gropius, Mies van der Rohe, and Le Corbusier (Charles Édouard Jeanneret-Gris), all but the last of whom resided in the United States and continued to plan and to build with undiminished vigor and excellence throughout the nineteen-fifties.[7]

In private home design the trend after 1946 was toward moderation. Several striking new houses embodied variations of the functional features emphasized by Wright and others years before—openness, spatial relationships, a blending of exterior and interior by extensive use of glass and of "balconies and horizontal strip walls floating out on graceful cantilevers." But in most private homes in the postwar era the traditional Cape Cod or Georgian styles gave way to modified forms, the so-called ranch and split-level types.

Innovation and imagination found their greatest outlet in the design of public buildings and commercial structures, where adaptation to the demands of the modern age was most sorely needed. The evolution of the skyscraper took a giant step forward in the fifties with the perfection and use of the all-glass curtain wall laced by metal grids. The idea and tentative use of the glass curtain wall dated back to the beginnings of the modern movement in architecture, but its effective utilization had to await not only a greater receptivity by the public but a host of technological advances in the metallurgical and plastics industries. Wartime and postwar demands spurred much of the technological advance and helped to rationalize, quicken, and cheapen the complex practice of building construction. By mid-century the public was ready for the new design. It found striking expression in the United Nations Secretariat in 1950, in Mies van der Rohe's Lake Shore apartment buildings in Chicago in 1951 and 1957, in the same architect's Seagram Building on Park Avenue in New York in 1958, and in Gordon Bunshaft's starkly handsome Lever Building, also on Park Avenue, in 1952.

Some critics voiced the fear as the sixties opened that the new popularity of the glass-walled rectilinear structures would result in dull uniformity in American cities, "an endless repetition of standard box-like units bring-

[6] Ian McCallum, *Architecture U.S.A.* (New York, 1959), p. 9.
[7] Frank Lloyd Wright died in 1959 at the age of ninety.

ing an end to character and the expression of the creative personality." [8]
But the imagination and resourcefulness of American architects in the
1960's were the best safeguard against this possibility. A swiftly advancing
technology, which had profited from the rapid development of prefabrica-
tion techniques and new processes and materials perfected during the Second World War, was expanding architectural horizons in a number of directions. An unprecedented scope and harmony in the planning and execution
of new projects were now possible thanks to the so-called umbrella method
adopted by many architectural firms. It thoroughly blended and coordinated the talents of architects, engineers, landscape and interior de-
signers, and other specialists.

Dramatic breakaways from the rectilinear pattern had come within
reach: the use of plastics and sprayed concrete and factory-made molded
structures that no longer required costly reinforced concrete combined to
provide an almost boundless sculptural freedom for American architects.
They began experimenting with revolutionary new forms in a host of exciting ways. Curved and folded shells, concrete barrel vaults suspended
from parabolic arches, sweeping curved façades and roof lines, and a bewildering variety of other unusual structural forms took shape upon the
drawing boards. Most of the designs were still in the blueprint and model
stage at the end of the fifties, but a few had been translated into reality, and
they offered startling vistas of what lay ahead: Frank Lloyd Wright's Guggenheim Museum in New York, Edward D. Stone's United States Pavilion
at the Brussels Exposition, Eero Saarinen's Kresge Auditorium at the
Massachusetts Institute of Technology, and Minoru Yamasaki's air terminal
in St. Louis, to mention only a few.

The new shapes, which promised to supplement rather than replace
the stark simplicity of the box-like office buildings and skyscrapers, were
being applied to churches, school and college buildings, sports arenas and
stadiums, transportation terminals, civic and cultural centers, research
laboratories, American embassies abroad, and private homes. Urban renewal projects and downtown civic centers embodying combinations of the
rectilinear and sculptured forms were fast appearing. If the precise directions and enduring styles in this architectural revolution remained in doubt
in 1960, what was happening guaranteed brilliant achievement and rapid
progress. It also held the promise that both aesthetic and functional deliverance from the unplanned, decaying ugliness of most American urban
centers was near at hand.

American music, too, retained its vitality and showed signs of increasing maturity in the postwar generation. The era was one of progress in almost every field. The quality of musical workshops and training in colleges
and universities was higher than ever, with distinguished composers in
residence at some of the leading institutions—Roger Sessions at Princeton,
Randall Thompson and Walter Piston at Harvard, Douglas Moore at Columbia, Paul Hindemith at Yale (until 1953), Ernest Bloch at California until
his death in 1959—providing unequaled opportunities for American music
students. Summer music festivals continued to flourish, while conservatories and the excellent Berkshire Music Center steadily advanced the level

[8] Ian McCallum, *Architecture U.S.A.*, p. 26.

of musical instruction. More and more school children were being exposed to systematic, competent training in both performance and appreciation.

Jazz remained the most distinctive and uniquely American musical product and enjoyed an ever widening circle of devout adherents. Perhaps the foremost jazz artist was the veteran trumpet player Louis Armstrong. He won tumultuous acclaim and made each of his tours abroad an international triumph. Each variation had its enthusiastic cult, from "hot" jazz to "cool" jazz, from the irregular "bop" to an uninspiring, repetitive rhythm that won favor among teen-agers under the descriptive title of rock-and-roll. Folk music in all its varieties was another area of continued American pre-eminence, its vogue much enhanced in the 1950's by the magnetic voice and presence of Harry Belafonte, a young Negro who took audiences across the country by storm.

Choral music, opera, and ballet all underwent a marked revival in the United States during the forties and fifties. The work of Robert Shaw and John Finley Williamson, the inspiring premiere of Bernard Rogers's oratorio *The Passion* in Cincinnati in 1944, the magnificent all-Negro Infantry Chorus of Leonard De Paur, and the gifted Trapp Family Singers from Austria all contributed to a renewed interest in choral music. American opera reached new heights with the works of Vittorio Giannini, Kurt Weill, Hugo Weisgall, and above all Gian-Carlo Menotti. His bold operatic compositions, notably *The Saint of Bleecker Street*, 1954, placed him in the first rank of younger American composers. Ballet began to come into its own in the United States with the formation of the Ballet Theater in 1939, the Ballet Society in 1946, and the New York City Center Ballet in 1948.

A versatile group of American composers, some already established and others just coming to prominence, made noteworthy contributions to the musical scene in the forties and fifties. In terms of virtuosity and range none could compare to the brilliant young Leonard Bernstein, conductor of the New York Philharmonic since 1958. His musical creations included ballets, an opera, symphonies, chamber music, musical comedies, and movie scores. Among the traditional writers, still interested in the classical forms, there were Walter Piston, Samuel Barber, and younger composers like David Diamond and Paul Nordoff. Virgil Thomson, Roger Sessions, William Schuman, and Paul Creston were eclectics who displayed, often in combination, both advanced and conservative musical form. Then there were pioneers along the sometimes controversial frontier of dissonance, polyphony, and the twelve-tone scale, which freed the musician—not always to his benefit—from the restriction of traditional chords and keys. Among these innovators were ardent experimentalists like Henry Brant, Elliott Carter, Alexei Haieff (of whose work a critic reported that "one leaves the concert hall feeling somewhat bruised and battered, if respectful"), and John Cage, who produced bizarre effects by employing electric buzzers, flowerpots, brake-bands, and other devices to supplement the more conventional instruments. Radical experimentalists also welcomed the possibilities of electronic music because it opened new vistas of a sort through manipulation of the tape recorder. By replaying a normal tape at faster or slower speeds, or backwards, and by splicing it, what one authority euphemistically described as "unusual groupings of sounds" could be produced.

The forties and fifties were the great golden age of musical drama in the United States. A glittering succession of smash hits delighted Broadway audiences during these years and met with equal enthusiasm on the road. They were a matchless blend of imaginative dance sequences, bright comedy, catchy tunes, and not a little music of enduring quality. Among the best were Irving Berlin's *Annie Get Your Gun*, 1946, and *Call Me Madam*, 1950; Cole Porter's *Kiss Me Kate*, 1948, and *Silk Stockings*, 1955; Leonard Bernstein's *West Side Story*, 1957; and Frederick Loewe's and Alan Jay Lerner's *Brigadoon*, 1947, *My Fair Lady*, 1956, probably the most brilliant and successful musical comedy of all time, and *Camelot*, 1960. Finally, there was the parade of unforgettable hits by "America's Gilbert and Sullivan," composer Richard Rodgers and librettist Oscar Hammerstein II: *Oklahoma!*, 1943, *Carousel*, 1945, *South Pacific*, 1949, *The King and I*, 1951, *Me and Juliet*, 1953, *Pipe Dream*, 1955, *Flower Drum Song*, 1958, and *The Sound of Music*, 1960. All in all, Americans of the postwar generation could take justifiable pride in the range, quality, and promise of their musical achievements.

211. *Motion Pictures and Television*

As popular art forms, neither the old motion picture industry nor the new television industry was able to demonstrate, save fitfully, that it was interested in much more than the lowest denominator of the mass entertainment market during the postwar era. Except for interesting developments in the early fifties in wide-angle photography and richer sound effects (Cinerama, Vistavision) and a short-lived and unfruitful experiment with three-dimensional movies, there were no technical advances of importance in the motion picture industry after 1940. Hollywood discreetly abandoned social themes during the war years and turned to the production of films to entertain and to inspire, or to educate the American people to an understanding of the Nazi menace and their new international responsibilities. There was also a marked revival during the war period of religious movies, the most notable of which were "The Song of Bernadette" and "Going My Way."

In the postwar era Hollywood faced new dangers and crises, the direst in the history of motion pictures. The most serious menace to the film's integrity was the determination of a vocal minority to purge Hollywood of alleged Communists and prevent the production of any films that attempted seriously to grapple with social questions. The campaign of suppression promptly frightened producers from certain controversial social themes and seriously hampered the creative impulses of many of the industry's ablest writers and technicians.

Hard on the heels of Hollywood's Red Scare, which declined somewhat with the waning of McCarthyism in the United States after 1955, came the impact of sharply falling attendance at the nation's motion picture theaters. Hit by television and other forms of entertainment and the refusal of many former movie-goers to face the inconveniences of parking shortages and baby sitters, thousands of movie theaters in small towns and big cities alike were forced out of business. Weekly attendance at the movies shrank from a peak of more than eighty million in the war and immediate postwar years to less than fifty million in 1953, with no upturn in sight by the end of the decade.[9]

Another change in the prewar pattern was the breakup of the monopoly of a few large producing companies centered in Hollywood, each with its "stable" of name stars and its sprawling acreage of elaborate sets and studios. Faced by rising costs of labor and production in addition to a declining market, the major studios were forced to retrench and to relinquish much of their former power. More and more stars broke away from their enthrallment to a particular company, while others joined with like-minded producers to establish small independent companies, which competed successfully, on lower budget and overhead costs, with the giant studios. Writers, scenarists, and other technicians also benefited from the diffusion of power in Hollywood, as well as from the new opportunities created by a rapidly expanding television industry.

These varied challenges and changes had a mixed effect upon the quality of postwar movies. On the one hand, Hollywood turned increasingly after 1945 to "safe" and uncontroversial films: musicals, frothy comedies, adaptations of popular dramas and best-selling novels, westerns, romantic extravaganzas, ornate spectaculars with a vague historical base like "The Ten Commandments," "Ben Hur," "Spartacus," or "King of Kings," and a line of unbelievably vapid horror shows for teen-age consumption. The level of technical competence in these standard offerings was high, and many postwar films were entertainment landmarks: topnotch mysteries like "Dial M for Murder" and "Witness for the Prosecution," superb comedies like "Born Yesterday," "The Moon Is Blue," and "Roman Holiday," the screen versions of "Hamlet" and "Julius Caesar," and the successful adaptation of stage musicals like "Guys and Dolls" and "The King and I," of Broadway dramas like "A Streetcar Named Desire" and "Come Back, Little Sheba," and of novels like "All the King's Men" and "The African Queen." Only the best of such films possessed more than passing artistic merit, however, and critics who enjoyed describing Hollywood as a vast cultural wasteland were not without evidence in support of their claim.

But it would be wrong to say that American producers lost all courage or imagination in the postwar era. Some turned to new social themes as old ones lost their relevance for the contemporary generation. "Crossfire" and "Gentleman's Agreement" explored the depths of anti-Semitism. "The Lost Week-End," "Man With the Golden Arm," and "Snake Pit" dealt courageously with the plight of alcoholics, drug addicts, and the mentally ill. "Pinkie," "Intruder in the Dust," "Lost Boundaries," and "The Defiant Ones" confronted the explosive subjects of race prejudice and miscegenation. And "The Best Years of Our Lives," "High Noon," and "Bad Day at Black Rock" symbolized the plight of the individual in a world of craven and corrupt men. Hollywood occasionally demonstrated genuine maturity and convinc-

<hr/>

[9] While total personal expenditures for recreation increased nearly 200 per cent between 1945 and 1958, family expenditures at the motion picture box office dropped nearly 20 per cent. National income originating in motion picture theaters declined 14 per cent during the same period, and corporate profits after taxes in the movie industry as a whole (including production, distribution, service industries, and theaters) plummeted from $181,000,000 in 1946 to *minus* $16,000,000 in 1956.

ing realism, creating films of enduring quality such as "On the Waterfront," "Stalag 17," "Marty," and "Bridge on the River Kwai," to say nothing of the artistic excellence of such spectaculars as Michael Todd's "Around the World in Eighty Days."

Many talented new stars took their places in the postwar firmament, including Marlon Brando, Paul Newman, Grace Kelly, Audrey Hepburn, William Holden, Gregory Peck, Jean Simmons, wartime crooner Frank Sinatra, and that inimitable American dream-girl, Marilyn Monroe. Although movie-goers mourned the passing, between 1957 and 1961, of such veteran favorites as Ronald Colman, Humphrey Bogart, Tyrone Power, Errol Flynn, Clark Gable, and Gary Cooper, a host of other prewar stars were still enlivening the quality of American films in the early sixties.

As for television, the first decade and a half of its existence as a major entertainment medium was largely a story of vast potential, mediocre performance, and deferred promise. Perhaps more could not be expected of so young an industry. But many critics saw less hope for the future of television in 1960 than they had thought existed five or ten years earlier. And most intellectuals, if they did not shun it entirely, frankly admitted that they turned to it as opiate rather than art. The majority of Americans, however, seemed content with the new medium. Nearly 45,000,000 sets had found their way into American homes by 1960, an average of almost one per family, and millions of people young and old continued to devote a startling number of hours each week to their favorite programs.

With some exceptions, these programs followed stock formulas that made the standard Hollywood fare seem almost imaginative by comparison: westerns, "private eye" mysteries and other suspense stories, situation comedies, soap operas, giveaway and quiz shows (the latter coming under a severe cloud with the eruption of the Van Doren scandals in 1959), news and weather programs, a multiplicity of sporting events, variety shows usually centering around a popular comedian or singer, old Hollywood films and cartoons, and so on. On the whole, this was dreary fare, offering endless rounds of violence, sticky comedy, shallow characterization, unlikely plots, long commercials, bathos, and banality. In its desperate desire to avoid offending any segment of its vast audience, the industry blazed few new trails, battled for few causes, ignored most social problems, and shunned controversial issues. The new writing, acting, and producing talent that television seemed on the verge of developing in its early years tended either to lose itself in the unimaginative program formats or to escape to the relatively greener fields of Hollywood and Broadway.

There were a few bright spots. News coverage of important current events was often excellent, and several competent news analysts and commentators achieved a deserved eminence in the medium, notably the sharp-tongued, laconic duo of Chet Huntley and David Brinkley. Panel discussions and interviews featuring distinguished public figures, writers, and intellectuals often focused on current problems with courage and insight. Television coverage of such explosive national problems as racial tension in the South brought these issues home to the public in effective and often salutary fashion. Tentative but visible strides were made in the field of educational television, which offered distinct possibilities in such subjects as mathematics, science, foreign languages, and literature. Concerts and other musical offerings were often capably presented, and a few plays written especially for television possessed real merit. The medium developed some comedians of great virtuosity and talent, notably Sid Caesar, George Gobel, Jackie Gleason, Steve Allen, Ernie Kovacs, and Art Carney, although few if any of these gifted performers could sustain the grueling pace of weekly comedy shows for an extended period. Such overexposure devoured imaginative comic material faster than it could be created. Dramatic series like Studio One, Playhouse 90, Kraft Theater, and Play of the Week attained occasional brilliance and demonstrated that the best in both classical and modern drama could be staged effectively on television, while millions enjoyed their first taste of Shakespeare's historical plays in the competent "Age of Kings" series in 1961.

Despite these and a few other hopeful signs, even friendly critics were afraid by 1960 that television's great potential as a cultural and educational medium had been hopelessly stultified by the joint and interacting timidity of television's ruling groups—the broadcasting networks, advertising agencies, and sponsors. They tended to prefer inoffensive mediocrity and low-level entertainment over boldness, experimentation, controversy, or excellent programs that lacked mass appeal. Detailed investigations by the FCC into the whole question of program content and control, beginning in 1961, promised to give needed publicity to the problem and possibly to inaugurate some overdue reform, but such hopes were confined to the future. Violence and shallow escapism continued to dominate the television scene at the beginning of the sixties.

212. *American Newspapers and Magazines*

The forties and fifties were years of challenge and mounting trouble for American newspapers, although the picture seemed bright enough on the surface. Despite problems of censorship, communication, and grave wartime shortages of labor and newsprint, the press won deserved laurels for its thorough, often brilliant coverage of military action during the Second World War. Outstanding among the many talented war reporters was the famed Ernie Pyle, whose eloquent descriptions of life at the front with "G.I. Joe" captivated millions of American readers until Pyle was killed by a Japanese sniper on Ie Shima in the spring of 1945.

The public thirst for news in the war and postwar years raised the combined circulation of American dailies from about 40,000,000 in 1940 to over 54,000,000 in 1950. This figure continued to climb, although at a much slower rate and far less rapidly than the population, to over 59,000,-000 in 1960. Total receipts, including those for weekly as well as daily papers, increased from $846,000,000 in 1939 to $3,491,000,000 in 1958, while advertising revenues shot up from $539,000,000 to $2,428,000,000 during the same period. Significant technological improvements after 1940 included the widespread use of color, a high degree of automation in the photoengraving field and in the newspaper mailing room, and new composing machines that more than doubled printing speed by using teletype tape instead of the linotype keyboard, and by using photography to assemble characters on transparent acetate film.

Despite such evidence of progress, the daily press had come to occupy an unenviable position by the postwar era. "On the whole," in the words of one authority, "the fifties were looked upon as a decade in which prosperity and peril marched shoulder to shoulder." [10] Newspapers were beset by steadily rising costs of labor and materials that tended to wipe out gains in gross income. Strikes were frequent and costly throughout the period. Dependence upon advertising for over 70 per cent of total revenues caused newspapers to suffer in even the mildest of recessions. Growing urban traffic jams vastly complicated the task of prompt circulation. High salaries drew more and more journalistic talent into public relations, magazines, and the electronic media. And a new threat was offered by the steady growth of suburban weekly newspapers after 1945. These suburban sheets competed successfully for local advertising and offered a type of community news coverage that the big metropolitan daily could not match.

Most important, the newspaper's primary function was being undermined by powerful competitors. On the one hand, the press was totally unable to match radio and television in the prompt presentation of up-to-the-minute news. On the other hand, it was overshadowed by the weekly news magazines and periodicals of opinion in the analysis and interpretation of major news events. As one critic succinctly put it: "A man no longer needs to read a daily newspaper in order to be well-informed. Conversely, no single newspaper, with two or three brilliant exceptions, will bring an educated man anything like all the news he needs to know of his city, the nation, and the world." [11]

The trend toward consolidation, so marked a feature of the newspaper business since the First World War, continued apace. The total number of daily papers declined during the war years, from 1,878 in 1940 to 1,749 in 1945, then held remarkably steady for the next decade and a half; the admission of Hawaii and Alaska brought the national total to 1,763 in 1960. The number of weekly and semiweekly publications declined from approximately 11,000 in 1940 to 9,300 by 1960, despite the emergence of the new suburban press. Over one hundred newspaper chains or "groups," the latter term signifying a high degree of autonomy permitted to member journals, owned over 30 per cent of the nation's daily papers by 1960, and accounted for an even higher percentage of daily circulation. Among the venerable journals suspended or absorbed in this period were the Philadelphia *Public Ledger*, the Boston *Post*, and the New York *Sun*. Some sixty so-called hyphenated dailies, serving two or more adjacent cities, had appeared by the end of the 1950's. Of all American cities in 1960, only sixty-five had competing papers. Four of the nation's twenty largest cities had all their papers under single ownership, and only five such cities enjoyed more than two papers.

Regardless of ownership, American newspapers more than ever reflected the fact that they were a big-business enterprise—in the essential sameness of their offerings, revealing an overdependence upon the wire services and nationally syndicated columns and features, and in the steady

[10] Frank Luther Mott, *American Journalism, A History: 1690–1960* (third edition, New York, 1962), p. 811.
[11] Carl E. Lindstrom, *The Fading American Newspaper* (New York, 1960), p. 13.

PART III: *Second World War and Uncertain Peace, 1941–1966*

growth of advertising ratio to total newspaper content, from 40 per cent in 1940 to over 60 per cent in 1960. With the exception of eminent "national" publications like the *New York Times,* the *Wall Street Journal,* and the *Christian Science Monitor,* together with a few outstanding metropolitan dailies, the American press offered grossly inadequate coverage of foreign news and exhibited a parochial uniformity that was the despair of many professional journalists. There were signs by the end of the 1950's, however, that public taste in newspapers was on the rise.

Several changes were manifest in the periodical press after 1940. As before, the industry was marked by many new ventures, a high mortality rate among both new and established magazines, and fierce competition for more advertising, which accounted for 55 per cent of gross periodical income in 1939 and 66 per cent in 1958. On the whole, magazines showed healthy circulation increases in the postwar era, and total receipts expanded from $409,000,000 in 1939 to $1,558,000,000 in 1958. Specialization became the watchword in this as in so many phases of American life. "In view of the diversity of the total general audience," one authority noted, "a magazine must establish in the public mind an idea of itself as designed for certain classes and therefore a selective market tailored for certain desirable advertisers. This adaptation of the 'image' technique was widely used by the big magazines, mainly to attract advertisers who wished to reach the higher economic segments of the mass audience." [12] The trend toward specialization could be seen on all sides—in the continued appeal of established "specialty" periodicals like *The New Yorker, Harper's,* and *Vogue,* and in the striking success of new ventures that aimed at a specific market, like *Holiday, Playboy,* the Negro magazine *Ebony,* the hard-cover *American Heritage* and *Horizon,* and a range of hobby, sporting, and "men's" magazines. At the same time, general magazines of wide circulation either readjusted their format and retailored their offering, as did the popular *Saturday Evening Post,* or passed into oblivion, as did such veteran favorites as *Collier's, Liberty,* and *American Magazine.*

The percentage of fiction in most magazines declined, while periodicals and articles emphasizing news, public affairs, home services, and personalities recorded gains. Shorter articles, in keeping with the tempo of the age, were more and more in evidence. The influence of advertising was shown by the adoption of "split-run" editions of consumer magazines, which enabled advertisers to reach certain portions or geographic segments of the total circulation. Multimillion circulation figures were maintained and enlarged by popular magazines whose "image" and appeal were well defined: *Reader's Digest* and *Coronet;* the picture magazines *Life* and *Look;* the weekly news journals like *Time* and *Newsweek;* the women's magazines —*McCall's, Ladies' Home Journal, Better Homes and Gardens;* and such varied specialties as *TV Guide, Popular Science Monthly, Photoplay, True Story,* and the venerable *National Geographic.*

That American reading taste retained its immature element was evidenced both by the perennial success of the comic magazine, a $150,000,-000 industry selling 90,000,000 copies per month in 1960, and by the sudden vogue of so-called polecat publications that skirted the bounds of ob-

[12] F. L. Mott, *American Journalism,* p. 829.

scenity and exploited real or imagined scandal in the lives of entertainment figures. But even here the trend was hopeful. Comic book publishers responded to criticism by cleaning up much of their product, and libel suits and post-office bans did much to chasten or subdue the offensive "polecats." In sum, it can be said that the magazine industry showed many more signs of health, vigor, and imagination than the newspaper industry during the postwar era.

213. *Crises in American Education, 1940–1960*

A few generalizations illustrate the main trends in American public education. From 1940 to 1960 the number of pupils enrolled in public elementary and secondary schools increased from 25,434,000 to 36,305,000, in private schools, from 2,611,000 to 6,100,000. Total expenditures for public education expanded during the same two decades from $2,344,000,000 to $14,234,000,000, expenditure per student, from $88.09 in 1940 to $341.14 in 1958. Finally, there were encouraging increases in the length of school term, average daily attendance, and in teachers' salaries.

These general statistics, however, obscure the severe problems and challenges that confronted American schools during the two decades following the attack on Pearl Harbor. Never before, it seemed, had American public education been beset by so many dangers. The war brought a series of crises to the public schools. Crowding in defense areas caused incredible strains, and authorities in many areas used abandoned buildings and put schools on double shift. School buildings fell into disrepair as it became impossible to find building materials and other equipment. But the worst problem of all was the exodus of men and women from the teaching profession. By 1945 some 350,000 teachers, or more than one third the number employed in 1941, had left for higher paying jobs in business, industry, and government. In many instances school administrators hired whoever they could find, and 109,000 teachers were employed by 1945 on emergency certificates. But it was not enough: "Schools were closed or were conducted for short terms; many subjects included in the high school curriculum had to be abandoned for lack of adequately prepared teachers." [13]

The situation got considerably worse in the postwar era before the tide began to turn. Surveying the national education scene in late 1946 and early 1947, the educational reporter for the *New York Times* revealed the dimensions of the crisis. The result of these and other disclosures was to generate such a crusade for education as the country had not witnessed since the 1920's. Groups like the NAM, Chamber of Commerce, AF of L, and CIO joined powerful teachers' lobbies and citizens' committees in nearly every community to demand increased school appropriations and new buildings. The results were encouraging but far from adequate to meet the crisis. Nearly 100,000 of the nation's 1,367,000 public school teachers had substandard credentials by 1959, and despite intensive construction during the fifties there remained an estimated shortage of 132,000 classrooms. On the other hand, the lot of the teacher had improved markedly since

[13] I. L. Kandel, *The Impact of the War Upon American Education* (Chapel Hill, N.C., 1948), p. 7.

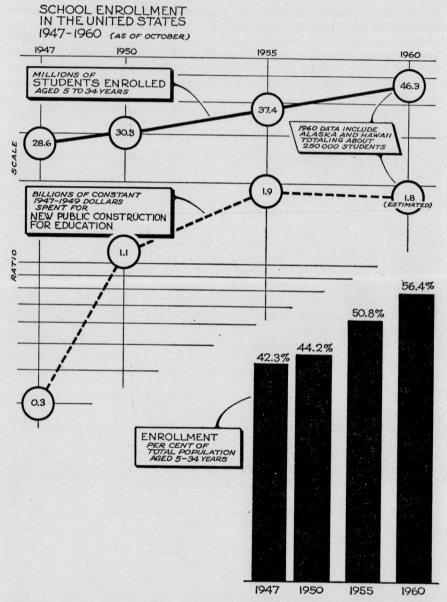

SCHOOL ENROLLMENT
IN THE UNITED STATES
1947–1960 *(AS OF OCTOBER)*

1940: average annual salaries for public school teachers increased faster than the cost of living, from $1,441 in 1940 to $4,940 in 1959.[14]

---

[14] Most critics agreed, however, that further improvement in teachers' salaries was needed if talented individuals were to be attracted to the teaching profession in sufficient numbers to cope with the swelling educational demands of the immediate future. Average family personal income in the United States was $6,520 in 1959—considerably higher than that for school teachers.

Emerging hand in hand with the postwar crusade for an expanded and modernized educational plant was a fundamental re-examination of current educational philosophy and practice. Both real and alleged deficiencies in the nation's school system were subjected to angry scrutiny as criticism mounted. The major focus of this critical onslaught was that unsystematized and poorly understood body of principles known as progressive education.

The progressive impulse in education, a product of the reform movements of the early twentieth century, had had a profound if uneven influence upon American schools in the generation between the two world wars. In a zealous attempt to apply the ideas of John Dewey and other pioneer reformers to the nation's classrooms, progressive-minded educators had wrought a host of changes, including many distinct improvements. There had been, for example, a revamped and expanded curriculum, with increased attention to vocational, cultural, and extracurricular activities; greater variation and flexibility in the grouping of students, based on intelligence and achievement tests; a new mobility and informality in the classroom, as "projects" competed with the rigidities of recitation and rote learning; fresher and more attractive textbooks and other educational materials; and improved facilities such as assembly rooms, gymnasiums, laboratories, shops, movable furniture and partitions, better lighting, and so on.

Despite these substantial accomplishments, progressive education came under heavy fire in the postwar era. The collapse of the movement, in view of the considerable prestige it had acquired since 1917, was dramatically swift. The end of its tenure as the reigning philosophy in American education was symbolized by the dissolution of the once powerful and influential Progressive Education Association in 1955. In the words of one authority, "a movement that had for half a century enlisted the enthusiasm, the loyalty, the imagination, and the energy of large segments of the American public and the teaching profession became, in the decade following World War II, anathema." [15]

The reason lay not so much in the strength of the assault as in the vulnerability of the target. It became increasingly clear in the postwar years that the progressive education movement had reached, at least temporarily, a dead end. Its weaknesses were many. Its intellectual vitality was largely gone. It lacked a clear and consistent program or philosophical base. It was torn by internal schisms and arid factional disputes, badly overprofessionalized, and inbred. Finally, it was too much addicted to jargon and slogans as a substitute for constructive thought and increasingly out of touch with the changes that had transformed American society since 1929.

The unprecedented strength of the postwar attack on progressive education derived from sources that had little connection with such chronic foes as traditionalists, superpatriots, witch-hunters, and reactionaries. These elements, to be sure, were in full voice in the postwar era. But the growing chorus of criticism after 1945 was led by intellectuals, academicians, and informed segments of the lay public—groups that were, by and

wwwwwwwwwwwwww

[15] Lawrence A. Cremin, *The Transformation of the School: Progressivism in American Education, 1876–1957* (New York, 1961), p. vii.

large, in sympathy with much that progressivism had sought to do in the field of education. These groups now felt that something had gone drastically wrong. The major theme in the indictment was sounded by Walter Lippmann as early as 1940. In the modern school, Lippmann noted angrily, "there is no common faith, no common body of principle, no common body of knowledge, no common moral and intellectual discipline."

This theme, with variations and refinements, was embellished by a vigorous group of writers in the postwar era. The most significant and penetrating attacks appeared in 1953—Albert Lynd's *Quackery in the Public Schools*, Robert M. Hutchins's *The Conflict in Education*, and especially Arthur Bestor's *Educational Wastelands*, revised two years later under the title *The Restoration of Learning*. The attack continued throughout the 1950's, reaching even greater intensity in the shock that followed the launching of Russia's Sputnik satellite in 1957.

In brief, the substance of the criticism was that modern progressivism, by emasculating scholarship and subject matter in the interests of pedagogic techniques and "life adjustment," had sapped much intellectual vitality, rigor, focus, and discipline from the school system—and hence from many young American minds. What was needed, the critics felt, was a fundamental shift in emphasis that would concentrate upon more rigorous intellectual training in the basic academic disciplines—English, history, mathematics, science, languages—and a clearer definition of the school's primary responsibilities, which involved, at bottom, teaching pupils how to think.

Progressive education utterly failed to produce a constructive response. It would be wrong, however, to assume that it had suffered either a total or a permanent defeat. The progressive influence upon American education had been, in many ways, profound, beneficial, and ineradicable. Moreover, American schools as a whole were probably less shot through with weakness than some of the critics claimed, and the real faults that did exist were not in every instance attributable solely or even primarily to the progressives. More important, beneath the movement's undoubted distortions, excesses, and contradictions lay a faith in human potential and a desire to train and develop human capacity to its utmost, to the lasting benefit of the individual and society alike. If, as many observers felt, a program of constructive reform was about to emerge from the welter of postwar criticism, such a program could hardly avoid basing itself in part, at least, upon certain essential features of the progressive educational philosophy.

For colleges and universities the two decades from 1940 to 1960 were a time of phenomenal growth and development. For example, enrollment increased from 1,500,000 to 3,402,000, expenditures from $605,755,000 to $3,447,000,000 between 1940 and 1956. But one crisis after another confronted higher education during these years. No sooner had colleges and universities recovered ground lost during the depression than they faced an even worse crisis when enrollments plummeted during the war. Then came the shock of a sudden increase in the number of students after the Japanese surrender, as veterans enjoying liberal public support returned to college or entered for the first time. As enrollments shot up from 1,155,272 in 1944 to 2,659,021 in 1950, the strain on housing, classroom, and library facilities became well-nigh unbearable.

The gravest danger to American higher education in the postwar era came not from overcrowding and deterioration of standards, but from the consequences of popular alarm regarding alleged Communists among the ranks of college and university teachers. Actually, there was little controversy over the question of whether Communists should be allowed to teach, either in the public schools or state colleges and universities. The Association of American Universities, National Education Association, and American Federation of Teachers had all taken firm stands by the end of 1953 against employment of Communist teachers. The grave danger to academic freedom, in higher education as well as among the public schools, stemmed rather from powerful campaigns in many states and cities aimed at driving nonconformist and progressive teachers from the classroom by identifying dissent and progressivism with Communism.

Exposure of a far-flung Communist espionage network in the United States in 1948–9 led many states and cities to impose test oaths on teachers and establish committees to examine textbooks for subversive materials. The University of Oklahoma virtually excluded any but native-born citizens from its staff; Kansas, Massachusetts, and Pennsylvania authorized schools to dismiss teachers for disloyalty; and Maryland, New York, and New Jersey forbade teachers to join certain proscribed organizations. However well-intentioned these efforts were, their chief effect was not to expose the infinitesimally small number of Communists in the classrooms but to impeach the integrity of the overwhelming majority of teachers and to cast a pall of fear over the schools. As conformity and blind acceptance of the *status quo* became synonymous in many minds with "Americanism," fear of being called a Communist drove thousands of teachers either into silence or to extremes of orthodoxy.[16]

Although crises kept intruding during the war and postwar years, the period was a time of continuing thoughtful inquiry into the philosophy, methods, and goals of higher education that culminated in a sweeping victory for the proponents of an integrated curriculum designed to afford a general education for American undergraduates. Leadership in the revolt against the intellectual chaos of the free elective system came in the thirties from Robert M. Hutchins, president of the University of Chicago. The revolt

wwwwwwwwwwwwww

[16] The dangers inherent in reckless assaults upon academic freedom and in the imposition of indiscriminate test oaths were illustrated by a tragic controversy that nearly wrecked the University of California and rocked academic circles in the United States from 1949 to 1952. In order to protect the university from attacks by certain demagogues in the legislature, the president and regents imposed a loyalty oath of their own on March 25, 1949. Forty-nine professors, among them the most distinguished scholars and teachers in the university, were discharged when they refused to sign the oath on the ground that it impeached their loyalty and integrity and affronted their dignity. In the battle that ensued the University of California suffered not only the loss of other professors who resigned in protest or refused to accept appointment but the respect of the entire academic world as well. Eventually, in 1951 and 1952, the regents rescinded the oath and reinstated the discharged professors who had not gone elsewhere.

came to a head with the publication of the Harvard committee's *General Education in a Free Society* in 1945. A milestone in the development of educational philosophy in the United States, the Harvard report was an eloquent plea for greater emphasis upon general education that would acquaint students with the whole of human experience rather than with isolated fragments. Harvard, Yale, and Princeton led the way in curriculum changes, and dozens of other institutions followed suit.

This searching self-examination of American higher education provoked changes in numerous other ways. There was, for example, widespread recognition of the importance of Judaism and Christianity in the development of western civilization, and this in turn gave rise to the establishment of religion departments in numerous institutions that had once gladly abandoned the study of religion. When a *New York Times* survey in 1943 revealed that most college students were appallingly ignorant of their country's history, several states required students in state-supported colleges and universities to take courses in American history. Recognition of America's new international responsibilities after 1941 stimulated a flowering of international studies, especially of institutes to promote study about Russia, the Far East, and the Middle East.

Looking back over the development of higher education in the United States since 1900, Americans might feel inclined to boast. Within sixty years they had freed themselves from cultural dependence upon Europe and built a system of higher education on the whole unexcelled anywhere else in the world. But the most significant fact was that the expansion of higher educational opportunities had gone hand in hand with steady improvement in standards. The American people were nearer than ever to the great goal of universal higher education for all men and women who could meet the standards imposed.

And yet, paradoxically, American education in the postwar era faced a challenge of such awesome proportions as to dwarf the progress of the past sixty years. Never in their history could the American people less afford to rest on their laurels. The social, technological, and scientific revolutions of the modern age were making unprecedented demands upon the nation's educational system. The challenges of the cold war and world Communism, of underdeveloped areas and a world population explosion, international trade and economic growth, the farm problem and the urban problem and the race problem, automation and the uses of atomic energy, presented a baffling kaleidoscope of change and ferment that could not be met or even endured without a steady increase in the size and quality of the educational plant. In the years ahead there would be a staggering need for individuals with the advanced professional skills that only higher education could provide.

214. *The Return to Religion*

Religious bodies grew remarkably in membership and material resources during the war and postwar years. Church membership in the United States from 1940 to 1958 increased from 64,502,000, or 49 per cent of the total population, to 109,558,000, or 63 per cent. But the general statistics obscure the important trends in growth. The onset of war and return of full prosperity abruptly reversed the downward plunge in church membership and influence in 1940–1; and the return to religion constituted one of the most significant social and intellectual movements in the United States during the following two decades.

Nearly all of the various religious bodies recorded substantial gains. Though Orthodox Judaism suffered a slight decline in membership, it became suffused with new vigor after 1945; and Conservative Judaism expanded its membership from 75,000 to 200,000 families, Reform Judaism from 50,000 to 255,000 families, between 1937 and 1956. All Protestant denominations grew faster than the general population; but the significant growth occurred among the bodies that made an aggressive appeal to the lower middle and lower classes. The Baptists, particularly the southern wing, made the most striking gains, increasing in numbers from 8,262,287 in 1936 to 23,525,000 in 1957. Moreover, the various bodies on the social frontier of Protestantism—the Church of the Nazarene, the several Churches of God, the Pentecostal Assemblies, and the Foursquare Gospel Movement—also grew rapidly and gave evidences of changing from fringe sects into established denominations.

Although the United States remained a predominantly Protestant country, a striking feature of the 1950's was the enormous gain in membership recorded by the Roman Catholic Church. Total Protestant membership increased by nearly 66 per cent between 1926 and 1950, from 31,512,000 to 51,080,000, as compared with a Catholic increase of 55 per cent, from 18,-605,000 to 28,635,000. But the Roman Church far outstripped Protestant denominations in rate of growth during the next decade. Protestant membership expanded from 51,080,000 to 61,505,000, or 20 per cent, from 1950 to 1958, Catholic membership from 28,635,000 to 39,510,000, or nearly 40 per cent. As a result of these recent gains, the proportion of Catholics in the total church population increased from 33 per cent in 1940 to almost 36 per cent in 1958.

Expanding church membership was only one evidence of the new interest in religion. The nation seemed to be undergoing a veritable "surge of piety," including much that was genuine, much that was superficial, and not a little that bordered on blasphemy.[17] A widespread yearning for relief from anxiety and insecurity produced a spate of sermons and religious books offering complete inner tranquillity, new self-confidence, heightened powers, and an end to worry through prayer and "positive thinking." Among the leading figures in this "cult of reassurance" were Rabbi Joshua Liebman, author of *Peace of Mind*, 1946; Monsignor Fulton J. Sheen, author of *Peace of Soul*, 1949; and above all the Reverend Norman Vincent Peale, whose parade of best-selling titles indicated the emphasis of the movement: *The Art of Living, A Guide to Confident Living, The Power of Positive Thinking, Stay Alive All Your Life*. The most spectacular manifestation of the postwar religious hunger was a new wave of revivalism, unprecedented

[17] As examples of the latter tendency, one might mention the prominent (and sincerely religious) Hollywood star who referred chummily to God as a "livin' doll," or the lush advertisements for the movie "A Man Called Peter," based on the life of the late Presbyterian minister Peter Marshall.

since Billy Sunday's triumphs in the early years of the century. The un-questioned champion of the modern revivalists was the Reverend Billy Graham, who swayed huge crowds in all parts of the world with his earnest, impassioned oratory, including 60,000 people in New York's Yankee Stadium in 1957, and persuaded thousands to come forward and declare for Christ. Elsewhere, dedicated laymen formed associations which enlisted the services of God and Christianity in behalf of freedom's crusade against Communism, or, in some instances, more specifically in behalf of limited government and a free enterprise economy.

It was difficult to escape reminders of the new religious impulse. Another layman's committee directed the "Religion in American Life" campaign, pursuing their objective with the help of millions of dollars' worth of free advertising in a variety of media. As a result, billboards and spot television and radio announcements repeatedly exhorted Americans to "attend and support the church or synagogue of their individual choice." The phrase "under God" was added to the pledge of allegiance that millions of American school children gave daily. A flood of religious and inspirational books enjoyed spectacular sales, and film extravaganzas like "The Ten Commandments" broke box-office records. Politicians seldom failed to pay tribute to church and religion in their campaign speeches. And the unremitting blare of the nation's juke boxes attested to the huge if ephemeral popularity of "hit" religious tunes like "The Man Upstairs" and "I Believe." Religion, as one authority wryly put it, had "come into vogue."

The causes for the return to religion were complex and often obscure. Prosperity after 1939 was in part responsible, but prosperity alone does not explain the phenomenon. The Second World War drew millions of American families to church or synagogue to pray for the safe return of sons, husbands, fathers, and brothers. Another important factor was the change in popular attitudes toward man, society, and God that took place during the late thirties and afterward. In brief, there occurred a metamorphosis from a prevailing optimism and humanism to a profound despair of man and his works, as the mass destruction of the Second World War, revelations of Nazi and Soviet inhumanity, and fear of future annihilation weakened public faith in automatic human progress and caused millions of Americans to seek understanding and hope in religion.

There were other factors, including a few whose connection with meaningful religion was tenuous, at best. The pressures of conformity and status undoubtedly played a role, although such drives are never easily separable from more genuine religious impulses. In any event, the social advantages of "belonging," and even the urge to advertise or confirm one's rising economic and social status by associating with a "respectable" denomination, were among the pressures operating in the new suburban communities that blossomed in the postwar era.

A somewhat deeper hypothesis was advanced by Will Herberg, a professor at Drew Theological Seminary, in *Protestant-Catholic-Jew*, 1955. He suggested that the great increase in church membership since 1940 was partly explainable in terms of a search for identity on the part of millions of Americans—particularly third-generation immigrants. The sons and daughters of the original immigrants, growing up in the new country and usually far more eager than their parents to be assimilated and "Americanized," had often abandoned the traditional family religion. But a third generation had come of age by the Second World War, and the pendulum swung back. This new generation lived in a highly mobile society that had effectively blurred ethnic, regional, and class differences. The religion of one's ancestors, whether Protestant, Catholic, or Jewish, offered the most convenient and satisfying path to social identity within the broader American framework.

Whether his thesis was basic or merely incidental in explaining the postwar religious phenomenon, Herberg observed one fact that was genuinely disquieting to orthodox believers from all three faiths. "By and large," he wrote, "the religion which actually prevails among Americans today has lost much of its authentic Christian (or Jewish) content. Even when they are thinking, feeling, or acting religiously, their thinking, feeling, and acting do not bear an unequivocal relation to the faiths they profess."[18] Other analysts of the current religious scene made similar observations: modern religion was strongly secular; doctrinal differences, especially among Protestants, were blurring or at least softening; and what one authority defined as "religion-in-general," a vague "national religion," was fast outstripping and eroding the three traditional faiths in competing for the loyalty of American believers.

The prevailing emphasis in much of the new religion, especially among Protestants, was not only secular but humanistic—so much so, as informed Protestant scholars and ministers were quick to point out, that the essence of the Christian doctrine was in danger of being lost. Too many of the popular religious themes were standing biblical truth on its head by putting God to work in the service of man. For such, in effect, was the message of the "positive thinking" advocates, who made religious experience something of an automatic bargain-counter operation in which God, in exchange for prayer, doled out peace of mind, worldly happiness, and worldly success. On a larger and more blatant scale, such also was the message of those ardent persons who identified God's will with the cause of democracy or free enterprise, in contravention of the scriptural reminders that the Almighty had purposes of His own, which men could at best know only in part. Even the revivalists, for all their emphasis upon salvation by conversion, implied that the vital act of conversion was the work of man rather than the unmerited gracious act of the Holy Spirit.

These theological critics neither denied nor belittled the positive elements in the return to religion, nor the obvious sincerity and good intent of most of its spokesmen and their followers. Clearly, untold millions of Americans had found greater peace, confidence, and strength from the preacher or church "of their individual choice," and the messages of God's love and understanding were infinitely preferable to much that was current in the postwar world. What worried the critics was the underlying trend of the new religion. True Christianity was giving way to a shallow, fuzzy, neatly packaged, humanistic faith that dangerously oversimplified when it did not distort. The God of Abraham and of Jacob had become The Man Upstairs-- friendly, manageable, at man's disposal, eager to serve.

᭐᭐᭐᭐᭐᭐᭐᭐᭐᭐᭐᭐᭐᭐᭐

[18] Will Herberg, *Protestant-Catholic-Jew* (revised edition, Garden City, New York, 1960), p. 3.

This was a harsh indictment of postwar religion, but the critics saw some grounds for hope. There were signs as the 1950's ended that the surge of ignorant piety had lost its fervor. By no means all of the churches had surrendered to a watered-down religion-in-general; responsible elements in Judaism, Catholicism, and Protestantism steadfastly refused to conform. There was hope, too, in the nation's seminaries, most of which had turned from the liberal, humanistic doctrines of the 1920's and 1930's toward Biblical theology and epistemology, building upon the neo-orthodox foundations laid by such outstanding Protestant theologians as Karl Barth, Paul Tillich, and Reinhold Niebuhr before the Second World War. (For details, see above, pp. 293–294.) Catholicism was similarly invigorated by the uncompromising theology of the French scholar Jacques Maritain, and Judaism found the basis for a sharper faith in the incisive theology of Martin Buber. The ecumenical movement, which brought American churchmen into prolonged intellectual contact with the ablest Christian theologians from other parts of the world, also promised to have a beneficial effect.

And finally, in the opinion of one authority, the people themselves were a great source of hope—"the people whom one meets in the more prosaic and more enduring life of the Church in local congregations everywhere. This 'hidden Church,' a little flock which no doubt numbers many millions, has profited from the revival and will certainly outlive it. Nowhere else is the Christian witness more sorely tempted; nowhere else is it more likely to survive." [19]

As significant as the sheer facts of growth in church membership and religious interest was the way in which the social character of the churches apparently changed. If we accept the assumption that Protestantism was the religion of the middle and upper classes before 1940 and that Catholicism was the religion of the city masses, then the realignment that took place in the forties was nothing less than revolutionary. A survey made in 1945–6 revealed that the "lower classes" constituted 56 per cent of the membership in all major bodies—66 per cent among the Catholics, 68 per cent among the Baptists, 53 per cent among the Lutherans, and 52 per cent among the Methodists. Even among the so-called upper-class denominations —Episcopalians, Presbyterians, and Congregationalists—the lower-class members were a large minority. A second survey revealed that 44 per cent of all American church members were urban manual workers, 17 per cent were farmers, 20 per cent were white-collar workers, and 19 per cent were from the business and professional classes. By mid-century, therefore, the American churches had ceased to be strongholds of social snobbery and middle-class conservatism and had become in large measure the spiritual homes of all people.

Of untold importance to the future of organized Christianity in the United States was the ecumenical movement. It had gathered headway in the 1920's and 1930's and moved by leaps and bounds after 1940. The number of intradenominational mergers proceeded apace. Two large Presbyterian bodies merged in 1958, and two branches of the Society of Friends came together in 1955. The Evangelical and Reformed Church merged with

[19] Martin E. Marty, *The New Shape of American Religion* (New York, 1958), p. 30.

the Congregational Christian Churches in 1957 to form the United Church of Christ. An important union among various Lutheran bodies was achieved in 1960, with a broader combination in store for the early sixties.

Meanwhile, the Federal Council of Churches of Christ in America continued to speak for a growing majority of American Protestant churches. The Federal Council combined with eight important interdenominational agencies in 1941; and the entire structure was reorganized in 1950 and reintegrated into the National Council of the Churches of Christ, which included every important Protestant denomination except the southern Baptists and the Missouri Synod Lutherans.

The final and most heartening outgrowth of the ecumenical spirit was the World Council of Churches, organized in Amsterdam in 1948 after years of preparation. It combined practically all the non-Roman Catholic churches of the world, including the Russian Orthodox Church by 1961, into a working fellowship. The Second Assembly of the World Council met in Evanston, Illinois, in 1954, the Third Assembly in New Delhi in 1961. The display of Christian unity and the earnest attempts to formulate a basic, all-embracing Christian creed were impressive; and continuing association among churchmen of varying beliefs and traditions held great promise for the future. Looking hopefully ahead to a time when the ecumenical spirit could win support of individual parish churches throughout the world, one authority predicted that the movement "might become one of the most important Christian developments since Pentecost." [20]

Despite an abundance of religious progress in other areas, many thoughtful Americans were dismayed by an unhappy development—the strong revival of old Protestant-Catholic antagonisms. There was a long background of mutual misunderstanding, but the most disturbing issues in the postwar era were federal aid to education and public support for parochial schools.

Public authorities in many northern and midwestern states furnished bus transportation, textbooks, and lunches to children attending parochial schools. As a consequence, Protestants charged that Catholics were working slowly toward full public support of parochial schools. During debates over federal aid to education in the postwar era, Catholics opposed any federal assistance unless aid to children attending parochial schools was also included. Protestants replied that Catholics were in principle opposed to public schools and had joined with reactionary groups to destroy the entire system of public education.

Protestant alarm at alleged Catholic aggressions took shape in the formation in 1948 of Protestants and Other Americans United for Separation of Church and State. The distinguished leaders who formed this group were not themselves religious bigots. But their propaganda was inevitably anti-Catholic, and it was a powerful factor in encouraging anti-Catholic antagonisms. The most vocal spokesman in the postwar Protestant crusade was Paul Blanshard, whose *American Freedom and Catholic Power,* 1949, and *Communism, Democracy, and Catholic Power,* 1952, stirred one of the live-

[20] Clifton E. Olmstead, *History of Religion in the United States* (Englewood Cliffs, N.J., 1960), p. 540.

liest controversies of the decade, especially after school boards in Newark and New York City banned *The Nation* from the public schools because it printed Blanshard's articles.

Several Catholic spokesmen answered Blanshard and other Protestant critics moderately. However, many distinguished Catholic leaders, including Francis Cardinal Spellman of New York, poured oil on the flames by charging that Protestant critics and opponents of public aid to parochial schools were Ku Kluxers, bigots, or subversives. Although the controversy grew less virulent in the middle and later 1950's, the tension and bitterness remained to disturb the American social scene.

It was hard to predict the course of this historic religious antagonism in the 1960's. On the one hand, Americans were encouraged by the comparative restraint and moderation with which most politicians and churchmen handled the religious issue in the election of 1960, when John F. Kennedy, the Democratic standard-bearer, became the first Roman Catholic presidential nominee since Al Smith in 1928. The conduct of this campaign contrasted favorably with that of 1928, and many saw in the election of America's first Catholic President a signal victory for religious tolerance and hope for an eventual end of the dispute. On the other hand, the firm intransigence of many Catholics and Protestants in the battle over President Kennedy's bill for federal aid to public schools in 1961 gave new cause for worry. (For details, see below, p. 869.) The vitally important school issue found the two faiths as bitterly opposed as ever before. Moderation and common sense, even when enforced by the prestige of a Catholic President who favored aid to public but not parochial schools and enjoyed widespread popularity in the nation at large, seemed powerless to find a way out of the deadlock. The school aid controversy promised to keep religious antagonism between Protestant and Catholic alive for many years to come.

CHANGE

27

Politics and Problems
of the Truman Era

NOT IN MANY YEARS had the American political scene seemed so confused as during the period between the end of the Second World War and the election of 1952. The Democratic party was torn by struggles over civil rights, labor policy, and measures to combat inflation. It was further weakened by a growing popular conviction that the Truman administration was riddled with corruption and tainted with Communism. The Republicans, although out of power in Washington except for a brief period during 1947 and 1948 when they controlled Congress, were beset by difficulties as perplexing if not as apparent as those that plagued their opponents. Republicans were torn by divisions between internationalists and neo-isolationists and between progressives and reactionaries, weakened by a long absence from power, and plagued by reckless irresponsibility. They gave no brighter promise of uniting the country and providing constructive leadership than did the Democrats.

Yet never before had the problems confronting the American people been so great. What shall we say of the achievements of the postwar period? The following chapter will attempt to answer that question. It must suffice to say here that, in spite of seeming chaos and undoubted intense partisanship, the American people and their leaders met the challenges of their time more courageously and with greater wisdom than their grandfathers had done during Reconstruction or their fathers during the decade following the Armistice of 1918.

215. *Harry S. Truman and the Progressive Movement*

A distraught man stood in the White House at 7:09 p.m. on April 12, 1945, and took the oath as President of the United States. Franklin D. Roosevelt had died a few hours before, and leadership was now entrusted to his Vice President, Harry S. Truman. For Roosevelt, as for Lincoln, death was a merciful deliverer, sparing him a host of troubles at the moment of his greatest triumph. For Truman, Roosevelt's passing meant a new life of trial and yet such opportunity as rarely comes to any man. "Who the hell is Harry Truman?" Admiral William D. Leahy had asked when Roosevelt told him of the vice-presidential nominee in the summer of 1944. That same question was repeated often if less profanely during the days of mourning that followed the war President's death. Harry S. Truman was born at Lamar, Missouri, on May 8, 1884, the grandson of pioneers from Kentucky, and grew up a son of the Middle Border in Grandview, Independence, and Kansas City. He worked as a bank clerk and farmer after being graduated from high school in 1901. He went to France with his National Guard field artillery regiment and rose to the rank of major by hard work and courageous service on the western front. He married his childhood sweetheart and entered the clothing business in Kansas City in 1919. Ruined by the postwar recession in 1922, Truman accepted nomination as county judge, or county commissioner, of eastern Jackson County from the Democratic machine of Kansas City. He was defeated for re-election in 1924, in part because of his opposition to the Ku Klux Klan, but he returned to the courthouse in Independence as presiding judge in 1927. During the next seven years he rebuilt the county's roads and courthouse, helped to plan a system of parkways for Kansas City, and earned a reputation as an able and incorruptible administrator.

Truman was nominated for the United States Senate in 1934 with the help of the Pendergast machine and won easily in the Democratic landslide in the autumn elections. In Washington, however, he was known as the "Gentleman from Pendergast"; and his political career seemed at an end when his patron, Tom Pendergast, was sentenced to federal prison in 1939 for income tax evasion. He surprised friends as well as enemies when he won re-election to the Senate on his own in 1940—by attracting the votes of workers, farmers, and Negroes in a campaign prophetic of his more famous battle eight years later.

Truman returned to Washington in December 1940 with increased political stature. It seemed that he was destined, not for greatness, but for a long and honorable career in the upper house. Then came the defense crisis and his first opportunity to render national service. Appalled by the waste in defense spending and the neglect of small business by the army in the awarding of contracts, he obtained appointment in 1941 as chairman of a special Senate committee to investigate the defense effort. The Truman Committee worked assiduously from 1941 to 1944 to prevent waste and favoritism. Truman's fairness and insistence upon constructive criticism won him the admiration of President Roosevelt and the vice-presidential nomination in 1944.

Even so, the country knew little of the character of Harry S. Truman when he entered the White House. Because he was uncommonly modest in demeanor, unpretentious in physical appearance, and obviously lacking in Roosevelt's histrionic abilities and patrician touch, many Americans assumed that Truman was the epitome of the average man. Never had the popular judgment been more mistaken, for in most aspects the new President was extraordinary indeed.

He was extraordinary in his personal warmth and charm, breadth of learning that often astonished scholars, and ability to understand difficult situations. He was extraordinary in his personal honesty and integrity. When he failed in business, for example, he refused to go into bankruptcy and paid his debts even though the effort was a long one. Although he had the support of a corrupt political organization, he never allowed the machine to use him, or misappropriated a single dollar of county funds. He was extraordinary in his devotion to duty and the general interest, and in his capacity for hard work. He was extraordinary in his hatred of pretense, feeling for the underdog, and broad sympathy that tolerated no racial or religious distinctions. But above all he was extraordinary in his courage— whether in defying the Ku Klux Klan in his home county, fighting a seemingly lost battle on the hustings, dismissing a renowned general, or leading his country in bold pursuit of peace and security.

There were, however, other traits that weakened Truman's force as a personal leader. He was President during a period of intense partisanship, and his own campaign oratory did little to elevate the tone of public discourse. He was usually cautious in matters of state, but he was often rash and impulsive in personal controversy and given to name-calling in public. Absolutely honest himself, he was so much a professional politician, who accepted the game as he found it, that he appeared unable to see dishonesty in others. This weakness came out especially in his loyalty to the Pendergast machine and in his refusal to reappoint the federal district attorney who had helped to uncover corruption in Kansas City.

Many of Truman's weaknesses stemmed in the beginning from his undue modesty and feeling of inadequacy for the great tasks ahead. "I don't know whether you fellows ever had a load of hay or a bull fall on you," he told reporters on April 13, 1945. "But last night the moon, the stars and all the planets fell on me." He had inherited a Cabinet and administration of strangers; and in his loneliness he turned at first to friends in the Senate and gathered around him a group of intimates known as the Missouri Gang. Some lowering of the tone of the public service following the war was inevitable, for corruption permeated city, state, and federal politics and administration. And yet Truman in some measure contributed to the deterioration of public morality. He trusted too much and refused to move hard and fast against corruption in high places. This was not without its political consequences, as we shall see.

Even so, historians have been kinder to Truman than were many Americans in his own day. They have forgiven him his personal excesses, just as they earlier forgave Lincoln his, and they have remembered his strength and courage and how in large matters he put the national interest above personal and party advantage. They have remembered his contributions, the most important of which was a farsighted foreign policy in Europe; the difficulties of his tasks; and his great growth in leadership.

In spite of early indecision, Truman became not only leader of his party but also the true heir of Bryan, Wilson, and the two Roosevelts in perpetuating and developing the progressive tradition in the United States. In the conviction that the President must be the one national spokesman and defender of the general interest, he preserved the executive branch against congressional assaults and even strengthened the office of President. He fought hard and for the most part successfully to prevent a normal postwar reaction from developing into a general repudiation of progressive ideals and practices. Indeed, he actually succeeded in extending the horizons of the American progressive movement. This was a task of considerable difficulty, for progressives were divided, confused, and uncertain at the end of the war. Some, like the spokesmen of the CIO and the non-Communist followers of Henry A. Wallace, wanted in varying degree a full-fledged collectivistic state, with widespread nationalization and comprehensive planning and economic controls. Others, especially many Southerners, demanded an end to further reform. Allying himself with neither extreme, Truman not only consolidated and enlarged the New Deal structure but also extended the frontiers of progressivism in the direction of civil rights, public health, and public power. As we shall see, his Fair Deal opened new vistas for progressives and provided a program for the future.

216. *Demobilization, Reconversion, and a New Federal Structure*

As we have seen in an earlier chapter, the immediate postwar years were characterized by inflation and widespread labor unrest, but withal by tremendous economic expansion and prosperity. (See above, pp. 586–630.) They were characterized also by growing international tension, which caused the problems of foreign policy to intrude into all the calculations of executive and legislative leaders. The historian looking back over the tumult of the years 1945–7 is astonished by the constructive things that were done in spite of the apparent chaos in Washington.

The first order of national business in 1945–6 was demobilization of the armed forces and conversion of the economy from a war to a peace footing. It was apparent to the new President and his military advisers even before the Japanese surrendered that the world was entering an uncertain period of potential conflict and realignment of power, and that national security demanded the retention of large armed forces. But the dimensions of the Soviet threat to peace were not clear in the autumn of 1945, while the popular and congressional demand for speedy and drastic demobilization was so overwhelming that probably no administration could have resisted it. As one writer has observed, "That rush to disarm in late 1945 was surely one of the most expensive economies—in terms of life and effort as well as of money—in which the United States ever indulged." [1] But it was inevitable.

The army began a limited demobilization in May 1945, and both armed services began discharging men as rapidly as possible once Japan had surrendered. The army slowed demobilization in January 1946, and there were riots among enlisted men abroad and frenzied protests at home. The Presi-

---

[1] Walter Millis (ed.), *The Forrestal Diaries* (New York, 1951), p. 110.

dent and the Army Chief of Staff, General Eisenhower, quieted the storm by appealing for patience and public support. Nonetheless, demobilization had to proceed inexorably in response to public and congressional demand. "The program we were following," Truman later wrote, "was no longer demobilization—it was disintegration of our armed forces." [2] By its completion in midsummer of 1946 the great wartime army and navy had been reduced to 1,500,000 and 700,000 men, respectively.

For the next four years the President and his military advisers pointed out time and again that American armed strength was barely sufficient to meet the country's minimum international responsibilities, much less provide for security in the event of new aggressions. Congress grudgingly extended a weak Selective Service from July 1, 1946, to May 31, 1947, and reinstituted the draft on a broader basis a year later. At the same time, the men on Capitol Hill refused to approve the administration's plan for universal military training and insisted upon even further reductions in armed strength from 1946 to 1948. There were momentary increases after the Communists seized power in Czechoslovakia and the Berlin blockade heightened Soviet-American tension in 1948. But the President and his new Secretary of Defense, Louis Johnson, joined the economy forces in Congress in 1949 to effect new reductions that brought American armed strength to a postwar low point. By the spring of 1950 they had imposed a $13,000,000,-000 ceiling on defense expenditures and reduced the army to 600,000 men and ten active divisions.

Meanwhile, the country had confronted the problems of reconversion. One major problem—assistance for veterans—was solved thoroughly and without a show of partisanship. All political leaders were determined that veterans should have generous help in finding jobs, adjusting to civilian life, and recovering lost educational opportunities. Congress in June 1944 had enacted the Servicemen's Readjustment Act, with good reason called the G.I. Bill of Rights,[3] and a grateful nation poured out its resources to help its former servicemen. Expenditures of the Veterans' Administration rose from $723,445,000 in 1944 to a peak of $9,278,000,000 in 1950. They then declined to about $6,000,000,000 in 1951 and 1952 and ran about $5,000,-000,000 annually through the balance of the decade. These later expenditures included outlays for veterans of the Korean War of 1950–3. The government during the peak period 1945–52 gave $13,548,765,000 for education and training alone, and nearly $4,000,000,000 for unemployment benefits and self-employment help. In addition, the Veterans' Administration guaranteed or insured nearly $16,500,000,000 in veterans' loans for homes, farms, and businesses and operated a chain of some 150 hospitals that served an average daily number of 108,038 patients in 1950.

Nor was there much partisan controversy over the desirability of tax reductions and assistance to industry in its conversion to civilian produc-

[2] H. S. Truman, *Memoirs by Harry S. Truman* (2 vols., New York, 1955), I, p. 509.

[3] It provided large sums for new veterans' hospitals and vocational rehabilitation for the wounded in body and spirit; guaranteed unemployment compensation of $20 weekly for a year to veterans who could not find work; provided substantial assistance to veterans in the purchase of homes, farms, and businesses; and offered free tuition, books, and subsistence to veterans for job training and four years of college or university education.

tion. For example, Congress responded to public pressure by reducing taxes nearly $6,000,000,000 in November 1945, while the administration disposed of most government-owned war plants in 1945–6. Together they represented a total investment of $15,000,000,000 and accounted for some 20 per cent of the nation's industrial capacity.

The overshadowing domestic fear in 1944–5 was dread of a catastrophic postwar depression that might end in national bankruptcy and world chaos. The government's success in marshaling industry and labor during the war stimulated bold ideas. The National Resources Planning Board led off in March 1943 with a massive report entitled *Security, Work, and Relief Policies*. Progressives like Henry A. Wallace and spokesmen of the C.I.O. followed, repudiating the assumption that the nation must inevitably career through alternating periods of "boom and bust." They proposed that the federal government assume responsibility for full employment through indirect stimulation of purchasing power and, if necessary, sufficient compensatory spending to prevent recession. The promise of "full employment" after the war became the major Democratic domestic pledge during the presidential campaign of 1944. It was reaffirmed by Truman on September 9, 1945, and set off the first full-fledged debate on postwar domestic policy.

The administration's plan was embodied in the Full Employment bill submitted by Senator James E. Murray, Democrat from Montana, soon afterward. It stipulated that the President and his staff should prepare an annual national production and employment budget—an estimate of the investment and production necessary to maintain full employment—and that a congressional joint committee on the national budget should assume responsibility for "federal investment and expenditure as will be sufficient to bring the aggregate volume . . . up to the level required to assure a full employment volume of production." To conservatives, the Murray bill meant nothing less than a permanent program of deficit spending through partisan agencies. They countered by proposing establishment of a nonpartisan National Economic Commission to advise the President and Congress on the state of the economy and measures necessary, as one conservative put it, "to foster private enterprise . . . and promote a high and stable level of employment."

Although conservatives and progressives disagreed on means, the significant aspect of the debate over the Murray bill was that both groups agreed in placing chief responsibility for economic stabilization upon the federal government. The outcome was the Employment Act of February 1946, a compromise that affirmed national responsibility for prosperity without prescribing an inflexible method to achieve it. It created, first, a three-man Council of Economic Advisers, presumably expert and nonpartisan, to study the economy for signs of weakness and advise the President and Congress on means of promoting national economic welfare, and, second, a congressional joint committee on the economic report to study and propose stabilization measures. It was, actually, a milestone in American progressivism. As the first chairman of the Council of Economic Advisers has said, it established machinery for "mobilizing all our organizational resources, public and private, within our system of free enterprise, for a sustained high level of national production and the correspondingly high level of national income." [4] Future experience would reveal that even "experts" on the Council could disagree, and that ultimate decisions had to be made by political agencies. Nonetheless, the Employment Act established machinery for the first time for systematic investigation and planning for national welfare.

Construction of a postwar policy for development of atomic energy was, as events turned out, considerably more urgent. Most Republicans and Democrats agreed that national security demanded retention of an absolute governmental monopoly on all aspects of research and production of fissionable materials, at least until effective international machinery had been established to prevent the manufacture of atomic bombs. On the issue of civilian or military control of the program, however, a heated controversy ensued when a special Senate committee set to work on an atomic energy bill in the autumn of 1945. The chairman, Senator Brien MacMahon of Connecticut, drafted a measure at Truman's urging establishing exclusive civilian control through an Atomic Energy Commission (AEC). It won the support of most progressives, scientists, and religious and educational leaders. On the other hand, Senator Arthur H. Vandenberg of Michigan suggested giving military and naval leaders a full voice, even a veto over civilian authorities, in determining atomic energy policies. He won the overwhelming support of the Senate committee.

The controversy came to a head in March and April 1946, after the committee adopted Vandenberg's amendment to the MacMahon bill providing for military participation. So violent was Truman's opposition and the public reaction that Vandenberg and his supporters agreed to a compromise amendment. It established a Military Liaison Committee to work with the AEC but placed exclusive control in civilian hands. Thus the Atomic Energy Act, approved by the President on August 1, 1946, preserved governmental monopoly on fissionable materials, vested complete control of research and production in the hands of a five-man AEC, and gave to the President alone the power to order the use of the atomic bomb in warfare. It also barred divulgence of information to foreign governments, even friendly ones, a provision that drew a sharp protest from the British.

One problem—unification of the armed services—was entirely nonpartisan but gave rise to one of the bitterest controversies of the postwar era. Almost everyone, including military and naval spokesmen, agreed that the Pearl Harbor disaster and wasteful interservice competition during the war had proved the need for common control and direction of the defense establishment. But violent disagreement arose on almost every practical suggestion for unification. The generals and the army's friends in Congress favored unification, but the admirals and the navy's champions feared that army domination of a unified defense structure would eliminate the Marine Corps and favor land-based air forces at the expense of sea power.

Partisans of the two services maneuvered and skirmished from the end of 1945 until the summer of 1947. The Secretary of the Navy, James V. Forrestal, although opposed to complete integration, supported greater unity than had hitherto existed and held rebellious admirals in check, while the President mediated skillfully. The result of the give and take was the Na-

ᴧᴧᴧᴧᴧᴧᴧᴧᴧᴧᴧᴧᴧᴧᴧᴧᴧᴧ

[4] Edwin G. Nourse, *The 1950's Come First* (New York, 1951), p. 8.

tional Security Act of July 26, 1947, which completely overhauled and strengthened the defense structure. It created a single Department and Secretary of Defense with Cabinet rank and supervision over Secretaries of the Army, Navy, and Air Force. It formalized the institution of the Joint Chiefs of Staff representing the three services, to prepare defense plans and consider matters of strategy. Finally, it created the Central Intelligence Agency to take supreme command of intelligence work and two additional agencies, the National Security Council and the National Security Resources Board, to advise the President and Congress on measures to promote national security.

ORGANIZATION FOR NATIONAL SECURITY
IN THE POSTWAR ERA

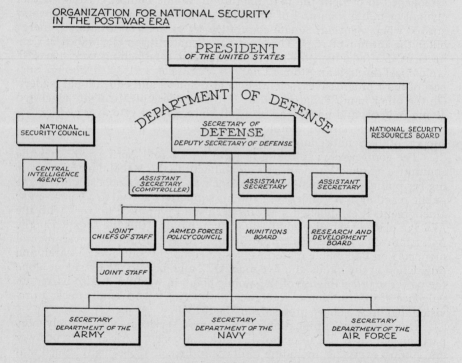

As Forrestal, the first Secretary of Defense, soon discovered, it was easier to erect the façade of a new defense structure than to compel genuine unification.[5] Even so, adoption of the National Security Act was one of the great accomplishments of the Truman era. If it had done nothing more than establish an independent Air Force and provide a framework for gradual unification, the measure would have justified all the great labor that went into its writing and adoption.

There was little partisan bickering and considerable agreement among all leaders on the need for a thorough overhaul of the federal administrative and legislative structures. They had grown wildly, often without plan or over-all purpose, during the New Deal and war periods. The most significant

ᵃᵃᵃᵃᵃᵃᵃᵃᵃᵃᵃᵃᵃᵃᵃᵃᵃᵃᵃ

[5] Forrestal, in fact, broke under the strain, resigned on March 2, 1949, and committed suicide soon afterward in a moment of depression.

step came in 1947, when the President, with Congress's approval, appointed a commission on executive reorganization headed by former President Herbert Hoover. It undertook a comprehensive study of the complicated executive machinery and issued eighteen reports, embodying recommendations for many consolidations, in the early months of 1949.[6]

Largely at Truman's insistence, Congress approved another major governmental change—the Presidential Succession Act of 1947. It placed the Speaker of the House and the President pro tempore of the Senate ahead of the Secretary of State and other Cabinet members in the line of presidential succession after the Vice President. A final constitutional alteration was the Twenty-Second Amendment. It forbade election to the presidency for more than two full terms, or the re-election of a President for more than one term if he had served over two years of an unfinished term. Passed by a Republican Congress in 1947 and approved by the thirty-sixth state on February 26, 1951, the Amendment came too late to achieve its major purpose—to prevent the re-election of Franklin D. Roosevelt; and it specifically exempted Truman from its interdiction. Nonetheless, it reflected a widespread conviction that the powers of the office were too great to justify the risk of having another perpetual President.

217. *Truman's Struggles with Congress, 1945–1948*

The President and Republicans in Congress, often joined by a minority of conservative Democrats, also engaged in bitter controversies over aspects of economic and social policy—continuation of aid to agriculture and public health and housing, for example, or economic controls and federal labor policies. Truman, by his gestures of friendship toward congressional leaders during the first months of his presidency, led conservatives to believe that he planned to preside over the liquidation of the progressive movement. This brief "honeymoon" came to an end on September 6, 1945, when the President sent his first important domestic message to the Capitol. "It was on that day and with this message," Truman later wrote, "that I first spelled out the details of the program of liberalism and progressivism which was to be the foundation of my administration." [7] He called for a full revival of progressive policies—extension of Social Security, increase in the minimum wage, national health insurance, renewal of the New Deal's war against

∿∿∿∿∿∿∿∿∿∿∿∿∿∿∿∿

[6] Among the most important recommendations were those suggesting reduction of the number of federal departments and agencies from sixty-five to twenty-three; establishment of a Department of Welfare to consolidate federal activities in the fields of public health, education, and social welfare; and thoroughgoing reorganization of the Post Office Department. Congress, in the Reorganization Act of June 20, 1949, authorized the President to submit plans for reorganization, which would go into effect unless Congress specifically disapproved. Truman submitted thirty-six reorganization plans in 1949–50. All of them were allowed to go into effect except a plan to establish a Department of Welfare. It was defeated in 1950 by Republicans and southern Democrats, who feared approval might imply acquiescence in the President's proposal for national health insurance. The plan for a Department of Health, Education, and Welfare was revived by President Eisenhower and approved by Congress early in 1953.

[7] *Memoirs by Harry S. Truman*, I, pp. 481–2.

slums, new regional developments like the TVA, a full employment bill, executive reorganization, and extension of wartime economic controls through the reconversion period.

Truman's manifesto of September 6 showed clearly enough that he knew what he wanted. It was not always easy, however, to find majority support in the Seventy-ninth Congress that sat during 1945 and 1946. On many nonpartisan issues Truman succeeded with relative ease; on others he won compromise solutions that conservatives could approve. A conservative coalition of Republicans and southern Democrats often controlled both houses of Congress and blocked the President on advanced measures of welfare and civil rights and defeated him in hard battles over economic controls and revision of federal labor policies.[8]

The President and Office of Price Administration announced soon after the Japanese surrender that they would undertake "continued stabilization of the national economy" by gradual relaxation of wartime controls over prices, wages, and scarce commodities. During the last months of 1945 and the first half of 1946 the OPA was able to end most rationing, continue priorities on scarce industrial materials, and hold wholesale prices to an increase of only 7 per cent and the general cost of living to an increase of 3 per cent. At the same time, inflationary pressures were mounting powerfully to burst the bonds of price controls. Consumers with extra billions were buying in black markets; organized labor was driving for higher wages; and manufacturers and farmers had combined with Republican leaders in Congress to demand an end to all controls.

A bitter battle raged in Congress all through the spring of 1946 over extension of the OPA. The conservative coalition on June 27 presented the embattled President with a Price Control bill that extended the agency for one year but severely weakened its power and commanded it to decontrol prices "as rapidly as possible." Instead of acquiescing in the inevitable compromise, Truman vetoed the bill on June 29 and allowed price controls to end altogether on July 1. Prices rose wildly in the severest inflation since 1942 while Congress debated a new measure. Congress approved a second bill extending price and rent controls for one year on July 25, 1946. But the damage was already done. Moreover, the new measure was, if anything, even weaker and more confusing than the bill that Truman had vetoed. The President gave up the fight after the Republican victory in the congressional elections in November 1946. He ended all controls on wages and prices, except on rents, sugar, and rice, on November 9, and the OPA began to wind up its affairs a month later.

The wild inflation occurred just as GOP leaders were beginning their campaign to capture Congress in the autumn elections. Republican speakers and advertisements all during the late summer and early autumn played on the theme of confusion and failure in the price control program. One incident was particularly damaging to Democratic fortunes. The OPA restored price ceilings on meat on August 21, and farmers withheld beef from the market in anticipation of a change in policy. While housewives waited in

<hr />

[8] For Truman's controversy with Congress over labor policy in 1946, see above, p. 620.

line in vain for hamburger at any price, Republicans pressed their telling question, "Had enough?"

Numerous other signs pointed to an overwhelming Republican victory that November. Truman, it seemed, had alienated almost every major group. Organized labor was embittered by his drastic bridling of John L. Lewis and his stern action in breaking the railroad strike in the spring of 1946. (See above, pp. 617–618.) Conservatives were already disenchanted by his vigorous advocacy of welfare and civil rights legislation. New Dealers, on the other hand, were disgruntled by two recent incidents that threatened to disrupt the Democratic party. The first was the dramatic resignation of the "old curmudgeon," Harold L. Ickes, as Secretary of the Interior, following Truman's appointment of Edwin Pauley as Undersecretary of the Navy.[9] The second was Truman's dismissal of Secretary of Commerce Henry A. Wallace on September 20, soon after the former Vice President had publicly attacked the administration's policy of stiffening resistance to Russian demands. The President, actually, had to choose between Wallace and his Secretary of State, James F. Byrnes, for Byrnes had threatened to resign if Wallace remained in office. But the Democratic party's chief liability in the autumn of 1946 was Truman himself. He had given millions of Americans an impression of total inability either to lead or govern.

Few observers were surprised, therefore, when the GOP won firm control of the House and Senate for the first time since 1928 and captured governorships in twenty-five of the thirty-two non-southern states on November 5, 1946. What was surprising was the dimension of the landslide and the sharp decrease in the urban Democratic vote. Party machines in cities like Boston, New York, and Chicago had obviously been weakened by prosperity and the movement of people into the suburbs, and the hitherto solidly Democratic labor bloc had momentarily disintegrated.

The significance of the Republican triumph became evident soon after the Eightieth Congress convened on January 3, 1947. There were many new faces and an entirely new conservative leadership in both houses, but above them all, at least in consideration of domestic matters, stood Robert A. Taft of Ohio, chairman of the Republican policy committee in the Senate, champion of the business interests, and trenchant foe of advanced progressivism. This son of a former President would lead such vigorous opposition during the next five years as to earn the title "Mr. Republican" and to come within a few votes of winning the presidential nomination in 1952.

Republican leaders in Congress fought with the President and his friends on Capitol Hill all during 1947 and the early months of 1948. The noise emanating from Washington might well have prompted a superficial observer to conclude that effective government was impossible in the melee. There was, actually, often considerable difference between appearance and reality. In foreign policy the President and Congress co-operated during 1947–8 to achieve a record unsurpassed during any comparable period in American history. Even so, sharp differences over domestic policies provided abundant grist for the mill of partisanship. Truman, for example, fought hard to defeat the Taft-Hartley bill (see above, pp. 620–621), even

᠁᠁᠁᠁᠁᠁᠁᠁

[9] Ickes accused Pauley of using improper influence to prevent the Justice Department from pressing suit to recover offshore oil deposits off California.

though he had moved severely against arrogant labor leaders. Adoption of
the Taft-Hartley measure over the President's veto in June 1947 was the
most important conservative triumph of the postwar era. A second long controversy centered on ways and means of combating inflation. The President
pleaded against further tax reduction, which he said would only increase inflationary pressures. But the Republicans, with their eyes on 1948, adopted
a tax bill over Truman's veto in July 1947 that gave greatest relief to persons
on low and middle incomes. When prices continued to rise during the summer and autumn, Truman called Congress into special session on November 17, 1947, to consider a ten-point anti-inflation program. Republican leaders responded in December with an Anti-Inflation bill that carefully avoided
giving the President effective power. Congress extended rent controls for another year in March 1948; at the same time, it added to inflationary pressures by adopting, again over Truman's veto, another measure for tax reduction, the third since the end of the war. The President and Congress fought
their last battles before the campaign of 1948 over housing and agricultural
policies. Truman and moderate Republicans, led on this occasion by Senator Taft, supported the Taft-Ellender-Wagner bill, which would have inaugurated a broad program of public housing designed to benefit lower income
groups. All that the Republican majority would permit, however, was a
measure, adopted June 19, 1948, that provided governmental credit only for
veterans' homes and co-operative housing projects. As for agriculture, Congress in June 1948 approved a measure continuing support of farm prices at
90 per cent of parity through 1949, to be followed by a program of flexible
supports ranging from 60 to 90 per cent of parity.

218.   *The Election of 1948*

Not for two decades had the GOP been so confident as it was during
the early months of 1948. Among Republican hopefuls the most eager candidate for the presidential nomination was former Governor Harold E. Stassen of Minnesota. He won widespread popular backing by his frank support
of progressive policies at home and vigorous American leadership in world
affairs. After his victories in the Wisconsin and Nebraska presidential primaries in April, it seemed that Stassen might be irresistible. As it turned out,
the party leaders knew otherwise. They preferred Robert A. Taft, whose conservatism had won the support of a large part of the business community,
particularly in the Middle West. Taft's chances, however, were fatally weakened by his isolationist record before 1942, his lukewarm support of postwar
internationalism, and above all the popular feeling that he was cold and a
poor campaigner. The Republican leaders were too eager for victory to run
such risks. They approached General Eisenhower, who refused to run. Then
they turned to their titular leader, Governor Thomas E. Dewey of New York,
who had gained a reputation as a progressive and strong internationalist.
The Republican national convention, meeting in Philadelphia on June 21,
1948, nominated Dewey on the third ballot and named Governor Earl Warren of California as his running mate. At the same time it adopted a brief
platform that approved the New Deal reform structure and the postwar bipartisan foreign policy. It also promised further tax reductions, greater effi-

ciency, and more legislation for civil rights, welfare, and public housing.

In the meantime, civil wars were apparently destroying the Democratic party. The chief rebel in the field was Henry A. Wallace. He had organized the Progressive Citizens of America in 1947 and was now busy trying to rally New Dealers behind an advanced collectivistic program and all Americans against the administration's policy of resistance to Soviet imperialism. He appealed especially to idealistic college students. When he announced, on December 29, 1947, that he would run for President on a third-party ticket, observers predicted that he would poll between five and eight million votes and blast Democratic chances in 1948.

While the nation watched to see what dimensions the Wallace rebellion would assume, Democratic progressives, now organized in Americans for Democratic Action (ADA), maneuvered desperately to avoid having to choose between Truman and Wallace. They tried alternately to force Truman to retire and to find a winning candidate in Justice William O. Douglas or General Eisenhower. The powerful Democratic leaders Frank Hague of Jersey City, Edward Flynn of New York, and Jacob Arvey of Chicago also joined the movement to oust Truman and draft Eisenhower. As if to make a party rupture certain, southern Democrats were up in arms against the President's civil rights program and threatened to bolt if the convention adopted a strong civil rights plank in the platform.

It was, therefore, a gloomy and contentious Democratic convention that assembled in Philadelphia from July 12 to 15, 1948. The ADA progressives, led by Mayor Hubert Humphrey of Minneapolis and supported by the big city leaders, were determined to draft a program for the future even while they expected defeat in 1948. They put through a platform that strongly reaffirmed the progressive tradition. Then, after a bitter floor fight, the convention adopted a civil rights plank demanding a Fair Employment Practices Commission and federal anti-lynching and anti-poll tax legislation. Finally, a harassed convention early in the morning of July 15 named Truman for President because it had no other choice. As his running mate the President chose Alben W. Barkley, President pro tempore of the Senate, after Justice Douglas had declined to run.

What Democratic leaders most feared, a party rupture, occurred a few days later. The rebel left wing met in Philadelphia from July 22 to 25, organized the Progressive party, and nominated Wallace for President and Senator Glen Taylor of Idaho for Vice President. Their platform demanded gradual nationalization of basic industries, an end to segregation, and reorientation of foreign policy toward friendship with Russia. This was, actually, the high point of Wallace's strength, for the convention revealed what many already suspected: The Progressive party organization was controlled by Communists and fellow travelers, and Wallace had allowed himself to be used in a Communist attempt to disrupt progressive ranks.[10] Few progressives went to the third-party convention; only one or two former New Deal leaders remained in the new party; and Wallace lost support the more he campaigned.

Meanwhile, the smoldering southern rebellion had also erupted. So-

---

[10] But see Karl M. Schmidt, *Henry A. Wallace: Quixotic Crusader* (Syracuse, N.Y., 1960), which argues (unconvincingly to the present writer) to the contrary.

called Dixiecrats met in Birmingham on July 17, waved Confederate flags, and formed the States' Rights Democratic party. They nominated Governor J. Strom Thurmond of South Carolina and Governor Fielding L. Wright of Mississippi on their "national" ticket. The "Dixiecrats' " opposition to the President's civil rights program had a powerful appeal to southern white sentiment and enabled them to control the Democratic party in Alabama, South Carolina, Mississippi, and Louisiana. But they failed to achieve their main objective—an all-southern rebellion, which would throw the election of the President into the House of Representatives.

Republican confidence mounted as the left and right wings of the Democracy pummeled President Truman. Governor Dewey conducted a mild and dignified campaign. He repeated old strictures against alleged Democratic incompetence, but he made it clear that he approved all the basic aspects of Democratic domestic and foreign policy. Dewey was so encouraged by the Gallup Poll, which showed him far in the lead, that he bestirred himself only to make plans for his inauguration. The mass of newspapers and magazines shared his confidence. The Chicago *Tribune*, for example, ran large headlines on its front page hailing Dewey as the victor.

Indeed, Truman was one of the few men in the country who thought that he had a chance to win. He startled the country at the Democratic convention by announcing that he would call the Eightieth Congress into special session and give the Republicans an opportunity to enact their platform into law. Congress met from July 26 to August 7 without, as Truman expected, adopting any important legislation. Then Truman went to the country in perhaps the most strenuous personal campaign in American history. Traveling more than 30,000 miles, he made 351 speeches, many of them "whistle-stop" talks in railroad yards from the rear platform of his car, to an estimated 12,000,000 people. "The technique I used . . ." he later wrote, "was simple and straightforward. . . . I had simply told the people in my own language that they had better wake up to the fact that it was their fight." [11] Castigating the "do-nothing" Eightieth Congress, he urged a bold and full resumption of progressive policies: repeal of the Taft-Hartley Act, strong civil rights protection for minority groups, national health insurance, new antitrust legislation, federal aid to education, broadening of social security benefits, an increase in the minimum wage, and continued high parity support for farm prices. Moreover, he went into Harlem to become the first presidential candidate ever to appeal in person for Negro votes.

The American people admired the President's courage in fighting hard alone and assumed that Dewey was bound to win. As one writer observed, Americans seemed willing to give Truman anything but the presidency. But he knew better than the pollsters and commentators, and he went to bed on election night, November 2, 1948, confident and serene. In the most surprising political upset in American history, Truman won 24,105,695 popular and 303 electoral votes, Dewey 21,969,170 popular and 189 electoral votes. Thurmond, with 1,169,021 popular and 39 electoral votes, and Wallace, with 1,156,103 popular votes, trailed far behind. Moreover, the Democrats won control of the next Congress by majorities of ninety-three in the House and twelve in the Senate.

[11] *Memoirs by Harry S. Truman*, II, p. 211.

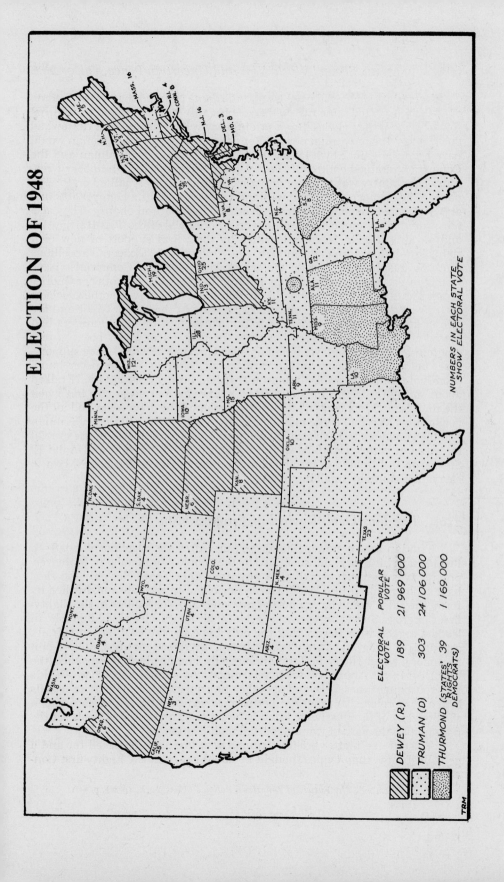

ELECTION OF 1948

	ELECTORAL VOTE	POPULAR VOTE
DEWEY (R)	189	21 969 000
TRUMAN (D)	303	24 106 000
THURMOND (STATES' RIGHTS DEMOCRATS)	39	1 169 000

NUMBERS IN EACH STATE SHOW ELECTORAL VOTE

ME. 5
N.H. 4
VT. 3
MASS. 16
R.I. 4
CONN. 8
N.Y. 47
N.J. 16
PA. 35
DEL. 3
MD. 8
W.VA. 8
VA. 11
N.C. 14
S.C. 8
GA. 12
FLA. 8
ALA. 11
MISS. 9
TENN. 11
KY. 11
OHIO 25
IND. 13
MICH. 19
ILL. 28
WIS. 12
MINN. 11
IOWA 10
MO. 15
ARK. 9
OKLA. 10
KAN. 8
NEBR. 6
S.DAK. 4
N.DAK. 4
TEXAS 23
COLO. 6
N. MEX. 4
WYO. 3
MONT. 4
UTAH 4
ARIZ. 4
IDAHO 4
NEV. 3
WASH. 8
OREG. 6
CALIF. 25

TRM

Republican critics like the Chicago *Tribune* charged that Dewey had no one but himself to blame for his debacle because he had offered no alternative to Democratic policies. But a careful survey later proved that Dewey had polled about the maximum normal Republican vote, and that Truman would have been the gainer by a larger turnout on election day. Truman and the Democrats retained control of the federal government for a number of reasons. The country was at peace, prosperous, and relatively united on foreign policy. The Democrats could thus stand as champions of a happy *status quo* and depict their opponents as the advocates of unnatural change. They also recaptured labor support by their advocacy of repeal of the Taft-Hartley Act and an almost solid Negro allegiance by their firm support of new civil rights legislation. Ironically enough, the Wallace and "Dixiecrat" rebellions probably assured Democratic victory by removing the Communist issue from the campaign and making it clear to Negroes and other minority groups that the southern wing did not dominate the party. Another decisive factor was the unexpected behavior of farmers in the Middle West and the Border states, all of which went for Truman except Indiana. Farmers had feared and expected a depression since the war. Farm prices began a precipitous decline in 1948, yet Republicans advocated "flexible" price supports that could mean disaster in the rural areas. Truman, on the other hand, promised maintenance of a program that had brought prosperity. "I talked about voting for Dewey all summer," one Iowa farmer declared, "but when the time came I just couldn't do it. I remembered the depression and all the good things that had come to me under the Democrats." [12] Finally, Truman had the good luck to have strong local Democratic candidates in the crucial midwestern states. Candidates like Humphrey in Minnesota and Adlai E. Stevenson in Illinois ran far ahead of Truman and probably helped him to carry their states by small majorities.

219.   *The Fair Deal: Revival of Progressivism*

Truman was a new political creature after the election of 1948—a President in his own right, sustained by the people's supreme gift. Moreover, progressives were happier than at any time since 1936. Not only did they have a champion in the White House dedicated to the cause of further reform; they also would have a host of new and vigorous leaders in the Eighty-first Congress. Surveying the wreckage of their hopes, chastened Republican leaders agreed with Dewey that the only hope for the GOP lay in a frank espousal of progressivism. Progressivism, therefore, seemed once again ascendant when Harry S. Truman formally launched what he called the Fair Deal in his Annual Message to Congress on January 20, 1949. In this and subsequent messages and speeches he consolidated his past proposals into a comprehensive program. Let us now see how his efforts to broaden the horizons of progressivism fared before a new international crisis set the nation upon the path of war and partial mobilization.

To state the matter briefly, Truman won less than he asked for and a good deal more than cynics thought he could get from the Eighty-first Con-

[12] Samuel Lubell, *The Future of American Politics* (New York, 1952), p. 161.

gress. For labor, he obtained in 1949 and 1950 an amendment to the Fair Labor Standards Act increasing the minimum wage from 40 to 75 cents an hour, plus amendments to the Social Security Act that brought 10,000,000 new beneficiaries into the system and increased benefits for retired workers by an average of 77.5 per cent. For the millions who lived in rented homes and apartments, he won extension of rent control to March 31, 1951. His greatest victory for labor and the poorer classes was the Housing Act of 1949, adoption of which marked the end of a bitter struggle that had raged since 1945. It provided large sums for slum clearance and authorized construction of 810,000 units for low-income families during the next six years.

The President and Congress co-operated in other ways to expand the economic and welfare activities of the federal government. Truman failed to win approval for the St. Lawrence Seaway, a Missouri Valley Authority, and other regional projects. But he obtained large increases for the Reclamation Bureau's ambitious hydroelectric, water-control, and irrigation program in the West. He won, also, increased appropriations for the TVA, the REA, and the Farmers' Home Administration, which since the war had continued the work of the Farm Security Administration in extending loans to farmers for rehabilitation and farm ownership. Finally, the President gained approval in June 1950 of a new Displaced Persons bill to admit some 400,000 European refugees.

However, in striving to achieve labor's most important goal—repeal of the Taft-Hartley Act—the President, the AF of L, and the CIO tried to gain too much and failed. Congress and the public were obviously unwilling to give up many features of the measure that unions condemned as a "slave labor" law. The Senate, with the approval of Senator Taft, did adopt a series of amendments that revised the measure substantially in labor's favor. But Truman and his labor allies, gambling on the future, ruined the opportunity by rejecting the compromise and demanding nothing less than complete repeal of the Taft-Hartley Act.

The President and his friends pushed too hard too fast on other important Fair Deal objectives. The administration's farsighted program for agriculture, the Brannan Plan,[13] was probably the best solution of the farm problem. But it aroused charges of regimentation and socialism and provoked bitter opposition from large farmers. In spite of the failure of the Brannan Plan, the administration could claim that the Agricultural Act approved by Congress in October 1949 not only redeemed Democratic pledges but also reaffirmed a progressive policy for agriculture. It continued rigid price supports at 90 per cent of parity through 1950 and provided for "flexible" price supports ranging from 75 to 90 per cent of parity afterward.

[13] The Brannan Plan was proposed by Secretary of Agriculture Charles Brannan in April 1949. It was the first serious effort since 1938 to eliminate the weaknesses in federal farm policy. It proposed to maintain a "farm income standard," or a dollar income as high as the average of the preceding ten years. To accomplish this goal, it would continue the program of price supports through loans and storage of nonperishable commodities. But for perishable commodities like meat, eggs, and dairy products it suggested a new method of distribution and maintenance of parity income—the immediate sale of all such commodities at whatever price the market would bring, followed by federal payments to the farmer to make up the difference between what he received and the official support price.

In other and more controversial projects of Fair Deal reform, Truman encountered bitter opposition and defeat. His proposal for national health insurance was defeated by the American Medical Association's gigantic campaign of newspaper advertising and lobbying. His plan for federal aid to education had substantial bipartisan support, but it ran afoul of the opposition of the Roman Catholic Church because it did not include certain subsidies to children in parochial schools.

It was in the field of civil rights that the President suffered his most discouraging defeats. He had appointed a Committee on Civil Rights in December 1946, composed of distinguished Southerners, Negroes, and leaders in church and education throughout the country. It was instructed to investigate and recommend "more adequate and effective means and procedures for the protection of the civil rights of the people of the United States." The Committee issued its report, *To Secure These Rights*, in 1947. It exposed the operation and consequences of the caste system and called for a systematic federal-state program to root out injustices based on race—by strengthening the Civil Rights Section of the Justice Department, using the FBI in cases involving violations of civil rights, enacting anti-lynching and anti-poll tax laws, establishing a permanent FEPC, and other such measures.

Truman appealed to Congress year in and year out to implement the Committee's recommendations, but he could never overcome the threat of a southern filibuster in the Senate. However, he had other recourses; and through them he struck hard blows at the caste system. He strengthened the Civil Rights Section. He began the practice of having the Justice Department assist private parties in civil rights cases. He invited Negroes to the inaugural reception and ball in 1949. He appointed the first Negro Governor of the Virgin Islands and the first Negro federal judge. Most important, he began abolition of segregation in governmental departments and the armed services in 1948.

Looking back over the first eighteen months of Truman's second term, the historian must wonder at how much, not how little, the Fair Deal accomplished during this period of prosperity and relative social and economic contentment. One fact of supreme importance stood out at mid-century: The vast majority of Americans, regardless of party affiliation, were so fundamentally progressive that their differences involved only the degree and speed of further movement toward the welfare state.

220.   *The Second Red Scare*

By that fateful day in June 1950 when the North Korean Communists invaded South Korea the American people were convulsed by fear of Communist infiltration of their government and institutions. This second Red Scare, so reminiscent of the hysteria of the years after the First World War, would grow to larger proportions before it began to ebb and would leave a residue of personal and partisan bitterness unparalleled since Reconstruction. For this reason its effects were tragically disruptive during a time when the American people desperately needed unity of will and purpose. Unhappily, in contrast to the Red Scare of 1919 and 1920, the fear of Communist infiltration following the Second World War was in some measure justified.

And because the fear was present and in part well grounded, millions of Americans turned receptive ears to demagogues who used the Communist issue to seek personal power and attack freedom in politics, the press, and education.

In an earlier chapter we noted the rise and decline of Communism in the United States during the 1930's and the success of underground party members in infiltrating into some key positions in the federal government. (See above, pp. 449–453.) That infiltration continued unabated during the war. As one writer has put it, "During the war years, Communists and fellow travelers had entered the government in droves. . . . During wartime, most government agencies had considered Communist affiliations to be unimportant. In the Office of Strategic Services, it was common knowledge that the employment of pro-Communists was approved at very high levels provided they were suited for specific jobs." [14]

The FBI undertook its first comprehensive investigation of Communist organizations, and the departments in Washington began their own disjointed and often ineffective investigations, in 1945 and 1946. However, the impetus for a full-scale drive to root Communists out of the American government came from two specific events at this time. The first was the *Amerasia* case. The Office of Strategic Services discovered early in 1945 that certain of its most secret documents had fallen into the hands of Philip J. Jaffe, editor of *Amerasia,* a Communist-sponsored monthly magazine established for the purpose of influencing American policy in the Far East. OSS officers raided the *Amerasia* offices on March 11, 1945, and discovered huge piles of diplomatic and military documents. A few days later jurisdiction was given to the FBI. It easily established an intimate connection between Jaffe and his associates and Soviet and Chinese Communist officials. The Justice Department prosecuted Jaffe and his fellow conspirators in order to destroy their ring, even though the Department knew that it could not make a strong case because it had taken evidence unlawfully. Jaffe and an accomplice subsequently received light fines for conspiring to receive government property illegally. Even more jarring was the report issued in 1946 by a Canadian royal commission appointed to investigate charges of Communist espionage. The commission proved that the Communist party in Canada was an arm of the Soviet government and exposed the operation of several Soviet spy rings. More important, it revealed that at least twenty-three Canadians in "positions of trust," one of them a member of Parliament, another a leading atomic scientist, were agents of the Communist ring and had sent atomic secrets and samples of uranium to Moscow.

These revelations spurred the FBI and security officers of Washington departments to a full-scale drive against Communists. President Truman issued an Executive Order in March 1947 inaugurating a comprehensive investigation of all federal employees by the FBI and the Civil Service Commission. Some features of the program evoked strong opposition from liberals. They charged that the government had introduced the principle of "guilt by association" and failed to provide adequate safeguards against discharge on account of rumors and unknown accusers. On the whole, however, the administration moved with regard for justice and civil rights dur-

[14] Nathaniel Weyl, *The Battle Against Disloyalty* (New York, 1951), p. 180.

ing its loyalty probe from 1947 to 1951. The gigantic task had been completed by the early months of 1951. The Civil Service Commission had cleared more than 3,000,000 federal employees. The FBI had made some 14,000 full-scale investigations of doubtful cases. Over 2,000 employees had resigned. And 212 persons had been dismissed on the ground that there was reasonable doubt as to their loyalty. In addition, the President approved a bill in August 1950 authorizing heads of ten so-called sensitive departments and agencies to dismiss persons who, though not necessarily disloyal, were deemed bad security risks. Persons thus accused might demand a hearing by the security board of their own agency but were denied the right of appeal to a review board.

In spite of the thoroughness, even the severity, of the administration's loyalty probe,[15] it was not enough to quiet popular alarm or prevent the Republicans from exploiting the issue. This was true not only because demagogues soon went to work, but also because sensational exposures after 1947 revealed the former extent of Communist infiltration and the devastating effectiveness of Soviet espionage in acquiring secrets vital to the security of the United States. It was true, most poignantly, because the President and a large body of public leaders were drawn into a compromising position in one of the most celebrated cases in American history—the trial of Alger Hiss, ostensibly for perjury but actually for Soviet espionage.

Hiss had been a member of the Ware group, the most important Communist cell in Washington, during the New Deal era, and had risen rapidly through various departments to a position of considerable trust in the State Department. He had in a sense become the model of the able young civil servant. Among a host of friends he could count a Justice of the Supreme Court and a future Secretary of State. He resigned from the State Department in 1947 to accept the presidency of the Carnegie Endowment for International Peace of New York City.

Whittaker Chambers, a former Soviet agent, had denounced Hiss and other Communists to the State Department in 1939 but had failed to offer proof or even to describe the espionage network of which Hiss was a member. Events subsequently convinced Chambers that democracy and Communism were engaged in a death grapple, and he told his story to the public and the House un-American activities committee in 1948. Hiss sued for libel, and Chambers produced microfilms of sixty-five State Department documents that he said Hiss had passed to him in early 1938. Called before a federal grand jury in New York, Hiss denied that he had ever delivered State Department documents to Chambers. He was then indicted for perjury and convicted on January 21, 1950, after a first trial had ended in a hung jury. Hiss's personal tragedy was awful enough. Even more tragic was his betrayal both of the President, who in the autumn of 1948 denounced the House committee's investigation as a "red herring," and of a large body of distinguished public leaders who testified to his integrity. The Hiss trials, more than any other event of the postwar era, contributed to the growing

---

[15] Perhaps the best testimony to the effectiveness of the program was the failure of the Justice Department, security officials, and congressional committees to find any Communists in the government after the Republicans came to power in 1953.

public conviction that the Roosevelt and Truman administrations had been oblivious to the danger of Communist subversion at home.

One effect of the Hiss trials was to rehabilitate the House un-American activities committee, long the whipping boy of liberals, and to spur it to new investigations in 1949 and 1950. In 1949, too, the country was shocked by the arrest, trial, and conviction of Judith Coplon, a young employee in the Justice Department, for passing vital information on the FBI's counter-espionage system to a Soviet agent. Virtual hysteria followed the revelation in 1950 that a group of Anglo-American agents had succeeded in delivering full information on the manufacture of the atomic bomb to the Soviet government from 1943 to 1947.[16]

These disclosures and their implications raised new fears and set the stage for the spectacular rise of Joseph R. McCarthy of Wisconsin and full-scale anti-Communist hysteria in the United States. Elected to the Senate in 1946, McCarthy had already acquired considerable reputation for moral callousness, doubtful integrity, and utter ruthlessness. He decided early in 1950 to use the issue of Communist infiltration to improve his ebbing political fortunes. By his indiscriminate and reckless attacks during the next four years he won clear title as the most unprincipled man in public life since Aaron Burr and the most successful demagogue since Huey Long. At the same time, he did more than any other living American to confuse and divide the people and discredit his country's good name abroad.

McCarthy opened what many thought was a campaign to win control of the Republican party on February 9, 1950, by announcing that he had the names of 205, or 57, Communists in the State Department. Unable to point out a single Communist then in the Department, McCarthy countered by naming Owen Lattimore of The Johns Hopkins University, an expert on the Far East, as the head of "the espionage ring in the State Department." When J. Edgar Hoover, head of the FBI, affirmed that there was no evidence to substantiate this charge,[17] a special Senate committee headed by Millard Tydings of Maryland gave Lattimore a clean bill of health. Such failure only stirred McCarthy to more brutal attacks. He turned next against Philip C. Jessup, American representative in the General Assembly of the United Nations, charging savagely that this distinguished public servant had Communist connections; against Senator Tydings, whom he helped defeat for re-election in the autumn of 1950; and finally against Generals George C.

~~~~~~~~~~~~~~~~~~~~

[16] All during the war Soviet agents made fantastic attempts to obtain information about all phases of the atomic energy program. Army intelligence and FBI agents frustrated most of these efforts but failed to discover the most important atomic spy ring. It was led by Dr. Klaus Fuchs, a German-born physicist and naturalized British subject. He had been sent to Los Alamos in 1944 to help make the atomic bomb and succeeded in delivering apparently complete information on the bomb to Soviet agents. The American people learned the shocking and frightening news of his betrayal when Fuchs was arrested in February 1950 and promptly confessed to British authorities, and when the FBI soon afterward arrested Fuchs's accomplices in the United States.

[17] Apparently the only serious charge brought against Lattimore was the allegation that he consciously sought to influence American far eastern policy in order to further Soviet interests. The Senate internal security committee, which reopened the Lattimore case during 1951 and 1952, made this accusation and obtained an indictment charging Lattimore with perjury. The indictment was later dismissed by a federal court.

Marshall and Dwight D. Eisenhower, both of whom he accused on June 15, 1951, of assisting the Russians in their drive for world domination.

McCarthy's smear campaign and use of the "big lie" tactic, so reminiscent of the methods of Adolf Hitler, filled many with loathing, but millions of Americans were so frightened by the revelations of Communist espionage and infiltration that they turned receptive ears to his propaganda. Moreover, Republican leaders encouraged the Wisconsin demagogue and used him with apparently telling effect in the congressional campaign of 1950. There would be a reckoning after the inauguration of the Republican administration in 1953, to be sure; but for a time it seemed that "McCarthyism" had won at least the approval, if not the open endorsement, of the great GOP.

221.   *Communism, the Courts, and Congress*

"McCarthyism" was only the most violent manifestation of the anti-Communist hysteria that engulfed the United States from 1948 to 1953. In varying degree it affected the press, schools, churches, courts, and Congress. It created an atmosphere of fear and stimulated the conviction that it was safer to conform than to disagree with the majority. To be sure, many bold voices pleaded for sanity and preservation of civil liberties, and the hysteria began to ebb in 1954. Meanwhile, however, the government had carried through and the courts had approved an anti-Communist program that greatly diminished traditional American civil liberty.

The Truman administration opened the drive in 1948 by obtaining the indictment of eleven high-ranking Communist leaders for conspiring, in violation of the Smith Act of 1940, to *teach* the violent overthrow of the United States. The government had prepared its case thoroughly; and during a long trial in 1949 it proved its charges by the testimony of a number of FBI agents and former Communists. The defense failed either to convince the public that the trial was unfair or to harry the long-suffering trial judge into insanity or suicide; and the Communist leaders were duly convicted and sentenced to varying terms in prison. After the Court of Appeals upheld the decision, the case—Dennis *et al. v.* United States—came before the Supreme Court for final review.

The court upheld the constitutionality of the Smith Act and confirmed the conviction of the eleven Communists by a vote of six to two on June 4, 1951. The charge was not conspiracy to overthrow the government by force, but conspiracy to teach or advocate revolution. Chief Justice Vinson spoke for the majority in one of the most important decisions in American history. He reconciled the conviction with the right of free speech by affirming that the government had proved that the Communist threat was sufficiently substantial to justify conviction under the doctrine of "clear and present danger." The Justice Department soon afterward obtained the conviction and imprisonment of some forty regional, state, and Hawaiian Communist leaders for violating the Smith Act. Defenders of civil liberties were further shocked by two Supreme Court decisions in 1951 and 1952 that seemed to condone police censorship and state suppression of free speech on broad grounds.[18] Indeed, many persons wondered whether the court had not been sucked into the vortex of the reaction against Communism.

Congress, too, reacted violently in 1950 by approving over the President's veto the McCarran Internal Security bill. It was easily the severest measure since the Sedition Act of 1918 and one of the most confused. It required Communist organizations to register with the Attorney General and furnish complete membership lists and financial statements. But it specifically declared that membership or officeholding in a Communist organization was not, per se, a crime. In a second breath, the Act made it illegal knowingly to conspire to perform "any act" that would "substantially" contribute to the establishment of a totalitarian dictatorship in the United States. It also forbade employment of Communists in defense plants or granting of passports to Communists; authorized the internment of Communists in the event of war; and established a bipartisan Subversive Activities Control Board to assist the Attorney General in exposing subversive organizations.

If, as the President charged in his veto message, the internal security provisions of the McCarran Act were mainly blundering and ineffective, then the provisions relating to immigration, deportation, and naturalization struck a serious blow at American security. By forbidding the entry into the United States of any person who had once been a member of a totalitarian organization, for example, the measure deprived the American government of its most effective means of inducing Russian and other Communist leaders to break with their governments and come into the free camp. Understandably, the Justice Department, Defense Department, and Central Intelligence Agency, as well as the President, opposed the McCarran bill.

Congressional determination to strike at Communism was reflected again two years later when the two houses passed over Truman's veto the McCarran-Walter Immigration and Nationality bill in June 1952. It rectified an old injustice by permitting the naturalization of resident Asiatics and the annual admission of some 2,000 Orientals on a quota basis. But the President and many liberals thought that its provisions for exclusion and deportation of aliens and control of American citizens abroad were unnecessarily harsh and subversive of fundamental rights.

[18] In the cases of Feiner *v.* New York and Beauharnais *v.* Illinois. Feiner had been arrested for disorderly conduct while making a soapbox speech in Syracuse, New York, during the campaign of 1948. The shocking aspect of the Supreme Court's verdict, which upheld the conviction, was the implication that the police were justified in arresting any person who *in their opinion* was provoking a riot. Beauharnais was head of the anti-Negro White Circle League of Chicago and was convicted of violating an Illinois statute forbidding the libeling of any person or group on account of race, color, creed, or religion. In upholding the conviction by a five-to-four majority, the Court specifically approved the new theory of "group libel" and thus further enlarged the state's control over speech and expression.

CHAPTER

28

Vain Struggles for a Brave New World

1945–1949

AMERICANS thanked God in the midsummer of 1945 that the war was over and hoped that a new world order would banish fears and rivalries upon which wars bred. Events soon made a mockery of these hopes. The Allied victory had raised a new menace—the threat of Soviet expansion— almost as great as the Nazi danger had been. The utter destruction of German and Japanese power had removed two counterbalances to Soviet power, and Americans were confronted with two unwelcome alternatives. They could either allow the Russians to fill the power vacuums in Europe and the Far East or build and support a new power structure to check Russian expansion.

In due time the people would learn that perils and hardships inevitably accompany leadership in world affairs. The grave danger during the period 1945–9 was that Americans were still so inexperienced and naive as to expect prompt and easy solutions, and that they would abandon leadership when their hopes were frustrated, as they had done in 1919 and 1920. Let us now see what triumphs and failures awaited the American people and their leaders during the postwar years, and how they groped toward effective leadership in the affairs of mankind.

222.   *The Brave New World*

President Roosevelt and Secretary Hull worked diligently after American entry into the Second World War to achieve their primary postwar objective, creation of an international organization to prevent aggression and preserve peace. They found an almost unanimous response in the United States; abroad they found disagreement only upon details. The leaders of the three great powers resolved their differences at the Dumbarton Oaks Conference in 1944 and the Yalta Conference in early 1945. (See above, pp. 572–575.) They also approved the structure of a United Nations and convoked an international conference to meet in San Francisco in April 1945 to draft a charter for the new organization.

It seemed for a time in March and April 1945 that Allied disagreement over Poland might disrupt the conference before it could meet. But President Truman made it clear to Foreign Minister Molotov on April 22, 1945, that the United States intended to take leadership in forming an international organization whether or not Russia co-operated, and the Soviets abruptly changed their attitude. Thus the conference opened on schedule on April 25, and representatives of forty-six nations met to transform a wartime alliance into a permanent structure for world peace.

The San Francisco Conference, however, was an inauspicious beginning for the reign of universal brotherhood. Almost from beginning to end the American and Russian delegates wrangled over questions large and small; and Truman saved the conference from disruption on one occasion only by appealing personally to Stalin. In the end, the Charter of the United Nations—signed on June 26, approved by the United States Senate on July 28, and promulgated on October 24, 1945—embodied a minimum of concessions to Soviet demands and every important objective for which the United States had contended. It was an American document in all its strengths and weaknesses—Wilson's League Covenant embellished and revised.

The Charter created a United Nations with a bicameral legislature. The Security Council, or "upper house," had initiative and authority in fundamental matters. It was composed of representatives of five powers with permanent seats [1] and six other members elected biennially by the other house. Procedural questions might be settled by the vote of any seven members, but action on substantive questions required the unanimous approval of the five permanent members. The General Assembly, or "lower house," in which each member nation might have as many as five delegates but only one vote,[2] was empowered to discuss any question and to recommend to the Security Council on any matter within the scope of the Charter, except in the case of a dispute already on the Council's agenda.

The Charter also created a Secretariat, headed by a Secretary-General, to perform routine tasks of administration, and an International Court of

[1] The United States, Great Britain, Russia, France, and China.

[2] The exception was Russia, which in effect had three votes. In return for Soviet concessions on other matters, the Ukrainian and Byelorussian "soviet republics," though actually an integral part of the USSR, were given seats in the General Assembly.

ORGANS OF T

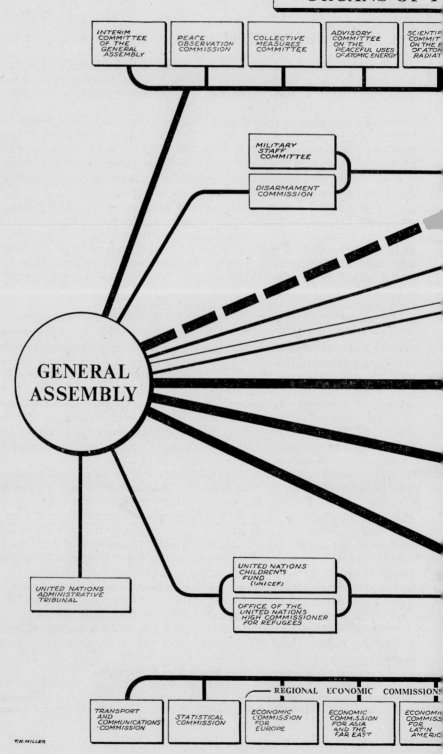

INTERIM COMMITTEE OF THE GENERAL ASSEMBLY

PEACE OBSERVATION COMMISSION

COLLECTIVE MEASURES COMMITTEE

ADVISORY COMMITTEE ON THE PEACEFUL USES OF ATOMIC ENERGY

SCIENTIF COMMIT ON THE E OF ATON RADIAT

MILITARY STAFF COMMITTEE

DISARMAMENT COMMISSION

GENERAL ASSEMBLY

UNITED NATIONS CHILDREN'S FUND (UNICEF)

OFFICE OF THE UNITED NATIONS HIGH COMMISSIONER FOR REFUGEES

UNITED NATIONS ADMINISTRATIVE TRIBUNAL

REGIONAL ECONOMIC COMMISSIONS

TRANSPORT AND COMMUNICATIONS COMMISSION

STATISTICAL COMMISSION

ECONOMIC COMMISSION FOR EUROPE

ECONOMIC COMMISSION FOR ASIA AND THE FAR EAST

ECONOMIC COMMISSION FOR LAT'N AMERIC

T.R.MILLER

UNITED NATIONS

RELIEF AND WORKS AGENCY FOR PALESTINE REFUGEES IN THE NEAR EAST

UNITED NATIONS KOREAN RECONSTRUCTION AGENCY

INTERNATIONAL LAW COMMISSION

COMMITTEE ON INFORMATION FROM NON-SELF-GOVERNING TERRITORIES

ADVISORY COMMITTEE ON ADMINISTRATIVE AND BUDGETARY QUESTIONS

COMMITTEE ON CONTRIBUTIONS

SECURITY COUNCIL

INTERNATIONAL ATOMIC ENERGY AGENCY

INTERNATIONAL COURT OF JUSTICE

TRUSTEESHIP COUNCIL

SECRETARIAT

ECONOMIC AND SOCIAL COUNCIL

ADMINISTRATIVE COMMITTEE ON CO-ORDINATION

TECHNICAL ASSISTANCE BOARD

SPECIALIZED AGENCIES

INTERNATIONAL LABOR ORGANIZATION

WORLD HEALTH ORGANIZATION

FOOD AND AGRICULTURE ORGANIZATION OF THE UNITED NATIONS

UNIVERSAL POSTAL UNION

UNITED NATIONS EDUCATIONAL, SCIENTIFIC, AND CULTURAL ORGANIZATION

INTERNATIONAL TELECOMMUNICATION UNION

INTERNATIONAL CIVIL AVIATION ORGANIZATION

WORLD METEOROLOGICAL ORGANIZATION

INTERNATIONAL MONETARY FUND

INTER-GOVERNMENTAL MARITIME CONSULTATIVE ORGANIZATION

INTERNATIONAL BANK FOR RECONSTRUCTION AND DEVELOPMENT

INTERNATIONAL FINANCE CORPORATION (AFFILIATE OF INTERNATIONAL BANK)

INTERNATIONAL TRADE ORGANIZATION (INTERIM COMMISSION)

COMMISSION HUMAN RIGHTS

SOCIAL COMMISSION

COMMISSION ON THE STATUS OF WOMEN

POPULATION COMMISSION

COMMISSION ON NARCOTIC DRUGS

COMMISSION ON INTERNATIONAL COMMODITY TRADE

Justice endowed with such jurisdiction as member states chose to grant. There were dozens of subsidiary and allied independent agencies: the United Nations Economic and Social Council, with its own numerous commissions; the Trusteeship Council, established to supervise old League mandates and territories taken from Japan and Italy; the International Monetary Fund, with total resources of nearly $9,000,000,000 for currency stabilization and expansion of world trade; and the International Bank for Reconstruction and Development, with subscribed capital of $9,100,000,-000, to facilitate long-term investment in war-ravaged and economically backward areas. There was, finally, the United Nations Relief and Rehabilitation Administration (UNRRA), eventually given nearly $4,000,000,000 to provide food and clothing for war-stricken peoples of Europe and Asia from 1945 to 1947.

It was an imposing structure, calculated to fit every need and please all but the most extreme nationalists. But it was a structure for world confederation and co-operation, not for effective world government. On paper the United Nations Charter inaugurated an era of universal peace, for all members agreed to follow the path of arbitration rather than the road to war. And yet the United Nations lacked power sufficient to its task. Like the American union established by the Articles of Confederation, the United Nations was an association of sovereign states, with no authority except such as the leading members condescended to let it use. Established primarily to prevent war, the United Nations could be blocked in performing this elementary function by the veto of one of the permanent members of the Security Council. In other words, the United Nations was powerless to prevent aggression by one of its leading members. In this respect it was a weaker peace instrument than the League of Nations. Nor was there much hope of reform and reorganization, for the Charter gave permanent members of the Security Council the right to veto any proposed amendments.

American leaders, notably Roosevelt and Hull, were in large measure responsible for these constitutional defects. They feared isolationist sentiment at home and were willing to make whatever concessions were necessary to obtain Russian membership. They insisted upon an agency that would not impair national sovereignty and could function effectively only so long as all the great powers agreed. Thus the veto was more an American than a Russian invention; the provision for "regional" defensive associations, creation of which later emphasized the weakness of the United Nations as a peace agency, was also included at American insistence.

These inherent weaknesses were only dimly perceptible as the people set to the task of helping to create a new and better world in 1945. To the first and most urgent task, that of relief for war-ravaged areas, Americans responded with commendable generosity. The United States contributed some $2,700,000,000 through UNRRA in food and supplies to the peoples of China and central and eastern Europe. In addition, the American Army assumed the burden of relief in Japan and the American zone of Germany, while the American Red Cross, church groups, and private organizations added several hundred million dollars' worth of clothing and food. Through the sale on credit of surplus property and Lend-Lease supplies and the extension of credits by the Export-Import Bank, the Washington government made some additional $4,700,000,000 available for relief and re-construction, chiefly to western Europe.

To the second task, restoration of foreign trade, the American government addressed itself with considerable boldness and success. The fundamental problem was Europe's continued dependence upon the United States for food, supplies, and industrial equipment, and her inability to pay in full, either in dollars, goods, or services, because of the abrupt termination of Lend-Lease assistance at the end of the war. Foreigners accumulated deficits of $19,182,000,000 in 1946–7. These deficits were so staggering that world trade would simply have collapsed without decisive support by the United States. The Washington government solved the problem before 1948 by stopgap expedients: UNRRA and other aid, loans by the Export-Import Bank, a credit loan of $3,750,000,000 to the British government in 1946, and the like. The world economy was not much healthier in 1948 than it had been in 1945; but stopgap aid had prevented the collapse of the international economic structure until a comprehensive reconstruction program could be launched.

The third and perhaps most difficult task was the reconstruction and reform of Germany and Japan and the punishment of individuals allegedly responsible for the war. It was an undertaking for which the American people were unprepared, and in retrospect many of the occupation policies seem unwise, unnecessarily harsh, and, above all, utopian. Not even during the bitterest days of Reconstruction had the American government practiced such terrible vengeance upon former enemies; not even during the heyday of Wilsonian missionary interventionism had the United States embarked upon so stupendous an effort to reform other nations.

American policy in Germany was determined in the beginning by the desire to visit condign punishment and then to remake the German people and institutions over in the American image. All four occupying powers were pledged to destroy Nazism and help build new democratic governments and institutions, but American authorities outshone all the others in zeal. The United States co-operated with the other powers in limiting German steel production to a low level, destroying armament plants and industries with a direct war potential, and dismantling other plants and sending them to Russia, Poland, and elsewhere as reparations. The result was to limit the German contribution to general European recovery and to aggravate the huge burden of relief for refugees, displaced persons, the homeless, and the unemployed.

By the middle of 1949, when "denazification" was completed, military authorities and German tribunals had punished 1,635 major and some 600,000 minor Nazi offenders. The culmination of Allied vengeance was the trial of some twenty-two high Nazi officials by an International Military Tribunal at Nuremberg from November 21, 1945, to October 1, 1946. The Tribunal acquitted three of the defendants and convicted nineteen, of whom twelve were sentenced to death.[3] The Tribunal tried hard to avoid

[3] The death sentence was executed by hanging on eight defendants. Another, Martin Bormann, was never apprehended and was presumed to be dead; another, Hermann Goering, cheated the hangman by committing suicide.

the appearance of a kangaroo court and observed some of the forms of justice. Even so, the trial violated nearly every tradition of Anglo-American jurisprudence. The conviction and execution of former political officials for planning and waging aggressive war, for example, violated the ancient prohibition against ex post facto laws. The execution of military commanders established the new and impossible doctrine that soldiers might be punished for obeying orders. Above all, the trial of defendants for war crimes and atrocities in a special military court instead of by regular courts established the principle that, as Churchill put it, "the leaders of a nation defeated in war shall be put to death by the victors."

The United States exercised complete control over occupation and reconstruction policies in Japan, vesting all authority in General Douglas MacArthur as the Supreme Commander for the Allied Powers. There was the inevitable purge of thousands of alleged militarists and supporters of aggression and the trial and execution of hundreds of military leaders for war crimes. Most important, some twenty-eight former high officials were prosecuted before an International Military Tribunal for the Far East, for waging aggressive war in violation of international law.[4] But MacArthur and his subordinates came to reform as well as to punish. They sought not only to destroy institutions and customs that had served the Japanese people for thousands of years, but also to create a new political, economic, and social order with roots deep in the American utopian traditions. This new order included renunciation even of defensive war, complete demilitarization, land distribution, an antitrust campaign, and social democracy. It aimed, in short, at nothing less than creation of a perfect state and society. A few "reactionaries" protested; a few "realists" suggested that utter destruction of Japanese power would only serve the interests of the Soviet Union in the Far East. But most Americans hailed the building of this new and better America in the far Pacific.

223.   *The Breakup of the Grand Alliance, 1945–1947*

President Roosevelt worked hard until his death to remove Soviet suspicions and create an atmosphere of mutual trust in which genuine collaboration could develop. There were increasing evidences of Russian bad faith and imperialistic ambitions, and warnings by the American Ambassador in Moscow, W. Averell Harriman, and his assistant, George F. Kennan, that such collaboration was impossible. Even so, President Truman and his new Secretary of State, James F. Byrnes,[5] continued Roosevelt's search for understanding during 1945 and 1946.

Russian action in imposing a Communist government on Rumania, bitter dissension over a government for Poland, and Stalin's accusation that

[4] This "trial" began in Tokyo on June 3, 1946, and ended on April 16, 1948. The Tribunal found all defendants guilty on November 11, 1948, and sentenced seven of them, including two former Premiers of Japan, to death by hanging. The sentences were executed in Tokyo on December 23, 1948.

[5] President Truman appointed Byrnes Secretary of State on June 30, 1945, to succeed Edward R. Stettinius, Jr.

Roosevelt and Churchill conspired during the last weeks of the war to make a separate peace with Germany had raised grave doubts about the permanence of the Grand Alliance even before the German surrender. The rift widened at the San Francisco Conference, and Truman sent Harry Hopkins to Moscow in May 1945 to join Harriman in frank talks with Stalin. The dictator was in an angry mood and accused the American government of insulting the USSR at San Francisco and of ending Lend-Lease aid abruptly after the German surrender in order to apply pressure on the Soviet government. Stalin mellowed in conversation and agreed to admit non-Communist Poles to the Polish government and to meet President Truman and Prime Minister Churchill in July for a full discussion of outstanding problems.

Truman, Stalin, Churchill, and Clement Attlee, soon to be Churchill's successor as head of a new Labour government, assembled in Potsdam, outside shattered Berlin, on July 17, 1945, for the last meeting of the chiefs of state of the Grand Alliance. The conferees quickly agreed to issue a Declaration demanding the immediate surrender of Japan and to establish a Council of Foreign Ministers to prepare peace treaties for Italy and the Balkan states that had joined in Hitler's attack against Russia. There was, however, almost interminable disagreement over the sensitive issues— reparations and implementing the Yalta Declaration on Liberated Countries. Under strong pressure from Truman and Churchill, the Russians finally agreed to permit Anglo-American observers in Rumania, Hungary, Bulgaria, and Finland to move about freely. In return, the American and British leaders approved Polish occupation and administration of German territory east of the Neisse River until a peace conference could settle German boundaries. As for reparations, which a commission had discussed earlier to no avail, Stalin accepted Secretary Byrnes's proposal that each power obtain reparations from its own zone, and that the Western Allies transfer 15 per cent of the capital equipment in their zones to Russia in exchange for food, coal, and other raw materials. Unsettled issues, like Russian demands for virtual control of the Dardanelles and Italy's north African colony of Tripolitania, were deferred for future discussion.

Byrnes and his advisers struggled during the next seventeen months, in the face of mounting obstacles, to reach agreement with the Russians on all outstanding problems—a united policy for Germany, peace treaties for Italy and the central European and Balkan countries, and international agreement for disarmament and control of atomic energy. Byrnes was imbued with Roosevelt's conviction that American co-operation with the Soviet Union was the indispensable cornerstone of postwar peace. He therefore sought to overcome Russian suspicion by concession and compromise. His failure to find understanding prepared the way for a bolder policy of firm support of western Europe and stern resistance to further Soviet aggrandizement.

Germany, that cockpit of Europe, was the source of greatest potential conflict. In order to destroy the German threat to European security and world peace, Roosevelt had envisaged and seemingly won Stalin's cordial support for united action in demilitarizing and thus neutralizing Germany for years to come. Byrnes urged the Russians at London in September 1945 and again at Moscow in the following December to join in a twenty-five-year alliance to prevent the resurgence of German militarism. When

Truman, Stalin, and the British and French Foreign Ministers approved, Byrnes hopefully prepared the treaty, only to encounter insuperable Russian opposition in the spring of 1946. Byrnes's successor, George C. Marshall, raised the proposal again in April 1947 and once more encountered Soviet opposition. By the time that the Grand Alliance had become permanently disrupted in the spring of 1947, Russian policy was clear. It was to keep Germany divided until the entire nation came under Soviet control.

Byrnes also worked with unflagging zeal on the peripheral issues of peace treaties for Hitler's erstwhile junior partners. The Russians stubbornly refused to approve an Austrian treaty, as such action would have compelled them to withdraw from a vital outpost in central Europe and destroyed their excuse for retaining troops in Hungary and Rumania. On the other hand, Byrnes finally obtained peace treaties for Italy, Hungary, Rumania, and Bulgaria, signed at Paris on February 10, 1947. They confirmed western Allied supremacy in Italy and North Africa and Soviet predominance in Hungary and the Balkans. It was perhaps the only settlement possible, but it ended with American recognition of Russian control of southeastern Europe and marked the beginning of the "sovietization" of that area.

On the other overshadowing issue of 1945–6—international disarmament and control of atomic energy—American leaders formulated a new plan to relieve the world's anxiety over atomic warfare and lay the foundations for future peace. With sole possession of atomic bombs from 1945 until the Russians detonated their first in the summer of 1949, Americans might have pursued "atomic imperialism," that is, policies of threat and coercion. Instead, they came forward with what was easily the most revolutionary disarmament proposal up to that time—the plan submitted to the United Nations Atomic Energy Commission by Bernard M. Baruch on June 14, 1946. Drafted mainly by Dean G. Acheson and David E. Lilienthal, the Baruch plan called for an International Atomic Development Authority. It would eventually own, control, and operate all uranium and thorium mines and production facilities and alone conduct research in atomic explosives. The Authority might permit use of atomic energy for peaceful purposes, but it would have full power, unrestrained by any veto, of inspection and punishment of violators of the international statute controlling atomic energy.

It was a breath-taking proposal, but it was more than the Russians believed they could safely approve. They correctly perceived that the Authority would be controlled by the United States and its friends. They therefore countered with a proposal simply to outlaw manufacture and use of the atomic bomb and to vest enforcement in the Security Council, where they might veto action against violators of the agreement. The Russians subsequently made important concessions by accepting unlimited international inspection, but they would never yield the power to veto punishment of violators. The American government was unwilling to accept any compromise that impaired the principle of effective international control; it rejected the Soviet overtures and in effect ended all serious hopes for atomic disarmament.

The failure of the Baruch plan merely underscored the larger failure of the United States and the Soviet Union to find a basis for common action

CENTRAL
AND EASTERN
EUROPE

TERRITORIAL CHANGES
1939-1947

300 MILES

NORTH CAPE

Petsamo

Murmansk

WHITE SEA

NORWAY

SWEDEN

FINLAND

GULF OF BOTHNIA

Oslo

Helsinki

LAKE LADOGA

PORKKALA-UDD
(LEASED TO
U.S.S.R.)

GULF OF FINLAND

Tallinn

Leningrad

Stockholm

ESTONIA

BALTIC SEA

S O V I E T

DENMARK

Riga

LATVIA

Moscow

Copen-
hagen

FORMER GERMAN
TERRITORY
ADMINISTERED
BY U.S.S.R.
AND POLAND

LITHUANIA

Gdansk
(DANZIG)

Kaunas

Vilna

ANNEXED BY THE
SOVIET UNION

POMERANIA

EAST
PRUSSIA

Minsk

WEST
(ALLIED
OCC.)

Szczecin
(STETTIN)

POLAND

Berlin

GERMANY

EAST
(U.S.S.R.
OCC.)

Warsaw

EASTERN
POLAND

Bonn

Wrocław
(BRESLAU)

GERMANY AND
AUSTRIA DIVIDED
AND OCCUPIED

Prague

Cracow

Kiev

BERLIN AND
VIENNA JOINTLY
OCCUPIED

CZECHOSLOVAKIA

U N I O N

(U.S.S.R.
OCC.)

Bratislava

Vienna

BRIDGE-
HEAD

SWITZ.

AUSTRIA

Budapest

SUB-
CARPATHIAN
RUTHENIA

NORTHERN
BUKOVINA

BESSARABIA

(ALLIED
OCC.)

HUNGARY

TRANSYLVANIA

Odessa

Trieste

VENEZIA
GIULIA

RUMANIA

FREE
TERRITORY
OF TRIESTE

ANNEXED
BY
YUGOSLAVIA

Belgrade

Bucharest

DOBRUJA

BLACK
SEA

Zara
(CEDED
TO YUGO.)

YUGOSLAVIA

Rome

LAGOSTA
IS.

Sofia

BULGARIA

ANNEXED BY
BULGARIA

ITALY

ALBANIA

Tirana

Istanbul

(TURK.)

SASENO
I.
(CEDED TO
ALBANIA)

TURKEY

GREECE

SICILY

Athens

TRM

on Germany, general disarmament, and creation of armed forces for the United Nations. Perhaps the Russians would have been more co-operative had the United States extended material aid for civilian reconstruction after the termination of Lend-Lease. Perhaps the American leaders confirmed Russian suspicions that the United States wanted to dominate the world by moving too boldly and quickly on disarmament. On the other hand, it does seem fair to say that the Russian leaders, out of ignorance, isolation, a distorted view of the nature of international politics, or desire to extend their own power, rejected American friendship and wrecked the world's best hopes for a stable peace.

224. *The Chinese Tragedy*

The Chinese Communist victory of 1949 upset the balance of power in the world and destroyed all American hopes for peace and stability in the Far East. It also had a supremely ironic quality. The American government had sought for half a century to maintain Chinese independence and give the Chinese what it regarded as the benefits of western civilization, democracy, and Christianity. The United States, among all the major powers in the Far East, had been the least imperialistic and self-seeking, and had defended Chinese integrity even to the point of a long and bloody war with Japan. Yet only five years after the Japanese surrender the American people found themselves at war with a Chinese government that hated and reviled them as China's most dangerous enemies. The dimensions of this tragedy are apparent, but the causes are still obscure.

The stage was set for the Communist triumph during the period 1941 to 1945. By the end of 1941 the Nationalist government at Chungking headed by Chiang Kai-shek was exhausted and nearly fatally weakened after four years of seemingly hopeless resistance to the Japanese. It managed to survive after 1941 only because the Japanese concluded that its final destruction was not worth the effort. The American government did its best to keep China in the war. The extension of a half-billion-dollar credit in 1942, the sending of supplies by air over the treacherous Himalayan Hump, and the dispatch of military advisers to Chungking were all manifestations of American good will. But they were totally inadequate to the main task of strengthening and supplying the Chinese armies. Allied armies in Burma finally broke the siege of China and opened a supply route from India to Kunming in early 1945. But the war was nearly over by this time, and the Nationalist government had been terribly weakened.

Meanwhile, Roosevelt and his advisers had been maturing plans to strengthen China after the war and establish her as a great power even while lifeblood drained from the Chungking regime. The President won Churchill's and Stalin's seeming approval, at Cairo and Teheran, of the Cairo Declaration, issued on December 1, 1943. It promised the return of Manchuria and Formosa to China. The President won a permanent seat on the Security Council for China and Stalin's promise of support for the Nationalist government at Yalta in early 1945. These were great plans but dangerous ones, unless the Soviets honored their promises and the United States was prepared to support and strengthen the Nationalists. Yet even while the leaders talked at Yalta, China stood on the verge of a civil war. Its outcome would make China a great power, to be sure, but allied with the Soviet Union and dedicated to the destruction of American influence in the Far East.

Chiang Kai-shek all through the war faced not only the outward Japanese menace but also the internal peril of Communist subversion and conquest. The Chinese Communists, driven out of southern China in 1934–35, had fought their way to Yenan, in the Shensi Province in northwestern China. There they established a precarious government, harassed but never conquered by the Nationalist forces. The Communists grew stronger after the Japanese invasion in 1937 and rejected Chiang's appeals that they submit to the central government and join in common defense of the motherland. The Communists were so strong by the beginning of 1944, in fact, that Chiang had diverted 400,000 of his best troops in order to contain the threatened Communist tide.

At this point the Allied need for manpower in Burma and the beginning of a new Japanese offensive in China caused the American government to try to unify the Chinese forces. Roosevelt was reassured by Stalin and Molotov that Russia had no interest in controlling China and that, in any event, Chinese Communists were not good Communists. The President then sent Vice President Wallace to Chungking in June 1944. Wallace urged Chiang to come to terms with the Communists so that all Chinese troops could combine against the common enemy. A short time later Roosevent sent General Patrick J. Hurley as his personal representative to Chiang. Hurley went by way of Moscow and learned from Molotov that the Kremlin was not interested in or responsible for the Chinese comrades and would take no part in the civil war.

But the more American leaders urged Chiang to come to agreement with his enemies, the more stubbornly did he insist that Chinese Communists were revolutionaries bent upon domination of China. And the more Chiang refused to approve unification upon any basis except the military submission of Yenan, the stronger the conviction grew in American circles that Chiang and his government were unreasonable, corrupt, incompetent, and unrepresentative of the Chinese people. Chiang did allow American newspaper reporters and official observers to go to Yenan in the spring of 1944. The naive reporters sent back glowing accounts of the Communists, while American Foreign Service officers in Yenan confirmed the newsmen's reports that the Communists were primarily agrarian reformers, extraordinarily efficient, and above all devoted to the cause of democracy in China. At the same time, these observers emphasized the obvious shortcomings of the Chungking regime so heavily that "The main effect of their reporting was . . . to weaken faith in the power of the Generalissimo [Chiang] and his group to govern China." [6]

A rational American policy toward China would have been difficult at best as the showdown between the Communists and Nationalists approached in 1945. It was, however, virtually impossible because of the incredibly irresponsible way that the Washington Administration was then doing business in China. Its two chief officials in that country—General

[6] Herbert Feis, *The China Tangle* (Princeton, 1953), p. 259.

Hurley, who became Ambassador in December 1944, and General Albert C. Wedemeyer, who succeeded General Joseph W. Stilwell as Chiang's Chief of Staff and commander of American forces in China in October 1944—tried hard to work with Chiang and mature a program of effective support of the Nationalists. The Foreign Service experts in China, on the other hand, argued that the Nationalist government was hopelessly corrupt and tyran- nical, and that the Communists would prevail because they were genuinely representative of the people. They appealed over Hurley's head to Wash- ington, urging that the United States should either compel Chiang to come to terms with the Communists or else, if he refused, join hands with the Yenan regime.

When Roosevelt supported Hurley at a showdown meeting in Wash- ington in March 1945, American policy toward China became reasonably clear. The United States would continue to support Chiang but would also seek to arrest the civil war by bringing the Nationalists and Communists together in some coalition government. The decision had Hurley's cordial support, for the Ambassador, like most Americans, was convinced that Russia would not intervene in China, and that the Chinese Communists were neither genuine Communists nor allied with Moscow.[7]

Hurley therefore set more intensively to the task of mediation upon his return to Chungking in May 1945. In Moscow Harry Hopkins received from Stalin an unequivocal pledge of support for the Nationalist government. Then the war in the Pacific suddenly ended, and the American government had to redefine its policy. It quickly came to Chiang Kai-shek's assistance in the first task ahead—accepting the surrender of Japanese forces and occupying key Chinese ports and cities before the Communists could occupy them. Thus, the American Army Air Forces moved three Chinese armies from the interior to eastern and northern provinces during Septem- ber and October 1945. The United States Navy later transported an addi- tional 400,000 Nationalist troops to Manchurian ports. Moreover, some 55,000 American marines occupied strategic cities like Tsingtao, Tientsin, and Peiping until the Nationalist troops could take over. By the end of 1945, therefore, American and Chinese troops had accepted the surrender of Japanese forces everywhere in China but Manchuria, and Chiang controlled the important cities of the southern and eastern provinces and of Man- churia.

Even so, the situation was fraught with danger. The Chinese Com- munists were powerfully entrenched in many parts of northern China and Manchuria and were secretly receiving huge quantities of former Japanese arms from Russian occupation forces in Manchuria. The Nationalist armies were fearfully overextended, while Chiang's political agents were often inexperienced, inefficient, and corrupt. Moreover, before the Russians with- drew from Manchuria in February 1946, they stripped that province of some $2,000,000,000 worth of industrial and railroad equipment, thus leaving the area useless to assist in the rebuilding of China. Worst of all, it

---

[7] Hurley's views were "confirmed" in Moscow by Stalin and Molotov in April 1945. It is only fair to add, however, that the American Ambassador, W. Averell Harriman, and his assistant, George F. Kennan, were not deceived by Stalin's assurances and warned the State Department against taking them seriously.

was obvious that China stood on the brink of full-scale civil war, the out-come of which might well decide the fate of Asia.

Clearly, this was a crucial moment of decision in Washington. Should the United States occupy China and Manchuria, at least with token forces, and give full material assistance to the Nationalists in their war against Yenan? Should it seek to halt the civil war through mediation and threaten to withdraw support if Chiang refused to co-operate? Or should it with-draw from China altogether and let the two opposing forces fight it out? These were the choices confronting American leaders in the late autumn of 1945.

The final decision was not adopted because of any lack of reliable in-formation. General Wedemeyer warned in a series of messages in late November that the task of unifying and pacifying China was too great for Chiang and his generally incompetent government to accomplish. Numer-ous other military observers confirmed Wedemeyer's analysis and agreed that abandoning Chiang meant abandoning China to the Communists. And yet there was no disposition in Washington or the country at large to give wholehearted support to Chiang's allegedly reactionary, inefficient, and corrupt regime in a war against what many thought was the honest, effi-cient, and democratic Communist regime. In fact, the administration's desire to stay out of the civil war enjoyed almost universal support in the United States.

Thus supported, the Washington leaders made their decision in late November and early December 1945. It was to send General Marshall to China to press for a truce and conduct mediation looking toward establish-ment of a coalition government in which both the Kuomintang, or Na-tionalist, and Communist parties would compete peacefully for power. Marshall received instructions on December 9, and the President explained the policy to the world six days later.

Marshall arrived in Chungking at the end of December 1945 and set to work at once to find a formula for peace and unity. It seemed for several months that he might succeed, as the opposing groups approved a cease-fire and a plan for governmental reorganization. Actually, Marshall merely delayed the inevitable full-scale war—inevitable because neither side would trust the other or yield on essential points—during a time when de-lay worked greatly to the advantage of the Communists. He abandoned his mission in January 1947 with a blast at Nationalist reactionaries and Communists alike, declaring that the hope of Chinese salvation lay with a liberal group who were without power and prestige in the Kuomintang.

Marshall returned to Washington to become Secretary of State, and the war in China began in earnest in January 1947. The Nationalists were well equipped [8] and greatly superior in numbers at the outset. But the Com-munist forces had the edge in training, discipline, and leadership, and the advantage of interior lines of communication, while the Nationalist com-manders were content to occupy isolated cities and seemed totally unable to wage aggressive campaigns. The tide was beginning to turn by mid-

[8] They had obtained the arms and equipment of some 1,235,000 Japanese soldiers and received some $700,000,000 worth of Lend-Lease supplies, in addition to large quantities of surplus military equipment, from the United States in 1945–6.

1947. Defeatism swept through the Nationalist armies, and Chiang's government at Nanking lost further popular support through its failure to
curb inflation, suppress war lords and bandits, and govern competently.

Resumption of the civil war forced the Washington government to
face a new situation. American leaders were convinced that the Nationalist
armies were adequately equipped, and that the Washington government
could do nothing more without running heavy risks of full-scale participation. Hence they simply withdrew all military forces, except a small
contingent of marines at Tsingtao, and refused to extend any large new
assistance to Chiang in 1947. However, President Truman did send General
Wedemeyer back to China in July to investigate and recommend. The
General explained the dangers of the Chinese situation in a report on
September 19, 1947. While admitting that "reactionary leadership, repression and corruption" had caused the people to lose faith in Chiang's
government, he held out the hope of genuine reform, provided that the
United States gave effective moral and material support to Nanking.
Wedemeyer then proceeded to say what others before him had either not
understood or had not had the courage to say: Communist control of
China would imperil American interests and peace in the Far East, because Chinese Communists were agents of Soviet expansion and domination in that area. The situation, Wedemeyer went on, was far from hopeless.
The United States should insist that the United Nations take control of
Manchuria to prevent that province from falling into the Soviet orbit. It
should also inaugurate a large program of "moral, advisory, and material"
assistance to China "to protect United States strategic interests against
militant forces which now threaten them."

In retrospect we can see that Wedemeyer offered the only possible
means of stemming the Communist tide in the Far East. Even such action
might not have sufficed. Indeed, most historians agree that the Nationalist
government was doomed, that only full-scale American military participation could have averted a Communist victory, and that the American people would not have tolerated sending large ground forces to China. Yet these
are unproved hypotheses. The administration not only refused to sanction
Wedemeyer's report but kept it secret until the Communists had driven
Chiang from the Chinese mainland, failing even to try to rally the American people to the peril of a Chinese Communist victory.

Indeed, the President and his advisers seemed overborne by a sense of
helplessness and despair. Congress appropriated $400,000,000 for aid to
China in April 1948 at Truman's request,[9] it is true; but in asking for this
piddling amount, only $125,000,000 of which could be spent for military
supplies, Secretary Marshall declared that there was nothing the United
States could do to "make the present Chinese Government capable of re-
establishing and then maintaining its control throughout all of China."
And Congress, in granting this assistance, made it plain that it assumed no
responsibility for the Nationalist regime.

Of course the small assistance under the China Aid Act of 1948 was too

wwwwwwwwwwwwww

[9] Actually, the President asked for $570,000,000 for aid to China over a fifteen-
month period.

little too late. The Communists captured Mukden in October 1948 and then swept on to victory with incredible speed, assisted by the rapid disintegration of the Nationalist government and armies. The Communists crossed the Yangtze in April 1949 and quickly captured Hankow, Shanghai, Canton, and other southern ports and cities. Chiang retired to Chungking in October and fled by air with the remnants of his government to Formosa in December. Meanwhile, Mao Tse-tung and Chou En-lai had established the People's Republic of China at Peking, declared their friendship for the USSR, and begun an intensive campaign to drive American officials, missionaries, and citizens from China and rally Asiatics in a great crusade to end American influence in the Far East.

225. *The Decline of the Good Neighbor Policy*

Evidences of the success of the Good Neighbor policy came within a few days after the Japanese struck at Pearl Harbor, as twelve Latin American governments either declared war upon, or broke diplomatic relations with, the Axis. "We were now to gather the fruits of patient cultivation at the conferences of Montevideo, Buenos Aires, Lima, Panama, and Havana," Hull afterward wrote, "and of our innumerable measures to apply and solidify the doctrine of the Good Neighbor." [10]

Two days after Pearl Harbor the State Department invited the other American republics to send delegates to Rio de Janeiro in January 1942 to consider joint action. Argentine spokesmen, more friendly to Germany than to the United States, raised sullen opposition. But Sumner Welles, chief of the American delegation at Rio, won approval of a resolution calling upon the American republics to break with the Axis and co-operate with their northern neighbor. All Latin American governments that had not already taken the step, except Argentina and Chile, either severed relations with or declared war upon the Axis powers soon afterward. [11]

The American republics joined hands in genuine collaboration as the war progressed. Brazil participated in the campaign against German U-boats, provided airfields for an "air ferry" to Africa, and sent a division to the Italian front. [12] Most other Latin American countries did what they could, by sending vital raw materials, offering air bases, and joining with American agents to root out Axis influences. The one important exception and the source of greatest danger was Argentina. Her leaders not only refused to break with the Axis but also maintained intimate relations with Nazi agents and were openly sympathetic to the German cause. A group of army officers seized control of the Buenos Aires government in June 1943 and launched a campaign to destroy the democratic opposition. A new President, General Edelmiro Farrell, consequently came to power in Febru-

---

[10] Cordell Hull, *The Memoirs of Cordell Hull*, 2 vols. (New York, 1948), II, p. 1139.

[11] Chile broke relations in January 1943; Argentina, in January 1944.

[12] Because of its large assistance, Brazil received the lion's share—$331,651,000 out of a total of $459,422,000—of American Lend-Lease aid to Latin America.

ary 1944, and the Washington government undertook to persuade the other American republics to withhold recognition and several months later froze Argentina's gold assets in the United States.

This action raised fears in Latin America that the United States would take even stronger unilateral measures. Hence the State Department called a special conference of the American states at war to meet in Mexico City in February 1945. The delegates first invited Argentina to return to the inter-American fold. Then they approved the Act of Chapultepec on March 3. It completed the mutualization of the Monroe Doctrine by declaring that any attack upon the territory or sovereignty of one American state would be met by the combined forces of all of them. The Argentine government soon afterward declared war on Germany and Japan, ratified the act of Chapultepec, and received the diplomatic recognition of the United States.

For a brief time the breach appeared healed, especially when the American delegation at the San Francisco Conference joined Latin American representatives in winning membership in the United Nations for Argentina. Actually, however, the American government was already hard at work on daring new stratagems. The State Department had good reason to distrust the Farrell government in Buenos Aires. It had suppressed free speech, opposition parties, and the press. The Washington government, however, did more than stand by in silent disapproval; it went so far as to attempt to destroy the militaristic regime. Its chief agent was Spruille Braden, American Ambassador in Buenos Aires. He worked secretly with leaders of the democratic opposition. More important, in speeches and public statements he virtually called upon *Argentinos* to change their government as the price for retaining American friendship.

The leader of the anti-democratic forces, Colonel Juan D. Perón, answered Braden's challenge by demanding a national election and by announcing on December 14, 1945, that he would be a candidate for the presidency. Then the State Department issued a so-called Argentine Blue Book on February 12, 1946, just two weeks before the election. It accused the militaristic clique of "aid to the enemy, deliberate misrepresentation and deception in promises of hemispheric cooperation, subversive activity against neighboring republics, and [forming] a vicious partnership of Nazi and native totalitarian forces." American faith in Argentina could be restored, the Blue Book warned, only when the Argentine people were represented by a government that commanded "full faith and confidence at home and abroad."

This intervention in the political affairs of a sovereign, suspicious, and proud people was stern but ill-fated diplomacy. In what was probably a fair election, *Argentinos* gave a large majority to Perón and a clear answer to their northern neighbor. The State Department had no alternative but to recall Braden and accept the verdict. At the same time, it refused to cooperate with the movement then under way to construct a regional defense association and declared that the United States would wait for evidences of the good faith of the new Perón government. Relations between the United States and Argentina remained tense enough during the remainder of 1946 to imperil the entire structure of hemispheric unity. Most Latin American governments disliked the Perón regime; but for obvious reasons they disliked American intervention in Argentine affairs even more. In the face of mounting criticism at home and in Latin America, President Truman and Secretary Marshall agreed that the now pointless feud must end. The President duly announced on June 3, 1947, that his government was ready to begin discussions looking toward a hemispheric defense pact.

In response, delegates from all twenty-one American republics gathered at Rio de Janeiro on August 15, 1947, to consider enforcement machinery for the Act of Chapultepec. What emerged was the Inter-American Treaty of Reciprocal Assistance, signed in the Brazilian capital on September 2, 1947. It obligated all signatories, when two thirds of the member states so voted, to sever diplomatic and economic relations with any internal or external violator of the Act of Chapultepec, but no party to the treaty would be required to use its armed forces without its consent. The treaty also specified a broad security zone around the North and South American continents, including Greenland and Alaska, and declared that an attack anywhere within this zone would constitute an attack against all American republics.

Moreover, a ninth Inter-American Conference assembled at Bogotá from March 30 to May 2, 1948, to reorganize the political machinery of the hemispheric system. It drafted a charter for an Organization of American States giving full constitutional status to the inter-American system.[13] Its Pact of Bogotá provided for the peaceful settlement of disputes. Finally, its agreement on economic co-operation pledged all signatories to treat foreign capital fairly and not to expropriate foreign-owned property without just compensation.

The mutual defense and political structures erected at Mexico City, Rio, and Bogotá were certainly signs that the Good Neighbor policy had been thoroughly mutualized. Even so, they provided more form than substance, for hemispheric co-operation actually declined in practice from 1945 to 1953. For one thing, the postwar era was a time of severe economic dislocation in Latin America, caused mainly by the region's inability to sell as much to the United States as it wished to buy, and by failure of American investors to help remedy the large "dollar gap" that threatened to disrupt inter-American trade. The Washington government, burdened by its huge financial commitments to Europe, gave scant attention to this problem. For another, the postwar era was a time of political unrest in Latin America unprecedented since the depression, as leaders of the downtrodden and illiterate masses and representatives of the privileged classes, usually military cliques, contended for power. Perhaps the chief cause of the decline of the Good Neighbor policy after 1945 was the fact that Latin America ceased to be of prime importance to the United States. The assumption that it was had been the cornerstone of American foreign policy and almost a popular obsession in the 1930's, supported alike by internationalists and isolationists. As the United States as-

[13] The charter established three representative bodies within the Organization— the Inter-American Conference, the Meeting of Consultation of Foreign Ministers, and the Council of the Organization—and constituted the Pan-American Union in Washington as its permanent secretariat.

sumed large new responsibilities after 1945, however, the direction of foreign policy and popular interest inevitably shifted to Europe and Asia, and this shift provoked bitter criticism south of the border.

Huge American purchases of raw materials following the outbreak of the Korean War momentarily solved Latin America's economic problems, it is true. Small amounts of American aid under the Mutual Security Act made possible the extension of some technical assistance. And the Export-Import and World banks furnished slight funds for internal development. Even so, Latin American economic, political, and social institutions remained so fundamentally unstable by 1952 that the Good Neighbor policy of superficial political and military co-operation would no longer suffice to preserve the peace of the hemisphere.

226. *Beginnings of Containment: The Truman Doctrine*

A change in American foreign policy occurred in the spring of 1947 that ranks in importance with the promulgation of the Monroe Doctrine and the decisions to enter the two world wars. The Truman administration, after struggling for nearly two years to find accommodation with Russia, undertook a bold program aimed at nothing less than halting further Soviet expansion in the Near East and Europe. The idea of containing Soviet expansion did not stem merely from irritation and disappointment over Russian behavior. It was a radical new departure grounded upon certain harsh assumptions and devised to meet the specific threat of Soviet control of the eastern Mediterranean.

Many leaders in the United States and Great Britain had abandoned the assumptions of collaboration with the Russians by the time that a policy of containment was put into effect. It is not possible to surmise from President Truman's memoirs precisely when he concluded that fruitful collaboration with Russia was impossible. Certainly he never fully shared Roosevelt's illusions about the chances of successful co-operation; he was fully aware of the danger of Soviet expansion in the Near East and Greece as early as January 1946. Admiral Leahy and Secretary Forrestal argued at this early date for the re-establishment of American naval power in the eastern Mediterranean in order to thwart Russian expansion in that area. Former Prime Minister Churchill warned the free world of the peril of Soviet aggression in his celebrated "iron curtain" speech at Fulton, Missouri, on March 5, 1946. Ambassador W. Averell Harriman admonished the State Department of Soviet plans and ambitions from his lonely outpost in Moscow.

However, it was George F. Kennan, Counselor of the American Embassy in Moscow, who first fully and frankly elaborated the assumptions behind the policy of containment. Stalin, on February 9, 1946, declared that international peace was impossible "under the present capitalist development of world economy" and called upon the Russian people to prepare for "any eventuality." This prompted Kennan to draft an eight-thousand-word dispatch to the State Department to clarify the character, tactics, motivation, and ambitions of the Soviet state and the international Communist movement. After exploring the historical background of

Russian distrust of the West, Kennan pointed up the immediate danger: "We have here a political force committed fanatically to the belief that with the U.S. there can be no permanent *modus vivendi*, that it is desirable and necessary that the internal harmony of our society be disrupted, our traditional way of life be destroyed, the international authority of our state be broken, if Soviet power is to be secure." [14]

If it were true, as Kennan and others asserted, that the leaders of the Soviet Union and its adherents throughout the world believed that Communism and democracy were at war with each other, and were at work to promote the violent overthrow of non-Communist governments, then how could the American government and people best meet the threat of Soviet imperialism and subversion? Again it was Kennan who best summarized what numerous other Americans were thinking in early 1947. He elaborated the doctrine of containment in an anonymous article in the July 1947 issue of *Foreign Affairs*. The United States could live at peace with the Soviet Union only by building its own strength and by erecting effective counterweights in order to contain Communist power at least in Europe. "It is clear," he continued, "that the main element of any United States policy toward the Soviet Union must be that of a long-term, patient but firm and vigilant containment of Russian expansive tendencies. . . . To avoid destruction the United States need only measure up to its own best traditions and prove itself worthy of preservation as a great nation."

Truman and his new Secretary of State, George C. Marshall,[15] were suddenly impelled toward an open policy of containment in the late winter of 1946–7 by the threat of Soviet expansion in the eastern Mediterranean and the Middle East. The Russians had attempted during the war to create a puppet regime in the Iranian province of Azerbaijan, withdrawing their troops early in 1946 only after the State Department protested sharply and Truman sent "a blunt message" to Stalin. The Russian threat to Iran had by no means passed by early 1947. Even more threatening was extraordinary Russian pressure on Turkey for cession of certain territory and the right to build naval bases in the Bosporus. The Soviet Foreign Office pressed these demands on the Ankara government from 1945 to 1947, while Russian propaganda warned of the dire consequences if Turkey refused to yield. In brief, the Communist leaders seemed determined to achieve an historic Russian objective—control of the Straits and the eastern Mediterranean.

Another dire threat was the possibility that Communist-Soviet forces would capture Greece, thus outflanking Turkey and imperiling the entire Middle East. The British had supported a rightist Greek government from late 1944 to early 1947 in a protracted and bloody effort to suppress a Communist-led faction known as the EAM. The British Ambassador informed Washington on February 24, 1947, that Great Britain could no longer bear the burden of resisting Communist expansion in the eastern Mediterranean and would soon have to withdraw entirely from Greece. This declaration marked the end of historic British supremacy in one of the most strategic areas in the world, and the President's response marked a fateful turning point in American foreign policy. He saw the implications

[14] Quoted in Walter Millis (ed.), *The Forrestal Diaries* (New York, 1951), pp. 138–9.
[15] President Truman appointed Marshall Secretary of State on January 7, 1947.

of inaction clearly enough: "If Greece was lost, Turkey would become an untenable outpost in a sea of Communism. Similarly, if Turkey yielded to Soviet demands, the position of Greece would be extremely endangered." [16] After discussions with Congressional leaders he went to Capitol Hill on March 12 to ask for $400,000,000 for military assistance to Greece and Turkey. Even more important was his bold enunciation of the so-called Truman doctrine, which went far beyond Kennan's concept of containment: "I believe that it must be the foreign policy of the United States to support free peoples who are resisting attempted subjugation by armed minorities or by outside pressures. . . . The free peoples of the world look to us for support in maintaining their freedoms. If we falter in our leadership, we may endanger the peace of the world—and we shall surely endanger the welfare of our own Nation."

The meaning of this pronouncement was clear and shocking to the American people, then inadequately prepared to assume such enormous new responsibilities in Europe and the Near East. But the administration stood firm against a barrage of charges that it was supporting British imperialism and needlessly provoking the Soviet Union. And with the crucial help of Senator Arthur Vandenberg of Michigan, chairman of the Senate foreign relations committee, the President won the support of a Republican Congress for his Greek-Turkish Aid bill in May 1947. Thus, as one writer has expressed it, "Congress took the plunge and, in taking it, confirmed a new departure in American foreign policy. The United States served notice that henceforward, to deny further strategic advantages to Russia, it would act to bolster up nations and governments resisting Soviet pressure and penetration." [17]

The United States did not falter during the following years in its effort to save Greece from Communist domination and strengthen the Turkish bastion on the Soviet southern flank. All told, the Washington government spent some $659,000,000 under the Greek-Turkish aid program from 1947 to 1950. The American task in Turkey was quickly and inexpensively accomplished, as the Turkish government was relatively honest and undisturbed by internal warfare. By giving some $350,000,000 in aid from 1947 to 1953, the United States helped the Turks to achieve economic stability and modernize their sizable army, without the slightest show of friction on either side.

The Greek problem, on the other hand, proved to be immensely difficult. The American government found itself in the embarrassing position of defending democracy in Greece by supporting a reactionary government that refused to do anything effective about the basic economic and social evils that stirred the masses to revolt. In any event, a military mission and enormous military supplies from the United States enabled a reorganized Greek army to undertake a determined campaign to end the civil war. It cleared the Peloponnesus of guerrillas and then turned northward toward the EAM stronghold. Success was assured when Yugoslavia broke with the Soviet bloc in 1948 and abandoned support of the Greek Communists in the

[16] *Memoirs by Harry S. Truman*, II, p. 100.

[17] John C. Campbell *et al.*, *The United States in World Affairs, 1947–1948* (New York, 1948), p. 48.

summer of 1949. The long civil war was over by October 1949, and the Greek people could turn to urgent problems of domestic reconstruction.

Thus the Truman Doctrine accomplished its first major objectives. American aid to Turkey won a powerful ally on Russia's southern flank and prevented Russian power from bursting into the eastern Mediterranean or threatening the Middle East. American aid to Greece saved that country from certain Communist conquest and at least gave the Greeks an opportunity to solve their internal problems in their own way.

227. To Save Western Europe: The Marshall Plan

As winter turned into spring in 1947 there were alarming signs that the Greco-Turkish situation was merely a reflection of a more momentous crisis that threatened all of western Europe. In a varying degree Britain, France, Italy, and other nations were staggering under nearly impossible burdens of reconstruction, careening from one economic crisis to another, and facing violent social upheaval if they failed to accomplish miracles of recovery. The United States had kept western Europe from near starvation and economic collapse since the war's end by an outlay of some $11,000,-000,000 in UNRRA aid, loans, credits, and assistance of various kinds. But this huge outpouring had mainly helped Europeans to find dollars for food, clothing, and other elementary necessities, not to build a sound recovery. The situation grew worse as the months passed in 1947, until it was clear that cessation of large-scale American aid might mean the triumph of Communism in France and Italy.

Leaders in Washington knew the problem in all its frightening dimensions. The Policy Planning Staff of the State Department, headed by Kennan, was also hard at work to devise a radical remedy. Undersecretary of State Dean Acheson, in a speech at Cleveland, Mississippi, on May 8, 1947, gave first public indication of its thinking. It was necessary, Acheson said, to strengthen governments that were "seeking to preserve their independence and democratic institutions and human freedoms against totalitarian pressures, either internal or external." Then, in an address at Harvard University on June 5, Secretary Marshall pointed up the solution. The European governments should work out a comprehensive program and tell America how it might best help in achieving lasting recovery. "Any government willing to assist in the task of reconstruction," he promised, "will find full co-operation on the part of the United States."

The Secretary envisaged nothing less than the rebuilding of the western European economy in order to provide a more stable social order. Indeed, he, Kennan, and others in the State Department thought that there was a chance that Russia might also be willing to co-operate in a gigantic European effort. Nothing but good could come of such an enterprise, they believed.

They were willing to run the risk that Russian co-operation would wreck the plan in Congress. But they must have realized that this danger was exceedingly remote. The Russians had been consolidating their economic control over eastern Europe since 1945. They were not likely to relinquish this control. Moreover, they had revealed, only two months before Marshall's speech, their determination to prevent solution of Europe's most urgent problem, unification and economic rehabilitation of Germany. Issuing an invitation to all European nations to join in a common effort must have seemed safe enough to men in Washington.

In any event, the showdown came soon after Marshall made his memorable address, when the British, French, and Russian Foreign Ministers met in Paris on June 27, 1947, to consider a proper reply. The British and French Ministers, Ernest Bevin and Georges Bidault, voiced the overwhelming enthusiasm and gratitude of western Europe, while Molotov expressed the sullen opposition of the Communist bloc and left the meeting when he could not disrupt it. Representatives from Britain, France, Italy, Turkey, and the other non-Communist nations of Europe met in Paris on July 12 and appointed a Committee of European Economic Cooperation. It submitted a master recovery plan two months later calling for $22,400,-000,000 in assistance and loans from the United States. By the autumn of 1947, therefore, the lines were drawn for "a struggle which was to be waged with weapons of politics and propaganda as well as with loans, grants and trade agreements." [18] That struggle was already particularly acute in France and Italy. Communists, expelled from coalition Cabinets early in the spring, were now working hard to destroy moderate governments by accusing them of abetting American imperialism and building up Germany in order to gain American dollars.

Meanwhile, lines were also being drawn in the United States between the champions of the European Recovery Program (ERP), as the Marshall Plan was called, and an incongruous company of opponents. Debate began in earnest when the President submitted the draft of an Economic Cooperation bill on December 19, 1947, calling for $17,000,-000,000 in aid during the next four years. Opponents of the measure, fatally handicapped by Communist opposition to it, were soon overwhelmed by a coalition that included important farm organizations, the AF of L and CIO, the NAM, and numerous other pressure groups. Any doubts that Congress would approve the Economic Cooperation bill were ended when a Communist minority in Czechoslovakia seized control in February 1948 and destroyed a democracy for which millions of Americans felt strong emotional attachment.

The main burden of leadership in Congress fell upon Senator Vandenberg. He insisted upon eliminating authorization of the full commitment and upon reducing the first appropriation from $6,800,000,000 for the first fifteen months to $5,300,000,000 for the first twelve months. After the hearings had ended, Vandenberg opened debate in the Senate on March 1, 1948, with an address that brought senators and spectators to their feet in applause. "The greatest nation on earth either justifies or surrenders its leadership," he declared. "We must choose. . . . The iron curtain must not come to the rims of the Atlantic either by aggression or by default."

The Senate approved the bill by a huge majority on March 13. Then, while the House dallied, the President and Secretary of State began a public campaign to point up the dangers of Soviet expansion and the immediate menace of a Communist victory in Italy if the House did not act before the

wwwwwwwwwwww

[18] J. C. Campbell *et al.*, *The United States in World Affairs, 1947–1948*, p. 444.

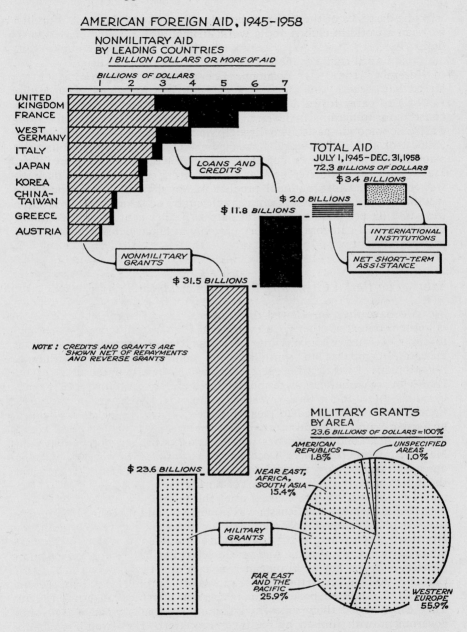

AMERICAN FOREIGN AID, 1945-1958

Italian elections on April 18. The popular pressure was almost irresistible; and the House approved the measure on March 31, and the President signed it on April 3, 1948. If there had ever been any doubts that the nation would falter because the task of saving western Europe seemed too great, those doubts were now ended. The launching of the ERP meant that hereafter the destinies of the American people were inextricably intertwined with the destinies of the free peoples who stood on the dangerous frontier between a world in chains and a world struggling for a new birth of freedom.

From April 1948 until it was supplanted by the Mutual Security Agency in December 1951, the Economic Cooperation Administration (ECA) joined hands with the Committee of European Economic Cooperation (CEEC) to carry forward one of the most ambitious and successful reconstruction programs in history. The American government gave some $12,000,000,000 in assistance through the ECA during this period, but the CEEC took the initiative and furnished the chief direction. Results were astonishing even by the end of 1950, before American rearmament following the outbreak of the Korean War gave a further economic stimulus to the western world. Gross national product in Marshall Plan countries as a whole increased 25 per cent from 1947 through 1950. Industrial production increased 64 per cent, agricultural output, 24 per cent, during the same period. In most categories recovery not only attained but far exceeded the prewar levels.

228. *The Berlin Crisis and the North Atlantic Treaty*

We have thus far viewed the European Recovery Program partially out of the context of other great events that were impelling western nations toward closer unity and driving the Soviet Union into opposition and a desperate campaign to consolidate its control over eastern Europe. Achievement of western European unity would depend upon the ability of European and American statesmen to agree upon a plan for rehabilitating Germany and tying it to the western community. American, British, and French leaders continued to plead for the unification and neutralization of Germany until the end of 1947. But the Russians made it clear at the Moscow and London meetings of the Council of Foreign Ministers in March–April and November–December of 1947 that they would approve no agreement on Germany that did not give them a large voice in the control of the Ruhr Valley, the industrial heart of Europe.

The western powers realized after the failure of the London Conference that agreement with Russia was impossible, and that the only alternative was to agree upon their own plan for Germany. This undertaking, by arousing French fears, might drive France into the arms either of extreme nationalists or Communists. And yet the effort had to be made, for German recovery was the key to European recovery, and the defense of Western Germany was the key to the defense of western Europe. British and American leaders, therefore, hastened to prepare new plans for western Germany. They consolidated their zones in February 1948 and created a German government with limited authority at Frankfort. They won French approval in June for a West German federal government with limited sovereignty. They also won French consent to sweeping currency reform in the three western zones and measures to include West Germany as a full partner in the ERP. The Germans organized state governments in October 1948, adopted a constitution for a German Federal Republic on May 8,

DIVIDED GERMANY AND AUSTRIA

FEDERAL REPUBLIC OF GERMANY
FULLY SOVEREIGN ON MAY 5, 1955

GERMAN DEMOCRATIC REPUBLIC

FORMERLY GERMAN TERRITORY
UNDER U.S.S.R. AND POLISH ADMIN.

SOVIET UNION

DENMARK

Danzig

EAST PRUSSIA

(U.S.)

Hamburg

Stettin

Bremen
(U.S.)

NETHERLANDS

BRITISH ZONE

Berlin
(JOINT OCCUR)

SOVIET ZONE

Warsaw

P O L A N D

Cologne

Leipzig

EAST

Bonn

LUX.

BELGIUM

Dresden

GERMANY

WEST

Frankfurt

Prague

CZECHOSLOVAKIA

SAAR

Nuremberg

UNITED STATES ZONE

FRENCH ZONE

Stuttgat

FRANCE

Freibourg

Munich

REPUBLIC OF AUSTRIA
REGAINED FULL SOVEREIGNTY JULY 27, 1955

(U.S.S.R.)

Vienna
(JOINT OCCUR.)

(U.S.)

SWITZERLAND

A U S T R I A

(FR.)

Graz

(BR.)

HUNG.

DIVIDED
GERMANY
AND
AUSTRIA

100 MILES

ITALY

YUGOSL.

AIR CORRIDORS
RAILROADS
HIGHWAYS
WATERWAYS

50 MILES

B A L T I C   S E A

Hamburg

Stettin

WEST

EAST

POLAND

WESER

ELBE

ODER

Hannover

BERLIN
(JOINT OCCUR)

Helmstedt

Potsdam

GERMANY

GERMANY

ELBE

Leipzig

FRENCH SECTOR

TEGEL AIRFIELD

BRITISH SECTOR

SOVIET SECTOR

GATOW AIRFIELD

TEMPELHOF AIRFIELD

SCHOENFIELD AIRFIELD

Frankfurt

UNITED STATES SECTOR

CZECHOSL.

DIVIDED
GREATER BERLIN

5 MILES

BERLIN'S CHANNELS TO THE WEST

TRM

1949, and elected a federal Diet that met at Bonn in September and organized a full-fledged constitutional government.

Soviet reaction to the Marshall Plan and to western measures for uniting and rehabilitating West Germany was immediate, and so violent as to threaten the peace of the world. To begin with, the Soviet leaders created the Cominform in October 1947 to unite eastern Europe in a campaign of complete "sovietization," that is, a final destruction of all anti-Communist elements in the countries east of the Iron Curtain. The Kremlin next launched a campaign of strikes and violence through Communist parties and Communist-controlled trades unions that impeded but did not prevent substantial Italian and French recovery. The Soviet government in February 1948 engineered the coup that overthrew a coalition government in Prague and established a totalitarian Communist regime in Czechoslovakia. On the other hand, Soviet efforts to control the Communist government of Yugoslavia headed by Marshal Tito backfired in a violent break between Belgrade and Moscow and the subsequent partial alignment of Yugoslavia with the West.

The grand and perilous climax was the Berlin blockade. Soviet authorities began on April 1, 1948, to restrict movement of people and freight from the western zones into Berlin, then under four-power control but isolated in the Russian-held eastern zone of Germany. This action provoked violent controversies in the Allied *Kommandatura,* the four-power control council for the German capital, and eventuated in Soviet withdrawal from that body on July 1. Meanwhile, Soviet authorities, in retaliation against Allied introduction of the new West German currency in Berlin, halted all traffic to Berlin from the western zones on June 23. Soviet propaganda made no effort to conceal the objectives of the Berlin blockade—either to force the Allies from their advanced position behind the Iron Curtain or else to compel them to abandon their plans for West German unification. Yet withdrawal from Berlin would signify surrender in the face of superior force, the end of Allied influence in the rest of Germany, and a diplomatic victory for the Soviet Union with catastrophic implications throughout the world. Free men everywhere turned to Washington for leadership in this first open test of strength between the West and the Soviet Union.

The thought of retreat apparently never troubled the mind of the stubborn Missourian in the White House. When army leaders raised the question of withdrawal on June 28, Truman "interrupted to say that there was no discussion on this point, we were going to stay." Rejecting the suggestion that the army send armed convoys and fight its way into Berlin if need be, the President instead approved a bolder plan—to supply West Berlin by air and thereby force the Russians to make the decision for peace or war. Soon afterward he approved the sending of two groups of B-29 bombers to English bases—an obvious warning to the Kremlin. At the same time he refused to give the Military Establishment physical possession of atomic bombs because, as he said, he did not propose "to have some dashing lieutenant colonel decide when would be the proper time to drop one."

While the siege of Berlin proceeded from June 1948 to mid-May of 1949 the British R.A.F. and the United States Air Force accomplished a miracle. The airlift by September 1948 was carrying a daily average of 4,000 tons of supplies, including huge quantities of coal, to the western sectors of Berlin. All told, British and American planes made 277,264 flights and carried nearly 2,500,000 tons of supplies, enough to sustain the outpost.

The airlift cheered free men as no other event since the end of the war had done, but it was no permanent solution. That solution would have to come through diplomacy. "Some voices," Truman later wrote, "were raised in America calling for a break with the Russians. These people did not understand that our choice was only between negotiations and war. There was no third way." [19] Thus the American, British, and French governments opened negotiations in July 1948 that forced the Soviet government to admit that it had instituted the blockade in retaliation against Allied policy in western Germany. In a full-dress meeting with Stalin, Molotov, and the British and French Ambassadors in Moscow on August 2, the American Ambassador, Walter Bedell Smith, warned the Russian leaders that the western powers would not be bullied, and that the Soviet threat "could not be allowed to succeed." Stalin was seemingly conciliatory, but efforts at compromise foundered during the next few months upon Russian insistence that the Allies abandon their plans for unification of western Germany without Soviet participation, and Allied refusal to discuss this larger issue so long as the Berlin blockade was in effect.

The Russians yielded in the end and lifted the blockade on May 12, 1949, in return for Allied agreement to hold a meeting of the Council of Foreign Ministers in Paris on May 23. It was a small price to pay for so large a victory in what was by this time called the cold war between the West and the East. The Paris conference brought no important agreement on Germany, but it did reveal considerable Soviet indecision and obvious unity among the Allied powers. As the new American Secretary of State, Dean Acheson, observed upon his return to Washington, "the position of the West has grown greatly in strength, and . . . the position of the Soviet Union in regard to the struggle for the soul of Europe has changed from the offensive to the defensive."

It was a masterful understatement, for by the time Acheson spoke the western European nations and the United States were united in a military alliance for common defense of the Atlantic community. Let us review the background of this momentous event.

The first major thrust toward Atlantic unity was the Marshall Plan. This project reflected a dramatic reversal of economic nationalism and a determination by American and western European statesmen to create an integrated economic community free from artificial barriers to trade and investment. The second thrust came at the height of the debate over the ERP. The British Foreign Secretary, Ernest Bevin, in a speech in the House of Commons on January 22, 1948, announced his country's readiness to join a western European union. Representatives of Britain, France, the Netherlands, Belgium, and Luxembourg signed a fifty-year treaty of economic co-operation and military alliance at Brussels on March 17. The Foreign Ministers of this so-called Brussels Union a month later established elaborate machinery to speed economic and military collaboration. The council of Europe was created on January 28, 1949. It included not

[19] *Memoirs by Harry S. Truman*, II, p. 128.

only the Brussels powers but Italy, Ireland, Denmark, Norway, Sweden, the Saar, and the German Federal Republic as well.[20]

The leaders of western Europe now turned to Washington. The Vandenberg Resolution, adopted by the Senate on June 11, 1948, had implicitly promised American co-operation with a western European alliance. Negotiations looking toward an Atlantic alliance began in the American capital in July 1948 and culminated in the completion of a draft treaty in the following December. It was signed in Washington on April 4, 1949, by representatives of the United States, Britain, France, Italy, the Netherlands, Belgium, Canada, Iceland, Luxembourg, Denmark, Norway, and Portugal. This, the North Atlantic Treaty, was the culmination of American and European efforts to create an effective counterweight to Soviet power. It declared that an armed attack against any member in Europe, North America, or the Algerian Department of France would be considered an attack against all signatories; and it looked forward to the creation of joint military forces. Thus, Congress in September 1949 approved the Mutual Defense Assistance Act appropriating $1,000,000,000 for arms and equipment for the signatories and an additional $211,000,000 for Greece and Turkey.

One meaning in these momentous events stood out above all others. In signing the North Atlantic Pact, the United States revealed its determination to abandon historic traditions against alliances and do what was necessary to protect western Europe from Soviet attack. President Truman and Secretary Acheson had wisely drawn Republican as well as Democratic senators into the negotiations. Consequently, a solid bipartisan phalanx overwhelmed the opposition when debate on the Treaty opened in the Senate on July 5, 1949. It ratified the Pact without reservation on July 21 by a vote of 82 to 13.

[20] The first important outcome of this drive toward European union was the approval of the so-called Schuman Plan, originated by Jean Monnet of France and pressed by Robert Schuman, French Foreign Minister. The treaty implementing the Schuman Plan was signed by representatives of France, Germany, Italy, the Netherlands, Belgium, and Luxembourg on March 19, 1951. It established a High Authority to pool all coal and steel resources, production, and distribution in the signatory countries.

CHAPTER

29

The Korean War and
the Election of 1952

T HE FOUR YEARS between the signing of the North Atlantic Treaty and
the inauguration of Dwight D. Eisenhower were a time of mounting international crises, domestic tension, and moral challenge rarely paralleled in
the experience of the American people. Catapulted into leadership of what
was commonly called the free world, they now had to demonstrate whether
they could lead courageously and wisely in an endless struggle for peace
and security. American policy won a series of victories in western Europe
from 1949 to 1952. On the other hand, the Communist victory in China
upset the precarious balance of power in the Far East and set the stage for
the direst menace to peace in the postwar era—the North Korean and
Chinese assaults upon South Korea.

229. Prelude to the Korean Crisis

The American people were convulsed and confused all during late
1949 and early 1950 by a bitter debate over foreign policy in general and
the failure of American far eastern policy in particular. Despite the marked
development of a neo-isolationism, especially in the Midwest, and of a conviction that the United States could not keep pouring billions into Europe,
the administration continued to enjoy large bipartisan support for its policy of assistance to western Europe. This was evidenced by approval of the
North Atlantic Treaty and enactment of the Mutual Defense Assistance
Act in 1949. In addition, the President mustered considerable Republican

support in 1950 in obtaining a $35,000,000 appropriation to launch his "bold new program" of preventing the spread of Communism by rendering technical assistance to underdeveloped areas.

Even so, there were numerous signs by early 1950 that the Republican leaders were eager to disrupt bipartisan unity and use foreign policy as a major issue in the congressional elections of 1950. The Republican leader on foreign policy in the Senate, Arthur H. Vandenberg, was so disturbed that he violated his doctor's orders after a severe lung operation and returned to Washington in January 1950 to head off the revolt. He succeeded momentarily; but his great services were ended by renewed illness that removed him from his post and took his life on April 18, 1951. Long before he died, his Republican colleagues had raised a violent storm over China that was subdued for a time by the Korean crisis, then renewed on an even greater scale when the Chinese intervened in Korea.

The Washington government had meanwhile been trying to formulate a policy to meet the situation in the Orient caused by the establishment of a Chinese People's Republic allied to the Soviet Union. The administration would perhaps have recognized the new Peking regime, as Britain, India, and other powers did, had it not launched a violent campaign in the autumn of 1949 to drive American diplomatic agents, missionaries, and private interests from China. Reaction in the United States was violent. Anti-Chinese Communist sentiment was further exacerbated by a so-called China lobby, and by a Republican-sponsored campaign to discredit the administration and force it to extend military assistance to the Chinese Nationalists on Formosa.

Meanwhile, the State Department had washed its hands of responsibility for the Chinese debacle by releasing a white paper that blamed the Nationalists for their defeat. The President, on January 5, 1950, reaffirmed his determination not to be drawn into the Chinese civil war, even if such a policy resulted in the capture of Formosa by the Chinese Communists. And a week later Secretary of State Dean Acheson announced what was in effect a new American policy in the Far East.[1] The American government, he declared, desired only to help the peoples of Asia to realize their democratic aspirations. The United States would protect a "defensive perimeter" that ran from the Aleutians to Japan, the Ryukyus, and the Philippines, but it could not attempt to defend other areas—Korea, Formosa, and Southeast Asia—from military attack. Aggression there, Acheson concluded, would have to be met by the peoples involved and by the United Nations.

Acheson's speech gave new impetus to the Republican attack. It took a violent turn as Senators McCarthy, Taft, Kenneth S. Wherry of Nebraska, and other GOP spokesmen opened a campaign to drive the Secretary from office and prove that the State Department was riddled with Communists and fellow travelers who, as Taft put it, had "surrendered to every demand of Russia . . . and promoted at every opportunity the Communist cause in China." So violent was this assault that it wrecked the bipartisan policy, made formulation of a rational far eastern policy impossible at the very time when it was most desperately needed, and raised grave doubts abroad whether the United States was capable of wise leadership.

[1] Acheson had succeeded Marshall on January 21, 1949.

These months were a time of trouble and soul-searching as well because thoughtful men began to wonder whether the world was heading straight for destruction. The President's revelation on September 23, 1949, that the Russians had detonated an atomic bomb upset all assumptions upon which American defensive strategy had been based since 1945. It also renewed a fierce debate in high administration circles, particularly between the scientists J. Robert Oppenheimer and Edward Teller, over the development of a hydrogen or tritium bomb, potentially 1,000 times more powerful than the atomic bombs that destroyed Hiroshima and Nagasaki. When the President announced on January 31, 1950, that he had ordered the Atomic Energy Commission to proceed with work on the hydrogen bomb, thoughtful Americans were stunned by the gloomy prospects even while they agreed that their government had no other recourse. Acheson tried to quiet the mounting fear but admitted that the American people were entering a new era of "total diplomacy," in which their fortitude and wisdom would be put to severe and numerous tests.

230. *The Korean Crisis*

Not many months after Acheson spoke, an invasion of South Korea threatened the peace of the world and sorely taxed the courage and capacities of the American people. The background of this story can be briefly told. Roosevelt and his advisers had decided that Korea should be freed from Japanese control at the end of the war, but they gave no thought to a postwar policy for Korea—this in spite of the fact that Japan and Russia had fought one war for control of this strategic peninsula in 1904–5, and that Russian dominance there would gravely threaten the future security of Japan. Russian troops entered northern Korea on August 10, 1945; American forces occupied southern Korea on September 8. The two governments agreed to divide their occupation zones at the thirty-eighth parallel, which runs north of the capital city, Seoul.

American leaders assumed in their early postwar naïveté that the Korean people would soon organize a government, and that occupation forces would thereupon be withdrawn. The Russians in fact approved, at the Moscow Conference in December 1945, a plan to create a Korean government under the guidance of a joint American-Soviet commission. But the Russian representatives on the commission blocked all efforts at unification, established a Communist "people's government" in North Korea, and trained and equipped an army of some 150,000 men. The United States then appealed to the United Nations Assembly, which established a Temporary Commission on Korea in November 1947. It visited Seoul in January 1948 and, after being denied entry into the Soviet zone, held elections in South Korea for a constituent assembly. The assembly met in July 1948, adopted a constitution for a new Republic of Korea, and elected Syngman Rhee as President. The United Nations Assembly, the United States, and other non-Communist powers recognized the South Korean regime as the only lawful government of Korea. The Washington government, following advice of the Joint Chiefs of Staff and General MacArthur in Japan, withdrew its last troops from South Korea in June 1949. It also gave substantial assistance to Rhee's government during 1949 and the first months of 1950.

This, in general, was the situation when North Korean forces crossed the thirty-eighth parallel in an all-out invasion of South Korea at 4 a.m., Korean time, on June 25, 1950. Precisely what part the Soviet government played in planning the invasion or what its objectives were, we cannot now say. In all likelihood, the withdrawal of American troops and Acheson's statement that Korea lay outside America's far eastern "defense perimeter" led the Kremlin to conclude that the United States would not fight to prevent Soviet control of the entire Korean peninsula. It is even more certain that the Russians came to this conclusion on account of general American military weakness and inability to fight a limited war on its defense perimeter.

News of the invasion reached Washington at 9:26 p.m., June 24, Washington time. Acheson held hurried conferences at the State Department and called the President, who was then in Independence, at about midnight. Truman agreed that the Secretary should bring the matter before the Security Council of the United Nations at once. By the following afternoon, when the Security Council met in emergency session, it was fully evident that the North Koreans had launched not a border raid but a full-scale war. With the Russian representative absent,[2] the Council by a vote of 9 to 0 adopted a resolution condemning the invasion as aggression and demanding withdrawal of Communist troops from South Korean territory.

The President arrived in Washington soon afterward and went straight to Blair House, the temporary presidential mansion, for a conference with his civilian and military advisers. The upshot was Truman's decision to order the Seventh Fleet to neutralize Formosa, and direct General MacArthur to furnish arms and limited air support to the South Koreans. The President conferred with intelligence and army officials all during the following day, June 26. Intelligence agents, it should be added, knew next to nothing about the strength of the North Korean forces or the object of their assault. That evening Truman called his advisers to Blair House and, after hearing their views, announced that American naval and air forces in the Far East would render full assistance to the South Koreans. "Everything I have done in the last five years," he declared, "has been to try to avoid making a decision such as I have had to make tonight."[3]

Events now moved swiftly to a climax. The President called congressional leaders of both parties to the White House on the morning of June 27 and told them of his decision to resist the Communist invasion and his determination to rally the United Nations in a bold collective effort to repel aggression and preserve the peace. The Security Council met in the afternoon and adopted an American-sponsored resolution calling upon member nations to render all necessary assistance to the Republic of Korea. And on June 29 and 30, after it had become evident that the Communists would

wwwwwwwwwwwwwww

[2] The Russians had boycotted the Security Council since the preceding January, because the Council had refused to seat a delegate from the Chinese Communist government.

[3] Beverly Smith, "Why We Went to War in Korea," *Saturday Evening Post,* CCXXIV (Nov. 10, 1951), p. 80.

quickly overrun the peninsula unless American troops stopped them, the President made the hardest decision of all—to send two divisions of ground troops from Japan to Korea and authorize a naval blockade of North Korea. The decision, incidentally, was approved by the Joint Chiefs of Staff, the State Department, General MacArthur, and other military advisers, all of whom assumed that limited American support would turn the tide, and that Russia and China would not intervene. In fact, it was the reception in Washington on June 29 of a Russian disclaimer of responsibility for the North Korean attack that "opened the way for the commitment of American ground troops." [4] Obviously, the full costs of the intervention were not known in advance.

231. *The Korean War: First Phase*

"This is the Greece of the Far East," Truman said to one reporter. "If we are tough enough now, there won't be any next step." The President's decision to call Stalin's hand was, as one writer put it, "like a gust of wind blowing away a fog of uncertainty and gloom. . . . Here at last was the courage to tackle an aggressor." [5] The Republican leaders Governor Dewey and John Foster Dulles were effusive in praise. Members of the House of Representatives stood and cheered on June 28 when they learned that the President had ordered air and naval forces to defend South Korea. Even Senator Taft declared that he would vote for a resolution authorizing use of American forces in Korea, even though he opposed the President's acting without congressional consent. Elsewhere men and governments rallied. The Security Council established a United Nations Command and requested the American government to name a commander in chief. Some nineteen nations had made a military contribution by the middle of September; by the end of 1950 British, Turkish, Australian, and Philippine troops were fighting beside Americans and South Koreans under the supreme commander, General MacArthur.

Meanwhile, however, it seemed that North Korean troops would overrun the entire peninsula before American power could be brought to bear. The Communists had pressed the defenders into the southeastern corner by September 12 and were threatening to drive them from Pusan, their remaining supply port. But Allied defenses stiffened and then held firm, and MacArthur brought in large American reinforcements to turn the tide. Opening an offensive on September 15 with a daring landing on the North Korean flank at Inchon, he soon recaptured Seoul, overran southern Korea, and destroyed or captured more than half the Communist invaders. United Nations forces had reached the thirty-eighth parallel by October 1 and were preparing to launch an invasion of North Korea.

The American people watched breathlessly during the first two months and went on a buying spree that caused violent price increases and momen-

~~~~~~~~~~~~~~~~~~~~~~~

[4] John W. Spanier, *The Truman-MacArthur Controversy and the Korean War* (Cambridge, Mass., 1959), p. 33.

[5] Albert L. Warner, "How the Korea Decision Was Made," *Harper's Magazine*, CCII (June 1951), p. 104.

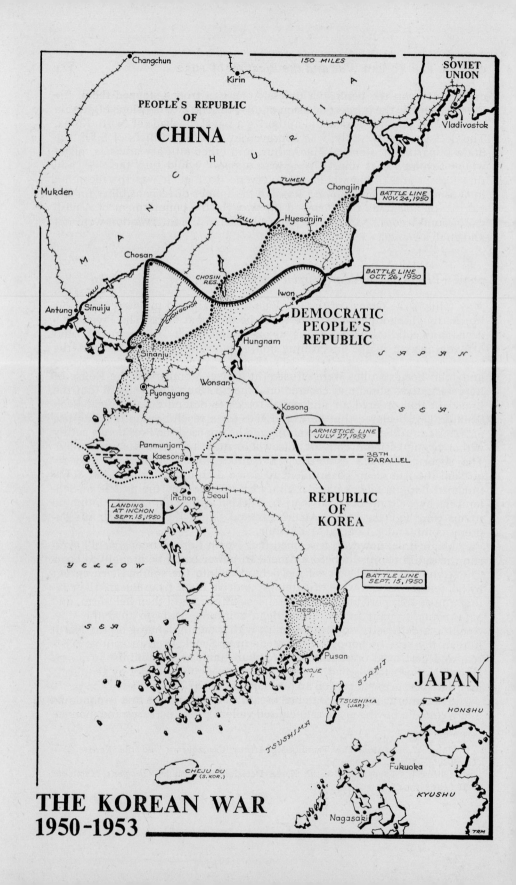

Changchun

Kirin

SOVIET
UNION

PEOPLE'S REPUBLIC
OF
CHINA

Vladivostok

Mukden

TUMEN

Chongjin

BATTLE LINE
NOV. 24, 1950

YALU

Hyesanjin

BATTLE LINE
OCT. 26, 1950

Chosan

CHOSIN
RES.

Iwon

Antung
Sinuiju

CHONGCHON

YALU

DEMOCRATIC
PEOPLE'S
REPUBLIC

Sinanju

Hungnam

Pyongyang

Wonsan

Kosong

ARMISTICE LINE
JULY 27, 1953

Panmunjom

Kaesong

38TH
PARALLEL

LANDING
AT INCHON
SEPT. 15, 1950

Inchon

Seoul

REPUBLIC
OF
KOREA

YELLOW

SEA

BATTLE LINE
SEPT. 15, 1950

Taegu

Pusan

JAPAN

KOJE
I.

TSUSHIMA
(JAP)

HONSHU

TSUSHIMA

CHEJU DU
(S. KOR.)

Fukuoka

KYUSHU

THE KOREAN WAR
1950-1953

Nagasaki

TRM

tary scarcities. But the most significant impact of the Korean incident was its awakening of Americans to the peril of new and more portentous Soviet aggressions, perhaps against the Middle East, perhaps against western Europe. And it was obvious that the peril was great precisely because the United States and western Europe lacked an effective counterforce. As one contemporary put it, "The vital question was whether time still remained to create the armed strength which alone might deter the Kremlin from undertaking further and even more dangerous adventures." [6]

Thus the chief issue was not *whether*, but *how*, the United States should prepare to meet unseen dangers. Resisting demands for all-out mobilization, the President and Congress moved swiftly to set a limited, orderly mobilization under way. Congress approved the basic legislation, the Defense Production Act, in August 1950. It announced American determination to "oppose acts of aggression and . . . to develop and maintain whatever military and economic strength is found to be necessary to carry out this purpose." This measure empowered the President to institute allocations and priorities, authorize tax incentives to encourage defense production, build industrial plants, and impose limited price and sweeping credit controls. Congress during September appropriated an additional $12,600,-000,000 for the defense establishment and approved plans to double the armed forces from 1,500,000 to 3,000,000 men by the middle of 1951. It also adopted a revenue bill designed to raise nearly $4,500,000,000 in additional income and corporate taxes, and appropriated over $5,000,000,000 for military assistance, chiefly to western Europe.

The President, assuming that the Korean War would soon be ended, did not establish special mobilization machinery or invoke the price control provisions of the Defense Production Act. He also assumed that the greatest danger was a Soviet invasion of western Europe. Hence the Washington government embarked upon a bold program during the summer and autumn of 1950 to stimulate western European rearmament and create a unified North Atlantic Treaty Organization (NATO) army with German units. With the promise of huge new Mutual Defense assistance, Britain, France, and the other NATO countries announced plans for rearmament. The North Atlantic Council met in Brussels in December 1950 and approved plans for unifying all NATO forces under the command of General Eisenhower. The American proposal for limited German rearmament foundered upon French opposition.

This summer and autumn of fear and crisis witnessed one of the bitterest congressional campaigns in American history. Republicans did not openly repudiate the Korean intervention, but they charged that Truman and Acheson had blundered so badly as to make the Korean War inevitable. They also warned of further inflation, socialization, and federal aggrandizement if the Truman policies were not abandoned. But the main Republican issue was Communism—the alleged Democratic failure to recognize and cope with Communist infiltration and influence in the State Department. Not all Republican leaders emulated the example of McCarthy, who used the issue to engineer the defeat of the veteran Democratic senator from

[6] Richard P. Stebbins *et al.*, *The United States in World Affairs, 1950* (New York, 1951), p. 244.

Maryland, Millard Tydings, or of Representative Richard M. Nixon, who exploited the popular fear in his successful campaign in California for election to the Senate. Even so, Republican campaigners highlighted the issue almost everywhere with considerable success.

The Democrats retained narrow control of both houses in the election of November 7, 1950, but the results were actually a smashing reversal for the administration. Two Fair Deal stalwarts in the Senate—Frank P. Graham of North Carolina and Claude W. Pepper of Florida—had been defeated earlier in the primaries by anti-Truman conservatives, and a whole host of the President's friends followed them into retirement after November 7. On the other hand, a spectacular Democratic effort to unseat Senator Taft in Ohio failed so dramatically as to make Taft a leading contender for the Republican presidential nomination in 1952. Even more important were the underlying developments—the return of the agrarian Middle West to the Republican fold; the obvious success of the Communist and inflation issues; and the fact that Republicans polled a larger vote than Democrats in contests for seats in the House of Representatives.

232.   *The Korean Crisis Threatens a Third World War*

The United Nations forces quickly cleared South Korea following their capture of Seoul on September 26, 1950, and drove to the thirty-eighth parallel. There they halted until the General Assembly, on October 7, called upon MacArthur to take all necessary steps to establish United Nations control throughout Korea. The Foreign Minister of the Chinese People's Republic had warned only a few days before that the Chinese would not "supinely tolerate seeing their neighbors being savagely invaded by imperialists." Moreover, he had told the Indian Ambassador in Peking on October 3 that "if the U.S. or U.N. forces crossed the Thirty-eighth Parallel, China would send troops to the Korean frontier to defend North Korea." But few leaders in the free world took the threat seriously. MacArthur, for example, assured the President at a conference on Wake Island on October 15 that there was little danger of Chinese intervention and promised a great slaughter if the Chinese armies entered the fight. Leaders in Washington shared his confidence. Indeed, Truman had approved military operations north of the thirty-eighth parallel as early as September 11. Western European leaders were equally enthusiastic for a drive to unify Korea.

MacArthur's troops drove triumphantly northward toward the Yalu River separating Korea from Manchuria. Just as it seemed that North Korean resistance had entirely collapsed, advanced American troops encountered large units of Chinese troops some fifty miles south of the Yalu on about October 30. Subsequent reconnaissance revealed that the Chinese had massed armies of some 850,000 men in Manchuria and moved advanced units into northern Korea. The entire western world waited to see what the future would bring. While Chinese "volunteers" skirmished defensively, the Security Council heard representatives of the Peking government demand prompt American withdrawal from Korea. But MacArthur launched a final great United Nations offensive on November 24 to drive the Chinese "volunteers" beyond the Yalu and end the war before Christmas. In this action he violated the spirit if not the letter of his instructions. It was Washington's policy to send only South Korean troops into this area in order to avoid provocation of the Chinese. MacArthur's decision was also a nearly fatal strategic blunder, for he drove his men into a huge trap. The Chinese counterattacked on November 26 and split the center of the United Nations line held by Republic of Korea troops. The United States Eighth Army on the western flank withdrew in an orderly retreat toward the thirty-eighth parallel, but the X Corps on the northeastern flank was isolated and cut off. After two weeks of desperate fighting the First Marine Division, the 3rd and 7th infantry divisions, and the ROK Capital Division fought their way to the port of Hungnam. From there they were evacuated and transferred to the main United Nations defensive line north of the thirty-eighth parallel. It was one of the most spectacular operations in the history of modern warfare.

The Washington government, in the meantime, had gravely accepted the challenge and begun to prepare the United States and the United Nations for a possible general war. "This new act of aggression," Secretary Acheson declared on November 29, "has created . . . a situation of unparalleled danger. . . . No one can guarantee that war will not come." The President denounced the Chinese intervention as unprovoked aggression on December 1 and outlined a vast new mobilization program in a broadcast on December 15. On the following day he declared a state of national emergency and announced creation of an Office of Defense Mobilization and beginning of production and stabilization controls.

The American mobilization effort proceeded smoothly and successfully on the whole during the next two years under the direction of Charles E. Wilson, former president of the General Electric Company. Congress opposed the President on nearly every other score, but it granted his requests for unprecedented peacetime appropriations for the military establishment, civilian defense, and military assistance to NATO countries.[7] The result was a sudden and spectacular increase in the military strength of the United States and its allies. The NATO countries had created forces probably capable of withstanding a Soviet invasion of western Europe by the end of 1952.

233. *The Second "Great Debate" and the MacArthur Affair*

It would be pleasant for the historian to record that the American people and their leaders met these new foreign threats calmly, wisely, and in firm conjunction with their European allies. The truth is, however, that the American people nearly lost their heads, the Truman administration

wwwwwwwwwwwww

[7] Congress appropriated nearly $57,000,000,000 for national defense and almost $7,500,000,000 for Mutual Security assistance during 1951–2 and nearly $47,000,000,-000 for national defense and some $6,500,000,000 for Mutual Security purposes during 1952–3.

nearly lost control of foreign policy, and the United States almost lost its allies as a result of the "great debate" and events that followed the Chinese intervention.

The "great debate" began on November 10, 1950, when Senator Taft, reacting to the President's announcement that he would send additional divisions to Europe, proposed a re-examination of the nation's foreign and military policies and raised the question whether defense of western Europe was essential to American security. Former President Hoover voiced the convictions of a large group of neo-isolationists on December 20. The United States, he declared, should defend the Atlantic and Britain, and the Pacific to Japan. But it should withdraw troops from western Europe and withhold further support until it had organized and equipped sufficient forces to withstand a Russian assault. These were only two indications of the surging growth of a Republican neo-isolationism based in large measure upon fear of huge expenditures for the military establishment and the expansion of presidential power.

The debate exploded with exceptional bitterness in Congress on January 8, 1951, when Senator Wherry offered a resolution declaring that "no ground forces of the United States should be assigned to duty in the European area for the purposes of the North Atlantic Treaty pending the adoption of a policy with respect thereto by Congress." Administration and military spokesmen replied frankly that defense of western Europe was essential to the defense of the United States. General Eisenhower returned from his command in Paris to report to Congress that the western European nations could build a strong anti-Russian barrier if the American people did not desert them. Even so, the debate raged and the issue was long in doubt, especially after a majority of House Republicans signed a manifesto endorsing Hoover's proposals on February 15. Resolution came on April 4, 1951, when the Senate reaffirmed American commitments under the North Atlantic Treaty, approved the sending of four more divisions to Europe, but warned the President not to send additional troops without "further Congressional approval."

The furor of this debate was nothing as compared to the fury that exploded following the President's recall of General MacArthur from his command in Tokyo. Indeed, few episodes in American history have been so extraordinary or revealing as the MacArthur affair. It brought to a head the Republican campaign against Truman and Acheson and the bitter conflict over the far eastern and European policies of the United States.

In the beginning the conflict between Truman and MacArthur centered around relations between the United States and Chiang Kai-shek's government on Formosa. MacArthur made an ostentatious visit to Formosa in July 1950. He then addressed a message to the annual convention of the Veterans of Foreign Wars in late August calling for incorporation of Formosa into the American security system and talking about "offensive strategy" in the Far East. Truman was shocked and considered relieving the General of his command. Instead, he met MacArthur on Wake Island on October 15, again explained that he had no intention of becoming involved in the Chinese civil war, and warned the General to make no more provocative statements.

MacArthur was silent for a time, but after the Chinese intervention he opened a campaign to force the administration to permit him to bomb Chinese bases in Manchuria. The President replied on December 6, forbidding the release of any statement on foreign policy by civilian or military officials without prior approval by the State Department. During the following weeks, when the Chinese and North Koreans seemed about to drive the United Nations forces from Korea, the President and Joint Chiefs of Staff deliberated the question of what to do should such a catastrophe occur. MacArthur, on December 29, 1950, suggested that the United States blockade the Chinese coast, bombard China by air and by sea, and support a Nationalist invasion from Formosa. Otherwise, he intimated, it might be necessary to evacuate his forces. The Joint Chiefs replied that such retaliatory actions could not then be permitted; at the same time they began to prepare for similar desperate measures should the United Nations be driven from Korea.

Events in Korea during the next few weeks decided the issue. The American Eighth Army, now under the command of General Matthew B. Ridgway, halted the enemy assault and began a limited offensive on January 26, 1951. Since it was now evident that the United Nations could remain in Korea, the President and Joint Chiefs quickly agreed upon a policy —to conduct a limited war for the limited objective of maintaining the integrity of South Korea. Such a policy would avert the danger of a general war with China—"the wrong war, at the wrong place, at the wrong time, and with the wrong enemy," General Omar N. Bradley, chairman of the Joint Chiefs, later called it. A war with China might require a shifting of all available manpower and resources to the Far East and thus invite a Russian attack on western Europe. Limited and essentially defensive operations in Korea would not destroy the Chinese Communist regime, the President and Joint Chiefs agreed. At the same time, those operations could inflict such terrible punishment on the Chinese and North Korean forces that they would have to abandon their aggression. By so doing they would acknowledge a defeat that would vindicate the principle of collective security. These were also the strong convictions of the NATO leaders. Prime Minister Attlee, for example, had come to Washington to press them in early December 1950.

MacArthur, however, was temperamentally incapable of accepting the concept of a limited war. He was prepared to abandon Europe to its inevitable doom, for he believed that future destiny lay with the Orient. He also believed that blundering, if not treasonable, political leadership was depriving the American people of an opportunity to settle the far eastern question for generations to come. He therefore resorted to desperate measures. The Joint Chiefs informed him on March 20 that the President was about to attempt to settle the Korean conflict by diplomacy. MacArthur replied with a public statement on March 24, 1951, aimed at preventing a peaceful settlement. Then, in reply to a letter from Joseph W. Martin, Jr., of Massachusetts, Republican minority leader in the House, the General called for a war to defeat Communism in the Far East. "We must win," he concluded. "There is no substitute for victory."

Martin read the letter to the House of Representatives on April 5. The

country was by now convulsed by a frenetic Republican campaign to force
the administration to adopt MacArthur's proposals for a victory offensive in
Korea and possible war against China. The publication of MacArthur's letter to Martin was an open challenge to the President's foreign policy by a
military commander who had joined hands with the administration's foes.
Reluctantly but resolutely the man from Independence took the inevitable
step: On April 10, 1951, he relieved MacArthur of his commands in Japan
and Korea and appointed General Ridgway as his successor. "I could do
nothing else and still be President of the United States," Truman wrote on
April 10. "Even the Chiefs of Staff came to the conclusion that civilian control of the military was at stake and I didn't let it stay at stake very long." [8]
"If I allowed him to defy the civil authorities in this manner," Truman afterward wrote of MacArthur, "I myself would be violating my oath to uphold
and defend the Constitution." [9]

The recall of a general who was the greatest living American in millions of eyes required a certain courage. But all the furies of hell seemed
abroad in the country in consequence. Republicans, the China lobby, and
many commentators poured out a stream of invective and abuse. Mac-
Arthur, with a large entourage, returned to his native land for the first time
in more than a decade. He made triumphal tours, like some Roman procon-
sul, in San Francisco, Chicago, New York, and Washington, and he basked
in the warmth of popular applause. His climax was a melodramatic address
before a joint session of Congress on April 19, calling for stern action
against the Chinese.

While the nation reverberated from the din, congressional leaders
agreed that the Senate armed services committee should investigate Mac-
Arthur's recall and review American far eastern policy. The committee
heard more than 2,000,000 words of testimony from MacArthur, Bradley,
Acheson, and dozens of other officials from May 3 to June 25, 1951. Chairman Richard B. Russell of Georgia would tolerate no nonsense, and the
committee acted neither like partisans, prosecutors, nor circus performers,
but rather like men who wanted only to learn the truth. As the hearings
ground on, the country recovered its senses, and at least the majority of
thoughtful Americans understood and probably approved the administration's policy.

In retrospect, we can see that the MacArthur affair cleared the air of
popular confusion over far eastern policy. As Secretary of Defense Marshall,
Secretary Acheson, and General Bradley sought to make clear, the United
States would neither adopt the MacArthur program nor evacuate Korea. It
would continue to "inflict the greatest number of casualties . . . in order
to break down not only the morale but the trained fabric of the Chinese armies." The unification of Korea remained a political and diplomatic objective; but as unification had never been a military objective, the United Nations would accept a compromise that provided for Communist withdrawal
north of the thirty-eighth parallel. In brief, the United States would fight a
limited war for limited objectives in order to avert the risk of world conflict.

---

[8] William Hillman, *Mr. President* (New York, 1952), p. 133.
[9] *Memoirs by Harry S. Truman*, II, p. 444.

234. *Decision in Korea: Truce and Armistice*

The Washington government had meanwhile moved on several fronts to convince the Chinese Communists that aggression did not pay. Secretary Acheson won United Nations approval of an embargo against the shipment of arms, munitions, and critical raw materials to China on May 18, 1951. Moreover, Acheson made it clear that the United States would strenuously oppose the Peking regime's effort to join the United Nations and would prevent Communist seizure of Formosa. In Korea, the United Nations forces repulsed two great offensives in April and May with staggering losses to the attackers. It was obvious by the middle of June that American policy was succeeding. The Communists had suffered an estimated 1,162,500 casualties; the best Chinese armies had been decimated; and China was isolated diplomatically and economically from the free world and had no hope of forcing a military decision.

Moreover, the Chinese intervention confirmed the American government's determination to conclude a peace treaty with Japan that would not only restore sovereignty to that conquered Empire but also make it the cornerstone of a new American security system in the far Pacific. Direction of negotiations was entrusted to John Foster Dulles, Republican adviser to the State Department. They proceeded smoothly among the former allied Pacific powers during 1950 and 1951. To be sure, the Russians objected, but their opposition only strengthened Anglo-American-Commonwealth unity and facilitated signing of a "peace of reconciliation" in San Francisco on September 8, 1951. The treaty stripped Japan of its overseas empire, but in all other respects it was extraordinarily generous. It imposed no restrictions upon the future development of the Japanese economy, levied no reparations, and recognized Japan's right to rearm.

The American government a short time before had begun to erect a new security system in the Pacific. The United States and the Philippines concluded a Mutual Defense Treaty on August 30, 1951. Two days later, the United States, Australia, and New Zealand signed a Tripartite Security Treaty. Finally, on the same day that the Japanese Peace Treaty was signed at San Francisco, the American and Japanese governments concluded a Security Treaty that gave the United States the right to maintain land, sea, and air bases in Japan.

While the American government was thus beginning to marshal Pacific countries in a broad anti-Communist front, the Communists showed the first sign of retreat in the Far East. Jacob A. Malik, head of the Russian delegation in the United Nations, declared on June 23, 1951, that the Korean conflict could be ended if the belligerents began discussions looking toward a "cease-fire and an armistice providing for the mutual withdrawal of forces from the 38th parallel." When Moscow endorsed the suggestion, General Ridgway opened truce negotiations with Chinese and North Korean officials on July 10. While the negotiators haggled at Kaesong and later at Panmunjom, the United Nations forces conducted defensive operations to hold their line north of the thirty-eighth parallel. It seems fairly certain that the strengthened United Nations armies could have cleared the decimated

Communist forces from North Korea in the summer of 1951, and that the Russians proposed truce talks chiefly to avert this catastrophe. Whether the Washington leaders knew this at the time, we cannot say. In any event, they instructed Ridgway and his successor, General Mark W. Clark, to maintain an impregnable defensive position and prevent a large build-up of Communist power through unrelenting air assaults upon North Korea.

Meanwhile, the truce negotiations proceeded amid charges and countercharges on both sides. The first break came on November 27, 1951, when the Communists yielded their demand for United Nations withdrawal southward to the thirty-eighth parallel and accepted the American demand for a demarcation line that coincided with the military line at the time an armistice was signed. Then the negotiators reached an impasse over the question of repatriation of prisoners of war. The Communists demanded the forcible delivery of some 46,000 Chinese and North Koreans who had signified that they would resist such repatriation. The Americans adamantly refused, and the Communists broke off discussions in October 1952.

The Eisenhower administration, inaugurated in early 1953, was determined to end the impasse even if this involved resumption of hostilities. The Communists responded by agreeing in March and April to exchange wounded prisoners, and armistice talks began again in earnest on April 26. The new Secretary of State, John Foster Dulles, now used what was later called "brinkmanship" to assure speedy conclusion. He intimated to Prime Minister Jawaharlal Nehru in New Delhi on May 21 that the United States meant to have peace by one means or another. The warning certainly went at once to Peking, and with prompt results. The Communist negotiators conceded all essential United Nations demands. Trouble now arose from Syngman Rhee, doughty President of the Republic of Korea, who threatened to withdraw his troops from the United Nations command and resume hostilities if his allies approved an armistice that left Chinese troops in North Korea. However, the South Korean President gave in and agreed to support the armistice even though he would not sign it. In return, the American government promised to train and equip a South Korean army of twenty divisions, extend some $1,000,000,000 in economic aid, and conclude a mutual security pact to protect South Korea against further Communist aggression. Negotiations ground to a successful conclusion at Panmunjom with the signing of an elaborate armistice on July 27, 1953. It vindicated every important objective for which the American people and their allies had been fighting.[10] Thus ended the Korean War. It had cost the United States 54,246 dead, 103,284 wounded, and billions of dollars.

[10] Specifically, the agreement established a demilitarized zone along a boundary that coincided with the military line and a joint United Nations–Communist Military Armistice Commission and a Neutral Nations Supervisory Commission to enforce a cease-fire and prevent violations of the armistice. To supervise the repatriation of prisoners of war and release of prisoners who refused to return to their homelands, the agreement established a Neutral Nations Repatriation Commission, composed of representatives of Sweden, Switzerland, Poland, Czechoslovakia, and India. India, moreover, would furnish troops to take charge of the prisoners of war. Finally, the signatories recommended to their respective governments a political conference within three months "to settle through negotiation the question of the withdrawal of all foreign forces from Korea, the peaceful settlement of the Korean question, etc."

235. Challenges to Democratic Supremacy

There were abundant signs from 1950 to 1952 of mounting popular discontent with administration policies at home and abroad. Indeed, probably a majority of Americans for one reason or another desired a change of government by early 1952. To begin with, not since Alfred E. Smith's nomination in 1928 had the South been so restive and resentful. Practically the entire white South was on the verge of revolt against the President's civil rights program and in a state of tense fear lest the Supreme Court outlaw segregation in the public schools. In addition, Democratic leaders and private interests in Texas, Oklahoma, Louisiana, and Florida were near rebellion because of presidential and northern Democratic opposition to their demands for state ownership of offshore oil lands and exclusive state regulation of the natural gas industry.

This was also the time when Senator McCarthy pressed his campaign to expose alleged Communist infiltration in high places in Washington. Other Republican leaders were less abusive than the Wisconsin demagogue, but they joined his attack by charging that Roosevelt had "sold out" to Stalin at Yalta and asserting that Communist sympathizers in the State Department had facilitated Communist victory in China. These persistent attacks had succeeded by the spring of 1952 in planting in millions of minds the suspicion that the Democratic party was tainted with treason and Communism.

Opposition to Democratic rule was also generated by revelations of widespread corruption in Washington. An investigation of the Reconstruction Finance Corporation by a Senate committee in 1951 revealed corrupt influences in the granting of loans and exposed a ring of so-called five per centers. Soon afterward came a sensational and nationally televised investigation of organized crime. A special Senate committee, headed by Estes Kefauver of Tennessee, exposed embarrassing connections between Democratic city machines and crime syndicates. The crowning blow came in late 1951 and early 1952. It was the revelation that the Bureau of Internal Revenue was literally riddled with corruption, and that the Assistant Attorney General in charge of income tax evasion cases had accepted large gifts, including two mink coats for his wife, from "fixers" and persons accused of income tax fraud.

Such revelations were of course good grist for the Republican mill, even though these scandals were insignificant as compared to the corruption that riddled the Grant and Harding administrations. Even more damaging to Democratic prestige was the President's failure to take dramatic leadership in ousting the corrupt element. To be sure, he reorganized the RFC and the Bureau of Internal Revenue; but he acted slowly and, it seemed, reluctantly. Truman finally launched a house-cleaning of other departments early in 1952. But the affair turned into a farce because his Attorney General, J. Howard McGrath, would not permit the special investigator to question employees of the Justice Department about their incomes. The investigator resigned when Truman upheld McGrath; Truman dismissed McGrath on April 3, 1952, and appointed James P. McGranery as Attorney General. McGranery quietly abandoned the project of a special investigation.

Economic developments during the Korean War also contributed to the general dissatisfaction. Wholesale prices increased 13 per cent from June 1950 to January 1952, and this spurred new rounds of wage demands and a sharp increase in the number of work stoppages. Although per capita disposable income kept pace with the increase in taxes and prices,[11] certain groups—persons on fixed incomes, for example, or farmers, whose costs increased more rapidly than income—suffered considerable hardship.

Ironically, however, the Korean War itself generated the greatest popular discontent. Almost the entire nation had cheered when the President intervened, but disillusionment and a kind of despair swept through large elements of the country following the Chinese intervention and the administration's refusal to take desperate measures to end the war quickly. Few Americans actually wanted to risk a third world war, but millions of them could not comprehend the concept of limited war and were certain that there must be some quick and easy way out of the stalemate. Casualties mounted while the truce talks ground on to no seeming end or purpose, and a tide of peace sentiment threatened to engulf the party in power.

236. *The Campaign and Election of 1952*

Republican leaders launched a campaign in late 1951 to capture the presidency and Congress. But basic disagreement between the two important wings of the GOP quickly erupted into a battle for control of that party. Senator Robert A. Taft had emerged since his smashing re-election in 1950 more than ever the unchallenged Republican leader in Congress, the spokesman of conservatives and neo-isolationists in the country at large, and the pre-eminent foe of the President's foreign and domestic policies. He had the support of powerful business interests, conservative-isolationist newspapers like the Chicago *Tribune,* and Republican state organizations in the South and Middle West. He seemed irresistible as he opened an all-out campaign to win the presidential nomination and wrest control from the eastern internationalist leaders who had guided the party since 1940.

The powerful eastern wing moved to counter the Taft challenge. Led by Governor Dewey of New York and the men who controlled Republican organizations in New England, Pennsylvania, New Jersey, and Maryland, the Easterners enjoyed a working alliance with West Coast GOP leaders. They were moderately progressive in domestic affairs and committed to preserving the New Deal reform structure. In foreign policy they were committed to support of the United Nations and the free world in the struggle against Communism. Their chief task was to find a candidate who could defeat Taft and then go on to win the presidency in the autumn.

At first it seemed to be an impossible undertaking. Former Governor Harold E. Stassen, now president of the University of Pennsylvania, was eager but unacceptable. Their most prominent spokesman, Governor Dewey, was disqualified by virtue of his defeats in 1944 and 1948. The eastern Republicans turned, therefore, to General Eisenhower, president of Columbia

wwwwwwwwwwww

[11] Per capita disposable personal income was, in constant 1953 dollars, $1,509 in 1950, $1,508 in 1951, and $1,517 in 1952.

University on leave and Supreme Commander of NATO forces in Europe, and implored him to run. Eisenhower reluctantly agreed to do so—only, as he told intimate friends, in order to prevent Taft's nomination and the triumph of isolationism in the Republican party.

The Republican preconvention campaign opened in January 1952, when Eisenhower's manager, Senator Henry Cabot Lodge, Jr., of Massachusetts, entered the General's name in the New Hampshire presidential primary, and Taft and his friends began a campaign to win the South and Middle West. Eisenhower won easily in New Hampshire, Pennsylvania, and New Jersey, but Taft won such impressive victories in Wisconsin, Nebraska, and elsewhere in the Midwest that Eisenhower resigned his NATO command, returned to the United States, and entered the campaign in person with a speech at his home town of Abilene, Kansas, in early June. Not since the William H. Taft–Theodore Roosevelt battle in 1912 had Republicans waged such a bitter and narrowly contested prenomination campaign. Taft and Eisenhower each garnered about 500 delegates. The nomination would go, therefore, to the candidate who won Minnesota and California, committed to favorite sons, and contested delegations with sixty-eight votes from Texas, Georgia, and Louisiana.

The Taft forces controlled the Republican National Committee when the convention opened in Chicago on July 7, 1952. But they were outmaneuvered by Dewey and Lodge in the struggle for the crucial contested delegates. The two Eisenhower managers won a bitter battle on the convention floor and were thereby able to nominate Eisenhower on the first ballot on July 11. It was an impressive victory but a potentially fatal one, for Taft and his embittered supporters were threatening to bolt the ticket. The fate of the party in the coming campaign would depend upon Eisenhower's success in closing the breach. Meanwhile, the convention had nominated Senator Richard M. Nixon of California for Vice President and adopted a platform broad enough to accommodate both wings of the GOP.[12]

The Democrats also had their own long and bitter campaign to determine party control and a presidential ticket. There were a host of Democratic contenders by January 1952—Senator Richard B. Russell of Georgia, Vice President Alben W. Barkley of Kentucky, W. Averell Harriman of New York, Senator Robert S. Kerr of Oklahoma, and Senator Estes Kefauver of Tennessee. Kefauver made the most vigorous campaign and scored the earliest successes by open opposition to the Truman administration. Even so, power rested with leaders of the northern and midwestern state organizations and in large measure with the President himself. Truman played a cautious game during the early months in order to head off a Kefauver boom. However, he announced on March 30 that he would not run again;

---

[12] It promised reductions in federal expenditures and taxes, extension of the Social Security system, maintenance of high farm price supports, and exclusive state control of the so-called tidelands. It condemned corruption in government; approved the Taft-Hartley Act but promised substantial revision favorable to labor; approved in principle an FEPC but declared that the states should have primary control of race relations; and denounced the President's alleged usurpation of the warmaking power by intervening in Korea without congressional consent. Finally, it announced a new policy of the "liberation" of peoples under Soviet domination, to replace the allegedly futile policy of containment.

and soon afterward he began a campaign among Democratic leaders to draft Governor Adlai E. Stevenson of Illinois. But Stevenson announced that he was not a candidate and continued his protestation until the very eve of the Democratic convention.

Truman and the party leaders therefore promised to support Barkley for the nomination. He left for the convention "with the assurances of party leaders from President Truman down, that Adlai Stevenson would not take the presidential nomination and that . . . [he] would be the convention's choice." [13] But on the eve of the convention a group of "certain self-anointed political labor leaders," including Walter Reuther and Jack Kroll of the CIO and George M. Harrison of the AF of L, told Barkley that he was too old to run and asked him to withdraw. They spoke without authority, but they gained their objective.

The Kefauver forces made a gallant effort when the Democrats assembled in Chicago on July 21. But Truman and his friends were in the driver's seat. They turned again to Stevenson. This time the Illinois governor consented, and won the nomination on the third ballot on July 25. The convention named Senator John J. Sparkman of Alabama as Stevenson's running mate and adopted a platform demanding repeal of the Taft-Hartley Act, enactment of a full civil rights program, including a compulsory FEPC, and maintenance of high price supports for farmers. The platform also promised continuation of the Truman administration's policies in Asia and full support of NATO.

Stevenson, once he accepted the nomination, acted like a man who wanted to win. In a series of addresses unparalleled for literary excellence since Wilson's day, he told the American people that there was no easy road to peace and security. On domestic issues he began the campaign as a moderate progressive, but he was drawn inevitably into full espousal of Fair Deal progressivism. He won the endorsement of the AF of L and CIO by demanding repeal of the Taft-Hartley Act. He won the support of a majority of Negroes by championing advanced civil rights legislation. He drew most intellectuals to his side by his high seriousness and obvious intellectual capacity. On the other hand, he was not as successful in bidding for crucial farm support, as many midwestern farmers were sick of the Korean War and refused to listen to a candidate tainted by association with the administration that had intervened.

Stevenson's great campaign and personal assets were not enough to withstand the tremendous Republican assault. Eisenhower took the lead. In August and early September he launched a "great crusade" for honest and efficient government at home and for "freedom in the world." Then he took up the theme of liberation of captive peoples, first developed by John Foster Dulles and included in the Republican platform. Condemning the Truman administration's "appalling and disastrous mismanagement" of foreign affairs, Eisenhower promised a surer road to peace than the policy of containment, although he was never precise in pointing to the new way. On domestic issues he talked in generalities broad enough to please almost all classes and interests.

Eisenhower during the early weeks of the campaign struck a posture of

[13] Alben W. Barkley, *That Reminds Me—* (New York, 1954), p. 233.

national leadership above the din of party battle. He soon persuaded himself, however, that national salvation lay as much in the sweeping triumph
of the Republican party as in his own election; and he shifted his ground
midway in the campaign in order to insure Republican unity and victory.
He invited Senator Taft to New York City to conciliate the right wing. At
their conference on September 12 Eisenhower signed Taft's articles of surrender and won the Ohioan's promise of co-operation.[14] Eisenhower soon
afterward opened a strongly partisan attack upon the Truman administration and the President personally. At the same time, he made it clear that he
agreed with Taft that one objective of his administration would be to destroy
such products of "creeping socialism" as the TVA and federal hydroelectric
projects in the Northwest. Finally, Eisenhower tried to cement party unity
by supporting all Republican candidates, including his bitter enemies, Senator McCarthy and Senator William Jenner of Indiana.

Eisenhower's most important shift occurred in October, when he took
up the Korean issue in a supreme effort to capitalize upon the overriding
popular desire for peace. He did not specifically say that the intervention
had been unwise. But he did charge that Truman's blundering had helped to
cause the conflict, and that the United States had walked into a Soviet trap
by agreeing to cease-fire negotiations in 1951. He struck the high note of his
campaign at Detroit on October 24 by promising to bring the Korean War to
"an early and honorable end." "That job," he continued, "requires a personal
trip to Korea. I shall make that trip. Only in that way could I learn how best
to serve the American people in the cause of peace. I shall go to Korea."

Meanwhile, a united Republican party had begun one of the most powerful and best financed campaigns in the history of the country. Utilizing all
the techniques of advertising through television, radio, and the press, Republican spokesmen mounted an attack that sent the Democrats reeling.
Practically all Republican campaigners used the Communist issue; a few,
like McCarthy, went so far as to charge that Stevenson was tainted with
Communist associations. Even more devastating was the Republican attack
on American participation in the Korean War. So vigorous and persistent
was this offensive that the Democrats were unable to defend their record,
much less make a successful counterattack.

The Republican momentum was halted only once. The Democratic National Committee on September 18 published proof that Nixon had enjoyed
access to a modest fund provided by friends in California. Eisenhower was
so furious that he commissioned Governor Dewey to ask Nixon to withdraw
from the ticket. But Nixon fought back, making an emotional television
broadcast on September 23 that won new support for the Republican ticket.
Eisenhower was convinced and rushed to a dramatic public reconciliation.

All signs pointed to a Republican victory on November 5, but the poll-

[14] Taft had earlier made it clear that he regarded Eisenhower as another Dewey, as
a "me-too" candidate who would carry the GOP to defeat by agreeing substantially with
the Democrats on all important points. At this New York conference, Eisenhower agreed
that the main issue of the campaign was "liberty against creeping socialization" and
promised to defend the basic principles of the Taft-Hartley Act and to treat Taft's followers fairly in dispensing the patronage. The two men, Taft explained after the conference, disagreed on foreign policy; but Taft added, "I think it is fair to say that our
differences are differences of degree."

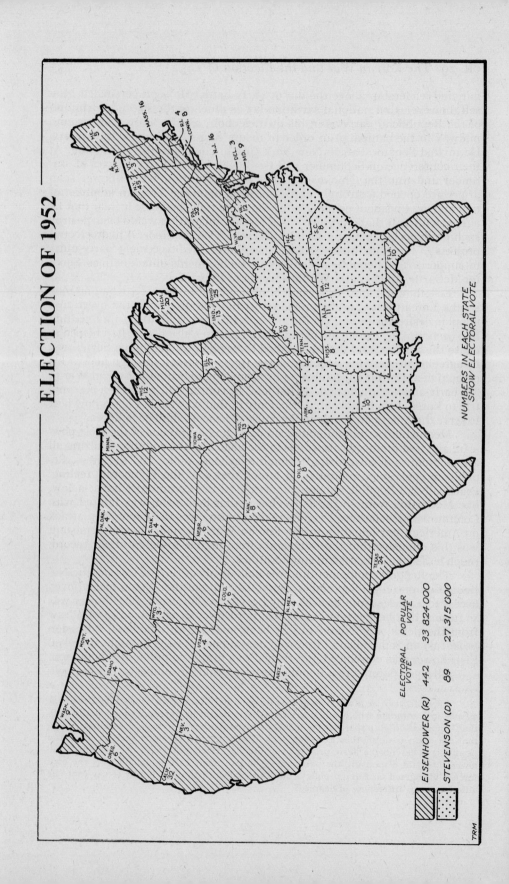

ELECTION OF 1952

NUMBERS IN EACH STATE
SHOW ELECTORAL VOTE

	ELECTORAL VOTE	POPULAR VOTE
EISENHOWER (R)	442	33 824 000
STEVENSON (D)	89	27 315 000

WASH. 9
OREG. 6
CALIF. 32
NEV. 3
IDAHO 4
MONT. 4
UTAH 4
ARIZ. 4
WYO. 3
COLO. 6
N. MEX. 4
N. DAK. 4
S. DAK. 4
NEBR. 6
KAN. 8
OKLA. 8
TEXAS 24
MINN. 11
IOWA 10
MO. 13
ARK. 8
LA. 10
WIS. 12
MICH. 20
ILL. 27
IND. 13
OHIO 25
KY. 10
TENN. 11
MISS. 8
ALA. 11
GA. 12
FLA. 10
S.C. 8
N.C. 14
VA. 12
W.VA. 8
PA. 32
N.Y. 45
ME. 5
N.H. 4
VT. 3
MASS. 16
R.I. 4
CONN. 8
N.J. 16
DEL. 3
MD. 9

TRM

sters were unsure of themselves, and Eisenhower and his campaigners fought hard to avert a last-minute swing to Stevenson. That swing did not occur, and Stevenson polled 27,314,987 popular votes and carried only North Carolina, West Virginia, Kentucky, South Carolina, Georgia, Alabama, Mississippi, Louisiana, and Arkansas, for a total of 89 electoral votes. In contrast, Eisenhower won 33,824,351 popular votes and carried thirty-nine states with a total electoral vote of 442.

Eisenhower's election was the perhaps inevitable personal triumph of a man who seemed to embody all the qualities that Americans most admired —honesty, simplicity, personal goodness, and decency; whose rise from humble origins gave testimony once again to the strength of the American democracy; and who had comported himself with dignity and earned the reputation of a leader of men since the North African campaign. In addition, the Republicans won because they were the opposition at a time when discontent over certain federal policies was great enough to destroy normal voting habits and break the Democratic coalition of farmers, workers, the lower middle classes, and Southerners. Many southern Democrats, including the Governors of Texas and South Carolina, voted as much against Truman's civil rights program and for state ownership of the tidelands as for Eisenhower. Many Democratic workers defected because as Catholics and persons of eastern European ancestry they were particularly susceptible to the Republican anti-Communist campaign and denunciation of Yalta. Midwestern farmers voted Republican, in part, because Eisenhower simply outbid the Democrats for their support. The lower middle classes and persons on fixed incomes were obsessed by the fear of further inflation.

But all observers agreed that the issue with the greatest impact was the Korean War. It crystallized all accumulated discontent. "In marking their ballots for Eisenhower," one analyst has written, "many persons, of course, hoped to bring their sons and husbands back home. Still, the election should not be interpreted as a vote for peace at any price. It was more a vote of impatience with the frustrating state of neither war nor peace." [15]

And yet we can easily exaggerate the meaning of the popular verdict by emphasizing only Eisenhower's triumph and the issues that divided the parties. The astonishing phenomenon was the continued strength of the Democratic party. In spite of Eisenhower's personal popularity, widespread discontent over the Truman policies, and the power of the Republican offensive, the Republicans only managed to elect a majority of eight in the House and, because of the defection of Senator Wayne Morse of Oregon from the GOP, to break even in the Senate. As Eisenhower ran far ahead of most other Republican candidates, it is a safe assumption that he carried the slight Republican majority in Congress along with him into office. Nor could reactionaries or neo-isolationists claim that the election signified a repudiation of either progressivism at home or the Truman policies abroad. Actually, the differences between the parties and the candidates on fundamental issues was slight as compared to their substantial agreement on the necessity of preserving the great New Deal reform structure and American security through a continuation of the alliance-assistance system inaugurated after 1945.

〰〰〰〰〰〰〰〰

[15] Samuel Lubell, "Who Elected Eisenhower?" *Saturday Evening Post*, CCXXV (Jan 10, 1953), p. 74.

CHAPTER

30

Politics and Problems
of the Eisenhower Era

THE CONFUSION and uncertainty that had permeated the American political scene during the Truman era were in no way resolved by the inauguration of a Republican President in January 1953. The GOP was back in power for the first time in twenty years, and Dwight D. Eisenhower had just received one of the most impressive personal mandates on record. But those Americans who believed that new leadership would bring deliverance from the anxieties of the postwar world were doomed to disappointment. The pressures, crises, and awful portents of the cold war continued undiminished. Mounting prosperity at home was threatened by inflation and recession. Heightened racial, religious, social, and ideological tensions added their disruptions to the normal problems of a mobile society. Social and economic changes vastly altered old voting patterns, and the period was one of flux and partial deadlock in politics. The emphasis had shifted somewhat, but doubt and uncertainty were as rife at the end of the Eisenhower era as they had been at the beginning.

Despite confusion and deadlock, there were positive gains during President Eisenhower's eight years in the White House. Before the end of his first term the nation had largely recovered from the excesses of its second Red Scare. There was genuine if uneven progress in the field of civil rights. The new administration prevented runaway inflation and presided over the most prosperous decade that Americans had ever known. Moreover, the GOP's return to power resulted in a cautious expansion of the New Deal reform structure, rather than its dismantling or destruction. The anticipated break with the Democratic era did not occur.

But these were not years of vigorous leadership or bold action in domestic affairs. Thoughtful Americans came to fear that the government's refusal to move more forcefully against the growing problems of technological unemployment, urban decay, education, transportation, and the farm surplus would bring dangerous crises in the near future. This inactivity stemmed from the overriding urgency of foreign affairs, a general public mood of complacency, fear of inflation and excessive governmental spending, and widespread disagreement over specific means and goals. Perhaps no leadership could have made appreciable headway in the face of such obstacles. But many critics said that the President's failure to use his enormous prestige and power more effectively in behalf of needed domestic reform amounted to an abdication of responsibility. Whether the dire consequences that they predicted would in fact flow from this lack of positive leadership, only the future could tell.

237. *The New Republican President*

Dwight David Eisenhower brought to the White House, and retained, a degree of popularity accorded to few if any of his predecessors. Not since Hoover had a new presidential candidate been as widely known and respected at the time of his nomination. Not since Grant had the American people turned so hopefully to a military hero.

Eisenhower was born in Denison, Texas, on October 14, 1890, and moved with his family to Abilene, Kansas, while only a few months old. Boyhood and high school in Abilene were followed by attendance at West Point and graduation from the Military Academy in 1915. Then followed twenty-seven years of routine duty at a succession of regular army posts, attendance at various service schools, and a tour of duty as aide to General MacArthur in the Philippines from 1935 to 1940. Eisenhower was a lieutenant colonel with the temporary rank of brigadier general when the United States entered the Second World War. During the next three years, after brief service as head of the War Plans Division of the War Department in 1942, he served as commander of United States forces in the European theater, directed the North African campaign, became Supreme Commander of the Allied Expeditionary Force that landed on Norman beaches in June 1944, and achieved the five stars of a General of the Army. After serving as commander of the American occupation forces in Germany following the Nazi surrender, he succeeded George C. Marshall as Army Chief of Staff in November 1945. He resigned from active service in 1948 to become president of Columbia University. At the end of 1950 he took leave of absence from Columbia to head the newly formed NATO forces as Supreme Commander of the Allied Powers in Europe.

How well had this long and distinguished military career prepared General Eisenhower for the nation's highest office? A certain amount of legitimate controversy will doubtless attend this question until future historians can make long-range assessments of his presidency. His lack of ordinary civilian experience was certainly a liability. No previous President —with the possible exception of Zachary Taylor, whose example was not overly comforting—had had a briefer exposure to civilian life prior to his election. Eisenhower's short tenure at Columbia University after the war did not do much to widen his horizons. He still knew little about the thousand problems that beset the American people in the postwar world.

Moreover, Eisenhower entered the campaign of 1952 with no experience and almost no working knowledge of the American political system and process. Indeed, his political views were so ill defined after the war that no one, including the General himself, was quite sure of his party preference, with the result that both parties besought his candidacy in 1948. This lack of deep-seated political commitment was in one sense a distinct asset, since it freed him, both in appearance and in fact, from the kind of intense partisanship that the nation had experienced all too frequently in recent years. But the lack of political sophistication that underlay his nonpartisan attitude before 1952 was a potential weakness. A long army career had grievously narrowed and insulated his intellectual horizons and taught him to rely too heavily upon the initiative and good judgment of subordinates.

However, military experience provided some training for leadership. In the army Eisenhower had learned to direct gigantic operations, developed a talent for working harmoniously with others and reconciling divergent viewpoints, and become accustomed to the burdens of large responsibility. At a time when questions of national defense were crucial, Eisenhower brought to the presidency a high level of professional competence in the field. His experiences in Europe during and after the war had also provided a mature internationalist outlook, an invaluable working familiarity with European leaders and problems, and a determination to maintain and strengthen the western alliance system and the free world generally in the struggle against Soviet-communist imperialism. This all gave a strength and a focus to his presidency that no specific errors or failures could altogether undermine.

The most significant key to understanding Eisenhower can be found in certain qualities and attitudes in the man himself. He was not an intellectual by any ordinary definition, nor was he given to serious reading in history, politics, or current affairs. "Eisenhower's mind is, like his personality, standard-American," one observer has written. "It is unschematic, distrustful of fine distinctions, given to overstatement, impatient with theory, eager to make translations into the realm of matter and things, concerned with the effect of ideas rather than with their validity." [1] He tended to express commonplace, almost platitudinous ideas in a syntax that was the despair of English teachers. Yet he spoke in terms and voiced sentiments that millions of Americans understood and shared.

Indeed, Eisenhower was "standard-American" almost to the point of caricature. He liked westerns, bourbon, bridge and poker, golf, fishing, gardening, and hunting. His admiration of the successful businessman was so unabashed that it reminded historians, rather uneasily, of U. S. Grant. In a generation that had experienced bewildering changes and longed for the real and imagined comforts of a vanished past, Eisenhower seemed to embody the traditional American virtues: fundamental decency, self-reliance, thrift, and individualism. The political views that began to emerge with his

[1] Richard H. Rovere, *Affairs of State: The Eisenhower Years* (New York, 1956), p. 17.

candidacy in 1952 smacked strongly of orthodox Republicanism: devotion to free enterprise and a balanced budget, a belief that liberty was more important than security, a respect for state rights, a distrust of "creeping socialism" and the welfare state. Yet he agreed that the essentials of the New Deal reform structure should be maintained.

This seemed like inconsistency and fuzzy thinking to critics, both progressive and conservative. However, it exemplified the middle-road position that Eisenhower consciously sought to occupy, and it was an excellent approximation of majority sentiment in the 1950's. Most Americans, in short, wanted freedom *and* security. Their new President was a perfect embodiment of these not always compatible goals. Moderation was the keynote of both the man and his administration.

Moderation also characterized his methods of leadership. A gifted coordinator, Eisenhower detested controversy and constantly sought to reconcile opposing viewpoints. He employed approaches that were by long experience second nature to him: persuasion, discussion, tact, charm, patience, sincere good will. Co-operative teamwork was the key to accomplishment in Eisenhower's formula. The leader's role was to harmonize the functioning of the team and ratify decisions and policies carefully prepared by responsible subordinates.

It was an agreeable method of leadership, but results were strangely disappointing. The military staff system, with its chains of command and sweeping delegations of pyramided authority, lent itself only moderately well to the ill-assorted operations of the federal executive. The teamwork and co-ordination that had made the Allied landings on D-Day so huge a success were poorly designed to absorb the frictions and pressures of the political process. Conciliation and compromise had a way of deferring or diluting clear-cut decision, and moderation began to look like drift.

The American presidency's proper functioning depends entirely upon the vigor and resolution of the man in command. Eisenhower seemed to lack both the will and the knowledge to make the executive branch operate efficiently. He disliked many of the normal tasks of the presidency and avoided, where possible, systematic exposure to the details, close political contacts, and daily burdens of the office. There were times when he seemed to think of himself as a constitutional monarch. He acquired some political competence, but he refused to grasp the immense possibilities that a combination of political skill, vigorous leadership, and his own prestige had placed at his disposal. Seldom was so intrinsically powerful an office more feebly used—or, as some interpreted it, more forcefully employed to restrict rather than expand the area of positive action.

And yet it can almost be said that, given the situation in 1952, an Eisenhower was both inevitable and necessary. His outlook, temperament, and style of leadership fitted the public mood like a tailored uniform. Americans wanted just such a President—a man above the political battle, an esteemed and respected figure, a cautious moderate, an embodiment of the "American way" and the old American virtues. Twenty years of one-party dominance had weakened the vitality and responsibility of Republicans and Democrats alike. The New Deal reform structure needed the kind of bipartisan ratification that only a well-disposed Republican administration could give it. The Republicans needed to learn, as only the possession of government could teach them, that both the New Deal and the postwar world could not be wished into oblivion.

238.   *The Waning of the Second Red Scare*

National alarm over alleged Communists in government, so paramount an issue during the latter portion of the Truman administration, persisted for about half of Eisenhower's first term. It threw up a host of accusers, ranging from the malevolent to the comic and grotesque. But the central figure during the heyday of the second Red Scare from 1950 to 1954, the man who did most to shape its course and stamp it with the unforgettable mark of his own personality and character, was Senator Joseph R. McCarthy of Wisconsin.

It was widely assumed as the Eisenhower administration took office in January 1953 that McCarthy's great days of power and influence were about to end. He had made his reputation as a savage and reckless critic of the party in power. Now that the Democrats were gone, taking with them their alleged softness toward communism, conspiracies, and twenty years of treason, there seemed to be no need for further assaults. "It is this newspaper's hope and belief that McCarthyism would disappear overnight if Eisenhower were elected," the Washington *Post* had said before the campaign of 1952. This confidence persisted for a few weeks after the election. Senator Taft, who disapproved strongly of McCarthy even though he had condoned McCarthy's scurrilous attacks on Democrats for the past three years, believed that GOP strategists could now contain and divert the Wisconsin demagogue. Even McCarthy, in the days following the election, saw a new role ahead for himself. "The picture has so infinitely changed," he told newspapermen. "Now it will be unnecessary for me to conduct a one-man campaign to expose Communists in government. We have a new President who doesn't want party-line thinkers or fellow travelers. He will conduct the fight." [2]

Taft planned to render McCarthy impotent by assigning the chairmanship of the Senate internal security committee, which would handle loyalty investigations, to the devoutly anti-Communist but thoroughly colorless William Jenner of Indiana. McCarthy would be safely pigeonholed as chairman of the hitherto innocuous committee on government operations. "We've got McCarthy where he can't do any harm," Taft concluded happily —as utterly mistaken a judgment as the astute Ohioan ever made. Part of McCarthy's new committee was a permanent subcommittee on investigations. Although the "investigations" were ostensibly directed at governmental contracts, McCarthy saw that the word was a convenient turret that could be aimed in any direction. Making himself chairman of the subcommittee, he quickly resumed his flamboyant crusade against Communists in government.

For the next year and a half McCarthy was rarely out of the headlines. He piled accusations, wild charges, sensational "disclosures," and widely

wwwwwwwwwwwww

[2] Quoted in Richard Rovere, *Senator Joe McCarthy* (New York, 1959), p. 187.

publicized investigations one upon another. His shadow seemed to grow ominously longer, and only the President of the United States wielded comparable influence. Few men in public life were willing to challenge him when opinion polls reported in early 1954 that 50 per cent of the people approved of McCarthy and another 21 per cent "did not know." The Senate was conspicuous in its reluctance to apply a halter, for McCarthy had demonstrated more than once what he could do against a senator in an election campaign.[3] Except for a small band of extreme conservatives, senators despised him—and feared him even more.

The President also stayed aloof as long as he could. This was not due to fear—Eisenhower's contempt and loathing for the man were manifest—but rather to the President's inveterate dislike of personal controversy and his desire for party harmony. He knew full well that any direct clash with McCarthy would be on the latter's level, which meant a virtual barroom brawl. "I will not get in the gutter with that guy," the President is reported to have snapped.[4] He also wished to avoid a complete break with the Republican right wing and apparently hoped that forbearance and time would solve the McCarthy problem with the least friction and damage.

The President's forbearance was sorely tested during his first eighteen months in office. McCarthy conducted a tirade against the appointment of Charles E. Bohlen as Ambassador to Russia in 1953. Taft finally intervened to secure Bohlen's confirmation, but at the price of a virtual agreement by the administration to make no further appointments that McCarthy disapproved. The State Department meekly chose what everyone regarded as a "McCarthy man" for its security officer. Thereafter the Senator from Wisconsin exercised a virtual veto over the Secretary of State in the personnel policy of the Department. McCarthy announced in March 1953 that he had "negotiated" an agreement with Greek shipowners to stop trading at Soviet and other Communist ports. When this drew from Harold Stassen, Director of Mutual Security, the indignant charge that McCarthy was usurping the functions of the executive branch and undermining American foreign policy, the administration made peace by issuing a mild rebuke to McCarthy and forcing Stassen to tone down his statement.

McCarthy charged ahead on many fronts. His subcommittee conducted a frantic search for alleged Communists in the Voice of America program, finding none but managing to destroy the efficiency and morale of that agency. He performed a similar operation in the summer of 1953 upon the State Department's overseas information program. In the process, two irresponsible young members of McCarthy's staff conducted a farcical "investigation" abroad and brought shame and despair to every American embassy in Europe. The State Department dutifully removed from its overseas libraries, and in some instances actually burned, books by authors whom the Mc-

---

[3] Millard Tydings of Maryland, William Benton of Connecticut, Scott Lucas of Illinois, and Ernest MacFarland of Arizona were among those defeated senators who counted themselves McCarthy's victims. Raymond Baldwin of Connecticut resigned his Senate seat in 1949 primarily because, as one authority put it, McCarthy had poured upon him "more abuse than he felt called upon to bear." R. Rovere, *McCarthy*, p. 37.

[4] Quoted in Robert J. Donovan, *Eisenhower: The Inside Story* (New York, 1956), p. 249.

Carthy subcommittee regarded as subversive.[5] Another member of McCarthy's staff wrote a magazine article charging that the American Protestant clergy was riddled with subversion. The administration did manage to take a stand against the book-burning and the attack on the clergy, but not in such fashion as to deter the freewheeling Senator from Wisconsin. Millions of Americans were too impressed by the range and variety of his charges to notice the fact that in four years of strenuous activity he had not unearthed a single Communist in the federal government or anywhere else.

Meanwhile, not to be outdone, the Justice Department and other federal agencies conducted energetic loyalty probes of their own. The government had become so hedged about with suspicion and security regulations that its very functioning was adversely affected, especially in the vital fields of scientific research, national defense, and foreign policy. Attacks on the State Department and Foreign Service, for example, shattered morale among loyal public servants and caused a sharp decline in the number of young men entering the diplomatic corps. Worse still was the damage done by one of the most frightful episodes of the postwar era. The Atomic Energy Commission, on the initiative of its new chairman, Lewis L. Strauss, barred J. Robert Oppenheimer, former director of the Los Alamos Laboratory and head of the Institute for Advanced Study, from access to classified materials on July 7, 1953, on the ground that he was a poor security risk. A special board affirmed Oppenheimer's loyalty in May 1954 but agreed that security regulations required that he be denied access to classified data. Perhaps the most revealing aspect of the entire affair was the fact that not a single individual prominent in political life raised his voice against these proceedings, not even after their shameful character had been laid bare by two journalists.[6]

The climax came with McCarthy's attack upon the army in the opening weeks of 1954. He discovered that a reserve corps dentist at Fort Monmouth had been promoted and given an honorable discharge despite his refusal to sign an army loyalty certificate. From this insignificant episode, which the army admitted having mishandled, came wild charges about subversion in the armed forces and a new round of subcommittee hearings. When McCarthy bullied and humiliated Brigadier General Ralph Zwicker, who had been the dentist's commanding officer, Secretary of the Army Robert Stevens rushed indignantly to the general's defense. He denounced the subcomittee, ordered Zwicker and several other officers not to testify before it, and prepared a strong statement which he planned to read before it himself. McCarthy, calling Stevens an "awful dupe," conferred with the Secretary at a luncheon arranged by other members of the subcommittee. He there obtained Stevens's signature to articles of surrender permitting Zwicker to tes-

wwwwwwwwwwwwww

[5] These "subversive" authors included Bert Andrews, chief of the Washington Bureau of the New York *Herald Tribune;* Richard Lauterbach, former European correspondent of *Time* magazine; Clarence Streit, long-time leader in a movement for the union of the western democracies; Walter White, distinguished Negro leader; and Foster Rhea Dulles, professor of history at Ohio State University and a cousin of the Secretary of State.

[6] Joseph and Stewart Alsop, "We Accuse!" *Harper's Magazine,* CCIX (October 1954), pp. 25–45.

tify after all. The army struck back on March 11, 1954, with the charge that McCarthy and his staff had attempted by various improper means to obtain preferential treatment for Private G. David Schine, former "consultant" to the subcommittee.

This embroilment led to televised hearings by the subcommittee that captivated millions for thirty-five days during the late spring of 1954. McCarthy dominated these proceedings as he had dominated all such affairs —interrupting, raising "points of order," evading questions, bullying witnesses, glowering, sneering, obstructing. Many Americans saw McCarthy in action for the first time. They saw uncouth arrogance, frank brutality, and a calloused disregard for established rules, law, the rights of others, and human decency. They saw the face of evil and recognized it.

Equally important, McCarthy's performance goaded both the Senate and the President into their first open defiance. The Democratic members of the McCarthy subcommittee could hardly acquiesce or look the other way before a national television audience, and bluntly opposed their chairman for the first time. President Eisenhower delivered an uncompromising blast from the White House. During the hearing, McCarthy had produced a letter containing secret material from the FBI files and announced that federal employees were "duty bound" to give him information "even though some bureaucrat may have stamped it secret." This was open aggression against the rights of the Executive, and the White House responded with the flat statement that executive responsibility could not "be usurped by any individual who may seek to set himself above the laws of our land or to override orders of the President of the United States." [7]

McCarthy's star was on the wane by the time the hearing ground to a close in June 1954. The hearings themselves ended in victory for neither side, but McCarthy was the real loser. His investigation of the army installation at Fort Monmouth had collapsed; he had lost his hitherto dictatorial control over the subcommittee; and both the Senate and the President had come out in open opposition. In August, following debate over a censure resolution introduced by Senator Ralph Flanders of Vermont, the Senate voted to appoint a special committee to investigate McCarthy's conduct as a senator. After prolonged hearings, in which McCarthy for once appeared as defendant rather than prosecutor, the committee submitted a 40,000-word report that recommended censure on two counts. By a vote of sixty-seven to twenty-two, the Senate adopted a resolution "condemning" certain of McCarthy's actions on December 2, 1954.

There followed a rapid downhill trail to obscurity and death. The Democratic victory in the election of 1954 cost McCarthy his committee chairmanships. The Senate thereafter ignored him. A host of physical ailments, apparently complicated by excessive drinking, drained his vitality. His will to resume the struggle seemed to have been sapped by the events of 1954, and he never again captured the headlines or strode dramatically into the limelight. A hard core of devoted followers remained loyal to the end—and afterward—but most Americans simply forgot about him. When McCarthy died on May 2, 1957, of complications induced by neuritis, hepatitis, and

[7] In reply, McCarthy referred again to the "evidence of treason that has been growing over the past twenty—twenty-*one* years."

inflammation of the liver, the era to which he had given his name was already dead.[8]

239. *The Anomaly of American Politics, 1953–1960*

Although the new President was instrumental in restoring a measure of unity and confidence to a nation torn by fear of Communism at home and abroad, the most striking feature of American politics during the 1950's was its confused and unstable condition. Eisenhower's huge majority in 1952 signaled the breakup of the Roosevelt coalition of laborers, farmers, urban minorities, and Southerners that had dominated American politics since the early thirties, but no new majority coalition of any stability or permanence took its place. The result was stalemate, and even a Roosevelt or a Wilson would have found it difficult to assert positive leadership in similar circumstances.

It was not merely that cleavages within and between the two major parties limited constructive action on domestic affairs. Consistency and recognizable patterns seemed to vanish from the political scene. Traditional party allegiance declined in almost every group, class, and section of the country. A huge "swing vote" appeared, varying in size and composition with each election. Millions of Americans adopted the practice of voting a split ticket, supporting a man or an issue rather than a party, and shifting sides repeatedly in response to circumstances. For the decade as a whole, the two parties were more nearly equal in voting strength than at any time since the early 1890's. Under the cumulative impact of depression, war, cold war, prosperity, and social change, an unstable and unpredictable equilibrium had become the political norm.

A brief analysis of the various pressures that shattered the Roosevelt coalition in 1952 will best illustrate the scope and nature of this political ferment. Fear of Communism in government and resentment over the Korean War, as noted in the preceding chapter, swung many traditionally Democratic votes into the Republican column in 1952. The extreme charges of Democratic disloyalty—"twenty years of treason," the alleged "sellout" at Yalta, and so on—had their most telling impact upon Americans of German descent, and upon Catholics generally. Genuinely fearful of Communism, these elements reacted more strongly to the loyalty issue perhaps because

~~~~~~~~~~~~~~~~~~~~~~~~

[8] McCarthy's decline was perhaps as much symptom as cause. Except for a determined minority on the far right, Americans were beginning to realize by 1955 that there were more important problems—or more interesting diversions—than the search for Communists in government. Common sense was reasserting itself, especially after the loyalty probes received a deadly blow in the early months of 1955. Harvey Matusow, a voluble ex-Communist who had been a prize witness in the government's case against certain individuals, suddenly went back on his former testimony, confessed to perjury, and admitted having lied about the individuals in question. A few other ex-Communists, some of whom had been retained by the Department of Justice as consultants in preparing cases against alleged subversives, also repudiated earlier testimony. The country could not help but laugh at the spectacle of committees actually trying to persuade these gentlemen that they were lying now about having lied earlier; the whole process of anti-Communist investigation was thrown into confusion and disrepute, and never fully recovered.

their own Americanism had been suspect in times past. Many clung to their suspicions or resentments long after the second Red Scare had subsided, and the Democratic party did not regain its old following among Catholic voters until the end of the decade.

Far more pervasive in its impact upon older voting habits was the mounting prosperity of the postwar years. Among farmers, for example, the dire economic plight that had produced Democratic majorities in most rural areas in the 1930's was largely gone. The farmer continued to rely upon governmental price supports and other New Deal benefits, but since 1941 he had exchanged problems of poverty for the worries of relative affluence. By midcentury the odds were that the tenant of fifteen years before (if he had not simply moved to the city) now owned his own farm, and that the owner of fifteen years before had paid off the mortgage and put cash in the bank. Debtor psychology had vanished. The steadily rising costs that accompanied the purchase and upkeep of farm machinery made inflation a matter of prime concern. Thus the farmer now disapproved of governmental spending—except, of course, for agricultural price supports—and tended to regard Democratic fiscal and welfare policies as more inflationary than those of the Republicans. Moreover, the rural voter was prey to the rather widespread public feeling that labor unions had grown too strong and exercised undue influence in the Democratic party.

Comparable pressures were at work in urban areas, where regular Democratic majorities of 60 and 70 per cent had been the rule in the 1930's and 1940's. The urban masses were joining the middle class. As millions of families moved from city slums to become suburban homeowners after 1945, fear of inflation often outweighed older class prejudices. As they began paying income and property taxes for the first time in their lives, many erstwhile tenement dwellers reconsidered their party loyalties. Voting returns suggested in the mid-fifties that a new Republican majority in the suburbs now offset the Democratic big-city vote. Moreover, urban political machines lost much of their cohesion and power as the federal government assumed larger shares of the welfare burden, and as once-submerged ethnic groups climbed the social ladder and challenged the dominance of former leaders. Among urban groups in the 1950's, only the Negro retained the staunch Democratic loyalty that the New Deal had fostered twenty years before.

Labor leaders were often unable to hold their members in line as a bulwark of Democratic power. The goals that had united labor politically during the thirties had long since been won, and Democratic allegiance was undermined by fear of inflation, dislike of taxes, resentment of the Korean War, and dissatisfaction with trade and tariff policies in certain industries. Attempts by AFL-CIO leaders to influence Democratic policy and marshal labor support for Democratic candidates alienated many non-union Democrats and frequently, as in the abortive campaign to unseat Senator Taft in 1950, backfired even among the union rank and file.

Political life changed even more in the South in the 1950's. The region was no longer blighted by backward one-crop agriculture, tenancy, rural poverty, and wool-hatted rustics. It now boasted of growing cities and plush modern suburbs, booming industries, a large urban middle class, newly prosperous farms, and an economy more nearly in tune with that of the nation as a whole than ever before in history. At the same time, the southern tradition of white supremacy faced a challenge unparalleled since Reconstruction. The nature and impact of this challenge, embodied in the drive for civil rights legislation, the Supreme Court's desegregation decision of 1954, and the growing determination of American Negroes to assert their rights and destroy the barriers of discrimination, will be discussed later. It should be noted here that the racial challenge, coinciding as it did with the impact of economic change, had a profoundly unsettling effect on southern politics.

The ultimate outcome of this political ferment remained in doubt by 1960. In presidential elections, at least, the "Solid South" was a thing of the past. The chances that a genuine two-party system would emerge looked brighter than at any time since the 1890's. Economic transformation and the assault upon segregation produced two insurgent factions in southern politics, both highly vocal and determined to register a protest. The first, drawing its main strength from the old "black belt" counties and the low-income urban wards, was frankly dedicated to preservation of white supremacy. The other consisted of the rising business and professional elements in southern cities who were increasingly resentful of their impotence in a one-party system.

An odd paradox resulted. These two rebellious factions had only one thing in common—vigorous opposition to the national Democratic party. Segregationists were arrayed against the national party's stand on civil rights; the southern business group resented dominance of the party by the northern urban-labor wing and were conservative on economic and social questions. Both factions began voting for Republican presidential candidates in the frank hope of depriving the Democrats of federal power. Even so, they could not combine for effective political co-operation. Many southern rural and labor voters who favored segregation were progressive on economic and welfare issues. The urban middle classes were not willing to jeopardize economic and moral progress by all-out resistance to increased civil rights for Negroes. As a result, the two factions could not co-operate effectively in state and local politics. The one-party system remained, ambiguous though it often was.

However, the break in southern Democratic solidarity in presidential elections during the 1950's was striking. The GOP carried four of the ex-Confederate states in 1952, five in 1956, and three in 1960. Even more startling were Republican gains in the southern popular vote. The GOP won a paltry 22 per cent of the major-party vote in the South in 1940, and 28 per cent in 1944. In contrast, it won 49 per cent in 1952, almost 51 per cent in 1956, and not quite 48 per cent in 1960.

Republicans were unable to construct a stable national majority of their own during the 1950's, in spite of the general erosion of Democratic strength. The Roosevelt coalition had been broken because the conditions that gave it birth were largely gone, but the Democrats still retained a majority of several million registered voters throughout the Eisenhower years. It was no longer a reliable majority, but the country remained "normally" Democratic, and neither prosperity, Eisenhower's popularity, nor the frustrations and resentments of the Korean War and the second Red Scare could make permanent Republicans out of the millions of Democrats who supported Eisenhower in 1952.

General prosperity had in effect created a nation of moderates who refused to give blind allegiance to either party. The American people had neither forgotten the Great Depression nor turned their backs on the New Deal. If prosperity had engendered a new sensitivity to inflation and opposition to governmental spending, depression memories prevented any return to the Republican "normalcy" of the 1920's and produced a reaction in favor of the Democrats in times of recession. Nor were registered Democrats alone in their new independent voting habits. Districts that had remained loyal to the GOP throughout the thirties suddenly went Democratic in the 1950's. Voters often self-consciously swung back and forth in order to keep the parties in approximate balance. "I voted for Eisenhower to turn the tide of too much reliance on government," an Illinois farmer explained in 1954. "Now I'm voting Democratic again to see that things don't go too far the other way." Or, as a Jersey City bus driver put it, "I'd like to see a different party in control of each part of Congress. Then they'll watch each other and won't let either party have things too much its own way." [9]

240. National Elections in the 1950's

The effect of shifting political alignments was felt most acutely in national elections. The GOP could do no better in 1952 than break even in the Senate and win a majority of eight in the House. The trend during the balance of the decade, with the exception of Eisenhower's vote in 1956, was toward a steady resurgence of Democratic strength. A mild recession, beginning in the early months of 1954, caused a rise in unemployment and touched off fears of depression. These alarms, when added to rural discontent over administration farm policy, contributed to a Republican reversal in the midterm elections of 1954. Although the President stumped for Republican candidates, the Democrats won a precarious majority in the Senate and regained control of the lower house by a margin of 232 to 203. Republicans could derive some comfort from the claim that their losses had been less than those normally suffered by the party in power in a midterm election. Moreover, fear of depression had not revived the huge Democratic majorities of New Deal days.

Even more indicative of the new political stalemate were the results in 1956. The only serious question on the Republican side was the President's health. He had suffered a major heart attack in the autumn of 1955 and had undergone an operation for ileitis in the late spring of 1956. His recovery in both cases had been so remarkable as to remove most doubts about his ability to serve a second term, and Republican leaders well knew that defeat impended if he did not run again. They were also determined to renominate the more controversial Nixon for the vice-presidency. Nixon had outraged Democrats and offended a few liberal Republicans by his vigorous use of the

ᴧᴧᴧᴧᴧᴧᴧᴧᴧᴧᴧᴧᴧᴧᴧᴧᴧᴧᴧ

[9] Both quotations are from Samuel Lubell, *Revolt of the Moderates* (New York, 1956), p. 118.

Communist issue in the campaigns of 1952 and 1954, but GOP strategists were convinced that he was the best link between the moderate and conservative wings of the party. There was a momentary flurry late in the preconvention period when Harold Stassen, the President's adviser on disarmament, suggested that the party should try to find a new vice-presidential candidate. It was not taken seriously, and a jubilant Republican convention met in San Francisco on August 20, 1956, and quickly renominated Eisenhower and Nixon. They adopted a platform promising flexible price supports for farmers, federal aid to schools, revision of the Taft-Hartley Act, and tax reductions if possible. As for civil rights, the platform approved the Supreme Court's desegregation decision of 1954 but opposed the use of force to implement it.

Meanwhile, the Democrats had met in Chicago on August 13 and renominated Adlai E. Stevenson of Illinois. Stevenson had retained most of his prestige and following within the party and had been its titular head and major spokesman since his loss to Eisenhower in 1952. But he did not win the second nomination without a struggle. Senator Estes Kefauver of Tennessee, a southern liberal whose national reputation was based largely upon his investigations of crime, announced in the spring of 1956 that he would enter certain Democratic primaries and seek the presidential nomination. A long, exhausting, and uninspiring primary battle between Stevenson and Kefauver then ensued. The Tennessean scored early successes in New Hampshire and Minnesota by dint of prodigious energy and much handshaking, then lost to Stevenson in the Florida, California, and Oregon primaries. When Democratic conventions in state after state named pro-Stevenson or favorite-son delegates to the national convention, Kefauver gave up the contest and came out for Stevenson's candidacy on August 1. Stevenson encountered a second challenge when former President Truman came to the convention to work for the candidacy of Governor Averell S. Harriman of New York. But the Stevenson forces were sufficiently well organized and powerful to beat down this threat, and the Illinoisan won the nomination on the first ballot.

The only unexpected development at the Democratic convention occurred in the selection of a running-mate. Stevenson announced soon after his renomination that he would leave the convention free to choose a vice-presidential candidate. A feverish battle for second place on the ticket immediately broke out, with several younger aspirants—notably Senators Hubert Humphrey of Minnesota, Albert Gore of Tennessee, and John F. Kennedy of Massachusetts—competing among the state delegates for support. Kefauver also entered the contest, which soon became a Kefauver-Kennedy duel. Kefauver won in the end, but the most noteworthy aspect was the willingness with which Southerners had supported Kennedy, a Roman Catholic.

The Democratic platform promised more generous and rigid price supports, a higher minimum wage law, and repeal of the Taft-Hartley Act. It also advocated a balanced budget, federal atomic energy plants, better conservation of natural resources, and tax reduction for lower-income groups. The civil rights plank cautiously endorsed the recent Supreme Court decision and called for continued efforts to wipe out discrimination, but it contained no pledge to implement desegregation and was distinctly weaker than its Republican counterpart. The platform also attacked the Eisenhower foreign and domestic policies. It claimed that the administration had weakened the defense establishment, damaged America's standing with her allies, increased the risk of war, and ignored the needs of farmers, small businessmen, low-income groups, and elderly citizens.

The second Eisenhower-Stevenson campaign was a dull affair. The Democrats, to be sure, labored under staggering disadvantages. The President was at the peak of his popularity and almost invulnerable to criticism, and Stevenson groped vainly for an issue. Charges that Eisenhower's uncertain health would impair his leadership made no visible impact whatever. Nothing in the Democratic arsenal could possibly match the Republican appeal of the twin themes of "peace and prosperity." Neither farm discontent nor unemployment was acute enough to cause a major political upheaval. No matter how they treated it, the civil rights question was more liability than asset to the Democrats. They did their best to make an issue out of Nixon, but the Vice President offered an unsatisfactory target. When Stevenson tried to discuss the perils of radioactive fallout and the need for a cessation of nuclear testing, the country seemed satisfied that the experienced Eisenhower knew best about such matters. As in 1952, the press was overwhelmingly Republican.

To make matters worse for the Democrats, Stevenson ran far less effectively than in 1952. He seemed unsure of himself and lacked much of the deft wit, courageous realism, and lofty eloquence that had marked his first campaign. And when he tried to adopt a more "folksy" manner and appeal to the "average" voters, the effect was disappointing. In retrospect, it is doubtful that anything Stevenson might have said or done would have affected the outcome. The sudden eruption of the Hungarian and Suez crises a few days before the election (for details, see below, pp. 820–1, 839–43) raised serious questions about the wisdom of recent American diplomacy, but the Democrats could not profit from the issue. Most Americans apparently believed that the soldier-statesman's experienced leadership was more necessary than ever now that threat of war seemed imminent.

The result on November 6 was an Eisenhower landslide of almost staggering proportions. The Republican candidate received a record number of 35,582,236 popular votes and carried forty-one states with 457 electoral votes. Stevenson, with 26,028,887 popular votes, won only the seventy-three electoral votes of Missouri, Arkansas, Alabama, Mississippi, Georgia, and the Carolinas. Only in Missouri, California, and a few of the western farm states did Eisenhower fail to run more strongly than in 1952.

Given the magnitude of this victory, the results in Congress were striking and quite without precedent. The Democrats carried both houses, retaining their narrow majority in the Senate and slightly enlarging their House margin to 234 to 201. Never before had a party won both branches of Congress while losing the presidency.[10] In part, of course, the outcome was a

[10] The Republicans failed to capture either house when Lincoln triumphed in 1860, but the opposition was divided, and no single party could claim a majority in the lower house. Zachary Taylor failed to carry either branch for the Whigs in 1848, but the Democrats were also a minority in the lower house: the balance of power was held by a small bloc of Free Soil congressmen.

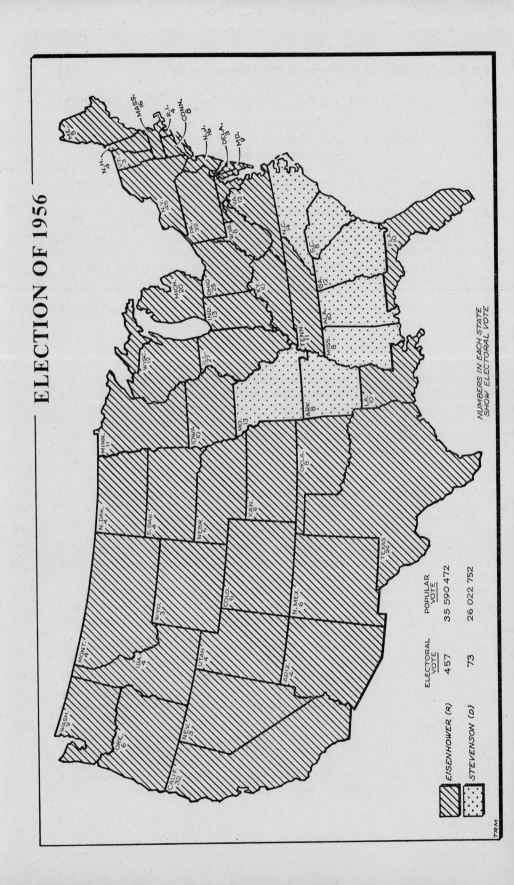

ELECTION OF 1956

NUMBERS IN EACH STATE
SHOW ELECTORAL VOTE

	ELECTORAL VOTE	POPULAR VOTE
EISENHOWER (R)	457	35 590 472
STEVENSON (D)	73	26 022 752

personal tribute to Eisenhower. It also indicated that the country retained a normal Democratic majority, but that this majority had utterly lost its cohesion at the national level.

Two years later the Republicans suffered one of the worst midterm defeats in American history. The country was shaken from its complacency by a series of events in 1957 and 1958 that gravely weakened public confidence in the Eisenhower administration; for the first time, even the President's own popularity declined. A recession beginning in late 1957 brought a sharp rise in unemployment and reawakened old fears of depression. The much-publicized launching of the Russian *Sputnik* satellites caused widespread alarm and dissatisfaction over the state of American education, science, and defense. The need to enforce desegregation by the use of federal troops in Little Rock, Arkansas, dramatized all of the unlovely possibilities of that explosive question. International crises in the Middle and Far East in 1958 vastly increased the threat of war. Finally, labor opposition solidified in response to Republican attempts to enact "right to work" laws and other anti-union measures in several states.

Beset by these liabilities,[11] the Republicans received a stunning rebuke at the polls in the fall of 1958. The Democrats enlarged their congressional majorities to a massive 64 to 34 in the Senate and 283 to 153 in the House, the largest since the heyday of the New Deal twenty-two years before. There was a resurgence of Democratic strength among white-collar workers, young voters, and suburbanites. Moreover, the campaign of 1958 revealed a strong revival of progressivism. Dozens of able young liberals in both parties swept into office, while a host of diehard conservatives, notably Republican Senators William Jenner of Indiana, William F. Knowland of California, John Bricker of Ohio, and George Malone of Nevada, retired or went down to defeat.

However, neither the fact of the huge Democratic majorities nor the new progressive impulse was sufficient to pull the nation from its middle course during the final two years of the Eisenhower era. The country emerged rapidly from the recession in the early months of 1959, and the President, warning against the dangers of inflation, made effective use of the veto to block what he regarded as overly ambitious or costly Democratic legislation. On most domestic matters the Democratic majority was less impressive than it looked. The southern Democratic-conservative Republican coalition, a powerful force in Congress since 1938, was often able to modify or defeat progressive measures. Moreover, the Democratic leaders in Con-

[11] To complete the Republicans' discomfiture, the public learned in the spring of 1958 that Sherman Adams, the dour-faced ex-Governor of New Hampshire, who since 1953 had wielded great power and influence in the administration as Assistant to the President—in effect the White House chief of staff—had accepted gifts and favors from a New England industrialist under compromising circumstances. Though hardly a flagrant or earth-shaking example of official misconduct, the episode was highly embarrassing to the administration—first, because the GOP had made clean government a major talking-point in every campaign, with Adams often hailed as the leading watchdog against corruptionists and influence-peddlers; and, second, because Eisenhower insisted upon retaining Adams in his post for months after the disclosure, despite a mounting chorus of criticism. "I need him," was the President's sole and none too comforting response to the critics. When Adams finally resigned in September as protests became too strenuous to ignore, the political damage had already been done.

gress—the Senate Majority Leader, Lyndon B. Johnson, and the veteran Speaker of the House, Sam Rayburn, both Texans and highly skilled politicians—followed a deliberate strategy of compromise and co-operation in their dealings with the White House. They were political realists, as moderate in many respects as the President himself. They preferred to keep party ranks intact and work for victory in 1960 rather than risk the internal disruption that an overly progressive program would cause between the northern and southern wings.

Moderation thus remained the keynote in American politics as the decade came to a close. Progressivism had stirred noticeably in 1958, and there were signs that increasing numbers of Americans were in a mood for more positive leadership as the need for domestic action in certain areas mounted. But complacency, fear of inflation and excessive spending, and uncertain political allegiance remained forces to reckon with. Few political experts felt overly confident in their predictions about the outcome of the 1960 campaign.

241. *Dynamic Conservatism: The Cabinet and Fiscal Policy*

It was generally expected that a rightward swing in domestic policy impended as the Eisenhower administration took office in January 1953. Actually, the new administration was to be far less conservative than many progressives feared and many Republicans hoped. Neither Eisenhower nor his closest advisers contemplated anything like a return to the business-as-usual policy of the 1920's. The emphasis would be, as the President expressed it, upon "dynamic conservatism"—caution in financial and economic matters, but careful attention to problems of human welfare.

In many respects, however, the early months of the Eisenhower administration were decidedly more conservative than dynamic. The new cabinet seemed, and to some extent was, a citadel of orthodox Republicanism. For the important post of Secretary of State, the President chose John Foster Dulles, experienced diplomat, leading Republican spokesman on foreign policy, and wealthy corporation lawyer. Two prominent corporation executives, George Humphrey of the M. A. Hanna Steel Company and Charles E. Wilson of General Motors, headed the Treasury and Defense departments. Ezra Taft Benson, conservative farm marketing specialist and Apostle of the Mormon Church, became Secretary of Agriculture. A New England industrialist, Sinclair Weeks, was appointed Secretary of Commerce, while an automobile distributor, Arthur E. Summerfield, became Postmaster General. Governor Douglas McKay of Oregon headed the Interior Department. The new Attorney General was Herbert Brownell, Jr., of New York, legal aide and close political ally of Thomas E. Dewey. For the Secretaryship of Labor, Eisenhower turned to the union leader Martin P. Durkin, president of the United Association of Journeymen Plumbers and Steamfitters.

So studded with wealth and business connections was the Eisenhower cabinet that the *New Republic*'s irreverent description—"eight millionaires and a plumber"—though not precisely accurate, enjoyed wide circulation in the early months of 1953, especially among Democrats. A ninth "millionaire" was added in April when the President appointed Mrs. Oveta Culp

Hobby, wartime commander of the WAC and wife of a wealthy Texas publisher, to head the newly created Department of Health, Education and Welfare.

The early statements and attitudes of some of the new cabinet members could not help but alarm progressives. Secretary Benson, for example, was a devout and outspoken believer in self-reliance, free enterprise, and rugged individualism; he wanted to reduce if not eliminate federal aid to farmers. Secretary Wilson delivered the first of several memorable utterances in the Senate hearings that attended confirmation of his appointment. Unable to see any potential conflict of interest between his new position in the Defense Department and his large holdings of General Motors stock, Wilson bluntly affirmed that "what was good for the country was good for General Motors, and vice versa." Secretary Humphrey, uncompromising advocate of a balanced budget, tighter credit, reduced spending, and lower taxes, seemed to provide the most symbolic gesture of all when he restored a portrait of Andrew W. Mellon, high priest of economic normalcy in the 1920's, to the wall of his office. And progressives exchanged more grim nods in the summer of 1953 when Secretary of Labor Durkin resigned, charging that the administration had not kept its promise to revise the Taft-Hartley Act.[12]

By and large, the cabinet was much less conservative than it looked or sounded. For all their orthodox talk, businessmen like Humphrey and Wilson were hardheaded realists whose basic approach to specific problems was pragmatic rather than doctrinaire. They had gained their business experience in the age of Franklin Roosevelt, not of McKinley, and they were accustomed to operating within the New Deal–Fair Deal framework. Adaptable and flexible, serving a president whose approach was as untheoretical as their own, they had no intention of trying to turn the clock back to 1921.

Even so, Republicans were determined to make it tick more slowly in certain areas of government activity. One of the first acts of the new administration was elimination of federal price, wage, rent, and other controls established during the Korean War. Twenty-eight federally owned synthetic rubber plants were sold to private corporations. The Reconstruction Finance Corporation, created by Herbert Hoover during the Great Depression, was allowed to go out of business in 1953.

Even more indicative of the early conservative trend was the administration's fiscal policy, which strongly reflected the views of Secretary Humphrey and Senator Taft. Tax reductions for individuals and corporations went into effect on January 1, 1954, and a vigorous attempt was made to bring the federal budget into balance. The attempt failed, but the Republicans did succeed in slashing federal expenditures in the fiscal year 1954 by fully $6,500,000,000 under the figure for the preceding year, a reduction of almost 10 per cent. At the same time, Secretary Humphrey, in co-operation with the Federal Reserve Board, moved to avert inflation by raising interest rates and tightening credit in the early months of 1953.

Despite this initial application of doctrinaire conservatism, the Eisen-

wwwwwwwwwwwwww

[12] Durkin was succeeded by a department store vice president, James P. Mitchell, experienced labor relations and manpower specialist who had served as director of industrial personnel in the War Department during the Second World War.

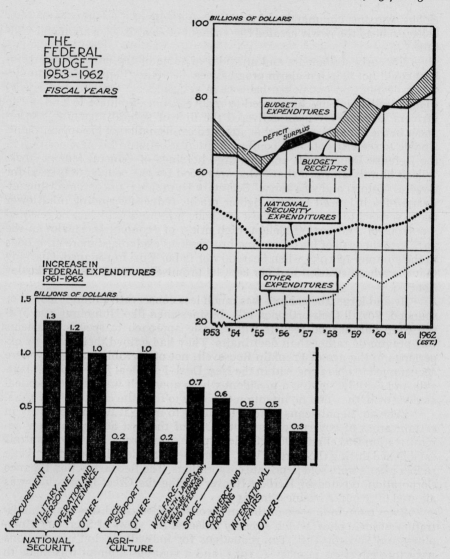

THE FEDERAL BUDGET 1953–1962
FISCAL YEARS

BILLIONS OF DOLLARS

100
80
60
40
20

BUDGET EXPENDITURES

DEFICIT   SURPLUS

BUDGET RECEIPTS

NATIONAL SECURITY EXPENDITURES

OTHER EXPENDITURES

1953 '54 '55 '56 '57 '58 '59 '60 '61 1962 (EST.)

INCREASE IN FEDERAL EXPENDITURES 1961–1962

BILLIONS OF DOLLARS

1.5
1.0
0.5

1.3 1.2 1.0   1.0   0.7 0.6 0.5 0.5   0.3
                0.2   0.2

PROCUREMENT MILITARY PERSONNEL OPERATION AND MAINTENANCE OTHER PRICE SUPPORT OTHER WELFARE (HEALTH, LABOR, WELFARE, EDUCATION, AND VETERANS) SPACE COMMERCE AND HOUSING INTERNATIONAL AFFAIRS OTHER

NATIONAL SECURITY   AGRI-CULTURE

hower administration's basic realism was nowhere more evident than in the realm of fiscal policy. Humphrey believed fervently in a balanced budget and tighter credit, yet he quickly learned that a too rigorous application of deflationary policies was both dangerous and, in the long run, impossible. Raising the interest rates on new government bond issues hurt the market price of older bonds and stirred complaint from bankers. A short time later tightened credit induced a slump in economic indices that contributed to a recession in 1954. As investment, employment, production, and corporate profits declined in 1954, federal tax revenues fell off, and balancing the budget became correspondingly more difficult. Furthermore, federal expenditures simply could not be slashed indefinitely; the government cut military appropriations by another $6,000,000,000 in the 1955 budget but could not hold the line elsewhere. Upon investigation, Humphrey realized that a continued high rate of economic aid to foreign countries was vital to American security, and he agreed to a 30 per cent increase in foreign aid for 1955. "Before coming in here," Humphrey admitted frankly, "I had no idea of the extent to which our own security was involved in whatever happens in the world." The demand for larger appropriations for veterans' benefits, welfare, agriculture, and housing was impossible to ignore. Thus the second Eisenhower budget ended with a larger deficit than the first.

The administration seemed to have learned its lesson and followed a flexible policy for the balance of the decade. Though still on guard against inflation, the Treasury Department and Federal Reserve Board were quick to ease credit and apply other "countercyclical" measures whenever the economy lagged—as in the recessions of 1954 and 1957–8. Rigid insistence on a balanced budget was frankly abandoned. The government showed a small surplus in 1956 and 1957, but it accepted a deficit in 1958 and a much larger one in 1959—the largest in thirteen years—as higher appropriations for defense, foreign aid, welfare, agriculture, and housing were approved in the face of decreased federal revenues. Balance was achieved again in 1960, only to disappear before a $4,000,000,000 deficit in 1961.

The administration also bowed to financial reality in the matter of tax reduction. Excise taxes were lowered slightly in 1954, and revision of the internal revenue code in that year relieved individuals and certain businesses of some $1,400,000,000 in income taxes during 1955. But thereafter, despite pressure from both business and labor for further reductions, the government maintained existing rates for excise taxes and individual and corporate incomes.

242. *Dynamic Conservatism: Natural Resources and Public Power*

The most "conservative" of the Eisenhower policies, and certainly one of the most controversial, involved the role of government in developing electrical power and natural resources. The power controversy had been important at least since Coolidge's time; the conservation question, since Theodore Roosevelt's; and President Eisenhower had firm views about each. Though by no means reactionary, he believed that too large a federal role in these areas resulted in waste and "creeping socialism," both of which he deplored. In regard to conservation, the President believed that government ownership of natural resources often infringed upon the rights of states and should be carefully circumscribed. On the power issue, Eisenhower advocated neither expansion nor withdrawal of federal activity, but rather a kind of partnership between government and private industry that would both serve the public interest and strengthen so-called free enterprise. The two subjects were most effectively dramatized by three specific controversies that arose during the Eisenhower era—the tidelands oil deposits, the Hell's Canyon Dam project, and the Dixon-Yates contract with the Atomic Energy Commission.

The tidelands oil controversy went back to the 1930's. Huge oil deposits had been discovered in the coastal areas off California and the Gulf states, and dispute immediately arose over ownership. The states fought the claims of the Roosevelt administration to the submerged lands, and the controversy remained unsettled during the Truman era. Congress adopted bills in 1946 and 1952 granting title to the states, but President Truman vetoed both; and Supreme Court decisions in 1947 and 1950 affirmed the "paramount rights" of the federal government to the offshore lands. President Eisenhower, however, was favorably disposed toward the state viewpoint. Sworn to oppose what he termed "federal encroachment upon the rights and affairs of the states," Eisenhower signed the Submerged Lands Act on May 22, 1953, after it had passed both houses of Congress by substantial majorities. The Act gave title to submerged coastal lands within their "historic boundaries" [13] to the states but recognized federal jurisdiction over the Continental Shelf extending beyond these boundaries. Denouncing the measure as a gigantic "giveaway," opponents of the new law agreed with its defenders that the principle of state rights had won a notable victory.

Meanwhile, the historic power controversy blazed merrily during the 1950's. Public power advocates wanted the government to build and operate a huge dam and hydroelectric plant in Hell's Canyon, on the Snake River in Idaho. Strongly averse to the expansion of federal activity in the power industry, the President opposed Democratic bills for the Hell's Canyon project and threw his support behind the counterproposal of a private firm, the Idaho Power Company, to develop power in the region by the erection of three smaller dams. After a bitter two-year battle, the Idaho company obtained a license from the FPC for its project in 1955. The Democrats renewed the attempt to pass a Hell's Canyon bill in the next two sessions of Congress, but could not hold their majority together. Rejecting one such measure in 1956, the Senate passed another in 1957 only to see it fail in the House, where a number of Democrats swung to the administration side and voted against the bill. An insurmountable veto would have awaited it in any case, the President having condemned federal development of the project as wasteful and fought the proposal at every step. Progressives were forced to accept Hell's Canyon as another major defeat.

The Dixon-Yates controversy began in 1953 over the means of providing increased electrical power to the AEC's atomic energy plant at Paducah, Kentucky. The Tennessee Valley Authority discovered that its hydroelectric installations could not supply the AEC's expanding needs. The TVA consequently asked Congress for $100,000,000 to erect a new steam plant at Fulton, Tennessee. Congress rejected this request, and the President, strongly opposed to the indefinite expansion of federal power projects in the Tennessee Valley, supported a proposal already under consideration by the AEC to obtain its power from private sources. A newly formed utility group, headed by Edgar H. Dixon, president of Middle South Utilities, and Eugene A. Yates, chairman of the Southern Company, had

---

[13] Three miles in the case of Louisiana, Alabama, and Mississippi, ten and a half (three leagues) in the case of Texas and Florida. Three Supreme Court decisions in 1960 upheld these differences on the grounds that only the two latter states had produced evidence that their historic boundaries extended beyond the normal three-mile limit.

offered to construct a new generating plant, with a capacity of 600,000 kilowatts, at West Memphis, Arkansas. The plant would sell its power to TVA, which could then divert more of its own electricity to the AEC.

The Dixon-Yates proposal immediately became the major issue in a slashing battle between friends and opponents of public power. Although Eisenhower, on June 17, 1954, directed the AEC to negotiate a twenty-five-year contract with the Dixon-Yates company (its terms had been approved by the Bureau of the Budget and the FPC), five months of heated controversy elapsed before the contract was signed. Three of the five members of the AEC at first opposed the contract, approval of which was also required by the Joint Congressional Committee on Atomic Energy. This committee found that there had been no competitive bidding, that an allegedly better offer from a New York group had been rejected, and that the TVA, which was bitterly opposed to the plan, had not been consulted until late in the proceedings. The Democrats were now attacking the Dixon-Yates project in full force, claiming that the administration was trying to scuttle the TVA and create a private power monopoly in its place. The administration won the first round when the AEC voted its approval of the Dixon-Yates contract and signed it on November 11, 1954. The Joint Congressional Committee on Atomic Energy also endorsed the contract seven days later by a strict party vote after a few revisions had been obtained.

New disclosures, mounting protests, and heightened opposition from the Democrats, who won control of Congress in 1954, brought defeat to the Dixon-Yates project in 1955. Among the leaders in the Democratic assault was Senator Kefauver of Tennessee, staunch defender of the TVA and a member of the Senate anti-monopoly subcommittee that conducted hearings on the Dixon-Yates contract. Republicans indignantly denied Kefauver's blunt assertion that the Dixon-Yates power company would be a "risk-free, government-granted, and government-guaranteed monopoly." But serious questions did exist as to the proposed method of financing the new company, its expected profits, and its ultimate effect upon TVA. The administration might have weathered these charges, but it could hardly ignore the implications of a new disclosure in the early months of 1955. This was the revelation that the special consultant who had advised the government to accept the Dixon-Yates contract in 1954 was a vice president of the investment firm that had been engaged to market the Dixon-Yates securities.

The whole affair had taken on a distinctly unsavory look, and President Eisenhower was quick to take advantage of an alternative. When the city of Memphis announced that it was ready to build a municipal power plant with ample capacity to supply the needed electricity, the President ordered cancellation of the Dixon-Yates contract on July 11, 1955. Later that year, on November 13, the AEC formally ruled that the contract had been invalid because of a possible conflict of interest in its negotiation. Public power advocates were much relieved at this defeat of an alleged threat to the TVA, while the President could take comfort from the fact that a municipal rather than a new federal power plant was being constructed.

One other phase of the power controversy, of which the Dixon-Yates question had in fact been a part, centered around the President's program for the development of atomic energy. In a celebrated "Atoms-for-Peace" address before the United Nations in December 1953, Eisenhower proposed the international pooling of atomic information and materials and the use of this common fund in peaceful pursuits. The plan was favorably received both at home and abroad. In the Atomic Energy Act of 1954, Congress included a provision authorizing the President to join other nations in creating an international atomic pool along the lines he had suggested.[14]

It was the domestic side of the President's atomic program, also implemented by the Atomic Energy Act of 1954, that rekindled the power controversy. Eisenhower's idea of sharing atomic information blended with his distrust of too much government to prompt the suggestion that American atomic development be opened under proper safeguards to private industry rather than remain a governmental monopoly. Battle lines formed immediately in Congress, and the private power clauses in the Atomic Energy Act did not pass without a long struggle that included a thirteen-day filibuster by Democratic opponents of the bill. As finally adopted, the Atomic Energy Act of 1954, approved by the President on August 30, made atomic material and production facilities available to private companies under AEC safeguards. It also authorized the AEC to license private construction of nuclear reactors and to pay a fair price for nuclear material produced in such reactors. All in all, though somewhat modified by Democratic revisions,[15] the Act was a victory for the President.

The Democrats were able gradually to expand the government's role in atomic developments despite opposition from the White House.[16] In the process of voting large appropriations in 1957 for the inauguration and continuation of various atomic projects, Congress debated a Democratic bill that called for federal construction of several large power reactors—a measure regarded as a blow at the Eisenhower "partnership" program. In the end a compromise bill was passed, including funds for three reactors

wwwwwwwwwwwwww

[14] The administration set to work at once, concluding an agreement, soon signed by representatives of seventy-nine other nations, creating an International Atomic Energy Agency. It was approved by the Senate in June 1957. The agency, which was to report annually to the United Nations, was designed to co-operate with other nations in peaceful atomic research, to disseminate information, and to establish safeguards preventing military misuse. The United States agreed to pay one third of the agency's administrative expense. The President was empowered to appoint American representatives to the agency, subject to Senate confirmation, and was instructed to report annually to Congress on the subject.

The United States in 1958 concluded an agreement with the New European Atomic Energy Community (Euratom)—France, West Germany, Italy, and the Benelux countries—to promote production of nuclear power in Europe. In this treaty the United States pledged a loan of $135 million and enough uranium to operate several reactors for a period of twenty years. These reactors, under a $100 million research program financed jointly by the United States and Euratom, were to be used to seek ways of cutting the cost of atomic power. Congress also amended the Atomic Energy Act in 1958 to permit greater exchange of atomic information and materials between the United States and its allies.

[15] The most important of these was a "patent-licensing" provision calling for compulsory sharing of commercial atomic patents for five years, to prevent the formation of patent monopolies.

[16] A Democratic bill to authorize federal pilot atomic reactors passed the Senate in 1956 but failed narrowly in the House. At the same time, the Democrats defeated two administration-sponsored measures to encourage private atomic power development.

which the administration did not want to build. They were to be constructed, maintained, and operated by the government, but the steam would be sold to co-operatives or public utilities to generate electricity.

243. *The Middle Road: Maintenance of the New Deal*

Eisenhower tried earnestly throughout his tenure to implement a moderate expansion of the New Deal economic and social policies. He was constantly hampered by conservatives who wanted no expansion at all, by progressives who wanted more than he was willing to approve, and by representatives of special interests with small concern for the general interest. Sectional, religious, and racial antagonisms often caused Congress to defeat or weaken important bills. The President's desire for an adequate welfare program was also circumscribed if not crippled by his own dislike of spending and of too much government. Yet he succeeded, despite setbacks in some areas and small results in others, in preserving and enlarging the complex body of welfare legislation initiated by Franklin Roosevelt and Harry Truman. Thus what is loosely called the New Deal was assimilated into bipartisan political tradition.

It was not easy going during Eisenhower's first two years in office, for conservative Republicans were firmly in the saddle in Congress. They liked "dynamic conservatism" no better than New Deal progressivism. They refused to permit revision of the Taft-Hartley Act, notwithstanding the pledge in the Republican platform of 1952. They rejected Eisenhower's proposals for federal support for health insurance systems, larger appropriations for highway construction, and limited federal aid to education. They nearly approved a constitutional amendment offered by Senator John W. Bricker of Ohio to limit the President's treaty-making power.[17] The tragic death of Senator Taft due to cancer in the early summer of 1953 only exacerbated this rift between the moderate and reactionary elements within the Republican Party, for Taft had supported the administration and used his great prestige and influence to win a measure of co-operation from the right wing during the early months of 1953.

On the whole, Eisenhower's programs fared better in the moderate and narrowly Democratic Eighty-fourth and Eighty-fifth Congresses (1955–8) than in the Republican Eighty-third (1953–4). The large Democratic majorities in the Eighty-sixth Congress of 1959–60 tended to be more progressive than the President, but here again the record was generally one of co-operation rather than obstruction. With the exception of the

~~~~~~~~~~~~~~~~~~~~~

[17] The Bricker amendment was prompted by both isolationist and state-rights sentiment. Specifically, it (1) invalidated all treaties dealing with matters constitutionally reserved to the states, unless individual state legislation gave specific approval of such treaties, and (2) gave Congress the power to regulate and pass upon all executive agreements with foreign nations and international organizations. Designed both to give Congress a dominant role in foreign policy and to prevent American participation in broad international agreements concerning human rights that might offend one or more of the states, the amendment was the subject of repeated hearings and acrid controversy throughout much of 1953 and 1954. It was finally rejected by the Senate on February 25, 1954, by a vote of fifty to forty-two.

power controversy, differences between Eisenhower and the Democrats on the broad questions of domestic reform and general welfare were differences of detail and degree, not of philosophy. Let us now see how various New Deal–Fair Deal policies fared at the hands of moderate congresses and a middle-of-the-road president.

Certainly the most difficult policy to maintain rationally was that of support for farm prices to assure parity income to agriculture. The nation's farmers were more efficient than ever before in history, but they were caught in an inexorable vise of rising costs of equipment, labor, and dis-

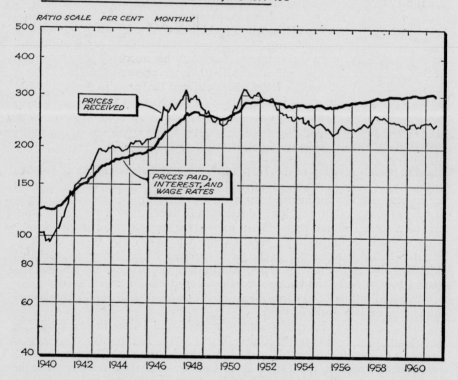

PRICES PAID AND RECEIVED BY FARMERS
DEPARTMENT OF AGRICULTURE DATA, 1910–1914=100

tribution. As a result, total net agricultural income declined by 35 per cent from 1947 to 1960, net income per farm by 12 per cent from 1947 to 1958.[18] The farmer's share of the retail cost of his product dropped from 51 per cent in 1947 to 39 per cent in 1960, and the parity ratio declined from 115 in 1947 to 100 in 1952, and to 79 in 1960. Large commercial farms were often prosperous, and farm tenancy had declined from 38.7 per cent in

[18] Net income per farm actually declined 29 per cent between 1947 and 1957, but higher prices for farm products in 1958 resulted in a gain in net income per farm from $2,060 in 1957 to $2,538 in 1958. A redefinition of "farm" in compiling data for 1959 and after renders comparison with earlier figures meaningless; but net income per farm held steady during the final three years of the Eisenhower administration.

1940 to 20.5 per cent in 1959. But all farmers—commercial, marginal, owner, and tenant—felt the price squeeze in one way or another.

It was generally agreed that overproduction was the major problem during the 1950's, as increasing use of machinery, fertilizer, and better scientific methods swelled the average yield per acre in startling fashion.[19] Farm prices sagged hopelessly beneath the weight of a gigantic surplus that overburdened the granaries and warehouses every year.[20] The government remained committed, as it had been since 1933, to the basic principle of farm price supports, but there was little agreement over the formula that would best achieve reduced production and fair prices. Whether governmental supports were raised or lowered, whether acreage allotments were increased or reduced, the farmer's natural tendency was to expand his yield to the fullest possible extent in order to achieve maximum profits. Hence total farm production mounted steadily.

Farm spokesmen were by no means unanimous on the subject, but they generally favored the highest price supports obtainable and opposed any reduction in the 90 per cent parity payments established by the Agricultural Act of 1949. The Eisenhower administration, on the other hand, followed the lead of Secretary Benson and advocated lower supports on a flexible sliding scale. Benson's basic theory was that high and rigid price supports only stimulated overproduction and thereby insured falling prices for the farmer and an ever costlier and less manageable surplus for the government. Congress, mindful of the farm vote, was cool to the Benson program, but the administration succeeded in making it the basis for the Agricultural Act of 1954. It established a flexible scale of price supports on basic commodities ranging from 82½ to 90 per cent of parity for the 1955 crop, and from 70 to 90 per cent in succeeding years. Rural dissatisfaction with Benson and his flexible program contributed not a little to the Republican defeat in the midterm elections of 1954.

Nevertheless, the administration continued to work for lower and more flexible price supports. The principle was retained in the Agricultural Act of 1956, which Eisenhower signed on May 28 after vetoing a Democratic bill on April 11 that re-established 90 per cent supports. The main feature of the Act of 1956 was the "soil bank" plan, which set up both acreage reserve and conservation reserve programs in an effort to reduce the farm surplus. Farmers who agreed to reduce their acreage below their normal allotments, or to devote a portion of their land to soil-conserving rather than commercial use, were eligible to receive governmental payments as compensation for the smaller crop. Although farmers set aside several million acres each year under the soil-bank program,[21] higher yields per acre produced a succession of record-breaking bumper crops from 1956 through 1960, and the formidable surpluses remained as large as ever.

∧∧∧∧∧∧∧∧∧∧∧∧∧∧∧∧∧∧∧

[19] For example, the yield per acre for corn was 41 per cent higher in 1958 than the average for 1946–50. For wheat, the comparable increase was 44 per cent; for cotton, 70 per cent; for potatoes, 38 per cent; for tobacco, 32 per cent.

[20] In 1960, for example, the government owned 1,146,000,000 bushels of wheat and 1,472,000,000 bushels of corn.

[21] The acreage reserve program was discontinued after 1958, but the more important conservation reserve program was expanded: farmers took nearly 29,000,000 acres out of production under this program in 1960 alone.

The last major farm legislation during the Eisenhower era was the Agricultural Act of 1958, signed on August 16 after another hard battle between proponents of rigid and flexible price supports. The Act was a compromise that represented a partial victory for the administration. It was achieved with the aid of Democratic votes after Eisenhower had vetoed a bill on March 31 freezing price supports at their existing level. Under the new law, supports were to be lowered gradually to a minimum of 65 per cent on most basic crops in 1961–2. Critics of the Eisenhower-Benson farm program claimed that a progressive lowering of price supports was self-defeating because it merely encouraged the farmers to produce more and thus create larger surpluses. Defenders responded that high supports had the same effect at greater cost to the taxpayer. The farm problem, surely one of the most intricate and urgent dilemmas confronting the American people, had clearly not been solved by 1960. Nor were experts appreciably closer to agreement on the answer.

The basic principle of general and substantial federal support of agriculture had, however, become permanently established, and the government under Eisenhower maintained and even expanded other forms of aid. Agricultural research programs continued their valuable work. The Rural Electrification Association celebrated its twenty-fifth birthday in 1960 with the proud announcement that 97 per cent of all American farms now had electricity, as compared with 11 per cent in 1935. The Farmers Home Administration was making and insuring farm loans at a rate of over $300,000,000 a year during the late 1950's. And a Rural Development Program, designed to provide opportunities for farmers and rural dwellers in low-income areas to improve their standard of living, was operating in 262 counties in thirty-one states by 1960, with more than 2,000 local improvement projects under way.

Meanwhile, the government began making beneficial use of the huge farm surpluses that accumulated in its warehouses under the price support program. In the Agricultural Trade Development and Assistance Act of 1954, renewed with larger appropriations and expanded provisions by nearly every succeeding Congress, the government was authorized to finance the sale and export of surplus farm products to other nations in exchange for foreign currencies, to make outright gifts of surplus food to needy nations, to provide milk for American school children, and, by an amendment in 1959, to make up to $1,000,000,000 in surplus food available to needy American families through the issuance of free stamps redeemable at grocery stores.

The Eisenhower administration also continued the liberal trade policy inaugurated during the New Deal era. Indeed, as its title suggested, one of the major purposes of the Agricultural Trade Development and Assistance Act of 1954 was the stimulation of America's foreign commerce.[22] The Trade Agreements Act of 1934, which had authorized the President to

---

[22] The Act of 1954 empowered the President to use the foreign currencies accruing from the sale of farm surplus to build new markets abroad. An amendment in 1957 permitted up to 25 per cent of such foreign currencies to be lent to American or foreign companies to promote expanded markets for American products. And the Act was further liberalized in 1958 to permit, among several other projects, the use of these foreign currencies to finance American participation in international trade fairs.

enter reciprocal agreements with other nations lowering specific duties by as much as 50 per cent without requiring the approval of Congress, was regularly extended throughout the 1950's.

Another important step to promote American trade was the creation of the St. Lawrence Seaway Development Corporation. The project of improving navigation on the St. Lawrence River by means of locks and dredging, in order to open the Great Lakes to large ocean-going vessels, had been advocated without success by Presidents Hoover, Roosevelt, and Truman. Eisenhower finally overcame the opposition and persuaded Congress to authorize American participation in the project in 1954. Jointly constructed by the Canadian and United States governments, the St. Lawrence Seaway was formally opened in the spring of 1959. Tonnage passing between Montreal and Lake Ontario during the first season was 75 per cent greater than in 1958, and several foreign shipping lines immediately took steps to inaugurate or enlarge direct trade between European and Great Lakes ports. The President justly regarded the Seaway as one of the most valuable achievements of his administration.[23]

Eisenhower's firm support of the St. Lawrence Seaway was one of several indications that he was more sympathetic to federal public works projects than progressives maintained. To be sure, he disapproved strongly of pork-barrel legislation and shared Secretary Humphrey's outspoken opposition to federal spending as an antidote to recession. He continued to favor federal "partnership" with state, local, and private enterprise whenever this was feasible. He insisted that the tests of legitimate need and fiscal responsibility be applied to all public works programs. And, as we have seen, he wanted to restrict government activity in the realm of power development. Yet within these limits Eisenhower supported a variety of public works measures. These included increased funds for flood control and other projects in the Columbia River Valley in 1953; a $1,000,000,000 appropriation for 183 river, harbor, and flood control projects in 1954; a gigantic Colorado River Storage Project, including reservoirs, power plants, and irrigation facilities, in 1956; similar undertakings in Texas, Oklahoma, Nevada, California, and the Missouri River Valley in 1956 and 1958; and an agreement to participate with the Mexican government in the construction of a huge dam and power plant on the Rio Grande in 1960.

Congress and the President generally saw eye to eye on the scope of the public works program until late in his second term. In 1959, however, the big Democratic majorities in the Eighty-sixth Congress ignored

[23] The Seaway had long been opposed by eastern railroad and other business interests which feared that they would be adversely affected by the project. But Eisenhower was able to overcome these and other congressional scruples by pointing, first, to the announced determination of the Canadian government to proceed with construction of the Seaway without American help; and, second, to the growing need of midwestern steel producers for Laurentian ore from Canada as the great Mesabi deposits neared exhaustion. Seven new locks (five constructed by Canada, two by the United States) formed the nucleus of the Seaway and permitted the passage of ships up to 750 feet in length with drafts up to 27 feet.

Power development was an important adjunct of the Seaway project. The administration compromised between public and private power advocates by turning over the development and distribution of Seaway power to the State of New York. The Canadian government worked out a similar arrangement with the Province of Ontario.

his plea for fiscal caution and adopted a large public works bill that included sixty-seven new flood control and reclamation projects. The President vetoed the measure on September 9, only to see his veto overridden on the following day. "The lure of the pork barrel was a little too much for Congress," the President commented wryly. But Eisenhower himself had done much to keep the public works program alive.

This was true, certainly, in the fields of housing and highway construction, although Congress again tended toward more liberal programs than the President thought advisable. New low-income housing units were authorized at an annual rate of approximately 35,000 during the Eisenhower years. Progressives denounced this figure as inadequate for American needs, and Congress occasionally—as in 1955 and 1957—enlarged the President's housing appropriation. Most of the housing legislation during the 1950's merely liberalized FHA terms for mortgages, interest rates, loan maturity, and down payments for the benefit of purchasers of low-income housing.

Eisenhower's plan for a massive federal-state highway project failed in 1955, but a compromise measure passed Congress in 1956 and was signed by the President on June 29. The Federal Aid Highway Act, as it was called, envisioned a 42,500-mile network of superhighways linking all major urban areas, with the government paying 90 per cent and the states 10 per cent of the estimated cost of $27,500,000,000.[24] Awareness of the need to overhaul the nation's transportation network was further reflected in the Transportation Act of 1958. It authorized the ICC to use up to $500,000,000 in guaranteeing loans to railroads for equipment and maintenance. The Act also attempted to tighten the ICC's control over discriminatory rates and stated specifically that all interstate commercial motor transportation was subject to the ICC's regulation. It was a feeble, tardy, but much-needed beginning of what would perforce become a systematic reappraisal of federal transportation policy.

Eisenhower also moved to expand the New Deal welfare legislation. Amendments to the Social Security Act in 1954 and 1956 extended coverage and benefits to millions not previously covered—salaried and self-employed professionals; religious, domestic, and clerical workers; farm operators and workers; and members of the armed forces. Congress also expanded federal contributions to state old-age and disability funds and increased appropriations for child welfare. Another amendment to the Social Security Act, though opposed by the administration, received support from both parties in Congress during 1958 and became law on January 1, 1959. It increased benefits by about 7 per cent by raising both the tax rate and the amount of individual income subject to tax. By the end of the decade, over 58,000,000 individuals were covered by social security legisla-

ᴧᴧᴧᴧᴧᴧᴧᴧᴧᴧᴧᴧᴧᴧᴧᴧᴧ

[24] Money for the thirteen-year program was to be raised by increased "user" taxes on gasoline, tires, diesel fuel, trucks, buses, and trailers. An additional $5,000,000,000 for primary and secondary roads was included in the Highway Act, the cost to be shared equally by the federal and state governments. The administration's insistence on "pay-as-you-go" financing, whereby construction would not start until user taxes were actually in the highway trust fund, was suspended by Congress in 1958 for two years in order to speed the work. Congress also increased the annual appropriation for the highway system in 1958, and the President accepted these changes "with serious misgivings."

tion. Moreover, Congress amended the Fair Labor Standards Act in 1955 to increase the minimum wage from seventy-five cents to one dollar an hour.[25] Though Congress refused in 1954 and 1956 to act on the President's request for a measure of federal participation in a national health insurance program, the level of federal spending on public health, medical research, hospital construction, and similar items increased steadily during the Eisenhower years—from $290,000,000 in 1954 to $971,000,000 in 1961.

244. *Expansion of the New Deal: Education and Civil Rights*

In response to obvious popular demand, the Eisenhower administration also worked to expand the New Deal reform structure in two vitally important and hitherto slighted areas—education and civil rights. Substantial progress was blocked or limited during the 1950's, sometimes by partisan disagreement over method or detail, but more often by conservative bipartisan coalitions in Congress. Nevertheless, the President could justly claim that significant beginnings had been made by 1960.

Mounting pressure on the nation's public school system, in consequence of the new high birth rate and a growing shortage of classrooms and qualified teachers, was one of the inescapable facts of the postwar era. (For details, see above, pp. 653–654.) State and local budgets were already strained to the utmost, and many authorities believed that only federal aid could prevent massive deterioration in educational standards.

Not one but several controversies raged over the school question. Many persons opposed federal aid on principle—alleging that it would result in federal control, infringe upon state and local rights, and cost too much money. Spokesmen for the nation's private schools, many of which were Catholic, feared that federal spending for public education would damage if not destroy the private schools unless they received a share of the funds. Conversely, the stoutest champions of federal aid were often irrevocably opposed to any measure that granted public funds to private education. Finally, Southerners tended to oppose federal aid because it offered a means of enforcing school desegregation, while many Negro leaders insisted that federal aid should not be extended to schools refusing to desegregate. All these groups were well represented in Congress. It is not surprising, therefore, that complex political maneuvering, repeated setbacks, and painfully slow progress marked the development of a school-aid program.

Eisenhower's first education bill, in 1956, proposed aid on a basis of per capita income and relative state expenditures on schools. The Democrats substituted a bill making population the basis for apportionment of aid. In a maneuver that was to be repeated, the House first adopted an amendment offered by Representative Adam Clayton Powell of New York,

[25] The President had asked for a minimum wage of 90 cents, but he signed the bill when Democratic majorities in both houses raised the level to one dollar. A bill to raise the hourly wage by progressive steps to $1.25 passed both houses of Congress in 1960 but was not reported from conference because of disagreement over a proposal to extend coverage to some 4,000,000 additional workers. The bill, sponsored by Senator John F. Kennedy of Massachusetts, was due for consideration by the Eighty-seventh Congress in 1961. (See below, p. 869.)

making compliance with the Supreme Court's desegregation decision a requisite for receiving school aid. Then a conservative Republican–southern Democratic majority defeated the measure altogether. A similar fate befell the administration's school-aid bill in 1957.

Eisenhower's lone accomplishment in this field came the following year, as the shock of *Sputnik* stirred national concern over alleged American educational deficiencies. The National Defense Education Act was signed by the President on September 2, 1958. It provided funds for long-term, low-interest loans to college students, with half the loan to be canceled if the student taught in elementary or secondary school for at least five years after graduation. It offered matching grants to public schools for laboratories, textbooks, and other facilities in the sciences, mathematics, and foreign languages, as well as funds for 5,500 fellowships for graduate students interested in college or university teaching. Finally, it provided grants to state agencies for counseling, vocational education, and other purposes.

The National Defense Education Act's major weakness, of course, was that it side-stepped the crucial issue of comprehensive federal aid for new classrooms and teachers' salaries. Bills containing such provisions were debated by Congress in 1959 and even more thoroughly in 1960. The Senate approved a bill on February 4, 1960, authorizing expenditure of $1,800,-000,000 over a two-year period for both construction and salaries. The House passed a bill on May 26 providing $325,000,000 a year over a four-year period, to be applied to construction only, but with Powell's anti-segregation amendment attached. Then the House and Senate conferees agreed informally to drop the Powell amendment and limit the fund to classroom construction, thus meeting both southern and administration objections. But the House rules committee, firmly controlled by its four Republican and three southern Democratic members, stubbornly refused to authorize the official House-Senate conference that was prepared to adjust differences between the two bills.

The record of achievement was, curiously, better in the more controversial field of civil rights, and adoption of a Civil Rights Act in 1957 was a landmark of the postwar era. It was attended, of course, by months of bickering and southern obstruction. But the southern senators abandoned their filibuster in the end, after winning minor concessions, and permitted enactment of the first federal civil rights legislation in eighty-two years. The Act, approved September 9, 1957, established a bipartisan Civil Rights Commission with power to subpoena witnesses and authority to investigate denial of voting rights and equal protection of the laws on account of color, race, religion, or national origin. The Act also provided for a new Assistant Attorney General who might initiate injunctive proceedings in federal district courts when voting rights were interfered with. Finally, the measure authorized such courts to issue injunctions and begin civil contempt proceedings to secure compliance with its orders.[26] Eisenhower appointed the

---

[26] These *civil* contempt proceedings were to be held without jury trial, thus bypassing the problem of selecting an unbiased jury. If the courts began *criminal* contempt proceedings, as punishment for actual violation of court orders, defendants could demand

Civil Rights Commission on November 7, 1957, and it set to work at once.

Various Negro movements for equality met increasing violence (for details, see below, pp. 781–783), but Congress did no more in 1959 than extend the life of the Civil Rights Commission for another two years. Democratic and Republican leaders then agreed, after much discussion, to postpone further action until the following year. It came after another long debate with adoption of the Civil Rights Act of 1960. In order to afford added protection of voting rights, the Act empowered federal courts to appoint referees to consider state voting-qualification laws whenever a petitioner had been deprived of the right to register or vote because of race or color.[27] It also imposed heavy penalties against illegal acts by private citizens. With what seemed to civil rights advocates like agonizing slowness, but nonetheless surely, the power of the federal government was finally being extended in behalf of fair and equal treatment for all Americans.

245. *The Warren Court: Civil Rights and Civil Liberties*

Less than nine months after taking the oath of office, President Eisenhower named Governor Earl Warren of California to succeed the late Fred M. Vinson as Chief Justice of the United States. Future historians may well decide that the new Chief Justice and his eight Associates did far more to shape the course of American history after midcentury than Eisenhower, Congress, or the political parties.

Civil rights and civil liberties had been the Supreme Court's major concern between the late 1930's and the accession of Chief Justice Warren. Decisions affecting the status of the Negro had gone a long way toward undermining the barriers of racial discrimination in the forties and early fifties. The New Deal court, for example, had eventually moved to open the polls to Negroes in the South. In Grovey *v.* Townsend, 1935, the court had unanimously agreed that state party organizations, acting on their own initiative, could exclude Negroes from party primaries without violating the Fourteenth and Fifteenth Amendments. But in Smith *v.* Allwright, 1944, the court reversed Grovey *v.* Townsend by declaring that

a jury trial if the judge imposed a fine of more than three hundred dollars or a jail term longer than forty-five days.

In United States *v.* Raines, 1960, the Supreme Court upheld the provision of the Civil Rights Act that permitted the Attorney General to obtain injunctions from the federal courts preventing state officials from discriminating against voting rights on grounds of race or color. The Raines decision also upheld the provision of the Act that permitted the Civil Rights Commission to conduct hearings without permitting persons accused of denying voting rights to be apprised of specific charges against them or the identity of their accusers. The court reasoned that this did not violate the due process clause of the Fifth Amendment because the Civil Rights Commission was an investigative and fact-finding agency; it did not violate the Sixth Amendment because the proceedings were not in the category of "criminal prosecutions."

[27] The Act also provided that petitioners might vote provisionally when an election took place before a given voting case had been decided. It permitted suits to be brought against states for violations, and required federal election officials, under penalty of fine or imprisonment, to preserve all election records for at least twenty-two months.

Negroes could not be denied the right to participate in party primaries, because they were in fact an integral part of the electoral process. When South Carolina tried to circumvent this ruling by removing all regulations for party primaries from its statute books, District Judge J. Waites Waring of Charleston refused to approve this subterfuge and ordered Democratic registrars to enroll qualified Negro voters in 1948. The Supreme Court upheld Waring's ruling by refusing to review the case. And in Terry *v.* Adams, 1953, the court outlawed a Texas organization known as the Jaybird Association, which limited its membership to whites and chose nominees for the local Democratic primary. Noting that the Jaybird candidates almost invariably won both the primary and the election, the court identified the device as another illegal method of circumventing the Allwright decision and excluding Negroes from voting. By thus taking a realistic view of southern political practices, the court destroyed the white primary and hastened the day when Negroes would be citizens in fact as well as in theory.[28]

It was on the educational front that the court found cause to strike down the historic "separate but equal" concept, the legalism upon which the southern states had built their elaborate system of Jim Crow legislation. Chief Justice Hughes had opened the assault in the Gaines decision in 1938 (for details, see above, pp. 444–445). In Sweatt *v.* Painter, 1950, the court decreed that separate law school facilities could never be really equal and ordered the University of Texas to admit a Negro student who had refused to attend the state law school for Negroes in Houston. The effect of the Sweatt decision was to compel many southern state universities to admit Negroes to law, medical, and graduate schools. More important was the clear implication of the Sweatt case: segregated public education on any level was unequal education. Thus encouraged, the National Association for the Advancement of Colored People stepped up its campaign to end segregation in public schools. Most southern states, equally mindful of the court's growing hostility to the legal fabric of Jim Crow, spent large sums improving Negro school facilities in an effort to achieve true equality within the separate system and thus, it was hoped, stave off the ruling that they feared.

Thus the stage was set for the Warren court's epochal decision in 1954. A number of cases challenging the legality of public school segregation came before the Vinson court in 1952. Unable to reach a decision, the justices ordered reargument of these cases in 1953 and requested counsel to answer certain key questions regarding the intent and meaning of the Fourteenth Amendment. With Warren on the bench during the reargument, the justices handed down their decision on a representative case—Brown *v.* Board of Education of Topeka—on May 17, 1954. A unanimous court held that public school segregation was unconstitutional under the Fourteenth Amendment, thus completely reversing the "separate but equal" doctrine

꙳꙳꙳꙳꙳꙳꙳꙳꙳꙳꙳꙳꙳꙳

[28] As compared with a negligible number of Negro voters in the South before 1944, an estimated 1,320,000 Negroes in eleven southern states, or 25 per cent of the adult Negro population of the area, had registered by 1959—chiefly in southern cities. The figure was far from adequate, and older patterns of pressure and discrimination against Negro voting persisted in rural areas and smaller cities, but the advance in fifteen years had been a significant one.

enunciated in Plessy *v*. Ferguson in 1896. Impressed by the trenchant logic of Thurgood Marshall, counsel for the NAACP, the justices emphasized sociological and psychological factors in their decision. "In the field of public education," Warren declared unequivocally, "the doctrine of 'separate but equal' has no place. Separate educational facilities are inherently unequal."

The court outlined the basic procedure for implementing the Brown decision a year later. It instructed federal district courts to order school desegregation in their respective areas and to require "good faith," "a prompt and reasonable start," and "all deliberate speed" from the local authorities. Though demanding compliance with the principle, these instructions duly recognized that the timing and mode of desegregation would vary according to local conditions, and they permitted district judges to use discretion in setting specific deadlines and other details. Nevertheless, the broad import of the Brown decision was momentous and unmistakable. Affecting the school systems of seventeen states and the District of Columbia,[29] it promised to alter the pattern of education for over 8,000,000 white and 2,500,000 Negro children, representing nearly 40 per cent of American public school enrollment. No one could deny that the Warren court had erected a historic landmark in American constitutional law.

Meanwhile legalized Jim Crow had been systematically obliterated in other fields. Having destroyed the "separate but equal" doctrine in public school education, the Warren court was quick to render it inapplicable elsewhere.[30] It steadily ruled in favor of Negroes seeking admission to southern colleges, universities, and professional graduate schools. As a result, out of 195 formerly all-white public institutions of higher learning in fourteen southern states, fully 124 had admitted Negro students by 1960. In a series of rulings in the wake of the Brown decision, the federal courts also invalidated segregation in parks, public housing, municipal golf courses, public beaches and bathhouses, intrastate buses, and bus, railway, and air terminals serving interstate passengers. The ICC in late 1955 proceeded on the basis of the Brown decision to order several railroads to end all rules and practices maintaining segregation. Like emancipation a century earlier, the long-overdue extension of equal justice under law to the American Negro in the 1950's was a beginning, not an end. It was, nevertheless, a forward step of lasting importance.

<hr/>

[29] Segregation in the nation's capital was actually invalidated by a companion decision, Bolling *v*. Sharpe, which the court pronounced immediately after handing down Brown *v*. Board of Education. The due process clause of the Fifth Amendment, rather than the Fourteenth, was held to forbid segregation in the federally administered District of Columbia.

In addition to the seventeen states where segregation was required by law, four other states that permitted it by local option were affected by the Brown decision.

[30] As with education, the way had been paved by recent decisions of the Vinson court. In 1946 it invalidated a Virginia statute requiring segregated seating in interstate buses by decreeing that such segregation was an undue burden on interstate commerce. Two years later it struck a heavy blow at residential segregation by ruling that covenants forbidding the sale of real estate to persons on account of race or color were not enforceable in the courts. Formerly all-white hotels, restaurants, and theaters in the District of Columbia were opened to Negroes in 1953.

A few years later, the Warren court handed down a decision that will rank with Brown *v.* Board of Education as a constitutional milestone of profound significance. In Baker *v.* Carr, 1962, the court ruled, six to two, that legislative apportionment by the states was subject to the scrutiny of the federal courts. The case involved representation in the legislature of Tennessee. In Tennessee, as in most other states, the make-up of the legislature reflected the rural-urban balance of forty or even sixty years earlier. Not wishing to lose their power, rural lawmakers had blocked reapportionment decade after decade, while their districts lost population and metropolitan areas mushroomed. Urban and suburban voters had become increasingly restive under this form of inequality, and when Baker *v.* Carr opened the question to judicial review, suits demanding reapportionment were immediately brought in over two dozen states. It would be years, obviously, before the complexities raised by legislative reapportionment could be adequately solved. But the Warren court had, as in the Brown decision, brought the nation face to face once again with the deeper implications of its democratic creed.

On the race question the court had moved with boldness, unanimity, and unswerving devotion to principle. On the closely related issue of civil liberties, involving reconciliation of individual freedoms with the demands of national security, the justices proceeded somewhat cautiously. The difference was understandable. The former question, though enormously complex, was essentially a contest between elementary justice and entrenched prejudice; the latter issue found legitimate needs and rights at stake on both sides. Rather than attempt to enunciate a fundamental principle that would guide and control future action, as it had in the Brown case, the court dealt with civil liberties on a pragmatic, *ad hoc* basis. It questioned procedure and the wording of specific laws, sought to curb excesses, and invited the legislative and executive branches to tighten and improve their loyalty programs. Often badly divided on specific details, the justices groped for the middle ground that would preserve the substance of individual liberties without crippling or destroying the government's right to protect itself from disloyalty and subversion.

The general timidity of the Vinson court, which sat during the rise and peak of the second Red Scare, has been noted in an earlier chapter. (For details, see above, pp. 686–687.) As McCarthyism declined after 1954 and the vigorous influence of the new Chief Justice began to make itself felt, the federal judiciary moved toward a bolder stand in defense of civil liberties. Two lower court decisions in 1956, for example, narrowed the investigative authority of the Senate committee on government operations by applying the standard of pertinency.[31] The Supreme Court in 1955 strongly upheld the controversial right of witnesses to avoid incrimination by invoking the Fifth Amendment before congressional committees. It added, moreover, that a "veiled claim" of the privilege was permissible in

<hr />

[31] In United States *v.* Kamin, a federal district judge held that a study of subversion in private defense plants was not within the authority of the committee. In United States *v.* Lamont, a federal circuit court found a similar lack of pertinency in the committee's inquiry into the length of time a writer had spent on a trip to Russia. Both of these cases had arisen out of contempt prosecutions initiated by the committee while McCarthy was its chairman.

view of the opprobrium often attached to its use. Congress attempted to circumvent the Fifth Amendment by passing the Immunity Act of 1954, under which witnesses could be granted immunity from criminal prosecution and then be *compelled* to testify before courts, grand juries, or congressional committees in national security cases. Not unmindful of the government's desire for facts in such cases, the court upheld the Immunity Act in Ullman *v.* United States, 1956. It warned, however, that the protection afforded by the Fifth Amendment must not be downgraded or diminished.

In a series of decisions from 1955 to 1959, the Warren court upset several actions of the executive branch in disloyalty proceedings: the compiling of a subversive list, the dismissal of certain federal employees, the denial of a passport, and so on. Though all of these cases raised constitutional issues, the court avoided them by settling each on narrow procedural grounds.[32] However, the effect of one decision—Greene *v.* McElroy, 1959—was to invalidate the government's industrial security program for private defense plants; the effect of another—Cole *v.* Young, 1956—was to render some 80 per cent of all federal employees immune from the security program by ruling that it applied only to "sensitive" government positions and agencies.

On the subject of the rights of aliens the court did not take a bold stand. In 1954 it broadly upheld the provision of the Internal Security Act of 1950 that required deportation of any alien who had been a member of the Communist party when he entered the United States or at any time thereafter. The effect of three later decisions in 1956 and 1957 was to limit and reform various governmental procedures in deportation and denaturalization cases. But in Jay *v.* Boyd, 1956, a five-to-four decision upheld the Department of Justice in a case involving deportation on the basis of confidential information not disclosed to the alien. The four dissenters included the Chief Justice and the veteran New Deal appointees—Felix Frankfurter, Hugo Black, and William O. Douglas. They variously objected to certain features of the case: undisclosed information, faceless informers, dubious delegation of authority, and the shifting of deportation trials from courts to temporary removable appointees like the hearing officer who had decided against the alien in question.

The high-water mark in the Warren court's defense of civil liberties came in 1957, with a spate of decisions that left legal experts breathless and conservatives enraged. In Jencks *v.* United States, the court held that in certain circumstances a defendant was entitled to inspect FBI reports

ᴡᴡᴡᴡᴡᴡᴡᴡᴡᴡᴡᴡᴡᴡᴡ

[32] Specifically, in Communist Party *v.* Subversive Activities Control Board, 1956, the court simply returned a subversive listing to the Board with the request that it base its findings on "untainted evidence." Peters *v.* Hobey, 1955, involved the problem of whether a federal employee might be discharged when the findings against him reflected statements of secret informers. The court side-stepped this issue and upset the dismissal on the technical ground that the Loyalty Review Board lacked authority to issue the dismissal order because the case had not been appealed to it properly. In Service *v.* Dulles, 1957, the court condemned the discharge of the diplomat John Stewart Service, on the ground that the State Department had violated its own regulations in dismissing him. And in Kent *v.* Dulles, 1958, the justices held that Congress had not authorized the Secretary of State to withhold a passport because of the applicant's political beliefs and associations.

used in his trial, and ordered the government to dismiss criminal action if it chose to withhold such reports. In Yates *v.* United States, the justices narrowed the meaning of the Smith Act by ruling that an individual might advocate the "abstract principle" of overthrowing the government so long as he did not advocate specific action to that end. And in Watkins *v.* United States, the court invalidated a contempt conviction by the House un-American activities committee because its legislative mandate was "loosely worded" and "excessively broad," and because it had failed to show the pertinency of its questions to the inquiry at hand. Detecting a threat to freedoms guaranteed by the First Amendment, the court took occasion in the Watkins ruling to remind Congress that it was not a law enforcement agency, and that an inquiry was not an end in itself but must be directly related to some legitimate congressional task.

In a companion set of decisions, the justices reviewed and set aside certain state actions against subversives. The most important of these rulings was Pennsylvania *v.* Nelson, 1956, in which the court invalidated Nelson's conviction under a state sedition law on the ground that Congress had in effect pre-empted the field of sedition, which was a national question, and had thus "superseded" state laws on this subject. The effect of the Nelson decision was to set aside, at least temporarily, anti-Communist laws in forty-two states. In Slochower *v.* Board of Higher Education of New York, 1956, the court ruled that a state could not discharge a teacher for using the privilege against self-incrimination in a congressional investigation, on the ground that the mere claim of the privilege had been construed by the state as "conclusive presumption of guilt." The court later invalidated two state decisions denying the admission of certain lawyers to the bar. It held that facts casting doubt on the loyalty of the applicants did not warrant denial of application on grounds of failure to demonstrate good moral character. And in Sweezy *v.* New Hampshire, 1957, the justices invalidated a state legislative inquiry into subversive activities.[33]

Although progressives hailed these decisions as a clarion reaffirmation of individual liberties, the loudest reaction came from the voices of dissent. Conservatives tended to feel, with varying degrees of intensity, that the Warren court had protected Communists, done great if not irreparable harm to the national security program, and encroached upon the rightful powers of the legislative and executive branches. "Well, Comrades," one newspaper remarked in 1957, "you've finally got what you wanted. The Supreme Court has handed it to you on a platter." [34] The Nelson and Sweezy

[33] The Warren court limited state and local authority in other fields as well. In 1955 and 1956 it held that federal labor legislation (1) pre-empted the right of a state supreme court to bar certain strikes by injunction, and (2) prevailed over a state "right to work" provision that had been used to bar a union-shop contract.

In the realm of censorship, the court in 1957 struck down a Chicago ordinance against "immoral and obscene" movies as unconstitutionally vague, and invalidated a similar New York statute in 1959 on the ground that it prevented the advocacy of an idea—in this case, that under certain conditions adultery may not be improper or immoral behavior. However, in 1957 the court upheld both a federal and a California anti-obscenity statute by excluding obscenity from the protections afforded by the First and Fourteenth Amendments.

[34] Quoted in Alpheus T. Mason, *The Supreme Court from Taft to Warren* (Baton Rouge, La., 1958), p. 4.

rulings, critics charged, had destroyed the ability of the states to combat subversion. J. Edgar Hoover, director of the FBI, lamented "the mounting success of criminal and subversive elements in employing loopholes, technicalities, and delays in the law to defeat the interests of jusice." [35] A conference of state governors in 1956, an assemblage of state chief justices in 1958, and the American Bar Association in 1959 all voiced criticism of recent Supreme Court decisions and asked for more judicial restraint. Extremists on the far right denounced the nine justices with a virulence unrivaled since the aftermath of the Dred Scott decision a century earlier.

Efforts to persuade Congress to bridle the court were not notably successful. Southern congressmen repeatedly introduced bills to nullify the desegregation decision of 1954. Among the more extreme and farfetched proposals, backed by an angry coalition of segregationists and reactionaries, were constitutional amendments aimed at destroying the power of judicial review, limiting the Supreme Court's appellate jurisdiction, and choosing justices by popular election or by vote of state supreme court judges. Such schemes got nowhere. One court-curbing bill sponsored by Senator Jenner of Indiana actually came to a vote and was defeated. Bills protecting state anti-subversion laws and broadening the "violent overthrow" provision of the Smith Act passed the House in 1959 but died in the Senate. Measures to strengthen the government's security program as it applied to private defense plants and "non-sensitive" federal positions failed to become law. The only positive enactment that emerged from the debate was a law adopted in August 1957. It protected the security of the FBI files against undue exposure, but it did not overturn the basic principle affirmed in the Jencks decision.

Congress failed to move more decisively, in part because of the natural reluctance of many members to tamper with the judiciary, and in part because anti-Communist hysteria ebbed more and more each year after 1955. Even more important, perhaps, were later decisons that did much to mollify conservative fears and provide additional leeway for anti-subversion measures. The court clarified and qualified its ruling in the Slochower decision of 1956 by twice declaring, in 1958, that state and city employees, including teachers, might be dismissed upon reasonable determination of "unfitness," even though alleged disloyalty was the root cause for dismissal.[36] In Uphaus v. New Hampshire, 1959, the court narrowed the implications of the Nelson and Sweezy decisions by sanctioning the efforts of the state attorney general to obtain information about subversive activities in New Hampshire. The states, it appeared, were not powerless in the battle against Communism after all. And in Barenblatt v. United States, 1959, the court ruled that a congressional committee *could* compel a witness to

~~~~~~~~~~~~~~~~~~~~~~~~~~

[35] Quoted in Leon I. Salomon (ed.), *The Supreme Court* (New York, 1961), p. 114.

[36] Beilan v. Board of Public Education of Philadelphia involved the dismissal of a teacher for incompetency after he had refused to tell a school superintendent whether he had held a position in the Communist party. Lerner v. Casey involved the discharge of a subway conductor by the City of New York as a person of doubtful trust and reliability because of his lack of candor in refusing to answer questions about membership in subversive organizations. In both instances a bare majority of the court agreed that the state had remained within legitimate bounds in finding against the employees in question.

answer its questions about his Communist affiliations, thus modifying the controversial Watkins decision of 1957. "The balance between the individual and the government interests here at stake," the court noted in the Barenblatt case, "must here be struck in favor of the latter."

Though doubt and confusion were sometimes created by the effect of various decisions, the court's general policy of avoiding broad constitutional pronouncements and requiring greater procedural care on the part of state and federal authorities was undoubtedly a wise approach to the problem. Few could deny by 1962 that the rights of the individual had on the whole been greatly strengthened by the exertions of the federal judiciary, yet not at the price of undermining the government's legitimate powers.

246. The Negro in the Nineteen Fifties

For American Negroes, the postwar era was one of unparalleled striving, ferment, and progress. It was also, inevitably, a time of heightened tension, as the Negro's determined onslaught against the barriers of racial discrimination challenged traditional attitudes, altered the *status quo*, and met the resistance born of prejudice, ignorance, and fear. The most significant feature in this changing pattern of race relations was not the Negro's specific progress. Nor was it the tension that accompanied his crusade for equal treatment, despite the gravity of racial antagonism in many areas. It was, rather, the fact that various developments at home and abroad had finally forced the nation, after generations of evasion and indifference, to come to serious grips with its most urgent social problem.

Such a confrontation could, it seemed, no longer be deferred. A few Americans had long been aware that the status of the Negro represented American democracy's most glaring failure. The New Deal, with its concern for the plight of all underprivileged citizens, emphasized the extent to which poverty and lack of opportunity were a way of life for the great majority of American Negroes. At the same time, as the nation recoiled in horror from the theory and practice of Nazi racist doctrines, the injustice of systematic racial discrimination at home became strikingly apparent. The unswerving loyalty with which Negroes supported the cause of democracy during the Second World War, and the implications of America's position as the leader of the free world after 1945, made the anachronism of second-class citizenship for 10 per cent of the country's inhabitants more insupportable than ever. The United States could manifestly never win the respect or co-operation of the emergent nations of Asia and Africa while it degraded its own darker-skinned minority. By midcentury, therefore, increasing numbers of white Americans were prepared to extend the benefits of democracy to all citizens regardless of race or color.

Even more important, the Negro himself had reached a point by 1950 where he was both able and determined to advance his own cause. The New Deal had provided the first relative economic security that millions of Negroes had ever known. They had shared largely in the new job opportunities and high wages of the war years, and they further expanded their economic strength in the postwar prosperity that followed. Their growing concentration in the urban centers of the North and West conferred a political power which both parties were forced to recognize. The federal courts, as we have seen, began to support the Negro's bid for equality. Though still far below the national average, the percentage of Negroes with comfortable incomes, white-collar jobs, high-school diplomas, college degrees, and advanced professional skills increased markedly after 1945.

Moreover, the Negro was now ready psychologically to launch a full-fledged campaign for first-class citizenship. Economic, political, and educational advances not only provided new strength and hope but spurred ambition for further gains. The Negro was keenly aware of the relevance, for him, of the values at stake in democracy's struggle against fascist and communist totalitarianism. His confidence was further stimulated in the postwar era by the efforts of President Truman and other national leaders in behalf of civil rights. The greatest emotional turning-point was undoubtedly the Warren court's desegregation decision of 1954. As a noted Negro psychologist, Kenneth Clark, put it: "For the first time every Negro *felt* that he was a man in his own right and that his government would help him prove it." [37]

There were other grounds for the belief that a new day was dawning. The entire Negro community was encouraged by the collapse of the color line in major league baseball in the late 1940's, and exulted in the achievements of Jackie Robinson, Roy Campanella, Willie Mays, and other Negro stars. They took pride, too, in the national distinction accorded increasing numbers of their race in the fields of music, literature, scholarship, entertainment, and sport. They were also stirred by momentous international developments after 1945—the steady breakup of European colonial empires, the growing power and influence of non-white nations like India and China, and above all the emergence of the new African countries from colonial subservience to independence and an uneasy but expanding place in the sun.

Hope for the future was matched by increasing dissatisfaction with the *status quo*. The retreat of white supremacy in most other parts of the world had become a rout; how long would it continue to be tolerated in the United States? The Negro's patience was wearing thin. By and large he bore little malice and sought to wage his campaign for equal treatment by legal and peaceful means. But a pressure for change had built up that would find other outlets if these were denied. As a group, American Negroes would never again be content with menial jobs, inferior schools, the urban ghetto, or the back of the bus.

The Negro's campaign was supported by the policies and actions of numerous public and private organizations. The federal government, as we have seen, instituted desegregation in both the civil service and the armed forces, promoted equal job opportunities, and eventually passed legislation designed to protect Negro voting rights. Most northern states passed or strengthened anti-discrimination laws aimed at removing inequities in employment, housing, and public accommodations.[38] National labor organiza-

---

[37] Quoted in Harry S. Ashmore, *The Other Side of Jordan* (New York, 1960), p. 121.

[38] New York state, with its large and politically powerful Negro population, was one of the leaders in this anti-discrimination movement. Its fair employment act of 1945, the first of such statutes, was amended in 1952 to cover discrimination in public

tions strove to end segregation and other discriminatory practices in union membership, although many local unions remained strongholds of prejudice. Corporations and other business firms evinced a growing willingness to hire qualified Negroes for positions formerly closed to them. Youth organizations, urban welfare agencies, and other groups were active in promoting racial harmony and combating the effects of prejudice.

Religious bodies, including nearly all of the great Protestant denominations, took a far more liberal and enlightened stand on the race question than in previous times. According to one historian, "every major church body in the South has made some pronouncement in agreement with the Supreme Court decision regarding segregation." [39] Ministers and religious leaders in all parts of the country reminded worshipers that prejudice and discrimination were a gross violation of the Christian law of love. Many churches attempted to practice what they preached by establishing interracial congregations.[40] Unquestionably, the moral weight of official religious pronouncements in behalf of tolerance, brotherhood, and equality did much to erode prejudice and racial tension.

Until late in the 1950's, the vanguard in the civil rights campaign was occupied by several important interracial organizations. In the South, for example, the Southern Regional Council, with headquarters in Atlanta, worked quietly but effectively to promote equal opportunity and extend the area of friendly contact between the races. The National Urban League, founded in the early years of the twentieth century, was operating in forty-one states by 1960. Moderate in method and approach, dependent largely upon local resources and contributions, the Urban League maintained a variety of services but concentrated primarily upon advancing employment opportunities for Negroes. A more recent organization, the Congress of Racial Equality (CORE), supported a wide range of anti-discrimination campaigns with emphasis upon direct though nonviolent action.

The most influential of these biracial groups was undoubtedly the National Association for the Advancement of Colored People. Supported by 350,000 members, white and Negro, the NAACP conducted an intensive

accommodations and in 1955–6 to include public housing. New York's State Commission Against Discrimination worked hard to investigate and remove discriminatory practices in employment, resort areas, and elsewhere. Massachusetts, Connecticut, Washington, Colorado, and Oregon led the way in combating discrimination in private housing.

[39] Thomas D. Clark, *The Emerging South* (New York, 1961), p. 260. Roman Catholic bishops in the South also took steps to begin the integration of parochial schools in the wake of the Brown decision, the latest such action being that of the Atlanta diocese in 1962. When certain white Roman Catholics in New Orleans, where the problem of integrated parochial schools was largest, attempted to defy the order, Archbishop Joseph F. Rummel did not hesitate to employ the weapon of excommunication to secure compliance.

[40] According to one authority, an estimated 10 per cent of all Protestant churches were interracial by 1957—a fivefold increase in ten years. Many large and wealthy churches in downtown areas, crippled by the mass migration of white parishioners to the suburbs, refused to close or relocate, choosing instead to welcome Negroes and other minorities and rebuild their congregations on an interracial basis. The once aristocratic Episcopal Church has had noteworthy success with this policy in several of its large urban parishes.

and highly successful legal campaign to destroy segregation in the postwar era. Victorious in all but four of its forty-six appeals to the Supreme Court, the NAACP was instrumental in the epochal decisions that advanced the Negro's voting rights, invalidated restrictive housing covenants, and upset the "separate but equal" doctrine in transportation, public facilities, and education.

Progress in the Negro's march toward first-class citizenship often seemed slow, but it was truly remarkable by comparison with any previous period. Even more gratifying was the fact that, in general, the northern white community did not respond to the Negro challenge with large-scale acts of violence. To be sure, racial tension mounted in many areas and found expression in sporadic outbreaks of vandalism, terrorism, and mob action, especially in urban neighborhoods undergoing racial transition and all-white suburban communities resisting the "invasion" of a single Negro family. Such incidents were numerous, and it would be fatuous to claim that harmony prevailed over old prejudices.

The over-all record, however, was surprisingly good. Comparable Negro migrations into new cities and neighborhoods during and after the First World War had been accompanied by some of the bloodiest race riots in the nation's history; and as late as 1943, the heavy wartime influx of both Negro and white job-seekers had touched off a major race riot in Detroit. But alert law-enforcement agencies and private citizens' groups managed, with amazing success, to keep racial incidents from getting out of hand in the postwar years, despite the continued movement of Negroes into and within the metropolitan areas. In some transitional neighborhoods, public officials and residents co-operated to reduce friction, prevent the "panic selling" by which such districts were quickly converted into new Negro ghettos, and establish relatively harmonious biracial communities. Here and there, white employees grew accustomed to working with Negroes in skilled, professional, and white-collar positions; restaurants, theaters, and other social facilities increasingly accepted colored patrons without incident. If success in all such areas was partial and uneven, it was substantial enough to indicate that racial bias was gradually diminishing, and that the Negro was measurably closer to acceptance as an equal citizen.

Inevitably, progress was slower in the South. Not only were notions of white supremacy and segregation far more deeply entrenched, but the full weight of state and local authority as well as custom was opposed to the Negro who attempted to cross the color line. Even in the South, however, a softening of traditional attitudes was observable in the years *preceding* the Brown decision of 1954. White Southerners were by no means prepared to grant full social equality, but large numbers of them had come to admit that the Negro was entitled to greater economic and educational opportunities. Most southern states made large strides in improving their Negro schools after 1945 as the "separate but equal" concept came under judicial fire. The devout bigotry of the old rural South was steadily being leavened by the more enlightened outlook of the new urban-industrial South, and a sizable body of moderate white opinion, typified by the religious and professional leaders who worked on the Southern Regional Council, now fairly offset the old uncompromising viewpoint. The Brown decision was greeted with alarm and shock in some quarters, but also with a rather widespread, if reluctant, willingness to comply with the law of the land.

Unfortunately, southern extremism triumphed over southern moderation within twelve months of the Brown ruling. Some observers blamed the federal government, and more particularly the President, for failing to exert positive leadership and moral influence in behalf of the decision in the crucial first months. Others simply concluded that moderate sentiment in the South was too timid to assert itself in the face of powerful adverse opinion. In any case, while the moderates spoke in muted tones or not at all, southern politicians on every level assumed varying postures of defiance, and segregationist opinion rapidly mobilized to meet the challenge.

Among the host of local organizations that were formed to oppose school desegregation,[41] the most important by far were the White Citizens Councils. The first of these was organized in Indianola, Mississippi, in the summer of 1954. The idea spread rapidly, especially in the black-belt regions of the lower South, until a network of Citizens Councils had appeared in several southern states. In contrast to the Ku Klux Klan—which, in spite of the real gravity of the postwar threat to white supremacy, never attained a fraction of the following or influence it had enjoyed in the 1920's —the Citizens Councils officially renounced violence, terrorism, and hooded night raids.[42] Instead, they employed the weapons of propaganda, pressure, persuasion, and vociferous agitation to solidify white opinion and resist integration. They relied heavily upon state-rights arguments and tirelessly denounced the Brown decision as unconstitutional. All of the familiar white-supremacy shibboleths, including many that were hoary in John C. Calhoun's time, were systematically circulated in a flood of pamphlets, books, speeches, letters, radio programs, and lectures. So effective a pressure group did the Citizens Councils become in most southern states that opposition was quickly silenced; even rational discussion of the problem soon became impossible. Few enlightened Southerners dared or cared to risk the ostracism, harassment, vilification, and economic loss that were usually the fate of dissenters.

The white South, of course, was not monolithic on this or any other question, and the speed and degree of compliance with the Brown decision varied greatly within the area concerned. On the whole, school integration was accomplished rapidly and without undue difficulty in the District of Columbia and the border states. "Token integration" was achieved in North Carolina, Tennessee, Arkansas, and Texas by 1957. In Virginia and the deep South, on the other hand, the viewpoint represented by the Citizens Councils was dominant, and little progress took place before the end of

---

[41] The names of a few of these organizations reveal the thought-processes at work: Federation of Constitutional Government; the Grass Roots League, Inc.; the Virginia League; The Federation of Defenders of State Sovereignty and Individual Liberties; The State's Rights Council of Georgia, Inc.; The Society for the Preservation of State Government and Racial Integrity; White American, Inc.

[42] Scattered evidence suggests, however, that some of the Citizens Councils used economic coercion, anonymous telephone calls, and other forms of intimidation against both Negro and white citizens. Moreover, the language and tactics of the Councils were sufficiently inflammatory to encourage acts of violence on the part of others and generally foster a spirit of defiance of law and order.

the decade. Southern legislatures passed a barrage of resolutions, laws, and constitutional amendments after 1954 designed to circumvent the Brown ruling. Among these enactments were measures that would permit or require state officials to close the public schools rather than allow integration. Every legal device, maneuver, and gambit that imaginative southern attorneys could conjure up was mobilized to delay or thwart the desegregation process.

Despite resistance from state authorities and the pressure of local opinion, federal district judges for the most part went resolutely about the task of implementing the Brown decision. Appellate courts were quick to sustain their integration orders or reverse lower court rulings and demand more vigorous action when district judges countenanced undue evasion or delay. The first major clash between federal and state authority occurred in Arkansas. Governor Orval E. Faubus posted state national guardsmen outside Central High School in Little Rock to bar the entry of nine Negro students in the fall of 1957. President Eisenhower immediately federalized the national guard and sent federal troops to Little Rock to preserve order and enforce integration. Openly encouraged by state policy during the next few months, aroused white citizens prepared to bar the re-entry of the Negro students in the fall of 1958. So threatening had the situation in Little Rock become that a federal district judge granted the local school board a two-and-a-half-year delay in integration in order to avoid violence. This order was quickly appealed, and the Supreme Court, in Cooper v. Aaron, September 1958, unanimously set aside the district judge's ruling. "Law and order," the Supreme Court announced, "are not here to be preserved by depriving the Negro children of their constitutional rights." The state of Arkansas thereupon closed the four Little Rock high schools but reopened them again in 1960 on a basis of limited integration.

Schools facing integration were also closed in 1958–9 in Virginia, another leading bastion of "massive resistance." But both state and federal courts in 1959 held that Virginia's school-closing law was unconstitutional, and local opinion in the districts affected soon swung to the position that a little integration was better than no schools at all. State authorities yielded, and token integration was peacefully accomplished in several Virginia schools in 1959 and 1960. Even in the deep South the wall was finally breached: a few Negroes began attending formerly all-white schools in Florida in 1959 and, despite an angry boycott by white parents, in Louisiana in 1960. When Georgia yielded, in 1961, to the extent of permitting its local school boards to comply with federal court orders if they chose, Atlanta drew up an integration plan, and nine Negro students entered a white school in that city in the fall of 1961. By the latter date, only South Carolina, Alabama, and Mississippi had failed to make at least a token compliance with the Brown decision.

Although the courts were methodically striking down most of the state laws designed to prevent desegregation,[43] it was obvious that anything be-

---

[43] In one important set of rulings from 1958 to 1961, the Supreme Court invalidated laws in several southern states that required the NAACP to disclose the names of its members to state or local authorities, on the ground that such laws were an invasion of freedom of association. These laws had been designed to thwart the efforts of the NAACP in the South to support the campaign against Jim Crow.

yond token and limited integration in the lower South would be a long time coming. White citizens were beginning to realize that they could better preserve the substance of segregation in practice by accepting a small measure of integration in principle. Devices to limit integration by "pupil placement" laws, permitting assignment to schools on some basis other than race—psychological factors, mental aptitude, availability of classrooms and teachers, and so on—appeared less apt to be struck down by the courts if carefully drawn. The Supreme Court held in 1958, for example, that an Alabama school-placement law was not unconstitutional on its face. As of 1960, six years after the Brown decision, only about 181,000, or 6 per cent, of some 3,000,000 Negro students in the South were actually attending public schools with white students, and all but a minute fraction of these were in the border states and the District of Columbia.

Meanwhile, however, the Negro was striking more directly and dramatically at other parts of the Jim Crow system. Many of these new protests were Negro-led, locally supported, and largely spontaneous direct-action movements that vividly underscored the black man's growing determination to destroy the barriers of caste by his own efforts.

A Negro Baptist minister, Martin Luther King of Montgomery, Alabama, founded the Montgomery Improvement Association in 1955 to protest segregated seating on local buses. Supported eventually by nearly all of Montgomery's 50,000 Negroes, the Association organized car pools and conducted a massive boycott against the bus company. Negroes unable to find a car pool walked to work or school for months in support of the campaign. Though exposed to harassment and indignities from local authorities and white citizens, King and his followers maintained the boycott for over a year and nearly drove the transit company into bankruptcy. A court decision in 1956 struck down segregated seating in local transportation, and Montgomery Negroes triumphantly returned to the buses to sit where they chose. Many other southern cities soon instituted desegregation in local transit.

The basis of King's philosophy, which received wide publicity during and after the Montgomery boycott, was the doctrine of nonviolent or passive resistance that Mohandas K. Gandhi had made famous in India many years before. Following King's example, a host of Negro college students proceeded to challenge Jim Crow by deliberately breaking local segregation ordinances in peaceful and orderly fashion. Seeking to dramatize the injustice of such laws, the demonstrators offered no resistance to violence and actually courted arrest. Major targets of this movement were southern department stores, which uniformly maintained segregated lunch counters while welcoming Negro trade in all other sections of the store. The first of the "sit-in" demonstrations occurred in Greensboro, North Carolina, in early 1960, when four Negro students sat at a Woolworth lunch counter, requested service, and continued to wait patiently after being refused.

The technique caught on immediately. Dozens of similar demonstrations took place in other southern cities in the weeks that followed. Many sit-ins were spontaneous and locally organized, while others were sponsored by CORE and similar groups. The idea particularly captured the imagination of college students, both Negro and white, who staged numerous demonstrations in the South and picketed northern chain stores in sympathetic protest. The demonstrators were often heckled, spat upon, chased, and beaten; scores were arrested for violating local ordinances, trespassing, or disturbing the peace. Nevertheless, the movement continued and soon bore successful results. Chain stores in dozens of southern communities desegregated their lunch counters during 1960 and 1961.

Even more provocative, in part because "outsiders" from the North played a major role, were the "freedom rides" that began in the spring of 1961. Sponsored by several interracial organizations, Negro and white citizens attacked segregation in interstate bus travel by chartering special buses and riding through the heart of the South, deliberately entering segregated restaurants and terminals en route. White resentment quickly boiled over. In Anniston, Alabama, one group of freedom riders was attacked and beaten, and a second freedom bus was halted, bombed, set afire, and destroyed by an angry mob. When the riders attempted to proceed from Anniston to Montgomery, the situation deteriorated still further. The Governor of Alabama, denouncing the riders as "rabble-rousers," made no attempt to curb the resentful citizens of Montgomery. Thus encouraged, they mobbed the freedom riders so ferociously that the federal government, in the absence of effective action by state or local authorities, was forced to intervene. Only after Attorney General Robert F. Kennedy sent several hundred federal marshals to Montgomery to prevent further violence did the Governor act, placing the city under martial law and employing state national guardsmen and police to restore order. It had been one of the most serious disturbances in the postwar era.

Yet the freedom rides continued. Bruised but unintimidated, most of the original group left Montgomery for Jackson, Mississippi, in a bus under heavy policy escort. Twenty-seven of them were arrested in Jackson for violating a segregation ordinance, but police officials were scrupulously careful to prevent further acts of mob violence. Thereafter, in fact, the freedom riders met with little more than epithets, angry stares, and occasional mass arrests. State authorities, keenly aware of the unfavorable publicity that the Anniston and Montgomery episodes had received in the northern press and the world at large, took steps in advance to avert similar outbreaks when the freedom buses appeared. One group was beaten by a mob in McComb, Mississippi, but most of the rides took place without incident.

Results came in late 1961 when the ICC ordered all bus companies to desegregate their interstate routes, post signs to that effect on every bus, and cease stopping at restaurants and terminals that maintained segregated facilities. The bus lines complied, and an increasing number of local terminals—though by no means all of them—took down the "white" and "colored" signs and grudgingly admitted Negroes who sought to enter the white section. As with the sit-ins, the freedom rides had resulted in partial rather than total victory, but another important area of Jim Crow practice had been broken.[44]

vvvvvvvvvvvvvvvvvvvvvv

[44] Recognizing the heavy expenses of posting bail and paying fines for the numerous arrests that greeted their forays, the groups sponsoring the freedom rides announced in June 1962 that they would henceforth concentrate upon court decisions and legislation in their drive for racial equality. However, CORE, the NAACP, and other groups

Notwithstanding the bitterness, fear, racial tension, and sporadic violence that attended the Negro's bid for equal treatment in the South, there
were grounds for cautious optimism. To begin with, the amount of actual
violence was relatively small—either by comparison with the record of past
decades, or when measured against the depth and variety of the postwar
challenge to old customs and attitudes.[45] A powerful if silent pressure,
hitherto insignificant in the South, was acting not only to restrain lawlessness and violence but to weaken the caste system. This pressure, of course,
was industrialization, which was impatient of Jim Crow and any other im-
pediment to the orderly transaction of business. Still dependent upon
northern investment capital and eager to attract more industry, southern
business leaders deplored and often worked to prevent mob outbreaks that
hurt trade and discouraged outside investment. In the second place, industrial development had drawn the Negro to southern as well as northern
cities; over half the Negroes *in the South* were urban dwellers before 1960.
Their purchasing power was incomparably greater than ever before, and
white merchants were increasingly loath to offend so large a bloc of cus-
tomers.

Not all of the voices of enlightened moderation had been stilled by
segregationist pressure. A few courageous ministers, writers, and editors
continued to speak forthrightly in favor of common sense, tolerance, obedience to law, and adjustment to the postwar world. Many Southerners,
though opposed to desegregation, were painfully aware of the bad name
their section had acquired in the rest of the country and abroad, and realized that some modification of the old order was necessary. Finally, even
the segregationists were not of one mind about the desirability of actually
closing the public schools to avoid integrating them; the experiences in Arkansas and Virginia had been sobering. Several southern communities, the
most striking example being Atlanta in 1961, showed that careful planning
could avert trouble and insure peaceful integration.

For all Southerners, Negro and white, this was a time of travail and
grinding readjustment; a social system in retreat cannot avoid displays of
extremism and angry resistance. But neither good will nor patience had
been permanently eclipsed. These qualities were present in both the Negro

still planned to challenge segregation in hotels, theaters, and public beaches by occasional "stand-ins," "wade-ins," and other direct-action methods—but these would be
subordinate to legal and legislative endeavor.

[45] There were, to be sure, a number of tragic episodes. Six Negroes were lynched
during the *decade* of the 1950's (as compared, however, with the dismal record of
1,100 Negroes lynched in the years 1900–17, and 70 in 1919 alone). In addition to the
brutality occasionally suffered by sit-in demonstrators and freedom riders, there were
vicious mob outbreaks in Nashville and Clinton, Tennessee, over school integration. Unruly white students forced a Negro girl off the campus of the University of Alabama in
1956 after she had attempted to enroll there. Several churches and synagogues were
bombed during the bus boycott and sit-in campaigns. Brutal economic coercion was
applied to several hundred Negroes in western Tennessee who sought to register. The
Klan burned crosses and made threats; there was much intimidation.

Without attempting to make light of these tragedies, it can be said that the record
was far less stained than it might have been—or would have been, fifty or even twenty
years earlier. The entire absence of racial incidents in integrated southern schools
throughout the academic year 1961–2 was an encouraging sign.

and white communities in sufficient quantity to suggest that the impulses for gradual but steady progress toward a satisfactory racial adjustment were stronger than the forces of reaction.

One further aspect of Negro protest in the postwar era remains to be noted. The sit-ins, the freedom rides, the bus boycott, and other recent episodes offered convincing proof that Negroes as a whole, and especially young people, were becoming impatient with the legal gradualism advocated by older leaders and favored some form of direct action to achieve more immediate results. A harmonious biracial society of equal citizens remained their goal, but one restless Negro element had set its sights in a far different direction. The phenomenon known as black nationalism, first observable in Marcus Garvey's "Back to Africa" campaign in the 1920's (for details, see above, pp. 241–242), was disturbingly in evidence during the 1950's. It was the extremist, uncompromising fringe of the Negro movement, and it offered a warning which the white community would ignore at its peril.

Black nationalism after 1945 was most powerfully represented by the so-called Black Muslims, a quasi-religious organization professing allegiance to its own version of Mohammedanism. There were other black nationalist groups, but the Muslims alone achieved a significant following. Founded originally in Detroit in the early 1930's, the Black Muslims soon passed under the leadership of a Georgia Negro named Elijah Poole, who adopted the name of Elijah Muhammad and achieved absolute authority over the movement. Under Muhammad's militant and aggressive guidance, the Black Muslims became a well-knit, dedicated body of over 100,000 adherents by 1960. Muhammad enforced a stern morality upon all members, organized a cadre of highly disciplined young Negroes as a sort of Praetorian guard, levied huge contributions from the faithful, acquired real estate and all manner of business enterprises for the organization, and had established, by 1960, over fifty temples in urban centers from coast to coast, South as well as North.

The core of Muslim doctrine was black supremacy—an explicit and uncompromising racism. Locally, Muhammad spoke of the day when American Negroes would have an entire culture and economy of their own in the United States, totally separate from the white. Ultimately, he predicted the downfall of white civilization and the dominance of the world by the colored races. He was deliberately vague as to just when and how all of this would take place, being careful to avoid openly seditious utterances or invitations to violence. Though he preached a race hatred as bitter and extreme as that of the most ardent Ku Klux Klansman, he insisted that all Black Muslims should avoid aggressive or hostile acts against white men. But the implications of eventual violence and race war were present in his message—and, some thought, in the paramilitary elite corps of disciplined young men who enforced order within the movement and were prepared to obey his every command with fanatic loyalty.

The significant feature of the Black Muslims was not their religious beliefs or their advocacy of a separate and economically independent Negro state in America, which was thoroughly unrealistic. It was that a message based firmly upon militant racism and hatred of the white man could attract so large a following. The Muslims had a vitality and a growth rate unmatched by any other Negro group. Their adherents were almost entirely from the urban lower class, and they were predominantly young people, with a high percentage of males. Negro intellectuals largely shunned the movement. So did the Negro middle class, which had consciously turned its back upon the black urban masses in order to move toward greater social acceptance by the white community. But these black urban masses could not be written off so easily. Their growing allegiance to Elijah Muhammad served to warn the American people that only by offering hope, opportunity, acceptance, and human dignity to this vital segment of the Negro community can the nation offset the Muslim appeal and guide the race problem toward ultimate solution.

CHAPTER

31

Defense Policies and
Nuclear Stalemate

THE UNITED STATES faced in Soviet Russia and her new Chinese ally the most powerful and unrelenting adversaries it had ever encountered. It had just fought Communist forces to a standstill in Korea. With the end of that struggle in July 1953, the nation undertook the task, in peacetime, of devising a defensive strategy and maintaining a military strength that would enable it to counter Communist aggression in any part of the free world. It set about this task during a period of rapid advances in military technology and revolutionary changes in weapons systems. The remorseless logic of the cold war forced a progressive development of American and Soviet nuclear arsenals even as the destructive capacity of the new weapons gave urgency to quests for disarmament and attempts to negotiate disputes that might lead to war. Taken together, the quests for military security, disarmament, and peace after 1953 were the most formidable, intricate, and costly programs ever undertaken by an American government. They were attended by repeated controversy, haunting uncertainty, and the omnipresent knowledge that miscalculation might mean ruinous setback or total annihilation.

247. *National Defense Policy in the Nuclear Age*

American defense policy and the effectiveness of the nation's military establishment became questions of overriding concern as the cold war grew in scope and deadly seriousness after 1953. Many of the potent weapons of the Second World War had become almost as obsolete as the crossbow and the flintlock musket. There seemed to be no limit to destructive power, no end to the constant, expensive changes and improvements required to keep a nation's armed forces in readiness for combat. And yet diplomacy, to say nothing of national security, depended upon the success or failure of defense policy.

The Eisenhower administration during its first year in office evolved a national defense policy which it pursued with unshaken confidence for more than four years. The cornerstone of this new policy, enunciated by Secretary of State Dulles in January 1954, was the controversial and easily misunderstood doctrine of "massive retaliation." It envisaged the kind of powerful deterrent force—accompanied by a well-advertised determination to use it—that would forestall aggression by making it too costly. A potential aggressor would supposedly cancel his plans if he knew that the retaliatory damage to himself would outweigh the anticipated gain.

One objective was flexibility: "a great capacity," as Dulles put it, "to retaliate, instantly, by means and at places of our choosing. That permits a selection of military means instead of a multiplication of means." Another objective was economy. Hereafter, the country would not need to guard against future Koreas by maintaining extensive ground forces, deployed to resist aggression by conventional means wherever the Communist bloc chose to make a thrust. Willingness to use massive retaliation would recapture initiative while permitting large reductions in spending on conventional forces. America's defense needs would be geared to what President Eisenhower termed the "long haul" concept—a steady, well-planned rate of expenditures rather than the "inefficient and expensive starts and stops" that had characterized defense spending and strained the economy in the past.

The doctrine of massive retaliation did not envisage abandonment of all armaments save strategic bombers equipped with nuclear weapons. It called instead for the replacement of old-style military forces by "highly mobile naval, air, and amphibious units" in combat readiness, poised to strike quickly, and equipped where feasible with a variety of tactical atomic weapons. These would be backed, of course, by the growing "massive deterrent" fleet of medium- and long-range bombers in the Strategic Air Command. As Admiral Arthur W. Radford, Chairman of the Joint Chiefs of Staff, put it: "We must be ready for tremendous, vast retaliatory and counteroffensive blows in event of a global war, and we must also be ready for lesser military actions short of all-out war." [1]

The Washington administration also realized that countries bordering the Communist empire would have to maintain conventional forces for defense against local aggression and subversion. The United States would continue to provide military and economic aid to nations that could not afford to maintain adequate defensive forces. But there would be a new allocation of effort and resources on the part of the free world, again aimed at efficiency and economy. The funds and manpower for local defensive

[1] Quoted in Richard P. Stebbins *et al., The United States in World Affairs, 1953* (New York, 1955), p. 359.

forces on the Communist perimeter would increasingly have to be provided by the nations concerned, while the major American contribution would be the protective umbrella provided by massive retaliation.

The outcome was a realignment of the American defense system that placed a heavy emphasis on the nuclear deterrent. As we shall see in a later section, the policy also set off numerous controversies over alleged deterioration in the nation's relative strength and strategic position. The desire for economy, which exercised an almost hypnotic fascination upon Republican leaders, seems to have overshadowed other goals for a time. The administration's budget for the fiscal year 1954 (July 1, 1953–June 30, 1954), prepared well before the Korean truce negotiations of 1953 were concluded, cut defense appropriations from the Truman estimate of $41,-200,000,000 to the $34,400,000,000 finally appropriated by Congress on July 29, 1953.[2] Actual defense expenditures during the fiscal year 1954 were nearly $3,500,000,000 less than in the preceding twelve months.

The most surprising feature of defense estimates in 1953 was the substantial reduction in the air force—from a projected 143 wings to 120, 114 of which would be activated and equipped by mid-1954.[3] In answer to criticism from Congress, which was distinctly partial to the air force, the Defense Department explained that the Truman estimate of 143 wings had been unnecessarily large and extravagant, that there was a huge backlog of $28,000,000,000 in unspent funds available for air power, and that the proposed reduction would eliminate much "fat" while preserving the "muscle" in this important branch of the service.

In any event, the reduction in the proposed size of the air force was a temporary expedient, prompted by budgetary concerns. The government cut defense expenditures another $6,300,000,000 in the fiscal year 1955 (July 1, 1954–June 30, 1955), but the axe fell entirely upon the army, navy, and marine corps, and on the foreign military aid program, while the air force actually spent $737,000,000 more than in the preceding year. The administration announced plans in 1954 for an increase in the number of military aircraft over the next three years from 33,000 to 40,000, including navy and marine planes, and an expansion of the air force to 137 wings. The Strategic Air Command, backbone of American retaliatory power, boasted fifty-three combat wings and 1,800 bombers by 1959. The Department of the Air Force had received little more than twenty-five cents of every defense dollar in 1950 and about thirty-four cents in 1953. Its share climbed to almost fifty cents in 1955 and stayed there for the balance of the

vvvvvvvvvvvvvvvvvvvv

[2] The Truman estimate of $41,200,000,000 for defense in fiscal 1954 was itself based on the assumption that the Korean War would soon end. The figure was markedly lower than the $52,400,000,000 requested by the Truman administration for fiscal 1953 or the $61,700,000,000 requested for fiscal 1952. The large additional reductions in defense appropriations made by Eisenhower and the Republican Congress for fiscal 1954 were not, therefore, explainable simply on the basis that the war was now over.

[3] A wing was an administrative unit that embraced not only a given number of planes and crews, but the necessary ground crews, bases, and support units. At this time, the air force put thirty aircraft in a heavy bomber wing, forty-five in a medium bomber wing, seventy-five in a fighter wing, and seventy-five in an interceptor wing. The new figure of 120 wings for 1954 compared with an actual strength of 103 wings in March 1953, ten of which had not yet received combat aircraft.

decade.[4] Atomic energy appropriations and the nation's nuclear stockpile also grew steadily.

Meanwhile, the army was progressively reduced from a postwar peak of 1,553,000 men and expenditures of $17,000,000,000 in 1953, to 873,000 men by 1960 and to annual expenditures averaging less than $10,000,000,-000 from 1955 to 1960. Though corresponding cuts were less drastic, the navy's personnel shrank from 795,000 to 618,000 men between 1953 and 1960; the marine corps', from 250,000 to 170,000. Naval expenditures declined from $11,875,000,000 in 1953 to less than $9,750,000,000 in 1955 and 1956, then climbed inexorably back toward the 1953 figure as rising costs defied attempts at further economy.

248. *Changes in the American Military Establishment*

The real justification for the reductions in the military establishment just described lay in the steady development and adoption of new equipment and weapons. Each branch of the service worked energetically to keep pace with the insatiable demands of modernization. All made phenomenal progress in warning and air defense systems by effective use of radio, radar, and electronic computers and control systems. The Defense Early Warning (DEW) Line, a string of radar stations above the Arctic Circle from Alaska to Baffin Island, was begun in 1955 and completed in 1958. It was later extended to Greenland and reinforced by the even more sensitive Ballistic Missile Early Warning System (BMEWS), which was under construction by 1960.[5] As we shall see in more detail below, each service made substantial progress in developing rockets and missiles after 1955.

The navy undertook a host of technological improvements.[6] U.S.S. *Forrestal,* first of a new class of six mammoth 60,000-ton supercarriers, joined the fleet in 1955. Several types of ships, beginning with the 13,000-ton cruiser *Canberra* in 1956, were equipped with guided missiles of both

᠎ᜌᜌᜌᜌᜌᜌᜌᜌᜌᜌᜌᜌᜌᜌᜌᜌᜌᜌ

[4] Since a sizable portion of naval expenditures was also devoted to aviation, the *total* share of the defense dollar consumed by air power was even higher. President Eisenhower claimed that sixty cents out of each defense dollar was so allocated as early as 1953, and this figure certainly did not diminish in succeeding years. Expenditures by the Department of the Air Force mounted steadily, from $15,085,000,000 in 1953 to $19,065,000,000 in 1960.

[5] This impressive progress in military defense against aerial attack was almost completely unmatched by any real effort in the field of civil defense. The President and other administration leaders advocated such a program more than once, but Congress appropriated trifling sums for the purpose, and the public was manifestly indifferent. As a result, the United States had little more than the rudiments of a civil defense program by 1960.

[6] Symbolic of the changed order of things, marking the end of a mighty era in naval history, was the decommissioning of U.S.S. *Wisconsin* in 1957, last battleship on active service in the United States navy. Britain had retired its last battleship a year earlier. As had been clear at least since 1945, this historic class of vessel—backbone of the world's fleets, both steam and sail, since the seventeenth century—had become obsolescent in the jet-atomic age, superseded after midcentury by the aircraft carrier and the submarine as the vital components of naval strength.

the surface-to-air and surface-to-surface variety. By 1958 the navy was per-fecting, among other potent new weapons, a rocket-assisted airborne atomic depth charge and a submersible guided missile.

The navy's most significant innovation was the nuclear-powered war-ship. A nuclear heavy cruiser, three nuclear frigates, and a nuclear carrier, U.S.S. *Enterprise*,[7] were nearing completion by the end of Eisenhower's second term. Even more important, the nuclear-powered submarine put in its appearance with the commissioning of U.S.S. *Nautilus* in 1955. It was, as one authority noted, "the first authentic submarine," capable of almost indefinite submersion because its engines did not require oxygen.

The new craft demonstrated their prowess repeatedly. *Nautilus* and *Skate* made pioneer reconnaissance voyages beneath the North Polar ice-cap, and *Seawolf* established a sixty-day submersion record in 1958, fol-lowed by *Triton's* eighty-four-day undersea voyage around the world in 1960. There followed the successful test launching of the new intermediate-range Polaris missile from a submerged submarine in July 1960; the com-missioning and stationing of the first two specially designed, Polaris-equipped nuclear submarines before the end of the year; and authorization for an entire fleet of such vessels. The navy was perfecting a powerful, highly mobile, and well-nigh invulnerable "nuclear deterrent."

The army also strove to supply its forces with modern equipment and techniques. Many improvements were effected in conventional weapons,[8] but it was in the fields of nuclear firepower, missiles, and organization that the ground forces registered the most striking progress. American troops in Europe, the United States, and the Far East were equipped with atomic cannon as early as 1955. The "Honest John" rocket and "Corporal" guided missile, expressly though not exclusively designed to carry nuclear war-heads, were operational by 1957 and deployed in newly created "atomic support" or missile commands. The Nike-Ajax surface-to-air missile, the pioneer antiaircraft rocket, was in use by 1955. The army's first Missile Group, featuring the new Redstone 200-mile surface-to-surface missile, was activated in 1957. The army organized a new, lightweight airborne divi-sion with atomic capability in 1956, underwent a basic reorganization into

---

[7] She was commissioned in 1961. Displacing 86,000 tons, 1,123 feet long and 252 feet wide, with a flight deck of four and a half acres, *Enterprise* is by far the largest and most complex warship ever built. Every statistic is a superlative. Costing $444,000,-000, with an undisclosed speed well in excess of forty knots, she carries over 100 attack and fighter planes, all with atomic-bomb-carrying capability. Eight nuclear reactors give *Enterprise* a range of 140,000 miles at full speed or fully 400,000 miles at 20 knots, making her more independent of shore bases or auxiliaries than any vessel since the age of sail. Electronic data-processing equipment make her virtually a push-button war-ship.

[8] Among these might be mentioned the 280-mm. cannon, designed for conventional or atomic ammunition, possessing better range and accuracy as well as greater fire-power than older artillery pieces; the light, mobile, 106-mm. recoilless antitank rifle, sup-posedly able to destroy any existing variety of tank; the M56 self-propelled 90-mm. gun; the new M14 all-purpose rifle; the M60 machine gun; and the M-60 tank. In addition, the army was developing and testing a whole variety of new equipment: an aerial jeep, a flying-crane helicopter, light weapons with great firepower, improved troop carriers and "off-road" vehicles, missile-firing light vehicles, and so on.

the so-called pentomic divisions beginning in 1957,[9] and set up the Strategic Army Corps (STRAC) in 1958. It consisted of three highly trained divisions maintained in instant combat readiness in the United States, and capable of quick dispatch to reinforce American and allied units overseas in the event of general war or to provide initial resistance wherever a limited war might break out.[10]

Reorganization was by no means limited to actual military units and commands. President Eisenhower repeatedly undertook an extensive overhaul of the entire defense establishment, in an attempt to achieve greater efficiency and reduce wasteful interservice duplication and rivalry. Such were the goals of the Defense Reorganization acts of 1953 and 1958, which attempted to co-ordinate and centralize the complex allocations of responsibility and authority within the Department of Defense.[11] The government attempted to cope systematically with the challenges of the space age by creating the National Aeronautics and Space Administration (NASA) out of the older National Advisory Commission for Aeronautics in 1958, and by assigning civilian space research projects to NASA and the military

[9] The new pentomic divisions, smaller and lighter in the case of airborne and infantry units than the conventional divisions which they supplanted, were composed of five mobile combat groups with artillery support, including Honest John rockets and atomic capability. The result was increased mobility, flexibility, and firepower. The innovations embodied in the pentomic concept constituted, in the opinion of one military authority, "the most revolutionary and rapid changes in warfare organization and tactics in modern history."

[10] In other organizational improvements, the army began streamlining its supply system in 1956 and established the Ordnance Missile Command, integrating the various agencies and units engaged in research, development, and testing of ballistic and guided missiles, in 1958.

[11] The Act of 1953, embodying the recommendations of an Eisenhower-appointed committee, centralized power and responsibility in the hands of the Secretary of Defense, eliminated the semi-autonomy of the three service departments (army, navy, air force), established a single chain of command within the Defense Department, and increased the authority of the Joint Chiefs of Staff, whose Chairman now became the actual director and co-ordinator of strategy and joint operations. Under the new system, the military staff could devote more time to actual combat matters, while the jurisdiction of high-ranking civilian officials was expanded to include operational matters as well as general policy and budgetary questions. The Act also abolished several independent agencies—the Munitions Board, the Research and Development Board, the Defense Supply Management Agency, and others—and transferred their functions to new assistant secretaries in the Defense Department.

The Act of 1958 sought to unify strategic planning and centralized operational direction of the armed forces, and was a response to the growing interservice jealousy of recent years. The effectiveness of "unified commands" (which included land, sea, and air units) was increased by giving eacl unified commander full authority over all units under his direction, and by requiring that only the Secretary of Defense could approve withdrawal from a unified command. The working staff of the Joint Chiefs of Staff was much enlarged, to permit that body to conduct more extensive and detailed strategic planning.

The best example of the "unified command" principle was the Composite Air Strike Force, developed in 1958 to cope with any type of limited war or internal unrest abroad that required American participation. The CASF demonstrated its effectiveness by the speed with which it deployed American troops in Lebanon during the Middle Eastern crisis of 1958.

space program to the Defense Department's Advanced Research Projects Agency.[12]

Notwithstanding these efforts to improve all aspects of the American defense effort, the administration's major emphasis was upon air power. The policy of massive retaliation seemed to require such an emphasis, and there was no gainsaying the favored position occupied by the United States Air Force during the 1950's.[13] Concentration upon the air arm was doubly attractive to policy makers and the general public: it seemed to offer vast savings in reduced equipment and manpower for the ground and naval forces, and it held out the hope that future Communist aggression could be met without the heavy commitment of American troops and attendant high casualties that had been the price of the Korean War.

The air force did in fact deploy an impressive and mounting array of strength during the 1950's. Organized, as it had been since 1946, into three basic structures—the Strategic Air Command (SAC) for massive long-range bombing, the Tactical Air Command (TAC) for support of ground operations, and the Air Defense Command (ADC) for interception of enemy bombing raids—the air force constantly improved its ability to carry out these vital tasks. Korea had convincingly demonstrated the jet airplane's superiority over the "horse and buggy" propeller-driven aircraft. The air force announced in 1954 that all its fighters were now jets. But the jet age, of course, was no more than a threshold. The famed F-86F "Sabrejet" and F-84G "Thunderjet" fighter-bombers, which had been the last word in aviation by the end of the Korean War, were being replaced by newer and better craft within eighteen months. The supersonic jet fighter, first achieved in the F-100 "Super Sabre" in 1953, rapidly became indispensable for both TAC and ADC operations as several models in this category went into production and became available after 1955. The entire interceptor force of the ADC was "supersonic" by 1960.

As air speeds increased steadily, approaching "Mach 2" (twice the speed of sound, or about 1,450 miles per hour) with the F-104 "Starfighter" and other types in 1957, the problem of perpetual and almost immediate obsolescence bulked large in air force planning. Greater range, maneuverability, and firepower likewise added to the rapid turnover in front-line combat planes: aerial refueling, all-weather navigational and bombing systems, and tactical attack planes that carried nuclear bombloads and fired air-to-air and air-to-surface rockets, were among the important advances in military aviation during the late 1950's.

While TAC fighters and attack planes and ADC interceptors became faster and more lethal each year,[14] SAC continually made its awesome de-

[12] Later, however, NASA took charge of all space-satellite projects, while the Advanced Research Projects Agency continued its development of air defense systems, rocket fuels and propellants, and similar items.

[13] Recognizing that the air force had become and would remain a co-ordinate (if not actually predominant) military arm, the administration implemented plans long in the making and established the Air Force Academy in 1954 (in temporary quarters at Lowry Air Force Base, Denver, until the Academy's new plant and campus near Colorado Springs were completed and ready for occupancy in 1958).

[14] The same was true, of course, of naval aircraft. The navy received its first swept-wing fighter-bomber (the F9F-6 "Cougar") in 1954, and two years later was testing

terrent power more "massive" than ever. Aside from missile development, SAC's biggest project during the Eisenhower era was a gradual but steady change-over from obsolescent propeller-driven bombers to faster, longer-range, and better equipped jet bombers carrying larger nuclear "payloads." By 1955 the stratojet B-47 medium bomber had completely replaced the piston-engined B-50 medium bomber as the principal SAC weapon.[15] The cumbersome, propeller-driven B-36, standard American heavy bomber, survived somewhat longer; the first squadron of 600-m.p.h. jet B-52 heavy bombers was activated in 1955, but the eleven heavy-bomber wings of the Strategic Air Command were not completely equipped with B-52s until 1960.[16] The first supersonic bomber, the turbojet B-58 "Hustler," was tested successfully in 1958 and went into its first operational unit in 1960. Designed to supersede the B-47 in the medium-bomber category, the delta-winged "Hustler" had twice the B-47's speed and a "non-refueled" range three thousand miles greater.

249.   *The Missile Age*

Constant improvements in manned aircraft were overshadowed toward the end of the decade by progress in missile development. Spurred by Soviet achievements in this field after 1957, each branch of the armed services had by 1960 designed and put into operation a whole range of missiles of varied range, type, and purpose. The most significant examples were in the "anti-missile missile" field, offering the hope that an effective defense against enemy nuclear rockets might be obtainable,[17] and in the

supersonic carrier-based fighters and attack planes like the A4D "Skyhawk," the A3D "Skywarrior," and the F8U-1 "Crusader," which had a speed of 1,000 m.p.h. Later and improved versions were constantly being added: the new "Skyhawk" of 1958, now a midget atom-bomber; the Grumman A2F-1, a low-level attack plane that purportedly avoided radar detection; and the F8U-2N of 1960, an all-weather fighter equipped with "Sidewinder" air-to-air missiles and a speed approaching Mach 2.

[15] Missiles aside, approximately three fourths of SAC's offensive units were medium bombers; the remainder were heavy bombers.

[16] An improved version of the B-52, the B-52G, began going into service in 1960. With a range 25 per cent greater than the B-52, the G model was equipped to fly non-stop, non-refueled, round-trip missions anywhere in the world with a full nuclear bomb-load plus two air-to-surface nuclear "Hound Dog" missiles under its wings for release hundreds of miles from the target. The B-52H, an even more capable version, was under construction. But the air force proposal to build a fleet of huge supersonic B-70 jet heavy bombers could not win final approval from either the Eisenhower or the Kennedy administration. By 1960 it was at least probable, if not certain, that the long-range missile had rendered the manned bomber obsolete.

[17] The most promising defensive missiles were the air force's "Bomarc" group and the army's "Nike" family, the latest versions of which were still in the advanced testing stage by 1960. Impressive in early tests against short-range and air-launched missiles, the Nike-Zeus scored its most spectacular success in the summer of 1962 by intercepting an Atlas ICBM that had been fired 5,000 miles away and was moving at a speed of 16,000 miles per hour. It yet remained doubtful whether Nike-Zeus or any other conceivable weapon could provide a truly effective defense against a large-scale missile attack. But air defense had become, together with the radar warning system, almost entirely a missile function by the early 1960's.

vital category of so-called intercontinental (ICBM) and intermediate range (IRBM) ballistic missiles that would first supplement, and perhaps eventually replace, the manned bombers of the Strategic Air Command as the nation's ultimate offensive weapon.

The armed services registered a host of triumphs in the field of strategic offensive missiles before the end of the Eisenhower administration. The success in 1960 of the navy's "Polaris" IRBM, fired from nuclear submarines, has already been noted. The army's "Jupiter" and the air force's "Thor," IRBM's with a range of 1,500–2,000 miles, completed their tests and went into production in 1958. Thor missile squadrons were deployed two years later at RAF bases in Great Britain, Jupiter squadrons at NATO bases in Italy and Turkey.

America's first ICBM was the air force "Atlas," [18] successfully test-fired at its full range of 6,325 miles in November 1958, and deployed in its first strategic missile squadron by 1960. Its maximum range was soon increased to 9,000 miles by reducing its weight and expanding the thrust of its liquid-fueled rocket engine. The "Titan," another air force ICBM with comparable range, became "war ready" in 1961, with an improved version already in production that boasted a storable liquid propellant and a jam-proof inertial guidance system. A total of thirteen Atlas squadrons and fourteen Titan squadrons were scheduled for activation between 1962 and 1964, while construction began in 1960 on several newly selected ICBM base sites in various parts of the country. The air force was also developing the "Minute Man," a simpler and less expensive ICBM that could be launched from underground silos and movable railroad cars. The first Minute Man squadron of fifty-five missiles was activated in 1962.

250. *Defense Controversy and Nuclear Arms Race*

Despite these remarkable achievements, the Eisenhower administration soon became embroiled in a nagging controversy over alleged shortcomings and failures in its defense policy. The controversy, in some ways more serious though less acrimonious than the Truman-MacArthur dispute of 1951, began to gather momentum early in Eisenhower's first term. Variations and extensions of the argument were still in progress when he left office.

At issue, essentially, was the entire policy of massive retaliation with its emphasis upon nuclear air power. The first reaction came from abroad, where the apparent implications of the policy met widespread condemnation. To many foreign observers, especially in neutral nations, this outspoken use of "nuclear diplomacy" vastly increased the possibility of total war and endangered all mankind. The NATO countries were similarly alarmed. The reduction in American ground forces, it was feared, would mean withdrawal of American contingents from Europe and other over-

[18] The first operational long-range missile was actually the "Snark," which was deployed in a strategic missile wing as early as 1957. The Snark was a jet-powered "air breathing" *guided* missile with a range of 5,000 miles, slower and less potent than the long-range *ballistic* missiles that followed it.

seas bases and a consequent invitation to Soviet aggression. At the same time, reliance upon the nuclear deterrent was simply "rattling the A-bomb" and condemning America's allies to "annihilation without representation."

Democratic critics, including Adlai E. Stevenson and former Secretary of State Dean Acheson, attacked the policy on substantive as well as partisan grounds. General Matthew B. Ridgway resigned as army Chief of Staff in 1955 out of disagreement with the policy. General Maxwell D. Taylor, who succeeded Ridgway as Chief of Staff in 1955, soon became as critical as his predecessor. Perhaps the most judicious and penetrating of the critics was Henry A. Kissinger, Associate Director of the Center for International Affairs at Harvard University, who questioned the massive-deterrent policy in a series of articles in 1955 and 1956 and finally in a book, *Nuclear Weapons and Foreign Policy*, 1957. His unfavorable verdict was echoed by Robert E. Osgood in *Limited War*, 1957, and by several other specialists in military and international affairs.

The essence of the indictment was that dependence upon massive retaliation placed American policy in a paralyzing and dangerous strait jacket. By reducing the nation's capacity to fight limited wars of the Korean variety, it positively encouraged the Communists to "nibble" at peripheral and remote areas. Since it was unlikely that the United States would bomb Moscow whenever such local aggression or subversive activity occurred, "massive retaliation" was no more than a patent bluff that would inevitably be called—had already been called, in fact, in Indochina in 1953–4. Aside from the case of direct Soviet attacks upon the United States or western Europe, critics argued, the policy was doubly harmful: it was useless as a deterrent because it lacked credibility, and the emphasis upon it deprived the country, when faced with lesser Communist thrusts, of any alternative save yielding.

This meant, to begin with, that Communist threats of limited aggression might be employed as a deliberate instrument of foreign policy. Since the United States would lack the non-nuclear means to contain them, such threats would "act as a powerful form of blackmail, which will tend to dissolve the political bonds of the free world and prepare the way for bloodless conquests, even while the Communists pose as the champions of peace and the United States incurs the onus of 'nuclear diplomacy.' " [19]

Worse still, the policy could easily lead to war by miscalculation—the very contingency Secretary Dulles was most determined to avoid. He hoped to prevent such miscalculation by making clear in advance how the nation would respond. Yet talk of massive retaliation made for ambiguity rather than clarity, and the ambiguity increased each time the deterrent was not actually employed. The Communist leaders might well shape their policy on the assumption that the American threat was pure bluff. Sooner or later, critics warned, they would act on this assumption once too often—in which case, as Kissinger remarked, "the reliance on 'massive retaliation' may bring about the total war it seeks to prevent."

It was perhaps ironical—and frightening to Dulles's critics—that the alleged policy of massive retaliation was promulgated at the very moment

∿∿∿∿∿∿∿∿∿∿∿∿∿

[19] Robert E. Osgood, *Limited War: The Challenge to American Strategy* (Chicago, 1957), p. 7.

that shifts in the military balance of power between the United States and the Soviet Union were rendering it altogether obsolete. When the Russians developed the hydrogen bomb in the summer of 1953—a bare nine months after the United States had done so—the "nuclear deterrent" became more than ever a two-edged sword. The arms race was on in earnest, and each year the possibility grew more remote that the United States could employ its nuclear striking power against the USSR without suffering damage equal to what it could inflict.

The Russians were now displaying, in fact, a formidable rate of progress in military technology. Already boasting the most powerful army in the world, they built a navy that was second only to America's after mid-century and a submarine fleet second to none. Their advances in strategic air power during the 1950's were of sufficient scope to alarm western observers. American superiority in the quality of equipment and trained personnel was still unsurpassed, but the Soviet had acquired, by 1956, a large enough fleet of long-range bombers and a sufficient nuclear stockpile to devastate the largest American cities in the event of all-out war. Soviet progress in the development of tactical atomic weapons and short-range rockets was equal to that of the United States. The most disturbing news came in 1957, first with the Russian claim that they had successfully test-fired an intercontinental ballistic missile in August, well over a year before "Atlas" proved its merit, and then with the launching of the Sputnik space satellites in October and November.

It was not a heartening prospect. Americans had barely adjusted to the idea that the Soviet Union could *match* their vaunted technological genius. Now they were faced with indisputable evidence that in certain vital military areas the Russians were *outdoing* them. To be sure, the United States launched an impressive number and variety of its own space satellites after Explorer I led the way in January 1958. Moreover, the technical equipment in these satellites, and the scientific information that they made available about outer space, demonstrated a superiority over the Russian ventures. But in one fundamental matter—development of a "thrust" sufficiently powerful to orbit large vehicles with heavy payloads—the Soviet Union was clearly far in advance of the United States.[20] Even the substantial American progress in long-range missile development after 1958 did not altogether quiet the fear that a dangerous "missile gap" was tipping the balance of nuclear power in Russia's favor. Critics now charged that emphasis upon air power had slowed the nation's missile program.

wwwwwwwwwwwwwww

[20] The Soviets continued to register a number of important "firsts" in space exploration from 1958 to 1962: the first satellite to hit the moon, the first to circle the moon and send back photographs of its dark side, the first to go into orbit around the sun—and, in 1961, the first manned flights around the earth, beginning with Major Yuri Gagarin's orbit, followed a few months later by Major Gherman Titov's seventeen-orbit flight. In the summer of 1962 the Russians launched an even more spectacular prelude to an eventual moon flight by placing two manned satellites into orbit in close proximity, where they circled the earth for several days. The United States, too, began to make progress in the "space race," with the increasingly successful flights of the American Astronauts in 1961–3: the sub-orbital trips of Alan Shepard and Virgil Grissom, the three-orbit trips of Lieutenant Colonel John Glenn and Lieutenant Commander M. Scott Carpenter, the six-orbit flight of Commander Walter M. Schirra, and finally, the impressive 22-orbit flight of Major Gordon Cooper in the spring of 1963.

Unfortunately, the furor over the alleged "missile gap" broke out just as the administration was making alarming discoveries about the cost of the defense program. The Defense Department realized in 1957 that it had seriously underestimated the current level of expenditures by the armed forces. All efforts at economy had not prevented the 1957 defense budget from rising nearly $3,000,000,000 over the $35,800,000,000 figure for the fiscal year 1956 (July 1, 1955–June 30, 1956), as expensive new weapons and research programs more than offset the money saved by reductions in troop strength and conventional equipment. Now it developed that expenditures for the fiscal year 1958 (July 1, 1957–June 30, 1958) would be even higher than the $39,000,000,000 estimate unless drastic new cuts were made.

The administration, mindful of Secretary Humphrey's dire warning that the country faced "a depression that will curl your hair" unless the budget and taxes were reduced, slashed its military program desperately in 1958. It ordered further troop reductions, shelving of defense contracts, abandonment or postponement of various research and development projects on missiles and other new weapons, retirement of nearly one hundred warships, and elimination of five tactical wings from the air force in the desperate new economy drive. Four existing army divisions, two proposed "missile" commands, and fifteen to twenty antiaircraft battalions were pared from the rolls between January 1957 and June 1958. All this coincided with the launching of Sputnik and the firing of the first Soviet ICBM.

With the administration now caught in a vicious cross fire between the irreconcilable demands of economy and military preparedness, the defense controversy took on new dimensions and flamed hotter than ever. The President, the Secretaries of State and Defense, and certain high-ranking military spokesmen had insisted all along that emphasis upon nuclear air power had in no way reduced the nation's capacity to fight limited or conventional wars. Now the government tried to assure restive congressmen and an anxious public that the reductions of 1957–8 would be effected "without impairment of our national security" and "without materially affecting our deployments of major combat units abroad."

But the evidence was profoundly disquieting. Two special reports on the military situation added to this anxiety: a top-secret document prepared for the administration in 1957 by a group headed by H. Rowan Gaither, Jr., that was known to take a gloomy view of relative Soviet and American armed strength; and a public report released by the Special Studies Project of the Rockefeller Brothers Fund in January 1958. Senator Stuart Symington of Missouri, Secretary of the Air Force under Truman and now chairman of the Senate armed forces subcommittee, added to the disquietude in 1959 by charging that the Eisenhower administration, "far from planning to close the current ICBM gap, . . . is actually allowing it to widen."

Critics were now accusing the government of multiple failure. Having first weakened the nation's conventional forces and limited-war capability in the twin interests of economy and nuclear air power, it had then fallen behind the Russians in missile development while failing to keep defense costs down. In the face of these charges and Soviet gains, defense expenditures climbed from $39,000,000,000 in 1958 to over $41,000,000,000 each year from 1959 through 1961, in addition to increased amounts for atomic research and military aid. They were the highest military budgets since the peak of the Korean War. Even so, public confidence had been severely shaken. Official statements that the American military position was fundamentally sound, even when they issued from the White House, seemed to lack the reassurance that they had had earlier in the decade. The "missile gap" and other alleged shortcomings in the defense effort became a major issue in the campaign of 1960, with even the Republicans promising improvements if re-elected.

Actually, the state of American defenses during the late 1950's was probably less critical than opponents of the Eisenhower administration claimed. Progress in certain aspects of missile development undoubtedly lagged behind Russia's, but American strength was clearly sufficient, at any time during the Eisenhower era, to deter an all-out Russian attack or retaliate with crushing effectiveness. It is probably true that less concern for economy in governmental spending would have advanced the missile and space programs and reassured the nation's allies about its ability to fight limited wars and repel Communist aggression by non-nuclear means. On the other hand, the settlement of the Korean and Indochinese conflicts in 1953 and 1954 marked the end of the sort of "limited wars" that the United States was accused of being unable to fight, while the speed and efficiency with which American forces occupied Lebanon in 1958 suggested that such operations were still within the nation's competence. One fact, however, overshadowed all the claims and counterclaims of the defense controversy during the 1950's. It was that both Russia and the United States were acquiring and enlarging nuclear arsenals capable of destroying each other, and possibly much of the rest of the world as well.

251. *America and the Soviet Union: Summit Diplomacy and Cold War*

The inauguration of President Eisenhower coincided almost exactly with the death, on March 5, 1953, of Joseph Stalin. The vacuum thus created at the top of the Soviet hierarchy, after twenty-five years of dictatorial rule, led to a struggle for power the outcome of which was not immediately apparent to foreign observers. The new Premier, Georgi M. Malenkov, shared power from the outset with such high-ranking Communist party officials as Vyacheslav M. Molotov, who once again headed the Foreign Office; Lavrenti P. Beria, Minister of Internal Affairs; Nikolai A. Bulganin, Minister of Defense; and Nikita S. Khrushchev, First Secretary of the Communist party's influential Central Committee.

Control shifted with bewildering frequency during the next five years. Beria was shot in 1953. Malenkov gave way as Premier to Bulganin in early 1955. Molotov resigned from the Foreign Office in June 1956 and was ousted from the Central Committee. Malenkov followed him in humiliation a year later. Many other figures, including Marshal Georgi K. Zhukov, eminent war hero, rose and fell during this turbulent period. Among the principal Soviet leaders by 1960 were Marshal Rodion Y. Malinovsky,

Defense Minister since 1957; Andrei Gromyko, who became Foreign Minister in 1957; and Anastas I. Mikoyan, First Deputy Premier. The man who solidified or enhanced his power with each shake-up and maneuvered his way adroitly to the top of the hazardous Russian pyramid was Khrushchev. He exercised virtual control during Bulganin's premiership, 1955–8, and formally succeeded Bulganin as Premier in March 1958. This volatile Russian, with his stocky figure, histrionic speeches, and expressive countenance, alternately beaming and glowering, became a familiar figure to Americans after 1955.

The violent struggle for power that followed Stalin's death had barely begun before the vying Russian leaders inaugurated a tactical change in Russian foreign policy. Underlying Communist objectives remained the same, but the men in the Kremlin apparently acted after March 1953 on the assumption that a less provocative diplomacy would best serve Russian interests. They talked of relaxing tensions, evinced a seeming willingness to negotiate hitherto deadlocked questions, and hinted at concessions. They also began to speak of the "peaceful coexistence" of the socialistic and capitalistic nations.

The Eisenhower administration responded cautiously, but the President was prompt in displaying a willingness to explore the possibilities of understanding. He tried, however, to make it clear that words were not enough. "We welcome every honest act of peace," he said on April 16. "We care nothing for mere rhetoric. We are only for sincerity of peaceful purpose attested by deeds." The Soviets did in fact make a series of conciliatory gestures during the spring and summer of 1953, the most notable of which was their prompt endorsement of the Chinese and North Korean Communist proposal on March 28 to resume the armistice negotiations at Panmunjom. These actions lent some weight to Premier Malenkov's assertion, in an address on August 8, that "there is not one dispute or undecided question that cannot be decided by peaceful means on the basis of mutual understanding of interested countries. This is our attitude toward all states, among them the U.S.A."

By and large, the United States wanted more assurances than these before it would accept the sincerity of Russian intentions. Prime Minister Churchill of Great Britain, in a speech to the House of Commons on May 11, again urged a four-power meeting of heads of government, or summit conference, a step he had been advocating for three years. But Eisenhower was loath, as Truman had been, to meet the Russians at the summit until some assurance of genuine progress and Soviet co-operation on certain outstanding questions could be had in advance.

Gradually, and with the kind of tortuous crabwise movements that American statesmen had grown used to in dealing with the Russians, the two sides maneuvered toward a position whence a path to the summit could be cleared. The first break in the diplomatic log jam occurred at a Foreign Ministers' Conference in Vienna in May 1955. The Russians finally agreed, after nearly a decade of haggling and stalling, to conclude a treaty that restored Austria's freedom and provided for withdrawal of the four-power occupation forces. It was the first time in the postwar era that the Soviets had consented to pull completely out of an area where their troops had established a foothold. It did much to persuade the western nations—

and particularly the United States, which had been the most dubious—that the new Russian leaders genuinely desired better relations.

Plans for a summit meeting were quickly drawn in the late spring of 1955, and President Eisenhower, Premier Bulganin, Prime Minister Anthony Eden of Great Britain, and Premier Edgar Faure of France met at Geneva from July 18 to July 23, to define and review the issues dividing East and West. Each leader was accompanied by his foreign minister and other advisers, with Khrushchev present in the Soviet delegation. It was the first time an American and Soviet chief of state had talked directly since Truman's meeting with Stalin at Potsdam ten years before. The encounter raised high hopes. Its relaxed atmosphere, stimulated by an abundance of vodka, martinis, and mutual cordiality, seemed to suggest that a major turn for the better in the troubled state of world affairs was taking place at last.

Actually, the goals of the conference were realistically modest, the results more modest still. It had been decided in advance that the heads of government would try to formulate rather than solve the pressing issues, and agree, if possible, only upon the methods to be followed. Substantive agreements would then be sought by a later conference of Foreign Ministers. The four leaders defined the paramount problems as German reunification, European security, disarmament, and greater contacts between East and West. They recommended free elections under proper conditions as the method of achieving German unification, a general treaty renouncing force or aid to aggressors as the primary means of safeguarding European security, the United Nations as the best vehicle for pursuing the goal of disarmament, and—as a final truism—the progressive elimination of barriers to the flow of people and ideas as a way of establishing more East-West contacts.

The bright but ephemeral feelings of good will generated by this conference, often invoked and widely hailed as the "spirit of Geneva," could not long conceal the fact that, measured by concrete results, the first summit meeting was a flat failure. The Foreign Ministers, at their "follow-up" conference in Geneva in October and November 1955, were totally unable to realize summit directives. Neither side was willing to make vital concessions, and what one put forth as a satisfactory solution, the other interpreted, almost by definition, as a threat. Harmony at the summit was preserved at the price of avoiding all public discussion of such explosive but important issues as freedom in eastern Europe and the admission of Communist China to the United Nations.

Nevertheless, the "spirit of Geneva" and hopes for some sort of East-West *détente* remained alive for over a year. The Russian leaders had made a favorable impression at the summit by smiling and talking of peace, and they refrained for months after the Geneva meeting from use of the bellicose language of the Stalin era. They had apparently been impressed in their turn by Eisenhower's manifest good will and desire for peace. A public correspondence between Premier Bulganin and President Eisenhower, initiated by the former in September 1955 and continuing for over two years, was devoted to further polite exchanges on the problems discussed at Geneva. Designed to impress world opinion rather than as serious diplomacy, these letters revealed that little if any basis for accord existed on vital issues. But the very fact of the exchange, together with the uniformly cordial tone of the letters, kept alive the impression that the two leaders were searching earnestly for peaceful solutions.

Hopes for peace received a sharp setback in October 1956, when rebellions broke out in Poland and Hungary, and the Suez crisis touched off an invasion of Egypt by Israeli, British, and French forces. (For details, see below, pp. 820–1, 839–43.) Chances that the two superpowers would reach an accord were obviously more remote than ever. When Switzerland proposed another summit meeting to halt the threat of war in the fall of 1956, Eisenhower replied that the crisis should be handled by the United Nations. There seemed little point at the moment in further top-level discussions with the men in the Kremlin.

The "spirit of Geneva" could not survive such awful violations, and the era of perpetual crisis returned after a brief and deceptively calm interlude. World-wide instability brought a new "freeze" to the cold war. Yet the Russians, while busily attempting to turn every new trouble spot to their advantage and hammering steadily at western unity, tried repeatedly to bring about a second summit meeting. They began this agitation late in 1957, fresh from the widely publicized triumph of *Sputnik,* and they finally induced a reluctant assent from Eisenhower and Dulles in March 1958. England and France also accepted the proposal, but the three western powers insisted that a top-level conference be preceded by conversations at the ambassadorial level and then among the Foreign Ministers.

Khrushchev replaced Bulganin as Soviet Premier just as the western leaders agreed to return to the summit, and there followed a period of bewildering reversals in the Russian attitude. Khrushchev's public criticisms of Eisenhower during the spring of 1958 seemed to destroy the chances of a summit meeting. But in response to multiple crises in the Middle East Khrushchev reversed his tactics and called for an immediate top-level conference that would include Prime Minister Nehru of India and Secretary-General Hammarskjold of the United Nations. It did not take place. Then Khrushchev's sudden challenge of western rights in Berlin in November 1958 (see below, pp. 823–824) provided new impetus to the movement for another heads-of-government conference. Khrushchev's challenge to West Berlin led directly to a Foreign Ministers' conference at Geneva from May 11 to August 5, 1959, and a visible relaxation of tension during the next few months. Khrushchev permitted the six-month deadline on Berlin, which he had earlier announced, to expire without incident, and later, following a visit to the United States in September 1959, dropped the time limit for a Berlin settlement. Eisenhower, who had steadfastly refused to go to the summit under the seeming duress of a Berlin deadline, forthwith consented to a heads-of-government conference. Despite one or two unpleasant episodes, Khrushchev's tour of the United States ended in such a friendly mood, induced especially by cordial private talks between the Premier and the President at Camp David, the latter's mountain retreat west of Washington, that observers began speaking hopefully of the "spirit of Camp David" before the end of the year.

This spirit proved even more illusory and short-lived than that of Geneva. Well in advance of the summit meeting, which was scheduled to open in Paris in May 1960, it became evident that little if anything would be achieved there. The powers had made some slight progress toward agreement on a nuclear test ban, but none whatever on German reunification, Berlin, or the broad question of arms control. Khrushchev's general posture during the weeks preceding the Paris meeting did not augur well for its success, and he was handed an opportunity to disrupt it on May 1, a bare fortnight before the conference was to meet.

This opportunity was the "U-2" affair, in which a high-altitude American reconnaissance plane was shot down far over the interior of Russia. The Washington administration at first claimed that a routine weather flight from one of its overseas bases near the Soviet border had gone astray. Then Khrushchev announced that the pilot had been captured and had freely confessed that aerial espionage was the real purpose of the flight. The American government not only admitted this fact; it added, in a display of frankness that amazed foreign diplomats, that such photo-reconaissance flights had been taking place over Soviet territory since 1956.

Khrushchev came to Paris in a dangerous temper. He voiced all manner of threats, not only against the United States but against nations that permitted such "spy flights" to take off or land on their soil. (The U-2 aircraft in question had actually been flying across Russia from Pakistan to Norway.) He demanded, as the price of his participation at the conference, that the President apologize for these violations of Soviet air space and promise their immediate discontinuance. He added, sneeringly, that whatever the United States did about the U-2 flights, it would be necessary to cancel Eisenhower's scheduled visit to Russia in June because the Soviet people were too upset by the recent episode to greet the American president with the proper "cordiality."

Eisenhower ordered suspension of the U-2 flights, but he refused to apologize. His own temper mounted wrathfully as Khrushchev's diatribes continued, and the efforts of Prime Minister Harold Macmillan of Great Britain and President Charles de Gaulle of France to restore harmony and save the summit meeting were to no avail. It broke up in mutual frustration and anger before it actually convened.

Many observers felt that Khrushchev had used the U-2 incident as a pretext for disrupting a conference he no longer saw advantage in attending. Certainly the propaganda value of the whole affair, which the Russians artfully exploited, was of greater benefit to them than the inevitable deadlock would have been. Despite his bellicose anger, the Soviet Premier did not renew the Berlin threat and even spoke in favor of a summit conference at some future date. But he made it clear that such a meeting could not take place while Eisenhower was President. Eisenhower left office, therefore, with Soviet-American relations at a low ebb and the record of summit diplomacy thus far a distinct failure.

252. *America and the Soviet Union: Nuclear Stalemate and the Quest for Disarmament*

A grim and apparently insoluble dilemma confronted American policy makers during the Eisenhower era, just as it had haunted President Truman and his advisers. The appalling destructive force of new thermonuclear weapons made their control and, if possible, their elimination a matter of increasing urgency. Tragically, the deep mutual distrust that underlay the world rivalry between the Communist bloc and the Western Alliance placed a seemingly insuperable obstacle in the path of a workable system of arms control. Given this distrust, the demands of national security impelled the United States and the Soviet Union, as we have seen, into the vicious ascending spiral of a nuclear arms race. Pressures to enlarge and contract the dread arsenals thus mounted simultaneously; quests for a controlled disarmament formula and more devastating weapons proceeded hand in hand. It was sadly true, moreover, that the effectiveness of modern science made the latter quest all too successful, while the limitations of cold war diplomacy compiled for the former a record of little save frustration, deadlock, and despair.

That record was, in fact, already seven years old when President Eisenhower and Secretary Dulles renewed the long-standing American quest for a workable agreement on arms control in 1953. Various commissions established by the United Nations had tried since 1946 to produce such agreements on both nuclear and conventional weapons, but progress had been consistently stymied by the unyielding attitudes of both Russia and the western powers. Though both camps ostensibly favored disarmament, the difference that separated the two points of view was fundamental. The western allies, not trusting Russia, had insisted all along that disarmament could neither begin nor proceed save under an effective system of international inspection and control. The Russians, on the other hand, had flatly rejected this approach and hammered away on a sweeping disarmament formula of their own: immediate abolition of all atomic weapons, a one-third across-the-board reduction in conventional forces by all countries, and abandonment by every nation of all military, naval, and air bases on foreign territory. The Soviets were in effect asking the United States to abolish the Strategic Air Command and emasculate NATO while the Red Army retained its decisive numerical superiority. Such a program was hardly acceptable to the West.

Though repeated shifts, new proposals, and partial concessions on both sides marked the growing complexity of disarmament negotiations from 1953 to 1960, there was no real change in the basic positions and hence no substantive progress during the Eisenhower era. The United Nations Disarmament Commission, having failed to accomplish anything since its creation in early 1952, delegated its task in 1954 to a five-power subcommittee composed of representatives of the United States, the Soviet Union, Great Britain, France, and Canada. The subcommittee held frequent private meetings in London from 1954 to 1957 and probed every facet of the subject. The talks centered around three important questions: an inspection system for controlling nuclear weapons, a method of preventing surprise attacks, and a ban on nuclear testing. At times the two sides seemed on the verge of bridging the gap that separated them. Invariably, however, some item that one side considered indispensable was regarded by the other as placing it at a disadvantage, and no agreement was reached.

None of the various allied proposals for "phased" and controlled disarmament or international inspection systems was acceptable to the Rus-

sians, whose deep-seated dislike of opening their country to foreign observation stemmed in part from fear that it was a cloak for espionage. For
the same reason they opposed all western suggestions for preventing surprise attacks. The most famous and comprehensive of these was the "open
skies" plan put forth by President Eisenhower at the Geneva summit conference in 1955. The President proposed that the United States and Russia
exchange complete information about military installations, equipment,
and organization, and allow monitored but unrestricted aerial reconnaissance and photography over each other's territory. It was an appealing
proposal, and one which the Soviets endorsed in principle. But later discussions of the matter by the disarmament subcommittee, and polite exchanges on the subject between Eisenhower and Soviet Premier Bulganin,
resulted in the customary failure to agree on matters of detail. Although
some of the Russian proposals for controlled and inspected reductions in
armament were quite similar to earlier formulas put forth by the western
allies, one or more of the western powers inevitably boggled over some point
on which the Russians refused to retreat; and the stalemate persisted. A
new group that convened at Geneva in November 1958 to examine methods
of preventing surprise attacks likewise adjourned in failure.

The powers made the most progress and came closest to genuine
accord on the issue of a nuclear test ban. World opinion justly regarded
this subject as the least difficult and most imperative aspect of the disarmament controversy, especially as repeated tests by the United States, the
Soviet Union, and Great Britain (which developed the hydrogen bomb in
1957) demonstrated the terrifying potential of the thermonuclear weapon.
Agitation for an immediate discontinuance of nuclear testing, initiated by
Prime Minister Nehru of India in 1954, mounted steadily in all parts of the
Globe.[21]

Scenting propaganda advantage, the Russians made a test ban one of
the principal items in their succession of disarmament proposals. They
used the issue effectively in appealing to the worried neutral countries,
particularly when President Eisenhower gave the impression of rejecting
the test ban by insisting that it be tied to a larger settlement and contain
adequate safeguards. Though the President's reaction was understandable,
given the widespread American distrust of Soviet intentions, it seemed
obstructive in other quarters and compared unfavorably with the Russian
proposal that a moratorium on testing precede rather than follow an inspection system or agreement on other issues.

Gradually the two sides moved toward a more constructive approach
to the problem. The Soviet demand for a test ban, repeated incessantly
since Nehru first advocated it in 1954, culminated in a dramatic announcement from the Kremlin in March 1958 that the USSR would suspend nu-

[21] There was a growing fear that the tests were highly dangerous in themselves,
and not merely as precursors of future holocaust, because of the increased amount of
radioactive "fallout" with which they poisoned the atmosphere. This was dramatized in
1954 when several crew members of a Japanese fishing boat that had strayed within
the "danger zone" of current American nuclear tests in the Pacific suffered burns. Hor-
rifying predictions of the genetic damage that a higher rate of present fallout could
wreak upon future generations strengthened the growing conviction that the nuclear
tests posed their own threat to human civilization.

clear tests, although it reserved the right to resume them if the other powers did not join the moratorium. The Washington administration countered with a plea for joint technical studies to examine methods of detecting violations of a test-ban agreement. The Russians agreed unenthusiastically. A panel of scientific experts, composed of delegations from four Communist states (the USSR, Poland, Czechoslovakia, Rumania) and four western nations (the United States, Britain, France, Canada), held closed meetings in Geneva during July and August 1958. Conducting their deliberations in a co-operative spirit and with remarkable objectivity, the scientists submitted a constructive and highly encouraging report. It was technically feasible, they agreed, to establish a workable control system that would detect violations of a nuclear test ban. The system would require numerous land-based control posts on every continent, including both Russian and American territory, plus naval and air patrols and mobile inspection groups, the whole to be operated by some form of international control agency.

The American and British governments now seized the initiative from the Soviet Union by promptly announcing their willingness to negotiate a three-power treaty that would establish an international control system and provide for the permanent cessation of nuclear tests. Moreover, the two western powers agreed to suspend their own tests for one year if the Russians accepted the principle of a controlled test ban and agreed to negotiate to that end. Both allied governments made it clear that they would conclude their present test series before invoking the proposed one-year suspension, and would resume testing if the Russians did so; otherwise, however, the suspensions would be subject to one-year extensions if the treaty negotiations made satisfactory progress.

Although the Russians were apparently then planning to resume testing, they could hardly refuse the western invitation to negotiate after years of urging a permanent test ban. The Soviet government accordingly accepted the offer on August 30, and the three-power Conference on the Discontinuance of Nuclear Weapons Tests duly assembled in Geneva on October 31, 1958. The prospects of ultimate success seemed bright for a time, then dimmed in 1960. As in almost all previous negotiations on every phase of disarmament, the issue of controls proved an unbridgeable gap. Despite agreement on the basic *principle* of controls, the Americans consistently held out for a more extensive system and a larger number of on-site inspections than the Russians were willing to grant.

The conferees continued the sessions in good spirit until the end of 1960, gradually narrowing their differences, then recessed to await the inauguration of the new American President. Even though a sizable number of American experts now doubted that an effective control system was possible, and favored a resumption of American testing, hope for an eventual test-ban treaty remained alive. As the decade ended, the unilateral suspensions that the three nuclear powers had proclaimed in 1958 were still being observed by the United States and Great Britain and—so far as anyone knew—by the USSR as well. The atmosphere had been untainted by new fallout for over two years.

Meanwhile, the powers had resumed their search for agreement on the broader issues of disarmament. In the momentary aura of good feeling that emerged during Premier Khrushchev's visit to the United States in the late summer of 1959, the Soviet leader had offered a sweeping four-year plan for "universal and complete" disarmament, and the Big Four Foreign Ministers had agreed upon a ten-nation disarmament conference to meet in Geneva in the following spring. It duly met in the historic Swiss city on March 15, 1960, to explore "avenues of possible progress" toward reducing armaments "under effective international control." Though established to operate outside the United Nations, the ten-nation committee was to report periodically to that body and had on its agenda the various disarmament proposals—including Khrushchev's—put forward at the last session of the General Assembly.

It soon became apparent, notwithstanding the generally co-operative tone of the deliberations, that the old stumbling blocks of inspection and control barred the road to agreement. Substitute and compromise proposals offered in turn by both factions could not conceal the fact that, to put it briefly, the West insisted upon adequate controls before disarmament could take place, while the Communists insisted that disarmament could begin at once, and a control system could be worked out later. Gradually, as the irreconcilable nature of this impasse took shape at Geneva, the talks degenerated into the kind of propaganda battle that so often passed for negotiations when the Soviets were present.

The conference recessed at the end of April 1960 in the hope that a forthcoming summit meeting in Paris would provide an improved basis for further discussion. But Paris was an utter fiasco (for details, see above, pp. 802–803), and the outlook was dim when the ten-nation conference reassembled in early June. The Soviets first juggled their current disarmament formula in an effort to split the NATO allies. Then, after the American delegate returned from special consultations in Washington with a revised counteroffer, the Communist delegations walked out without listening to it, charging that the western powers had not negotiated in good faith. The ten-nation conference, like the summit meeting, thus ended in shambles. Khrushchev announced on June 27 that further meetings were useless, and that the disarmament problem should be referred to the next session of the General Assembly. The Eisenhower era closed with no agreements reached and few in sight on one of the most pressing questions of the day.

CHAPTER

32

The United States in a Turbulent World

1953–1960

AMERICANS had become well acquainted with crisis and tension in international affairs by the time that Eisenhower came to the presidency. But the winds of adversity and change were blowing with stronger force in every corner of the globe. The Soviet Union worked to undermine western unity and laid claim to the loyalty of impoverished but aspiring millions in Asia, Africa, and Latin America. The United States and its allies worked earnestly if not always harmoniously to preserve their security and contain the spread of Communism. Border quarrels, political upheavals, and social revolutions in the remotest parts of the world thus became bound up with the limitless scope of East-West rivalry and the cold war.

253. The "New Look" in American Foreign Policy

As we have seen in an earlier chapter, the Republican landslide in 1952 in large measure reflected widespread public dissatisfaction with recent Democratic foreign policy. Some Americans believed McCarthy's charges of Democratic treason and betrayal. Others, though they did not like the Wisconsin demagogue, believed that Roosevelt's and Truman's blunders had brought the nation to its plight. The American government after 1945, they thought, had permitted the Russians to repudiate the Yalta

agreement and solidify their control in eastern Europe, take over Czechoslovakia, and develop the atomic bomb. It had permitted Communist triumph
in China. It was mired in indecisive war in Korea. Its basic response—the
policy of containment—now seemed to these distraught Americans defensive and almost defeatist in tone: a far cry from the splendid old American
objectives of total victory and unconditional surrender.

Republican spokesmen in 1952 understandably stressed the need for a
"new look" in American foreign policy and promised to recapture the initiative that the Democrats had allegedly lost to the Soviets. Eisenhower's
pledge to go to Korea, if elected, and work for a satisfactory conclusion to
that stalemate was undoubtedly the most effective and appealing statement
of the entire campaign. GOP leaders, stimulated by their triumph at the
polls and aware of the public desire for a change, continued to speak confidently of new departures in foreign policy during the next few months.
The Republican administration launched the "new look" in highly auspicious fashion by negotiating a truce in Korea in July 1953 (for details, see
above, pp. 729–730).

Chief spokesman and virtual embodiment of the "new look" was John
Foster Dulles, who served as Secretary of State from 1953 until a fatal illness forced his retirement in 1959. An experienced diplomat and international lawyer, grandson of one Secretary of State and nephew of another,
Dulles was eminently qualified for his important post. He had served his
apprenticeship as observer at the Second Hague Conference in 1907 and
as legal adviser on reparations at Paris in 1919 and Berlin in 1933. He had
been a delegate at the San Francisco Conference that created the United
Nations in 1945, a member of the American delegation to the General Assembly in the late 1940's, and an adviser at four Foreign Ministers' conferences from 1945 to 1949. Most significantly, he had been the major
architect of the Japanese Peace Treaty of 1951 and the security treaties
with New Zealand, Australia, the Philippines, and Japan in 1950–1.

Dulles also had an abundance of energy, keen intelligence, profound
self-assurance, and a domineering personality. He was seldom plagued by
doubt, and it was often difficult to distinguish between his moral certitude
and self-righteousness. He traveled nearly half a million miles during his
six years in office, visited some forty-six countries, and dominated the State
Department so completely that he was described, with only slight exaggeration, as carrying foreign policy under his hat. In shaping policy he relied
primarily upon his own ideas and knowledge. As a result, subordinates,
including ambassadors and members of the Policy Planning Staff, declined
in importance. He enjoyed the complete confidence of President Eisenhower, with whom his relationship was harmonious and close from beginning to end. All in all, he was one of the most forceful, influential, and
controversial Secretaries of State in American history.

Much of the controversy stemmed from the fact that Dulles found it
hard to resist the temptation to make phrases and snappy slogans. They
were largely responsible for the general expectation that the new administration would completely reshape American foreign policy. In the Republican platform of 1952, which he drafted, Dulles condemned Yalta by
promising to repudiate all "secret understandings," indicted the Roosevelt
and Truman administrations for "neglect of the Far East," and promised

that Republicans would find a "dynamic" substitute for the "negative, futile and immoral" policy of containment. In ensuing months he spoke confidently, if somewhat vaguely, of a "rollback" of Soviet power in eastern Europe and "liberation" of countries under Communist domination. He also helped to popularize the notion that Chiang Kai-shek and his Nationalist forces on Taiwan would be "unleashed" to attack the Chinese mainland.

Responsibility did not seem to restrain the urge to make phrases after 1953, even when Dulles was announcing what seemed to be major alterations in foreign policy. First came "agonizing reappraisal," Dulles's warning in December 1953 that France's failure to approve German rearmament in a European army would force the United States to make an "agonizing reappraisal" of its commitments on the continent—a thinly veiled threat to withdraw American troops and leave Europe to its own devices. Next came "massive retaliation," which Dulles enunciated in January 1954. It suggested that the United States would hereafter rely upon nuclear weapons instead of ground forces in responding to any and all Communist aggressions, and it was promptly translated and widely publicized by other slogan-makers as "a bigger bang for the buck." Finally, there was Dulles's statement, made in 1956, that he had taken the United States to "the brink of war" on three occasions since 1953 in order to preserve the peace. It was derisively called "brinkmanship" by Democrats during the presidential campaign of 1956.

Ironically, the "new look" for the most part consisted of old policies obscured by new language. Bold promises of change were given mainly to assuage public dissatisfaction and the neo-isolationist wing of the Republican party. The Eisenhower administration did not have a workable alternative to containment. In fact, the fundamental principles of Truman-Acheson diplomacy—regional alliances, collective security, foreign aid, and support of the UN—were not only maintained but extended during the Eisenhower era. Continuity rather than change marked the transition from Democratic to Republican rule.

It could hardly have been otherwise. Both Eisenhower and Dulles had participated in a major way in formulating American policy and strategy during and after the Second World War. Both were firmly committed to the postwar system of alliances, treaties, and mutual obligations. This meant, for instance, that Dulles, while threatening France with "agonizing reappraisal," had not the remotest intention of withdrawing American troops from Europe. The kind of extreme revision loudly advocated by neo-isolationists—whose agenda variously called for elimination of foreign aid, abandonment of the United Nations, retreat to a highly armed "fortress America," instant nuclear response to Communist aggression, attacks on China, and even preventive war—was totally unacceptable to the new President and Secretary of State. Any changes that they undertook were bound to be made within the general framework of internationalism and collective security.

Even more important, the reality of the world situation in the 1950's simply precluded most of the actions that Dulles forecast so confidently in announcing the "new look." The Secretary meant much less, in fact, than his phrases implied. He quickly saw that repudiation of "secret understandings" like Yalta would merely afford the Soviet Union opportunities for further repudiations of her own. Attempts to end the alleged "neglect of the Far East" did not prevent further deterioration in that area. Notwithstanding rebellious outbreaks in some of the Russian satellite countries during the 1950's, the United States could manifestly do nothing to "roll back" Soviet power or "liberate" captive nations without courting a third world war, and Dulles was careful not to go to the brink when vital Soviet interests were at stake. As for "unleashing" Chiang Kai-shek, administration leaders knew that the Nationalists could not invade the mainland without massive American support, which they never seriously contemplated providing.

Reality likewise negated or reduced the significance of "massive retaliation." This phrase obviously could not mean that the United States would rely solely upon nuclear weapons to respond to any and all Communist aggressions. As we have seen, Republican defense policy aimed at achieving the power to deter most attacks and the flexibility to counter all. In short, the Eisenhower administration was unswervingly committed to defense of the entire free world and containment of Communism, by whatever means seemed most appropriate. This differed from the policy of the Truman administration by not so much as a hair.

The historian can only conclude that it was unfortunate that the new administration felt obliged to conceal continuity in foreign policy by misleading phrases. The task confronting the United States after midcentury was certainly formidable, and many of the free world's reverses during the 1950's were caused by circumstances beyond American control. But in retrospect it seems obvious that the Eisenhower administration compounded ordinary difficulties. There was frustration and disillusionment at home and abroad when the champion of liberation could do no more than protest while Soviet tanks brutally crushed popular uprisings in East Germany in 1953 and in Hungary in 1956. Moreover, rash pronouncements from the State Department bred controversy at home and aroused fear and hostility in allied and neutral countries. Internationalists criticized Dulles because of the seeming recklessness of his utterances; isolationists, because nothing ever came of them. Among America's allies, Dulles encouraged a suspicion that the United States planned to withdraw its troops and "protect" Europe and other targets of Soviet imperialism solely by nuclear retaliation—a form of protection which they regarded as militarily useless, diplomatically unreliable, and morally repulsive. His phrasemaking and penchant for moralizing created an image generally held by foreigners of a reckless and self-righteous diplomatist who viewed the world in terms of simple moral absolutes, treated neutrals as enemies and allies as satellites, and used sermons and nuclear threats in lieu of diplomacy.

This image persisted in many quarters even though it was almost totally false. Actually, Dulles was a flexible, patient, canny diplomat with a realistic view of world affairs. In many ways—promoting the cause of European unity, upholding and extending the principle of collective security, and demonstrating repeatedly an authentic commitment to the defense of freedom—he revealed vision and courage. Moreover, as we shall see, he was not always unsuccessful.

254. *Europe and the United States in the Nineteen Fifties*

Europe remained the central battleground in the cold war. The strength and solidarity of the North Atlantic alliance continued to be the primary concern of American foreign policy; the weakening or disruption of that alliance retained a high priority among Soviet goals. There was not the slightest doubt in either Washington or Moscow that the renascent countries of western Europe, with their booming economies, vast industrial and human resources, and quickening sense of unity, were the pivot in the world balance of power. Conversely, maintenance of the adjoining satellite empire in eastern Europe was of crucial importance to the Kremlin. Overarching the problems of NATO and eastern Europe, essential to the security of both, was the future status of divided Germany and Berlin.

The NATO allies had concluded by midcentury that they could not rely solely upon American strategic air power to deter a Russian attack on western Europe. Conventional ground forces would also be necessary, although numerical parity with the Soviet bloc in eastern Europe was never contemplated. It was hoped, rather, to raise and equip a sufficient number of divisions—the so-called defensive shield—to prevent Europe from being overrun before American retaliatory bombing—NATO's "striking sword"—could turn the tide.

The alliance promptly took steps to formulate a defensive strategy, improve its military organization, and raise an army. Backed by a flood of American supplies, NATO countries evolved an integrated command system for western Europe and pushed rearmament programs. By 1953 NATO could deploy five thousand tactical aircraft and had large stockpiles of weapons and equipment. Actual troop strength was another matter. NATO's main reliance was on a handful of well-equipped divisions—mainly American, British, and French—backed by a larger number of undermanned reserve divisions. The entire NATO army was at best less than half the size of the forces immediately available to the Soviet bloc. Nevertheless, the new "defensive shield" had become strong enough by 1953 to provide western Europe with at least a measure of military security.

The real problems lay just ahead. The Eisenhower era was a time of prolonged trial, frustration, and uncertainty for NATO. Its unity and effectiveness were badly strained by three concurrent challenges: the changing emphases of Soviet policy after Stalin, the lengthening of the thermonuclear shadow, and the violent cresting of the nationalist wave in Asia, Africa, and the Middle East. These challenges magnified the divisive tendencies inherent in any peacetime coalition, and the outstanding fact was not that NATO encountered vast difficulties after 1953 but that it survived at all.

One important key to NATO's success was Germany. The Atlantic allies, faced since 1945 with a persistent Soviet refusal to permit German reunification on terms that they could accept, had adopted the alternative in 1948–9 of uniting the three western zones in the West German Federal Republic. (For details, see above, pp. 712–714.) When the NATO countries undertook their campaign for rearmament and joint military reorganization in 1950, West Germany immediately became a decisive element in their planning.

To begin with, the "forward strategy" adopted by the NATO high command called for including West Germany within the allied defense perimeter and meeting a Soviet thrust at or near the Communist border. The United States, playing upon European fears that the Korean War might be the prelude to a Soviet offensive in the West, put forth specific proposals at a NATO Council meeting in September 1950 for a West German army. The American government, then and later, could see no other solution to the problem of defending western Europe.

The question of German rearmament threatened to disrupt the North Atlantic alliance for the next four years. No European country could view the prospect of Germans in uniform without misgiving so soon after Hitler's Reich. The strongest opposition came, understandably, from the French. Even so, the European members of NATO agreed reluctantly with the American view that German manpower was indispensable, and the first major design for rearming West Germany came from the French Premier, René Pleven, in late 1950. His plan called for a highly integrated European Defense Community (EDC), linked to NATO, with West German units submerged in a supranational army under joint control of the member nations. Once EDC went into force, the joint occupation would be ended, and a larger measure of sovereignty would be granted to the Federal Republic.

A treaty creating the EDC was signed in Paris on May 27, 1952, by France, Belgium, the Netherlands, Luxembourg, Italy, and West Germany, but the French National Assembly rejected the treaty on August 30, 1954, after more than two years of debates and delays. Neither firmer British pledges to EDC, nor assurances from President Eisenhower that American troops would remain on the continent, nor Secretary Dulles's dire threats of "agonizing reappraisal" were sufficient to muster a French majority in favor of the treaty. Dulles, who had probably labored harder than any other statesman to make this blueprint for European unity a reality, termed defeat of EDC a "shattering blow." "It looked," he said in October 1954, "as though the whole North Atlantic treaty structure, its whole system, might be undermined and even swept away by political indecisions and uncertainties." [1]

Fortunately, Prime Minister Eden of Great Britain came forward with an alternative which soon won acceptance from all quarters. The British proposal was hammered into final form in London in September 1954, signed in Paris in October, ratified by the nations concerned during the next few months, and put into force in May 1955. In brief, the Paris agreement ended the joint occupation, restored full sovereignty to the West German government, and admitted West Germany to NATO. It also provided for the contribution of a maximum of twelve West German divisions to NATO forces and expanded NATO's authority over the armed forces of all member nations.

~~~~~~~~~~~~~~~~~~~~~

[1] Quoted in Richard P. Stebbins *et al.*, *The United States in World Affairs*, 1954 (New York, 1956), p. 150.

COLLECTIVE DEFEN.

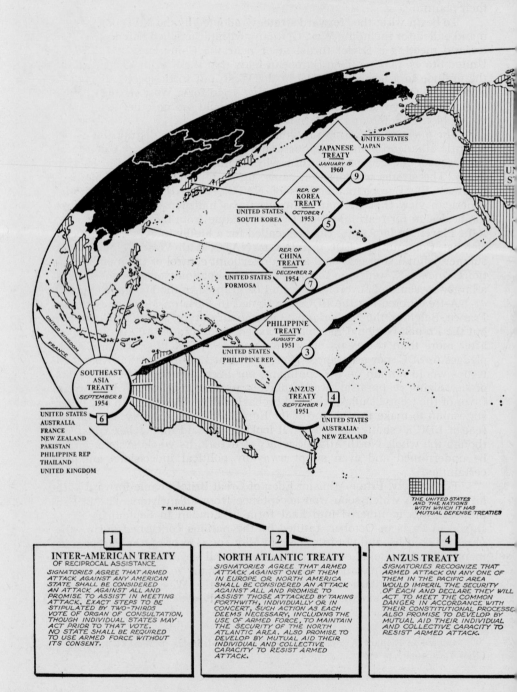

UNITED STATES
JAPAN

JAPANESE TREATY
JANUARY 19 1960
9

REP. OF
KOREA TREATY
OCTOBER 1 1953
UNITED STATES
SOUTH KOREA
5

REP. OF
CHINA TREATY
DECEMBER 2 1954
UNITED STATES
FORMOSA
7

PHILIPPINE TREATY
AUGUST 30 1951
UNITED STATES
PHILIPPINE REP.
3

UNITED KINGDOM
FRANCE

SOUTHEAST ASIA TREATY
SEPTEMBER 8 1954
6

UNITED STATES
AUSTRALIA
FRANCE
NEW ZEALAND
PAKISTAN
PHILIPPINE REP
THAILAND
UNITED KINGDOM

ANZUS TREATY
SEPTEMBER 1 1951
4
UNITED STATES
AUSTRALIA
NEW ZEALAND

T R MILLER

THE UNITED STATES
AND THE NATIONS
WITH WHICH IT HAS
MUTUAL DEFENSE TREATIES

1

INTER-AMERICAN TREATY
OF RECIPROCAL ASSISTANCE

SIGNATORIES AGREE THAT ARMED
ATTACK AGAINST ANY AMERICAN
STATE SHALL BE CONSIDERED
AN ATTACK AGAINST ALL AND
PROMISE TO ASSIST IN MEETING
ATTACK. EXACT STEPS TO BE
STIPULATED BY TWO-THIRDS
VOTE OF ORGAN OF CONSULTATION,
THOUGH INDIVIDUAL STATES MAY
ACT PRIOR TO THAT VOTE.
NO STATE SHALL BE REQUIRED
TO USE ARMED FORCE WITHOUT
ITS CONSENT.

2

NORTH ATLANTIC TREATY

SIGNATORIES AGREE THAT ARMED
ATTACK AGAINST ONE OF THEM
IN EUROPE OR NORTH AMERICA
SHALL BE CONSIDERED AN ATTACK
AGAINST ALL AND PROMISE TO
ASSIST THOSE ATTACKED BY TAKING
FORTHWITH, INDIVIDUALLY OR IN
CONCERT, SUCH ACTION AS EACH
DEEMS NECESSARY, INCLUDING THE
USE OF ARMED FORCE, TO MAINTAIN
THE SECURITY OF THE NORTH
ATLANTIC AREA. ALSO PROMISE TO
DEVELOP BY MUTUAL AID THEIR
INDIVIDUAL AND COLLECTIVE
CAPACITY TO RESIST ARMED
ATTACK.

4

ANZUS TREATY

SIGNATORIES RECOGNIZE THAT
ARMED ATTACK ON ANY ONE OF
THEM IN THE PACIFIC AREA
WOULD IMPERIL THE SECURITY
OF EACH AND DECLARE THEY WILL
ACT TO MEET THE COMMON
DANGER IN ACCORDANCE WITH
THEIR CONSTITUTIONAL PROCESSE.
ALSO PROMISE TO DEVELOP BY
MUTUAL AID THEIR INDIVIDUAL
AND COLLECTIVE CAPACITY TO
RESIST ARMED ATTACK.

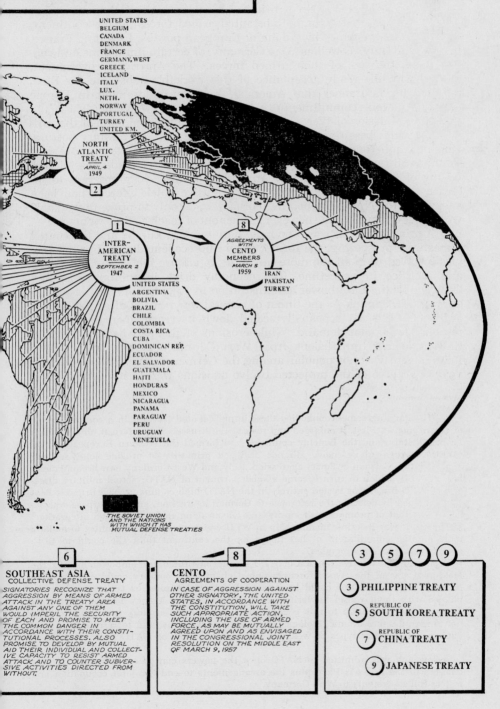

RRANGEMENTS, 1961

UNITED STATES
BELGIUM
CANADA
DENMARK
FRANCE
GERMANY, WEST
GREECE
ICELAND
ITALY
LUX.
NETH.
NORWAY
PORTUGAL
TURKEY
UNITED KM.

NORTH
ATLANTIC
TREATY
*APRIL 4
1949*

2

INTER-
AMERICAN
TREATY
*SEPTEMBER 2
1947*

1

8

AGREEMENTS
WITH
CENTO
MEMBERS
*MARCH 5
1959*

IRAN
PAKISTAN
TURKEY

UNITED STATES
ARGENTINA
BOLIVIA
BRAZIL
CHILE
COLOMBIA
COSTA RICA
CUBA
DOMINICAN REP.
ECUADOR
EL SALVADOR
GUATEMALA
HAITI
HONDURAS
MEXICO
NICARAGUA
PANAMA
PARAGUAY
PERU
URUGUAY
VENEZUELA

THE SOVIET UNION
AND THE NATIONS
WITH WHICH IT HAS
MUTUAL DEFENSE TREATIES

6

SOUTHEAST ASIA
COLLECTIVE DEFENSE TREATY

*SIGNATORIES RECOGNIZE THAT
AGGRESSION BY MEANS OF ARMED
ATTACK IN THE TREATY AREA
AGAINST ANY ONE OF THEM
WOULD IMPERIL THE SECURITY
OF EACH AND PROMISE TO MEET
THE COMMON DANGER IN
ACCORDANCE WITH THEIR CONSTI-
TUTIONAL PROCESSES. ALSO
PROMISE TO DEVELOP BY MUTUAL
AID THEIR INDIVIDUAL AND COLLECT-
IVE CAPACITY TO RESIST ARMED
ATTACK AND TO COUNTER SUBVER-
SIVE ACTIVITIES DIRECTED FROM
WITHOUT.*

8

CENTO
AGREEMENTS OF COOPERATION

*IN CASE OF AGGRESSION AGAINST
OTHER SIGNATORY, THE UNITED
STATES, IN ACCORDANCE WITH
THE CONSTITUTION, WILL TAKE
SUCH APPROPRIATE ACTION,
INCLUDING THE USE OF ARMED
FORCE, AS MAY BE MUTUALLY
AGREED UPON AND AS ENVISAGED
IN THE CONGRESSIONAL JOINT
RESOLUTION ON THE MIDDLE EAST
OF MARCH 9, 1957*

3 **5** **7** **9**

3 PHILIPPINE TREATY

REPUBLIC OF
5 SOUTH KOREA TREATY

REPUBLIC OF
7 CHINA TREATY

9 JAPANESE TREATY

The most revolutionary features of the Paris agreement were, first, a positive commitment by Great Britain—far more binding than its earlier pledges to EDC—to maintain substantial armed forces on the continent; and, second, acceptance by the major European powers, including France, Britain, and Italy, as well as West Germany, of certain limitations and controls upon the size of their armed forces.[2] The American government, pleased with the ready acceptance of this workable substitute for EDC, repeated its assurances that American troops would remain in Europe under the nation's commitment to NATO.

The admission of West Germany, however, alleviated none of the various difficulties besetting the North Atlantic alliance. Its military posture, which the adherence of the Federal Republic was designed to improve, had begun to slip well before the Paris agreement of 1954 made possible the raising of German contingents. An ambitious three-year program to increase the size and strength of the "defensive shield" forces had been adopted by the NATO Council in February 1952, only to prove unworkable within a few months and slide ever further out of reach as time went on.

A primary reason was economic. Both western Europe and the United States were prospering, the former at an unprecedented rate, but the peoples involved were all the more unwilling to endure high taxes, austerity, and sacrifice in peacetime. The economy drive in military spending launched by the Eisenhower administration in 1953 had its counterpart in every NATO capital. As the threat of general war receded after the Korean armistice, each ally repeatedly scaled down its rearmament program in response to popular demand. While erosions of this sort became chronic, the anticipated transfusions from West Germany were slow to arrive. Rearmament was not popular among the German people. As late as mid-1957 only three of the projected twelve divisions were ready to take their

ᄿᄿᄿᄿᄿᄿᄿᄿᄿᄿᄿᄿᄿ

[2] The Paris agreement embodied these unprecedented features in a complex series of arrangements. First, it enlarged and revised the Brussels Pact of 1948, under which France, Britain, and the Benelux countries had formed the Western European Union (WEU), a regional defensive alliance designed primarily to provide joint security against future German or Soviet aggression. Italy and West Germany now became members of WEU, which in turn became a subdepartment of NATO; actual military direction of WEU forces was vested entirely in the NATO high command. The Brussels Pact was amended by deleting the reference to German aggression, and its purpose was redefined as that of promoting the unity and encouraging the "progressive integration" of Europe. It was Britain's membership in WEU which enabled that country to make a more binding commitment of her troops on the continent than she could to EDC, of which she was not a member.

The old Consultative Council of WEU was reconstituted and empowered to fix the maximum size of the armed forces which each member country could contribute to NATO. These limitations could be increased only by unanimous consent, and compliance with them would be verified by a newly created Agency for the Control of Armaments. In addition to this general limitation, West Germany specifically agreed not to manufacture atomic, biological, or chemical weapons, and to refrain from producing certain other types of weapons save upon request of NATO with approval of WEU.

Germany was admitted to NATO once the powers concerned had ratified these changes in the Brussels Pact, plus the arrangements to end the joint occupation and restore full sovereignty to West Germany.

place in the NATO command structure.[3] Indeed, NATO never achieved the thirty-division strength described by its commanders in 1958 as the necessary minimum.

This failure was accompanied by a progressive weakening of NATO's diplomatic solidarity. By 1955 the circumstances and international climate that had given birth to NATO were considerably altered. Western Europe's economic recovery since 1948 had instilled new confidence in European leaders and lessened European dependence upon the United States. Prosperity had alleviated popular discontent and stabilized national politics to the point where local Communist parties, though still a potent force in states like Italy and France, no longer threatened any European government with paralysis, civil war, or mastery through subversion or triumph at the polls. And changes in Russian foreign policy after the death of Stalin had dissipated the fear of war.

This last development was probably the most significant. The "peace offensive" launched by Stalin's successors had an unsettling effect upon European opinion. A substantial minority, eager to avoid war and not unsympathetic to Marxist ideology, gave credence to Soviet talk of peaceful coexistence, relaxation of tensions, disarmament, and willingness to negotiate. Responsible European statesmen were far from accepting these Russian blandishments at face value, but they felt strongly that western policy needed overhauling in order to respond effectively to new Soviet strategy.

This quest for a more flexible and imaginative approach to the cold war agitated western Europe most strongly during 1955 and 1956, when hopes raised by the Austrian treaty and the Geneva summit conference were at their height. Unfortunately, European leaders could agree upon the need for a new departure but not upon a specific policy, and the principal effect was an erosion of NATO solidarity. The Soviets redoubled their effort to cripple the alliance by harping on their desire for peace, warning that western Europe would suffer most in a future war, advancing disarmament formulas that would eliminate American bases on the continent, and proposing a new all-European security pact led by Russia and excluding the United States.

European dissatisfaction with American policies and leadership became more outspoken. The feeling grew that the United States was too rigid in its approach to Russia, unreasonable in its refusal to recognize Communist China, overly obsessed with internal security and military preparedness, unwilling to give proper attention to economic and political developments, and intolerant of the particular needs and problems of its allies. Americans in their turn sometimes felt that the European countries were too "soft" on Communism (or at least not sufficiently alarmed by it), too prone to trust and even appease the Soviets, and unwilling to assume a fairer share of the joint western defense effort. European trade with Communist China vexed the United States, while liberal opinion in Europe disapproved of America's close military ties with the Fascist regime of Generalissimo Francisco Franco in Spain.[4]

‎꜖꜖꜖꜖꜖꜖꜖꜖꜖꜖꜖꜖꜖꜖꜖꜖
[3] Seven German divisions were available by 1959.

[4] The United States and Spain concluded agreements in 1953 whereby the former undertook a program of substantial economic and military aid to the Franco government

Other quarrels also took their toll. The most nagging was the problem of Germany. Distrust of a resurgent Germany remained strong even after the Federal Republic joined NATO in the spring of 1955. It fed on such developments as the sporadic manifestations of neo-Nazi sentiment on the fringe of German society, the growing power of the new West German army, and Bonn's attempt, without first consulting its allies, to conclude an agreement with Spain in 1959 that would permit German troops to conduct combat maneuvers on Spanish soil. The Federal Republic's mounting economic influence, the chance that it would embrace neutralism or seek accord with Moscow in order to reunite with East Germany, and its desire to equip its troops with tactical atomic weapons all added to European apprehensions during the latter 1950's.

The Soviet government naturally did its best to exploit these fears. It also made a desperate effort to prevent German rearmament. When this failed, it promptly created a regional grouping of its own patterned directly after the North Atlantic alliance. This was the Warsaw Pact of May 1955, binding Albania, Bulgaria, Czechoslovakia, East Germany, Hungary, Poland, and Rumania to the USSR in close military alliance. Still hopeful of driving a wedge between America and western Europe, the Soviets later renewed their proposal to form an all-European security system by excluding the United States from a merger of the NATO and Warsaw Pact alliances.

While exploiting European fear of Germany on the one hand, Soviet leaders also sought to woo the Federal Republic. Reunification was the Soviet trump card, and all western efforts to reach agreement with Moscow on this important issue ended in failure. From the very beginnning, the Eisenhower administration had pursued the twin goals of rearming the Federal Republic within NATO and unifying the two Germanys through free elections. These were not easily reconcilable goals, and achievement of the former made the latter more remote than ever. The western allies had urged reunification upon Russia at the Berlin conference in early 1954 without success. They renewed the quest at the Geneva summit meeting in July 1955 and did obtain Bulganin's agreement that free elections should be the basis for future settlement of the German problem. But the post-summit conference of Foreign Ministers that autumn showed that Soviet intransigence was unabated.

The Soviets first insisted that the two German governments negotiate directly, in order to guarantee East Germany a voice in any united government formed by such negotiations. Next came the so-called Rapacki plan, suggested by the Polish Foreign Minister, Adam Rapacki, in October 1957. It called for a ban on production or stockpiling of nuclear weapons in both Germanys, Poland, and Czechoslovakia, to bring about the military disengagement of central Europe. Another Soviet proposal, put forth in 1959, demanded withdrawal of all foreign troops from German soil, restricted German armaments, and forbade a reunited Germany to join any alliance

in return for the right to build and maintain air and naval bases in Spain. Relations between the two countries remained cordial throughout the decade as the new military installations south of the Pyrenees became a vital component in the American system of overseas bases.

that did not include the Western Big Three and the USSR. The two sides remained far apart, and the existing boundary between the two Germanys seemed more permanent than ever before.

Another serious challenge to western unity was colonialism. The breakup of European colonial empires under the hammer blows of nationalist and independence movements in Asia and Africa was a truly epochal development of the postwar era. Whether by war and revolution or patient negotiation—or both—most of the colonies and protectorates in the once extensive empires of Great Britain, France, and the Netherlands either won independence or advanced to its threshold between 1945 and 1962. By the latter date only Portugal, oldest of the imperial powers, still clung tenaciously to the bulk of its overseas possessions. All in all, some thirty-five new countries, with a total population of over 600,000,000 people, emerged from some form of colonial status during the postwar years.

It was a difficult transition at best. For the European powers, the economic and psychological readjustments demanded by the steady and sometimes violent dismantling of their empires were enormous. To add to their burden, public opinion elsewhere in the world was overwhelmingly opposed to even the vestiges of colonialism. The newly freed nations clamored incessantly, while the Communist bloc, for obvious reasons, quickly took up the cry and posed as the enemy of imperialism and the champion of self-determination.

NATO suffered because it included all the major imperial powers, and, equally importantly, because Americans strongly opposed colonialism on grounds of both principle and expediency. The United States, seeking to combat the rising anti-western sentiment that was a by-product of European imperialism, was not always patient in urging decolonization upon its allies. The imperial powers, in turn, felt that the American government failed to appreciate the complexity of their problems and was oversensitive to the frequently unreasonable demands of the anti-colonial nations. This tension laid foundations for a rupture that almost destroyed NATO in the autumn of 1956.

Meanwhile, the solidarity of the eastern European bloc was also crumbling. The first break in the monolithic Communist structure had occurred in 1948, when the Yugoslav leader, Marshal Tito, defied Stalin and embarked upon independent foreign and domestic policies. He adhered to a policy of noncommitment, although the intensity of Russian hostility during Stalin's final years very nearly drove Yugoslavia into the western camp. The American government was so encouraged that it provided economic and military aid to Yugoslavia during the 1950's and pursued a policy of restrained friendship toward this unaligned Communist state.

Soviet leaders soon after Stalin's death relaxed somewhat their control over their satellites. They also abandoned all hostility toward Yugoslavia and attempted to effect a reconciliation with Tito through friendly overtures. Tito welcomed better relations with Moscow but hewed steadfastly to his policies of neutrality in foreign affairs and independence in domestic matters.

The satellite nations, encouraged by Tito's example and emboldened by the new leeway that Moscow now permitted, stirred restlessly from 1953 to 1956. Their peoples dreamed variously of self-government within a

Communist framework, improved economic conditions, increased national independence, and possibly even freedom from Communism itself. Popular hopes in eastern Europe rose higher than ever when Tito made a state visit to Russia in June 1956 and won Soviet approval of a joint declaration that every country should be permitted to choose its own road to socialism without interference from outside. They were further heightened by the partial but outspoken repudiations of Stalinism that poured from the Kremlin during early 1956.

Pent-up economic and political discontent in some of the satellite nations burst forth in the summer and fall of 1956. First, unorganized riots by workers demanding "bread and freedom" broke out in the Polish industrial city of Poznan in late June, and demands for an end to Soviet control over Polish armed forces and internal affairs reached revolutionary proportions by October. With strong public support, a major element within the Polish Communist party moved to free the Warsaw government from Soviet domination, by elevating Wladyslaw Gomulka, who had once been jailed in a Stalinist purge, to the important post of First Secretary. Top Soviet leaders, including Khrushchev, hastened to Warsaw to face down this challenge to their authority. They were backed by fresh units of Soviet troops moving into Poland from Russia and East Germany. Minor clashes between Polish and Russian military formations seemed to presage an imminent full-scale war within the Communist empire.

Polish nationalism won a notable victory in the ensuing tense discussions in Warsaw. The Soviets backed down on October 20, withdrawing their troops and acquiescing in the installation of Gomulka as First Secretary and head of the Polish government. He won enough concessions from Moscow to launch Poland on a "national Communist" policy along Titoist lines.

Gomulka's victory was barely won when nationalist dissent erupted in Hungary. This revolt, which began in Budapest on October 23–24, led to bloodshed and intervention by Soviet military forces almost immediately, and then proceeded to get out of hand. The Hungarians lacked a leader of Gomulka's stature and ability, and what had begun as another "Titoist" bid for national Communist autonomy soon broadened into a sweeping, ill-organized movement to overthrow Communist rule altogether. The Hungarian Communist regime replaced unpopular leaders with moderates who made concession after concession to the rebels—now backed by an almost nationwide general strike—and virtually dismantled the Communist edifice in Hungary. In what sounded like a major retreat, Moscow announced on October 30 that it would withdraw all Soviet troops at Hungary's request and re-examine its entire policy of military and economic influence in the affairs of fellow-Communist states.

President Eisenhower undoubtedly spoke for most of the West when he hailed these developments as "the dawning of a new day" in eastern Europe. But the situation in Hungary quickly passed from bright hope to darkest tragedy. Whether or not the Soviets originally intended to carry out their sweeping promises of October 30, the Hungarians proceeded to seal their own fate by asking for more than Russia could possibly grant. While anti-Soviet strikes and demonstrations continued, the Hungarian government informed the Soviet ambassador on November 1 that Hungary was about to renounce the Warsaw Pact, declare its neutrality, and appeal to the United Nations for support. This bold attempt to withdraw entirely from the Communist bloc was met by the prompt dispatch of Soviet divisions to Budapest and bloody suppression of the revolt. In less than a week the movement had been crushed and a new puppet government installed.

The West was horrified, but it could not intervene without risking a third world war. Appeals and condemnation from the United Nations and expressions of sympathy and relief appropriations from the United States were no more effective than the poorly armed Hungarian rebels in fending off Russian tanks and bayonets.

Whatever diplomatic or propaganda advantages the West might otherwise have derived from the Hungarian tragedy were offset by the Anglo-French-Israeli invasion of Egypt in early November 1956. We will tell this story in a later section. It is important to note here that the events leading to the Suez crisis revealed a basic disparity of viewpoint between the United States and its major European allies on the colonial question. The crisis itself transformed this disparity into a split that almost wrecked the Atlantic alliance. The United States not only refused to back its allies in their desperate assault on Egypt but joined the Soviet Union and most other countries in the United Nations in condemning it. The final result was a pall of suspicion and animosity over the western camp that dissipated but slowly.

However, Soviet bellicosity in both Hungary and Suez had effectively dramatized the need for continued western unity, and allied statesmen and diplomats worked patiently to heal the breach in the months that followed. As resentments engendered by Suez gradually subsided on either side of the Atlantic, the western powers restored a reasonably harmonious relationship and renewed their search for security against the Communist threat. The dawning of the missile age in 1957—with Russia visibly in the lead— demanded a fundamental readjustment in western strategy. The United States proposed to strengthen western defenses by equipping its NATO contingents with tactical atomic weapons and installing intermediate-range missile bases on the territory of its European allies. Control over the nuclear warheads for these weapons would remain in American hands.

This policy, together with the appearance of Soviet intercontinental missiles after 1957 and threats of instant retaliation against any country that permitted the launching of nuclear missiles from its soil, raised twin questions in the minds of European statesmen. Now that American cities could be devastated by Russian rockets, would the United States be willing any longer to employ its own nuclear force in response to a Soviet attack *on western Europe*? Secondly, did European countries dare to permit deployment of American tactical atomic arms and missile bases on the continent, thus increasing both the risk and the destructive scope of a future war, without some voice in the decision to use these weapons?

Europeans, fearful that the United States might either refuse to defend Europe or fatally involve its NATO allies in a nuclear war without their consent, grew restive under America's nuclear preponderance. Seeking to escape it, the British succeeded during the 1950's in developing their own atomic and nuclear capability.[5] France, determined to follow suit, conducted successful atomic explosions in the Sahara desert in 1960, despite objections from her allies and widespread criticism from neutral quarters.

But neither Britain nor France, much less the "non-atomic" members of the western alliance, could develop anything like an adequate nuclear or missile arsenal in the near future unless the United States shared closely guarded scientific information and fissionable materials. If these were not forthcoming, European countries wanted at least a measure of control over any decision to employ America's nuclear striking power if their territories were in any way involved. Distrust of the United States would continue so long as some such co-operation was withheld.

For a time, and for comparable reasons, Americans wanted to retain their near-monopoly in the nuclear field almost as badly as Europeans wanted to break it. But the necessity to repair the damage done by the Suez imbroglio demanded concessions on the American side. Eisenhower agreed in 1957 to a larger measure of collaboration with Great Britain in missile and atomic research and development. Further, the United States began providing its allies with more nuclear information as soon as Congress made this possible by amending the Atomic Energy Act in 1958. European contingents in NATO began to receive limited instruction and training in the use of American tactical atomic weapons and rockets, and the United States built large stockpiles of nuclear warheads for these weapons in Europe, to be available to the "shield" forces in the event of war.[6] In return, Great Britain agreed in 1958 to permit establishment of Thor IRBM squadrons on British soil.[7] Italy and Turkey concluded missile-base agreements with the United States a year later.

But real accord within the alliance on the touchy nuclear question had not been achieved. No other NATO ally was willing to allow American missile bases on its soil, and the United States retained full control over nuclear warheads for the missiles and tactical weapons it deployed in Europe. President Charles de Gaulle, almost from the moment that he came to power in France in 1958, voiced dissatisfaction with NATO and proposed creation of a three-power *directoire* (France, Britain, and the United States) to direct alliance policy. When this plan was rebuffed, de Gaulle refused to place French units at the complete disposal of the NATO Supreme Commander and adopted a generally unco-operative attitude. Meanwhile, proposals in 1960 for a combined "nuclear striking force" under

ʌʌʌʌʌʌʌʌʌʌʌʌʌʌʌʌʌʌʌ

[5] With the perfection of her own hydrogen bomb in 1957, Britain immediately followed the American example and launched a sweeping overhaul of her defensive strategy with heavy emphasis upon nuclear striking power and corresponding reductions in conventional armament.

[6] Even the new German forces, despite objections from other NATO countries, resistance within the Federal Republic itself, and violent protests from the USSR, demanded and began to receive instruction in the use of Honest John rockets and other tactical weapons. The United States retained control over nuclear warheads, and over the decision actually to provide the Federal Republic and other nations with full use of these weapons. But their employment by NATO forces in the event of large-scale hostilities seemed a certainty by 1960.

[7] The British government also agreed in 1960 to permit American Polaris submarines to operate from a base in Scotland.

NATO jurisdiction were not translated into action. NATO's strategic adjustment to the nuclear age, and indeed its inner cohesiveness as an effective supranational force, were thus far from complete by 1960.

Of special significance for America's relations with western Europe, and indeed with the entire world, were two developments that had their formal origins in 1958—the Berlin crisis and the Common Market. Berlin was still nominally under four-power control, with small American, British, French, and Soviet garrisons each occupying a sector of the city. Actually, there were only two Berlins in 1958, divided by a line running irregularly north and south along city streets. On one side was East Berlin, Soviet sector since 1945 and capital of the German Democratic Republic since its formation in October 1949. Its million and a quarter inhabitants lived drably amid a few well-lit modern avenues and vast dismal neighborhoods that still carried the scars of war. Across the street lay West Berlin, embracing the three Anglo-American-French sectors. It was a prosperous beehive, its two and a quarter million inhabitants full of exuberant energy.

West Berlin was both an affront and a menace to the entire Communist system. It afforded an easy escape route for the thousands of East Germans who deserted the unpopular puppet state each year, and its very existence kept discontent alive among those who remained. It thus contributed substantially to East Germany's shortage of manpower, relative economic stagnation, and mounting political instability. The Soviets viewed this situation with understandable nervousness. They had had to quell one East German uprising in 1953. Since then they had experienced major difficulties in Poland and Hungary. Chronic unrest in the German Democratic Republic remained strong.

One further development set the stage for the crisis of 1958. Three years earlier the Russians had transferred to East Germany the power to supervise civilian traffic and freight on the surface arteries that linked West Berlin to the Federal Republic. Russian troops continued to inspect military traffic supplying the allied garrisons in West Berlin, but after 1955 East Germany possessed the ability to harass, delay, or block the heavy flow of civilian goods upon which West Berlin's prosperity depended. The three western powers, which had never recognized the East German regime, responded in 1955 with the warning that they would continue to hold Russia accountable for any disruption of the Berlin traffic or any infringement of their right of access to the city.

Three years passed without major incident. Then Khrushchev told a Moscow audience in November 1958 that four-power occupation of Berlin was out of date and should be terminated. Russia, he said, would shortly hand over all its functions in the city to the East German government. If they did not follow suit, the western allies would henceforth have to deal directly with East Germany. Russia would meet forcible western resistance to this new arrangement with force. The western governments promptly reiterated their right to remain in Berlin until a peace treaty with a reunited Germany had been concluded. They also renewed their promise to protect West Berlin.

Khrushchev then turned the vise. He notified the western allies on November 27, 1958, that Russia no longer recognized any western right of access to or presence in Berlin. He charged that continued occupation was a threat to the security of East Germany, the Soviet Union, and the entire Communist bloc. As an alternative to absorbing all of Berlin into East Germany, Khrushchev offered to make West Berlin a disarmed and neutralized "free city." But a satisfactory adjustment in Berlin's present status was imperative, the Premier added, and Russia would sign a separate peace treaty with East Germany in six months if no such adjustment had been made by that date. The peace treaty, of course, would transfer to the East German government all controls then exercised by the Red Army in and about Berlin. Thereafter a showdown over access or occupation rights would confront the allies with the unpalatable choices of abandoning West Berlin, recognizing the East German regime, or war.

The West met this challenge with uncompromising firmness. Three times before the end of 1958 the British, French, and American governments made it clear that they did not recognize Russia's right to act unilaterally in altering the four-power occupation, that they would not abandon the citizens of West Berlin, and that negotiation of the city's status would be possible only in connection with the entire German question and in the absence of an ultimatum. Tension eased in early 1959 after visits by Deputy Premier Mikoyan to the United States and Prime Minister Macmillan to Moscow, and the six-month deadline set by Khrushchev in November 1958 expired without incident.

Absolutely no progress, however, could be made toward a definitive settlement. Negotiations at the Geneva Conference of Foreign Ministers from May to August 1959 ended in the usual impasse. Package offers that included minor concessions never reconciled Russian insistence upon allied withdrawal and western determination to stay until the entire German problem was settled. Khrushchev wanted to discuss Berlin at the summit. He also wanted to visit the United States and have informal conversations with President Eisenhower, and Russian demands were toned down somewhat before and during his visit in September 1959. In his talks with the President at Camp David the Soviet Premier agreed that no new time limit should be imposed upon a solution to the Berlin problem, thus removing the ultimatum that had barred a path to the summit. (For further details of Khrushchev's visit, see above, pp. 802–803.)

There was no real change in the Soviet or western position between September 1959 and May 1960, when the ill-fated Paris summit meeting took place. Khrushchev apparently realized by the early spring of 1960 that the summit would produce no allied concessions on Berlin and hence no settlement of the dispute. This might have persuaded him to write off the summit meeting even before the U-2 incident gave him an opportunity to blame the United States for the ensuing disruption of that gathering. (For details, see above, pp. 802–803.)

The Soviet Premier, having despaired of winning concessions from Eisenhower, laid the groundwork for pressure upon his successor by announcing that Russia would not sign a separate peace treaty with East Germany until after the American presidential election. As this event drew nearer, Khrushchev in October 1960 set April 1961 as a new deadline for settlement of the Berlin question. Since Russia would accept no settlement that did not include withdrawal of allied troops, it was clear by the end of 1960 that another test of western firmness had been prepared for the incom-

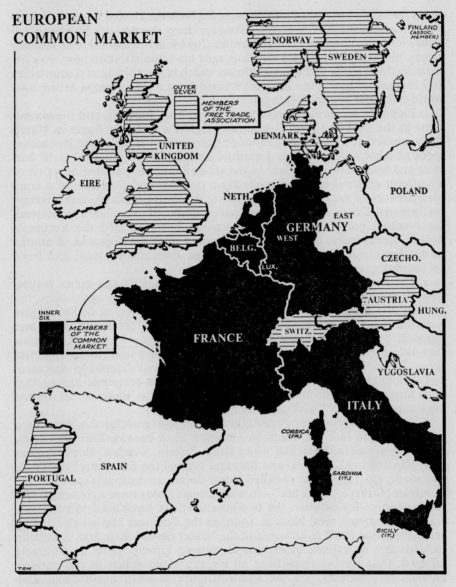

EUROPEAN
COMMON MARKET

NORWAY

SWEDEN

FINLAND
(ASSOC.
MEMBER)

OUTER
SEVEN

MEMBERS
OF THE
FREE TRADE
ASSOCIATION

DENMARK

UNITED
KINGDOM

EIRE

NETH.

POLAND

EAST
GERMANY
WEST

BELG.

LUX.

CZECHO.

INNER
SIX

MEMBERS
OF THE
COMMON
MARKET

AUSTRIA

HUNG.

SWITZ.

FRANCE

YUGOSLAVIA

ITALY

CORSICA
(FR)

SPAIN

SARDINIA
(IT.)

PORTUGAL

SICILY
(IT.)

TRM

ing American President. The fear grew stronger that both sides, while not
wanting war over Berlin, had assumed irreconcilable positions from which
neither dared to retreat.

If hardening attitudes on Berlin gave cause for profound concern as
the sixties began, the early success of the Common Market cast a bright ray
of hope across the European scene. The Common Market was a direct outgrowth of the European Coal and Steel Community. (See above, p. 716.)
Farsighted European statesmen and experts had been laying plans
ever since its inception to broaden the area of economic unity. New im-

petus was added when resentment against both the United States and Russia in the aftermath of Suez and Hungary drew the western European nations closer together. As French Premier Guy Mollet expressed it in January 1957: "Between an America which is now too impulsive and now too slow to understand perils and a Soviet Union which is disquieting and sometimes still menacing, how often have we wished for a united Europe acting as a world force, not neutral, but independent." [8]

Plans for economic integration went quickly forward, and the six nations in the Coal and Steel Community signed a treaty in Rome in March 1957 creating the European Economic Community. It called for free movement of labor and capital and gradual abolition of all internal tariff barriers and trade restrictions within the six-nation area; eventual adoption of a uniform external tariff on goods from outside; and direction by a complex network of supranational executive, legislative, judicial, and advisory institutions. The agreement was purposely designed to provide a framework for eventual political union. A companion treaty formed the European Atomic Community, or Euratom, to conduct joint development of atomic power for economic and industrial purposes. Both treaties went into force on January 1, 1958.

The first 10 per cent reduction in internal tariffs and quota restrictions took place in January 1959, the second in January 1960. More important, the ability of the various supranational governing bodies to prepare sound long-range programs, resolve complex technical questions, and harmonize conflicting national economic policies gave tangible evidence that this experiment in economic unity had the power to survive and grow. Individual economies of the member nations flourished spectacularly under the integrated system. A powerful new economic aggregation with human and industrial resources on a par with those of the United States and the Soviet Union was emerging in Europe.

The new arrangement inevitably posed problems for the West as a whole. Plans to link the Common Market with a broader European trade area were temporarily stalled when Great Britain, Sweden, Norway, Denmark, Switzerland, Austria, and Portugal formed the European Free Trade Association in 1959—the so-called Outer Seven, as distinguished from the Common Market's "Inner Six"—in a somewhat looser trade agreement. Differences in policy between the two organizations threatened to become a trade war between rival blocs in 1960, as the Common Market effected its second internal tariff reduction and the "Outer Seven" their first. American concern that its volume of exports to western Europe would be adversely affected, thus further imperiling an already acute deficit in the nation's balance of payments, led the administration to warn against exclusive economic policies that might damage world trade and place other nations at an unfair disadvantage.

The Common Market's striking economic success and bright political promise showed signs of overcoming most of these troubles in the early 1960's. The British government, which had been loath to associate with the "Inner Six" for fear its important economic ties with the Common-

[8] Richard P. Stebbins *et al., The United States in World Affairs, 1957* (New York, 1958), p. 104.

wealth nations might be endangered, reversed a historic policy and bade for full membership in the Common Market in 1961. In the United States, respect for the Market led in 1962 to adoption of one of the most liberal and far-reaching trade bills in American history—foreshadowing, some thought, a gradual economic fusion of the entire Atlantic community. (See below, p. 868.)

Perhaps the clearest proof of the organization's success came from the Soviet Union. In a not unfamiliar pattern, the Soviets revealed their respect for this capitalist device by first denouncing it and then copying it. The Soviet bloc's Council for Mutual Economic Assistance, or Comecon, began duplicating Common Market institutions and procedures in wholesale fashion in the autumn of 1962. This was the sincerest form of flattery, and it confirmed the growing belief of observers in every continent that the Common Market, whether or not it presaged a dawning United States of Europe, might well mark a turning point in the history of the modern world.

255. Recurrent Troubles in the Far East

The signing of the Korean armistice in July 1953 marked the end of major military action involving American armed forces in the Far East. But termination of the Korean War brought neither peace nor stability to the troubled Orient and solved none of the basic problems that kept the area in ferment. Most of the tension in the Far East stemmed from antagonism between Communist China and the United States. Because China's emergence as a great power under Communist auspices was an ironic perversion of long-standing American hopes, and because they felt partially responsible for what had happened there, Americans tended to view all matters pertaining to China after 1949 in frustration and resentment. Every triumph of the militant People's Republic was in effect a blow to American hopes and a setback for American diplomacy.

The government of Mao Tse-tung demonstrated its hostility toward the West from the very outset. It intervened in the Korean War and assisted the Indochinese rebels in their struggle against the French. It defied the United Nations, mistreated prisoners of war, and showed a cynical disregard for international law and human rights. It confiscated American property, imprisoned American citizens, conducted a steady barrage of virulent anti-American propaganda, and accused the United States of aggression and use of germ warfare. It loudly proclaimed its intention to "liberate" Formosa and the smaller offshore islands held by the Nationalist government of Chiang Kai-shek. And it repeatedly violated the terms of the Korean armistice after July 1953.

For these reasons, both the Truman and Eisenhower administrations pursued a policy of rigid opposition to the Chinese People's Republic. Although this course did not lack critics at home or abroad, the prevailing mood of the American people and the uniform hostility emanating from Peking seemed to leave no reasonable alternative. The policy toward China had two components, one for each of the rival governments that claimed sovereignty over China's vast territory and population. On the one hand, the United States continued, under Eisenhower as under Truman, to withhold recognition from the Peking regime, and used all its influence to block admission of the People's Republic to the United Nations. Save for Secretary Dulles's grudging confrontation with Chinese Premier Chou En-lai at Geneva in 1954, the United States kept its diplomatic contacts with Peking on an indirect and subordinate level.[9] As a further attempt to isolate and weaken its Oriental foe, the United States refused to trade with Communist China and tried to persuade its allies to maintian the broad embargo on strategic materials recommended by the United Nations in May 1951.

The American government adhered to this policy even though several of its allies abandoned it. Many countries, including Great Britain and most other western European states, sooner or later accorded recognition and accepted Peking's sovereignty as an accomplished fact. The majority mustered by the United States against admitting Communist China to the United Nations dwindled each year in the General Assembly. Britain acted unilaterally to ease the embargo on strategic materials in 1957. A year later Japan and most of the NATO countries agreed—without American participation —upon a general reduction in the number of strategic items that could not be sold to the Communist bloc.

The Eisenhower administration also gave firm support to the Chinese Nationalist government of Chiang Kai-shek. Though Chiang and his followers had been confined since 1949 to Taiwan (Formosa) and smaller islands off the Chinese coast, the United States continued to recognize his regime as the legitimate government of all of China and upheld Chiang's envoy in the United Nations as the proper occupant of China's permanent seat on the Security Council. Nationalist military strength was bolstered by a continuous flow of American arms and equipment.

This much was a continuation of Truman's policy, but the Republicans, mindful of their campaign promise to end alleged neglect of the Far East, attempted to do more. First, they encouraged the belief that a Nationalist reconquest of the Chinese mainland was imminent. President Eisenhower announced in February 1953 that the United States Seventh Fleet would no longer be used to "shield" Communist China from a possible Nationalist offensive. Second, Secretary Dulles moved to bring Taiwan more formally within the western defensive perimeter by negotiating a mutual defense pact with the Nationalist government. It was signed in December 1954 and approved by the Senate two months later.

By the time the treaty with Nationalist China was being drawn, however, the administration had ceased to look for an alternative to containment in the Far East. Abandoning even the pretense of a possible Nationalist invasion of the mainland, the American government took pains to insure that Chiang Kai-shek would undertake no major offensive operations against Communist China without American consent. An exchange of letters between Dulles and Chiang, together with senatorial reservations to the mutual security treaty, kept the agreement defensive in nature and removed the danger of unilateral offensive action by the aging Nationalist leader. In the treaty, Taiwan and the adjacent Pescadores were

<hr />

[9] During the attempts to negotiate a cease-fire in Formosa Strait in 1958, for example, the United States carried on its talks with Communist China in Warsaw through the two countries' respective ambassadors to Poland.

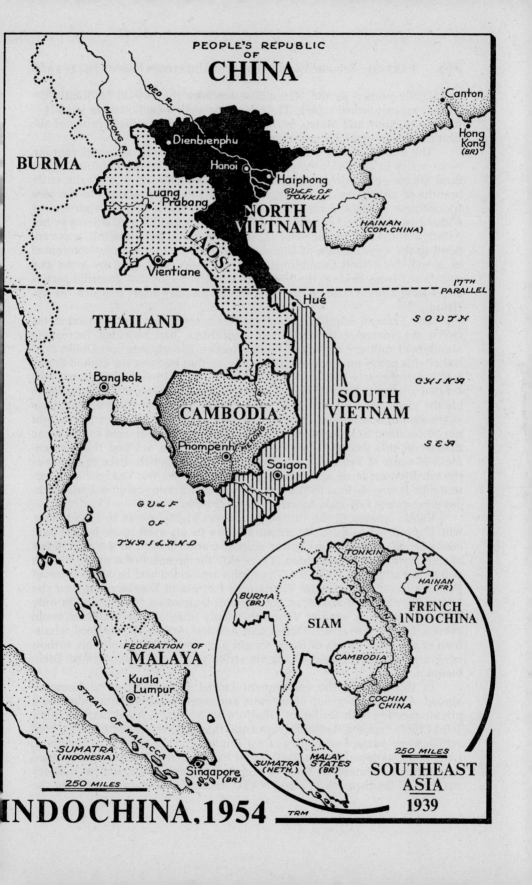

PEOPLE'S REPUBLIC
OF
CHINA

Canton

Hong Kong (BR)

BURMA

Dienbienphu

Hanoi

Haiphong

GULF OF TONKIN

Luang Prabang

NORTH VIETNAM

HAINAN (COM. CHINA)

LAOS

Vientiane

17TH PARALLEL

THAILAND

Hué

SOUTH

Bangkok

CAMBODIA

MEKONG R.

SOUTH VIETNAM

CHINA

Phompenh

Saigon

SEA

GULF OF THAILAND

FEDERATION OF MALAYA

TONKIN

HAINAN (FR)

BURMA (BR)

LAOS

FRENCH INDOCHINA

SIAM

Kuala Lumpur

CAMBODIA

STRAIT OF MALACCA

SUMATRA (INDONESIA)

COCHIN CHINA

Singapore (BR)

SUMATRA (NETH.)

MALAY STATES (BR)

250 MILES

250 MILES

SOUTHEAST ASIA
1939

INDOCHINA, 1954

TRM

specifically named as the Nationalist territory that would be jointly defended against armed attack. The other Nationalist-held offshore islands—notably Quemoy and Matsu, within actual sight and artillery range of the Chinese coast—were not mentioned.

The importance of adhering more closely to a strengthened containment policy in the Orient was brought home to the administration by the final stages and ultimate outcome of the Indochinese war in the early months of 1954. France, reluctant to grant full independence to the new Indochinese states of Laos, Vietnam, and Cambodia, had been struggling without success since 1947 to put down local nationalist movements in her Asiatic colony. The strongest of these movements, the Vietminh, was centered in the coastal state of Vietnam and became increasingly dominated by a well-disciplined Communist element. Heavily assisted by arms and equipment from Peking, the Vietminh employed effective guerrilla tactics and successfully resisted a growing French military effort to crush the uprising.

The Truman administration, quickly recognizing the connection between the struggles in Korea and Indochina, had provided increasing amounts of military aid to the French forces. Eisenhower and Dulles continued this policy on an even larger scale, so that by 1953 the United States was bearing nearly half the cost of France's Indochinese campaign. Fearful that a truce in Korea would enable Communist China to divert troops to aid the Vietminh, Secretary Dulles warned in September 1953 that Chinese aggression in Southeast Asia would have "grave consequences which might not be confined to Indochina." But Mao Tse-tung did not need to intervene directly in this struggle. Despite massive American aid and the commitment of some of France's best troops, an all-out French drive to suppress the rebellion made no appreciable progress, and the war dragged on interminably. It was obvious by the end of 1953 that France could not win without more or less full-scale American participation.

Public opinion in the United States was highly averse to such a step, which promised to mire American soldiers in an even more remote and costly Korea, but the Eisenhower administration moved to the very brink of military action in Indochina. There was the prospect of a major French defeat in early 1954 when the Vietminh surrounded and besieged some of France's finest troops in the Vietnamese fortress of Dienbienphu near the Laotian border. The American government learned on March 20 that only a heavy air attack against Vietminh supply lines and siege forces could avert a French surrender. Dulles and Admiral Arthur W. Radford, chairman of the Joint Chiefs of Staff, sought a congressional resolution authorizing an American carrier-based air strike to aid the defenders of Dienbienphu.

In this venture the government lacked support either at home or abroad. A bipartisan group of senators and representatives, summoned to a private meeting with Dulles and Radford on April 3, learned that the other Joint Chiefs opposed Radford's views and that the British had not been consulted. They advised strongly against sending such a request to Congress. Later consultations between Dulles and British Prime Minister Eden failed to produce agreement on Dulles's proposal to form an immediate military coalition in Southeast Asia along NATO lines. Mutual distrust between the two Atlantic allies grew when Dulles then tried to go ahead with this project against Eden's express wishes. It grew still further when the American Secretary of State suddenly proposed dispatch of a token Anglo-American military force to Indochina. The British government wanted no part of an operation that seemed to risk a third world war.

The possibility of American intervention ended when the French forces in Dienbienphu surrendered in May 1954, and the Foreign Ministers' Conference then sitting in Geneva soon managed to end the Indochinese war. Eisenhower had warned that Communist victory in Indochina might topple other free governments in Asia like a row of dominoes, but the growing supremacy of the Vietminh in most of Vietnam and the French government's determination to come to terms after Dienbienphu precluded any chance of continuing the struggle.

The armistice signed in July 1954 duly recognized Communist military successes in Indochina. Vietnam was divided at the seventeenth parallel, with Vietminh Communists in control of the northern "Democratic Republic" and the western-backed regime of President Ngo Dinh Diem installed in South Vietnam.[10] Cease-fire arrangements were to be directed by an international truce commission. All the Indochinese states became fully independent. Although Laos and Cambodia lost no territory and retained non-Communist governments, they were in effect neutralized by agreeing not to join regional alliances or allow foreign bases on their soil. Parties to the Geneva agreement, which included Communist China but not the United States, promised to respect the independence and territorial integrity of the Indochinese states. The settlement was generally unsatisfactory to the American government. Dulles acquiesced in it because he had no choice, but he avoided actually endorsing it and announced that the United States would resist future Communist attempts to overrun Southeast Asia.

Anxious to forestall this possibility, Dulles strove earnestly to erect a regional defense system for the area. The result of his effort was the Southeast Asia Collective Defense Treaty, signed by eight nations in Manila on September 8, 1954. Transformed into the Southeast Asia Treaty Organization, or SEATO, a few weeks later, the Manila Pact included the United States, Great Britain, France, Australia, New Zealand, the Philippines, Thailand, and Pakistan in its membership. Each signatory agreed that its own safety would be endangered by an armed attack upon any other member within the carefully defined treaty area, or upon any additional state or territory in that area which the members, acting unanimously, might later designate. The signatories promised to consult in the event of threatened subversion, and to act together against the common danger in accordance with their respective constitutional processes. The pact also

ᴧᴧᴧᴧᴧᴧᴧᴧᴧᴧᴧᴧᴧᴧᴧᴧᴧᴧ

[10] The armistice called for internationally supervised elections in 1956 to determine the reunification of Vietnam. When the time came, however, the United States supported President Diem of South Vietnam in refusing to join in the procedure despite prodding from the Communist regime in North Vietnam. Neither Diem nor the American government saw any likelihood of genuinely free elections involving Communist participation. Thus Vietnam, like Germany and Korea, remained divided between a Communist and a pro-western regime with few prospects of peaceful reunification.

called for economic co-operation among members and strengthening of free institutions and military defenses by each. A declaration endorsing equal rights and self-determination, designed to remove any colonialist taint, was signed in conjunction with the treaty. A SEATO Council with headquarters at Bangkok was soon established, charged with the formidable tasks of promoting social and economic welfare and preventing invasion and subversion within the treaty area. Another instrument of containment had been forged—on paper, at least.

Dulles hailed SEATO as the capstone of the already elaborate Pacific regional defense system. SEATO, however, was far from being a replica of NATO. Its weaknesses were many. It possessed no military forces of its own and no centralized command system. More than half of SEATO's members were far removed from the actual treaty area, and no two of those within it were geographically contiguous. Strategically, the region posed enormous defensive problems, especially for the United States, upon whom the main burden of defense would necessarily fall. Finally, the alliance was crippled by the absence of India, Burma, and Indonesia, all of whose governments believed neutralism a safer course than military alignment with the West.

The Indochina armistice had scarcely been concluded before a new threat to peace loomed in the Far East. Focus of this latest crisis was Formosa Strait. Fresh from the triumph of its Vietminh proteges in Indochina, the Chinese People's Republic talked menacingly of an early liberation of Taiwan. President Eisenhower countered with the blunt statement that an invasion from the mainland "would have to run over the Seventh Fleet." Rather than risk such a major clash, the Peking government tested American intentions in September 1954 by opening a bombardment of Quemoy and Matsu, Chiang's tiny outposts off the Chinese mainland.

The American government postponed decision to defend these islands until the extent of the Communist assault could be determined. The first American reply to the bombardment was the signing of the bilateral security treaty with Nationalist China in December. As we have seen, this committed the United States to the defense of Taiwan but deliberately omitted specific mention of the offshore islands. Probing still further, Communist forces in January 1955 captured one of the Tachen Islands, northernmost group of the Nationalist-held offshore chain. The President, concluding that the remote Tachens were not necessary to the defense of Taiwan, ordered the Seventh Fleet to cover the evacuation of the 11,000 Nationalist troops stationed on the Tachens. At the same time, Eisenhower warned Peking that attacks on the other offshore islands might encounter American resistance. To make the country's position clear, he asked Congress on January 25 for a resolution authorizing him to use armed force to defend not only Taiwan and the nearby Pescadores, already covered in the security treaty, but also certain unidentified "closely related localities." Congress, by huge majorities, granted him this broad discretionary authority within three days and stipulated that the resolution would remain in effect until the President deemed it no longer necessary.

The intermittent bombardment of Quemoy and Matsu continued for another three months, but the Peking government did not expand its military action, and the American government carefully dissociated itself from

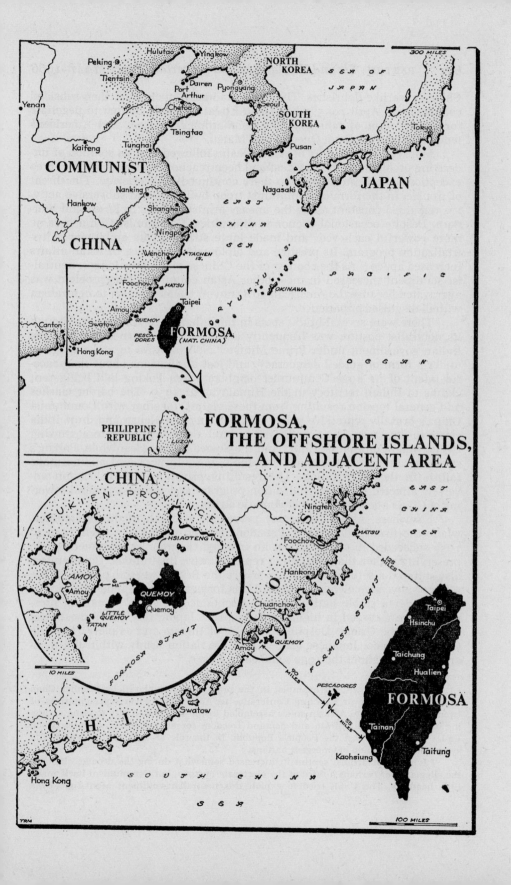

300 MILES

Yenan
Peking
Hulutao
Yingkow
NORTH KOREA
SEA OF JAPAN
Tientsin
Port Arthur
Dairen
Pyongyang
Kaifeng
Tunghai
Chefoo
Seoul
SOUTH KOREA
Tokyo
Tsingtao
COMMUNIST
Pusan
JAPAN
Nanking
Nagasaki
Hankow
Shanghai
EAST
Ningpo
CHINA
CHINA
Wenchow
SEA
TACHEN IS.
Foochow
MATSU
RYUKYU IS.
PACIFIC
Amoy
Taipei
OKINAWA
Canton
Swatow
QUEMOY
FORMOSA
PESCA-
DORES
(NAT. CHINA)
Hong Kong
OCEAN

PHILIPPINE REPUBLIC
LUZON

FORMOSA,
THE OFFSHORE ISLANDS,
AND ADJACENT AREA

CHINA
EAST
CHINA
FUKIEN PROVINCE
Ningteh
SEA
HSIAOTENG I.
Foochow
MATSU
AMOY
125 MILES
Hankong
Amoy
6 MI.
QUEMOY
Quemoy
Chuanchow
LITTLE QUEMOY
TATAN
QUEMOY
Taipei
COAST
Amoy
QUEMOY
Hsinchu
FORMOSA STRAIT
10 MILES
FORMOSA STRAIT
Taichung
Hualien
PESCADORES
CHINA
Swatow
515 MILES
FORMOSA
Tainan
SOUTH CHINA
Kaohsiung
Taitung
Hong Kong
SEA

100 MILES

TRM

Chiang's warlike flourishes. The crisis gradually tapered off, then subsided completely in April 1955, when Chou En-lai suddenly offered to negotiate for a relaxation of tensions. The bombardment ceased, and Americans temporarily forgot about Quemoy and Matsu.

More than three years of relative calm followed. But no solution of underlying problems in the Far East had been reached, and, with two or three exceptions, the western position there continued to deteriorate. The threat of trouble, in the form of Communist troop build-ups and subversive activity, remained constant along the uneasy armistice lines in Korea and Vietnam. Despite occasional economic difficulties, Communist China became more powerful each year and made large strides in its ambitious industrialization program. Its prestige and diplomatic influence in Asian affairs increased apace.[11] As the shadow of the Chinese giant grew longer, neutralist sentiment increased in most other Asian countries. This problem was aggravated because the American government tended to react to neutralism with ill-disguised impatience.

There were several bright spots in this otherwise dark picture. Though its neutralist posture was frequently annoying to western diplomats, the Indian government under Prime Minister Nehru strove to make progress under a form of guided democracy, and lost all illusions about the peaceful intent of its huge Communist neighbor when Peking laid belligerent claims to Indian territory in the Himalayas in 1959. The border clashes and general tension resulting from these claims, together with Communist China's brutally repressive policy in Tibet, angered Nehru and drew India closer to the West. The Sino-Indian quarrel also contributed to a growing rift between Communist China and the Soviet Union. Meanwhile, Peking's sweeping attempt to communize Chinese agriculture proved an enormous failure in the early 1960's. The resulting privation and dislocation adversely affected the industrialization program and forced a general lowering of China's economic and diplomatic sights.

Elsewhere, Asian democracy proved its strength in the Philippines, where the firm leadership of President Ramon Magsaysay from 1953 to 1957 succeeded in stamping out an internal Communist movement while preserving rather than curtailing representative institutions. Communism also suffered a setback in Malaya, where the British were able to eradicate a large subversive element and lead this former colony to independence in 1957 under a stable native regime. Economic gains and mounting prosperity were recorded in highly industrialized Japan, the West's most vital bastion in the Orient. Despite a mixture of threats and cajolery from the Communist bloc, Japanese leaders kept the nation firmly within the western orbit throughout the 1950's and early 1960's.[12]

∿∿∿∿∿∿∿∿∿∿∿∿∿∿∿

[11] This was shown, for example, in the prominent role played by Premier Chou En-lai at the important Bandung Conference in April 1955, when representatives of twenty-nine Asian and African states assembled in the Indonesian city to issue a ringing anti-colonialist manifesto and demand freedom for all remaining colonies. Chou En-lai successfully cast the People's Republic in the role of anti-colonial leader and sympathetic champion of emergent nations.

[12] Japanese neutralist sentiment increased somewhat during the decade, claiming the allegiance of perhaps a third of the electorate by 1960, but Communism itself made little headway. The USSR tried to exploit this neutralist sentiment after 1956 by a

Acute crisis returned to the Far East when the Chinese Communists abruptly resumed bombardment of the offshore islands in August 1958. The American government met the new threat firmly. It would be unwise to assume, Dulles warned, that an invasion of the offshore islands could be a "limited operation." He added on September 4 that the congressional resolution of January 1955 might apply to Quemoy and Matsu. The administration assembled a huge naval and air striking force in Formosa Strait, and American warships escorted Nationalist supply convoys from Taiwan to Quemoy. Tension mounted when Khrushchev promised Russian support to the People's Republic in any clash with the United States and called for an end to American intervention in what he said were China's internal affairs.

The possibility of major war over Quemoy and Matsu set off an adverse public reaction in the United States and expressions of alarm from western Europe, and both sides quickly showed signs of retreat. Dulles announced on September 30 that the American government had no commitment to defend Quemoy and Matsu and spoke in favor of reducing Nationalist forces on the islands. A dependable cease-fire, the Secretary added, would make such a withdrawal possible. At the same time, the Chinese Communists seemed almost to welcome the chance to call off what had become a profitless venture. Peking first suspended the bombardment for a total of three weeks beginning October 6, then proclaimed the bizarre policy of not shelling Quemoy on even-numbered days while reserving the right to do so on odd ones. The Chinese Communists kept up an intermittent and rather desultory shelling of Quemoy for some months and then abandoned the effort.

Meanwhile, another problem was steadily assuming ominous proportions in Southeast Asia. Domestic political conflict in the landlocked kingdom of Laos became an issue in the cold war before the end of the decade, and the ordinary tranquillity of life in this remote land was soon shattered by the cumbersome maneuvering of the great powers and their agents. Laos, although insignificant in size, population, and actual or potential wealth, possessed strategic importance because it adjoined Communist China, North Vietnam, and the four non-Communist states of Burma, Thailand, Cambodia, and South Vietnam.

policy of friendship and co-operation, supporting Japan's bid to join the United Nations (Japan became the eightieth member of that organization in December 1956), and pointing out the disadvantages and dangers in Japan's alliance with the United States.

Recognizing the problem, the American government soon agreed to revision of the 1951 security treaty in Japan's favor. The new treaty, negotiated in 1958–9 and signed in January 1960, placed Japan on a more equal footing in a variety of ways. Most important, it gave the Japanese a voice in the placing of American military units—including the touchy questions of missile bases and reconnaissance planes—on Japanese soil.

Japanese Premier Kishi, a leader of the pro-western Liberal Democratic party, succeeded in the face of stiff neutralist opposition and domestic turmoil in obtaining approval of the new treaty by the Japanese Diet. Anti-treaty demonstrations were so riotous that a projected visit to Japan by President Eisenhower in the spring of 1960 had to be canceled. Order was soon restored, and elections in the fall of 1960 kept the Liberal Democrats in power under Kishi's successor, Hayato Ikeda, but the strong Socialist party continued its opposition to the treaty and the western alliance.

Forbidden by the Geneva armistice of 1954 to join regional alliances or solicit military aid from either East or West, Laos was largely occupied after the armistice in pacifying its pro-Communist political faction, known as the Pathet Lao. This group continued to receive aid from the Vietminh Communists in North Vietnam. After years of effort, Prince Souvanna Phouma, neutralist Premier of Laos, managed to bring Pathet Lao leaders into a unified national government in July 1958. Souvanna Phouma then resigned in favor of another middle-of-the-road Premier, Phoui Sananikone.

The political situation in Laos worsened steadily during the next two years. Neither the Communist bloc nor the United States had approved the strict neutralist policy of Souvanna Phouma. With his departure both sides —in unabashed contravention of the Geneva armistice—maneuvered for advantage in the tiny kingdom. Communist pressure on Laos mounted steadily during the Quemoy crisis of 1958. The United States countered with an expanding program of military and economic assistance. Thus strengthened, the new Premier first excluded all Communist elements from his cabinet, then tried in early 1959 to subdue the Pathet Lao altogether. Fighting spread as increasing numbers of guerrillas crossed into Laos from North Vietnam, and the royal government announced in July 1959 that the reinforced Pathet Lao was endangering the kingdom.

This internal struggle, temporarily quieted by a United Nations inquiry and a subsequent investigation by Secretary-General Hammarskjold in November 1959, gradually took on dimensions of an international crisis in 1960. A pro-western general, Phoumi Nosavan, ousted Premier Sananikone in January and supported a new pro-American government which made certain that subsequent elections went against the Pathet Lao faction. Then an enterprising neutralist captain named Kong Le engineered a military coup in August which returned Souvanna Phouma to power. Souvanna continued to argue that only a government of all factions—pro-American, neutralist, and pro-Communist—could restore peace. The Eisenhower administration disagreed, and when neither diplomacy nor a clumsy form of economic pressure dissuaded Souvanna Phouma from his coalition policy, American support was thrown behind a counterrevolution recently launched by General Nosavan. Nosavan's army, after defeating Kong Le's forces in a violent battle near the capital, installed a pro-western government under Prince Boun Oum on December 1, 1960. Souvanna Phouma, still recognized by Russia as the rightful Laotian Premier, went into exile in Cambodia, while Kong Le and his followers joined the Pathet Lao.

The tide quickly turned against the new pro-American government. Laotian Communists controlled large segments of the kingdom by early 1961 and threatened the capital itself, defeating Boun Oum's forces decisively whenever they met. Boun Oum's complete collapse was clearly imminent, and the Eisenhower administration in its closing weeks sought the neutralist compromise it had earlier helped to defeat. But Souvanna Phouma, still in exile, blamed the impending disaster on Washington and refused to co-operate, while the resurgent Pathet Lao scented total victory and rejected all compromise proposals.

As the Kennedy administration prepared to take office in January 1961, it appeared that only large-scale American intervention, with obvious risk of counteraction by the major Communist powers, could save strife-torn Laos for the West. The stability of Ngo Dinh Diem's government in neighboring South Vietnam was already menaced by Vietminh guerrilla bands infiltrating through Communist-held portions of Laos. The "row of dominoes" to which Eisenhower had likened the fragile governments of Southeast Asia six years before seemed already to be toppling.

256. *The Middle East and Africa*

The spread of the cold war to the Middle East and later to sub-Saharan Africa during the 1950's raised new threats to world peace and drew the United States diplomatically into areas it had hitherto relegated to secondary importance or virtually ignored. The Middle East was by no means remote to the American people, but responsibility for protecting large western interests in the region had largely been borne by Britain and France until about 1950. The economic and political realities of the postwar world forced these nations to abandon or reduce imperial commitments in the area. Their disengagement was far enough advanced by 1950 to encourage Soviet penetration and prompt American activity in response.

The Middle East was made to order for Communist exploitation. It included historic land and sea routes connecting three continents and the richest known oil deposits in the world. It was composed of underdeveloped countries ruled by inexperienced, unstable, or reactionary regimes. It fairly seethed with resentments born of poverty, anti-colonial bitterness, popular unrest, extremist agitation, clashing nationalist ambitions, and religious strife.

The specific ingredients that, along with Soviet meddling, combined to brew incipient crisis in the Middle East were Arab-Israeli antagonism, American attempts to erect a regional defensive system, inept western diplomacy, and the ambitions of the new Egyptian strong man, Gamal Abdel Nasser. The mortal conflict between Arab and Jew, probably the bitterest international quarrel of the postwar era, stemmed from the irreconcilable determination of Israel to protect her hard-won independence and of her Arab neighbors to destroy the new Jewish state. Boundaries between Israel and the encircling ring of hostile Arab nations had been set by an armistice that ended the Arab-Israeli war of 1948–9, and the armistice lines were supervised by a UN truce team and upheld by an Anglo-American-French pledge of 1950. But neither armistice nor pledge brought peace to the troubled region. Although the United States worked to prevent an arms race after 1950, Israel became a virtual garrison state whose well-trained, well-equipped forces were an object of envy, alarm, and attempted duplication by her implacable neighbors. There were constant raids, counterraids, and terrorism by both sides across the armistice lines. These episodes kept mutual hatred and suspicion at fever pitch, defied all outside efforts to harmonize or soothe the deep-seated quarrel, and threatened at almost any moment to touch off a second Arab-Israeli war.

Western diplomacy in the Middle East, in which the United States had begun to play a major role after announcement of the Truman Doctrine in 1947, faced a well-nigh impossible task. It wanted to preserve peace and remain neutral in the Arab-Israeli impasse while courting Arab favor in erecting a Middle Eastern defensive system against possible Soviet aggression. Its efforts were seriously hampered by touchy nationalist and anti-colonial feelings in every Middle Eastern country, directed primarily at Britain and France, and by Arab resentment over western sponsorship of Israel in the late 1940's, directed primarily against the United States.

Secretary Acheson had hoped to forestall Soviet penetration by creating a Middle East Command along NATO lines, but his successor in the State Department did not consider this project immediately realizable. Instead, Dulles sought Arab friendship by promoting settlement of an Anglo-Egyptian dispute over Britain's huge base at Suez. His efforts were crowned by a treaty between England and Egypt in October 1954, whereby the former gave up her rights to the base and agreed to evacuate all her armed forces from the canal zone within twenty months. Egypt agreed in return to keep the Suez base in combat readiness and permit re-entry of British forces in the event of attack by an outside power against Turkey or any of the Arab states. Western defenses were weakened by this abandonment of Suez, but both Dulles and Eden hoped that Egypt under Nasser's newly installed regime would co-operate in reducing Arab-Israeli tensions and building a collective defense system in the Middle East. American offers of economic and military aid to Egypt under the Mutual Security Act followed immediately upon conclusion of the Anglo-Egyptian treaty of 1954.

Nasser was loath to align himself with the West. He wanted arms, but primarily for use against Israel and not at the price of the pledges demanded in return for American Mutual Security aid. He professed to see in this program a potential new form of western imperialism, and he did not share American alarm about the menace of Communism in the Middle East. Moreover, Nasser aspired to establish Egyptian primacy in the Arab world. He deeply resented the rival aspirations of pro-western Iraq and suspected that Iraq's interest in strengthening her western ties was designed to bolster her bid for Arab leadership.

Events in 1955 embarked Nasser on the international high road to adventure and trouble. A large-scale raid by Israeli armed units on the Egyptian territory of Gaza in late February revealed the relative weakness of Nasser's military forces and whetted his desire for preparedness against Israel. At the same time, Dulles's efforts to create a regional defense system in the "northern tier" of Middle Eastern states were rewarded with a defensive alliance between Turkey and Iraq, signed at Baghdad on February 24. The Baghdad Pact was soon expanded by the adherence of Great Britain, Pakistan, and Iran. This new alliance, which the United States encouraged and aided but did not formally join, seemed to close the ring of containment around the Communist perimeter.[13] But it also infuriated Nasser, worried the other Arab states, and evoked protests and warnings from Russia.

Nasser took advantage of Soviet resentment, and concluded a gigantic arms agreement with the Communist bloc in September 1955. It called for exchange of Czechoslovakian tanks, planes, artillery, and other equipment for Egyptian rice and cotton. Arab nationalists in every country now turned

[13] The Baghdad Pact was linked to NATO through Turkey and to SEATO through Pakistan, while Great Britain was a member of all three.

to Nasser for leadership against Israel. Egypt concluded defensive alliances and joint military arrangements with Syria and Saudi Arabia in October 1955. The Israelis, alarmed by this prospective enhancement of Arab military strength, began laying specific plans to strike while the advantage still lay in their favor. Armed clashes and raids across the tense armistice lines during 1955 were bloodier than any since the end of the Arab-Israeli war in 1949.

Nasser now moved more boldly into the center of East-West rivalries in 1956. This time he attempted to work both sides in obtaining foreign loans for a high dam across the Nile at Aswan, 800 miles above Cairo. It was an ambitious but worthwhile project, designed to increase Egypt's supply of arable land and stimulate industrial expansion. The British and American governments had already made a trial offer, totaling $200,000,-000, to underwrite initial construction on the Aswan Dam, and the World Bank was prepared to advance an additional $200,000,000 when preliminary work was completed. Nasser rejected the Anglo-American offer in January 1956, claiming that it threatened Egyptian independence, and hinted that better terms were available in Moscow.

By this time Nasser was also conducting an intensive anti-western propaganda campaign in the Middle East, plotting against the pro-western governments of Iraq and Jordan, aiding the Algerian rebels in their war against France, proclaiming the doom of Israel, and praising the USSR. Soviet and East German technicians were much in evidence in Cairo, and Syrian Communists were exercising a strong and potentially decisive voice in the government of that Arab state. Though Nasser continued to proclaim his neutralism in the cold war, he had all but mortgaged Egypt's economy to the Communist bloc in exchange for arms, and Egypt seemed on the verge of becoming a new Soviet satellite.

Secretary Dulles acted following rumors in June 1956 of a twenty-year $1,000,000,000 Russian loan to finance the Aswan Dam. He informed the Egyptian ambassador on July 19, 1956, that the United States had decided not to participate in the Aswan Dam project. Events quickly led to the most serious international crisis since Korea. Stung by Dulles's public rebuff, the Egyptian President cast about for a new way to finance his cherished dam. He found it by nationalizing the Suez Canal Company on July 26. Its net annual profits of $30,000,000 would provide money for the dam. Assuming adequate compensation to the shareholders, which the Egyptian government readily promised, there was nothing illegal in Nasser's action. The canal lay in Egyptian territory, and the company that operated it held an Egyptian charter and was subject to Egyptian law. The company's concession, in any case, was due to expire and revert to Egypt in 1968.

What made Nasser's abrupt maneuver so alarming, from the European point of view, was the economic and strategic importance of the Suez Canal. It carried over 100,000,000 tons of cargo a year, three fifths of which was Middle Eastern oil bound for western Europe, and its continued efficient operation had become a mainstay of European prosperity, NATO's security, and the international economy. Nasser took pains to announce that in operating the canal the Egyptian government would abide by the terms of the Constantinople Convention of 1888, which guaranteed all nations free navigation in peace and war.

The British and French governments took no comfort from these assurances. Constantinople Convention and protests from the United Nations notwithstanding, Nasser had barred Israeli shipping from the Suez for years. The British doubted that Egypt could operate the canal efficiently. The French had long detested Nasser for his open support of the Algerian rebels. Both governments regarded Nasser's act as a blow to their prestige and a threat to their security, and they determined to tolerate neither. Prime Minister Eden cabled Eisenhower on July 27 that Britain was prepared to use force as a last resort if Egypt did not relinquish the canal.

Two and a half months of intricate, futile negotiations followed. Painstaking efforts by Dulles and other would-be mediators failed utterly to produce agreement. Nasser refused to accept any scheme of outright international control of the canal, and Britain and France refused to accept any system that left unfettered control in Nasser's hands. Partial concessions from both sides seemed at last to place agreement within sight, but a final uncompromise resolution containing guarantees acceptable to the European allies was killed by a Russian veto in the Security Council on October 13.

The most disturbing aspect of the negotiations was the failure of the Atlantic allies to co-ordinate their policy or, in the end, even to communicate. Dulles had initially conceded that Nasser must be made to "disgorge" the canal and had not ruled out force if all other measures failed. But his view soon changed. The American government did not share the Anglo-French sense of urgency or think that vital principles were at stake, and it insisted that settlement by negotiation was both possible and imperative. Eisenhower, on September 11, declared his unwillingness to be a party to aggression, and Dulles insisted two days later that the United States would not "try to shoot its way through the Canal." Britain and France went ahead now with their plans in full knowledge that they would lack American support. Indeed, after October 13, when actual preparation for an attack on Egypt was begun, London and Paris concealed news of the operation from Washington.

The attack began with a sudden invasion of Egypt by Israeli forces on October 29, 1956—the preventive war that Israel had contemplated for some time. Many persons suspected that it was launched in direct collusion with the British and French, and the evidence was impressive, to say the least. The rapid Israeli invasion of the Sinai Peninsula toward the canal gave Britain and France a pretext for their own assault. Justifying intervention as a means of insulating the canal from Israeli-Egyptian hostilities in Sinai, the European allies sent an ultimatum to Cairo and Tel Aviv on October 30. They demanded an end to fighting, a ten-mile withdrawal of all military forces from the canal, and the right temporarily to occupy key positions along the route in order to safeguard free transit. England and France vetoed American and Soviet resolutions in the Security Council calling upon all members to refrain from use of force, and opened an aerial bombardment of Cairo and the Canal area on October 31 when Egypt ignored the ultimatum. The attack coincided almost exactly with the ill-fated Hungarian revolt.

American leaders, caught completely off guard, were nettled because they had not been consulted or even notified in advance, and embarrassed

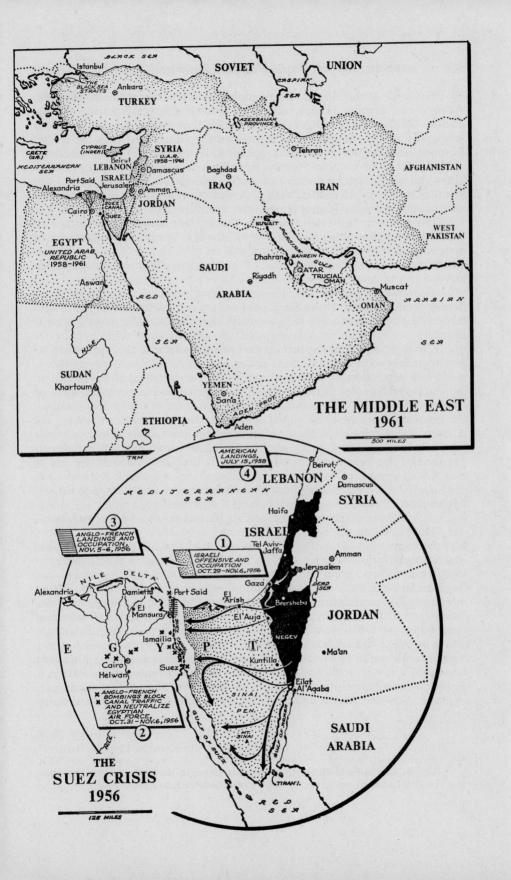

THE MIDDLE EAST
1961

500 MILES

THE
SUEZ CRISIS
1956

125 MILES

by this attack at the climax of a presidential campaign at home. They recognized that Britain, France, and Israel were acting under extreme provocation, but they could not condone an action that betrayed so many American and western commitments. It violated the charters of both the United
Nations and the North Atlantic Alliance. It flouted an Anglo-American-
French pledge of 1950 to oppose any breach in the Arab-Israeli armistice
lines and an American promise of April 1956 to "support and assist" any
country under attack in that region. It was contrary to the American policies of separating the Canal controversy from the Arab-Israeli conflict and
excluding Russia from the area. The Washington administration took its
stand against the allied assault regretfully but firmly. "There can be no
peace without law," Eisenhower declared on October 31. "There can be no
law if we work to invoke one code of international conduct for those who
oppose us and another for our friends."

Events followed swiftly during the first week of November. Israeli
forces occupied most of the Sinai peninsula within a few days. The Anglo-
French invasion was mounted so slowly, however, that Egypt had time to
block the canal with sunken ships before allied troops could occupy the
route. Syrian saboteurs cut Britain's oil pipelines from Iraq. Meanwhile, an
emergency session of the General Assembly passed an American-sponsored
cease-fire resolution by a huge majority on November 2 and renewed its
appeal two days later. It then created an international emergency force on
November 5 to "secure and supervise the cessation of hostilities." Belligerent threats from Moscow added materially to the growing tension. The
United States rejected Bulganin's proposal for joint Soviet-American military action to end the fighting, but the Kremlin avowed its own readiness to
"crush the aggressors and restore peace in the East through the use of
force" and spoke of recruiting "volunteers" to aid the Egyptians. The
threat of some such enlargement of the conflict led Eisenhower to order a
global alert of American armed forces on November 6.

The British government decided on that same day to accept a cease-
fire. The Israeli government, having gained most of its military objectives,
did the same, and the French had no choice but to follow suit. Arrival of
the United Nations Emergency Force (UNEF) enabled the invaders to
withdraw without complete humiliation.[14] Actually, their operation had
been a complete fiasco. They had not only failed to destroy Nasser, but his
prestige in Egypt and throughout the Arab world was higher than ever. Their
offensive had been mounted too slowly to prevent obstruction of the canal
and called off too soon to guarantee their possession at the time of the
cease-fire. The Suez Canal not only remained in Egypt's hands but was
closed to all traffic until obstructions could be removed, forcing Europe in
the interim to rely upon American oil and the costly route around Africa.

Anglo-French prestige was at an all-time low, and anti-colonial sentiment in Asia and Africa had been fanned to new heat. The United States

[14] Anglo-French withdrawal took place in December 1956 when the UNEF arrived
to stabilize the area, but Israel was not persuaded to relinquish the Egyptian territory it
had occupied until March 1957. By this time the Israelis were convinced of UNEF's
effectiveness and had established their shipping rights in the Gulf of Aqaba, the opening of which had been another major objective of the attack on Egypt.

had won approval in neutral and anti-colonial quarters for its resolute opposition to the assault, but the western position as a whole had been badly
weakened, and the Atlantic alliance was a shambles. Russia had reaped
huge advantages in the Middle East by posing as the defender of Arab
nationalism against imperialist aggression. Afro-Asian opinion could overlook Soviet brutality in Hungary in its greater sensitivity to what seemed
like a resurgence of European colonialism.

The Middle East remained a major storm center in international politics for the next two years. The UNEF ultimately proved an effective means
of maintaining relative peace and stability in and about Suez and the Arab-
Israeli armistice area, and a UN salvage team succeeded in removing all
obstructions and reopening the canal by April 1957. Contrary to European
fears, Egypt thereafter proved surprisingly co-operative in not interfering
with canal traffic (save Israel's) and surprisingly efficient in administering
and operating the busy waterway. But dangerous political ferment was on
the rise in other quarters. Moscow-backed Communist elements and Nasser-
supported nationalist elements enlarged their influence in every Arab state.
They dominated the Syrian government and endangered shaky pro-western
regimes in Iraq, Jordan, and Lebanon.

America's first response, in the dazed and tense aftermath of the Suez
crisis, was the so-called Eisenhower Doctrine. A joint congressional resolution of March 9, 1957, authorized the President to use up to $200,000,000
in Mutual Security funds for economic and military assistance to Middle
Eastern nations that desired it, asserted America's vital interest in preserving the independence and integrity of all countries in the Middle East, and
offered American armed assistance upon the request of any such nation
facing "armed aggression from any country controlled by international
communism."

As an attempt to deter aggression and clarify American policy in the
Middle East, the Eisenhower Doctrine contained certain large ambiguities
and omissions. It deliberately left the Suez and Arab-Israeli disputes to the
United Nations. It did not precisely define the area covered by the resolu-
tion. It could not be applied until a nation requested it. It did not cover
Communist subversion, which many regarded as a far greater danger to the
Middle East than outside aggression. The new doctrine was denounced by
the Soviet bloc, described as an imperialist plot by Egypt, hailed by pro-
western Iraq, Iran, and Turkey, and received with cautious approval in
Jordan, Lebanon, and Saudi Arabia.

Alarm signals flashed again and again during 1957. Young King Hussein of Jordan, who had recently cut traditional ties with Britain under
pressure from anti-western elements, abruptly ousted his pro-Nasser cabinet in April 1957 and appealed to loyal Bedouin tribes to protect his throne.
Eisenhower moved to forestall Soviet exploitation and possible Nasserite
intervention, by pronouncing Jordan's independence "vital" and ordering
the Sixth Fleet to the eastern Mediterranean. This action momentarily
stabilized Hussein's throne, but charges of American plotting in Communist-dominated Syria culminated in October with a blast from Moscow and
a new war scare. The Soviets accused the United States of inciting a Turkish
attack upon Syria and threatened Turkey with rocket attacks. Syria requested a United Nations investigation while the American and Soviet dele-

gates exchanged accusations, and Egypt sent troops to reinforce Syrian concentrations along the Turkish border. King Saud of Saudi Arabia stepped forward to mediate the Turko-Syrian dispute before UN action was necessary.

American intervention, threats of war, and new western setbacks followed in 1958. Syria and Egypt merged to form the United Arab Republic in February and stepped up their subversive activities against the pro-western Arab regimes. A Nasserite revolt broke out in Lebanon in May. The Lebanese government accused Egypt and Syria of border violations and interference in its internal affairs and requested a United Nations investigation. An observation group dispatched by Secretary-General Hammarskjold was unable to seal the frontier, stop the fighting, or probe deeply enough to substantiate Lebanese charges. When appeals to the Arab League also failed, Lebanon asked for American assistance.

The President, loath to risk a clash between Americans and Arabs and fearful of Russian intervention, hesitated at first. Then a nationalist group that included pro-Nasser elements, led by General Abdel Karim al-Kassim, overthrew the pro-western regime in Baghdad on July 14, 1958. Even before Kassim signed a mutual defense pact with Nasser on July 19, Iraq's withdrawal from the West and into the Egyptian or even the Soviet orbit seemed imminent. Such a shift threatened to produce comparable results in Lebanon, Jordan, and Saudi Arabia. Thoroughly alarmed, both Lebanon and Jordan sent out desperate calls for western help.

President Eisenhower, after hurried conferences with advisers and congressmen, ordered the Sixth Fleet to deploy off Lebanon for an amphibious landing. Some 8,000 American troops streamed unopposed into the little country between July 15 and July 19, "to encourage the Lebanese government in defense of Lebanese sovereignty and integrity," while Britain sent 3,000 men to Jordan in response to Hussein's appeal. The operations were executed brilliantly, but diplomatic reactions were ominous. Nasser flew to Moscow, and Russia responded with warnings and charges of aggression. Khrushchev, saying that the world was on the "brink of disaster," demanded an immediate conference at Geneva with Eisenhower, Macmillan, de Gaulle, Nehru, and Hammarskjold. "I am not aware," Eisenhower replied drily on July 22, "of any factual basis for your extravagantly expressed fear." In the Security Council, where the American delegate had already agreed to transfer responsibility for order in Lebanon to the world organization, attempts to stabilize the situation along those lines encountered Soviet vetoes. The United States thereupon asked for an emergency session of the General Assembly.

The Middle Eastern outlook had brightened somewhat when the Assembly convened in emergency session on August 8. Khrushchev had been quoted as saying that Russia had no intention of sending "volunteers" or regular troops to the area in present circumstances. There had been no bloodshed in Lebanon, and a new president acceptable to all factions had been found. The United States had quieted Arab fears of intervention in Iraq by recognizing the Kassim regime. While the General Assembly argued over Soviet demands for immediate Anglo-American withdrawal and American proposals for a condemnation of indirect aggression, the entire bloc of Arab states presented a resolution on August 21 that passed unanimously. It accepted assurances that none of those states would take "any action calculated to change established systems of government," asked members of the United Nations to refrain from interfering in the internal affairs of other states, and requested the Secretary-General to "make . . . such practical arrangements as would adequately help in upholding the purposes and principles of the Charter in relation to Lebanon and Jordan." Such measures would "facilitate" the speedy withdrawal of American and British troops. Hammarskjold was able to arrange matters so effectively that all American and British units had withdrawn from Lebanon and Jordan by early November 1958.

Relative calm descended upon the strife-torn Middle East during the remainder of the Eisenhower era. The United States and the Soviet Union continued to maneuver for advantage in the region, but no large-scale violence or major war scares occurred in 1959 and 1960. The Arab-Israeli dispute remained unsettled, but fewer bloody incursions disturbed the impasse. Ships continued to pass undisturbed through the Suez Canal.

Actually, genuine neutrality undoubtedly gained ground at the expense of both East and West. Iraq withdrew from the Baghdad Pact in March 1959, and the alliance was transformed five months later into the Central Treaty Organization, or CENTO, with headquarters at Ankara. Like its predecessor, CENTO was strongly supported and encouraged, but not formally joined, by the United States. It also, like SEATO, lacked a unified command or armed forces of its own, and was more a symbol than a bastion of western power in the Middle East. Nasser remained strong in Egypt and influential in the Arab world, but he concentrated more on internal affairs and less on high international adventure after the Lebanese crisis. Although he accepted a twelve-year $100,000,000 loan from Russia in December 1958 and began work on the Aswan Dam with help from Russian engineers, his neutralism grew steadily less belligerent and less aligned with Moscow. Indeed, he clamped down ruthlessly on Communist activity in Egypt. Kassim's shaky regime in Iraq encountered grave economic troubles but managed to maintain itself without sliding under control of either Egypt or Russia. It was overthrown by an anti-Communist group in early 1963, and Kassim was executed. Lebanon became neutral after 1958, and Hussein still occupied an uncertain throne in Jordan, but both countries preserved more independence than had seemed possible in 1958. Syria severed ties with Egypt in 1962.

Meanwhile, the world spotlight was turning toward Africa, where the movement for independence was fully under way in the late 1950's. As late as 1955 there were only five independent nations in Africa. Twenty-eight new nations had joined their number by the end of 1962. Only a few British dependencies in the east and south, two large Portuguese colonies, tiny French Somaliland, Saharan Algeria, and the small Spanish and Portuguese possessions along the west coast were still under European rule by this date.

American diplomatic interest in Africa was passive, to say the least, until about 1958. The United States had been content, before that time, to express good will, friendship, and humanitarian interest toward the peoples

of Africa, while marring its generally favorable image in African eyes by
racial discrimination at home. Africa remained primarily a European responsibility until the end of the 1950's.

The generalization did not apply to North Africa, because it was close
enough to the main theaters of the cold war to possess strategic value. The
former Italian colony of Libya graduated from a UN mandate to independence in 1953; Morocco and Tunisia achieved independence from France in
1956. In Tunisia the pro-western orientation of President Habib Bourguiba,
an influential figure in the Arab world, was an important counterweight to
Nasser. Libya's continued friendship became vital in 1954 when that country signed a sixteen-year lease of the huge Wheelus Air Force base near
Tripoli to the United States. Morocco figured even more prominently in
American strategic planning because of the four airfields and the naval base
that the United States had built there in 1950–1. Libya remained well disposed, but Morocco demanded cancellation of American bases on its soil
once it achieved independence. These demands became so insistent that the
American government promised in 1959 to relinquish all of its Moroccan
bases by the end of 1963. The agreement was made possible by completion
of the new network of American bases in Spain in 1960.

Between Tunisia and Morocco lay the French colony of Algeria, oldest
and richest possession in France's diminishing empire. American concern
for Algeria stemmed from the diplomatic and military ramifications of
France's prolonged efforts to put down the Moslem rebellion that broke out
in Algeria in late 1954. The war became one of the West's biggest liabilities
as time went on. It crippled NATO's military strength by draining off nearly
all French contingents, strained French relations with her allies, embarrassed western standing with neutral and ex-colonial nations, and transformed Bourguiba from pro-western champion to outspoken neutralist. The
American government was torn between loyalty to an ally, on the one hand,
and sympathy for the Algerian rebels and concern for anti-colonial opinion,
on the other. Its scrupulous attempts to offend neither side inevitably ended
by displeasing both, and it was no more able than Bourguiba, the United Nations, or any other third party to effect a settlement. France ultimately
found a leader, General de Gaulle, who was able to terminate the bitter
struggle in 1962 by granting independence to Algeria. Only time could reveal whether the long struggle had fatally weakened western influence in
North Africa.

Meanwhile, the cold war had sucked sub-Saharan Africa into its vortex.
Soviet attacks on western imperialism and white supremacy in this vast region began in earnest in 1958, as the first new nations began to emerge from
colonial status. Ghana, for example, maintained a policy of nonalignment
but espoused a pan-African nationalism that frequently arrayed her against
the West. Guinea went much further toward direct alignment with Moscow.
The Soviets, unencumbered by any liabilities of imperialism in Africa or traditions of white supremacy, enjoyed great advantage over the western powers in bidding for the friendship of the new African nations. The United
States again found itself caught between sympathy for African aspirations
and the demands of its NATO partners with colonies in the area.

The first real test of whether Soviet Communism could subvert the African independence movement came when Belgium hastily granted freedom

to the Congo in June 1960. Congolese leaders had barely taken the reins of government before mutiny in the native army and widespread looting and violence broke out. Belgium, alarmed for the safety of its nationals still on the scene, hastily reinforced the handful of white troops remaining in the Congo and thereby touched off new violence. The Congolese Premier, Patrice Lumumba, asked the United Nations on July 10 for assistance against "external aggression" and hinted that he would seek help elsewhere if the UN did not provide it.

Chaos quickly engulfed the unhappy Congo. The province of Katanga, from whose rich mineral resources and prosperous mining companies the new republic planned to derive much of its revenue, seceded on July 11 under the leadership of Moise Tshombe. Part of neighboring Kasai did the same a month later. Lumumba, seeking a unified state under a strong central government, tried to put down the secessionist movements and soon won the support of Ghana, Guinea, and the Soviet Union. Indeed, he welcomed technicians and military equipment sent by the Soviet bloc. Joseph Kasavubu, the Congolese President, grew alarmed at Lumumba's Communist leanings and dismissed the Premier in September 1960. The so-called parliament restored him to power, but the army disbanded parliament, arrested Lumumba in December, ousted the Soviet and Czechoslovakian missions, and endeavored to come to terms with secessionist Katanga and Kasai. The internal struggle became three-cornered when the followers of Lumumba, still recognized by the Soviets as Premier, organized a new separatist movement in Eastern and Kivu provinces. Virtual anarchy prevailed in much of the country.

The United Nations did what it could to deal with the problem. The Security Council on July 14 asked Belgium to withdraw its troops and authorized creation of a multinational peace force by the Secretary-General. A resolution of July 22 urged more haste upon Belgium and recommended that all states refrain from interfering. While the Soviets accused NATO of plotting to restore colonialism in the Congo, and affirmed their readiness to combat this move, Moscow and Washington exchanged blunt warnings about keeping troops out of the new republic. In assembling the peace force Hammarskjold was careful to draw largely upon African and Asian contingents and sought no aid from the major powers.

Tshombe's recalcitrance added to the general difficulty. The Katangan leader first defied, and then proved unco-operative in his dealings with the central government; refused to permit the United Nations forces to enter Katanga; and drew threats from Ghana and Russia to force his adherence to a unified Congo. This produced another resolution from the Security Council on August 7, proclaiming that the UN command would have to enter Katanga but must not be employed, as Lumumba and the Soviets obviously wished, to assist any party in the Congo's internal dispute.

This last proved an impossible directive. The United Nations force, eventually totaling nearly 20,000 men, could not restore peace to the Congo without inadvertently aiding one faction or another. Khrushchev was convinced that the United Nations had connived against Lumumba in favor of Kasavubu, especially after the General Assembly voted on November 22 to seat Kasavubu's delegates instead of Lumumba's. When Congolese factionalism became more sharply three-cornered after Lumumba's arrest in December 1960, the Soviets supported his cause against both the central government and Katanga and wanted the UN command to do the same. The West backed the Kasavubu regime, and the United Nations troops tried to avoid partisanship in coping with an impossible situation. The cost of maintaining its force in the Congo threatened the United Nations with bankruptcy when the Communist bloc and several other countries refused to contribute to its support. Involvement also led to tragic death for Hammarskjold. He was killed when his airplane crashed in Northern Rhodesia on September 18, 1961, on a flight to Katanga.

High melodrama was added in the same year when Lumumba escaped from prison, was recaptured and confined in Katanga, and was later murdered in mysterious circumstances that suggested Tshombe's connivance. Soviet and African leaders demanded extreme measures, but Lumumba's Communist-oriented movement gradually faded into impotence. Tshombe's Katanga, however, steadfastly refused to submit to the authority of the central government and eventually offered armed resistance to the UN command. Cyrille Adoula, the new Congolese Premier appointed in 1961, proved an able moderate who won support from both western and African governments, and he was finally able with the help of UN troops to bring Tshombe to terms.

Even so, the situation remained confused and unstable in the early 1960's, with likelihood of further violence and few prospects for an early solution to Congolese problems. The Congo had vividly illustrated both the disruptive effects of East-West rivalry upon local conditions and the internal difficulties that threatened the stability and progress of emergent Africa. Other new states in sub-Saharan Africa managed during their first two or three years of existence to avoid anarchy or civil war. Their relative stability at least raised the hope that the inevitable difficulties confronting them might be faced without ruinous exposure to international politics or the cold war. But progress on the long road to domestic security and well-being had barely begun for most of Africa.

257. *The Western Hemisphere*

The New World, oldest and until recently the paramount sphere of American diplomatic activity, was largely overshadowed after 1945 by the greater urgency of new commitments in other continents. The United States, in its preoccupation with NATO, the Marshall Plan, Germany, Korea, SEATO, the Baghdad Pact, and Suez paid relatively less attention to the Monroe Doctrine, the Good Neighbor policy, or the Organization of American States. But conditions in Latin America offered a tempting target for Communist exploitation, and geographic remoteness proved no barrier. Poverty, overpopulation, social discontent, reactionary or unstable governments, sensitive nationalism, and hatred of imperialism—in this case focused entirely upon the United States—were facts of life in most countries south of the Rio Grande. The *status quo,* here as in other areas, was under massive assault. The United States did not awaken to the full implications of this process in the New World until Communism established a firm beachhead in the very center of the hemisphere in 1960.

In its failure the United States was partly negligent and partly a victim of circumstances. It could not change the fact that its wealth was a source of envy, its power a source of alarm, its diplomacy in the early twentieth century a source of resentment, and its necessary footholds in Panama and Guantánamo, Cuba, a source of irritation south of the border. There were no easy solutions to Latin America's underlying economic problems: a rate of population increase that nullified gains in productivity; and overdependence upon foreign trade, the United States market, and a single-export commodity subject to fluctuating world prices.[15] A wave of revolutions in Latin America during the 1950's swept away traditional military dictatorships in favor of more or less democratic governments, but the very dictates of a well-intentioned Good Neighbor policy often meant that the United States lost rather than gained by these upheavals. In the interests of hemispheric solidarity, the American government cultivated friendly relations with despotic regimes and thereby antagonized democratic leaders who came to power later. Careful adherence by the United States to the doctrine of non-intervention, upon which Latin America insisted, meant that triumphs over dictatorship were achieved without help from Washington. Though it often had no real alternative in such cases, the United States was widely criticized for alleged lack of sympathy with Latin American democratic movements.

The United States government occasionally contributed more actively to this Latin American image of a reactionary and neo-imperialist "colossus of the North." It was sometimes unduly lavish in its praise of Latin tyrants. It often seemed to prefer an orderly dictatorship, however unpopular and repressive, to an unstable or radically inclined democracy. It did not always act promptly in suspending arms shipments when such weapons were used to suppress domestic opposition to authoritarian regimes. And it persisted, until late in the decade, in stressing the importance of private investment rather than its own aid as the best means of promoting Latin American economies.[16] Although the large volume of United States private investment

∿∿∿∿∿∿∿∿∿∿∿∿∿∿∿∿

[15] A few figures suggest the economic dilemma faced by many Latin American countries. Economic growth rate for the region as a whole was high—approximately 5.5 per cent each year in the decade 1946–56, as opposed to 5 per cent in western Europe and 4 per cent in the United States; and there was an estimated increase in gross product from $32.2 billion in 1946 to $47.2 billion ten years later. But these gains were largely canceled by inequitable distribution, inflation, and population increases that kept per capita income low.

Dependence on foreign trade was shown by the fact that, whereas the United States normally exported about 10 per cent of its total production, many Latin American countries exported as much as 80 per cent. Dependence on the United States market was shown by the fact that this country took about 80 per cent of Latin America's copper; 70 per cent of its coffee, lead, and zinc; and large percentages of other basic products. And nearly every Latin American country depended largely upon a single product, such as coffee, sugar, copper, or tin, in its export trade. Latin American requests that the Washington government grant preferential treatment and stabilize prices of these commodities lacked appeal in Washington, since any such action would mean higher consumer prices in the United States.

[16] Aid to Latin America under the Mutual Security Act was minuscule compared to the huge amounts expended in Europe and Asia. For example, 3 per cent of the $2.76 billion mutual security appropriation for 1955 was allocated south of the Rio Grande.

south of the border conferred undeniable benefits, Latin Americans were far from satisfied with the over-all results.[17]

Communism acquired its first foothold in the New World in the Central American republic of Guatemala, where a long overdue social revolution in 1944 had overthrown a reactionary regime. Guatemala, eager for reform, moved farther to the left after the election of Jacobo Arbenz in 1950, and a small Communist party had won effective control of the government by 1953. It immediately sought to expropriate foreign assets in Guatemala and launched subversive movements in neighboring countries.

Dulles wanted the Organization of American States to consider some form of joint action or strong protest, but Latin American respect for nonintervention limited the possibilities. The Secretary of State could obtain no more than a resolution, passed at the Tenth Inter-American Conference in Caracas in March 1954, defining "domination or control of the political institutions of any American State by the international communist movement" as a threat to the "sovereignty and political independence of the American States, endangering the peace of America." Unabashed, Guatemalan leaders obtained a shipment of Czechoslovakian military equipment and fomented major strikes in neighboring Honduras in May 1954. Dulles denounced these actions and accused Guatemala of planning aggression, and the Defense Department furnished weapons to Honduras and Nicaragua under recent mutual defense pacts.

Arbenz invoked martial law in Guatemala on June 8 and claimed that a foreign plot to overthrow him was under way. A few days later a small force of exiles crossed into the country from Honduras and united with dissident army units to challenge the Communist regime. Guatemala demanded an emergency meeting of the Security Council, charging Honduras and Nicaragua with aggression "at the instigation of certain foreign monopolies." A heated debate followed, with Russia demanding instant action and vetoing an American-supported resolution to refer the problem to the Organization of American States. While the Soviet delegate charged that the OAS was controlled in Washington, the American delegate angrily warned the Russians to "stay out of this hemisphere." The Council finally passed a French resolution calling for immediate cessation of hostilities, then met again a

The United States also provided valuable technical assistance, short-run aid in the form of stabilization programs and emergency credits, and indirect aid through public institutions like the Export-Import Bank, International Monetary Fund, and World Bank. But public assistance was neither substantial enough nor comprehensive enough to meet the basic capital or welfare needs of Latin American countries.

[17] On the positive side, the $6,556,000,000 of private United States investment in Latin America in 1955 (the figure reached $9,000,000,000 by 1957) was responsible for producing goods and services with an annual market value of $5,000,000,000. In 1955, United States companies produced 30 per cent of Latin America's exports and 20 per cent of its industrial output, paid over $1,000,000,000 in taxes to Latin American governments, and employed over 600,000 Latin American citizens.

However, critics argued that this private investment was unevenly applied (45 per cent confined to Venezuela and Brazil, for example, and 30 per cent in the petroleum industry alone). To radical reformers it smacked of imperialism and a form of economic thralldom to the United States. It certainly did not provide the kind of balanced, comprehensive, long-range economic assistance that most Latin American countries needed.

few days later when Guatemala and Russia charged that the resolution had not been complied with.

Over Soviet protests, the Council decided to defer action until an investigation by the Inter-American Peace Committee (a mediatory adjunct of the OAS) had been completed. Before this happened, Arbenz had fled and Guatemala had come under control of a strongly authoritarian anti-Communist government approved by the United States. The Eisenhower administration denied complicity in the movement to overthrow Arbenz, but there is little doubt that sympathy and at least indirect support from Washington made it possible for the little rebellion to succeed.

Communism did not duplicate its temporary achievement in Guatemala until the end of the decade, but Communist agitation in other parts of Latin America continued. It was backed by the strategy of cultural and economic penetration that Russia and Communist China were pursuing in other areas, and the United States was awakened to the danger when Communist-inspired mobs assaulted Vice President Nixon in Peru and Venezuela in 1958. In the meantime, the Washington government had revised its treaty with Panama in 1955 in response to Panamanian demand [18] and was endeavoring within certain limits to promote economic progress and better relations south of the border. But its unwillingness to provide large-scale economic aid or modify certain trade and tariff policies remained a continual source of irritation below the Rio Grande. Economic and social discontent in many countries had clearly passed the point where assurances, palliatives, or stopgap aid would serve. Nixon warned the administration upon his return that there were many non-Communists in the crowds that menaced him in Lima and Caracas. The United States began re-examining and liberalizing its economic policies, promoted regional free trade agreements in Latin America, and supported an international program to stabilize the price of coffee. Most important, it agreed in 1959 to participate in an Inter-American Development Bank with a capital of $1,000,000,000, of which the United States subscribed 25 per cent and guaranteed an additional 20 per cent, for both commercial and "soft" loans to Latin American countries.

But time was running out for the United States. Communism found its next major opportunity with the overthrow of Fulgencio Batista's harsh dictatorship in Cuba on January 1, 1959. The successful revolutionary movement was led by Fidel Castro, whose new regime veered with unexpected rapidity down the path of extremism and Communist alignment. Castro had announced a sweeping land reform program that worried foreign investors, and he had never concealed his antipathy toward the United States for its tolerance of Batista and other dictators. The American government was therefore prepared for difficulty even after extending prompt recognition and friendly gestures to the new Cuban government, but not for the intensity of Castro's anti-American policy or the violence of his assault upon the *status quo* in the Western Hemisphere.

While Castro leaned more and more toward views held by Communist

---

[18] The revised treaty of 1955 increased the annuity paid by the United States to Panama from $430,000 to $1,930,000, enabled Panama to tax its citizens who worked in the Canal Zone, transferred certain Canal Zone lands back to Panama, and altered in Panama's favor several American economic privileges in and about the Zone.

supporters in the Cuban revolutionary movement, and became increasingly virulent in his denunciations of the United States, Cuba became a vast head-quarters for Communist intrigue and subversive planning. Communists and radical exiles from other Caribbean republics converged on the island to plot and prepare invasions, accumulate weapons, and conduct training exercises. Reports of armed expeditions and imminent invasions led to an inter-American Foreign Ministers' meeting in August 1959, but Secretary of State Christian Herter's [19] hopes for joint action were reduced to a pair of resolutions condemning totalitarianism and reaffirming democratic principles. Meanwhile, Castro accused the United States of harboring and equipping his enemies, inciting sabotage and counterrevolutionary activity, and permitting air attacks on Cuba. His domestic reform program moved markedly leftward, and Cuban seizures of American property totaled $1,000,000,-000 by mid-1960. Relations between the two countries worsened steadily.

The American government grew increasingly exasperated, but it pursued a patient policy toward Castro for eighteen months. The United States was in a dilemma. Military retaliation was unthinkable, and economic retaliation would provoke cries of dollar diplomacy and imperialism throughout Latin America. Yet continued passivity in the face of Castro's sweeping property confiscations might encourage other Latin demagogues to follow suit. American patience weakened when Castro abandoned the hemispheric bloc in the General Assembly and proclaimed a neutralism that echoed the Soviet position; signed an extensive five-year trading agreement with Russia in February 1960; and hinted at a military alliance with the USSR. Eisenhower's patience snapped altogether when Castro, in response to an American memorandum to the Inter-American Peace Committee accusing Cuba of "systematic and provocative" slander, seized a $25,000,000 Texaco refinery in June 1960 for refusing to process Russian crude oil. The President retaliated in early July by cutting American imports of Cuban sugar, thus depriving the island of an annual income of $90,000,000.

The shadow of the cold war was lengthening inexorably across the Western Hemisphere. While Cuba complained of American action before the Security Council, Khrushchev entered the controversy on July 9 with a typical gasconade. He declared that "Soviet artillerymen can support Cuba with rocket fire" in event of an American attack on the island. The Soviet Premier struck at the very cornerstone of America's New World policy a few days later by proclaiming that the Monroe Doctrine was obsolete, had "died a natural death," and should not be permitted to "poison the air by its decay." The State Department replied on July 14 with the flat statement that the Doctrine was as valid in 1960 as it had been in 1823, and that attempts to extend the Russian system to the New World would be considered dangerous to the peace and safety of the United States. The Soviets continued their denunciation of the Doctrine in the Security Council, calling it a cloak for American territorial greed. The Council voted to refer the United States–Cuba dispute to the Organization of American States.

The OAS was badly torn by the turmoil that seemed about to engulf Latin America. Unstable democratic governments were being threatened from both left and right, as Castro's subversive activities were matched by

――――――――――――――――――

[19] Herter had succeeded the stricken Dulles in April 1959.

similar plots emanating from Rafael S. Trujillo's dictatorship in the Dominican Republic. An attempt by the latter to overthrow the democratic regime of Romulo Betancourt in Venezuela was sharply condemned in August 1960 by the inter-American Foreign Ministers. They voted unanimously to break off diplomatic relations and impose sanctions on the Dominican Republic.

But the OAS could not bring itself to take similar action against Castro. They condemned Sino-Soviet meddling in hemispheric affairs and criticized Cuba indirectly for allowing the Soviets to exploit its internal situation, but the resolutions contained neither overt condemnation nor sanctions. Although the other Latin nations disapproved Cuba's military flirtation with the Soviet Union, many of them sympathized with the broad social objectives of Castro's revolution. A few secretly admired his successful defiance of the "colossus of the North." Those who might otherwise have condemned him were frankly fearful of the effects of such a move upon restive Castro elements in their homelands. For Castro was the spearhead, if not of Communism in the New World, then of widespread social and economic unrest that simmered from Lower California to the Straits of Magellan.

Castro was unintimidated by the tepid OAS resolution, and the United States, deprived of any hope of joint inter-American action, did all it could unilaterally short of military intervention. It imposed an embargo in October 1960 on all exports to Cuba save food, medicine, and medical supplies; set up a naval patrol in the Caribbean in November to prevent rumored Cuban invasions of Nicaragua and Guatemala; and formally severed relations in January 1961. Castro had, in the meantime, recognized Communist China, continued vilifying the United States, expropriated what remained of American businesses in Cuba, threatened to seize the naval base at Guantánamo, and drilled his militia in preparation for an alleged American invasion. It was revealed in January 1961 that American personnel were training anti-Castro Cubans at a secret camp in Guatemala. The American public did not yet know that the Central Intelligence Agency had begun a more systematic program of aiding Cuban exiles in Florida for a military assault on Castro.

As the decade ended, the United States was finally preparing to undertake the broad program of social and economic assistance that might yet prevent other Latin American countries from going the way of Fidel Castro. But it also was faced with a choice between tolerating a Communist outpost on its very doorstep or courting obloquy and world war by trying to destroy it.

258. *The Changing United Nations*

Fittingly enough, the United Nations in the 1950's reflected both the political developments that had remade the postwar world and the pervasive disruptions and tensions generated by the cold war. The organization underwent a variety of changes, demonstrated certain promise, and came finally under an attack that threatened its effectiveness if not its very existence.

One change, already in process during the Truman era, was a continued decline in the importance and usefulness of the Security Council. The presence of the Soviet Union and the western Big Three as permanent members of that body made unanimity on major questions virtually impossible. This meant, for one thing, that Article 43 in the United Nations Charter, which provided for placing military forces at the Council's disposal, was never implemented. It meant, moreover, that constructive action was repeatedly crippled by use of the veto power, available to all permanent members on nonprocedural matters. Russia's persistent and familiar use of this device was irritating but understandable, since western representation on the Council outnumbered that of the Communist bloc. The result was virtual negation of the Council's ability to mediate important disputes or take action against major threats to peace. The organization as a whole, in fact, was not an effective device for settling big issues involving the great powers, and disputes of this sort were increasingly negotiated outside the UN framework.

As the Security Council declined, there was a corresponding if limited expansion in the role of the General Assembly. Its size and composition, especially toward the end of the Eisenhower era, made it more a debating forum for the airing of grievances than a formulator of international policy. But the Assembly on occasion was able to break log jams created by the Security Council. The device that made this possible was a "Uniting for Peace" Resolution of 1950 by which questions deadlocked in the Council might be considered and resolved by the Assembly. Specifically, the resolution provided that seven members of the Council or a majority of all UN members could request an emergency session of the General Assembly on a day's notice. It also invited members to maintain and train military units for special UN duty and provided for a Peace Observation Commission and a recommendatory Collective Security Committee, but these devices proved unimportant. The provision for an emergency session was, however, used effectively during the Suez and Lebanon crises to help settle those disputes.

Far more important than the Assembly's increased influence was its increased size and altered balance. Membership in the United Nations grew slowly, from fifty-one nations to sixty, during the first decade of its existence. In this period the United States was able to muster majorities on important resolutions through the support it normally commanded from its thirteen NATO allies and the twenty Latin American republics. American influence dwindled, however, with the rapid expansion from sixty to 111 members between 1955 and the end of 1962. Five new Communist countries, seven Asian nations, and twenty-eight new African states were included in this influx, which meant that western voting power was increasingly overshadowed by a large Afro-Asian neutralist bloc. Although the Communist bloc often voted with Afro-Asian members on questions involving colonialism and other matters reflecting on the West, the basic shift arising from enlarged membership was the growing influence of the neutral nations as a third force between East and West. The growth of the neutralist bloc encouraged use of the Assembly for propaganda purposes and the introduction of sweeping resolutions, but it also forced both parties in the cold war to take greater cognizance of neutral opinion. And the importance with which the new countries viewed the United Nations augured well for its future survival.

The most significant development during the 1950's was the key role played by the Secretary-General on several important occasions. The first to hold this office was Trygve Lie of Norway, whose attempts to make positive use of it ran afoul of Soviet opposition during the Korean War and thus hampered his effectiveness. Lie was replaced in April 1953 by Dag Hammarskjold of Sweden, whose skill and impartiality soon won the confidence of all parties and enabled him to find solutions to a number of problems. He was able, for example, to secure the release of several American fliers from Communist China in 1955. More important, he engineered a cease-fire between the Arabs and Israel in April 1956, planned the Emergency Force that stabilized conditions after Suez, made arrangements that permitted withdrawal of British and American troops from Jordan and Lebanon in the autumn of 1958, temporarily eased the situation in Laos in 1959, and created the UN Peace Force that went to the Congo in 1960. Hammarskjold's own prestige and ability, together with the machinery that he was able to employ, suggested for a time that the United Nations might be evolving an effective instrument for easing tensions and preserving peace.

Hammarskjold's important role in the Congo crisis, however, roused Soviet ire and soon inspired a Russian campaign to reduce the United Nations to impotence, if not to dissolve it. The refusal of the UN Peace Force to work in Premier Lumumba's behalf in the Congo dispute led Russia to denounce Hammarskjold as a friend of the "NATO colonialists." The Soviets now feared that the recent growth in UN peacekeeping ability through the office of the Secretary-General would work to western advantage and interfere with Communist penetration in underdeveloped areas. They accordingly demanded Hammarskjold's resignation and subjected him to the same attacks and denunciations that had nullified Lie's work. Hammarskjold refused to resign, but Russian opposition led to a decline in his influence. His leadership was already impaired when tragic death overtook him in Africa in 1961, and there was little hope that his successor, U Thant of Burma, would be granted the joint East-West support or emergency authority that Hammarskjold had turned to such good advantage.

Not content with personal attacks on Hammarskjold, the Russians introduced measures that would render the United Nations impotent. They proposed to replace the Secretary-General with a three-man directorate, nicknamed *troika* after the Russian three-horse carriage, representing the East, the West, and the neutralist bloc. Since each director would possess a veto on all action, the Soviets obviously sought to prevent the organization from doing anything against Communist wishes, which would convert it entirely into a useless forum for Soviet agitation and propaganda. The *troika* proposition was temporarily shelved during the selection and incumbency of U Thant as Acting Secretary-General to fill out Hammarskjold's unexpired term, but the Russians reintroduced the idea as the time for a new election in 1963 approached. If they failed to obtain their *troika*, it was probable that they would either block the election of any candidate who might oppose them or prevent the filling of the office altogether. This Russian campaign, together with their generally disruptive tactics at UN sessions and refusal to contribute to the cost of the Congo operation; threatened to subvert the organization entirely to the quarrelsome maneuvers of the cold war.

Despite America's own declining influence in the United Nations, the Eisenhower administration followed Truman's example and gave it firm and unwavering support. The President was necessarily forced to seek solutions to many important problems outside its framework, but he lost no opportunity to affirm his belief in the organization and recommend adherence to its principles. His insistence upon placing observance of the UN Charter over loyalty to his allies during the Suez crisis was eloquent testimony to this faith. Although the Soviet assault in 1960 confronted the international body with its gravest challenge as Eisenhower left office, it was probably still true that the United Nations remained, as he termed it, "the soundest hope for peace in the world."

CHAPTER

33

New Frontiers and
The Great Society

THE 1960's saw the return of the Democratic party to power in Washington. A young and vigorous President, John F. Kennedy, defining programs to deal with the increasing complexities of American society, asked for renewed dedication and sacrifice from the people. Congress was slow to heed the call, and the President's major tasks lay unfinished at the time of his tragic death in the streets of Dallas. However, under the leadership of Lyndon B. Johnson, a vast new scheme of social legislation, comparable in scope to the New Deal and the New Freedom, was enacted. The first years of the decade also saw the United States approach the brink of nuclear war with Russia. Although amicable relations with the Soviet Union were restored following the crisis, a war in Southeast Asia soon brought dissension at home and the danger of a direct confrontation with Communist China.

259. The Election of 1960

The American people undertook preparations for the presidential election of 1960 against a backdrop of economic uncertainty at home and setbacks and challenges in international affairs. The Democrats, encouraged by the certainty that they would not be facing Eisenhower in a presidential race again, thanks to the Twenty-Second Amendment, engaged in one of their customary uninhibited contests for the presidential nomination. Four Democratic candidates had formally entered the race by the early months of 1960: Senators Hubert H. Humphrey of Minnesota, John F. Kennedy of Massachusetts, Lyndon B. Johnson of Texas, and Stuart Symington of Missouri. There was also considerable support for the party's nominee in 1952 and 1956, Adlai Stevenson. Stevenson never became a formal candidate in 1960, but he was amenable to a draft.

The forty-two-year-old Kennedy, first Roman Catholic to contend seriously for the presidency since 1928, quickly emerged as Democratic front runner. His triumph over Humphrey in the Wisconsin primary by a six-to-four margin on April 5 was inconclusive, since most Kennedy support came from Wisconsin's strongly Catholic districts. But five weeks later, in heavily Protestant West Virginia, Kennedy's well-run and generously financed campaign ended with a decisive triumph over the Minnesotan. Humphrey thereupon withdrew, and Kennedy went on to record impressive primary victories in Nebraska, Maryland, and Oregon. These victories, together with earlier successes in New Hampshire and Indiana, caused Democratic leaders in the East and Midwest to climb on his bandwagon. Kennedy and his managers also worked unceasingly during May and June for support in other areas. They came to the Democratic convention in Los Angeles on July 11 confident of at least 600 of the 761 votes necessary for the nomination.

Delegates converged on Los Angeles in a perplexed and sober mood, shaken by recent international events. The party platform, adopted on July 12, proclaimed that an enduring peace could be obtained only by restoring American "military, economic and moral" strength. Charging the Eisenhower administration with having lost America's "position of pre-eminence," it promised to "recast" national military capacity along more effective lines. Other Democratic pledges included more systematic planning for disarmament, reshaping of American foreign aid, with new emphasis upon economic assistance and long-range international co-operation, promotion of economic growth without inflation, and an end to the Republican "high-interest, tight-money policy" that had allegedly stifled economic expansion in recent years. The platform also contained the strongest civil rights plank in American history.[1]

The convention then proceeded, after the most intricate and strenuous political maneuvering, to nominate John F. Kennedy on the first ballot. Symington's chances had faded with Kennedy's victory in West Virginia; Johnson's, with his failure to build substantial western support for his candidacy. Determined efforts by Stevenson strategists to win support from favorite-son candidates in a few key states and break the tenuous allegiance of certain Kennedy delegates elsewhere proved unsuccessful against the well-disciplined Kennedy organization. In a move that

---

[1] It pledged full use of federal power and leadership to assure equal rights and opportunities in housing, employment, schools, public facilities, and voting. The civil rights plank also promised to move toward elimination of literacy tests and poll taxes as voting requirements, called upon every state affected by the Brown decision of 1954 to submit desegregation plans by 1963, and openly endorsed the recent "sit-in" demonstrations and similar peaceful protests by Negro citizens.

surprised veteran politicians and the public alike, Kennedy then requested and obtained Johnson's nomination for the vice presidency.

"The world is changing," Kennedy proclaimed in his acceptance speech on July 15. "The old era is ending . . . and we stand today on the edge of a New Frontier—the frontier of the 1960's—a frontier of unknown opportunities and perils—a frontier of unfulfilled hopes and threats. . . . But the New Frontier of which I speak is not a set of promises— it is a set of challenges. It sums up, not what I intend to offer the American people, but what I intend to ask of them."

No comparable struggle for the presidential nomination took place within the Republican party. It had been clear for months that Vice President Richard M. Nixon enjoyed overwhelming support from party regulars in all parts of the country. His only serious contender was Governor Nelson A. Rockefeller of New York, a progressive Republican who had won national prominence with an impressive victory over Governor Averell Harriman in 1958. Rockefeller formed an organization and sought party support during 1959. He was popular among independents and liberals within his party, but he quickly discovered that Republican regulars and important financial backers were firmly committed to Nixon. Rockefeller formally announced his withdrawal as an avowed candidate in December 1959.

Rockefeller could not win the nomination, but he was able to exert decisive influence on the party platform. Disturbed by recent international developments, and convinced that the Eisenhower administration had permitted America's military, economic, and diplomatic strength to deteriorate, Rockefeller on June 8 submitted a sweeping program for reform and improvement in these and other areas, including civil rights. It was tantamount to frank repudiation of many Eisenhower policies. The Governor let it be known indirectly that he would accept a draft and threatened an open fight for his program on the convention floor if his views were not incorporated in the GOP platform.

Nixon privately agreed with much of Rockefeller's indictment and dreaded an open rupture with the Governor's wing of the party. Yet he did not dare to join Rockefeller in a virtual repudiation of Eisenhower. Rockefeller flatly rejected a compromise draft platform offered by the Nixon forces. Then the Vice President met the Governor secretly at the latter's New York apartment three days before the GOP convention opened in Chicago on July 25, and accepted nearly all of Rockefeller's demands. They were embodied in the "Compact of Fifth Avenue," published in the press on July 23. It called for a more imaginative foreign policy, a much-accelerated defense program, reorganization of the executive branch "to cope effectively with modern problems and challenges," stimulation of the economy, strong federal action in behalf of civil rights, a program of medical care for the aged, and aid to education.

News of the Compact immediately touched off angry explosions within the GOP. The platform committee, made up entirely of conservatives, felt betrayed and rebelled openly for a time. Senator Barry M. Goldwater of Arizona, leading spokesman of the Republican right wing, denounced the Compact as the "Munich of the Republican Party." And from President Eisenhower, then on vacation in Newport, Rhode Island, came angry retorts.

The Nixon forces used every ounce of political leverage they possessed to placate the conservatives and then to force partial acceptance of the Compact. The GOP platform, adopted on July 27, represented a complete victory for Rockefeller in the field of civil rights: its plank was almost as strong as that of the Democrats. The platform praised the Eisenhower record in foreign affairs and national defense but pledged thorough modernization and acceleration of military programs in all fields and promised not to let budgetary concerns put a "price ceiling on America's security." The economic plank, while giving due praise to the prosperity of the past eight years, admitted the need for a higher growth rate. Warning against "massive new Federal spending," the document promised to stimulate economic expansion through tax reform, a stable dollar, an end to featherbedding, and other stimulants to private initiative and investment. All in all, the Republican platform of 1960 was a far more progressive and vigorous document than it would have been without Rockefeller's intervention. The platform crisis over, the convention proceeded on the following day, July 28, to nominate Nixon by acclamation on the first ballot. With equal celerity it nominated the man designated by Nixon as his choice for the vice presidency—Henry Cabot Lodge, Jr., of Massachusetts, Ambassador to the United Nations.

Personalities and emotions played a more important role than issues in the campaign that ensued. This was true, in part, because the two candidates seemed to agree basically on most major questions. Both were internationalists in foreign policy and moderate progressives on social and economic matters; their programs differed in detail and emphasis but hardly in kind. Kennedy's central theme was the need for positive leadership, public sacrifice, and bold national effort to "get America moving again." Nixon denied that the military and economic situation was as grave as his opponent claimed. But Nixon also repeatedly affirmed that the United States could not afford to stand still or rest upon past laurels, and he repudiated complacency with earnest sincerity.

The advantage lay with Nixon during the first phase of the campaign. Kennedy was tied down in Congress until early September by the futile, barren, postconvention session of the Eighty-sixth Congress. Nixon was meanwhile free to launch his campaign. Moveover, Nixon at the outset was far better known in the country at large because of his active role in the Eisenhower administration. He emphasized this point throughout the campaign (abandoning the narrow partisanship and hardhitting tactics of his early career), and for a time he made telling use of the argument that Nixon and Lodge were far more qualified for the awesome task of national leadership than the youthful, inexperienced Kennedy. Nixon enjoyed a substantial lead in late-summer public opinion polls.

The picture changed drastically, however, on account of an innovation that may have been the most decisive single feature of the campaign: four nationally televised debates between Nixon and Kennedy from September 26 to October 21. The two men were unable to explore issues thoughtfully or at length, and few clear distinctions in their basic positions emerged. But Kennedy profited enormously from these encounters. The polls in October showed him in the lead, and veteran reporters were increasingly impressed by the size and enthusiasm of the crowds that turned out to see him. Democratic confidence and Republican gloom waxed steadily as election time neared. But effective stump speeches by President Eisenhower and a massive Republican television effort during the last week of the campaign produced a marked resurgence of Nixon strength and reduced Kennedy's margin to the vanishing point.

Early returns from the East and South on election night, November 8, 1960, indicated a Kennedy landslide. But his early lead dwindled steadily as returns from the midwestern, prairie, mountain, and Pacific states came in. The decision remained in doubt until the morning of November 9. Then complete returns from Illinois, Texas, and Minnesota gave these states and the presidency to Kennedy by a narrow margin. He received, all told, 34,227,000 popular and 303 electoral votes; Nixon, 34,108,000 popular and 219 electoral votes.[2] Kennedy's popular majority was 120,000 votes, or less than one fifth of 1 per cent of the total cast! The Democrats retained control of Congress, although their large majorities of 1958 were slightly reduced by a loss of two seats in the Senate and twenty-two in the House. The new Democratic majorities were 64 to 36 and 263 to 174, respectively.

The election of 1960 provided endless material for analysis and controversy. Voting patterns displayed, superficially at least, a marked sectional hue. The historic Democratic coalition of East and South provided Kennedy with the bulk of his electoral support. He swept the populous Northeast, losing only Maine, New Hampshire, and Vermont. In the South, Texas and Louisiana renewed their Democratic allegiance, thanks largely to Lyndon Johnson's presence on the ticket, and five other states returned Democratic majorities, although Nixon duplicated Eisenhower's triumphs in Virginia, Florida, and Tennessee. In the border region, Kennedy lost Kentucky but won handily in West Virginia and narrowly in Missouri. Michigan, Illinois, and Minnesota were Kennedy's only triumphs in the Middle West. And Nixon carried every state, except Nevada, New Mexico, and Hawaii, in the region west of the hundredth meridian.

But sectionalism was both inadequate and deceptive as a key to American sentiment in this complex presidential campaign. Closer examination revealed that changes in popular voting habits observable during the 1950's—increased ticket splitting, independent voting, erosion of traditional party loyalties in all regions—were more pronounced than ever. Both candidates ran ahead of their tickets in some areas and behind in others. The returns proved that the disappearance of the "Solid South" in presidential elections was no temporary phenomenon dependent upon Eisenhower's popularity. The anti-Democratic coalition that had emerged in the South after midcentury gave Nixon nearly half of the southern popular vote—almost as large a share as Eisenhower had received in 1952 and 1956. Conversely, Kennedy ran surprisingly well in such traditionally Republican areas as northern New England, parts of the Middle West, and the suburbs. Negroes and other minority groups voted heavily for the

[2] Six of Alabama's eleven Democratic electors, and all eight of Mississippi's, were unpledged. They cast their votes for Senator Harry F. Byrd of Virginia, who also received one vote from a defecting Republican elector in Oklahoma.

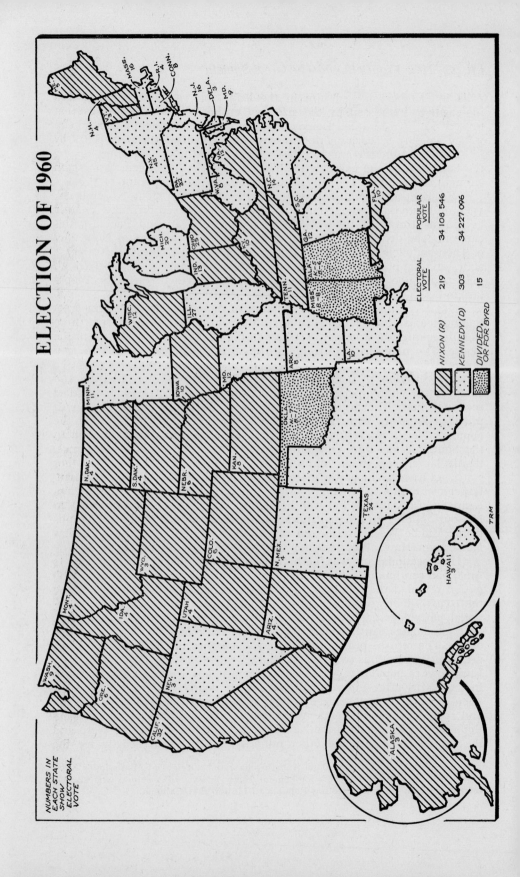

ELECTION OF 1960

NUMBERS IN
EACH STATE
SHOW
ELECTORAL
VOTE

	ELECTORAL VOTE	POPULAR VOTE
NIXON (R)	219	34 108 546
KENNEDY (D)	303	34 227 096
DIVIDED, OR FOR BYRD	15	

Democratic candidate. The results also proved that a Roman Catholic was no longer automatically barred from winning the nation's highest office.

260. New Frontiers at Home

Thousands of Americans lined the streets of Washington on January 20, 1961, and millions more watched on television as John F. Kennedy's inaugural procession moved down Pennsylvania Avenue from the White House to the climactic ceremony at the east front of the Capitol. A heavy snow had blanketed the city the night before, and the day was windy and raw. Chief Justice Warren administered the oath of office. Then the new President turned to face the audience and delivered his inaugural address to an expectant nation and a curious world.

"Let the word go forth from this time and place, to friend and foe alike," he proclaimed, "that the torch has been passed to a new generation of Americans—born in this century, tempered by war, disciplined by a hard and bitter peace, proud of our ancient heritage." Pledging loyalty to America's allies, firm support to the United Nations, and generous aid to underdeveloped countries, Kennedy called for a "grand and global alliance" against "the common enemies of man: tyranny, poverty, disease and war itself." To "those nations who would make themselves our adversary," he suggested that "both sides begin anew the quest for peace."

He concluded with an eloquent appeal: "In your hands, my fellow citizens, more than mine, will rest the final success or failure of our course. . . . In the long history of the world, only a few generations have been granted the role of defending freedom in its hour of maximum danger. . . . The energy, the faith, the devotion which we bring to this endeavor will light our country and all who serve it—and the glow from that fire can truly light the world. And so, my fellow Americans: ask not what your country can do for you—ask what you can do for your country."

Admirers and detractors alike agreed that the man who acceded to leadership in January 1961 was a fascinating and remarkable individual. As presidential backgrounds go, his was both unusual and instructive. John Fitzgerald Kennedy was born in Brookline, Massachusetts, on May 29, 1917, the second of nine children. Both his grandfathers were Irish Catholic immigrants' sons who rose to prominence in Boston's Irish Democratic politics. His father, Joseph P. Kennedy, made a large fortune in banking, stocks, and real estate, later supported Franklin Roosevelt, and served as Ambassador to Great Britain during the late 1930's.

John F. Kennedy was graduated *cum laude* from Harvard in 1940 and published his first book, an outgrowth of his senior thesis, that summer. A junior naval officer during the Second World War, Kennedy won the Navy and Marine Corps Medal for rescuing the surviving crew members of his PT boat after a Japanese destroyer had sunk it off the Solomon Islands in 1943. He entered Democratic politics after the war and was elected in 1946 to the House of Representatives from Massachusetts' Eleventh District, in the Boston area. Six years later he ran for the Senate against the Republican incumbent, Henry Cabot Lodge, Jr. It was a formidable undertaking. Lodge, with a distinguished name and record, was also campaign manager for the Republican presidential candidate, Eisenhower.

The young Democrat stumped Massachusetts with tireless energy and defeated Lodge by 70,000 votes, while Eisenhower carried the state by over 200,000.

Kennedy's congressional career was marked by moderate progressivism, broadening national awareness, ambition, and remarkable vote-getting ability. He was re-elected to the Senate in 1958 by 875,000 votes, the largest majority in Massachusetts history. Almost from the moment of his defeat for the vice-presidential nomination in 1956, Kennedy launched an unrelenting campaign for the presidency that culminated first with his convention victory at Los Angeles in July 1960 and finally with his narrow triumph over Nixon in November.

Kennedy, the youngest man ever elected to the presidency, displayed an impressive, if frequently baffling, combination of personal qualities. It was impossible to tell, at the outset of his tenure, whether they added up to greatness, but there was a compelling quality about the new President that suggested large potential. Impressed observers, looking perhaps too hard for parallels in an age that demanded wise leadership, found certain resemblances to illustrious predecessors. He shared Theodore Roosevelt's magnetism, dash, and robust energy, and Woodrow Wilson's keen intelligence and eloquence. His poise, charm, wit, self-assurance, and political skill were reminiscent of Franklin Roosevelt. He had something of Andrew Jackson's cold anger and no-quarter combativeness when challenged. His sensitive awareness of the American political process was almost on a par with Lincoln's. He shared with all of them a leader's fascination for political power.

The parallels were probably forced. John F. Kennedy resembled none of these men, nor all of them together, and the style and ability that he brought to the presidency were uniquely his own. He was well informed, incisive, and articulate, and he respected these qualities in others. He was eager to accept responsibility. Critics detected a streak of ruthlessness and feared that his ambition and love of power were excessive. Though he inspired fierce devotion and loyalty among his followers, even admirers sometimes expressed a certain doubt. Coolly level-headed, he was able at all times to view situations, associates, enemies, and himself with remarkable detachment. This was a practical asset, but some believed that it might also reflect a basic limitation. He was a realist, a believer in the art of the possible; his wife once defined him as "an idealist without illusions." Kennedy's progressivism, his desire to promote human welfare at home and abroad, were undoubtedly genuine, but they seemed to represent an intellectual rather than an emotional commitment.

Kennedy's Cabinet, carefully chosen in pre-inaugural weeks, was formally announced on January 20, 1961. Among the more surprising appointments was that of Dean Rusk, then president of the Rockefeller Foundation, as Secretary of State. Rusk was an experienced diplomat, but his name had not been among those mentioned for this important post. Adlai Stevenson, mentioned frequently and favored by liberal Democrats for the office of Secretary of State, was named instead as Ambassador to the UN. Another surprise, aimed at reassuring "sound money" conservatives, was the appointment of the New York banker, C. Douglas Dillon, Eisenhower's Under Secretary of State, as Secretary of the Treasury,

Another Republican, Robert S. McNamara, left the presidency of Ford Motor Company to become Secretary of Defense.

Most of the other posts went to experienced Democratic politicians. They included the President's brother, Robert F. Kennedy, as Attorney General; J. Edward Day of California, Postmaster General; former Representative Stewart L. Udall of Arizona, Secretary of the Interior; former Governor Orville L. Freeman of Minnesota, Secretary of Agriculture; former Governor Luther H. Hodges of North Carolina, Secretary of Commerce; and former Governor Abraham A. Ribicoff of Connecticut, Secretary of Health, Education and Welfare. The Secretaryship of Labor went to Arthur J. Goldberg, prominent labor lawyer.[3]

As Kennedy had hoped, public imagination was quickly stirred by the vigor, spirit, and industry of the new administration. Public opinion polls taken a few weeks after the inauguration indicated that fully 75 per cent of the people "approved" of their new President—a popularity rating as high as Eisenhower ever achieved. But this popularity, he soon discovered, could not be easily translated into congressional support for his ambitious legislative program. The major roadblock in his path was the coalition of conservative Republican and southern Democratic congressmen that had been powerful enough to defeat or weaken much welfare legislation since 1938. Kennedy usually had a reliable working majority in the Senate. But the 261 Democrats in the lower house included some 100 Southerners, at least half of whom voted consistently with the Republicans against progressive measures. Keeping this coalition from mustering a majority against any given bill required every ounce of pressure and persuasive skill that the administration could bring to bear.

The only parts of Kennedy's program that came through this gauntlet relatively unscathed during the Eighty-seventh Congress of 1961–2 were those pertaining to national defense and foreign policy. The recognizable menace of Communist aggression enabled the President to command strong legislative support for nearly all his proposals to strengthen the free world. Congress readily appropriated nearly $47,000,000,000 for defense in 1961 and over $48,000,000,000 in 1962, on both occasions actually exceeding the amount Kennedy had asked for. The President requested and obtained authority in 1961 to call as many as 250,000 reservists into the armed forces for twelve months. Congress renewed this authority, reducing the figure to 150,000 in 1962. It readily approved his request of May 25, 1961, for a space program designed to put a man on the moon before 1970. Congress also authorized, in September 1961, creation of the Arms Control and Disarmament Agency, an independent planning and advisory body responsible to the State Department.

The President encountered more resistance to his far-reaching aid and trade programs, but he obtained much of what he wanted. Congress disappointed him on only three items. They cut $870,000,000 from the

[3] There were only three changes during the Kennedy administration. Ribicoff resigned as Secretary of HEW in July 1962 in order to run for the Senate, and was succeeded by Mayor Anthony J. Celebrezze of Cleveland. Secretary of Labor Goldberg, appointed to the Supreme Court in August 1962, was succeeded by the Under Secretary of Labor, W. Willard Wirtz. Postmaster General J. Edward Day was replaced by John A. Gronouski in September 1963.

$5,000,000,000 that he requested for foreign aid in 1961, and over $1,000,000,000 from the $5,000,000,000 that he asked for in 1962. And they refused to approve his request for long-term borrowing authority, which would have enabled him to avoid the annual battle for new appropriations and develop foreign aid projects on a long-range rather than year-to-year basis.

But these defeats were more than offset by a number of substantial triumphs. Congressmen responded to his proposal for a five-year program of aid to underdeveloped countries by creating the Development Loan Fund in 1961. They authorized $1,200,000,000 for the Fund in its first year and annual appropriations of $1,500,000,000 over the next four. At Kennedy's urging, they appropriated $600,000,000 for loans to Latin American countries, implementing a program authorized by the Eisenhower administration in 1960. Meanwhile, Kennedy proposed a far more comprehensive program for Latin American aid in March 1961. This was the Alliance for Progress, formally launched at an Inter-American Conference in Uruguay on August 16, 1961, and signed by all the American republics except Cuba. The Alliance, envisaging a massive ten-year program for economic and social improvement in Latin America, promised at least $20,000,000,000 in foreign aid, over half to be provided by the United States, and the balance by international agencies, European countries, and private capital.

There were other victories. The Senate consented to the ratification of a treaty in March 1961 making the United States a member of the newly created Organization for Economic Cooperation and Development (OECD). Including the United States, Canada, and eighteen western European countries in its membership, the OECD was designed to improve world trade, promote closer economic ties among members, and evolve a program allocating the future foreign aid contributions to be made by member states to underdeveloped countries. The most dramatic of Kennedy's aid proposals was the Peace Corps, which he created by executive order on March 1, 1961, to train volunteers for educational and technical service abroad wherever skilled manpower was needed. Thousands of Americans volunteered, and Congress, in a bill approved on September 22, 1961, established the Peace Corps on a permanent basis.

Kennedy's biggest legislative achievement was passage of the Trade Expansion Act in September 1962. Designed to establish closer ties with, and win reciprocal tariff concessions from, the European Common Market, this measure permitted him to reduce tariffs by 50 per cent, and by as much as 100 per cent on articles in which the United States and Common Market countries together accounted for four fifths of world trade. Another major feature of the Act was a system of "trade adjustment assistance." It provided federal aid to American firms and workers adversely affected by lower tariffs. The Trade Expansion Act was a significant landmark in the history of American tariff legislation.

In fiscal matters the new administration proceeded cautiously. Kennedy's economic views were distinctly moderate: his plans to stimulate the economy did not envisage massive federal spending or a marked increase in the role of government. Moreover, at the outset of this term he was caught in an acute financial dilemma that jeopardized almost any course of action. On the one hand, the recession that had begun in the autumn of 1960 was growing worse: business investment and construction had declined, and unemployment was rising. On the other hand, the country was faced with a near-crisis in its international balance of payments. During the last three years of the Eisenhower administration, money spent abroad (for imports, economic and military aid, private investment) had exceeded income *from* abroad (from exports, interest, and services) by a total of $11,000,000,000. The result was an outflow of gold that was increased after the election by the action of European speculators who feared that the incoming administration would devalue the dollar. The crisis over balance of payments and "flight from the dollar" would become more acute if Kennedy attacked the recession through large-scale resort to New Deal pump-priming measures. The President moved swiftly but circumspectly to ease both problems. Instead of asking for large congressional appropriations, he countered the recession through a variety of executive actions that did not weaken confidence in the dollar.[4] At the same time, he took action to restore the balance of payments without resorting to the remedies of raising tariffs or reducing foreign aid.

Announcement of these measures, together with Kennedy's financial restraint in domestic policy and his appointment of the conservative Dillon as Secretary of the Treasury, quickly restored European confidence in the dollar and ended the speculation in gold. The balance of payments deficit began to decrease as Kennedy's policies took effect and American exports rose sharply. And whether despite or because of his executive actions at home, the country began climbing steadily from the recession in the second quarter of 1961 and continued to improve, albeit slowly, for the balance of the year.

With the economy expanding again, the President took pains to reassure a suspicious American business community that he was not an irresponsible "spender." He was genuinely eager to avoid inflationary action that would nullify returning prosperity. It was ironic, and extremely galling to the President, that the first real assault upon a relatively stable price level came from an important segment of the business community. Negotiations between the major steel companies and the United Steelworkers over a new wage contract broke down in early March 1962. Kennedy and Secretary of Labor Goldberg were instrumental in persuading the two sides to renew negotiations, and they were heartened when a noninflationary two-year wage contract was signed on March 31. Kennedy, with assurances from the steel executives that the agreement obviated the need for a price rise, praised both labor and management for their "industrial statesmanship" in holding the line against inflation. Ten days later, however, Roger M. Blough, chairman of the board of United States Steel, the

---

[4] For example, he reduced the interest rate on FHA loans to stimulate housing construction, released $274,000,000 in highway improvement funds, ordered early payment of $258,000,000 in veterans' insurance dividends, and accelerated governmental procurement and construction programs in depressed areas. The Defense Department was able to release $690,000,000 of ready funds for this latter purpose, and the Federal Home Loan Bank Board liberalized its lending rules for federal savings and loan associations and thus released over $1,000,000,000 in credit to stimulate residential building.

nation's biggest producer, called upon the President to announce that his company was raising its prices by six dollars a ton. Five other major steel companies announced an identical increase on the following day, April 11.

Feeling betrayed, Kennedy scathingly denounced the steel companies in his press conference on April 11. Quoting figures, he denied any justification for the rise in prices. He was shocked, he said, that "a tiny handful of steel executives, whose pursuit of private power and profit exceeds their sense of public responsibility, can show such utter contempt for the interest of 185,000,000 Americans." The President did more than denounce. The nation looked in awe as he mobilized the massive power of the federal government. The Federal Trade Commission launched an inquiry into the possibility of collusive price-fixing. The Treasury Department spoke of a tax investigation. The Department of Justice announced that it would see whether the antitrust laws had been violated. The Defense Department hinted that its purchases of steel would be made from companies that had not raised their prices.

The offending steel companies quickly surrendered. Bethlehem Steel announced on April 13 that it was rescinding its price rise. The others followed suit on April 14, and the inflationary threat to the wage-price level was over. Kennedy's careful attempts to cultivate better relations with the business community suffered heavily, but the public on the whole was impressed by the President's firmness under pressure. Andrew Jackson, when challenged by the Second Bank of the United States, had acted no more forcefully.

But Kennedy's ability to deal with the steel companies had not changed the situation in Congress. The New Frontier, as defined by the President in his first message to Congress on January 30, 1961, was designed to bring the country out of recession, stimulate economic growth, and assist various needy groups by economic and social welfare measures. The conservative coalition in Congress, however, continued to oppose much of the program.

Administration Democrats, led by the venerable Sam Rayburn, powerful Speaker of the House of Representatives, moved early in 1961 to render the coalition less effective by striking at one of its strongest bastions—the House rules committee. This committee was composed of eight Democrats and four Republicans. Its chairman and one other Democrat were southern conservatives, and they had consistently voted with the four Republican members to deadlock the committee and bottle up progressive bills. Rayburn, after a bitter contest, was able to gain House acceptance on January 31, 1961, of a resolution enlarging the rules committee from twelve members to fifteen. He then appointed two pro-administration Democrats and one Republican to the new seats, thereby making possible an eight-to-seven administration majority. Kennedy had won the first round.

Administration forces then waged a succession of hard-fought battles over each item in the Kennedy program, usually winning or losing by a handful of votes. Honors were about evenly divided between the President and the conservative coalition during the two sessions of the Eighty-seventh Congress. Conservatives scored a major triumph in the first session by defeating the administration's ambitious school-aid bill. It called for a federal grant of $2,300,000,000 to the states over a three-year period for school construction and teachers' salaries, and the allocation of another $3,300,000,000 for colleges, universities, and federal scholarships over a five-year period. The bill passed the Senate without difficulty in May 1961, but Roman Catholic bishops then demanded that parochial schools receive aid on an equal basis with public schools. Kennedy refused to accept this amendment, and the search for a compromise proved futile. Two Catholic Democrats on the rules committee joined with the conservatives to bury Kennedy's bill, and the House later defeated a weak substitute measure by a vote of 242 to 170.

On other measures, however, the New Frontier recorded a series of victories during the 1961 session. One was an important new Housing Act authorizing nearly $5,000,000,000 for local urban renewal projects over a four-year period. Secondly, strenuous administration efforts finally mustered a Democratic majority in favor of a higher minimum wage bill. The new law, which went into effect on September 3, 1961, raised the minimum in two stages over a two-year period from $1 to $1.25 an hour for the 24,000,000 workers already covered, and extended the same coverage to some 3,625,000 new workers, primarily in certain retail and service industries. A third administration triumph was the Area Redevelopment Act, signed on May 1, 1961. It provided nearly $400,000,000 in federal loans and grants for assistance to 675 "distressed areas" of economic stagnation and high unemployment. Kennedy also obtained an extension of emergency unemployment compensation, liberalization of Social Security provisions and benefits, and new funds for the Federal Water Pollution Control Act that permitted construction of sewage treatment plants.

The record was far different in the 1962 session. Speaker Rayburn, stricken by a fatal cancer near the end of the first session, died on November 16, 1961. His successor was far less able to enforce House discipline in the administration's behalf, and the unrepentant southern chairman of the rules committee was once again able to keep several bills from coming to a vote. Aside from the Trade Expansion Act, the New Frontier scored few successes during 1962. Drug control legislation, an increase in postal rates, and funds for retraining displaced workers were minor victories, totally outweighed by the defeat or crippling of key administration measures.

Three such measures were finally passed, but without the provisions that Kennedy wanted most. One, the Revenue Act of 1962, granted business $1,000,000,000 a year in special tax credits to encourage new outlays for industrial machinery and equipment. But the measure omitted Kennedy's proposals for withholding income taxes on dividends and interest and curtailing expense account deductions. The second was a farm bill designed to impose strict production controls on wheat and feed grains. The administration bill was beaten in the House on June 21, 1962, and a weak substitute measure merely extended the existing voluntary control program for another year. In a third compromise, Congress authorized the President to channel $900,000,000 in public works projects into areas with high unemployment but denied his request for stand-by authority to initiate a $2,000,000,000 anti-recession public works program.

Even more important were the measures defeated by the conservative coalition during 1962. The most important was a bill to provide health insurance for the aged through the Social Security system. This so-called Medicare program, strongly advocated by Kennedy since the summer of 1960, was killed in the Senate on July 17, 1962, by a vote of 52 to 48. Another major loss was the defeat of Kennedy's plan to create a new Cabinet Department of Urban Affairs. The House rules committee stifled two youth employment bills, a program for commuter transit assistance, a bill to aid medical schools through construction grants and student loans, and a bill to aid migrant workers. All in all, the legislative record of Kennedy's first two years compared favorably with that of most postwar Congresses but fell considerably short of fulfilling the New Frontier program.

Nor did the President's difficulties with Congress appear headed for improvement as the midterm election approached. If the past was any guide, the Democrats could expect to lose at least forty seats in the House and six in the Senate. None of these losses was likely to occur in the South. Kennedy was inclined to fight for a more amenable Congress, but as Franklin Roosevelt and Dwight Eisenhower could testify, presidential intervention was fraught with dangers. Nevertheless, the President said, Republicans had been negative on domestic programs of social reform; they had to be defeated. September witnessed the beginnings of what promised to be the most energetic intervention by any President in a midterm election. Ignoring the warnings of his advisers, Kennedy campaigned across the country, placing the full prestige of his office behind Democratic candidates. The effects of this bold move will never be fully known. In mid-October, Kennedy abruptly ended his tour in the face of the greatest crisis of his administration—the confrontation with Russia over Cuba. Although the Democrats went on to score the most impressive midterm victory since 1934, gaining four seats in the Senate and losing only two in the House, the results could not be interpreted either as approval of the President's election activities or as a mandate for his domestic program. More likely, it reflected public endorsement of his firm stand against the Russian thrust into the Western Hemisphere.

A time of peace and prosperity appeared at hand as the President faced the new Congress in January 1963. Russian-American relations had passed the crisis of Cuba; West Berlin was quiet; Southeast Asia, although continuing to simmer, was relatively tranquil; and the economy was humming. "In short," Kennedy noted in his annual State of the Union message, "both at home and abroad, there may be a temptation to relax." But this was no time for excessive optimism or complacency, the President warned. The deeply rooted problems of American society persisted. Material prosperity was only one side of the coin. "The quality of American life," he emphasized, "must keep pace with the quantity of American goods." The United States had to be strengthened by investing in its youth, by safeguarding the health of its citizens, by protecting the basic rights of all the people, and by the prudent use of its resources and facilities. Furthermore, the rate of economic growth had to be sustained, and unemployment had to be reduced. To accomplish these goals, the President urged, "one step, above all, is essential—the enactment this year of a substantial reduction and revision in Federal income taxes."

The administration's program, however, was not destined to fare any better in the first session of the Eighty-eighth Congress than it had in the Eighty-seventh. The fight for a reduction in federal income taxes pointed the way.

The President was determined to sustain a rate of economic growth of at least 5 per cent. The economy, presidential advisers argued, could be stimulated either through large-scale governmental spending, or through a tax reduction which would increase consumer purchasing power. Kennedy chose the latter course. The details of his proposal were spelled out in a special message to Congress in late January. Tax rates would be cut so as to reduce federal revenues by $11,000,000,000 from individuals and $2,600,000,000 from corporations. A tightening of existing tax schedules would raise an additional $3,400,000,000, thus making a net tax reduction of $10,200,000,000. The President's plan immediately came under fire from all sides. Labor demanded further cuts favoring lower income groups; business claimed discrimination against middle income groups; and Congress complained that federal revenues could not be cut when the budget for fiscal 1964 of $97,700,000,000 envisioned a deficit of $8,300,000,000.

Despite the administration's request for prompt action, Congress moved at a snail's pace. The House ways and means committee did not order the bill reported until September. The lower chamber finally passed the measure, substantially in the form requested by the President, on September 25, 1963, but there was no action forthcoming from the Senate during the first session of the Eighty-eighth Congress.

The administration fared little better on appropriations for foreign aid and space programs. Kennedy initially requested a foreign aid program of $4,900,000,000 for fiscal 1964, later reduced to $4,500,000,000. Congress appropriated only $3,000,000,000. The space program suffered a similar, if less drastic fate. The National Aeronautics and Space Administration's request for $5,700,000,000 came under critical review in Congress. Perhaps, it was argued, placing a man on the moon by 1970 was not worth the expense. Congress proceeded to cut NASA's budget by more than $600,000,000.

On the other hand, Kennedy's program for increasing the quality of American life scored several modest but notable successes. Congress approved $150,000,000 to be spent over fiscal 1965–7 in grants to states for the construction of nonprofit community health centers, designed to prevent, diagnose, treat, and rehabilitate the mentally ill. Other programs enacted or extended included federal aid for building medical and dental schools; loans for students of these schools; increased efforts to control and prevent air pollution; a one-year extension of the National Defense Education Act; and an expanded vocational education program.

Yet 1963 was not a very productive year. The first session of the Eighty-eighth Congress in fact enacted the lowest amount of requested legislation of any Kennedy Congress. The President viewed the first three years of his term in office as chiefly educative and preparative, and he looked forward to the passage of additional legislation during the second session of Congress. Above all, he anticipated the fruition of his program during his second term.

261. Kennedy and the Negro Revolution

One of President Kennedy's—and the American nation's—most pressing problems was discontent among American Negroes that was growing
by leaps and bounds. Nearly one hundred years after the Emancipation
Proclamation, Negroes were far from free. In the South, the Negro met
segregation and discrimination at every turn. He could not eat in a restau-
rant or stay at the same hotel with whites. And his children, despite a
Supreme Court decision to the contrary, could not usually attend the same
schools as whites. Furthermore, in many southern counties and some
states he lacked the political power to redress these grievances: he could
not vote. Conditions in the North were no better. In fact, in many slum
areas, they were far worse. Negroes had the least education, the most
unemployed, and the highest rate of disease of any segment of the population.

Kennedy was sincerely committed to equality for Negroes, but his
performance during his first two years in office was, as civil rights leader
Martin Luther King, Jr., observed, "essentially cautious and defensive."
There were, however, some gains. The President named many Negroes to
positions of high responsibility, including the selection of Robert C.
Weaver for the sensitive post of Federal Housing Administrator. Kennedy
also created a new Committee on Equal Employment Opportunity, headed
by Vice President Johnson. The committee, given much broader enforcement powers than similar committees had received from Eisenhower,
Truman, or Roosevelt, persuaded more than fifty of the nation's largest
defense contractors to sign "Plans for Progress" embodying agreements to
provide equal opportunity. Later, all firms holding governmental contracts
in excess of $10,000 were required to file periodic reports with the commit-
tee proving compliance with the President's anti-discrimination order.
Kennedy also issued an executive order on November 20, 1962, prohibiting
racial and religious discrimination in all housing built or purchased with
federal aid.

Above all, the President acted with dispatch in the case of James H.
Meredith. Meredith, a Negro citizen of Mississippi, had instituted a suit in
federal court charging racial bias after his two applications to enroll at the
University of Mississippi had been rejected. A variety of legal means to
force Meredith's admission all failed in the face of Governor Ross Barnett's
defiance of judicial authority. Finally, after Meredith's fourth attempt to
register was rebuffed by 200 state police on September 27, 1962, the
United States Circuit Court in New Orleans announced that its powers
were exhausted. Further action, it declared, was now up to the executive
branch. President Kennedy moved to insure compliance with the court's
orders. Several hundred federal marshals accompanied Meredith to the
university campus in Oxford, Mississippi, on Sunday, September 30.
On the same day, Kennedy ordered federal troops to a base at nearby
Memphis, Tennessee, and federalized the Mississippi National Guard.
That evening a mob of students and bystanders attacked the marshals
with rocks and occasional rifle fire, and a fierce riot ensued until dawn of

the following day. The state police withdrew, and only the prompt arrival of federal troops saved the lightly armed and outnumbered marshals. Two civilians were killed and seventy wounded before order was restored. State resistance thereupon melted away as federal bayonets kept order. James Meredith was formally registered on October 1 and began attending classes under heavy armed guard.

President Kennedy moved for a new civil rights law following the midterm election. In February 1963 he requested legislation to broaden existing laws for protection of Negroes' voting rights and to authorize federal technical assistance to areas in the process of desegregating their schools. The President also called for a four-year extension of the Civil Rights Commission. This moderate program was hardly calculated to please civil rights leaders demanding "Freedom Now."

Two months later, Dr. King began a campaign to end discrimination in shops, restaurants, and employment in Birmingham, the center of deep southern resistance. The protest, small at first, began with "sit-ins" at lunch counters, picketing, and demonstrations. The mood became increasingly ugly as King was met with the full force of Birmingham law enforcement authorities, led by Police Commissioner Eugene "Bull" Connor. The climax came on May 3, when a Negro protest march was broken up by the use of firehoses and police dogs. This action was immediately forced on the nation's attention as television screens followed events in Birmingham. The white middle class conscience was aroused as demonstrations now spread to other parts of the South and into the North. In the ten weeks following Birmingham, there were 758 demonstrations across the nation, bringing 13,786 arrests in eleven southern states alone.

Convinced that the federal government now had to act, Kennedy addressed the nation on June 11. "We face," he declared, "a moral crisis as a country and as a people." Negro aspirations could no longer be denied. The United States could not preach freedom abroad and practice discrimination at home. "This is one country," the President emphasized. "It has become one country because all of us and all the people who came here had an equal chance to develop their talents." This had not been true of the Negro. Something had to be done, and done at once.

The President submitted a new civil rights bill to Congress one week later. It contained all the features of his February proposal, plus many additional provisions. The government, under its terms, would be permitted to file suits to desegregate schools and could cut off funds for federal programs in areas where discrimination was practiced in their application. The bill also strengthened existing machinery for the prevention of employment discrimination by governmental contractors, and it established a Community Relations Service, designed to help local communities resolve racial disputes. The heart of the new bill was a section guaranteeing Negroes equal access to public accommodations.

Demonstrations, continuing while Congress considered the President's plan, were climaxed by a "March on Washington" on August 28. Many feared that this remonstrance would lead to violence and would only serve to alienate Congress. But the march, with over 200,000 participants, was notable for its decorum and dignity.

Meanwhile, a House judiciary subcommittee, headed by liberals, drafted a bill that went far beyond the scope of the administration's proposal. Under its provisions, the Justice Department would be given almost unlimited powers to file suits against civil rights violators. Kennedy registered concern at this action. The bill, he feared, would not have broad enough appeal to attract the Republican votes needed for passage. Conferences with administration officials followed, and a compromise was reached. The Justice Department would now be authorized to enter any civil rights suit pending in federal courts. The Justice Department would also be given authority to initiate suits to desegregate public facilities. This compromise virtually assured passage in the House, but little action was forthcoming from the Senate, where the bill was being held in the judiciary committee, headed by Senator James O. Eastland of Mississippi. Although a hard fight loomed ahead, and a Senate filibuster attempt was certain, Kennedy could look forward with optimism to the enactment of civil rights legislation during the second session of the Eighty-eighth Congress.

262. *The Cold War Continues*

President Kennedy's domestic strivings were largely overshadowed during 1961–3 by foreign crises. The first was in Southeast Asia, where externally supported native Communist movements threatened pro-western regimes in Laos and South Vietnam. (See above, pp. 836–837.) Three rival "governments" contended for primacy in Laos. The right-wing faction of Prince Boun Oum, despite strong diplomatic and material support from the United States, was suffering defeat after defeat at the hands of the Communist Pathet Lao movement led by Prince Souphanouvong, and seemed not far from collapse. Other Laotians continued to support the neutralist regime of the exiled Premier, Prince Souvanna Phouma. The situation was further complicated by the fact that the Soviet Union was airlifting large quantities of equipment to the Pathet Lao but still recognized Souvanna Phouma as the rightful ruler of Laos.

Only large-scale American intervention could save Boun Oum, and Kennedy chose to avoid this course of action. Instead, he affirmed the goal of a "neutral and independent Laos" and pressed for a diplomatic solution along that line. But when the Russians temporized in order to permit continuation of the Pathet Lao offensive, Kennedy warned in March 1961 that "no one should doubt" American determination to prevent a Communist triumph in Laos. The Soviets finally agreed, in late April, to discuss the Laotian problem at an international conference and join other powers in requesting a cease-fire.

All three Laotian Princes and representatives of thirteen nations—the western Big Three, the Soviet Union, Communist China, Canada, Poland, India, Burma, Thailand, Cambodia, and North and South Vietnam—assembled in Geneva on May 16, 1961. The conference remained in session almost without interruption for fourteen months. After hammering out terms for an international agreement safeguarding Laotian neutrality and independence, the conferees sought to persuade the three Princes to form a coalition government. The latter proved more difficult to achieve than East-West accord. The Princes, especially Boun Oum, were refractory and suspicious, and the Pathet Lao repeatedly violated the cease-fire in order to improve their strategic position. Communist subversive activity from Laos became so menacing in the spring of 1962 that Kennedy sent naval units and 5,000 marines to Thailand in May to prevent border violations.

Boun Oum's persistent refusal to co-operate led the United States to suspend aid to his government in March 1962 and virtually forced him to come to agreement. Souphanouvong, Souvanna Phouma, and General Phoumi Nosavan, who had replaced Boun Oum, signed a compact on June 12 establishing a "troika" coalition government under the premiership of Souvanna Phouma. The new coalition cabinet was installed on June 22 and approved a genuine cease-fire two days later.

The Geneva conference thereupon resumed its sessions and approved two neutrality pacts, signed by all fourteen nations on July 23, 1962. The first was a joint declaration pledging respect for the neutrality, territorial integrity, and independence of Laos. The second was a joint protocol specifying procedures for the withdrawal of all foreign troops and the safeguarding of Laotian neutrality in the future.[5] The United States began withdrawing its troops from Thailand on July 1, 1962. With at least ostensible support from all the powers concerned, tiny Laos and its new coalition government once again resumed the search for peace and neutrality.

Meanwhile, the situation in neighboring South Vietnam had been deteriorating steadily. Despite American economic aid, the pro-western government of Ngo Dinh Diem was unable to cope with the mounting subversive activities of Vietcong guerrillas who were infiltrating from North Vietnam and Communist-held territory in Laos. After a fact-finding visit to South Vietnam by Vice President Johnson in May 1961, the United States embarked upon an ambitious program of expanded economic assistance and military training. The training program was enlarged in October 1961, and by early 1962 over 4,000 American military personnel were on the scene, instructing, indeed assisting, Vietnamese troops in more efficient supply and combat operations. One year later, the commitment rose to 11,000 personnel. During 1963 sixty American soldiers were killed in action, and the costs of supporting the South Vietnamese regime had risen to $1,500,000 per day. Kennedy, in May 1963, expressed hope that the United States could begin withdrawing some of its forces by the end of the year. But as the military scene brightened, the political situation deteriorated. The Buddhist leadership, dissatisfied with the Diem regime, rose in protest in June. Diem crushed the uprising. The Buddhists then turned to the tactic of suicide by fire in hopes of mobilizing public opinion

wwwwwwwwwwwwwww

[5] This agreement prohibited re-entry of foreign troops, forbade Laos to join or accept protection from SEATO or any other regional alliance, and re-established the International Commission for Supervision and Control (composed of Indian, Polish, and Canadian truce teams) that had overseen Laotian neutrality after the Geneva armistice of 1954.

behind their cause. Diem responded by declaring martial law and attacking the Buddhist pagodas. Diem successfully stifled public protests, but
three months later, in November, he fell victim to a military coup, led by
General Duong Van Minh. As the year ended, the situation in South
Vietnam was anything but promising.

President Kennedy had barely formulated his Laotian and Vietnamese policies in early 1961 when he was forced to make a crucial
decision about Cuba. His long-range plans for Latin America found best
expression in the Alliance for Progress (see above, p. 866), extensive
preparations for which were launched as soon as the new administration
took office. But the orderly hemispheric progress and development envisaged by this comprehensive aid program were seriously menaced by the
disruptive effects of Fidel Castro's foreign and domestic policies. The
Cuban dictator was determined to export his radical social and economic
revolution throughout the Western Hemisphere, and few Latin American
governments were sufficiently stable, popular, and progressive to feel
immune. At the same time, the unmistakable trend in Castro's domestic
program, and the elaborate network of economic, military, and technical
agreements that he had recently concluded with the Soviet bloc, stamped
him a Communist and his country a Communist satellite in all but name.
Informed observers were of the opinion that his subversive activities and
radical doctrines, if unchecked, would lead to Communist gains all over
Latin America.

The United States government, months before Kennedy came to
power, had concluded that the only feasible prospect of overthrowing the
Castro regime lay in supporting the thousands of anti-Castro Cubans who
had fled from their homeland after 1959. The Eisenhower administration
therefore decided, as early as March 1960, to provide equipment and
military training for Cuban refugees in camps in Central America and the
southern United States under the auspices of the Central Intelligence
Agency. The CIA was convinced that a well-timed assault upon Cuba by
these refugees would set off a massive general uprising of disaffected
Cubans and topple the Castro regime. Blueprints for such an invasion,
prepared before Eisenhower left office, awaited only Kennedy's approval
before being put into action.

Kennedy, despite some misgivings, ordered the assault to take place.
He did so against the advice of several White House staff members and
Senator J. William Fulbright, chairman of the foreign relations committee.
He thus became responsible for one of the most dismally planned, care-
lessly managed, and ineptly executed episodes in American history. Cuban
airfields were attacked on the morning of April 15 by B-26 fighter-bombers,
which the United States claimed were flown by defecting Cuban air force
pilots, but which were later revealed to have taken off from a refugee base
in Central America. The actual landing took place before dawn on April 17
in the *Bahía de Cochinos*—the Bay of Pigs—on the southern coast of
Cuba. An estimated 1,500 Cuban refugees took part in the landing, which
in the absence of air or naval artillery cover was pinned down and
overwhelmed within three days by Castro's armed forces. Contact with the
underground was not made, and the anticipated anti-Castro uprising did
not occur.

The fiasco inevitably had disastrous repercussions. The United States suffered almost universal condemnation and heavy loss of prestige. Khrushchev combined threats of possible Soviet armed intervention in defense of Cuba with pious lectures to Kennedy on good conduct and the importance of observing international law. Castro, strengthened rather than weakened by the episode both at home and abroad, proceeded to make Cuba an even greater storm center in hemispheric affairs. He reaffirmed his ties with Russia, claimed that only Soviet offers of armed assistance had deterred further American assaults, formally proclaimed Cuba a "socialist" country, and quickened the pace of socialization in all phases of Cuban life. Other Latin American governments, disturbed by this apparent recrudescence of Yankee imperialism, refused to co-operate with Washington's attempts to induce inter-American accord or action against the Communist menace in Cuba. The only benefit accruing to the United States from the Bay of Pigs disaster was its effect upon the President. Shaken and sobered but not demoralized, he publicly accepted full responsibility for the failure and obviously learned much from the experience.[6]

Cuba was only the first of sobering international experiences in store for President Kennedy. The second was his conference with Premier Khrushchev in Vienna on June 3–4, 1961. It was not a summit meeting but a private encounter, permitting the two leaders to exchange views and take each other's measure. Khrushchev handed Kennedy a memorandum explicitly defining the Soviet position on Berlin. Without setting an actual deadline, it renewed demands for an "immediate" peace treaty with Germany and a consequent end to the present four-power occupation of Berlin. The Soviet leader made it plain that he would sign such a treaty with East Germany whether the western allies participated or not, thus forcing them to negotiate their rights in Berlin directly with a government they were determined not to recognize.

Berlin had once again become the focus of a crisis that could lead to war. Months of almost unbroken tension followed the Vienna meeting. The western allies were uncertain and divided as to how much, if anything, was negotiable in this tangled controversy. But they were united and firm on one central point: they would not back down. Their responses, in the East-West diplomatic exchange that followed the Vienna meeting, contained a flat rejection of any solution to the Berlin problem that did not guarantee western presence, western access, and unhampered freedom for the citizens of West Berlin. President Kennedy drew the line most sharply in a broadcast to the American people on July 25, 1961. "We do not want to fight, but we have fought before," he said gravely. "We cannot and will not permit the Communists to drive us out of Berlin, either gradually or by force."

The situation grew steadily more ominous. Both the United States and

---

[6] The overconfidence with which Kennedy and his youthful advisers had approached foreign affairs in previous weeks promptly gave way to sober caution. Determined never again to be so dependent upon a single source of information, Kennedy ordered a re-examination of the intelligence-gathering and policy-making functions of the CIA and appointed General Maxwell D. Taylor to the White House Staff as special military adviser.

the USSR announced increases in their armed forces and military budgets in the summer of 1961. The East German government, determined to block the accelerating flow of refugees to the West, closed the boundary between the eastern and western sectors of Berlin on August 13, 1961, while Soviet troops surrounded the city. Transit to and within the city by West Berliners, West Germans, and allied personnel was theoretically unaffected by the maneuver, which was aimed at controlling the movement of East Germans and thus shutting their escape hatch to the free world. Yet all but twelve—soon all but seven—of the eighty crossing points between the sectors were completely closed, and new restrictions on August 22 further encroached upon western rights of free movement in East Berlin. While the Soviets ignored stern allied notes protesting against the illegality of this action, East German authorities physically sealed off the entire Berlin border by a wall of concrete blocks and barbed wire running across the city. To many, the Berlin wall was a perfect symbol of the barrier that divided East and West, a fitting monument to Communism's ultimate failure in the battle for the mind of man.

The wall and the city it bisected were scenes of violent, tragic, and highly dangerous incidents for more than a year. To reassure the anxious West Berliners, who feared that allied acquiescence in the building of the wall heralded their abandonment of Berlin to the Communists, President Kennedy provided three eloquent tokens of western determination to remain. He sent Vice President Johnson on a quick visit to the city to renew American pledges of support. He appointed General Lucius D. Clay, symbol of western firmness during the airlift crisis of 1948–9, as his personal representative in West Berlin. And, in a dramatic move, Kennedy reinforced the American garrison by dispatching a battle group of 1,500 American troops down the 100-mile *Autobahn* from West Germany to Berlin.

Although diplomatic exchanges between East and West utterly failed to break the impasse, tension eased somewhat when Premier Khrushchev announced on October 17 that he would no longer insist upon a settlement of the German question before the end of the year. Soviet harassment of allied air corridors was halted in March 1962. General Clay, expressing the belief that Berlin was no longer in immediate peril, returned to the United States on May 8. The danger of war over Berlin had receded, but the problem of Berlin remained.

While tensions over Berlin relaxed, the Cuban situation grew worse. By early 1962 the island had become an appendage of the Communist system and a Soviet military base, capable of supporting guerrilla operations and subversive activities all over Latin America. The other Latin republics became sufficiently worried about Castro to vote Cuba's exclusion from the inter-American system on January 30. The United States tightened its trade embargo against the Castro regime in February and again in March. In response, large numbers of Soviet technicians began to arrive in Cuba during the summer of 1962.

There was considerable sentiment in the United States in favor of stronger action against the Cuban dictator, and Republican spokesmen began to criticize the administration for failing to prevent the Cuban arms build-up or cause Castro's fall. Kennedy replied in August 1962 that he was opposed to an armed invasion of Cuba, adding that the United States would take no stronger action so long as arms shipments to Cuba from the Soviet bloc remained "defensive" in nature. He received explicit assurances from Soviet Foreign Minister Andrei Gromyko in a White House meeting on October 18 that all such arms were in fact defensive. But four days earlier, the President had learned from aerial reconnaissance that medium-range ballistic missiles were already present in Cuba, and that the construction of launching pads was nearing completion.

Reporters detected unusual activity and an air of incipient crisis in Washington during the week of Gromyko's visit. Then the White House announced on Monday afternoon, October 22, that the President would address the nation at seven o'clock that evening in a message of "national urgency." He began this address by announcing that the crisis concerned Cuba. He then proceeded to stun the world with a series of uncompromising statements. "Within the past week," he said, "unmistakable evidence has established the fact that a series of offensive missile sites is now in preparation" on Cuban soil. Announcing establishment of a "strict quarantine of all offensive military equipment under shipment to Cuba," the President asserted that the United States would demand "prompt dismantling and withdrawal" of all offensive bases at an emergency meeting of the Security Council and would maintain the quarantine—actually a selective blockade—until the bases had been removed.

Kennedy put the issue squarely in one of the most chilling statements of intent ever uttered by an American president: "It shall be the policy of this nation to regard any nuclear missile launched from Cuba against any nation in the Western Hemisphere as an attack by the Soviet Union on the United States requiring a full retaliatory response on the Soviet Union." He also made it clear that the United States was not thinking solely of the Caribbean: "Any hostile move anywhere in the world against the safety and freedom of peoples to whom we are committed, including in particular the brave people of West Berlin, will be met with whatever action is needed."

It was the most direct and ominous confrontation in the history of Soviet-American relations, and the world hovered on the brink of war for a few tense days. The Soviets, caught off balance by the American move, replied hesitantly and with unaccustomed restraint. The Acting Secretary-General of the UN, U Thant called upon Khrushchev and Kennedy to suspend both the Cuban missile build-up and the blockade and begin peaceful negotiation of the dispute. Kennedy's reply did not close the door to negotiations but insisted that suspension of the blockade depended upon the removal of offensive bases and international inspection of Cuba to insure compliance. American warships and planes in the Atlantic and Caribbean began the quarantine patrol and prepared to intercept all vessels bearing offensive equipment to Cuba.

The American people, their western allies, and the OAS all rallied overwhelmingly behind President Kennedy, and the Soviets backed steadily away from the American challenge. American reconnaissance planes in the Atlantic reported on October 24 that Soviet vessels carrying jet aircraft and other "contraband" had altered course away from Cuba. Two Cuban-bound Soviet ships bearing no offensive equipment submitted to American inspection and were permitted to proceed. Khrushchev first offered to remove Russian bases in Cuba in exchange for American evacuation of its bases in Turkey. When Kennedy refused, the Russian Premier agreed to the substance of the President's demands in a message on October 28. The USSR would remove all offensive weapons and submit to international inspection if the United States would pledge not to invade Cuba. The President agreed to these terms and suspended the blockade, while U Thant went to Havana on October 29 to arrange details for the inspection. Dismantling and removal of the missile bases took place promptly.

Cuba proved the decisive test for John F. Kennedy. Khrushchev, grossly underestimating the determination of the American people and their President, had found both willing to go to the brink of nuclear war to defend the vital interests of the United States. Soviet-American relations improved considerably after Cuba as Khrushchev shifted back to the shadow war of "peaceful" coexistence. The two nations, in fact, soon appeared on the verge of a new era of friendly relations. The control of nuclear testing provided the key to a *détente*.

The Soviet Union, at the height of the Berlin crisis in the summer of 1961, had announced the resumption of atmospheric nuclear testing on an unprecedented scale. The first detonation in the new Russian series occurred on September 1, 1961, and nearly two dozen others, including one massive superbomb in the fifty-megaton range (equivalent to 50,000,000 tons of TNT), took place in Soviet Asia and the Arctic during the next two months. The United States responded in March 1962 by announcing plans for its own atmospheric tests. However, President Kennedy stipulated that the United States would cancel the series if Russia agreed to a test ban treaty. When Moscow refused, American authorities conducted extensive atmospheric and underwater tests in the Pacific during the spring of 1962. Meanwhile, the tripartite test ban conference, responding to appeals from the United Nations, had resumed its sessions in Geneva on November 28, 1961. The talks collapsed on January 29, 1962, began again on March 15, and proceeded intermittently until September. The two sides were totally unable to reach agreement on the crucial question of inspection.

Following its Cuban misadventure, the Soviet Union showed signs of willingness to reopen negotiations. Private talks began in January 1963, but they bogged down on the question of inspection. The United States, with improved methods of detection, had lowered its previous demand for twenty on-site inspections per year to seven. Russia, heretofore unwilling to accept any inspections, now conceded that two or three might be allowed. The two nations, however, were unable to bridge the narrow gap that now separated their two positions. Meanwhile, at the Geneva Disarmament discussions, the first progress was made in years. Although the point was a minor one—an agreement to install a "hot line" for direct communications between Moscow and Washington—it was a significant indication of the trend in Soviet-American relations.

President Kennedy took the initiative in a speech delivered at American University on June 10, 1963. He called for a re-examination of American attitudes toward the Soviet Union and toward the cold war. The negotiation of a test ban treaty, he emphasized, was the first step along the road to peace. The following month he dispatched Under Secretary of State Averell Harriman, one of the ablest and most experienced of American negotiators, to Moscow. Harriman found the Russians both willing and eager to conclude a treaty. The question of underground testing, which would require on-site inspections, was put aside in favor of an agreement banning atmospheric explosions. The treaty was initialed on July 25. It provided that there should be no testing in the atmosphere or under water, and it banned other tests which would spread radioactive debris outside the territorial limits of the testing state. Also, both nations pledged to refrain from "causing, encouraging, or in any way participating in" tests anywhere else. Either party could withdraw from the agreement if its supreme interests were in jeopardy by giving three months' notice. Eventually, more than 100 nations signed the treaty, but the two powers closest to a nuclear capacity, France and China, refused to sign.

The test ban treaty was favorably received in the United States. Despite dissenting voices claiming that the agreement endangered American security, most Americans appeared to be willing to accept this potential danger in return for the tangible benefits afforded by the agreement. The Senate consented to ratification by a vote of 80 to 19 on September 24, 1963.

Other signs of lessening tensions between the world's two greatest powers followed. In September, President Kennedy proposed a joint Soviet-American expedition to the moon. The following month he authorized the sale, through private channels, of American wheat to the Soviet Union. Indeed, as the year ended, Russian-American relations were more cordial than at any time since the Second World War. It remained to be seen whether this represented a brief respite in a continuing storm or the dawn of a new era.

263. *Tragedy at Dallas*

In the autumn of 1963, President Kennedy's thoughts turned to the election of 1964. The past three years had been a time of preparation. He confidently expected re-election, a clear mandate from the people, and the fulfillment of his legislative program. He journeyed to Texas in late November, in the company of the Vice President, for the purpose of mending political fences. Texas was badly split between the liberal Democratic forces of Senator Ralph W. Yarborough, and a conservative faction led by Governor John B. Connally. Kennedy sought unity for the coming election. The President arrived in Dallas—a center of extremist right-wing activities—on the morning of November 22. The previous month, Ambassador Stevenson had attended the celebration of United Nations Day in the city. He had met an ugly reception, had been spat upon, and had been hit by a picket sign. But there was no sign of hostility as the President's motorcade proceeded from Love Field to downtown Dallas. In fact, the streets were lined with friendly, cheering people. Twice, Kennedy halted the motorcade to greet the crowds. At 12:30 p.m., CST, just as the motorcade turned on to Elm Street, past the Texas Book Depository Building, shots rang out. The first hit Kennedy in the back of the neck, exiting through his throat. The President stiffened, then lurched slightly forward in his seat. Governor Connally, sitting in front of the President, was also hit. Then Kennedy received a bullet in the back of the head. He fell into his wife's lap. The President was sped to Parkland Memorial Hospital, four miles away, but it was too late. He was pronounced dead at 1:00 p.m.

The President's assassin, Lee Harvey Oswald, was soon captured by police. A special presidential commission, headed by Chief Justice Warren, concluded that Oswald's guilt was certain beyond any reasonable doubt. Oswald was a twenty-four-year-old malcontent, with a record of emotional disturbance and grievance against society. The Warren Commission found no evidence that Oswald "was part of any conspiracy, domestic or foreign, to assassinate President Kennedy." He had acted as an individual. Oswald's own end came two days later at the hand of another assassin.

No single event in American history had ever caused such trauma as the young President's assassination. The President's body, taken to the White House, remained there until Sunday, when it was placed in the Rotunda of the Capitol on the same catafalque that had held the body of Abraham Lincoln nearly one hundred years before. More than a quarter of a million people passed by to pay their last respects.

Monday, November 25, was clear and cold, and a million people lined the streets of Washington to view the funeral, while many millions more watched on television. Eight heads of state, ten prime ministers, and most of the world's remaining royalty attended the funeral, adding to the pomp and pageantry of the somber occasion. The cortege moved from the Capitol to St. Matthew's Cathedral, where a funeral mass was said by Richard Cardinal Cushing, Archbishop of Boston, and a lifelong friend of the late President. The funeral procession then moved down Connecticut Avenue to Constitution Avenue, past the Lincoln Memorial, and over Memorial Bridge to Arlington National Cemetery. There, on a hill overlooking the city of Washington, John F. Kennedy was laid to his final rest.

264. *Johnson Takes the Helm*

The eyes of the world now turned to the new leader of the American people, Lyndon Baines Johnson. Born near Stonewall, Texas on August 27, 1908, Johnson had known much adversity as a youth. He completed his education at Southwest Texas State Teachers College and then taught school for a year. Politics, however, strongly attracted the young man. Both his father and grandfather had served in the Texas legislature, and he soon developed his own political ambitions. Johnson first came to Washington in 1932 as secretary to Representative Richard M. Kleberg. Four years later, at the age of twenty-seven, he was appointed National Youth Administrator for the State of Texas. This office proved a springboard for his election to the House of Representatives in 1937. Johnson was a stanch supporter of the New Deal, and in return received President Roosevelt's attention and patronage. The rising politician won the Texas senatorial primary, tantamount to election, in 1948, defeating his opponent by eighty-seven votes. The Texan's political talents were quickly recognized in the Senate, and he was elected Minority Leader in 1953—a rare tribute to a freshman senator. Johnson compiled a distinguished record as Majority Leader from 1955 to 1960.

Johnson made a serious bid for the presidential nomination in 1960 but was swept aside by the Kennedy bandwagon. Kennedy, well aware of the strength that Johnson would bring to the Democratic ticket, offered him the vice-presidential nomination. Few, including Kennedy, believed that Johnson would abandon his powerful position in the Senate for the less influential post of Vice President. But Johnson, ignoring the advice of his closest friends, accepted because he wanted to become a national instead of a sectional figure. Johnson proved a loyal lieutenant to his young chief, and Kennedy, in turn, treated Johnson with respect and kept him fully informed. While it is undoubtedly true, as President Kennedy once said, that there is no adequate preparation for the presidency, no man ever came to the office with greater knowledge and mastery of the national political process than Lyndon Johnson.

But what of the man? Johnson, one astute political commentator has observed, was "the first uninhibited product of the American frontier to take over since Andrew Jackson." [7] There was much truth in this statement. The new President was direct and earthy, and his speeches frequently sounded like the homilies of a rural preacher. Yet he was much more complex than his style seemed to indicate. He was vain and sensitive; he desired constant praise and approval, or what he termed a national consensus. Unquestionably, the President's most striking personal characteristics were immense energy, drive, and determination. This energy he channeled entirely into politics, for he lacked outside interests. In political philosophy, he was totally unideological, yet he had a deep and passionate concern for the poor, the elderly, and the downtrodden. Government, he believed, existed to serve people and do for them what they were unable to do for themselves. Thus, even more than Kennedy, Johnson was a direct inheritor of the New Deal tradition and its passionate commitment to social and economic justice.

The new President, upon assuming office, said that his first task was to complete the Kennedy program. Johnson well knew that economy had been Congress' main excuse for rejecting his predecessor's proposals. The President thereupon ordered an immediate review of all federal programs, warning that expenditures had to be pared wherever possible. His final figure of $97,900,000,000 for fiscal 1965 envisioned a deficit of only $4,900,000,000, down from an estimated deficit of $10,000,000,000 for 1964. This, the President reassured Congress, was "an important first step toward a balanced budget."

Johnson's strategy succeeded so well that Kennedy's program now swept through Congress. The tax reduction bill (see above, p. 870–871) passed in February. A variety of conservation measures were enacted, including the incorporation of federal wilderness areas into a National Wilderness Preservation System. Congress appropriated $375,000,000 to aid in planning and developing area-wide urban transit systems. Appropriations for foreign aid gave the best evidence of the administration's suc-

wwwwwwwwwwwwww

[7] Michael Davie, *LBJ: A Foreign Observer's Viewpoint* (New York, 1966), p. 5.

cess. For more than a decade, Congress had evidenced increasing re-luctance to support foreign aid, and large reductions had become common. Johnson, taking a new tack, submitted a "bare bones" program calling for the expenditure of $3,500,000,000, or $1,100,000,000 less than the previous year's request. In return, Congress reduced the request by only $250,000,000, the lowest percentage cut in the seventeen-year history of the foreign aid program. In fact, the second session of the Eighty-eighth Congress approved $106,000,000,000 of the administration's total requests of $110,000,000,000.

President Johnson also continued the fight for civil rights legisla-tion—and continued it with grim and unrelenting determination. "No memorial oration or eulogy," he stated in his first address to Congress, "could more eloquently honor President Kennedy's memory than the earliest possible passage of the civil rights bill for which he fought so long." The bill passed the House easily enough on February 10, 1964, but there was delay in the Senate once a southern filibuster began in late March. However, only nineteen Southerners participated, and many of them were old men. Moreover, the ablest of the group, Richard B. Russell of Georgia, did not seem to have his heart in the struggle. The bill's managers, Majority Whip Hubert H. Humphrey of Minnesota and Minority Whip Thomas H. Kuchel of California, maintained unrelenting pressure all through the spring. Two senators were always on the floor, and enough supporters were kept on hand to answer quorum calls. Finally, on June 10, fifty-seven days after formal consideration of the bill had begun, the Senate voted cloture on a civil rights debate for the first time in its history. The bill passed handily one week later by a vote of 76 to 18.

The measure signed by the President on July 2 contained all the major provisions originally requested by the Kennedy administration, plus the strengthening features added by the House in the previous October (see above, p. 871). While a few changes had been made in the Senate in order to mobilize the widest possible support for the bill, the Act of 1964 remained the most far-reaching civil rights law since Reconstruction.

President Johnson could not only look back with pride to remarkable progress in a brief time but could also point to a major legislative triumph of his own. The President, in his first State of the Union message in January 1964, had declared "unconditional war on poverty in America." One fifth of the nation was impoverished in an affluent society, and legislation was urgently needed to combat illiteracy, unemployment, and the lack of public services. Congress responded with the Economic Oppor-tunity Act of 1964, authorizing the expenditure of $947,500,000 in fiscal 1965 to begin a three-year program. It provided, among other things, for a Job Corps to train youths in conservation camps and urban areas; a community action program conducted by state and local agencies aimed at job training and the improvement of health and housing; and a domestic peace corps to co-operate with state and local authorities in combating poverty. The Act also established the Office of Economic Opportunity in the Executive Office of the President to supervise the program. R. Sargent Shriver, Jr., Director of the Peace Corps, was named head of the new agency in October.

265. The Election of 1964

While Johnson consolidated his hold on the presidency, Republicans searched for a candidate to oppose him in 1964. Volunteers for the GOP presidential nomination did not abound. The early favorites for the nomination, Senator Barry M. Goldwater of Arizona and Governor Nelson A. Rockefeller of New York, had their first confrontation in the New Hampshire Republican presidential primary campaign in March. To everyone's surprise, the voters rejected both men, writing in the name of Henry Cabot Lodge, Jr., Ambassador to South Vietnam. Goldwater, who had advocated voluntary participation in Social Security and had suggested the advisability of granting NATO commanders as well as the President the right to order the use of nuclear weapons, had acquired a reputation for irresponsibility, whether deserved or not. Rockefeller, on the other hand, had been hurt by a recent divorce and remarriage.

Lodge was the front runner as the Republican aspirants faced Oregon's voters in May. Rockefeller, however, came out on top after a vigorous campaign. With the Lodge boom deflated, Rockefeller and Goldwater again faced each other, and the presidential primary in California became the crucial test. Goldwater, who had been working effectively at the grass-roots level since 1961, already controlled a large number of delegates to the Republican national convention. But he had to prove his popularity with the voters before he could capitalize on this advantage. A victory for Rockefeller in California might not guarantee him the nomination, but it would assuredly give him a decisive voice in naming the presidential candidate and in writing the Republican platform. The California presidential primary campaign was thus a major showdown, bitter and intense. On June 2 California Republicans chose Goldwater by a narrow margin.

Although the Arizona Senator's nomination was now virtually assured, the more liberal elements of the party, headed by Governor William W. Scranton of Pennsylvania, rallied in a last-minute "Stop Goldwater" movement. It was too late. The Republican convention, meeting in San Francisco on July 13, was a Goldwater affair all the way. This first became apparent when the platform committee, drafting the most conservative major party platform in modern times, pledged "limited, frugal and efficient" government at home and "a dynamic strategy aimed at victory" abroad. Rebuffed in committee, the party liberals carried the fight to the convention floor. They offered three amendments to the platform to strengthen the civil rights provision, condemn by name extremist groups of the left and right, and reaffirm the President's exclusive control over nuclear weapons. They were booed, heckled, and raucously shouted down, and Goldwater was nominated on the first ballot on July 15. Showing no inclination to heal wounds, Goldwater chose Representative William E. Miller of New York, a former GOP national chairman known for his conservative views, as his running mate. Moreover, Goldwater in his acceptance speech further exacerbated the division between the two wings of his party. "Any who join us in all sincerity," he said, "we welcome. Those who do not care for our cause we do not expect to enter our ranks in any case." Finally, in a statement destined to become widely quoted by the Democrats during the coming campaign, Goldwater declared: *"I would remind you that extremism in the defense of liberty is no vice. And let me remind you also that moderation in the pursuit of justice is no virtue."*

Goldwater had sounded the battle cry, saying that he had embarked upon a crusade, not a campaign. The western conservative wing of the GOP, after years of frustration, had finally nominated one of their own. The Arizonan's political views left little role for the federal government in coping with the problems of modern society. Big government was unnecessary and usually corrupt. The American people had to stand on their own feet and deal with problems in the same forthright manner as that exhibited by their forefathers on the frontier. In foreign relations, the United States had to stand firm against the Soviet Union. There would be no more "capitulation" through fear of nuclear catastrophe. Freedom could not be compromised.

The Democratic convention, held in Atlantic City in late August, was an anti-climax to the spectacle at San Francisco. Johnson, who managed the affair from beginning to end, was duly nominated. Some Democrats wanted Robert Kennedy for Vice President, but Johnson turned instead to Hubert Humphrey, an old friend and stanch liberal. The convention ratified the President's choice on August 26. To no one's surprise, the Democratic platform endorsed the Great Society.

What had promised to be an exciting presidential campaign soon degenerated into an extraordinarily dull affair. From the beginning, the polls indicated an overwhelming triumph for the Democrats. Even so, Goldwater's supporters gave the appearance of having some hope in the belief that a silent conservative majority might carry their candidate to victory. Goldwater's managers also hoped to capitalize on the white reaction, called the "backlash," against the Negro revolution. Governor George C. Wallace of Alabama had demonstrated that such a "backlash" did exist. In the Democratic presidential primaries, the Governor, a strident segregationist, had captured 33.8 per cent of the vote in Wisconsin, 29.8 per cent in Indiana, and 42.8 per cent in Maryland. Republican hopes of profiting from the "blacklash" rose when a series of riots erupted in Negro areas of northern cities during the summer. The first occurred in Harlem on July 18–23, leaving 1 dead, 140 injured, and causing millions of dollars of damage. The riots spread like wildfire to Rochester, Jersey City, Philadelphia, and Dixmoor, a suburb of Chicago. But as the presidential campaign got under way, civil rights leaders worked diligently and effectively to quiet the Negro population. Many of Goldwater's supporters wanted him to exploit this potentially explosive situation, but he steadfastly refused to do so.

Johnson, shrewdly reading the signs, conducted a limited and restrained campaign. Only one incident seemed to jeopardize his victory. Walter Jenkins, one of the President's chief assistants, was arrested in early October on a morals charge, thus appearing to lend credence to Goldwater's charge that the Johnson administration was ridden by moral decay. The nation's attention, however, was soon diverted by dramatic events abroad. On October 15, Premier Khrushchev was ousted from power in the Kremlin, and China exploded its first nuclear device on the follow-

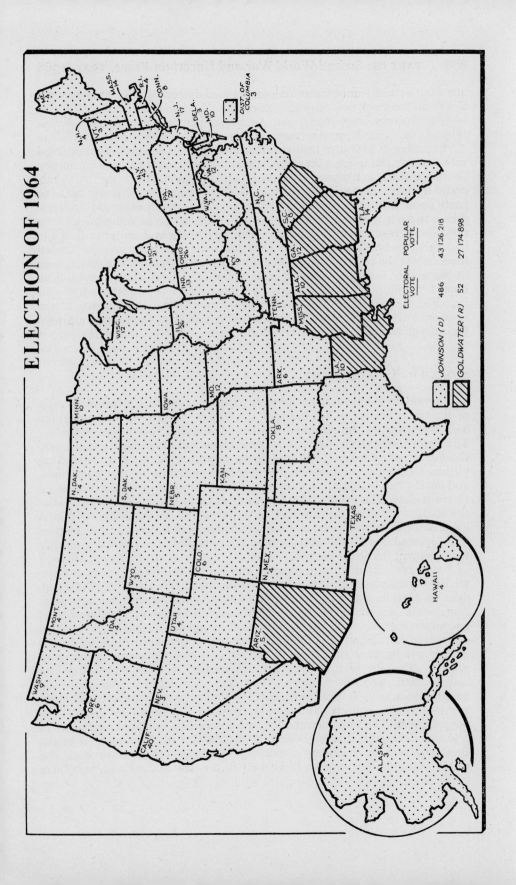

ELECTION OF 1964

	ELECTORAL VOTE	POPULAR VOTE
JOHNSON (D)	486	43 126 218
GOLDWATER (R)	52	27 174 898

ME. 4
N.H. 4
VT. 3
MASS. 14
R.I. 4
CONN. 8
N.Y. 43
N.J. 17
PA. 29
DELA. 3
MD. 10
DIST. OF COLUMBIA 3
W.VA. 12
VA. 12
N.C. 13
S.C. 8
GA. 12
ALA. 10
MISS. 7
TENN. 11
KY. 9
OHIO 26
IND. 13
ILL. 26
MICH. 21
WIS. 12
FLA. 14
LA. 10
ARK. 6
MO. 12
IOWA 9
MINN. 10
N.DAK. 4
S.DAK. 4
NEBR. 5
KAN. 7
OKLA. 8
TEXAS 25
COLO. 6
N.MEX. 4
WYO. 3
MONT. 4
IDA. 4
UTAH 4
ARIZ. 5
NEV. 3
CALIF. 40
ORE. 6
WASH. 9
HAWAII 4
ALASKA 3

ing day. National uneasiness redounded in Johnson's favor, and only the size of his majority now remained in doubt.

On November 3, 1964, the American people accorded Lyndon B. Johnson the largest popular vote, 43,000,000, ever given to any presidential candidate. Goldwater trailed far behind with 27,000,000. The electoral vote stood at 486 to 52, with the Arizonan carrying only Alabama, Georgia, South Carolina, Louisiana, Mississippi, and Arizona. The sweeping Democratic triumph cut so deeply into the GOP's strength at all levels that the party was left in shambles. The Democrats gained thirty-eight House seats, giving them a 295 to 140 margin in the next, or Eighty-ninth Congress; they also gained two seats in the Senate, giving them a majority of 68 to 32 in that body. In addition, the GOP lost over 500 seats in state legislatures across the country. A few Republican leaders pointed to their inroads in the South, but these were Pyrrhic victories. There seemed to be little hope for building party strength by appealing to segregationists. Other Republican spokesmen frankly acknowledged the real significance of the election returns—that the American people had overwhelmingly affirmed their allegiance to the progressive tradition.

266. *The Great Society*

President Johnson, buoyed by his popular mandate, set forth the goals of the Great Society in his State of the Union message of January 1965. The Great Society, he observed, rested on abundance and liberty for all. The opportunities enjoyed by most Americans had to be opened to all, and the quality of everyone's life had to be improved. This could be accomplished by stimulating the economy, continuing the antipoverty programs, and developing imaginative solutions for the complex problems of modern urban society. The control of water and air pollution was imperative, and the country's natural beauty had to be preserved. Above all, a new and expanded program of federal aid to education was needed. In the months that followed, the President submitted a large number of specific proposals to implement the Great Society.

Congress acted with an alacrity and enthusiasm rarely seen on Capitol Hill. The Appalachian Regional Development Act, signed by the President in March, was the first major domestic program to be approved. Appalachia, extending from Pennsylvania to northern Alabama and encompassing 182,000 square miles and 17,000,000 people, was a region of poverty in a nation of abundance. Per capita income in Appalachia was 40 per cent lower than the national average; unemployment, 50 per cent greater. The President's program emphasized economic development rather than welfare support. Thus the Appalachian Act provided $1,100,000,000 in federal subsidies for highway construction, establishment of health centers, and development of the area's resources. The program would be implemented by an Appalachian Regional Commission, a joint federal-state agency headed by a federal member appointed by the President and by members appointed by Appalachian governors. The states would design projects to fit their own needs and then submit them for consideration by the Commission. Once approved, they would be executed by state authorities.

The decay of the nation's urban areas was, in many ways, an even more pressing problem, for there was little opportunity and less hope in rapidly expanding city slums. The administration sought to alleviate one aspect of this plight with the Housing and Urban Development Act of 1965. This measure, representing the most comprehensive legislation since the Housing Act of 1949, extended the major programs of the Housing and Home Finance Agency for four years, provided assistance for the construction of approximately 240,000 additional units of low-rent public housing, and authorized $2,900,000,000 in federal grants for urban renewal over a four-year period. There was controversy only over provisions for payment of direct federal rent supplements to low income families. Although Congress failed to approve funds for this portion of the program before adjourning in October, the necessary money was furnished by a supplementary appropriation in May 1966. Congress, at the President's request, also created a Cabinet-level Department of Housing and Urban Development to administer the provisions of the Act and related programs. Robert C. Weaver, the first Negro ever named to the Cabinet, was sworn in as head of the new agency in January 1966.

A further milestone was reached in 1965 with passage of the most significant piece of welfare legislation since the New Deal. President Truman had proposed a comprehensive plan for medical care for the aged, to be financed through Social Security, in 1945. During the next twenty years, the proposal had faced the vehement and successful opposition of the American Medical Association. But Johnson, having made the program a major issue in his campaign, now had both a mandate and the necessary votes on Capitol Hill. The House and Senate approved the bill by large majorities, and it was signed into law by President Johnson, with Truman at his side, on July 30 in Independence, Missouri.[8]

Education, the President emphasized on many occasions, was the key to the Great Society. Although school and college enrollment soared to approximately 54,000,000 in 1965 and the nation spent a record $39,000,000,000 on education during the 1964–5 school year, many Americans remained unable to provide their children with full educational opportunities. President Johnson was determined to help their need. The Elementary and Secondary Education Act of 1965, passed by Congress in April, was an historic breakthrough, settling a twenty-year controversy over the use of large-scale federal funds to support primary and secondary education. The $1,300,000,000 program was designed primarily to furnish federal assistance to schools with large numbers of children from low income families. The Act contained a formula for handling the thorny

~~~~~~~~~~~~~~~~~~~~~

[8] The Act, covering most persons sixty-five and older, included a basic health plan which provided up to 90 days of hospital care, 100 days of nursing home care, and 100 home health-care visits. A supplementary plan, available to those over sixty-five who elected to pay a premium of $3 a month, covered 80 per cent of the costs of a variety of health services, including doctors' fees, after a standard deduction of $50. The program would be funded by general revenues and an increased Social Security tax, rising in steps from 8.4 per cent in 1966 to 11.3 per cent in 1987.

issue of federal aid to parochial schools: assistance would be supplied to children attending both private and public schools, but expenditures would be controlled by public agencies. The President, in addition, won approval of the Higher Education Act of 1965 to expand federal aid on another level of education. It made scholarships averaging $500 available to more than 140,000 capable but needy college students. The measure also authorized a National Teachers Corps to provide qualified personnel for schools in poverty-striken areas at the expense of the federal government. Funds to initiate this part of the program were approved in 1966.

Meanwhile, the Negro revolution continued unabated. Protest demonstrations began in Selma, Alabama, the center of Dr. King's campaign for voter registration, in January 1965. After two months of intense effort by civil rights workers, local registrars had added only fifty Negroes to the voting list. King decided to publicize the plight of the Negro in the Deep South by staging a protest march from Selma to the state capitol in Montgomery, a distance of fifty miles. The Negroes started their journey on March 7. It was quickly broken up by state and local police using billy clubs and electric cattle prods. Federal Judge Frank M. Johnson, Jr., ordered Governor Wallace to permit the march and to protect the marchers. When Wallace claimed that the state was unable to implement this order, President Johnson called the Alabama National Guard into federal service. The march took place without incident on March 21–25, culminating in a rally of 25,000 persons in front of the first capitol of the Confederacy. But there was no end to white violence against civil rights workers in the Deep South. James J. Reeb, a Unitarian minister from Boston, died on March 11 after being beaten on the streets of Selma. Viola Liuzzo, a civil rights worker from Detroit, was shot and killed on March 25 while driving her car on an Alabama highway immediately after the march to Montgomery.

Events in Selma, like those in Birmingham, were the catalyst for new federal action. The President, appearing before a joint session of Congress on March 15, used the vocabulary of the Negro revolution in an impassioned plea for justice. "Their cause must be our cause too," he said. "Because it is not just Negroes, but really it is all of us who must overcome the crippling legacy of bigotry and injustice. And we shall overcome." Negroes must not be denied their basic constitutional rights. "This time, on this issue," he continued, "there must be no delay, or no hesitation or no compromise."

There was none. Twenty weeks later Congress passed the Civil Rights Act of 1965, suspending literacy and other voter tests and authorizing federal supervision of registration in states and counties where such tests or devices had been employed prior to November 1, 1964, and where less than half of the adult residents had been registered to vote or had voted in the presidential election of 1964. In the event that state officials refused to register qualified applicants, federal examiners were empowered to do so.

The last great legislative step guaranteeing the right to vote to the Negro had been taken. But other problems plagued the racial front. This was demonstrated during the week of August 11–16, when riots convulsed the Watts section of Los Angeles; 34 persons were killed, over

1,000 were injured, and the damage was estimated to be in excess of $40,000,000. A minor incident had provoked the riots, but the real causes lay deeper. As a special commission headed by John A. McCone, former Director of the CIA, pointed out, the trouble was rooted in chronic unemployment, insufficient schooling, hatred of police as symbols of authority, and seething discontent. Although state and federal officials were making efforts to improve conditions, the Watts riots were only part of the price being paid by the nation for decades of neglect.

Although President Johnson's legislative program had met generally smooth sailing in Congress, there were several defeats. Labor legislation was the most notable failure. The President had pledged during the campaign to work for the repeal of Section 14(b), the "right to work" provision, of the Taft-Hartley Act. The measure passed the House but ran aground on a filibuster in the Senate. Efforts to revive the repeal measure in 1966 were equally unsuccessful. Congress, in addition, failed to pass the President's home rule bill for the District of Columbia.

Johnson planned to continue and expand his Great Society programs in 1966. Addressing Congress in January of that year, he called for an intensification of the war on poverty, creation of a new Cabinet-level Transportation Department, and the beginning of a massive reconstruction of cities. The President also asked for a new civil rights law to prohibit discrimination in the selection of federal and state juries, empower the Attorney General to initiate suits to desegregate schools and public accommodations, ban discrimination in the sale and rental of housing, and punish persons committing violence against Negroes and civil rights workers. But by mid-1966, as the President faced difficulties both at home and abroad, none of his major requests had been approved by Congress. The administration had only obtained sanction of its tax proposal, designed to dampen inflationary pressures and furnish additional revenue for the war in Vietnam.[9]

267. *The Supreme Court Enlarges Its Revolution*

The Supreme Court continued to affirm its new role as protector of individual rights—as opposed to its earlier role as protector of property rights—under Presidents Kennedy and Johnson. Landmark decisions were handed down on civil rights, due process in criminal cases, and, above all, the nature of the electoral process. In fact, the court's decisions in these areas were as significant as any legislation adopted by Congress during the same period.

Problems raised by the Negro revolution occupied much of the court's time. Most of the cases coming before the high bench involved the review of convictions obtained by state and local authorities on trespass or crimi-

[9] This measure was expected to raise $1,100,000,000 in fiscal 1966 and $4,800,-000,000 in 1967. It provided for increased withholding of individual income taxes, an accelerated payment of corporate taxes, and the suspension in 1966 and 1967 of the reduction in federal excise taxes on automobiles and telephone service that had been approved earlier.

nal mischief statutes against Negroes and civil rights workers for "sit-ins," protest marches, and demonstrations. The court, in Burton *v.* Wilmington Parking Authority, 1961, expanded the coverage of the Fourteenth Amendment by ruling against the exclusion of Negroes by private owners of restaurants located on state property. An even more significant decision—Peterson *v.* City of Greenville, 1963—extended this principle, under certain conditions, to privately-owned facilities. In Cox *v.* Louisiana, 1964, the court reversed the conviction of a civil rights leader under a Louisiana statute prohibiting disturbance of the peace. Such laws, designed to punish public demonstrations protesting against discrimination and segregation, were an infringement of the rights of free speech and assembly. But this decision, the court carefully pointed out, should not be interpreted as approving riotous conduct, or even peaceful demonstrations, which conflicted with honest state and local efforts to promote law and order, regulate traffic, and safeguard private and public property.

Federal civil rights legislation also fared well in the court. The validity of the public accommodations section of the Civil Rights Act of 1964 was sustained in Heart of Atlanta Motel *v.* United States, 1964. The federal government's prohibitions against racial discrimination by hotels providing lodging to transient guests, the court ruled, constituted a legitimate exercise of its power to regulate interstate commerce. The same principle was applied to restaurants in Katzenbach *v.* McClung, 1964. The court, on March 7, 1966, unanimously dismissed South Carolina *v.* Katzenbach, a suit challenging the validity of the Civil Rights Act of 1965. In a related matter, the court struck down the Virginia poll tax in *state* and *local* elections. Such a tax, the court ruled in Harper *v.* Virginia State Board of Education, 1966, violated the "equal protection" clause of the Fourteenth Amendment. The Twenty-Fourth Amendment, passed in 1964, had banned poll taxes in *federal* elections.

Indigent defendants in criminal cases often found it difficult to make full use of the judicial process to protect their legal rights and obtain review of convictions. The court moved to rectify this situation in a number of historic decisions. In Gideon *v.* Wainwright, 1963, the court held that a state—Florida in this instance—was obliged to supply defense counsel to indigent defendants even in non-capital prosecutions. The court, in fact, overruled a previous case—Betts *v.* Brady, 1942—with such alacrity that Justice Tom C. Clark commented in a concurring opinion: "I agree that *Betts* should be overruled, but consider it entitled to a more respectful burial than has been accorded." The Gideon decision applied retroactively to all convicts who had been tried and found guilty of non-capital offenses without benefit of counsel.

In Fay *v.* Noia, 1963, the court expanded the right of prisoners to obtain federal judicial review of questionable state court procedures used in their trial. Prisoners who had failed to exercise their right of appeal through the state court system, the Supreme Court ruled, might still seek later federal review. The court also continued to expand the coverage of the Fourteenth and Fifth amendments in protecting the individual against the harsh administration of criminal law. The court, in Escobedo *v.* Illinois, 1964, decreed that a conviction was invalid when the police had either refused to permit a suspect to have counsel during interrogation or had failed to inform him of his right to remain silent.

The court, in a series of decisions on June 13, 1966, established clear guidelines for the police in the treatment of arrested persons. Such persons had to be advised of their right to remain silent or have a lawyer present during interrogation, and counsel had to be provided, even at state expense, if requested by the suspect. This last decision, applying the privileges of the Fifth Amendment to the police station, provoked vigorous dissent from several members of the court. Justice John M. Harlan termed the ruling a dangerous experiment in view of the increasing crime rate. "Nothing in the letter or spirit of the Constitution or in the precedents," he maintained, "squares with the heavy-handed and one-sided action that is so precipitously taken by the Court in the name of fulfilling its constitutional responsibilities." Chief Justice Warren, speaking for the majority, countered that the right against self-incrimination was enshrined in the Constitution. "That right," he added, "cannot be abridged."

These important decisions affecting civil rights and criminal due process were overshadowed by the court's further application of the "one man, one vote" principle, first annunciated in Baker *v.* Carr, 1962 (see above, p. 772). The first significant case to be decided involved the legality of Georgia's county unit system, used in primary elections for state offices and United States Senate seats. The court struck down this system in Gray *v.* Sanders, 1963, as a violation of the "equal protection" clause of the Fourteenth Amendment. Undue weight, the court ruled, had been accorded rural votes. In Wesberry *v.* Sanders, 1964, the court declared that the "one man, one vote" mandate was inherent in Article I of the Constitution as applied to seats in the United States House of Representatives. States were instructed to draw the boundaries of their congressional districts so that members of Congress would represent districts of roughly equal population. The high water mark of the court's rulings came with Reynolds *v.* Sims, 1964, and a series of related cases. The court now held that both houses of *state* legislatures had to be composed of representatives elected from districts having roughly equal population. Following this decision, the court was widely criticized for having exceeded its prerogatives and usurping the functions assigned to the legislative branch under the Constitution. Chief Justice Warren disagreed. Speaking for the court in Reynolds *v.* Sims, he had commented: "Legislators represent people, not trees or acres. Legislators are elected by voters, not farms or cities or economic interests. As long as ours is a representative form of government, and our legislators are those instruments of government elected directly by and directly representative of the people, the right to elect legislators in a free and unimpaired fashion is a bedrock of our political system."

Two decisions, Engel *v.* Vitale, 1962, and School District of Abington Township *v.* Schempp, 1963, outlawed local or state laws requiring Bible reading and prayers in public schools on the ground that such practices constituted an establishment of religion contrary to the First Amendment. These decisions set off much public furor and a movement to reverse the court's rulings by a constitutional amendment. This movement quickly ran aground on a national conviction, expressed officially by several major Protestant denominations, that the court was right. A similar campaign for an amendment to restore exclusive control over apportionment to the states did not seem destined to succeed by the end of 1966.

268.   *Continued Perplexities in a Changing World*

President Johnson had taken great strides toward constructing the Great Society at home, but his administration faced mounting problems abroad in meeting the responsibilities of America's great power. The unity of the Atlantic community threatened to collapse; there was unrest in Latin America; and, in Asia, the United States was drawn into its first undeclared war since Korea.

The North Atlantic Treaty Alliance appeared on the verge of disintegration by the mid-1960's. The United States had long advocated a unified Europe and one in close partnership with its American ally for common defense. The nations of Western Europe had taken steps in this direction with the formation of the Common Market and by participation in the unified NATO command structure. Although control of nuclear weapons had raised many difficulties, the United States hoped to solve these, and foster European unity at the same time, by creating a multilateral nuclear force—a fleet manned by mixed crews and equipped with atomic weapons. But the American "Grand Design" met considerable opposition, first from Great Britain, then from France.

During the late 1950's and early 1960's, the British had put up the chief obstacles to Atlantic unity. They were reluctant to enter the Common Market and thus loosen their ties with their Commonwealth partners. More important, they hesitated to surrender their independent nuclear capability. The United States sympathized with the British attitude. In fact, in 1960 President Eisenhower had pledged that Great Britain could share the Skybolt missile system—a bomber-launched ballistic missile with a 1,000-mile range—then being developed by the United States Government. As Skybolt would extend the life of obsolete British V-bombers to 1970, thus providing an independent deterrent at the least cost, the British canceled development of their own medium-range ballistic missile. Skybolt, however, proved a slow and costly project. By the time of President Kennedy's election, it was clear that Skybolt would not be worth its cost to the United States in view of the increasing effectiveness of the Minuteman and Polaris missile systems. Therefore, Secretary of Defense McNamara, with Kennedy's approval, canceled the project. The British were understandably upset. Kennedy, attempting to restore harmony in Anglo-American relations, met with Prime Minister Macmillan in Nassau in December 1962. The President first suggested that the American and British governments share the costs of Skybolt's further development. When this was refused, he offered to give Polaris missiles to Britain, on the condition that the British agreed to assign their Polaris-equipped forces to NATO. Macmillan objected at first, then agreed, with the proviso that Britain's Polaris missiles could be withdrawn from NATO if Britain decided that its national security was in extreme jeopardy.

The United States also offered to supply Polaris missiles to France under comparable conditions. President De Gaulle, in a news conference on January 14, 1963, flatly rejected this proposal, adding that France would continue to develop its own nuclear weapons. Furthermore, he registered strong opposition to Britain's belated bid to enter the Common Market. A unified Europe, if it should come, De Gaulle implied, would be led by France, not Britain.

Franco-American relations continued downhill following President Kennedy's death. The new administration in Washington continued to press for the multilateral nuclear force, but the French President would not budge from his opposition. The dénouement came on March 12, 1966, when France informed the fourteen other NATO members that all French troops would be withdrawn from that organization. De Gaulle also requested the removal of NATO headquarters and American military personnel and installations from French soil. He did not, however, denounce the Treaty, due for renegotiation in 1969. President Johnson, in turn, affirmed America's determination to maintain NATO, even without France. "We shall not," he said, "abandon an institution which has proved itself in the hour of peril."

A resurgent French nationalism, fed by President De Gaulle, precipitated the Atlantic crisis, but the reasons for the threatened breakup of NATO lay deeper. Paradoxically, NATO's difficulties reflected the accomplishments of the Alliance. The United States, determined to reconstruct Europe following the Second World War, had poured its treasure into the continent. The resultant economic prosperity testified to the effectiveness of America's efforts. Yet, as a strong and vital community emerged, it became less dependent upon American aid and protection. Disunity seemed the price of success.

Latin American unrest presented more immediate problems for the Johnson administration, with Panama affording the first serious crisis. Relations between Panamanians and American residents of the Canal Zone, long strained, broke out in violence on January 9, 1964, when Panamanian students demanded that the Panamanian flag be flown alongside the American flag at Balboa High School in the Canal Zone. The riots that followed lasted three and a half days and resulted in the death of twenty-one Panamanians and three American soldiers. A genuine feeling of resentment triggered the riots, but the violence was encouraged by ultranationalistic and Communist elements. Panama promptly broke off diplomatic relations with the United States. The two nations, after tempers had cooled, agreed to permit the Inter-American Peace Committee of the OAS to mediate the dispute. The OAS's efforts, reinforced by secret talks between Panama and the United States, resulted in the signing of a joint declaration on April 3, 1964. It called for an immediate resumption of diplomatic intercourse, followed by "the prompt elimination of the cause of the conflict between the two countries without limitations or preconditions of any kind."

More serious trouble erupted in the Dominican Republic. The United States had become deeply involved in that island's affairs following the overthrow of the dictatorial Trujillo regime in 1961. Economic aid was poured into the country as the Kennedy administration attempted to make it a showpiece of the Alliance for Progress. The United States, in addition, had encouraged an election which led to the victory of Juan Bosch, a distinguished novelist and political liberal, in December 1962. Bosch tried to deal with his country's chronic social and economic problems, but he proved to be an inefficient administrator and leader. His failure led to his overthrow by military leaders in September 1963. President Kennedy, disturbed that his efforts to bring stability to the island had gone awry, withheld recognition from the new regime and suspended American economic aid.

President Johnson, although restoring diplomatic relations in December 1963, maintained an attitude of cautious reserve toward Dominican affairs. Donald Reid Cabral, head of the civilian junta that came to power after Bosch's fall, was no more successful than his predecessor. Sabotage, strikes, and underground resistance kept the country in continuous turmoil. Any hope of solving the Republic's economic difficulties vanished when the price of sugar, the island's major product, dropped precipitously in 1964. Cabral sought to forestall economic chaos by canceling the traditional Christmas bonus for workers, cutting payrolls in the sugar industry, and reducing the military budget. This sensible policy only served to fuse all elements of the population in opposition to his regime. The anti-government forces, led by the army, rebelled on April 24, 1965, toppling Cabral. However, pro-Bosch elements of the coalition distrusted the army's promise to hold free elections. They demanded that the constitution of 1963 be restored and that Bosch resume the presidency. When the army failed to meet these demands, violence broke out in Santo Domingo. The Dominican army, led by General Elias Wessin y Wessin, responded by attacking the city. Meanwhile, the rebels elected Colonel Francisco Caamaño Deñó as "provisional President."

Events in the Dominican Republic caused consternation in Washington. The administration knew that Communist elements had infiltrated the rebel forces, but it was difficult to judge the extent of their influence. The Washington government feared that the Communists might profit from the turbulent situation by seizing power and turning the island into another Cuba. Determined to prevent such an outcome, President Johnson landed a contingent of marines at Santo Domingo on April 28, 1965. Over 20,000 American troops soon followed.

The United States attempted to generate support for the intervention by requesting the creation of an Inter-American Peace Force. The OAS, with some reluctance, approved the request on May 6. Subsequently, American forces on the island were joined by units from Paraguay, Nicaragua, Honduras, and Brazil.

On September 3 the United States installed a provisional President, Héctor García-Godoy, to serve until elections could be held. The rebels, reduced to their last stronghold in central Santo Domingo, had no choice but to submit. The army, although reluctant to accept García-Godoy, capitulated after the United States threatened to cut off its funds. Unrest continued to simmer below the surface, occasionally erupting in violence, but the situation remained under control. The provisional President, backed by American troops, assigned the military and rebel leaders to diplomatic posts abroad. The way was now clear for free elections, sched-

VIETNAM, 1966

uled for June 1, 1966. Juan Bosch, who had returned from exile, was favored to win, but Joaquin Balaguer, a moderate, scored a surprising victory. Bosch's popular strength apparently had been overestimated. The Dominican people, especially those living in the countryside, had voted for peace and stability.

European and Latin American problems pale into insignificance when compared with perplexities in South Vietnam. America's role in that truncated nation had been limited before 1961 to supplying economic aid and military equipment. This commitment was expanded by President Kennedy to include American military technicians and advisers; by the time of Kennedy's death the United States had over 16,500 military personnel in South Vietnam (see above, p. 875). President Johnson pledged continued assistance to South Vietnam, but conditions grew worse daily. The military situation was precarious: North Vietnam, exhausting its cadres of trained Southerners, infiltrated increasing numbers of its own troops across the border. Worse still, the political situation was chaotic: there had been a procession of nine governments in the sixteen months following Diem's overthrow in November 1963. A Communist victory was in sight.

Johnson evidenced his concern over Vietnam in selecting replacements for the leading American diplomatic and military officials in the country. General Maxwell D. Taylor, Chairman of the Joint Chiefs of Staff, took over as Ambassador in June 1964 when Henry Cabot Lodge returned to the political wars in the United States. U. Alexis Johnson, the State Department's highest ranking career diplomat, was appointed to the newly-created post of Deputy Ambassador. General William C. Westmoreland was named to head the American military mission.

While American policy came under review in Washington, North Vietnam challenged United States naval power in the South China Sea. On August 2, 1964, three North Vietnamese motor patrol boats attacked U.S.S. *Maddox*, a destroyer cruising in the Gulf of Tonkin some thirty miles off the coast of North Vietnam. No damage resulted. Two days later, the *Maddox* and another vessel came under fire, again without result, this time while steaming sixty miles off the coast. North Vietnam's motives for these attacks were unclear. They may have been made in retaliation for South Vietnamese guerrilla raids; perhaps they were meant to test American reaction. In any event, the United States quickly responded. American aircraft struck North Vietnam on August 4–5, destroying approximately two dozen patrol boats and supporting facilities.

The President, at the same time, asked Congress to support his actions. The House passed a resolution of approval on August 7 by a vote of 416 to 0. In the Senate, Wayne Morse of Oregon alone opposed the resolution, claiming that the United States had provoked the attacks. Senator J. William Fulbright, chairman of the foreign relations committee, replied that North Vietnam was guilty of aggression. The United States, Fulbright said, had no choice but to fight back and make it clear to the Communists "that their aggressive and expansionist ambitions, wherever advanced, will meet precisely that degree of American opposition which is necessary to frustrate them." The Senate speedily approved the resolution.

American forces maintained their advisory role following the Gulf of Tonkin incident, and there were no further raids on the North. The administration was still pondering a course of action when, again, events in Southeast Asia prompted a decision to escalate American participation. The Vietcong attacked American barracks and installations at Pleiku on the night of February 8, 1965, killing 8 American soldiers and wounding more than 100. United States aircraft retaliated the next day by bombing just north of the 17th Parallel dividing North Vietnam and South Vietnam. The Vietcong struck next on February 11, blowing up an American billet at Quinhon. Twenty-one Americans were found dead in the rubble. Events began to move swiftly. A sustained air offensive against North Vietnam was opened in March. The first elements of two reinforced marine battalions landed at Danang during the same month. American troops numbered 190,000 by the end of 1965 and increased to more than 275,000 by mid-1966. The United States was at war, in fact if not in name.

While wielding the sword with one hand, President Johnson held out the olive branch with the other. In a major policy address at the The Johns Hopkins University on April 7, 1965, the President, while reaffirming America's determination to halt aggression, also expressed willingness to negotiate. In addition, he advocated a vast program of aid for Southeast Asia, including development of the Mekong Valley along the lines of the TVA. The President invited the Communists to participate in the project. Bombing raids on the North were halted in the following month while the President called for "unconditional negotiations." Although North Vietnam did not respond to these overtures, and American bombing was soon resumed, the administration continued to search for a peaceful solution to the conflict. In late December 1965, the air attacks were again suspended while American diplomats around the world sought a basis for negotiation. There was still no reply, and the air offensive was renewed on January 31, 1966.

The Communists' silence may have been due to their confidence in a military victory. Before the summer of 1965, their forces roamed most of South Vietnam at will, and the size of their attacks had reached the regimental level. American military power, however, was quickly brought to bear. In August 1965, American marines attacked a Vietcong main-force regiment dug in on the Chu Lai peninsula, just south of the major American base at Danang. Although the marines suffered more than 200 casualties, the Communist regiment was destroyed. An even more important engagement took place in November, when the First Cavalry Division (Airmobile) clashed with North Vietnamese regular troops in the Iadrang Valley of the strategically important Central Highlands. After a fierce four-day battle, American troops claimed 2,200 Communist dead at the cost of 600 American casualties. The war was far from won by the end of 1965, but a Communist military victory no longer seemed imminent. After another year of the same kind of fighting, the war still continued, but a Communist victory now no longer seemed possible.

American officials were aware that military power alone would not bring victory. "The war," President Johnson observed, "must be won on two fronts. One front is military. The other front is the struggle against social injustice; against hunger, disease and ignorance; against political apathy and indifference." Accordingly, the President personally led an American delegation to Hawaii in February 1966 to meet with the Premier of South Vietnam, Nguyen Cao Ky. Johnson urged the South Vietnamese leader to undertake an extensive program of social and economic reform, especially in the rural areas. Ky agreed to give this problem his full attention. The Premier, however, returned home to face renewed opposition to his government from dissident Buddhist elements. Political unrest continued to vitiate efforts for reform.

President Johnson also faced growing—if less violent—discontent at home. His administration had made little progress in explaining the motives and objectives of policy in South Vietnam to the American people. The Senate foreign relations committee, under the prodding of Chairman Fulbright, took matters in hand when hearings began, in late January 1966, on the President's request for additional funds for the war. The proceedings were given wide publicity, with much of the testimony carried over national television. General Taylor, Secretary Rusk, and David E. Bell, Administrator of the Agency for International Development (AID), defended the administration. Their views were challenged by, among others, General James M. Gavin, former Ambassador to France, and by George F. Kennan, specialist on Soviet affairs.

While the Senate hearings provided a forum for discussion of American policy in Asia, college campuses across the nation became focal points for discontent. In 1965 "teach-ins" had characterized the protest movement; during the following year, protest was marked by less discussion and more demonstration. No issue had so convulsed the academic community since Munich.

Americans had become increasingly divided by mid-1966. Some voices called for complete American withdrawal from South Vietnam; others urged an expansion of the war; still others counseled a middle course of continued effort to assist South Vietnam to repel aggression and enjoy self-determination without, however, risking a direct confrontation with North Vietnam's supporter, Red China. The President continued to steer this middle course. But the dilemma of South Vietnam remained far from solved. It continued to be the most perplexing—and the most dangerous—problem facing the Johnson administration and the American people.

SUGGESTED ADDITIONAL

READING

———

INDEX

SUGGESTED ADDITIONAL READING

1. American Politics from Theodore Roosevelt to Herbert Hoover

A.   Aspects of the Progressive Revolt, 1897–1917

For origins and the immediate background, see Charles A. Barker, *Henry George* (1955); Sidney Fine, *Laissez Faire and the General Welfare State* (1956); and Harold U. Faulkner, *Politics, Reform, and Expansion, 1890–1900* (1959). We now have a number of general accounts of varying quality and different emphases. Among them are Samuel P. Hays, *The Response to Industrialism, 1885–1914* (1957); Eric F. Goldman, *Rendezvous with Destiny* (1953); H. U. Faulkner, *The Quest for Social Justice, 1898–1914* (1931); Russel B. Nye, *Midwestern Progressive Politics* (1951); and C. Vann Woodward, *Origins of the New South, 1877–1913* (1951). See also Richard Hofstadter, *The Age of Reform* (1955), which should be read with Norman Pollack, *The Populist Response to Industrial America: Midwestern Populist Thought* (1962), and Walter T. K. Nugent, *The Tolerant Populists: Kansas Populism and Nativism* (1963). S. P. Hays, *Conservation and the Gospel of Efficiency: The Progressive Conservation Movement, 1890–1920* (1959); Robert H. Wiebe, *Businessmen and Reform: A Study of the Progressive Movement* (1962); and Samuel Haber, *Efficiency and Uplift: Scientific Management in the Progressive Era, 1890–1920* (1964), illuminate significant phases.

Still the classic accounts of progressive revolt in the cities and states are Lincoln Steffens's *The Shame of the Cities* (1904) and *The Struggle for Self-Government* (1906). They should be read with *The Autobiography of Lincoln Steffens* (1931). Excellent state studies include Ransome E. Noble, Jr., *New Jersey Progressivism Before Wilson* (1946); George E. Mowry, *The California Progressives* (1951); Robert S. Maxwell, *La Follette and the Rise of the Progressives in Wisconsin* (1956); Richard M. Abrams, *Conservatism in a Progressive Era: Massachusetts Politics, 1900–1912* (1964); and Hoyt Landon Warner, *Progressivism in Ohio, 1897–1917* (1964). Among the biographies of city and state leaders, the following range far beyond the scope of this section: Alpheus T. Mason, *Brandeis: A Free Man's Life* (1946); Belle C. and Fola La Follette, *Robert M. La Follette* (2 vols., 1953); Aubrey L. Brooks and H. T. Lefler (eds.), *The Papers of Walter Clark* (2 vols., 1948–50); Dewey W. Grantham, *Hoke Smith and the Politics of the New South* (1958); Oliver H. Orr, Jr., *Charles Brantley Aycock* (1961); William Larsen, *Montague of Virginia, the Making of a Southern Progressive* (1965); and Richard Lowitt, *George W. Norris, the Making of a Progressive, 1861–1912* (1963). Daniel Levine, *Varieties of Reform Thought* (1964), dealing with Jane Addams, Samuel Gompers, Robert La Follette, and others, is an important contribution to our understanding of this period.

We are now well on the way toward a comprehensive history of the social justice movement. Don D. Lescohier, "Working Conditions," and Elizabeth Brandeis, "Labor Legislation," in John R. Commons *et al.*, *History of Labour in the United States* (4 vols., 1918–35), vol. III, contain much of the basic information. Robert H. Bremner, *From the Depths: The Discovery of Poverty in the United States* (1956), is a rich and eloquent general account, supplemented by his brief *American Philanthropy* (1960). Roy Lubove, *The Professional Altruist: The Emergence of Social Work as a Career,*

1880–1930 (1965), is an important study. Josephine C. Goldmark, *Impatient Crusader: Florence Kelley's Life Story* (1953), and Louise C. Wade, *Graham Taylor: Pioneer for Social Justice, 1851–1938* (1964), record the work of two of the pioneers. See also the following memoirs by a leader in the movement: Jane Addams, *Twenty Years at Hull-house* (1910) and *The Second Twenty Years at Hull-house* (1930).

On the muckrakers there is a rich literature: Cornelius C. Regier, *The Era of the Muckrakers* (1932); Louis Filler, *Crusaders for American Liberalism* (1939); Daniel Aaron, *Men of Good Hope* (1951); and Lloyd R. Morris, *Postscript to Yesterday* (1947). The writings of the muckrakers and the literature of the revolt are discussed in this volume, Sections 34–35.

We have no general history of intellectual progressivism, but Henry S. Commager, *The American Mind* (1950); Maurice M. Vance, *Charles Richard Van Hise: Scientist Progressive* (1960); Joseph Dorfman, *Thorstein Veblen and His America* (1934); David W. Noble, *The Paradox of Progressive Thought* (1958); Charles Forcey, *The Crossroads of Liberalism: Croly, Weyl, Lippmann and the Progressive Era, 1900–1925* (1961); and Goldman, *Rendezvous with Destiny*, and Mason, *Brandeis,* both cited above, provide invaluable insight. For the most important contributions by the intellectual progressives, see Section 36 of this volume.

The literature on Socialism and left-wing unionism is large and excellent: David A. Shannon, *The Socialist Party of America: A History* (1955); Donald D. Egbert and S. Persons (eds.), *Socialism and American Life* (2 vols., 1952); Howard H. Quint, *The Forging of American Socialism* (1953); Ira Kipnis, *The American Socialist Movement, 1897–1912* (1952); Paul F. Brissenden, *The I.W.W.* (1919); and Ray Ginger, *The Bending Cross, A Biography of Eugene Victor Debs* (1940).

B. *The Republican Era, 1901–1913*

George E. Mowry, *The Era of Theodore Roosevelt, 1900–1912* (1958), has filled the need for a good concise political history of the Republican era. Mark Sullivan, *Our Times, the United States, 1900–1925* (6 vols., 1926–35), vols. I–IV, is racy and informative. For legislative issues and battles, see Frank W. Taussig, *Tariff History of the United States* (1931 edn.); Sidney Ratner, *American Taxation* (1942); M. Nelson McGeary, *Gifford Pinchot, Forester-Politician* (1960); Hans Thorelli, *The Federal Antitrust Policy* (1954); William Z. Ripley, *Railroads: Rates and Regulation* (1912); Paul P. Van Riper, *History of the United States Civil Service* (1958); and Oscar E. Anderson, Jr., *The Health of a Nation: Harvey W. Wiley and the Fight for Pure Food* (1958).

The general biographical literature of this period grows increasingly richer. Henry F. Pringle, *Theodore Roosevelt, A Biography* (1931), long the standard, has now been supplanted by William H. Harbaugh, *Power and Responsibility, The Life and Times of Theodore Roosevelt* (1961). No student should overlook Elting E. Morison and J. M. Blum (eds.), *The Letters of Theodore Roosevelt* (8 vols., 1951–54), and John M. Blum, *The Republican Roosevelt* (1954), for new information and insights. H. F. Pringle, *The Life and Times of William Howard Taft* (2 vols., 1939), covers the entire period and beyond. For other political leaders in the period, see Philip C. Jessup, *Elihu Root* (2 vols., 1938); Richard W. Leopold, *Elihu Root and the Conservative Tradition* (1954); Merlo J. Pusey, *Charles Evans Hughes* (2 vols., 1951); John A. Garraty, *Henry Cabot Lodge* (1953); Francis B. Simkins, *Pitchfork Ben Tillman* (1944); Claude G. Bowers, *Beveridge and the Progressive Era* (1932); Hermann Hagedorn, *Leonard Wood* (2 vols., 1931); Elting E. Morison, *Turmoil and Tradition: A Study of the Life and Times of Henry L. Stimson* (1960); Paul W. Glad, *The Trumpet Soundeth: William Jennings Bryan and His Democracy, 1896–1912* (1960); and Paola E. Coletta, *William Jennings Bryan: Political Evangelist, 1860–1908* (1964). G. E. Mowry, *Theodore Roosevelt and the Progressive Movement* (1946), and A. T. Mason, *Bureaucracy Convicts Itself: The Ballinger-Pinchot Controversy of 1910* (1941), are excellent for the rise of the insurgents and rupture of the GOP. J. Rogers Hollingsworth, *The Whirligig of Politics: The*

Democracy of Cleveland and Bryan (1963), relates the fortunes of the Democratic party.

C.   *The Wilson Era*

The only general works on the period 1912–21 are Frederick L. Paxson, *The American Democracy and the World War* (3 vols., 1936–48), and Arthur S. Link, *Woodrow Wilson and the Progressive Era* (1954). For aspects of domestic history, see Henry P. Willis, *The Federal Reserve System* (1923), and J. Laurence Laughlin, *The Federal Reserve Act* (1933), for the background and writing of the Federal Reserve bill; and John D. Clark, *The Federal Trust Policy* (1931), for the writing of the Clayton and Federal Trade Commission bills.

The most voluminous and sometimes the best literature on the Wilson period are the biographies and memoirs of the leaders of that period. Arthur Walworth, *Woodrow Wilson* (2 vols., 1958), is a good personal biography. A. S. Link, *Wilson: The Road to the White House* (1947), *Wilson: The New Freedom* (1956), *Wilson: The Struggle for Neutrality* (1960), *Wilson: Confusions and Crises, 1915–1916* (1964), and *Wilson: Campaigns for Progressivism and Peace, 1916–1917* (1965), cover the public career in some detail from 1902 to 1917. A. S. Link, *Woodrow Wilson, A Brief Biography* (1963); J. M. Blum, *Woodrow Wilson and the Politics of Morality* (1956); and J. A. Garraty, *Woodrow Wilson* (1956), are brief studies. R. S. Baker and W. E. Dodd (eds.), *The Public Papers of Woodrow Wilson* (6 vols., 1925–27), prints speeches and public papers, while John Wells Davidson (ed.), *A Crossroads of Freedom: The 1912 Campaign Speeches of Woodrow Wilson* (1956), is a significant addition. An indispensable source is Charles Seymour (ed.), *The Intimate Papers of Colonel House* (4 vols., 1926–28).

Biographies about leaders in the Wilson era include: J. M. Blum, *Joe Tumulty and the Wilson Era* (1951); Frank Freidel, *Franklin D. Roosevelt: The Apprenticeship* (1952); C. H. Cramer, *Newton D. Baker, A Biography* (1961); Margaret L. Coit, *Mr. Baruch* (1957); Stanley Coben, *A. Mitchell Palmer: Politician* (1963); and Lawrence W. Levine, *Defender of the Faith, William Jennings Bryan: The Last Decade, 1915–1925* (1965), which are all helpful although of varying quality.

D.   *Demobilization and the Politics and Problems of the Twenties*

For general histories, none of which is comprehensive, see John D. Hicks, *Republican Ascendancy, 1921–1933* (1960); William E. Leuchtenburg, *The Perils of Prosperity, 1914–1932* (1958); Paxson, *The American Democracy and the World War,* vol. III, and Sullivan, *Our Times,* vols. V–VI, cited above, which cover demobilization and the Harding era; H. U. Faulkner, *From Versailles to the New Deal* (1950), a brief survey; Preston W. Slosson, *The Great Crusade and After, 1914–1928* (1930); and James R. Mock and E. Thurber, *Report on Demobilization* (1944).

Valuable for Republican politics and policies of the period are Samuel H. Adams, *Incredible Era: The Life and Times of Warren Gamaliel Harding* (1939), a scathing account; Andrew Sinclair, *The Available Man: The Life Behind the Masks of Warren Gamaliel Harding* (1965); William A. White, *A Puritan in Babylon* (1938), a superb biography of Coolidge; and Herbert Hoover, *Memoirs* (3 vols., 1951–52), vol. II. William T. Hutchinson, *Lowden of Illinois* (2 vols., 1957), is particularly good on the Republican preconvention fight of 1920, but see especially the fine general study by Wesley M. Bagby, *The Road to Normalcy: The Presidential Campaign and Election of 1920* (1962). The literature on Democratic politics in the twenties is sparse. F. Friedel, *Franklin D. Roosevelt: The Ordeal* (1954), is significant and perceptive; James M. Cox, *Journey through My Years* (1946), is good for the campaign of 1920; H. F. Pringle, *Alfred E. Smith* (1927), is still the best biography of the leading Democrat of the period, but see the brief work, Oscar Handlin, *Al Smith and His America* (1958), and the excellent study, Edmund A. Moore, *A Catholic Runs for President: The Campaign*

of 1928 (1956). Humes D. Joy, *Oswald Garrison Villard, Liberal of the 1920's* (1960);
Arthur Mann, *La Guardia: A Fighter Against His Times, 1882–1933* (1959) and *La
Guardia Comes to Power, 1933* (1965); and Howard Zinn, *La Guardia in Congress*
(1959), add much to our knowledge of liberal politics of the period. J. Joseph
Huthmacher, *Massachusetts People and Politics, 1919–1933* (1959), is a pioneering
state study.

There is an abundant and fast-growing literature on specific problems of the
post-Armistice decade. For the first Red Scare, Zechariah Chafee, Jr., *Free Speech in
the United States* (1941), is indispensable, but see also S. Coben, *A. Mitchell Palmer*,
cited above; Robert K. Murray, *Red Scare: A Study in National Hysteria, 1919–1920*
(1955); and Frederick Lewis Allen, *Only Yesterday, An Informal History of the
Nineteen-Twenties* (1931). Theodore Draper, *The Roots of American Communism*
(1957) and *American Communism and Soviet Russia during the Formative Period*
(1960), are superb new contributions. Major aspects of postwar intolerance and
bigotry are related by David M. Chalmers, *Hooded Americanism: The First Century of
the Ku Klux Klan, 1865–1965* (1965); Walter Lippmann, *American Inquisitors* (1928);
and Howard K. Beale, *Are American Teachers Free?* (1936). The facts and significance
of the greatest legal *cause célèbre* of the twenties are related in Felix Frankfurter, *The
Case of Sacco and Vanzetti* (1927), and G. Louis Joughin and E. M. Morgan, *The
Legacy of Sacco and Vanzetti* (1948). Norman F. Furniss's judicious *The Fundamentalist Controversy, 1918–1931* (1954), is the best work on that subject, but see also Ray
Ginger, *Six Days or Forever? Tennessee v. John Thomas Scopes* (1958), for a detailed
study of the Scopes trial. For the origins of the twentieth-century prohibition move-
ment, see Peter H. Odegard, *Pressure Politics, the Story of the Anti-Saloon League*
(1928). The failure of the "noble experiment" is recounted by Herbert Asbury, *The
Great Illusion, an Informal History of Prohibition* (1950). Burl Noggle, *Teapot Dome:
Oil and Politics in the 1920's* (1962), focuses on a major issue of the period.

For three major legislative issues of the twenties—tariff, taxes, and federal policy
toward the electric power industry—see F. Taussig, *Tariff History*, and S. Ratner,
American Taxation, both cited above, and George W. Norris, *Fighting Liberal* (1945).
Judson King, *The Conservation Fight: From Theodore Roosevelt to the Tennessee
Valley Authority* (1959), is highly condemnatory of the private utilities. Preston J.
Hubbard, *Origins of the TVA, the Muscle Shoals Controversy, 1920–1932* (1961), is a
superb scholarly account of the greatest single power fight of the twenties. The farm
problem, revival of insurgency, and the Progressive party of 1924 are amply treated in
R. Nye, *Midwestern Progressive Politics*, cited above; Theodore Saloutos and J. D.
Hicks, *Agrarian Discontent in the Middle West, 1900–1939* (1951); and T. Saloutos,
Farmer Movements in the South, 1865–1933 (1960). See also James H. Shideler, Farm
Crisis, 1919–1932 (1957); Robert L. Morlan, *Political Prairie Fire: The Nonpartisan
League, 1915–1922* (1955); and Kenneth C. MacKay, *The Progressive Movement of
1924* (1947). Clarke A. Chambers, *Seedtime of Reform: American Social Service and
Social Action, 1918–1933* (1963), provides a provocative answer to the question, What
happened to progressivism in the twenties?

E.   *The Supreme Court and Social Economic Policy,*
1897–1929

Charles Warren, *The Supreme Court in United States History* (2 vols., 1937), is a
general survey, but Louis B. Boudin, *Government by Judiciary* (2 vols., 1932), gives
more attention to the Supreme Court and social and economic legislation. Alfred H.
Kelly and W. A. Harbison, *The American Constitution* (1963 edn.), is a briefer survey
but is adequate for the general reader. For the Supreme Court during the twenties, see
Alpheus T. Mason, *The Supreme Court from Taft to Warren* (1958) and *William
Howard Taft, Chief Justice* (1965). In addition, there are some excellent biographies
of leaders in the Court for this period: Pringle, *Taft*, Pusey, *Hughes*, and Mason,
Brandeis, already cited; A. T. Mason's monumental *Harlan Fiske Stone* (1956),

perhaps the finest judicial biography in our literature; and Max Lerner (ed.), *The Mind and Faith of Justice Holmes* (1943).

2. American Politics from Hoover to Johnson, 1929–1966

A. *Hoover and the Great Depression*

For brief and objective surveys of the Hoover period, see Hicks, *Republican Ascendancy*, and Leuchtenburg, *Perils of Prosperity*, both cited earlier. Arthur M. Schlesinger, Jr., *The Age of Roosevelt: The Crisis of the Old Order, 1919–1933* (1957)—the first volume in a monumental series noted more fully below—marks the beginning of a re-evaluation of the Hoover administration, as does Harris G. Warren, *Herbert Hoover and the Great Depression* (1959), and Albert U. Romasco, *The Poverty of Abundance: Hoover, the Nation, the Depression* (1965).

For vivid accounts of the impact of the depression on American life, thought, and politics, see Clarence J. Enzler, *Some Social Aspects of the Depression* (1939); Dixon Wecter, *The Age of the Great Depression, 1929–1941* (1948); and F. L. Allen, *Since Yesterday: The Nineteen-Thirties in America* (1940). Broadus Mitchell, *Depression Decade* (1947), analyzes the causes and problems of the depression in a general way, but the following are useful for specific aspects: Brookings Institution, *The Recovery Problem in the United States* (1936); Charles S. Johnson *et al.*, *The Collapse of Cotton Tenancy* (1935); Maurice Levin *et al.*, *America's Capacity to Consume* (1934); and Edwin G. Nourse *et al.*, *America's Capacity to Produce* (1934).

B. *Franklin D. Roosevelt and American Politics*

The literature on the era of Franklin Roosevelt, already richer than that dealing with any other comparable period in American history since 1865, is constantly growing. The best introduction to this period is Dr. Schlesinger's multivolume *The Age of Roosevelt*, which is both excellent history and great literature. He has published *The Crisis of the Old Order* (1957), *The Coming of the New Deal* (1958), and *The Politics of Upheaval* (1960). W. E. Leuchtenburg, *Franklin D. Roosevelt and the New Deal, 1932–1940* (1963), is a superb brief survey. D. Wexter, *Age of the Great Depression*, cited above, is good for the social impact of New Deal policies, but B. Mitchell, *Depression Decade*, cited earlier, sometimes sounds as if the author were lecturing from a Socialist soapbox. Samuel Lubell, *The Future of American Politics* (1952), shrewdly analyzes the impact of the New Deal on party loyalties and the party structure, while Matthew Josephson, *Sidney Hillman: Statesman of American Labor* (1952), is useful for understanding the New Deal's impact on labor politics.

Biographies of Roosevelt and memoirs of his friends and enemies are numerous enough to fill a special volume, and we will mention only the most important of them. We might begin with the most important, Robert E. Sherwood, *Roosevelt and Hopkins* (1948), a fascinating biography-memoir of Harry L. Hopkins, Roosevelt's closest adviser from 1935 to 1945. The first two volumes of F. Freidel's objective biography have already been cited; his third, *Franklin D. Roosevelt: The Triumph* (1956), carries the story through the election of 1932. Rexford G. Tugwell, *The Democratic Roosevelt* (1957), is a good one-volume biography, while James M. Burns, *Roosevelt: The Lion and the Fox* (1956), is a superb study of Roosevelt the politician. Thomas H. Greer, *What Roosevelt Thought* (1958), and Daniel R. Fusfield, *The Economic Thought of Franklin D. Roosevelt* (1956), are helpful special works. No serious student should ignore Edgar E. Robinson, *The Roosevelt Leadership, 1933–1945* (1955), which raises some challenging questions. Among the best of the numerous memoirs are Samuel I. Rosenman, *Working with Roosevelt* (1952), and Frances Perkins, *The Roosevelt I Knew* (1946). Raymond B. Moley, *After Seven Years* (1939), is critical and indispensable for understanding the First New Deal. See also John M. Blum (ed.), *From the*

Morgenthau Diaries: Years of Crisis, 1928–1938 (1959) and *From the Morgenthau Diaries: Years of Urgency, 1938–1941* (1965).

C. Aspects of the New Deal

1. *Financial Reform and the Problem of Recovery.* Ferdinand Pecora, *Wall Street Under Oath* (1939), and J. T. Flynn, *Security Speculation* (1934), demonstrate the need for financial reform. Marriner S. Eccles, *Beckoning Frontiers: Public and Personal Recollections* (1951), tells the story of the writing of the Banking Act of 1935, while Marion L. Ramsay, *Pyramids of Power: The Story of Roosevelt, Insull and the Utility Wars* (1937), covers the Holding Company Act of 1935 and the effort to regulate the securities exchange. The Treasury's monetary policies and the administration's experiments in "pump-priming" are adequately discussed in G. Griffith Johnson, Jr., *Treasury and Monetary Policy* (1939), and John K. Galbraith and G. G. Johnson, Jr., *The Economic Effects of the Federal Public Works Expenditure, 1933–1938* (1940). The best study of the NRA is Leverett S. Lyon *et al.*, *The National Recovery Administration* (1935), but see Merle Fainsod and L. Gordon, *Government and the American Economy* (1948 edn.), for an incisive analysis. For the work of the RFC, see Jesse H. Jones, *Fifty Billion Dollars: My Thirteen Years with the RFC, 1932–1945* (1951). Ellis W. Hawley, *The New Deal and the Problem of Monopoly, 1933–1939* (1965), is a monumental new study.

2. *The New Deal and Relief, Social Security, and Public Housing.* Mitchell, *Depression Decade,* cited above, includes an excellent summary of these phases of New Deal policy. Frances Perkins tells the story of the writing of the Social Security Act in *The Roosevelt I Knew,* cited above, as does Edwin E. Witte, *Development of the Social Security Act* (1962). Searle F. Charles, *Minister of Relief: Harry Hopkins and the Depression* (1963), is an important study. Nathan Straus, *Seven Myths of Housing* (1944), surveys the New Deal's housing program. An excellent recent addition is Paul K. Conkin, *Tomorrow a New World: The New Deal Community Program* (1959).

3. *The New Deal and Agriculture, 1933–1941.* Saloutos and Hicks, *Agrarian Discontent,* and Nye, *Midwestern Progressive Politics,* both cited earlier, are excellent for the farm problem in 1932 and 1933. For the AAA and its program, see E. G. Nourse *et al.*, *Three Years of the Agricultural Adjustment Administration* (1937), and Murray R. Benedict, *Farm Policies of the United States, 1790–1950* (1953). Dean Albertson, *Roosevelt's Farmer: Claude R. Wickard in the New Deal* (1961), is excellent for the later stages of New Deal farm policy.

4. *The South, the Concept of the Region, and the TVA.* Rupert B. Vance, *All These People, the Nation's Human Resources in the South* (1945), is comprehensive, while F. Freidel, *F.D.R. and the South* (1965), is a series of provocative lectures. V. O. Key, Jr., *Southern Politics in State and Nation* (1949), is a superb study. H. W. Odum and H. E. Moore, *American Regionalism* (1938), is the pioneer work in developing the regional concept. Robert E. Burke, *Olson's New Deal for California* (1953), reveals the impact of the New Deal in a single state. For the TVA, see C. Herman Pritchett, *The Tennessee Valley Authority: A Study in Public Administration* (1943), a dispassionate study, and David E. Lilienthal, *The Journals of David E. Lilienthal: The TVA Years, 1939–1945* (1965).

5. *Opposition to the New Deal.* There is, unfortunately, no study of Republican politics in the 1930's, but Lubell, *Future of American Politics,* cited above, analyzes the causes for the GOP's weakness. Morton Keller, *In Defense of Yesterday: James M. Beck and the Politics of Conservatism, 1861–1936* (1959), reflects the conservative Republican reaction to the New Deal. Even more revealing is the study of the American Liberty League by George Wolfskill, *Revolt of the Conservatives, A History of the American Liberty League, 1934–1940* (1962). Donald B. Johnson, *The Republican Party and Wendell Willkie* (1960), discusses the Republican situation in the late thirties. For non-Communist left-wing opposition to the New Deal, see Donald R. McCoy, *Angry Voices: Left-of-Center Politics in the New Deal Era* (1958); Allan P. Sindler, *Huey Long's Louisiana* (1956); and Charles J. Tull, *Father Coughlin and the New Deal* (1965). Egbert and Persons (eds.), *Socialism and American Life,* cited earlier,

contains the best brief survey of the rise and decline of Communism in the United States in the thirties. Wilson Record, *The Negro and the Communist Party* (1951), is thorough and balanced, as are three volumes in the superb "Communism in American Life" series: Ralph L. Roy, *Communism and the Churches* (1960); Robert W. Iverson, *The Communists and the Schools* (1959); and Daniel Aaron, *Writers on the Left* (1961).

6. *The Supreme Court Controversy, the New Deal Court, and Afterward.* Mason, *The Supreme Court from Taft to Warren*, cited earlier, covers the entire period. For the New Deal Court, see C. H. Pritchett, *The Roosevelt Court* (1948). Samuel Hendel's *Charles Evans Hughes and the Supreme Court* (1951), is a scholarly study of the Court controversy. There are some excellent biographies of leaders in the Court during the New Deal: Pusey, *Hughes*, Mason, *Brandeis* and *Stone*, all cited earlier. For the Court during the Truman era and after, see C. H. Pritchett, *Civil Liberties and the Vinson Court* (1954); and Walter F. Murphy, *Congress and the Court,* an important analysis of congressional opposition to interpretations in the late 1950's. Henry M. Christman (ed.), *The Public Papers of Chief Justice Earl Warren* (1966 edn.), is helpful.

D. Harry S. Truman and American Politics, 1945–1952

The literature of the Truman period is beginning to take form, and we now have enough scholarly work to be able to write fairly confidently on this period. Herbert Agar, *The Price of Power: America Since 1945* (1957); Eric F. Goldman, *The Crucial Decade and After, 1945–1960* (1961); and Walter Johnson, *1600 Pennsylvania Avenue* (1960), are good brief introductions. Among the biographies of Truman, Jonathan Daniels, *The Man of Independence* (1951), is the best but carries the story only to 1949. William Hillman (ed.), *Mr. President* (1952), contains brief excerpts from Truman's diaries and letters. Morris B. Schnapper (ed.), *The Truman Program* (1949), is a collection of Truman's speeches on all major Fair Deal policies. Harry S. Truman, *Memoirs by Harry S. Truman* (2 vols., 1955–56), is a storehouse of documentary and other information. Walter Millis and E. S. Duffield (eds.), *The Forrestal Diaries* (1951), is especially revealing on military and naval policies. D. E. Lilienthal, *The Journals of David E. Lilienthal: The Atomic Energy Years, 1945–1950* (1965), adds considerably to our understanding of this period. Arthur H. Vandenberg, Jr. (ed.), *The Private Papers of Senator Vandenberg* (1952), deals mainly with foreign affairs but reveals the tensions that divided the Republican party. For the campaign and election of 1948, see A. M. Schlesinger, Jr., *The Vital Center* (1949); Lindsay Rogers, *The Pollsters* (1949); William S. White, *The Taft Story* (1954); Karl M. Schmidt, *Henry A. Wallace: Quixotic Crusade* (1960); and Lubell, *Future of American Politics,* and Key, *Southern Politics,* both cited earlier. John W. Spanier, *The Truman-MacArthur Controversy and the Korean War* (1965 edn.), is superb and says much about partisan controversies of 1950–51. The best analysis of the campaign of 1952 is S. Lubell, "Who Elected Eisenhower?" *Saturday Evening Post,* January 10, 1953, and *The Revolt of the Moderates* (1956).

For economic issues in the postwar era, the best single volume is George A. Steiner, *Government's Role in Economic Life* (1953). Lester V. Chandler, *Inflation in the United States, 1940–1948* (1950), is comprehensive and clearly written. On the writing and significance of the Employment Act of 1946, see Stephen K. Bailey, *Congress Makes a Law* (1957); E. G. Nourse, *The 1950's Come First* (1951) and *Economics in the Public Service* (1953); and S. E. Harris, *Economic Planning* (1949). For the mobilization following the outbreak of the Korean War, see L. V. Chandler and D. H. Wallace (eds.), *Economic Mobilization and Stabilization* (1951); S. E. Harris, *The Economics of Mobilization and Inflation* (1951); and Steiner, *Government's Role in Economic Life,* just cited.

Charles W. Tobey, *The Return to Morality* (1952); Paul H. Douglas, *Ethics in Government* (1952); Blair Bolles, *How to Get Rich in Washington* (1952); H. Hubert Wilson, *Congress: Corruption and Compromise* (1951); and Karl Schriftgiesser, *The Lobbyists* (1951), describe the causes and consequences of corruption during the Truman era. The President's Committee on Civil Rights, *To Secure These Rights*

(1947); Robert K. Carr, *Federal Protection of Civil Rights* (1947); Milton R. Konvitz, *The Constitution and Civil Rights* (1947); and Morroe Berger, *Equality by Statute* (1952), highlight the postwar drive for an FEPC, antilynching, and other civil rights measures. Also see the titles listed below on Negro rights and the segregation controversy.

The literature on Communism, civil liberties, and so-called McCarthyism is large and steadily growing. On Communism in the United States, see the works cited above in *Opposition to the New Deal* and David A. Shannon, *The Decline of American Communism* (1959), the best general work for the postwar period. Alistair Cooke, *A Generation on Trial* (1950), is a balanced analysis of the Hiss trials and their consequences. Robert E. Cushman, *Civil Liberties in the United States* (1956), is a dispassionate survey. R. K. Carr, *The House Committee on Un-American Activities, 1945-1950* (1952); Clair Wilcox (ed.), *Civil Liberties Under Attack* (1951); and John W. Caughey, *In Clear and Present Danger* (1958), condemn the excessive fear of internal Communism and call for a reaffirmation of faith in democracy. Most of the works cited above deal with McCarthyism, but see also Richard H. Rovere, *Senator Joe McCarthy* (1959), and William F. Buckley, Jr. and L. B. Bozell, *McCarthy and His Enemies, the Record and Its Meaning* (1954).

E.   *Eisenhower and Normalcy*

The literature specifically on the politics of the Eisenhower era is of course still scanty. Goldman, *Crucial Decade*, and Johnson, *1600 Pennsylvania Avenue*, both cited earlier, are broad surveys. The most important sources for this period are Dwight D. Eisenhower, *The White House Years: Mandate for Change* (1963) and *The White House Years: Waging Peace, 1956-1961* (1965). Emmet John Hughes, *The Ordeal of Power: A Political Memoir of the Eisenhower Years* (1963), is candid. Three journalistic studies contain useful information about the first term: Merlo J. Pusey, *Eisenhower the President* (1956); Robert J. Donovan, *Eisenhower, the Inside Story* (1956); and Richard H. Rovere, *Affairs of State: The Eisenhower Years* (1956). Sherman Adams, *First-Hand Report* (1961), and Richard M. Nixon, *Six Crises* (1962), are "inside" stories to be read with some caution. Most of the specialized works on the Truman administration cited above also relate to the Eisenhower period, but see also Aaron Wildavsky, *Dixon-Yates: A Study in Power Politics* (1962), for a major controversy of the Eisenhower era. Theodore S. White, *The Making of the President, 1960* (1961), is a brilliant account of the campaign of 1960.

F.   *The New Frontier and the Great Society*

Although the Kennedy administration would normally be too recent to expect any studies worthy of note, we are fortunate in having two excellent works on this period: Arthur M. Schlesinger, Jr., *A Thousand Days: John F. Kennedy in the White House* (1965), a monumental study that will remain the basic work for the politics of the Kennedy administration for many years to come; and Theodore C. Sorensen, *Kennedy* (1965), an important memoir written by the man closest to the President. T. H. White, *The Making of the President, 1964* (1965), ably recounts the campaign of 1964, while Richard Harris, *The Real Voice* (1964), dealing with the drug industry bill, is the only significant study of the legislative history of the Kennedy era. There has been nothing substantial written on the Johnson administration, but see Michael Davie, *LBJ: A Foreign Observer's Viewpoint* (1966), for an incisive portrait of the President.

3. The United States and Its World Relations, 1898–1966

A.   *General*

Samuel F. Bemis and Robert H. Ferrell (eds.), *The American Secretaries of State and Their Diplomacy* (15 vols., 1927-29, 1963-66); Selig Adler, *The Isolationist Impulse*

(1959); Foster R. Dulles, *America's Rise to World Power, 1898–1954* (1955); H. C. Allen, *Great Britain and the United States* (1955); George F. Kennan, *American Diplomacy, 1900–1950* (1951); and Norman A. Graebner (ed.), *An Uncertain Tradition, American Secretaries of State in the Twentieth Century* (1961), are good surveys for readers deficient in background. But incomparably the best general work is Richard W. Leopold, *The Growth of American Foreign Policy* (1962).

B.   The War with Spain, Imperialism, and the United States and Europe and Asia, 1901–1914

Walter Millis, *The Martial Spirit* (1931), is a popular history of the war with Spain, while Howard K. Beale, *Theodore Roosevelt and the Rise of America to World Power* (1956), F. R. Dulles, *The Imperial Years* (1956), and Ernest R. May, *Imperial Democracy* (1961), treat that war and related events in a broader context. Valuable supplements are Julius W. Pratt, *Expansionists of 1898* (1936), and Harold and M. Sprout, *The Rise of American Naval Power* (1939).

There is no good book-length study of the controversy over imperialism, but J. W. Pratt, *America's Colonial Experiment* (1950), is a splendid survey of the rise, governing, and decline of the American colonial empire, while Robert E. Osgood, *Ideals and Self-Interest in America's Foreign Relations* (1953), includes a thoughtful analysis of the impact on American thought of the rise of the United States to world power.

We lack any general study of American relations with Europe from 1901 to 1914. Beale, *Roosevelt*, Garraty, *Lodge*, Leopold, *Root*, Jessup, *Root*, Pringle, *Roosevelt* and *Taft*, all cited earlier, Tyler Dennett, *John Hay* (1933), and Allan Nevins, *Henry White: Thirty Years of American Diplomacy* (1930), are valuable for the diplomacy of the Roosevelt-Taft period. Richard R. Heindel, *The American Impact on Great Britain, 1898–1914* (1940); Charles S. Campbell, Jr., *Anglo-American Understanding, 1898–1903* (1961); Alexander E. Campbell, *Great Britain and the United States, 1895–1903* (1961); and Clara E. Schieber, *The Transformation of American Sentiment toward Germany, 1870–1914* (1923), are excellent monographs.

In contrast to the paucity of good works on American-European relations from 1901 to 1914 stands a large body of general and monographic studies dealing with the United States and the Far East during the same period. A. Whitney Griswold, *The Far Eastern Policy of the United States* (1938); Edwin O. Reischauer, *The United States and Japan* (1965 edn.), and John K. Fairbank, *The United States and China* (1958 edn.), are the best surveys, but G. F. Kennan, *American Diplomacy*, cited above, and Louis J. Halle, *Dream and Reality: Aspects of American Foreign Policy* (1958), make some provocative observations. For important monographs, see T. Dennett, *Roosevelt and the Russo-Japanese War* (1925); Thomas A. Bailey, *Theodore Roosevelt and the Japanese-American Crisis* (1934); John A. White, *The Diplomacy of the Russo-Japanese War* (1964); Beale, *Roosevelt*, cited above; and Paul A. Varg, *Missionaries, Chinese, and Diplomats* (1954). Pringle, *Taft*, cited above, Herbert Croly, *Willard Straight* (1924), and Charles Vevier, *The United States and China, 1906–1913* (1955), are useful for Taft's "dollar diplomacy" in the Far East, while L. Ethan Ellis, *Reciprocity, 1911* (1939), relates Taft's ill-fated effort to win a reciprocal trade agreement with Canada. The most concise survey of Wilson's far eastern policy before 1917 is in A. S. Link, *Woodrow Wilson and the Progressive Era*, cited earlier, but see also his *Wilson: The New Freedom* and *Wilson: The Struggle for Neutrality*, both cited above.

C.   The United States and Latin America, 1900–1933

S. F. Bemis, *The Latin American Policy of the United States* (1943), covers the entire period and is the only general survey. For general works on the United States and the Caribbean, see Dexter Perkins, *Hands Off: A History of the Monroe Doctrine* (1941) and *The United States and the Caribbean* (1947), and Pratt, *America's Colonial Experiment*, cited above. Dana G. Munro, *Intervention and Dollar Diplomacy in the Caribbean, 1900–1921* (1964), is excellent. Link, *Woodrow Wilson and the Progressive*

Era, cited earlier, has the best summary of Wilson's Caribbean and Mexican policies, but see also the chapters in his *Wilson: The New Freedom, Wilson: The Struggle for Neutrality, Wilson: Confusions and Crises*, and *Wilson: Campaigns for Progressivism and Peace*, all cited earlier.

The decline of American intervention in Mexico and the Caribbean area in the 1920's has been well related by Bemis, *Latin American Policy of the United States*, cited above; Howard F. Cline, *The United States and Mexico* (1953); Pusey, *Hughes*, cited earlier; Harold Nicolson, *Dwight Morrow* (1935); and Alexander de Conde, *Herbert Hoover's Latin-American Policy* (1951).

D.   *The First Road to War, 1914–1917*

Among the general studies, Charles Seymour, *American Diplomacy during the World War* (1934) and *American Neutrality, 1914–1917* (1935), as well as Ernest R. May, *The World War and American Isolation* (1950), and Edward H. Buehrig, *Woodrow Wilson and the Balance of Power* (1955), are the best. Seymour (ed.), *The Intimate Papers of Colonel House*, cited earlier, includes materials indispensable to understanding Wilson's policies. Link, *Woodrow Wilson and the Progressive Era*, cited above, is also a useful summary, but see also his *Wilson: The Struggle for Neutrality, Wilson: Confusions and Crises*, and *Wilson: Campaigns for Progressivism and Peace*, all cited above, and the same author's *Wilson the Diplomatist* (1957 and 1963).

Special studies on this subject abound, and we will mention only a few of them: Karl E. Birnbaum, *Peace Moves and U-Boat Warfare* (1958), one of the best monographs in modern diplomatic history; Laurence W. Martin, *Peace Without Victory: Woodrow Wilson and the British Liberals* (1958), useful for the entire period 1914–19; Horace C. Peterson, *Propaganda for War* (1939), which overrates the influence of Allied propaganda; George S. Viereck, *Spreading Germs of Hate* (1930), excellent for German propaganda activities; and Carl Wittke, *German-Americans and the World War* (1936).

R. E. Osgood, *Ideals and Self-Interest in America's Foreign Relations*, cited earlier, presents an incisive analysis of American reactions to the challenges of the First World War. For the preparedness controversy and the peace movement from 1914 to 1917, see H. Hagedorn, *The Bugle that Woke America* (1940), a study of Theodore Roosevelt and the preparedness crisis; E. E. Morison, *Admiral Sims and the Modern American Navy* (1942); H. Hagedorn, *Leonard Wood*, cited earlier; and A. S. Link, *Wilson: Confusions and Crises*, cited above.

Almost all the biographies and memoirs cited in preceding sections have chapters on the background of America's first intervention. To these should be added Robert Lansing, *War Memoirs of Robert Lansing* (1935); Burton J. Hendrick, *The Life and Letters of Walter H. Page* (3 vols., 1922–25); and Stephen Gwynn (ed.), *Letters and Friendships of Sir Cecil Spring Rice* (2 vols., 1929).

E.   *The War, the Versailles Conference, and the Great Betrayal*

We are now beginning to have an excellent literature on American diplomacy during the First World War. Seymour, *American Diplomacy during the World War*, cited above, based on the House Papers and somewhat limited, is now supplemented by the following excellent works: Arno J. Mayer, *Political Origins of the New Diplomacy, 1917–1918* (1959); Harry R. Rudin, *Armistice, 1918* (1944); Louis L. Gerson, *Woodrow Wilson and the Rebirth of Poland* (1953); Victor S. Mamatey, *The United States and East Central Europe, 1914–1918* (1957); George F. Kennan's monumental *Russia Leaves the War* (1956) and *The Decision to Intervene* (1958), and his briefer but incisive *Russia and the West under Lenin and Stalin* (1961); and David F. Trask, *The United States in the Supreme War Council* (1961).

The early American movement for a League of Nations is related by Ruhl J. Bartlett, *The League to Enforce Peace* (1944), the background of the Peace Conference by Seymour, *American Diplomacy during the World War,* cited above, and Lawrence E. Gelfand, *The Inquiry: American Preparations for Peace, 1917–1919* (1963). R. S. Baker, *Woodrow Wilson and World Settlement* (3 vols., 1922), is a friendly account of the Paris Conference, rich in source materials. Also sympathetic to Wilson are Paul Birdsall, *Versailles Twenty Years After* (1941), and Seth P. Tillman, *Anglo-American Relations at the Paris Peace Conference* (1961). T. A. Bailey, *Woodrow Wilson and the Lost Peace* (1944), is more critical. Russell H. Fifield, *Woodrow Wilson and the Far East* (1952), relates Wilson's struggles with the Japanese at Versailles.

The best accounts of the Treaty fight in the United States are T. A. Bailey, *Woodrow Wilson and the Great Betrayal* (1945), and Denna F. Fleming, *The United States and the League of Nations, 1918–1920* (1932). Bailey emphasizes Wilson's responsibility for the failure of the Treaty; Fleming emphasizes Lodge's role. Blum, *Tumulty,* Garraty, *Lodge,* Link, *Wilson the Diplomatist,* Leopold, *Root,* Jessup, *Root,* and Seymour, *Intimate Papers of Colonel House,* all cited above, have significant chapters on the Treaty fight.

F.   *The Twenties: Futile Search for Isolation*

The most comprehensive general history of American foreign policy in the 1920's is D. F. Fleming, *The United States and World Organization, 1920–1933* (1938), but see also S. Adler, *The Uncertain Giant: 1921–1941* (1965). Fleming's *The United States and the World Court* (1945) is specialized but discusses an issue that persisted throughout the entire period. Studies of Secretaries of State include Pusey, *Hughes,* cited above; L. E. Ellis, *Frank B. Kellogg and American Foreign Relations, 1925–1929* (1961), which is also the best general work on the foreign policies of the second Coolidge administration; and Robert H. Ferrell, *Frank B. Kellogg/Henry L. Stimson* (1963).

The postwar naval race, Japanese-American tension, the American Siberian interventions, and Russo-American relations from 1918 to 1933 are discussed by H. and M. Sprout, *Toward a New Order of Sea Power* (1940); Betty M. Unterberger, *America's Siberian Adventure, 1918–1920* (1956); G. F. Kennan, *The Decision to Intervene* and *Russia and the West,* just cited; Robert P. Browder, *The Origins of Soviet-American Diplomacy* (1953); and William A. Williams, *American-Russian Relations, 1781–1947* (1952).

For the Washington Naval Conference and further efforts at naval disarmament, see Pusey, *Hughes,* Sprout and Sprout, *Toward a New Order of Sea Power,* and Griswold, *Far Eastern Policy of the United States,* all cited above; and Merze Tate, *The United States and Armaments* (1948). Robert H. Ferrell, *Peace in Their Time* (1952), is an excellent account of the American peace crusade of the twenties and the negotiation of the Kellogg-Briand Pact. For American international economic policy during the twenties, see Herbert Feis, *The Diplomacy of the Dollar: First Era, 1919–1932* (1950).

G.   *The United States and the Collapse of the International Structure, 1931–1936*

The best general work on the foreign policy of the Hoover administration is R. H. Ferrell, *American Diplomacy in the Great Depression: Hoover-Stimson Foreign Policy, 1929–1933* (1957), but see also Council on Foreign Relations, *Survey of American Foreign Relations, 1928–1931* (4 vols., 1928–31) and *The United States in World Affairs, 1931–1933* (3 vols., 1932–34). For the Manchurian crisis, see Reginald Bassett, *Democracy and Foreign Policy, the Sino-Japanese Dispute, 1931–1933* (1952); Henry L. Stimson and M. Bundy, *On Active Service in Peace and War* (1948); Richard N. Current, *Secretary Stimson* (1954), a severe criticism; and Armin Rappaport, *Henry L. Stimson and Japan, 1931–33* (1963).

The shifting pattern of Franklin D. Roosevelt's international economic policies comes out clearly in R. B. Moley, *After Seven Years,* cited earlier; Cordell Hull,

Memoirs (2 vols., 1948); and J. W. Pratt, *Cordell Hull, 1933–1944* (2 vols., 1964). Hull, *Memoirs*, and Sumner Welles, *The Time for Decision* (1944), are basic sources for the Good Neighbor policy by its two chief architects, but see also Bryce Wood, *The Making of the Good Neighbor Policy* (1961). Cline, *The United States and Mexico*, cited above, should be read with Josephus Daniels, *Shirt-Sleeve Diplomat* (1947), and especially E. David Cronon, *Josephus Daniels in Mexico* (1960), for Mexican-American controversies and conciliation in the 1930's.

There is no good history of the antiwar crusade of the 1930's, but the volumes of *The United States in World Affairs* for the years 1934 to 1939 contain a wealth of information on public opinion, while T. A. Bailey, *The Man in the Street* (1948), and S. Adler, *The Isolationist Impulse*, cited earlier, have relevant chapters. For the enactment and significance of the neutrality legislation, see Edwin M. Borchard and W. P. Lage, *Neutrality for the United States* (1937), and Robert A. Divine, *The Illusion of Neutrality* (1962).

H.   *The Second Road to War, 1937–1941*

The body of literature on the background of American participation in the Second World War is immense, and we will mention only the most important. The two outstanding works on the subject are William L. Langer and S. E. Gleason, *The Challenge to Isolation, 1937–1940* (1952) and *The Undeclared War, 1940–1941* (1953), which rank among the finest products of American historical scholarship. Sherwood, *Roosevelt and Hopkins*, cited earlier, and Winston S. Churchill, *The Gathering Storm* (1948) and *Their Finest Hour* (1949), are valuable sources. See also Charles A. Beard, *American Foreign Policy in the Making, 1932–1940* (1946) and *President Roosevelt and the Coming of the War, 1941* (1948), "revisionist" studies deserving of serious consideration.

Relations with Japan during the 1930's are examined by Griswold, *Far Eastern Policy*, cited earlier; Dorothy Borg, *The United States and the Far East Crises of 1933–1938* (1964); and Joseph C. Grew, *Turbulent Era, a Diplomatic Record of Forty Years, 1904–1945* (2 vols., 1952), the memoirs of the American Ambassador in Tokyo during the thirties. The Langer and Gleason volumes contain the fullest account of the rupture in Japanese-American relations, but see also H. Feis, *The Road to Pearl Harbor* (1950), an excellent and objective study. Paul W. Schroeder, *The Axis Alliance and Japanese-American Relations, 1941* (1958), and Robert J. C. Butow, *Tojo and the Coming of the War* (1961), add much new evidence on the Japanese side. Roberta Wohlstetter, *Pearl Harbor: Warning and Decision* (1962), is the most scholarly account of that controversial episode.

For the first Great Debate over American policy toward the war, we now have adequate studies for both the internationalist and isolationist organizations—Walter Johnson, *The Battle against Isolation* (1944), a study of the Committee to Defend America by Aiding the Allies, and Wayne S. Cole, *America First, the Battle against Intervention, 1940–1941* (1953), a study of the America First Committee.

I.   *The Diplomacy of the Second World War, 1941–1945*

Herbert Feis, *Churchill, Roosevelt, Stalin* (1957), is the best one-volume account of wartime diplomacy, but see also W. S. Churchill's magisterial *The Grand Alliance* (1950), *The Hinge of Fate* (1950), *Closing the Ring* (1951), and *Triumph and Tragedy* (1953). For the Yalta Conference, see John L. Snell (ed.), *The Meaning of Yalta* (1956). The Potsdam Conference and the end of the war are covered by H. Feis, *Between War and Peace: The Potsdam Conference* (1960) and *Japan Subdued* (1961); and R. J. C. Butow, *Japan's Decision to Surrender* (1954). H. Feis, *The China Tangle* (1953), is a superb account of American wartime relations with China. W. L. Langer, *Our Vichy Gamble* (1947); Robert Murphy, *Diplomat Among Warriors* (1964); and J. H. Hayes, *Wartime Mission in Spain, 1942–1945* (1947), treat the problems of France and Franco's Spain.

J.   The Brave New World, the Cold War, and the Korean Crisis

The basic, indispensable general works on American foreign relations since the Second
World War are the volumes in the Council on Foreign Relations, *The United States in
World Affairs, 1945–1965* (20 vols., 1947–1966). They are thorough in coverage and
objective in tone. The best general survey of American foreign policy in the postwar
period is John W. Spanier, *American Foreign Policy Since World War II* (1960).
Richard L. Walker and George Curry, *E. R. Stettinius, Jr., and James F. Byrnes* (1965),
and R. H. Ferrell, *George C. Marshall* (1966), study Truman's Secretaries of State.
There is nothing comparable on Dean Acheson, but see McGeorge Bundy (ed.), *The
Pattern of Responsibility* (1952), a collection of Acheson's major speeches. Arnold
Wolfers, *Alliance Policy in the Cold War* (1959); George Liska, *The New Statecraft:
Foreign Aid in American Foreign Policy* (1960); and H. Bradford Westerfield, *Foreign
Policy and Party Politics: Pearl Harbor to Korea* (1955), are valuable for aspects of
diplomacy during the Truman administration and beyond.

For the United Nations and American international economic policies in the
immediate postwar period, see Leland M. Goodrich, *The United Nations* (1959);
Abraham H. Feller, *United Nations and World Community* (1952); Raymond F.
Mikesell, *United States Economic Policy and International Relations* (1952); Brian
Tew, *International Monetary Cooperation, 1945–1952* (1952); and C. Wilcox, *A
Charter for World Trade* (1949). Hajo Holborn, *American Military Government*
(1947), and Eugene Davidson, *The Death and Life of Germany: An Account of the
American Occupation* (1959), are useful for American occupation policies in Germany.
There has been no good study of the Nuremberg trial, but see Robert H. Jackson, *The
Case Against the Nazi War Criminals* (1946) and *The Nuremberg Case* (1947), for a
justification of the proceedings. Hugh Borton *et al.*, *The Far East, 1942–1946* (1955),
and Kazuo Kawai, *Japan's American Interlude* (1960), reveal the dimensions of the
American experiment in Japan.

The causes of the disruption of the Grand Alliance have been told many times.
Churchill, *Triumph and Tragedy;* Sherwood, *Roosevelt and Hopkins;* and Feis, *Churchill, Roosevelt, Stalin; Between War and Peace;* and *Japan Subdued,* all cited earlier,
discuss the beginnings of the tension between the western democracies and the Soviet
Union, as does William H. McNeill, *America, Britain, and Russia: Their Co-operation
and Conflict, 1941–1946* (1953). James F. Byrnes, *Speaking Frankly* (1947), relates
the Secretary's futile struggle for understanding and friendship. There are a few
glimpses of Truman's private views in Hillman, *Mr. President,* and detailed discussions
of the growing tension in Millis and Duffield (eds.), *The Forrestal Diaries,* and Vandenberg (ed.), *The Private Papers of Senator Vandenberg,* all cited previously. Truman,
Memoirs, already cited, is indispensable. Kennan, *American Diplomacy,* cited above,
contains an incisive chapter on the Truman doctrine and Kennan's own influential
articles on containment. For the Berlin crisis, see Lucius D. Clay, *Decision in Germany*
(1950), and W. Phillips Davison, *The Berlin Blockade* (1958).

The debate over the failure of American policy in China has stimulated the
printing of most of the basic documents and the writing of some first-rate scholarly
studies on recent American policy in the Far East. Department of State, *United States
Relations with China* (1949), is the White Paper that presents the official version and
the documents. H. Feis, *The China Tangle,* cited above, goes through the end of the
Marshall mission, while Tang Tsou's excellent *America's Failure in China, 1941–50*
(1963), carries the story to the outbreak of the Korean War.

For the Cold War, see the works cited for the causes of the disruption of the
Grand Alliance, especially the volumes in *The United States in World Affairs* series
and the Truman *Memoirs.* Joseph M. Jones, *The Fifteen Weeks* (1955), analyzes the
change in opinion during the development of the Greek-Turkish aid program and the
Marshall Plan. Harry B. Price, *The Marshall Plan and Its Meaning* (1955), is the best
work on that topic. T. H. White, *Fire in the Ashes* (1953) is a moving record of
American success in the Cold War in western Europe. Halford L. Hoskins, *The Atlantic*

Pact (1949), and Drew Middleton, *Defense of Western Europe* (1952), recount the movement toward Atlantic unity and the development of plans for mutual defense after 1949.

American policies in the Middle East after 1945 are discussed by W. H. McNeill, *The Greek Dilemma* (1947); Ephraim A. Speiser, *The United States and the Near East* (1947); L. V. Thomas and R. N. Frye, *The United States and Turkey and Iran* (1951); and James G. McDonald, *My Mission in Israel, 1948–1951* (1951).

The best general work on the Korean War is David Rees, *Korea: The Limited War* (1964), but see especially Spanier, *The Truman-MacArthur Controversy*, cited above, for the recall of General MacArthur. R. E. Osgood, *Limited War* (1957), considers important strategic discussions and decisions, while Allen S. Whiting, *China Crosses the Yalu* (1960), treats the question of Chinese intervention. Mark W. Clark, *From the Danube to the Yalu* (1954), recounts events of the last months of the Korean War and the armistice negotiations.

H.   Diplomacy Under Eisenhower, Kennedy, and Johnson

The volumes in *The United States in World Affairs* series, already cited, discuss foreign affairs during these years. The basic sources for the Eisenhower period are Eisenhower, *Mandate for Change* and *Waging Peace*, cited above. Roscoe Drummond and G. Coblentz, *Duel at the Brink: John Foster Dulles' Command of American Power* (1960), is an appraisal of Eisenhower's Secretary of State, while Andrew H. Berding, *Dulles on Diplomacy* (1965), recounts conversations with the Secretary. Schlesinger, *A Thousand Days*, and Sorensen, *Kennedy*, both cited above, are the best accounts of Kennedy's foreign policy. Ernest K. Lindley (ed.), *The Winds of Freedom* (1963), is a selection from the speeches and statements of Secretary of State Dean Rusk. It is much too early for scholarly accounts of Lyndon B. Johnson's foreign policy, but see John Bartlow Martin, *Overtaken by Events* (1966), for a firsthand appraisal of events in the Dominican Republic; and Bernard B. Fall, *The Two Viet-Nams* (1965 edn.), and Robert Shaplen, *The Lost Revolution* (1966 edn.), for the background of the major dilemma of the Johnson administration.

4. The American People During Two World Wars

A.   The American Military and Naval Contributions in the First World War

The best summaries of military operations are John J. Pershing, *Final Report* (1919), and Leonard P. Ayres, *The War with Germany* (1919). J. J. Pershing, *My Experiences in the World War* (2 vols., 1931), and James G. Harbord, *The American Army in France, 1917–1919* (1936), are candid memoirs by two American commanders. On the American naval contributions, see Thomas G. Frothingham, *The Naval History of the World War* (3 vols., 1924–26), and Morison, *Admiral Sims*, cited above.

B.   The American Home Front, 1917–1918

The American home front during the war is treated by Seward W. Livermore, *Politics Is Adjourned: Woodrow Wilson and the War Congress, 1916–1918* (1966), Frederick Palmer, *Newton D. Baker: America at War* (2 vols., 1931), and Daniel R. Beaver, *Newton D. Baker and the American War Effort, 1917–1919* (1966). Bernard M. Baruch, *American Industry in War* (1941 edn.), discusses the problems of industrial mobilization. For special studies, see Alexander D. Noyes, *The War Period of American Finance, 1908–1925* (1926); Walker D. Hines, *War History of American Railroads* (1928); Edward N. Hurley, *The Bridge to France* (1927); Frank M. Surface and R. L. Bland, *American Food in the World War and Reconstruction Period* (1931); George Creel, *How We Advertised America* (1920); James R. Mock and C. Larson, *Words that*

Won the War: The Story of the Committee on Public Information, 1917–1919 (1939); and H. C. Peterson and G. C. Fite, *Opponents of War, 1917–1918* (1957).

C.   The American Military and Naval Effort, 1941–1945

Hundreds of volumes exist on virtually all aspects of the American military effort in the Second World War, and the list that follows is a selection of the works most useful to the general reader.

Among the general studies, Churchill's volumes, previously cited, include brilliant summaries of all major operations. Chester Wilmot, *The Struggle for Europe* (1952), is excellent on Allied operations in Europe. The Department of the Army's Office of Military History has published numerous volumes in its large and generally excellent series. Samuel E. Morison, *History of United States Naval Operations in World War II* (15 vols., 1947–62), is the definitive account of the American navy during the war. Kent Roberts Greenfield (ed.), *Command Decisions* (1959), contains a number of brilliant analyses of crucial military events, and also reveals how considerations of military strategy affected diplomacy. K. R. Greenfield, *American Strategy in World War II: A Reconsideration* (1963), contains provocative essays on military affairs. Forrest C. Pogue, *George C. Marshall: Ordeal and Hope, 1939–1942* (1966), is an important new study. Accounts by American military leaders include Dwight D. Eisenhower, *Crusade in Europe* (1948); Douglas MacArthur, *Reminiscences* (1964); Omar N. Bradley's candid *A Soldier's Story* (1951); Henry H. Arnold, *Global Mission* (1949); Joseph W. Stilwell's salty *The Stilwell Papers* (1948); Ernest J. King and W. M. Whitehill, *Fleet Admiral King* (1952); William D. Leahy, *I Was There* (1950); and Millis and Duffield (eds.), *The Forrestal Diaries*, cited above.

D.   The Home Front during the Second World War

There is no adequate study of domestic politics during this period. Jack Goodman (ed.), *While You Were Gone: A Report on Wartime Life in the United States* (1946), contains some good essays. The story of American industrial mobilization has not been told by an impartial historian. Donald M. Nelson, *Arsenal of Democracy* (1946), is an "official" history. Frederick C. Lane *et al.*, *Ships for Victory* (1951), is excellent for the shipbuilding program; E. R. Stettinius, Jr., *Lend-Lease, Weapon of Victory* (1944), is good for the export of matériel; James P. Baxter, 3rd, *Scientists Against Time* (1944), is a superb account of American scientific achievement during wartime; and Leslie R. Groves, *Now It Can Be Told* (1962), is the story of the Manhattan Project by its leader. Walter W. Wilcox, *The Farmer in the Second World War* (1947), is excellent, while Randolph E. Paul, *Taxation for Prosperity* (1947), recounts wartime tax struggles with considerable objectivity. Dorothy S. Thomas and R. S. Nishimoto, *The Spoilage* (1946), and D. S. Thomas *et al.*, *The Salvage* (1952), are scholarly studies of the evacuation of Japanese-Americans from the West Coast.

5. The American People and Their Economic Institutions, 1897–1966

A.   The American People: Demographic Changes and Wealth

The handiest references for general economic and social data are Bureau of the Census, *Historical Statistics of the United States* (1960) and *Statistical Abstract of the United States*, published annually. Warren S. Thompson, *Population Problems* (1953 edn.), is the best recent survey. Earlier and more comprehensive demographic studies are President's Research Committee, *Recent Social Trends in the United States* (2 vols., 1933); W. S. Thompson and P. K. Whelpton, *Population Trends in the United States* (1933); National Resources Committee, *Problems of a Changing Population* (1938); Walter F. Wilcox, *Studies in American Demography* (1940); and R. B. Vance,

Research Memorandum on Population Redistribution (1938). However, the best sources for decennial demographic changes are the summary volumes of the *Census*.

There are a number of excellent studies of wealth, income, and income distribution in the United States since the 1890's. For discussions in the broad context of economic development, see H. U. Faulkner, *The Decline of Laissez Faire, 1897–1917* (1951); George Soule, *Prosperity Decade: From War to Depression, 1917–1929* (1947); Mitchell, *Depression Decade*, cited previously; Ralph E. Freeman (ed.), *Postwar Economic Trends in the United States* (1960); and Harold G. Vatter, *The U.S. Economy in the 1950's: An Economic History* (1963). Milton Friedman and A. J. Schwartz, *A Monetary History of the United States, 1867–1960* (1963), is a monumental study, while Robert F. Martin, *National Income in the United States, 1799–1938* (1939), is an excellent statistical summary. Charles B. Spahr, *An Essay on the Present Distribution of Wealth* (1896); Wilford I. King, *The Wealth and Income of the People of the United States* (1915); and Wesley C. Mitchell *et al.*, *Income in the United States . . . 1909–1919* (2 vols., 1921–22), discuss income distribution from the late nineties to the twenties. For changing patterns of income distribution since 1920, see President's Conference on Unemployment, *Recent Economic Changes in the United States* (2 vols., 1929); Frederick C. Mills, *Economic Tendencies in the United States* (1932); M. Leven *et al.*, *America's Capacity to Consume*, cited above; E. G. Nourse *et al.*, *America's Capacity to Produce*, cited earlier; Simon Kuznets, *National Income* (1946) and *Shares of Upper Income Groups in Income and Savings* (1953); and Robert J. Lampman, *The Share of Top Wealth-holders in National Wealth, 1922–1956* (1962). S. Kuznets, *Capital in the American Economy* (1961), and Raymond W. Goldsmith, *The National Wealth of the United States* (1962), are more general studies.

B.   *The Problems of Labor, 1897–1966*

There are brief discussions in Faulkner, *Decline of Laissez Faire*, Soule, *Prosperity Decade*, and Mitchell, *Depression Decade*, all cited above, and in Foster R. Dulles, *Labor in America* (1949). However, the third and fourth volumes of J. R. Commons *et al.*, *History of Labour*, cited above, are the best general works for the period 1897–1932, while Philip Taft, *Organized Labor in American History* (1964), Henry Pelling, *American Labor* (1960), and Joseph G. Raybeck, *A History of American Labor* (1959), cover the entire period in a more general way.

For detailed specialized studies of unionization, union politics, and labor struggles, see Lewis L. Lorwin, *The American Federation of Labor* (1933), Leo Wolman, *The Growth of American Trade Unions, 1880–1923* (1924) and *Ebb and Flow in Trade Unionism* (1936); Marguerite Green, *The National Civic Federation and the American Labor Movement, 1900–1925* (1956); Marc Karson, *American Labor Unions and Politics, 1900–1918* (1958); James O. Morris, *Conflict within the AFL: A Study of Craft versus Industrial Unionism, 1901–1938* (1958); P. Taft, *The A. F. of L. from the Death of Gompers to the Merger* (1959); Walter Galenson, *The CIO Challenge to the AFL: A History of the American Labor Movement, 1935–1941* (1960); Richard A. Lester, *As Unions Mature* (1958); Sidney Lens, *The Crisis of American Labor* (1961); Joel I. Seidman, *American Labor from Defense to Reconversion* (1953); Louis Adamic, *Dynamite, the Story of Class Violence in America* (rev. edn., 1934); Samuel Yellen, *American Labor Struggles* (1936); Interchurch World Movement, Commission of Inquiry, *Report on the Steel Strike of 1919* (1920) and *Public Opinion and the Steel Strike* (1921); Robert R. R. Brooks, *As Steel Goes* (1940); Paul M. Angle, *Bloody Williamson* (1952); and David Brody, *Steelworkers in America: The Nonunion Era* (1960). Robert F. Kennedy, *The Enemy Within* (1960), is an analysis of labor racketeering.

Most of the general works just cited have chapters on wages, hours, working conditions, and the health of American workers. For specialized studies, however, see Brody, *Steelworkers in America*, just cited; Irving Bernstein, *The Lean Years: A History of the American Worker, 1920–1933* (1960); Solomon Fabricant, *Employment in Manufacturing, 1899–1939* (1942); Albert Rees, *Real Wages in Manufacturing, 1890–1914* (1961); and Robert M. Woodbury, *Workers' Health and Safety* (1927).

The history of the labor movement since the 1890's is writ large in the memoirs and biographies of its leaders. Samuel Gompers, *Seventy Years of Life and Labor* (2 vols., 1925), is one of the great autobiographies in American literature. Elsie Glück, *John Mitchell, Miner* (1929), and Hyman Weintraub, *Andrew Furuseth: Emancipator of Seaman* (1959), illuminate the careers of two wise leaders. James A. Wechsler, *Labor Baron: A Portrait of John L. Lewis* (1944), and Saul D. Alinsky, *John L. Lewis: An Unauthorized Biography* (1949), present radically different portraits of the stormy petrel of the twentieth century labor movement. M. Josephson, *Sidney Hillman,* cited earlier, is an important if uncritical contribution, while Charles A. Madison, *American Labor Leaders* (1950), is also useful. C. Wright Mills, *The New Men of Power* (1948), and Eli Ginzberg, *The Labor Leader* (1948), are sociological studies of the rise of a new labor leadership since the enactment of the Wagner Act.

C. Government and Labor

All the general and many of the special studies cited in the preceding section include discussions of the development of public policy and judicial interpretation concerning labor unions. For judicial interpretation, the following monographs are excellent: F. Frankfurter and N. Greene, *The Labor Injunction* (1930); Edward Berman, *Labor and the Sherman Act* (1930); Charles O. Gregory, *Labor and the Law* (1946); and Elias Lieberman, *Unions Before the Bar* (1950). A. S. Link, *Woodrow Wilson and the Progressive Era,* and the volumes in the same author's biography of Wilson, all cited earlier, discuss the labor policies of the Wilson administration until the First World War. For labor during the war, see Pringle, *Taft,* cited above, and Alexander M. Bing, *War-time Strikes and Their Adjustment* (1921). Harry A. Millis and E. C. Brown, *From the Wagner Act to Taft-Hartley* (1950), covers the development of federal policy from 1935 to 1946, but Seidman, *American Labor from Defense to Reconversion,* cited above, is more comprehensive. For postwar labor, state and federal, see Charles C. Killingsworth, *State Labor Relations Acts* (1948); Millis and Brown, cited above; Emily C. Brown, *National Labor Policy* (1950); and Fred A. Hartley, Jr., *Our New National Labor Policy* (1948).

D. The Changing Tides of Immigration

Carl Wittke, *We Who Built America* (1939), and George M. Stephenson, *History of American Immigration, 1820–1924* (1926), are standard surveys, but J. R. Commons, *Races and Immigrants in America* (1907), is still useful. Oscar Handlin, *The Uprooted* (1951), and L. Adamic, *From Many Lands* (1940) and *A Nation of Nations* (1945), highlight the impact of the uprooting upon the immigrants and the immigrant contribution to American life. Good specialized studies are O. Handlin, *The American People in the Twentieth Century* (1954) and *The Newcomers: Negroes and Puerto Ricans in a Changing Metropolis* (1959); Rowland T. Berthoff, *British Immigrants in Industrial America, 1790–1950* (1953); T. Saloutos, *They Remember America: The Story of the Repatriated Greek-American* (1956); and C. Wittke, *The Irish in America* (1956). William I. Thomas and Florian Znaniecki, *The Polish Peasant in Europe and America* (2 vols., 1927 edn.), is a classic.

Most of the works on immigration policy reflect the controversial aspects of the issue, but Roy L. Garis, *Immigration Restriction* (1927), and William S. Bernard, *American Immigration Policy* (1950), are thorough and objective. John Higham, *Strangers in the Land, Patterns of American Nativism, 1860–1925* (1955), is superb for nativism in the twentieth century, as is the more specialized work, Barbara M. Solomon, *Ancestors and Immigrants: A Changing New England Tradition* (1956). For another controversial aspect, see Roger Daniels, *The Politics of Prejudice: The Anti-Japanese Movement in California, and the Struggle for Japanese Exclusion* (1962).

Bernard, *American Immigration Policy*, cited above, and President's Commission, *Whom Shall We Welcome?* (1953) are the best surveys of immigration policy since 1945.

E.   The Growth of American Industry, 1897–1966

Faulkner, *Decline of Laissez Faire*, Soule, *Prosperity Decade*, and Mitchell, *Depression Decade*, all cited above, include chapters on the growth of industry from 1897 to 1941, while chapters from Harold F. Williamson (ed.), *The Growth of the American Economy* (1957 edn.), bring the story to the mid-fifties. Thomas C. Cochran, *The American Business System, 1900–1950* (1957), is a thoughtful general analysis, but see also Freeman (ed.), *Postwar Economic Trends*, cited earlier.

For developments in the late nineteenth century and early twentieth century, see Thomas C. Cochran and W. Miller, *The Age of Enterprise* (1942), and Louis M. Hacker, *The Triumph of American Capitalism* (1940). More specialized studies include Edmund E. Day and W. Thomas, *The Growth of Manufactures, 1899 to 1923* (1928); John W. Kendrick, *Productivity Trends in the United States* (1961); Gabriel Kolko, *Railroads and Regulation, 1877–1916* (1965); S. Fabricant, *The Output of Manufacturing Industries, 1899–1937* (1940); and National Resources Committee, *The Structure of the American Economy* (2 vols., 1939–40). Editors of Fortune, *U.S.A., the Permanent Revolution* (1951), is excellent for the rise of new industries in the period after 1945, while B. and G. S. Mitchell, *The Industrial Revolution in the South* (1930); Calvin B. Hoover and B. U. Ratchford, *Economic Resources and Policies of the South* (1951); Princeton University Conference, *The Industrialization of the South* (1960); and Thomas D. Clark, *The Emerging South* (1961), are excellent for the growth of southern industry since the 1890's.

The past decade has witnessed the burgeoning of a new type of American economic history—histories of individual companies, sponsored by the companies themselves but prepared under strict scholarly canons. The following examples greatly enrich our knowledge: Ralph W. and Muriel E. Hidy, *Pioneering in Big Business, 1882–1911: History of the Standard Oil Company (New Jersey)* (1955); George S. Gibb and Evelyn H. Knowlton, *The Resurgent Years, 1911–1927: History of the Standard Oil Company (New Jersey)* (1956); Paul H. Giddens, *Standard Oil Company (Indiana): Oil Pioneer of the Middle West* (1955); Henrietta M. Larson and K. W. Porter, *History of Humble Oil and Refining Company* (1959); and Forrest McDonald, *Let There Be Light: The Electric Utility Industry in Wisconsin, 1881–1955* (1957).

Biographies are often the most palatable form of economic history of the general reader. F. L. Allen, *The Great Pierpont Morgan* (1949), and Lewis Corey, *The House of Morgan* (1930), reveal different points of view about the leading financier of the twentieth century. A. Nevins, *Study in Power: John D. Rockefeller, Industrialist and Philanthropist* (2 vols., 1953), is as much a history of the American oil industry as a biography of its master builder. A. Nevins, *Ford, the Times, the Man, the Company* (1954), is a saga of the rise of the automobile in the twentieth century.

F.   Concentration and Competition in the American Economy

The best survey of the concentration movement in American industry from 1870 to the 1920's is Seager and Gulick, *Trust and Corporation Problems*, cited earlier, but Arthur R. Burns, *The Decline of Competition* (1936), Ralph L. Nelson, *Merger Movements in American Industry, 1895–1956* (1959), G. Warren Nutter, *The Extent of Enterprise Monopoly in the United States, 1899–1939* (1951), Adolf A. Berle, Jr. and G. C. Means, *The Modern Corporation and Private Property* (1932), and Federal Trade Commission, *The Merger Movement* (1948), are excellent general surveys. John Moody, *The Truth About the Trusts* (1904), is the best source for the merger movement from 1897 to 1903. James C. Bonbright and G. C. Means, *The Holding Company* (1932), analyzes the chief instrument of consolidation in the 1920's. Harry W. Laidler, *Concentration of Control in American Industry* (1931), describes the extent of concentration in 1930, while Clair Wilcox, *Competition and Monopoly in American Industry* (1940), David Lynch, *Concentration of Economic Power* (1946), and E. W. Hawley, *The New Deal and the Problem of Monopoly,* cited earlier, describe the situation in the late thirties.

For developments during and after the Second World War, see J. K. Galbraith, *American Capitalism* (1952); Adolf A. Berle, Jr., *The 20th Century Capitalist Revolution* (1954) and *Power without Property, A New Development in American Political Economy* (1959); Federal Trade Commission, *The Merger Movement,* cited above, *Interlocking Directorates* (1951), and *The Concentration of Productive Facilities* (1949); and Wassily W. Leontief, *Studies in the Structure of the American Economy* (1953). Thurman W. Arnold, *The Bottlenecks of Business* (1940); Walton H. Hamilton, *Antitrust in Action* (1940); and Corwin D. Edwards, *Maintaining Competition* (1949), are excellent for the philosophy and achievements of the second antitrust crusade from 1938 to 1952. Richard B. Wilson, "The Eisenhower Antitrust Policy," *Rocky Mountain Law Review,* XXXII (February 1960), 1–25, and "Antitrust Policy and Constitutional Theory," *Cornell Law Quarterly,* XLVI (Summer 1961), 505–531, carry the story through the Eisenhower era.

G. *Financial Institutions and Developments Since the 1890's*

The best survey for the general reader, F. L. Allen, *The Lords of Creation* (1935), gives special attention to the financial leaders. Faulkner, *Decline of Laissez Faire,* Soule, *Prosperity Decade,* Mitchell, *Depression Decade,* and Williamson (ed.), *Growth of the American Economy,* all cited earlier, give considerable attention to financial institutions and policies from 1897 to 1950. An indispensable general work for the serious student is George W. Edwards, *The Evolution of Finance Capitalism* (1938).

Among the specialized works, Louis D. Brandeis, *Other People's Money, and How the Bankers Use It* (1914), summarizes the findings of the Pujo Committee in 1913; Henry L. Staples and A. T. Mason, *The Fall of a Railroad Empire* (1947), the story of Morgan and the New Haven Railroad, is a case study in banker mismanagement; W. Z. Ripley, *Main Street and Wall Street* (1927), discusses banking developments in the 1920's; and F. Pecora, *Wall Street Under Oath,* and J. T. Flynn, *Security Speculation,* both cited earlier, highlight the bankers' contributions to the stock market crash of 1929. S. E. Harris, *Twenty Years of Federal Reserve Policy* (2 vols., 1933), and Paul M. Warburg, *The Federal Reserve System* (2 vols., 1930), are excellent for monetary policies before the New Deal. Friedman and Schwartz, *Monetary History of the United States,* cited earlier, is indispensable.

H. *The Technological Revolution*

Excellent surveys and special studies are John W. Oliver, *History of American Technology* (1956); Leonard S. Silk, *The Research Revolution* (1960); Harry Jerome, *Mechanization in Industry* (1934); National Resources Committee, *Technological Trends and National Policy* (1937); L. L. Lorwin, *Technology in Our Economy* (1941); S. Fabricant, *Labor Savings in American Industry, 1899–1939* (1945); Spurgeon Bell, *Productivity, Wages, and National Income* (1940); G. J. Stigler, *Trends in Output and Employment* (1947); and Kendrick, *Productivity Trends in the United States,* cited earlier.

6. Social and Intellectual Main Currents in American Life, 1897–1966

A. *Social Trends and Changes*

Faulkner, *The Quest for Social Justice.* Slosson, *The Great Crusade and After,* and Wecter, *The Age of the Great Depression,* all cited earlier, are excellent general works that together cover the years from 1897 to 1941. L. R. Morris, *Postscript to Yesterday,* cited above, and *Not So Long Ago* (1949), cover the same ground but emphasize manners and ideas; M. Sullivan, *Our Times*, cited earlier, contains a wealth of social history, as does Walter Lord, *The Good Years: From 1900 to the First World War* (1960), while F. L. Allen, *The Big Change: America Transforms Itself, 1900–1950* (1952), surveys the half century in a panoramic fashion. Most helpful for understanding prewar social and intellectual currents is Henry F. May, *The End of American Innocence: A Study of the First Years of Our Own Time, 1912–1917* (1959).

President's Committee, *Recent Social Trends in the United States*, cited earlier, is the best general work for the period 1919–32, but also excellent for changing social patterns in the twenties are F. L. Allen, *Only Yesterday*, cited above; Robert S. and H. M. Lynd, *Middletown* (1929); and Sigmund Diamond, *The Reputation of the American Businessman* (1955). For the impact of the depression and the New Deal, see Allen, *Since Yesterday*, already cited; Ruth Lindquist, *The Family in the Present Social Order* (1931); R. S. and H. M. Lynd, *Middletown in Transition* (1937); H. E. Stearns (ed.), *America Now* (1938); and White House Conference, *Children in a Democracy* (1940). Francis E. Merrill, *Social Problems on the Home Front* (1948), is an excellent analysis of social tensions and changes during the Second World War.

Sociologists, social psychologists, foreign observers, and other scholars have written a multitude of works on the postwar social scene in the United States. Harold J. Laski, *The American Democracy* (1948), is the commentary of a British Socialist. John W. Chase (ed.), *Years of the Modern* (1949); D. Wecter *et al.*, *Changing Patterns in American Civilization* (1949); and Editors of Fortune, *U.S.A., the Permanent Revolution*, cited earlier, comment on the changing mores. David Riesman, *The Lonely Crowd* (1950) and *Faces in the Crowd* (1952), are penetrating studies of mass behavior. National Conference on Family Life, *The American Family* (1953), and Ruth S. Cavan, *The American Family* (1953), are the best surveys for the postwar era.

Among the specialized works on aspects of social change, see Sophonisba P. Breckinridge, *Women in the Twentieth Century* (1933); Eleanor Flexner, *Century of Struggle: The Woman's Rights Movement in the United States* (1959); F. R. Dulles, *America Learns to Play* (1940); G. J. Stigler, *Domestic Servants in the United States, 1900–1940* (1946); Kenneth E. Boulding, *The Organizational Revolution* (1953); Sidney H. Ditzion, *Marriage, Morals, and Sex in America* (1953); and Alfred E. Kinsey *et al.*, *Sexual Behavior in the Human Male* (1948) and *Sexual Behavior in the Human Female* (1953).

B.   *Currents of American Thought*

Herbert W. Schneider, *A History of American Philosophy* (1946); M. Curti, *The Growth of American Thought* (1951 edn.); and Ralph H. Gabriel, *The Course of American Democratic Thought* (1958 edn.), discuss important developments since the 1890's. H. S. Commager, *The American Mind*, cited earlier, is also general in scope. Richard Hofstadter, *Social Darwinism in American Thought, 1860–1915* (1944); Morton G. White, *Social Thought in America* (1949), and J. Dorfman, *The Economic Mind in American Civilization* (5 vols., 1946–59), are all indispensable, if specialized. Stearns (ed.), *Civilization in the United States*, cited earlier, Joseph W. Krutch, *The Modern Temper* (1929), and W. Lippmann, *A Preface to Morals* (1929), summarize the intellectual discontent of the 1920's.

For representative American philosophers, see Schneider, *American Philosophy*, cited above, and Ralph B. Perry, *The Thought and Character of William James* (1935); Sidney Hook, *John Dewey* (1939); and writings of James, Dewey, Josiah Royce, and George Santayana.

C.   *The Growth of American Education, 1897–1966*

Of all the major fields of American history, the history of education is most neglected. Among the general surveys, Ellwood P. Cubberley, *Public Education in the United States* (1934 edn.); Stuart G. Noble, *A History of American Education* (1938); and Edgar W. Knight, *Education in the United States* (1951 edn.), are the best. Isaac L.

Kandel (ed.), *Twenty-Five Years of American Education* (1924), has excellent chapters on development during the quarter century after 1897, but see especially his thoughtful *American Education in the Twentieth Century* (1957). Lawrence A. Cremin, *The Transformation of the School: Progressivism in American Education, 1876–1957* (1961), is excellent social history. For the twenties, see President's Committee, *Recent Social Trends*, cited earlier. Malcolm W. Willey (ed.), *Depression, Recovery, and Higher Education* (1937); David S. Hill and F. J. Kelly, *Economy in Higher Education* (1933); I. L. Kandel, *The End of an Era* (1941); and Hollis P. Allen, *The Federal Government and Education* (1950), are useful for the depression and the impact of federal aid in the 1930's; I. L. Kandel, *The Impact of the War Upon American Education* (1948), for the Second World War period.

There is no general study of educational developments since 1945, but the following highlight the postwar crises: Benjamin Fine, *Our Children Are Cheated: The Crisis in American Education* (1947); James B. Conant, *The American High School Today* (1959) and *The Education of American Teachers* (1963); Arthur E. Bestor, Jr., *Educational Wastelands* (1953) and *The Restoration of Learning* (1955); and Albert Lynd, *Quackery in the Public Schools* (1953).

The development of educational philosophies and the debate over general education are revealed in Cremin, *Transformation of the School*, cited above; M. Curti, *The Social Ideas of American Educators* (1935); John Dewey, *Democracy and Education* (1916); George S. Counts *et al.*, *The Social Foundations of Education* (1934); Robert M. Hutchins, *Higher Learning in America* (1936) and *Education for Freedom* (1943); Alexander Meiklejohn, *Education Between Two Worlds* (1942); and Harvard Committee, *General Education in a Free Society* (1945).

For the development of American scholarship since 1897, see M. Curti (ed.), *American Scholarship in the Twentieth Century* (1953), and the following biographies and memoirs: Henry James, *Charles W. Eliot* (2 vols., 1930); Henry A. Yeomans, *Abbott Lawrence Lowell* (1948); Nicholas M. Butler, *Across the Busy Years* (2 vols., 1939); J. R. Commons, *Myself* (1934); Richard T. Ely, *Ground Under Our Feet* (1938); Alvin S. Johnson, *Pioneer's Progress* (1952); Arthur F. Burns, *Wesley Clair Mitchell* (1952); Samuel Tenenbaum, *William Heard Kilpatrick* (1951); and H. K. Beale (ed.), *Charles A. Beard, An Appraisal* (1954).

D. *American Religious Institutions and Thought Since 1897*

James W. Smith and A. Leland Jamison (eds.), *Religion in American Life* (4 vols., 1961), is the best introduction to American religious history. The two bibliographical volumes in this series are especially helpful. William W. Sweet, *The Story of Religion in America* (1939), Jerald C. Brauer, *Protestantism in America* (1953), and Clifton E. Olmstead, *History of Religion in the United States* (1960), cover the twentieth century, but more detailed are H. W. Schneider, *Religion in 20th Century America* (1952), and Willard L. Sperry, *Religion in America* (1945). Other useful surveys are Theodore Maynard, *The Story of American Catholicism* (1941); Will Herberg, *Protestant, Catholic, Jew* (1955); John T. Ellis, *American Catholicism* (1956); Nathan Glazer, *American Judaism* (1957); Winthrop S. Hudson, *American Protestantism* (1961); and Kenneth K. Bailey, *Southern White Protestantism in the Twentieth Century* (1964).

Charles H. Hopkins, *The Rise of the Social Gospel in American Protestantism, 1865–1915* (1940); Aaron I. Abell, *The Urban Impact on American Protestantism, 1865–1900* (1943); Henry F. May, *Protestant Churches and Industrial America* (1949); A. I. Abell, *American Catholicism and Social Action* (1960); Herbert A. Wisbey, Jr., *Soldiers without Swords: A History of the Salvation Army in the United States* (1955); C. H. Hopkins, *History of the Y.M.C.A. in North America* (1951); Robert M. Miller, *American Protestantism and Social Issues, 1919–1939* (1958); and Paul A. Carter, *The Decline and Revival of the Social Gospel, 1920–1940* (1956), are excellent for the awakening of the church's social conscience. Personal studies on twentieth-century religious leaders are scarce, but the following mark a beginning: J.

T. Ellis, *The Life of James Cardinal Gibbons* (2 vols., 1952); Ira V. Brown, *Lyman Abbott, Christian Evolutionist* (1953); William G. McLoughlin, Jr., *Billy Sunday Was His Real Name* (1955); Dores R. Sharpe, *Walter Rauschenbusch* (1942); and Harry E. Fosdick, *The Living of These Days* (1956). Bernard A. Weisberger, *They Gathered at the River* (1958), and W. G. McLoughlin, Jr., *Modern Revivalism: Charles Grandison Finney to Billy Graham* (1959), are superb on twentieth-century revivalism. Charles S. Braden, *These Also Believe* (1949), is an account of the sects along the frontier of Protestantism. Ralph L. Roy, *Apostles of Discord* (1953), is a study of Protestant bigotry and fundamentalism at mid-century. For the renewal of Protestant-Catholic antagonisms and the struggle over religion in the schools in the postwar years, see Roy, *Apostles of Discord*, just cited; Conrad H. Moehlman, *The Wall of Separation between Church and State* (1951); Paul Blanshard, *American Freedom and Catholic Power* (1949) and *Communism, Democracy, and Catholic Power* (1951); and James M. O'Neill, *Catholicism and American Freedom* (1952). Martin E. Marty, *The New Shape of American Religion* (1959), and Arthur R. Eckhardt, *The Surge of Piety in America* (1958), raise some important questions about the so-called return to religion in the fifties.

Gerald B. Smith (ed.), *Religious Thought in the Last Quarter-Century* (1927); Arnold S. Nash (ed.), *Protestant Thought in the Twentieth Century* (1951); and Donald B. Meyer, *The Protestant Search for Political Realism, 1919–1941* (1960), are good surveys, but no student should overlook the work of the leading neo-orthodox theologian, Reinhold Niebuhr, especially *Moral Man and Immoral Society* (1932) and *The Nature and Destiny of Man* (2 vols., 1941–43), and the synthesis of latter-day liberal thought, Henry N. Wieman *et al.*, *Religious Liberals Reply* (1947).

E. American Literature, 1897–1966

For significant work in fiction, poetry, and drama, see the relevant sections in this volume. The following list includes only general works and omits biographies and critical studies of individual writers.

The basic general history is Robert E. Spiller *et al.*, *Literary History of the United States* (1953 edn.), which contains discussions of virtually every American writer worthy of mention, lengthy essays on the major writers, and a good general bibliography. For general works on fictional writing, see Leon Howard, *Literature and the American Tradition* (1960), Willard Thorp, *American Writing in the Twentieth Century* (1960), and Frederick J. Hoffman, *The Modern Novel in America, 1900–1950* (1956), all brief but incisive surveys; Walter F. Taylor, *The Economic Novel in America* (1942), and Walter B. Rideout, *The Radical Novel in the United States, 1900–1954* (1956), useful for the literature of protest; Alfred Kazin, *On Native Grounds* (1942), excellent for American naturalism; Granville Hicks, *The Great Tradition* (1935), a survey of left-wing and proletarian writers; and F. J. Hoffman, *Freudianism and the Literary Mind* (1945).

Among the special and period studies, the following are helpful: Van Wyck Brooks, *The Confident Years, 1885–1915* (1952); Malcolm Cowley, *Exile's Return: A Literary Odyssey of the 1920's* (1951); Wilbur M. Frohock, *The Novel of Violence in America, 1920–1950* (1950); Maxwell D. Geismar, *The Last of the Provincials: The American Novel, 1915–1925* (1947); John W. Aldridge, *After the Lost Generation* (1951); Leo Gurko, *The Angry Decade* (1947); and Louis D. Rubin and R. D. Jacobs (eds.), *Southern Renascence: The Literature of the Modern South* (1953).

For the growth of literary criticism in the twentieth century, see F. J. Hoffman *et al.*, *The Little Magazine* (1946); Irene and A. Cleaton, *Books & Battles* (1937); Charles I. Glicksberg (ed.), *American Literary Criticism, 1900–1950* (1952); and especially William V. O'Conner, *An Age of Criticism, 1900–1950* (1952). Alan S. Downer, *Fifty Years of American Drama, 1900–1950* (1951), and Louise Bogan, *Achievement in American Poetry, 1900–1950* (1951), cover the main currents in their respective fields.

F.   Art, Architecture, and Music

Oliver W. Larkin, *Art and Life in America* (1949), is a splendid general history that relates the American achievement in painting, architecture, sculpture, and photography to the main currents of thought and politics. Another excellent if more specialized survey is Virgil Barker, *American Painting, History and Interpretation* (1950). John I. H. Baur, *Revolution and Tradition in Modern American Art* (1951), and E. P. Richardson, *Painting in America* (1956), emphasize recent trends, while Thomas H. Benton, *An Artist in America* (1937), sets forth the philosophy of the "American" school.

James M. Fitch, *American Building* (1948), and Larkin, *Art and Life in America*, just cited, are excellent for main trends in American architecture and especially for the social and intellectual forces that shaped it, but see also Ian McCallum, *Architecture U.S.A.* (1959). Carl W. Condit, *The Rise of the Skyscraper* (1952), discusses the Chicago pioneers who developed the skyscraper form. For vigorous enunciations of the functional philosophy, see Frank L. Wright, *Modern Architecture* (1931) and *Autobiography* (1932), and Lewis Mumford (ed.), *Roots of Contemporary American Architecture* (1952) and *The Culture of Cities* (1938). Finis Farr, *Frank Lloyd Wright* (1961), is a helpful if not monumental biography of that irascible pioneer.

John T. Howard, *Our American Music* (1946 edn.), and John Culshaw, *A Century of Music* (1952), review the American achievement in the field of so-called serious music, while Aaron Copland, *Our New Music* (1941), defends the modern school. For ragtime, jazz, and other popular music since 1900, there is a large and excellent literature: Sigmund Spaeth, *A History of Popular Music in America* (1948); Rudi Blesh and H. Janis, *They All Played Rag-time* (1950); R. Blesh, *Shining Trumpets* (1946); William C. Handy, *Father of the Blues* (1941); Douglas Gilbert, *Lost Chords* (1942); Robert Goffin, *Jazz* (1944); Winthrop Sargeant, *Jazz* (1946); Eddie Condon, *We Called It Music* (1947); and Deems Taylor, *Some Enchanted Evenings* (1953).

G.   Main Trends in American Journalism, 1897–1966

Frank L. Mott, *American Journalism: A History* (1960 edn.), is a comprehensive survey. James E. Pollard, *The Presidents and the Press* (1947), covers a little known aspect of presidential and journalistic history. Oswald G. Villard, *Some Newspapers and Newspaper-men* (1923) and *The Disappearing Daily* (1944), are excellent for twentieth-century developments, while Simon M. Bessie, *Jazz Journalism* (1938), is a good account of tabloid newspapers. Commission on Freedom of the Press, *A Free and Responsible Press* (1947), and M. L. Ernst, *The First Freedom* (1946), discuss developments since the 1930's, particularly the consolidation movement and the impact of pressure groups on newspaper policies. The origins and growth of magazine journalism are magnificently covered in F. L. Mott, *A History of American Magazines* (4 vols., 1938–57); James P. Wood, *Magazines in the United States* (1956); and Theodore Peterson, *Magazines in the Twentieth Century* (1956).

Biographies and memoirs of editors and newspapermen help to recreate the history of American journalism since the 1890's. See, for example, L. Steffens, *Autobiography*, cited earlier; George Creel, *Rebel at Large* (1947); Joseph F. Wall, *Henry Watterson: Unreconstructed Rebel* (1956); Warren F. Kuehl, *Hamilton Holt* (1960); Oliver Carlson and E. S. Bates, *Hearst, Lord of San Simeon* (1936); W. A. Swanberg, *Citizen Hearst* (1961); Willis F. Johnson, *George Harvey* (1929); R. S. Baker, *American Chronicle* (1945); and O. G. Villard, *Fighting Years, Memoirs of a Liberal Editor* (1939).

H.   The American Negro from Serfdom to Citizenship

In no field of American history or sociology is there a more rewarding literature than in the area of the Negro and race relations in the United States. Rayford W. Logan,

The Negro in American Life and Thought: The Nadir, 1877–1901 (1954), and C. V. Woodward, *The Strange Career of Jim Crow* (1955), provide background discussions for twentieth-century developments. General histories abound, but the best are John H. Franklin, *From Slavery to Freedom: A History of American Negroes* (1956), E. Franklin Frazier, *The Negro in the United States* (1949), and J. Saunders Redding, *Lonesome Road: The Story of the Negro's Part in America* (1958). Gunnar Myrdal, *An American Dilemma* (2 vols., 1944), is a massive, penetrating study of all phases of the race question. Arnold M. Rose, *The Negro in America* (1948), is an abridgment of Myrdal's volumes. F. B. Simkins, *A History of the South* (1953), E. F. Frazier, *The Negro Family in the United States* (1939), and C. S. Johnson, *Patterns of Negro Segregation* (1943), are other general studies.

For Negro movements and the Negro in politics since 1900, see Samuel R. Spencer, Jr., *Booker T. Washington* (1955); August Meier, *Negro Thought in America, 1880–1915* (1963); Francis L. Broderick, *W. E. B. Du Bois: Negro Leader in a Time of Crisis* (1959); William E. B. Du Bois, *Dusk of Dawn* (1940); Robert L. Jack, *History of the National Association for the Advancement of Colored People* (1943); E. D. Cronon, *Black Moses: The Story of Marcus Garvey* (1955); Walter White, *A Man Called White* (1948); Elbert L. Tatum, *The Changed Political Thought of the Negro, 1915–1940* (1951); Henry L. Moon, *Balance of Power, the Negro Vote* (1948); V. O. Key, Jr., *Southern Politics*, cited above; the excellent C. E. Lincoln, *The Black Muslims in America* (1961); and E. U. Essien-Udom, *Black Nationalism* (1962).

Louise V. Kennedy, *The Negro Peasant Turns Cityward* (1930), and Ira DeA. Reid, *The Negro Immigrant* (1939), are excellent for the black migration from the South during and after the First World War; Walter White, *Rope & Faggot* (1929), and A. F. Raper, *The Tragedy of Lynching* (1933), for lynching in the twentieth century; Horace R. Cayton and G. S. Mitchell, *Black Workers and the New Unions* (1939), and Herbert R. Northrup, *Organized Labor and the Negro* (1944), for the integration of Negroes into the ranks of organized labor; and Louis R. Harlan, *Separate and Unequal: Public School Campaigns and Racism in the Southern Seaboard States, 1901–1915* (1958), for early difficulties over Negro education.

For general developments in the period after 1945, Arnold M. Rose, *The Negro in Postwar America* (1950), is the best survey, but see also Bucklin Moon, *The High Cost of Prejudice* (1947); Frank S. Loescher, *The Protestant Church and the Negro* (1948); Dwight W. Culver, *Negro Segregation in the Methodist Church* (1953); J. Saunders Redding, *On Being Negro in America* (1951); Carl T. Rowan, *South of Freedom* (1952); E. Franklin Frazier, *Black Bourgeoisie* (1957); Jack Greenberg, *Race Relations and American Law* (1959); and Margaret Price, *The Negro and the Ballot in the South* (1959).

I. *The Segregation Controversy*

Bernard H. Nelson, *The Fourteenth Amendment and the Negro Since 1920* (1946); Pritchett, *The Roosevelt Court* and *The Vinson Court*, both cited earlier; Robert J. Harris, *The Quest for Equality* (1960); Harry S. Ashmore, *The Negro and the Schools* (1954); and Benjamin Muse, *Ten Years of Prelude: The Story of Integration Since the Supreme Court's 1954 Decision* (1964), are all excellent general introductions. For various aspects of the segregation controversy following the schools decision of 1954, see John B. Martin, *The Deep South Says "Never"* (1957); Benjamin Muse, *Virginia's Massive Resistance* (1961); Harry S. Ashmore, *The Other Side of Jordan* (1960); J. W. Peltason, *58 Lonely Men* (1961), on southern federal district judges and desegregation; James W. Silver, *Mississippi: The Closed Society* (1964); and Russell H. Barrett, *Integration at Old Miss* (1965).

INDEX

DATE DUE

GAYLORD			PRINTED IN U.S.A.